First Amendment Law

First Amendment Law

Freedom of Expression and Freedom of Religion

FOURTH EDITION

Arthur D. Hellman
Sally Ann Semenko Endowed Chair
University of Pittsburgh School of Law

William D. Araiza
Professor of Law
Brooklyn Law School

Thomas E. Baker
Professor of Law
Florida International University College of Law

Ashutosh A. Bhagwat
Martin Luther King Jr. Professor of Law
University of California at Davis
School of Law

Carolina Academic Press
Durham, North Carolina

LCCN: 2018933299
ISBN: 978-1-5310-0940-3
eISBN: 978-1-53100-941-0

Carolina Academic Press, LLC
700 Kent Street
Durham, North Carolina 27701
Telephone (919) 489-7486
Fax (919) 493-5668
www.cap-press.com

Printed in the United States of America

Contents

PART ONE

FREEDOM OF EXPRESSION

Table of Cases

Preface to the Fourth Edition

The First Edition of our Casebook was published in 2006. As we explained in the Preface to that work (reprinted immediately following), the book's content and organization were shaped by our belief that, from a lawyer's perspective, the First Amendment is above all else *law* — albeit a special kind of law. One thing that is special is that First Amendment law is found primarily in the decisions of the Supreme Court of the United States. Close analysis of those precedents is thus the principal tool that lawyers must rely on when seeking to persuade a judge or when negotiating with an adversary on behalf of a client. One purpose of our book was to help students learn how to best deploy that tool. To that end, we provided versions of the opinions that were relatively complete; we also organized the cases in accordance with the Court's own categories and the temporal development of the doctrines within those categories.

The Second and Third Editions of the book were published in 2010 and 2014, respectively. While the Third Edition added a new section (in Chapter 3) highlighting the sequence of decisions in which the Court steadfastly refused to expand the universe of unprotected speech, the Second and Third Editions otherwise hewed closely to the organization of the First Edition.

This Fourth Edition adheres to the organizational *principle* that has guided us through the prior editions, but because the Court's decisions have moved in some new directions, the organization itself features some significant changes. Most notably, while the first four chapters (Chapters 1–4) retain their pre-existing pride of place, the next four chapters (Chapters 5–8) now cover, respectively, the rule against content discrimination; time, place, and manner regulations; expressive conduct and the secondary effects doctrine; and the public forum doctrine. We moved up this material primarily to reflect the increased emphasis the Court has placed on the content-neutrality rule, especially in the new leading case of *Reed v. Town of Gilbert* (2015). That change, in turn, prompted us to move up our discussions of the doctrines that follow from that rule. Simply put, the content-neutrality rule has achieved a sufficiently central status in First Amendment doctrine that it merits students' early and careful attention, after they have encountered the historically foundational cases addressing unprotected speech categories (Chapters 1 and 2), partially or potentially unprotected categories (Chapter 3), and prior restraints, vagueness, and overbreadth (Chapter 4). Our belief is that early exposure to concepts such as content neutrality and strict scrutiny will make the later materials more accessible to students.

A second organizational change is to give campaign finance regulation its own chapter (Chapter 11), in recognition of the growing (and largely self-contained) body of First Amendment doctrine governing that subject. This new chapter immediately follows the chapter on freedom of association, consistent with the grounding of the doctrine in "the right to associate with the political party of one's choice" in *Buckley v. Valeo* (1976). By contrast, we retired the earlier editions' chapter on new technologies and distributed its most important content among Chapter 3 (*FCC v. Pacifica Foundation* (1978)) and Chapter 15 (*Packingham v. North Carolina* (2017)). We made this change partly to keep the book at a manageable length, but primarily because some of the cases in that now-deleted chapter (most notably the spectrum scarcity cases growing out of *Red Lion Broadcasting v. FCC* (1969)) have likely become sufficiently marginalized and irrelevant to students' experiences as to become less important and pedagogically satisfying.

Chapter 15 concludes Part I of the book, and focuses on three areas that each implicate multiple, cross-cutting aspects of free speech law. The section on "hate speech" remains from the corresponding chapter from the earlier editions, and it is followed by *Matal v. Tam* (2017), the decision that struck down the disparagement provision of federal trademark law, and *Packingham v. North Carolina* (2017), which invalidated the state's law against convicted sex offenders accessing social media. The debate over "hate speech" undoubtedly remains current today in the popular culture. *Matal* engages that debate, while also broaching the fascinating and pedagogically important question of how to analyze, for First Amendment purposes, programs such as the federal trademark regime. Finally, *Packingham* features potentially broad language about the importance of social media in the marketplace of ideas as well as musings about the First Amendment-protected status of the Internet as a public forum—along with a pointed caution about those musings from the concurring Justices.

Overall, the organization and the structure of Part Two on Freedom of Religion have required little change over three editions, but the Fourth Edition incorporates modest modifications to reflect the Supreme Court's recent handiwork. In Chapter 16 ("The History and Purposes of the Religion Clauses") we added a new section to introduce students to the values underlying the Religion Clauses. Chapter 17 ("The Establishment Clause") includes a new section on Legislative Prayer that features *Town of Greece v. Galloway* (2014). In Chapter 18 ("The Free Exercise Clause") an extensive new note summarizes various statutory provisions that are important other protections of religious liberty. Chapter 19 ("Interrelationships Among the Clauses") has been revamped to emphasize the line of precedents that includes *Locke v. Davey* (2004) and the very recent decision in *Trinity Lutheran Church of Columbia v. Comer* (2017).

In addition to these organizational and structural changes, the Fourth Edition, like those before it, features smaller-scale alterations to reflect recent developments and also to ensure that material is presented as compactly as possible. In particular, following a practice that we initiated for the Third Edition, some principal cases have been condensed down to essential extracts in extended Notes. We have done this because we want to keep the foundational older opinions that define the landscape of First Amendment law but also to include the significant recent decisions that alter the contours or expand the boundaries—all the while allowing the Justices to speak for themselves. It is simply not possible to do all that and treat every important case as a principal case. But even when we have condensed some cases to Notes, we have endeavored, as much as possible, to present the material through extended quotations from the Justices' own language. We believe these Note versions are sufficiently complete to support meaningful class discussion.

We also continue to include Problems as a key pedagogical tool. These Problems have been carefully designed to require students to analyze the cases and use them as lawyers do to make or respond to arguments. For this edition, we reviewed all of the Problems in the Third Edition. Most of them have worked well in the classroom, and we have kept them, sometimes with minor updating or tweaking. But we have dropped Problems that did not work well or that seemed outdated and have added some new ones.

With this edition Professors Hellman, Araiza, and Baker welcome as a co-author Professor Ashutosh A. Bhagwat of the University of California at Davis School of Law. The three incumbent authors are delighted that he has joined the book and they extend their great appreciation for his many contributions to the Fourth Edition.

ARTHUR D. HELLMAN
hellman@pitt.edu

WILLIAM D. ARAIZA
bill.araiza@brooklaw.edu

THOMAS E. BAKER
thomas.baker@fiu.edu

ASHUTOSH A. BHAGWAT
aabhagwat@ucdavis.edu

Preface to the First Edition

The title of our new First Amendment casebook is "First Amendment Law." The emphasis on "law" is not simply a matter of nomenclature. The First Amendment can be viewed as history, as policy, and as theory, but from a lawyer's perspective, it is above all *law*—albeit a special kind of law. One thing that is special is that the governing texts have receded into the background. *The law is the cases, and the cases are the law.* Close analysis of precedent is therefore the principal tool of argumentation and adjudication. The purpose of this book is to help students to learn the law in a way that will enable them to use it in the service of clients. This process entails skills as well as knowledge.

Constitutional topics like the First Amendment are not often thought of as vehicles for skills training, but they can be, and we hope that in our book they will be. Moreover, the skills we seek to impart will be valuable to students not just in the realm of the First Amendment, but in any area where lawyers must rely on close analysis of precedent when seeking to persuade a judge or an adversary on behalf of a client. Four principal features of the book will help students to master these skills.

First, the cases have been edited with a relatively light hand. If students read cases in severely abridged versions that include only the essential passages, they will be greatly handicapped when they are required to use cases in their sprawling unabridged original form. Supreme Court opinions are so long today that some abridgement is necessary, but our versions are generally more complete than those of other casebooks.

Second, the structure of the book has been designed to reinforce the students' understanding of what the cases establish and what they leave open. Commentators—and sometimes casebook authors—attempt to impose their own structure on the law of the First Amendment. But for a lawyer seeking to persuade a judge or an adversary, the structure that matters is the structure that the Supreme Court has created. Using that structure as the starting point (while raising questions about it in the note material) enables students to see how the cases build upon one another—or move in new directions.

Third, the book concentrates on the main lines of development and their implications for future disputes rather than traveling down every byway of doctrinal refinement. Each year, the Supreme Court adds as many as 10 new decisions to the already-voluminous body of precedent interpreting the First Amendment. No one can possibly master all of that law through a single law school course. Nor is there any need to do so; if the student is familiar with the principal lines of doctrine, the refinements can easily be fitted into the mental picture that those lines delineate.

Finally, in editing the cases we have acted upon the premise that the Justices' own treatment of precedent can provide a uniquely valuable perspective for gaining an understanding of First Amendment doctrines — their content, their evolution, and their interrelationships. This is so, in part, because not all precedents are equal. While the total number of Supreme Court decisions is large, the body of precedents that the Justices invoke outside their immediate context for more than platitudes or abstractions is relatively small. Most of those cases are included in this Casebook. And in editing the Justices' opinions, we have retained all references to those cases (other than string cites and the like). This enables students to see how the Justices use precedent to build their arguments; it also reinforces students' understanding of the doctrines and ideas covered in previous chapters. As students encounter the landmark precedents again and again, each time approaching them from a different direction, they will come to appreciate the First Amendment landscape as a whole as well as the contours of its individual features.

Supporting materials. As the preceding account suggests, our overriding principle in designing the casebook has been to give primacy to the Justices' own words and the Court's own doctrinal structure. But we have also provided guidance in working with the opinions. Ultimately students will have to learn to work with lengthy cases entirely on their own, but a casebook can help. The notes and questions in this book direct students' attention to critical language in Court opinions, to apparent inconsistencies between decisions addressing similar issues, and to point-counterpoint face-offs between majorities and dissents.

The notes and questions make use of a variety of sources. For example, we have drawn on the rich material now available in the archives from the private papers of the Justices — preliminary drafts of opinions, memorandum exchanges between Justices, and even notes of the Justices' private conferences. These shed light on what was established by existing precedents and how a new decision changes (or does not change) the law.

We also exploit another of the characteristics that makes First Amendment law special: the law is made by a small number of individuals — the Justices of the Supreme Court — and bears the imprint of their individual philosophies as well as their collective judgments. Tracing the views of individual Justices can contribute to an understanding of the larger issues that the members of the Court address in different contexts over a period of years. This provides a vehicle for seeing the connections between doctrines that is internal rather than external.

To assist in that endeavor, Appendix B lists the Justices serving on the Court in every Term starting with 1946. Knowing the volume of the United States Reports in which an opinion is published, you can find who was on the Court at that time. And by seeing who dissented or concurred, you can see which Justices joined in the majority.

Finally, the book includes some problems. These problems have been designed from the overall perspective of the book; their primary purpose is to encourage a close reading of precedent and an understanding of what that precedent stands for. Most of the problems are based on actual cases.

As is evident, we have cast our net widely in writing and compiling the non-case material in this casebook. In part, this is because different approaches work better for different topics. But we also believe that the variety itself makes the course more interesting for the teacher as well as the student. However, the goal remains the same: to enhance the student's understanding of—and ability to use—the law of the First Amendment.

Legal eloquence. There are special rewards in studying the First Amendment. No other area of law has so often inspired the Justices of the Supreme Court to write opinions marked by eloquence and passion. And because words are the lawyer's stock in trade, study of these opinions is a profitable enterprise even for the student who will never litigate a First Amendment case.

Most of the great opinions have been written in defense of First Amendment rights; here you will find memorable language from Holmes, Brandeis, Hughes, Jackson, Harlan, and Brennan—to name only some of the Justices of the past. But there is eloquence on the other side as well, perhaps best illustrated by the writings of Frankfurter and (again) Jackson.

Editing of cases. Although we have gone further than most casebooks in retaining the content of the Justices' opinions, we have not hesitated to adjust matters of format in the interest of readability. (Thus, the cases should not be used for research purposes.) In this, we have followed familiar conventions. Specifically: Omissions are indicated by brackets or ellipses; alterations are indicated by brackets. Most footnotes have been omitted; however, footnotes in opinions and other quoted material retain their original numbers. Citations to cases other than those in the Casebook have generally been deleted. Brackets and internal quotation marks have been omitted from quoted material within cases. Lengthy paragraphs have sometimes been broken up to promote readability.

Acknowledgments

Professor Hellman expresses his thanks for the dedicated efforts of Faculty Secretary Patricia Blake and research assistance by Linda Tashbook of the Library staff. He expresses his appreciation for research support from the University of Pittsburgh School of Law.

Professor Araiza thanks his research assistants: Marvin Espana, Giancarlo Martinez, Rebecca Meyer, and Michael Tal, as well as his faculty assistants: Simone Clemente and Maria Raneri. He also expresses his deep appreciation to Dean Nick Allard of Brooklyn Law School for encouraging his work even while he served as Vice Dean.

Professor Baker appreciates the dedicated efforts of his research assistants: Andrew Figueroa—who performed yeoman service with the copyright permissions—along with Andrew Balthazor, Patrick Brady, Tal Knight, Tucker Pryor, and George Zeckler. He also thanks Veronica Torres for her unfailing staff support. Finally, he does not take for granted the research support of the Florida International University College of Law and the encouragement of former Dean R. Alexander Acosta.

Professor Bhagwat thanks the UC Davis School of Law as well as Deans Kevin Johnson and Madhavi Sunder for generous and unflagging support.

Special thanks go from all of the authors for the dedicated efforts of the staff of the Document Technology Center at the University of Pittsburgh School of Law: LuAnn Driscoll, Barbara Salopek, Karen Knochel, Darleen Mocello, and Vicki DiDomenico.

Permissions

Epstein, Steven B., *Rethinking the Constitutionality of Ceremonial Deism*, 96 COLUM. L. REV. 2083, 2084–85 (1996). Copyright © 1996 Columbia Law Review. All rights reserved. Reprinted by permission.

Excerpt from ACTIVE LIBERTY: INTERPRETING OUR DEMOCRATIC CONSTITUTION by Stephen Breyer, Copyright © 2005 by Stephen Breyer. Used by permission of Alfred A. Knopf, an imprint of the Knopf Doubleday Publishing Group, a division of Random House LLC. All rights reserved.

THE SUPREME COURT IN CONFERENCE: THE PRIVATE DISCUSSIONS BEHIND NEARLY 300 SUPREME COURT DECISIONS (1940–1985), at 433 (Del

Dickson ed., 2001). Copyright © 2001 Oxford University Press. Reprinted by Permission of Oxford University Press, USA.

- For Electronic Edition — The Supreme Court in Conference — The Private Discussions Behind Nearly 300 Supreme Court Decisions (1940–1985) 433 (Del Dickson ed., 2001). Copyright © 2001 Oxford University Press. Reprinted by Permission of Oxford University Press, USA. www.oup.com.

William P. Marshall, *Truth and the Religion Clauses*, 43 DePaul L. Rev. 243, 244-56 & 260-68 (1994). Copyright DePaul Law Review. Reprinted with permission.

Part One

Freedom of Expression

Chapter 1

The Problem of Subversive Advocacy

A. First Encounters

World War I began in Europe in August 1914. The United States remained neutral until the spring of 1917, when German submarines sank several American ships. On April 6, 1917, the United States declared war on Germany. At first, members of Congress resisted the idea of a draft; however, before the month was out, both Houses had approved President Wilson's plan for conscription. Two months later, Congress passed the Espionage Act of 1917. Section 3 of the Act provided as follows:

> Whoever, when the United States is at war, shall willfully make or convey false reports or false statements with intent to interfere with the operation or success of the military or naval forces of the United States or to promote the success of its enemies and whoever, when the United States is at war, shall willfully cause or attempt to cause insubordination, disloyalty, mutiny, or refusal of duty, in the military or naval forces of the United States, or shall willfully obstruct the recruiting or enlistment service of the United States, to the injury of the service or of the United States, shall be punished by a fine of not more than $10,000 or imprisonment for not more than twenty years, or both.

In August 1917, Charles Schenck, general secretary of the Socialist Party, supervised the printing and distribution of leaflets attacking the draft. Schenck was convicted of violating the Act. His case came before the Supreme Court in early 1919, two months after the Armistice ended the war.

Schenck v. United States
249 U.S. 47 (1919)

MR. JUSTICE HOLMES delivered the opinion of the Court.

This is an indictment in three counts. The first charges a conspiracy to violate the Espionage Act of June 15, 1917, § 3, by causing and attempting to cause insubordination, &c., in the military and naval forces of the United States, and to obstruct the recruiting and enlistment service of the United States, when the United States was at war with the German Empire, to-wit, that the defendant wilfully conspired to have printed and circulated to men who had been called and accepted for military service under the Act of May 18, 1917, a document set forth and alleged to be calculated to cause such insubordination and obstruction. The count alleges overt acts in pursuance of the conspiracy, ending in the distribution of the document set forth. [The other two counts alleged the use of the mails to transmit the same documents.] The defendants were found guilty on all the counts. They set up the First Amendment to the Constitution forbidding Congress to make any law abridging the freedom of speech, or of the press, [as a defense]. . . .

The document in question upon its first printed side recited the first section of the Thirteenth Amendment, said that the idea embodied in it was violated by the Conscription Act and that a conscript is little better than a convict. In impassioned language it intimated that conscription was despotism in its worst form and a monstrous wrong against humanity in the interest of Wall Street's chosen few. It said, "Do not submit to intimidation," but in form at least confined itself to peaceful measures such as a petition for the repeal of the act. The other and later printed side of the sheet was headed "Assert Your Rights." It stated reasons for alleging that any one violated the Constitution when he refused to recognize "your right to assert your opposition to the draft," and went on "If you do not assert and support your rights, you are helping to deny or disparage rights which it is the solemn duty of all citizens and residents of the United States to retain." It described the arguments on the other side as coming from cunning politicians and a mercenary capitalist press, and even silent consent to the conscription law as helping to support an infamous conspiracy. It denied the power to send our citizens away to foreign shores to shoot up the people of other lands, and added that words could not express the condemnation such cold-blooded ruthlessness deserves, &c., &c., winding up, "You must do your share to maintain, support and uphold the rights of the people of this country." Of course the document would not have been sent unless it had been intended to have some effect, and we do not see what effect it could be expected to have upon persons subject to the draft except to influence them to obstruct the carrying of it out. The defendants do not deny that the jury might find against them on this point.

But it is said, suppose that that was the tendency of this circular, it is protected by the First Amendment to the Constitution. Two of the strongest expressions are said to be quoted respectively from well-known public men. It well may be that the prohibition of laws abridging the freedom of speech is not confined to previous restraints, although to prevent them may have been the main purpose, as intimated in *Patterson v. Colorado*, 205 U.S. 454, 462 (1907). We admit that in many places and in ordinary times the defendants in saying all that was said in the circular would have been within their constitutional rights. But the character of every act depends upon the circumstances in which it is done. The most stringent protection of free speech would not protect a man in falsely shouting fire in a theatre and causing a panic. It does not even protect a man from an injunction against uttering words that may have all the effect of force. *Gompers v. Bucks Stove & Range Co.*, 221 U.S. 418, 439 (1911). The question in every case is whether the words used are used in such circumstances and are of such a nature as to create a clear and present danger that they will bring about the substantive evils that Congress has a right to prevent. It is a question of proximity and degree. When a nation is at war many things that might be said in time of peace are such a hindrance to its effort that their utterance will not be endured so long as men fight and that no Court could regard them as protected by any constitutional right. It seems to be admitted that if an actual obstruction of the recruiting service were proved, liability for words that produced that effect might be enforced. The statute of 1917 . . . punishes conspiracies to obstruct as well as actual obstruction. If the act, (speaking, or circulating a paper,) its tendency and the intent with which it is done are the same, we perceive no ground for saying that success alone warrants making the act a crime. *Goldman v. United States*, 245 U.S. 474, 477 (1918). Indeed that case might be said to dispose of the present contention if the precedent covers all *media concludendi*. But as the right to free speech was not referred to specially, we have thought fit to add a few words. . . .

Judgments affirmed.

————

Note: Schenck *and Its Antecedents*

1. The discussion of the First Amendment in *Schenck* is contained in the single long paragraph set forth above. What part does precedent play in the holding? Toward the end of the opinion, the Court cites its recent decision in *Goldman v. United States*, 245 U.S. 474, 477 (1918), adding that *Goldman* "might be said to dispose of the present contention if the precedent covers all *media concludendi*," i.e., all steps in the argument. In *Goldman*, the defendants were convicted of conspiring to induce individuals to disobey the law by refusing to register for the draft. The Supreme Court affirmed the convictions. At the page cited in *Schenck*, the Court said:

> [Defendants argue] that no crime results from an unlawful conspiracy to bring about an illegal act joined with the doing of overt acts in furtherance of the conspiracy unless the conspiracy has accomplished its unlawful purpose by causing the illegal act to be committed. This, however, but disregards the settled doctrine that an unlawful conspiracy . . . to bring about an illegal act and the doing of overt acts in furtherance of such conspiracy is in and of itself inherently and substantively a crime punishable as such irrespective of whether the result of the conspiracy has been to accomplish its illegal end.

Is the Court saying that the holding in *Goldman* necessarily embraced rejection of the First Amendment claim in *Schenck*? Is that a plausible reading of *Goldman*?

2. In *Gompers v. Bucks Stove & Range Co.*, 221 U.S. 418 (1911), members of the American Federation of Labor were found in contempt of court by the Supreme Court of the District of Columbia. They had published material in violation of an earlier injunction that barred all boycotts and statements that Bucks Stove & Range was on the "Unfair" or "We don't patronize" lists. The Supreme Court held that such behavior was not constitutionally protected:

> In the case of an unlawful conspiracy, the agreement to act in concert when the signal is published gives the words "Unfair," "We don't patronize,"

or similar expressions, a force not inhering in the words themselves, and therefore exceeding any possible right of speech which a single individual might have. Under such circumstances they become what have been called "verbal acts," and as much subject to injunction as the use of any other force whereby property is unlawfully damaged.

How strong a precedent was this for the holding in *Schenck*?

3. The Court briefly cites the decision in *Patterson v. Colorado*, 205 U.S. 454 (1907). Patterson was the owner and editor of several newspapers in Colorado. The Colorado Supreme Court had invalidated a referendum providing home rule to the city of Denver, and Patterson's newspapers published editorials and cartoons ridiculing the court's decision. Upon application of the state attorney general, Patterson was convicted of criminal contempt. The state supreme court upheld the conviction, holding that it was "entirely immaterial whether the matter published is true or false."

Patterson appealed to the United States Supreme Court, asserting that under the Fourteenth Amendment he had a right to prove the truth of the articles he published. The Court, in an opinion by Justice Holmes, found no violation of the federal Constitution. Justice Holmes wrote:

> We leave undecided the question whether there is to be found in the Fourteenth Amendment a prohibition similar to that in the First. But even if we were to assume that freedom of speech and freedom of the press were protected from abridgments on the part not only of the United States but also of the states, still we should be far from the conclusion that the [defendant] would have us reach. In the first place, the main purpose of such constitutional provisions is "to prevent all such previous restraints upon publications as had been practiced by other governments," and they do not prevent the subsequent punishment of such as may be deemed contrary to the public welfare. The preliminary freedom extends as well to the false as to the true; the subsequent punishment may extend as well to the true as to the false.

Two Justices dissented. Justice Harlan asserted that "the privileges of free speech and of a free press, belonging to every citizen of the United States, constitute essential parts of every man's liberty, and are protected against violation by" the due process clause of the Fourteenth Amendment.

4. Assume that no other Supreme Court precedents were relevant to the issue presented by *Schenck*. What other approaches might the Court have taken to the decision of the case?

5. A few weeks after the *Schenck* decision came down, Holmes wrote to his friend Frederick Pollock, "As it happens I should go farther probably than the majority in favor of [free speech], and I daresay it was partly on that account that the [Chief Justice] assigned the case to me." II HOLMES-POLLOCK LETTERS 7 (Mark DeWolfe Howe ed., 1942). What principle of opinion assignment does this comment suggest? Why might a Chief Justice follow such a practice?

6. On March 18, 1919, another of Holmes's correspondents, Professor Harold J. Laski, wrote to him, "Your analogy of a cry of fire in a crowded theater is, I think, excellent." I HOLMES-LASKI LETTERS 191 (Mark DeWolfe Howe ed., 1953). Do you agree?

————

Note: The "Unrevised Holmes" and Baltzer v. United States

One of Justice Holmes's recent biographers, Sheldon M. Novick, discovered an unpublished dissent by Justice Holmes in *Baltzer v. United States*, a draft obstruction case that was argued two months before *Schenck*. The conviction was ultimately reversed upon the Government's confession of error, so Holmes's dissent became moot. In it he said:

> The only evidence against the [defendants] is that the petition set forth in the indictment was signed and sent by them to the Governor of the State. . . . [The petition] demands that the Governor should stand for a referendum on the draft and advocates the notion that no more expense should be incurred for the war than could be paid for in cash and that war debts should be repudiated. It demands an answer and action or resignation on penalty of defeat at the polls. . . .
>
> It seems to me that this petition to an official by ignorant persons who suppose him to possess power of revision and change that he does not, and demand of him as the price of votes, of course assumed to be sufficient to turn the next election, that he make these changes, was nothing in the world but the foolish exercise of a right. . . .
>
> Real obstructions of the law, giving real aid and comfort to the enemy, I should have been glad to see punished more summarily and severely than they sometimes were. But I think that our intention to put out all our powers in aid of success in war should not hurry us into intolerance of opinions and speech that could not be imagined to do harm, although opposed to our own. It is better for those who have unquestioned and almost unlimited power in their hands to err on the side of freedom. We have enjoyed so much freedom for so long that perhaps we are in danger of forgetting that the bill of rights which cost so much blood to establish still is worth fighting for, and that no tittle of it should be abridged. I agree that freedom of speech is not abridged unconstitutionally in those cases of subsequent punishment with which this court has had to deal from time to time. But the emergency would have to be very great before I could be persuaded that an appeal for political action through legal channels, addressed to those supposed to have power to take such action was an act that the Constitution did not protect as well after as before.

Sheldon M. Novick, *The Unrevised Holmes and Freedom of Expression*, 1991 SUP. CT. REV. 303, 388–90. Novick argues that "Nothing in the *Baltzer* dissent is inconsistent with Holmes's opinion in *Schenck*." Sheldon M. Novick, *Book Review*, 33 WM. & MARY L. REV. 1219, 1231 (1992). Do you agree?

Frohwerk v. United States
249 U.S. 204 (1919)

MR. JUSTICE HOLMES delivered the opinion of the Court.

This is an indictment in thirteen counts. The first alleges a conspiracy between the plaintiff in error and one Carl Gleeser, they then being engaged in the preparation and publication of a newspaper, the Missouri Staats Zeitung, to violate the Espionage Act of June 15, 1917. It alleges as overt acts the preparation and circulation of twelve articles, &c. in the said newspaper at different dates from July 6, 1917, to December 7 of the same year. The other counts allege attempts to cause disloyalty, mutiny and refusal of duty in the military and naval forces of the United States, by the same publications, each count being confined to the publication of a single date. . . . There was a trial and Frohwerk was found guilty on [twelve counts]. He was sentenced to a fine and to ten years [imprisonment].

. . . The absence of a bill of exceptions and the suggestions in the application for mandamus have caused us to consider the case with more anxiety than if it presented only the constitutional question which was the theme of the principal argument here. With regard to that argument we think it necessary to add to what has been said in *Schenck v. United States*, only that the First Amendment while prohibiting legislation against free speech as such cannot have been, and obviously was not, intended to give immunity for every possible use of language. We venture to believe that neither Hamilton nor Madison, nor any other competent person then or later, ever supposed that to make criminal the counselling of a murder within the jurisdiction of Congress would be an unconstitutional interference with free speech.

Whatever might be thought of the other counts on the evidence, if it were before us, we have decided in *Schenck* that a person may be convicted of a conspiracy to obstruct recruiting by words of persuasion. . . . [And] so far as the language of the articles goes there is not much to choose between expressions to be found in them and those before us in *Schenck*.

The first begins by declaring it a monumental and inexcusable mistake to send our soldiers to France, says that it comes no doubt from the great trusts, and later that it appears to be outright murder without serving anything practical; speaks of the unconquerable spirit and undiminished strength of the German nation, and characterizes its own discourse as words of warning to the American people. . . . Later, on August 3, came discussion of the causes of the war, laying it to the administration and saying "that a few men and corporations might amass unprecedented fortunes we sold our honor, our very soul," with the usual repetition that we went to war to protect the loans of Wall Street. Later, after more similar discourse, comes "We say therefore, cease firing."

Next, on August 10, after deploring "the draft riots in Oklahoma and elsewhere" in language that might be taken to convey an innuendo of a different sort, it is said that the previous talk about legal remedies is all very well for those who are past the draft age and have no boys to be drafted, and the paper goes on to give a picture, made as moving as the writer was able to make it, of the sufferings of a drafted man, of his then recognizing that his country is not in danger and that he is being sent to a foreign land to fight in a cause that neither he nor any one else knows anything of, and reaching the conviction that this is but a war to protect some rich men's money. Who then, it is asked, will pronounce a verdict of guilty upon him if he stops reasoning and follows the first impulse of nature: self-preservation; and further, whether, while technically he is wrong in his resistance, he is not more sinned against than sinning; and yet again whether the guilt of those who voted the unnatural sacrifice is not greater than the wrong of those who now seek to escape by ill-advised resistance. . . . On August 31 with more of the usual discourse, it is said that the sooner the public wakes up to the fact that we are led and ruled by England, the better; that our sons, our taxes and our sacrifices are only in the interest of England. . . . Later follow some compliments to Germany and a statement that the Central Powers are carrying on a defensive war. There is much more to the general effect that we are in the wrong and are giving false and hypocritical reasons for our course, but the foregoing is enough to indicate the kind of matter with which we have to deal.

It may be that all this might be said or written even in time of war in circumstances that would not make it a crime. We do not lose our right to condemn either measures or men because the Country is at war. It does not appear that there was any special effort to reach men who were subject to the draft; and if the evidence should show that the defendant was a poor man, turning out copy for Gleeser, his employer, at less than a day laborer's pay, for Gleeser to use or reject as he saw fit, in a newspaper of small circulation, there would be a natural inclination to test every question of law to be found in the record very thoroughly before upholding the very severe penalty imposed. But we must take the case on the record as it is, and on that record it is impossible to say that it might not have been found that the circulation of the paper was in quarters where a little breath would be enough to kindle a flame and that the fact was known and relied upon by those who sent the paper out. Small compensation would not exonerate the defendant if it were found that he expected the result, even if pay were his chief desire. When we consider that we do not know how strong the Government's evidence may have been we find ourselves unable to say that the articles could not furnish a basis for a conviction upon the first count at least. . . . *Judgment affirmed.*

Debs v. United States

249 U.S. 211 (1919)

Mr. Justice Holmes delivered the opinion of the Court.

This is an indictment under the Espionage Act of June 15, 1917, as amended by the Act of May 16, 1918. [The indictment was based on a public speech given by Debs at Canton, Ohio, on June 16, 1918. The fourth count alleged that by delivering the speech Debs obstructed and attempted to obstruct the recruiting and enlistment service of the United States, with intent to do so. Debs was sentenced to ten years' imprisonment.]

The main theme of the speech was socialism, its growth, and a prophecy of its ultimate success. With that we have nothing to do, but if a part or the manifest intent of the more general utterances was to encourage those present to obstruct the recruiting service and if in passages such encouragement was directly given, the immunity of the general theme may not be enough to protect the speech. The speaker began by saying that he had just returned from a visit to the workhouse in the neighborhood where three of their most loyal comrades were paying the penalty for their devotion to the working class — these being Wagenknecht, Baker and Ruthenberg, who had been convicted of aiding and abetting another in failing to register for the draft. He said that he had to be prudent and might not be able to say all that he thought, thus intimating to his hearers that they might infer that he meant more, but he did say that those persons were paying the penalty for standing erect and for seeking to pave the way to better conditions for all mankind. Later he added further eulogies and said that he was proud of them. He then expressed opposition to Prussian militarism in a way that naturally might have been thought to be intended to include the mode of proceeding in the United States.

After considerable discourse that it is unnecessary to follow, he took up the case of Kate Richards O'Hare, convicted of obstructing the enlistment service, praised her for her loyalty to socialism and otherwise, and said that she was convicted on false testimony, under a ruling that would seem incredible to him if he had not had some experience with a Federal Court. . . . The defendant spoke of other cases, and then, after dealing with Russia, said that the master class has always declared the war and the subject class has always fought the battles — that the subject class has had nothing to gain and all to lose, including their lives; that the working class, who furnish the corpses, have never yet had a voice in declaring war and never yet had a voice in declaring peace. "You have your lives to lose; you certainly ought to have the right to declare war if you consider a war necessary." The defendant next mentioned Rose Pastor Stokes, convicted of attempting to cause insubordination and refusal of duty in the military forces of the United States and obstructing the recruiting service. He said that she went out to render her service to the cause in this day of crises, and they sent her to the penitentiary for ten years; that she had said no more than the speaker had said that afternoon; that if she was guilty so was he, and that he would not be cowardly enough to plead his innocence; but that her message that opened the eyes of the people must be suppressed, and so after a mock trial before a packed jury and a corporation tool on the bench, she was sent to the penitentiary for ten years.

There followed personal experiences and illustrations of the growth of socialism, a glorification of minorities, and a prophecy of the success of the international socialist crusade, with the interjection that "you need to know that you are fit for something better than slavery and cannon fodder." The rest of the discourse had only the indirect though not necessarily ineffective bearing on the offences alleged that is to be found in the usual contrasts between capitalists and laboring men, sneers at the advice to cultivate war gardens, attribution to plutocrats of the high price of coal, &c., with the implication running through it all that the working men are not concerned in the war, and a final exhortation, "Don't worry about the charge of treason to your masters; but be concerned about the treason that involves yourselves." The defendant addressed the jury himself, and while contending that his speech did not warrant the charges said, "I have been accused of obstructing the war. I admit it. Gentlemen, I abhor war. I would oppose the war if I stood alone." The statement was not necessary to warrant the jury in finding that one purpose of the speech, whether incidental or not does not matter, was to oppose not only war in general but this war, and that the opposition was so expressed that its natural and intended effect would be to obstruct recruiting. If that was intended and if, in all the circumstances, that would be its probable effect, it would not be protected by reason of its being part of a general program and expressions of a general and conscientious belief.

[Defendant relies on the First Amendment to the Constitution, but that defense was] disposed of in *Schenck*.

There was introduced [into evidence] an "Anti-War Proclamation and Program" adopted at St. Louis in April, 1917, coupled with testimony that about an hour before his speech the defendant had stated that he approved of that platform in spirit and in substance.... This document contained the usual suggestion that capitalism was the cause of the war and that our entrance into it "was instigated by the predatory capitalists in the United States." It alleged that the war of the United States against Germany could not "be justified even on the plea that it is a war in defence of American rights or American 'honor.'" It said: "We brand the declaration of war by our Government as a crime against the people of the United States and against the nations of the world. In all modern history there has been no war more unjustifiable than the war in which we are about to engage." Its first recommendation was, "continuous, active, and public opposition to the war, through demonstrations, mass petitions, and all other means within our power." Evidence that the defendant accepted this view and this declaration of his duties at the time that he made his speech is evidence that if in that speech he used words tending to obstruct the recruiting service he meant that they should have that effect. The principle is too well established and too manifestly good sense to need citation of the books. We should add that the jury were most carefully instructed that they could not find the defendant guilty for advocacy of any of his opinions unless the words used had as their natural tendency and reasonably probable effect to obstruct the recruiting service, &c., and unless the defendant had the specific intent to do so in his mind.

Without going into further particulars we are of opinion that the verdict on the fourth count, for obstructing and attempting to obstruct the recruiting service of the United States, must be sustained....

———

Note: Frohwerk *and* Debs

1. The decisions in *Frohwerk* and *Debs* were handed down one week after the decision in *Schenck*. Are the two cases simply applications of *Schenck*, or do they go further? What light do they shed on what Holmes meant by "clear and present danger"?

2. Eugene V. Debs was the leader of the Socialist Party in the United States. He ran as the party's candidate for president in five elections starting in 1900. In 1920 he conducted his campaign from inside prison while serving his sentence on the Espionage Act conviction affirmed by the Supreme Court. He received nearly one million votes. On Christmas Day of 1921, the winning candidate, President Warren G. Harding, commuted Debs' sentence and ordered his release from prison.

3. In *Frohwerk*, Holmes refers to the views of Hamilton and Madison. What might have prompted this reference, and what sort of argument is Holmes making?

B. The *Abrams* Case and the Holmes Dissent
Abrams v. United States
250 U.S. 616 (1919)

[*Schenck, Frohwerk*, and *Debs* were argued and decided in the Court's 1918–19 Term. In October 1919, the Court heard argument in *Abrams v. United States. Abrams* was a prosecution under the Espionage Act as amended in 1918. The 1918 amendment, sometimes referred to as the "Sedition Act," greatly expanded section 3 of the 1917 Act (set forth on the first page of this chapter). Among other things, the Act made it a crime, when the United States was at war, to

> willfully utter, print, write, or publish any language intended to incite, provoke, or encourage resistance to the United States or to promote the cause of its enemies . . . [or to] willfully by utterance, writing, printing, publication, or language spoken, urge, incite, or advocate any curtailment of production in this country of any thing or things, product or products, necessary or essential to the prosecution of the war in which the United States may be engaged, with intent by such curtailment to cripple or hinder the United States in the prosecution of the war . . . .]

[There were four counts to the indictment. The Court affirmed the conviction under counts three and four, which tracked the language of the prohibitions quoted above.]

Mr. Justice Holmes dissenting.

This indictment is founded wholly upon the publication of two leaflets which I shall describe in a moment. The third count alleges a conspiracy to encourage resistance to the United States in the [war with Germany] and to attempt to effectuate the purpose by publishing the same leaflets. The fourth count lays a conspiracy to incite curtailment of production of things necessary to the prosecution of the war and to attempt to accomplish it by publishing the second leaflet to which I have referred.

The first of these leaflets says that the President's cowardly silence about the intervention in Russia reveals the hypocrisy of the plutocratic gang in Washington. It intimates that "German militarism combined with allied capitalism to crush the Russian revolution"—goes on that the tyrants of the world fight each other until they see a common enemy—working class enlightenment, when they combine to crush it; and that now militarism and capitalism combined, though not openly, to crush the Russian revolution. It says that there is only one enemy of the workers of the world and that is capitalism; that it is a crime for workers of America, &c., to fight the workers' republic of Russia, and ends "Awake! Awake, you workers of the world! Revolutionists." A note adds "It is absurd to call us pro-German. We hate and despise German militarism more than do you hypocritical tyrants. We have more reason for denouncing German militarism than has the coward of the White House."

The other leaflet, headed "Workers—Wake Up," with abusive language says that America together with the Allies will march for Russia to help the Czecko-Slovaks in their struggle against the Bolsheviki, and that this time the hypocrites shall not fool the Russian emigrants and friends of Russia in America. It tells the Russian emigrants that they now must spit in the face of the false military propaganda by which their sympathy and help to the prosecution of the war have been called forth and says that with the money they have lent or are going to lend "they will make bullets not only for the Germans but also for the Workers Soviets of Russia," and further, "Workers in the ammunition factories, you are producing bullets, bayonets, cannon to murder not only the Germans, but also your dearest, best, who are in Russia and are fighting for freedom." It then appeals to the same Russian emigrants at some length not to consent to the "inquisitionary expedition to Russia," and says that the destruction of the Russian revolution is "the politics of the march to Russia." The leaflet winds up by saying "Workers, our reply to this barbaric intervention has to be a general strike!," and after a few words on the spirit of revolution, exhortations not to be afraid, and some usual tall talk ends "Woe unto those who will be in the way of progress. Let solidarity live! The Rebels."

. . . With regard to [the fourth count] it seems too plain to be denied that the suggestion to workers in the ammunition factories that they are producing bullets to murder their dearest, and the further advocacy of a general strike, both in the second leaflet, do urge curtailment of production of things necessary to the prosecution of the war within the meaning of the [1918 Act]. But to make the conduct criminal that statute requires that it should be "with intent by such curtailment to cripple or hinder the United States in the prosecution of the war." It seems to me that no such intent is proved.

I am aware of course that the word intent as vaguely used in ordinary legal discussion means no more than knowledge at the time of the act that the consequences said to be intended will ensue. . . . But, when words are used exactly, a deed is not done with intent to produce a consequence unless that consequence is the aim of the deed. . . .

It seems to me that this statute must be taken to use its words in a strict and accurate sense. They would be absurd in any other. A patriot might think that we were wasting money on aeroplanes, or making more cannon of a certain kind than we needed, and might advocate curtailment with success, yet even if it turned out that the curtailment hindered and was thought by other minds to have been obviously likely to hinder the United States in the prosecution of the war, no one would hold such conduct a crime. I admit that my illustration does not answer all that might be said but it is enough to show what I think and to let me pass to a more important aspect of the case. I refer to the [First Amendment].

I never have seen any reason to doubt that the questions of law that alone were before this Court in the cases of *Schenck, Frohwerk*, and *Debs*, were rightly decided. I do not doubt for a moment that by the same reasoning that would justify punishing persuasion to murder, the United States constitutionally may punish speech that produces or is intended to produce a clear and imminent danger that it will bring about forthwith certain substantive evils that the United States constitutionally may seek to prevent. The power undoubtedly is greater in time of war than in time of peace because war opens dangers that do not exist at other times.

But as against dangers peculiar to war, as against others, the principle of the right to free speech is always the same. It is only the present danger of immediate evil or an intent to bring it about that warrants Congress in setting a limit to the expression of opinion where private rights are not concerned. Congress certainly cannot forbid all effort to change the mind of the country. Now nobody can suppose that the surreptitious publishing of a silly leaflet by an unknown man, without more, would present any immediate danger that its opinions would hinder the success of the government arms or have any appreciable tendency to do so. Publishing those opinions for the very purpose of obstructing, however, might indicate a greater danger and at any rate would have the quality of an attempt. So I assume that the second leaflet if published for the purposes alleged in the fourth count might be punishable. . . .

I do not see how anyone can find the intent required by the statute in any of the defendant's words. The second leaflet is the only one that affords even a foundation for the charge, and there, without invoking the hatred of German militarism expressed in the former one, it is evident from the beginning to the end that the only object of the paper is to help Russia and stop American intervention there against the popular government—not to impede the United States in the war that it was carrying on. . . .

In this case sentences of twenty years imprisonment have been imposed for the publishing of two leaflets that I believe the defendants had as much right to publish as the Government has to publish the Constitution of the United States now vainly invoked by them. Even if I am technically wrong and enough can be squeezed from these poor and puny anonymities to turn the color of legal litmus paper; I will add, even if what I think the necessary intent were shown; the most nominal punishment seems to me all that possibly could be inflicted, unless the defendants are to be made to suffer not for what the indictment alleges but for the creed that they avow—a creed that I believe to be the creed of ignorance and immaturity when honestly held, as I see no reason to doubt that it was held here, but which, although made the subject of examination at the trial, no one has a right even to consider in dealing with the charges before the Court.

Persecution for the expression of opinions seems to me perfectly logical. If you have no doubt of your premises or your power and want a certain result with all your heart you naturally express your wishes in law and sweep away all opposition. To allow opposition by speech seems to indicate that you think the speech impotent, as when a man says that he has squared the circle, or that you do not care whole-heartedly for the result, or that you doubt either your power or your premises. But when men have realized that time has upset many fighting faiths, they may come to believe even more than they believe the very foundations of their own conduct that the ultimate good desired is better reached by free trade in ideas—that the best test of truth is the power of the thought to get itself accepted in the competition of the market, and that truth is the only ground upon which their wishes safely can be carried out. That at any rate is the theory of our Constitution. It is an experiment, as all life is an experiment. Every year if not every day we have to wager our salvation upon some prophecy based upon imperfect knowledge. While that experiment is part of our system I think that we should be eternally vigilant against attempts to check the expression of opinions that we loathe and believe to be fraught with death, unless they so imminently threaten immediate interference with the lawful and pressing purposes of the law that an immediate check is required to save the country.

I wholly disagree with the argument of the Government that the First Amendment left the common law as to seditious libel in force. History seems to me against the notion. I had conceived that the United States through many years had shown its repentance for the Sedition Act of 1798, by repaying fines that it imposed. Only the emergency that makes it immediately dangerous to leave the correction of evil counsels to time warrants making any exception to the sweeping command, "Congress shall make no law . . . abridging the freedom of speech." Of course I am speaking only of expressions of opinion and exhortations, which were all that were uttered here, but I regret that I cannot put into more impressive words my belief that in their conviction upon this indictment the defendants were deprived of their rights under the Constitution of the United States.

———

Note: The Abrams Dissent and Seditious Libel

1. Only Justice Brandeis joined Justice Holmes' dissent in *Abrams*. The other seven Justices joined the majority opinion, which stated:

> It will not do to say, as is now argued, that the only intent of these defendants was to prevent injury to the Russian cause. Men must be held to have intended, and to be accountable for, the effects which their acts were likely to produce. Even if their primary purpose and intent was to aid the cause of the Russian Revolution, the plan of action which they adopted necessarily involved, before it could be realized, defeat of the war program of the United States, for the obvious effect of this appeal, if it should become effective, as they hoped it might, would be to persuade persons of character such as those whom they regarded themselves as addressing, not to aid government loans and not to work in ammunition factories, where their work would produce "bullets, bayonets, cannon" and other munitions of war, the use of which would cause the "murder" of Germans and Russians. . . .

. . . [W]hile the immediate occasion for this particular outbreak of lawlessness, on the part of the defendant alien anarchists, may have been resentment caused by our Government sending troops into Russia as a strategic operation against the Germans on the eastern battle front, yet the plain purpose of their propaganda was to excite, at the supreme crisis of the war, disaffection, sedition, riots, and, as they hoped, revolution, in this country for the purpose of embarrassing and if possible defeating the military plans of the Government in Europe. . . .

2. Justice Holmes' dissent does not describe the circumstances surrounding the distribution of the leaflets. The Court's opinion states that 5000 circulars were printed. Some were thrown from the window of a building where one of the defendants was employed. Others were distributed secretly in New York City. The Court notes that the leaflets were "circulated in the greatest port of our land, from which great numbers of soldiers were at the time taking ship daily, and in which great quantities of war supplies of every kind were at the time being manufactured for transportation overseas." For a vivid account of the events underlying the prosecution, see RICHARD POLENBERG, FIGHTING FAITHS 43–153 (1987).

3. Justice Holmes rejects the Government's argument "that the First Amendment left the common law as to seditious libel in force." He then refers to the Sedition Act of 1798. That Act, signed by President John Adams, made it a crime, punishable by a $5,000 fine and five years in prison, "if any person shall write, print, utter or publish . . . any false, scandalous and malicious writing or writings against the government of the United States, or either house of the Congress . . . , or the President . . . , with intent to defame . . . or to bring them, or either of them, into contempt or disrepute; or to excite against them, or either or any of them, the hatred of the good people of the United States."

More than four decades after *Abrams*, the Supreme Court agreed with Holmes' position: "Although the Sedition Act was never tested in this Court, the attack upon its validity has carried the day in the court of history." *New York Times Co. v. Sullivan*, 376 U.S. 254, 273–76 (1964) (Chapter 2). But is it so clear that punishing Abrams for violation of the Espionage Act is equivalent to punishing him for seditious libel?

C. Learned Hand and the *Masses* Case

Masses Publishing Co. v. Patten

244 Fed. 535 (S.D.N.Y. 1917)

LEARNED HAND, DISTRICT JUDGE.

The plaintiff applies for a preliminary injunction against the postmaster of New York to forbid his refusal to accept its magazine in the mails under the following circumstances: The plaintiff is a publishing company in the city of New York engaged in the production of a monthly revolutionary journal called "The Masses," containing both text and cartoons . . . .

In July, 1917, the postmaster of New York, acting upon the direction of the Postmaster General, advised the plaintiff that the August number to which he had had access would be denied the mails under the Espionage Act of June 15, 1917. [This was the statute under which Schenck, Frohwerk, and Debs were convicted. Under section 12 of the Act, any publication in violation of any of the other provisions of the Act was declared to be nonmailable matter.] . . . [The postmaster,] while objecting generally that the whole purport of the number was in violation of the law, since it tended to produce a violation of the law, to encourage the enemies of the United States, and to hamper the government in the conduct of the war, specified four cartoons and four pieces of text as especially falling within [the statute]. . . .

. . . In this case there is no dispute of fact which the plaintiff can successfully challenge except the meaning of the words and pictures in the magazine. As to these the query must be: What is the extreme latitude of the interpretation which must be placed upon them, and whether that extremity certainly falls outside any of the provisions of the act of June 15, 1917. Unless this be true, the decision of the postmaster must stand. It will be necessary, first, to interpret the law, and, next, the words and pictures.

It must be remembered at the outset [that] no question arises touching the war powers of Congress. . . . It may be that the peril of war, which goes to the very existence of the state, justifies any measure of compulsion, any measure of suppression, which Congress deems necessary to its safety, the liberties of each being in subjection to the liberties of all. . . . Here is presented solely the question of how far Congress after much discussion has up to the present time seen fit to exercise a power which may extend to measures not yet even considered, but necessary to the existence of the state as such. . . .

Coming to the act itself, [the defendant's position is that plaintiff violates section 3 of title 1]. That section contains three provisions. The first is, in substance, that no one shall make any false statements with intent to interfere with the operation or success of the military or naval forces of the United States or to promote the success of its enemies. The defendant says that the cartoons and text of the magazine, constituting, as they certainly do, a virulent attack upon the war and those laws which have been enacted to assist its prosecution, may interfere with the success of the military forces of the United States. . . .

[The defendant's position on this point is correct, but the question is] whether such an attack is a willfully false statement. That phrase properly includes only a statement of fact which the utterer knows to be false, and it cannot be maintained that any of these statements are of fact, or that the plaintiff believes them to be false. They are all within the range of opinion and of criticism; they are all certainly believed to be true by the utterer. As such they fall within the scope of that right to criticise either by temperate reasoning, or by immoderate and indecent invective, which is normally the privilege of the individual in countries dependent upon the free expression of opinion as the ultimate source of authority. The argument may be trivial in substance, and violent and perverse in manner, but so long as it is confined to abuse of existing policies or laws, it is impossible to class it as a false statement of facts of the kind here in question. To modify this provision, so clearly intended to prevent the spreading of false rumors which may embarrass the military, into the prohibition of any kind of propaganda, honest or vicious, is to disregard the meaning of the language, established by legal construction and common use, and to raise it into a means of suppressing intemperate and inflammatory public discussion, which was surely not its purpose.

The next phrase relied upon is that which forbids any one from willfully causing insubordination, disloyalty, mutiny, or refusal of duty in the military or naval forces of the United States. The defendant's position is that to arouse discontent and disaffection among the people with the prosecution of the war and with the draft tends to promote a mutinous and insubordinate temper among the troops. This, too, is true; men who become satisfied that they are engaged in an enterprise dictated by the unconscionable selfishness of the rich, and effectuated by a tyrannous disregard for the will of those who must suffer and die, will be more prone to insubordination than those who have faith in the cause and acquiesce in the means. Yet to interpret the word "cause" so broadly would, as before, involve necessarily as a consequence the suppression of all hostile criticism, and of all opinion except what encouraged and supported the existing policies, or which fell within the range of temperate argument. It would contradict the normal assumption of democratic government that the suppression of hostile criticism does not turn upon the justice of its substance or the decency and propriety of its temper. Assuming that the power to repress such opinion may rest in Congress in the throes of a struggle for the very existence of the state, its exercise is so contrary to the use and wont of our people that only the clearest expression of such a power justifies the conclusion that it was intended.

The defendant's position, therefore, in so far as it involves the suppression of the free utterance of abuse and criticism of the existing law, or of the policies of the war, is not, in my judgment, supported by the language of the statute. Yet there has always been a recognized limit to such expressions, incident indeed to the existence of any compulsive power of the state itself. One may not counsel or advise others to violate the law as it stands. Words are not only the keys of persuasion, but the triggers of action, and those which have no purport but to counsel the violation of law cannot by any latitude of interpretation be a part of that public opinion which is the final source of government in a democratic state. The defendant asserts not only that the magazine indirectly through its propaganda leads to a disintegration of loyalty and a disobedience of law, but that in addition it counsels and advises resistance to existing law, especially to the draft. The consideration of this aspect of the case more properly arises under the third phrase of section 3, which forbids any willful obstruction of the recruiting or enlistment service of the United States, but, as the defendant urges that the magazine falls within each phrase, it is as well to take it up now.

To counsel or advise a man to an act is to urge upon him either that it is his interest or his duty to do it. While, of course, this may be accomplished as well by indirection as expressly, since words carry the meaning that they impart, the definition is exhaustive, I think, and I shall use it. Political agitation, by the passions it arouses or the convictions it engenders, may in fact stimulate men to the violation of law.

Detestation of existing policies is easily transformed into forcible resistance of the authority which puts them in execution, and it would be folly to disregard the causal relation between the two. Yet to assimilate agitation, legitimate as such, with direct incitement to violent resistance, is to disregard the tolerance of all methods of political agitation which in normal times is a safeguard of free government. The distinction is not a scholastic subterfuge, but a hard-bought acquisition in the fight for freedom, and the purpose to disregard it must be evident when the power exists. If one stops short of urging upon others that it is their duty or their interest to resist the law, it seems to me one should not be held to have attempted to cause its violation. If that be not the test, I can see no escape from the conclusion that under this section every political agitation which can be shown to be apt to create a seditious temper is illegal. I am confident that by such language Congress had no such revolutionary purpose in view.

It seems to me, however, quite plain that none of the language and none of the cartoons in this paper can be thought directly to counsel or advise insubordination or mutiny, without a violation of their meaning quite beyond any tolerable understanding. I come, therefore, to the third phrase of the section, which forbids any one from willfully obstructing the recruiting or enlistment service of the United States. . . . Here [again,] since the question is of the expression of opinion, I construe the sentence, so far as it restrains public utterance, as I have construed the other two, and as therefore limited to the direct advocacy of resistance to the recruiting and enlistment service. If so, the inquiry is narrowed to the question whether any of the challenged matter may be said to advocate resistance to the draft, taking the meaning of the words with the utmost latitude which they can bear.

As to the cartoons it seems to me quite clear that they do not fall within such a test. Certainly the nearest is that entitled "Conscription," and the most that can be said of that is that it may breed such animosity to the draft as will promote resistance and strengthen the determination of those disposed to be recalcitrant. There is no intimation that, however hateful the draft may be, one is in duty bound to resist it, certainly none that such resistance is to one's interest. . . .

The text offers more embarrassment. The poem to Emma Goldman and Alexander Berkman, at most, goes no further than to say that they are martyrs in the cause of love among nations. Such a sentiment holds them up to admiration, and hence their conduct to possible emulation. The paragraph in which the editor offers to receive funds for their appeal also expresses admiration for them, but goes no further. The paragraphs upon conscientious objectors are of the same kind. They go no further than to express high admiration for those who have held and are holding out for their convictions even to the extent of resisting the law. It is plain enough that the paper has the fullest sympathy for these people, that it admires their courage, and that it presumptively approves their conduct. Indeed, in the earlier numbers and before the draft went into effect the editor urged resistance. . . .

Moreover, these passages . . . occur in a magazine which attacks with the utmost violence the draft and the war. That such comments have a tendency to arouse emulation in others is clear enough, but that they counsel others to follow these examples is not so plain. . . . One may admire and approve the course of a hero without feeling any duty to follow him. There is not the least implied intimation in these words that others are under a duty to follow. The most that can be said is that, if others do follow, they will get the same admiration and the same approval. Now, there is surely an appreciable distance between esteem and emulation; and unless there is here some advocacy of such emulation, I cannot see how the passages can be said to fall within the law. . . .

. . . The question before me is quite the same as what would arise upon a motion to dismiss an indictment at the close of the proof: Could any reasonable man say, not that the indirect result of the language might be to arouse a seditious disposition, for that would not be enough, but that the language directly advocated resistance to the draft? I cannot think that upon such language any verdict would stand. Of course, the language of the statute cannot have one meaning in an indictment and another when the case comes up here, because by hypothesis, if this paper is nonmailable under section 3 of title 1, its editors have committed a crime in uttering it. . . .

The defendant's action was based, as I understand it, not so much upon the narrow question whether these four passages actually advocated resistance, though that point was distinctly raised, as upon the doctrine that the general tenor and animus of the paper as a whole were subversive to authority and seditious in effect. I cannot accept this test under the law as it stands at present. The tradition of English-speaking freedom has depended in no small part upon the merely procedural requirement that the state point with exactness to just that conduct which violates the law. . . .

It follows that the plaintiff is entitled to the usual preliminary injunction.

————

Note: The Opinion in Masses

1. Although Judge Hand parses the language of the 1917 Act with great care, his opinion has generally been read as articulating—and indeed relying on—constitutional principles. For example, Hand refers to "that right to criticize . . . which is normally the privilege of the individual in countries dependent upon the free expression of opinion as the ultimate source of authority." In a similar vein, he suggests that "public opinion . . . is the final source of government in a democratic state."

What theory of the First Amendment does Judge Hand embrace, and how does he derive the test that he applies from that theory? Consider, in particular, the passages quoted immediately above.

2. Judge Hand's approach to the First Amendment resembles one that is often associated with James Madison. Almost four decades after *Masses*, the Supreme Court drew upon Madison's speeches and writings in explaining how the attack on the validity of the Sedition Act of 1798 had "carried the day in the court of history." (See the Note following *Abrams*.) Justice Brennan wrote for the Court:

Madison prepared [a] Report in support of the protest [against the Act]. His premise was that the Constitution created a form of government under which "The people, not the government, possess the absolute sovereignty." . . .

Earlier, in a debate in the House of Representatives, Madison had said: "If we advert to the nature of Republican Government, we shall find that the censorial power is in the people over the Government, and not in the Government over the people." 4 ANNALS OF CONGRESS, p. 934 (1794).

New York Times Co. v. Sullivan, 376 U.S. 254 (1964) (Chapter 2). As you analyze the issues raised by the cases in this and subsequent chapters, consider how Madison's premise bears on the free-speech claims presented.

3. Note that Judge Hand makes no mention of the speaker's intent. This was not inadvertent. Shortly after reading the opinion in *Debs*, Judge Hand — continuing a prior correspondence — wrote to Justice Holmes:

> All I say is, that since the cases actually occur when men are excited and since juries are especially clannish groups, . . . it is very questionable whether the test of motive is not a dangerous test. Juries wont [sic] much regard the difference between the probable result of the words and the purposes of the utterer. In any case, unless one is rather set in conformity, it will serve to intimidate,—throw a scare into,—many a man who might moderate the storms of popular feeling. I know it did in 1918.

Quoted in Gerald Gunther, *Learned Hand and the Origins of Modern First Amendment Doctrine: Some Fragments of History*, 27 STAN. L. REV. 719, 759 (1975). As you read the cases that follow, consider whether the Supreme Court has adopted Judge Hand's position.

4. Three months after Judge Hand issued the injunction, the Court of Appeals for the Second Circuit reversed. *Masses Publishing Co. v. Patten*, 246 Fed. 24 (1917). The court rejected Judge Hand's view of the law:

> If the natural and reasonable effect of what is said to encourage resistance to a law, and the words are used in an endeavor to persuade to resistance, it is immaterial that the duty to resist is not mentioned, or the interest of the persons addressed in resistance is not suggested. That one may willfully obstruct the enlistment service, without advising in direct language against enlistments, and without stating that to refrain from enlistment is a duty or in one's interest, seems to us too plain for controversy. To obstruct the recruiting or enlistment service, within the meaning of the statute, it is not necessary that there should be a physical obstruction. Anything which impedes, hinders, retards, restrains, or puts an obstacle in the way of recruiting is sufficient. . . .

———

Problem: Protesting a U.S. Military Action

Last year, the United States initiated a military action against the Middle Eastern nation of Saddaq. In announcing the move, the President said, "For several years, terrorists supported by the Saddaqi government have launched deadly raids into peaceful neighboring countries. This aggression must be stopped, and it will be."

On October 13, combat troops and other American military personnel arrived at Andrews Air Force Base near Washington, D.C., from bases throughout the country. Over the next few days, they would be flown to the Middle East to begin combat operations.

On the evening of October 13, a group of American citizens, organized as the Middle Eastern Peace Committee, held a protest rally on the Mall in Washington. The rally was extensively covered on local television. Rosa Stringfellow, one of the organizers of the rally, made a speech that included the following language:

> The President says he is sending troops to stop Saddaqi aggression. That is only a smokescreen. The real purpose is to gain control of the Saddaqi oil fields. Innocent women and children will be killed by American bombs so that American oil companies can dominate the world oil market. Any American citizen who takes part in this slaughter is no better than the German soldiers who helped to run the Nazi concentration camps.

On the basis of that speech, Stringfellow was prosecuted and convicted for violating a statute that provides in relevant part: "Whoever, when the United States is engaged in a military action, shall wilfully cause or attempt to cause insubordination, disloyalty, mutiny, or refusal of duty, in the military forces of the United States" is guilty of a felony.

Would Judge Hand uphold the conviction? Would Justice Holmes?

D. *Gitlow, Whitney*, and the Cases of the Thirties

Today we tend to think of the 1920s as a carefree, even innocent, era. This picture is not entirely inaccurate, but there were also darker currents. The war with Germany had hardly ended when many Americans came to believe that the peace and security of the country were threatened, not by foreign aggression, but by "agitators" and "revolutionaries" within our own borders. Socialists, Communists, anarchists, and others—generally on the political "left"—were subjected to raids, roundups, seizures, and prosecutions.

Two of the prosecutions generated major Supreme Court decisions. Benjamin Gitlow, a member of the Left Wing Section of the Socialist Party, was charged with violating New York's Criminal Anarchy Act. This statute, enacted in the wake of the assassination of President McKinley in 1901, had lain largely unused since then. California invoked its Criminal Syndicalism Act of 1919 against Anita Whitney for helping to organize the Communist Labor Party of California.

Gitlow v. New York
268 U.S. 652 (1925)

Mr. Justice Sanford delivered the opinion of the Court.

[Benjamin Gitlow was convicted of the statutory crime of criminal anarchy. The New York courts affirmed.] The contention here is that the statute, by its terms and as applied in this case, is repugnant to the due process clause of the Fourteenth Amendment. Its material provisions are:

§ 160. *Criminal anarchy defined.* Criminal anarchy is the doctrine that organized government should be overthrown by force or violence, or by assassination of the executive head or of any of the executive officials of government, or by any unlawful means. The advocacy of such doctrine either by word of mouth or writing is a felony.

§ 161. Advocacy of criminal anarchy. Any person who:

1. By word of mouth or writing advocates, advises or teaches the duty, necessity or propriety of overthrowing or overturning organized government by force or violence, or by assassination of the executive head or of any of the executive officials of government, or by any unlawful means; or,

2. Prints, publishes, edits, issues or knowingly circulates, sells, distributes or publicly displays any book, paper, document, or written or printed matter in any form, containing or advocating, advising or teaching the doctrine that organized government should be overthrown by force, violence or any unlawful means . . . .

Is guilty of a felony and punishable [by imprisonment or fine, or both].

The indictment was in two counts. The first charged that the defendant had advocated, advised and taught the duty, necessity and propriety of overthrowing and overturning organized government by force, violence and unlawful means, by certain writings therein set forth entitled "The Left Wing Manifesto"; the second that he had printed, published and knowingly circulated and distributed a certain paper called "The Revolutionary Age," containing the writings set forth in the first count. . . .

. . . The sole contention here is, essentially, that as there was no evidence of any concrete result flowing from the publication of the Manifesto or of circumstances showing the likelihood of such result, the statute as construed and applied by the trial court penalizes the mere utterance, as such, of "doctrine" having no quality of incitement, without regard either to the circumstances of its utterance or to the likelihood of unlawful sequences; and that, as the exercise of the right of free expression with relation to government is only punishable "in circumstances involving likelihood of substantive evil," the statute contravenes the due process clause of the Fourteenth Amendment. . . .

The statute does not penalize the utterance or publication of abstract "doctrine" or academic discussion having no quality of incitement to any concrete action. It is not aimed against mere historical or philosophical essays. It does not restrain the advocacy of changes in the form of government by constitutional and lawful means. What it prohibits is language advocating, advising or teaching the overthrow of organized government by unlawful means. These words imply urging to action. Advocacy is defined in the Century Dictionary as: "1. The act of pleading for, supporting, or recommending; active espousal." It is not the abstract "doctrine" of overthrowing organized government by unlawful means which is denounced by the statute, but the advocacy of action for the accomplishment of that purpose. . . .

The Manifesto, plainly, is neither the statement of abstract doctrine nor, as suggested by counsel, mere prediction that industrial disturbances and revolutionary mass strikes will result spontaneously in an inevitable process of evolution in the economic system. It advocates and urges in fervent language mass action which shall progressively foment industrial disturbances and through political mass strikes and revolutionary mass action overthrow and destroy organized parliamentary government. It concludes with a call to action in these words: "The proletariat revolution and the Communist reconstruction of society — *the struggle for these* — is now indispensable. . . . The Communist International calls the proletariat of the world to the final struggle!" This is not the expression of philosophical abstraction, the mere prediction of future events; it is the language of direct incitement.

The means advocated for bringing about the destruction of organized parliamentary government, namely, mass industrial revolts usurping the functions of municipal government, political mass strikes directed against the parliamentary state, and revolutionary mass action for its final destruction, necessarily imply the use of force and violence, and in their essential nature are inherently unlawful in a constitutional government of law and order. That the jury were warranted in finding that the Manifesto advocated not merely the abstract doctrine of overthrowing organized government by force, violence and unlawful means, but action to that end, is clear.

For present purposes we may and do assume that freedom of speech and of the press — which are protected by the First Amendment from abridgment by Congress — are among the fundamental personal rights and "liberties" protected by the due process clause of the Fourteenth Amendment from impairment by the States. We do not regard the incidental statement in *Prudential Ins. Co. v. Cheek*, 259 U.S. 530, 543 (1922), that the Fourteenth Amendment imposes no restrictions on the States concerning freedom of speech, as determinative of this question. . . .

By enacting the present statute the State has determined, through its legislative body, that utterances advocating the overthrow of organized government by force, violence and unlawful means, are so inimical to the general welfare and involve such danger of substantive evil that they may be penalized in the exercise of its police power. That determination must be given great weight. Every presumption is to be indulged in favor of the validity of the statute. . . . That utterances inciting to the overthrow of organized government by unlawful means, present a sufficient danger of substantive evil to bring their punishment within the range of legislative discretion, is clear. Such utterances, by their very nature, involve danger to the public peace and to the security of the State. They threaten breaches of the peace and ultimate revolution. And the immediate danger is none the less real and substantial, because the effect of a given utterance cannot be accurately foreseen. The State cannot reasonably be required to measure the danger from every such utterance in the nice balance of a jeweler's scale. A single revolutionary spark may kindle a fire that, smouldering for a time, may burst into a sweeping and destructive conflagration. It cannot be said that the State is acting arbitrarily or unreasonably when in the exercise of its judgment as to the measures necessary to protect the public peace and safety, it seeks to extinguish the spark without waiting until it has enkindled the flame or blazed into the conflagration. It cannot reasonably be required to defer the adoption of measures for its own peace and safety until the revolutionary utterances lead to actual disturbances of the public peace or imminent and immediate danger of its own destruction; but it may, in the exercise of its judgment, suppress the threatened danger in its incipiency. . . .

We cannot hold that the present statute is an arbitrary or unreasonable exercise of the police power of the State unwarrantably infringing the freedom of speech or press; and we must and do sustain its constitutionality.

This being so it may be applied to every utterance — not too trivial to be beneath the notice of the law — which is of such a character and used with such intent and purpose as to bring it within the prohibition of the statute. . . . In other words, when the legislative body has determined generally, in the constitutional exercise of its discretion, that utterances of a certain kind involve such danger of substantive evil that they may be punished, the question whether any specific utterance coming within the prohibited class is likely, in and of itself, to bring about the substantive evil, is not open to consideration. It is sufficient that the statute itself be constitutional and that the use of the language comes within its prohibition.

It is clear that the question in such cases is entirely different from that involved in those cases where the statute merely prohibits certain acts involving the danger of substantive evil, without any reference to language itself, and it is sought to apply its provisions to language used by the defendant for the purpose of bringing about the prohibited results. There, if it be contended that the statute cannot be applied to the language used by the defendant because of its protection by the freedom of speech or press, it must necessarily be found, as an original question, without any previous determination by the legislative body, whether the specific language used involved such likelihood of bringing about the substantive evil as to deprive it of the constitutional protection. In such case it has been held that the general provisions of the statute may be constitutionally applied to the specific utterance of the defendant if its natural tendency and probable effect was to bring about the substantive evil which the legislative body might prevent. *Schenck; Debs.* And the general statement in the *Schenck* case that the "question in every case is whether the words used are used in such circumstances and are of such a nature as to create a clear and present danger that they will bring about the substantive evils," — upon which great reliance is placed in the defendant's argument — was manifestly intended, as shown by the context, to apply only in cases of this class, and has no application to those like the present, where the legislative body itself has previously determined the danger of substantive evil arising from utterances of a specified character.

[None of the rulings of the trial court] involved any invasion of the constitutional rights of the defendant. It was not necessary, within the meaning of the statute, that the defendant should have advocated "some definite or immediate act or acts" of force, violence or unlawfulness. It was sufficient if such acts were advocated in general terms; and it was not essential that their immediate execution should have been advocated. Nor was it necessary that the language should have been "reasonably and ordinarily calculated to incite certain persons" to acts of force, violence or unlawfulness. The advocacy need not be addressed to specific persons. . . .

Affirmed.

MR. JUSTICE HOLMES, dissenting.

Mr. Justice Brandeis and I are of opinion that this judgment should be reversed. The general principle of free speech, it seems to me, must be taken to be included in the Fourteenth Amendment, in view of the scope that has been given to the word — liberty — as there used, although perhaps it may be accepted with a somewhat larger latitude of interpretation than is allowed to Congress by the sweeping language that governs or ought to govern the laws of the United States. If I am right then I think that the criterion sanctioned by the full Court in *Schenck* applies: "The question in every case is whether the words used are used in such circumstances and are of such a nature as to create a clear and present danger that they will bring about the substantive evils that [the State] has a right to prevent." It is true that in my opinion this criterion was departed from in *Abrams*, but the convictions that I expressed in that case are too deep for it to be possible for me as yet to believe that it [has] settled the law. If what I think the correct test is applied it is manifest that there was no present danger of an attempt to overthrow the government by force on the part of the admittedly small minority who shared the defendant's views. It is said that this manifesto was more than a theory, that it was an incitement. Every idea is an incitement. It offers itself for belief and if believed it is acted on unless some other belief outweighs it or some failure of energy stifles the movement at its birth. The only difference between the expression of an opinion and an incitement in the narrower sense is the speaker's enthusiasm for the result. Eloquence may set fire to reason. But whatever may be thought of the redundant discourse before us it had no chance of starting a present conflagration. If in the long run the beliefs expressed in proletarian dictatorship are destined to be accepted by the dominant forces of the community, the only meaning of free speech is that they should be given their chance and have their way.

If the publication of this document had been laid as an attempt to induce an uprising against government at once and not at some indefinite time in the future it would have presented a different question. The object would have been one with which the law might deal, subject to the doubt whether there was any danger that the publication could produce any result, or in other words, whether it was not futile and too remote from possible consequences. But the indictment alleges the publication and nothing more.

————

Note: Gitlow *and* Lochner

1. In his famous dissent in *Lochner v. New York*, 198 U.S. 45, 75–76 (1905), Justice Holmes declared:

This case is decided upon an economic theory which a large part of the country does not entertain. If it were a question whether I agreed with that theory, I should desire to study it further and long before making up my mind. But I do not conceive that to be my duty, because I strongly believe that my agreement or disagreement has nothing to do with the right of a majority to embody their opinions in law. It is settled by various decisions of this court that state constitutions and state laws may regulate life in many ways which we as legislators might think as injudicious, or if you like as tyrannical, as this, and which, equally with this, interfere with the liberty to contract. Sunday laws and usury laws are ancient examples. A more modern one is the prohibition of lotteries. . . .

. . . Every opinion tends to become a law. I think that the word "liberty," in the Fourteenth Amendment, is perverted when it is held to prevent the natural outcome of a dominant opinion, unless it can be said that a rational and fair man necessarily would admit that the statute proposed would infringe fundamental principles as they have been understood by the traditions of our people and our law. It does not need research to show that no such sweeping condemnation can be passed upon the statute before us. . . .

Can Holmes' dissent in *Gitlow* be reconciled with this view? Note in particular the standard articulated in the second quoted paragraph. Does Holmes' dissent in *Gitlow* attempt to show that New York's criminal anarchy law "would infringe fundamental principles as they have been understood by the traditions of our people and our law"? Does the last paragraph of the dissent in *Abrams* furnish material for such an argument?

2. If the two dissents represent different approaches to judicial review, is there a way of reconciling them? Consider the implications of Holmes's reference in the *Lochner* dissent to "the natural outcome of a dominant opinion."

Whitney v. California
274 U.S. 357 (1927)

Mr. Justice Sanford delivered the opinion of the Court.

[The Criminal Syndicalism Act of California defined "criminal syndicalism" as "any doctrine or precept advocating, teaching or aiding and abetting the commission of crime, sabotage (which word is hereby defined as meaning willful and malicious physical damage or injury to physical property), or unlawful acts of force and violence or unlawful methods of terrorism as a means of accomplishing a change in industrial ownership or control or effecting any political change." Anita Whitney was convicted on one count of violating the Act. The information charged that she "did [willfully] organize and assist in organizing, and was, is, and knowingly became a member of an organization, society, group and assemblage of persons organized and assembled to advocate, teach, aid and abet criminal syndicalism." The intermediate appellate court affirmed the conviction.]

The following facts, among many others, were established on the trial by undisputed evidence: The defendant, a resident of [Oakland, California,] had been a member of the Local Oakland branch of the Socialist Party. This Local sent delegates to the national convention of the Socialist Party held in Chicago in 1919, which resulted in a split between the "radical" group and the old-wing Socialists. The "radicals"—to whom the Oakland delegates adhered—being ejected, went to another hall, and formed the Communist Labor Party of America. . . . In its "Platform and Program" the Party declared [that] its purpose was "to create a unified revolutionary working class movement in America," organizing the workers as a class, in a revolutionary class struggle to conquer the capitalist state, for the overthrow of capitalist rule, the conquest of political power and the establishment of a working class government, the Dictatorship of the Proletariat. . . .

Shortly thereafter the Local Oakland withdrew from the Socialist Party, and sent accredited delegates, including the defendant, to a convention held in Oakland in November 1919, for the purpose of organizing a California branch of the Communist Labor Party. The defendant, after taking out a temporary membership in the Communist Labor Party, attended this convention as a delegate and took an active part in its proceedings. . . .

While it is not denied that the evidence warranted the jury in finding that the defendant became a member of and assisted in organizing the Communist Labor Party of California, and that this was organized to advocate, teach, aid or abet criminal syndicalism as defined by the Act, it is urged that the Act, as here construed and applied, deprived the defendant of her liberty without due process of law in that it has made her action in attending the Oakland convention unlawful by reason of "a subsequent event brought about against her will, by the agency of others," with no showing of a specific intent on her part to join in the forbidden purpose of the association, and merely because, by reason of a lack of "prophetic" understanding, she failed to foresee the quality that others would give to the convention. . . . This contention, while advanced in the form of a constitutional objection to the Act, is in effect nothing more than an effort to review the weight of the evidence for the purpose of showing that the defendant did not join and assist in organizing the Communist Labor Party of California with a knowledge of its unlawful character and purpose. This question, which is foreclosed by the verdict of the jury, . . . is one of fact merely which is not open to review in this Court, involving as it does no constitutional question whatever. . . .

Nor is the Syndicalism Act as applied in this case repugnant to the due process clause as a restraint of the rights of free speech, assembly, and association. . . .

By enacting the provisions of the Syndicalism Act the State has declared, through its legislative body, that to knowingly be or become a member of or assist in organizing an association to advocate, teach or aid and abet the commission of crimes or unlawful acts of force, violence or terrorism as a means of accomplishing industrial or political changes, involves such danger to the public peace and the security of the State, that these acts should be penalized in the exercise of its police power. That determination must be given great weight. [The statute] may not be declared unconstitutional unless it is an arbitrary or unreasonable attempt to exercise the authority vested in the State in the public interest.

The essence of the offense denounced by the Act is the combining with others in an association for the accomplishment of the desired ends through the advocacy and use of criminal and unlawful methods. It partakes of the nature of a criminal conspiracy. That such united and joint action involves even greater danger to the public peace and security than the isolated utterances and acts of individuals, is clear. We cannot hold that, as here applied, the Act is an unreasonable or arbitrary exercise of the police power of the State, unwarrantably infringing any right of free speech, assembly or association, or that those persons are protected from punishment by the due process clause who abuse such rights by joining and furthering an organization thus menacing the peace and welfare of the State.

[*Judgment affirmed.*]

Mr. Justice Brandeis, concurring. . . .

Despite arguments to the contrary which had seemed to me persuasive, it is settled that the due process clause of the Fourteenth Amendment applies to matters of substantive law as well as to matters of procedure. Thus all fundamental rights comprised within the term liberty are protected by the Federal Constitution from invasion by the States. The right of free speech, the right to teach and the right of assembly are, of course, fundamental rights. See *Meyer v. Nebraska*, 262 U.S. 390 (1923); *Pierce v. Society of Sisters*, 268 U.S. 510 (1925); *Gitlow v. New York*, 268 U.S. 652, 666 (1925). These may not be denied or abridged. But, although the rights of free speech and assembly are fundamental, they are not in their nature absolute. Their exercise is subject to restriction, if the particular restriction proposed is required in order to protect the state from destruction or from serious injury, political, economic or moral. That the necessity which is essential to a valid restriction does not exist unless speech would produce, or is intended to produce, a clear and imminent danger of some substantive evil which the State constitutionally may seek to prevent has been settled. See *Schenck*.

It is said to be the function of the Legislature to determine whether at a particular time and under the particular circumstances the formation of, or assembly with, a society organized to advocate criminal syndicalism constitutes a clear and present danger of substantive evil; and that by enacting the law here in question the legislature of California determined that question in the affirmative. Compare *Gitlow*. The legislature must obviously decide, in the first instance, whether a danger exists which calls for a particular protective measure. But where a statute is valid only in case certain conditions exist, the enactment of the statute cannot alone establish the facts which are essential to its validity. Prohibitory legislation has repeatedly been held invalid, because unnecessary, where the denial of liberty involved was that of engaging in a particular business. The power of the courts to strike down an offending law are no less when the interests involved are not property rights, but the fundamental personal rights of free speech and assembly.

This Court has not yet fixed the standard by which to determine when a danger shall be deemed clear; how remote the danger may be and yet be deemed present; and what degree of evil shall be deemed sufficiently substantial to justify resort to abridgement of free speech and assembly as the means of protection. To reach sound conclusions on these matters, we must bear in mind why a State is, ordinarily, denied the power to prohibit dissemination of social, economic and political doctrine which a vast majority of its citizens believes to be false and fraught with evil consequence.

Those who won our independence believed that the final end of the State was to make men free to develop their faculties; and that in its government the deliberative forces should prevail over the arbitrary. They valued liberty both as an end and as a means. They believed liberty to be the secret of happiness and courage to be the secret of liberty. They believed that freedom to think as you will and to speak as you think are means indispensable to be discovery and spread of political truth; that without free speech and assembly discussion would be futile; that with them, discussion affords ordinarily adequate protection against the dissemination of noxious doctrine; that the greatest menace to freedom is an inert people; that public discussion is a political duty; and that this should be a fundamental principle of the American government. They recognized the risks to which all human institutions are subject. But they knew that order cannot be secured merely through fear of punishment for its infraction; that it is hazardous to discourage thought, hope and imagination; that fear breeds repression; that repression breeds hate; that hate menaces stable government; that the path of safety lies in the opportunity to discuss freely supposed grievances and proposed remedies; and that the fitting remedy for evil counsels is good ones. Believing in the power of reason as applied through public discussion, they eschewed silence coerced by law—the argument of force in its worst form. Recognizing the occasional tyrannies of governing majorities, they amended the Constitution so that free speech and assembly should be guaranteed.

Fear of serious injury cannot alone justify suppression of free speech and assembly. Men feared witches and burnt women. It is the function of speech to free men from the bondage of irrational fears. To justify suppression of free speech there must be reasonable ground to fear that serious evil will result if free speech is practiced. There must be reasonable ground to believe that the danger apprehended is imminent. There must be reasonable ground to believe that the evil to be prevented is a serious one. Every denunciation of existing law tends in some measure to increase the probability that there will be violation of it. [Here Justice Brandeis cited Judge Hand's opinion in *Masses*.] Condonation of a breach enhances the probability. Expressions of approval add to the probability. Propagation of the criminal state of mind by teaching syndicalism increases it. Advocacy of law-breaking heightens it still further. But even advocacy of violation, however reprehensible morally, is not a justification for denying free speech where the advocacy falls short of incitement and there is nothing to indicate that the advocacy would be immediately acted on. The wide difference between advocacy and incitement, between preparation and attempt, between assembling and conspiracy, must be borne in mind. In order to support a finding of clear and present danger it must be shown either that immediate serious violence was to be expected or was advocated, or that the past conduct furnished reason to believe that such advocacy was then contemplated.

Those who won our independence by revolution were not cowards. They did not fear political change. They did not exalt order at the cost of liberty. To courageous, self-reliant men, with confidence in the power of free and fearless reasoning applied through the processes of popular government, no danger flowing from speech can be deemed clear and present, unless the incidence of the evil apprehended is so imminent that it may befall before there is opportunity for full discussion. If there be time to expose through discussion the falsehood and fallacies, to avert the evil by the processes of education, the remedy to be applied is more speech, not enforced silence. Only an emergency can justify repression. Such must be the rule if authority is to be reconciled with freedom. Such, in my opinion, is the command of the Constitution. It is therefore always open to Americans to challenge a law abridging free speech and assembly by showing that there was no emergency justifying it.

Moreover, even imminent danger cannot justify resort to prohibition of these functions essential to effective democracy, unless the evil apprehended is relatively serious. Prohibition of free speech and assembly is a measure so stringent that it would be inappropriate as the means for averting a relatively trivial harm to society. A police measure may be unconstitutional merely because the remedy, although effective as means of protection, is unduly harsh or oppressive. Thus, a state might, in the exercise of its police power, make any trespass upon the land of another a crime, regardless of the results or of the intent or purpose of the trespasser. It might, also, punish an attempt, a conspiracy, or an incitement to commit the trespass. But it is hardly conceivable that this Court would hold constitutional a statute which punished as a felony the mere voluntary assembly with a society formed to teach that pedestrians had the moral right to cross unenclosed, unposted, waste lands and to advocate their doing so, even if there was imminent danger that advocacy would lead to a trespass. The fact that speech is likely to result in some violence or in destruction of property is not enough to justify its suppression. There must be the probability of serious injury to the State. Among free men, the deterrents ordinarily to be applied to prevent crime are education and punishment for violations of the law, not abridgment of the rights of free speech and assembly. . . .

[A declaration of emergency in the Syndicalism Act] satisfies the requirement of the constitution of the State concerning emergency legislation. But it does not preclude inquiry into the question whether, at the time and under the circumstances, the conditions existed which are essential to validity under the Federal Constitution. As a statute, even if not void on its face, may be challenged because invalid as applied, the result of such an inquiry may depend upon the specific facts of the particular case. Whenever the fundamental rights of free speech and assembly are alleged to have been invaded, it must remain open to a defendant to present the issue whether there actually did exist at the time a clear danger; whether the danger, if any, was imminent; and whether the evil apprehended was one so substantial as to justify the stringent restriction interposed by the legislature. The legislative declaration, like the fact that the statute was passed and was sustained by the highest court of the State, creates merely a rebuttable presumption that these conditions have been satisfied.

Whether in 1919, when Miss Whitney did the things complained of, there was in California such clear and present danger of serious evil, might have been made the important issue in the case. [However, Miss Whitney] did not claim that [the statute] was void because there was no clear and present danger of serious evil, nor did she request that the existence of these [conditions] be passed upon by the court or a jury. On the other hand, there was evidence on which the court or jury might have found that such danger existed. I am unable to assent to the suggestion in the opinion of the Court that assembling with a political party, formed to advocate the desirability of a proletarian revolution by mass action at some date necessarily far in the future, is not a right within the protection of the Fourteenth Amendment. In the present case, however, there was other testimony which tended to establish the existence of a conspiracy, on the part of members of the International Workers of the World, to commit present serious crimes; and likewise to show that such a conspiracy would be furthered by the activity of the society of which Miss Whitney was a member. Under these circumstances the judgment of the state court cannot be disturbed.

Our power of review in this case [from a state court] is limited not only to the question whether a right guaranteed by the Federal Constitution was denied, but to the particular claims duly made below, and denied. . . . Because we may not inquire into the errors now alleged I concur in affirming the judgment of the state court.

Mr. Justice Holmes joins in this opinion.

––––––––––

Note: Why Protect Freedom of Speech?

1. In his dissent in *Abrams*, Justice Holmes gave us the "marketplace" metaphor: "the theory of our constitution" is that "free trade in ideas" is valuable because it provides "the best test of truth." Is that the thrust of Justice Brandeis's concurring opinion in *Whitney*? Does Justice Brandeis rely on the theory of free speech embraced by Judge Learned Hand in the *Masses* opinion?

2. Professor Ronald Dworkin has suggested that the justifications for protecting freedom of speech fall into two broad categories. One group of theories "treats free speech as important *instrumentally*, that is, not because people have any intrinsic moral right to say what they wish, but because allowing them to do so will produce good effects for the rest of us." The *Abrams* dissent exemplifies this approach. A second group of theories posits "that freedom of speech is valuable, not just in virtue of the consequences it has, but because it is an essential and 'constitutive' feature of a just political society that government treat all its adult members . . . as responsible moral agents." The essence of this "constitutive" approach is that "Government insults its citizens, and denies their moral responsibility, when it decrees that they cannot be trusted to hear opinions that might persuade them to dangerous or offensive convictions." Ronald Dworkin, Freedom's Law 199–200 (1996) (essay originally published in 1992).

Does the concurring opinion in *Whitney* embrace "constitutive" as well as "instrumental" arguments for protecting free speech? How would a judge — or anyone else — determine whether such arguments are relevant to resolving claims under the First Amendment?

3. As you think about the various content-based restrictions treated in this and later chapters, consider the relevance of "constitutive" and "instrumental" arguments. To what extent are these theories reflected in the Justices' opinions?

————

Note: Organizational Advocacy and Individual Responsibility

1. Under what circumstances may an *individual* be prosecuted for activities on behalf of, or connected to, an *organization* that may have engaged in unprotected advocacy? That is a recurring question in First Amendment law. (What answer does *Whitney* give?) Three decisions of the Court in the 1920s and 1930s addressed the question in different contexts. All reversed convictions under state law.

2. *Fiske v. Kansas*, 274 U.S. 380 (1927). In this case, decided on the same day as *Whitney*, the Court unanimously reversed a conviction under the Kansas Criminal Syndicalism Act. The conviction was based on an information (equivalent to an indictment) that accused Fiske of violating the Act by soliciting membership in the Industrial Workers of the World (IWW). The only evidence offered by the state as to the doctrines advocated by the IWW was a copy of the preamble to the IWW constitution. The information quoted three passages from that preamble:

> [The] working class and the employing class have nothing in common, [and] there can be no peace so long as hunger and want are found among millions of working people and the few who make up the employing class have all the good things of life.

> Between these two classes a struggle must go on until the workers of the World organize as a class, take possession of the earth, and the machinery of production and abolish the wage system.

> Instead of the conservative motto, "A fair day's wages for a fair day's work," we must inscribe on our banner the revolutionary watchword, "Abolition of the wage system." By organizing industrially we are forming the structure of the new society within the shell of the old.

The Court said, "No substantial inference [can] be drawn from the language of this preamble, that the organization taught, advocated or suggested the duty, necessity, propriety, or expediency of crime, criminal syndicalism, sabotage, or other unlawful acts or methods. . . . The result is that the Syndicalism Act has been applied in this case to sustain the conviction of the defendant, without any charge or evidence that the organization in which he secured members advocated any crime, violence or other unlawful acts or methods as a means of effecting industrial or political changes or revolution. Thus applied the Act is an arbitrary and unreasonable exercise of the police power of the State, unwarrantably infringing the liberty of the defendant in violation of the due process clause of the Fourteenth Amendment."

The opinion — by Justice Sanford, the author of both *Gitlow* and *Whitney* — makes no mention of freedom of speech. The only discussion of those cases is in the following passage:

> [The] language of the preamble is essentially different from that of the manifesto involved in *Gitlow*, and lacks the essential elements which brought that document under the condemnation of the law. And it is not as if the preamble were shown to have been followed by further statements or declarations indicating that it was intended to mean, and to be understood as advocating, that the ends outlined therein would be accomplished or brought about by violence or other related unlawful acts or methods. Compare *Whitney* [this day decided].

3. The *Fiske* case is best known today for its holding on Supreme Court review of state court findings of fact:

> [T]his Court will review the finding of facts by a State court where a Federal right has been denied as the result of a finding shown by the record to be without evidence to support it; or where a conclusion of law as to a Federal right and a finding of fact are so intermingled as to make it necessary, in order to pass upon the Federal question, to analyze the facts.

This rule of "independent examination" has been extended to review by federal courts of appeals of findings of fact by federal district courts in First Amendment cases. *See Bose Corp. v. Consumers Union of United States, Inc.*, 466 U.S. 485, 499–511 (1984).

4. *De Jonge v. Oregon*, 299 U.S. 353 (1937). The Court unanimously reversed a conviction under the Criminal Syndicalism Law of Oregon. The indictment, as construed by the state supreme court, charged "that the defendant presided at, conducted and assisted in conducting an assemblage of persons, organization, society and group, to-wit, the Communist Party, [which] was unlawfully teaching and advocating in Multnomah county the doctrine of criminal syndicalism and sabotage." The indictment did not charge that criminal syndicalism or sabotage was advocated at the meeting, either by De Jonge or by anyone else. However, De Jonge did not dispute that the Communist Party as such did advocate the doctrine of criminal syndicalism.

Chief Justice Hughes, writing for the Court, began by specifying more precisely the nature of the charges upon which De Jonge was convicted:

> [While De Jonge] was a member of the Communist Party, he was not indicted for participating in its organization, or for joining it, or for soliciting members or for distributing its literature. He was not charged with teaching or advocating criminal syndicalism or sabotage or any unlawful acts, either at the meeting or elsewhere. . . . His sole offense as charged, and for which he was convicted and sentenced to imprisonment for seven years, was that he had assisted in the conduct of a public meeting, albeit otherwise lawful, which was held under the auspices of the Communist Party.

The Chief Justice then reviewed the precedents and explained why "none of our decisions go to the length of sustaining such a curtailment of the right of free speech and assembly as the Oregon statute demands in its present application." For example, in *Whitney*, "the defendant was found guilty of willfully and deliberately assisting in the forming of an organization for the purpose of carrying on a revolutionary class struggle by criminal methods." The opinion continued:

> Freedom of speech and of the press are fundamental rights which are safe-guarded by the due process clause of the Fourteenth Amendment of the Federal Constitution. *Gitlow* [and other cases]. The right of peaceable assembly is a right cognate to those of free speech and free press and is equally fundamental. . . . These rights may be abused by using speech or press or assembly in order to incite to violence and crime. . . . [But the] rights themselves must not be curtailed. . . .

> . . .

> It follows from these considerations that, consistently with the Federal Constitution, peaceable assembly for lawful discussion cannot be made a crime. . . . If the persons assembling have committed crimes elsewhere, if they have formed or are engaged in a conspiracy against the public peace and order, they may be prosecuted for their conspiracy or other violation of valid laws. But it is a different matter when the State, instead of prosecuting them for such offenses, seizes upon mere participation in a peaceable assembly and a lawful public discussion as the basis for a criminal charge.

> We are not called upon to review the findings of the state court as to the objectives of the Communist Party. Notwithstanding those objectives, the defendant still enjoyed his personal right of free speech and to take part in a peaceable assembly having a lawful purpose, although called by that party.

5. *Herndon v. Lowry*, 301 U.S. 242 (1937). Herndon was convicted of attempting to incite insurrection by violence, in violation of section 56 of the Georgia Penal Code. The Supreme Court reversed by a vote of 5 to 4 in an opinion by Justice Owen Roberts. The Court found that the evidence failed to show that Herndon engaged in the forbidden advocacy. The Court also held, apparently as an independent ground for reversing the conviction, that the statute, as construed and applied in Herndon's trial, did "not furnish a sufficiently ascertainable standard of guilt." Under the state court's construction, a defendant could be convicted if a jury believed that "he ought to have foreseen that his utterances might contribute in any measure to some future forcible resistance to the existing government."

Although the *Herndon* decision is of historical interest, it has played almost no role in the later development of First Amendment law.

E. The Smith Act Prosecutions

In 1945, America's "Greatest Generation" returned home after defeating the Nazi regime in Germany and the empire of Japan. The country's future looked bright. But it was not long before many people began to perceive new threats to peace, security, and even liberty in the United States. The principal source of this concern was the emergence of the Soviet Union as a world power under a Communist government that promoted Communist revolutions in other countries.

By 1951, when the *Dennis* case was decided by the Supreme Court, much had happened to reinforce this concern. An "Iron Curtain" had descended over Eastern Europe as one country after another fell to Soviet domination. Particularly shocking was the 1948 Communist coup in Czechoslovakia. In addition, the Soviet Union had detonated a nuclear weapon, ending America's monopoly of nuclear capability. Alger Hiss—a protégé of Justice Holmes and Felix Frankfurter—had been convicted of perjury for denying that he had engaged in spying for Russia while an official of the State Department. Committees in Congress had begun their investigations of Communist infiltration of newspapers, film-making, and other American institutions.

In the midst of these ominous developments, President Truman's Justice Department brought conspiracy charges against the leaders of the Communist Party of the United States. The Government invoked sections 2 and 3 of the Smith Act, passed by Congress in June 1940 as part of the misleadingly named Alien Registration Act.

Dennis v. United States
341 U.S. 494 (1951)

Mr. Chief Justice Vinson announced the judgment of the Court and an opinion in which Mr. Justice Reed, Mr. Justice Burton and Mr. Justice Minton join.

Petitioners were indicted in July, 1948, for violation of the conspiracy provisions of the Smith Act, during the period of April, 1945, to July, 1948. . . . A verdict of guilty as to all the petitioners was returned by the jury on October 14, 1949. The Court of Appeals affirmed the convictions. We granted certiorari, limited to the following two questions: (1) Whether either § 2 or § 3 of the Smith Act, inherently or as construed and applied in the instant case, violates the First Amendment and other provisions of the Bill of Rights; (2) whether either § 2 or § 3 of the Act, inherently or as construed and applied in the instant case, violates the First and Fifth Amendments because of indefiniteness.

Sections 2 and 3 of the Smith Act provide as follows:

Sec. 2. (a) It shall be unlawful for any person—

(1) to knowingly or willfully advocate, abet, advise, or teach the duty, necessity, desirability, or propriety of overthrowing or destroying any government in the United States by force or violence, or by the assassination of any officer of any such government;

(2) with intent to cause the overthrow or destruction of any government in the United States, to print, publish, edit, issue, circulate, sell, distribute, or publicly display any written or printed matter advocating, advising, or teaching the duty, necessity, desirability, or propriety of overthrowing or destroying any government in the United States by force or violence;

(3) to organize or help to organize any society, group, or assembly of persons who teach, advocate, or encourage the overthrow or destruction of any government in the United States by force or violence; or to be or become a member of, or affiliate with, any such society, group, or assembly of persons, knowing the purposes thereof. . . .

SEC. 3. It shall be unlawful for any person to attempt to commit, or to conspire to commit, any of the acts prohibited by the provisions of . . . this title.

The indictment charged the petitioners with wilfully and knowingly conspiring (1) to organize as the Communist Party of the United States of America a society, group and assembly of persons who teach and advocate the overthrow and destruction of the Government of the United States by force and violence, and (2) knowingly and wilfully to advocate and teach the duty and necessity of overthrowing and destroying the Government of the United States by force and violence. The indictment further alleged that §2 of the Smith Act proscribes these acts and that any conspiracy to take such action is a violation of §3 of the Act.

The trial of the case extended over nine months, six of which were devoted to the taking of evidence, resulting in a record of 16,000 pages. Our limited grant of the writ of certiorari has removed from our consideration any question as to the sufficiency of the evidence to support the jury's determination that petitioners are guilty of the offense charged. Whether on this record petitioners did in fact advocate the overthrow of the Government by force and violence is not before us, and we must base any discussion of this point upon the conclusions stated in the opinion of the Court of Appeals, which treated the issue in great detail.

[The Court of Appeals held that the record supports the following broad conclusions:] that the Communist Party is a highly disciplined organization, adept at infiltration into strategic positions, use of aliases, and double-meaning language; that the Party is rigidly controlled; that Communists, unlike other political parties, tolerate no dissension from the policy laid down by the guiding forces, but that the approved program is slavishly followed by the members of the Party; that the literature of the Party and the statements and activities of its leaders, petitioners here, advocate, and the general goal of the Party was, during the period in question, to achieve a successful overthrow of the existing order by force and violence. . . .

The obvious purpose of the [Smith Act] is to protect existing Government, not from change by peaceable, lawful and constitutional means, but from change by violence, revolution and terrorism. That it is within the *power* of the Congress to protect the Government of the United States from armed rebellion is a proposition which requires little discussion. . . . The question with which we are concerned here is not whether

Congress has such *power*, but whether the *means* which it has employed conflict with the First and Fifth Amendments to the Constitution. . . .

[In *Gitlow*, Justices Holmes and Brandeis in dissent] made no distinction between a federal statute which made certain acts unlawful, the evidence to support the conviction being speech, and a statute which made speech itself the crime. In [the *Whitney* concurrence Justices Brandeis and Holmes] repeated that even though the legislature had designated certain speech as criminal, this could not prevent the defendant from showing that there was no danger that the substantive evil would be brought about.

Although no case subsequent to *Whitney* and *Gitlow* has expressly overruled the majority opinions in those cases, there is little doubt that subsequent opinions have inclined toward the Holmes-Brandeis rationale. . . .

In this case we are squarely presented with the application of the "clear and present danger" test, and must decide what that phrase imports. We first note that many of the cases in which this Court has reversed convictions by use of this or similar tests have been based on the fact that the interest which the State was attempting to protect was itself too insubstantial to warrant restriction of speech. . . . Overthrow of the Government by force and violence is certainly a substantial enough interest for the Government to limit speech. . . . If, then, this interest may be protected, the literal problem which is presented is what has been meant by the use of the phrase "clear and present danger" of the utterances bringing about the evil within the power of Congress to punish.

Obviously, the words cannot mean that before the Government may act, it must wait until the *putsch* is about to be executed, the plans have been laid and the signal is awaited. If Government is aware that a group aiming at its overthrow is attempting to indoctrinate its members and to commit them to a course whereby they will strike when the leaders feel the circumstances permit, action by the Government is required. The argument that there is no need for Government to concern itself, for Government is strong, it possesses ample powers to put down a rebellion, it may defeat the revolution with ease needs no answer. For that is not the question. Certainly an attempt to overthrow the Government by force, even though doomed from the outset because of inadequate numbers or power of the revolutionists, is a sufficient evil for Congress to prevent. The damage which such attempts create both physically and politically to a nation makes it impossible to measure the validity in terms of the probability of success, or the immediacy of a successful attempt.

In the instant case the trial judge charged the jury that they could not convict unless they found that petitioners intended to overthrow the Government "as speedily as circumstances would permit." This does not mean, and could not properly mean, that they would not strike until there was certainty of success. What was meant was that the revolutionists would strike when they thought the time was ripe. We must therefore reject the contention that success or probability of success is the criterion.

The situation with which Justices Holmes and Brandeis were concerned in *Gitlow* was a comparatively isolated event, bearing little relation in their minds to any substantial threat to the safety of the community. Such also is true of cases like *Fiske* and *DeJonge*. They were not confronted with any situation comparable to the instant one—the development of an apparatus designed and dedicated to the overthrow of the Government, in the context of world crisis after crisis.

Chief Judge Learned Hand, writing for the majority below, interpreted the phrase as follows: "In each case [courts] must ask whether the gravity of the 'evil,' discounted by its improbability, justifies such invasion of free speech as is necessary to avoid the danger." We adopt this statement of the rule. As articulated by Chief Judge Hand, it is as succinct and inclusive as any other we might devise at this time. It takes into consideration those factors which we deem relevant, and relates their significances. More we cannot expect from words.

Likewise, we are in accord with the court below, which affirmed the trial court's finding that the requisite danger existed. The mere fact that from the period 1945 to 1948 petitioners' activities did not result in an attempt to overthrow the Government by force and violence is of course no answer to the fact that there was a group that was ready to make the attempt. The formation by petitioners of such a highly organized conspiracy, with rigidly disciplined members subject to call when the leaders, these petitioners, felt that the time had come for action, coupled with the inflammable nature of world conditions, similar uprisings in other countries, and the touch-and-go nature of our relations with countries with whom petitioners were in the very least ideologically attuned, convince us that their convictions were justified on this score. And this analysis disposes of the contention that a conspiracy to advocate, as distinguished from the advocacy itself, cannot be constitutionally restrained, because it comprises only the preparation. It is the existence of the conspiracy which creates the danger. If the ingredients of the reaction are present, we cannot bind the Government to wait until the catalyst is added.

Although we have concluded that the finding that there was a sufficient danger to warrant the application of the statute was justified on the merits, there remains the problem of whether the trial judge's treatment of the issue was correct. He charged the jury, in relevant part, as follows:

> In further construction and interpretation of the statute I charge you that it is not the abstract doctrine of overthrowing or destroying organized government by unlawful means which is denounced by this law, but the teaching and advocacy of action for the accomplishment of that purpose, by language reasonably and ordinarily calculated to incite persons to such action. Accordingly, you cannot find the defendants or any of them guilty of the crime charged unless you are satisfied beyond a reasonable doubt that they conspired to organize a society, group and assembly of persons who teach and advocate the overthrow or destruction of the Government of the United States by force and violence and to advocate and teach the duty and necessity of overthrowing or destroying the Government of the United States by force and violence, with the intent that such teaching and advocacy be of a rule or principle of action and by language reasonably and ordinarily

calculated to incite persons to such action, all with the intent to cause the overthrow or destruction of the Government of the United States by force and violence as speedily as circumstances would permit.

If you are satisfied that the evidence establishes beyond a reasonable doubt that the defendants, or any of them, are guilty of a violation of the statute, as I have interpreted it to you, I find as matter of law that there is sufficient danger of a substantive evil that the Congress has a right to prevent to justify the application of the statute under the First Amendment of the Constitution. . . .

[The defendants argue] that a jury must decide a question of the application of the First Amendment. We do not agree. . . . The doctrine that there must be a clear and present danger of a substantive evil that Congress has a right to prevent is a judicial rule to be applied as a matter of law by the courts. . . .

We hold that §§ 2(a)(1), 2(a)(3) and 3 of the Smith Act do not inherently, or as construed or applied in the instant case, violate the First Amendment and other provisions of the Bill of Rights. . . . Petitioners intended to overthrow the Government of the United States as speedily as the circumstances would permit. Their conspiracy to organize the Communist Party and to teach and advocate the overthrow of the Government of the United States by force and violence created a "clear and present danger" of an attempt to overthrow the Government by force and violence. They were properly and constitutionally convicted for violation of the Smith Act. The judgments of conviction are *affirmed*.

Mr. Justice Clark took no part in the consideration or decision of this case.

Mr. Justice Frankfurter, concurring in affirmance of the judgment.

. . . The appellants maintain that they have a right to advocate a political theory, so long, at least, as their advocacy does not create an immediate danger of obvious magnitude to the very existence of our present scheme of society. On the other hand, the Government asserts the right to safeguard the security of the Nation by such a measure as the Smith Act. . . .

But how are competing interests to be assessed? Since they are not subject to quantitative ascertainment, the issue necessarily resolves itself into asking, who is to make the adjustment?—who is to balance the relevant factors and ascertain which interest is in the circumstances to prevail? Full responsibility for the choice cannot be given to the courts. Courts are not representative bodies. They are not designed to be a good reflex of a democratic society. Their judgment is best informed, and therefore most dependable, within narrow limits. Their essential quality is detachment, founded on independence. History teaches that the independence of the judiciary is jeopardized when courts become embroiled in the passions of the day and assume primary responsibility in choosing between competing political, economic and social pressures. . . .

. . . Free-speech cases are not an exception to the principle that we are not legislators, that direct policy-making is not our province. How best to reconcile competing interests is the business of legislatures, and the balance they strike is a judgment not to be displaced by ours, but to be respected unless outside the pale of fair judgment. . . .

. . . Not every type of speech occupies the same position on the scale of values. . . . The defendants have been convicted of conspiring to organize a party of persons who advocate the overthrow of the Government by force and violence. The jury has found that the object of the conspiracy is advocacy as "a rule or principle of action," "by language reasonably and ordinarily calculated to incite persons to such action," and with the intent to cause the overthrow "as speedily as circumstances would permit." On any scale of values which we have hitherto recognized, speech of this sort ranks low.

Throughout our decisions there has recurred a distinction between the statement of an idea which may prompt its hearers to take unlawful action, and advocacy that such action be taken. . . . It is true that there is no divining rod by which we may locate "advocacy." Exposition of ideas readily merges into advocacy. . . . But there is underlying validity in the [distinction,] and we do not discard a useful tool because it may be misused. That such a distinction could be used unreasonably by those in power against hostile or unorthodox views does not negate the fact that it may be used reasonably against an organization wielding the power of the centrally controlled international Communist movement. The object of the conspiracy before us is so clear that the chance of error in saying that the defendants conspired to advocate rather than to express ideas is slight. Mr. Justice Douglas quite properly points out that the conspiracy before us is not a conspiracy to overthrow the Government. But it would be equally wrong to treat it as a seminar in political theory.

These general considerations underlie decision of the case before us.

On the one hand is the interest in security. The Communist Party was not designed by these defendants as an ordinary political party. . . . The jury found that the Party rejects the basic premise of our political system — that change is to be brought about by nonviolent constitutional process. . . .

In finding that the defendants violated the statute, we may not treat as established fact that the Communist Party in this country is of significant size, well-organized, well-disciplined, conditioned to embark on unlawful activity when given the command. But in determining whether application of the statute to the defendants is within the constitutional powers of Congress, we are not limited to the facts found by the jury. . . . We may take judicial notice that the Communist doctrines which these defendants have conspired to advocate are in the ascendency in powerful nations who cannot be acquitted of unfriendliness to the institutions of this country. . . . In sum, [the evidence at trial and matters of common knowledge] would amply justify a legislature in concluding that recruitment of additional members for the Party would create a substantial danger to national security. . . .

On the other hand is the interest in free speech. The right to exert all governmental powers in aid of maintaining our institutions and resisting their physical overthrow does not include intolerance of opinions and speech that cannot do harm although opposed and perhaps alien to dominant, traditional opinion. . . . It is better for those who have almost unlimited power of government in their hands to err on the side of freedom. We have enjoyed so much freedom for so long that we are perhaps in danger of forgetting how much blood it cost to establish the Bill of Rights.

. . . A public interest is not wanting in granting freedom to speak their minds even to those who advocate the overthrow of the Government by force. For, as the evidence in this case abundantly illustrates, coupled with such advocacy is criticism of defects in our society. . . . Suppressing advocates of overthrow inevitably will also silence critics who do not advocate overthrow but fear that their criticism may be so construed. No matter how clear we may be that the defendants now before us are preparing to overthrow our Government at the propitious moment, it is self-delusion to think that we can punish them for their advocacy without adding to the risks run by loyal citizens who honestly believe in some of the reforms these defendants advance. It is a sobering fact that in sustaining the convictions before us we can hardly escape restriction on the interchange of ideas. . . .

It is not for us to decide how we would adjust the clash of interests which this case presents were the primary responsibility for reconciling it ours. Congress has determined that the danger created by advocacy of overthrow justifies the ensuing restriction on freedom of speech. The determination was made after due deliberation, and the seriousness of the congressional purpose is attested by the volume of legislation passed to effectuate the same ends. . . .

To make validity of legislation depend on judicial reading of events still in the womb of time—a forecast, that is, of the outcome of forces at best appreciated only with knowledge of the topmost secrets of nations—is to charge the judiciary with duties beyond its equipment. . . .

. . . The too easy transition from disapproval of what is undesirable to condemnation as unconstitutional, has led some of the wisest judges to question the wisdom of our scheme in lodging such authority in courts. But it is relevant to remind that in sustaining the power of Congress in a case like this nothing irrevocable is done. The democratic process at all events is not impaired or restricted. . . . All the Court says is that Congress was not forbidden by the Constitution to pass this enactment and that a prosecution under it may be brought against a conspiracy such as the one before us.

The wisdom of the assumptions underlying the legislation and prosecution is another matter. In finding that Congress has acted within its power, a judge does not remotely imply that he favors the implications that lie beneath the legal issues. . . .

Civil liberties draw at best only limited strength from legal guaranties. Preoccupation by our people with the constitutionality, instead of with the wisdom, of legislation or of executive action is preoccupation with a false value. . . . Much that should be rejected as illiberal, because repressive and envenoming, may well be not unconstitutional. . . .

Mr. Justice Jackson, concurring.

. . . The principal reliance of the defense in this Court is that the conviction cannot stand under the Constitution because the conspiracy of these defendants presents no "clear and present danger" of imminent or foreseeable overthrow. . . .

The Communist Party . . . does not seek its strength primarily in numbers. Its aim is a relatively small party whose strength is in selected, dedicated, indoctrinated, and rigidly disciplined members. . . . It seeks members that are, or may be, secreted in strategic posts in transportation, communications, industry [and government]. . . . Through these placements in positions of power it seeks a leverage over society that will make up in power of coercion what it lacks in power of persuasion. . . .

. . . Communist technique in the overturn of a free government was disclosed by the *coup d'etat* in which they seized power in Czechoslovakia. There the Communist Party during its preparatory stage claimed and received protection for its freedoms of speech, press, and assembly. [Here Justice Jackson described in detail the various stages by which the Communists took control of governmental and other essential functions.] A virtually bloodless abdication by the elected government admitted the Communists to power, whereupon they instituted a reign of oppression and terror, and ruthlessly denied to all others the freedoms which had sheltered their conspiracy. . . .

I would save [the "clear and present danger" test], unmodified, for application as a "rule of reason" in the kind of case for which it was devised. When the issue is criminality of a hot-headed speech on a street corner, or circulation of a few incendiary pamphlets, or parading by some zealots behind a red flag, or refusal of a handful of school children to salute our flag, it is not beyond the capacity of the judicial process to gather, comprehend, and weigh the necessary materials for decision whether it is a clear and present danger of substantive evil or a harmless letting off of steam. . . . [But if] we must decide that this Act and its application are constitutional only if we are convinced that petitioner's conduct creates a "clear and present danger" of violent overthrow, we must appraise imponderables, including international and national phenomena which baffle the best informed foreign offices and our most experienced politicians. We would have to foresee and predict the effectiveness of Communist propaganda, opportunities for infiltration, whether, and when, a time will come that they consider propitious for action, and whether and how fast our existing government will deteriorate. And we would have to speculate as to whether an approaching Communist *coup* would not be anticipated by a nationalistic fascist movement. . . .

The authors of the clear and present danger test never applied it to a case like this, nor would I. If applied as it is proposed here, it means that the Communist plotting is protected during its period of incubation; its preliminary stages of organization and preparation are immune from the law; the Government can move only after imminent action is manifest, when it would, of course, be too late. . . . I think direct incitement [to violent overthrow] by speech or writing can be made a crime, and I think there can be a conviction without also proving that the odds favored its success by 99 to 1, or some other extremely high ratio. . . .

I do not suggest that Congress could punish conspiracy to advocate something, the doing of which it may not punish. Advocacy or exposition of the doctrine of communal property ownership, or any political philosophy unassociated with advocacy of its imposition by force or seizure of government by unlawful means could not be reached through conspiracy prosecution. But it is not forbidden to put down force or violence, it is not forbidden to punish its teaching or advocacy, and the end being punishable, there is no doubt of the power to punish conspiracy for the purpose. . . .

MR. JUSTICE BLACK, dissenting.

. . . [T]he other opinions in this case show that the only way to affirm these convictions is to repudiate directly or indirectly the established "clear and present danger" rule. This the Court does in a way which greatly restricts the protections afforded by the First Amendment. . . .

So long as this Court exercises the power of judicial review of legislation, I cannot agree that the First Amendment permits us to sustain laws suppressing freedom of speech and press on the basis of Congress' or our own notions of mere "reasonableness." Such a doctrine waters down the First Amendment so that it amounts to little more than an admonition to Congress. . . .

MR. JUSTICE DOUGLAS, dissenting.

If this were a case where those who claimed protection under the First Amendment were teaching the techniques of sabotage, the assassination of the President, the filching of documents from public files, the planting of bombs, the art of street warfare, and the like, I would have no doubts. . . . But the fact is that no such evidence was introduced at the trial. . . .

So far as the present record is concerned, what petitioners did was to organize people to teach and themselves teach the Marxist-Leninist doctrine contained chiefly in four books: STALIN, FOUNDATIONS OF LENINISM (1924); MARX AND ENGELS, THE COMMUNIST MANIFESTO (1848); LENIN, THE STATE AND REVOLUTION (1917); HISTORY OF THE COMMUNIST PARTY OF THE SOVIET UNION (B.) (1939). . . .

The opinion of the Court does not outlaw these texts nor condemn them to the fire, as the Communists do literature offensive to their creed. But if the books themselves are not outlawed, if they can lawfully remain on library shelves, by what reasoning does their use in a classroom become a crime? . . . The Act, as construed, requires the element of intent—that those who teach the creed believe in it. The crime then depends not on what is taught but on who the teacher is. That is to make freedom of speech turn not on *what is said*, but on the *intent* with which it is said. . . .

There comes a time when even speech loses its constitutional immunity. Speech innocuous one year may at another time fan such destructive flames that it must be halted in the interests of the safety of the Republic. That is the meaning of the clear and present danger test. When conditions are so critical that there will be no time to avoid the evil that the speech threatens, it is time to call a halt. Otherwise, free speech which is the strength of the Nation will be the cause of its destruction. . . .

. . . This record, however, contains no evidence whatsoever showing that the acts charged *viz.*, the teaching of the Soviet theory of revolution with the hope that it will be realized, have created any clear and present danger to the Nation. . . . If we are to take judicial notice of the threat of Communists within the nation, it should not be difficult to conclude that *as a political party* they are of little consequence. . . . Communism in the world scene is no bogeyman; but Communism as a political faction or party in this country plainly is. Communism has been so thoroughly exposed in this country that it has been crippled as a political force. Free speech has destroyed it as an effective political party. . . .

How it can be said that there is a clear and present danger that this advocacy will succeed is, therefore, a mystery. Some nations less resilient than the United States, where illiteracy is high and where democratic traditions are only budding, might have to take drastic steps and jail these men for merely speaking their creed. But in America they are miserable merchants of unwanted ideas; their wares remain unsold. . . .

The political impotence of the Communists in this country does not, of course, dispose of the problem. Their numbers; their positions in industry and government; the extent to which they have in fact infiltrated the police, the armed services, transportation, stevedoring, power plants, munitions works, and other critical places—these facts all bear on the likelihood that their advocacy of the Soviet theory of revolution will endanger the Republic. But the record is silent on these facts. . . . On this record no one can say that petitioners and their converts are in such a strategic position as to have even the slightest chance of achieving their aims. . . .

———

Note: Dennis *and Revolutionary Speech*

1. As noted at the outset of the plurality opinion, the Court limited its grant of certiorari to two of the questions presented by the petitioners. Excluded from the grant was the question whether "as to each of the petitioners, the evidence was sufficient to sustain the conviction." Also excluded was the question whether the trial court "prejudicially erred in the admission and reception of evidence." (Petition for Certiorari at 10.) What do you think was the effect on the decisional process of excluding these questions—particularly the first—from those that the Court had to decide?

2. Professor Harry Kalven once commented: "No one advocates violent overthrow of the government without advancing some premises in favor of his conclusion. It is the premises and not the conclusion that are worth protecting." Harry Kalven, *The Metaphysics of the Law of Obscenity*, 1960 SUP. CT. REV. 1, 11 (1961). Do you agree with Kalven's characterization of "revolutionary speech"? Does the *Dennis* Court? Did the *Dennis* Court succeed in protecting the Communists' right to advance their premises?

3. Justice Douglas, in dissent, says that in America the Communists "are miserable merchants of unwanted ideas; their wares remain unsold." It's a great phrase, but is it responsive to the arguments made by the majority? Consider particularly the two concurring opinions.

Note: Yates, Scales, *and* Noto

1. The *Dennis* decision was handed down in June 1951. Six months later, the Government filed an indictment charging a different group of individuals with conspiring to commit offenses prohibited by the Smith Act. The defendants were convicted, and the convictions came before the Supreme Court in *Yates v. United States*, 354 U.S. 298 (1957).

As summarized by the Court, the indictment in *Yates* charged the defendants with:

> conspiring (1) to advocate and teach the duty and necessity of overthrowing the Government of the United States by force and violence, and (2) to organize, as the Communist Party of the United States, a society of persons who so advocate and teach, all with the intent of causing the overthrow of the Government by force and violence as speedily as circumstances would permit. The conspiracy is alleged to have originated in 1940 and continued down to the date of the indictment in 1951.
>
> The indictment charged that in carrying out the conspiracy the defendants and their co-conspirators would (a) become members and officers of the Communist Party, with knowledge of its unlawful purposes, and assume leadership in carrying out its policies and activities; (b) cause to be organized units of the Party in California and elsewhere; (c) write and publish, in the "Daily Worker" and other Party organs, articles on the proscribed advocacy and teaching; (d) conduct schools for the indoctrination of Party members in such advocacy and teaching; and (e) recruit new Party members, particularly from among persons employed in the key industries of the nation. Twenty-three overt acts in furtherance of the conspiracy were alleged.

The lower courts believed that *Dennis* was controlling, but the Supreme Court disagreed. Justice Harlan, writing for the Court, purported to decide the case as a matter of statutory construction. He explained:

> The legislative history of the Smith Act and related bills shows beyond all question that Congress was aware of the distinction between the advocacy or teaching of abstract doctrine and the advocacy or teaching of action, and that it did not intend to disregard it. The statute was aimed at the advocacy and teaching of concrete action for the forcible overthrow of the Government, and not of principles divorced from action. . . .
>
> There can be no doubt from the record that in . . . instructing the jury the court regarded as immaterial, and intended to withdraw from the jury's consideration, any issue as to the character of the advocacy in terms of its capacity to stir listeners to forcible action. . . . We are thus faced with the question whether the Smith Act prohibits advocacy and teaching of forcible overthrow as an abstract principle, divorced from any effort to instigate action to that end, so long as such advocacy or teaching is engaged in with evil intent. We hold that it does not.
>
> The distinction between advocacy of abstract doctrine and advocacy directed at promoting unlawful action is one that has been consistently recognized in the opinions of this Court. . . .
>
> In failing to distinguish between advocacy of forcible overthrow as an abstract doctrine and advocacy of action to that end, the District Court appears

to have been led astray by the holding in *Dennis* that advocacy of violent action to be taken at some future time was enough. . . . The essence of the *Dennis* holding was that indoctrination of a group in preparation for future violent action, as well as exhortation to immediate action, by advocacy found to be directed to "action for the accomplishment" of forcible overthrow, to violence as "a rule or principle of action," and employing "language of incitement," is not constitutionally protected when the group is of sufficient size and cohesiveness, is sufficiently oriented towards action, and other circumstances are such as reasonably to justify apprehension that action will occur. This is quite a different thing from the view of the District Court here that mere doctrinal justification of forcible overthrow, if engaged in with the intent to accomplish overthrow, is punishable *per se* under the Smith Act. That sort of advocacy, even though uttered with the hope that it may ultimately lead to violent revolution, is too remote from concrete action to be regarded as the kind of indoctrination preparatory to action which was condemned in *Dennis*. . . .

In light of the foregoing we are unable to regard the District Court's charge upon this aspect of the case as adequate. The jury was never told that the Smith Act does not denounce advocacy in the sense of preaching abstractly the forcible overthrow of the Government. . . . The essential distinction is that those to whom the advocacy is addressed must be urged to *do* something, now or in the future, rather than merely to *believe* in something. . . .

The Court then reviewed the evidence in the record against the 14 convicted defendants. The Court concluded that the evidence against five petitioners was "so clearly insufficient that their acquittal should be ordered," but that as to nine other petitioners, a retrial would be permissible.

Justice Clark dissented alone. He quoted the Court's statement (above) of the "essence of the *Dennis* holding" and commented: "I have read this statement over and over but do not seem to grasp its meaning for I see no resemblance between it and what the respected Chief Justice wrote in *Dennis*, nor do I find any such theory in the concurring opinions." Justice Brennan and Justice Whittaker, who joined the Court after the case was argued, took no part in the decision.

2. Four years after *Yates*, in *Scales v. United States*, 367 U.S. 203 (1961), the Court considered a conviction under the membership clause of the Smith Act. Again Justice Harlan wrote for the Court, but this time the Court affirmed the conviction. The Court began by outlining the substance of the membership clause and the relationship between membership and advocacy:

The [membership clause] makes a felony the acquisition or holding of knowing membership in any organization which advocates the overthrow of the Government of the United States by force or violence. The indictment charged that from January 1946 to the date of its filing (November 18, 1954) the Communist Party of the United States was such an organization, and that petitioner throughout that period was a member thereof, with knowledge of the Party's illegal purpose and a specific intent to accomplish overthrow "as speedily as circumstances would permit." . . .

. . . It was settled in *Dennis* that the advocacy with which we are here concerned is not constitutionally protected speech, and it was further established that a combination to promote such advocacy, albeit under the aegis of what purports to be a political party, is not such association as is protected by the First Amendment. We can discern no reason why membership, when it constitutes a purposeful form of complicity in a group engaging in this same forbidden advocacy, should receive any greater degree of protection from the guarantes of that Amendment. . . .

[The] membership clause, as here construed, . . . does not make criminal all association with an organization which has been shown to engage in illegal advocacy. There must be clear proof that a defendant "specifically intend[s] to accomplish [the aims of the organization] by resort to violence." *Noto v. United States*, 367 U.S. 290, 299 (1961) [decided simultaneously with *Scales*; *see infra* this Note].

The Court then reviewed the evidence against Scales, drawing on the exposition of the standard in *Yates*:

The *Yates* opinion . . . indicates what type of evidence is needed to permit a jury to find that (a) there was "advocacy of action" and (b) the Party was responsible for such advocacy.

First, *Yates* makes clear what type of evidence is not *in itself* sufficient to show illegal advocacy. This category includes evidence of the following: the teaching of Marxism-Leninism and the connected use of Marxist "classics" as textbooks; the official general resolutions and pronouncements of the Party at past conventions; dissemination of the Party's general literature, including the standard outlines on Marxism; the Party's history and organizational structure; the secrecy of meetings and the clandestine nature of the Party generally; statements by officials evidencing sympathy for and alliance with U.S.S.R. However, this kind of evidence, while insufficient in itself to sustain a conviction, is not irrelevant. Such evidence, in the context of other evidence, may be of value in showing illegal advocacy.

Second, the *Yates* opinion also indicates what kind of evidence is sufficient. . . . Viewed together, [the] events described in *Yates* indicate at least two patterns of evidence sufficient to show illegal advocacy: (a) the teaching of forceful overthrow, accompanied by directions as to the type of illegal action which must be taken when the time for the revolution is reached; and (b) the teaching of forceful overthrow, accompanied by a contemporary, though legal, course of conduct clearly undertaken for the specific purpose of rendering effective the later illegal activity which is advocated. Compare *Noto v. United States* [discussed below] . . .

> We conclude that [the] evidence sufficed to make a case for the jury on the issue of illegal Party advocacy. *Dennis* and *Yates* have definitely laid at rest any doubt that present advocacy of *future* action for violent overthrow satisfies statutory and constitutional requirements equally with advocacy of *immediate* action to that end. Hence this record cannot be considered deficient because it contains no evidence of advocacy for immediate overthrow.

The Court also found that the advocacy "was sufficiently broadly based to permit its attribution to the Party." Four Justices dissented, though only two reached the First Amendment question.

3. In a companion case to *Scales*, the Court unanimously reversed a conviction under the membership clause of the Smith Act. The case was *Noto v. United States*, 367 U.S. 290 (1961), and again Justice Harlan wrote for the Court. He said:

> [The evidence] fails to establish that the Communist Party was an organization which presently advocated violent overthrow of the Government now or in the future, for that is what must be proven. The most that can be said is that the evidence as to [the "industrial concentration"] program might justify an inference that the leadership of the Party was preparing the way for a situation in which future acts of sabotage might be facilitated, but there is no evidence that such acts of sabotage were presently advocated; and it is present advocacy, and not an intent to advocate in the future or a conspiracy to advocate in the future once a groundwork has been laid, which is an element of the crime under the membership clause.

4. In contrast to *Dennis*, the opinions in *Yates*, *Scales*, and *Noto* do not apply a "clear and present danger" test to the defendants' advocacy. What test replaces it? Consider the Problem below.

Problem: "Warriors for Earth"

"Warriors for Earth" is the name adopted by a loosely organized group of individuals who believe that "industrial civilization is a threat to the survival of everything, and it has to be destroyed." Among other actions, the Warriors have taken "credit" for a string of fires last year that burned down luxury homes under construction in a Colorado forest; the destruction by fire of a lumber company office in Oregon; and a $12 million fire that stopped the expansion of a Utah ski resort into threatened lynx habitat. Earlier this year, members of the group attempted to blow up a fish and game club building in Maine. They rigged the propane system to set off an explosion, but the first person to notice something was wrong was a firefighter who disabled the explosive device.

Law enforcement authorities have learned that the Warriors operate in "cells," small groups of two to five people who maintain their anonymity even with each other. The group appears to be controlled by "traveling evangelists," who travel from state to state providing activists with instructions and materials.

State authorities have identified one such "traveling evangelist," William Watson. They have evidence that Watson distributed materials that included tips on how to commit arson, detailed instructions for the construction and placement of explosive devices, and advice on what to do when the FBI comes calling. Watson is the author of a recent manifesto that stated, "Industrial civilization must be destroyed so that the earth can be restored to its natural balance. This year we are committed to an escalation in tactics against capitalism and industry."

Watson has been indicted under a recent statute that provides in relevant part:

> It shall be unlawful for any person to teach or demonstrate the making or use of incendiary devices or explosive materials if the person intends or knows or has reason to know that such devices or materials will likely be used for, or in furtherance of, injury to persons or unlawful destruction of property.

Under *Yates*, *Scales*, and *Noto*, does the prosecution meet First Amendment standards? If so, does *Brandenburg*, the next principal case, change the result?

F. *Brandenburg v. Ohio* and Its Implications
Brandenburg v. Ohio
395 U.S. 444 (1969)

Per Curiam.

The appellant, a leader of a Ku Klux Klan group, was convicted under the Ohio Criminal Syndicalism statute for "advocat[ing] . . . the duty, necessity, or propriety of crime, sabotage, violence, or unlawful methods of terrorism as a means of accomplishing industrial or political reform" and for "voluntarily assembl[ing] with any society, group, or assemblage of persons formed to teach or advocate the doctrines of criminal syndicalism." He was fined $1,000 and sentenced to one to 10 years' imprisonment. The appellant challenged the constitutionality of the criminal syndicalism statute under the First and Fourteenth Amendments to the United States Constitution, but the intermediate appellate court of Ohio affirmed his conviction without opinion. The Supreme Court of Ohio dismissed his appeal, *sua sponte*, "for the reason that no substantial constitutional question exists herein." It did not file an opinion or explain its conclusions. Appeal was taken to this Court, and we noted probable jurisdiction. We reverse.

The record shows that a man, identified at trial as the appellant, telephoned an announcer-reporter on the staff of a Cincinnati television station and invited him to come to a Ku Klux Klan "rally" to be held at a farm in Hamilton County. With the cooperation of the organizers, the reporter and a cameraman attended the meeting and filmed the events. Portions of the films were later broadcast on the local station and on a national network.

The prosecution's case rested on the films and on testimony identifying the appellant as the person who communicated with the reporter and who spoke at the rally. The State also introduced into evidence several articles appearing in the film, including a pistol, a rifle, a shotgun, ammunition, a Bible, and a red hood worn by the speaker in the films.

One film showed 12 hooded figures, some of whom carried firearms. They were gathered around a large wooden cross, which they burned. No one was present other than the participants and the newsmen who made the film. Most of the words uttered during the scene were incomprehensible when the film was projected, but scattered phrases could be understood that were derogatory of Negroes and, in one instance, of Jews.[1] Another scene on the same film showed the appellant, in Klan regalia, making a speech. The speech, in full, was as follows:

> This is an organizers' meeting. We have had quite a few members here today which are — we have hundreds, hundreds of members throughout the State of Ohio. I can quote from a newspaper clipping from the Columbus, Ohio Dispatch, five weeks ago Sunday morning. The Klan has more members in the State of Ohio than does any other organization. We're not a revengent organization, but if our President, our Congress, our Supreme Court, continues to suppress the white, Caucasian race, it's possible that there might have to be some revengeance taken.

> We are marching on Congress July the Fourth, four hundred thousand strong. From there we are dividing into two groups, one group to march on St. Augustine, Florida, the other group to march into Mississippi. Thank you.

The second film showed six hooded figures one of whom, later identified as the appellant, repeated a speech very similar to that recorded on the first film. The reference to the possibility of "revengeance" was omitted, and one sentence was added: "Personally, I believe the nigger should be returned to Africa, the Jew returned to Israel." Though some of the figures in the films carried weapons, the speaker did not.

The Ohio Criminal Syndicalism Statute was enacted in 1919. From 1917 to 1920, identical or quite similar laws were adopted by 20 States and two territories. E. DOWELL, A HISTORY OF CRIMINAL SYNDICALISM LEGISLATION IN THE UNITED STATES 21 (1939). In 1927, this Court sustained the constitutionality of California's Criminal Syndicalism Act, the text of which is quite similar to that of the laws of Ohio. *Whitney v. California.* The Court upheld the statute on the ground that, without more, "advocating" violent means to effect political and economic change involves such danger to the security of the State that the State may outlaw it. *Cf. Fiske v. Kansas.* But *Whitney* has been thoroughly discredited by later decisions. *See Dennis v. United States.* These later decisions have fashioned the principle that the constitutional guarantees of free speech and free press do not permit a State to forbid or proscribe advocacy of the use of force or of law violation except where such advocacy is directed to inciting or producing imminent lawless action and is likely to incite or produce such action.[2] As we said in *Noto v. United*

---

1. The significant portions that could be understood were: "How far is the nigger going to — yeah." "This is what we are going to do to the niggers." "A dirty nigger." "Send the Jews back to Israel." "Let's give them back to the dark garden." "Save America." "Let's go back to constitutional betterment." "Bury the niggers." "We intend to do our part." "Give us our state rights." "Freedom for the whites." "Nigger will have to fight for every inch he gets from now on."

2. It was on the theory that the Smith Act embodied such a principle and that it had been applied only in conformity with it that this Court sustained the Act's constitutionality. *Dennis v. United States.*

States, "the mere abstract teaching . . . of the moral propriety or even moral necessity for a resort to force and violence, is not the same as preparing a group for violent action and steeling it to such action." *See also Herndon v. Lowry.* A statute which fails to draw this distinction impermissibly intrudes upon the freedoms guaranteed by the First and Fourteenth Amendments. It sweeps within its condemnation speech which our Constitution has immunized from governmental control. *Cf. Yates v. United States; De Jonge v. Oregon.*

Measured by this test, Ohio's Criminal Syndicalism Act cannot be sustained. The Act punishes persons who "advocate or teach the duty, necessity, or propriety" of violence "as a means of accomplishing industrial or political reform"; or who publish or circulate or display any book or paper containing such advocacy; or who "justify" the commission of violent acts "with intent to exemplify, spread or advocate the propriety of the doctrines of criminal syndicalism"; or who "voluntarily assemble" with a group formed "to teach or advocate the doctrines of criminal syndicalism." Neither the indictment nor the trial judge's instructions to the jury in any way refined the statute's bald definition of the crime in terms of mere advocacy not distinguished from incitement to imminent lawless action.

Accordingly, we are here confronted with a statute which, by its own words and as applied, purports to punish mere advocacy and to forbid, on pain of criminal punishment, assembly with others merely to advocate the described type of action. Such a statute falls within the condemnation of the First and Fourteenth Amendments. The contrary teaching of *Whitney v. California* cannot be supported, and that decision is therefore overruled.

MR. JUSTICE BLACK, concurring.

I agree with the views expressed by Mr. Justice Douglas in his concurring opinion in this case that the "clear and present danger" doctrine should have no place in the interpretation of the First Amendment. I join the Court's opinion, which, as I understand it, simply cites *Dennis v. United States,* but does not indicate any agreement on the Court's part with the "clear and present danger" doctrine on which *Dennis* purported to rely.

MR. JUSTICE DOUGLAS, concurring.

. . . Though I doubt if the "clear and present danger" test is congenial to the First Amendment in time of a declared war, I am certain it is not reconcilable with the First Amendment in days of peace. . . . I see no place in the regime of the First Amendment for any "clear and present danger" test, whether strict and tight as some would make it, or free-wheeling as the Court in *Dennis* rephrased it.

When one reads the opinions closely and sees when and how the "clear and present danger" test has been applied, great misgivings are aroused. First, the threats were often loud but always puny and made serious only by judges so wedded to the *status*

That this was the basis for Dennis was emphasized in *Yates v. United States,* in which the Court overturned convictions for advocacy of the forcible overthrow of the Government under the Smith Act, because the trial judge's instructions had allowed conviction for mere advocacy, unrelated to its tendency to produce forcible action.

quo that critical analysis made them nervous. Second, the test was so twisted and perverted in *Dennis* as to make the trial of those teachers of Marxism an all-out political trial which was part and parcel of the cold war that has eroded substantial parts of the First Amendment. . . .

The example usually given by those who would punish speech is the case of one who falsely shouts fire in a crowded theatre. This is, however, a classic case where speech is brigaded with action. . . . Apart from rare instances of that kind, speech is, I think, immune from prosecution. Certainly there is no constitutional line between advocacy of abstract ideas as in *Yates* and advocacy of political action as in *Scales*. The quality of advocacy turns on the depth of the conviction; and government has no power to invade that sanctuary of belief and conscience.

————

Note: Brandenburg *and Its Antecedents*

1. Although the *Brandenburg* opinion is brief, it is obviously a major step in First Amendment law, if only because it explicitly overrules the landmark precedent of *Whitney v. California*. Why then was the opinion issued *per curiam*—a form usually reserved for routine decisions? Here are some clues. The case was argued on February 27, 1969, and decided on June 9, 1969. Other clues will be found in the chart showing the membership of the Court [Appendix].

2. The Court says that decisions subsequent to *Whitney* "have fashioned the principle that the constitutional guarantees of free speech and free press do not permit a State to forbid or proscribe advocacy of the use of force or of law violation except where such advocacy is directed to inciting or producing imminent lawless action and is likely to incite or produce such action." Reread the Note on *Yates, Scales,* and *Noto.* Is this an accurate description of the law established by those cases? Does the language quoted from *Noto* in the *Brandenburg* opinion establish the "principle" that the Court says has been "fashioned" by later decisions?

Hess v. Indiana
414 U.S. 105 (1973)

PER CURIAM.

Gregory Hess appeals from his conviction in the Indiana courts for violating the State's disorderly conduct statute. [Hess's federal constitutional contentions were rejected by the state courts.]

The events leading to Hess' conviction began with an antiwar demonstration on the campus of Indiana University. In the course of the demonstration, approximately 100 to 150 of the demonstrators moved onto a public street and blocked the passage of vehicles. When the demonstrators did not respond to verbal directions from the sheriff to clear the street, the sheriff and his deputies began walking up the street, and the demonstrators in their path moved to the curbs on either side, joining a large number of spectators who had gathered. Hess was standing off the street as the sheriff passed him.

The sheriff heard Hess utter the word "fuck" in what he later described as a loud voice and immediately arrested him on the disorderly conduct charge. It was later stipulated that what appellant had said was "We'll take the fucking street later," or "We'll take the fucking street again." Two witnesses who were in the immediate vicinity testified, apparently without contradiction, that they heard Hess' words and witnessed his arrest. They indicated that Hess did not appear to be exhorting the crowd to go back into the street, that he was facing the crowd and not the street when he uttered the statement, that his statement did not appear to be addressed to any particular person or group, and that his tone, although loud, was no louder than that of the other people in the area.

Indiana's disorderly conduct statute was applied in this case to punish only spoken words. It hardly needs repeating that "[t]he constitutional guarantees of freedom of speech forbid the States to punish the use of words or language not within 'narrowly limited classes of speech.'" . . .

The Indiana Supreme Court placed primary reliance on the trial court's finding that Hess' statement "was intended to incite further lawless action on the part of the crowd in the vicinity of appellant and was likely to produce such action." At best, however, the statement could be taken as counsel for present moderation; at worst, it amounted to nothing more than advocacy of illegal action at some indefinite future time. This is not sufficient to permit the State to punish Hess' speech. Under our decisions, "the constitutional guarantees of free speech and free press do not permit a State to forbid or proscribe advocacy of the use of force or of law violation except where such advocacy is directed to inciting or producing *imminent* lawless action and is likely to incite or produce such action." *Brandenburg v. Ohio* (1969). (Emphasis added.) Since the uncontroverted evidence showed that Hess' statement was not directed to any person or group of persons, it cannot be said that he was advocating, in the normal sense, any action. And since there was no evidence or rational inference from the import of the language, that his words were intended to produce, and likely to produce, imminent disorder, those words could not be punished by the State on the ground that they had "a 'tendency to lead to violence.'"

Accordingly, the motion to proceed in forma pauperis is granted and the judgment of the Supreme Court of Indiana is reversed.

MR. JUSTICE REHNQUIST, with whom THE CHIEF JUSTICE [BURGER] and MR. JUSTICE BLACKMUN join, dissenting.

The Court's per curiam opinion rendered today aptly demonstrates the difficulties inherent in substituting a different complex of factual inferences for the inferences reached by the courts below. Since it is not clear to me that the Court has a sufficient basis for its action, I dissent.

It should be noted at the outset that the case was tried de novo in the Superior Court of Indiana upon a stipulated set of facts, and, therefore, the record is perhaps unusually colorless and devoid of life. . . .

[The summaries of testimony establish] that "Hess was standing off the street on the eastern curb of Indiana Avenue" and that he said, in the words of the trial court,

"We'll take the fucking street later (or again)." The two female witnesses testified, as the majority correctly observes, that they were not offended by Hess' statement, that it was said no louder than statements by other demonstrators, "that Hess *did not appear* to be exhorting the crowd to go back into the street," that he was facing the crowd, and "that his statement *did not appear* to be addressed to any particular person or group." (Emphasis added.)

The majority makes much of this "uncontroverted evidence," but I am unable to find anywhere in the opinion an explanation of why it must be believed. Surely the sentence "We'll take the fucking street later (or again)" is susceptible of characterization as an exhortation, particularly when uttered in a loud voice while facing a crowd. The opinions of two defense witnesses cannot be considered *proof* to the contrary, since the trial court was perfectly free to reject this testimony if it so desired. Perhaps, as these witnesses and the majority opinion seem to suggest, appellant was simply expressing his views to the world at large, but that is surely not the only rational explanation.

The majority also places great emphasis on appellant's use of the word "later," even suggesting at one point that the statement "could be taken as counsel for present moderation." The opinion continues: "[A]t worst, it amounted to nothing more than advocacy of illegal action at some indefinite future time." From that observation, the majority somehow concludes that the advocacy was not directed towards inciting imminent action. But whatever other theoretical interpretations may be placed upon the remark, there are surely possible constructions of the statement which would encompass more or less immediate and continuing action against the harassed police. They should not be rejected out of hand because of an unexplained preference for other acceptable alternatives.

The simple explanation for the result in this case is that the majority has interpreted the evidence differently from the courts below. In doing so, however, I believe the Court has exceeded the proper scope of our review. . . .

Note: The Summary Reversal in Hess

The *Hess* case was a summary reversal, i.e., it was decided on the application for review and response, without briefing or oral argument. Summary reversal "is a rare and exceptional disposition, usually reserved by [the Supreme Court] for situations in which the law is well settled and stable, the facts are not in dispute, and the decision below is clearly in error." ROBERT STERN ET AL., SUPREME COURT PRACTICE 321 (8th ed. 2002) (citation and internal quotation marks omitted). Does *Hess* fit that description?

NAACP v. Claiborne Hardware Company
458 U.S. 886 (1982)

JUSTICE STEVENS delivered the opinion of the Court.

The term "concerted action" encompasses unlawful conspiracies and constitutionally protected assemblies. The "looseness and pliability" of legal doctrine applicable to concerted action led Justice Jackson to note that certain joint activities have a "chameleon-like" character. The boycott of white merchants in Claiborne County, Miss., that gave rise to this litigation had such a character; it included elements of criminality and elements of majesty. Evidence that fear of reprisals caused some black citizens to withhold their patronage from respondents' businesses convinced the Supreme Court of Mississippi that the entire boycott was unlawful and that each of the 92 petitioners was liable for all of its economic consequences. Evidence that persuasive rhetoric, determination to remedy past injustices, and a host of voluntary decisions by free citizens were the critical factors in the boycott's success presents us with the question whether the state court's judgment is consistent with the Constitution of the United States.

In March 1966, black citizens of Port Gibson, Miss., and other areas of Claiborne County presented white elected officials with a list of particularized demands for racial equality and integration. The complainants did not receive a satisfactory response and, at a local National Association for the Advancement of Colored People (NAACP) meeting at the First Baptist Church, several hundred black persons voted to place a boycott on white merchants in the area. On October 31, 1969, several of the merchants filed suit in state court to recover losses caused by the boycott and to enjoin future boycott activity. We recount first the course of that litigation and then consider in more detail the events that gave rise to the merchants' claim for damages. [Most of the Court's detailed account is omitted.]

On April 19, Charles Evers spoke to a group assembled at the First Baptist Church and led a march to the courthouse where he demanded the discharge of the entire Port Gibson Police Force. When this demand was refused, the boycott was reimposed on all white merchants. One of Evers' speeches on this date was recorded by the police. [In that speech] Evers stated that boycott violators would be "disciplined" by their own people and warned that the Sheriff could not sleep with boycott violators at night.

On April 20, Aaron Henry came to Port Gibson, spoke to a large gathering, urged moderation, and joined local leaders in a protest march and a telegram sent to the Attorney General of the United States. On April 21, Evers gave another speech to several hundred people, in which he again called for a discharge of the police force and for a total boycott of all white-owned businesses in Claiborne County. Although this speech was not recorded, the chancellor [in the state court] found that Evers stated: "If we catch any of you going in any of them racist stores, we're gonna break your damn neck."

As noted, this lawsuit was filed in October 1969. No significant events concerning the boycott occurred after that time. The chancellor identified no incident of violence that occurred after the suit was brought. He did identify, however, several significant incidents of boycott-related violence that occurred some years earlier.

Before describing that evidence, it is appropriate to note that certain practices generally used to encourage support for the boycott were uniformly peaceful and orderly. The few marches associated with the boycott were carefully controlled by black leaders. Pickets used to advertise the boycott were often small children. The police made no arrests—and no complaints are recorded—in connection with the picketing and occasional demonstrations supporting the boycott. Such activity was fairly irregular, occurred primarily on weekends, and apparently was largely discontinued around the time the lawsuit was filed.

One form of "discipline" of black persons who violated the boycott appears to have been employed with some regularity. Individuals stood outside of boycotted stores and identified those who traded with the merchants. Some of these "store watchers" were members of a group known as the "Black Hats" or the "Deacons." The names of persons who violated the boycott were read at meetings of the Claiborne County NAACP and published in a mimeographed paper entitled the "Black Times." As stated by the chancellor, those persons "were branded as traitors to the black cause, called demeaning names, and socially ostracized for merely trading with whites."

The chancellor also concluded that a quite different form of discipline had been used against certain violators of the boycott. He specifically identified 10 incidents that "strikingly" revealed the "atmosphere of fear that prevailed among blacks from 1966 until 1970." The testimony concerning four incidents convincingly demonstrates that they occurred because the victims were ignoring the boycott. In two cases, shots were fired at a house; in a third, a brick was thrown through a windshield; in the fourth, a flower garden was damaged. None of these four victims, however, ceased trading with white merchants. . . .

[Respondents point to Evers' speeches] as justification for the chancellor's damages award. Since respondents would impose liability on the basis of a public address—which predominantly contained highly charged political rhetoric lying at the core of the First Amendment—we approach this suggested basis of liability with extreme care.

There are three separate theories that might justify holding Evers liable for the unlawful conduct of others. First, a finding that he authorized, directed, or ratified specific tortious activity would justify holding him responsible for the consequences of that activity. Second, a finding that his public speeches were likely to incite lawless action could justify holding him liable for unlawful conduct that in fact followed within a reasonable period. Third, the speeches might be taken as evidence that Evers gave other specific instructions to carry out violent acts or threats.

While many of the comments in Evers' speeches might have contemplated "discipline" in the permissible form of social ostracism, it cannot be denied that references to the possibility that necks would be broken and to the fact that the Sheriff could not sleep with boycott violators at night implicitly conveyed a sterner message. In the passionate atmosphere in which the speeches were delivered, they might have been understood as inviting an unlawful form of discipline or, at least, as intending to create a fear of violence whether or not improper discipline was specifically intended.

. . . This Court has made clear, however, that mere *advocacy* of the use of force or violence does not remove speech from the protection of the First Amendment. [The Court quoted from *Brandenburg* and *Noto*.]

The emotionally charged rhetoric of Charles Evers' speeches did not transcend the bounds of protected speech set forth in *Brandenburg*. The lengthy addresses generally contained an impassioned plea for black citizens to unify, to support and respect each other, and to realize the political and economic power available to them. In the course of those pleas, strong language was used. If that language had been followed by acts of violence, a substantial question would be presented whether Evers could be held liable for the consequences of that unlawful conduct. In this case, however — with the possible exception of [one] incident — the acts of violence identified in 1966 occurred weeks or months after the April 1, 1966, speech; the chancellor made no finding of any violence after the challenged 1969 speech. Strong and effective extemporaneous rhetoric cannot be nicely channeled in purely dulcet phrases. An advocate must be free to stimulate his audience with spontaneous and emotional appeals for unity and action in a common cause. When such appeals do not incite lawless action, they must be regarded as protected speech. To rule otherwise would ignore the "profound national commitment" that "debate on public issues should be uninhibited, robust, and wide-open." *New York Times Co. v. Sullivan*, 376 U.S. 254, 270 (1964).

For these reasons, we conclude that Evers' addresses did not exceed the bounds of protected speech. If there were other evidence of his authorization of wrongful conduct, the references to discipline in the speeches could be used to corroborate that evidence. But any such theory fails for the simple reason that there is no evidence — apart from the speeches themselves — that Evers authorized, ratified, or directly threatened acts of violence. The chancellor's findings are not sufficient to establish that Evers had a duty to "repudiate" the acts of violence that occurred. The findings are constitutionally inadequate to support the damages judgment against him. . . .

[JUSTICE REHNQUIST concurred in the result only. JUSTICE MARSHALL took no part in the consideration or decision of the case. There were no dissents or separate opinions.]

––––––––

Problem: Encouraging Participation in a "Jihad"

The United States filed an indictment against Muhammad Khan for violation of several federal statutes, including the conspiracy statute. The indictment was based on statements made by Khan at a meeting in Virginia five days after the President announced an increase in the size of the United States military force in Afghanistan. The indictment alleged that Khan unlawfully counseled and induced several young Muslim men to commit various offenses including "willfully and unlawfully supplying and attempting to supply services to the Taliban."

By way of background, the indictment explained that a "jihad" describes a religious obligation of Muslims to struggle for the defense and advancement of Islam, and "mujahideen" are warriors engaged in violent jihad. The Taliban is a military-political entity that controlled the territory of Afghanistan for many years and is now seeking to regain control. President Clinton, President George W. Bush, and President Obama have all identified the Taliban as a terrorist organization and a threat to the United

States. As authorized by various federal statutes, all three Presidents have prohibited United States persons (i.e., American citizens and resident aliens) from aiding the Taliban.

The indictment also described the activities of an organization known as LET. LET too has been classified as a terrorist organization. LET is the "military wing" of an organization that operates training camps for individuals from around the world seeking to be mujahideen. It claims to have trained thousands to fight in Afghanistan, Kashmir, Bosnia, Chechnya, Kosovo, and the Philippines.

The indictment also provided background about Khan, stating that he was the primary lecturer at an Islamic center in Virginia that focused on teaching in the English language about Islamic faith, practice, and civilization. Khan was highly respected by the students at the center as a scholar who had lectured around the world on topics related to Islam.

According to the indictment, Khan told the young men at the meeting that the time had come for them to go abroad to join the mujahideen engaged in violent jihad in Afghanistan. He expressed anger at the President's decision to send additional American troops to Afghanistan and said that the moment these troops touched down on Afghan soil, they would be "legitimate targets" of the jihad. Khan advised the young men on how to reach the LET camp undetected and urged them to obtain military-style training at the camp.

Within two weeks after this meeting, six of the young men traveled to the LET camp. They obtained military-style training there, learning to use AK-47 rifles, machine guns, anti-aircraft guns, and rocket-propelled grenades. Meanwhile, American military forces continued to fight the Taliban in various parts of Afghanistan. However, for various reasons none of the young men actually took part in any armed engagements against American forces.

Khan moved to dismiss the indictment on First Amendment grounds, but the trial court denied the motion. Khan was convicted after a bench trial. Assume that the evidence is sufficient for conviction under the indictment. Does the conviction violate the First Amendment?

———

Problem: Advice to a Street Gang

The State of Oceana has enacted a statute that makes it a crime to "participate in a criminal syndicate." Among the acts prohibited is "furnishing advice or direction in the conduct, financing or management of a criminal syndicate's affairs with the intent to promote or further the criminal objectives of a criminal syndicate." "Criminal syndicate" is defined to include "criminal street gang."

James Williams was convicted after a jury trial of participating in a criminal syndicate in violation of the statute. The evidence showed that Williams was a member of a gang in California during the late 1990s. Last year he moved from California to Bay City, the largest city in Oceana. In Bay City he became acquainted with his girlfriend's son and a number of his friends who belonged to a street gang called the Sharks.

Williams' conviction was based on statements he made at a meeting of the Sharks at the son's house. Several of the Sharks testified that Williams spoke to them about his experiences in the California gang. He advised them to formalize their gang by electing officers, collecting money to establish a bail fund for members, and spray-painting more gang graffiti to make their presence known in their territory. He also advised them to "jump in" more loyal members and "jump out" those who were not loyal. There was testimony explaining that "jumping" or "courting" meant initiating a new member or removing a current member by means of a group beating in which a number of members participated in beating or kicking the person "jumped" or "courted." Finally, Williams advised the Sharks to establish friendly relations with other gangs who would support them.

The trial court denied Williams' post-trial acquittal motion, concluding that the evidence was sufficient to prove his knowledge of the Oceana gang's criminal activities and his intent to promote those activities. The court also rejected Williams' argument that the statute violated the First Amendment because it prohibited constitutionally protected speech.

Williams has appealed his conviction, raising the First Amendment challenge. How should the court rule?

———

G. The "True Threat"

Note: Watts, Black, and the "True Threat"

1. After *Brandenburg* was argued, but before it was decided, the Supreme Court handed down its summary per curiam decision in *Watts v. United States*, 394 U.S. 705 (1969). Watts was convicted under 18 U.S.C. § 871(a), a statute that prohibits any person from "knowingly and willfully . . . [making] any threat to take the life of or to inflict bodily harm upon the President of the United States . . . ."

The Court described the circumstances leading up to the conviction as follows:

> The incident which led to petitioner's arrest occurred on August 27, 1966, during a public rally on the Washington Monument grounds. The crowd present broke up into small discussion groups and petitioner joined a gathering scheduled to discuss police brutality. Most of those in the group were quite young, either in their teens or early twenties. Petitioner, who himself was 18 years old, entered into the discussion after one member of the group suggested that the young people present should get more education before expressing their views. According to an investigator for the Army Counter Intelligence Corps who was present, petitioner responded: "They always holler at us to get an education. And now I have already received my draft classification as 1-A and I have got to report for my physical this Monday coming. I am not going. If they ever make me carry a rifle the first man I want to get in my sights is L.B.J." "They are not going to make me kill my black

brothers." On the basis of this statement, the jury found that petitioner had committed a felony by knowingly and willfully threatening the President.

The Court upheld the constitutionality of the statute in an analysis that reads in its entirely as follows:

> Certainly the statute under which petitioner was convicted is constitutional on its face. The Nation undoubtedly has a valid, even an overwhelming, interest in protecting the safety of its Chief Executive and in allowing him to perform his duties without interference from threats of physical violence. *See* H.R. Rep. No. 652, 64th Cong., 1st Sess. (1916).

The Court nevertheless reversed the conviction, stating:

> [A] statute such as this one, which makes criminal a form of pure speech, must be interpreted with the commands of the First Amendment clearly in mind. What is a threat must be distinguished from what is constitutionally protected speech.

> The judges in the Court of Appeals differed over whether or not the "willfullness" requirement of the statute implied that a defendant must have intended to carry out his "threat." . . . But whatever the "willfullness" requirement implies, the statute initially requires the Government to prove a true "threat." We do not believe that the kind of political hyperbole indulged in by petitioner fits within that statutory term. For we must interpret the language Congress chose "against the background of a profound national commitment to the principle that debate on public issues should be uninhibited, robust, and wide-open, and that it may well include vehement, caustic, and sometimes unpleasantly sharp attacks on government and public officials." *New York Times Co. v. Sullivan*, 376 U.S. 254 (1964) [Chapter 2]. The language of the political arena, like the language used in labor disputes, is often vituperative, abusive, and inexact. We agree with petitioner that his only offense here was "a kind of very crude offensive method of stating a political opposition to the President." Taken in context, and regarding the expressly conditional nature of the statement and the reaction of the listeners, we do not see how it could be interpreted otherwise.

Only five Justices joined the per curiam opinion. Justice Stewart would have denied the petition for certiorari. Justice White dissented without explanation. Justice Fortas, joined by Justice Harlan, dissented, saying: "The Court holds, without hearing, that this statute is constitutional and that it is here wrongly applied. Neither of these rulings should be made without hearing, even if we assume that they are correct." How would *Watts* be analyzed under *Brandenburg*?

2. In *Virginia v. Black*, 538 U.S. 343 (2003) (set forth more fully in Chapter 11), the Court discussed the "true threat" as an example of speech that is not protected by the First Amendment. The Court began by saying: "The protections afforded by the First Amendment [are] not absolute, and we have long recognized that the government may regulate certain categories of expression consistent with the Constitution." After quoting *Brandenburg*'s holding on incitement, the Court continued by citing *Watts* for the proposition that "the First Amendment also permits a State to ban a 'true threat.'" The Court explained:

> "True threats" encompass those statements where the speaker means to communicate a serious expression of an intent to commit an act of unlawful violence to a particular individual or group of individuals. See *Watts* ("political hyperbole" is not a true threat). The speaker need not actually intend to carry out the threat. Rather, a prohibition on true threats "protect[s] individuals from the fear of violence" and "from the disruption that fear engenders," in addition to protecting people "from the possibility that the threatened violence will occur." Intimidation in the constitutionally proscribable sense of the word is a type of true threat, where a speaker directs a threat to a person or group of persons with the intent of placing the victim in fear of bodily harm or death.

The *Black* opinion indicates that the Court views *Brandenburg* and *Watts* as defining distinct categories of unprotected speech. What is the relationship between them?

3. What are the criteria for determining whether expression constitutes an unprotected "true threat"? The *Black* opinion tells us that the speaker "need not actually intend to carry out the threat." Does this mean that the speaker's subjective intent is irrelevant?

In *Elonis v. United States*, 135 S. Ct. 2001 (2015), the Court granted certiorari to consider the question whether, under *Black* and the First Amendment, conviction of threatening another person requires proof of the defendant's subjective intent to threaten. The Court did not decide that question; instead, it reversed the conviction on statutory grounds, holding that the jury was improperly instructed that the Government need prove only that a reasonable person would regard the defendant's communications as threats.

How should the constitutional question be resolved? Should it be enough to show that the defendant acted recklessly — i.e., that he or she consciously disregarded the risk that the communication transmitted would be interpreted as a true threat? Or must the government show, as two circuits have held, that "the defendant *intended* the recipient of the threat to feel threatened"? *See United States v. Heineman*, 767 F.3d 970 (10th Cir. 2014).

Should courts distinguish between statements made in the context of a public protest and purely private threats? Must a true threat meet the *Brandenburg* standard for imminence?

Consider these questions in the context of the Problem that follows.

Problem: Anti-Abortion Website

The Freedom of Access to Clinic Entrances Act (FACE Act) provides in part: "Whoever . . . by force or threat of force . . . intentionally injures, intimidates or interferes with or attempts to injure, intimidate or interfere with any person . . . in order to intimidate [any] person or any class of persons from obtaining or providing reproductive health services . . . shall be subject to the penalties provided in subsection (b) and the civil remedies provided in subsection (c)." The penalties in subsection (c) include monetary damages.

Abortion providers brought suit under the FACE Act against the operators of "Nuremberg 2019," a site on the World Wide Web. The Website (no longer active) was named for the German city in which Nazis were put on trial for war crimes after World War II. The home page of the Website had the headline, "Nuremberg 2019: Visualize Abortionists on Trial." The page was illustrated with a picture of fetus parts with simulated blood dripping from them. The text read: "A coalition of concerned citizens throughout the United States is cooperating in collecting dossiers on abortionists in anticipation that one day we will be able to hold them on trial for crimes against humanity. We anticipate the day when these people will be charged in perfectly legal courts once the tide of this nation's opinion turns against the wanton slaughter of God's children."

A link on the home page, labeled "main archive," led the visitor to a page with the title "Guilty of Crimes Against Humanity." That page contained the names and addresses of dozens of doctors and clinic workers around the country who provide abortions. A few doctors had a red line though their names; other names were shown in gray. A note explained that the red line meant that the doctor has been killed; the gray indicated that the doctor had been wounded. The names of physicians continuing to perform abortions were printed in black type.

The website did not contain any explicitly threatening language. However, the plaintiffs' complaint asserts that the physicians who were the subjects of the Nuremberg Files nonetheless feared for their safety, because the personal information and photographs made them easily identifiable and because three other physicians had recently been killed after they were identified in similar web postings.

The plaintiffs' complaint asserts that during the last two decades there have been 7 killings, 15 attempted murders, 99 acid attacks, 154 arson incidents, and 39 bombings involving abortion clinics or workers. The complaint does not assert that the any of these acts were the direct result of any communication on the Website.

The complaint seeks up to $200 million in damages.

The defendants have moved to dismiss the complaint on the ground that the Website is protected by the First Amendment. How should the court rule on the motion?

H. A Last Word from Justice Holmes

United States v. Schwimmer

279 U.S. 644 (1929)

[Rosika Schwimmer, a well-known pacifist, filed a petition for naturalization as a citizen of the United States. The District Court denied the application on the ground that Schwimmer could not take the prescribed oath of allegiance without mental reservation and was not attached to the principles of the United States Constitution. The Supreme Court held by a vote of 6 to 3 that the District Court acted properly, because Schwimmer had not met her burden to show "that her opinions and beliefs would not prevent or impair the true faith and allegiance required by the [naturalization] act." Justice Holmes disagreed in what proved to be his last great dissent.]

Mr. Justice Holmes, dissenting.

The applicant seems to be a woman of superior character and intelligence, obviously more than ordinarily desirable as a citizen of the United States. It is agreed that she is qualified for citizenship except so far as the views set forth in a statement of facts "may show that the applicant is not attached to the principles of the Constitution of the United States and well disposed to the good order and happiness of the same, and except in so far as the same may show that she cannot take the oath of allegiance without a mental reservation." The views referred to are an extreme opinion in favor of pacifism and a statement that she would not bear arms to defend the Constitution. So far as the adequacy of her oath is concerned I hardly can see how that is affected by the statement, inasmuch as she is a woman over fifty years of age, and would not be allowed to bear arms if she wanted to. And as to the opinion the whole examination of the applicant shows that she holds none of the now-dreaded creeds but thoroughly believes in organized government and prefers that of the United States to any other in the world. Surely it cannot show lack of attachment to the principles of the Constitution that she thinks that it can be improved. I suppose that most intelligent people think that it might be. Her particular improvement looking to the abolition of war seems to me not materially different in its bearing on this case from a wish to establish cabinet government as in England, or a single house, or one term of seven years for the President. To touch a more burning question, only a judge mad with partisanship would exclude because the applicant thought that the Eighteenth Amendment should be repealed.

Of course the fear is that if a war came the applicant would exert activities such as were dealt with in *Schenck v. United States*, 249 U.S. 47. But that seems to me unfounded. Her position and motives are wholly different from those of Schenck. She is an optimist and states in strong and, I do not doubt, sincere words her belief that war will disappear and that the impending destiny of mankind is to unite in peaceful leagues. I do not share that optimism nor do I think that a philosophic view of the world would regard war as absurd. But most people who have known it regard it with horror, as a last resort, and even if not yet ready for cosmopolitan efforts, would welcome any practicable combinations that would increase the power on the side of peace. The notion that the applicant's optimistic anticipations would make her a worse citizen is sufficiently answered by her examination which seems to me a better argument for her admission than any that I can offer. Some of her answers might excite popular prejudice, but if there is any principle of the Constitution that more imperatively calls for attachment than any other it is the principle of free thought—not free thought for those who agree with us but freedom for the thought that we hate. I think that we should adhere to that principle with regard to admission into, as well as to life within this country. And recurring to the opinion that bars this applicant's way, I would suggest that the Quakers have done their share to make the country what it is, that many citizens agree with the applicant's belief and that I had not supposed hitherto that we regretted our inability to expel them because they believed more than some of us do in the teachings of the Sermon on the Mount.

————

Note: "Freedom for the Thought that We Hate"

1. In his last great First Amendment dissent, Holmes instructs us that if "the principle of free thought" is to be given meaning, it must be interpreted to protect, not the ideas we agree with, but "the thought that we hate." Consider the relevance of this admonition as you read the cases in the chapters that follow. In particular, you will see statements that take the form "This category of speech generally warrants protection, *but . . .*" Ask: what is the basis of the "but"? Is it—implicitly or explicitly—the belief that a particular idea is *really* hateful?

2. Apart from the force of his ideas, Holmes remains a vivid presence in American legal culture, in no small part because of his powers as a writer. Indeed, Holmes's rhetorical skills are so great that he can easily lead us (as in *Schenck*) to a conclusion which, upon analysis, proves to be quite flawed. But whether or not you agree with Holmes's reasoning, you can learn from his skill as writer. The *Schwimmer* dissent is an excellent example. (You might start by reading the opinion aloud.)

Chapter 2

Unprotected Speech:
The *Chaplinsky* Exclusions

In *Chaplinsky v. New Hampshire*, 315 U.S. 568 (1942), a unanimous Supreme Court introduced what Professor Harry Kalven later called the "two-level approach" to the First Amendment. "There are," said the Court, "certain well-defined and narrowly limited *classes* of speech, the prevention and punishment of which have never been thought to raise any Constitutional problem." When speech falls into one of these classes, no balancing or further inquiry is required; the speech is outside the protection of the First Amendment.

Chaplinsky itself involved "fighting words"—words "which by their very utterance inflict injury or tend to incite an immediate breach of the peace." Section A of this chapter traces the later development of the "fighting words" doctrine.

Two of *Chaplinsky*'s other "classes" were "the libelous" and "the lewd and obscene." In 1964, however, the Court announced that "libel can claim no talismanic immunity from constitutional limitations." Section B explores the Court's treatment of libel and other tort claims under the First Amendment.

In contrast, the Court has reaffirmed that "obscenity is *not* within the area of constitutionally protected speech or press." The critical question thus becomes: What is obscene? Section C examines the Court's efforts to answer that question.

A. "Fighting Words"
Chaplinsky v. New Hampshire
315 U.S. 568 (1942)

Mr. Justice Murphy delivered the opinion of the Court.

Appellant, a member of the sect known as Jehovah's Witnesses, was convicted in the municipal court of Rochester, New Hampshire, for violation of Chapter 378, § 2, of the Public Laws of New Hampshire: "No person shall address any offensive, derisive or annoying word to any other person who is lawfully in any street or other public place, nor call him by any offensive or derisive name . . ."

The complaint charged that appellant, "with force and arms, in a certain public place in said city of Rochester, to wit, on the public sidewalk on the easterly side of Wakefield Street, near unto the entrance of the City Hall, did unlawfully repeat, the words following, addressed to the complainant, that is to say, 'You are a God damned racketeer' and 'a damned Fascist and the whole government of Rochester are Fascists or agents of Fascists,' the same being offensive, derisive and annoying words and names." [Chaplinsky was found guilty, and the judgment of conviction was affirmed by the New Hampshire Supreme Court.]

There is no substantial dispute over the facts. Chaplinsky was distributing the literature of his sect on the streets of Rochester on a busy Saturday afternoon. Members of the local citizenry complained to the City Marshal, Bowering, that Chaplinsky was denouncing all religion as a "racket." Bowering told them that Chaplinsky was lawfully engaged, and then warned Chaplinsky that the crowd was getting restless. Some time later, a disturbance occurred and the traffic officer on duty at the busy intersection started with Chaplinsky for the police station, but did not inform him that he was under arrest or that he was going to be arrested. On the way, they encountered Marshal Bowering, who had been advised that a riot was under way and was therefore hurrying to the scene. Bowering repeated his earlier warning to Chaplinsky, who then addressed to Bowering the words set forth in the complaint.

Chaplinsky's version of the affair was slightly different. He testified that, when he met Bowering, he asked him to arrest the ones responsible for the disturbance. In reply, Bowering cursed him and told him to come along. Appellant admitted that he said the words charged in the complaint, with the exception of the name of the Deity. . . .

It is now clear that "Freedom of speech and freedom of the press, which are protected by the First Amendment from infringement by Congress, are among the fundamental personal rights and liberties which are protected by the Fourteenth Amendment from invasion by state action." *Lovell v. City of Griffin*, 303 U.S. 444, 450 (1938) . . . .

Allowing the broadest scope to the language and purpose of the Fourteenth Amendment, it is well understood that the right of free speech is not absolute at all times and under all circumstances. There are certain well-defined and narrowly limited classes of speech, the prevention and punishment of which have never been thought to raise any Constitutional problem. These include the lewd and obscene, the profane, the libelous, and the insulting or "fighting" words—those which by their very utterance inflict injury or tend to incite an immediate breach of the peace.[4] It has been well observed that such utterances are no essential part of any exposition of ideas, and are of such slight social value as a step to truth that any benefit that may be derived from them is clearly outweighed by the social interest in order and morality.[5] "Resort to epithets or personal abuse is not in any proper sense communication of information or opinion safeguarded by the Constitution, and its punishment as a criminal act would raise no question under that instrument." *Cantwell v. Connecticut*, 310 U.S. 296, 309–10 (1940) . . . .

---

4. Chafee, *Free Speech in the United States* 149 (1941).
5. Chafee, *op. cit.*, 150.

On the authority of its earlier decisions, the state court declared that the statute's purpose was to preserve the public peace, no words being "forbidden except such as have a direct tendency to cause acts of violence by the person to whom, individually, the remark is addressed." It was further said: "The word 'offensive' is not to be defined in terms of what a particular addressee thinks . . . . The test is what men of common intelligence would understand would be words likely to cause an average addressee to fight . . . . The English language has a number of words and expressions which by general consent are 'fighting words' when said without a disarming smile . . . . Such words, as ordinary men know, are likely to cause a fight. So are threatening, profane or obscene revilings. Derisive and annoying words can be taken as coming within the purview of the statute as heretofore interpreted only when they have this character-istic of plainly tending to excite the addressee to a breach of the peace . . . . The stat-ute, as construed, does no more than prohibit the face-to-face words plainly likely to cause a breach of the peace by the addressee, words whose speaking constitute a breach of the peace by the speaker — including 'classical fighting words,' words in current use less 'classical' but equally likely to cause violence, and other disorderly words, includ-ing profanity, obscenity and threats."

We are unable to say that the limited scope of the statute as thus construed contra-venes the constitutional right of free expression. It is a statute narrowly drawn and limited to define and punish specific conduct lying within the domain of state power, the use in a public place of words likely to cause a breach of the peace. Cf. *Cantwell v. Connecticut*, 310 U.S. 296, 311 (1940). This conclusion necessarily disposes of appel-lant's contention that the statute is so vague and indefinite as to render a conviction thereunder a violation of due process. A statute punishing verbal acts, carefully drawn so as not unduly to impair liberty of expression, is not too vague for a criminal law.

Nor can we say that the application of the statute to the facts disclosed by the rec-ord substantially or unreasonably impinges upon the privilege of free speech. Argu-ment is unnecessary to demonstrate that the appellations "damned racketeer" and "damned Fascist" are epithets likely to provoke the average person to retaliation, and thereby cause a breach of the peace. . . .

Affirmed.

———

Note: Chaplinsky *and Its Implications*

1. *Chaplinsky v. New Hampshire* is one of the most often-cited of all First Amendment opinions, and the portion of *Chaplinsky* that has been quoted most frequently is the passage beginning, "There are certain well-defined and narrowly limited classes of speech . . . ." What authority does the Court cite for the proposi-tions put forth in this passage?

2. In 2010, almost seven decades after the decision in *Chaplinsky*, the Court told us that this oft-quoted statement, and similar statements in later cases, are merely "descriptive. They do not set forth a test that may be applied as a general matter to permit the Government to imprison any speaker so long as his speech is deemed valueless or unnecessary, or so long as an ad hoc calculus of costs and benefits tilts in a statute's favor." *United States v. Stevens*, 559 U.S. 460 (2010) (Chapter 3).

3. At the end of the same paragraph in *Chaplinsky*, the Court quotes from *Cantwell v. Connecticut*, 310 U.S. 296 (1940) (Chapter 8). Cantwell was convicted of the common-law offense of inciting a breach of the peace. As summarized by the Court, the facts were as follows: "Jesse Cantwell . . . stopped two men in the street, asked, and received, permission to play a phonograph record, and played the record 'Enemies,' which attacked the religion and church of the two men, who were Catholics. Both were incensed by the contents of the record and were tempted to strike Cantwell unless he went away. On being told to be on his way he left their presence. There was no evidence that he was personally offensive or entered into any argument with those he interviewed." In a unanimous opinion by Justice Roberts, the Court concluded:

> Although the contents of the record not unnaturally aroused animosity, we think that, in the absence of a statute narrowly drawn to define and punish specific conduct as constituting a clear and present danger to a substantial interest of the State, the petitioner's communication, considered in the light of the constitutional guarantees, raised no such clear and present menace to public peace and order as to render him liable to conviction of the common law offense in question.

En route to this conclusion, the Court voiced the caveat quoted in the *Chaplinsky* opinion, adding, "We find in the instant case no assault or threatening of bodily harm, no truculent bearing, no intentional discourtesy, no personal abuse." How strong an authority was *Cantwell* for the decision in *Chaplinsky*?

4. The Court defines "fighting words" as "those which by their very utterance inflict injury or tend to incite an immediate breach of the peace." Is the Court describing one category of speech, or two? Which categorization applies to the language used by *Chaplinsky*?

Note: *"Fighting Words" Today*

1. The Court has not affirmed a "fighting words" conviction since *Chaplinsky*. A typical decision is *Gooding v. Wilson*, 405 U.S. 518 (1972), authored by Justice Brennan. In that case, the defendant was convicted under a Georgia statute that provided: "Any person who shall, without provocation, use to or of another, and in his presence . . . opprobrious words or abusive language, tending to cause a breach of the peace . . . shall be guilty of a misdemeanor."

The Georgia statute might seem to fall squarely within the ambit of *Chaplinsky*, and indeed that was the position of the state. However, the United States Supreme Court, making its own examination of Georgia cases, found that Georgia appellate decisions had construed the statute to apply to utterances that were not "fighting" words as *Chaplinsky* defined them. For example, in one case a conviction under the statute was sustained for awakening 10 women scout leaders on a camp-out by shouting, "Boys, this is where we are going to spend the night," and "Get the G—d—bed rolls out . . . let's see how close we can come to the G—d—tents." The Georgia statute was therefore overbroad and unconstitutional.

The overbreadth doctrine is considered in Chapter 4.

2. In *City of Houston v. Hill*, 482 U.S. 451 (1987) (Chapter 4), the Court, in another opinion by Justice Brennan, struck down an ordinance of the City of Houston that made it a crime "for any person to assault, strike or in any manner oppose, molest, abuse or interrupt any policeman in the execution of his duty, or any person summoned to aid in making an arrest." Although the decision in *City of Houston v. Hill* rested on the overbreadth doctrine, it also contained a holding on the scope of protected speech: "the First Amendment protects a significant amount of verbal criticism and challenge directed at police officers." It went on to cite with approval a concurring opinion by Justice Powell in a previous "fighting words" case for the proposition that "the 'fighting words' exception recognized in *Chaplinsky* might require a narrower application in cases involving words addressed to a police officer," since trained police officers should be expected to exercise restraint in the face of provocation. How far does this holding cut into the "fighting words" doctrine? Under what circumstances does the First Amendment not protect "verbal criticism and challenge directed at police officers"? In footnote 12, the Court states: "The freedom verbally to challenge police action is not without limits, of course; we have recognized that 'fighting words' which 'by their very utterance inflict injury or tend to incite an immediate breach of the peace' are not constitutionally protected." Does the rationale for the decision, as stated in the text, support such an exception? Can you draft a statute that would satisfy the Court's standards?

3. If one were to look solely at Supreme Court decisions, one might conclude that the "fighting words" doctrine exists more in name than in reality. However, a different picture emerges if we look at cases in the state courts. There, convictions have been affirmed, and some (indeed, most) have involved abusive language directed at police officers. To be sure, the cases often involve explicit threats of violence. But not all do.

Consider the cases summarized in the Problems that follow. Would affirmance of the convictions be consistent with Supreme Court case law?

4. The dissent in one recent case quoted a commentator who condemned the fighting words doctrine as "a hopeless anachronism that mimics the macho code of barroom brawls." Assume that the cases summarized below are representative of those in which convictions are upheld under the doctrine. Does the preservation of the doctrine threaten First Amendment values?

———

Problems: The "Callahan Epithet" and Other Expletives

1. In *People v. Callahan*, 168 Cal. App. 3d 631 (1985), *cert. denied*, 474 U.S. 1081 (1986), the facts are stated as follows:

> A California highway patrolman arrested Gerald Callahan for interfering with the performance of his duty (Pen. Code, § 148), the sole charged

offense. A jury found Callahan not guilty of violating section 148, but guilty of uttering offensive words in public which were inherently likely to provoke an immediate violent reaction (Pen. Code, §415, subd. (3)), a lesser related offense. [Section 415 provides in relevant part: "Every person who maliciously and wilfully disturbs the peace . . . by tumultuous or offensive conduct or [uses] any vulgar, profane, or indecent language within the presence or hearing of women or children, in a loud or boisterous manner, is guilty of a misdemeanor . . . ."]

Soon after midnight Highway Patrolman George received a message to investigate a traffic collision in Solana Beach. He found a truck had struck two parked cars. The truck driver was seated in a lawn chair being attended by several persons, including Callahan's wife. George thought the driver had a superficial scratch on his forehead. The driver stubbornly refused going to the hospital. George returned to the collision site, anxious to clear the area to eliminate a traffic hazard for persons about to be leaving nearby bars.

When George returned to the truck driver for his statement, Callahan announced he was a doctor, he had examined the driver and thought he required medical attention. Callahan appeared to be intoxicated. George told Callahan the driver had declined medical attention. When Callahan argued with George, the officer again asked the driver if he wanted medical attention. After Callahan's wife and another person said "Yes," the driver agreed. George radioed for an ambulance and returned to the collision scene.

While George gathered statements from witnesses, Callahan interrupted and inquired about the ambulance. George said one was on the way. Callahan responded, "Oh bull-shit! Don't give me that fucking shit." George warned Callahan not to interfere and turned away to complete his investigation. Callahan followed him, yelling and uttering profanities, interrupting him as he spoke to witnesses, stepping in front of him several times yelling for the ambulance. At least twice he was so close to the officer that he spat in his face as he argued for medical attention.

Three times George warned Callahan to stop interfering or he would arrest him for delaying a police officer in violation of Penal Code section 148. After the third warning, when Callahan called the officer a "fucking asshole," the officer arrested him. [In a footnote, the court adds: "To avoid continuous repetition of the phrase which arguably would assist its passage into parlor parlance, we refer to it as the 'Callahan epithet.'"]

The entire confrontation lasted between 10 and 20 minutes. There was no direct physical contact between Callahan and George. The officer testified Callahan's language did not provoke a violent reaction.

Under the Supreme Court's precedents, is the conviction under section 415 valid? Could Callahan have been validly convicted of interfering with a police officer?

2. In *In re Rowena V.*, an unpublished decision, the facts were as follows (as described in the *Callahan* opinion):

> Rowena, traveling south on Interstate 5, shouted, "You ask me if I give a fuck" to some boys in the next lane. Mrs. Reitsma, a stranger, overheard the phrase and became upset. Reitsma followed Rowena, caused a security officer to stop her, and in the officer's presence, Reitsma, wrought with righteous rectitude, wrathfully requested Rowena to repeat the rude and revolting remark. Rowena readily responded with a reprise. Reitsma filed a citizen's complaint against Rowena. Rowena was convicted of disturbing the peace (Pen. Code, § 415), and was imprisoned.

Is the conviction consistent with the Supreme Court's precedents?

3. In *State v. Clay*, 1999 Minn. App. LEXIS 1059 (Sept. 14, 1999), the defendant was convicted of disorderly conduct. The conviction rested on the following facts, as set forth by the court:

> After midnight, on May 10, 1998, the Winona Police Department received a report of a fight. An officer responded and saw one of the suspects, appellant Nathan Webb Clay, walking down the street with his hand bleeding. When the officer asked him what happened, appellant said that he had been jumped by four men but had "kicked their asses." Appellant then became agitated and called the officer a "white racist motherf—ker." When a second officer arrived on the scene, appellant also accused the second officer of racism and told the officers that he wished their mothers would die. It was Mother's Day weekend, and one of the officers had recently lost his father. During the encounter, appellant was swinging his arms in a threatening manner. The first officer testified that although he was concerned for his safety and feared that appellant might strike out, none of the swings came close to being a blow.
>
> The officers arrested appellant when he began to walk away from them. Both officers testified that despite appellant's behavior, they did not consider retaliation.

Under Supreme Court precedent, can the conviction stand?

4. In *State v. Read*, 680 A.2d 944 (Vt. 1996), defendant was convicted of disorderly conduct in violation of a statute that provided in relevant part:

> A person who, with intent to cause public inconvenience, or annoyance or recklessly creating a risk thereof . . . in a public place uses [abusive language] shall be imprisoned for not more than 60 days or fined not more than $500.00 or both.

The facts leading to the conviction were as follows:

> On May 20, 1993, at approximately 2:00 a.m., Trooper Michael Roj of the Vermont State Police responded to a single-car [accident]. Trooper Roj found defendant, whom the trooper knew, at the scene. Defendant told the trooper, "Mike, I fucked up." The trooper took no offense at defendant's language, but

considered the comment to be "street language." The trooper detected the odor of alcohol on defendant's breath, and defendant stated that he had consumed a beer after the accident. The trooper, observing that defendant had suffered multiple facial lacerations, persuaded defendant to seek treatment for his injuries, and summoned an ambulance, which transported defendant to the emergency room of the Southwestern Vermont Medical Center.

At approximately 3:00 a.m., Trooper Roj arrived at the medical center to continue his accident investigation. [In the examining room, he] asked defendant several questions about the accident; defendant responded in a cooperative manner. Trooper Roj then told defendant that, because he believed defendant had been driving under the influence of intoxicating beverages, he would be processing defendant for DUI. He immediately observed that defendant went "from being very cooperative and very personable to being very uncooperative, very aggressive, very argumentative, very insulting, very profane, and displaying a number of very aggressive mannerisms." Specifically, defendant shouted: "You're a fucking piece of shit . . . . You're a fucking asshole . . . . I want you to get out of my face. You're dead." Defendant's tone of voice was very loud, and Trooper Roj observed that defendant's arms were flexed and rigid, his fists were clenched, his teeth were grinding, and his facial expression was rigidly set in what the trooper called "the thousand-mile stare."

Trooper Roj attempted to calm defendant down, and advised him that there were a number of other people in the emergency room who should not be subjected to defendant's tone of voice or language. The trooper also told defendant that he could face criminal charges for his behavior. Defendant became even angrier, and shouted: "Go ahead, you fucking pig. You're a stupid fucking pig. You're not even here, you pig." Trooper Roj felt "a sense of great anger built up within me based upon not only the words that were used, but the voice, the aggressive voice in which they were used," and felt "afraid of the possibilities of an imminent attack by Mr. Read upon me," particularly after defendant told the trooper, "You're dead." During defendant's tirade, the door of the examining room was open. When Trooper Roj left the room, he observed a physician seated in an adjacent room with its door open, and a nurse seated forty-five feet from the examining room.

On appeal, should the conviction be sustained?

5. In *State v. Robinson*, 82 P.3d 27 (Mont. 2003), *cert. denied*, 541 U.S. 1037 (2004), the Montana Supreme Court described the facts as follows:

On October 8, 2000, at approximately midnight, Malachi Robinson was crossing the intersection of Broadway and Higgins in Missoula, Montana. Missoula County Sheriff's Deputy David McGinnis (McGinnis) was seated in a marked patrol car stopped at the traffic light. As Robinson crossed the intersection, which was crowded with several other pedestrians also crossing the street, Robinson glared at McGinnis and said, "fucking pig." McGinnis stated that this was said in a loud voice, prompting several pedestrians to take note and to move away from Robinson.

When Robinson reached the other side of the street, McGinnis parked his patrol car and approached Robinson on foot. He claims he told Robinson that "he now had my attention and asked him if there was anything he wanted to talk about." Robinson, stretching his vocabulary to its fullest, replied, "Fuck off, asshole." McGinnis arrested Robinson for disorderly conduct.

The state's disorderly conduct statute provides that "[a] person commits the offense of disorderly conduct if he knowingly disturbs the peace by . . . (c) using threatening, profane, or abusive language." The Montana Supreme Court had previously construed the statute to apply only to "fighting words." It upheld Robinson's conviction.

Was this decision correct as a matter of federal constitutional law? Robinson filed a petition for certiorari in the United States Supreme Court, but the petition was denied. Should we give any weight to that denial?

B. "The Libelous"—or Otherwise Tortious

In *Chaplinsky*, the Court identified "the libelous" as among the categories of speech long considered outside First Amendment protection. Until the decision that follows, courts accepted this without much question. Indeed, in *Beauharnais v. Illinois*, 343 U.S. 250 (1952) the Court extended this principle to uphold a statute criminalizing "any publication or exhibition [which] portrays depravity, criminality, unchastity, or lack of virtue of a class of citizens, of any race, color, creed or religion which said publication or exhibition exposes the citizens of any race, color, creed or religion to contempt, derision, or obloquy or which is productive of breach of the peace or riots . . ." In a crucial passage, the Court analogized this statute to laws barring libel of individuals, holding that "if an utterance directed at an individual may be the object of criminal sanctions, we cannot deny to a State power to punish the same utterances directed at a defined group, unless we can say that this is a willful and purposeless restriction unrelated to the peace and well-being of the State."

Is the analogy *Beauharnais* draws between individual and "group libel" convincing? *Beauharnais* has never been overruled. Consider, in light of the cases that follow (especially in Chapter 15), whether it is still good law.

Four Justices dissented in *Beauharnais*, on a variety of grounds. Toward the end of his dissent, Justice Douglas had the following warning: "Today a white man stands convicted for protesting in unseemly language against our decisions invalidating restrictive covenants. Tomorrow a Negro will be haled before a court for denouncing lynch law in heated terms." It was not "tomorrow," but a few years later, that the Court was presented with a case that came very close to fitting Justice Douglas's description.

[1] The Constitutionalization of Defamation

New York Times Co. v. Sullivan

376 U.S. 254 (1964)

Mr. Justice Brennan delivered the opinion of the Court.

We are required in this case to determine for the first time the extent to which the constitutional protections for speech and press limit a State's power to award damages in a libel action brought by a public official against critics of his official conduct.

Respondent L. B. Sullivan is one of the three elected Commissioners of the City of Montgomery, Alabama. He testified that he was "Commissioner of Public Affairs and the duties are supervision of the Police Department, Fire Department, Department of Cemetery and Department of Scales." He brought this civil libel action against the four individual petitioners, who are Negroes and Alabama clergymen, and against petitioner the New York Times Company, a New York corporation which publishes the New York Times, a daily newspaper. A jury in the Circuit Court of Montgomery County awarded him damages of $500,000, the full amount claimed, against all the petitioners, and the Supreme Court of Alabama affirmed.

Respondent's complaint alleged that he had been libeled by statements in a full-page advertisement that was carried in the New York Times on March 29, 1960. Entitled "Heed Their Rising Voices," the advertisement began by stating that "As the whole world knows by now, thousands of Southern Negro students are engaged in widespread non-violent demonstrations in positive affirmation of the right to live in human dignity as guaranteed by the U.S. Constitution and the Bill of Rights." It went on to charge that "in their efforts to uphold these guarantees, they are being met by an unprecedented wave of terror by those who would deny and negate that document which the whole world looks upon as setting the pattern for modern [freedom]." Succeeding paragraphs purported to illustrate the "wave of terror" by describing certain alleged events. The text concluded with an appeal for funds for three purposes: support of the student movement, "the struggle for the right-to-vote," and the legal defense of Dr. Martin Luther King, Jr., leader of the movement, against a perjury indictment then pending in Montgomery.

The text appeared over the names of 64 persons, many widely known for their activities in public affairs, religion, trade unions, and the performing arts. Below these names, and under a line reading "We in the south who are struggling daily for dignity and freedom warmly endorse this appeal," appeared the names of the four individual petitioners and of 16 other persons, all but two of whom were identified as clergymen in various Southern cities. The advertisement was signed at the bottom of the page by the "Committee to Defend Martin Luther King and the Struggle for Freedom in the South," and the officers of the Committee were listed.

Of the 10 paragraphs of text in the advertisement, the third and a portion of the sixth were the basis of respondent's claim of libel. They read as follows:

Third paragraph: "In Montgomery, Alabama, after students sang 'My Country, 'Tis of Thee' on the State Capitol steps, their leaders were expelled from school, and truckloads of police armed with shotguns and tear-gas ringed the Alabama State College Campus. When the entire student body protested to state authorities by refusing to re-register, their dining hall was padlocked in an attempt to starve them into submission."

Sixth paragraph: "Again and again the Southern violators have answered Dr. King's peaceful protests with intimidation and violence. They have bombed his home almost killing his wife and child. They have assaulted his person. They have arrested him seven times — for 'speeding,' 'loitering' and similar 'offenses.' And now they have charged him with 'perjury' — a felony under which they could imprison him for ten [years]."

Although neither of these statements mentions respondent by name, he contended that the word "police" in the third paragraph referred to him as the Montgomery Commissioner who supervised the Police Department, so that he was being accused of "ringing" the campus with police. He further claimed that the paragraph would be read as imputing to the police, and hence to him, the padlocking of the dining hall in order to starve the students into submission. As to the sixth paragraph, he contended that since arrests are ordinarily made by the police, the statement "They have arrested [Dr. King] seven times" would be read as referring to him; he further contended that the "They" who did the arresting would be equated with the "They" who committed the other described acts and with the "Southern violators." Thus, he argued, the paragraph would be read as accusing the Montgomery police, and hence him, of answering Dr. King's protests with "intimidation and violence," bombing his home, assaulting his person, and charging him with perjury. Respondent and six other Montgomery residents testified that they read some or all of the statements as referring to him in his capacity as Commissioner.

It is uncontroverted that some of the statements contained in the two paragraphs were not accurate descriptions of events which occurred in Montgomery. Although Negro students staged a demonstration on the State Capital steps, they sang the National Anthem and not "My Country, 'Tis of Thee." Although nine students were expelled by the State Board of Education, this was not for leading the demonstration at the Capitol, but for demanding service at a lunch counter in the Montgomery County Courthouse on another day. Not the entire student body, but most of it, had protested the expulsion, not by refusing to register, but by boycotting classes on a single day; virtually all the students did register for the ensuing semester. The campus dining hall was not padlocked on any occasion, and the only students who may have been barred from eating there were the few who had neither signed a preregistration application nor requested temporary meal tickets. Although the police were deployed near the campus in large numbers on three occasions, they did not at any time "ring" the campus, and they were not called to the campus in connection with the demonstration on the State Capitol steps, as the third paragraph implied. Dr. King had not been arrested seven times, but only four; and although he claimed to have been assaulted some years earlier in connection with his arrest for loitering outside a courtroom, one of the officers who made the arrest denied that there was such an assault.

On the premise that the charges in the sixth paragraph could be read as referring to him, respondent was allowed to prove that he had not participated in the events described. Although Dr. King's home had in fact been bombed twice when his wife and child were there, both of these occasions antedated respondent's tenure as Commissioner, and the police were not only not implicated in the bombings, but had made every effort to apprehend those who were. Three of Dr. King's four arrests took place before respondent became Commissioner. Although Dr. King had in fact been indicted (he was subsequently acquitted) on two counts of perjury, each of which carried a possible five-year sentence, respondent had nothing to do with procuring the indictment.

Respondent made no effort to prove that he suffered actual pecuniary loss as a result of the alleged libel.[3] One of his witnesses, a former employer, testified that if he had believed the statements, he doubted whether he "would want to be associated with anybody who would be a party to such things that are stated in that ad," and that he would not re-employ respondent if he believed "that he allowed the Police Department to do the things that the paper say he did." But neither this witness nor any of the others testified that he had actually believed the statements in their supposed reference to respondent.

The [advertisement was] published by the Times upon an order from a New York advertising agency acting for the signatory Committee. . . . The manager of the Advertising Acceptability Department testified that he had approved the advertisement for publication because he knew nothing to cause him to believe that anything in it was false, and because it bore the endorsement of "a number of people who are well known and whose reputation" he "had no reason to question." Neither he nor anyone else at the Times made an effort to confirm the accuracy of the advertisement, either by checking it against recent Times news stories relating to some of the described events or by any other means. . . .

Because of the importance of the constitutional issues involved, we granted the separate petitions for certiorari of the individual petitioners and of the Times. We reverse the judgment. We hold that the rule of law applied by the Alabama courts is constitutionally deficient for failure to provide the safeguards for freedom of speech and of the press that are required by the First and Fourteenth Amendments in a libel action brought by a public official against critics of his official conduct. We further hold that under the proper safeguards the evidence presented in this case is constitutionally insufficient to support the judgment for respondent. . . .

---

3. Approximately 394 copies of the edition of the Times containing the advertisement were circulated in Alabama. Of these, about 35 copies were distributed in Montgomery County. The total circulation of the Times for that day was approximately 650,000 copies.

I.

We may dispose at the outset of two grounds asserted to insulate the judgment of the Alabama courts from constitutional scrutiny. The first is the proposition relied on by the State Supreme Court—that "The Fourteenth Amendment is directed against State action and not private action." That proposition has no application to this case. Although this is a civil lawsuit between private parties, the Alabama courts have applied a state rule of law which petitioners claim to impose invalid restrictions on their constitutional freedoms of speech and press. It matters not that that law has been applied in a civil action and that it is common law only, though supplemented by statute. The test is not the form in which state power has been applied but, whatever the form, whether such power has in fact been exercised. See *Ex parte Virginia*, 100 U.S. 339 (1879).

The second contention is that the constitutional guarantees of freedom of speech and of the press are inapplicable here, at least so far as the Times is concerned, because the allegedly libelous statements were published as part of a paid, "commercial" advertisement. The argument relies on *Valentine v. Chrestensen*, 316 U.S. 52 (1942) [Chapter 3], where the Court held that a city ordinance forbidding street distribution of commercial and business advertising matter did not abridge the First Amendment freedoms, even as applied to a handbill having a commercial message on one side but a protest against certain official action on the other. The reliance is wholly misplaced. . . .

The publication here was not a "commercial" advertisement in the sense in which the word was used in *Chrestensen*. It communicated information, expressed opinion, recited grievances, protested claimed abuses, and sought financial support on behalf of a movement whose existence and objectives are matters of the highest public interest and concern. That the Times was paid for publishing the advertisement is as immaterial in this connection as is the fact that newspapers and books are sold. . . .

II.

Under Alabama law as applied in this case, a publication is "libelous per se" if the words "tend to injure a person * * * in his reputation" or to "bring [him] into public contempt". . . . The jury must find that the words were published "of and concerning" the plaintiff, but where the plaintiff is a public official his place in the governmental hierarchy is sufficient evidence to support a finding that his reputation has been affected by statements that reflect upon the agency of which he is in charge. Once "libel per se" has been established, the defendant has no defense as to stated facts unless he can persuade the jury that they were true in all their particulars. His privilege of "fair comment" for expressions of opinion depends on the truth of the facts upon which the comment is based. Unless he can discharge the burden of proving truth, general damages are presumed, and may be awarded without proof of pecuniary injury. A showing of actual malice is apparently a prerequisite to recovery of punitive damages, and the defendant may in any event forestall a punitive award by a retraction meeting the statutory requirements. Good motives and belief in truth do not negate an inference of malice, but are relevant only in mitigation of punitive damages if the jury chooses to accord them weight.

The question before us is whether this rule of liability, as applied to an action brought by a public official against critics of his official conduct, abridges the freedom of speech and of the press that is guaranteed by the First and Fourteenth Amendments.

Respondent relies heavily, as did the Alabama courts, on statements of this Court to the effect that the Constitution does not protect libelous publications. Those statements do not foreclose our inquiry here. None of the cases sustained the use of libel laws to impose sanctions upon expression critical of the official conduct of public officials. . . . [In *Beauharnais*] the Court was careful to note that it "retains and exercises authority to nullify action which encroaches on freedom of utterance under the guise of punishing libel"; for "public men, are, as it were, public property," and "discussion cannot be denied and the right, as well as the duty, of criticism must not be stifled." . . . In deciding the question now, we are compelled by neither precedent nor policy to give any more weight to the epithet "libel" than we have to other "mere labels" of state law. Like insurrection, contempt, advocacy of unlawful acts, breach of the peace, obscenity, solicitation of legal business, and the various other formulae for the repression of expression that have been challenged in this Court, libel can claim no talismanic immunity from constitutional limitations. It must be measured by standards that satisfy the First Amendment.

The general proposition that freedom of expression upon public questions is secured by the First Amendment has long been settled by our decisions. . . .

Thus we consider this case against the background of a profound national commitment to the principle that debate on public issues should be uninhibited, robust, and wide-open, and that it may well include vehement, caustic, and sometimes unpleasantly sharp attacks on government and public officials. See *Terminiello v. Chicago* (1949) [Chapter 8]; *De Jonge v. Oregon* (1937) [Chapter 1 Note]. The present advertisement, as an expression of grievance and protest on one of the major public issues of our time, would seem clearly to qualify for the constitutional protection. The question is whether it forfeits that protection by the falsity of some of its factual statements and by its alleged defamation of respondent.

Authoritative interpretations of the First Amendment guarantees have consistently refused to recognize an exception for any test of truth — whether administered by judges, juries, or administrative officials — and especially one that puts the burden of proving truth on the speaker. The constitutional protection does not turn upon "the truth, popularity, or social utility of the ideas and beliefs which are offered." [E]rroneous statement is inevitable in free debate, and [it] must be protected if the freedoms of expression are to have the 'breathing space' that they "need [to] survive." *N.A.A.C.P. v. Button*, 371 U.S. 415 (1963). . . .

Injury to official reputation affords no more warrant for repressing speech that would otherwise be free than does factual error. Where judicial officers are involved, this Court has held that concern for the dignity and reputation of the courts does not justify the punishment as criminal contempt of criticism of the judge or his decision. This is true even though the utterance contains "half-truths" and "misinformation."

Such repression can be justified, if at all, only by a clear and present danger of the obstruction of justice. If judges are to be treated as "men of fortitude, able to thrive in a hardy climate," surely the same must be true of other government officials, such as elected city commissioners. Criticism of their official conduct does not lose its constitutional protection merely because it is effective criticism and hence diminishes their official reputations.

If neither factual error nor defamatory content suffices to remove the constitutional shield from criticism of official conduct, the combination of the two elements is no less inadequate. This is the lesson to be drawn from the great controversy over the Sedition Act of 1798, which first crystallized a national awareness of the central meaning of the First Amendment. See Levy, *Legacy of Suppression* (1960), at 258 *et seq.*; Smith, *Freedom's Fetters* (1956), at 426, 431 and *passim*. That statute made it a crime, punishable by a $5,000 fine and five years in prison, "if any person shall write, print, utter or publish * * * any false, scandalous and malicious writing or writings against the government of the United States, or either house of the Congress * * *, or the President * * *, with intent to defame * * * or to bring them, or either of them, into contempt or disrepute; or to excite against them, or either or any of them, the hatred of the good people of the United States." The Act allowed the defendant the defense of truth, and provided that the jury were to be judges both of the law and the facts. Despite these qualifications, the Act was vigorously condemned as unconstitutional in an attack joined in by Jefferson and Madison. . . .

Although the Sedition Act was never tested in this Court, the attack upon its validity has carried the day in the court of history. Fines levied in its prosecution were repaid by Act of Congress on the ground that it was unconstitutional. . . . Jefferson, as President, pardoned those who had been convicted and sentenced under the Act and remitted their fines, stating: "I discharged every person under punishment or prosecution under the sedition law, because I considered, and now consider, that law to be a nullity, as absolute and as palpable as if Congress had ordered us to fall down and worship a golden image." The invalidity of the Act has also been assumed by Justices of this Court. See Holmes, J., dissenting and joined by Brandeis, J., in *Abrams v. United States* [Chapter 1]; Jackson, J., dissenting in *Beauharnais v. Illinois*; Douglas, *The Right of the People* 47 (1958). . . . These views reflect a broad consensus that the Act, because of the restraint it imposed upon criticism of government and public officials, was inconsistent with the First Amendment.

There is no force in respondent's argument that the constitutional limitations implicit in the history of the Sedition Act apply only to Congress and not to the States. . . . [This] distinction was eliminated with the adoption of the Fourteenth Amendment and the application to the States of the First Amendment's restrictions.

What a State may not constitutionally bring about by means of a criminal statute is likewise beyond the reach of its civil law of libel. The fear of damage awards under a rule such as that invoked by the Alabama courts here may be markedly more inhibiting than the fear of prosecution under a criminal statute. . . . The judgment awarded in this case—without the need for any proof of actual pecuniary loss—was one thousand times greater than the maximum fine provided by the Alabama criminal statute, and one hundred times greater than that provided by the Sedition Act. And since there is no double-jeopardy limitation applicable to civil lawsuits, this is not the only judgment that may be awarded against petitioners for the same publication.[18] Whether or not a newspaper can survive a succession of such judgments, the pall of fear and timidity imposed upon those who would give voice to public criticism is an atmosphere in which the First Amendment freedoms cannot survive. Plainly the Alabama law of civil libel is "a form of regulation that creates hazards to protected freedoms markedly greater than those that attend reliance upon the criminal law."

The state rule of law is not saved by its allowance of the defense of truth.... A rule compelling the critic of official conduct to guarantee the truth of all his factual assertions—and to do so on pain of libel judgments virtually unlimited in amount— leads [to] "self-censorship." Allowance of the defense of truth, with the burden of proving it on the defendant, does not mean that only false speech will be deterred. Even courts accepting this defense as an adequate safeguard have recognized the difficulties of adducing legal proofs that the alleged libel was true in all its factual particulars. Under such a rule, would-be critics of official conduct may be deterred from voicing their criticism, even though it is believed to be true and even though it is in fact true, because of doubt whether it can be proved in court or fear of the expense of having to do so. They tend to make only statements which "steer far wider of the unlawful zone." *Speiser v. Randall*, 357 U.S. 513 (1958). The rule thus dampens the vigor and limits the variety of public debate. It is inconsistent with the First and Fourteenth Amendments.

The constitutional guarantees require, we think, a federal rule that prohibits a public official from recovering damages for a defamatory falsehood relating to his official conduct unless he proves that the statement was made with "actual malice"—that is, with knowledge that it was false or with reckless disregard of whether it was false or not....

Such a privilege for criticism of official conduct is appropriately analogous to the protection accorded a public official when he is sued for libel by a private citizen. In *Barr v. Matteo*, 360 U.S. 564 (1959), this Court held the utterance of a federal official to be absolutely privileged if made "within the outer perimeter" of his duties.... [T]he threat of damage suits would otherwise "inhibit the fearless, vigorous, and effective administration of policies of government" and "dampen the ardor of all but the most resolute, or the most irresponsible, in the unflinching discharge of their duties." Analogous considerations support the privilege for the citizen-critic of government.... It would give public servants an unjustified preference over the public they serve, if critics of official conduct did not have a fair equivalent of the immunity granted to the officials themselves.

---

18. The Times states that four other libel suits based on the advertisement have been filed against it by others who have served as Montgomery City Commissioners and by the Governor of Alabama; that another $500,000 verdict has been awarded in the only one of these cases that has yet gone to trial; and that the damages sought in the other three total $2,000,000.

We conclude that such a privilege is required by the First and Fourteenth Amendments.

III.

We hold today that the Constitution delimits a State's power to award damages for libel in actions brought by public officials against critics of their official conduct. Since this is such an action,[23] the rule requiring proof of actual malice is applicable. While Alabama law apparently requires proof of actual malice for an award of punitive damages, where general damages are concerned malice is "presumed." Such a presumption is inconsistent with the federal rule. . . . Since the trial judge did not instruct the jury to differentiate between general and punitive damages, . . . the judgment must be reversed and the case remanded.

Since respondent may seek a new trial, we deem that considerations of effective judicial administration require us to review the evidence in the present record to determine whether it could constitutionally support a judgment for respondent. . . . We must "make an independent examination of the whole record," so as to assure ourselves that the judgment does not constitute a forbidden intrusion on the field of free expression.

Applying these standards, we consider that the proof presented to show actual malice lacks the convincing clarity which the constitutional standard demands, and hence that it would not constitutionally sustain the judgment for respondent under the proper rule of law. The case of the individual petitioners requires little discussion. Even assuming that they could constitutionally be found to have authorized the use of their names on the advertisement, there was no evidence whatever that they were aware of any erroneous statements or were in any way reckless in that regard. The judgment against them is thus without constitutional support.

As to the Times, we similarly conclude that the facts do not support a finding of actual malice. The statement by the Times' Secretary that, apart from the padlocking allegation, he thought the advertisement was "substantially correct," affords no constitutional warrant for the Alabama Supreme Court's conclusion that it was a "cavalier ignoring of the falsity of the advertisement [from which], the jury could not have but been impressed with the bad faith of The Times, and its maliciousness inferable therefrom." The statement does not indicate malice at the time of the publication; even if the advertisement was not "substantially correct," . . . that opinion was at least a reasonable one, and there was no evidence to impeach the witness' good faith in holding it. . . .

---

23. We have no occasion here to determine how far down into the lower ranks of government employees the "public official" designation would extend for purposes of this rule, or otherwise to specify categories of persons who would or would not be included. Nor need we here determine the boundaries of the "official conduct" concept. It is enough for the present case that respondent's position as an elected city commissioner clearly made him a public official, and that the allegations in the advertisement concerned what was allegedly his official conduct as Commissioner in charge of the Police Department. . . .

Finally, there is evidence that the Times published the advertisement without checking its accuracy against the news stories in the Times' own files. The mere presence of the stories in the files does not, of course, establish that the Times "knew" the advertisement was false, since the state of mind required for actual malice would have to be brought home to the persons in the Times' organization having responsibility for the publication of the advertisement. With respect to the failure of those persons to make the check, the record shows that they relied upon their knowledge of the good reputation of many of those whose names were listed as sponsors of the advertisement, and upon the letter from A. Philip Randolph, known to them as a responsible individual, certifying that the use of the names was authorized. . . . We think the evidence against the Times supports at most a finding of negligence in failing to discover the misstatements, and is constitutionally insufficient to show the recklessness that is required for a finding of actual malice.

We also think the evidence was constitutionally defective in another respect: it was incapable of supporting the jury's finding that the allegedly libelous statements were made "of and concerning" respondent. . . . [The Supreme Court of Alabama relied on the bare fact of respondent's official position. But that would transmute] criticism of government, however impersonal it may seem on its face, into personal criticism, and hence potential libel, of the officials of whom the government is composed. . . .

[The] judgment of the Supreme Court of Alabama is reversed and the case is remanded to that court for further proceedings not inconsistent with this opinion.

Mr. Justice Black, with whom Mr. Justice Douglas joins, concurring.

I base my vote to reverse on the belief that the First and Fourteenth Amendments not merely "delimit" a State's power to award damages to "public officials against critics of their official conduct" but completely prohibit a State from exercising such a power. . . . "Malice," even as defined by the Court, is an elusive, abstract concept, hard to prove and hard to disprove. The requirement that malice be proved provides at best an evanescent protection for the right critically to discuss public affairs and certainly does not measure up to the sturdy safeguard embodied in the First Amendment. Unlike the Court, therefore, I vote to reverse exclusively on the ground that the Times and the individual defendants had an absolute, unconditional constitutional right to publish in the Times advertisement their criticisms of the Montgomery agencies and officials. . . .

This record certainly does not indicate that any different verdict would have been rendered here whatever the Court had charged the jury about "malice," "truth," "good motives," "justifiable ends," or any other legal formulas which in theory would protect the press. Nor does the record indicate that any of these legalistic words would have caused the courts below to set aside or to reduce the half-million-dollar verdict in any amount.

[S]ince the adoption of the Fourteenth Amendment a State has no more power than the Federal Government to use a civil libel law or any other law to impose damages for merely discussing public affairs and criticizing public officials. The power of the United States to do that is, in my judgment, precisely nil. Such was the general view held when the First Amendment was adopted and ever since. . . .

This Nation, I suspect, can live in peace without libel suits based on public discussions of public affairs and public officials. But I doubt that a country can live in freedom where its people can be made to suffer physically or financially for criticizing their government, its actions, or its officials. . . .

Mr. Justice Goldberg, with whom Mr. Justice Douglas joins, concurring in the result.

. . . The impressive array of history and precedent marshaled by the Court . . . confirms my belief that the Constitution affords greater protection than that provided by the Court's standard to citizen and press in exercising the right of public criticism.

In my view, the First and Fourteenth Amendments to the Constitution afford to the citizen and to the press an absolute, unconditional privilege to criticize official conduct despite the harm which may flow from excesses and abuses. The prized American right "to speak one's mind," about public officials and affairs needs "breathing space to survive." The right should not depend upon a probing by the jury of the motivation of the citizen or press. . . .

. . . It may be urged that deliberately and maliciously false statements have no conceivable value as free speech. That argument, however, is not responsive to the real issue presented by this case, which is whether that freedom of speech which all agree is constitutionally protected can be effectively safeguarded by a rule allowing the imposition of liability upon a jury's evaluation of the speaker's state of mind. If individual citizens may be held liable in damages for strong words, which a jury finds false and maliciously motivated, there can be little doubt that public debate and advocacy will be constrained. And if newspapers, publishing advertisements dealing with public issues, thereby risk liability, there can also be little doubt that the ability of minority groups to secure publication of their views on public affairs and to seek support for their causes will be greatly diminished. . . .

The conclusion that the Constitution affords the citizen and the press an absolute privilege for criticism of official conduct does not leave the public official without defenses against unsubstantiated opinions or deliberate misstatements. "Under our system of government, counterargument and education are the weapons available to expose these matters, not abridgment [of free speech]." *Wood v. Georgia*, 370 U.S. 375, 389. The public official certainly has equal if not greater access than most private citizens to media of communication. . . .

———

Note: The Holding of New York Times

1. The Court rejects Sullivan's argument that statements in prior opinions "foreclose [the] inquiry" in this case. None of the precedents, the Court says, "sustained the use of libel laws to impose sanctions upon expression critical of the official

conduct of public officials." Does this response take adequate account of the rationale of *Beauharnais*?

2. In *Near v. Minnesota*, 283 U.S. 697 (1931) (Chapter 4), the county attorney of Hennepin county sued to enjoin publication of what was described as a "malicious, scandalous and defamatory newspaper." Although the state court granted the injunction, the United States Supreme Court reversed, establishing a broad rule against prior restraints. In the course of its opinion the Court said:

> [The] fact that for approximately one hundred and fifty years there has been almost an entire absence of attempts to impose previous restraints upon publications relating to the malfeasance of public officers is significant of the deep-seated conviction that such restraints would violate constitutional right. Public officers, whose character and conduct remain open to debate and free discussion in the press, find their remedies for false accusations in actions under libel laws providing for redress and punishment, and not in proceedings to restrain the publication of newspapers and periodicals. . . .

The Court in *Near* thus assumed that a "public officer" who is subjected to false accusations in the press could find a remedy in state libel laws. That assumption provided some of the support for the Court's holding that the official could not pursue proceedings in the nature of a prior restraint. The Alabama courts relied on *Near* (among other decisions), but Justice Brennan responds: "None of the cases sustained the use of libel laws to impose sanctions upon expression critical of the official conduct of public officials." Is that a persuasive basis for distinguishing *Near*?

3. Justice Brennan says that "the great controversy over the Sedition Act of 1798 . . . first crystallized a national awareness of the central meaning of the First Amendment." However, he never quite spells out what that "central meaning" is. Based on the *New York Times* opinion, what is it?

4. Justice Goldberg, in his concurring opinion, states that the right to criticize official conduct "should not depend upon a probing by the jury of the motivation of the citizen or the press." Similarly, he expresses concern that, under the Court's rule, liability can be imposed "upon a jury's evaluation of the speaker's state of mind." Is his concern well founded? Does "malice," as defined by the Court, embrace an inquiry into the motivation or "state of mind" of the speaker or writer?

5. Does the *New York Times* decision go too far in protecting freedom of speech at the expense of reputation? Justice White joined the Court's opinion, but two decades later he began to have second thoughts. In his concurring opinion in *Dun & Bradstreet, Inc. v. Greenmoss Builders, Inc.*, 472 U.S. 749 (1985), he wrote:

> I have [become] convinced that the Court struck an improvident balance in the *New York Times* case between the public's interest in being fully informed about public officials and public affairs and the competing interest of those who have been defamed in vindicating their reputation. . . . [First] Amendment values are not at all served by circulating false statements of

fact about public officials. On the contrary, erroneous information frustrates these values. They are even more disserved when the statements falsely impugn the honesty of those men and women and hence lessen the confidence in government. . . .

Even if the plaintiff sues, he frequently loses on summary judgment or never gets to the jury because of insufficient proof of malice. If he wins before the jury, verdicts are often overturned by appellate courts for failure to prove malice. . . . Also, by leaving the lie uncorrected, the *New York Times* rule plainly leaves the public official without a remedy for the damage to his reputation. . . .

We are not talking in these cases about mere criticism or opinion, but about misstatements of fact that seriously harm the reputation of another, by lowering him in the estimation of the community or to deter third persons from associating or dealing with him. The necessary breathing room for speakers can be ensured by limitations on recoverable damages; it does not also require depriving many public figures of any room to vindicate their reputations sullied by false statements of fact. . . . [Other] commercial enterprises in this country not in the business of disseminating information must pay for the damage they cause as a cost of doing business, and it is difficult to argue that the United States did not have a free and vigorous press before the rule in *New York Times* was announced. . . .

Do you agree that replacing the *New York Times* rule with "limitations on recoverable damages" would give the "necessary breathing room for speakers"? Is it only the prospect of a large damages award that would influence decisions about whether to publish material that criticizes the activities or character of a public official?

————

Note: Proving "Malice"

1. The Court held in *New York Times* that a public official may not recover damages for a defamatory falsehood relating to his official conduct "unless he proves that the statement was made with 'actual malice'—that is, with knowledge that it was false or with reckless disregard of whether it was false or not." In Part III of the opinion, the Court reviewed the evidence in the record and concluded that "the proof presented to show actual malice lacks the convincing clarity which the constitutional standard demands."

How might a libel plaintiff satisfy the burden that *New York Times* imposes? This Note considers that question.

2. Four years after *New York Times*, the Court applied the malice standard in *St. Amant v. Thompson*, 390 U.S. 727 (1968). St. Amant was a candidate for public office who, in a speech, had made comments accusing Herman Thompson, a deputy sheriff, of criminal conduct. St. Amant's comments relied heavily on an affidavit signed by a union member named Albin. Thompson won a libel judgment against St. Amant,

and the Louisiana court affirmed. The Louisiana court held that St. Amant had broadcast false information about Thompson recklessly, though not knowingly. As the United States Supreme Court explained:

> Several reasons were given for this conclusion. St. Amant had no personal knowledge of Thompson's activities; he relied solely on Albin's affidavit although the record was silent as to Albin's reputation for veracity; he failed to verify the information with those in the union office who might have known the facts; he gave no consideration to whether or not the statements defamed Thompson and went ahead heedless of the consequences; and he mistakenly believed he had no responsibility for the broadcast because he was merely quoting Albin's words.

The United States Supreme Court reversed, saying: "These considerations fall short of proving St. Amant's reckless disregard for the accuracy of his statements about Thompson." The Court explained:

> [Reckless conduct] is not measured by whether a reasonably prudent man would have published, or would have investigated before publishing. There must be sufficient evidence to permit the conclusion that the defendant in fact entertained serious doubts as to the truth of his publication. . . .

> The defendant in a defamation action brought by a public official cannot, however, automatically insure a favorable verdict by testifying that he published with a belief that the statements were true. The finder of fact must determine whether the publication was indeed made in good faith. Professions of good faith will be unlikely to prove persuasive, for example, where a story is fabricated by the defendant, is the product of his imagination, or is based wholly on an unverified anonymous telephone call. Nor will they be likely to prevail when the publisher's allegations are so inherently improbable that only a reckless man would have put them in circulation. Likewise, recklessness may be found where there are obvious reasons to doubt the veracity of the informant or the accuracy of his reports.

3. A rare case in which the Supreme Court found the malice standard satisfied is *Harte-Hanks Communications, Inc. v. Connaughton*, 491 U.S. 657 (1989). Plaintiff Connaughton was the unsuccessful candidate for a state judicial position. The defendant newspaper supported the reelection of the incumbent. Several weeks before the election, a member of the incumbent's staff resigned and was arrested on bribery charges. A grand jury initiated an investigation. One week before the election, the newspaper ran a front-page story quoting Alice Thompson, a grand jury witness, as stating that Connaughton had used "dirty tricks" and offered her and her sister jobs and a trip to Florida "in appreciation" for their help in the investigation. Connaughton sued for libel and won a jury verdict.

The Supreme Court, in an opinion that painstakingly analyzed the evidence submitted to the jury, affirmed. Although the Court reviewed the record "in its entirety," it gave particular emphasis to some of the things the defendant newspaper did *not* do:

By the time the November 1 story appeared, six witnesses had consistently and categorically denied Thompson's allegations, yet the newspaper chose not to interview the one witness that both Thompson and Connaughton claimed would verify their conflicting accounts of the relevant events. The newspaper's decision not to listen to the tapes of [an interview with that witness] in Connaughton's home also supports the finding of actual malice. . . . Much of what Thompson had said about the interview could easily have been verified or disproved by listening to the tapes. . . . Although failure to investigate will not alone support a finding of actual malice, the purposeful avoidance of the truth is in a different category.

4. *Problem.* The city's Director of Public Health has been accused by a local newspaper of misusing public funds for his personal benefit. The accusations were based primarily on interviews with the Director's former secretary and with an individual who carried out city health programs under contract with the Director's department. Assume that you could show that the accusations are false and defamatory. How would you go about showing that they were made with "malice"?

———

Note: *"Public Officials" and "Official Conduct"*

1. Footnote 23 of the Court's opinion in *New York Times* reserved the question "how far down into the lower ranks of government employees the 'public official' designation would extend" for purposes of the *New York Times* rule. The footnote was added at the suggestion of Justice Harlan. As he explained in his letter to Justice Brennan after a draft of the opinion was circulated, "I would not want to foreclose a cop, a clerk or some other minor public official from ordinary libel suits without a great deal more thought." *See* ANTHONY LEWIS, MAKE NO LAW: THE *SULLIVAN* CASE AND THE FIRST AMENDMENT 172 (1991).

2. Two years after *New York Times*, the Court considered a suit brought by the supervisor of a county recreation area. This was *Rosenblatt v. Baer*, 383 U.S. 75 (1966). Because the case had been tried before the *New York Times* decision came down, the Court did not decide whether the plaintiff was a "public official" for purposes of the *New York Times* rule. However, the opinion — again by Justice Brennan — did offer some guidance:

The motivating force for the decision in *New York Times* was twofold. . . . There is, first, a strong interest in debate on public issues, and, second, a strong interest in debate about those persons who are in a position significantly to influence the resolution of those issues. . . . It is clear, therefore, that the "public official" designation applies at the very least to those among the hierarchy of government employees who have, or appear to the public to have, substantial responsibility for or control over the conduct of governmental affairs. . . .

Where a position in government has such apparent importance that the public has an independent interest in the qualifications and performance of the person who holds it, beyond the general public interest in the qualifications and performance of all government employees, both elements we identified in *New York Times* are present and the *New York Times* malice standards apply.

[A concurring opinion suggests] that this test might apply to a night watchman accused of stealing state secrets. But a conclusion that the *New York Times* malice standards apply could not be reached merely because a statement defamatory of some person in government employ catches the public's interest; that conclusion would virtually disregard society's interest in protecting reputation. The employee's position must be one which would invite public scrutiny and discussion of the person holding it, entirely apart from the scrutiny and discussion occasioned by the particular charges in controversy.

3. Recall that in *New York Times*, Justice Goldberg, in his concurring opinion, commented: "The public official certainly has equal if not greater access than most private citizens to media of communication." The Court in *Rosenblatt* made no mention of that factor. Should "access to media of communication" be given any weight in determining whether a particular plaintiff should be considered a "public official" under *New York Times*?

4. In *New York Times*, the Court held that the "malice" standard must be applied in actions brought by public officials "against critics of their official conduct." What kinds of accusations fall within that description? In *Monitor Patriot Co. v. Roy*, 401 U.S. 265 (1971), the Court considered a libel action based on a newspaper story that characterized a candidate for the United States Senate as a "former small-time bootlegger." The Court first held that "publications concerning *candidates* must be accorded at least as much protection under the First and Fourteenth Amendments as those concerning *occupants* of public office." (Emphasis added.) The Court continued:

> The public-official rule protects the paramount public interest in a free flow of information to the people concerning public officials, their servants. To this end, anything which might touch on an official's fitness for office is relevant. . . .
>
> The principal activity of a candidate in our political system, his "office," so to speak, consists in putting before the voters every conceivable aspect of his public and private life that he thinks may lead the electorate to gain a good impression of him. . . . [A] charge of criminal conduct, no matter how remote in time or place, can never be irrelevant to an official's or a candidate's fitness for office for purposes of application of the "knowing falsehood or reckless disregard" rule of *New York Times Co. v. Sullivan*.

5. Which, if any, of the following should be deemed "public officials" for purposes of the *New York Times* rule? (Assume that the statements are false and defamatory.)

(a) A police lieutenant who was accused by a newspaper, based on allegations in an unfiled complaint, of fondling a woman while she was handcuffed during a strip search.

(b) A public high school teacher who was the subject of a newspaper story reporting accusations by parents that she is disorganized, erratic, forgetful and unfair; that she returns graded papers weeks late and absents herself from the classroom for long periods; and that she repeatedly demeans and humiliates students.

(c) A child protective care specialist in the Department of Human Resources who was the subject of a newspaper article stating that she did not petition for removal of an allegedly neglected and abused child for three years after gaining access to police files that described the child as a shoplifter, runaway, truant, and curfew violator.

————

Note: Beyond "Public Officials"

1. Consider this scenario. A newspaper has published a series of articles alleging that three star players on a major league baseball team have used steroids. The articles also alleged that the owner of the team helped the players to acquire the drugs. The players and the owner have sued the newspaper for libel, asserting that the accusations were false and defamatory. Must the plaintiffs meet the *New York Times* "malice" standard?

Obviously, the players and the owner are not "public officials." But is that dispositive? The Court confronted that issue three years after *New York Times* in *Curtis Publishing Co. v. Butts*, 388 U.S. 130 (1967). The opinion resolved a pair of cases that were argued and decided together. In *Butts*, the plaintiff was the former athletic director of the University of Georgia. Although the University is a state university, Butts was employed by the Georgia Athletic Association, a private corporation, rather than by the state itself. He sued Curtis for libel after an article published in the Saturday Evening Post accused him of conspiring to fix a football game. The jury awarded compensatory and punitive damages.

The companion case, *Associated Press v. Walker*, "arose out of the distribution of a news dispatch giving an eyewitness account of events on the campus of the University of Mississippi on the night of September 30, 1962, when a massive riot erupted because of federal efforts to enforce a court decree ordering the enrollment of a Negro, James Meredith, as a student in the University. The dispatch stated that [plaintiff] Walker, who was present on the campus, had taken command of the violent crowd and had personally led a charge against federal marshals sent there to effectuate the court's decree and to assist in preserving order." Walker sued for libel; he too won a jury verdict that was affirmed by the lower court.

At the Court's conference after oral argument, Justice Harlan observed: "We are at a turning point. Can the *Times* rule be contained in terms of public officials?" The Supreme Court in Conference 384. Ultimately all members of the Court agreed that the answer was "no." A majority joined an opinion by Chief Justice Warren explaining why:

> To me, differentiation between "public figures" and "public officials" and adoption of separate standards of proof for each have no basis in law, logic, or First Amendment policy. Increasingly in this country, the distinctions between governmental and private sectors are blurred. . . . [Many individuals] who do not hold public office at the moment are nevertheless

intimately involved in the resolution of important public questions or, by reason of their fame, shape events in areas of concern to society at large.

Viewed in this context, then, it is plain that although they are not subject to the restraints of the political process, "public figures," like "public officials," often play an influential role in ordering society. And surely as a class these "public figures" have as ready access as "public officials" to mass media of communication, both to influence policy and to counter criticism of their views and activities. Our citizenry has a legitimate and substantial interest in the conduct of such persons, and freedom of the press to engage in uninhibited debate about their involvement in public issues and events is as crucial as it is in the case of "public officials." The fact that they are not amenable to the restraints of the political process only underscores the legitimate and substantial nature of the interest, since it means that public opinion may be the only instrument by which society can attempt to influence their conduct.

The Court held that both Walker and Butts were "public figures" for First Amendment purposes.

2. Does Chief Justice Warren's analysis give sufficient weight to the rationale of *New York Times*? Justice Harlan, writing for four members of the Court, took note of differences as well as similarities between "public figures" and "public officials." He said:

In *New York Times* we were adjudicating in an area which lay close to seditious libel, and history dictated extreme caution in imposing liability. . . . In the cases we decide today none of the particular considerations involved in *New York Times* is present. These actions cannot be analogized to prosecutions for seditious libel. Neither plaintiff has any position in government which would permit a recovery by him to be viewed as a vindication of governmental policy. Neither was entitled to a special privilege protecting his utterances against accountability in libel. . . .

[On the other hand,] the public interest in the circulation of the materials here involved, and the publisher's interest in circulating them, is not less than that involved in *New York Times*. And both Butts and Walker commanded a substantial amount of independent public interest at the time of the publications; both, in our opinion, would have been labeled "public figures" under ordinary tort rules. Butts may have attained that status by position alone and Walker by his purposeful activity amounting to a thrusting of his personality into the "vortex" of an important public controversy, but both commanded sufficient continuing public interest and had sufficient access to the means of counterargument to be able "to expose through discussion the falsehood and fallacies" of the defamatory statements. *Whitney* (Brandeis, J., dissenting [sic]).

Justice Harlan thus concluded that "libel actions of the present kind cannot be left entirely to state libel laws," but that the burden on the plaintiff should not be as demanding as the *New York Times* "malice" standard. As already noted, the Court rejected that view.

3. Having established that a "public figure" must meet the same standard as a "public official," the Court was faced with the task of defining the "public figure." The task proved to be a difficult one, as the next case demonstrates.

[2] "Public Figures" and Private Plaintiffs

Gertz v. Robert Welch, Inc.

418 U.S. 323 (1974)

MR. JUSTICE POWELL delivered the opinion of the Court.

This Court has struggled for nearly a decade to define the proper accommodation between the law of defamation and the freedoms of speech and press protected by the First Amendment. With this decision we return to that effort. We granted certiorari to reconsider the extent of a publisher's constitutional privilege against liability for defamation of a private citizen.

I

In 1968 a Chicago policeman named Nuccio shot and killed a youth named Nelson. The state authorities prosecuted Nuccio for the homicide and ultimately obtained a conviction for murder in the second degree. The Nelson family retained petitioner Elmer Gertz, a reputable attorney, to represent them in civil litigation against Nuccio.

Respondent publishes American Opinion, a monthly outlet for the views of the John Birch Society. Early in the 1960s the magazine began to warn of a nationwide conspiracy to discredit local law enforcement agencies and create in their stead a national police force capable of supporting a Communist dictatorship. As part of the continuing effort to alert the public to this assumed danger, the managing editor of American Opinion commissioned an article on the murder trial of Officer Nuccio. For this purpose he engaged a regular contributor to the magazine. In March 1969 respondent published the resulting article under the title "FRAME-UP: Richard Nuccio And The War On Police." The article purports to demonstrate that the testimony against Nuccio at his criminal trial was false and that his prosecution was part of the Communist campaign against the police.

In his capacity as counsel for the Nelson family in the civil litigation, petitioner attended the coroner's inquest into the boy's death and initiated actions for damages, but he neither discussed Officer Nuccio with the press nor played any part in the criminal proceeding. Notwithstanding petitioner's remote connection with the prosecution of Nuccio, respondent's magazine portrayed him as an architect of the "frame-up." According to the article, the police file on petitioner took "a big, Irish cop to lift." The article stated that petitioner had been an official of the "Marxist League for Industrial Democracy, originally known as the Intercollegiate Socialist Society, which has advocated the violent seizure of our government." It labeled Gertz a "Leninist" and a

"Communist-fronter." It also stated that Gertz had been an officer of the National Lawyers Guild, described as a Communist organization that "probably did more than any other outfit to plan the Communist attack on the Chicago police during the 1968 Democratic Convention."

These statements contained serious inaccuracies. The implication that petitioner had a criminal record was false. Petitioner had been a member and officer of the National Lawyers Guild some 15 years earlier, but there was no evidence that he or that organization had taken any part in planning the 1968 demonstrations in Chicago. There was also no basis for the charge that petitioner was a "leninist" or a "Communist-fronter." And he had never been a member of the "Marxist League for Industrial Democracy" or the "Intercollegiate Socialist Society."

The managing editor of American Opinion made no effort to verify or substantiate the charges against petitioner. Instead, he appended an editorial introduction stating that the author had "conducted extensive research into the Richard Nuccio Case." And he included in the article a photograph of petitioner and wrote the caption that appeared under it: "Elmer Gertz of Red Guild harasses Nuccio." Respondent placed the issue of American Opinion containing the article on sale at newsstands throughout the country and distributed reprints of the article on the streets of Chicago. . . .

[Gertz filed a diversity action for libel in federal court. In the course of the lengthy proceedings, the District Court instructed the jury that some statements in the article constituted libel *per se*. On that basis, the jury awarded $50,000 to Gertz. Upon further reflection, however, the District Court concluded that the *New York Times* standard should govern the case even though Gertz was not a public official or public figure. The court entered judgment notwithstanding the verdict for the defendant. The court of appeals affirmed.] For the reasons stated below, we reverse.

II

The principal issue in this case is whether a newspaper or broadcaster that publishes defamatory falsehoods about an individual who is neither a public official nor a public figure may claim a constitutional privilege against liability for the injury inflicted by those statements. The Court considered this question on the rather different set of facts presented in *Rosenbloom v. Metromedia, Inc.*, 403 U.S. 29 (1971). [In *Rosenbloom*,] no majority could agree on a controlling rationale. The eight Justices who participated . . . announced their views in five separate opinions, none of which commanded more than three votes. [A plurality opinion by Justice Brennan took the position that the *New York Times* privilege should extend to defamatory falsehoods relating to private persons if the statements concerned matters of general or public interest.] The several statements not only reveal disagreement about the appropriate result in that case, they also reflect divergent traditions of thought about the general problem of reconciling the law of defamation with the First Amendment. One approach has been to extend the *New York Times* test to an expanding variety of situations. Another has been to vary the level of constitutional privilege for defamatory falsehood with the status of the person defamed. And a third view would grant to the press and broadcast media absolute immunity from liability for defamation. . . .

III

[A]

We begin with the common ground. Under the First Amendment there is no such thing as a false idea. However pernicious an opinion may seem, we depend for its correction not on the conscience of judges and juries but on the competition of other ideas. But there is no constitutional value in false statements of fact. Neither the intentional lie nor the careless error materially advances society's interest in "uninhibited, robust, and wide-open" debate on public issues. They belong to that category of utterances which "are no essential part of any exposition of ideas, and are of such slight social value as a step to truth that any benefit that may be derived from them is clearly outweighed by the social interest in order and morality." *Chaplinsky v. New Hampshire*, 315 U.S. 568, 572 (1942).

Although the erroneous statement of fact is not worthy of constitutional protection, it is nevertheless inevitable in free debate. . . . And punishment of error runs the risk of inducing a cautious and restrictive exercise of the constitutionally guaranteed freedoms of speech and press. Our decisions recognize that a rule of strict liability that compels a publisher or broadcaster to guarantee the accuracy of his factual assertions may lead to intolerable self-censorship. Allowing the media to avoid liability only by proving the truth of all injurious statements does not accord adequate protection to First Amendment liberties. . . . The First Amendment requires that we protect some falsehood in order to protect speech that matters.

The need to avoid self-censorship by the news media is, however, not the only societal value at issue. If it were, this Court would have embraced long ago the view that publishers and broadcasters enjoy an unconditional and indefeasible immunity from liability for defamation. Such a rule would, indeed, obviate the fear that the prospect of civil liability for injurious falsehood might dissuade a timorous press from the effective exercise of First Amendment freedoms. Yet absolute protection for the communications media requires a total sacrifice of the competing value served by the law of defamation.

The legitimate state interest underlying the law of libel is the compensation of individuals for the harm inflicted on them by defamatory falsehood. We would not lightly require the State to abandon this purpose, for, as Mr. Justice Stewart has reminded us, the individual's right to the protection of his own good name "reflects no more than our basic concept of the essential dignity and worth of every human being—a concept at the root of any decent system of ordered liberty. The protection of private personality, like the protection of life itself, is left primarily to the individual States under the Ninth and Tenth Amendments. But this does not mean that the right is entitled to any less recognition by this Court as a basic of our constitutional system." *Rosenblatt v. Baer*, 383 U.S. 75 (1966) (concurring opinion).

[B]

Some tension necessarily exists between the need for a vigorous and uninhibited press and the legitimate interest in redressing wrongful injury. . . . In our continuing effort to define the proper accommodation between these competing concerns, we have been especially anxious to assure to the freedoms of speech and press that "breathing space" essential to their fruitful exercise. To that end this Court has extended a measure of strategic protection to defamatory falsehood.

The *New York Times* standard defines the level of constitutional protection appropriate to the context of defamation of a public person. Those who, by reason of the notoriety of their achievements or the vigor and success with which they seek the public's attention, are properly classed as public figures and those who hold governmental office may recover for injury to reputation only on clear and convincing proof that the defamatory falsehood was made with knowledge of its falsity or with reckless disregard for the truth. This standard administers an extremely powerful antidote to the inducement to media self-censorship of the common-law rule of strict liability for libel and slander. And it exacts a correspondingly high price from the victims of defamatory falsehood. Plainly many deserving plaintiffs, including some intentionally subjected to injury, will be unable to surmount the barrier of the *New York Times* test. Despite this substantial abridgment of the state law right to compensation for wrongful hurt to one's reputation, the Court has concluded that the protection of the *New York Times* privilege should be available to publishers and broadcasters of defamatory falsehood concerning public officials and public figures. *New York Times Co. v. Sullivan; Curtis Publishing Co. v. Butts.*

We think that these decisions are correct, but we do not find their holdings justified solely by reference to the interest of the press and broadcast media in immunity from liability. Rather, we believe that the *New York Times* rule states an accommodation between this concern and the limited state interest present in the context of libel actions brought by public persons. For the reasons stated below, we conclude that the state interest in compensating injury to the reputation of private individuals requires that a different rule should obtain with respect to them.

Theoretically, of course, the balance between the needs of the press and the individual's claim to compensation for wrongful injury might be struck on a case-by-case basis. . . . But this approach would lead to unpredictable results and uncertain expectations, and it could render our duty to supervise the lower courts unmanageable. [We must therefore] lay down broad rules of general application. . . . [We do so even though] not all of the considerations which justify adoption of a given rule will obtain in each particular case decided under its authority.

[C]

With that caveat we have no difficulty in distinguishing among defamation plaintiffs. The first remedy of any victim of defamation is self-help—using available opportunities to contradict the lie or correct the error and thereby to minimize its adverse impact on reputation. Public officials and public figures usually enjoy significantly greater access to the channels of effective communication and hence have a more realistic opportunity to counteract false statements then private individuals normally enjoy.[9] Private individuals are therefore more vulnerable to injury, and the state interest in protecting them is correspondingly greater.

More important than the likelihood that private individuals will lack effective opportunities for rebuttal, there is a compelling normative consideration underlying the distinction between public and private defamation plaintiffs. An individual who decides to seek governmental office must accept certain necessary consequences of that involvement in public affairs. He runs the risk of closer public scrutiny than might otherwise be the case. And society's interest in the officers of government is not strictly limited to the formal discharge of official duties. As the Court pointed out in *Garrison v. Louisiana*, 379 U.S. at 77, the public's interest extends to "anything which might touch on an official's fitness for [office]. . . ."

Those classed as public figures stand in a similar position. Hypothetically, it may be possible for someone to become a public figure through no purposeful action of his own, but the instances of truly involuntary public figures must be exceedingly rare. For the most part those who attain this status have assumed roles of especial prominence in the affairs of society. Some occupy positions of such persuasive power and influence that they are deemed public figures for all purposes. More commonly, those classed as public figures have thrust themselves to the forefront of particular public controversies in order to influence the resolution of the issues involved. In either event, they invite attention and comment.

Even if the foregoing generalities do not obtain in every instance, the communications media are entitled to act on the assumption that public officials and public figures have voluntarily exposed themselves to increased risk of injury from defamatory falsehood concerning them. No such assumption is justified with respect to a private individual. He has not accepted public office or assumed an "influential role in ordering society." *Curtis Publishing Co. v. Butts* (Warren, C.J., concurring in result). He has relinquished no part of his interest in the protection of his own good name, and consequently he has a more compelling call on the courts for redress of injury inflicted by defamatory falsehood. Thus, private individuals are not only more vulnerable to injury than public officials and public figures; they are also more deserving of recovery.

For these reasons we conclude that the States should retain substantial latitude in their efforts to enforce a legal remedy for defamatory falsehood injurious to the reputation of a private individual. The extension of the *New York Times* test proposed by the *Rosenbloom* plurality would abridge this legitimate state interest to a degree that we find unacceptable. And it would occasion the additional difficulty of forcing state and federal judges to decide on an ad hoc basis which publications address issues of

---

9. Of course, an opportunity for rebuttal seldom suffices to undo harm of defamatory falsehood. Indeed, the law of defamation is rooted in our experience that the truth rarely catches up with a lie. But the fact that the self-help remedy of rebuttal, standing alone, is inadequate to its task does not mean that it is irrelevant to our inquiry.

"general or public interest" and which do not—to determine, in the words of Mr. Justice Marshall, "what information is relevant to self-government." We doubt the wisdom of committing this task to the conscience of judges. Nor does the Constitution require us to draw so thin a line between the drastic alternatives of the *New York Times* privilege and the common law of strict liability for defamatory error. . . .

We hold that, so long as they do not impose liability without fault, the States may define for themselves the appropriate standard of liability for a publisher or broadcaster of defamatory falsehood injurious to a private individual. This approach provides a more equitable boundary between the competing concerns involved here. It recognizes the strength of the legitimate state interest in compensating private individuals for wrongful injury to reputation, yet shields the press and broadcast media from the rigors of strict liability for defamation. At least this conclusion obtains where, as here, the substance of the defamatory statement "makes substantial danger to reputation apparent." This phrase places in perspective the conclusion we announce today. Our inquiry would involve considerations somewhat different from those discussed above if a State purported to condition civil liability on a factual misstatement whose content did not warn a reasonably prudent editor or broadcaster of its defamatory potential. Such a case is not now before us, and we intimate no view as to its proper resolution.

IV

Our accommodation of the competing values at stake in defamation suits by private individuals allows the States to impose liability on the publisher or broadcaster of defamatory falsehood on a less demanding showing than that required by *New York Times*. This conclusion is not based on a belief that the considerations which prompted the adoption of the *New York Times* privilege for defamation of public officials and its extension to public figures are wholly inapplicable to the context of private individuals. Rather, we [believe that] the strong and legitimate state interest in compensating private individuals for injury to reputation [extends] no further than compensation for actual injury. For the reasons stated below, we hold that the States may not permit recovery of presumed or punitive damages, at least when liability is not based on a showing of knowledge of falsity or reckless disregard for the truth.

The common law of defamation is an oddity of tort law, for it allows recovery of purportedly compensatory damages without evidence of actual loss. Under the traditional rules pertaining to actions for libel, the existence of injury is presumed from the fact of publication. . . . [This doctrine] invites juries to punish unpopular opinion rather than to compensate individuals for injury sustained by the publication of a false fact. More to the point, the States have no substantial interest in securing for plaintiffs such as this petitioner gratuitous awards of money damages far in excess of any actual injury.

We would not, of course, invalidate state law simply because we doubt its wisdom, but here we are attempting to reconcile state law with a competing interest grounded in the constitutional command of the First Amendment. It is therefore appropriate to require that state remedies for defamatory falsehood reach no farther than is necessary to protect the legitimate interest involved. It is necessary to restrict defamation plaintiffs who do not prove knowledge of falsity or reckless disregard for the truth to compensation for actual injury.... [Actual injury] is not limited to out-of-pocket loss. Indeed, the more customary types of actual harm inflicted by defamatory falsehood include impairment of reputation and standing in the community, personal humiliation, and mental anguish and suffering....

We also find no justification for allowing awards of punitive damages against publishers and broadcasters held liable under state-defined standards of liability for defamation.... Like the doctrine of presumed damages, jury discretion to award punitive damages unnecessarily exacerbates the danger of media self-censorship, but, unlike the former rule, punitive damages are wholly irrelevant to the state interest that justifies a negligence standard for private defamation actions.... In short, the private defamation plaintiff who establishes liability under a less demanding standard than that stated by *New York Times* may recover only such damages as are sufficient to compensate him for actual injury.

V

Notwithstanding our refusal to extend the *New York Times* privilege to defamation of private individuals, respondent contends that we should affirm the judgment below on the ground that petitioner is either a public official or a public figure. There is little basis for the former assertion. Several years prior to the present incident, petitioner had served briefly on housing committees appointed by the mayor of Chicago, but at the time of publication he had never held any remunerative governmental position. Respondent admits this but argues that petitioner's appearance at the coroner's inquest rendered him a "de facto public official." Our cases recognized no such concept. Respondent's suggestion would sweep all lawyers under the *New York Times* rule as officers of the court and distort the plain meaning of the "public official" category beyond all recognition. We decline to follow it.

Respondent's characterization of petitioner as a public figure raises a different question. That designation may rest on either of two alternative bases. In some instances an individual may achieve such pervasive fame or notoriety that he becomes a public figure for all purposes and in all contexts. More commonly, an individual voluntarily injects himself or is drawn into a particular public controversy and thereby becomes a public figure for a limited range of issues. In either case such persons assume special prominence in the resolution of public questions.

Petitioner has long been active in community and professional affairs. He has served as an officer of local civic groups and of various professional organizations, and he has published several books and articles on legal subjects. Although petitioner was consequently well known in some circles, he had achieved no general fame or notoriety in the community. None of the prospective jurors called at the trial had ever heard of petitioner prior to this litigation, and respondent offered no proof that this response was atypical of the local population. We would not lightly assume that a citizen's participation in community and professional affairs rendered him a public figure for all purposes. Absent clear evidence of general fame or notoriety in the community, and pervasive involvement in the affairs of society, an individual should not be deemed a public personality for all aspects of his life. It is preferable to reduce the public-figure question to a more meaningful context by looking to the nature and extent of an individual's participation in the particular controversy giving rise to the defamation.

In this context it is plain that petitioner was not a public figure. He played a minimal role at the coroner's inquest, and his participation related solely to his representation of a private client. He took no part in the criminal prosecution of Officer Nuccio. Moreover, he never discussed either the criminal or civil litigation with the press and was never quoted as having done so. He plainly did not thrust himself into the vortex of this public issue, nor did he engage the public's attention in an attempt to influence its outcome. We are persuaded that the trial court did not err in refusing to characterize petitioner as a public figure for the purpose of this litigation.

We therefore conclude that the *New York Times* standard is inapplicable to this case and that the trial court erred in entering judgment for respondent. Because the jury was allowed to impose liability without fault and was permitted to presume damages without proof of injury, a new trial is necessary. We reverse and remand for further proceedings in accord with this opinion.

Mr. Chief Justice Burger, dissenting.

In today's opinion the Court abandons the traditional thread so far as the ordinary private citizen is concerned and introduces the concept that the media will be liable for negligence in publishing defamatory statements with respect to such persons. . . . I would prefer to allow this area of law to continue to evolve as it has up to now with respect to private citizens rather than embark on a new doctrinal theory which has no jurisprudential ancestry. . . .

I would reverse the judgment of the Court of Appeals and remand for reinstatement of the verdict of the jury and the entry of an appropriate judgment on that verdict.

Mr. Justice Douglas, dissenting.

. . . Discussion of public affairs is often marked by highly charged emotions, and jurymen, not unlike us all, are subject to those emotions. It is indeed this very type of speech which is the reason for the First Amendment since speech which arouses little emotion is little in need of protection. The vehicle for publication in this case was the American Opinion, a most controversial periodical which disseminates the views of the John Birch Society, an organization which many deem to be quite offensive. The subject matter involved "Communist plots," "conspiracies against law enforcement agencies," and the killing of a private citizen by the police. With any such amalgam of controversial elements pressing upon the jury, a jury determination, unpredictable in the most neutral circumstances, becomes for those who venture to discuss heated issues, a virtual roll of the dice separating them from liability for often massive claims of damage.

It is only the hardy publisher who will engage in discussion in the face of such risk, and the Court's preoccupation with proliferating standards in the area of libel increases the risks. It matters little whether the standard be articulated as "malice" or "reckless disregard of the truth" or "negligence," for jury determinations by any of those criteria are virtually unreviewable. This Court, in its continuing delineation of variegated mantles of First Amendment protection, is, like the potential publisher, left with only speculation on how jury findings were influenced by the effect the subject matter of the publication had upon the minds and viscera of the jury. The standard announced today leaves the States free to "define for themselves the appropriate standard of liability for a publisher or broadcaster" in the circumstances of this case. This of course leaves the simple negligence standard as an option, with the jury free to impose damages upon a finding that the publisher failed to act as "a reasonable man." With such continued erosion of First Amendment protection, I fear that it may well be the reasonable man who refrains from speaking.

Since in my view the First and Fourteenth Amendments prohibit the imposition of damages upon respondent for this discussion of public affairs, I would affirm the judgment below.

MR. JUSTICE BRENNAN, dissenting.

. . . I adhere to my view expressed in *Rosenbloom v. Metromedia, Inc.*, that we strike the proper accommodation between avoidance of media self-censorship and protection of individual reputations only when we require States to apply the *New York Times* knowing-or-reckless-falsity standard in civil libel actions concerning media reports of the involvement of private individuals in events of public or general interest.

The teaching to be distilled from our prior cases is that, while public interest in events may at times be influenced by the notoriety of the individuals involved, "[t]he public's primary interest is in the event, [the] conduct of the participant and the content, effect, and significance of the [conduct]." *Rosenbloom.* Matters of public or general interest do not "suddenly become less so merely because a private individual is involved, or because in some sense the individual did not 'voluntarily' choose to become involved." . . .

The Court does not discount altogether the danger that jurors will punish for the expression of unpopular opinions. This probability accounts for the Court's limitation that "the States may not permit recovery of presumed or punitive damages, at least when liability is not based on a showing of knowledge of falsity or reckless disregard for the truth." But plainly a jury's latitude to impose liability for want of due care poses a far greater threat of suppressing unpopular views than does a possible recovery of presumed or punitive damages. Moreover, the Court's broad-ranging examples of "actual injury," including impairment of reputation and standing in the community, as well as personal humiliation, and mental anguish and suffering, inevitably allow a jury bent on punishing expression of unpopular views a formidable weapon for doing so. Finally, even a limitation of recovery to "actual injury"—however much it reduces the size or frequency of recoveries—will not provide the necessary elbowroom for First Amendment expression.

"It is not simply the possibility of a judgment for damages that results in self-censorship. The very possibility of having to engage in litigation, an expensive and protracted process, is threat enough to cause discussion and debate to 'steer far wider of the unlawful zone' thereby keeping protected discussion from public [cognizance]. Too, a small newspaper suffers equally from a substantial damage award, whether the label of the award be 'actual' or 'punitive.'"

MR. JUSTICE WHITE, dissenting.

For some 200 years — from the very founding of the Nation — the law of defamation and right of the ordinary citizen to recover for false publication injurious to his reputation have been almost exclusively the business of state courts and legislatures. [But now, the Court] has federalized major aspects of libel law by declaring unconstitutional in important respects the prevailing defamation law in all or most of the 50 States. That result is accomplished by requiring the plaintiff in each and every defamation action to prove not only the defendant's culpability beyond his act of publishing defamatory material but also actual damage to reputation resulting from the publication. Moreover, punitive damages may not be recovered by showing malice in the traditional sense of ill will; knowing falsehood or reckless disregard of the truth will not be required.

I assume these sweeping changes will be popular with the press, but this is not the road to salvation for a court of law. As I see it, there are wholly insufficient grounds for scuttling the libel laws of the States in such wholesale fashion, to say nothing of deprecating the reputation interest of ordinary citizens and rendering them powerless to protect themselves.

[Justice White's detailed critique of the Court's decision is omitted. He concluded by saying:] I would reverse the judgment of the Court of Appeals and reinstate the jury's verdict.

———

Note: Who Is a "Public Figure"?

1. The Court in *Gertz* says that there are two kinds of "public figures." First, "an individual may achieve such pervasive fame or notoriety that he becomes a public figure for all purposes and in all contexts." Second and more commonly, an individual may "voluntarily [inject himself or be drawn] into a particular public controversy" and thus become "a public figure for a limited range of issues."

Who in public life today might be considered "a public figure for all purposes and in all contexts"?

2. A year after *Gertz*, in *Time Inc. v. Firestone*, 424 U.S. 448 (1975), the Court considered a libel judgment based on an item appearing in Time Magazine that purported to describe the result of marital dissolution litigation between the plaintiff, Mary Alice Firestone, and her husband. One of the questions was whether Mrs. Firestone was a "public figure." Justice Marshall — who had joined the Court's opinion in *Gertz* — argued that she was. He said:

> [Mrs. Firestone] was prominent among the "400" of Palm Beach society, and an "active member of the sporting set" whose activities predictably attracted the

attention of a sizable portion of the public. Indeed, Mrs. Firestone's appearances in the press were evidently frequent enough to warrant her subscribing to a press-clipping service.

Mrs. Firestone brought suit for separate maintenance, with reason to know of the likely public interest in the proceedings. As the Supreme Court of Florida noted, Mr. and Mrs. Firestone's "marital difficulties were . . . well-known," and the lawsuit became "a veritable cause celebre in social circles across the country." The 17-month trial and related events attracted national news coverage, and elicited no fewer than 43 articles in the Miami Herald and 45 articles in the Palm Beach Post and Palm Beach Times. Far from shunning the publicity, Mrs. Firestone held several press conferences in the course of the proceedings.

These facts are sufficient to warrant the conclusion that Mary Alice Firestone was a "public figure" for purposes of reports on the judicial proceedings she initiated. . . .

If *Gertz* is to have any meaning at all, the focus of analysis must be on the actions of the individual, and the degree of public attention that had already developed, or that could have been anticipated, before the report in question. Under this approach, the class of public figures must include an individual like Mrs. Firestone, who acquired a social prominence that could be expected to attract public attention, initiated a lawsuit that predictably attracted more public attention, and held press conferences in the course of and in regard to the lawsuit.

However, a majority of the Court disagreed and held that Mrs. Firestone was *not* a public figure:

[Mrs. Firestone] did not assume any role of especial prominence in the affairs of society, other than perhaps Palm Beach society, and she did not thrust herself to the forefront of any particular public controversy in order to influence the resolution of the issues involved in it. . . .

Dissolution of a marriage through judicial proceedings is not the sort of "public controversy" referred to in *Gertz*, even though the marital difficulties of extremely wealthy individuals may be of interest to some portion of the reading public. Nor did respondent freely choose to publicize issues as to the propriety of her married life. She was compelled to go to court by the State in order to obtain legal release from the bonds of matrimony. . . . Her actions, both in instituting the litigation and in its conduct, were quite different from those of General Walker in *Curtis Publishing Co.* She assumed no "special prominence in the resolution of public questions."

3. In *Hutchinson v. Proxmire*, 443 U.S. 111 (1979), the Court further clarified the *Gertz* standard. Hutchinson was a research behavioral scientist who sued Senator William Proxmire for defamation arising out of Proxmire's giving what he called his "Golden Fleece" award. Proxmire had initiated the monthly award to publicize what he perceived to be the most egregious examples of wasteful governmental spending. This particular "award" went to federal agencies that had sponsored Hutchinson's research. Hutchinson alleged that in making the award and publicizing it nation-wide, Proxmire had libeled him.

The lower courts found that Hutchinson was a public figure for the limited purpose of comment on his receipt of federal funds for research projects. The Supreme Court reversed, saying:

> [The lower courts'] conclusion was based upon two factors: first, Hutchinson's successful application for federal funds and the reports in local newspapers of the federal grants; second, Hutchinson's access to the media, as demonstrated by the fact that some newspapers and wire services reported his response to the announcement of the Golden Fleece Award. Neither of those factors demonstrates that Hutchinson was a public figure prior to the controversy engendered by the Golden Fleece Award; his access, such as it was, came after the alleged libel.
>
> On this record, Hutchinson's activities and public profile are much like those of countless members of his profession. His published writings reach a relatively small category of professionals concerned with research in human behavior. To the extent the subject of his published writings became a matter of controversy, it was a consequence of the Golden Fleece Award. Clearly, those charged with defamation cannot, by their own conduct, create their own defense by making the claimant a public figure.
>
> Hutchinson did not thrust himself or his views into public controversy to influence others. [The defendants] have not identified such a particular controversy; at most, they point to concern about general public expenditures. But that concern is shared by most and relates to most public expenditures; it is not sufficient to make Hutchinson a public figure. . . .
>
> Moreover, Hutchinson at no time assumed any role of public prominence in the broad question of concern about expenditures. Neither his applications for federal grants nor his publications in professional journals can be said to have invited that degree of public attention and comment on his receipt of federal grants essential to meet the public figure level. . . .
>
> Finally, we cannot agree that Hutchinson had such access to the media that he should be classified as a public figure. Hutchinson's access was limited to responding to the announcement of the Golden Fleece Award. He did not have the regular and continuing access to the media that is one of the accouterments of having become a public figure.

4. Since 1979, the Supreme Court has heard very few libel cases and has given little additional guidance about who is a "public figure." However, in *Bartnicki v. Vopper*, 532 U.S. 514 (2001) (*infra* this chapter Note), a case involving a claim of invasion of privacy, a concurring opinion briefly addressed the point. The plaintiffs in *Bartnicki* were the president of a local teacher's union and the union's chief negotiator. Justice

Breyer, joined by Justice O'Connor, said that the plaintiffs were "'limited public figures,' for they voluntarily engaged in a public controversy. They thereby subjected themselves to somewhat greater public scrutiny and had a lesser interest in privacy than an individual engaged in purely private affairs."

———

Note: *"Public Figures" in the Lower Courts*

As the preceding Note indicates, the Supreme Court has been reluctant to find that a private individual has become a "public figure," even for a limited purpose. However, numerous cases in the lower courts have held that particular plaintiffs fall within the category. A few examples are given in this Note. Do you agree that the plaintiffs in these cases satisfy the criteria articulated by the Supreme Court?

1. *Lohrenz v. Donnelly*, 350 F.3d 1272 (D.C. Cir. 2003). The plaintiff became one of the first two women combat pilots in the United States Navy at a time when there was a public controversy about the appropriateness of women serving in combat roles. The defendant was an organization opposed to women in combat; it published various statements asserting that the plaintiff was an incompetent combat pilot. The court held that Lohrenz was a limited-purpose public figure:

> Lohrenz's evidence shows that she chose the F-14 combat jet while well aware of the public controversy over women in combat roles. . . . [When,] as a result of that choice, she became one of the first two women combat pilots, a central role in the public controversy came with the territory. Having assumed the risk when she chose combat jets that she would in fact receive a combat assignment, Lt. Lohrenz attained a position of special prominence in the controversy when she "suited up" as an F-14 combat pilot.

2. *Medure v. New York Times Co.*, 60 F. Supp. 2d 477 (W.D. Pa. 1999). The plaintiff was a businessman who owned companies that managed gaming casinos on Indian reservations. He was involved in a partnership to develop another gaming resort in California. The defendant newspaper published two articles about the proposed casino that reported concerns about the influence of organized crime on Indian casinos. The court found that the plaintiff was a limited-purpose public figure:

> Medure thrust himself to the forefront of a broad public controversy over gaming casinos on Indian property, and [this] controversy encompassed more than just the isolated Fountaingrove project. . . . Indeed, in trying to gain official and community approval for the Fountaingrove Casino plan through media and public relations events, Medure helped to create the controversy and became, as an individual and a businessman, a significant part of it. . . .

> The allegedly defamatory statements were made regarding a matter of public controversy, with "foreseeable and substantial ramifications for non-participants." Furthermore, by his involvement in the Fountaingrove casino project, Medure injected himself into the events which were the

subject of the articles at issue, and attempted to influence the outcome of the controversy itself.

3. *Dameron v. Washington Magazine, Inc.*, 779 F.2d 736 (D.C. Cir. 1985). The plaintiff was an air traffic controller who was the sole controller on duty at Dulles Airport at the time of an air crash. The defendant magazine published a lengthy article on aviation safety. The article stated that air traffic controllers "have been assigned partial blame in a few accidents," including the accident at Dulles. The court held that Dameron had become an "involuntary public figure":

> By sheer bad luck, Dameron happened to be the controller on duty at the time of the Mt. Weather crash. As in *Gertz*, Dameron "assumed a special prominence in the resolution of [a] public question." He became embroiled, through no desire of his own, in the ensuing controversy over the causes of the accident. He thereby became well known to the public in this one very limited connection. The numerous press reports on the Mt. Weather crash introduced by the defendants in their motion for summary judgment amply demonstrate this.

———————

Note: Suits by Private Plaintiffs

1. There are two groups of dissenters in *Gertz*. Justice Douglas and Justice Brennan think the Court does not go far enough in protecting defamatory falsehoods about persons who are not public figures, though they differ in where they would draw the line. Chief Justice Burger and Justice White think the Court has gone too far in imposing new burdens on non-public figure plaintiffs. Does the Court make a persuasive case for drawing the lines that it does?

2. After *Gertz*, the Court continued to refine the First Amendment doctrines applicable to libel actions by plaintiffs who are neither public officials nor public figures. Three decisions are of particular importance. Two are discussed in this Note; the third, in the Note that follows.

3. Recall that in *Gertz* the Court held that a private individual must prove "actual malice" in order to recover presumed or punitive damages for false and defamatory statements if the libel involved a matter of public concern. In *Dun & Bradstreet, Inc. v. Greenmoss Builders, Inc.*, 472 U.S. 749 (1985), the question was whether this rule applies when the false and defamatory statements did not involve matters of public concern. The Court held that the answer is "No." A plurality opinion by Justice Powell explained:

> [To answer this question, we] must employ the approach approved in *Gertz* and balance the State's interest in compensating private individuals for injury to their reputation against the First Amendment interest in protecting this type of expression. This state interest is identical to the one weighed in *Gertz*. . . .
>
> The First Amendment interest, on the other hand, is less [important]. . . . We have long recognized that not all speech is of equal First Amendment

importance. It is speech on matters of public concern that is "at the heart of the First Amendment's protection." ... In contrast, speech on matters of purely private concern is of less First Amendment concern. ... [In such cases,] "there is no threat to the free and robust debate of public issues; there is no potential interference with a meaningful dialogue of ideas concerning self-government; and there is no threat of liability causing a reaction of self-censorship by the press." ...

In *Gertz*, we found that the state interest in awarding presumed and punitive damages was not "substantial" in view of their effect on speech at the core of First Amendment concern. This interest, however, is "substantial" relative to the incidental effect these remedies may have on speech of significantly less constitutional interest. The rationale of the common-law rules has been the experience and judgment of history that "proof of actual damage will be impossible in a great many cases where, from the character of the defamatory words and the circumstances of publication, it is all but certain that serious harm has resulted in fact." ... In light of the reduced constitutional value of speech involving no matters of public concern, we hold that the state interest adequately supports awards of presumed and punitive damages — even absent a showing of "actual malice."

The libel suit in *Dun & Bradstreet* was based on a report that the defendant sent to five subscribers falsely stating that Greenmoss, a construction contractor, had filed a voluntary petition for bankruptcy. The Court held that this credit report did not involve a matter of public concern. The Court drew on its decision in *Connick v. Myers*, 461 U.S. 138 (1983), a case involving the free-speech rights of public employees. (*See* Chapter 12.) The Court said:

"[Whether speech] addresses a matter of public concern must be determined by [the expression's] content, form, and context ... as revealed by the whole record." *Connick*. These factors indicate that petitioner's credit report concerns no public issue. It was speech solely in the individual interest of the speaker and its specific business audience. This particular interest warrants no special protection when — as in this case — the speech is wholly false and clearly damaging to the victim's business reputation. Moreover, since the credit report was made available to only five subscribers, who, under the terms of the subscription agreement, could not disseminate it further, it cannot be said that the report involves any "strong interest in the free flow of commercial information." There is simply no credible argument that this type of credit reporting requires special protection to ensure that "debate on public issues [will] be uninhibited, robust, and wide-open."

Four dissenting Justices, in an opinion by Justice Brennan, acknowledged that the credit report was "not at the essence of self-government," but argued that it fell "within the range of speech that *Gertz* sought to protect from the chill of unrestrained presumed and punitive damage awards."

4. The First Amendment claim enjoyed greater success in *Philadelphia Newspapers, Inc. v. Hepps*, 475 U.S. 767 (1986). A bare majority held that "at least where a newspaper publishes speech of public concern, a private-figure plaintiff cannot recover damages without also showing that the statements at issue are false." The Court explained:

> Here, as in *Gertz*, the plaintiff is a private figure and the newspaper articles are of public concern. In *Gertz*, as in *New York Times*, the common-law rule was superseded by a constitutional rule. We believe that the common law's rule on falsity — that the defendant must bear the burden of proving truth — must similarly fall here to a constitutional requirement that the plaintiff bear the burden of showing falsity, as well as fault, before recovering damages. . . .

> Because the burden of proof is the deciding factor only when the evidence is ambiguous, we cannot know how much of the speech affected by the allocation of the burden of proof is true and how much is false. . . . To ensure that true speech on matters of public concern is not deterred, we hold that the common-law presumption that defamatory speech is false cannot stand when a plaintiff seeks damages against a media defendant for speech of public concern.

––––––––

Note: "Fact" and "Opinion"

1. Some of the language in the *Gertz* opinion (notably the opening paragraph of Part III) led many courts to conclude that the Court drew a distinction between "fact" and "opinion," and that the First Amendment provides absolute immunity for any expression of "opinion." In *Milkovich v. Lorain Journal Co.*, 497 U.S. 1 (1990), the Supreme Court rejected that proposition. The Court explained:

> [The breathing space which freedoms of expression require in order to survive] is adequately secured by existing constitutional doctrine without the creation of an artificial dichotomy between "opinion" and fact.

> Foremost, we think *Hepps* [discussed in the Note above] stands for the proposition that a statement on matters of public concern must be provable as false before there can be liability under state defamation law, at least in situations, like the present, where a media defendant is involved . . . . *Hepps* ensures that a statement of opinion relating to matters of public concern which does not contain a provably false factual connotation will receive full constitutional protection.

> Next, [another line of cases] provides protection for statements that cannot "reasonably [be] interpreted as stating actual facts" about an individual. This provides assurance that public debate will not suffer for lack of "imaginative expression" or the "rhetorical hyperbole" which has traditionally added much to the discourse of our Nation. [This line of cases includes *Hustler Magazine v. Falwell*, 485 U.S. 46 (1988), discussed in the next subsection.]

The *New York Times-Butts-Gertz* culpability requirements further ensure that debate on public issues remains "uninhibited, robust, and wide-open." Thus, where a statement of "opinion" on a matter of public concern reasonably implies false and defamatory facts regarding public figures or officials, those individuals must show that such statements were made with knowledge of their false implications or with reckless disregard of their truth. Similarly, where such a statement involves a private figure on a matter of public concern, a plaintiff must show that the false connotations were made with some level of fault as required by *Gertz*.

2. The libel suit in *Milkovich* was based on signed article published by the defendant newspaper "implying that Milkovich, a local high school wrestling coach, lied under oath in a judicial proceeding about an incident involving [Milkovich] and his team which occurred at a wrestling match." The article included the following sentence: "Anyone who attended the meet, whether he be from Maple Heights, Mentor, or impartial observer, knows in his heart that Milkovich and [the school superintendent] lied at the hearing after each having given his solemn oath to tell the truth." The Supreme Court, after rejecting the argument that any expression of "opinion" is protected, continued:

> The dispositive question in the present case then becomes whether a reasonable factfinder could conclude that the statements in the [newspaper] column imply an assertion that petitioner Milkovich perjured himself in a judicial proceeding. We think this question must be answered in the affirmative. As the Ohio Supreme Court itself observed: "The clear impact in some nine sentences and a caption is that [Milkovich] 'lied at the hearing after . . . having given his solemn oath to tell the truth.'" This is not the sort of loose, figurative, or hyperbolic language which would negate the impression that the writer was seriously maintaining that petitioner committed the crime of perjury. Nor does the general tenor of the article negate this impression.
>
> We also think the connotation that petitioner committed perjury is sufficiently factual to be susceptible of being proved true or false. A determination whether petitioner lied in this instance can be made on a core of objective evidence by comparing, inter alia, petitioner's testimony before the [athletic association] board with his subsequent testimony before the trial court.

3. One of the leading pre-*Milkovich* cases in the lower courts was *Ollman v. Evans*, 750 F.2d 970 (D.C. Cir. 1984). The plaintiff in that case was a political science professor who sued for libel based on a newspaper column published under the title "The Marxist Professor's Intentions." The column included the following statements, which the plaintiff asserted were false and defamatory:

> While Ollman is described in news accounts as a "respected Marxist scholar," he is widely viewed in his profession as a political activist . . . . [His] pamphleteering is hooted at by one political scientist in a major eastern university, whose scholarship and reputation as a liberal are well known. "Ollman has no status within the profession, but is a pure and simple activist," he said.

The D.C. Circuit concluded that all of the challenged statements in the column were protected as "opinion." How would they be analyzed under *Milkovich*?

[3] "Outrage" and Emotional Distress

Snyder v. Phelps

562 U.S. 443 (2011)

Chief Justice Roberts delivered the opinion of the Court.

A jury held members of the Westboro Baptist Church liable for millions of dollars in damages for picketing near a soldier's funeral service. The picket signs reflected the church's view that the United States is overly tolerant of sin and that God kills American soldiers as punishment. The question presented is whether the First Amendment shields the church members from tort liability for their speech in this case.

I

A

Fred Phelps founded the Westboro Baptist Church in Topeka, Kansas, in 1955. The church's congregation believes that God hates and punishes the United States for its tolerance of homosexuality, particularly in America's military. The church frequently communicates its views by picketing, often at military funerals. In the more than 20 years that the members of Westboro Baptist have publicized their message, they have picketed nearly 600 funerals.

Marine Lance Corporal Matthew Snyder was killed in Iraq in the line of duty. Lance Corporal Snyder's father selected the Catholic church in the Snyders' hometown of Westminster, Maryland, as the site for his son's funeral. Local newspapers provided notice of the time and location of the service.

Phelps became aware of Matthew Snyder's funeral and decided to travel to Maryland with six other Westboro Baptist parishioners (two of his daughters and four of his grandchildren) to picket. On the day of the memorial service, the Westboro congregation members picketed on public land adjacent to public streets near the Maryland State House, the United States Naval Academy, and Matthew Snyder's funeral. The Westboro picketers carried signs that were largely the same at all three locations. They stated, for instance: "God Hates the USA/Thank God for 9/11," "America is Doomed," "Don't Pray for the USA," "Thank God for IEDs," "Thank God for Dead Soldiers," "Pope in Hell," "Priests Rape Boys," "God Hates Fags," "You're Going to Hell," and "God Hates You."

The church had notified the authorities in advance of its intent to picket at the time of the funeral, and the picketers complied with police instructions in staging their demonstration. The picketing took place within a 10- by 25-foot plot of public land adjacent to a public street, behind a temporary fence. That plot was approximately 1,000 feet from the church where the funeral was held. Several buildings separated the picket site from the church. The Westboro picketers displayed their signs for about

30 minutes before the funeral began and sang hymns and recited Bible verses. None of the picketers entered church property or went to the cemetery. They did not yell or use profanity, and there was no violence associated with the picketing.

The funeral procession passed within 200 to 300 feet of the picket site. Although Snyder testified that he could see the tops of the picket signs as he drove to the funeral, he did not see what was written on the signs until later that night, while watching a news broadcast covering the event.

B

Snyder filed suit against Phelps, Phelps's daughters, and the Westboro Baptist Church (collectively Westboro or the church) in the United States District Court for the District of Maryland under that court's diversity jurisdiction. [Snyder alleged five state tort law claims, including intentional infliction of emotional distress. A trial was held on that claim and two others. At trial, Snyder described the severity of his emotional injuries. He testified that he is unable to separate the thought of his dead son from his thoughts of Westboro's picketing, and that he often becomes tearful, angry, and physically ill when he thinks about it. Expert witnesses testified that Snyder's emotional anguish had resulted in severe depression and had exacerbated pre-existing health conditions.

[A jury found for Snyder and held Westboro liable for $2.9 million in compensatory damages and $8 million in punitive damages. The District Court remitted the punitive damages award to $2.1 million, but left the jury verdict otherwise intact. The Court of Appeals reversed, holding that the church was entitled to judgment as a matter of law because the First Amendment fully protected Westboro's speech.]

II

To succeed on a claim for intentional infliction of emotional distress in Maryland, a plaintiff must demonstrate that the defendant intentionally or recklessly engaged in extreme and outrageous conduct that caused the plaintiff to suffer severe emotional distress. The Free Speech Clause of the First Amendment—"Congress shall make no law . . . abridging the freedom of speech"—can serve as a defense in state tort suits, including suits for intentional infliction of emotional distress. See, *e.g., Hustler Magazine, Inc. v. Falwell*, 485 U.S. 46 (1988).

Whether the First Amendment prohibits holding Westboro liable for its speech in this case turns largely on whether that speech is of public or private concern, as determined by all the circumstances of the case. "[S]peech on 'matters of public concern' . . . is 'at the heart of the First Amendment's protection.'" *Dun & Bradstreet, Inc. v. Greenmoss Builders, Inc.* (1985) (opinion of Powell, J.). The First Amendment reflects "a profound national commitment to the principle that debate on public issues should be uninhibited, robust, and wide-open." *New York Times Co. v. Sullivan* (1964) . . . . Accordingly, "speech on public issues occupies the highest rung of the hierarchy of First Amendment values, and is entitled to special protection." *Connick v. Myers* (1983) [Chapter 12].

"'[N]ot all speech is of equal First Amendment importance,'" however, and where matters of purely private significance are at issue, First Amendment protections are often less rigorous. *Hustler* (quoting *Dun & Bradstreet*); see *Connick*. That is because restricting speech on purely private matters does not implicate the same constitutional concerns as limiting speech on matters of public interest: "[T]here is no threat to the free and robust debate of public issues; there is no potential interference with a meaningful dialogue of ideas"; and the "threat of liability" does not pose the risk of "a reaction of self-censorship" on matters of public import. *Dun & Bradstreet.*

We noted a short time ago, in considering whether public employee speech addressed a matter of public concern, that "the boundaries of the public concern test are not well defined." *San Diego v. Roe* (2004) [Chapter 12 Note]. Although that remains true today, we have articulated some guiding principles, principles that accord broad protection to speech to ensure that courts themselves do not become inadvertent censors.

Speech deals with matters of public concern when it can "be fairly considered as relating to any matter of political, social, or other concern to the community," *Connick*, or when it "is a subject of legitimate news interest; that is, a subject of general interest and of value and concern to the public," *San Diego*. The arguably "inappropriate or controversial character of a statement is irrelevant to the question whether it deals with a matter of public concern." *Rankin v. McPherson,* 483 U.S. 378 (1987).

Our opinion in *Dun & Bradstreet*, on the other hand, provides an example of speech of only private concern. In that case we held, as a general matter, that information about a particular individual's credit report "concerns no public issue." The content of the report, we explained, "was speech solely in the individual interest of the speaker and its specific business audience." That was confirmed by the fact that the particular report was sent to only five subscribers to the reporting service, who were bound not to disseminate it further. To cite another example, we concluded in *San Diego v. Roe* that, in the context of a government employer regulating the speech of its employees, videos of an employee engaging in sexually explicit acts did not address a public concern; the videos "did nothing to inform the public about any aspect of the [employing agency's] functioning or operation."

Deciding whether speech is of public or private concern requires us to examine the "'content, form, and context'" of that speech, "'as revealed by the whole record.'" *Dun & Bradstreet* (quoting *Connick*). As in other First Amendment cases, the court is obligated "to 'make an independent examination of the whole record' in order to make sure that 'the judgment does not constitute a forbidden intrusion on the field of free expression.'" *Bose Corp. v. Consumers Union of United States, Inc.*, 466 U.S. 485, 499 (1984). In considering content, form, and context, no factor is dispositive, and it is necessary to evaluate all the circumstances of the speech, including what was said, where it was said, and how it was said.

The "content" of Westboro's signs plainly relates to broad issues of interest to society at large, rather than matters of "purely private concern." *Dun & Bradstreet*. The placards read "God Hates the USA/Thank God for 9/11," "America is Doomed," "Don't

Pray for the USA," "Thank God for IEDs," "Fag Troops," "Semper Fi Fags," "God Hates Fags," "Maryland Taliban," "Fags Doom Nations," "Not Blessed Just Cursed," "Thank God for Dead Soldiers," "Pope in Hell," "Priests Rape Boys," "You're Going to Hell," and "God Hates You." While these messages may fall short of refined social or political commentary, the issues they highlight—the political and moral conduct of the United States and its citizens, the fate of our Nation, homosexuality in the military, and scandals involving the Catholic clergy—are matters of public import. The signs certainly convey Westboro's position on those issues, in a manner designed, unlike the private speech in *Dun & Bradstreet*, to reach as broad a public audience as possible. And even if a few of the signs—such as "You're Going to Hell" and "God Hates You"—were viewed as containing messages related to Matthew Snyder or the Snyders specifically, that would not change the fact that the overall thrust and dominant theme of Westboro's demonstration spoke to broader public issues.

Apart from the content of Westboro's signs, Snyder contends that the "context" of the speech—its connection with his son's funeral—makes the speech a matter of private rather than public concern. The fact that Westboro spoke in connection with a funeral, however, cannot by itself transform the nature of Westboro's speech. Westboro's signs, displayed on public land next to a public street, reflect the fact that the church finds much to condemn in modern society. Its speech is "fairly characterized as constituting speech on a matter of public concern," *Connick*, and the funeral setting does not alter that conclusion.

Snyder argues that the church members in fact mounted a personal attack on Snyder and his family, and then attempted to "immunize their conduct by claiming that they were actually protesting the United States' tolerance of homosexuality or the supposed evils of the Catholic Church." We are not concerned in this case that Westboro's speech on public matters was in any way contrived to insulate speech on a private matter from liability. Westboro had been actively engaged in speaking on the subjects addressed in its picketing long before it became aware of Matthew Snyder, and there can be no serious claim that Westboro's picketing did not represent its "honestly believed" views on public issues. There was no pre-existing relationship or conflict between Westboro and Snyder that might suggest Westboro's speech on public matters was intended to mask an attack on Snyder over a private matter. Contrast *Connick* (finding public employee speech a matter of private concern when it was "no coincidence that [the speech] followed upon the heels of [a] transfer notice" affecting the employee).

Snyder goes on to argue that Westboro's speech should be afforded less than full First Amendment protection "not only because of the words" but also because the church members exploited the funeral "as a platform to bring their message to a broader audience." There is no doubt that Westboro chose to stage its picketing at the Naval Academy, the Maryland State House, and Matthew Snyder's funeral to increase publicity for its views and because of the relation between those sites and its views—in the case of the military funeral, because Westboro believes that God is killing American soldiers as punishment for the Nation's sinful policies.

Westboro's choice to convey its views in conjunction with Matthew Snyder's funeral made the expression of those views particularly hurtful to many, especially to Matthew's father. The record makes clear that the applicable legal term — "emotional distress" — fails to capture fully the anguish Westboro's choice added to Mr. Snyder's already incalculable grief. But Westboro conducted its picketing peacefully on matters of public concern at a public place adjacent to a public street. Such space occupies a "special position in terms of First Amendment protection." *United States v. Grace*, 461 U.S. 171, 180 (1983). "[W]e have repeatedly referred to public streets as the archetype of a traditional public forum," noting that "'[t]ime out of mind' public streets and sidewalks have been used for public assembly and debate." *Frisby v. Schultz* (1988) [Chapter 6].

That said, "[e]ven protected speech is not equally permissible in all places and at all times." *Id.* Westboro's choice of where and when to conduct its picketing is not beyond the Government's regulatory reach — it is "subject to reasonable time, place, or manner restrictions" that are consistent with the standards announced in this Court's precedents. Maryland now has a law imposing restrictions on funeral picketing, as do 43 other States and the Federal Government. To the extent these laws are content neutral, they raise very different questions from the tort verdict at issue in this case. Maryland's law, however, was not in effect at the time of the events at issue here, so we have no occasion to consider how it might apply to facts such as those before us, or whether it or other similar regulations are constitutional . . . .

Simply put, the church members had the right to be where they were. Westboro alerted local authorities to its funeral protest and fully complied with police guidance on where the picketing could be staged. The picketing was conducted under police supervision some 1,000 feet from the church, out of the sight of those at the church. The protest was not unruly; there was no shouting, profanity, or violence . . . .

Given that Westboro's speech was at a public place on a matter of public concern, that speech is entitled to "special protection" under the First Amendment. Such speech cannot be restricted simply because it is upsetting or arouses contempt . . . .

The jury here was instructed that it could hold Westboro liable for intentional infliction of emotional distress based on a finding that Westboro's picketing was "outrageous." "Outrageousness," however, is a highly malleable standard with "an inherent subjectiveness about it which would allow a jury to impose liability on the basis of the jurors' tastes or views, or perhaps on the basis of their dislike of a particular expression." *Hustler* . . . . What Westboro said, in the whole context of how and where it chose to say it, is entitled to "special protection" under the First Amendment, and that protection cannot be overcome by a jury finding that the picketing was outrageous.

For all these reasons, the jury verdict imposing tort liability on Westboro for intentional infliction of emotional distress must be set aside . . . .

IV

Our holding today is narrow. We are required in First Amendment cases to carefully review the record, and the reach of our opinion here is limited by the particular facts before us . . . .

Westboro believes that America is morally flawed; many Americans might feel the same about Westboro. Westboro's funeral picketing is certainly hurtful and its contribution to public discourse may be negligible. But Westboro addressed matters of public import on public property, in a peaceful manner, in full compliance with the guidance of local officials. The speech was indeed planned to coincide with Matthew Snyder's funeral, but did not itself disrupt that funeral, and Westboro's choice to conduct its picketing at that time and place did not alter the nature of its speech.

Speech is powerful. It can stir people to action, move them to tears of both joy and sorrow, and — as it did here — inflict great pain. On the facts before us, we cannot react to that pain by punishing the speaker. As a Nation we have chosen a different course — to protect even hurtful speech on public issues to ensure that we do not stifle public debate. That choice requires that we shield Westboro from tort liability for its picketing in this case.

The judgment of the United States Court of Appeals for the Fourth Circuit is affirmed.

JUSTICE BREYER, concurring.

. . . While I agree with the Court's conclusion that the picketing addressed matters of public concern, I do not believe that our First Amendment analysis can stop at that point. A State can sometimes regulate picketing, even picketing on matters of public concern. See *Frisby v. Schultz* (1988) [Chapter 6]. Moreover, suppose that A were physically to assault B, knowing that the assault (being newsworthy) would provide A with an opportunity to transmit to the public his views on a matter of public concern. The constitutionally protected nature of the end would not shield A's use of unlawful, unprotected means. And in some circumstances the use of certain words as means would be similarly unprotected. See *Chaplinsky v. New Hampshire* (1942) ("fighting words") . . . .

The dissent requires us to ask whether our holding unreasonably limits liability for intentional infliction of emotional distress — to the point where A (in order to draw attention to his views on a public matter) might launch a verbal assault upon B, a private person, publicly revealing the most intimate details of B's private life, while knowing that the revelation will cause B severe emotional harm. Does our decision leave the State powerless to protect the individual against invasions of, *e.g.*, personal privacy, even in the most horrendous of such circumstances?

As I understand the Court's opinion, it does not hold or imply that the State is always powerless to provide private individuals with necessary protection. Rather, the Court has reviewed the underlying facts in detail, as will sometimes prove necessary where First Amendment values and state-protected (say, privacy-related) interests seriously conflict. That review makes clear that Westboro's means of communicating its views consisted of picketing in a place where picketing was lawful and in compliance with all police directions. The picketing could not be seen or heard from the funeral ceremony itself. And Snyder testified that he saw no more than the tops of the picketers' signs as he drove to the funeral. To uphold the application of state law in these circumstances would punish Westboro for seeking to communicate its views on matters of public concern without proportionately advancing the State's interest in protecting its citizens against severe emotional harm. Consequently, the First Amendment protects Westboro. As I read the Court's opinion, it holds no more.

Justice Alito, dissenting.

Our profound national commitment to free and open debate is not a license for the vicious verbal assault that occurred in this case . . . .

I

Respondents and other members of their church have strong opinions on certain moral, religious, and political issues, and the First Amendment ensures that they have almost limitless opportunities to express their views . . . . And they may express their views in terms that are "uninhibited," "vehement," and "caustic." *New York Times Co. v. Sullivan* (1964).

It does not follow, however, that they may intentionally inflict severe emotional injury on private persons at a time of intense emotional sensitivity by launching vicious verbal attacks that make no contribution to public debate. To protect against such injury, "most if not all jurisdictions" permit recovery in tort for the intentional infliction of emotional distress (or IIED). *Hustler Magazine, Inc. v. Falwell* (1988).

This is a very narrow tort with requirements that "are rigorous, and difficult to satisfy." . . . [But] respondents long ago abandoned any effort to show that those tough standards were not satisfied here . . . . They did not dispute that Mr. Snyder suffered "'wounds that are truly severe and incapable of healing themselves.'" Nor did they dispute that their speech was "'so outrageous in character, and so extreme in degree, as to go beyond all possible bounds of decency, and to be regarded as atrocious, and utterly intolerable in a civilized community.'" Instead, they maintained that the First Amendment gave them a license to engage in such conduct. They are wrong.

II

It is well established that a claim for the intentional infliction of emotional distress can be satisfied by speech . . . . And although this Court has not decided the question, I think it is clear that the First Amendment does not entirely preclude liability for the intentional infliction of emotional distress by means of speech.

This Court has recognized that words may "by their very utterance inflict injury" and that the First Amendment does not shield utterances that form "no essential part of any exposition of ideas, and are of such slight social value as a step to truth that any benefit that may be derived from them is clearly outweighed by the social interest in order and morality." *Chaplinsky v. New Hampshire* (1942). When grave injury is intentionally inflicted by means of an attack like the one at issue here, the First Amendment should not interfere with recovery.

III

In this case, respondents brutally attacked Matthew Snyder, and this attack, which was almost certain to inflict injury, was central to respondents' well-practiced strategy for attracting public attention.

On the morning of Matthew Snyder's funeral, respondents could have chosen to stage their protest at countless locations . . . . But of course, a small group picketing at [locations such as a public park or the White House] would have probably gone unnoticed.

The Westboro Baptist Church, however, has devised a strategy that remedies this problem. As the Court notes, church members have protested at nearly 600 military funerals. They have also picketed the funerals of police officers, firefighters, and the victims of natural disasters, accidents, and shocking crimes. And in advance of these protests, they issue press releases to ensure that their protests will attract public attention . . . .

In this case, respondents implemented the Westboro Baptist Church's publicity-seeking strategy. Their press release stated that they were going "to picket the funeral of Lance Cpl. Matthew A. Snyder" because "God Almighty killed Lance Cpl. Snyder. He died in shame, not honor — for a fag nation cursed by God . . . . Now in Hell — sine die." This announcement guaranteed that Matthew's funeral would be transformed into a raucous media event and began the wounding process. It is well known that anticipation may heighten the effect of a painful event.

On the day of the funeral, respondents, true to their word, displayed placards that conveyed the message promised in their press release . . . .

. . . Since respondents chose to stage their protest at Matthew Snyder's funeral and not at any of the other countless available venues, a reasonable person would have assumed that there was a connection between the messages on the placards and the deceased. Moreover, since a church funeral is an event that naturally brings to mind thoughts about the afterlife, some of respondents' signs — *e.g.*, "God Hates You," "Not Blessed Just Cursed," and "You're Going to Hell" — would have likely been interpreted as referring to God's judgment of the deceased.

Other signs would most naturally have been understood as suggesting — falsely — that Matthew was gay. Homosexuality was the theme of many of the signs. There were signs reading "God Hates Fags," "Semper Fi Fags," "Fags Doom Nations," and "Fag Troops." Another placard depicted two men engaging in anal intercourse. A reasonable bystander seeing those signs would have likely concluded that they were meant to suggest that the deceased was a homosexual.

After the funeral, the Westboro picketers reaffirmed the meaning of their protest. They posted an online account entitled "The Burden of Marine Lance Cpl. Matthew A. Snyder. The Visit of Westboro Baptist Church to Help the Inhabitants of Maryland Connect the Dots!" [Albert Snyder discovered the posting, referred to by the parties as the "epic," during an Internet search for his son's name.] Belying any suggestion that they had simply made general comments about homosexuality, the Catholic Church, and the United States military, the "epic" addressed the Snyder family directly:

> God blessed you, Mr. and Mrs. Snyder, with a resource and his name was Matthew. He was an arrow in your quiver! In thanks to God for the comfort the child could bring you, you had a DUTY to prepare that child to serve

the LORD his GOD—PERIOD! You did JUST THE OPPOSITE—you raised him for the devil.

. . . .

Albert and Julie RIPPED that body apart and taught Matthew to defy his Creator, to divorce, and to commit adultery. They taught him how to support the largest pedophile machine in the history of the entire world, the Roman Catholic monstrosity. Every dime they gave the Roman Catholic monster they condemned their own souls. They also, in supporting satanic Catholicism, taught Matthew to be an idolater.

. . . .

Then after all that they sent him to fight for the United States of Sodom, a filthy country that is in lock step with his evil, wicked, and sinful manner of life, putting him in the cross hairs of a God that is so mad He has smoke coming from his nostrils and fire from his mouth! How dumb was that?

In light of this evidence, it is abundantly clear that respondents, going far beyond commentary on matters of public concern, specifically attacked Matthew Snyder because (1) he was a Catholic and (2) he was a member of the United States military. Both Matthew and petitioner were private figures, and this attack was not speech on a matter of public concern. While commentary on the Catholic Church or the United States military constitutes speech on matters of public concern, speech regarding Matthew Snyder's purely private conduct does not . . . .

IV

The Court concludes that respondents' speech was protected by the First Amendment for essentially three reasons, but none is sound.

First—and most important—the Court finds that "the overall thrust and dominant theme of [their] demonstration spoke to" broad public issues. As I have attempted to show, this portrayal is quite inaccurate; respondents' attack on Matthew was of central importance. But in any event, I fail to see why actionable speech should be immunized simply because it is interspersed with speech that is protected. The First Amendment allows recovery for defamatory statements that are interspersed with nondefamatory statements on matters of public concern, and there is no good reason why respondents' attack on Matthew Snyder and his family should be treated differently.

Second, the Court suggests that respondents' personal attack on Matthew Snyder is entitled to First Amendment protection because it was not motivated by a private grudge, but I see no basis for the strange distinction that the Court appears to draw. Respondents' motivation—"to increase publicity for its views,"—did not transform their statements attacking the character of a private figure into statements that made a contribution to debate on matters of public concern . . . .

Third, the Court finds it significant that respondents' protest occurred on a public street, but this fact alone should not be enough to preclude IIED liability. . . . A physical assault may occur without trespassing; it is no defense that the perpetrator had "the right to be where [he was]." And the same should be true with respect to unprotected speech. Neither classic "fighting words" nor defamatory statements are immunized when they occur in a public place, and there is no good reason to treat a verbal assault based on the conduct or character of a private figure like Matthew Snyder any differently . . . .

[Funerals] are unique events at which special protection against emotional assaults is in order. At funerals, the emotional well-being of bereaved relatives is particularly vulnerable. Exploitation of a funeral for the purpose of attracting public attention . . . may permanently stain [relatives'] memories of the final moments before a loved one is laid to rest. Allowing family members to have a few hours of peace without harassment does not undermine public debate. I would therefore hold that, in this setting, the First Amendment permits a private figure to recover for the intentional infliction of emotional distress caused by speech on a matter of private concern . . . .

Note: Intentional Infliction of Emotional Distress and the First Amendment

1. At several points the opinion in *Snyder* cites the decision in *Hustler Magazine v. Falwell*, 485 U.S. 46 (1988). *Hustler*, like *Snyder*, was a tort suit litigated in federal court. The plaintiff was Jerry Falwell, described by the Court as "a nationally known minister who has been active as a commentator on politics and public affairs." Falwell sued Hustler and its publisher, Larry Flynt, to recover damages for (*inter alia*) libel and intentional infliction of emotional distress (IIED). The suit was based on an item published in the November 1983 issue of Hustler magazine:

> The inside front cover of the [issue] featured a "parody" of an advertisement for Campari Liqueur that contained the name and picture of [Falwell] and was entitled "Jerry Falwell talks about his first time." This parody was modeled after actual Campari ads that included interviews with various celebrities about their "first times." Although it was apparent by the end of each interview that this meant the first time they sampled Campari, the ads clearly played on the sexual double entendre of the general subject of "first times." Copying the form and layout of these Campari ads, Hustler's editors chose [Falwell] as the featured celebrity and drafted an alleged "interview" with him in which he states that his "first time" was during a drunken incestuous rendezvous with his mother in an outhouse. The Hustler parody portrays [Falwell] and his mother as drunk and immoral, and suggests that [Falwell] is a hypocrite who preaches only when he is drunk. In small print at the bottom of the page, the ad contains the disclaimer, "ad parody — not to be taken seriously." The magazine's table of contents also lists the ad as "Fiction; Ad and Personality Parody."

The jury found against Falwell on the libel claim but ruled in his favor on the IIED claim. Hustler appealed to the Fourth Circuit, which affirmed. The Supreme Court unanimously reversed.

Chief Justice Rehnquist wrote the Court's opinion. He began by reviewing basic principles and the law established by the *New York Times* line of cases:

> The sort of robust political debate encouraged by the First Amendment is bound to produce speech that is critical of [public officials and public figures] . . . . Such criticism, inevitably, will not always be reasoned or moderate . . . . Of course, this does not mean that [such speech] is immune from sanction in the form of damages. Since *New York Times Co. v. Sullivan* we have consistently ruled that a public figure may hold a speaker liable for the damage to reputation caused by publication of a defamatory falsehood, but only if the statement was made "with knowledge that it was false or with reckless disregard of whether it was false or not."

Falwell argued that intent to cause injury was the gravamen of the tort of IIED, and that a different standard was therefore justified. The Court disagreed:

> [In] the world of debate about public affairs, many things done with motives that are less than admirable are protected by the First Amendment . . . . [While a] bad motive may be deemed controlling for purposes of tort liability in other areas of the law, we think the First Amendment prohibits such a result in the area of public debate about public figures.

After canvassing other First Amendment decisions, including *Chaplinsky*, the opinion ended with these paragraphs:

> We conclude that public figures and public officials may not recover for the tort of intentional infliction of emotional distress by reason of publications such as the one here at issue without showing in addition that the publication contains a false statement of fact which was made with "actual malice," i.e., with knowledge that the statement was false or with reckless disregard as to whether or not it was true. This is not merely a "blind application" of the *New York Times* standard, it reflects our considered judgment that such a standard is necessary to give adequate "breathing space" to the freedoms protected by the First Amendment.
>
> Here it is clear that [Falwell] is a "public figure" for purposes of First Amendment law. The jury found against [Falwell] on his libel claim when it decided that the Hustler ad parody could not "reasonably be understood as describing actual facts about [Falwell] or actual events in which [he] participated." The Court of Appeals interpreted the jury's finding to be that the ad parody "was not reasonably believable," and in accordance with our custom we accept this finding. [Falwell] is thus relegated to his claim for damages awarded by the jury for the intentional infliction of emotional distress by "outrageous" conduct. But for reasons heretofore stated this claim cannot, consistently with the First Amendment, form a basis for the award of damages when the conduct in question is the publication of a caricature such as the ad parody involved here. The judgment of the Court of Appeals is accordingly [reversed].

2. Suppose that Falwell's mother sued for intentional infliction of emotional distress based on the same ad parody. Assume that she is neither a public figure nor a public official. Under *Hustler*, must she show "actual malice"? Would *Snyder* bar her claim?

3. Although *Hustler* was the Supreme Court's only prior decision on an IIED claim, the *Snyder* opinion devotes surprisingly little attention to it. What is the relationship between the two decisions? Are there any IIED claims that would be barred by *Hustler* but not by *Snyder*?

4. As Justice Alito notes, a few weeks after the funeral of Matthew Snyder, one of the picketers posted a message on the Westboro Baptist Church Website entitled "The Burden of Marine Lance Cpl. Matthew A. Snyder. The Visit of Westboro Baptist Church to Help the Inhabitants of Maryland Connect the Dots!" The message (referred to as the "epic") addressed the Snyder family directly. (*See* the extracts in the dissenting opinion.)

The majority, in holding that the church members were shielded from tort liability by the First Amendment, refused to consider the "epic" because it was not discussed in Snyder's petition for certiorari. Justice Alito responded by saying that the "epic" was "not a distinct claim but a piece of evidence that the jury considered in imposing liability for the claims now before this Court. The protest and the epic are parts of a single course of conduct that the jury found to constitute intentional infliction of emotional distress."

Suppose that the jury handed down a verdict finding Westboro liable for intentional infliction of emotional distress based on the "epic," and that the validity of the verdict was squarely presented to the Supreme Court. Would that verdict withstand scrutiny under the First Amendment?

Problem: An Obsessive Blogger

Alan Grogan is a graduate of the University of Illiana. Six months ago, he launched a blog centered on James Wilkins, who had just been elected as president of the student government association at the University.

"Welcome to 'James Wilkins Watch,'" Grogan wrote in his inaugural blog post. "This is a site for concerned University of Illiana alumni, students and others who oppose the recent election of James Wilkins—a RADICAL HOMOSEXUAL ACTIVIST, RACIST, ELITIST, & LIAR—as the new head of student government at our beloved University."

Subsequent blog posts—appearing two or three times each week over a period of months—contained numerous attacks, both verbal and pictorial, against Wilkins. These included the following:

- "Wilkins is an outright anti-Christian bigot who openly mocks God, the Bible, and the sanctity of unborn human life."
- Wilkins is "Satan's representative" and "a viciously militant homosexual activist."

- Wilkins suffers a "narcissistic personality," is an "elite pervert," and a "privileged pervert."
- Wilkins harbors a "severe contempt" for others' civil rights and has views "much like Nazi Germany's leaders."
- A picture of Wilkins with "Pervert" written over his face.
- A swastika superimposed over a gay pride flag, with an arrow pointing toward Wilkins.

(This is only a small sample of the posts.)

Wilkins has brought suit against Grogan asserting a variety of state-law tort claims including intentional infliction of emotional distress. The complaint recites a total of 85 particular statements similar to the examples above and asserts that Grogan's conduct was "beyond all possible bounds of decency," "not for any proper purpose," and "of such a character as to be intolerable in a civilized society." Wilkins seeks compensatory and punitive damages and also an injunction requiring Grogan to cease and desist from posting similar content in the future.

Grogan has moved to dismiss the IIED count on the ground that it is barred by the First Amendment. How should the court rule?

[4] Invasion of Privacy

A recurring theme in First Amendment doctrine is the quest for "truth." Holmes defended freedom of speech on the ground that "the competition of the market" provides "the best test of truth." *New York Times* and its progeny give broad protection to defamatory falsehoods on the theory any other rule would suppress some speech that is true.

Does it follow that the ability of speakers to disseminate truthful information outweighs all state interests that might be invoked in support of regulation? In particular, what about state efforts to protect individual privacy? After all, it was Justice Brandeis—the great champion of free speech—who wrote the landmark article on "the right to privacy," and who later described "the right to be let alone" as "the right most valued by civilized men." What happens when one person's claim to privacy comes into conflict with another person's claim of a right to speak?

The Court has confronted this question in several cases. In one major case, *The Florida Star v. B.J.F.*, 491 U.S. 524 (1989), the newspaper asked the Court "to hold broadly that truthful publication may never be punished consistently with the First Amendment." The Court declined the invitation, saying that "the sensitivity and significance of the interests presented in clashes between First Amendment and privacy rights counsel relying on limited principles that sweep no more broadly than the appropriate context of the [particular] case."

Florida Star involved a Florida statute that made it unlawful to "print, public or broadcast . . . in any instrument of mass communication" the name of a victim of a sexual offense. The Court held that the newspaper could not be subjected to civil liability for publishing the name of a rape victim which the newspaper had obtained from a publicly released police report.

Quoting a previous case involving disclosure of the name of a juvenile defendant that the press also won, the Court described the scope of its holding as follows: "[i]f a newspaper lawfully obtains truthful information about a matter of public significance then state officials may not constitutionally punish publication of the information, absent a need to further a state interest of the highest order" (quoting *Smith v. Daily Mail Pub. Co.*, 443 U.S. 97, 103 (1979)). Three Justices dissented, but they acknowledged that the Court's ruling was consistent with the course charted by previous decisions. Indeed, the dissenters could not point to a single case—nor has one yet arisen—in which the Court allowed the state to penalize a speaker for truthful publication. Do you agree that the identity of a rape victim is "a matter of public significance"? Why is the state's interest in protecting the victim's privacy not "a state interest of the highest order" justifying the imposition of liability on a newspaper?

In *Bartnicki v. Vopper*, 532 U.S. 514 (2001), the Court continued its pattern of refusing to impose liability on the press for disclosure of truthful information lawfully obtained by the press—though with a twist. In *Bartnicki*, an unknown party illegally intercepted a cell phone conversation between the president and chief negotiator of a teachers' union (all Justices agreed the interception itself could be criminalized). The speakers expressed frustration with the local school board (with whom the union was in labor negotiations), and the president commented "we're gonna have to go to their, their homes. . . . To blow off their front porches, we'll have to do some work on some of these guys." The interceptor mailed a tape of the conversation to the head of a local taxpayer's organization, who in turn passed the tape on to Vopper, a radio commentator. Vopper played the tape on the air, and was sued by the union officials pursuant to federal and state statutes creating civil liability for the knowing disclosure of the contents of illegally intercepted oral communications. Quoting *Smith v. Daily Mail*, the Court ruled for Vopper because the content of the intercepted conversation constituted "truthful information of public concern." The Court emphasized, however, that it was not deciding whether the state's interest in protecting privacy "is strong enough to justify the application of [the statute] to disclosures of trade secrets or domestic gossip or other information of purely private concern." Justice Breyer, joined by Justice O'Connor, concurred, emphasizing the narrowness of the Court's holding. Chief Justice Rehnquist, joined by Justices Scalia and Thomas, dissented on the grounds that the privacy interests at stake justified imposing liability on the press, because the consequence of not protecting privacy is to deter private speech.

Problem: A Wrestler and a Sex Tape

Harry Johnson is a retired professional wrestler. During his career, under the stage name "Slammin' Sam" Johnson was world famous, and after retirement he remained a prominent celebrity who appeared in a number of Hollywood movies. Throughout his career, Johnson actively sought press attention, and occasionally boasted of his sexual prowess.

In 2005, Johnson had an affair with a married co-star of one of his movies. Johnson made a videotape of himself having sex with his co-star, which he intended to keep private. Several years later, however, the tape was inadvertently disclosed to the public, and came into the possession of a number of media outlets. In 2015, the tape was obtained by the Internet media website Hawker, which specializes in stories about celebrities. Hawker posted a short clip from the Johnson tape onto its website, as part of a story about celebrity sex tapes. Johnson immediately contacted Hawker to complain and demand that the excerpt be taken down, but Hawker refused.

Johnson sues Hawker in state court for invasion of privacy and intentional infliction of emotional distress. Hawker files a motion to dismiss, arguing that its actions were protected by the First Amendment. How should the court rule?

C. "The Lewd and Obscene"

[1] Initial Development of the Law

As we have seen, the decision in *New York Times v. Sullivan* emphatically repudiated the *Chaplinsky* dictum that treated "the libelous" as one of the "classes of speech" that raise no constitutional problems. Seven years earlier, the Court considered the constitutional status of another of the *Chaplinsky* exclusions, "the lewd and obscene." As in *Sullivan*, the Court spoke through Justice William J. Brennan. But the Court's response was quite different.

Roth v. United States
Alberts v. California
354 U.S. 476 (1957)

Mr. Justice Brennan delivered the opinion of the Court.

The constitutionality of a criminal obscenity statute is the question in each of these cases. In *Roth*, the primary constitutional question is whether the federal obscenity statute[1] violates the provision of the First Amendment that "Congress shall make no law . . . abridging the freedom of speech, or of the press. . . ." In *Alberts*, the primary constitutional question is whether the obscenity provisions of the California Penal Code[2] invade the freedoms of speech and press as they may be incorporated in the

---

1. The federal obscenity statute provided, in pertinent part:
   "Every obscene, lewd, lascivious, or filthy book, pamphlet, picture, paper, letter, writing, print, or other publication of an indecent character; . . .
   "Is declared to be nonmailable matter and shall not be conveyed in the mails or delivered from any post office or by any letter carrier.
   "Whoever [uses the mails to distribute or circulate nonmailable matter] shall be fined not more than $5,000 or imprisoned not more than five years, or both."
2. The California Penal Code provides, in pertinent part:
   "Every person who wilfully and lewdly, either:

liberty protected from state action by the Due Process Clause of the Fourteenth Amendment. . . .

Roth conducted a business in New York in the publication and sale of books, photographs and magazines. He used circulars and advertising matter to solicit sales. He was convicted [by a jury] upon 4 counts of a 26-count indictment charging him with mailing obscene circulars and advertising, and an obscene book, in violation of the federal obscenity statute. His conviction was affirmed by the Court of Appeals for the Second Circuit. . . .

Alberts conducted a mail-order business from Los Angeles. He was convicted by the Judge of the Municipal Court of the Beverly Hills Judicial District (having waived a jury trial) under a misdemeanor complaint which charged him with lewdly keeping for sale obscene and indecent books, and with writing, composing and publishing an obscene advertisement of them, in violation of the California Penal Code. The conviction was affirmed by the Appellate Department of the [California] Superior Court. . . .

The dispositive question is whether obscenity is utterance within the area of protected speech and press.[8] Although this is the first time the question has been squarely presented to this Court, either under the First Amendment or under the Fourteenth Amendment, expressions found in numerous opinions indicate that this Court has always assumed that obscenity is not protected by the freedoms of speech and press. [E.g.,] *Chaplinsky v. New Hampshire* (1942) [*supra* this chapter].

The guaranties of freedom of expression in effect in 10 of the 14 States which by 1792 had ratified the Constitution, gave no absolute protection for every utterance. Thirteen of the 14 States provided for the prosecution of libel, and all of those States made either blasphemy or profanity, or both, statutory crimes. As early as 1712, Massachusetts made it criminal to publish "any filthy, obscene, or profane song, pamphlet, libel or mock sermon" in imitation or mimicking of religious services. Thus, profanity and obscenity were related offenses.

In light of this history, it is apparent that the unconditional phrasing of the First Amendment was not intended to protect every utterance. This phrasing did not prevent this Court from concluding that libelous utterances are not within the area of constitutionally protected speech. *Beauharnais v. Illinois*, 343 U.S. 250, 266 (1952) [*supra* this chapter Note]. At the time of the adoption of the First Amendment, obscenity law was not as fully developed as libel law, but there is sufficiently contemporaneous evidence to show that obscenity, too, was outside the protection intended for speech and press.

"3. Writes, composes, stereotypes, prints, publishes, sells, distributes, keeps for sale, or exhibits any obscene or indecent writing, paper, or book; or designs, copies, draws, engraves, paints, or otherwise prepares any obscene or indecent picture or print; or molds, cuts, casts, or otherwise makes any obscene or indecent figure; or,

"4. Writes, composes, or publishes any notice or advertisement of any such writing, paper, book, picture, print or figure; . . .

"6. [is] guilty of a misdemeanor. . . ."

8. No issue is presented in either case concerning the obscenity of the material involved.

The protection given speech and press was fashioned to assure unfettered inter-change of ideas for the bringing about of political and social changes desired by the people. . . . All ideas having even the slightest redeeming social importance — unorthodox ideas, controversial ideas, even ideas hateful to the prevailing climate of opinion — have the full protection of the guaranties, unless excludable because they encroach upon the limited area of more important interests. But implicit in the history of the First Amendment is the rejection of obscenity as utterly without redeeming social importance. This rejection for that reason is mirrored in the universal judgment that obscenity should be restrained, reflected in the international agreement of over 50 nations, in the obscenity laws of all of the 48 States, and in the 20 obscenity laws enacted by the Congress from 1842 to 1956. This is the same judgment expressed by this Court in *Chaplinsky*:

> . . . There are certain well-defined and narrowly limited classes of speech, the prevention and punishment of which have never been thought to raise any Constitutional problem. *These include the lewd and obscene. . . . It has been well observed that such utterances are no essential part of any exposition of ideas, and are of such slight social value as a step to truth that any benefit that may be derived from them is clearly outweighed by the social interest in order and morality. . . .* (Emphasis added.)

We hold that obscenity is not within the area of constitutionally protected speech or press.

It is strenuously urged that these obscenity statutes offend the constitutional guaranties because they punish incitation to impure sexual *thoughts*, not shown to be related to any overt antisocial conduct which is or may be incited in the persons stimulated to such thoughts. In *Roth*, the trial judge instructed the jury: "the words 'obscene, lewd and lascivious' as used in the law, signify that form of immorality which has relation to sexual impurity and has a tendency to excite lustful *thoughts*." (Emphasis added.) In *Alberts*, the trial judge applied the test laid down in *People v. Wepplo*, 78 Cal. App. 2d Supp. 959 (1947), namely, whether the material has "a substantial tendency to deprave or corrupt its readers by inciting lascivious *thoughts* or arousing lustful desires." (Emphasis added.) It is insisted that the constitutional guaranties are violated because convictions may be had without proof either that obscene material will perceptibly create a clear and present danger of antisocial conduct, or will probably induce its recipients to such conduct. But, in light of our holding that obscenity is not protected speech, the complete answer to this argument is in the holding of this Court in *Beauharnais*:

> Libelous utterances not being within the area of constitutionally protected speech, it is unnecessary, either for us or for the State courts, to consider the issues behind the phrase "clear and present danger." Certainly no one would contend that obscene speech, for example, may be punished only upon a showing of such circumstances. Libel, as we have seen, is in the same class.

However, sex and obscenity are not synonymous. Obscene material is material which deals with sex in a manner appealing to prurient interest.[20] The portrayal of sex, e.g., in art, literature and scientific works, is not itself sufficient reason to deny material the constitutional protection of freedom of speech and press. Sex, a great and mysterious motive force in human life, has indisputably been a subject of absorbing interest to mankind through the ages; it is one of the vital problems of human interest and public concern. . . .

The fundamental freedom of speech and press have contributed greatly to the development and well-being of our free society and are indispensable to its continued growth. Ceaseless vigilance is the watchword to prevent their erosion by Congress or by the States. The door barring federal and state intrusion into this area cannot be left ajar; it must be kept tightly closed and opened only the slightest crack necessary to prevent encroachment upon more important interests. It is therefore vital that the standards for judging obscenity safeguard the protection of freedom of speech and press for material which does not treat sex in a manner appealing to prurient interest.

The early leading standard of obscenity allowed material to be judged merely by the effect of an isolated excerpt upon particularly susceptible persons. *Regina v. Hicklin*, (1868) L.R. 3 Q.B. 360. Some American courts adopted this standard but later decisions have rejected it and substituted this test: whether to the average person, applying contemporary community standards, the dominant theme of the material taken as a whole appeals to prurient interest. The *Hicklin* test, judging obscenity by the effect of isolated passages upon the most susceptible persons, might well encompass material legitimately treating with sex, and so it must be rejected as unconstitutionally restrictive of the freedoms of speech and press. On the other hand, the substituted standard provides safeguards adequate to withstand the charge of constitutional infirmity.

Both trial courts below sufficiently followed the proper standard. Both courts used the proper definition of obscenity. . . .

It is argued that the statutes do not provide reasonably ascertainable standards of guilt and therefore violate the constitutional requirements of due process. . . . Many decisions have recognized that [the] terms of obscenity statutes are not precise. This Court, however, has consistently held that lack of precision is not itself offensive to the requirements of due process. . . . These words, applied according to the proper

---

20. I.e., material having a tendency to excite lustful thoughts. *Webster's New International Dictionary* (Unabridged, 2d ed. 1949) defines prurient, in pertinent part, as follows:

> . . . Itching; longing; uneasy with desire or longing; of persons, having itching, morbid, or lascivious longings; of desire, curiosity, or propensity, lewd. . . .

> We perceive no significant difference between the meaning of obscenity developed in the case law and the definition of the A.L.I., Model Penal Code, § 207.10(2) (Tent. Draft No. 6, 1957), viz.:

> . . . A thing is obscene if, considered as a whole, its predominant appeal is to prurient interest, i.e., a shameful or morbid interest in nudity, sex, or excretion, and if it goes substantially beyond customary limits of candor in description or representation of such matters. . . .

standard for judging obscenity, already discussed, give adequate warning of the conduct proscribed . . .

The judgments are *affirmed*.

MR. CHIEF JUSTICE WARREN, concurring in the result.

. . . It is not the book that is on trial [in these cases]; it is a person. The conduct of the defendant is the central issue, not the obscenity of a book or picture. The nature of the materials is, of course, relevant as an attribute of the defendant's conduct, but the materials are thus placed in context from which they draw color and character. A wholly different result might be reached in a different setting. . . .

The defendants in both these cases were engaged in the business of purveying textual or graphic matter openly advertised to appeal to the erotic interest of their customers. They were plainly engaged in the commercial exploitation of the morbid and shameful craving for materials with prurient effect. I believe that the State and Federal Governments can constitutionally punish such conduct. That is all that these cases present to us, and that is all we need to decide. . . .

MR. JUSTICE HARLAN, concurring in the result in [*Alberts*], and dissenting in [*Roth*].

I regret not to be able to join the Court's opinion. I cannot do so because I find lurking beneath its disarming generalizations a number of problems which not only leave me with serious misgivings as to the future effect of today's decisions, but which also, in my view, call for different results in these two cases.

I.

My basic difficulties with the Court's opinion are threefold. First, the opinion paints with such a broad brush that I fear it may result in a loosening of the tight reins which state and federal courts should hold upon the enforcement of obscenity statutes. Second, the Court fails to discriminate between the different factors which, in my opinion, are involved in the constitutional adjudication of state and federal obscenity cases. Third, relevant distinctions between the two obscenity statutes here involved, and the Court's own definition of "obscenity," are ignored.

. . . Proceeding from the premise that "no issue is presented in either case, concerning the obscenity of the material involved," the Court finds the "dispositive question" to be "whether obscenity is utterance within the area of protected speech and press," and then holds that "obscenity" is not so protected because it is "utterly without redeeming social importance." This sweeping formula appears to me to beg the very question before us. The Court seems to assume that "obscenity" is a peculiar genus of "speech and press," which is as distinct, recognizable, and classifiable as poison ivy is among other plants. On this basis the constitutional question before us simply becomes, as the Court says, whether "obscenity," as an abstraction, is protected by the First and Fourteenth Amendments, and the question whether a particular book may be suppressed becomes a mere matter of classification, of "fact," to be entrusted to a fact-finder and insulated from independent constitutional judgment. But surely the problem cannot be solved in such a generalized fashion. Every communication has an individuality and "value" of its own. The suppression of a particular writing or other tangible form of expression is, therefore, an individual matter, and in the nature of things every such suppression raises an individual constitutional problem, in which a reviewing court must determine for itself whether the attacked expression is suppressable within constitutional standards. . . .

I do not think that reviewing courts can escape this responsibility by saying that the trier of the facts, be it a jury or a judge, has labeled the questioned matter as "obscene," for, if "obscenity" is to be suppressed, the question whether a particular work is of that character involves not really an issue of fact but a question of constitutional judgment of the most sensitive and delicate kind. Many juries might find that Joyce's "Ulysses" or Bocaccio's "Decameron" was obscene, and yet the conviction of a defendant for selling either book would raise, for me, the gravest constitutional problems, for no such verdict could convince me, without more, that these books are "utterly without redeeming social importance." In short, I do not understand how the Court can resolve the constitutional problems now before it without making its own independent judgment upon the character of the material upon which these convictions were based. . . .

My second reason for dissatisfaction with the Court's opinion is that the broad strides with which the Court has proceeded has led it to brush aside with perfunctory ease the vital constitutional considerations which, in my opinion, differentiate these two cases. It does not seem to matter to the Court that in one case we balance the power of a State in this field against the restrictions of the Fourteenth Amendment, and in the other the power of the Federal Government against the limitations of the First Amendment. I deal with this subject more particularly later.

Thirdly, the Court has not been bothered by the fact that the two cases involve different statutes. . . .

II.

I concur in the judgment of the Court in No. 61, *Alberts v. California.* . . .

In judging the constitutionality of this conviction, we should remember that our function in reviewing state judgments under the Fourteenth Amendment is a narrow one. . . . We can inquire only whether the state action so subverts the fundamental liberties implicit in the Due Process Clause that it cannot be sustained as a rational exercise of power. . . .

What, then, is the purpose of this California statute? Clearly the state legislature has made the judgment that printed words can "deprave or corrupt" the reader—that words can incite to anti-social or immoral action. The assumption seems to be that the distribution of certain types of literature will induce criminal or immoral sexual conduct. It is well known, of course, that the validity of this assumption is a matter of dispute among critics, sociologists, psychiatrists, and penologists. . . . [But nothing] in the Constitution requires California to accept as truth the most advanced and sophisticated psychiatric opinion. It seems to me clear that it is not irrational, in our present state of knowledge, to consider that pornography can induce a type of sexual conduct which a State may deem obnoxious to the moral fabric of society. In fact the very division of opinion on the subject counsels us to respect the choice made by the State.

Furthermore, even assuming that pornography cannot be deemed ever to cause, in an immediate sense, criminal sexual conduct, other interests within the proper cognizance of the States may be protected by the prohibition placed on such materials. The State can reasonably draw the inference that over a long period of time the indiscriminate dissemination of materials, the essential character of which is to degrade sex, will have an eroding effect on moral standards. And the State has a legitimate interest in protecting the privacy of the home against invasion of unsolicited obscenity. . . .

What has been said, however, does not dispose of the case. It still remains for us to decide whether the state court's determination that this material should be suppressed is consistent with the Fourteenth Amendment; and that, of course, presents a federal question as to which we, and not the state court, have the ultimate responsibility. And so, in the final analysis, I concur in the judgment because, upon an independent perusal of the material involved, and in light of the considerations discussed above, I cannot say that its suppression would so interfere with the communication of "ideas" in any proper sense of that term that it would offend the Due Process Clause. I therefore agree with the Court that appellant's conviction must be affirmed.

III.

I dissent in No. 582, *Roth v. United States.*

We are faced here with the question whether the federal obscenity statute, as construed and applied in this case, violates the First Amendment to the Constitution. To me, this question is of quite a different order than one where we are dealing with state legislation under the Fourteenth Amendment. . . .

The Constitution differentiates between those areas of human conduct subject to the regulation of the States and those subject to the powers of the Federal Government. . . . Congress has no substantive power over sexual morality. Such powers as the Federal Government has in this field [are] not of the same nature as those possessed by the States, which bear direct responsibility for the protection of the local moral fabric. . . .

Not only is the federal interest in protecting the Nation against pornography attenuated, but the dangers of federal censorship in this field are far greater than anything the States may do. . . . The danger is perhaps not great if the people of one State, through their legislature, decide that "Lady Chatterley's Lover" goes so far beyond the acceptable standards of candor that it will be deemed offensive and non-sellable, for the State next door is still free to make its own choice. At least we do not have one uniform standard. But the dangers to free thought and expression are truly great if the Federal Government imposes a blanket ban over the Nation on such a book. The prerogative of the States to differ on their ideas of morality will be destroyed, the ability of States to experiment will be stunted. The fact that the people of one State cannot read some of the works of D. H. Lawrence seems to me, if not wise or desirable, at least acceptable. But that no person in the United States should be allowed to do so seems to me to be intolerable, and violative of both the letter and spirit of the First Amendment.

I judge this case, then, in view of what I think is the attenuated federal interest in this field, in view of the very real danger of a deadening uniformity which can result from nation-wide federal censorship, and in view of the fact that the constitutionality of this conviction must be weighed against the First and not the Fourteenth Amendment. So viewed, I do not think that this conviction can be upheld. The petitioner was convicted under a statute which, under the judge's charge, makes it criminal to sell books which "tend to stir sexual impulses and lead to sexually impure thoughts." I cannot agree that any book which tends to stir sexual impulses and lead to sexually impure thoughts necessarily is "utterly without redeeming social importance." Not only did this charge fail to measure up to the standards which I understand the Court to approve, but as far as I can see, much of the great literature of the world could lead to conviction under such a view of the statute. Moreover, in no event do I think that the limited federal interest in this area can extend to mere "thoughts." The Federal Government has no business, whether under the postal or commerce power, to bar the sale of books because they might lead to any kind of "thoughts."

It is no answer to say, as the Court does, that obscenity is not protected speech. The point is that this statute, as here construed, defines obscenity so widely that it encompasses matters which might very well be protected speech. I do not think that the federal statute can be constitutionally construed to reach other than what the Government has termed as "hard-core" pornography. Nor do I think the statute can fairly be read as directed only at persons who are engaged in the business of catering to the prurient minded, even though their wares fall short of hard-core pornography. Such a statute would raise constitutional questions of a different order. That being so, and since in my opinion the material here involved cannot be said to be hard-core pornography, I would reverse this case with instructions to dismiss the indictment.

MR. JUSTICE DOUGLAS, with whom JUSTICE BLACK concurs, dissenting.

When we sustain these convictions, we make the legality of a publication turn on the purity of thought which a book or tract instills in the mind of the reader. I do not think we can approve that standard and be faithful to the command of the First Amendment. . . .

[I reject] the implication that problems of freedom of speech and of the press are to be resolved by weighing against the values of free expression, the judgment of the Court that a particular form of that expression has "no redeeming social importance." The First Amendment, its prohibition in terms absolute, was designed to preclude courts as well as legislatures from weighing the values of speech against silence. . . .

Freedom of expression can be suppressed if, and to the extent that, it is so closely brigaded with illegal action as to be an inseparable part of it. *Giboney v. Empire Storage & Ice Co.*, 336 U.S. 490, 498 (1949). As a people, we cannot afford to relax that standard. For the test that suppresses a cheap tract today can suppress a literary gem tomorrow.

All it need do is to incite a lascivious thought or arouse a lustful desire. The list of books that judges or juries can place in that category is endless.

I would give the broad sweep of the First Amendment full support. I have the same confidence in the ability of our people to reject noxious literature as I have in their capacity to sort out the true from the false in theology, economics, politics, or any other field.

————

Note: Roth *and Its Antecedents*

1. The Court states (footnote 8), "No question is presented in either case concerning the obscenity of the material involved." The petition for certiorari in *Roth* included eight "Questions Presented." The last of these was, "Were the publications, when considered in their entirety, obscene?" Petition for Certiorari at 2. In the body of the petition, Roth argued, "The publication American Aphrodite when considered in its entirety was not obscene." *Id.* at 53. In reply to the Government's Brief in Opposition, Roth stated, "It is the petitioner's contention that . . . , however coarse, however obnoxious, however vulgar [the publications] may be to any segment of the population, they are not obscene as a matter of law." Reply Brief at 2.

Certiorari was granted in *Roth* on January 14, 1957. The order limited the grant to three of Roth's eight questions, excluding the question whether American Aphrodite or any of Roth's other publications were obscene.

What were the consequences of limiting the grant of certiorari? Recall that the Court took the same action in *Dennis*, and compare Justice Harlan's approach with that of the majority.

2. In explaining why "obscenity is not within the area of constitutionally protected speech or press," Justice Brennan invokes both history (the practices of the states at the time the First Amendment was adopted) and precedent (including *Chaplinsky* and *Beauharnais*). How did the Court — again speaking through Justice Brennan — treat these same materials seven years later in *New York Times v. Sullivan*?

3. In *Dennis* and *Beauharnais*, the Court devoted considerable attention to the governmental interests underlying the challenged laws. Does the Court in *Roth* explain the governmental interests underlying obscenity laws? What are they?

4. Justice Douglas, in dissent, expresses confidence that people will reject "noxious literature" of a sexual nature just as they can "sort out the true from the false in theology, economics, politics, or any other field." Does the Court respond to this argument? If not, what response might it have made?

————

Note: "Ideas" and "Entertainment"

In explaining why obscenity is not protected by the First Amendment, Justice Brennan emphasizes that freedom of speech and press is designed "to assure unfettered exchange of *ideas* for the bringing about of political and social changes desired by the people." (Emphasis added.) Is he saying that protection of the First Amendment is *limited* to ideas?

Almost a decade before *Roth*, the Court seemed to reject that proposition. In *Winters v. New York*, 333 U.S. 507 (1948), the Court considered the constitutionality of a New York statute that prohibited the distribution of magazines or other printed material "devoted to the publication, and principally made up of criminal news, police reports, or accounts of criminal deeds, or pictures, or stories of deeds of bloodshed, lust or crime." The highest court of New York construed the statute to apply only to collections of criminal deeds of bloodshed or lust "so massed as to become vehicles for inciting violent and depraved crimes against the person." The Supreme Court held that the statute as construed was vague and indefinite and thus unconstitutional under the Due Process clause. In the course of its opinion (by Justice Reed), the Court said:

> We do not accede to [the state's] suggestion that the constitutional protection for a free press applies only to the exposition of ideas. The line between the informing and the entertaining is too elusive for the protection of that basic right. Everyone is familiar with instances of propaganda through fiction. What is one man's amusement, teaches another's doctrine. Though we can see nothing of any possible value to society in these magazines, they are as much entitled to the protection of free speech as the best of literature. They are equally subject to control if they are lewd, indecent, obscene or profane.

Is the opinion in *Roth* consistent with this analysis? On what basis would the Court decide whether, and to what extent, the protections of the First Amendment extend beyond "the exposition of ideas"?

———

Note: "I Know It When I See It"?

1. In his separate opinion in *Roth*, Justice Harlan insisted that the problem of obscenity could not be "solved" by means of the "disarming generalizations" proffered by the majority. Time soon proved him correct. As Justice Harlan himself observed, in words often quoted by other Justices, obscenity cases "produced a variety of views among the members of the Court unmatched in any other course of constitutional adjudication." *Interstate Circuit, Inc. v. Dallas*, 390 U.S. 676, 704–05 (1968) (separate opinion).

One member of the Court, Justice Potter Stewart took the position that governmental power to regulate obscenity was limited to "hard core pornography." In *Jacobellis v. Ohio*, 378 U.S. 184, 197 (1964), Justice Stewart uttered the words which, he later said, he feared would be engraved on his tombstone:

> I have reached the conclusion, which I think is confirmed at least by negative implication in the Court's decisions since *Roth* and *Alberts*, that under the First and Fourteenth Amendments criminal laws in this area are constitutionally limited to hard-core pornography. I shall not today attempt further

to define the kinds of material I understand to be embraced within that shorthand description; and perhaps I could never succeed in intelligibly doing so. But I know it when I see it, and the motion picture involved in this case is not that.

2. A decade after *Roth*, the Court abandoned any attempt to develop a jurisprudence of obscenity. Instead, as Justice Brennan later explained, the Court "began the practice in *Redrup v. New York*, 386 U.S. 767 (1967), of per curiam reversals of convictions for the dissemination of materials that at least five members of the Court, applying their separate tests, deemed not to be obscene." This was, to say the least, an unsatisfactory—and unstable—regime. In 1969, the Court appeared to be moving toward a reconsideration of *Roth*.

Stanley v. Georgia
394 U.S. 557 (1969)

MR. JUSTICE MARSHALL delivered the opinion of the Court.

An investigation of appellant's alleged bookmaking activities led to the issuance of a search warrant for appellant's home. Under authority of this warrant, federal and state agents secured entrance. They found very little evidence of bookmaking activity, but while looking through a desk drawer in an upstairs bedroom, one of the [agents] found three reels of eight-millimeter film. Using a projector and screen found in an upstairs living room, they viewed the films. The state officer concluded that they were obscene and seized them. [Appellant was indicted and convicted for "knowingly hav[ing] possession of . . . obscene matter" in violation of Georgia law. The Supreme Court of Georgia affirmed.]

Appellant raises several challenges to the validity of his conviction.[2] We find it necessary to consider only one. . . . For reasons set forth below, we agree that the mere private possession of obscene matter cannot constitutionally be made a crime.

. . . Georgia concedes that the present case appears to be one of "first impression . . . on this exact point,"[3] but contends that since "obscenity is not within the area of constitutionally protected speech or press," *Roth v. United States*, the States are free, subject to the limits of other provisions of the Constitution, to deal with it any way deemed necessary, just as they may deal with possession of other things thought to be detrimental to the welfare of their citizens. If the State can protect the body of a citizen, may it not, argues Georgia, protect his mind?

---

2. Appellant does not argue that the films are not obscene. For the purpose of this opinion, we assume that they are obscene under any of the tests advanced by members of this Court. *See Redrup v. New York*, 386 U.S. 767 (1967).

3. The issue was before the Court in *Mapp v. Ohio*, 367 U.S. 643 (1961), but that case was decided on other grounds. Mr. Justice Stewart, although disagreeing with the majority opinion in *Mapp*, would have reversed the judgment in that case on the ground that the Ohio statute proscribing mere possession of obscene material was "not 'consistent with the rights of free thought and expression assured against state action by the Fourteenth Amendment.'"

It is true that *Roth* does declare, seemingly without qualification, that obscenity is not protected by the First Amendment. That statement has been repeated in various forms in subsequent cases. . . . However, neither *Roth* nor any subsequent decision of this Court dealt with the precise problem involved in the present case. . . . Indeed, with one exception, we have been unable to discover any case in which the issue in the present case has been fully considered.

In this context, we do not believe that this case can be decided simply by citing *Roth*. . . . *Roth* and the cases following it discerned [an] "important interest" in the regulation of commercial distribution of obscene material. That holding cannot foreclose an examination of the constitutional implications of a statute forbidding mere private possession of such material.

It is now well established that the Constitution protects the right to receive information and ideas. . . . Moreover, in the context of this case — a prosecution for mere possession of printed or filmed matter in the privacy of a person's own home — that right takes on an added dimension. For also fundamental is the right to be free, except in very limited circumstances, from unwanted governmental intrusions into one's privacy. "The makers of our Constitution . . . conferred, as against the government, the right to be let alone — the most comprehensive of rights and the right most valued by civilized man." *Olmstead v. United States*, 277 U.S. 438, 478 (1928) (Brandeis, J., dissenting).

These are the rights that appellant is asserting in the case before us. He is asserting the right to read or observe what he pleases — the right to satisfy his intellectual and emotional needs in the privacy of his own home. He is asserting the right to be free from state inquiry into the contents of his library. Georgia contends that appellant does not have these rights, that there are certain types of materials that the individual may not read or even possess. Georgia justifies this assertion by arguing that the films in the present case are obscene. But we think that mere categorization of these films as "obscene" is insufficient justification for such a drastic invasion of personal liberties guaranteed by the First and Fourteenth Amendments. Whatever may be the justifications for other statutes regulating obscenity, we do not think they reach into the privacy of one's own home. If the First Amendment means anything, it means that a State has no business telling a man, sitting alone in his own house, what books he may read or what films he may watch. Our whole constitutional heritage rebels at the thought of giving government the power to control men's minds.

And yet, in the face of these traditional notions of individual liberty, Georgia asserts the right to protect the individual's mind from the effects of obscenity. We are not certain that this argument amounts to anything more than the assertion that the State has the right to control the moral content of a person's thoughts.[8] To some, this may

---

8. "Communities believe, and act on the belief, that obscenity is immoral, is wrong for the individual, and has no place in a decent society. They believe, too, that adults as well as children are corruptible in morals and character, and that obscenity is a source of corruption that should be eliminated. Obscenity is not suppressed primarily for the protection of others. Much of it is suppressed for the purity of the community and for the salvation and welfare of the 'consumer.'

be a noble purpose, but it is wholly inconsistent with the philosophy of the First Amendment. . . . Nor is it relevant that obscene materials in general, or the particular films before the Court, are arguably devoid of any ideological content. The line between the transmission of ideas and mere entertainment is much too elusive for this Court to draw, if indeed such a line can be drawn at all. Whatever the power of the state to control public dissemination of ideas inimical to the public morality, it cannot constitutionally premise legislation on the desirability of controlling a person's private thoughts.

Perhaps recognizing this, Georgia asserts that exposure to obscene materials may lead to deviant sexual behavior or crimes of sexual violence. There appears to be little empirical basis for that assertion. But more important, if the State is only concerned about printed or filmed materials inducing antisocial conduct, we believe that in the context of private consumption of ideas and information we should adhere to the view that "[a]mong free men, the deterrents ordinarily to be applied to prevent crime are education and punishment for violations of the law. . . ." *Whitney v. California* (Brandeis, J., concurring). Given the present state of knowledge, the State may no more prohibit mere possession of obscene matter on the ground that it may lead to antisocial conduct than it may prohibit possession of chemistry books on the ground that they may lead to the manufacture of homemade spirits.

It is true that in *Roth* this Court rejected the necessity of proving that exposure to obscene material would create a clear and present danger of antisocial conduct or would probably induce its recipients to such conduct. But that case dealt with public distribution of obscene materials and such distribution is subject to different objections. For example, there is always the danger that obscene material might fall into the hands of children, or that it might intrude upon the sensibilities or privacy of the general public. No such dangers are present in this case.

Finally, we are faced with the argument that prohibition of possession of obscene materials is a necessary incident to statutory schemes prohibiting distribution. That argument is based on alleged difficulties of proving an intent to distribute or in producing evidence of actual distribution. We are not convinced that such difficulties exist, but even if they did we do not think that they would justify infringement of the individual's right to read or observe what he pleases. Because that right is so fundamental to our scheme of individual liberty, its restriction may not be justified by the need to ease the administration of otherwise valid criminal laws.

We hold that the First and Fourteenth Amendments prohibit making mere private possession of obscene material a crime. *Roth* and the cases following that decision are not impaired by today's holding. As we have said, the States retain broad power to regulate obscenity; that power simply does not extend to mere possession by the individual in the privacy of his own home. Accordingly, the judgment of the court below

---

Obscenity, at bottom, is not crime. Obscenity is sin." Henkin, *Morals and the Constitution: The Sin of Obscenity*, 63 Colum. L. Rev. 391, 395 (1963).

is reversed and the case is remanded for proceedings not inconsistent with this opinion.

MR. JUSTICE BLACK, concurring. [Omitted.]

MR. JUSTICE STEWART, with whom MR. JUSTICE BRENNAN and MR. JUSTICE WHITE join, concurring in the result.

. . . In affirming the appellant's conviction, the Georgia Supreme Court specifically determined that the films had been lawfully seized. The appellant correctly contends that this determination was clearly wrong under established principles of constitutional law. But the Court today disregards this preliminary issue in its hurry to move on to newer constitutional frontiers. I cannot so readily overlook the serious inroads upon Fourth Amendment guarantees countenanced in this case by the Georgia courts. . . .

————

Note: The Implications of Stanley

1. The Court insists in *Stanley* that "*Roth* and the cases following [it] are not impaired by today's decision." Consider the arguments put forth by the state of Georgia and rejected by the Court. To what extent would the Court's response apply to laws prohibiting the sale or distribution of obscene material?

2. In *Karalexis v. Byrne*, 306 F. Supp. 1363 (D. Mass. 1969), *vacated on other grounds*, 401 U.S. 216 (1971), a three-judge district court considered the implications of *Stanley* for a case in which "possibly obscene" movies were exhibited to "paying adult members of the public." The court said:

> We confess that no oracle speaks to [the theater owner] unambiguously. Nonetheless, we think it probable that *Roth* remains intact only with respect to public distribution in the full sense, and that restricted distribution, adequately controlled, is no longer to be condemned. It is difficult to think that if Stanley has a constitutional right to view obscene films, the Court would intend its exercise to be only at the expense of a criminal act on behalf of the only logical source, the professional supplier. A constitutional right to receive a communication would seem meaningless if there were no coextensive right to make it. If a rich Stanley can view a film, or read a book, in his home, a poorer Stanley should be free to visit a protected theatre or library. We see no reason for saying he must go alone.

3. In *United States v. Reidel*, 402 U.S. 351 (1971), another lower court embraced the "rich Stanley, poor Stanley" argument. The Supreme Court, speaking through Justice White, reversed, saying:

> To extrapolate from Stanley's right to have and peruse obscene material in the privacy of his own home a First Amendment right in Reidel to sell it to him would effectively scuttle *Roth*, the precise result that the *Stanley* opinion abjured. Whatever the scope of the "right to receive" referred to in *Stanley*, it is not so broad as to immunize the dealings in obscenity in

which Reidel engaged here — dealings that *Roth* held unprotected by the First Amendment.

> The right Stanley asserted was "the right to read or observe what he pleases — the right to satisfy his intellectual and emotional needs in the privacy of his own home." . . . The focus of [the language in *Stanley*] was on freedom of mind and thought and on the privacy of one's home. It does not require that we fashion or recognize a constitutional right in people like Reidel to distribute or sell obscene materials. The personal constitutional rights of those like Stanley to possess and read obscenity in their homes and their freedom of mind and thought do not depend on whether the materials are obscene or whether obscenity is constitutionally protected. Their rights to have and view that material in private are independently saved by the Constitution.

> Reidel is in a wholly different position. He has no complaints about governmental violations of his private thoughts or fantasies, but stands squarely on a claimed First Amendment right to do business in obscenity and use the mails in the process. But *Roth* has squarely placed obscenity and its distribution outside the reach of the First Amendment and they remain there today. *Stanley* did not overrule *Roth* and we decline to do so now.

Does the Court adequately answer the argument that if a rich Stanley can view a film in his home, a poorer Stanley should be free to view the same movie in a theater with others? Justice Black, dissenting in *Reidel* and a companion case, observed wryly that that "perhaps in the future [*Stanley*] will be recognized as good law only when a man writes salacious books in his attic, prints them in his basement, and reads them in his living room." Consider, in light of the cases that follow, whether Justice Black's prediction has proved accurate.

[2] Current Doctrine

Miller v. California
413 U.S. 15 (1973)

Mr. Chief Justice Burger delivered the opinion of the Court.

This is one of a group of "obscenity-pornography" cases being reviewed by the Court in a re-examination of standards enunciated in earlier cases involving what Mr. Justice Harlan called "the intractable obscenity problem."

Appellant conducted a mass mailing campaign to advertise the sale of illustrated books, euphemistically called "adult" material. After a jury trial, he was [convicted of] knowingly distributing obscene matter, and the [appellate court] summarily affirmed the judgment without opinion. Appellant's conviction was specifically based on his conduct in causing five unsolicited advertising brochures to be sent through the mail in an envelope addressed to a restaurant in Newport Beach, California. The envelope was opened by the manager of the restaurant and his mother. They had not requested the brochures; they complained to the police.

The brochures advertise four books entitled "Intercourse," "Man-Woman," "Sex Orgies Illustrated," and "An Illustrated History of Pornography," and a film entitled "Marital Intercourse." While the brochures contain some descriptive printed material, primarily they consist of pictures and drawings very explicitly depicting men and women in groups of two or more engaging in a variety of sexual activities, with genitals often prominently displayed.

I

This case involves the application of a State's criminal obscenity statute to a situation in which sexually explicit materials have been thrust by aggressive sales action upon unwilling recipients who had in no way indicated any desire to receive such materials. This Court has recognized that the States have a legitimate interest in prohibiting dissemination or exhibition of obscene material[2] when the mode of dissemination carries with it a significant danger of offending the sensibilities of unwilling recipients or of exposure to juveniles. *Stanley v. Georgia*, 394 U.S. 557, 567 (1969). . . .

II

This much has been categorically settled by the Court, that obscene material is unprotected by the First Amendment. . . . We acknowledge, however, the inherent dangers of undertaking to regulate any form of expression. State statutes designed to regulate obscene materials must be carefully limited. As a result, we now confine the permissible scope of such regulation to works which depict or describe sexual conduct. That conduct must be specifically defined by the applicable state law, as written or authoritatively construed. A state offense must also be limited to works which, taken as a whole, appeal to the prurient interest in sex, which portray sexual conduct in a patently offensive way, and which, taken as a whole, do not have serious literary, artistic, political, or scientific value.

The basic guidelines for the trier of fact must be: (a) whether "the average person, applying contemporary community standards" would find that the work, taken as a whole, appeals to the prurient interest; (b) whether the work depicts or describes, in a patently offensive way, sexual conduct specifically defined by the applicable state law; and (c) whether the work, taken as a whole, lacks serious literary, artistic, political, or scientific value. We do not adopt as a constitutional standard the "*utterly* without redeeming social value" test of *Memoirs v. Massachusetts*, 383 U.S. 413 (1966); that

---

2. This Court has defined "obscene material" as "material which deals with sex in a manner appealing to prurient interest," but the *Roth* definition does not reflect the precise meaning of "obscene" as traditionally used in the English language. . . . The material we are discussing in this case is more accurately defined as "pornography" or "pornographic material." "Pornography" derives from the Greek (*porne*, harlot, and *graphos*, writing). The word now means "1: a description of prostitutes or prostitution 2: a depiction (as in writing or painting) of licentiousness or lewdness: a portrayal of erotic behavior designed to cause sexual excitement." Webster's Third New International Dictionary. Pornographic material which is obscene forms a subgroup of all "obscene" expression, but not the whole, at least as the word "obscene" is now used in our language. We note, therefore, that the words "obscene material," as used in this case, have a specific judicial meaning which derives from the *Roth* case, i.e., obscene material "which deals with sex."

concept has never commanded the adherence of more than three Justices at one time.[7] If a state law that regulates obscene material is thus limited, as written or construed, the First Amendment values applicable to the States through the Fourteenth Amendment are adequately protected by the ultimate power of appellate courts to conduct an independent review of constitutional claims when necessary.

We emphasize that it is not our function to propose regulatory schemes for the States. That must await their concrete legislative efforts. It is possible, however, to give a few plain examples of what a state statute could define for regulation under part (b) of the standard announced in this opinion, *supra*:

(a) Patently offensive representations or descriptions of ultimate sexual acts, normal or perverted, actual or simulated.

(b) Patently offensive representation or descriptions of masturbation, excretory functions, and lewd exhibition of the genitals.

Sex and nudity may not be exploited without limit by films or pictures exhibited or sold in places of public accommodation any more than live sex and nudity can be exhibited or sold without limit in such public places. At a minimum, prurient, patently offensive depiction or description of sexual conduct must have serious literary, artistic, political, or scientific value to merit First Amendment protection. For example, medical books for the education of physicians and related personnel necessarily use graphic illustrations and descriptions of human anatomy. In resolving the inevitably sensitive questions of fact and law, we must continue to rely on the jury system, accompanied by the safeguards that judges, rules of evidence, presumption of innocence, and other protective features provide, as we do with rape, murder, and a host of other offenses against society and its individual members.

[Mr. Justice Brennan] has abandoned his former position and now maintains that no formulation of this Court, the Congress, or the States can adequately distinguish obscene material unprotected by the First Amendment from protected expression. Paradoxically, Mr. Justice Brennan indicates that suppression of unprotected obscene material is permissible to avoid exposure to unconsenting adults, as in this case, and to juveniles, although he gives no indication of how the division between protected and nonprotected materials may be drawn with greater precision for these purposes than for regulation of commercial exposure to consenting adults only. Nor does he indicate where in the Constitution he finds the authority to distinguish between a willing "adult" one month past the state law age of majority and a willing "juvenile" one month younger.

Under the holdings announced today, no one will be subject to prosecution for the sale or exposure of obscene materials unless these materials depict or describe patently offensive "hard core" sexual conduct specifically defined by the regulating state law, as written or construed. We are satisfied that these specific prerequisites will provide

---

7. "A quotation from Voltaire in the flyleaf of a book will not constitutionally redeem an otherwise obscene publication . . ." *Kois v. Wisconsin*, 408 U.S. 229, 231 (1972). We also reject, as a constitutional standard, the ambiguous concept of "social importance."

fair notice to a dealer in such materials that his public and commercial activities may bring prosecution. If the inability to define regulated materials with ultimate, god-like precision altogether removes the power of the States or the Congress to regulate, then "hard core" pornography may be exposed without limit to the juvenile, the passerby, and the consenting adult alike, as, indeed, Mr. Justice Douglas contends. . . . In this belief, however, Mr. Justice Douglas now stands alone.

Mr. Justice Brennan also emphasizes "institutional stress" in justification of his change of view. . . . It is certainly true that the absence, since *Roth*, of a single majority view of this Court as to proper standards for testing obscenity has placed a strain on both state and federal courts. But today, for the first time since *Roth* was decided in 1957, a majority of this Court has agreed on concrete guidelines to isolate "hard core" pornography from expression protected by the First Amendment. Now we may abandon the casual practice of *Redrup v. New York*, 386 U.S. 767 (1967), and attempt to provide positive guidance to federal and state courts alike. . . .

III

Under a National Constitution, fundamental First Amendment limitations on the powers of the States do not vary from community to community, but this does not mean that there are, or should or can be, fixed, uniform national standards of precisely what appeals to the "prurient interest" or is "patently offensive." These are essentially questions of fact, and our Nation is simply too big and too diverse for this Court to reasonably expect that such standards could be articulated for all 50 States in a single formulation, even assuming the prerequisite consensus exists. When triers of fact are asked to decide whether "the average person, applying contemporary community standards" would consider certain materials "prurient," it would be unrealistic to require that the answer be based on some abstract formulation. The adversary system, with lay jurors as the usual ultimate factfinders in criminal prosecutions, has historically permitted triers of fact to draw on the standards of their community, guided always by limiting instructions on the law. To require a State to structure obscenity proceedings around evidence of a *national* "community standard" would be an exercise in futility. . . .

It is neither realistic nor constitutionally sound to read the First Amendment as requiring that the people of Maine or Mississippi accept public depiction of conduct found tolerable in Las Vegas, or New York City. . . . We hold that the requirement that the jury evaluate the materials with reference to "contemporary standards of the State of California" serves this protective purpose and is constitutionally adequate.

IV

The dissenting Justices sound the alarm of repression. But, in our view, to equate the free and robust exchange of ideas and political debate with commercial exploitation of obscene material demeans the grand conception of the First Amendment and its high purposes in the historic struggle for freedom. . . . The First Amendment protects works which, taken as a whole, have serious literary, artistic, political, or scientific value, regardless of whether the government or a majority of the people approve of the ideas these works represent. "The protection given speech and press was fashioned to assure unfettered interchange of *ideas* for the bringing about of political and social changes desired by the people," *Roth v. United States* (emphasis added). But the public portrayal of hard-core sexual conduct for its own sake, and for the ensuing commercial gain, is a different matter.

There is no evidence, empirical or historical, that the stern 19th century American censorship of public distribution and display of material relating to sex, in any way limited or affected expression of serious literary, artistic, political, or scientific ideas. . . .

Mr. Justice Brennan finds "it is hard to see how state-ordered regimentation of our minds can ever be forestalled." These doleful anticipations assume that courts cannot distinguish commerce in ideas, protected by the First Amendment, from commercial exploitation of obscene material. Moreover, state regulation of hard-core pornography so as to make it unavailable to nonadults, a regulation which Mr. Justice Brennan finds constitutionally permissible, has all the elements of "censorship" for adults; indeed even more rigid enforcement techniques may be called for with such dichotomy of regulation. One can concede that the "sexual revolution" of recent years may have had useful byproducts in striking layers of prudery from a subject long irrationally kept from needed ventilation. But it does not follow that no regulation of patently offensive "hard core" materials is needed or permissible; civilized people do not allow unregulated access to heroin because it is a derivative of medicinal morphine.

In sum, we (a) reaffirm the *Roth* holding that obscene material is not protected by the First Amendment; (b) hold that such material can be regulated by the States, subject to the specific safeguards enunciated above, without a showing that the material is "*utterly* without redeeming social value"; and (c) hold that obscenity is to be determined by applying "contemporary community standards," not "national standards." The judgment of the [California court] is vacated and the case remanded to that court for further proceedings not inconsistent with the First Amendment standards established by this opinion.

Mr. Justice Douglas, dissenting. [Omitted.]

Mr. Justice Brennan, with whom Mr. Justice Stewart and Mr. Justice Marshall join, dissenting.

[It] is clear that under my dissent in *Paris Adult Theatre I* [which follows], the statute under which the prosecution was brought is unconstitutionally overbroad, and therefore invalid on its face. . . .

Paris Adult Theatre I v. Slaton
413 U.S. 49 (1973)

Mr. Chief Justice Burger delivered the opinion of the Court.

Petitioners are two Atlanta, Georgia, movie theaters and their owners and managers, operating in the style of "adult" theaters. On December 28, 1970, respondents, the local state district attorney and the solicitor for the local state trial court, filed civil complaints in that court alleging that petitioners were exhibiting to the public for paid admission two allegedly obscene films, contrary to Georgia Code Ann. § 26-2101. The two films in question, "Magic Mirror" and "It All Comes Out in the End," depict sexual conduct characterized by the Georgia Supreme Court as "hard core pornography" leaving "little to the imagination." . . .

The two films were exhibited to the trial court. The only other state evidence was testimony by criminal investigators that they had paid admission to see the films and that nothing on the outside of the theater indicated the full nature of what was shown. In particular, nothing indicated that the films depicted—as they did—scenes of simulated fellatio, cunnilingus, and group sex intercourse. There was no evidence presented that minors had ever entered the theaters. Nor was there evidence presented that petitioners had a systematic policy of barring minors, apart from posting signs at the entrance. [Photographs show a conventional, inoffensive theater entrance, without any pictures, but with signs indicating that the theaters exhibit "Atlanta's Finest Mature Feature Films." On the door itself is a sign saying: "Adult Theatre—You must be 21 and able to prove it. If viewing the nude body offends you, Please Do Not Enter."]

[The Georgia Supreme Court] assumed that the adult theaters in question barred minors and gave a full warning to the general public of the nature of the films shown, but held that the films were without protection under the First Amendment. . . . After viewing the films, the Georgia Supreme Court held that their exhibition should have been enjoined, stating: "The films in this case leave little to the imagination. It is plain what they purport to depict, that is, conduct of the most salacious character. We hold that these films are also hard core pornography, and the showing of such films should have been enjoined since their exhibition is not protected by the first amendment."

[Today,] in *Miller v. California*, we have sought to clarify the constitutional definition of obscene material subject to regulation by the States, and we vacate and remand this case for reconsideration in light of *Miller*. . . .

II

We categorically disapprove the theory . . . that obscene, pornographic films acquire constitutional immunity from state regulation simply because they are exhibited for consenting adults only. . . . Although we have often pointedly recognized the high importance of the state interest in regulating the exposure of obscene materials to juveniles and unconsenting adults, this Court has never declared these to be the only legitimate state interests permitting regulation of obscene material. The States have a long-recognized legitimate interest in regulating the use of obscene material in local commerce and in all places of public accommodation, as long as these regulations do not run afoul of specific constitutional prohibitions. . . .

In particular, we hold that there are legitimate state interests at stake in stemming the tide of commercialized obscenity, even assuming it is feasible to enforce effective safeguards against exposure to juveniles and to passersby. Rights and interests "other than those of the advocates are involved." These include the interest of the public in the quality of life and the total community environment, the tone of commerce in the great city centers, and, possibly, the public safety itself. The Hill-Link Minority Report of the Commission on Obscenity and Pornography indicates that there is at least an arguable correlation between obscene material and crime. Quite apart from sex crimes, however, there remains one problem of large proportions aptly described by Professor Bickel:

> It concerns the tone of the society, the mode, or to use terms that have perhaps greater currency, the style and quality of life, now and in the future. A man may be entitled to read an obscene book in his room, or expose himself indecently there. . . . We should protect his privacy. But if he demands a right to obtain the books and pictures he wants in the market, and to foregather in public places—discreet, if you will, but accessible to all—with others who share his tastes, *then to grant him his right is to affect the world about the rest of us, and to impinge on other privacies.* Even supposing that each of us can, if he wishes, effectively avert the eye and stop the ear (which, in truth, we cannot), what is commonly read and seen and heard and done intrudes upon us all, want it or not. 22 THE PUBLIC INTEREST 25–26 (Winter 1971). (Emphasis added.)

As Mr. Chief Justice Warren stated, there is a "right of the Nation and of the States to maintain a decent society . . . ," *Jacobellis v. Ohio*, 378 U.S. 184, 199 (1964) (dissenting opinion).

But, it is argued, there are no scientific data which conclusively demonstrate that exposure to obscene material adversely affects men and women or their society. It is urged on behalf of the petitioners that, absent such a demonstration, any kind of state regulation is "impermissible." We reject this argument. It is not for us to resolve empirical uncertainties underlying state legislation, save in the exceptional case where that legislation plainly impinges upon rights protected by the Constitution itself. . . . Although there is no conclusive proof of a connection between antisocial behavior and obscene material, the legislature of Georgia could quite reasonably determine that such a connection does or might exist. In deciding *Roth*, this Court implicitly accepted that a legislature could legitimately act on such a conclusion to protect "*the social interest in order and morality.*" *Roth*, quoting *Chaplinsky* (emphasis added in *Roth*).

From the beginning of civilized societies, legislators and judges have acted on various unprovable assumptions. Such assumptions underlie much lawful state regulation of commercial and business affairs. The same is true of the federal securities and antitrust laws and a host of federal regulations. . . . Understandably those who entertain an absolutist view of the First Amendment find it uncomfortable to explain why rights of association, speech, and press should be severely restrained in the marketplace of goods and money, but not in the marketplace of pornography. . . .

[If we accept] the well nigh universal belief that good books, plays, and art lift the spirit, improve the mind, enrich the human personality, and develop character, can we then say that a state legislature may not act on the corollary assumption that commerce in obscene books, or public exhibitions focused on obscene conduct, have a tendency to exert a corrupting and debasing impact leading to antisocial behavior? . . .

The sum of experience, including that of the past two decades, affords an ample basis for legislatures to conclude that a sensitive, key relationship of human existence, central to family life, community welfare, and the development of human personality, can be debased and distorted by crass commercial exploitation of sex. Nothing in the Constitution prohibits a State from reaching such a conclusion and acting on it legislatively simply because there is no conclusive evidence or empirical data. . . .

[It is asserted] that standards for evaluating state commercial regulations are inapposite in the present context, as state regulation of access by consenting adults to obscene material violates the constitutionally protected right to privacy enjoyed by petitioners' customers. . . . Nothing, however, in this Court's decisions intimates that there is any "fundamental" privacy right "implicit in the concept of ordered liberty" to watch obscene movies in places of public accommodation.

If obscene material unprotected by the First Amendment in itself carried with it a "penumbra" of constitutionally protected privacy, this Court would not have found it necessary to decide *Stanley* on the narrow basis of the "privacy of the home," which was hardly more than a reaffirmation that "a man's home is his castle." Moreover, we have declined to equate the privacy of the home relied on in *Stanley* with a "zone" of "privacy" that follows a distributor or a consumer of obscene materials whatever he goes. *United States v. Reidel.* The idea of a "privacy" right and a place of public accommodation are, in this context, mutually exclusive. Conduct or depictions of conduct that the state police power can prohibit on a public street do not become automatically protected by the Constitution merely because the conduct is moved to a bar or a "live" theater stage, any more than a "live" performance of a man and woman locked in a sexual embrace at high noon in Times Square is protected by the Constitution because they simultaneously engage in a valid political dialogue.

It is also argued that the State has no legitimate interest in "control [of] the moral content of a person's thoughts," *Stanley v. Georgia*, and we need not quarrel with this. But we reject the claim that the State of Georgia is here attempting to control the minds or thoughts of those who patronize theaters. Preventing unlimited display or distribution of obscene material, which by definition lacks any serious literary, artistic, political, or scientific value as communication, *Miller v. California*, is distinct from a control of reason and the intellect. Where communication of ideas, protected by the First Amendment, is not involved, or the particular privacy of the home protected by *Stanley*, or any of the other "areas or zones" of constitutionally protected privacy, the mere fact that, as a consequence, some human "utterances" or "thoughts" may be incidentally affected does not bar the State from acting to protect legitimate state interests. The fantasies of a drug addict are his own and beyond the reach of government, but government regulation of drug sales is not prohibited by the Constitution.

Finally, petitioners argue that conduct which directly involves "consenting adults" only has, for that sole reason, a special claim to constitutional protection. Our Constitution establishes a broad range of conditions on the exercise of power by the States, but for us to say that our Constitution incorporates the proposition that conduct involving consenting adults only is always beyond state regulation, is a step we are unable to take.[15] Commercial exploitation of depictions, descriptions, or exhibitions of obscene conduct on commercial premises open to the adult public falls within a State's broad power to regulate commerce and protect the public environment. The issue in this context goes beyond whether someone, or even the majority, considers the conduct depicted as "wrong" or "sinful." The States have the power to make a morally neutral judgment that public exhibition of obscene material, or commerce in such material, has a tendency to injure the community as a whole, to endanger the public safety, or to jeopardize in Mr. Chief Justice Warren's words, the States' "right . . . to maintain a decent society."

To summarize, we have today reaffirmed the basic holding of *Roth v. United States* that obscene material has no protection under the First Amendment. We have directed our holdings, not at thoughts or speech, but at depiction and description of specifically defined sexual conduct that States may regulate within limits designed to prevent infringement of First Amendment rights. We have also reaffirmed the [holding] of *United States v. Reidel* that commerce in obscene material is unprotected by any constitutional doctrine of privacy. In this case we hold that the States have a legitimate interest in regulating commerce in obscene material and in regulating exhibition of obscene material in places of public accommodation, including so-called "adult" theaters from which minors are excluded.

In light of these holdings, nothing precludes the State of Georgia from the regulation of the allegedly obscene material exhibited in Paris Adult Theatre I or II, provided that the applicable Georgia law, as written or authoritatively interpreted by the Georgia courts, meets the First Amendment standards set forth in *Miller v. California*. The judgment is vacated and the case remanded to the Georgia Supreme Court for further proceedings not inconsistent with this opinion and *Miller v. California*.

MR. JUSTICE DOUGLAS, dissenting.

. . . "Obscenity" at most is the expression of offensive ideas. . . . I am sure I would find offensive most of the books and movies charged with being obscene. But in a life that has not been short, I have yet to be trapped into seeing or reading something that would offend me. I never read or see the materials coming to the Court under charges of "obscenity," because I have thought the First Amendment made it unconstitutional for me to act as a censor. I see ads in bookstores and neon lights over theaters that resemble bait for those who seek vicarious exhilaration. As a parent or a

---

15. The state statute books are replete with constitutionally unchallenged laws against prostitution, suicide, voluntary self-mutilation, brutalizing "bare fist" prize fights, and duels, although these crimes may only directly involve "consenting adults." Statutes making bigamy a crime surely cut into an individual's freedom to associate, but few today seriously claim such statutes violate the First Amendment or any other constitutional provision. See also the summary of state statutes prohibiting bearbaiting, cock-fighting, and other brutalizing animal "sports," in STEVENS, FIGHTING AND BAITING, IN ANIMALS AND THEIR LEGAL RIGHTS 112–27 (Leavitt ed., 1970). As Professor Irving Kristol has observed: "Bearbaiting and cockfighting are prohibited only in part out of compassion for the suffering animals; the main reason they were abolished was because it was felt that they debased and brutalized the citizenry who flocked to witness such spectacles." ON THE DEMOCRATIC IDEA IN AMERICA 33 (1972).

priest or as a teacher I would have no compunction in edging my children or wards away from the books and movies that did no more than excite man's base instincts. But I never supposed that government was permitted to sit in judgment on one's tastes or beliefs — save as they involved action within the reach of the police power of government. . . .

Mr. Justice Brennan, with whom Mr. Justice Stewart and Mr. Justice Marshall join, dissenting.

. . . I am convinced that the approach initiated 16 years ago in *Roth v. United States*, and culminating in the Court's decision today, cannot bring stability to this area of the law without jeopardizing fundamental First Amendment values, and I have concluded that the time has come to make a significant departure from that approach. . . .

. . . The essence of our problem in the obscenity area is that we have been unable to provide "sensitive tools" to separate obscenity from other sexually oriented but constitutionally protected speech, so that efforts to suppress the former do not spill over into the suppression of the latter. . . . Although we have assumed that obscenity does exist and that we "know it when [we] see it," we are manifestly unable to describe it in advance except by reference to concepts so elusive that they fail to distinguish clearly between protected and unprotected speech. . . .

The severe problems arising from the lack of fair notice, from the chill on protected expression, and from the stress imposed on the state and federal judicial machinery persuade me that a significant change in direction is urgently required. I turn, therefore, to the alternatives that are now open.

[We could hold] that any depiction or description of human sexual organs, irrespective of the manner or purpose of the portrayal, is outside the protection of the First Amendment and therefore open to suppression by the States. . . . But such a standard would be appallingly overbroad . . . Yet short of that extreme it is hard to see how any choice of words could reduce the vagueness problem to tolerable proportions, so long as we remain committed to the view that some class of materials is subject to outright suppression by the State.

The alternative adopted by the Court today recognizes that a prohibition against any depiction or description of human sexual organs could not be reconciled with the guarantees of the First Amendment. [But the Court's approach] necessarily assumes that some works will be deemed obscene — even though they clearly have *some* social value — because the State was able to prove that the value, measured by some unspecified standard, was not sufficiently "serious" to warrant constitutional protection. That result is not merely inconsistent with our holding in *Roth*; it is nothing less than a rejection of the fundamental First Amendment premises and rationale of the *Roth* opinion and an invitation to widespread suppression of sexually oriented speech. . . .

In any case, even if the Court's approach left undamaged the conceptual framework of *Roth*, and even if it clearly barred the suppression of works with at least some social value, I would nevertheless be compelled to reject it. . . . Ultimately, the reformulation must fail because it still leaves in this Court the responsibility of determining in each case whether the materials are protected by the First Amendment. . . . I am convinced that a definition of obscenity in terms of physical conduct cannot provide sufficient clarity to afford fair notice, to avoid a chill on protected expression, and to minimize the institutional stress, so long as that definition is used to justify the outright suppression of any material that is asserted to fall within its terms.

I have also considered the possibility of reducing our own role, and the role of appellate courts generally, in determining whether particular matter is obscene. Thus, we might conclude that juries are best suited to determine obscenity *vel non* and that jury verdicts in this area should not be set aside except in cases of extreme departure from prevailing standards. [But while that approach] would mitigate the institutional stress produced by the *Roth* approach, it would neither offer nor produce any cure for the other vices of vagueness. . . . And the approach would expose much protected, sexually oriented expression to the vagaries of jury determinations.

Finally, I have considered the view, urged so forcefully since 1957 by our Brothers Black and Douglas, that the First Amendment bars the suppression of any sexually oriented expression. That position would [strip] the States of power to an extent that cannot be justified by the commands of the Constitution, at least so long as there is available an alternative approach that strikes a better balance between the guarantee of free expression and the States' legitimate interests. . . .

At the outset it should be noted that virtually all of the interests that might be asserted in defense of suppression, laying aside the special interests associated with distribution to juveniles and unconsenting adults, were also posited in *Stanley v. Georgia*, where we held that the State could not make the "mere private possession of obscene material a crime." That decision presages the conclusions I reach here today.

In *Stanley* we pointed out that "[t]here appears to be little empirical basis for" the assertion that "exposure to obscene materials may lead to deviant sexual behavior or crimes of sexual violence."[26] . . .

If, as the Court today assumes, "a state legislature may . . . act on the . . . assumption that commerce in obscene books, or public exhibitions focused on obscene conduct, have a tendency to exert a corrupting and debasing impact leading to antisocial behavior," then it is hard to see how state-ordered regimentation of our minds can ever be forestalled. . . .

In short, while I cannot say that the interests of the State—apart from the question of juveniles and unconsenting adults—are trivial or nonexistent, I am compelled to conclude that these interests cannot justify the substantial damage to constitutional

---

26. Indeed, since *Stanley* was decided, the President's Commission on Obscenity and Pornography has concluded: "In sum, empirical research designed to clarify the question has found no evidence to date that exposure to explicit sexual materials plays a significant role in the causation of delinquent or criminal behavior among youth or adults. The Commission cannot conclude that exposure to erotic materials is a factor in the causation of sex crime or sex delinquency." REPORT OF THE COMMISSION ON OBSCENITY AND PORNOGRAPHY 27 (1970). . . .

rights and to this Nation's judicial machinery that inevitably results from state efforts to bar the distribution even of unprotected material to consenting adults. I would hold, therefore, that at least in the absence of distribution to juveniles or obtrusive exposure to unconsenting adults, the First and Fourteenth Amendments prohibit the State and Federal Governments from attempting wholly to suppress sexually oriented materials on the basis of their allegedly "obscene" contents. . . .

———

Note: The 1973 "Restatement"

1. Justice Douglas, dissenting in *Paris Adult*, says that obscenity "at most is the expression of ideas." What "ideas" are expressed by hard core pornography? At the other extreme, the Court (in footnote 15) compares obscenity laws to laws against suicide and cock-fighting. Would anyone argue that suicide and cock-fighting are protected by the First Amendment?

2. The Court twice quotes Chief Justice Warren's reference to "the right of the Nation and of the State to maintain a decent society." What is the injury to "a decent society" when willing adults read or view hard core pornography?

3. Justice Brennan, in dissent, argues that it is impossible to define and prosecute obscenity in a way that will not "chill" protected expression. States have been free to prosecute "obscenity," as defined in *Miller*, since 1973. Has time vindicated Justice Brennan's position?

4. A year after *Miller*, in *Jenkins v. Georgia*, 418 U.S. 153 (1974), the Court reversed the obscenity conviction of a movie theater owner for showing the film "Carnal Knowledge." In a crucial paragraph, the Court explained its reasoning as follows:

> Our own viewing of the film satisfies us that "Carnal Knowledge" could not be found under the *Miller* standards to depict sexual conduct in a patently offensive way. Nothing in the movie falls within either of the two examples given in *Miller* of material which may constitutionally be found to meet the "patently offensive" element of those standards, nor is there anything sufficiently similar to such material to justify similar treatment. While the subject matter of the picture is, in a broader sense, sex, and there are scenes in which sexual conduct including "ultimate sexual acts" is to be understood to be taking place, the camera does not focus on the bodies of the actors at such times. There is no exhibition whatever of the actors' genitals, lewd or otherwise, during these scenes. There are occasional scenes of nudity, but nudity alone is not enough to make material legally obscene under the *Miller* standards.

5. *Patent offensiveness.* In the four decades since *Jenkins*, the Supreme Court has given little guidance about what materials may be deemed "patently offensive" for purposes of the *Miller* test. During that time, sensibilities and standards have changed enormously, and the Internet and the World Wide Web have revolutionized communication. What kind of material might be found "patently offensive" today?

6. *Lack of serious value.* In *Pope v. Illinois*, 481 U.S. 497 (1987), the Court addressed the third prong of the *Miller* test. That prong requires the trier of fact to determine "whether the work, taken as a whole, lacks serious literary, artistic, political, or scientific value." The issue in *Pope* was whether, in a prosecution for the sale of allegedly obscene materials, the jury may be instructed to apply community standards in deciding the value question. The Court held that, unlike the first and second prongs, the third prong is *not* tested by community standards. The Court said:

> There is no suggestion in our cases that the question of the value of an allegedly obscene work is to be determined by reference to community standards. . . . In *Miller* itself, the Court was careful to point out that "[t]he First Amendment protects works which, taken as a whole, have serious literary, artistic, political, or scientific value, regardless of whether the government or a majority of the people approve of the ideas these works represent." Just as the ideas a work represents need not obtain majority approval to merit protection, neither, insofar as the First Amendment is concerned, does the value of the work vary from community to community based on the degree of local acceptance it has won. The proper inquiry is not whether an ordinary member of any given community would find serious literary, artistic, political, or scientific value in allegedly obscene material, but whether a reasonable person would find such value in the material, taken as a whole.

Justice Stevens, joined by Justice Brennan and Justice Marshall, argued that this standard did not adequately protect First Amendment interests:

> In my judgment, communicative material of this sort is entitled to the protection of the First Amendment if *some reasonable persons* could consider it as having serious literary artistic, political, or scientific value. . . . The purpose of the third element of the *Miller* test is to ensure that the obscenity laws not be allowed to "'level' the available reading matter to the majority or lowest common denominator of the population. . . . It is obvious that neither *Ulysses* nor *Lady Chatterley's Lover* would have literary appeal to the majority of the population." F. SCHAUER, THE LAW OF OBSCENITY 144 (1976). A juror asked to create "a reasonable person" in order to apply the standard that the Court announces today might well believe that the majority of the population who find no value in such a book are more reasonable than the minority who do find value. First Amendment protection surely must not be contingent on this type of subjective determination.

Justice Stevens added:

> The problems with the Court's formulation are accentuated when expert evidence is adduced about the value that the material has to a discrete segment of the population—be they art scholars, scientists, or literary critics. Certainly a jury could conclude that although those people reasonably find value in the material, the ordinary "reasonable person" would not.

Justice Scalia, in a concurring opinion, disagreed with this analysis:

I join the Court's opinion with regard to an "objective" or "reasonable person" test of "serious literary, artistic, political, or scientific value," because I think that the most faithful assessment of what *Miller* intended, and because we have not been asked to reconsider *Miller* in the present case. I must note, however, that in my view it is quite impossible to come to an objective assessment of (at least) literary or artistic value, there being many accomplished people who have found literature in Dada, and art in the replication of a soup can.

The approach proposed [by Justice Stevens] does not eliminate this difficulty, but arguably aggravates it. It is a refined enough judgment to estimate whether a reasonable person *would* find literary or artistic value in a particular publication; it carries refinement to the point of meaninglessness to ask whether he *could* do so. Taste being . . . unpredictable, the answer to the question must always be "yes"—so that there is little practical difference between that proposal and Part III of Justice Stevens' dissent, which asserts more forthrightly that "government may not constitutionally criminalize mere possession or sale of obscene literature, absent some connection to minors, or obtrusive display to unconsenting adults."

———

Note: *"Community Standards" and the Internet*

As *Jenkins* and *Spokane Arcades* make clear, two of the three prongs of the test for obscenity—patent offensiveness and appeal to prurient interest—are measured by "contemporary community standards." In *Hamling v. United States*, 418 U.S. 87 (1974) (decided on the same day as *Jenkins*), the Court elaborated on this point, holding that a juror sitting in an obscenity case may "draw on knowledge of *the community or vicinage from which he comes* in deciding what conclusion 'the average person, applying contemporary community standards' would reach in a given case." (Emphasis added.) But how can courts apply "community standards" to material on the Internet and the World Wide Web? Should they even try?

The Justices debated these questions, but did not provide definitive answers, in *Ashcroft v. American Civil Liberties Union*, 535 U.S. 564 (2002). The case involved a facial challenge to the Child Online Protection Act (COPA). Under COPA, it was a crime to use the World Wide Web to "knowingly . . . make[] any communication for commercial purposes that is available to any minor and that includes any material that is harmful to minors." In defining "material that is harmful to minors," the statute called for the application of "contemporary community standards" to determine whether the material appealed to prurient interest.

The Third Circuit held that this reliance on "contemporary community standards" in the context of "the electronic medium of the Web" rendered the statute unconstitutionally overbroad. The Supreme Court rejected the Third Circuit's position, but without a majority opinion.

Justice Thomas, writing for a three-Justice plurality, acknowledged that juries in different sections of the country would apply different standards in prosecutions under

COPA; he acknowledged, too, that "Web publishers currently lack the ability to limit access to their sites on a geographic basis." But he rejected the argument that forcing Web publishers "to cope with the community standards of every hamlet into which their goods [might] wander" would result in "debilitating self-censorship that abridges the First Amendment rights of the people." And he saw no reason to modify "this Court's community standards jurisprudence" in the context of Internet transmissions:

> [We] do not believe that [the "unique characteristics" of the Internet] justify adopting a different approach than that set forth in [the Court's precedents]. If a publisher chooses to send its material into a particular community, this Court's jurisprudence teaches that it is the publisher's responsibility to abide by that community's standards. The publisher's burden does not change simply because it decides to distribute its material to every community in the Nation. Nor does it change because the publisher may wish to speak only to those in a "community where avant garde culture is the norm," but nonetheless utilizes a medium that transmits its speech from coast to coast. If a publisher wishes for its material to be judged only by the standards of particular communities, then it need only take the simple step of utilizing a medium that enables it to target the release of its material into those communities.

Justice O'Connor and Justice Breyer concurred in the judgment but disagreed with Justice Thomas's analysis of the community standards issue; both took the position that the Court should adopt a national standard for defining obscenity on the Internet. Justice O'Connor wrote:

> [Given] Internet speakers' inability to control the geographic location of their audience, expecting them to bear the burden of controlling the recipients of their speech, as we did in *Hamling* . . . , may be entirely too much to ask, and would potentially suppress an inordinate amount of expression. For these reasons, adoption of a national standard is necessary in my view for any reasonable regulation of Internet obscenity.

Justice Breyer was even more direct. He said:

> To read the statute as adopting the community standards of every locality in the United States would provide the most puritan of communities with a heckler's Internet veto affecting the rest of the Nation. The technical difficulties associated with efforts to confine Internet material to particular geographic areas make the problem particularly serious. And these special difficulties also potentially weaken the authority of prior cases in which they were not present. *Cf. Hamling.*

Justice Kennedy, in an opinion joined by Justice Souter and Justice Ginsburg, edged toward that position but stopped short of adopting it. He said that the Third Circuit "may have been correct . . . to conclude that in practical effect COPA imposes the most puritanical community standard on the entire country," and he also observed:

"The national variation in community standards constitutes a particular burden on Internet speech." But he agreed to a remand because "[w]e cannot know whether variation in community standards renders the Act substantially overbroad without first assessing the extent of the speech covered and the variations in community standards with respect to that speech."

Justice Stevens, who dissented alone, insisted that the precedents relied on by Justice Thomas were distinguishable:

> If the material were forwarded through the mails or over the telephone [as in *Hamling* and the other cases cited by Justice Thomas], the sender could avoid destinations with the most restrictive standards. . . . Given the undisputed fact that a provider who posts material on the Internet cannot prevent it from entering any geographic community, a law that criminalizes a particular communication in just a handful of destinations effectively prohibits transmission of that message to all of the 176.5 million Americans that have access to the Internet. In light of this fundamental difference in technologies, the rules applicable to the mass mailing of an obscene montage or to obscene dial-a-porn should not be used to judge the legality of messages on the World Wide Web.

On remand, the Third Circuit again affirmed the grant of a preliminary injunction against enforcement of COPA. This time the Supreme Court also affirmed. After a full trial the Third Circuit held the statute unconstitutional, and the Supreme Court denied certiorari. The question of "community standards" in obscenity prosecutions for material distributed via the Internet thus remains open. How should the question be resolved? Should the Court distinguish between material disseminated by email and material posted on websites?

Chapter 3

New Candidates for Categorical Exclusion or Limited Protection

A. Offensive Language and Images

Cohen v. California

403 U.S. 15 (1971)

Mr. Justice Harlan delivered the opinion of the Court.

This case may seem at first blush too inconsequential to find its way into our books, but the issue it presents is of no small constitutional significance.

Appellant Paul Robert Cohen was convicted in the Los Angeles Municipal Court of violating that part of California Penal Code § 415 which prohibits "maliciously and willfully disturb[ing] the peace or quiet of any neighborhood or person . . . by . . . offensive conduct . . . ." He was given 30 days' imprisonment. The facts upon which his conviction rests are detailed in the opinion of the Court of Appeal of California, Second Appellate District, as follows:

> On April 26, 1968, the defendant was observed in the Los Angeles County Courthouse in the corridor outside of division 20 of the municipal court wearing a jacket bearing the words "Fuck the Draft" which were plainly visible. There were women and children present in the corridor. The defendant was arrested. The defendant testified that he wore the jacket knowing that the words were on the jacket as a means of informing the public of the depth of his feelings against the Vietnam War and the draft. The defendant did not engage in, nor threaten to engage in, nor did anyone as the result of his conduct in fact commit or threaten to commit any act of violence. The defendant did not make any loud or unusual noise, nor was there any evidence that he uttered any sound prior to his arrest.

In affirming the conviction the Court of Appeal held that "offensive conduct" means "behavior which has a tendency to provoke others to acts of violence or to in turn disturb the peace," and that the State had proved this element because, on the facts of this case, "[i]t was certainly reasonably foreseeable that such conduct might cause others to rise up to commit a violent act against the person of the defendant or attempt to forceably remove his jacket." The California Supreme Court declined review by a divided vote . . . . We now reverse . . . .

I

In order to lay hands on the precise issue which this case involves, it is useful first to canvass various matters which this record does not present.

The conviction quite clearly rests upon the asserted offensiveness of the words Cohen used to convey his message to the public. The only "conduct" which the State sought to punish is the fact of communication. Thus, we deal here with a conviction resting solely upon "speech," not upon any separately identifiable conduct which allegedly was intended by Cohen to be perceived by others as expressive of particular views but which, on its face, does not necessarily convey any message and hence arguably could be regulated without effectively repressing Cohen's ability to express himself. *Cf. United States v. O'Brien*, 391 U.S. 367 (1968) [Chapter 7]. Further, the State certainly lacks power to punish Cohen for the underlying content of the message the inscription conveyed. At least so long as there is no showing of an intent to incite disobedience to or disruption of the draft, Cohen could not, consistently with the First and Fourteenth Amendments, be punished for asserting the evident position on the inutility or immorality of the draft his jacket reflected. *Yates v. United States* (1957) [Chapter 1 Note].

Appellant's conviction, then, rests squarely upon his exercise of the "freedom of speech" protected from arbitrary governmental interference by the Constitution and can be justified, if at all, only as a valid regulation of the manner in which he exercised that freedom, not as a permissible prohibition on the substantive message it conveys. This does not end the inquiry, of course, for the First and Fourteenth Amendments have never been thought to give absolute protection to every individual to speak whenever or wherever he pleases or to use any form of address in any circumstances that he chooses. In this vein, too, however, we think it important to note that several issues typically associated with such problems are not presented here.

In the first place, Cohen was tried under a statute applicable throughout the entire State. Any attempt to support this conviction on the ground that the statute seeks to preserve an appropriately decorous atmosphere in the courthouse where Cohen was arrested must fail in the absence of any language in the statute that would have put appellant on notice that certain kinds of otherwise permissible speech or conduct would nevertheless, under California law, not be tolerated in certain places . . . .[3]

In the second place, as it comes to us, this case cannot be said to fall within those relatively few categories of instances where prior decisions have established the power of government to deal more comprehensively with certain forms of individual expression simply upon a showing that such a form was employed. This is not, for example, an obscenity case. Whatever else may be necessary to give rise to the States' broader power to prohibit obscene expression, such expression must be, in some significant

---

3. It is illuminating to note what transpired when Cohen entered a courtroom in the building. He removed his jacket and stood with it folded over his arm. Meanwhile, a policeman sent the presiding judge a note suggesting that Cohen be held in contempt of court. The judge declined to do so and Cohen was arrested by the officer only after he emerged from the courtroom.

way, erotic. It cannot plausibly be maintained that this vulgar allusion to the Selective Service System would conjure up such psychic stimulation in anyone likely to be confronted with Cohen's crudely defaced jacket.

This Court has also held that the States are free to ban the simple use, without a demonstration of additional justifying circumstances, of so-called "fighting words," those personally abusive epithets which, when addressed to the ordinary citizen, are, as a matter of common knowledge, inherently likely to provoke violent reaction. *Chaplinsky v. New Hampshire* (1942) [Chapter 2]. While the four-letter word displayed by Cohen in relation to the draft is not uncommonly employed in a personally provocative fashion, in this instance it was clearly not "directed to the person of the hearer." *Cantwell v. Connecticut* (1940) [Chapter 8]. No individual actually or likely to be present could reasonably have regarded the words on appellant's jacket as a direct personal insult. Nor do we have here an instance of the exercise of the State's police power to prevent a speaker from intentionally provoking a given group to hostile reaction. *Cf. Feiner v. New York* (1951) [Chapter 8 Note]; *Terminiello v. Chicago* (1949) [Chapter 8]. There is, as noted above, no showing that anyone who saw Cohen was in fact violently aroused or that appellant intended such a result.

Finally, in arguments before this Court much has been made of the claim that Cohen's distasteful mode of expression was thrust upon unwilling or unsuspecting viewers, and that the State might therefore legitimately act as it did in order to protect the sensitive from otherwise unavoidable exposure to appellant's crude form of protest. Of course, the mere presumed presence of unwitting listeners or viewers does not serve automatically to justify curtailing all speech capable of giving offense. While this Court has recognized that government may properly act in many situations to prohibit intrusion into the privacy of the home of unwelcome views and ideas which cannot be totally banned from the public dialogue, we have at the same time consistently stressed that "we are often 'captives' outside the sanctuary of the home and subject to objectionable speech." The ability of government, consonant with the Constitution, to shut off discourse solely to protect others from hearing it is, in other words, dependent upon a showing that substantial privacy interests are being invaded in an essentially intolerable manner. Any broader view of this authority would effectively empower a majority to silence dissidents simply as a matter of personal predilections.

In this regard, persons confronted with Cohen's jacket were in a quite different posture than, say, those subjected to the raucous emissions of sound trucks blaring outside their residences. Those in the Los Angeles courthouse could effectively avoid further bombardment of their sensibilities simply by averting their eyes. And, while it may be that one has a more substantial claim to a recognizable privacy interest when walking through a courthouse corridor than, for example, strolling through Central Park, surely it is nothing like the interest in being free from unwanted expression in the confines of one's own home.

Given the subtlety and complexity of the factors involved, if Cohen's "speech" was otherwise entitled to constitutional protection, we do not think the fact that some unwilling "listeners" in a public building may have been briefly exposed to it can serve to justify this breach of the peace conviction where, as here, there was no evidence that persons powerless to avoid appellant's conduct did in fact object to it, and where that portion of the statute upon which Cohen's conviction rests evinces no concern . . . with the special plight of the captive auditor, but, instead, indiscriminately sweeps within its prohibitions all "offensive conduct" that disturbs "any neighborhood or person."

II

Against this background, the issue flushed by this case stands out in bold relief. It is whether California can excise, as "offensive conduct," one particular scurrilous epithet from the public discourse, either upon the theory of the court below that its use is inherently likely to cause violent reaction or upon a more general assertion that the States, acting as guardians of public morality, may properly remove this offensive word from the public vocabulary.

The rationale of the California court is plainly untenable. At most it reflects an "undifferentiated fear or apprehension of disturbance [which] is not enough to overcome the right to freedom of expression." *Tinker v. Des Moines Indep. Community School Dist.* (1969) [Chapter 12]. We have been shown no evidence that substantial numbers of citizens are standing ready to strike out physically at whoever may assault their sensibilities with execrations like that uttered by Cohen. There may be some persons about with such lawless and violent proclivities, but that is an insufficient base upon which to erect, consistently with constitutional values, a governmental power to force persons who wish to ventilate their dissident views into avoiding particular forms of expression. The argument amounts to little more than the self-defeating proposition that to avoid physical censorship of one who has not sought to provoke such a response by a hypothetical coterie of the violent and lawless, the States may more appropriately effectuate that censorship themselves.

Admittedly, it is not so obvious that the First and Fourteenth Amendments must be taken to disable the States from punishing public utterance of this unseemly expletive in order to maintain what they regard as a suitable level of discourse within the body politic. We think, however, that examination and reflection will reveal the shortcomings of a contrary viewpoint.

At the outset, we cannot overemphasize that, in our judgment, most situations where the State has a justifiable interest in regulating speech will fall within one or more of the various established exceptions, discussed above but not applicable here, to the usual rule that governmental bodies may not prescribe the form or content of individual expression. Equally important to our conclusion is the constitutional backdrop against which our decision must be made. The constitutional right of free expression is powerful medicine in a society as diverse and populous as ours. It is designed and intended to remove governmental restraints from the arena of public discussion, putting the decision as to what views shall be voiced largely into the hands of each of us, in the hope that use of such freedom will ultimately produce a more capable citizenry and more perfect polity and in the belief that no other approach would comport with the premise of individual dignity and choice upon which our political system rests. *See Whitney v. California* (1927) (Brandeis, J., concurring) [Chapter 1].

To many, the immediate consequence of this freedom may often appear to be only verbal tumult, discord, and even offensive utterance. These are, however, within established limits, in truth necessary side effects of the broader enduring values which the process of open debate permits us to achieve. That the air may at times seem filled with verbal cacophony is, in this sense not a sign of weakness but of strength. We cannot lose sight of the fact that, in what otherwise might seem a trifling and annoying instance of individual distasteful abuse of a privilege, these fundamental societal values are truly implicated . . . .

Against this perception of the constitutional policies involved, we discern certain more particularized considerations that peculiarly call for reversal of this conviction. First, the principle contended for by the State seems inherently boundless. How is one to distinguish this from any other offensive word? Surely the State has no right to cleanse public debate to the point where it is grammatically palatable to the most squeamish among us. Yet no readily ascertainable general principle exists for stopping short of that result were we to affirm the judgment below. For, while the particular four-letter word being litigated here is perhaps more distasteful than most others of its genre, it is nevertheless often true that one man's vulgarity is another's lyric. Indeed, we think it is largely because governmental officials cannot make principled distinctions in this area that the Constitution leaves matters of taste and style so largely to the individual.

Additionally, we cannot overlook the fact, because it is well illustrated by the episode involved here, that much linguistic expression serves a dual communicative function: it conveys not only ideas capable of relatively precise, detached explication, but otherwise inexpressible emotions as well. In fact, words are often chosen as much for their emotive as their cognitive force. We cannot sanction the view that the Constitution, while solicitous of the cognitive content of individual speech has little or no regard for that emotive function which practically speaking, may often be the more important element of the overall message sought to be communicated . . . .

Finally, and in the same vein, we cannot indulge the facile assumption that one can forbid particular words without also running a substantial risk of suppressing ideas in the process. Indeed, governments might soon seize upon the censorship of particular words as a convenient guise for banning the expression of unpopular views. We have been able, as noted above, to discern little social benefit that might result from running the risk of opening the door to such grave results.

It is, in sum, our judgment that, absent a more particularized and compelling reason for its actions, the State may not, consistently with the First and Fourteenth Amendments, make the simple public display here involved of this single four-letter expletive a criminal offense. Because that is the only arguably sustainable rationale for the conviction here at issue, the judgment below must be reversed.

MR. JUSTICE BLACKMUN, with whom THE CHIEF JUSTICE [BURGER] and MR. JUSTICE BLACK join.

I dissent, and I do so for two reasons:

1. Cohen's absurd and immature antic, in my view, was mainly conduct and little speech. *See* [e.g.] *Giboney v. Empire Storage & Ice Co.*, 336 U.S. 490, 502 (1949) . . . . Further, the case appears to me to be well within the sphere of *Chaplinsky v. New Hampshire*, where Mr. Justice Murphy, a known champion of First Amendment freedoms, wrote for a unanimous bench. As a consequence, this Court's agonizing over First Amendment values seem misplaced and unnecessary.

2. I am not at all certain that the California Court of Appeal's construction of § 415 is now the authoritative California construction. . . . Inasmuch as this Court does not dismiss this case, it ought to be remanded to the California Court of Appeal for reconsideration in the light of [a subsequent] decision by the State's highest tribunal.

MR. JUSTICE WHITE concurs in Paragraph 2 of MR. JUSTICE BLACKMUN's dissenting opinion.

––––––––

Note: *The Implications of* Cohen

1. Review Justice Harlan's account of the "more particularized considerations that peculiarly call for reversal of [Cohen's] conviction." To what extent can these arguments be made in the context of obscenity prosecutions? Does the rationale of *Cohen* cast doubt on the soundness of the Court's approach to obscenity?

2. At the Court's initial conference on *Cohen*, Justice White explained his vote to affirm by saying, "California can prevent people from tapping a woman on the shoulder and saying 'fuck you.'" THE SUPREME COURT IN CONFERENCE at 351. Does the *Cohen* opinion foreclose prosecution under those facts?

Rosenfeld v. New Jersey

408 U.S. 901 (1972)

[This case was decided without oral argument or full briefing; the Court had before it only the jurisdictional statement (the equivalent of the petition for certiorari) and the appellee's motion to dismiss or affirm. The Court's disposition reads in its entirety as follows.]

Appeal from Superior Court of New Jersey. Judgment vacated and case remanded for reconsideration in light of *Cohen v. California*, 403 U.S. 15 (1971), and *Gooding v. Wilson*, 405 U.S. 518 (1972) [Chapter 2 Note].

MR. JUSTICE POWELL, with whom THE CHIEF JUSTICE [BURGER] and MR. JUSTICE BLACKMUN join, dissenting . . . .

This case presents an example of gross abuse of the respected privilege in this country of allowing every citizen to speak his mind. Appellant addressed a public school board meeting attended by about 150 people, approximately 40 of whom were children and 25 of whom were women. In the course of his remarks he used the adjective "m _____ f_____" on four occasions, to describe the teachers, the school board, the town and his own country.

For using this language under these circumstances, appellant was prosecuted and convicted under a New Jersey statute which provides: "Any person who utters loud and offensive or profane or indecent language in any public street or other public place, public conveyance, or place to which the public is invited . . . [i]s a disorderly person." Prior to appellant's prosecution, the Supreme Court of New Jersey had limited the statute's coverage as follows: "[T]he words must be spoken loudly, in a public place and must be of such a nature as to be likely to incite the hearer to an immediate breach of the peace or to be likely, in the light of the gender and age of the listener and the setting of the utterance, to affect the sensibilities of a hearer. The words must be spoken with the intent to have the above effect or with a reckless disregard of the probability of the above consequences."

The Court today decides to vacate and remand this case for reconsideration in light of *Gooding v. Wilson* and *Cohen v. California*. As it seems to me that neither of these cases is directly relevant, and that considerations not present in those cases are here controlling, I respectfully dissent.

Perhaps appellant's language did not constitute "fighting words" within the meaning of *Chaplinsky*. While most of those attending the school board meeting were undoubtedly outraged and offended, the good taste and restraint of such an audience may have made it unlikely that physical violence would result. Moreover, the offensive words were not directed at a specific individual. But the exception to First Amendment protection recognized in *Chaplinsky* is not limited to words whose mere utterance entails a high probability of an outbreak of physical violence. It also extends to the willful use of scurrilous language calculated to offend the sensibilities of an unwilling audience.

. . . [A] verbal assault on an unwilling audience may be so grossly offensive and emotionally disturbing as to be the proper subject of criminal proscription, whether under a statute denominating it disorderly conduct, or more accurately, a public nuisance . . . .

The decision in *Gooding v. Wilson* turned largely on an application of the First Amendment overbreadth doctrine, and the Court's remand order suggests that the overbreadth doctrine should be applied in this case . . . . In my view, the doctrine is not applicable in this case.

The New Jersey statute was designed to prohibit the public use of language such as that involved in this case, and certainly the State has an interest — perhaps a compelling one — in protecting non-assenting citizens from vulgar and offensive verbal assaults. A statute directed narrowly to this interest does not impinge upon the values of protected free speech . . . .

The line between [legitimate First Amendment rights] and the type of conduct proscribed by the New Jersey statute is difficult to draw. The preservation of the right of free and robust speech is accorded high priority in our society and under the Constitution. Yet, there are other significant values. One of the hallmarks of a civilized society is the level and quality of discourse. We have witnessed in recent years a disquieting deterioration in standards of taste and civility in speech. For the increasing number of persons who derive satisfaction from vocabularies dependent upon filth and obscenities, there are abundant opportunities to gratify their debased tastes. But our free society must be flexible enough to tolerate even such a debasement provided it occurs without subjecting unwilling audiences to the type of verbal nuisance committed in this case. The shock and sense of affront, and sometimes the injury to mind and spirit, can be as great from words as from some physical attacks.

I conclude in this case that appellant's utterances fall within the proscription of the New Jersey statute, and are not protected by the First Amendment . . . .

[JUSTICE REHNQUIST dissented separately.]

———

Note: "The Willful Use of Scurrilous Language"

1. In his dissent in *Rosenfeld*, Justice Powell explicitly separates the "breach of the peace" and "inflict injury" prongs of *Chaplinsky*. He argues that "utterances . . . which may amount to a public nuisance" fall outside the protection of the First Amendment even if they do not "threaten physical violence." Professor Zechariah Chafee — whose analysis provided the basis for the *Chaplinsky* dictum — took a similar position. Chafee wrote, "The man who swears in a street car is as much of a nuisance as the man who smokes there." ZECHARIAH CHAFEE, JR., FREE SPEECH IN THE UNITED STATES 150 (1941). Is the analogy persuasive as a ground for rejecting a First Amendment defense?

2. Consider the proposition advanced by Justice Powell: the First Amendment does not protect "the willful use of scurrilous language calculated to offend the sensibilities of an unwilling audience." The Supreme Court has never accepted this proposition, nor has the Court rejected it. Is the proposition sound? Does Justice Powell adequately answer Justice Harlan's question in *Cohen*: "How is one to distinguish this from any other offensive word?"

3. Simultaneously with *Rosenfeld*, the Court issued a similar order in *Brown v. Oklahoma*, 408 U.S. 914 (1972). The facts of *Brown* were described as follows in the dissenting opinion of Justice Rehnquist:

> Appellant [spoke] to a large group of men and women gathered in the University of Tulsa chapel. During a question and answer period he referred to some policemen as "m___ f___ fascist pig cops" and to a particular Tulsa police officer as that ". . . black m___ f___ pig ___." Brown was convicted of violating an Oklahoma statute that prohibited the utterance of "any obscene or lascivious language or word in any public place, or in the presence of females . . . ."

Justice Powell concurred in the result in *Brown*, stating:

The statute involved in this case is considerably broader than the statute involved in *Rosenfeld v. New Jersey*, and it has not been given a narrowing construction by the Oklahoma courts. Moreover, the [record indicates] that the language for which appellant was prosecuted was used in a political meeting to which appellant had been invited to present the Black Panther viewpoint. In these circumstances language of the character charged might well have been anticipated by the audience.

Do you agree that the facts of the two cases warrant different results?

————

Note: Protecting the Unwilling Audience

1. Two years after his dissent in *Rosenfeld*, Justice Powell had the opportunity to write for the Court in *Erznoznik v. City of Jacksonville*, 422 U.S. 205 (1975). The defendant challenged the facial validity of a city ordinance that prohibited drive-in movie theaters from showing films containing nudity if the movie screen was visible from a public street or place. The city conceded that its ordinance swept "far beyond the permissible restraints on obscenity," but it tried to persuade the Court that "any movie containing nudity which is visible from a public place may be suppressed as a nuisance." The Court rejected the contention, saying:

> [The city's] primary argument is that it may protect its citizens against unwilling exposure to materials that may be offensive. Jacksonville's ordinance, however, does not protect citizens from all movies that might offend; rather it singles out films containing nudity, presumably because the lawmakers considered them especially offensive to passersby . . . .
>
> A State or municipality may protect individual privacy by enacting reasonable time, place, and manner regulations applicable to all speech irrespective of content. But when the government, acting as censor, undertakes selectively to shield the public from some kinds of speech on the ground that they are more offensive than others, the First Amendment strictly limits its power. Such selective restrictions have been upheld only when the speaker intrudes on the privacy of the home, or the degree of captivity makes it impractical for the unwilling viewer or auditor to avoid exposure.
>
> The plain, if at times disquieting, truth is that in our pluralistic society, constantly proliferating new and ingenious forms of expression, "we are inescapably captive audiences for many purposes." Much that we encounter offends our esthetic, if not our political and moral, sensibilities. Nevertheless, the Constitution does not permit government to decide which types of otherwise protected speech are sufficiently offensive to require protection for the unwilling listener or viewer. Rather, absent the narrow circumstances described above, the burden normally falls upon the viewer to "avoid further bombardment of [his] sensibilities simply by averting [his] eyes." *Cohen.*

In a footnote, Justice Powell addressed the concerns he had raised in his *Rosenfeld* dissent:

> It has [been] suggested that government may proscribe, by a properly framed law, "the willful use of scurrilous language calculated to offend the sensibilities of an unwilling audience." ... In the present case, however, appellant is not trying to reach, much less shock, unwilling viewers. Appellant manages a commercial enterprise which depends for its success on paying customers, not on freeloading passersby. Presumably, where economically feasible, the screen of a drive-in theater will be shielded from those who do not pay.

2. Do *Cohen* and *Erznoznik* leave any room for legislation designed to protect unwilling listeners or viewers from offensive language or displays in public places? Is it the law that, outside the home, the burden *always* falls upon the offended individual to "avoid further bombardment of his sensibilities" by averting his eyes (or closing his ears)? If so, is that a sound interpretation of the First Amendment? Consider the Problems that follow.

––––––––

Problem: Foul Language in a Neighborhood Park

Linwood Park is the only park in the western section of Bayport, a medium-sized city. For many years, parents have taken their children to the park in the daytime and in the early evening. However, during the last several months local teenagers have been congregating in the park at all hours of day and night, using foul language that includes all of George Carlin's "filthy words" and more. The teenagers are loud, and it sometimes seems that they cannot utter a single sentence without using one or more of the words.

The parents are outraged; they feel that the park has been stolen from them. At a recent meeting of the Bayport City Council, a group of parents exhorted the lawmakers to pass an ordinance that would allow the police to remove and arrest youths who use foul language in Linwood Park.

You are the city attorney. Can you draft an ordinance that would meet the parents' concerns without violating the First Amendment?

––––––––

Problem: The Cursing Canoeist

William Bradshaw was convicted of violating section 213.04 of the state criminal code, which provides as follows:

> Any person who shall use any indecent, immoral, obscene, vulgar or insulting language in the presence or hearing of any woman or child shall be guilty of a misdemeanor.

Bradshaw's conviction arose out of events that occurred on the Mullarkee River about a year ago. A group of people were canoeing down the river when Bradshaw, one of the canoeists, fell out of his canoe and into the river. Witness Harry Nelson was canoeing down the river with his wife and two children approximately 40 yards behind Bradshaw's party. He testified that Bradshaw loudly uttered a stream of profanities as he slapped the water and threw his hands into the air.

Martin Krupke, a road patrol deputy for the Boone County Sheriff's Department, happened to be on duty at the river that day. He testified that he heard a "loud commotion" and "vulgar language" coming from approximately one-quarter mile up the river. Krupke looked up and saw Bradshaw chasing a group of canoes, splashing water at them with his paddle, and repeatedly swearing at them. Krupke and Nelson both testified that the river was crowded with families and children, and that Bradshaw would have been able to see Nelson's two children, who were under five years old. Krupke issued Bradshaw a citation for violating section 213.04.

Bradshaw appeals, arguing that the statute violates the First Amendment on its face and as applied. How should the court rule?

FCC v. Pacifica Foundation
438 U.S. 726 (1978)

Mr. Justice Stevens delivered the opinion of the Court (Parts I, II, III and IV-C) and an opinion in which The Chief Justice and Mr. Justice Rehnquist joined (Parts IV-A and IV-B).

This case requires that we decide whether the Federal Communications Commission has any power to regulate a radio broadcast that is indecent but not obscene.

A satiric humorist named George Carlin recorded a 12-minute monologue entitled "Filthy Words" before a live audience in a California theater. He began by referring to his thoughts about "the words you couldn't say on the public, ah, airwaves, um, the ones you definitely wouldn't say, ever." He proceeded to list those words and repeat them over and over again in a variety of colloquialisms. The transcript of the recording, which is appended to this opinion, indicates frequent laughter from the audience.*

———————

* [*Editor's note.* The appendix is omitted. Here are some excerpts from the opening portion of the monologue: "Okay, I was thinking one night about the words you couldn't say on the public, ah, airwaves, um, the ones you definitely wouldn't say, ever, [']cause I heard a lady say bitch one night on television, and it was cool like she was talking about, you know, ah, well, the bitch is the first one to notice that in the litter Johnie right (murmur) Right. And, uh, bastard you can say, and hell and damn so I have to figure out which ones you couldn't say ever and it came down to seven but the list is open to amendment, and in fact, has been changed, uh, by now, ha, a lot of people pointed things out to me, and I noticed some myself. The original seven words were, shit, piss, fuck, cunt, cocksucker, motherfucker, and tits. Those are the ones that will curve your spine, grow hair on your hands and (laughter) maybe, even bring us, God help us, peace without honor (laughter) um, and a bourbon. (laughter) And now the first thing that we noticed was that word fuck was really repeated in there because the word motherfucker is a compound word and it's another form of the word fuck. (laughter) You want to be a purist it doesn't really — it can't be on the list of basic words. Also, cocksucker is a compound word and neither half of that is really dirty. The word — the half sucker that's merely suggestive (laughter) and the word cock is a half-way dirty word, 50% dirty — dirty half the time, depending on what you mean by it. (laughter)."]

At about 2 o'clock in the afternoon on Tuesday, October 30, 1973, a New York radio station, owned by respondent Pacifica Foundation, broadcast the "Filthy Words" monologue. A few weeks later a man, who stated that he had heard the broadcast while driving with his young son, wrote a letter complaining to the Commission. He stated that, although he could perhaps understand the "record's being sold for private use, I certainly cannot understand the broadcast of same over the air that, supposedly, you control." . . .

On February 21, 1975, the Commission issued a declaratory order granting the complaint and holding that Pacifica "could have been the subject of administrative sanctions." The Commission did not impose formal sanctions, but it did state that the order would be "associated with the station's license file, and in the event that subsequent complaints are received, the Commission will then decide whether it should utilize any of the available sanctions it has been granted by Congress." . . .

. . . [The] Commission found a power to regulate indecent broadcasting in . . . 18 U.S.C. § 1464, which forbids the use of "any obscene, indecent, or profane language by means of radio communication." . . .

After the order issued, the Commission was asked to clarify its opinion by ruling that the broadcast of indecent words as part of a live newscast would not be prohibited. The Commission issued another opinion in which it pointed out that it "never intended to place an absolute prohibition on the broadcast of this type of language, but rather sought to channel it to times of day when children most likely would not be exposed to it." The Commission noted that its "declaratory order was issued in a specific factual context," and declined to comment on various hypothetical situations presented by the petition. . . .

The United States Court of Appeals for the District of Columbia Circuit reversed. . . .

Having granted the Commission's petition for certiorari, we must decide: [whether] the broadcast was indecent within the meaning of § 1464; [and] whether the order violates the First Amendment of the United States Constitution.

[The Court first held that the afternoon broadcast of the "Filthy Words" monologue "was indecent within the meaning of § 1464."]

IV

Pacifica makes two constitutional attacks on the Commission's order. First, it argues that the Commission's construction of the statutory language broadly encompasses so much constitutionally protected speech that reversal is required even if Pacifica's broadcast of the "Filthy Words" monologue is not itself protected by the First Amendment. Second, Pacifica argues that inasmuch as the recording is not obscene, the Constitution forbids any abridgment of the right to broadcast it on the radio.

A

The first argument fails because our review is limited to the question whether the Commission has the authority to proscribe this particular broadcast. . . . That approach is appropriate for courts as well as the Commission when regulation of indecency is at stake, for indecency is largely a function of context—it cannot be adequately judged in the abstract. . . .

B

When the issue is narrowed to the facts of this case, the question is whether the First Amendment denies government any power to restrict the public broadcast of indecent language in any circumstances. For if the government has any such power, this was an appropriate occasion for its exercise.

The words of the Carlin monologue are unquestionably "speech" within the meaning of the First Amendment. It is equally clear that the Commission's objections to the broadcast were based in part on its content. The order must therefore fall if, as Pacifica argues, the First Amendment prohibits all governmental regulation that depends on the content of speech. Our past cases demonstrate, however, that no such absolute rule is mandated by the Constitution.

The classic exposition of the proposition that both the content and the context of speech are critical elements of First Amendment analysis is Mr. Justice Holmes' statement for the Court in *Schenck v. United States* (1919) [Chapter 1]:

[Justice Stevens quoted *Schenck*'s "falsely shouting fire in a theater" and "clear and present danger" language. He also cited several other constitutionally-approved "distinctions based on content," including the denial of First Amendment protection for "speech calculated to provoke a fight" (citing *Chaplinsky v. New Hampshire* (1942)) [Chapter 2], "the commonsense differences between commercial speech and other varieties," the constitutional difference between "libels against private citizens . . . [and] libels against public officials" (citing *Gertz v. Robert Welch, Inc.* (1974)) [Chapter 2], and obscenity (citing *Miller v. California* (1973)) [Chapter 2].]

The question in this case is whether a broadcast of patently offensive words dealing with sex and excretion may be regulated because of its content. Obscene materials have been denied the protection of the First Amendment because their content is so offensive to contemporary moral standards. *Roth v. United States* (1957) [Chapter 2]. But the fact that society may find speech offensive is not a sufficient reason for suppressing it. Indeed, if it is the speaker's opinion that gives offense, that consequence is a reason for according it constitutional protection. For it is a central tenet of the First Amendment that the government must remain neutral in the marketplace of ideas. If there were any reason to believe that the Commission's characterization of the Carlin monologue as offensive could be traced to its political content—or even to the fact that it satirized contemporary attitudes about four-letter words—First Amendment protection might be required. But that is simply not this case. These words offend for the same reasons that obscenity offends. Their place in the hierarchy of First Amendment values was aptly sketched by Mr. Justice Murphy when he said: "Such utterances are no essential part of any exposition of ideas, and are of such slight social value as a step to truth that any benefit that may be derived from them is clearly outweighed by the social interest in order and morality." *Chaplinsky.*

Although these words ordinarily lack literary, political, or scientific value, they are not entirely outside the protection of the First Amendment. . . . Nonetheless, the constitutional protection accorded to a communication containing such patently offensive sexual and excretory language need not be the same in every context. It is a characteristic of speech such as this that both its capacity to offend and its "social value," to use Mr. Justice Murphy's term, vary with the circumstances. Words that are commonplace in one setting are shocking in another. To paraphrase Mr. Justice Harlan, one occasion's lyric is another's vulgarity. *Cf. Cohen v. California* (1971) [*supra* this chapter].

In this case it is undisputed that the content of Pacifica's broadcast was "vulgar," "offensive," and "shocking." Because content of that character is not entitled to absolute constitutional protection under all circumstances, we must consider its context in order to determine whether the Commission's action was constitutionally permissible.

C

We have long recognized that each medium of expression presents special First Amendment problems. *Joseph Burstyn, Inc. v. Wilson*, 343 U.S. 495 (1952). And of all forms of communication, it is broadcasting that has received the most limited First Amendment protection. Thus, although other speakers cannot be licensed except under laws that carefully define and narrow official discretion, a broadcaster may be deprived of his license and his forum if the Commission decides that such an action would serve "the public interest, convenience, and necessity." Similarly, although the First Amendment protects newspaper publishers from being required to print the replies of those whom they criticize, *Miami Herald Publishing Co. v. Tornillo* (1974) [Note *infra* this chapter], it affords no such protection to broadcasters; on the contrary, they must give free time to the victims of their criticism. *Red Lion v. FCC* (1969) [Note *infra* this chapter].

The reasons for these distinctions are complex, but two have relevance to the present case. First, the broadcast media have established a uniquely pervasive presence in the lives of all Americans. Patently offensive, indecent material presented over the airwaves confronts the citizen, not only in public, but also in the privacy of the home, where the individual's right to be left alone plainly outweighs the First Amendment rights of an intruder. Because the broadcast audience is constantly tuning in and out, prior warnings cannot completely protect the listener or viewer from unexpected program content.

To say that one may avoid further offense by turning off the radio when he hears indecent language is like saying that the remedy for an assault is to run away after the first blow. One may hang up on an indecent phone call, but that option does not give the caller a constitutional immunity or avoid a harm that has already taken place.

Second, broadcasting is uniquely accessible to children, even those too young to read. Although Cohen's written message might have been incomprehensible to a first grader, Pacifica's broadcast could have enlarged a child's vocabulary in an instant. Other forms of offensive expression may be withheld from the young without restricting the expression at its source. Bookstores and motion picture theaters, for example, may be prohibited from making indecent material available to children. We held in *Ginsberg v. New York*, 390 U.S. 629 (1968), that the government's interest in the "well-being of its youth" and in supporting "parents' claim to authority in their own household" justified the regulation of otherwise protected expression. The ease with which children may obtain access to broadcast material, coupled with the concerns recognized in *Ginsberg*, amply justify special treatment of indecent broadcasting.

It is appropriate, in conclusion, to emphasize the narrowness of our holding. This case does not involve a two-way radio conversation between a cab driver and a dispatcher, or a telecast of an Elizabethan comedy. We have not decided that an occasional expletive in either setting would justify any sanction or, indeed, that this broadcast would justify a criminal prosecution. The Commission's decision rested entirely on a nuisance rationale under which context is all-important.

The concept requires consideration of a host of variables. The time of day was emphasized by the Commission. The content of the program in which the language is used will also affect the composition of the audience, and differences between radio, television, and perhaps closed-circuit transmissions, may also be relevant. As Mr. Justice Sutherland wrote, a "nuisance may be merely a right thing in the wrong place,—like a pig in the parlor instead of the barnyard." *Euclid v. Ambler Realty Co.*, 272 U.S. 365 (1926). We simply hold that when the Commission finds that a pig has entered the parlor, the exercise of its regulatory power does not depend on proof that the pig is obscene.

The judgment of the Court of Appeals is *reversed*.

MR. JUSTICE POWELL, with whom MR. JUSTICE BLACKMUN joins, concurring in part and concurring in the judgment.

I join Parts I, II, III, and IV-C of Mr. Justice Stevens' opinion. . . .

I also agree with much that is said in Part IV of Mr. Justice Stevens' opinion, and with its conclusion that the Commission's holding in this case does not violate the First Amendment. Because I do not subscribe to all that is said in Part IV, however, I state my views separately.

I

It is conceded that the monologue at issue here is not obscene in the constitutional sense. . . . But it also is true that the language employed is, to most people, vulgar and offensive. . . .

The issue [is] whether the Commission may impose civil sanctions on a licensee radio station for broadcasting the monologue at two o'clock in the afternoon. The Commission's primary concern was to prevent the broadcast from reaching the ears of unsupervised children who were likely to be in the audience at that hour. In essence, the Commission sought to "channel" the monologue to hours when the fewest unsupervised children would be exposed to it. In my view, this consideration provides strong support for the Commission's holding.

The Court has recognized society's right to "adopt more stringent controls on communicative materials available to youths than on those available to adults." *Erznoznik v. Jacksonville*, 422 U.S. 205 (1975); *see also, e.g., Miller v. California* (1973) [Chapter 2]; *Ginsberg v. New York*, 390 U.S. 629 (1968). This recognition stems in large part from the fact that "a child . . . is not possessed of that full capacity for individual choice which is the presupposition of First Amendment guarantees." *Ginsberg* (Stewart, J., concurring in result). Thus, children may not be able to protect themselves from speech which, although shocking to most adults, generally may be avoided by the unwilling through the exercise of choice. At the same time, such speech may have a deeper and more lasting negative effect on a child than on an adult. . . .

In most instances, the dissemination of this kind of speech to children may be limited without also limiting willing adults' access to it. Sellers of printed and recorded matter and exhibitors of motion pictures and live performances may be required to shut their doors to children, but such a requirement has no effect on adults' access. The difficulty is that such a physical separation of the audience cannot be accomplished in the broadcast media. During most of the broadcast hours, both adults and unsupervised children are likely to be in the broadcast audience, and the broadcaster cannot reach willing adults without also reaching children. This, as the Court emphasizes, is one of the distinctions between the broadcast and other media to which we often have adverted as justifying a different treatment of the broadcast media for First Amendment purposes. See [e.g.] *Red Lion Broadcasting Co. v. FCC* (1969) [Note *infra* this chapter]. In my view, the Commission was entitled to give substantial weight to this difference in reaching its decision in this case.

A second difference, not without relevance, is that broadcasting—unlike most other forms of communication—comes directly into the home, the one place where people ordinarily have the right not to be assaulted by uninvited and offensive sights and sounds. [E.g.] *Cohen v. California* [*supra* this chapter]. Although the First Amendment may require unwilling adults to absorb the first blow of offensive but protected speech when they are in public before they turn away, a different order of values obtains in the home. . . . The Commission also was entitled to give this factor appropriate weight in the circumstances of the instant case. . . .

It is argued that despite society's right to protect its children from this kind of speech, and despite everyone's interest in not being assaulted by offensive speech in the home, the Commission's holding in this case is impermissible because it prevents willing adults from listening to Carlin's monologue over the radio in the early afternoon hours. It is said that this ruling will have the effect of "reduc[ing] the adult population . . . to [hearing] only what is fit for children." *Butler v. Michigan* (1957). This argument is not without force.

The Commission certainly should consider it as it develops standards in this area. But it is not sufficiently strong to leave the Commission powerless to act in circumstances such as those in this case.

The Commission's holding does not prevent willing adults from purchasing Carlin's record, from attending his performances, or, indeed, from reading the transcript reprinted as an appendix to the Court's opinion. On its face, it does not prevent respondent Pacifica Foundation from broadcasting the monologue during late evening hours when fewer children are likely to be in the audience, nor from broadcasting discussions of the contemporary use of language at any time during the day. The Commission's holding, and certainly the Court's holding today, does not speak to cases involving the isolated use of a potentially offensive word in the course of a radio broadcast, as distinguished from the verbal shock treatment administered by respondent here. In short, I agree that on the facts of this case, the Commission's order did not violate respondent's First Amendment rights.

II

As the foregoing demonstrates, my views are generally in accord with what is said in Part IV-C of Mr. Justice Stevens' opinion. I therefore join that portion of his opinion. I do not join Part IV-B, however, because I do not subscribe to the theory that the Justices of this Court are free generally to decide on the basis of its content which speech protected by the First Amendment is most "valuable" and hence deserving of the most protection, and which is less "valuable" and hence deserving of less protection. In my view, the result in this case does not turn on whether Carlin's monologue, viewed as a whole, or the words that constitute it, have more or less "value" than a candidate's campaign speech. This is a judgment for each person to make, not one for the judges to impose upon him.

The result turns instead on the unique characteristics of the broadcast media, combined with society's right to protect its children from speech generally agreed to be inappropriate for their years, and with the interest of unwilling adults in not being assaulted by such offensive speech in their homes. Moreover, I doubt whether today's decision will prevent any adult who wishes to receive Carlin's message in Carlin's own words from doing so, and from making for himself a value judgment as to the merit of the message and words. These are the grounds upon which I join the judgment of the Court as to Part IV.

Mr. Justice Brennan, with whom Mr. Justice Marshall joins, dissenting. . . .

I

. . . [T]he Court refuses to embrace the notion, completely antithetical to basic First Amendment values, that the degree of protection the First Amendment affords protected speech varies with the social value ascribed to that speech by five Members of this Court. See opinion of Mr. Justice Powell. . . . Yet despite the Court's refusal to create a sliding scale of First Amendment protection calibrated to this Court's perception of the worth of a communication's content, and despite our unanimous agreement that the Carlin monologue is protected speech, a majority of the Court nevertheless finds that, on the facts of this case, the FCC is not constitutionally barred from imposing sanctions on Pacifica for its airing of the Carlin monologue. This majority apparently believes that the FCC's disapproval of Pacifica's afternoon broadcast of Carlin's "Dirty Words" recording is a permissible time, place, and manner regulation. *Kovacs v. Cooper* (1949) [Chapter 6 Note]. Both the opinion of my Brother

Stevens and the opinion of my Brother Powell rely principally on two factors in reaching this conclusion: (1) the capacity of a radio broadcast to intrude into the unwilling listener's home, and (2) the presence of children in the listening audience. Dispassionate analysis, removed from individual notions as to what is proper and what is not, starkly reveals that these justifications, whether individually or together, simply do not support even the professedly moderate degree of governmental homogenization of radio communications — if, indeed, such homogenization can ever be moderate given the pre-eminent status of the right of free speech in our constitutional scheme — that the Court today permits.

A

Without question, the privacy interests of an individual in his home are substantial and deserving of significant protection. In finding these interests sufficient to justify the content regulation of protected speech, however, the Court commits two errors. First, it misconceives the nature of the privacy interests involved where an individual voluntarily chooses to admit radio communications into his home. Second, it ignores the constitutionally protected interests of both those who wish to transmit and those who desire to receive broadcasts that many — including the FCC and this Court — might find offensive.

. . . I am in wholehearted agreement with my Brethren that an individual's right "to be let alone" when engaged in private activity within the confines of his own home . . . is entitled to the greatest solicitude. *Stanley v. Georgia* (1969) [Chapter 2]. However, I believe that an individual's actions in switching on and listening to communications transmitted over the public airways and directed to the public at large do not implicate fundamental privacy interests, even when engaged in within the home. Instead, because the radio is undeniably a public medium, these actions are more properly viewed as a decision to take part, if only as a listener, in an ongoing public discourse. . . .

Even if an individual who voluntarily opens his home to radio communications retains privacy interests of sufficient moment to justify a ban on protected speech if those interests are "invaded in an essentially intolerable manner," the very fact that those interests are threatened only by a radio broadcast precludes any intolerable invasion of privacy; for unlike other intrusive modes of communication, such as sound trucks, "[t]he radio can be turned off" — and with a minimum of effort. . . .

The Court's balance, of necessity, fails to accord proper weight to the interests of listeners who wish to hear broadcasts the FCC deems offensive. It permits majoritarian tastes completely to preclude a protected message from entering the homes of a receptive, unoffended minority. . . .

B

. . . Because the Carlin monologue is obviously not an erotic appeal to the prurient interests of children, the Court, for the first time, allows the government to prevent minors from gaining access to materials that are not obscene, and are therefore protected, as to them. . . . This result violates in spades the principle of *Butler v. Michigan* (1957). . . .

Where, as here, the government may not prevent the exposure of minors to the suppressed material, the principle of *Butler* applies a *fortiori*. The opinion of my Brother Powell acknowledges that there lurks in today's decision a potential for "'reduc[ing] the adult population . . . to [hearing] only what is fit for children,'" but expresses faith that the FCC will vigilantly prevent this potential from ever becoming a reality. I am far less certain than my Brother Powell that such faith in the Commission is warranted, and even if I shared it, I could not so easily shirk the responsibility assumed by each Member of this Court jealously to guard against encroachments on First Amendment freedoms. . . .

C

As demonstrated above, neither of the factors relied on by both the opinion of my Brother Powell and the opinion of my Brother Stevens—the intrusive nature of radio and the presence of children in the listening audience—can, when taken on its own terms, support the FCC's disapproval of the Carlin monologue. These two asserted justifications are further plagued by a common failing: the lack of principled limits on their use as a basis for FCC censorship. No such limits come readily to mind, and neither of the opinions constituting the Court serve to clarify the extent to which the FCC may assert the privacy and children-in-the-audience rationales as justification for expunging from the airways protected communications the Commission finds offensive. . . .

In order to dispel the specter of the possibility of so unpalatable a degree of censorship, . . . the FCC insists that it desires only the authority to reprimand a broadcaster on facts analogous to those present in this case. . . . The opinions of both my Brother Powell and my Brother Stevens take the FCC at its word. . . . To insure that the FCC's regulation of protected speech does not exceed these bounds, my Brother Powell is content to rely upon the judgment of the Commission while my Brother Stevens deems it prudent to rely on this Court's ability accurately to assess the worth of various kinds of speech. For my own part, even accepting that this case is limited to its facts, I would place the responsibility and the right to weed worthless and offensive communications from the public airways where it belongs and where, until today, it resided: in a public free to choose those communications worthy of its attention from a marketplace unsullied by the censor's hand. . . .

Mr. Justice Stewart, with whom Mr. Justice Brennan, Mr. Justice White, and Mr. Justice Marshall join, dissenting [omitted].

———

Note: The Medium and the Message

1. In *Pacifica Foundation*, the Court relies heavily on the need to protect children from foul language to uphold the FCC's "Indecency" policy as applied to the George Carlin monologue. Yet in *Cohen*, after acknowledging that "children were present in the corridor" the Court reversed Cohen's conviction for exposing those children to the phrase "Fuck the Draft" on his jacket. Justice Stevens and the FCC emphasize that the Carlin broadcast was at 2:00 in the afternoon, but presumably so were Cohen's actions, since courthouses are not open at night. Are the Justices' efforts in *Pacifica Foundation* to reconcile the two cases convincing?

2. The primary difference distinguishing *Pacifica* from *Cohen* appears to be the medium through which the message was conveyed—a jacket in a public place versus a radio broadcast. *Pacifica* thus grants a lesser degree of protection to the broadcast medium than speech in public places. In this respect, the Court builds on a previous decision, *Red Lion Broadcasting Co. v. FCC*, 395 U.S. 367 (1969). In *Red Lion*, the Court upheld the FCC's "Fairness Doctrine," which required broadcast television and radio stations to give the opposing side on an issue a chance to present its views when the station took a position on a public issue. In his opinion for the Court, Justice White emphasized that broadcast frequencies were "scarce" (i.e., limited in number), and that therefore in order to prevent interference the government necessarily had to allocate licenses to use frequencies to a limited number of broadcasters. For this reason, Justice White concluded that, in assessing regulation of broadcasters, "[i]t is the right of the views and listeners, not the right of the broadcasters, which is paramount." As the *Pacifica* Court notes, however, five years after *Red Lion*, the Court struck down a similar statute directed at print newspapers because of the differences between the print and broadcast mediums. *Miami Herald Publishing Co. v. Tornillo*, 418 U.S. 241 (1974).

3. The reasoning of *Pacifica* has not been extended to other more modern communications technology, including most notably the Internet. In *Reno v. American Civil Liberties Union*, 521 U.S. 844 (1997), the Court unanimously struck down the "Communications Decency Act of 1996," which criminalized the knowing sending or displaying of "patently offensive messages" on the Internet knowing they would be available to minors. Then, in *Ashcroft v. ACLU*, 542 U.S. 656 (2004), the Court by a 5-4 vote struck down the "Child Online Protection Act" or "COPA," a congressional effort to regulate Internet websites in order to restrict minors' access to sexually explicit materials. The Court concluded that the burden on adult speech by COPA was too great, because Congress could achieve its goals with less restrictive regulatory means such as encouraging the use of blocking and filtering software.

4. *Pacifica* has never been overruled, and the FCC continues to enforce its indecency policy. Given the ongoing migration of entertainment to cable television and the Internet, does *Pacifica* make sense anymore? *See Fox Television Stations v. FCC*, 556 U.S. 502 (2009) (Thomas, J., concurring).

———

Problem: The Over-Excited Actress

Every year the Chinchilla Broadcasting Network (CBN) carries live the annual Screen Actors and Musicians Awards Show (the "Sammys"). Last year Chastity Nott, a well-known actress, won the award for best actress in a musical comedy. She is well-known for her trademark line, "This is so incredibly awesome!" Unfortunately, Chastity got caught up in her own elation at winning a Sammy, and at the start of her acceptance speech blurted out, "This is so incredibly f***ing awesome!" Even though CBN broadcasts the Sammys on a seven-second delay to allow censors to bleep out inappropriate content, CBN censors were caught off-guard and they failed to bleep out the offending word. The Federal Communications Commission fines CBN. Is the fine constitutional?

Is the result different if Nott makes the comment during an interview on CBN's live morning news show?

Is the result different if Nott makes the comment in an interview during *The CBN Not-Quite-Real News Hour*, a scripted comedy show that reports real news developments with satirical commentary and ends with a live, unscripted interview with a famous personality?

Assume that CBN is a cable network, rather than a traditional broadcaster. Is the result any different under any of these three scenarios?

Is the result different if the expletive was uttered by an actress winning a local theater award, with the ceremony broadcast on a local public television station that did not have the financial capability to employ monitoring censors with bleeping technology, with the result that the fine caused the local station to cancel any future broadcasts of the ceremony?

B. Child Pornography

Starting in the 1970s, states began to pass laws aimed at combating the exploitative use of children in the production of pornography. Were these "child pornography" laws to be tested by the same standard as obscenity laws? The Supreme Court soon confronted the issue.

New York v. Ferber

458 U.S. 747 (1982)

Justice White delivered the opinion of the Court.

At issue in this case is the constitutionality of a New York criminal statute which prohibits persons from knowingly promoting sexual performances by children under the age of 16 by distributing material which depicts such performances.

I

In recent years, the exploitive use of children in the production of pornography has become a serious national problem.[1] The Federal Government and 47 States have sought to combat the problem with statutes specifically directed at the production of

---

1. "[C]hild pornography and child prostitution have become highly organized, multimillion dollar industries that operate on a nationwide scale." S. Rep. No. 95-438, 5 (1977). One researcher has documented the existence of over 260 different magazines which depict children engaging in sexually explicit conduct. "Such magazines depict children, some as young as three to five years of age . . . . The activities featured range from lewd poses to intercourse, fellatio, cunnilingus, masturbation, rape, incest and sado-masochism." . . .

child pornography. At least half of such statutes do not require that the materials produced be legally obscene. Thirty-five States and the United States Congress have also passed legislation prohibiting the distribution of such materials; 20 States prohibit the distribution of material depicting children engaged in sexual conduct without requiring that the material be legally obscene.

New York is one of the 20. In 1977, the New York Legislature enacted Article 263 of its Penal Law .... [At issue in this case is §263.15, defining a class D felony: "A person is guilty of promoting a sexual performance by a child when, knowing the character and content thereof, he produces, directs or promotes any performance which includes sexual conduct by a child less than sixteen years of age."]

A "[s]exual performance" is defined as "any performance or part thereof which includes sexual conduct by a child less than sixteen years of age." "Sexual conduct" is in turn defined [as] "actual or simulated sexual intercourse, deviate sexual intercourse, sexual bestiality, masturbation, sado-masochistic abuse, or lewd exhibition of the genitals." A performance is defined as "any play, motion picture, photograph or dance" or "any other visual representation exhibited before an audience."

To "promote" is also defined: "'Promote' means to procure, manufacture, issue, sell, give, provide, lend, mail, deliver, transfer, transmute, publish, distribute, circulate, disseminate, present, exhibit or advertise, or to offer or agree to do the same." A companion provision [§263.10] bans only the knowing dissemination of obscene material.

This case arose when Paul Ferber, the proprietor of a Manhattan bookstore specializing in sexually oriented products, sold two films to an undercover police officer. The films are devoted almost exclusively to depicting young boys masturbating .... After a jury trial, Ferber was acquitted of [two] counts of promoting an obscene sexual performance, but found guilty of [two] counts under §263.15, which did not require proof that the films were obscene .... The New York Court of Appeals reversed, holding that §263.15 violated the First Amendment ....

II

The Court of Appeals proceeded on the assumption that the standard of obscenity incorporated in §263.10, which follows the guidelines enunciated in *Miller v. California* (1973) [Chapter 2], constitutes the appropriate line dividing protected from unprotected expression by which to measure a regulation directed at child pornography ... [That] assumption was not unreasonable in light of our decisions. This case, however, constitutes our first examination of a statute directed at and limited to depictions of sexual activity involving children. We believe our inquiry should begin with the question of whether a State has somewhat more freedom in proscribing works which portray sexual acts or lewd exhibitions of genitalia by children ....

... Like obscenity statutes, laws directed at the dissemination of child pornography run the risk of suppressing protected expression by allowing the hand of the censor to become unduly heavy. For the following reasons, however, we are persuaded that the States are entitled to greater leeway in the regulation of pornographic depictions of children.

First. It is evident beyond the need for elaboration that a State's interest in "safe-guarding the physical and psychological well-being of a minor" is "compelling." . . . Accordingly, we have sustained legislation aimed at protecting the physical and emotional well-being of youth even when the laws have operated in the sensitive area of constitutionally protected rights. [The Court cited, *inter alia, Ginsberg v. New York,* 390 U.S. 629 (1968) and *FCC v. Pacifica Foundation* (1978) [*supra* this chapter].]

The prevention of sexual exploitation and abuse of children constitutes a government objective of surpassing importance . . . . We shall not second-guess this legislative judgment. Respondent has not intimated that we do so . . . .

Second. The distribution of photographs and films depicting sexual activity by juveniles is intrinsically related to the sexual abuse of children in at least two ways. First, the materials produced are a permanent record of the children's participation and the harm to the child is exacerbated by their circulation. Second, the distribution network for child pornography must be closed if the production of material which requires the sexual exploitation of children is to be effectively controlled. Indeed, there is no serious contention that the legislature was unjustified in believing that it is difficult, if not impossible, to halt the exploitation of children by pursuing only those who produce the photographs and movies. While the production of pornographic materials is a low-profile, clandestine industry, the need to market the resulting products requires a visible apparatus of distribution. The most expeditious if not the only practical method of law enforcement may be to dry up the market for this material by imposing severe criminal penalties on persons selling, advertising, or otherwise promoting the product . . . .

Respondent does not contend that the State is unjustified in pursuing those who distribute child pornography. Rather, he argues that it is enough for the State to prohibit the distribution of materials that are legally obscene under the *Miller* test. While some States may find that this approach properly accommodates its interests, it does not follow that the First Amendment prohibits a State from going further. The *Miller* standard, like all general definitions of what may be banned as obscene, does not reflect the State's particular and more compelling interest in prosecuting those who promote the sexual exploitation of children. Thus, the question under the *Miller* test of whether a work, taken as a whole, appeals to the prurient interest of the average person bears no connection to the issue of whether a child has been physically or psychologically harmed in the production of the work. Similarly, a sexually explicit depiction need not be "patently offensive" in order to have required the sexual exploitation of a child for its production. In addition, a work which, taken on the whole, contains serious literary, artistic, political, or scientific value may nevertheless embody the hardest core of child pornography . . . . We therefore cannot conclude that the *Miller* standard is a satisfactory solution to the child pornography problem.

Third. The advertising and selling of child pornography provide an economic motive for and are thus an integral part of the production of such materials, an activity illegal throughout the Nation. "It rarely has been suggested that the constitutional freedom for speech and press extends its immunity to speech or writing used as an integral part of conduct in violation of a valid criminal statute." *Giboney v. Empire Storage & Ice Co.*, 336 U.S. 490, 498 (1949).[14] We note that were the statutes outlawing the employment of children in these films and photographs fully effective, and the constitutionality of these laws has not been questioned, the First Amendment implications would be no greater than that presented by laws against distribution: enforceable production laws would leave no child pornography to be marketed.

Fourth. The value of permitting live performances and photographic reproductions of children engaged in lewd sexual conduct is exceedingly modest, if not de minimis. We consider it unlikely that visual depictions of children performing sexual acts or lewdly exhibiting their genitals would often constitute an important and necessary part of a literary performance or scientific or educational work. [If] it were necessary for literary or artistic value, a person over the statutory age who perhaps looked younger could be utilized. Simulation outside of the prohibition of the statute could provide another alternative. Nor is there any question here of censoring a particular literary theme or portrayal of sexual activity. The First Amendment interest is limited to that of rendering the portrayal somewhat more "realistic" by utilizing or photographing children.

Fifth. Recognizing and classifying child pornography as a category of material outside the protection of the First Amendment is not incompatible with our earlier decisions. "The question whether speech is, or is not protected by the First Amendment often depends on the content of the speech." *Young v. American Mini Theatres, Inc.* (1976) [Chapter 7 Note] (plurality opinion). Leaving aside the special considerations when public officials are the target, *New York Times Co. v. Sullivan* (1964) [Chapter 2], a libelous publication is not protected by the Constitution. *Beauharnais v. Illinois* (1951) [Chapter 2 Note]. Thus, it is not rare that a content-based classification of speech has been accepted because it may be appropriately generalized that within the confines of the given classification, the evil to be restricted so overwhelmingly outweighs the expressive interests, if any, at stake, that no process of case-by-case adjudication is required. When a definable class of material, such as that covered by § 263.15, bears so heavily and pervasively on the welfare of children engaged in its production, we think the balance of competing interests is clearly struck and that it is permissible to consider these materials as without the protection of the First Amendment.

There are, of course, limits on the category of child pornography which, like obscenity, is unprotected by the First Amendment. As with all legislation in this sensitive area, the conduct to be prohibited must be adequately defined by the applicable state

---

14. In *Giboney*, a unanimous Court held that labor unions could be restrained from picketing a firm in support of a secondary boycott which a State had validly outlawed. In *Pittsburgh Press Co. v. Pittsburgh Comm'n on Human Relations*, 413 U.S. 376 (1973), the Court allowed an injunction against a newspaper's furtherance of illegal sex discrimination by placing of job advertisements in gender-designated columns. The Court stated: "Any First Amendment interest which might be served by advertising an ordinary commercial proposal and which might arguably outweigh the governmental interest supporting the regulation is altogether absent when the commercial activity itself is illegal and the restriction on advertising is incidental to a valid limitation on economic activity."

law, as written or authoritatively construed. Here the nature of the harm to be combated requires that the state offense be limited to works that visually depict sexual conduct by children below a specified age. The category of "sexual conduct" proscribed must also be suitably limited and described.

The test for child pornography is separate from the obscenity standard enunciated in *Miller*, but may be compared to it for the purpose of clarity. The *Miller* formulation is adjusted in the following respects: A trier of fact need not find that the material appeals to the prurient interest of the average person; it is not required that sexual conduct portrayed be done so in a patently offensive manner; and the material at issue need not be considered as a whole. We note that the distribution of descriptions or other depictions of sexual conduct, not otherwise obscene, which do not involve live performance or photographic or other visual reproduction of live performances, retains First Amendment protection. As with obscenity laws, criminal responsibility may not be imposed without some element of scienter on the part of the defendant.

Section 263.15's prohibition incorporates a definition of sexual conduct that comports with the above-stated principles. . . . We hold that § 263.15 sufficiently describes a category of material the production and distribution of which is not entitled to First Amendment protection . . . .

III

It remains to address the claim that the New York statute is unconstitutionally overbroad because it would forbid the distribution of material with serious literary, scientific, or educational value or material which does not threaten the harms sought to be combated by the State. Respondent prevailed on that ground below, and it is to that issue that we now turn . . . .

[Under the First Amendment overbreadth doctrine] we have allowed persons to attack overly broad statutes even though the conduct of the person making the attack is clearly unprotected and could be proscribed by a law drawn with the requisite specificity. [However, we have] insisted that the overbreadth involved be "substantial" before the statute involved will be invalidated on its face.

[W]e hold that § 263.15 is not substantially overbroad. We consider this the paradigmatic case of a state statute whose legitimate reach dwarfs its arguably impermissible applications . . . . While the reach of the statute is directed at the hard core of child pornography, the Court of Appeals was understandably concerned that some protected expression, ranging from medical textbooks to pictorials in the National Geographic would fall prey to the statute. How often, if ever, it may be necessary to employ children to engage in conduct clearly within the reach of § 263.15 in order to produce educational, medical, or artistic works cannot be known with certainty. Yet we seriously doubt, and it has not been suggested, that these arguably impermissible applications of the statute amount to more than a tiny fraction of the materials within the statute's reach. Nor will we assume that the New York courts will widen the possibly invalid reach of the statute by giving an expansive construction to the proscription on "lewd exhibition[s] of the genitals." Under these circumstances, § 263.15 is "not substantially overbroad . . . ."

IV

Because § 263.15 is not substantially overbroad, it is unnecessary to consider its application to material that does not depict sexual conduct of a type that New York may restrict consistent with the First Amendment. As applied to Paul Ferber and to others who distribute similar material, the statute does not violate the First Amendment as applied to the States through the Fourteenth. The judgment of the New York Court of Appeals is [reversed].

JUSTICE BLACKMUN concurs in the result.

JUSTICE O'CONNOR, concurring.

Although I join the Court's opinion, I write separately to stress that the Court does not hold that New York must except "material with serious literary, scientific, or educational value," from its statute. The Court merely holds that, even if the First Amendment shelters such material, New York's current statute is not sufficiently overbroad to support respondent's facial attack. The compelling interests identified in today's opinion suggest that the Constitution might in fact permit New York to ban knowing distribution of works depicting minors engaged in explicit sexual conduct, regardless of the social value of the depictions. For example, a 12-year-old child photographed while masturbating surely suffers the same psychological harm whether the community labels the photograph "edifying" or "tasteless." The audience's appreciation of the depiction is simply irrelevant to New York's asserted interest in protecting children from psychological, emotional, and mental harm.

An exception for depictions of serious social value, moreover, would actually increase opportunities for the content-based censorship disfavored by the First Amendment. As drafted, New York's statute does not attempt to suppress the communication of particular ideas. The statute permits discussion of child sexuality, forbidding only attempts to render the "portrayal[s] somewhat more 'realistic' by utilizing or photographing children." Thus, the statute attempts to protect minors from abuse without attempting to restrict the expression of ideas by those who might use children as live models.

On the other hand, it is quite possible that New York's statute is overbroad because it bans depictions that do not actually threaten the harms identified by the Court. For example, clinical pictures of adolescent sexuality, such as those that might appear in medical textbooks, might not involve the type of sexual exploitation and abuse targeted by New York's statute. Nor might such depictions feed the poisonous "kiddie porn" market that New York and other States have attempted to regulate. Similarly, pictures of children engaged in rites widely approved by their cultures, such as those that might appear in issues of the National Geographic, might not trigger the compelling interests identified by the Court. It is not necessary to address these possibilities further today, however, because this potential overbreadth is not sufficiently substantial to warrant facial invalidation of New York's statute.

JUSTICE BRENNAN, with whom JUSTICE MARSHALL joins, concurring in the judgment.

. . . [I agree] with the Court that the "tiny fraction," of material of serious artistic, scientific, or educational value that could conceivably fall within the reach of the [New York] statute is insufficient to justify striking the statute on the grounds of overbreadth.

But in my view application of § 263.15 or any similar statute to depictions of children that in themselves do have serious literary, artistic, scientific, or medical value, would violate the First Amendment. As the Court recognizes, the limited classes of speech, the suppression of which does not raise serious First Amendment concerns, have two attributes. They are of exceedingly "slight social value," and the State has a compelling interest in their regulation. *See Chaplinsky v. New Hampshire* (1942) [chapter 2]. The First Amendment value of depictions of children that are in themselves serious contributions to art, literature, or science, is, by definition, simply not "de minimis." At the same time, the State's interest in suppression of such materials is likely to be far less compelling. For the Court's assumption of harm to the child resulting from the "permanent record" and "circulation" of the child's "participation," lacks much of its force where the depiction is a serious contribution to art or science. . . . In short, it is inconceivable how a depiction of a child that is itself a serious contribution to the world of art or literature or science can be deemed "material outside the protection of the First Amendment." . . .

JUSTICE STEVENS, concurring in the judgment.

Two propositions seem perfectly clear to me. First, the specific conduct that gave rise to this criminal prosecution is not protected by the Federal Constitution; second, the state statute that respondent violated prohibits some conduct that is protected by the First Amendment. The critical question, then, is whether this respondent, to whom the statute may be applied without violating the Constitution, may challenge the statute on the ground that it conceivably may be applied unconstitutionally to others in situations not before the Court. I agree with the Court's answer to this question but not with its method of analyzing the issue . . . .

. . . On a number of occasions, I have expressed the view that the First Amendment affords some forms of speech more protection from governmental regulation than other forms of speech. Today the Court accepts this view, putting the category of speech described in the New York statute in its rightful place near the bottom of this hierarchy. Although I disagree with the Court's position that such speech is totally without First Amendment protection, I agree that generally marginal speech does not warrant the extraordinary protection afforded by the overbreadth doctrine.

———

Note: A New Category of Unprotected Speech

1. In *Ferber*, the Court self-consciously recognizes a new category of unprotected speech. The Court gives five reasons. Under "Fifth," the Court says it is "not rare" that an entire "class of material" has been excluded from the First Amendment "because it may be appropriately generalized that within the confines of the given classification, the evil to be restricted so overwhelmingly outweighs the expressive interests, if any,

at stake, that no process of case-by-case adjudication is required." How strongly do the cases cited by the Court support that proposition?

2. In the paragraph marked "Third," the Court invokes the principle of *Giboney v. Empire Storage & Ice Co.*, 336 U.S. 490 (1949): the First Amendment does not protect "speech or writing used as an integral part of conduct in violation of a valid criminal statute." Or, as stated elsewhere in *Giboney*, "it has never been deemed an abridgement of freedom of speech or press to make a course of conduct illegal merely because the conduct was in part initiated, evidenced, or carried out by means of language, either spoken, written, or printed." The holding in *Giboney* explains why prosecutions of crimes such as price-fixing, or solicitation of murder, which are carried out primarily through words have never been thought to raise First Amendment concerns.

In *United States v. Stevens* (2010) (*infra* this chapter), the Court described/reinterpreted *Ferber* as a simple application of the *Giboney* principle and nothing more. As the Court notes, *Giboney* involved picketing by a labor union in support of a secondary boycott. Do you agree that the distribution of child pornography falls within the *Giboney* principle? How about possession of child pornography? Note also the reliance on *Giboney* in *Osborne v. Ohio*, the child pornography possession case described in the Note immediately following.

3. The Court says that the test for child pornography is an "adjusted" version of the *Miller* test for obscenity. The implication is that the difference is not great. Is the implication correct?

Note: Private Possession of Child Pornography

1. Under *Miller* and *Stanley*, the government can prohibit the *distribution* of material that is obscene, but it may not criminalize "mere *possession* [of obscene material] by the individual in the privacy of his own home." *Ferber* established that the government can prohibit the distribution of child pornography. Does the First Amendment protect the right to possess and view child pornography "in the privacy of [the] home"?

That question came before the Court in *Osborne v. Ohio*, 495 U.S. 103 (1990). Osborne was convicted under the Ohio child pornography statute and sentenced to six months in prison after the Columbus, Ohio, police, pursuant to a valid search, found four photographs in his home. Each photograph depicted a nude male adolescent posed in a sexually explicit position.

Osborne argued that under *Stanley*, the state may not constitutionally proscribe the possession and viewing of child pornography. The Supreme Court disagreed. Justice White, writing for the Court, said:

> *Stanley* should not be read too broadly. We have previously noted that *Stanley* was a narrow holding, see *United States v. 12 200-ft. Reels of Film*, 413 U.S. 123 (1973), and, since the decision in that case, the value of permitting child pornography has been characterized as "exceedingly modest, if not de minimis." *Ferber*. But assuming, for the sake of argument, that *Osborne* has a First Amendment interest in viewing and possessing child pornography,

we nonetheless find this case distinct from *Stanley* because the interests underlying child pornography prohibitions far exceed the interests justifying the Georgia law at issue in *Stanley* . . . .

In *Stanley*, Georgia primarily sought to proscribe the private possession of obscenity because it was concerned that obscenity would poison the minds of its viewers. We responded that "[w]hatever the power of the state to control public dissemination of ideas inimical to the public morality, it cannot constitutionally premise legislation on the desirability of controlling a person's private thoughts." The difference here is obvious: [T]he State does not rely on a paternalistic interest in regulating Osborne's mind. Rather, Ohio has enacted § 2907.323(A)(3) in order to protect the victims of child pornography; it hopes to destroy a market for the exploitative use of children.

[It is] surely reasonable for the State to conclude that it will decrease the production of child pornography if it penalizes those who possess and view the product, thereby decreasing demand. In *Ferber*, where we upheld a New York statute outlawing the distribution of child pornography, we found a similar argument persuasive . . . . "It rarely has been suggested that the constitutional freedom for speech and press extends its immunity to speech or writing used as an integral part of conduct in violation of a valid criminal statute." *Giboney v. Empire Storage & Ice Co.* (1949).

Osborne contends that the State should use other measures, besides penalizing possession, to dry up the child pornography market. Osborne points out that in *Stanley* we rejected Georgia's argument that its prohibition on obscenity possession was a necessary incident to its proscription on obscenity distribution. This holding, however, must be viewed in light of the weak interests asserted by the State in that case. *Stanley* itself emphasized that we did not "mean to express any opinion on statutes making criminal possession of other types of printed, filmed, or recorded materials . . . . In such cases, compelling reasons may exist for overriding the right of the individual to possess those materials."

Given the importance of the State's interest in protecting the victims of child pornography, we cannot fault Ohio for attempting to stamp out this vice at all levels in the distribution chain. According to the State, since the time of our decision in *Ferber*, much of the child pornography market has been driven underground; as a result, it is now difficult, if not impossible, to solve the child pornography problem by only attacking production and distribution. Indeed, 19 States have found it necessary to proscribe the possession of this material.

Other interests also support the Ohio law. First, as *Ferber* recognized, the materials produced by child pornographers permanently record the victim's abuse. The pornography's continued existence causes the child victims continuing harm by haunting the children in years to come. The State's ban on possession and viewing encourages the possessors of these materials to destroy them. Second, encouraging the destruction of these materials is also desirable because evidence suggests that pedophiles use child pornography to seduce other children into sexual activity.

> Given the gravity of the State's interests in this context, we find that Ohio may constitutionally proscribe the possession and viewing of child pornography.

Justice Brennan, joined by Justices Marshall and Stevens, dissented from the Court's holding. He wrote:

> *Ferber* held only that child pornography is "a category of material the *production and distribution* of which is not entitled to First Amendment protection" (emphasis added); our decision did not extend to private possession . . . . *Ferber* did nothing more than place child pornography on the same level of First Amendment protection as obscene adult pornography, meaning that its production and distribution could be proscribed. The distinction established in *Stanley* between what materials may be regulated and how they may be regulated still stands.

> The Court today finds *Stanley* inapposite on the ground that "the interests underlying child pornography prohibitions far exceed the interests justifying the Georgia law at issue in *Stanley*." The majority's analysis does not withstand scrutiny. While the sexual exploitation of children is undoubtedly a serious problem, Ohio may employ other weapons to combat it. Indeed, the State already has enacted a panoply of laws prohibiting the creation, sale, and distribution of child pornography and obscenity involving minors. Ohio has not demonstrated why these laws are inadequate and why the State must forbid mere possession as well.

2. As Professor Harry Kalven observed in his discussion of *Beauharnais* (Chapter 2 Note), "competition among analogies [is] the essential circumstance of legal reasoning." *Osborne* provides another good example. Justice Brennan in dissent argued that the case was controlled by *Stanley v. Georgia*; the majority held that *Stanley* was inapplicable and that arguments similar to those accepted in *Ferber* carried the day. Which analogy do you find more persuasive?

3. In 1990, when *Osborne* was decided, the Internet was in its infancy. The Court could assume that child pornography would be found in fixed media—photographs like the ones in Osborne's home or perhaps videotapes. Today, prosecutions for possession of child pornography generally involve digital files downloaded from the Internet. Does this development strengthen or weaken the argument for applying *Stanley*'s rationale to child pornography? Reconsider this question after reading *Free Speech Coalition*, the next principal case, and the Notes following it.

––––––

Problem: "Child Pornography" in a Journal

Three years ago, William Rylands was convicted of possessing child pornography. The conviction was based on Rylands' ownership of several photographs of under-age children engaging in sexual activities. Rylands was sentenced to a term of probation. As a condition of probation, he agreed to allow searches of his home.

Two months ago, in a routine search of Rylands' home, his probation officer found a 24-page journal that Rylands had written during the preceding year. The journal contained fictional stories about three children, ages 10 and 11, being caged in a basement, sexually molested, and tortured. The journal was not illustrated in any way.

The probation officer brought the journal to the local prosecutor, who took the matter to a grand jury. Rylands' stories were so disturbing that grand jurors asked a detective to stop reading after two pages. Ultimately the jurors read or heard the entire text, and they indicted Rylands for the offense of "pandering obscenity involving a minor." The offense is defined in section 2907.321 of the State Penal Code, which makes it a crime, *inter alia*, to (1) "create, reproduce, or publish any obscene material that has a minor as one of its participants or portrayed observers"; or to (5) "buy, procure, possess, or control any obscene material that has a minor as one of its participants." (The statute has a scienter requirement and some exceptions that are not applicable to Rylands.)

Rylands moves to dismiss the charges on the ground that application of the law to his conduct violates the First Amendment. How should the court rule? Does the *Free Speech Coalition* case shed light on the question?

Ashcroft v. Free Speech Coalition
535 U.S. 234 (2002)

JUSTICE KENNEDY delivered the opinion of the Court.

We consider in this case whether the Child Pornography Prevention Act of 1996 (CPPA) abridges the freedom of speech. The CPPA extends the federal prohibition against child pornography to sexually explicit images that appear to depict minors but were produced without using any real children. The statute prohibits, in specific circumstances, possessing or distributing these images, which may be created by using adults who look like minors or by using computer imaging. The new technology, according to Congress, makes it possible to create realistic images of children who do not exist.

By prohibiting child pornography that does not depict an actual child, the statute goes beyond *New York v. Ferber* (1982) [*supra* this chapter], which distinguished child pornography from other sexually explicit speech because of the State's interest in protecting the children exploited by the production process. As a general rule, pornography can be banned only if obscene, but under *Ferber*, pornography showing minors can be proscribed whether or not the images are obscene under the definition set forth in *Miller v. California* (1973) [Chapter 2] . . . .

The principal question to be resolved [is] whether the CPPA is constitutional where it proscribes a significant universe of speech that is neither obscene under *Miller* nor child pornography under *Ferber*.

I

Before 1996, Congress defined child pornography as the type of depictions at issue in *Ferber*, images made using actual minors. The CPPA retains that prohibition at 18 U.S.C. § 2256(8)(A) and adds three other prohibited categories of speech, of which the first, § 2256(8)(B), and the third, § 2256(8)(D), are at issue in this case. Section 2256(8)(B) prohibits "any visual depiction, including any photograph, film, video, picture, or computer or computer-generated image or picture" that "is, or appears to be, of a minor engaging in sexually explicit conduct." The prohibition on "any visual depiction" does not depend at all on how the image is produced. The section captures a range of depictions, sometimes called "virtual child pornography," which include computer-generated images, as well as images produced by more traditional means. For instance, the literal terms of the statute embrace a Renaissance painting depicting a scene from classical mythology, a "picture" that "appears to be, of a minor engaging in sexually explicit conduct." The statute also prohibits Hollywood movies, filmed without any child actors, if a jury believes an actor "appears to be" a minor engaging in "actual or simulated . . . sexual intercourse."

These images do not involve, let alone harm, any children in the production process; but Congress decided the materials threaten children in other, less direct, ways. Pedophiles might use the materials to encourage children to participate in sexual activity . . . . Furthermore, pedophiles might "whet their own sexual appetites" with the pornographic images, "thereby increasing the creation and distribution of child pornography and the sexual abuse and exploitation of actual children." Under these rationales, harm flows from the content of the images, not from the means of their production. In addition, Congress identified another problem created by computer-generated images: Their existence can make it harder to prosecute pornographers who do use real minors. As imaging technology improves, Congress found, it becomes more difficult to prove that a particular picture was produced using actual children . . . .

Section 2256(8)(C) prohibits a more common and lower tech means of creating virtual images, known as computer morphing. Rather than creating original images, pornographers can alter innocent pictures of real children so that the children appear to be engaged in sexual activity. Although morphed images may fall within the definition of virtual child pornography, they implicate the interests of real children and are in that sense closer to the images in *Ferber*. Respondents do not challenge this provision, and we do not consider it.

Respondents do challenge § 2256(8)(D). Like the text of the "appears to be" provision, the sweep of this provision is quite broad. Section 2256(8)(D) defines child pornography to include any sexually explicit image that was "advertised, promoted, presented, described, or distributed in such a manner that conveys the impression" it depicts "a minor engaging in sexually explicit conduct." . . .

[Fearing that the CPPA threatened the activities of its members, respondent Free Speech Coalition and others challenged the statute in federal court. The Court of Appeals for the Ninth Circuit held the CPPA to be substantially overbroad because it bans materials that are neither obscene nor produced by the exploitation of real children as in *Ferber*.]

II

. . . The CPPA's penalties are indeed severe. [For example, a] first offender may be imprisoned for 15 years . . . . [This] case provides a textbook example of why we permit facial challenges to statutes that burden expression. With these severe penalties in force, few legitimate movie producers or book publishers, or few other speakers in any capacity, would risk distributing images in or near the uncertain reach of this law. The Constitution gives significant protection from overbroad laws that chill speech within the First Amendment's vast and privileged sphere. Under this principle, the CPPA is unconstitutional on its face if it prohibits a substantial amount of protected expression. *See Broadrick v. Oklahoma*, 413 U.S. 601 (1973).

The sexual abuse of a child is a most serious crime and an act repugnant to the moral instincts of a decent people . . . . Congress may pass valid laws to protect children from abuse, and it has. The prospect of crime, however, by itself does not justify laws suppressing protected speech . . . .

As a general principle, the First Amendment bars the government from dictating what we see or read or speak or hear. The freedom of speech has its limits; it does not embrace certain categories of speech, including defamation, incitement, obscenity, and pornography produced with real children. While these categories may be prohibited without violating the First Amendment, none of them includes the speech prohibited by the CPPA. In his dissent from the opinion of the Court of Appeals, Judge Ferguson recognized this to be the law and proposed that virtual child pornography should be regarded as an additional category of unprotected speech. It would be necessary for us to take this step to uphold the statute.

As we have noted, the CPPA is much more than a supplement to the existing federal prohibition on obscenity . . . . [The CPPA] extends to images that appear to depict a minor engaging in sexually explicit activity without regard to the *Miller* requirements. The materials need not appeal to the prurient interest. Any depiction of sexually explicit activity, no matter how it is presented, is proscribed. The CPPA applies to a picture in a psychology manual, as well as a movie depicting the horrors of sexual abuse. It is not necessary, moreover, that the image be patently offensive. Pictures of what appear to be 17-year-olds engaging in sexually explicit activity do not in every case contravene community standards.

The CPPA prohibits speech despite its serious literary, artistic, political, or scientific value. The statute proscribes the visual depiction of an idea—that of teenagers engaging in sexual activity—that is a fact of modern society and has been a theme in art and literature throughout the ages . . . .

Both themes—teenage sexual activity and the sexual abuse of children—have inspired countless literary works. William Shakespeare created the most famous pair of teenage lovers, one of whom is just 13 years of age. *See Romeo and Juliet*, act I, sc. 2, l. 9 ("She hath not seen the change of fourteen years"). In the drama, Shakespeare portrays the relationship as something splendid and innocent, but not juvenile. The work has inspired no less than 40 motion pictures, some of which suggest that the teenagers consummated their relationship. Shakespeare may not have written sexually explicit scenes for the Elizabethan audience, but were modern directors to adopt a less conventional approach, that fact alone would not compel the conclusion that the work was obscene.

Contemporary movies pursue similar themes. Last year's Academy Awards featured the movie, Traffic, which was nominated for Best Picture. The film portrays a teenager, identified as a 16-year-old, who becomes addicted to drugs. The viewer sees the degradation of her addiction, which in the end leads her to a filthy room to trade sex for drugs. The year before, American Beauty won the Academy Award for Best Picture. In the course of the movie, a teenage girl engages in sexual relations with her teenage boyfriend, and another yields herself to the gratification of a middle-aged man. The film also contains a scene where, although the movie audience understands the act is not taking place, one character believes he is watching a teenage boy performing a sexual act on an older man.

Our society, like other cultures, has empathy and enduring fascination with the lives and destinies of the young. Art and literature express the vital interest we all have in the formative years we ourselves once knew, when wounds can be so grievous, disappointment so profound, and mistaken choices so tragic, but when moral acts and self-fulfillment are still in reach. Whether or not the films we mention violate the CPPA, they explore themes within the wide sweep of the statute's prohibitions. If these films, or hundreds of others of lesser note that explore those subjects, contain a single graphic depiction of sexual activity within the statutory definition, the possessor of the film would be subject to severe punishment without inquiry into the work's redeeming value. This is inconsistent with an essential First Amendment rule: The artistic merit of a work does not depend on the presence of a single explicit scene . . . .

The Government seeks to address this deficiency by arguing that speech prohibited by the CPPA is virtually indistinguishable from child pornography, which may be banned without regard to whether it depicts works of value. Where the images are themselves the product of child sexual abuse, *Ferber* recognized that the State had an interest in stamping it out without regard to any judgment about its content. The production of the work, not its content, was the target of the statute . . . .

In contrast to the speech in *Ferber*, speech that itself is the record of sexual abuse, the CPPA prohibits speech that records no crime and creates no victims by its production. Virtual child pornography is not "intrinsically related" to the sexual abuse of children, as were the materials in *Ferber*. While the Government asserts that the images can lead to actual instances of child abuse, the causal link is contingent and indirect. The harm does not necessarily follow from the speech, but depends upon some unquantified potential for subsequent criminal acts.

The Government says these indirect harms are sufficient because, as *Ferber* acknowledged, child pornography rarely can be valuable speech. This argument, however, suffers from two flaws. First, *Ferber*'s judgment about child pornography was based upon how it was made, not on what it communicated. The case reaffirmed that where the speech is neither obscene nor the product of sexual abuse, it does not fall outside the protection of the First Amendment.

The second flaw in the Government's position is that *Ferber* did not hold that child pornography is by definition without value. On the contrary, the Court recognized some works in this category might have significant value, but relied on virtual images — the very images prohibited by the CPPA — as an alternative and permissible means of expression: "If it were necessary for literary or artistic value, a person over the statutory age who perhaps looked younger could be utilized. Simulation outside of the prohibition of the statute could provide another alternative." *Ferber*, then, not only referred to the distinction between actual and virtual child pornography, it relied on it as a reason supporting its holding. *Ferber* provides no support for a statute that eliminates the distinction and makes the alternative mode criminal as well.

III

The CPPA, for reasons we have explored, is inconsistent with *Miller* and finds no support in *Ferber*. The Government seeks to justify its prohibitions in other ways. It argues that the CPPA is necessary because pedophiles may use virtual child pornography to seduce children. There are many things innocent in themselves, however, such as cartoons, video games, and candy, that might be used for immoral purposes, yet we would not expect those to be prohibited because they can be misused. The Government, of course, may punish adults who provide unsuitable materials to children, and it may enforce criminal penalties for unlawful solicitation. The precedents establish, however, that speech within the rights of adults to hear may not be silenced completely in an attempt to shield children from it. [E.g.] *Reno v. ACLU* (1997) [Note *supra* this chapter].

Here, the Government wants to keep speech from children not to protect them from its content but to protect them from those who would commit other crimes. The principle, however, remains the same: The Government cannot ban speech fit for adults simply because it may fall into the hands of children. The evil in question depends upon the actor's unlawful conduct, conduct defined as criminal quite apart from any link to the speech in question. This establishes that the speech ban is not narrowly drawn. The objective is to prohibit illegal conduct, but this restriction goes well beyond that interest by restricting the speech available to law-abiding adults.

The Government submits further that virtual child pornography whets the appetites of pedophiles and encourages them to engage in illegal conduct. This rationale cannot sustain the provision in question. The mere tendency of speech to encourage unlawful acts is not a sufficient reason for banning it. The government "cannot constitutionally premise legislation on the desirability of controlling a person's private thoughts." *Stanley v. Georgia* (1969) [Chapter 2]. First Amendment freedoms are most in danger when the government seeks to control thought or to justify its laws for that impermissible end. The right to think is the beginning of freedom, and speech must be protected from the government because speech is the beginning of thought.

To preserve these freedoms, and to protect speech for its own sake, the Court's First Amendment cases draw vital distinctions between words and deeds, between ideas and conduct. The government may not prohibit speech because it increases the chance an unlawful act will be committed "at some indefinite future time." *Hess v. Indiana* (1973) [Chapter 1]. The government may suppress speech for advocating the use of force or a violation of law only if "such advocacy is directed to inciting or producing imminent lawless action and is likely to incite or produce such action." *Brandenburg v. Ohio* (1969) [Chapter 1]. There is here no attempt, incitement, solicitation, or conspiracy. The Government has shown no more than a remote connection between speech that might encourage thoughts or impulses and any resulting child abuse. Without a significantly stronger, more direct connection, the Government may not prohibit speech on the ground that it may encourage pedophiles to engage in illegal conduct.

The Government next argues that its objective of eliminating the market for pornography produced using real children necessitates a prohibition on virtual images as well. Virtual images, the Government contends, are indistinguishable from real ones; they are part of the same market and are often exchanged. In this way, it is said, virtual images promote the trafficking in works produced through the exploitation of real children. The hypothesis is somewhat implausible. If virtual images were identical to illegal child pornography, the illegal images would be driven from the market by the indistinguishable substitutes. Few pornographers would risk prosecution by abusing real children if fictional, computerized images would suffice.

In the case of the material covered by *Ferber*, the creation of the speech is itself the crime of child abuse; the prohibition deters the crime by removing the profit motive . . . . [Here,] there is no underlying crime at all. Even if the Government's market deterrence theory were persuasive in some contexts, it would not justify this statute.

Finally, the Government says that the possibility of producing images by using computer imaging makes it very difficult for it to prosecute those who produce pornography by using real children. Experts, we are told, may have difficulty in saying whether the pictures were made by using real children or by using computer imaging. The necessary solution, the argument runs, is to prohibit both kinds of images. The argument, in essence, is that protected speech may be banned as a means to ban unprotected speech. This analysis turns the First Amendment upside down.

The Government may not suppress lawful speech as the means to suppress unlawful speech. Protected speech does not become unprotected merely because it resembles the latter. The Constitution requires the reverse. The overbreadth doctrine prohibits the Government from banning unprotected speech if a substantial amount of protected speech is prohibited or chilled in the process . . . .

In sum, § 2256(8)(B) covers materials beyond the categories recognized in *Ferber* and *Miller*, and the reasons the Government offers in support of limiting the freedom of speech have no justification in our precedents or in the law of the First Amendment. The provision abridges the freedom to engage in a substantial amount of lawful speech. For this reason, it is overbroad and unconstitutional.

IV

[In this part of the opinion, the Court held that § 2256(8)(D), the pandering provision, was unconstitutional. See discussion in the Note: *U.S. v. Williams* and "Purported" Child Pornography.]

V

For the reasons we have set forth, the prohibitions of §§ 2256(8)(B) and 2256(8)(D) are overbroad and unconstitutional. The judgment of the Court of Appeals is affirmed.

JUSTICE THOMAS, concurring in the judgment.

In my view, the Government's most persuasive asserted interest in support of the CPPA is the prosecution rationale—that persons who possess and disseminate pornographic images of real children may escape conviction by claiming that the images are computer-generated, thereby raising a reasonable doubt as to their guilt. At this time, however, the Government asserts only that defendants *raise* such defenses, not that they have done so successfully. In fact, the Government points to no case in which a defendant has been acquitted based on a "computer-generated images" defense. While this speculative interest cannot support the broad reach of the CPPA, technology may evolve to the point where it becomes impossible to enforce actual child pornography laws because the Government cannot prove that certain pornographic images are of real children. In the event this occurs, the Government should not be foreclosed from enacting a regulation of virtual child pornography that contains an appropriate affirmative defense or some other narrowly drawn restriction.

The Court suggests that the Government's interest in enforcing prohibitions against real child pornography cannot justify prohibitions on virtual child pornography, because "[the Government] may not suppress lawful speech as the means to suppress unlawful speech." But if technological advances thwart prosecution of "unlawful speech," the Government may well have a compelling interest in barring or otherwise regulating some narrow category of "lawful speech" in order to enforce effectively laws against pornography made through the abuse of real children ....

JUSTICE O'CONNOR, with whom THE CHIEF JUSTICE and JUSTICE SCALIA join as to Part II, concurring in the judgment in part and dissenting in part ....

This litigation involves a facial challenge to the CPPA's prohibitions of pornographic images that "appear to be ... of a minor" and of material that "conveys the impression" that it contains pornographic images of minors. While I agree with the Court's judgment that the First Amendment requires that the latter prohibition be struck down, I disagree with its decision to strike down the former prohibition in its entirety. The "appears to be ... of a minor" language in § 2256(8)(B) covers two categories of speech: pornographic images of adults that look like children ("youthful adult pornography") and pornographic images of children created wholly on a computer, without using any actual children ("virtual child pornography"). The Court concludes, correctly, that the CPPA's ban on youthful adult pornography is overbroad. In my view, however, respondents fail to present sufficient evidence to demonstrate that the ban on virtual child pornography is overbroad. Because invalidation due to overbreadth is such "strong medicine," I would strike down the prohibition of pornography that "appears to be" of minors only insofar as it is applied to the class of youthful adult pornography.

I

. . . The Government [requests] that the Court exclude youthful adult and virtual child pornography from the protection of the First Amendment. I agree with the Court's decision not to grant this request . . . . I also agree with the Court's decision to strike down the CPPA's ban on material presented in a manner that "conveys the impression" that it contains pornographic depictions of actual children ("actual child pornography"). The Government fails to explain how this ban serves any compelling state interest. Any speech covered by § 2256(8)(D) that is obscene, actual child pornography, or otherwise indecent is prohibited by other federal statutes . . . .

II

I disagree with the Court, however, that the CPPA's prohibition of virtual child pornography is overbroad. Before I reach that issue, there are two preliminary questions: whether the ban on virtual child pornography fails strict scrutiny and whether that ban is unconstitutionally vague. I would answer both in the negative.

[The Government's] concern is the prospect that defendants indicted for the production, distribution, or possession of actual child pornography may evade liability by claiming that the images attributed to them are in fact computer-generated. Respondents may be correct that no defendant has successfully employed this tactic. But, given the rapid pace of advances in computer-graphics technology, the Government's concern is reasonable . . . . Anyone who has seen, for example, the film "Final Fantasy: The Spirits Within" can understand the Government's concern. Moreover, this Court's cases do not require Congress to wait for harm to occur before it can legislate against it.

Respondents argue that, even if the Government has a compelling interest to justify banning virtual child pornography, the "appears to be . . . of a minor" language is not narrowly tailored to serve that interest. They assert that the CPPA would capture even cartoon sketches or statues of children that were sexually suggestive. Such images surely could not be used, for instance, to seduce children. I agree. A better interpretation of "appears to be . . . of" is "virtually indistinguishable from"—an interpretation that would not cover the examples respondents provide . . . . [This] narrowing interpretation avoids constitutional problems such as overbreadth and lack of narrow tailoring.

The Court concludes that the CPPA's ban on virtual child pornography is overbroad. The basis for this holding is unclear . . . . [Respondents have not demonstrated] that the regulation forbids a substantial amount of valuable or harmless speech . . . . [They] provide no examples of films or other materials that are wholly computer-generated and contain images that "appear to be . . . of minors" engaging in indecent conduct, but that have serious value or do not facilitate child abuse. Their overbreadth challenge therefore fails.

III

Although in my view the CPPA's ban on youthful adult pornography appears to violate the First Amendment, the ban on virtual child pornography does not . . . . Although 18 U.S.C. § 2256(8)(B) does not distinguish between youthful adult and virtual child pornography, the CPPA elsewhere draws a line between these two classes of speech . . . . Drawing a line around, and striking just, the CPPA's ban on youthful adult pornography not only is consistent with Congress' understanding of the categories of speech encompassed by § 2256(8)(B), but also preserves the CPPA's prohibition of the material that Congress found most dangerous to children.

In sum, I would strike down the CPPA's ban on material that "conveys the impression" that it contains actual child pornography, but uphold the ban on pornographic depictions that "appear to be" of minors so long as it is not applied to youthful adult pornography.

Chief Justice Rehnquist, with whom Justice Scalia [joins], dissenting.

I agree with Part II of Justice O'Connor's opinion. Congress has a compelling interest in ensuring the ability to enforce prohibitions of actual child pornography, and we should defer to its findings that rapidly advancing technology soon will make it all but impossible to do so. I also agree with Justice O'Connor that serious First Amendment concerns would arise were the Government ever to prosecute someone for simple distribution or possession of a film with literary or artistic value, such as "Traffic" or "American Beauty." I write separately, however, because the CPPA need not be construed to reach such materials.

We normally do not strike down a statute on First Amendment grounds "when a limiting instruction has been or could be placed on the challenged statute." . . . Other than computer generated images that are virtually indistinguishable from real children engaged in sexually explicitly conduct, the CPPA can be limited so as not to reach any material that was not already unprotected before the CPPA. The CPPA's definition of "sexually explicit conduct" is quite explicit in this regard. It makes clear that the statute only reaches "visual depictions" of:

> Actual or simulated . . . sexual intercourse, including genital-genital, oral-genital, anal-genital, or oral-anal, whether between persons of the same or opposite sex; . . . bestiality; . . . masturbation; . . . sadistic or masochistic abuse; . . . or lascivious exhibition of the genitals or pubic area of any person.

The Court and Justice O'Connor suggest that this very graphic definition reaches the depiction of youthful looking adult actors engaged in suggestive sexual activity, presumably because the definition extends to "simulated" intercourse. Read as a whole, however, I think the definition reaches only the sort of "hard core of child pornography" that we found without protection in *Ferber*. So construed, the CPPA bans visual depictions of youthful looking adult actors engaged in *actual* sexual activity; mere *suggestions* of sexual activity, such as youthful looking adult actors squirming under a blanket, are more akin to written descriptions than visual depictions, and thus fall outside the purview of the statute . . . .

In sum, while potentially impermissible applications of the CPPA may exist, I doubt that they would be "substantial . . . in relation to the statute's plainly legitimate sweep." For these reasons, I would construe the CPPA in a manner consistent with the First Amendment [and] uphold the statute in its entirety.

————

Note: *"Virtual Child Pornography"*

1. In *Free Speech Coalition*, the Court says that in order to uphold the statute it would be necessary to recognize "virtual child pornography" as "an additional category of unprotected speech." The dissenting judge in the Ninth Circuit would have taken that step. Is that the position of Chief Justice Rehnquist and Justice Scalia in their dissent from the Supreme Court decision?

2. Less than a year after the Supreme Court decision in *Free Speech Coalition*, Congress passed the Prosecutorial Remedies and Other Tools to end the Exploitation of Children Today Act of 2003. In the "findings" section of the Act, Congress noted that the decision greatly impeded the Government's ability to prosecute child pornography offenders. It said that if Congress did not act, the difficulties would increase. Congress explained: "The mere prospect that the technology exists to create composite or computer-generated depictions that are indistinguishable from depictions of real children will allow defendants who possess images of real children to escape prosecution; for it threatens to create a reasonable doubt in every case of computer images even when a real child was abused. This threatens to render child pornography laws that protect real children unenforceable."

The 2003 Act included a number of provisions that addressed this problem. One provision substantially revised the definition of virtual child pornography. Another added a new prohibition on pandering and soliciting child pornography. That provision is discussed in the Note that follows.

Note: U.S. v. Williams *and "Purported" Child Pornography*

1. Although most of the opinion in *Free Speech Coalition* focuses on "virtual child pornography," the Court also struck down a second provision of the CPPA. Section 2256(8)(D) prohibited depictions of sexually explicit conduct that are "advertised, promoted, presented, described, or distributed in such a manner that conveys the impression that the material is or contains a visual depiction of a minor engaging in sexually explicit conduct." The Court explained:

> One Committee Report identified the provision as directed at sexually explicit images pandered as child pornography. The statute is not so limited in its reach, however, as it punishes even those possessors who took no part in pandering. Once a work has been described as child pornography, the taint remains on the speech in the hands of subsequent possessors, making possession unlawful even though the content otherwise would not be objectionable . . . .

Under § 2256(8)(D), the work must be sexually explicit, but otherwise the content is irrelevant. Even if a film contains no sexually explicit scenes involving minors, it could be treated as child pornography if the title and trailers convey the impression that the scenes would be found in the movie. The determination turns on how the speech is presented, not on what is depicted . . . .

Section 2256(8)(D) does more than prohibit pandering. It prohibits possession of material described, or pandered, as child pornography by someone earlier in the distribution chain. The provision prohibits a sexually explicit film containing no youthful actors, just because it is placed in a box suggesting a prohibited movie . . . . The First Amendment requires a more precise restriction. For this reason, § 2256(8)(D) is substantially overbroad and in violation of the First Amendment.

2. Congress responded to this holding in 2003 by enacting a new pandering and solicitation prohibition. The 2003 law makes it a crime to knowingly distribute, promote, or solicit "any material or purported material in a manner that reflects the belief, or that is intended to cause another to believe, that the material or purported material is, or contains" child pornography.

The Eleventh Circuit held that the new statute was unconstitutionally overbroad, but in *United States v. Williams*, 553 U.S. 285 (2008), the Supreme Court reversed. Justice Scalia, writing for the Court, acknowledged that the 2003 law "does not require the actual existence of child pornography." He explained:

In this respect, [the 2003 law] differs from the statutes in *Ferber, Osborne,* and *Free Speech Coalition*, which prohibited the possession or distribution of child pornography. Rather than targeting the underlying material, this statute bans the collateral speech that introduces such material into the child-pornography distribution network. Thus, an Internet user who solicits child pornography from an undercover agent violates the statute, even if the officer possesses no child pornography. Likewise, a person who advertises virtual child pornography as depicting actual children also falls within the reach of the statute.

The Supreme Court nevertheless held that the statute did not violate the First Amendment. The Court relied in part on *Giboney*:

Offers to engage in illegal transactions are categorically excluded from First Amendment protection. *Giboney v. Empire Storage & Ice Co.* (1949). One would think that this principle resolves the present case, since the statute criminalizes only offers to provide or requests to obtain contraband—child obscenity and child pornography involving actual children, both of which are proscribed, and the proscription of which is constitutional . . . .

To be sure, there remains an important distinction between a proposal to engage in illegal activity and the abstract advocacy of illegality. *See Brandenburg v. Ohio; see also NAACP v. Claiborne Hardware Co.* [both in

Chapter 1]. The Act before us does not prohibit advocacy of child pornography, but only offers to provide or requests to obtain it. There is no doubt that this prohibition falls well within constitutional bounds. The constitutional defect we found in the pandering provision at issue in *Free Speech Coalition* was that it went beyond pandering to prohibit possession of material that could not otherwise be proscribed . . . .

The Eleventh Circuit believed it a constitutional difficulty that no child pornography need exist to trigger the statute. In its view, the fact that the statute could punish a "braggart, exaggerator, or outright liar" rendered it unconstitutional. That seems to us a strange constitutional calculus. Although we have held that the government can ban both fraudulent offers *and* offers to provide illegal products, the Eleventh Circuit would forbid the government from punishing *fraudulent offers to provide illegal products*. We see no logic in that position; if anything, such statements are doubly excluded from the First Amendment.

Justice Souter, joined by Justice Ginsburg, dissented. He emphasized that the 2003 law criminalizes offers and solicitations relating to material that does not depict an actual child model, as long as the defendant expresses or encourages a belief that that the material does show an actual child. The result, he said, is that *Ferber* and *Free Speech Coalition* "are left as empty as if the Court overruled them formally." He wrote:

No one can seriously assume that after today's decision the Government will go on prosecuting defendants for selling child pornography (requiring a showing that a real child is pictured, under *Free Speech Coalition*); it will prosecute for merely proposing a pornography transaction manifesting or inducing the belief that a photo is real child pornography, free of any need to demonstrate that any extant underlying photo does show a real child. If the Act can be enforced, it will function just as it was meant to do, by merging the whole subject of child pornography into the offense of proposing a transaction, dispensing with the real-child element in the underlying subject. And eliminating the need to prove a real child will be a loss of some consequence. This is so not because there will possibly be less pornography available owing to the greater ease of prosecuting, but simply because there must be a line between what the Government may suppress and what it may not, and a segment of that line will be gone. This Court went to great pains to draw it in *Ferber* and *Free Speech Coalition*; it was worth drawing and it is worth respecting now in facing the attempt to end-run that line through the provisions of the Act . . . .

3. Justice Stevens, who joined the Court's opinion in *Williams*, also wrote a concurring opinion that responded to Justice Souter's dissent. He acknowledged that the statute would encompass some "proposals to transact in constitutionally protected material," including pornographic but not obscene representations that do not depict real children. But he said that any constitutional concerns are answered by the fact that under the Court's interpretation of the statute, "proposing a transaction in such material would not give rise to criminal liability under the statute unless the defendant actually believed, or intended to induce another to believe, that the material in question depicted real children." Does that adequately answer the dissent's argument?

4. In *Free Speech Coalition*, the Court said that "the CPPA prohibits speech that records no crime and creates no victims by its production." Is that also true of the statute challenged in *Williams*? If so, why isn't that statute unconstitutional?

————

C. Commercial Speech

When Justice Murphy in *Chaplinsky v. New Hampshire* (1942) (Chapter 2) listed the categories of speech "the prevention and punishment of which have never been thought to raise any Constitutional problem," he made no mention of "commercial speech." One month later, however, in *Valentine v. Chrestensen*, 316 U.S. 52 (1942), the Court announced that "commercial advertising" did not receive constitutional protection. The opinion was very brief; it did not cite *Chaplinsky* or any other precedents, nor did it explain why "the freedom of communicating information and disseminating opinion" did not extend to "purely commercial advertising."

For more than three decades, commercial speech remained outside the ambit of the First Amendment. Today the law is quite different. Has this development been a healthy one? That is one of the themes explored in this section.

Virginia State Board of Pharmacy v. Virginia Citizens Consumer Council, Inc.

425 U.S. 748 (1976)

Mr. Justice Blackmun delivered the opinion of the Court.

The plaintiff-appellees in this case attack, as violative of the First and Fourteenth Amendments, that portion of § 54-524.35 of Va. Code Ann. (1974), which provides that a pharmacist licensed in Virginia is guilty of unprofessional conduct if he "(3) publishes, advertises or promotes, directly or indirectly, in any manner whatsoever, any amount, price, fee, premium, discount, rebate or credit terms . . . for any drugs which may be dispensed only by prescription." The three-judge District Court declared the quoted portion of the statute "void and of no effect," and enjoined [the Virginia State Board of Pharmacy] from enforcing it. [In the District Court's view, the expression in *Valentine v. Chrestensen* to the effect that "purely commercial advertising" is not protected had been tempered, by later decisions of this Court, to the point that First Amendment interests in the free flow of price information could be found to outweigh the countervailing interests of the State.] We noted probable jurisdiction of the appeal.

IV

The appellants contend that the advertisement of prescription drug prices is outside the protection of the First Amendment because it is "commercial speech." There can be no question that in past decisions the Court has given some indication that commercial speech is unprotected. [The Court cited *Valentine v. Chrestensen.*] . . . . Further support for a "commercial speech" exception to the First Amendment may perhaps be found in *Breard v. Alexandria*, 341 U.S. 622 (1951), where the Court upheld a conviction for violation of an ordinance prohibiting door-to-door solicitation of magazine subscriptions . . . .

Since the decision in *Breard*, however, the Court has never denied protection on the ground that the speech in issue was "commercial speech." That simplistic approach, which by then had come under criticism or was regarded as of doubtful validity by Members of the Court, was avoided in *Pittsburgh Press Co. v. Human Relations Comm'n*, 413 U.S. 376 (1973). There the Court upheld an ordinance prohibiting newspapers from listing employment advertisements in columns according to whether male or female employees were sought to be hired. The Court, to be sure, characterized the advertisements as "classic examples of commercial speech," and a newspaper's printing of the advertisements as of the same character. The Court, however, upheld the ordinance on the ground that the restriction it imposed was permissible because the discriminatory hirings proposed by the advertisements, and by their newspaper layout, were themselves illegal.

Last Term, in *Bigelow v. Virginia*, 421 U.S. 809 (1975), the notion of unprotected "commercial speech" all but passed from the scene. We reversed a conviction for violation of a Virginia statute that made the circulation of any publication to encourage or promote the processing of an abortion in Virginia a misdemeanor. The defendant had published in his newspaper the availability of abortions in New York . . . . We rejected the contention that the publication was unprotected because it was commercial. *Chrestensen*'s continued validity was questioned and its holding was described as "distinctly a limited one" that merely upheld "a reasonable regulation of the manner in which commercial advertising could be distributed." . . .

Some fragment of hope for the continuing validity of a "commercial speech" exception arguably might have persisted because of the subject matter of the advertisement in *Bigelow*. [Among other things,] the advertisement related to activity with which, at least in some respects, the State could not interfere. *See Roe v. Wade*, 410 U.S. 113 (1973) . . . . Here, in contrast, the question whether there is a First Amendment exception for "commercial speech" is squarely before us. Our pharmacist does not wish to editorialize on any subject, cultural, philosophical, or political. He does not wish to report any particularly newsworthy fact, or to make generalized observations even about commercial matters. The "idea" he wishes to communicate is simply this: "I will sell you the X prescription drug at the Y price." Our question, then, is whether this communication is wholly outside the protection of the First Amendment.

V

We begin with several propositions that already are settled or beyond serious dispute. It is clear, for example, that speech does not lose its First Amendment protection because money is spent to project it, as in a paid advertisement of one form or another. [E.g.,] *New York Times Co. v. Sullivan* (1964) [Chapter 2]. Speech likewise is protected even though it is carried in a form that is "sold" for profit, and even though it may involve a solicitation to purchase or otherwise pay or contribute money.

If there is a kind of commercial speech that lacks all First Amendment protection, therefore, it must be distinguished by its content. Yet the speech whose content deprives it of protection cannot simply be speech on a commercial subject. No one would contend that our pharmacist may be prevented from being heard on the subject of whether, in general, pharmaceutical prices should be regulated, or their advertisement forbidden. Nor can it be dispositive that a commercial advertisement is noneditorial, and merely reports a fact. Purely factual matter of public interest may claim protection.

Our question is whether speech which does "no more than propose a commercial transaction," *Pittsburgh Press Co. v. Human Relations Comm'n*, is so removed from any "exposition of ideas," *Chaplinsky*, and from "'truth, science, morality, and arts in general, in its diffusion of liberal sentiments on the administration of Government,'" *Roth v. United States* (1957) [Chapter 2], that it lacks all protection. Our answer is that it is not.

Focusing first on the individual parties to the transaction that is proposed in the commercial advertisement, we may assume that the advertiser's interest is a purely economic one. That hardly disqualifies him from protection under the First Amendment. The interests of the contestants in a labor dispute are primarily economic, but it has long been settled that both the employee and the employer are protected by the First Amendment when they express themselves on the merits of the dispute in order to influence its outcome . . . .

As to the particular consumer's interest in the free flow of commercial information, that interest may be as keen, if not keener by far, than his interest in the day's most urgent political debate . . . . Those whom the suppression of prescription drug price information hits the hardest are the poor, the sick, and particularly the aged. A disproportionate amount of their income tends to be spent on prescription drugs; yet they are the least able to learn, by shopping from pharmacist to pharmacist, where their scarce dollars are best spent. When drug prices vary as strikingly as they do, information as to who is charging what becomes more than a convenience. It could mean the alleviation of physical pain or the enjoyment of basic necessities.

Generalizing, society also may have a strong interest in the free flow of commercial information. Even an individual advertisement, though entirely "commercial," may be of general public interest . . . . Obviously, not all commercial messages contain the same or even a very great public interest element. There are few to which such an element, however, could not be added. Our pharmacist, for example, could cast himself as a commentator on store-to-store disparities in drug prices, giving his own and those of a competitor as proof. We see little point in requiring him to do so, and little difference if he does not.

Moreover, there is another consideration that suggests that no line between publicly "interesting" or "important" commercial advertising and the opposite kind could ever be drawn. Advertising, however tasteless and excessive it sometimes may seem, is nonetheless dissemination of information as to who is producing and selling what product, for what reason, and at what price. So long as we preserve a predominantly free enterprise economy, the allocation of our resources in large measure will be made through numerous private economic decisions. It is a matter of public interest that those decisions, in the aggregate, be intelligent and well informed. To this end, the free flow of commercial information is indispensable. And if it is indispensable to the proper allocation of resources in a free enterprise system, it is also indispensable to the formation of intelligent opinions as to how that system ought to be regulated or altered. Therefore, even if the First Amendment were thought to be primarily an instrument to enlighten public decisionmaking in a democracy, we could not say that the free flow of information does not serve that goal.

Arrayed against these substantial individual and societal interests are a number of justifications for the advertising ban. These have to do principally with maintaining a high degree of professionalism on the part of licensed pharmacists . . . .

Price advertising, it is argued, will place in jeopardy the pharmacist's expertise and, with it, the customer's health. It is claimed that the aggressive price competition that will result from unlimited advertising will make it impossible for the pharmacist to supply professional services in the compounding, handling, and dispensing of prescription drugs. Such services are time consuming and expensive; if competitors who economize by eliminating them are permitted to advertise their resulting lower prices, the more painstaking and conscientious pharmacist will be forced either to follow suit or to go out of business . . . . It is further claimed that advertising will lead people to shop for their prescription drugs among the various pharmacists who offer the lowest prices, and the loss of stable pharmacist-customer relationships will make individual attention and certainly the practice of monitoring impossible . . . .

The strength of these proffered justifications is greatly undermined by the fact that high professional standards, to a substantial extent, are guaranteed by the close regulation to which pharmacists in Virginia are subject. And this case concerns the retail sale by the pharmacist more than it does his professional standards. Surely, any pharmacist guilty of professional dereliction that actually endangers his customer will promptly lose his license. At the same time, we cannot discount the Board's justifications entirely. The Court regarded justifications of this type sufficient to sustain the advertising bans challenged on due process and equal protection grounds in *Williamson v. Lee Optical Co.*, 348 U.S. 483 (1955) [and other cases].

The challenge now made, however, is based on the First Amendment. This casts the Board's justifications in a different light, for on close inspection it is seen that the State's protectiveness of its citizens rests in large measure on the advantages of their being kept in ignorance. The advertising ban does not directly affect professional standards one way or the other. It affects them only through the reactions it is assumed people will have to the free flow of drug price information. There is no claim that the advertising ban in any way prevents the cutting of corners by the pharmacist who is so inclined. That pharmacist is likely to cut corners in any event. The only effect the advertising ban has on him is to insulate him from price competition and to open the way for him to make a substantial, and perhaps even excessive, profit in addition to providing an inferior service. The more painstaking pharmacist is also protected but, again, it is a protection based in large part on public ignorance.

It appears to be feared that if the pharmacist who wishes to provide low cost, and assertedly low quality, services is permitted to advertise, he will be taken up on his offer by too many unwitting customers. They will choose the low-cost, low-quality service and drive the "professional" pharmacist out of business. They will respond only to costly and excessive advertising, and end up paying the price. They will go from one pharmacist to another, following the discount, and destroy the pharmacist-customer relationship. They will lose respect for the profession because it advertises. All this is not in their best interests, and all this can be avoided if they are not permitted to know who is charging what.

There is, of course, an alternative to this highly paternalistic approach. That alternative is to assume that this information is not in itself harmful, that people will perceive their own best interests if only they are well enough informed, and that the best means to that end is to open the channels of communication rather than to close them. If they are truly open, nothing prevents the "professional" pharmacist from marketing his own assertedly superior product, and contrasting it with that of the low-cost, high-volume prescription drug retailer. But the choice among these alternative approaches is not ours to make or the Virginia General Assembly's. It is precisely this kind of choice, between the dangers of suppressing information, and the dangers of its misuse if it is freely available, that the First Amendment makes for us. Virginia is free to require whatever professional standards it wishes of its pharmacists; it may subsidize them or protect them from competition in other ways. But it may not do so by keeping the public in ignorance of the entirely lawful terms that competing pharmacists are offering. In this sense, the justifications Virginia has offered for suppressing the flow of prescription drug price information, far from persuading us that the flow is not protected by the First Amendment, have reinforced our view that it is. We so hold.

VI

In concluding that commercial speech, like other varieties, is protected, we of course do not hold that it can never be regulated in any way. Some forms of commercial speech regulation are surely permissible. We mention a few only to make clear that they are not before us and therefore are not foreclosed by this case.

There is no claim, for example, . . . that prescription drug price advertisements are forbidden because they are false or misleading in any way. Untruthful speech, commercial or otherwise, has never been protected for its own sake. *Gertz v. Robert Welch, Inc.* (1974) [Chapter 2]. Obviously, much commercial speech is not provably false, or even wholly false, but only deceptive or misleading. We foresee no obstacle to a State's dealing effectively with this problem. The First Amendment, as we construe it today does not prohibit the State from insuring that the stream of commercial information flow cleanly as well as freely.

Also, there is no claim that the transactions proposed in the forbidden advertisements are themselves illegal in any way. Finally, the special problems of the electronic broadcast media are likewise not in this case.

What is at issue is whether a State may completely suppress the dissemination of concededly truthful information about entirely lawful activity, fearful of that information's effect upon its disseminators and its recipients. Reserving other questions, we conclude that the answer to this one is in the negative.

The judgment of the District Court is *affirmed*.

Mr. Justice Stevens took no part in the consideration or decision of this case.

Mr. Chief Justice Burger, concurring. [Omitted.]

Mr. Justice Stewart, concurring.

[The] Court's decision calls into immediate question the constitutional legitimacy of every state and federal law regulating false or deceptive advertising. I write separately to explain why I think today's decision does not preclude such governmental regulation . . . .

The principles recognized in the libel decisions suggest that government may take broader action to protect the public from injury produced by false or deceptive price or product advertising than from harm caused by defamation. In contrast to the press, which must often attempt to assemble the true facts from sketchy and sometimes conflicting sources under the pressure of publication deadlines, the commercial advertiser generally knows the product or service he seeks to sell and is in a position to verify the accuracy of his factual representations before he disseminates them. The advertiser's access to the truth about his product and its price substantially eliminates any danger that governmental regulation of false or misleading price or product advertising will chill accurate and nondeceptive commercial expression. There is, therefore, little need to sanction "some falsehood in order to protect speech that matters." . . .

The Court's determination that commercial advertising of the kind at issue here is not "wholly outside the protection of" the First Amendment indicates by its very phrasing that there are important differences between commercial price and product advertising, on the one hand, and ideological communication on the other . . . . Commercial price and product advertising differs markedly from ideological expression because it is confined to the promotion of specific goods or services. The First Amendment protects the advertisement because of the "information of potential interest and value" conveyed, rather than because of any direct contribution to the interchange of ideas. Since the factual claims contained in commercial price or product advertisements relate to tangible goods or services, they may be tested empirically and corrected to reflect the truth without in any manner jeopardizing the free dissemination of thought. Indeed, the elimination of false and deceptive claims serves to promote the one facet of commercial price and product advertising that warrants First Amendment protection its contribution to the flow of accurate and reliable information relevant to public and private decisionmaking.

MR. JUSTICE REHNQUIST, dissenting.

The logical consequences of the Court's decision in this case, a decision which elevates commercial intercourse between a seller hawking his wares and a buyer seeking to strike a bargain to the same plane as has been previously reserved for the free marketplace of ideas, are far reaching indeed. Under the Court's opinion the way will be open not only for dissemination of price information but for active promotion of prescription drugs, liquor, cigarettes, and other products the use of which it has previously been thought desirable to discourage. Now, however, such promotion is protected by the First Amendment so long as it is not misleading or does not promote an illegal product or enterprise. In coming to this conclusion, the Court has overruled a legislative determination that such advertising should not be allowed . . . [The Court] extends the protection of [the First] Amendment to purely commercial endeavors which its most vigorous champions on this Court had thought to be beyond its pale . . . .

There are undoubted difficulties with an effort to draw a bright line between "commercial speech" on the one hand and "protected speech" on the other, and the Court does better to face up to these difficulties than to attempt to hide them under labels. In this case, however, the Court has unfortunately substituted for the wavering line previously thought to exist between commercial speech and protected speech a no more satisfactory line of its own that between "truthful" commercial speech, on the one hand, and that which is "false and misleading" on the other. The difficulty with this line is not that it wavers, but on the contrary that it is simply too Procrustean to take into account the congeries of factors which I believe could, quite consistently with the First and Fourteenth Amendments, properly influence a legislative decision with respect to commercial advertising.

The Court insists that the rule it lays down is consistent even with the view that the First Amendment is "primarily an instrument to enlighten public decisionmaking in a democracy." I had understood this view to relate to public decisionmaking as to political, social, and other public issues, rather than the decision of a particular individual as to whether to purchase one or another kind of shampoo. It is undoubtedly arguable that many people in the country regard the choice of shampoo as just as important as who may be elected to local, state, or national political office, but that does not automatically bring information about competing shampoos within the protection of the First Amendment . . . .

In the case of "our" hypothetical pharmacist, he may now presumably advertise not only the prices of prescription drugs, but may attempt to energetically promote their sale so long as he does so truthfully. Quite consistently with Virginia law requiring prescription drugs to be available only through a physician, "our" pharmacist might run any of the following representative advertisements in a local newspaper: "Pain getting you down? Insist that your physician prescribe Demerol. You pay a little more than for aspirin, but you get a lot more relief." "Can't shake the flu? Get a prescription for Tetracycline from your doctor today." "Don't spend another sleepless night. Ask your doctor to prescribe Seconal without delay."

Unless the State can show that these advertisements are either actually untruthful or misleading, it presumably is not free to restrict in any way commercial efforts on the part of those who profit from the sale of prescription drugs to put them in the widest possible circulation. But such a line simply makes no allowance whatever for what appears to have been a considered legislative judgment in most States that while prescription drugs are a necessary and vital part of medical care and treatment, there are sufficient dangers attending their widespread use that they simply may not be promoted in the same manner as hair creams, deodorants, and toothpaste . . . .

Both Congress and state legislatures have by law sharply limited the permissible dissemination of information about some commodities because of the potential harm resulting from those commodities, even though they were not thought to be sufficiently demonstrably harmful to warrant outright prohibition of their sale. Current prohibitions on television advertising of liquor and cigarettes are prominent in this category, but apparently under the Court's holding so long as the advertisements are not deceptive they may no longer be prohibited . . . .

———

Note: First Amendment Protection for Commercial Speech

1. *Virginia Pharmacy Board* holds that commercial speech enjoys First Amendment protection, but the Court does not say that henceforth commercial speech will be treated like other forms of protected speech. On the contrary, the Court adds (in a footnote): "There are commonsense differences between speech that does 'no more than propose a commercial transaction' and other varieties." One difference, says the Court, is that the truth of commercial speech "may be more easily verifiable by its disseminator than, let us say, news reporting or political commentary, in that ordinarily the advertiser seeks to disseminate information about a specific product or service that he himself provides and presumably knows more about than anyone else." Justice Stewart elaborates on this point in his concurring opinion. How accurate is the Court's generalization? How does it justify treating commercial speech differently from "other varieties" of speech?

2. A second difference, says the Court, is that "commercial speech may be more durable than other kinds." Thus, "there is little likelihood of its being chilled by proper regulation and forgone entirely." Is this generalization valid? Does the Court generally assume that "other varieties" of speech are fragile?

3. In another footnote, the Court emphasizes that "we have considered in this case the regulation of commercial advertising by pharmacists. Although we express no opinion as to other professions, the distinctions, historical and functional, between professions, may require consideration of quite different factors." Not surprisingly, challenges to regulation of commercial advertising by other professionals soon reached the Court. In *Bates v. State Bar of Arizona*, 433 U.S. 350 (1977), the Court struck down a disciplinary rule that prohibited advertising by attorneys. Since then, lawyer advertising has generated its own body of jurisprudence. Many regulations have been struck down, but some have survived. For an illustrative application, see *Florida Bar v. Went*

For It, Inc., 515 U.S. 618 (1995), upholding (by a vote of 5-4) rules prohibiting personal injury lawyers from sending targeted direct-mail solicitations to victims and their relatives for 30 days following an accident or disaster.

4. Justice Rehnquist predicted that under the Court's decision in *Virginia Pharmacy Board*, "the way will be open . . . for active promotion of prescription drugs, liquor, cigarettes, and other products the use of which it has previously been thought desirable to discourage." Has that prediction been borne out? If so, does that cast doubt on the soundness of the decision?

Central Hudson Gas & Electric Corp. v. Public Service Commission
447 U.S. 557 (1980)

Mr. Justice Powell delivered the opinion of the Court.

This case presents the question whether a regulation of the Public Service Commission of the State of New York violates the First and Fourteenth Amendments because it completely bans promotional advertising by an electrical utility.

I

[In December 1973, during a fuel shortage, the Commission ordered electric utilities in New York State to cease all advertising that "promot[es] the use of electricity." Four years later, when the fuel shortage had eased, the Commission issued a Policy Statement that divided advertising expenses "into two broad categories: promotional—advertising intended to stimulate the purchase of utility services—and institutional and informational, a broad category inclusive of all advertising not clearly intended to promote sales." The Commission declared all promotional advertising contrary to the national policy of conserving energy.]

The Commission's order explicitly permitted "informational" advertising designed to encourage "*shifts* of consumption" from peak demand times to periods of low electricity demand. (Emphasis in original.) Informational advertising would not seek to increase aggregate consumption, but would invite a leveling of demand throughout any given 24-hour period. The agency offered to review "specific proposals by the companies for specifically described [advertising] programs that meet these criteria." . . .

Appellant challenged the order in state court, arguing that the Commission had restrained commercial speech in violation of the First and Fourteenth Amendments. The New York Court of Appeals [upheld the order, concluding] that the governmental interest in the prohibition outweighed the limited constitutional value of the commercial speech at issue. [We reverse.]

II

The Commission's order restricts only commercial speech, that is, expression related solely to the economic interests of the speaker and its audience. The First Amendment [protects] commercial speech from unwarranted governmental regulation. Nevertheless, our decisions have recognized "the 'commonsense' distinction between speech proposing a commercial transaction, which occurs in an area traditionally subject to government regulation, and other varieties of speech." The Constitution therefore accords a lesser protection to commercial speech than to other constitutionally guaranteed expression . . . .

The First Amendment's concern for commercial speech is based on the informational function of advertising. Consequently, there can be no constitutional objection to the suppression of commercial messages that do not accurately inform the public about lawful activity. The government may ban forms of communication more likely to deceive the public than to inform it, or commercial speech related to illegal activity.

If the communication is neither misleading nor related to unlawful activity, the government's power is more circumscribed. The State must assert a substantial interest to be achieved by restrictions on commercial speech. Moreover, the regulatory technique must be in proportion to that interest. The limitation on expression must be designed carefully to achieve the State's goal. Compliance with this requirement may be measured by two criteria. First, the restriction must directly advance the state interest involved; the regulation may not be sustained if it provides only ineffective or remote support for the government's purpose. Second, if the governmental interest could be served as well by a more limited restriction on commercial speech, the excessive restrictions cannot survive . . . .

In commercial speech cases, then, a four-part analysis has developed. At the outset, we must determine whether the expression is protected by the First Amendment. For commercial speech to come within that provision, it at least must concern lawful activity and not be misleading. Next, we ask whether the asserted governmental interest is substantial. If both inquiries yield positive answers, we must determine whether the regulation directly advances the governmental interest asserted, and whether it is not more extensive than is necessary to serve that interest.

III

We now apply this four-step analysis for commercial speech to the Commission's arguments in support of its ban on promotional advertising . . . .

The Commission offers two state interests as justifications for the ban on promotional advertising. The first concerns energy conservation. Plainly, [this interest] is substantial.

The Commission also argues that promotional advertising will aggravate inequities caused by the failure to base the utilities' rates on marginal cost . . . . The choice among rate structures involves difficult and important questions of economic supply and distributional fairness. The State's concern that rates be fair and efficient represents a clear and substantial governmental interest.

Next, we focus on the relationship between the State's interests and the advertising ban. Under this criterion, the Commission's laudable concern over the equity and efficiency of appellant's rates does not provide a constitutionally adequate reason for restricting protected speech. The link between the advertising prohibition and appellant's rate structure is, at most, tenuous. The impact of promotional advertising on the equity of appellant's rates is highly speculative. Advertising to increase off-peak usage would have to increase peak usage, while other factors that directly affect the fairness and efficiency of appellant's rates remained constant. Such conditional and remote eventualities simply cannot justify silencing appellant's promotional advertising.

In contrast, the State's interest in energy conservation is directly advanced by the Commission order at issue here. There is an immediate connection between advertising and demand for electricity. Central Hudson would not contest the advertising ban unless it believed that promotion would increase its sales. Thus, we find a direct link between the state interest in conservation and the Commission's order.

We come finally to the critical inquiry in this case: whether the Commission's complete suppression of speech ordinarily protected by the First Amendment is no more extensive than necessary to further the State's interest in energy conservation. The Commission's order reaches all promotional advertising, regardless of the impact of the touted service on overall energy use. But the energy conservation rationale, as important as it is, cannot justify suppressing information about electric devices or services that would cause no net increase in total energy use. In addition, no showing has been made that a more limited restriction on the content of promotional advertising would not serve adequately the State's interests . . . .

The Commission's order prevents appellant from promoting electric services that would reduce energy use by diverting demand from less efficient sources, or that would consume roughly the same amount of energy as do alternative sources. In neither situation would the utility's advertising endanger conservation or mislead the public. To the extent that the Commission's order suppresses speech that in no way impairs the State's interest in energy conservation, the Commission's order violates the First and Fourteenth Amendments and must be invalidated.

The Commission also has not demonstrated that its interest in conservation cannot be protected adequately by more limited regulation of appellant's commercial expression. To further its policy of conservation, the Commission could attempt to restrict the format and content of Central Hudson's advertising. It might, for example, require that the advertisements include information about the relative efficiency and expense of the offered service, both under current conditions and for the foreseeable future. In the absence of a showing that more limited speech regulation would be ineffective, we cannot approve the complete suppression of Central Hudson's advertising . . . .

Accordingly, the judgment of the New York Court of Appeals is *reversed*.

Mr. Justice Brennan, concurring in the judgment. [Omitted.]

Mr. Justice Blackmun, with whom Mr. Justice Brennan joins, concurring in the judgment.

. . . I concur only in the Court's [judgment], because I believe the test now evolved and applied by the Court is not consistent with our prior cases and does not provide adequate protection for truthful, nonmisleading, noncoercive commercial speech.

The Court asserts that "a four-part analysis has developed" from our decisions concerning commercial speech . . . . I agree with the Court that this level of intermediate scrutiny is appropriate for a restraint on commercial speech designed to protect consumers from misleading or coercive speech, or a regulation related to the time, place, or manner of commercial speech. I do not agree, however, that the Court's four-part test is the proper one to be applied when a State seeks to suppress information about a product in order to manipulate a private economic decision that the State cannot or has not regulated or outlawed directly . . . .

I seriously doubt whether suppression of information concerning the availability and price of a legally offered product is ever a permissible way for the State to "dampen" demand for or use of the product. Even though "commercial" speech is involved, such a regulatory measure strikes at the heart of the First Amendment. This is because it is a covert attempt by the State to manipulate the choices of its citizens, not by persuasion or direct regulation, but by depriving the public of the information needed to make a free choice. As the Court recognizes, the State's policy choices are insulated from the visibility and scrutiny that direct regulation would entail and the conduct of citizens is molded by the information that government chooses to give them.

MR. JUSTICE STEVENS, with whom MR. JUSTICE BRENNAN joins, concurring in the judgment.

. . . This case involves a governmental regulation that completely bans promotional advertising by an electric utility. This ban encompasses a great deal more than mere proposals to engage in certain kinds of commercial transactions. It prohibits all advocacy of the immediate or future use of electricity. It curtails expression by an informed and interested group of persons of their point of view on questions relating to the production and consumption of electrical energy — questions frequently discussed and debated by our political leaders. For example, an electric company's advocacy of the use of electric heat for environmental reasons, as opposed to wood-burning stoves, would seem to fall squarely within New York's promotional advertising ban and also within the bounds of maximum First Amendment protection. The breadth of the ban thus exceeds the boundaries of the commercial speech concept, however that concept may be defined.

The justification for the regulation is nothing more than the expressed fear that the audience may find the utility's message persuasive. Without the aid of any coercion, deception, or misinformation, truthful communication may persuade some citizens to consume more electricity than they otherwise would. I assume that such a consequence would be undesirable and that government may therefore prohibit and punish the unnecessary or excessive use of electricity. But if the perceived harm associated with greater electrical usage is not sufficiently serious to justify direct regulation, surely it does not constitute the kind of clear and present danger that can justify the suppression of speech.

In sum, I concur in the result because I do not consider this to be a "commercial speech" case. Accordingly, I see no need to decide whether the Court's four-part analysis adequately protects commercial speech — as properly defined — in the face of a blanket ban of the sort involved in this case.

MR. JUSTICE REHNQUIST, dissenting.

. . . The Court's decision today fails to give due deference to [the] subordinate position of commercial speech. The Court in so doing returns to the bygone era of *Lochner v. New York*, 198 U.S. 45 (1905), in which it was common practice for this Court to strike down economic regulations adopted by a State based on the Court's own notions of the most appropriate means for the State to implement its considered policies. . . .

I doubt there would be any question as to the constitutionality of New York's conservation effort if the Public Service Commission had chosen to raise the price of electricity, to condition its sale on specified terms, or to restrict its production. In terms of constitutional values, I think that such controls are virtually indistinguishable from the State's ban on promotional advertising. . . .

I remain of the view that the Court unlocked a Pandora's Box when it "elevated" commercial speech to the level of traditional political speech by according it First Amendment protection in *Virginia Pharmacy Board v. Virginia Citizens Consumer Council* (1976) [*supra* this chapter]. The line between "commercial speech," and the kind of speech that those who drafted the First Amendment had in mind, may not be a technically or intellectually easy one to draw, but it surely produced far fewer problems than has the development of judicial doctrine in this area since *Virginia Board*. For in the world of political advocacy and its marketplace of ideas, there is no such thing as a "fraudulent" idea: there may be useless proposals, totally unworkable schemes, as well as very sound proposals that will receive the imprimatur of the "marketplace of ideas" through our majoritarian system of election and representative government. The free flow of information is important in this context not because it will lead to the discovery of any objective "truth," but because it is essential to our system of self-government.

The notion that more speech is the remedy to expose falsehood and fallacies is wholly out of place in the commercial bazaar, where if applied logically the remedy of one who was defrauded would be merely a statement, available upon request, reciting the Latin maxim "caveat emptor." But since "fraudulent speech" in this area is to be remediable under *Virginia Pharmacy Board*, the remedy of one defrauded is a lawsuit or an agency proceeding based on common-law notions of fraud that are separated by a world of difference from the realm of politics and government. What time, legal decisions, and common sense have so widely severed, I declined to join in *Virginia Pharmacy Board*, and regret now to see the Court reaping the seeds that it there sowed. For in a democracy, the economic is subordinate to the political, a lesson that our ancestors learned long ago, and that our descendants will undoubtedly have to relearn many years hence.

———

Note: Identifying Commercial Speech

1. In *Virginia Pharmacy Board*, the Court defined commercial speech as speech that does "no more than propose a commercial transaction." However, in *Central Hudson Gas*, the Court uses an alternative definition: "expression related solely to the economic interests of the speaker and its audience." That broader definition has

not survived in more recent cases, and the Court has now said that "the proposal of a commercial transaction" is *the test* for identifying commercial speech." *City of Cincinnati v. Discovery Network, Inc.* (1993) (emphasis in the original) (Note *infra* this chapter).

2. How should courts deal with speech that has both commercial and noncommercial elements? The Court gave some guidance on this point in *Bolger v. Youngs Drug Products Corp.*, 463 U.S. 60 (1983). A federal statute prohibited the mailing of unsolicited advertisements for contraceptives. Youngs wanted to mail various materials relating to contraceptives it manufactured, but the Postal Service notified the company that the proposed mailings would violate the statute. Youngs brought suit challenging the constitutionality of the law.

The first step for the Court was to determine whether the material in question constituted commercial speech. For most of the proposed mailings, the answer was clearly "yes." Two informational pamphlets presented a closer question. One of these, "Plain Talk about Venereal Disease," was an 8-page pamphlet discussing at length the problem of venereal disease and the use and advantages of condoms in aiding the prevention of venereal disease. The only identification of Youngs or its products was at the bottom of the last page of the pamphlet, which stated that the pamphlet was contributed as a public service by Youngs, the distributor of Trojan-brand prophylactics.

The Supreme Court acknowledged that the pamphlets could not be characterized "merely as proposals to engage in commercial transactions." But that was not the end of the analysis.

> The mere fact that these pamphlets are conceded to be advertisements clearly does not compel the conclusion that they are commercial speech. *See New York Times v. Sullivan* (1964) [Chapter 2]. Similarly, the reference to a specific product does not by itself render the pamphlets commercial speech. Finally, the fact that Youngs has an economic motivation for mailing the pamphlets would clearly be insufficient by itself to turn the materials into commercial speech.

> The combination of *all* these characteristics, however, provides strong support for [the] conclusion that the informational pamphlets are properly characterized as commercial speech. The mailings constitute commercial speech notwithstanding the fact that they contain discussions of important public issues such as venereal disease and family planning. [Advertising] which "links a product to a current public debate" is not thereby entitled to the constitutional protection afforded noncommercial speech. A company has the full panoply of protections available to its direct comments on public issues, so there is no reason for providing similar constitutional protection when such statements are made in the context of commercial transactions. Advertisers should not be permitted to immunize false or misleading product information from government regulation simply by including references to public issues.

The Court went on to apply the test of *Central Hudson Gas*. It found that the speech was protected and that the statute was unconstitutional as applied.

3. Does the category of commercial speech, as defined by the Court, make sense from the perspective of First Amendment values? Consider the following example, found in Alex Kozinzki & Stuart Banner, *Who's Afraid of Commercial Speech?*, 76 Va. L. Rev. 627, 646 n.66 (1990):

> On January 17, 1990, page A7 of the New York Times was occupied entirely by an advertisement for Kent cigarettes. The ad consisted of a blown-up clipping from the previous week's Wall Street Journal, which described the use of Kents as a black market currency in Romania. Underneath the clipping ran the legend "In Romania, Kents are too valuable to smoke. Fortunately, we live in America." Commercial speech? News reporting? Editorial commentary? Does it make any sense to be asking these questions?

Consider also the Problem that follows.

———

Problem: "Commercial" Speech and Public Debate

Beginning in 1996, Nike, Inc., the well-known manufacturer of sporting gear and clothing, came under attack by human rights and labor groups, newspaper editorial writers, and others who alleged that the company was mistreating and underpaying workers at foreign facilities. Nike responded to these charges in numerous ways, such as by sending out press releases, writing letters to the editors of various newspapers around the country, and mailing letters to university presidents and athletic directors.

In April 1998, Marc Kasky, a California resident, sued Nike under California laws that authorize a private individual, acting as a "private attorney general," effectively to prosecute a business for unfair competition or false advertising. Kasky alleged that Nike made false or misleading commercial statements. He based his claim on statements that Nike made in nine specific documents, including press releases and letters to the editor of a newspaper, to institutional customers, and to representatives of nongovernmental organizations. The documents included:

- a letter from Nike's Director of Sports Marketing to university presidents and athletic directors presenting "facts" about Nike's labor practices;

- a 30-page illustrated pamphlet about those practices;

- a letter from Nike's Director of Labor Practices to the Chief Executive Officer of YWCA of America, discussing criticisms of its labor practices; and

- a letter to the editor of The New York Times taking issue with a columnist's criticisms of Nike's practices.

The lower courts dismissed Kasky's claim without leave to amend, but the California Supreme Court reversed. The court held that the speech at issue fell within the category of "commercial speech" and that the First Amendment did not protect

Nike's statements insofar as they were false or misleading—regardless of whatever role they played in a public debate.

Is this a correct application of the Supreme Court's precedents? (The Supreme Court granted review of the California Supreme Court decision, but dismissed the writ without ruling on the merits.)

————

Note: Discovery Network *and the "Reasonable Fit"*

1. In *Central Hudson Gas*, the Court said that the First Amendment "accords a lesser protection to commercial speech than to other constitutionally guaranteed expression." Does this mean that governments can enforce regulations against commercial speech while leaving noncommercial speech unregulated? Not necessarily.

In *City of Cincinnati v. Discovery Network, Inc.*, 507 U.S. 410 (1993), the city initially authorized the plaintiff corporations to install freestanding newsracks on public property to distribute their commercial publications. A year later, however, the city revoked its authorization and ordered the plaintiffs to remove their newsracks. The city was motivated by its interest in safety and the attractive appearance of its streets and sidewalks, but the city took no steps to regulate newsracks that disseminated noncommercial speech. The city's prohibition would have resulted in the removal of 62 newsracks, while about 1,500–2,000 would have remained in place.

The Court held that the city's action violated the First Amendment. Justice Stevens, writing for six members of the Court, began by reviewing propositions that were not in dispute:

> There is no claim in this case that there is anything unlawful or misleading about the contents of respondents' publications. Moreover, respondents do not challenge their characterization as "commercial speech." Nor do respondents question the substantiality of the city's interest in safety and esthetics. It was, therefore, proper for the [lower courts] to judge the validity of the city's prohibition under the standards we set forth in *Central Hudson* and *Board of Trustees of State University of N.Y. v. Fox*, 492 U.S. 469 (1989). It was the city's burden to establish a "reasonable fit" between its legitimate interests in safety and esthetics and its choice of a limited and selective prohibition of newsracks as the means chosen to serve those interests.

In *Fox*, the Court reviewed its decisions applying the *Central Hudson* test and synthesized them as follows:

> What our decisions require is a "fit" between the legislature's ends and the means chosen to accomplish those ends—a fit that is not necessarily perfect, but reasonable; that represents not necessarily the single best disposition but one whose scope is in proportion to the interest served; that employs not necessarily the least restrictive means but, as we have put it in [other contexts], a means narrowly tailored to achieve the desired objective. Within those bounds we leave it to governmental decisionmakers to judge what manner

of regulation may best be employed. . . . Here we require the government goal to be substantial, and the cost to be carefully calculated. Moreover, since the State bears the burden of justifying its restrictions, it must affirmatively establish the reasonable fit we require.

Applying this standard in *Discovery Network*, the Court found that the city did not "establish the reasonable fit we require." "The fact that the city failed to address [its concern] about newsracks by regulating their size, shape, appearance, or number indicates that it has not 'carefully calculated' the costs and benefits associated with the burden on speech imposed by its prohibition." The Court agreed with the lower courts that "[t]he benefit to be derived from the removal of 62 newsracks while about 1,500–2,000 remain in place" was "minute" or "paltry."

The Court then addressed the city's argument that a categorical prohibition on the use of newsracks to disseminate *commercial* messages satisfied the requirements of *Central Hudson* and *Fox*:

> The city argues that there is a close fit between its ban on newsracks dispensing "commercial handbills" and its interests in safety and esthetics because every decrease in the number of such dispensing devices necessarily effects an increase in safety and an improvement in the attractiveness of the cityscape. In the city's view, the prohibition is thus entirely related to its legitimate interests in safety and esthetics.

> . . . The major premise supporting the city's argument is the proposition that commercial speech has only a low value. Based on that premise, the city contends that the fact that assertedly more valuable publications are allowed to use newsracks does not undermine its judgment that its esthetic and safety interests are stronger than the interest in allowing commercial speakers to have similar access to the reading public.

> We cannot agree. In our view, the city's argument attaches more importance to the distinction between commercial and noncommercial speech than our cases warrant and seriously underestimates the value of commercial speech. . . .

> [For] the purpose of deciding this case, we assume that all of the speech barred from Cincinnati's sidewalks is what we have labeled "core" commercial speech and that no such speech is found in publications that are allowed to use newsracks. We nonetheless agree with the Court of Appeals that Cincinnati's actions in this case run afoul of the First Amendment. Not only does Cincinnati's categorical ban on commercial newsracks place too much importance on the distinction between commercial and noncommercial speech, but in this case, the distinction bears no relationship *whatsoever* to the particular interests that the city has asserted. It is therefore an impermissible means of responding to the city's admittedly legitimate interests. . . .

> The city has asserted an interest in esthetics, but respondent publishers' newsracks are no greater an eyesore than the newsracks permitted to remain

on Cincinnati's sidewalks. Each newsrack, whether containing "newspapers" or "commercial handbills," is equally unattractive. . . . In fact, the newspapers are arguably the greater culprit because of their superior number.

Cincinnati has not asserted an interest in preventing commercial harms by regulating the information distributed by respondent publishers' newsracks, which is, of course, the typical reason why commercial speech can be subject to greater governmental regulation than noncommercial speech. . . .

In the absence of some basis for distinguishing between "newspapers" and "commercial handbills" that is relevant to an interest asserted by the city, we are unwilling to recognize Cincinnati's bare assertion that the "low value" of commercial speech is a sufficient justification for its selective and categorical ban on newsracks dispensing "commercial handbills."

Chief Justice Rehnquist, joined by Justice White and Justice Thomas, dissented. He wrote:

Despite its protestations to the contrary, [the Court's] argument rests on the discredited notion that the availability of "less restrictive means" to accomplish the city's objectives renders its regulation of commercial speech unconstitutional. As we observed in *Fox*, "almost all of the restrictions disallowed under *Central Hudson*'s fourth prong have been substantially excessive, disregarding far less restrictive and more precise means." That there may be other—less restrictive—means by which Cincinnati could have gone about addressing its safety and esthetic concerns, then, does not render its prohibition against respondents' newsracks unconstitutional.

Nor does the fact that, if enforced, the city's prohibition would result in the removal of only 62 newsracks from its street corners. . . . The relevant inquiry [is] not the degree to which the locality's interests are furthered in a particular case, but rather the relation that the challenged regulation of commercial speech bears to the "overall problem" the locality is seeking to alleviate. . . . [Every] newsrack that is removed from the city's sidewalks marginally enhances the safety of its streets and esthetics of its cityscape. . . .

The Court offers an alternative rationale for invalidating the city's policy: viz., the distinction Cincinnati has drawn (between commercial and noncommercial speech) in deciding which newsracks to regulate "bears no relationship *whatsoever* to the particular interests that the city has asserted." . . . [The] Court refuses "to recognize Cincinnati's bare assertion that the 'low value' of commercial speech is a sufficient justification for its selective and categorical ban on newsracks dispensing 'commercial handbills.'" . . .

If (as I am certain) Cincinnati may regulate newsracks that disseminate commercial speech based on the interests it has asserted, I am at a loss as to why its scheme is unconstitutional because it does not also regulate newsracks that disseminate noncommercial speech. One would have thought that the city, perhaps even following the teachings of our commercial speech juris-prudence, could have decided to place the burden of its regulatory scheme on less protected speech (i.e., commercial handbills) without running afoul of the First Amendment. Today's decision, though, places the city in the position of having to decide between restricting more speech — fully protected speech — and allowing the proliferation of newsracks on its street corners to continue unabated. It scarcely seems logical that the First Amendment compels such a result. . . .

2. Chief Justice Rehnquist argues in dissent that the city can satisfy the "reasonable fit" requirement by placing the burden of its regulatory scheme solely on commercial speech. The Court rejects this view, partly on the ground that the city can justify its regulation only by invoking "an interest in preventing *commercial harms*." Which of these views is more consistent with the treatment of commercial speech in *Virginia Pharmacy Board* and *Central Hudson*?

3. Could the city simply prohibit the placement of *all* newsracks on public property? We will consider this question in Chapter 6.

———

Lorillard Tobacco Co. v. Reilly

533 U.S. 525 (2001)

Justice O'Connor delivered the opinion of the Court.

In January 1999, the Attorney General of Massachusetts promulgated comprehensive regulations governing the advertising and sale of cigarettes, smokeless tobacco, and cigars. Petitioners, a group of cigarette, smokeless tobacco, and cigar manufacturers and retailers, filed suit in Federal District Court claiming that the regulations violate federal law and the United States Constitution. In large measure, the District Court determined that the regulations are valid and enforceable. The United States Court of Appeals for the First Circuit affirmed in part and reversed in part, concluding that the regulations are not pre-empted by federal law and do not violate the First Amendment. The first question presented for our review is whether certain cigarette advertising regulations are pre-empted by the Federal Cigarette Labeling and Advertising Act (FCLAA). The second question presented is whether certain regulations governing the advertising and sale of tobacco products violate the First Amendment. . . .

I

In January 1999, pursuant to his authority to prevent unfair or deceptive practices in trade, the Massachusetts Attorney General (Attorney General) promulgated regulations governing the sale and advertisement of cigarettes, smokeless tobacco, and cigars. The purpose of the cigarette and smokeless tobacco regulations [is to reduce the use of tobacco products by children under legal age]. . . . The regulations place a variety of restrictions on outdoor advertising, point-of-sale advertising, retail sales transactions, transactions by mail, promotions, sampling of products, and labels for cigars.

The cigarette and smokeless tobacco regulations being challenged before this Court provide:

"(2) *Retail Outlet Sales Practices.* Except as otherwise provided in [§ 21.04(4)], it shall be an unfair or deceptive act or practice for any person who sells or distributes cigarettes or smokeless tobacco products through a retail outlet located within Massachusetts to engage in any of the following retail outlet sales practices:

. . . .

"(c) Using self-service displays of cigarettes or smokeless tobacco products;

"(d) Failing to place cigarettes and smokeless tobacco products out of the reach of all consumers, and in a location accessible only to outlet personnel." §§ 21.04(2)(c)-(d).

"(5) *Advertising Restrictions.* Except as provided in [§ 21.04(6)], it shall be an unfair or deceptive act or practice for any manufacturer, distributor or retailer to engage in any of the following practices:

"(a) Outdoor advertising, including advertising in enclosed stadiums and advertising from within a retail establishment that is directed toward or visible from the outside of the establishment, in any location that is within a 1,000 foot radius of any public playground, playground area in a public park, elementary school or secondary school;

"(b) Point-of-sale advertising of cigarettes or smokeless tobacco products any portion of which is placed lower than five feet from the floor of any retail establishment which is located within a one thousand foot radius of any public playground, playground area in a public park, elementary school or secondary school, and which is not an adult-only retail establishment." §§ 21.04(5)(a)–(b).

The cigar regulations that are still at issue [place similar restrictions on cigar advertising]. . . .

* * *

II

[The Court held that federal law preempted Massachusetts' restrictions on cigarette advertising.]

III

By its terms, the FCLAA's pre-emption provision only applies to cigarettes. Accordingly, we must evaluate the smokeless tobacco and cigar petitioners' First Amendment challenges to the State's outdoor and point-of-sale advertising regulations. The cigarette petitioners did not raise a pre-emption challenge to the sales practices regulations. Thus, we must analyze the cigarette as well as the smokeless tobacco and cigar petitioners' claim that certain sales practices regulations for tobacco products violate the First Amendment.

A

For over 25 years, the Court has recognized that commercial speech does not fall outside the purview of the First Amendment. *See, e.g., Virginia Bd. of Pharmacy* [*supra* this chapter]. Instead, the Court has afforded commercial speech a measure of First Amendment protection "'commensurate'" with its position in relation to other constitutionally guaranteed expression. In recognition of the "distinction between speech proposing a commercial transaction, which occurs in an area traditionally subject to government regulation, and other varieties of speech," *Central Hudson* [*supra* this chapter], we developed a framework for analyzing regulations of commercial speech that is "substantially similar" to the test for time, place, and manner restrictions. The analysis contains four elements: [the Court quotes the *Central Hudson* test].

Petitioners urge us to reject the Central Hudson analysis and apply strict scrutiny. They are not the first litigants to do so. Admittedly, several Members of the Court have expressed doubts about the *Central Hudson* analysis and whether it should apply in particular cases. But we see "no need to break new ground. *Central Hudson*, as applied in our more recent commercial speech cases, provides an adequate basis for decision."

⋆ ⋆ ⋆

Only the last two steps of *Central Hudson*'s four-part analysis are at issue here. The Attorney General has assumed for purposes of summary judgment that petitioners' speech is entitled to First Amendment protection. With respect to the second step, none of the petitioners contests the importance of the State's interest in preventing the use of tobacco products by minors.

The third step of *Central Hudson* concerns the relationship between the harm that underlies the State's interest and the means identified by the State to advance that interest. It requires that

> the speech restriction directly and materially advanc[e] the asserted governmental interest. 'This burden is not satisfied by mere speculation or conjecture; rather, a governmental body seeking to sustain a restriction on commercial speech must demonstrate that the harms it recites are real and that its restriction will in fact alleviate them to a material degree. . . .'

The last step of the *Central Hudson* analysis "complements" the third step, "asking whether the speech restriction is not more extensive than necessary to serve the interests that support it." We have made it clear that "the least restrictive means" is not the standard; instead, the case law requires a reasonable "'fit between the legislature's ends and the means chosen to accomplish those ends, . . . a means narrowly tailored to achieve the desired objective.'" *Board of Trustees of State Univ. of N.Y. v. Fox* [*supra* Note this chapter]. Focusing on the third and fourth steps of the *Central Hudson* analysis, we first address the outdoor advertising and point-of-sale advertising regulations for smokeless tobacco and cigars. We then address the sales practices regulations for all tobacco products.

B

The outdoor advertising regulations prohibit smokeless tobacco or cigar advertising within a 1,000-foot radius of a school or playground. The District Court and Court of Appeals concluded that the Attorney General had identified a real problem with underage use of tobacco products, that limiting youth exposure to advertising would combat that problem, and that the regulations burdened no more speech than necessary to accomplish the State's goal. The smokeless tobacco and cigar petitioners take issue with all of these conclusions.

1

The smokeless tobacco and cigar petitioners contend that the Attorney General's regulations do not satisfy *Central Hudson*'s third step. They maintain that although the Attorney General may have identified a problem with underage cigarette smoking, he has not identified an equally severe problem with respect to underage use of smokeless tobacco or cigars. . . .

Our review of the record reveals that the Attorney General has provided ample documentation of the problem with underage use of smokeless tobacco and cigars. In addition, we disagree with petitioners' claim that there is no evidence that preventing targeted campaigns and limiting youth exposure to advertising will decrease underage use of smokeless tobacco and cigars. On this record and in the posture of summary judgment, we are unable to conclude that the Attorney General's decision to regulate advertising of smokeless tobacco and cigars in an effort to combat the use of tobacco products by minors was based on mere "speculation [and] conjecture."

2

Whatever the strength of the Attorney General's evidence to justify the outdoor advertising regulations, however, we conclude that the regulations do not satisfy the fourth step of the *Central Hudson* analysis. The final step of the *Central Hudson* analysis, the "critical inquiry in this case," requires a reasonable fit between the means and ends of the regulatory scheme. The Attorney General's regulations do not meet this standard. The broad sweep of the regulations indicates that the Attorney General did not "carefully calculat[e] the costs and benefits associated with the burden on speech imposed" by the regulations. *Cincinnati v. Discovery Network, Inc.* (1993) [Note *supra* this chapter].

The outdoor advertising regulations prohibit any smokeless tobacco or cigar advertising within 1,000 feet of schools or playgrounds. In the District Court, petitioners maintained that this prohibition would prevent advertising in 87% to 91% of Boston, Worcester, and Springfield, Massachusetts. The 87% to 91% figure appears to include not only the effect of the regulations, but also the limitations imposed by other generally applicable zoning restrictions. The Attorney General disputed petitioners' figures but "concede[d] that the reach of the regulations is substantial. . . ."

In some geographical areas, these regulations would constitute nearly a complete ban on the communication of truthful information about smokeless tobacco and cigars to adult consumers. The breadth and scope of the regulations, and the process by which the Attorney General adopted the regulations, do not demonstrate a careful calculation of the speech interests involved.

First, the Attorney General did not seem to consider the impact of the 1,000-foot restriction on commercial speech in major metropolitan areas. . . . In addition, the range of communications restricted seems unduly broad. For instance, it is not clear from the regulatory scheme why a ban on oral communications is necessary to further the State's interest. Apparently that restriction means that a retailer is unable to answer inquiries about its tobacco products if that communication occurs outdoors. Similarly, a ban on all signs of any size seems ill suited to target the problem of highly visible billboards, as opposed to smaller signs. To the extent that studies have identified particular advertising and promotion practices that appeal to youth, tailoring would involve targeting those practices while permitting others. As crafted, the regulations make no distinction among practices on this basis.

The State's interest in preventing underage tobacco use is substantial, and even compelling, but it is no less true that the sale and use of tobacco products by adults is a legal activity. We must consider that tobacco retailers and manufacturers have an interest in conveying truthful information about their products to adults, and adults have a corresponding interest in receiving truthful information about tobacco products. . . .

In some instances, Massachusetts' outdoor advertising regulations would impose particularly onerous burdens on speech. For example, we disagree with the Court of Appeals' conclusion that because cigar manufacturers and retailers conduct a limited amount of advertising in comparison to other tobacco products, "the relative lack of cigar advertising also means that the burden imposed on cigar advertisers is correspondingly small." If some retailers have relatively small advertising budgets, and use few avenues of communication, then the Attorney General's outdoor advertising regulations potentially place a greater, not lesser, burden on those retailers' speech. Furthermore, to the extent that cigar products and cigar advertising differ from that of other tobacco products, that difference should inform the inquiry into what speech restrictions are necessary.

In addition, a retailer in Massachusetts may have no means of communicating to passersby on the street that it sells tobacco products because alternative forms of advertisement, like newspapers, do not allow that retailer to propose an instant transaction in the way that onsite advertising does. The ban on any indoor advertising that is visible from the outside also presents problems in establishments like convenience stores, which have unique security concerns that counsel in favor of full visibility of the store from the outside. It is these sorts of considerations that the Attorney General failed to incorporate into the regulatory scheme.

We conclude that the Attorney General has failed to show that the outdoor advertising regulations for smokeless tobacco and cigars are not more extensive than necessary to advance the State's substantial interest in preventing underage tobacco use. . . .

C

Massachusetts has also restricted indoor, point-of-sale advertising for smokeless tobacco and cigars. Advertising cannot be "placed lower than five feet from the floor of any retail establishment which is located within a one thousand foot radius of" any school or playground. . . .

We conclude that the point-of-sale advertising regulations fail both the third and fourth steps of the *Central Hudson* analysis. A regulation cannot be sustained if it "'provides only ineffective or remote support for the government's purpose,'" or if there is "little chance" that the restriction will advance the State's goal. As outlined above, the State's goal is to prevent minors from using tobacco products and to curb demand for that activity by limiting youth exposure to advertising. The 5-foot rule does not seem to advance that goal. Not all children are less than 5 feet tall, and those who are certainly have the ability to look up and take in their surroundings. . . .

Massachusetts may wish to target tobacco advertisements and displays that entice children, much like floor-level candy displays in a convenience store, but the blanket height restriction does not constitute a reasonable fit with that goal. . . . We conclude that the restriction on the height of indoor advertising is invalid under *Central Hudson*'s third and fourth prongs.

D

The Attorney General also promulgated a number of regulations that restrict sales practices by cigarette, smokeless tobacco, and cigar manufacturers and retailers. Among other restrictions, the regulations bar the use of self-service displays and require that tobacco products be placed out of the reach of all consumers in a location accessible only to salespersons. . . .

Massachusetts' sales practices provisions regulate conduct that may have a communicative component, but Massachusetts seeks to regulate the placement of tobacco products for reasons unrelated to the communication of ideas. We conclude that the State has demonstrated a substantial interest in preventing access to tobacco products by minors and has adopted an appropriately narrow means of advancing that interest. *See United States v. O'Brien* [Chapter 7] . . . .

We conclude that the sales practices regulations withstand First Amendment scrutiny. The means chosen by the State are narrowly tailored to prevent access to tobacco products by minors, are unrelated to expression, and leave open alternative avenues for vendors to convey information about products and for would-be customers to inspect products before purchase.

IV

We have observed that "tobacco use, particularly among children and adolescents, poses perhaps the single most significant threat to public health in the United States." From a policy perspective, it is understandable for the States to attempt to prevent minors from using tobacco products before they reach an age where they are capable of weighing for themselves the risks and potential benefits of tobacco use, and other adult activities. Federal law, however, places limits on policy choices available to the States.

In these cases, Congress enacted a comprehensive scheme to address cigarette smoking and health in advertising and pre-empted state regulation of cigarette advertising that attempts to address that same concern, even with respect to youth. The First Amendment also constrains state efforts to limit advertising of tobacco products, because so long as the sale and use of tobacco is lawful for adults, the tobacco industry has a protected interest in communicating information about its products and adult customers have an interest in receiving that information.

To the extent that federal law and the First Amendment do not prohibit state action, States and localities remain free to combat the problem of underage tobacco use by appropriate means. The judgment of the United States Court of Appeals for the First Circuit is therefore affirmed in part and reversed in part, and the cases are remanded for further proceedings consistent with this opinion.

* * *

JUSTICE KENNEDY, with whom JUSTICE SCALIA joins, concurring in part and concurring in the judgment. [Omitted.]

JUSTICE THOMAS, concurring in part and concurring in the judgment.

I join the opinion of the Court (with the exception of Part III-B-1) because I agree that the Massachusetts cigarette advertising regulations are pre-empted by the Federal Cigarette Labeling and Advertising Act. I also agree with the Court's disposition of the First Amendment challenges to the other regulations at issue here, and I share the Court's view that the regulations fail even the intermediate scrutiny of *Central Hudson Gas*. At the same time, I continue to believe that when the government seeks to restrict truthful speech in order to suppress the ideas it conveys, strict scrutiny is appropriate, whether or not the speech in question may be characterized as "commercial." I would subject all of the advertising restrictions to strict scrutiny and would hold that they violate the First Amendment.

I

At the heart of this litigation is a Massachusetts regulation that imposes a sweeping ban on speech about tobacco products. . . . The regulations here are concerned with the advertising's primary effect, which is to induce those who view the advertisements to purchase and use tobacco products. In other words, it seeks to suppress speech about tobacco because it objects to the content of that speech. We have consistently applied strict scrutiny to such content-based regulations of speech.

A

There was once a time when this Court declined to give any First Amendment protection to commercial speech. . . . That position was repudiated in *Virginia Bd. of Pharmacy v. Virginia Citizens Consumer Council, Inc.*, (1976) [*supra* this chapter], which explained that even speech "which does 'no more than propose a commercial transaction'" is protected by the First Amendment. Since then, the Court has followed an uncertain course—much of the uncertainty being generated by the malleability of the four-part balancing test of *Central Hudson*.

I have observed previously that there is no "philosophical or historical basis for asserting that 'commercial' speech is of 'lower value' than 'noncommercial' speech." Indeed, I doubt whether it is even possible to draw a coherent distinction between commercial and noncommercial speech.

It should be clear that if these regulations targeted anything other than advertising for commercial products—if, for example, they were directed at billboards promoting political candidates—all would agree that the restrictions should be subjected to strict scrutiny. In my view, an asserted government interest in keeping people ignorant by suppressing expression "is *per se* illegitimate and can no more justify regulation of 'commercial' speech than it can justify regulation of 'noncommercial' speech." That is essentially the interest asserted here, and I would subject the Massachusetts regulations to strict scrutiny.

B

Even if one accepts the premise that commercial speech generally is entitled to a lower level of constitutional protection than are other forms of speech, it does not follow that the regulations here deserve anything less than strict scrutiny. Although we have recognized several categories of speech that normally receive reduced First Amendment protection, or no First Amendment protection at all, we have never held that the government may regulate speech within those categories in any way that it wishes. Rather, we have said "that these areas of speech can, consistently with the First Amendment, be regulated *because of their constitutionally proscribable content.*" *R.A.V. v. St. Paul* (1992) [Chapter 15]. Even when speech falls into a category of reduced constitutional protection, the government may not engage in content discrimination for reasons unrelated to those characteristics of the speech that place it within the category. . . .

In explaining the distinction between commercial speech and other forms of speech, we have emphasized that commercial speech is both "more easily verifiable by its disseminator" and less likely to be "chilled by proper regulation." *Virginia Bd.* These characteristics led us to conclude that, in the context of commercial speech, it is "less necessary to tolerate inaccurate statements for fear of silencing the speaker," and also that it is more "appropriate to require that a commercial message appear in such a form, or include such additional information, warnings, and disclaimers, as are necessary to prevent its being deceptive." Whatever the validity of this reasoning, it is limited to the peculiarly *commercial* harms that commercial speech can threaten—*i.e.*, the risk of deceptive or misleading advertising. Whatever power the State may have to regulate commercial speech, it may not use that power to limit the content of commercial speech, as it has done here, "for reasons unrelated to the preservation of a fair bargaining process." Such content-discriminatory regulation—like all other content-based regulation of speech—must be subjected to strict scrutiny. . . .

II

Under strict scrutiny, the advertising ban may be saved only if it is narrowly tailored to promote a compelling government interest. If that interest could be served by an alternative that is less restrictive of speech, then the State must use that alternative instead. Applying this standard, the regulations here must fail. . . .

* * *

No legislature has ever sought to restrict speech about an activity it regarded as harmless and inoffensive. Calls for limits on expression always are made when the specter of some threatened harm is looming. The identity of the harm may vary. People will be inspired by totalitarian dogmas and subvert the Republic. They will be inflamed by racial demagoguery and embrace hatred and bigotry. Or they will be enticed by cigarette advertisements and choose to smoke, risking disease. It is therefore no answer for the State to say that the makers of cigarettes are doing harm: perhaps they are. But in that respect they are no different from the purveyors of other harmful products, or the advocates of harmful ideas. When the State seeks to silence them, they are all entitled to the protection of the First Amendment.

* * *

JUSTICE SOUTER, concurring in part and dissenting in part. [Omitted.]

JUSTICE STEVENS, with whom JUSTICE GINSBURG and JUSTICE BREYER join, and with whom JUSTICE SOUTER joins as to Part I, concurring in part, concurring in the judgment in part, and dissenting in part.

This suit presents two separate sets of issues. The first—involving pre-emption—is straightforward. The second—involving the First Amendment—is more complex. Because I strongly disagree with the Court's conclusion that the Federal Cigarette Labeling and Advertising Act of 1965 precludes States and localities from regulating the location of cigarette advertising, I dissent from Parts II-A and II-B of the Court's opinion. On the First Amendment questions, I agree with the Court both that the outdoor advertising restrictions imposed by Massachusetts serve legitimate and important state interests and that the record does not indicate that the measures were properly tailored to serve those interests. Because the present record does not enable us to adjudicate the merits of those claims on summary judgment, I would vacate the decision upholding those restrictions and remand for trial on the constitutionality of the outdoor advertising regulations. Finally, because I do not believe that either the point-of-sale advertising restrictions or the sales practice restrictions implicate significant First Amendment concerns, I would uphold them in their entirety.

* * *

II

On the First Amendment issues raised by petitioners, my disagreements with the majority are less significant. I would, however, reach different dispositions as to the 1,000-foot rule and the height restrictions for indoor advertising, and my evaluation of the sales practice restrictions differs from the Court's.

The 1,000-Foot Rule

I am in complete accord with the Court's analysis of the importance of the interests served by the advertising restrictions. As the Court lucidly explains, few interests are more "compelling," than ensuring that minors do not become addicted to a dangerous drug before they are able to make a mature and informed decision as to the health risks associated with that substance. Unlike other products sold for human consumption, tobacco products are addictive and ultimately lethal for many long-term users. When that interest is combined with the State's concomitant concern for the effective enforcement of its laws regarding the sale of tobacco to minors, it becomes clear that Massachusetts' regulations serve interests of the highest order and are, therefore, immune from any ends-based challenge, whatever level of scrutiny one chooses to employ.

Nevertheless, noble ends do not save a speech-restricting statute whose means are poorly tailored. Such statutes may be invalid for two different reasons. First, the means chosen may be insufficiently related to the ends they purportedly serve. Alternatively, the statute may be so broadly drawn that, while effectively achieving its ends, it unduly restricts communications that are unrelated to its policy aims. . . .

To my mind, the 1,000-foot rule does not present a tailoring problem of the first type. For reasons cogently explained in our prior opinions and in the opinion of the Court, we may fairly assume that advertising stimulates consumption and, therefore, that regulations limiting advertising will facilitate efforts to stem consumption. Furthermore, if the government's intention is to limit consumption by a particular segment of the community — in this case, minors — it is appropriate, indeed necessary, to tailor advertising restrictions to the areas where that segment of the community congregates — in this case, the area surrounding schools and playgrounds.

However, I share the majority's concern as to whether the 1,000-foot rule unduly restricts the ability of cigarette manufacturers to convey lawful information to adult consumers. This, of course, is a question of line-drawing. While a ban on all communications about a given subject would be the most effective way to prevent children from exposure to such material, the State cannot by fiat reduce the level of discourse to that which is "fit for children". . . .

Finding the appropriate balance is no easy matter. Though many factors plausibly enter the equation when calculating whether a child-directed location restriction goes too far in regulating adult speech, one crucial question is whether the regulatory scheme leaves available sufficient "alternative avenues of communication." Because I do not think the record contains sufficient information to enable us to answer that question, I would vacate the award of summary judgment upholding the 1,000-foot rule and remand for trial on that issue. Therefore, while I agree with the majority that the Court of Appeals did not sufficiently consider the implications of the 1,000-foot rule for the lawful communication of adults, I dissent from the disposition reflected in Part III-B-2 of the Court's opinion.

There is no doubt that the 1,000-foot rule prohibits cigarette advertising in a substantial portion of Massachusetts' largest cities. Even on that question, however, the parties remain in dispute as to the percentage of these urban areas that is actually off limits to tobacco advertising. Moreover, the record is entirely silent on the impact of the regulation in other portions of the Commonwealth. The dearth of reliable statistical information as to the scope of the ban is problematic.

More importantly, the Court lacks sufficient qualitative information as to the areas where cigarette advertising is prohibited and those where it is permitted. The fact that 80% or 90% of an urban area is unavailable to tobacco advertisements may be constitutionally irrelevant if the available areas are so heavily trafficked or so central to the city's cultural life that they provide a sufficient forum for the propagation of a manufacturer's message. One electric sign in Times Square or at the foot of the Golden Gate Bridge may be seen by more potential customers than a hundred signs dispersed in residential neighborhoods.

Finally, the Court lacks information as to other avenues of communication available to cigarette manufacturers and retailers. For example, depending on the answers to empirical questions on which we lack data, the ubiquity of print advertisements hawking particular brands of cigarettes might suffice to inform adult consumers of the special advantages of the respective brands. Similarly, print advertisements, circulars mailed to people's homes, word of mouth, and general information may or may not be sufficient to imbue the adult population with the knowledge that particular stores, chains of stores, or types of stores sell tobacco products. . . .

The Sales Practice and Indoor Advertising Restrictions

After addressing petitioners' challenge to the sales practice restrictions imposed by the Massachusetts statute, the Court concluded that these provisions did not violate the First Amendment. I concur in that judgment, but write separately on this issue to make two brief points.

First, I agree with the District Court and the Court of Appeals that the sales practice restrictions are best analyzed as regulating conduct, not speech. . . .

Second, though I admit the question is closer, I would, for similar reasons, uphold the regulation limiting tobacco advertising in certain retail establishments to the space five feet or more above the floor. When viewed in isolation, this provision appears to target speech. Further, to the extent that it does target speech it may well run into constitutional problems, as the connection between the ends the statute purports to serve and the means it has chosen are dubious. Nonetheless, I am ultimately persuaded that the provision is unobjectionable because it is little more than an adjunct to the other sales practice restrictions. As the Commonwealth of Massachusetts can properly legislate the placement of products and the nature of displays in its convenience stores, I would not draw a distinction between such restrictions and height restrictions on related product advertising. I would accord the Commonwealth some latitude in imposing restrictions that can have only the slightest impact on the ability of adults to purchase a poisonous product and may save some children from taking the first step on the road to addiction.

III

Because I strongly disagree with the Court's conclusion on the pre-emption issue, I dissent from Parts II-A and II-B of its opinion. Though I agree with much of what the Court has to say about the First Amendment, I ultimately disagree with its disposition or its reasoning on each of the regulations before us.

Note: The Normalization of Commercial Speech

1. In *Posadas de Puerto Rico Associates v. Tourism Co. of P.R.*, 478 U.S. 328 (1986), the Court upheld a Puerto Rico statute that forbade local casinos from using advertising addressed at local inhabitants. Originally, the case was widely understood to create a "vice" exception to the general commercial speech doctrine that permitted states to bar commercial speech as a means to reducing demand for "vice" products such as gambling. However, 10 years later in *44 Liquormart, Inc. v. Rhode Island*, 517 U.S. 484 (1996), the Court in a highly splintered set of opinions unanimously struck down a Rhode Island statute prohibiting price advertising of alcoholic beverages. While there was wide disagreement among the Justices regarding the continuing viability of the *Central Hudson* test, at least as applied to truthful, nonmisleading commercial speech (a disagreement reflected in Justice Thomas's opinion in *Lorillard*), all appeared to agree that *Posadas* was wrongly decided. *Lorillard* appears to confirm that no such "vice" exception exists. Note, however, that states remain free to completely ban vices such as casino gambling and alcohol (as many do). And presumably, they could then ban advertising for those products, since the commercial speech doctrine does not protect advertising of illegal products. Why, then, will the Court not permit states to take the less restrictive path of permitting a product, but banning advertising for it?

2. In the *44 Liquormart* case, the Rhode Island Liquor Stores Association — an organization that represented the interests of small liquor stores — intervened as a *defendant* in the suit challenging the laws that prohibited price advertising. How might this bear on the First Amendment issue?

3. In *Lorillard*, the majority acknowledges criticisms of *Central Hudson* expressed by numerous Justices, but then declines to adopt strict scrutiny as the test for regulations of truthful, nonmisleading commercial speech. Instead, the Court says that "*Central Hudson*, as applied in our more recent commercial speech cases, provides an adequate basis for decision." What does the Court mean by the phrase "as applied in our more recent commercial speech decisions"?

4. In applying the fourth prong of the *Central Hudson* test, the Court cites and purports to follow the narrow tailoring analysis set out in *Board of State Univ. of N.Y. v. Fox*, which requires only a "reasonable fit," not that the state use "the least restrictive means." Does the *Lorillard* majority really follow *SUNY v. Fox*? Or is something more going on here?

5. In his concurring opinion Justice Thomas says that "there is no 'philosophical or historical basis for asserting that "commercial speech" is of "lower value" than "non-commercial" speech'" (he is quoting his separate opinion in *44 Liquormart*). Is his statement true? And what does it mean? Does it mean that he would entirely abandon the "commercial speech" doctrine, and instead treat commercial speech the same as, say, political speech? Is that possible or plausible?

6. Justice Thomas also argues that whatever the status of false or misleading commercial speech, strict scrutiny is the appropriate standard when a regulation limits commercial speech but is not targeting commercial harms—i.e., when the purpose of the regulation is to combat the tendency of advertising to convince the audience. This might be called the "anti-paternalism" approach to commercial speech. Note, however, that Massachusetts' concern in *Lorillard* was not that adults would be convinced to buy tobacco products, but rather that children would. Would Justice Thomas extend his anti-paternalism approach to children? Consider in this regard what the word "paternalism" means.

7. Does *Lorillard* doom all ordinances that substantially restrict outdoor advertising of tobacco products? Consider the following hypothetical.

The City of Bayport recently adopted Ordinance 307. The ordinance prohibits the placement of any sign that "advertises tobacco products in a publicly visible location," i.e., on "outdoor billboards, sides of buildings, and free standing signboards." However, the ordinance includes exceptions that allow for tobacco product advertising on buses, taxicabs, commercial vehicles used to transport tobacco product, and signs at businesses licensed to sell tobacco products, including professional sports stadiums. Ordinance 307 also contains an exception permitting such advertising in certain commercially and industrially zoned areas of the City. Is the ordinance constitutional?

8. *44 Liquormart* was decided in 1996, more than 20 years ago. *Lorillard* was decided in 2001, more than 15 years ago. As the case discussed in the next Note demonstrates, however, the disputes over the proper treatment of commercial speech, and the continuing viability of *Central Hudson*, remain very much alive.

———

Problem: Attacking Childhood Obesity

A committee of the United States Senate recently held hearings on the problem of obesity, particularly among children. The committee issued a report that included the following findings.* Obesity is the second largest contributor to mortality rates in the United States. (Tobacco use is the first.) Although the growth of obesity over the last few decades has had many causes, a significant factor has been the increased availability of large quantities of high-calorie, high-fat foods. Such foods have been aggressively marketed and promoted by fast food companies, with much of the advertising directed at children. The effect of advertising on children's eating habits is significant for two reasons. First, childhood obesity is a serious health problem in its own right.

_____

* This summary is taken from Justice Thomas's concurring opinion in *Lorillard*.

Second, eating preferences formed in childhood tend to persist in adulthood. Thus, even though fast food is not addictive in the same way tobacco is, children's exposure to fast food advertising can have deleterious consequences that are difficult to reverse.

Against this background, the committee proposes legislation that would prohibit the advertising of high-calorie, high-fat "snack foods" (defined in the legislation) on broadcast or cable television (a) during the hours 7 a.m. to noon on Saturday and Sunday; (b) on programs that feature animated cartoons and are broadcast from 7 a.m. to 9 p.m.; and (c) on programs directed at children. The legislation directs the Federal Communications Committee to flesh out the prohibitions through regulations that will give adequate guidance to broadcasters and advertisers.

Is the proposed legislation constitutional?

————

Note: Sorrell *and the Continued Ferment over Commercial Speech*

After *44 Liquormart* and *Lorillard*, the Court appeared to be on its way to assimilating commercial speech into the mainstream of First Amendment law. However, more recent decisions make clear that the Court remains deeply divided on how far to take the protection of commercial speech, and indeed over what kinds of expression fall within the category. A decade after *Lorillard*, with four new Justices sitting, the Court split 6-3 over whether to apply "heightened judicial scrutiny" to a regulation that the dissent viewed as a form of commercial regulation.

The case was *Sorrell v. IMS Health Inc.*, 564 U.S. 552 (2011). *Sorrell* arose out of a process called "detailing," used by pharmaceutical manufacturers to promote their drugs to doctors. "Detailing" typically involves a scheduled visit to a doctor's office to persuade the doctor to prescribe a particular pharmaceutical. Detailers can be more effective if they know the prescription practices of particular doctors. To get that information, they turn to "data miners." *Data miners* are firms that analyze prescriber-identifying information and produce reports on prescriber behavior. They obtain the information by buying it from pharmacies which, as a matter of business routine and federal law, receive the information when processing prescriptions.

Vermont passed a law that prohibited pharmacies and certain other entities from selling records containing prescriber-identifying information or from allowing the use of such records for marketing purposes. The law also prohibited pharmaceutical marketers from using such information for marketing. The Supreme Court, in an opinion by Justice Kennedy, held that the law violated the First Amendment. The Court began by analyzing the nature of the regulation:

> On its face, Vermont's law enacts content- and speaker-based restrictions on the sale, disclosure, and use of prescriber-identifying information. The provision first forbids sale subject to exceptions based in large part on the content of a purchaser's speech. For example, those who wish to engage in certain "educational communications" may purchase the information. The measure then bars any disclosure when recipient speakers will use the information for

marketing. Finally, the provision's second sentence prohibits pharmaceutical manufacturers from using the information for marketing. The statute thus disfavors marketing, that is, speech with a particular content.

More than that, the statute disfavors specific speakers, namely pharmaceutical manufacturers. As a result of these content- and speaker-based rules, detailers cannot obtain prescriber-identifying information, even though the information may be purchased or acquired by other speakers with diverse purposes and viewpoints. Detailers are likewise barred from using the information for marketing, even though the information may be used by a wide range of other speakers. For example, it appears that Vermont could supply academic organizations with prescriber-identifying information to use in countering the messages of brand-name pharmaceutical manufacturers and in promoting the prescription of generic drugs. But [the law] leaves detailers no means of purchasing, acquiring, or using prescriber-identifying information. The law on its face burdens disfavored speech by disfavored speakers.

The Court then looked at "the record and . . . formal legislative findings." The legislative findings stated that detailers—in particular those who promote brand-name drugs—convey messages that "are often in conflict with the goals of the state." Justice Kennedy said that this language showed that the legislature "designed [the law] to target those speakers and their messages for disfavored treatment." Thus, "in its practical operation," Vermont's law went "even beyond mere content discrimination, to actual viewpoint discrimination."

The Court next considered the appropriate level of scrutiny:

[The Vermont law] is designed to impose a specific, content-based burden on protected expression. It follows that heightened judicial scrutiny is warranted. . . . The First Amendment requires heightened scrutiny whenever the government creates "a regulation of speech because of disagreement with the message it conveys." *Ward v. Rock Against Racism* (1989) [Chapter 6] . . . Commercial speech is no exception. *See Discovery Network*. . . .

In the ordinary case it is all but dispositive to conclude that a law is content-based and, in practice, viewpoint-discriminatory. The State argues that a different analysis applies here because, assuming [the statute] burdens speech at all, it at most burdens only commercial speech. As in previous cases, however, the outcome is the same whether a special commercial speech inquiry or a stricter form of judicial scrutiny is applied. For the same reason there is no need to determine whether all speech hampered by [the statute] is commercial, as our cases have used that term.

This brought the Court to a "commercial speech inquiry." The state asserted two kinds of justifications for the law. The first centered on medical privacy; the second, on "policy objectives—namely, improved public health and reduced healthcare costs." The Court found that neither justification withstood scrutiny.

As for the privacy interests, the Court was willing to assume "that, for many reasons, physicians have an interest in keeping their prescription decisions confidential." But the statute was not narrowly drawn to serve that interest. The Court said:

> Vermont made prescriber-identifying information available to an almost limitless audience. The explicit structure of the statute allows the information to be studied and used by all but a narrow class of disfavored speakers. Given the information's widespread availability and many permissible uses, the State's asserted interest in physician confidentiality does not justify the burden that [the statute] places on protected expression.

The Court then turned to the state's other argument—that the statute "advance[d] important public policy goals by lowering the costs of medical services and promoting public health." In the Court's reading of the legislative findings, the state's position was that "[i]f prescriber-identifying information were available for use by detailers, ... then detailing would be effective in promoting brand-name drugs that are more expensive and less safe than generic alternatives." The opinion continued:

> While Vermont's stated policy goals may be proper, [the statute] does not advance them in a permissible way. ... The State seeks to achieve its policy objectives through the indirect means of restraining certain speech by certain speakers—that is, by diminishing detailers' ability to influence prescription decisions. ... But the "fear that people would make bad decisions if given truthful information" cannot justify content-based burdens on speech. ...
>
> As Vermont's legislative findings acknowledge, the premise of [the law] is that the force of speech can justify the government's attempts to stifle it. Indeed the State defends the law by insisting that "pharmaceutical marketing has a strong influence on doctors' prescribing practices." Brief for Petitioners 49–50. This reasoning is incompatible with the First Amendment. In an attempt to reverse a disfavored trend in public opinion, a State could not ban campaigning with slogans, picketing with signs, or marching during the daytime. Likewise the State may not seek to remove a popular but disfavored product from the marketplace by prohibiting truthful, nonmisleading advertisements that contain impressive endorsements or catchy jingles. That the State finds expression too persuasive does not permit it to quiet the speech or to burden its messengers. ...
>
> Vermont may be displeased that detailers who use prescriber-identifying information are effective in promoting brand-name drugs. The State can express that view through its own speech. [Here the Court cited another provision of the Vermont law that established a prescription drug educational program.] But a State's failure to persuade does not allow it to hamstring the opposition. The State may not burden the speech of others in order to tilt public debate in a preferred direction. ...
>
> When it enacted § 4631(d), the Vermont Legislature found that the "marketplace for ideas on medicine safety and effectiveness is frequently one-sided in that brand-name companies invest in expensive pharmaceutical

marketing campaigns to doctors." "The goals of marketing programs," the legislature said, "are often in conflict with the goals of the state." The text of §4631(d), associated legislative findings, and the record developed in the District Court establish that Vermont enacted its law for this end. The State has burdened a form of protected expression that it found too persuasive. At the same time, the State has left unburdened those speakers whose messages are in accord with its own views. This the State cannot do.

Justice Breyer, joined by Justice Ginsburg and Justice Kagan, dissented. He wrote:

> The Vermont statute before us adversely affects expression in one, and only one, way. It deprives pharmaceutical and data-mining companies of data, collected pursuant to the government's regulatory mandate, that could help pharmaceutical companies create better sales messages. In my view, this effect on expression is inextricably related to a lawful governmental effort to regulate a commercial enterprise. The First Amendment does not require courts to apply a special "heightened" standard of review when reviewing such an effort. And, in any event, the statute meets the First Amendment standard this Court has previously applied when the government seeks to regulate commercial speech. For any or all of these reasons, the Court should uphold the statute as constitutional.

In *Sorrell*, the Court said that the Vermont law "imposes a burden based on the content of the speech and the identity of the speaker." This suggested that the law was subject to strict scrutiny. The dissent said that the effect of the law on expression was "inextricably related to a lawful governmental effort to regulate a commercial enterprise." This meant that "heightened scrutiny" was "out of place."

Is the Court's characterization of the Vermont law necessarily inconsistent with the dissent's? If both are permissible, how does a court decide which one should control?

––––––––

Note: A Return to Lochner?

1. Justice Rehnquist, dissenting in *Central Hudson Gas*, argued that in protecting commercial speech the Court had "return[ed] to the bygone era of *Lochner*." Is that a persuasive characterization? For example, assume that the state's goal is to encourage the conservation of energy. If the state acts through price controls, its legislation would be judged with extreme deference under modern due process cases. But does it follow that the same standard should be applied when the state, instead, bans advertising aimed at increasing the use of energy?

2. In *Sorrell*, the dissent by Justice Breyer echoed the concern voiced by Justice Rehnquist three decades earlier. Justice Breyer wrote:

> Regulatory programs necessarily draw distinctions on the basis of content. . . . Nor, in the context of a regulatory program, is it unusual for particular rules to be "speaker-based," affecting only a class of entities, namely, the

regulated firms. . . . [Given] the sheer quantity of regulatory initiatives that touch upon commercial messages, the Court's vision of its reviewing task threatens to return us to a happily bygone era when judges scrutinized legislation for its interference with economic liberty. History shows that the power was much abused and resulted in the constitutionalization of economic theories preferred by individual jurists. *See Lochner v. New York* (1905) (Holmes, J., dissenting) [Chapter 1 Note].

By inviting courts to scrutinize whether a State's legitimate regulatory interests can be achieved in less restrictive ways whenever they touch (even indirectly) upon commercial speech, today's majority risks repeating the mistakes of the past in a manner not anticipated by our precedents. *See Central Hudson* (Rehnquist, J., dissenting).

Is the analogy persuasive? Do decisions like *Sorrell* and *44 Liquormart* indicate that the Court has "return[ed] to the bygone era of *Lochner*"?

D. The End of Categorical Balancing

"There are," the Court famously said in *Chaplinsky v. New Hampshire* (1942) (Chapter 2), "certain well-defined and narrowly limited *classes* of speech, the prevention and punishment of which have never been thought to raise any Constitutional problem." Four decades later, in *Ferber v. New York* (1982), the Court followed *Chaplinsky*'s approach and recognized a new "category of material outside the protection of the First Amendment"—child pornography. More recently, however, the Court has emphatically rejected the argument that "new categories of unprotected speech may . . . be added to the list by a legislature that concludes certain speech is too harmful to be tolerated." This line of cases begins with *United States v. Stevens*, decided in 2010.

United States v. Stevens

559 U.S. 460 (2010)

CHIEF JUSTICE ROBERTS delivered the opinion of the Court.

Congress enacted 18 U.S.C. § 48 to criminalize the commercial creation, sale, or possession of certain depictions of animal cruelty. The statute does not address underlying acts harmful to animals, but only portrayals of such conduct. The question presented is whether the prohibition in the statute is consistent with the freedom of speech guaranteed by the First Amendment.

I

Section 48 establishes a criminal penalty of up to five years in prison for anyone who knowingly "creates, sells, or possesses a depiction of animal cruelty," if done "for commercial gain" in interstate or foreign commerce. § 48(a). A depiction of "animal cruelty" is defined as one "in which a living animal is intentionally maimed, mutilated, tortured, wounded, or killed," if that conduct violates federal or state law where "the creation, sale, or possession takes place." § 48(c)(1). In what is referred to as the "exceptions clause," the law exempts from prohibition any depiction "that has serious religious, political, scientific, educational, journalistic, historical, or artistic value." § 48(b).

The legislative background of § 48 focused primarily on the interstate market for "crush videos." According to the House Committee Report on the bill, such videos feature the intentional torture and killing of helpless animals, including cats, dogs, monkeys, mice, and hamsters. Crush videos often depict women slowly crushing animals to death "with their bare feet or while wearing high heeled shoes," sometimes while "talking to the animals in a kind of dominatrix patter" over "[t]he cries and squeals of the animals, obviously in great pain." Apparently these depictions "appeal to persons with a very specific sexual fetish who find them sexually arousing or otherwise exciting." The acts depicted in crush videos are typically prohibited by the animal cruelty laws enacted by all 50 States and the District of Columbia. But crush videos rarely disclose the participants' identities, inhibiting prosecution of the underlying conduct.

This case, however, involves an application of § 48 to depictions of animal fighting. Dogfighting, for example, is unlawful in all 50 States and the District of Columbia, and has been restricted by federal law since 1976. Respondent Robert J. Stevens ran a business, "Dogs of Velvet and Steel," and an associated Web site, through which he sold videos of pit bulls engaging in dogfights and attacking other animals. Among these videos were Japan Pit Fights and Pick-A-Winna: A Pit Bull Documentary, which include contemporary footage of dogfights in Japan (where such conduct is allegedly legal) as well as footage of American dogfights from the 1960's and 1970's. A third video, Catch Dogs and Country Living, depicts the use of pit bulls to hunt wild boar, as well as a "gruesome" scene of a pit bull attacking a domestic farm pig. On the basis of these videos, Stevens was indicted on three counts of violating § 48.

[The jury convicted Stevens on all counts, but the en banc Third Circuit, over a three-judge dissent, vacated the conviction, holding that § 48 is facially unconstitutional. The Supreme Court granted the Government's petition for certiorari.]

II

The Government's primary submission is that § 48 necessarily complies with the Constitution because the banned depictions of animal cruelty, as a class, are categorically unprotected by the First Amendment. We disagree.

The First Amendment provides that "Congress shall make no law . . . abridging the freedom of speech." "[A]s a general matter, the First Amendment means that government has no power to restrict expression because of its message, its ideas, its subject matter, or its content." *Ashcroft v. American Civil Liberties Union* (2002) [Chapter 2 Note]. Section 48 explicitly regulates expression based on content: The statute restricts "visual [and] auditory depiction[s]," such as photographs, videos, or sound recordings, depending on whether they depict conduct in which a living animal is intentionally harmed. As such, § 48 is "'presumptively invalid,' and the Government bears the burden to rebut that presumption." *United States v. Playboy Entertainment Group, Inc.*, 529 U.S. 803, 817 (2000) (quoting *R.A.V. v. St. Paul* (1992) [Chapter 15]).

"From 1791 to the present," however, the First Amendment has "permitted restrictions upon the content of speech in a few limited areas," and has never "include[d] a freedom to disregard these traditional limitations." *R.A.V.* These "historic and traditional categories long familiar to the bar," *Simon & Schuster, Inc. v. Members of N.Y. State Crime Victims Bd.* (1991) [Chapter 7 Note] (Kennedy, J., concurring in judgment)—including obscenity, *Roth v. United States* (1957) [Chapter 2], defamation, *Beauharnais v. Illinois* (1952) [Chapter 2 Note], fraud, *Virginia Bd. of Pharmacy v. Virginia Citizens Consumer Council, Inc.* (1976) [*supra* this chapter], incitement, *Brandenburg v. Ohio* (1969) [Chapter 1], and speech integral to criminal conduct, *Giboney v. Empire Storage & Ice Co.* (1949)—are "well-defined and narrowly limited classes of speech, the prevention and punishment of which have never been thought to raise any Constitutional problem." *Chaplinsky v. New Hampshire* (1942) [Chapter 2].

The Government argues that "depictions of animal cruelty" should be added to the list. It contends that depictions of "illegal acts of animal cruelty" that are "made, sold, or possessed for commercial gain" necessarily "lack expressive value," and may accordingly "be regulated as *unprotected* speech." Brief for United States 10 (emphasis added). The claim is not just that Congress may regulate depictions of animal cruelty subject to the First Amendment, but that these depictions are outside the reach of that Amendment altogether—that they fall into a "First Amendment Free Zone."

As the Government notes, the prohibition of animal cruelty itself has a long history in American law, starting with the early settlement of the Colonies. But we are unaware of any similar tradition excluding *depictions* of animal cruelty from "the freedom of speech" codified in the First Amendment, and the Government points us to none.

The Government contends that "historical evidence" about the reach of the First Amendment is not "a necessary prerequisite for regulation today," and that categories of speech may be exempted from the First Amendment's protection without any long-settled tradition of subjecting that speech to regulation. Instead, the Government points to Congress's "legislative judgment that . . . depictions of animals being intentionally tortured and killed [are] of such minimal redeeming value as to render [them] unworthy of First Amendment protection," and asks the Court to uphold the ban on the same basis. The Government thus proposes that a claim of categorical exclusion should be considered under a simple balancing test: "Whether a given category of speech enjoys First Amendment protection depends upon a categorical balancing of the value of the speech against its societal costs." Brief for United States 8.

As a free-floating test for First Amendment coverage, that sentence is startling and dangerous. The First Amendment's guarantee of free speech does not extend only to categories of speech that survive an ad hoc balancing of relative social costs and benefits. The First Amendment itself reflects a judgment by the American people that the benefits of its restrictions on the Government outweigh the costs. Our Constitution forecloses any attempt to revise that judgment simply on the basis that some speech is not worth it. The Constitution is not a document "prescribing limits, and declaring that those limits may be passed at pleasure." *Marbury v. Madison*, 1 Cranch 137, 178 (1803).

To be fair to the Government, its view did not emerge from a vacuum. As the Government correctly notes, this Court has often *described* historically unprotected categories of speech as being "'of such slight social value as a step to truth that any benefit that may be derived from them is clearly outweighed by the social interest in order and morality.'" *R.A.V.* (quoting *Chaplinsky*). In *New York v. Ferber* (1982) [*supra* this chapter], we noted that within these categories of unprotected speech, "the evil to be restricted so overwhelmingly outweighs the expressive interests, if any, at stake, that no process of case-by-case adjudication is required," because "the balance of competing interests is clearly struck." The Government derives its proposed test from these descriptions in our precedents.

But such descriptions are just that—descriptive. They do not set forth a test that may be applied as a general matter to permit the Government to imprison any speaker so long as his speech is deemed valueless or unnecessary, or so long as an ad hoc calculus of costs and benefits tilts in a statute's favor.

When we have identified categories of speech as fully outside the protection of the First Amendment, it has not been on the basis of a simple cost-benefit analysis. In *Ferber*, for example, we classified child pornography as such a category. We noted that the State of New York had a compelling interest in protecting children from abuse, and that the value of using children in these works (as opposed to simulated conduct or adult actors) was *de minimis*. But our decision did not rest on this "balance of competing interests" alone. We made clear that *Ferber* presented a special case: The market for child pornography was "intrinsically related" to the underlying abuse, and was therefore "an integral part of the production of such materials, an activity illegal throughout the Nation." As we noted, "'[i]t rarely has been suggested that the constitutional freedom for speech and press extends its immunity to speech or writing used as an integral part of conduct in violation of a valid criminal statute.'" *Ferber* (quoting *Giboney*). *Ferber* thus grounded its analysis in a previously recognized, long-established category of unprotected speech, and our subsequent decisions have shared this understanding. *See Osborne v. Ohio* (1990) (describing *Ferber* as finding "persuasive" the argument that the advertising and sale of child pornography was "an integral part" of its unlawful production); *Ashcroft v. Free Speech Coalition* (noting that distribution and sale "were intrinsically related to the sexual abuse of children," giving the speech at issue "a proximate link to the crime from which it came").

Our decisions in *Ferber* and other cases cannot be taken as establishing a freewheeling authority to declare new categories of speech outside the scope of the First Amendment. Maybe there are some categories of speech that have been historically unprotected, but have not yet been specifically identified or discussed as such in our case law. But if so, there is no evidence that "depictions of animal cruelty" is among them. We need not foreclose the future recognition of such additional categories to reject the Government's highly manipulable balancing test as a means of identifying them.

III

[The Court held that § 48 was constitutionally overbroad. It thus affirmed the Third Circuit's judgment vacating the defendant's conviction. See Chapter 4 for a discussion of the overbreadth doctrine.]

JUSTICE ALITO, dissenting.

[Justice Alito's dissent rested on two propositions. First, he argued that "§ 48 may reasonably be construed not to reach almost all, if not all, of the depictions that the Court finds constitutionally protected"—notably, hunting videos. Second, he asserted that "§ 48 may validly be applied to at least two broad real-world categories of expression covered by the statute: crush videos and dogfighting videos." Here is part of his opinion addressing the second proposition.]

Crush videos present a highly unusual free speech issue because they are so closely linked with violent criminal conduct. The videos record the commission of violent criminal acts, and it appears that these crimes are committed for the sole purpose of creating the videos. In addition, . . . Congress was presented with compelling evidence that the only way of preventing these crimes was to target the sale of the videos. Under these circumstances, I cannot believe that the First Amendment commands Congress to step aside and allow the underlying crimes to continue.

The most relevant of our prior decisions is *Ferber*, which concerned child pornography. The Court there held that child pornography is not protected speech, and I believe that *Ferber*'s reasoning dictates a similar conclusion here.

In *Ferber*, an important factor—I would say the most important factor—was that child pornography involves the commission of a crime that inflicts severe personal injury to the "children who are made to engage in sexual conduct for commercial purposes." The *Ferber* Court repeatedly described the production of child pornography as child "abuse," "molestation," or "exploitation." As later noted in *Ashcroft v. Free Speech Coalition* (2002), in *Ferber* "[t]he production of the work, not its content, was the target of the statute."

Second, *Ferber* emphasized the fact that these underlying crimes could not be effectively combated without targeting the distribution of child pornography. . . .

Third, the *Ferber* Court noted that the value of child pornography "is exceedingly modest, if not *de minimis*," and that any such value was "overwhelmingly outweigh[ed]" by "the evil to be restricted." . . .

All three of these characteristics are shared by § 48, as applied to crush videos. First, the conduct depicted in crush videos is criminal in every State and the District of Columbia. Thus, any crush video made in this country records the actual commission of a criminal act that inflicts severe physical injury and excruciating pain and ultimately results in death. Those who record the underlying criminal acts are likely to be criminally culpable, either as aiders and abettors or conspirators. And in the tight and secretive market for these videos, some who sell the videos or possess them with the intent to make a profit may be similarly culpable. To the extent that § 48 reaches such persons, it surely does not violate the First Amendment.

Second, the criminal acts shown in crush videos cannot be prevented without targeting the conduct prohibited by § 48 — the creation, sale, and possession for sale of depictions of animal torture with the intention of realizing a commercial profit. The evidence presented to Congress posed a stark choice: Either ban the commercial exploitation of crush videos or tolerate a continuation of the criminal acts that they record. Faced with this evidence, Congress reasonably chose to target the lucrative crush video market.

Finally, the harm caused by the underlying crimes vastly outweighs any minimal value that the depictions might conceivably be thought to possess. Section 48 reaches only the actual recording of acts of animal torture; the statute does not apply to verbal descriptions or to simulations. And, unlike the child pornography statute in *Ferber* or its federal counterpart, § 48(b) provides an exception for depictions having any "serious religious, political, scientific, educational, journalistic, historical, or artistic value."

It must be acknowledged that § 48 differs from a child pornography law in an important respect: preventing the abuse of children is certainly much more important than preventing the torture of the animals used in crush videos. . . . But while protecting children is unquestionably *more* important than protecting animals, the Government also has a compelling interest in preventing the torture depicted in crush videos.

The animals used in crush videos are living creatures that experience excruciating pain. Our society has long banned such cruelty, which is illegal throughout the country. In *Ferber*, the Court noted that "virtually all of the States and the United States have passed legislation proscribing the production of or otherwise combating 'child pornography,'" and the Court declined to "second-guess [that] legislative judgment." Here, likewise, the Court of Appeals erred in second-guessing the legislative judgment about the importance of preventing cruelty to animals.

Section 48's ban on trafficking in crush videos also helps to enforce the criminal laws and to ensure that criminals do not profit from their crimes. . . . In short, *Ferber* is the case that sheds the most light on the constitutionality of Congress' effort to halt the production of crush videos. Applying the principles set forth in *Ferber*, I would hold that crush videos are not protected by the First Amendment.

Application of the *Ferber* framework also supports the constitutionality of § 48 as applied to depictions of brutal animal fights. [Justice Alito's analysis of the statute's application to animal fights was very similar to his discussion of the statute as applied to crush videos.]

Note: The Implications of Stevens

1. In Part II of his opinion, Chief Justice Roberts lists the "historic and traditional" categories of speech where the First Amendment permits restrictions on content. (All of the cases that he cites as exemplifying the categories are set forth in this and the preceding chapters, either as principal cases or as the subject of a Note.) Are there any categories that you would expect to find on the list but that are not there? Are you surprised by any of the cases cited by the Chief Justice?

2. The Chief Justice says that *Chaplinsky*'s oft-quoted description of "historically unprotected categories of speech" is "just that"—a description. And the Court emphatically repudiates the Government's argument that *Chaplinsky* and its progeny provide "a test that may be applied as a general matter" to identify new categories of unprotected speech. Based on pre-*Stevens* precedents, is the Court persuasive in saying that the *Chaplinsky* language did no more than describe the Court's holdings?

3. The Court rejects the Government's plea to recognize "depictions of animal cruelty" as a new category of unprotected speech. It does not address Justice Alito's arguments that crush videos and depictions of brutal animal fights can be proscribed without violating the First Amendment. Is Justice Alito persuasive in saying that the reasoning in *Ferber* "dictates a similar conclusion" with respect to these materials?

Brown v. Entertainment Merchants Association
564 U.S. 786 (2011)

JUSTICE SCALIA delivered the opinion of the Court.

We consider whether a California law imposing restrictions on violent video games comports with the First Amendment.

I

California Assembly Bill 1179 (2005) (Act), prohibits the sale or rental of "violent video games" to minors, and requires their packaging to be labeled "18." The Act covers games "in which the range of options available to a player includes killing, maiming, dismembering, or sexually assaulting an image of a human being, if those acts are depicted" in a manner that "[a] reasonable person, considering the game as a whole, would find appeals to a deviant or morbid interest of minors," that is "patently offensive to prevailing standards in the community as to what is suitable for minors," and that "causes the game, as a whole, to lack serious literary, artistic, political, or scientific value for minors." Violation of the Act is punishable by a civil fine of up to $1,000.

Respondents, representing the video-game and software industries, brought a preenforcement challenge to the Act in the United States District Court for the Northern District of California. That court concluded that the Act violated the First Amendment and permanently enjoined its enforcement. The Court of Appeals affirmed, and we granted certiorari.

II

California correctly acknowledges that video games qualify for First Amendment protection. The Free Speech Clause exists principally to protect discourse on public matters, but we have long recognized that it is difficult to distinguish politics from entertainment, and dangerous to try. "Everyone is familiar with instances of propaganda through fiction. What is one man's amusement, teaches another's doctrine." *Winters v. New York* (1948) [Chapter 2 Note]. Like the protected books, plays, and movies that preceded them, video games communicate ideas—and even social messages—through many familiar literary devices (such as characters, dialogue, plot, and music) and through features distinctive to the medium (such as the player's interaction with the virtual world). That suffices to confer First Amendment protection. . . . And whatever the challenges of applying the Constitution to ever-advancing technology, "the basic principles of freedom of speech and the press, like the First Amendment's command, do not vary" when a new and different medium for communication appears. *Joseph Burstyn, Inc. v. Wilson*, 343 U.S. 495 (1952).

The most basic of those principles is this: "[A]s a general matter, . . . government has no power to restrict expression because of its message, its ideas, its subject matter, or its content." *Ashcroft v. American Civil Liberties Union* (2002) [Chapter 2 Note]. There are of course exceptions. "'From 1791 to the present,' . . . the First Amendment has 'permitted restrictions upon the content of speech in a few limited areas,' and has never 'include[d] a freedom to disregard these traditional limitations.'" *United States v. Stevens* (2010) [*supra* this chapter]. These limited areas—such as obscenity, *Roth v. United States* (1957) [Chapter 2], incitement, *Brandenburg v. Ohio* (1969) [Chapter 1], and fighting words, *Chaplinsky v. New Hampshire* (1942) [Chapter 2]— represent "well-defined and narrowly limited classes of speech, the prevention and punishment of which have never been thought to raise any Constitutional problem."

Last Term, in *Stevens*, we held that new categories of unprotected speech may not be added to the list by a legislature that concludes certain speech is too harmful to be tolerated. *Stevens* concerned a federal statute purporting to criminalize the creation, sale, or possession of certain depictions of animal cruelty. . . . We held [the] statute to be an impermissible content-based restriction on speech. There was no American tradition of forbidding the *depiction of* animal cruelty—though States have long had laws against *committing* it.

The Government argued in *Stevens* that lack of a historical warrant did not matter; that it could create new categories of unprotected speech by applying a "simple balancing test" that weighs the value of a particular category of speech against its social costs and then punishes that category of speech if it fails the test. We emphatically rejected that "startling and dangerous" proposition. . . .

That holding controls this case. As in *Stevens*, California has tried to make violent-speech regulation look like obscenity regulation by appending a saving clause required for the latter. That does not suffice. Our cases have been clear that the obscenity exception to the First Amendment does not cover whatever a legislature finds shocking, but only depictions of "sexual conduct," *Miller v. California* (1973) [Chapter 2]. *See also Cohen v. California* (1971) [*supra* this chapter]; *Roth v. United States* (1957) [Chapter 2].

Stevens was not the first time we have encountered and rejected a State's attempt to shoehorn speech about violence into obscenity. In *Winters*, we considered a New York criminal statute "forbid[ding] the massing of stories of bloodshed and lust in such a way as to incite to crime against the person." The New York Court of Appeals upheld the provision as a law against obscenity. "[T]here can be no more precise test of written indecency or obscenity," it said, "than the continuing and changeable experience of the community as to what types of books are likely to bring about the corruption of public morals or other analogous injury to the public order." That is of course the same expansive view of governmental power to abridge the freedom of speech based on interest-balancing that we rejected in *Stevens*. Our opinion in *Winters*, which concluded that the New York statute failed a heightened vagueness standard applicable to restrictions upon speech entitled to First Amendment protection, made clear that violence is not part of the obscenity that the Constitution permits to be regulated. The speech reached by the statute contained "no indecency or obscenity in any sense heretofore known to the law."

Because speech about violence is not obscene, it is of no consequence that California's statute mimics the New York statute regulating obscenity-for-minors that we upheld in *Ginsberg v. New York,* 390 U.S. 629 (1968). That case approved a prohibition on the sale to minors of *sexual* material that would be obscene from the perspective of a child. We held that the legislature could "adjus[t] the definition of obscenity 'to social realities by permitting the appeal of this type of material to be assessed in terms of the sexual interests . . .' of . . . minors." And because "obscenity is not protected expression," the New York statute could be sustained so long as the legislature's judgment that the proscribed materials were harmful to children "was not irrational."

The California Act is something else entirely. It does not adjust the boundaries of an existing category of unprotected speech to ensure that a definition designed for adults is not uncritically applied to children. California does not argue that it is empowered to prohibit selling offensively violent works *to adults*—and it is wise not to, since that is but a hair's breadth from the argument rejected in *Stevens*. Instead, it wishes to create a wholly new category of content-based regulation that is permissible only for speech directed at children.

That is unprecedented and mistaken. "[M]inors are entitled to a significant measure of First Amendment protection, and only in relatively narrow and well-defined circumstances may government bar public dissemination of protected materials to them." *Erznoznik v. Jacksonville* (1975) [Note *supra* this chapter]. No doubt a State possesses legitimate power to protect children from harm, *Ginsberg; Prince v. Massachusetts*, 321 U.S. 158, 165 (1944), but that does not include a free-floating power to restrict the ideas to which children may be exposed. "Speech that is neither obscene as to youths nor subject to some other legitimate proscription cannot be suppressed solely to protect the young from ideas or images that a legislative body thinks unsuitable for them." *Erznoznik*.

California's argument would fare better if there were a longstanding tradition in this country of specially restricting children's access to depictions of violence, but there is none. Certainly the *books* we give children to read—or read to them when they are younger—contain no shortage of gore. Grimm's Fairy Tales, for example, are grim indeed. As her just deserts for trying to poison Snow White, the wicked queen is made to dance in red hot slippers "till she fell dead on the floor, a sad example of envy and jealousy." Cinderella's evil stepsisters have their eyes pecked out by doves. And Hansel and Gretel (children!) kill their captor by baking her in an oven.

High-school reading lists are full of similar fare. Homer's Odysseus blinds Polyphemus the Cyclops by grinding out his eye with a heated stake. . . . In the *Inferno*, Dante and Virgil watch corrupt politicians struggle to stay submerged beneath a lake of boiling pitch, lest they be skewered by devils above the surface. And Golding's *Lord of the Flies* recounts how a schoolboy called Piggy is savagely murdered *by other children* while marooned on an island.[4]

This is not to say that minors' consumption of violent entertainment has never encountered resistance. In the 1800's, dime novels depicting crime and "penny dreadfuls" (named for their price and content) were blamed in some quarters for juvenile delinquency. When motion pictures came along, they became the villains instead. "The days when the police looked upon dime novels as the most dangerous of textbooks in the school for crime are drawing to a close . . . . They say that the moving picture machine . . . tends even more than did the dime novel to turn the thoughts of the easily influenced to paths which sometimes lead to prison." *Moving Pictures as Helps to Crime*, N.Y. TIMES, Feb. 21, 1909. For a time, our Court did permit broad censorship of movies because of their capacity to be "used for evil," see *Mutual Film Corp. v. Industrial Comm'n of Ohio*, 236 U.S. 230, 242 (1915), but we eventually reversed course, *Joseph Burstyn, Inc.*, 343 U.S. at 502; *see also Erznoznik* (invalidating a drive-in movies restriction designed to protect children). Radio dramas were next, and then came comic books. Many in the late 1940's and early 1950's blamed comic books for fostering a "preoccupation with violence and horror" among the young, leading to a rising juvenile crime rate. But efforts to convince Congress to restrict comic books failed.[5] And, of course, after comic books came television and music lyrics.

California claims that video games present special problems because they are "interactive," in that the player participates in the violent action on screen and determines its outcome. . . . [But as] Judge Posner has observed, all literature is interactive. "[T]he better it is, the more interactive. Literature when it is successful draws the reader into the story, makes him identify with the characters, invites him to judge them and quarrel with them, to experience their joys and sufferings as the reader's own."

---

4. Justice Alito accuses us of pronouncing that playing violent video games "is not different in 'kind'" from reading violent literature. Well of course it is different in kind, but not in a way that causes the provision and viewing of violent video games, unlike the provision and reading of books, not to be expressive activity and hence not to enjoy First Amendment protection. Reading Dante is unquestionably more cultured and intellectually edifying than playing Mortal Kombat. But these cultural and intellectual differences are not *constitutional* ones. Crudely violent video games, tawdry TV shows, and cheap novels and magazines are no less forms of speech than *The Divine Comedy*, and restrictions upon them must survive strict scrutiny—a question to which we devote our attention in Part III, *infra*. Even if we can see in them "nothing of any possible value to society . . . , they are as much entitled to the protection of free speech as the best of literature." *Winters*.

5. The crusade against comic books was led by a psychiatrist, Frederic Wertham, who told the Senate Judiciary Committee that "as long as the crime comic books industry exists in its present forms there are no secure homes." Wertham's objections extended even to Superman comics, which he described as "particularly injurious to the ethical development of children." Wertham's crusade did convince the New York Legislature to pass a ban on the sale of certain comic books to minors, but it was vetoed by Governor Thomas Dewey on the ground that it was unconstitutional given our opinion in *Winters*.

Justice Alito has done considerable independent research to identify video games in which "the violence is astounding." . . . Justice Alito recounts all these disgusting video games in order to disgust us — but disgust is not a valid basis for restricting expression. And the same is true of Justice Alito's description of those video games he has discovered that have a racial or ethnic motive for their violence — "'ethnic cleansing' [of] . . . African Americans, Latinos, or Jews." To what end does he relate this? Does it somehow increase the "aggressiveness" that California wishes to suppress? Who knows? But it does arouse the reader's ire, and the reader's desire to put an end to this horrible message. Thus, ironically, Justice Alito's argument highlights the precise danger posed by the California Act: that the *ideas* expressed by speech — whether it be violence, or gore, or racism — and not its objective effects, may be the real reason for governmental proscription.

III

Because the Act imposes a restriction on the content of protected speech, it is invalid unless California can demonstrate that it passes strict scrutiny — that is, unless it is justified by a compelling government interest and is narrowly drawn to serve that interest. *R.A.V. v. St. Paul* (1992) [Chapter 15]. The State must specifically identify an "actual problem" in need of solving, and the curtailment of free speech must be actually necessary to the solution, see *R.A.V.* That is a demanding standard. "It is rare that a regulation restricting speech because of its content will ever be permissible."

California cannot meet that standard. At the outset, it acknowledges that it cannot show a direct causal link between violent video games and harm to minors. . . . California relies primarily on [studies that] purport to show a connection between exposure to violent video games and harmful effects on children. These studies have been rejected by every court to consider them, and with good reason: They do not prove that violent video games cause minors to act aggressively (which would at least be a beginning). Instead, "[n]early all of the research is based on correlation, not evidence of causation, and most of the studies suffer from significant, admitted flaws in methodology." . . .

[The remainder of the Court's analysis is omitted. The Court concluded:]

California's effort to regulate violent video games is the latest episode in a long series of failed attempts to censor violent entertainment for minors. . . . We have no business passing judgment on the view of the California Legislature that violent video games (or, for that matter, any other forms of speech) corrupt the young or harm their moral development. Our task is only to say whether or not such works constitute a "well-defined and narrowly limited clas[s] of speech, the prevention and punishment of which have never been thought to raise any Constitutional problem," *Chaplinsky* (the answer plainly is no); and if not, whether the regulation of such works is justified by that high degree of necessity we have described as a compelling state interest (it is not). Even where the protection of children is the object, the constitutional limits on governmental action apply.

California's legislation straddles the fence between (1) addressing a serious social problem and (2) helping concerned parents control their children. Both ends are legitimate, but when they affect First Amendment rights they must be pursued by means that are neither seriously underinclusive nor seriously overinclusive. As a means of protecting children from portrayals of violence, the legislation is seriously underinclusive, [both] because it excludes portrayals other than video games [and also] because it permits a parental or avuncular veto. And as a means of assisting concerned parents it is seriously overinclusive because it abridges the First Amendment rights of young people whose parents (and aunts and uncles) think violent video games are a harmless pastime. And the overbreadth in achieving one goal is not cured by the underbreadth in achieving the other. Legislation such as this, which is neither fish nor fowl, cannot survive strict scrutiny.

We affirm the judgment below.

JUSTICE ALITO, with whom THE CHIEF JUSTICE joins, concurring in the judgment.

[Justice Alito agreed with the video game industry that the California law was impermissibly vague and did not provide the fair notice that the Constitution requires. He therefore saw "no need to reach the broader First Amendment issues addressed by the Court." However, his opinion went on to discuss some of his reasons for "questioning the wisdom of the Court's approach." These included the Court's use of the *Stevens* decision and the special characteristics of video games.]

A

The Court is wrong in saying that the holding in *United States v. Stevens* "controls this case." First, the statute in *Stevens* differed sharply from the statute at issue here. *Stevens* struck down a law that broadly prohibited *any person* from creating, selling, or possessing depictions of animal cruelty for commercial gain. The California law involved here, by contrast, is limited to the sale or rental of violent video games *to minors*. The California law imposes no restriction on the creation of violent video games, or on the possession of such games by anyone, whether above or below the age of 18. The California law does not regulate the sale or rental of violent games by adults. And the California law does not prevent parents and certain other close relatives from buying or renting violent games for their children or other young relatives if they see fit.

Second, *Stevens* does not support the proposition that a law like the one at issue must satisfy strict scrutiny. The portion of *Stevens* on which the Court relies rejected the Government's contention that depictions of animal cruelty were categorically outside the range of *any* First Amendment protection. Going well beyond *Stevens*, the Court now holds that any law that attempts to prevent minors from purchasing violent video games must satisfy strict scrutiny instead of the more lenient standard applied in *Ginsberg v. New York* (1968), our most closely related precedent. As a result of today's decision, a State may prohibit the sale to minors of what *Ginsberg* described as "girlie magazines," but a State must surmount a formidable (and perhaps insurmountable) obstacle if it wishes to prevent children from purchasing the most violent and depraved video games imaginable.

Third, *Stevens* expressly left open the possibility that a more narrowly drawn statute targeting depictions of animal cruelty might be compatible with the First Amendment. In this case, the Court's sweeping opinion will likely be read by many, both inside and outside the video-game industry, as suggesting that no regulation of minors' access to violent video games is allowed—at least without supporting evidence that may not be realistically obtainable given the nature of the phenomenon in question. . . .

C

[The] Court is far too quick to dismiss the possibility that the experience of playing video games (and the effects on minors of playing violent video games) may be very different from anything that we have seen before. . . .

Today's most advanced video games create realistic alternative worlds in which millions of players immerse themselves for hours on end. These games feature visual imagery and sounds that are strikingly realistic, and in the near future video-game graphics may be virtually indistinguishable from actual video footage. . . . It is also forecast that video games will soon provide sensory feedback. . . . Persons who play video games also have an unprecedented ability to participate in the events that take place in the virtual worlds that these games create. . . .

These present-day and emerging characteristics of video games must be considered together with characteristics of the violent games that have already been marketed.

In some of these games, the violence is astounding. . . . It also appears that there is no antisocial theme too base for some in the video-game industry to exploit. There are games in which a player can take on the identity and reenact the killings carried out by the perpetrators of the murders at Columbine High School and Virginia Tech. The objective of one game is to rape a mother and her daughters; in another, the goal is to rape Native American women. There is a game in which players engage in "ethnic cleansing" and can choose to gun down African-Americans, Latinos, or Jews. . . .

If the technological characteristics of the sophisticated games that are likely to be available in the near future are combined with the characteristics of the most violent games already marketed, the result will be games that allow troubled teens to experience in an extraordinarily personal and vivid way what it would be like to carry out unspeakable acts of violence. . . .

When all of the characteristics of video games are taken into account, there is certainly a reasonable basis for thinking that the experience of playing a video game may be quite different from the experience of reading a book, listening to a radio broadcast, or viewing a movie. And if this is so, then for at least some minors, the effects of playing violent video games may also be quite different. The Court acts prematurely in dismissing this possibility out of hand. . . .

JUSTICE THOMAS, dissenting.

The Court's decision today does not comport with the original public understanding of the First Amendment. . . . The practices and beliefs of the founding generation establish that "the freedom of speech," as originally understood, does not include a right to speak to minors (or a right of minors to access speech) without going through the minors' parents or guardians. I would hold that the law at issue is not facially unconstitutional under the First Amendment, and reverse and remand for further proceedings. . . .

[Justice Thomas went on to support his conclusion with a detailed historical analysis.]

JUSTICE BREYER, dissenting.

. . . Applying traditional First Amendment analysis, I would uphold the [California] statute as constitutional on its face and would consequently reject the industries' facial challenge. . . .

I

A facial challenge to this statute based on the First Amendment can succeed only if "a substantial number of its applications are unconstitutional, judged in relation to the statute's plainly legitimate sweep." *United States v. Stevens* (2010). . . . I shall focus here upon an area within which I believe the State can legitimately apply its statute, namely sales to minors under the age of 17 (the age cutoff used by the industry's own ratings system), of highly realistic violent video games, which a reasonable game maker would know meet the Act's criteria. That area lies at the heart of the statute. I shall assume that the number of instances in which the State will enforce the statute within that area is comparatively large, and that the number outside that area (for example, sales to 17-year-olds) is comparatively small. And the activity the statute regulates combines speech with action (a virtual form of target practice). . . .

The majority's claim that the California statute, if upheld, would create a "new categor[y] of unprotected speech" is overstated. No one here argues that depictions of violence, even extreme violence, *automatically* fall outside the First Amendment's protective scope as, for example, do obscenity and depictions of child pornography. We properly speak of *categories* of expression that lack protection when, like "child pornography," the category is broad, when it applies automatically, and when the State can prohibit everyone, including adults, from obtaining access to the material within it. But where, as here, careful analysis must precede a narrower judicial conclusion (say, denying protection to a shout of "fire" in a crowded theater, or to an effort to teach a terrorist group how to peacefully petition the United Nations), we do not normally describe the result as creating a "new category of unprotected speech." *See Schenck v. United States* (1919) [Chapter 1]. . . .

II

In my view, California's statute provides "fair notice of what is prohibited," and consequently it is not impermissibly vague. [Discussion omitted.]

III

. . . Like the majority, I believe that the California law must be "narrowly tailored" to further a "compelling interest," without there being a "less restrictive" alternative that would be "at least as effective." I would not apply this strict tandard "mechanically." Rather, in applying it, I would evaluate the degree to which the statute injures speech-related interests, the nature of the potentially-justifying "compelling interests," the degree to which the statute furthers that interest, the nature and effectiveness of possible alternatives, and, in light of this evaluation, whether, overall, "the statute works speech-related harm . . . out of proportion to the benefits that the statute seeks to provide." . . .

A

California's law imposes no more than a modest restriction on expression. The statute prevents no one from playing a video game, it prevents no adult from buying a video game, and it prevents no child or adolescent from obtaining a game provided a parent is willing to help. All it prevents is a child or adolescent from buying, without a parent's assistance, a gruesomely violent video game of a kind that the industry *itself* tells us it wants to keep out of the hands of those under the age of 17. . . .

B

The interest that California advances in support of the statute is compelling. As this Court has previously described that interest, it consists of both (1) the "basic" parental claim "to authority in their own household to direct the rearing of their children," which makes it proper to enact "laws designed to aid discharge of [parental] responsibility," and (2) the State's "independent interest in the well-being of its youth." And where these interests work in tandem, it is not fatally "underinclusive" for a State to advance its interests in protecting children against the special harms present in an interactive video game medium through a default rule that still allows parents to provide their children with what their parents wish.

Both interests are present here. . . . [And] there is considerable evidence that California's statute significantly furthers [the State's compelling interest in "protecting the physical and psychological well-being of minors."] . . . .

California argues that . . . extremely violent games can harm children by rewarding them for being violently aggressive in play, and thereby often teaching them to be violently aggressive in life. And video games can cause more harm in this respect than can typically passive media, such as books or films or television programs.

There are many scientific studies that support California's views. Social scientists, for example, have found *causal* evidence that playing these games results in harm. Longitudinal studies, which measure changes over time, have found that increased exposure to violent video games causes an increase in aggression over the same period. . . .

Experts debate the conclusions of all these studies. . . . I, like most judges, lack the social science expertise to say definitively who is right. But associations of public health professionals who do possess that expertise have reviewed many of these studies and found a significant risk that violent video games, when compared with more passive media, are particularly likely to cause children harm. . . .

Unlike the majority, I would find sufficient grounds in these studies and expert opinions for this Court to defer to an elected legislature's conclusion that the video games in question are particularly likely to harm children. This Court has always thought it owed an elected legislature some degree of deference in respect to legislative facts of this kind, particularly when they involve technical matters that are beyond our competence, and even in First Amendment cases. . . . The majority, in reaching its own, opposite conclusion about the validity of the relevant studies, grants the legislature no deference at all.

C

I can find no "less restrictive" alternative to California's law that would be "at least as effective." The majority points to a voluntary alternative: The industry tries to prevent those under 17 from buying extremely violent games by labeling those games with an "M" (Mature) and encouraging retailers to restrict their sales to those 17 and older. But this voluntary system has serious enforcement gaps. . . .

IV

The upshot is that California's statute, as applied to its heartland of applications (i.e., buyers under 17; extremely violent, realistic video games), imposes a restriction on speech that is modest at most. That restriction is justified by a compelling interest (supplementing parents' efforts to prevent their children from purchasing potentially harmful violent, interactive material). And there is no equally effective, less restrictive alternative. California's statute is consequently constitutional on its face — though litigants remain free to challenge the statute as applied in particular instances, including any effort by the State to apply it to minors aged 17.

I add that the majority's different conclusion creates a serious anomaly in First Amendment law. *Ginsberg* makes clear that a State can prohibit the sale to minors of depictions of nudity; today the Court makes clear that a State cannot prohibit the sale to minors of the most violent interactive video games. But what sense does it make to forbid selling to a 13-year-old boy a magazine with an image of a nude woman, while protecting a sale to that 13-year-old of an interactive video game in which he actively, but virtually, binds and gags the woman, then tortures and kills her? What kind of First Amendment would permit the government to protect children by restricting sales of that extremely violent video game *only* when the woman — bound, gagged, tortured, and killed — is also topless?

This anomaly is not compelled by the First Amendment. It disappears once one recognizes that extreme violence, where interactive, and *without literary, artistic, or similar justification*, can prove at least as, if not more, harmful to children as photographs of nudity. And the record here is more than adequate to support such a view. That is why I believe that *Ginsberg* controls the outcome here *a fortiori*. And it is why I believe California's law is constitutional on its face. . . .

For these reasons, I respectfully dissent.

[Justice Breyer supplemented his opinion with two extensive appendices "listing peer-reviewed academic journal articles on the topic of psychological harm resulting from playing violent video games." The appendices fill more than 14 pages in the U.S. Reports.]

Note: Violence, Interactivity, and the Protection of Children

1. The Court says that *United States v. Stevens* "controls this case." Justice Alito, who concurs in the judgment only on vagueness grounds, says the Court "is wrong." How persuasive are the distinctions drawn by Justice Alito? Note that Chief Justice Roberts, the author of *Stevens*, joins Justice Alito's opinion. Does that mean that Justice Alito is correct?

2. The Court places heavy reliance on the largely forgotten 1948 decision in *Winters v. New York* (Chapter 2 Note). The Court cites *Winters* for the proposition that although the Free Speech Clause "exists primarily to protect discourse on public matters, . . . it is difficult to distinguish politics from entertainment, and dangerous to try." Consider the rationales for protecting speech articulated by Holmes, Brandeis, Hand, and Brennan. How strongly do they support the protection of "entertainment"? Does the Court in *Brown* give up too easily on the possibility of drawing the distinction between "entertainment" and "politics"?

3. As one of its reasons for concluding that the California statute fails to satisfy strict scrutiny, the Court says that the legislation is seriously underinclusive: it seeks to protect children from portrayals of violence, but it excludes portrayals other than video games. Justice Breyer, in dissent, relies on "experts" who have "found a significant risk that violent video games, when compared with more passive media, are particularly likely to cause children harm." Should the Court have given more weight to these "expert" studies?

4. The Court and Justice Alito debate the significance of the "interactive" nature of video games. The majority, quoting Judge Richard Posner, says that "all literature is interactive." Justice Alito responds (in an omitted passage) by comparing the experience of role-playing in a video game with that of a reader who reads Dostoyevsky's description of Raskolnikov's murder of the old pawnbroker. "For most people," he says, "the two experiences will not be the same." Do you agree?

5. Justice Breyer, in dissent, argues that the Court opinion "creates a serious anomaly in First Amendment law." Under *Ginsberg*, "a State can prohibit the sale to minors of depictions of nudity," but after *Brown*, "a State cannot prohibit the sale to minors of the most violent interactive video games." Does the Court adequately justify the different treatment of sexual content and violent content, especially in the context of distribution to minors?

United States v. Alvarez

567 U.S. 709 (2012)

JUSTICE KENNEDY announced the judgment of the Court and delivered an opinion, in which THE CHIEF JUSTICE, JUSTICE GINSBURG, and JUSTICE SOTOMAYOR join.

Lying was his habit. Xavier Alvarez, the respondent here, lied when he said that he played hockey for the Detroit Red Wings and that he once married a starlet from Mexico. But when he lied in announcing he held the Congressional Medal of Honor, respondent ventured onto new ground; for that lie violates a federal criminal statute, the Stolen Valor Act of 2005. 18 U.S.C. § 704.

In 2007, respondent attended his first public meeting as a board member of the Three Valley Water District Board. The board is a governmental entity with head-quarters in Claremont, California. He introduced himself as follows: "I'm a retired marine of 25 years. I retired in the year 2001. Back in 1987, I was awarded the Congressional Medal of Honor. I got wounded many times by the same guy." None of this was true. For all the record shows, respondent's statements were but a pathetic attempt to gain respect that eluded him. The statements do not seem to have been made to secure employment or financial benefits or admission to privileges reserved for those who had earned the Medal.

Respondent was [convicted] under the Stolen Valor Act for lying about the Congressional Medal of Honor at the meeting. . . . The United States Court of Appeals for the Ninth Circuit, in a decision by a divided panel, found the Act invalid under the First Amendment and reversed the conviction. This Court granted certiorari. . . .

It is right and proper that Congress, over a century ago, established an award so the Nation can hold in its highest respect and esteem those who, in the course of carry-ing out the "supreme and noble duty of contributing to the defense of the rights and honor of the nation," have acted with extraordinary honor. . . . The Government contends the criminal prohibition is a proper means to further its purpose in creat-ing and awarding the Medal. When content-based speech regulation is in question, however, exacting scrutiny is required. Statutes suppressing or restricting speech must be judged by the sometimes inconvenient principles of the First Amendment. By this measure, the statutory provisions under which respondent was convicted must be held invalid, and his conviction must be set aside.

I

Respondent's claim to hold the Congressional Medal of Honor was false. There is no room to argue about interpretation or shades of meaning. On this premise, respon-dent violated § 704(b); and, because the lie concerned the Congressional Medal of Honor, he was subject to an enhanced penalty under subsection (c). Those statutory provisions are as follows:

(b) FALSE CLAIMS ABOUT RECEIPT OF MILITARY DECORATIONS OR MEDALS.—
   Whoever falsely represents himself or herself, verbally or in writing, to have

been awarded any decoration or medal authorized by Congress for the Armed Forces of the United States . . . shall be fined under this title, imprisoned not more than six months, or both.

(c) Enhanced Penalty for Offenses Involving Congressional Medal of Honor.—

(1) In General.—If a decoration or medal involved in an offense under subsection (a) or (b) is a Congressional Medal of Honor, in lieu of the punishment provided in that subsection, the offender shall be fined under this title, imprisoned not more than 1 year, or both.

Respondent challenges the statute as a content-based suppression of pure speech, speech not falling within any of the few categories of expression where content-based regulation is permissible. The Government defends the statute as necessary to preserve the integrity and purpose of the Medal, an integrity and purpose it contends are compromised and frustrated by the false statements the statute prohibits. It argues that false statements "have no First Amendment value in themselves," and thus "are protected only to the extent needed to avoid chilling fully protected speech." Although the statute covers respondent's speech, the Government argues that it leaves breathing room for protected speech, for example speech which might criticize the idea of the Medal or the importance of the military. The Government's arguments cannot suffice to save the statute.

II

"[A]s a general matter, the First Amendment means that government has no power to restrict expression because of its message, its ideas, its subject matter, or its content." As a result, the Constitution "demands that content-based restrictions on speech be presumed invalid . . . and that the Government bear the burden of showing their constitutionality."

In light of the substantial and expansive threats to free expression posed by content-based restrictions, this Court has rejected as "startling and dangerous" a "free-floating test for First Amendment coverage . . . [based on] an ad hoc balancing of relative social costs and benefits." *United States v. Stevens* (2010) [*supra* this chapter]. Instead, content-based restrictions on speech have been permitted, as a general matter, only when confined to the few "historic and traditional categories [of expression] long familiar to the bar." *Id.* Among these categories are advocacy intended, and likely, to incite imminent lawless action, *see Brandenburg v. Ohio* (1969) [Chapter 1]; obscenity, *see, e.g., Miller v. California* (1973) [Chapter 2]; defamation, *see, e.g., New York Times Co. v. Sullivan* (1964) (providing substantial protection for speech about public figures) [Chapter 2]; *Gertz v. Robert Welch, Inc.* (1974) (imposing some limits on liability for defaming a private figure) [Chapter 2]; speech integral to criminal conduct, *see, e.g., Giboney v. Empire Storage & Ice Co.* (1949) [Note *supra* this chapter]; so-called "fighting words," *see Chaplinsky v. New Hampshire* (1942) [Chapter 2]; child pornography, *see New York v. Ferber* (1982) [*supra* this chapter]; fraud, *see Virginia Bd. of Pharmacy v. Virginia Citizens Consumer Council, Inc.* (1976) [*supra* this chapter]; true threats, *see Watts v. United States* (1969) [Chapter 1 Note]; and speech presenting some grave and imminent threat the government has the power to prevent, *see Near v. Minnesota* (1931) [Chapter 4], although a restriction under the last category is most difficult to sustain, *see New York Times Co. v. United States* (1971) [Chapter 4]. These categories have a historical foundation in the Court's free speech tradition. The vast realm of free speech and thought always protected in our tradition can still thrive, and even be furthered, by adherence to those categories and rules.

Absent from those few categories where the law allows content-based regulation of speech is any general exception to the First Amendment for false statements. This comports with the common understanding that some false statements are inevitable if there is to be an open and vigorous expression of views in public and private conversation, expression the First Amendment seeks to guarantee.

The Government disagrees with this proposition. It cites language from some of this Court's precedents to support its contention that false statements have no value and hence no First Amendment protection. These isolated statements in some earlier decisions do not support the Government's submission that false statements, as a general rule, are beyond constitutional protection. That conclusion would take the quoted language far from its proper context. For instance, the Court has stated "[f]alse statements of fact are particularly valueless [because] they interfere with the truth-seeking function of the marketplace of ideas," *Hustler Magazine, Inc. v. Falwell* (1988) [Chapter 2 Note]. . . . *See also, e.g., Virginia Bd. of Pharmacy* ("Untruthful speech, commercial or otherwise, has never been protected for its own sake").

These quotations all derive from cases discussing defamation, fraud, or some other legally cognizable harm associated with a false statement, such as an invasion of privacy or the costs of vexatious litigation. In those decisions the falsity of the speech at issue was not irrelevant to our analysis, but neither was it determinative. The Court has never endorsed the categorical rule the Government advances: that false statements receive no First Amendment protection. Our prior decisions have not confronted a measure, like the Stolen Valor Act, that targets falsity and nothing more.

Even when considering some instances of defamation and fraud, moreover, the Court has been careful to instruct that falsity alone may not suffice to bring the speech outside the First Amendment. The statement must be a knowing or reckless falsehood. *See Sullivan* (prohibiting recovery of damages for a defamatory falsehood made about a public official unless the statement was made "with knowledge that it was false or with reckless disregard of whether it was false or not"); *Illinois ex rel. Madigan v. Telemarketing Associates, Inc.*, 538 U.S. 600, 620 (2003) ("False statement alone does not subject a fundraiser to fraud liability").

The Government thus seeks to use this principle for a new purpose. It seeks to convert a rule that limits liability even in defamation cases where the law permits recovery for tortious wrongs into a rule that expands liability in a different, far greater realm of discourse and expression. That inverts the rationale for the exception. The requirements of a knowing falsehood or reckless disregard for the truth as the condition for recovery in certain defamation cases exists to allow more speech, not less. A rule designed to tolerate certain speech ought not blossom to become a rationale for a rule restricting it.

The Government then gives three examples of regulations on false speech that courts generally have found permissible: first, the criminal prohibition of a false statement made to a Government official, 18 U.S.C. §1001; second, laws punishing perjury; and third, prohibitions on the false representation that one is speaking as a Government official or on behalf of the Government, *see, e.g.*, §912; §709. These restrictions, however, do not establish a principle that all proscriptions of false statements are exempt from exacting First Amendment scrutiny. . . .

[For example, perjury] undermines the function and province of the law and threatens the integrity of judgments that are the basis of the legal system. Unlike speech in other contexts, testimony under oath has the formality and gravity necessary to remind the witness that his or her statements will be the basis for official governmental action, action that often affects the rights and liberties of others. Sworn testimony is quite distinct from lies not spoken under oath and simply intended to puff up oneself. . . .

As our law and tradition show, then, there are instances in which the falsity of speech bears upon whether it is protected. Some false speech may be prohibited even if analogous true speech could not be. This opinion does not imply that any of these targeted prohibitions are somehow vulnerable. But it also rejects the notion that false speech should be in a general category that is presumptively unprotected.

Although the First Amendment stands against any "freewheeling authority to declare new categories of speech outside the scope of the First Amendment," *Stevens*, the Court has acknowledged that perhaps there exist "some categories of speech that have been historically unprotected . . . but have not yet been specifically identified or discussed . . . in our case law." Before exempting a category of speech from the normal prohibition on content-based restrictions, however, the Court must be presented with "persuasive evidence that a novel restriction on content is part of a long (if heretofore unrecognized) tradition of proscription," *Brown v. Entertainment Merchants Assn.* (2011) [*supra* this chapter]. The Government has not demonstrated that false statements generally should constitute a new category of unprotected speech on this basis.

III

The probable, and adverse, effect of the Act on freedom of expression illustrates, in a fundamental way, the reasons for the Law's distrust of content-based speech prohibitions.

The Act by its plain terms applies to a false statement made at any time, in any place, to any person. It can be assumed that it would not apply to, say, a theatrical performance. Still, the sweeping, quite unprecedented reach of the statute puts it in conflict with the First Amendment. Here the lie was made in a public meeting, but the statute would apply with equal force to personal, whispered conversations within a home. The statute seeks to control and suppress all false statements on this one subject in almost limitless times and settings. And it does so entirely without regard to whether the lie was made for the purpose of material gain.

Permitting the government to decree this speech to be a criminal offense, whether shouted from the rooftops or made in a barely audible whisper, would endorse government authority to compile a list of subjects about which false statements are punishable. That governmental power has no clear limiting principle. Our constitutional tradition stands against the idea that we need Oceania's Ministry of Truth. *See* G. ORWELL, NINETEEN EIGHTY-FOUR (1949) (Centennial ed. 2003). Were this law to be sustained, there could be an endless list of subjects the National Government or the States could single out. Where false claims are made to effect a fraud or secure moneys or other valuable considerations, say offers of employment, it is well established that the Government may restrict speech without affronting the First Amendment. But the Stolen Valor Act is not so limited in its reach. Were the Court to hold that the interest in truthful discourse alone is sufficient to sustain a ban on speech, absent any evidence that the speech was used to gain a material advantage, it would give government a broad censorial power unprecedented in this Court's cases or in our constitutional tradition. The mere potential for the exercise of that power casts a chill, a chill the First Amendment cannot permit if free speech, thought, and discourse are to remain a foundation of our freedom.

IV

The previous discussion suffices to show that the Act conflicts with free speech principles. But even when examined within its own narrow sphere of operation, the Act cannot survive. In assessing content-based restrictions on protected speech, the Court has not adopted a free-wheeling approach, see *Stevens*, but rather has applied the "most exacting scrutiny." Although the objectives the Government seeks to further by the statute are not without significance, the Court must, and now does, find the Act does not satisfy exacting scrutiny.

The Government is correct when it states military medals "serve the important public function of recognizing and expressing gratitude for acts of heroism and sacrifice in military service," and also "foste[r] morale, mission accomplishment and esprit de corps among service members." . . .

These interests are related to the integrity of the military honors system in general, and the Congressional Medal of Honor in particular. . . .

But to recite the Government's compelling interests is not to end the matter. The First Amendment requires that the Government's chosen restriction on the speech at issue be "actually necessary" to achieve its interest. *Brown.* There must be a direct causal link between the restriction imposed and the injury to be prevented. The link between the Government's interest in protecting the integrity of the military honors system and the Act's restriction on the false claims of liars like respondent has not been shown. . . .

It must be acknowledged that when a pretender claims the Medal to be his own, the lie might harm the Government by demeaning the high purpose of the award, diminishing the honor it confirms, and creating the appearance that the Medal is awarded more often than is true. Furthermore, the lie may offend the true holders of the Medal. From one perspective it insults their bravery and high principles when falsehood puts them in the unworthy company of a pretender.

Yet these interests do not satisfy the Government's heavy burden when it seeks to regulate protected speech. The Government points to no evidence to support its claim that the public's general perception of military awards is diluted by false claims such as those made by Alvarez. As one of the Government's *amici* notes "there is nothing that charlatans such as Xavier Alvarez can do to stain [the Medal winners'] honor." This general proposition is sound, even if true holders of the Medal might experience anger and frustration.

The lack of a causal link between the Government's stated interest and the Act is not the only way in which the Act is not actually necessary to achieve the Government's stated interest. The Government has not shown, and cannot show, why counterspeech would not suffice to achieve its interest. The facts of this case indicate that the dynamics of free speech, of counterspeech, of refutation, can overcome the lie. Respondent lied at a public meeting. Even before the FBI began investigating him for his false statements "Alvarez was perceived as a phony." Once the lie was made public, he was ridiculed online, his actions were reported in the press, and a fellow board member called for his resignation. There is good reason to believe that a similar fate would befall other false claimants. . . .

The remedy for speech that is false is speech that is true. This is the ordinary course in a free society. The response to the unreasoned is the rational; to the uninformed, the enlightened; to the straightout lie, the simple truth. . . .

The First Amendment itself ensures the right to respond to speech we do not like, and for good reason. Freedom of speech and thought flows not from the beneficence of the state but from the inalienable rights of the person. And suppression of speech by the government can make exposure of falsity more difficult, not less so. Society has the right and civic duty to engage in open, dynamic, rational discourse. These ends are not well served when the government seeks to orchestrate public discussion through content-based mandates. . . .

. . . Only a weak society needs government protection or intervention before it pursues its resolve to preserve the truth. Truth needs neither handcuffs nor a badge for its vindication.

In addition, when the Government seeks to regulate protected speech, the restriction must be the "least restrictive means among available, effective alternatives." There is, however, at least one less speech-restrictive means by which the Government could likely protect the integrity of the military awards system. A Government-created database could list Congressional Medal of Honor winners. Were a database accessible through the Internet, it would be easy to verify and expose false claims. It appears some private individuals have already created databases similar to this, and at least one database of past winners is online and fully searchable.

The Solicitor General responds that although Congress and the Department of Defense investigated the feasibility of establishing a database in 2008, the Government "concluded that such a database would be impracticable and insufficiently comprehensive." Without more explanation, it is difficult to assess the Government's claim, especially when at least one database of Congressional Medal of Honor winners already exists.

The Government may have responses to some of these criticisms, but there has been no clear showing of the necessity of the statute, the necessity required by exacting scrutiny. . . .

The judgment of the Court of Appeals is *affirmed*.

JUSTICE BREYER, with whom JUSTICE KAGAN joins, concurring in the judgment.

I agree with the plurality that the Stolen Valor Act of 2005 violates the First Amendment. But I do not rest my conclusion upon a strict categorical analysis. Rather, I base that conclusion upon the fact that the statute works First Amendment harm, while the Government can achieve its legitimate objectives in less restrictive ways.

I

In determining whether a statute violates the First Amendment, this Court has often found it appropriate . . . to determine whether the statute works speech-related harm that is out of proportion to its justifications. Sometimes the Court has referred to this approach as "intermediate scrutiny," sometimes as "proportionality" review, sometimes as an examination of "fit," and sometimes it has avoided the application of any label at all. . . . [In this case,] the Court's term "intermediate scrutiny" describes what I think we should do.

As the dissent points out, "there are broad areas in which any attempt by the state to penalize purportedly false speech would present a grave and unacceptable danger of suppressing truthful speech." Laws restricting false statements about philosophy, religion, history, the social sciences, the arts, and the like raise such concerns, and in many contexts have called for strict scrutiny. But this case does not involve such a law. The dangers of suppressing valuable ideas are lower where, as here, the regulations concern false statements about easily verifiable facts that do not concern such subject matter. Such false factual statements are less likely than are true factual statements to make a valuable contribution to the marketplace of ideas. And the government often has good reasons to prohibit such false speech. But its regulation can nonetheless threaten speech-related harms. Those circumstances lead me to apply what the Court has termed "intermediate scrutiny" here.

II

A

. . . I would read the [Stolen Valor Act] favorably to the Government as criminalizing only false factual statements made with knowledge of their falsity and with the intent that they be taken as true. As so interpreted the statute covers only lies. But although this interpretation diminishes the extent to which the statute endangers First Amendment values, it does not eliminate the threat.

I must concede, as the Government points out, that this Court has frequently said or implied that false factual statements enjoy little First Amendment protection.

But these judicial statements cannot be read to mean "no protection at all." False factual statements can serve useful human objectives, for example: in social contexts, where they may prevent embarrassment, protect privacy, shield a person from prejudice, provide the sick with comfort, or preserve a child's innocence; in public contexts, where they may stop a panic or otherwise preserve calm in the face of danger; and even in technical, philosophical, and scientific contexts, where (as Socrates' methods suggest) examination of a false statement (even if made deliberately to mislead) can promote a form of thought that ultimately helps realize the truth.

Moreover, as the Court has often said, the threat of criminal prosecution for making a false statement can inhibit the speaker from making true statements, thereby "chilling" a kind of speech that lies at the First Amendment's heart. Hence, the Court emphasizes *mens rea* requirements that provide "breathing room" for more valuable speech by reducing an honest speaker's fear that he may accidentally incur liability for speaking.

Further, the pervasiveness of false statements, made for better or for worse motives, made thoughtlessly or deliberately, made with or without accompanying harm, provides a weapon to a government broadly empowered to prosecute falsity without more. And those who are unpopular may fear that the government will use that weapon selectively, say by prosecuting a pacifist who supports his cause by (falsely) claiming to have been a war hero, while ignoring members of other political groups who might make similar false claims.

I also must concede that many statutes and common-law doctrines make the utterance of certain kinds of false statements unlawful. Those prohibitions, however, tend to be narrower than the statute before us, in that they limit the scope of their application, sometimes by requiring proof of specific harm to identifiable victims; sometimes by specifying that the lies be made in contexts in which a tangible harm to others is especially likely to occur; and sometimes by limiting the prohibited lies to those that are particularly likely to produce harm. . . .

Statutes prohibiting trademark infringement present, perhaps, the closest analogy to the present statute. . . . But trademark statutes are focused upon commercial and promotional activities that are likely to dilute the value of a mark. Indeed, they typically require a showing of likely confusion, a showing that tends to assure that the feared harm will in fact take place.

. . . [Few] statutes, if any, simply prohibit without limitation the telling of a lie, even a lie about one particular matter. Instead, in virtually all these instances limitations of context, requirements of proof of injury, and the like, narrow the statute to a subset of lies where specific harm is more likely to occur. The limitations help to make certain that the statute does not allow its threat of liability or criminal punishment to roam at large, discouraging or forbidding the telling of the lie in contexts where harm is unlikely or the need for the prohibition is small.

The statute before us lacks any such limiting features. It may be construed to prohibit only knowing and intentional acts of deception about readily verifiable facts within the personal knowledge of the speaker, thus reducing the risk that valuable speech is chilled. But it still ranges very broadly. And that breadth means that it creates a significant risk of First Amendment harm. As written, it applies in family, social, or other private contexts, where lies will often cause little harm. It also applies in political contexts, where although such lies are more likely to cause harm, the risk of censorious selectivity by prosecutors is also high. Further, given the potential haziness of individual memory along with the large number of military awards covered (ranging from medals for rifle marksmanship to the Congressional Medal of Honor), there remains a risk of chilling that is not completely eliminated by *mens rea* requirements; a speaker might still be worried about being *prosecuted* for a careless false statement, even if he does not have the intent required to render him liable. And so the prohibition may be applied where it should not be applied, for example, to bar stool braggadocio or, in the political arena, subtly but selectively to speakers that the Government does not like. These considerations lead me to believe that the statute as written risks significant First Amendment harm.

B

Like both the plurality and the dissent, I believe the statute nonetheless has substantial justification. . . . To permit those who have not earned [military] honors to claim otherwise dilutes the value of the awards. . . . Thus, the statute risks harming protected interests but only in order to achieve a substantial countervailing objective.

C

We must therefore ask whether it is possible substantially to achieve the Government's objective in less burdensome ways. In my view, the answer to this question is "yes." Some potential First Amendment threats can be alleviated by interpreting the statute to require knowledge of falsity, etc. But other First Amendment risks, primarily risks flowing from breadth of coverage, remain. As is indicated by the limitations on the scope of the many other kinds of statutes regulating false factual speech, it should be possible significantly to diminish or eliminate these remaining risks by enacting a similar but more finely tailored statute. For example, not all military awards are alike. Congress might determine that some warrant greater protection than others. And a more finely tailored statute might, as other kinds of statutes prohibiting false factual statements have done, insist upon a showing that the false statement caused specific harm or at least was material, or focus its coverage on lies most likely to be harmful or on contexts where such lies are most likely to cause harm. . . .

The Government has provided no convincing explanation as to why a more finely tailored statute would not work. . . . That being so, I find the statute as presently drafted works disproportionate constitutional harm. It consequently fails intermediate scrutiny, and so violates the First Amendment.

For these reasons, I concur in the Court's judgment.

JUSTICE ALITO, with whom JUSTICE SCALIA and JUSTICE THOMAS join, dissenting.

Only the bravest of the brave are awarded the Congressional Medal of Honor, but the Court today holds that every American has a constitutional right to claim to have received this singular award. The Court strikes down the Stolen Valor Act of 2005, which was enacted to stem an epidemic of false claims about military decorations. These lies, Congress reasonably concluded, were undermining our country's system of military honors and inflicting real harm on actual medal recipients and their families.

Building on earlier efforts to protect the military awards system, Congress responded to this problem by crafting a narrow statute that presents no threat to the freedom of speech. The statute reaches only knowingly false statements about hard facts directly within a speaker's personal knowledge. These lies have no value in and of themselves, and proscribing them does not chill any valuable speech.

By holding that the First Amendment nevertheless shields these lies, the Court breaks sharply from a long line of cases recognizing that the right to free speech does not protect false factual statements that inflict real harm and serve no legitimate interest. I would adhere to that principle and would thus uphold the constitutionality of this valuable law.

I

. . . . Properly construed, [the Stolen Valor Act] is limited in five significant respects. First, the Act applies to only a narrow category of false representations about objective facts that can almost always be proved or disproved with near certainty. Second, the Act concerns facts that are squarely within the speaker's personal knowledge. Third, as the Government maintains, and both the plurality and the concurrence seemingly accept, a conviction under the Act requires proof beyond a reasonable doubt that the speaker actually knew that the representation was false. Fourth, the Act applies only to statements that could reasonably be interpreted as communicating actual facts; it does not reach dramatic performances, satire, parody, hyperbole, or the like. Finally, the Act is strictly viewpoint neutral. The false statements proscribed by the Act are highly unlikely to be tied to any particular political or ideological message. In the rare cases where that is not so, the Act applies equally to all false statements, whether they tend to disparage or commend the Government, the military, or the system of military honors.

The Stolen Valor Act follows a long tradition of efforts to protect our country's system of military honors. . . .

Congress passed the Stolen Valor Act in response to a proliferation of false claims concerning the receipt of military awards. For example, in a single year, *more than 600* Virginia residents falsely claimed to have won the Medal of Honor. An investigation of the 333 people listed in the online edition of WHO'S WHO as having received a top military award revealed that fully a third of the claims could not be substantiated. When the Library of Congress compiled oral histories for its Veterans History Project, 24 of the 49 individuals who identified themselves as Medal of Honor recipients had not actually received that award. . . .

As Congress recognized, the lies proscribed by the Stolen Valor Act inflict substantial harm. In many instances, the harm is tangible in nature: Individuals often falsely represent themselves as award recipients in order to obtain financial or other material rewards, such as lucrative contracts and government benefits. . . . In other cases, the harm is less tangible, but nonetheless significant. The lies proscribed by the Stolen Valor Act tend to debase the distinctive honor of military awards. . . .

It is well recognized in trademark law that the proliferation of cheap imitations of luxury goods blurs the "'signal' given out by the purchasers of the originals." . . . Surely it was reasonable for Congress to conclude that the goal of preserving the integrity of our country's top military honors is at least as worthy as that of protecting the prestige associated with fancy watches and designer handbags.

Both the plurality and Justice Breyer argue that Congress could have preserved the integrity of military honors by means other than a criminal prohibition, but Congress had ample reason to believe that alternative approaches would not be adequate. The chief alternative that is recommended is the compilation and release of a comprehensive list or database of actual medal recipients. . . .

This remedy, unfortunately, will not work. The Department of Defense has explained that the most that it can do is to create a database of recipients of certain top military honors awarded since 2001.

Because a sufficiently comprehensive database is not practicable, lies about military awards cannot be remedied by what the plurality calls "counterspeech." Without the requisite database, many efforts to refute false claims may be thwarted, and some legitimate award recipients may be erroneously attacked. In addition, a steady stream of stories in the media about the exposure of imposters would tend to increase skepticism among members of the public about the entire awards system. This would only exacerbate the harm that the Stolen Valor Act is meant to prevent.

The plurality and the concurrence also suggest that Congress could protect the system of military honors by enacting a narrower statute. . . . But much damage is caused, both to real award recipients and to the system of military honors, by false statements that are not linked to any financial or other tangible reward. Unless even a small financial loss—say, a dollar given to a homeless man falsely claiming to be a decorated veteran—is more important in the eyes of the First Amendment than the damage caused to the very integrity of the military awards system, there is no basis for distinguishing between the Stolen Valor Act and the alternative statutes that the plurality and concurrence appear willing to sustain. . . .

II

A

Time and again, this Court has recognized that as a general matter false factual statements possess no intrinsic First Amendment value. *See,* [*e.g.,*] *Gertz v. Robert Welch, Inc.* (1974) (There is "no constitutional value in false statements of fact").

Consistent with this recognition, many kinds of false factual statements have long been proscribed without "rais[ing] any Constitutional problem." Laws prohibiting fraud, perjury, and defamation, for example, were in existence when the First Amendment was adopted, and their constitutionality is now beyond question. . . .

It is true, as Justice Breyer notes, that many in our society either approve or condone certain discrete categories of false statements, including false statements made to prevent harm to innocent victims and so-called "white lies." But respondent's false claim to have received the Medal of Honor did not fall into any of these categories. . . .

. . . The lies covered by the Stolen Valor Act have no intrinsic value and thus merit no First Amendment protection unless their prohibition would chill other expression that falls within the Amendment's scope. I now turn to that question.

B

While we have repeatedly endorsed the principle that false statements of fact do not merit First Amendment protection for their own sake, we have recognized that it is sometimes necessary to "exten[d] a measure of strategic protection" to these statements in order to ensure sufficient "breathing space" for protected speech. *Gertz.* [*See also New York Times Co. v. Sullivan.* . . .]

These examples by no means exhaust the circumstances in which false factual statements enjoy a degree of instrumental constitutional protection. On the contrary, there are broad areas in which any attempt by the state to penalize purportedly false speech would present a grave and unacceptable danger of suppressing truthful speech. Laws restricting false statements about philosophy, religion, history, the social sciences, the arts, and other matters of public concern would present such a threat. The point is not that there is no such thing as truth or falsity in these areas or that the truth is always impossible to ascertain, but rather that it is perilous to permit the state to be the arbiter of truth. . . .

Allowing the state to proscribe false statements in these areas also opens the door for the state to use its power for political ends. Statements about history illustrate this point. If some false statements about historical events may be banned, how certain must it be that a statement is false before the ban may be upheld? And who should make that calculation? . . .

In stark contrast to hypothetical laws prohibiting false statements about history, science, and similar matters, the Stolen Valor Act presents no risk at all that valuable speech will be suppressed. The speech punished by the Act is not only verifiably false and entirely lacking in intrinsic value, but it also fails to serve any instrumental purpose that the First Amendment might protect. Tellingly, when asked at oral argument what truthful speech the Stolen Valor Act might chill, even respondent's counsel conceded that the answer is none.

C

Neither of the two opinions endorsed by Justices in the majority claims that the false statements covered by the Stolen Valor Act possess either intrinsic or instrumental value. Instead, those opinions appear to be based on the distinct concern that the Act suffers from overbreadth. But to strike down a statute on the basis that it is overbroad, it is necessary to show that the statute's "overbreadth [is] *substantial*, not only in an absolute sense, but also relative to [its] plainly legitimate sweep." *United States v. Williams* (2008) [Note *supra* this chapter]. The plurality and the concurrence do not even attempt to make this showing.

The plurality additionally worries that a decision sustaining the Stolen Valor Act might prompt Congress and the state legislatures to enact laws criminalizing lies about "an endless list of subjects." The plurality apparently fears that we will see laws making it a crime to lie about civilian awards such as college degrees or certificates of achievement in the arts and sports.

This concern is likely unfounded. . . . In any event, if the plurality's concern is not entirely fanciful, it falls outside the purview of the First Amendment. . . . . If there is a problem with, let us say, a law making it a criminal offense to falsely claim to have been a high school valedictorian, the problem is not the suppression of speech but the misuse of the criminal law, which should be reserved for conduct that inflicts or threatens truly serious societal harm. The objection to this hypothetical law would be the same as the objection to a law making it a crime to eat potato chips during the graduation ceremony at which the high school valedictorian is recognized. The safeguard against such laws is democracy, not the First Amendment. Not every foolish law is unconstitutional. . . .

Note: Knowingly False Statements of Fact

1. First *Stevens*, then *Brown*, now *Alvarez*: for the third time in three years, the Court considers whether to recognize a new category of unprotected speech, and it declines to do so. Or does it? Certainly Justice Kennedy does, but he speaks only for a plurality. Is there a holding of the Court on that point?

2. "After *Alvarez*, governments can punish people for making false statements of fact only when . . . ." How would you finish that sentence?

3. Justice Kennedy says that if the Stolen Valor Act were to be upheld, "there could be an endless list of subjects the National Government or the States could single out." Justice Alito, in dissent, responds that the plurality's concern "falls outside the purview of the First Amendment," and that the safeguard against foolish criminalizing of false statements "is democracy." Is this a persuasive response?

4. Justice Breyer reads the Stolen Valor Act "favorably to the Government as criminalizing only false factual statements made with knowledge of their falsity and with the intent that they be taken as true." Does the plurality also read the statute that way?

5. What other laws prohibiting false statements would be unconstitutional under *Alvarez*? Consider these examples.

   (a) A Michigan statute provides: "Any person who advertises or uses in any campaign material ... the words incumbent, re-elect, re-election, or otherwise indicates, represents, or gives the impression that a candidate for public office is the incumbent, when in fact the candidate is not the incumbent, is guilty of a [misdemeanor]." *See Treasurer of the Committee to Gerald D. Lostracco v. Fox*, 389 N.W.2d 446 (Mich. Ct. App. 1986).

   (b) A Wisconsin statute provides: "No person may knowingly make or publish, or cause to be made or published, a false representation pertaining to a candidate or referendum which is intended or tends to affect voting at an election."

   (c) A Minnesota statute provides: "A person is guilty of a gross misdemeanor who intentionally participates in the preparation, dissemination, or broadcast of paid political advertising or campaign material ... with respect to the effect of a ballot question, that is designed or tends to ... promote or defeat a ballot question, that is false, and that the person knows is false or communicates to others with reckless disregard of whether it is false." *See 281 Care Committee v. Arneson*, 638 F.3d 621 (8th Cir. 2011).

   (d) A Florida statute (now repealed) provided:

No person in the state may claim, either orally or in writing, to possess an academic degree, as defined in [another statute], or the title associated with said degree, unless the person has, in fact, been awarded said degree from an institution that is:

      (a) Accredited by a [recognized] regional or professional accrediting agency;

      (b) Provided, operated, and supported by a state government or any of its political subdivisions or by the Federal Government;

      (c) A school, institute, college, or university chartered outside the United States, the academic degree from which has been validated by an accrediting agency approved by the United States Department of Education as equivalent to the baccalaureate or post-baccalaureate degree conferred by a regionally accredited college or university in the United States;

      (d) Licensed by the [State] or exempt from licensure pursuant to [another statute] or

      (e) A religious seminary, institute, college, or university which offers only educational programs that prepare students for a religious vocation, career, occupation, profession, or lifework, and the nomenclature of whose certificates, diplomas, or degrees clearly identifies the religious character of the educational program.

Violations of the statute were punishable as a misdemeanor.

Problem: The Stolen Valor Act of 2013

Even before the Supreme Court handed down its decision in *Alvarez*, a new bill was introduced in the Senate "to establish a criminal offense relating to fraudulent claims about military service." That bill was not enacted, but in the spring of 2013 Congress passed, and President Obama signed, the Stolen Valor Act of 2011, Pub. Law No. 113-12. The new law replaces subsection (b) of 18 U.S.C. § 704 — quoted in the Court's opinion — with the following rewritten subsection:

> (b) Fraudulent Representations About Receipt of Military Decorations or Medals. — Whoever, with intent to obtain money, property, or other tangible benefit, fraudulently holds oneself out to be a recipient of a decoration or medal described in subsection (c)(2) or (d) shall be fined under this title, imprisoned not more than one year, or both.

Subsections (c)(2) and (d) refer to the Congressional Medal of Honor and certain other decorations including the Purple Heart.

Under *Alvarez*, is the new law constitutional?

Chapter 4

Trans-Substantive Doctrines

A. Prior Restraints
Note: An Introduction to Prior Restraints

As Justice Holmes noted in *Schenck* (Chapter 1), early writings suggested that the main purpose of the First Amendment was to prevent what he called "previous restraints" upon speech. Indeed, Blackstone's Commentaries—one of the most influential sources of guidance in the Founding Era—took the position that freedom of the press was *limited* to preventing governmental restraints prior to publication. Of course the Court has long since rejected that narrow view. But the Blackstonian tradition has left its imprint on First Amendment law. As the Court stated in *Bantam Books, Inc. v. Sullivan*, 372 U.S. 58 (1963), "Any system of prior restraints of expression comes to this Court bearing a heavy presumption against its constitutional validity." The implication is that some kinds of speech might be subject to punishment after publication but could not be regulated by a "system of prior restraints."

Against this background, it becomes important to distinguish between prior restraints (or "previous restraints," as they are sometimes called) and other forms of governmental regulation. But that is not always an easy task. Justice Kennedy, dissenting in *Alexander v. United States*, 509 U.S. 544 (1993), wrote:

> In its simple, most blatant form, a prior restraint is a law which requires submission of speech to an official who may grant or deny permission to utter or publish it based upon its contents. . . . In contrast are laws which punish speech or expression only after it has occurred and been found unlawful. While each mechanism, once imposed, may abridge speech in a direct way by suppressing it, or in an indirect way by chilling its dissemination, we have interpreted the First Amendment as providing greater protection from prior restraints than from subsequent punishments. In *Southeastern Promotions, Ltd. v. Conrad*, 420 U.S. 546 (1975), we explained that "[b]ehind the distinction is a theory deeply etched in our law: a free society prefers to punish the few who abuse rights of speech after they break the law than to throttle them and all others beforehand."
>
> It has been suggested that the distinction between prior restraints and subsequent punishments may have slight utility, see [M. Nimmer, Nimmer on Freedom of Speech] § 4.04, at 4-18 to 4-25, for in a certain sense every criminal obscenity statute is a prior restraint because of the caution a speaker

or bookseller must exercise to avoid its imposition. . . . To be sure, the term prior restraint is not self-defining. One problem, of course, is that some governmental actions may have the characteristics both of punishment and prior restraint. A historical example is the sentence imposed on Hugh Singleton in 1579 after he had enraged Elizabeth I by printing a certain tract. *See* F. Siebert, Freedom of the Press in England, 1476–1776, at 91–92 (1952). Singleton was condemned to lose his right hand, thus visiting upon him both a punishment and a disability encumbering all further printing. Though the sentence appears not to have been carried out, it illustrates that a prior restraint and a subsequent punishment may occur together.

[1] Licensing

As the preceding discussion indicates, the scope of the "prior restraint" doctrine remains open to debate. One kind of regulation, however, clearly falls within the doctrine: a law that requires individuals to obtain a license from the government before publishing a book or other written work. But does the doctrine apply to all government regulation of expressive activity? The Court's first encounter with a licensing law came more than 75 years ago.

Lovell v. City of Griffin
303 U.S. 444 (1938)

Mr. Chief Justice Hughes delivered the opinion of the Court.

Appellant, Alma Lovell, was convicted in the recorder's court of the City of Griffin, Ga., of the violation of a city ordinance and was sentenced to imprisonment for fifty days in default of the payment of a fine of $50. [The state courts affirmed.] The case comes here on appeal.

The ordinance in question is as follows:

Section 1. That the practice of distributing, either by hand or otherwise, circulars, handbooks, advertising, or literature of any kind, whether said articles are being delivered free, or whether same are being sold, within the limits of the City of Griffin, without first obtaining written permission from the City Manager of the City of Griffin, such practice shall be deemed a nuisance, and punishable as an offense against the City of Griffin.

Section 2. The Chief of Police of the City of Griffin and the police force of the City of Griffin are hereby required and directed to suppress the same and to abate any nuisance as is described in the first section of this ordinance.

The violation, which is not denied, consisted of the distribution without the required permission of a pamphlet and magazine in the nature of religious tracts, setting forth the gospel of the "Kingdom of Jehovah." Appellant did not apply for a permit, as she regarded herself as sent "by Jehovah to do His work" and that such an application would have been "an act of disobedience to His commandment." [Lovell challenged the ordinance as an abridgement of freedom of religion as well as freedom of the press, but the state courts rejected her arguments.]

Freedom of speech and freedom of the press, which are protected by the First Amendment from infringement by Congress, are among the fundamental personal rights and liberties which are protected by the Fourteenth Amendment from invasion by state action. *Gitlow v. New York* (1925) [*supra* Chapter 1]; *see also Palko v. Connecticut*, 302 U.S. 319 (1937).

The ordinance in its broad sweep prohibits the distribution of "circulars, handbooks, advertising, or literature of any kind." It manifestly applies to pamphlets, magazines and periodicals. The evidence against appellant was that she distributed a certain pamphlet and a magazine called the "Golden Age." Whether in actual administration the ordinance is applied, as apparently it could be, to newspapers does not appear. The City Manager testified that "every one applies to me for a license to distribute literature in this City. None of these people (including defendant) secured a permit from me to distribute literature in the City of Griffin." The ordinance is not limited to "literature" that is obscene or offensive to public morals or that advocates unlawful conduct. There is no suggestion that the pamphlet and magazine distributed in the instant case were of that character. The ordinance embraces "literature" in the widest sense.

The ordinance is comprehensive with respect to the method of distribution. It covers every sort of circulation "either by hand or otherwise." There is thus no restriction in its application with respect to time or place. It is not limited to ways which might be regarded as inconsistent with the maintenance of public order, or as involving disorderly conduct, the molestation of the inhabitants, or the misuse or littering of the streets. The ordinance prohibits the distribution of literature of any kind at any time, at any place, and in any manner without a permit from the City Manager.

We think that the ordinance is invalid on its face. Whatever the motive which induced its adoption, its character is such that it strikes at the very foundation of the freedom of the press by subjecting it to license and censorship. The struggle for the freedom of the press was primarily directed against the power of the licensor. It was against that power that John Milton directed his assault by his "Appeal for the Liberty of Unlicensed Printing." And the liberty of the press became initially a right to publish "*without* a license what formerly could be published only *with* one." While this freedom from previous restraint upon publication cannot be regarded as exhausting the guaranty of liberty, the prevention of that restraint was a leading purpose in the adoption of the constitutional provision. *See Patterson v. Colorado*, 205 U.S. 454 (1907) [Note *supra* Chapter 1]; *Near v. Minnesota* (1931) [*infra* this chapter]. Legislation of the type of the ordinance in question would restore the system of license and censorship in its baldest form.

The liberty of the press is not confined to newspapers and periodicals. It necessarily embraces pamphlets and leaflets. These indeed have been historic weapons in the defense of liberty, as the pamphlets of Thomas Paine and others in our own history abundantly attest. The press in its historic connotation comprehends every sort of publication which affords a vehicle of information and opinion. What we have had recent occasion to say with respect to the vital importance of protecting this essential liberty from every sort of infringement need not be repeated. *Near v. Minnesota*, 283 U.S. 697 (1931); *De Jonge v. Oregon*, 299 U.S. 353 (1937) [Note *supra* Chapter 1].

The ordinance cannot be saved because it relates to distribution and not to publication. "Liberty of circulating is as essential to that freedom as liberty of publishing; indeed, without the circulation, the publication would be of little value." *Ex parte Jackson*, 96 U.S. 727 (1878). The license tax in *Grosjean v. American Press Company*, 297 U.S. 233 (1936) [*infra* Chapter 14], was held invalid because of its direct tendency to restrict circulation.

As the ordinance is void on its face, it was not necessary for appellant to seek a permit under it. She was entitled to contest its validity in answer to the charge against her. *Smith v. Cahoon*, 283 U.S. 553 (1931).

The judgment is reversed and the cause is remanded for further proceedings not inconsistent with this opinion.

Mr. Justice Cardozo took no part in the consideration and decision of this case.

————

Note: Licensing Schemes and the Freedman Requirements

A. The Implications of *Lovell*

1. The Court in *Lovell v. City of Griffin* says that legislation like the Lovell ordinance "would restore the system of license and censorship in its baldest form." Does the Court adequately consider the differences between the Lovell ordinance and the "power of the licensor" in Milton's England?

2. After an initial mention of freedom of speech, the Court focuses on the "freedom" (or "liberty") of "the press." And the Court offers a capacious definition of what is protected, saying: "The press in its historic connotation comprehends every sort of publication which affords a vehicle of information and opinion." What are the implications of this proposition for regulation of new modes of communication like Twitter or Facebook?

3. As we shall see in Chapter 8, the decision in *Lovell* played an important role in the development of the public forum doctrine. Here we consider the implications of *Lovell* for licensing requirements for activities related to communication.

4. The broad language of *Lovell* might suggest that any legislation that requires individuals to obtain a license before engaging in communicative activities is necessarily a violation of the First Amendment. But that is not the law. Only three years after *Lovell*, the Court sustained the constitutionality of a state statute that prohibited a "parade or procession" upon a public street without a special license. The case was *Cox v. New Hampshire*, 312 U.S. 569 (1941), and Chief Justice Hughes, the author of *Lovell*, wrote the Court's unanimous opinion. *See* Chapter 8.

B. The *Freedman* Requirements

5. It is not surprising that the Court would uphold a licensing requirement for parades and processions on public streets; after all, you can't have two parades on the same street at the same time. But permissible licensing requirements are not limited to public streets. One of the most important precedents in the development of the law in this area involved a licensing system for motion pictures. The case is *Freedman v. Maryland*, 380 U.S. 51 (1965). In a later opinion, the Supreme Court outlined the Maryland licensing system and the Court's holding:

> In *Freedman v. Maryland*, we confronted a state law that ... required that every motion picture film be submitted to a Board of Censors before the film was shown anywhere in the State. The board enjoyed authority to reject films that it considered "obscene" or that "tended, in the judgment of the Board, to debase or corrupt morals or incite to crimes," characteristics defined by the statute in broad terms. The statute punished the exhibition of a film not submitted to the board for advance approval, even where the film would have received a license had it been properly submitted. It was no defense that the content of the film was protected by the First Amendment.
>
> We recognized in *Freedman* that a scheme conditioning expression on a licensing body's prior approval of content "presents peculiar dangers to constitutionally protected speech." "[T]he censor's business is to censor," and a licensing body likely will overestimate the dangers of controversial speech when determining, without regard to the film's actual effect on an audience, whether speech is likely "to incite" or to "corrupt [the] morals." In response to these grave "dangers of a censorship system," we held that a film licensing process must contain certain procedural safeguards in order to avoid constituting an invalid prior restraint: "(1) any restraint prior to judicial review can be imposed only for a specified brief period during which the status quo must be maintained; (2) expeditious judicial review of that decision must be available; and (3) the censor must bear the burden of going to court to suppress the speech and must bear the burden of proof once in court."

Thomas v. Chicago Park District, 534 U.S. 316 (2002).

6. It is hard to imagine that any state or municipality today would establish a Board of Censors and require a license for the exhibition of motion pictures. But governments can and do require licenses for other forms of communicative activity. And when licensing schemes are challenged in the courts, *Freedman* remains an important precedent. Here we look at the Court's treatment of *Freedman* in two contemporary contexts: sexually oriented businesses and expressive activities in public parks.

C. Licensing of Sexually Oriented Businesses

7. In *FW/PBS, Inc. v. Dallas*, 493 U.S. 215 (1990), the Court considered the applicability of the *Freedman* standards to a municipal ordinance requiring a license for the operation of a sexually oriented business. The Court held that the Dallas

licensing scheme violated the First Amendment because it did not provide the procedural safeguards required by Supreme Court precedents. But there was no majority
opinion on the principal issues in the case. A majority agreed that "the first two
[*Freedman*] safeguards are essential: the licensor must make the decision whether to
issue the license within a specified and reasonable time period during which the status quo is maintained, and there must be the possibility of prompt judicial review in
the event that the license is erroneously denied." A different majority (including one
Justice who would have held that the details of the ordinance did not have to satisfy
the First Amendment at all) held that the third *Freedman* requirement did not apply.
The plurality concluded that "the First Amendment does not require that the city
bear the burden of going to court to effect the denial of a license application or that
it bear the burden of proof once in court."

8. What is meant by the requirement of "prompt judicial review"? In *Freedman*
itself, the Court, illustrating what it meant by "prompt," set forth a "model" that
involved a "hearing one day after joinder of issue" and a "decision within two days
after termination of the hearing." But in the aftermath of *FW/PBS*, lower courts differed over how that model applies to licensing schemes for sexually oriented businesses. Some courts held that the requirement of "prompt judicial review" means
that the unsuccessful applicant for an adult business license must be assured a prompt
judicial *determination* on the merits of the permit denial. Others concluded that the
Constitution requires only prompt *access* to judicial review. After almost 15 years of
litigation, the Supreme Court gave its answer.

In *City of Littleton v. Z.J. Gifts D-4, L.L.C.*, 541 U.S. 774 (2004), the Court rejected
the city's argument that a licensing scheme for adult businesses must provide "only
an assurance of speedy access to the courts, not an assurance of a speedy court
decision." But the Court found that the Littleton ordinance satisfied the requirement of a prompt judicial determination. In an opinion by Justice Breyer, the Court
said:

> Littleton, in effect, argues that we should modify *FW/PBS*, withdrawing
> its implication that *Freedman*'s special judicial review rules apply in this
> case. And we accept that argument. In our view, Colorado's ordinary judicial
> review procedures suffice as long as the courts remain sensitive to the need
> to prevent First Amendment harms and administer those procedures
> accordingly. And whether the courts do so is a matter normally fit for case-
> by-case determination rather than a facial challenge.

The Court noted that "ordinary court procedural rules and practices, in Colorado
as elsewhere, provide reviewing courts with judicial tools sufficient to avoid delay-
related First Amendment harm." Moreover, "we have no reason to doubt the willingness of Colorado's judges to exercise these powers wisely."

The Court also emphasized that "the typical First Amendment harm at issue here
differs from that at issue in *Freedman*, diminishing the need in the typical case for
special procedural rules imposing special 2- or 3-day decisionmaking time limits."
The opinion explained:

[In *Freedman*], the Court considered a scheme with rather subjective standards and where a denial likely meant complete censorship. In contrast, the ordinance at issue here does not seek to censor material. And its licensing scheme applies reasonably objective, nondiscretionary criteria unrelated to the content of the expressive materials that an adult business may sell or display.

The ordinance says that an adult business license "*shall*" be denied if the applicant (1) is underage; (2) provides false information; (3) has within the prior year had an adult business license revoked or suspended; (4) has operated an adult business determined to be a state law "public nuisance" within the prior year; (5) (if a corporation) is not authorized to do business in the State; (6) has not timely paid taxes, fees, fines, or penalties; (7) has not obtained a sales tax license (for which zoning compliance is required, or (8) has been convicted of certain crimes within the prior five years. (Emphasis added).

These objective criteria are simple enough to apply and their application simple enough to review that their use is unlikely in practice to suppress totally the presence of any specific item of adult material in the Littleton community. Some license applicants will satisfy the criteria even if others do not; hence the community will likely contain outlets that sell protected adult material. A supplier of that material should be able to find outlets; a potential buyer should be able to find a seller.

Do you agree that these features of the Littleton ordinance sufficiently address the First Amendment concerns? How does the objective nature of the criteria for denial of a license diminish the need for "special procedural rules imposing special 2- or 3-day decisionmaking time limits" when a license is denied?

9. Note that the ordinance applies only to an "adult business." A commercial establishment falls into this category if, as judged by percentage of stock-in-trade, revenue, or advertising, it is primarily devoted to the sale of materials that are characterized by the depiction or description of "specified sexual activities" or "specified anatomical areas." (Both terms are defined in graphic detail in the ordinance.) Does this cast doubt on the soundness of the holding of *City of Littleton*?

D. *Freedman* in the Parks

10. In *Thomas v. Chicago Park District*, 534 U.S. 316 (2002), the Court considered whether a Park District ordinance requiring individuals to obtain a permit before conducting large-scale events in a city park must provide the procedural safeguards described in *Freedman*. The Court held that the *Freedman* requirements did not apply.

The ordinance was challenged by individuals who had applied to the District on several occasions for permits to hold rallies advocating the legalization of marijuana. The District granted some permits and denied others. The Supreme Court, after summarizing the *Freedman* requirements in the paragraphs quoted above, continued:

Petitioners contend that the Park District, like the Board of Censors in *Freedman*, must initiate litigation every time it denies a permit and that the ordinance must specify a deadline for judicial review of a challenge to a permit denial. We reject those contentions. *Freedman* is inapposite because the licensing scheme at issue here is not subject-matter censorship but content-neutral time, place, and manner regulation of the use of a public forum. The Park District's ordinance does not authorize a licensor to pass judgment on the content of speech: None of the grounds for denying a permit has anything to do with what a speaker might say. Indeed, the ordinance (unlike the classic censorship scheme) is not even directed to communicative activity as such, but rather to *all* activity conducted in a public park. The picnicker and soccer player, no less than the political activist or parade marshal, must apply for a permit if the 50-person limit is to be exceeded. And the object of the permit system (as plainly indicated by the permissible grounds for permit denial) is not to exclude communication of a particular content, but to coordinate multiple uses of limited space, to assure preservation of the park facilities, to prevent uses that are dangerous, unlawful, or impermissible under the Park District's rules, and to assure financial accountability for damage caused by the event.

We have never required that a content-neutral permit scheme regulating speech in a public forum adhere to the procedural requirements set forth in *Freedman*. . . . Regulations of the use of a public forum that ensure the safety and convenience of the people are not "inconsistent with civil liberties but . . . [are] one of the means of safeguarding the good order upon which [civil liberties] ultimately depend." *Cox v. New Hampshire* (1941). Such a traditional exercise of authority does not raise the censorship concerns that prompted us to impose the extraordinary procedural safeguards on the film licensing process in *Freedman*.

Of course even content-neutral time, place, and manner restrictions can be applied in such a manner as to stifle free expression. Where the licensing official enjoys unduly broad discretion in determining whether to grant or deny a permit, there is a risk that he will favor or disfavor speech based on its content. *See Forsyth County v. Nationalist Movement* (1992) [*infra* Chapter 8]. We have thus required that a time, place, and manner regulation contain adequate standards to guide the official's decision and render it subject to effective judicial review. Petitioners contend that the Park District's ordinance fails this test.

We think not. [The Park District] may deny a permit only for one or more of the reasons set forth in the ordinance. It may deny, for example, when the application is incomplete or contains a material falsehood or misrepresentation; when the applicant has damaged Park District property on prior occasions and has not paid for the damage; when a permit has been granted to an earlier applicant for the same time and place; when the intended use would present an unreasonable danger to the health or safety of park users or Park District employees; or when the applicant has violated the terms of a prior permit. Moreover, the Park District must process applications within 28 days and must clearly explain its reasons for any denial.

These grounds are reasonably specific and objective, and do not leave the decision "to the whim of the administrator." *Forsyth County*. They provide "narrowly drawn, reasonable and definite standards" to guide the licensor's determination. And they are enforceable on review-first by appeal to the General Superintendent of the Park District, and then by writ of common-law certiorari in the Illinois courts, which provides essentially the same type of review as that provided by the Illinois administrative procedure act,

11. In *FW/PBS, Inc.*, the Court held that a modified version of the *Freedman* requirements applied to the licensing of a sexually oriented business on private property, but in *Thomas* the Court held that the requirements did not apply at all when a group sought a permit to hold a rally in a public park seeking a change in the law—core political speech. Can both decisions be correct?

E. Facial Challenges to Licensing Laws

12. At the end of the opinion in *Lovell*, the Court states: "As the ordinance is void on its face, it was not necessary for appellant to seek a permit under it. She was entitled to contest its validity in answer to the charge against her." In *Freedman*, the Court indicated that this principle is specific to First Amendment challenges:

> In the area of freedom of expression it is well established that one has standing to challenge a statute on the ground that it delegates overly broad licensing discretion to an administrative office, whether or not his conduct could be proscribed by a properly drawn statute, and whether or not he applied for a license. . . . Standing is recognized in such cases because of the "danger of tolerating, in the area of First Amendment freedoms, the existence of a penal statute susceptible of sweeping and improper application."

Half a century after *Lovell*, in *City of Lakewood v. Plain Dealer Publishing Co.*, 486 U.S. 750 (1988), the Court divided sharply over the applicability of the "*Lovell-Freedman* line of cases," and, in particular, over the question: when may a person who is subject to a licensing law challenge the law facially without the necessity of applying for, and being denied, a license?

The majority held that a facial challenge lies when two conditions are met: the licensing law "gives a government official or agency substantial power to discriminate based on the content or viewpoint of speech by suppressing disfavored speech or disliked speakers"; and the law has "a close enough nexus to expression, or to conduct commonly associated with expression, to pose a real and substantial threat of the identified censorship risks."

Applying this rule to the case before it, the Court held that the plaintiff, the publisher of a daily newspaper, could bring a facial challenge to a city ordinance that required a permit—renewable annually—for placing newsracks on city property. The Court went on to hold that the ordinance violated the First Amendment because it lacked "the standards necessary to bound a licensor's discretion": the ordinance gave the mayor power to grant or deny permits, but did not specify grounds on which an application for a permit could be denied. Nor was the ordinance saved by the availability of judicial review, because there was no requirement of "reasonable dispatch" in the review process. The Court did not decide whether a city could constitutionally *prohibit* the placement of newsracks on city property.

Justice White, for the dissenters, argued that "where an activity that could be forbidden altogether (without running afoul of the First Amendment) is subjected to a local license requirement, the mere presence of administrative discretion in the licensing scheme will not render it invalid *per se*," nor does the *Lovell-Freedman* doctrine apply. Rather, "our usual rules concerning the permissibility of discretionary local licensing laws (and facial challenges to those laws) must prevail." This approach required Justice White to consider whether the newspaper had "a constitutional right to distribute its papers by means of dispensing devices or newsboxes, affixed to the public sidewalks." Justice White concluded that the answer was "no." Thus the newspaper could not pursue a facial challenge without first applying for a permit.

13. The Supreme Court has not yet decided whether a city could simply prohibit the placement of newsracks on city property. We will consider this issue in Chapter 6.

---

[2] Injunctions and Other Remedies

Near v. Minnesota

283 U.S. 697 (1931)

Mr. Chief Justice Hughes delivered the opinion of the Court.

Chapter 285 of the Session Laws of Minnesota for the year 1925 provides for the abatement, as a public nuisance, of a "malicious, scandalous and defamatory newspaper, magazine or other periodical." Section 1 of the act [states that anyone who publishes such a periodical "is guilty of a nuisance." Section 2 provides that, whenever any such nuisance is committed or exists, the County Attorney may maintain an action in state court to enjoin perpetually the persons committing or maintaining any such nuisance from further committing or maintaining it. Upon such evidence as the court shall deem sufficient, a temporary injunction may be granted.]

Under this statute, the County Attorney of Hennepin County brought this action to enjoin the publication of what was described as a "malicious, scandalous and defamatory newspaper, magazine or other periodical," known as "The Saturday Press," published by the defendants in the city of Minneapolis. The complaint alleged that the defendants, on September 24, 1927, and on eight subsequent dates in October and November, 1927, published and circulated editions of that periodical which were "largely devoted to malicious, scandalous and defamatory articles" . . . .

[T]he articles charged in substance that a Jewish gangster was in control of gambling, bootlegging, and racketeering in Minneapolis, and that law enforcing officers and agencies were not energetically performing their duties. Most of the charges were directed against the Chief of Police; he was charged with gross neglect of duty, illicit relations with gangsters, and with participation in graft. . . . A special grand jury and a special prosecutor were demanded to deal with the situation in general, and, in particular, to investigate an attempt to assassinate one Guilford, one of the original defendants, who, it appears from the articles, was shot by gangsters after the first issue of the periodical had been published. There is no question but that the articles made serious accusations against the public officers named and others in connection with the prevalence of crimes and the failure to expose and punish them.

[Upon the filing of the verified complaint, the trial court entered an order forbidding the defendants to publish, circulate, or have in their possession any editions of the periodical from September 24, 1927, to November 19, 1927, inclusive, and from publishing, circulating or having in their possession, "any future editions of said The Saturday Press" and "any publication, known by any other name whatsoever containing malicious, scandalous and defamatory matter of the kind alleged in plaintiff's complaint herein or otherwise."]

[The trial court] made findings of fact, which followed the allegations of the complaint . . . . Judgment was thereupon entered adjudging that "the newspaper, magazine and periodical known as The Saturday Press," as a public nuisance, "be and is hereby abated." The judgment perpetually enjoined the defendants "from producing, editing, publishing, circulating, having in their possession, selling or giving away any publication whatsoever which is a malicious, scandalous or defamatory newspaper, as defined by law," and also "from further conducting said nuisance under the name and title of said The Saturday Press or any other name or title." [The state Supreme Court affirmed.] . . .

If we cut through mere details of procedure, the operation and effect of the statute in substance is that public authorities may bring the owner or publisher of a newspaper or periodical before a judge upon a charge of conducting a business of publishing scandalous and defamatory matter — in particular that the matter consists of charges against public officers of official dereliction — and, unless the owner or publisher is able and disposed to bring competent evidence to satisfy the judge that the charges are true and are published with good motives and for justifiable ends, his newspaper or periodical is suppressed and further publication is made punishable as a contempt. This is of the essence of censorship.

The question is whether a statute authorizing such proceedings in restraint of publication is consistent with the conception of the liberty of the press as historically conceived and guaranteed. In determining the extent of the constitutional protection, it has been generally, if not universally, considered that it is the chief purpose of the guaranty to prevent previous restraints upon publication. The struggle in England, directed against the legislative power of the licenser, resulted in renunciation of the censorship of the press. The liberty deemed to be established was thus described by Blackstone: "the liberty of the press is indeed essential to the nature of a free state; but this consists in laying no previous restraints upon publications, and not in freedom from censure for criminal matter when published. Every freeman has an undoubted right to lay what sentiments he pleases before the public; to forbid this, is to destroy the freedom of the press; but if he publishes what is improper, mischievous or illegal, he must take the consequence of his own temerity." 4 Bl. Com. 151, 152. See Story on the Constitution, §§ 1884, 1889. . . .

The criticism upon Blackstone's statement has not been because immunity from previous restraint upon publication has not been regarded as deserving of special emphasis, but chiefly because that immunity cannot be deemed to exhaust the conception of the liberty guaranteed by state and federal constitutions. . . . In the present case, we have no occasion to inquire as to the permissible scope of subsequent punishment. For whatever wrong the appellant has committed or may commit, by his publications, the state appropriately affords both public and private redress by its libel laws. As has been noted, the statute in question does not deal with punishments; it provides for no punishment, except in case of contempt for violation of the court's order, but for suppression and injunction, that is, for restraint upon publication.

The objection has also been made that the principle as to immunity from previous restraint is stated too broadly, if every such restraint is deemed to be prohibited. That is undoubtedly true; the protection even as to previous restraint is not absolutely unlimited. But the limitation has been recognized only in exceptional cases. . . . No one would question but that a government might prevent actual obstruction to its recruiting service or the publication of the sailing dates of transports or the number and location of troops. On similar grounds, the primary requirements of decency may be enforced against obscene publications. The security of the community life may be protected against incitements to acts of violence and the overthrow by force of orderly government. The constitutional guaranty of free speech does not "protect a man from an injunction against uttering words that may have all the effect of force." *Schenck v. United States* (1919) [*supra* Chapter 1]. These limitations are not applicable here. Nor are we now concerned with questions as to the extent of authority to prevent publications in order to protect private rights according to the principles governing the exercise of the jurisdiction of courts of equity.

The exceptional nature of its limitations places in a strong light the general conception that liberty of the press, historically considered and taken up by the Federal Constitution, has meant, principally although not exclusively, immunity from previous restraints or censorship. The conception of the liberty of the press in this country had broadened with the exigencies of the colonial period and with the efforts to secure freedom from oppressive administration. That liberty was especially cherished for the immunity it afforded from previous restraint of the publication of censure of public officers and charges of official misconduct. . . .

The fact that for approximately one hundred and fifty years there has been almost an entire absence of attempts to impose previous restraints upon publications relating to the malfeasance of public officers is significant of the deep-seated conviction that such restraints would violate constitutional right. Public officers, whose character and conduct remain open to debate and free discussion in the press, find their remedies for false accusations in actions under libel laws providing for redress and punishment, and not in proceedings to restrain the publication of newspapers and periodicals. . . .

In attempted justification of the statute, it is said that it deals not with publication *per se*, but with the "business" of publishing defamation. If, however, the publisher has a constitutional right to publish, without previous restraint, an edition of his newspaper charging official derelictions, it cannot be denied that he may publish subsequent editions for the same purpose. He does not lose his right by exercising it. If his right exists, it may be exercised in publishing nine editions, as in this case, as well as in one edition. If previous restraint is permissible, it may be imposed at once; indeed, the wrong may be as serious in one publication as in several. Characterizing the publication as a business, and the business as a nuisance, does not permit an invasion of the constitutional immunity against restraint. . . .

The statute in question cannot be justified by reason of the fact that the publisher is permitted to show, before injunction issues, that the matter published is true and is published with good motives and for justifiable ends. If such a statute, authorizing suppression and injunction on such a basis, is constitutionally valid, it would be equally permissible for the legislature to provide that at any time the publisher of any newspaper could be brought before a court, or even an administrative officer (as the constitutional protection may not be regarded as resting on mere procedural details), and required to produce proof of the truth of his publication, or of what he intended to publish and of his motives, or stand enjoined. If this can be done, the legislature may provide machinery for determining in the complete exercise of its discretion what are justifiable ends and restrain publication accordingly. And it would be but a step to a complete system of censorship. . . .

Equally unavailing is the insistence that the statute is designed to prevent the circulation of scandal which tends to disturb the public peace and to provoke assaults and the commission of crime. Charges of reprehensible conduct, and in particular of official malfeasance, unquestionably create a public scandal, but the theory of the constitutional guaranty is that even a more serious public evil would be caused by authority to prevent publication. . . .

For these reasons we hold the statute, so far as it authorized the proceedings in this [action], to be an infringement of the liberty of the press guaranteed by the Fourteenth Amendment. . . .

Judgment reversed.

Mr. Justice Butler, dissenting.

. . . The record shows, and it is conceded, that defendants' regular business was the publication of malicious, scandalous, and defamatory articles concerning the principal public officers, leading newspapers of the city, many private persons, and the Jewish race. It also shows that it was their purpose at all hazards to continue to carry on the business. In every edition slanderous and defamatory matter predominates to the practical exclusion of all else. Many of the statements are so highly improbable as to compel a finding that they are false. The articles themselves show malice. . . .

The Court quotes Blackstone in support of its condemnation of the statute as imposing a previous restraint upon publication. But the *previous restraints* referred to by him subjected the press to the arbitrary will of an administrative officer. He describes the practice (Book IV, p. 152): "To subject the press to the restrictive power of a licenser, as was formerly done, both before and since the revolution [of 1688], is to subject all freedom of sentiment to the prejudices of one man, and make him the arbitrary and infallible judge of all controverted points in learning, religion, and government." . . .

The Minnesota statute does not operate as a *previous* restraint on publication within the proper meaning of that phrase. It does not authorize administrative control in advance such as was formerly exercised by the licensers and censors but prescribes a remedy to be enforced by a suit in equity. In this case there was previous publication made in the course of the business of regularly producing malicious, scandalous, and defamatory periodicals. The business and publications unquestionably constitute an abuse of the right of free press. The statute denounces the things done as a nuisance on the ground, as stated by the state Supreme Court, that they threaten morals, peace, and good order. There is no question of the power of the state to denounce such transgressions. The restraint authorized is only in respect of continuing to do what has been duly adjudged to constitute a nuisance. . . . There is nothing in the statute purporting to prohibit publications that have not been adjudged to constitute a nuisance. It is fanciful to suggest similarity between the granting or enforcement of the decree authorized by this statute to prevent *further* publication of malicious, scandalous, and defamatory articles and the *previous restraint* upon the press by licensers as referred to by Blackstone and described in the history of the times to which he alludes. . . .

It is well known, as found by the state supreme court, that existing libel laws are inadequate effectively to suppress evils resulting from the kind of business and publications that are shown in this case. The doctrine that measures such as the one before us are invalid because they operate as previous restraints to infringe freedom of press exposes the peace and good order of every community and the business and private affairs of every individual to the constant and protracted false and malicious assaults of any insolvent publisher who may have purpose and sufficient capacity to contrive and put into effect a scheme or program for oppression, blackmail or extortion.

The judgment should be affirmed.

Mr. Justice Van Devanter, Mr. Justice McReynolds, and Mr. Justice Sutherland concur in this opinion.

————

Note: The Decision in Near

1. The opinion of the Court describes Near's publications but does not quote them. The dissent includes a sample from the last edition of the Saturday Press, dated November 19, 1927. Here are excerpts:

FACTS NOT THEORIES.

"I am a bosom friend of Mr. Olson," snorted a gentleman of Yiddish blood, "and I want to protest against your article," and blah, blah, blah, ad infinitum, ad nauseam.

I am not taking orders from men of Barnett faith, at least right now. There have been too many men in this city and especially those in official life, who HAVE been taking orders and suggestions from JEW GANGSTERS, therefore we HAVE Jew Gangsters, practically ruling Minneapolis. . . .

It is Jewish men and women—pliant tools of the Jew gangster, Mose Barnett, who stand charged with having falsified the election records and returns in the Third ward. And it is Mose Barnett himself, who, indicted for his part in the Shapiro assault, is a fugitive from justice today.

Practically every vendor of vile hooch, every owner of a moonshine still, every snake-faced gangster and exbryonic yegg in the Twin Cities is a JEW. . . .

It is Jew, Jew, Jew, as long as one cares to comb over the records.

I am launching no attack against the Jewish people AS A RACE. I am merely calling attention to a FACT. And if the people of that race and faith wish to rid themselves of the odium and stigma THE RODENTS OF THEIR OWN RACE HAVE BROUGHT UPON THEM, they need only to step to the front and help the decent citizens of Minneapolis rid the city of these criminal Jews. . . .

We will call for a special grand jury and a special prosecutor within a short time, as soon as half of the staff can navigate to advantage, and then we'll show you what a real grand jury can do. Up to the present we have been merely tapping on the window. Very soon we shall start smashing glass.

2. Neither the majority nor the dissent in *Near* cite any precedents as controlling or even helpful. Chapter 1 includes all of the major First Amendment decisions that had been handed down at the time of *Near*. Would any of them have provided substantial support for either the majority or the dissent?

3. There is some irony in the fact that the opinion of the Court, ruling in favor of Near, was joined by the Court's only Jewish member, Justice Brandeis, while the dissent was endorsed by Justice McReynolds, a notorious anti-Semite.

4. Justice Butler, dissenting in *Near*, insists that the Minnesota statute "does not operate as a *previous* restraint on publication within the proper meaning of the phrase." Does the Court adequately respond to the dissent on this point?

5. In *Organization for a Better Austin v. Keefe*, 402 U.S. 415 (1971), the petitioner was an organization whose stated purpose was to "stabilize" the racial ratio in the Austin (Illinois) area. Respondent Keefe was a real estate broker. The organization contended that Keefe had engaged in tactics known as "blockbusting"—"specifically, that he aroused the fears of the local white residents that Negroes were coming into

the area and then, exploiting the reactions and emotions so aroused, was able to secure listings and sell homes to Negroes." Members of the organization distributed leaflets criticizing Keefe's alleged practices.

Keefe filed suit in state court seeking an injunction against the organization's activities. After an adversary hearing, the trial court entered a temporary injunction enjoining the organization "from passing out . . . literature of any kind . . . anywhere in the City of Westchester, Illinois." The intermediate appellate court affirmed. It found that the organization's activities in Westchester had invaded Keefe's right of privacy, had caused irreparable harm, and were without adequate remedy at law.

The United States Supreme Court reversed. The Court said:

> Under *Near v. Minnesota*, the injunction, so far as it imposes prior restraint on speech and publication, constitutes an impermissible restraint on First Amendment rights. Here, as in that case, the injunction operates, not to redress alleged private wrongs, but to suppress, on the basis of previous publications, distribution of literature "of any kind" in a city of 18,000.

Does this suggest that injunctions that operate only "to redress alleged private wrongs" do not fall within the prior restraint doctrine? Consider the "recalcitrant defamer" Problem that follows.

———

Problem: A Recalcitrant Defamer

In 1983, Ulysses Tory retained attorney Johnnie Cochran to represent him in a personal injury action. Tory became unhappy with the manner in which Cochran was representing him, and ultimately Cochran withdrew as Tory's lawyer. In July 1995, after many years of silence, Tory wrote to Cochran, demanding that he return certain moneys. In the interim, Cochran had received a great deal of publicity as one of the defense lawyers in the O.J. Simpson criminal trial.

In the mid-1990s, Tory and a troop of people began picketing outside Cochran's office and outside the Los Angeles Superior Court, carrying placards with statements that included: "Johnny is a crook, a liar and a thief." and "Attorney Cochran, We have no Use for Illegal Abuse." Tory continued to write to Cochran demanding money.

Cochran sued Tory in state court alleging causes of action for defamation and invasion of privacy. The trial court concluded that Tory's claim that Cochran owed him money was without foundation, that Tory had engaged in a continuous pattern of libelous and slanderous activity, and that Tory had used false and defamatory speech to "coerce" Cochran into paying "amounts of money to which Tory was not entitled" as a "tribute" or a "premium" for "desisting" from this libelous and slanderous activity.

After noting that Tory had indicated that he would continue to engage in this activity in the absence of a court order, the trial court issued a permanent injunction. The injunction, among other things, prohibited Tory and his "agents" or "representatives" from "picketing," from "displaying signs, placards or other written or printed material," and from "orally uttering statements" about Johnnie L. Cochran, Jr., and about Cochran's law firm in "any public forum."

Tory argued that this portion of the injunction was an unconstitutional prior restraint. The state intermediate appellate court disagreed, saying:

> Although a prior restraint can be presumptively unconstitutional, that rule has no application where, as here, an injunction against a private person operates "to redress alleged private wrongs," not to suppress a legitimate publication. *Organization for a Better Austin v. Keefe*, 402 U.S. 415 (1971). The injunction in this case was issued based on the trial court's findings—after a full trial on the merits—that Tory's statements were both libelous and slanderous within the meaning of [the California Civil Code], and that pecuniary compensation would not afford an adequate remedy. As a result, the [quoted paragraph of the injunction] "was issued only after the trial court determined that Tory had engaged in unlawful activity, and the order simply precludes Tory from continuing his unlawful activity." . . .

> Once there has been a final adjudication on the merits that the speech is unprotected, an injunction restraining that speech does not constitute an impermissible prior restraint.

Tory filed a certiorari petition in the United States Supreme Court, and the Court granted review. However, Cochran died after oral argument. The Court found that the case was not moot, but it decided the case on very narrow grounds. It concluded that the injunction had lost its underlying rationale and thus "now amount[ed] to an overly broad prior restraint upon speech, lacking plausible justification." The Court declined to address Tory's basic claims, "namely (1) that the First Amendment forbids the issuance of a permanent injunction in a defamation case, at least when the plaintiff is a public figure, and (2) that the injunction (considered prior to Cochran's death) was not properly tailored and consequently violated the First Amendment." *Tory v. Cochran*, 544 U.S. 734 (2005).

Assume that a similar case arises in the future and that the record supports findings by the trial court similar to those quoted above. In particular, assume that the defendant has engaged in a pattern of unprotected libelous speech against a public figure and has indicated that he will continue to engage in this activity unless restrained by a court order. How should the questions posed by the Supreme Court be resolved?

New York Times Co. v. United States
(The "Pentagon Papers" Case)
403 U.S. 713 (1971)

[The "Pentagon Papers" case was a consolidation of two separate proceedings. In each proceeding, the United States sought to enjoin a newspaper from publishing classified documents involving United States participation in the Vietnam war. In both cases the district courts refused to issue an injunction. On appeal, the government prevailed in the Second Circuit (the *New York Times* case), but lost in the District of

Columbia (the *Washington Post* case). The cases then went to the Supreme Court. In his dissent, Justice Harlan described the "frenzied train of events" leading to the Court's decision:

> Both the Court of Appeals for the Second Circuit and the Court of Appeals for the District of Columbia Circuit rendered judgment on June 23 [1971]. The New York Times' petition for certiorari, its motion for accelerated consideration thereof, and its application for interim relief were filed in this Court on June 24 at about 11 a.m. The application of the United States for interim relief in the Post case was also filed here on June 24 at about 7:15 p.m. This Court's order setting a hearing before us on June 26 at 11 a.m., a course which I joined only to avoid the possibility of even more peremptory action by the Court, was issued less than 24 hours before. The record in the Post case was filed with the Clerk shortly before 1 p.m. on June 25; the record in the Times case did not arrive until 7 or 8 o'clock that same night. The briefs of the parties were received less than two hours before argument on June 26.

The Court issued its decision on June 30, four days after oral argument.]

Per Curiam.

We granted certiorari in these cases in which the United States seeks to enjoin the New York Times and the Washington Post from publishing the contents of a classified study entitled "History of U.S. Decision-Making Process on Viet Nam Policy."

"Any system of prior restraints of expression comes to this Court bearing a heavy presumption against its constitutional validity." *Bantam Books, Inc. v. Sullivan*, 372 U.S. 58 (1963); *see also Near v. Minnesota* (1931) [*supra* this chapter]. The Government "thus carries a heavy burden of showing justification for the imposition of such a restraint." *Organization for a Better Austin v. Keefe*, 402 U.S. 415 (1971) [Note *supra* this chapter]. The District Court for the Southern District of New York in the *New York Times* case and the District Court for the District of Columbia and the Court of Appeals for the District of Columbia Circuit in the *Washington Post* case held that the Government had not met that burden. We agree.

The judgment of the Court of Appeals for the District of Columbia Circuit is therefore affirmed. The order of the Court of Appeals for the Second Circuit is reversed and the case is remanded with directions to enter a judgment affirming the judgment of the District Court for the Southern District of New York. The stays entered June 25, 1971, by the Court are vacated. The judgments shall issue forthwith.

Mr. Justice Black, with whom Mr. Justice Douglas joins, concurring.

[T]he Government's case against the Washington Post should have been dismissed and . . . the injunction against the New York Times should have been vacated without oral argument when the cases were first presented to this Court. I believe that every moment's continuance of the injunctions against these newspapers amounts to a flagrant, indefensible, and continuing violation of the First Amendment . . . . In my view it is unfortunate that some of my Brethren are apparently willing to hold that the publication of news may sometimes be enjoined. Such a holding would make a shambles of the First Amendment.

. . . Madison and the other Framers of the First Amendment, able men that they were, wrote in language they earnestly believed could never be misunderstood: "Congress shall make no law * * * abridging the freedom * * * of the press * * *." Both the history and language of the First Amendment support the view that the press must be left free to publish news, whatever the source, without censorship, injunctions, or prior restraints. . . .

In the First Amendment the Founding Fathers gave the free press the protection it must have to fulfill its essential role in our democracy. The press was to serve the governed, not the governors. The Government's power to censor the press was abolished so that the press would remain forever free to censure the Government. The press was protected so that it could bare the secrets of government and inform the people. Only a free and unrestrained press can effectively expose deception in government. And paramount among the responsibilities of a free press is the duty to prevent any part of the government from deceiving the people and sending them off to distant lands to die of foreign fevers and foreign shot and shell. In my view, far from deserving condemnation for their courageous reporting, the New York Times, the Washington Post, and other newspapers should be commended for serving the purpose that the Founding Fathers saw so clearly. In revealing the workings of government that led to the Vietnam war, the newspapers nobly did precisely that which the Founders hoped and trusted they would do.

The Government's case here is based on premises entirely different from those that guided the Framers of the First Amendment. The Solicitor General has carefully and emphatically stated: "Now, Mr. Justice [Black], your construction of * * * [the First Amendment] is well known, and I certainly respect it. You say that no law means no law, and that should be obvious. I can only say, Mr. Justice, that to me it is equally obvious that 'no law' does not mean 'no law', and I would seek to persuade the Court that that is true. * * * [T]here are other parts of the Constitution that grant powers and responsibilities to the Executive, and * * * the First Amendment was not intended to make it impossible for the Executive to function or to protect the security of the United States."

And the Government argues in its brief that in spite of the First Amendment, "[t]he authority of the Executive Department to protect the nation against publication of information whose disclosure would endanger the national security stems from two interrelated sources: the constitutional power of the President over the conduct of foreign affairs and his authority as Commander-in-Chief."

In other words, we are asked to hold that despite the First Amendment's emphatic command, the Executive Branch, the Congress, and the Judiciary can make laws enjoining publication of current news and abridging freedom of the press in the name of "national security." The Government does not even attempt to rely on any act of Congress. Instead it makes the bold and dangerously far-reaching contention that the courts should take it upon themselves to "make" a law abridging freedom of the press in the name of equity, presidential power and national security, even when the representatives of the people in Congress have adhered to the command of the First Amendment and refused to make such a law. To find that the President has "inherent power" to halt the publication of news by resort to the courts would wipe out the First Amendment and destroy the fundamental liberty and security of the very people the Government hopes to make "secure." No one can read the history of the adoption of the First Amendment without being convinced beyond any doubt that it was injunctions like those sought here that Madison and his collaborators intended to outlaw in this Nation for all time.

The word "security" is a broad, vague generality whose contours should not be invoked to abrogate the fundamental law embodied in the First Amendment. The guarding of military and diplomatic secrets at the expense of informed representative government provides no real security for our Republic. The Framers of the First Amendment, fully aware of both the need to defend a new nation and the abuses of the English and Colonial Governments, sought to give this new society strength and security by providing that freedom of speech, press, religion, and assembly should not be abridged. This thought was eloquently expressed in 1937 by Mr. Chief Justice Hughes—great man and great Chief Justice that he was—when the Court held a man could not be punished for attending a meeting run by Communists. "The greater the importance of safeguarding the community from incitements to the overthrow of our institutions by force and violence, the more imperative is the need to preserve inviolate the constitutional rights of free speech, free press and free assembly in order to maintain the opportunity for free political discussion, to the end that government may be responsive to the will of the people and that changes, if desired, may be obtained by peaceful means. Therein lies the security of the Republic, the very foundation of constitutional government." *De Jonge v. Oregon*, 299 U.S. 353 (1937) [Note *supra* Chapter 1].

MR. JUSTICE DOUGLAS, with whom MR. JUSTICE BLACK joins, concurring....

[T]he First Amendment ... leaves, in my view, no room for governmental restraint on the press.

There is, moreover, no statute barring the publication by the press of the material which the Times and the Post seek to use.... So any power that the Government possesses must come from its "inherent power."...

These disclosures[3] may have a serious impact. But that is no basis for sanctioning a previous restraint on the press....

The Government says that it has inherent powers to go into court and obtain an injunction to protect the national interest, which in this case is alleged to be national

---

3. There are numerous sets of this material in existence and they apparently are not under any controlled custody. Moreover, the President has sent a set to the Congress. We start then with a case where there already is rather wide distribution of the material that is destined for publicity, not secrecy. I have gone over the material listed in the in camera brief of the United States. It is all history, not future events. None of it is more recent than 1968.

security. *Near v. Minnesota* repudiated that expansive doctrine in no uncertain terms. . . .

The stays in these cases that have been in effect for more than a week constitute a flouting of the principles of the First Amendment as interpreted in *Near v. Minnesota.*

Mr. Justice Brennan, concurring.

I

I write separately in these cases only to emphasize what should be apparent: that our judgments in the present cases may not be taken to indicate the propriety, in the future, of issuing temporary stays and restraining orders to block the publication of material sought to be suppressed by the Government. So far as I can determine, never before has the United States sought to enjoin a newspaper from publishing information in its possession. The relative novelty of the questions presented, the necessary haste with which decisions were reached, the magnitude of the interests asserted, and the fact that all the parties have concentrated their arguments upon the question whether permanent restraints were proper may have justified at least some of the restraints heretofore imposed in these cases. . . . But [that proposition] has no bearing upon the propriety of similar judicial action in the future. To begin with, there has now been ample time for reflection and judgment . . . . More important, the First Amendment stands as an absolute bar to the imposition of judicial restraints in circumstances of the kind presented by these cases.

II

The error that has pervaded these cases from the outset was the granting of any injunctive relief whatsoever, interim or otherwise. The entire thrust of the Government's claim throughout these cases has been that publication of the material sought to be enjoined "could," or "might," or "may" prejudice the national interest in various ways. But the First Amendment tolerates absolutely no prior judicial restraints of the press predicated upon surmise or conjecture that untoward consequences may result.* Our cases, it is true, have indicated that there is a single, extremely narrow class of cases in which the First Amendment's ban on prior judicial restraint may be overridden. Our cases have thus far indicated that such cases may arise only when the Nation "is at war," *Schenck v. United States* (1919) [*supra* Chapter 1], during which times "no one would question but that a government might prevent actual obstruction to its recruiting service or the publication of the sailing dates of transports or the number and location of troops." *Near v. Minnesota.* Even if the present world situation were assumed to be tantamount to a time of war, or if the power of presently available armaments would justify even in peacetime the suppression of information that would set

---

* *Freedman v. Maryland,* 380 U.S. 51 (1965) [Note *supra* this chapter] and similar cases regarding temporary restraints of allegedly obscene materials are not in point. For those cases rest upon the proposition that "obscenity is not protected by the freedoms of speech and press." *Roth v. United States* (1957) [*supra* Chapter 2]. Here there is no question but that the material sought to be suppressed is within the protection of the First Amendment; the only question is whether, notwithstanding that fact, its publication may be enjoined for a time because of the presence of an overwhelming national interest. . . .

in motion a nuclear holocaust, in neither of these actions has the Government presented or even alleged that publication of items from or based upon the material at issue would cause the happening of an event of that nature. . . .

Thus, only governmental allegation and proof that publication must inevitably, directly, and immediately cause the occurrence of an event kindred to imperiling the safety of a transport already at sea can support even the issuance of an interim restraining order. In no event may mere conclusions be sufficient: for if the Executive Branch seeks judicial aid in preventing publication, it must inevitably submit the basis upon which that aid is sought to scrutiny by the judiciary. And therefore, every restraint issued in this case, whatever its form, has violated the First Amendment—and not less so because that restraint was justified as necessary to afford the courts an opportunity to examine the claim more thoroughly. Unless and until the Government has clearly made out its case, the First Amendment commands that no injunction may issue.

Mr. Justice Stewart, with whom Mr. Justice White joins, concurring.

In the governmental structure created by our Constitution, the Executive is endowed with enormous power in the two related areas of national defense and international relations. . . .

In the absence of the governmental checks and balances present in other areas of our national life, the only effective restraint upon executive policy and power in the areas of national defense and international affairs may lie in an enlightened citizenry—in an informed and critical public opinion which alone can here protect the values of democratic government. For this reason, it is perhaps here that a press that is alert, aware, and free most vitally serves the basic purpose of the First Amendment. For without an informed and free press there cannot be an enlightened people.

Yet it is elementary that the successful conduct of international diplomacy and the maintenance of an effective national defense require both confidentiality and secrecy. . . .

I think there can be but one answer to this dilemma, if dilemma it be. The responsibility must be where the power is. If the Constitution gives the Executive a large degree of unshared power in the conduct of foreign affairs and the maintenance of our national defense, then under the Constitution the Executive must have the largely unshared duty to determine and preserve the degree of internal security necessary to exercise that power successfully . . . [It] is clear to me that it is the constitutional duty of the Executive—as a matter of sovereign prerogative and not as a matter of law as the courts know law—through the promulgation and enforcement of executive regulations, to protect the confidentiality necessary to carry out its responsibilities in the fields of international relations and national defense.

This is not to say that Congress and the courts have no role to play. Undoubtedly Congress has the power to enact specific and appropriate criminal laws to protect government property and preserve government secrets. Congress has passed such laws, and several of them are of very colorable relevance to the apparent circumstances of these cases. . . .

But in the cases before us we are asked neither to construe specific regulations nor to apply specific laws. We are asked, instead, to perform a function that the Constitution gave to the Executive, not the Judiciary. We are asked, quite simply, to prevent the publication by two newspapers of material that the Executive Branch insists should not, in the national interest, be published. I am convinced that the Executive is correct with respect to some of the documents involved. But I cannot say that disclosure of any of them will surely result in direct, immediate, and irreparable damage to our Nation or its people. That being so, there can under the First Amendment be but one judicial resolution of the issues before us. I join the judgments of the Court.

Mr. Justice White, with whom Mr. Justice Stewart joins, concurring.

I concur in today's judgments, but only because of the concededly extraordinary protection against prior restraints enjoyed by the press under our constitutional system. I do not say that in no circumstances would the First Amendment permit an injunction against publishing information about government plans or operations. Nor, after examining the materials the Government characterizes as the most sensitive and destructive, can I deny that revelation of these documents will do substantial damage to public interests. Indeed, I am confident that their disclosure will have that result. But I nevertheless agree that the United States has not satisfied the very heavy burden that it must meet to warrant an injunction against publication in these cases, at least in the absence of express and appropriately limited congressional authorization for prior restraints in circumstances such as these.

The Government's position is simply stated: The responsibility of the Executive for the conduct of the foreign affairs and for the security of the Nation is so basic that the President is entitled to an injunction against publication of a newspaper story whenever he can convince a court that the information to be revealed threatens "grave and irreparable" injury to the public interest; and the injunction should issue whether or not the material to be published is classified, whether or not publication would be lawful under relevant criminal statutes enacted by Congress, and regardless of the circumstances by which the newspaper came into possession of the information.

At least in the absence of legislation by Congress, based on its own investigations and findings, I am quite unable to agree that the inherent powers of the Executive and the courts reach so far as to authorize remedies having such sweeping potential for inhibiting publications by the press. Much of the difficulty inheres in the "grave and irreparable danger" standard suggested by the United States. . . . To sustain the Government in these cases would start the courts down a long and hazardous road that I am not willing to travel, at least without congressional guidance and direction.

It is not easy to reject the proposition urged by the United States and to deny relief on its good-faith claims in these cases that publication will work serious damage to the country. But that discomfiture is considerably dispelled by the infrequency of prior-restraint cases. Normally, publication will occur and the damage be done before the Government has either opportunity or grounds for suppression. So here, publication has already begun and a substantial part of the threatened damage has already occurred. The fact of a massive breakdown in security is known, access to the documents by many unauthorized people is undeniable, and the efficacy of equitable relief against these or other newspapers to avert anticipated damage is doubtful at best.

What is more, terminating the ban on publication of the relatively few sensitive documents the Government now seeks to suppress does not mean that the law either requires or invites newspapers or others to publish them or that they will be immune from criminal action if they do. Prior restraints require an unusually heavy justification under the First Amendment; but failure by the Government to justify prior restraints does not measure its constitutional entitlement to a conviction for criminal publication. That the Government mistakenly chose to proceed by injunction does not mean that it could not successfully proceed in another way. . . .

Congress has addressed itself to the problems of protecting the security of the country and the national defense from unauthorized disclosure of potentially damaging information. It has not, however, authorized the injunctive remedy against threatened publication. It has apparently been satisfied to rely on criminal sanctions and their deterrent effect on the responsible as well as the irresponsible press. I am not, of course, saying that either of these newspapers has yet committed a crime or that either would commit a crime if it published all the material now in its possession. That matter must await resolution in the context of a criminal proceeding if one is instituted by the United States. In that event, the issue of guilt or innocence would be determined by procedures and standards quite different from those that have purported to govern these injunctive proceedings.

Mr. Justice Marshall, concurring.

The Government contends that the only issue in these cases is whether in a suit by the United States, "the First Amendment bars a court from prohibiting a newspaper from publishing material whose disclosure would pose a grave and immediate danger to the security of the United States." With all due respect, I believe the ultimate issue in this case is even more basic than the one posed by the Solicitor General. The issue is whether this Court or the Congress has the power to make law. . . .

Either the Government has the power under statutory grant to use traditional criminal law to protect the country or, if there is no basis for arguing that Congress has made the activity a crime, it is plain that Congress has specifically refused to grant the authority the Government seeks from this Court. In either case this Court does not have authority to grant the requested relief. It is not for this Court to fling itself into every breach perceived by some Government official nor is it for this Court to take on itself the burden of enacting law, especially a law that Congress has refused to pass.

Mr. Chief Justice Burger, dissenting.

. . . In these cases, the imperative of a free and unfettered press comes into collision with another imperative, the effective functioning of a complex modern government and specifically the effective exercise of certain constitutional powers of the Executive. Only those who view the First Amendment as an absolute in all circumstances—a view I respect, but reject—can find such cases as these to be simple or easy.

These cases are not simple for another and more immediate reason. We do not know the facts of the cases. . . .

Why are we in this posture, in which only those judges to whom the First Amendment is absolute and permits of no restraint in any circumstances or for any reason, are really in a position to act? . . .

It is not disputed that the Times has had unauthorized possession of the documents for three to four months, during which it has had its expert analysts studying them, presumably digesting them and preparing the material for publication. . . .

Would it have been unreasonable, since the newspaper could anticipate the Government's objections to release of secret material, to give the Government an opportunity to review the entire collection and determine whether agreement could be reached on publication? . . . To me it is hardly believable that a newspaper long regarded as a great institution in American life would fail to perform one of the basic and simple duties of every citizen with respect to the discovery or possession of stolen property or secret government documents. That duty, I had thought—perhaps naively—was to report forthwith, to responsible public officers. This duty rests on taxi drivers, Justices, and the New York Times. The course followed by the Times, whether so calculated or not, removed any possibility of orderly litigation of the issues. If the action of the judges up to now has been correct, that result is sheer happenstance.[2] . . .

The consequence of all this melancholy series of events is that we literally do not know what we are acting on. . . . I agree generally with Mr. Justice Harlan and Mr. Justice Blackmun but I am not prepared to reach the merits.

I would affirm the Court of Appeals for the Second Circuit and allow the District Court to complete the trial aborted by our grant of certiorari, meanwhile preserving the status quo in the *Post* case. I would direct that the District Court on remand give priority to the *Times* case to the exclusion of all other business of that court but I would not set arbitrary deadlines.

I should add that I am in general agreement with much of what Mr. Justice White has expressed with respect to penal sanctions concerning communication or retention of documents or information relating to the national defense. . . .

MR. JUSTICE HARLAN, with whom THE CHIEF JUSTICE and MR. JUSTICE BLACKMUN join, dissenting.

. . . With all respect, I consider that the Court has been almost irresponsibly feverish in dealing with these cases. . . .

---

2. Interestingly the Times explained its refusal to allow the Government to examine its own purloined documents by saying in substance this might compromise its sources and informants! The Times thus asserts a right to guard the secrecy of its sources while denying that the Government of the United States has that power.

[The frenzied train of events in these cases] took place in the name of the presumption against prior restraints created by the First Amendment. Due regard for the extraordinarily important and difficult questions involved in these litigations should have led the Court to shun such a precipitate timetable. In order to decide the merits of these cases properly, some or all of the following questions should have been faced:

1. Whether the Attorney General is authorized to bring these suits in the name of the United States. Compare *In re Debs*, 158 U.S. 564 (1895), with *Youngstown Sheet & Tube Co. v. Sawyer*, 343 U.S. 579 (1952). This question involves as well the construction and validity of a singularly opaque statute—the Espionage Act, 18 U.S.C. § 793(e).

2. Whether the First Amendment permits the federal courts to enjoin publication of stories which would present a serious threat to national security. *See Near v. Minnesota* (1931) (dictum) [*supra* this chapter].

3. Whether the threat to publish highly secret documents is of itself a sufficient implication of national security to justify an injunction on the theory that regardless of the contents of the documents harm enough results simply from the demonstration of such a breach of secrecy.

4. Whether the unauthorized disclosure of any of these particular documents would seriously impair the national security.

5. What weight should be given to the opinion of high officers in the Executive Branch of the Government with respect to questions 3 and 4.

6. Whether the newspapers are entitled to retain and use the documents notwithstanding the seemingly uncontested facts that the documents, or the originals of which they are duplicates, were purloined from the Government's possession and that the newspapers received them with knowledge that they had been feloniously acquired.

7. Whether the threatened harm to the national security or the Government's possessory interest in the documents justifies the issuance of an injunction against publication in light of—

   a. The strong First Amendment policy against prior restraints on publication;

   b. The doctrine against enjoining conduct in violation of criminal statutes; and

   c. The extent to which the materials at issue have apparently already been otherwise disseminated. . . .

Forced as I am to reach the merits of these cases, I dissent from the opinion and judgments of the Court. . . .

I agree that, in performance of its duty to protect the values of the First Amendment against political pressures, the judiciary must review the initial Executive determination to the point of satisfying itself that the subject matter of the dispute does lie within the proper compass of the President's foreign relations power. Constitutional considerations forbid "a complete abandonment of judicial control." Moreover the judiciary may properly insist that the determination that disclosure of the subject matter would irreparably impair the national security be made by the head of the Executive Department concerned—here the Secretary of State or the Secretary of Defense—after actual personal consideration by that officer. . . . .

But in my judgment the judiciary may not properly go beyond these two inquiries and redetermine for itself the probable impact of disclosure on the national security. . . .

Even if there is some room for the judiciary to override the executive determination, it is plain that the scope of review must be exceedingly narrow. I can see no indication in the opinions of either the District Court or the Court of Appeals in the *Post* litigation that the conclusions of the Executive were given even the deference owing to an administrative agency, much less that owing to a co-equal branch of the Government operating within the field of its constitutional prerogative. . . .

Pending further hearings in each case conducted under the appropriate ground rules, I would continue the restraints on publication. I cannot believe that the doctrine prohibiting prior restraints reaches to the point of preventing courts from maintaining the status quo long enough to act responsibly in matters of such national importance as those involved here.

Mr. Justice Blackmun, dissenting.

I join Mr. Justice Harlan in his dissent. I also am in substantial accord with much that Mr. Justice White says, by way of admonition, in the latter part of his opinion. . . .

The First Amendment, after all, is only one part of an entire Constitution. Article II of the great document vests in the Executive Branch primary power over the conduct of foreign affairs and places in that branch the responsibility for the Nation's safety. Each provision of the Constitution is important, and I cannot subscribe to a doctrine of unlimited absolutism for the First Amendment at the cost of downgrading other provisions. . . . What is needed here is a weighing, upon properly developed standards, of the broad right of the press to print and of the very narrow right of the Government to prevent. Such standards are not yet developed. The parties here are in disagreement as to what those standards should be. But even the newspapers concede that there are situations where restraint is in order and is constitutional. . . .

Judge Wilkey, dissenting in the District of Columbia case, after a review of only the affidavits before his court (the basic papers had not then been made available by either party), concluded that there were a number of examples of documents that, if in the possession of the Post, and if published, "could clearly result in great harm to the nation," and he defined "harm" to mean "the death of soldiers, the destruction of alliances, the greatly increased difficulty of negotiation with our enemies, the inability of our diplomats to negotiate * * *." I, for one, have now been able to give at least some cursory study not only to the affidavits, but to the material itself. I regret to say that from this examination I fear that Judge Wilkey's statements have possible foundation. I therefore share his concern. I hope that damage has not already been done. If, however, damage has been done, and if, with the Court's action today, these newspapers proceed to publish the critical documents and there results therefrom "the death of soldiers, the destruction of alliances, the greatly increased difficulty of negotiation with our enemies, the inability of our diplomats to negotiate," to which list I might add the factors of prolongation of the war and of further delay in the freeing of United States prisoners, then the Nation's people will know where the responsibility for these sad consequences rests.

———

Note: Injunctions Against Speech

1. "When a fragmented Court decides a case and no single rationale explaining the result enjoys the assent of five Justices, the holding of the Court may be viewed as that position taken by those Members who concurred in the [judgment] on the narrowest grounds." *Marks v. United States*, 430 U.S. 188, 193 (1977). Under this principle, what is the "holding" of the *Pentagon Papers* case?

2. Justice Douglas argues that the case is squarely controlled by *Near v. Minnesota*. Is he persuasive on this point?

3. In *Near*, Chief Justice Hughes emphasized that for 150 years "there has been almost an entire absence of attempts to impose previous restraints upon publications relating to the malfeasance of public officers." Similarly, in the *Pentagon Papers* case, Justice Brennan notes that "never before has the United States sought to enjoin a newspaper from publishing information in its possession." How much weight should be given, in a First Amendment analysis, to the absence of historical precedent for a particular restraint on speech?

———

Note: "The H-Bomb Secret"

1. In the spring of 1979, a magazine called *The Progressive* prepared to publish an article entitled "The H-Bomb Secret: How We Got It, Why We're Telling It." The editors asserted that their purpose was to alert the people of the United States to "the false illusion of security created by the government's futile efforts at secrecy." They asserted that publication would provide the people with needed information to make informed decisions on an urgent issue of public concern.

The magazine submitted a copy of the manuscript to the Department of Energy (DOE) and asked it to confirm the accuracy of certain enclosures. Based on their review of the article, DOE officials determined that a significant portion of the article contained information that the Atomic Energy Act requires to be classified as Secret Restricted Data.

Several days of discussions between Government officials and representatives of The Progressive ensued. DOE assured the magazine's representatives that it did not want to stop the publication of the entire manuscript but only those portions which contained Secret Restricted Data. Counsel for The Progressive stated that publication would proceed unless the United States promptly obtained a temporary restraining order (TRO).

The Government immediately filed a complaint in the United States District Court for the Eastern District of Wisconsin. The Government based its suit on section 2274 of the Atomic Energy Act, which prohibits anyone from communicating, transmitting, or disclosing any restricted data to any person "with reason to believe such data will be utilized to injure the United States or to secure an advantage to any foreign nation." The Government also relied on section 2280 of the Act, which authorizes applications for injunctive relief.

The Government asked for a TRO, and after a hearing, the court granted it. The court then held a hearing on the request for a preliminary injunction. Based on testimony and evidentiary materials, the district court issued the injunction. *United States v. The Progressive, Inc.*, 467 F. Supp. 990 (W.D. Wis. 1979). In its findings of fact, the court concluded:

> 15. . . . Although the Restricted Data portions of the article also contain some information that has been previously disclosed in scattered public sources, the article provides a more comprehensive, accurate, and detailed analysis of the overall construction and operation of a thermonuclear weapon than any publication to date in the public literature. Although various information in the public realm suggests a number of possible designs for a thermonuclear weapon, nowhere in the public domain is there a correct description of the type of design used in United States thermonuclear weapons.
>
> 16. Publication of the Restricted Data contained in the Morland article would be extremely important to a nation seeking a thermonuclear capability, for it would provide vital information on key concepts involved in the construction of a practical thermonuclear weapon. Once basic concepts are learned, the remainder of the process may easily follow. The article could provide sufficient information to allow a medium-size nation to move faster in developing a hydrogen weapon.
>
> 17. Publication of the Restricted Data contained in the article could materially reduce the time required by certain countries to achieve a thermonuclear weapon capability.

Assume that the court of appeals would hold that these "findings of fact" were not clearly erroneous. Under *Near* and the Pentagon Papers case, was the grant of injunctive relief proper?

2. Professor Tribe reports that the actual case was mooted when another magazine published the same material. He adds: "At this writing, the world has not ended." Lawrence H. Tribe, American Constitutional Law 1054 n.53 (2d ed. 1988). Does that prove that the district court was wrong in issuing the preliminary injunction?

————

Problems: Disclosure of NSA Monitoring

1. In 2005, the New York Times published a news story reporting that the President "secretly authorized the National Security Agency (NSA) to eavesdrop on Americans

and others inside the United States to search for evidence of terrorist activity without the court-approved warrants ordinarily required for domestic spying." According to the story, the program involved the monitoring of international telephone calls and international e-mail messages "in an effort to track possible 'dirty numbers' linked to" the terrorist organization al Qaeda.

The Times acknowledged that Administration officials had asked the newspaper not to publish the story, "arguing that it could jeopardize continuing investigations and alert would-be terrorists that they might be under scrutiny." After meeting with some of those officials, the Times delayed publication and omitted "[s]ome information that administration officials argued could be useful to terrorists."

Suppose that the Government, upon learning that the Times was prepared to publish information that "could jeopardize continuing investigations and alert would-be terrorists that they might be under scrutiny," were to ask a federal district court to enjoin publication of that information. Under the First Amendment, would the injunction be permissible?

2. A federal criminal law, 18 U.S.C. § 798, provides in part: "Whoever knowingly and willfully . . . *publishes* . . . any classified information . . . concerning the communication intelligence activities of the United States" shall be fined or imprisoned. Assume that the Government could prove, beyond a reasonable doubt, that the New York Times' disclosures of NSA monitoring violated § 798. Under the opinions in the Pentagon Papers case, would the criminal prosecution be permissible under the First Amendment?

B. Overbreadth and Vagueness

In several of the cases in the preceding chapters the Court considered an argument that a statute or ordinance was unconstitutionally "overbroad." Here, we examine the scope and application of the overbreadth doctrine. Also considered here is the related doctrine of vagueness.

New York v. Ferber
458 U.S. 747 (1982)

JUSTICE WHITE delivered the opinion of the Court.

At issue in this case is the constitutionality of a New York criminal statute which prohibits persons from knowingly promoting sexual performances by children under the age of 16 by distributing material which depicts such performances. [Parts I–IV of the opinion are set forth in Chapter 3, section B. The opinion continued:]

The traditional rule is that a person to whom a statute may constitutionally be applied may not challenge that statute on the ground that it may conceivably be applied unconstitutionally to others in situations not before the Court. [E.g.,] *Broadrick v. Oklahoma*, 413 U.S. 601, 610 (1973). In *Broadrick*, we recognized that this rule reflects two cardinal principles of our constitutional order: the personal nature of constitutional rights, and prudential limitations on constitutional adjudication. In *United States v. Raines*, 362 U.S. 17 (1960), we noted the "incontrovertible proposition" that it "would indeed be undesirable for this Court to consider every conceivable situation which might possibly arise in the application of complex and comprehensive legislation." By focusing on the factual situation before us, and similar cases necessary for development of a constitutional rule, we face "flesh-and-blood" legal problems with data "relevant and adequate to an informed judgment." This practice also fulfills a valuable institutional purpose: it allows state courts the opportunity to construe a law to avoid constitutional infirmities.

What has come to be known as the First Amendment overbreadth doctrine is one of the few exceptions to this principle and must be justified by "weighty countervailing policies." The doctrine is predicated on the sensitive nature of protected expression: "persons whose expression is constitutionally protected may well refrain from exercising their rights for fear of criminal sanctions by a statute susceptible of application to protected expression." It is for this reason that we have allowed persons to attack overly broad statutes even though the conduct of the person making the attack is clearly unprotected and could be proscribed by a law drawn with the requisite specificity. [E.g.,] *Dombrowski v. Pfister*, 380 U.S. 479 (1965); *Thornhill v. Alabama*, 310 U.S. 88 (1940).

The scope of the First Amendment overbreadth doctrine, like most exceptions to established principles, must be carefully tied to the circumstances in which facial invalidation of a statute is truly warranted. Because of the wide-reaching effects of striking down a statute on its face at the request of one whose own conduct may be punished despite the First Amendment, we have recognized that the overbreadth doctrine is "strong medicine" and have employed it with hesitation, and then "only as a last resort." We have, in consequence, insisted that the overbreadth involved be "substantial" before the statute involved will be invalidated on its face.

In *Broadrick*, we explained the basis for this requirement:

> [T]he plain import of our cases is, at the very least, that facial overbreadth adjudication is an exception to our traditional rules of practice and that its function, a limited one at the outset, attenuates as the otherwise unprotected behavior that it forbids the State to sanction moves from "pure speech" toward conduct and that conduct — even if expressive — falls within the scope of otherwise valid criminal laws that reflect legitimate state interests in maintaining comprehensive controls over harmful, constitutionally unprotected conduct. Although such laws, if too broadly worded, may deter protected speech to some unknown extent, there comes a point where that effect — at best a prediction — cannot, with confidence, justify invalidating a statute on its face and so prohibiting a State from enforcing the statute against conduct that is admittedly within its power to proscribe.

We accordingly held that "particularly where conduct and not merely speech is involved, we believe that the overbreadth of a statute must not only be real, but substantial as well, judged in relation to the statute's plainly legitimate sweep."

Broadrick examined a regulation involving restrictions on political campaign activity, an area not considered "pure speech," and thus it was unnecessary to consider the proper overbreadth test when a law arguably reaches traditional forms of expression such as books and films. As we intimated in *Broadrick*, the requirement of substantial overbreadth extended "at the very least" to cases involving conduct plus speech. This case, which poses the question squarely, convinces us that the rationale of *Broadrick* is sound and should be applied in the present context involving the harmful employment of children to make sexually explicit materials for distribution.

The premise that a law should not be invalidated for overbreadth unless it reaches a substantial number of impermissible applications is hardly novel. On most occasions involving facial invalidation, the Court has stressed the embracing sweep of the statute over protected expression. Indeed, Justice Brennan observed in his dissenting opinion in *Broadrick*:

> We have never held that a statute should be held invalid on its face merely because it is possible to conceive of a single impermissible application, and in that sense a requirement of substantial overbreadth is already implicit in the doctrine.

The requirement of substantial overbreadth is directly derived from the purpose and nature of the doctrine. While a sweeping statute, or one incapable of limitation, has the potential to repeatedly chill the exercise of expressive activity by many individuals, the extent of deterrence of protected speech can be expected to decrease with the declining reach of the regulation. This observation appears equally applicable to the publication of books and films as it is to activities, such as picketing or participation in election campaigns, which have previously been categorized as involving conduct plus speech. . . .

This requirement of substantial overbreadth may justifiably be applied to statutory challenges which arise in defense of a criminal prosecution as well as civil enforcement or actions seeking a declaratory judgment. Indeed, the Court's practice when confronted with ordinary criminal laws that are sought to be applied against protected conduct is not to invalidate the law *in toto*, but rather to reverse the particular conviction. We recognize, however, that the penalty to be imposed is relevant in determining whether demonstrable overbreadth is substantial. We simply hold that the fact that a criminal prohibition is involved does not obviate the need for the inquiry or *a priori* warrant a finding of substantial overbreadth.

B

Applying these principles, we hold that § 263.15 is not substantially overbroad. We consider this the paradigmatic case of a state statute whose legitimate reach dwarfs its arguably impermissible applications. New York, as we have held, may constitutionally prohibit dissemination of material specified in § 263.15. While the reach of the statute is directed at the hard core of child pornography, the Court of Appeals was understandably concerned that some protected expression, ranging from medical textbooks to pictorials in the National Geographic would fall prey to the statute. How often, if ever, it may be necessary to employ children to engage in conduct clearly within the reach of § 263.15 in order to produce educational, medical, or artistic works cannot be known with certainty. Yet we seriously doubt, and it has not been suggested, that these arguably impermissible applications of the statute amount to more than a tiny fraction of the materials within the statute's reach. Nor will we assume that the New York courts will widen the possibly invalid reach of the statute by giving an expansive construction to the proscription on "lewd exhibition[s] of the genitals." Under these circumstances, § 263.15 is "not substantially overbroad and . . . whatever overbreadth may exist should be cured through case-by-case analysis of the fact situations to which its sanctions, assertedly, may not be applied." *Broadrick.*

City of Houston v. Hill
482 U.S. 451 (1987)

Justice Brennan delivered the opinion of the Court.

This case presents the question whether a municipal ordinance that makes it unlawful to interrupt a police officer in the performance of his or her duties is unconstitutionally overbroad under the First Amendment . . . .

Code of Ordinances, City of Houston, Texas, § 34-11(a) (1984), reads:

> (a) It shall be unlawful for any person to assault, strike or in any manner oppose, molest, abuse or interrupt any policeman in the execution of his duty, or any person summoned to aid in making an arrest.

[Hill, a local activist, was arrested for violating the ordinance after an incident in Montrose, described by the Court as "a 'diverse and eclectic neighborhood' that is the center of gay political and social life in Houston." Following his acquittal, Hill brought suit in federal court seeking declaratory and injunctive relief against the enforcement of the ordinance. The Court of Appeals applied the doctrine of First Amendment overbreadth, as set forth in *Broadrick v. Oklahoma*, 413 U.S. 601 (1973). The court found that "[a] significant range of protected speech and expression is punishable and might be deterred by the literal wording of the statute." The statute was therefore substantially overbroad.]

. . . The elements of First Amendment overbreadth analysis are familiar. Only a statute that is substantially overbroad may be invalidated on its face. [The city argues] that the ordinance does not inhibit the exposition of ideas, and that it bans "core criminal conduct" not protected by the First Amendment . . . .

We disagree with the city's characterization for several reasons. First, the enforceable portion of the ordinance deals not with core criminal conduct, but with speech. As the city has conceded, the language in the ordinance making it unlawful for any person to "assault" or "strike" a police officer is pre-empted by the Texas Penal Code . . . . Accordingly, the enforceable portion of the ordinance makes it "unlawful for any person to . . . in any manner oppose, molest, abuse or interrupt any policeman in the execution of his duty," and thereby prohibits verbal interruptions of police officers.

Second, contrary to the city's contention, the First Amendment protects a significant amount of verbal criticism and challenge directed at police officers . . . . In *Lewis v. City of New Orleans*, 415 U.S. 130 (1974), for example, the appellant was found to have yelled obscenities and threats at an officer who had asked appellant's husband to produce his driver's license. Appellant was convicted under a municipal ordinance that made it a crime "'for any person wantonly to curse or revile or to use obscene or opprobrious language toward or with reference to any member of the city police while in the actual performance of his duty.'" We vacated the conviction and invalidated the ordinance as facially overbroad. Critical to our decision was the fact that the ordinance "punish[ed] only spoken words" and was not limited in scope to fighting words that "'by their very utterance inflict injury or tend to incite an immediate breach of the peace.'" *Lewis*, quoting *Gooding v. Wilson*, 405 U.S. 518 (1972). Moreover, in a concurring opinion in *Lewis*, Justice Powell suggested that even the "fighting words" exception recognized in *Chaplinsky* might require a narrower application in cases involving words addressed to a police officer, because "a properly trained officer may reasonably be expected to 'exercise a higher degree of restraint' than the average citizen, and thus be less likely to respond belligerently to 'fighting words.'"

The Houston ordinance is much more sweeping than the municipal ordinance struck down in *Lewis*. It is not limited to fighting words nor even to obscene or opprobrious language, but prohibits speech that "in any manner . . . interrupt[s]" an officer. The Constitution does not allow such speech to be made a crime.[11] The freedom of individuals verbally to oppose or challenge police action without thereby risking arrest is one of the principal characteristics by which we distinguish a free nation from a police state.[12]

---

11. Justice Powell suggests that our analysis of protected speech sweeps too broadly. But if some constitutionally unprotected speech must go unpunished, that is a price worth paying to preserve the vitality of the First Amendment. . . .

In any case, today's decision does not leave municipalities powerless to punish physical obstruction of police action. For example, Justice Powell states that "a municipality constitutionally may punish an individual who chooses to stand near a police officer and persistently attempt to engage the officer in conversation while the officer is directing traffic at a busy intersection." We agree, however, that such conduct might constitutionally be punished under a properly tailored statute, such as a disorderly conduct statute that makes it unlawful to fail to disperse in response to a valid police order or to create a traffic hazard. What a municipality may not do, however, and what Houston has done in this case, is to attempt to punish such conduct by broadly criminalizing speech directed to an officer — in this case, by authorizing the police to arrest a person who in any manner verbally interrupts an officer.

Justice Powell also observes that "contentious and abusive" speech can interrupt an officer's investigation, and offers as an example a person who "run[s] beside [an officer pursuing a felon] in a public street shouting at the officer." But what is of concern in that example is not simply contentious speech, but rather the possibility that by shouting and running beside the officer the person may physically obstruct the officer's investigation. Although that person might constitutionally be punished under a tailored statute that prohibited individuals from physically obstructing an officer's investigation, he or she may not be punished under a broad statute aimed at speech.

12. . . . The freedom verbally to challenge police action is not without limits, of course; we have recognized that "fighting words" which "by their very utterance inflict injury or tend to incite an immediate breach of the peace" are not constitutionally protected . . . .

The city argues, however, that even if the ordinance encompasses some protected speech, its sweeping nature is both inevitable and essential to maintain public order . . . .

This Houston ordinance, however, is not narrowly tailored to prohibit only disorderly conduct or fighting words . . . . Although we appreciate the difficulties of drafting precise laws, we have repeatedly invalidated laws that provide the police with unfettered discretion to arrest individuals for words or conduct that annoy or offend them. In *Lewis*, Justice Powell elaborated the basis for our concern with such sweeping, dragnet laws:

> This ordinance, as construed by the Louisiana Supreme Court, confers on police a virtually unrestrained power to arrest and charge persons with a violation. Many arrests are made in "one-on-one" situations where the only witnesses are the arresting officer and the person charged. All that is required for conviction is that the court accept the testimony of the officer that obscene or opprobrious language had been used toward him while in the performance of his duties.* . . .
>
> Contrary to the city's argument, it is unlikely that limiting the ordinance's application to genuine 'fighting words' would be incompatible with the full and adequate performance of an officer's duties . . . . [I]t is usually unnecessary [to charge a person] with the less serious offense of addressing obscene words to the officer. The present type of ordinance tends to be invoked only where there is no other valid basis for arresting an objectionable or suspicious person. The opportunity for abuse, especially where a statute has received a virtually open-ended interpretation, is self-evident.
>
> * The facts in this case, and particularly the direct conflict of testimony as to "who said what," well illustrate the possibility of abuse.

Houston's ordinance criminalizes a substantial amount of constitutionally protected speech, and accords the police unconstitutional discretion in enforcement. The ordinance's plain language is admittedly violated scores of times daily, yet only some individuals — those chosen by the police in their unguided discretion — are arrested . . . . [The] ordinance is susceptible of regular application to protected expression. We conclude that the ordinance is substantially overbroad, and that the Court of Appeals did not err in holding it facially invalid. . . .

JUSTICE BLACKMUN, concurring.

I join the Court's opinion and its judgment except that I do not agree with any implication — if one exists — that *Gooding v. Wilson* and *Lewis v. City of New Orleans* are good law in the context of their facts, or that they lend any real support to the judgment under review in this case. I dissented in *Gooding* and *Lewis*, in the conviction that the legislation there under consideration was related to "fighting words," within the teaching and reach of *Chaplinsky*. I am still of that view, and I therefore disassociate myself from any possible suggestion that those cases are controlling authority here. The Houston ordinance before us, however, as is evident from its very language, and as the Court demonstrates, is far more broad and more offensive to First Amendment values and is susceptible of regular application to protected expression.

JUSTICE SCALIA, concurring in the judgment. [Omitted.]

JUSTICE POWELL, [joined by JUSTICE O'CONNOR and JUSTICE SCALIA, concurring in the judgment].

. . . I agree with the Court's conclusion that the ordinance violates the Fourteenth Amendment, but do not join the Court's reasoning.

The Court finds that the ordinance "deals not with core criminal conduct, but with speech." This view of the ordinance draws a distinction where none exists. The terms of the ordinance—"oppose, molest, abuse or interrupt any policeman in the execution of his duty"—include general words that can apply as fully to conduct as to speech. It is in this respect that *Lewis v. City of New Orleans* is clearly distinguishable. In that case the New Orleans ordinance made it a breach of the peace for:

> any person wantonly to curse or revile or to use obscene or opprobrious language toward or with reference to any member of the city police while in the actual performance of his duty.

On its face, the New Orleans ordinance criminalizes only the use of language . . . . By contrast, the ordinance presented in this case could be applied to activity that involves no element of speech or communication. For example, the ordinance evidently would punish individuals who—without saying a single word—obstructed an officer's access to the scene of an ongoing public disturbance, or indeed the scene of a crime. Accordingly, I cannot agree with the Court that this ordinance punishes only speech.

I do agree that the ordinance can be applied to speech in some cases. And I also agree that the First Amendment protects a good deal of speech that may be directed at police officers. On occasion this may include verbal criticism, but I question the implication of the Court's opinion that the First Amendment generally protects verbal "challenge[s] directed at police officers." A "challenge" often takes the form of opposition or interruption of performance of duty. In many situations, speech of this type directed at police officers will be functionally indistinguishable from conduct that the First Amendment clearly does not protect. For example, I have no doubt that a municipality constitutionally may punish an individual who chooses to stand near a police officer and persistently attempt to engage the officer in conversation while the officer is directing traffic at a busy intersection. Similarly, an individual, by contentious and abusive speech, could interrupt an officer's investigation of possible criminal conduct. A person observing an officer pursuing a person suspected of a felony could run beside him in a public street shouting at the officer. Similar tactics could interrupt a policeman lawfully attempting to interrogate persons believed to be witnesses to a crime . . . .

Despite the concerns expressed above, I nevertheless agree that the ambiguous terms of this ordinance "confe[r] on police a virtually unrestrained power to arrest and charge persons with a violation . . . ." The opportunity for abuse, especially where a statute has received a virtually open-ended interpretation, is self-evident." *Lewis* (Powell, J., concurring in result). No Texas court has placed a limiting construction on the ordinance. Also, it is clear that Houston has made no effort to curtail the wide discretion of police officers under the present ordinance. . . . When government protects society's interests in a manner that restricts some speech the law must be framed more precisely than the ordinance before us. Accordingly, I agree with the Court that the Houston ordinance is unconstitutional.

CHIEF JUSTICE REHNQUIST, dissenting. [Omitted.]

Ashcroft v. Free Speech Coalition
535 U.S. 234 (2002)

[The report of this case is set forth in Chapter 3, section B.]

Note: The Overbreadth Doctrine

1. As Justice White notes in *Ferber*, the overbreadth doctrine "allow[s] persons to attack overly broad statutes even though the conduct of the person making the attack is clearly unprotected and could be proscribed by a law drawn with the requisite specificity." The earliest case cited for that proposition is *Thornhill v. Alabama*, 310 U.S. 88 (1940).

Thornhill was convicted under a statute that prohibited loitering or picketing for the purpose of injuring the business of another. The Court held that the statute was invalid on its face. En route to that conclusion, the Court said:

> Proof of an abuse of power in the particular case has never been deemed a requisite for attack on the constitutionality of a statute purporting to license the dissemination of ideas. [E.g.,] *Lovell v. Griffin* (1938) [*supra* this chapter]. . . . [The rule] derives from an appreciation of the character of the evil inherent in a licensing system. The power of the licensor against which John Milton directed his assault by his "Appeal for the Liberty of Unlicensed Printing" is pernicious not merely by reason of the censure of particular comments but by reason of the threat to censure comments on matters of public concern. It is not merely the sporadic abuse of power by the censor but the pervasive threat inherent in its very existence that constitutes the danger to freedom of discussion. *See Near v. Minnesota* (1931) [*supra* this chapter]. . . .

> A like threat is inherent in a penal statute, like that in question here, which does not aim specifically at evils within the allowable area of State control but, on the contrary, sweeps within its ambit other activities that in ordinary circumstances constitute an exercise of freedom of speech or of the press. The existence of such a statute, which readily lends itself to harsh and discriminatory enforcement by local prosecuting officials, against particular groups deemed to merit their displeasure, results in a continuous and pervasive restraint on all freedom of discussion that might reasonably be regarded as within its purview.

2. The *Thornhill* opinion explicitly suggests that an overbroad statute is analogous to a prior restraint. Is the analogy persuasive? Is it helpful in understanding the overbreadth doctrine? Consider this question as you read cases like *Ferber* and *Free Speech Coalition*.

3. Justice White's opinion in *Ferber* presents an exposition of the overbreadth doctrine as the Court now applies it, including the requirement that the overbreadth must be "substantial" before a statute or ordinance will be invalidated on its face. In *Ferber*, the law survives an overbreadth attack; in *Houston v. Hill* and *Ashcroft v. Free Speech Coalition*, the laws are held unconstitutional. Has the Court drawn a clear line in applying the doctrine?

4. Is the analysis primarily quantitative? In *Board of Airport Commissioners v. Jews for Jesus*, 482 U.S. 569 (1987), the Court considered a resolution banning all "First Amendment activities" at Los Angeles International Airport (LAX). The Court unanimously held that the resolution was substantially overbroad: "On its face, the resolution . . . reaches the universe of expressive activity, and, by prohibiting all protected expression, purports to create a virtual 'First Amendment Free Zone' at LAX." In *Ferber* it was equally clear (at least to the Court) that protected expression constituted no more than "a tiny fraction of the materials within the statute's reach." The statute therefore withstood the overbreadth attack.

5. Not all cases will be so easy. Consider, for example, an ordinance that provides: "A person commits an offense if, with intent to prevent or disrupt a lawful meeting, procession, or gathering, he obstructs or interferes with the meeting, procession, or gathering by physical action or verbal utterance." Assume that the ordinance applies only to official government meetings. Is it substantially overbroad?

6. Even if a law is impermissibly overbroad on its face, a state court can generally avoid invalidating the law if there is a narrowing construction that will save its constitutionality. However, this authority does not extend to "rewriting" a statute. If the ordinance above is overbroad as written, is it susceptible to a narrowing construction?

7. Two limitations on the overbreadth doctrine deserve mention. "Rarely, if ever, will an overbreadth challenge succeed against a law or regulation that is not specifically addressed to speech or to conduct necessarily associated with speech (such as picketing or demonstrating)." *Virginia v. Hicks*, 539 U.S. 113 (2003). And the overbreadth doctrine does not apply to commercial speech. E.g., *Bates v. State Bar of Arizona*, 433 U.S. 350, 380–81 (1977).

Note: The Vagueness Doctrine

1. In *Jews for Jesus* (discussed in the Note above), the plaintiffs challenged a resolution banning all "First Amendment activities" at Los Angeles International Airport (LAX). The Board attempted to defeat an overbreadth challenge by arguing that the regulation was intended to reach "only expressive activity *unrelated to airport-related purposes*." (Emphasis added.) The Supreme Court responded by saying that "the vagueness of this suggested construction itself presents serious constitutional difficulty."

As this passage suggests, the vice of vagueness is closely related to the flaw of overbreadth. Both doctrines are often invoked by the same challenger. However, the doctrines are distinct.

The vagueness doctrine originated as a doctrine of due process in settings far removed from the First Amendment. Indeed, the classic statement of the rule comes from a case involving a state minimum wage requirement. The Court said that "a statute which either forbids or requires the doing of an act in terms so vague that men of common intelligence must necessarily guess at its meaning and differ as to its application violates the first essential of due process of law." *Connally v. General Construction Co.*, 269 U.S. 385, 391 (1926).

The Court has advanced two principal reasons for the rule against vagueness in all contexts. "First, [vague laws] may trap the innocent by not providing fair warning. Second, if arbitrary and discriminatory enforcement is to be prevented, laws must provide explicit standards for those who apply them. A vague law impermissibly delegates basic policy matters to policemen, judges, and juries for resolution on an ad hoc and subjective basis, with the attendant dangers of arbitrary and discriminatory application." *Grayned v. City of Rockford*, 408 U.S. 104 (1972).

2. The vagueness doctrine operates with particular bite when a statute implicates First Amendment rights. As the Court explained in *Grayned*, "Uncertain meanings inevitably lead citizens to steer far wider of the unlawful zone than if the boundaries of the forbidden areas were clearly marked."

The Court in *Jews for Jesus* implied that a regulation prohibiting expressive activity unrelated to "airport-related purposes" would be void for vagueness. On the other hand, in *Grayned*, the Court rejected a vagueness challenge to an "antinoise" ordinance that read in relevant part as follows:

> [N]o person, while on public or private grounds adjacent to any building in which a school or any class thereof is in session, shall willfully make or assist in the making of any noise or diversion which disturbs or tends to disturb the peace or good order of such school session or class thereof.

The Court viewed the vagueness issue as "close," but found that the ordinance fell on the lawful side of the line:

> Condemned to the use of words, we can never expect mathematical certainty from our language. The words of the Rockford ordinance are marked by "flexibility and reasonable breadth, rather than meticulous specificity," but we think it is clear what the ordinance as a whole prohibits. . . . [Based on Illinois case law], we think it proper to conclude that the Supreme Court of Illinois would interpret the Rockford ordinance to prohibit only actual or imminent interference with the "peace or good order" of the school.
>
> Although the prohibited quantum of disturbance is not specified in the ordinance, it is apparent from the statute's announced purpose that the measure is whether normal school activity has been or is about to be disrupted. We do not have here a vague, general "breach of the peace" ordinance, but a statute written specifically for the school context, where the prohibited disturbances are easily measured by their impact on the normal activities of the school. Given this "particular context," the ordinance gives

"fair notice to those to whom [it] is directed." Although the Rockford ordinance may not be as precise as the statute we upheld in *Cameron v. Johnson*, 390 U.S. 611 (1968)—which prohibited picketing "in such a manner as to obstruct or unreasonably interfere with free ingress or egress to and from" any courthouse—we think that, as in *Cameron*, the ordinance here clearly "delineates its reach in words of common understanding."

The defendant in *Grayned* relied on two cases in which the Supreme Court had found ordinances to be unconstitutionally vague. The Court said that both cases were distinguishable:

> *Cox v. Louisiana*, 379 U.S. 536 (1965), and *Coates v. Cincinnati*, 402 U.S. 611 (1971), on which appellant particularly relies, presented completely different situations. In *Cox*, a general breach of the peace ordinance had been construed by state courts to mean "to agitate, to arouse from a state of repose, to molest, to interrupt, to hinder, to disquiet." The Court correctly concluded that, as construed, the ordinance permitted persons to be punished for merely expressing unpopular views. In *Coates*, the ordinance punished the sidewalk assembly of three or more persons who "conduct themselves in a manner annoying to persons passing by . . . ." We held [that] the ordinance was impermissibly vague because enforcement depended on the completely subjective standard of "annoyance."

> In contrast, Rockford's antinoise ordinance does not permit punishment for the expression of an unpopular point of view, and it contains no broad invitation to subjective or discriminatory enforcement. Rockford does not claim the broad power to punish all "noises" and "diversions." The vagueness of these terms, by themselves, is dispelled by the ordinance's requirements that (1) the "noise or diversion" be actually incompatible with normal school activity; (2) there be a demonstrated causality between the disruption that occurs and the "noise or diversion"; and (3) the acts be "willfully" done. "Undesirables" or their "annoying" conduct may not be punished.

For further discussion of *Grayned*, see Chapter 8, section C.

3. In *United States v. Williams*, 553 U.S. 285 (2008) [Note *supra* Chapter 3], the Court, in addressing a claim of unconstitutional vagueness, observed that prior decisions had struck down statutes "that tied criminal culpability to whether the defendant's conduct was 'annoying' or 'indecent'—wholly subjective judgments without statutory definitions, narrowing context, or settled legal meanings."

What other regulatory language might fall within this description? Consider a municipal ordinance that prohibits vending on city sidewalks but provides exceptions for (a) "the sale of newspapers, magazines, periodicals, or other printed matter commonly sold or disposed of by news vendors"; and (b) "the sale of merchandise constituting, carrying or making a religious, political, philosophical or ideological message or statement which is inextricably intertwined with the merchandise." Are any of the terms used in the ordinance vulnerable to a vagueness challenge?

Chapter 5

Content-Based Regulation

Outside the area of "low-value" speech discussed in Chapters 2 and 3, at the core of the Court's modern free-speech doctrine is a distinction between regulations that are "content-based" and those that are "content-neutral." Regulations that are "content-based" must meet a more stringent standard than those that are not. But as we shall see in this and the following chapter, there can be intense disagreement as to whether a particular law is "content-based" or "content-neutral." This chapter examines the principle of content discrimination and the corollary doctrines the Court has developed in applying it.

A. The Principle

Police Department of Chicago v. Mosley
408 U.S. 92 (1972)

Mr. Justice Marshall delivered the opinion of the Court.

At issue in this case is the constitutionality of the following Chicago ordinance:

> A person commits disorderly conduct when he knowingly: . . . "(i) Pickets or demonstrates on a public way within 150 feet of any primary or secondary school building while the school is in session and one-half hour before the school is in session and one-half hour after the school session has been concluded, provided, that this subsection does not prohibit the peaceful picketing of any school involved in a labor dispute. . . ."

The suit was brought by Earl Mosley, a federal postal employee, who for seven months prior to the enactment of the ordinance had frequently picketed Jones Commercial High School in Chicago. During school hours and usually by himself, Mosley would walk the public sidewalk adjoining the school, carrying a sign that read: "Jones High School practices black discrimination. Jones High School has a black quota." His lonely crusade was always peaceful, orderly, and quiet, and was conceded to be so by the city of Chicago.

. . . We hold that the ordinance is unconstitutional because it makes an impermissible distinction between labor picketing and other peaceful picketing.

I

The city of Chicago exempts peaceful labor picketing from its general prohibition on picketing next to a school.[2] The question we consider here is whether this selective exclusion from a public place is permitted. Our answer is "No."

Because Chicago treats some picketing differently from others, we analyze this ordinance in terms of the Equal Protection Clause of the Fourteenth Amendment. Of course, the equal protection claim in this case is closely intertwined with First Amendment interests; the Chicago ordinance affects picketing, which is expressive conduct; moreover, it does so by classifications formulated in terms of the subject of the picketing. As in all equal protection cases, however, the crucial question is whether there is an appropriate governmental interest suitably furthered by the differential treatment. *See Reed v. Reed*, 404 U.S. 71 (1971). . . .

The central problem with Chicago's ordinance is that it describes permissible picketing in terms of its subject matter. Peaceful picketing on the subject of a school's labor-management dispute is permitted, but all other peaceful picketing is prohibited. The operative distinction is the message on a picket sign. But, above all else, the First Amendment means that government has no power to restrict expression because of its message, its ideas, its subject matter, or its content. [The Court cited, *inter alia*, *Cohen v. California* (1971) [Chapter 3], *New York Times Co. v. Sullivan* (1964) [Chapter 2], and *De Jonge v. Oregon* (1937) [Chapter 1 Note]]. Any restriction on expressive activity because of its content would completely undercut the "profound national commitment to the principle that debate on public issues should be uninhibited, robust, and wide-open." *New York Times*.

Necessarily, then, under the Equal Protection Clause, not to mention the First Amendment itself, government may not grant the use of a forum to people whose views it finds acceptable, but deny use to those wishing to express less favored or more controversial views. And it may not select which issues are worth discussing or debating in public facilities. . . . Selective exclusions from a public forum may not be based on content alone, and may not be justified by reference to content alone.

Guided by these principles, we have frequently condemned such discrimination among different users of the same medium for expression. In *Niemotko v. Maryland*, 340 U.S. 268 (1951), a group of Jehovah's Witnesses were denied a permit to use a city park for Bible talks, although other political and religious groups had been allowed to put the park to analogous uses. Concluding that the permit was denied because of the city's "dislike for or disagreement with the Witnesses or their views," this Court held that the permit refusal violated "[t]he right to equal protection of the laws, in the exercise of those freedoms of speech and religion protected by the First and Fourteenth Amendments." . . .

---

2. By its terms, the statute exempts "the peaceful picketing of any school involved in a labor dispute." It is undisputed that this exemption applies only to labor picketing of a school involved in a labor dispute.

II

This is not to say that all picketing must always be allowed. We have continually recognized that reasonable "time, place and manner" regulations of picketing may be necessary to further significant governmental interests. Similarly, under an equal protection analysis, there may be sufficient regulatory interests justifying selective exclusions or distinctions among pickets. Conflicting demands on the same place may compel the State to make choices among potential users and uses. And the State may have a legitimate interest in prohibiting some picketing to protect public order. But these justifications for selective exclusions from a public forum must be carefully scrutinized. Because picketing plainly involves expressive conduct within the protection of the First Amendment, discriminations among pickets must be tailored to serve a substantial governmental interest.

III

In this case, the ordinance itself describes impermissible picketing not in terms of time, place, and manner, but in terms of subject matter. The regulation "thus slip[s] from the neutrality of time, place, and circumstance into a concern about content." Kalven, *The Concept of the Public Forum:* Cox v. Louisiana, 1965 SUP. CT. REV. 29. This is never permitted. In spite of this, Chicago urges that the ordinance is not improper content censorship, but rather a device for preventing disruption of the school. Cities certainly have a substantial interest in stopping picketing which disrupts a school. "The crucial question, however, is whether [Chicago's ordinance] advances that objective in a manner consistent with the commands of the Equal Protection Clause." *Reed v. Reed*. It does not.

Although preventing school disruption is a city's legitimate concern, Chicago itself has determined that peaceful labor picketing during school hours is not an undue interference with school. Therefore, under the Equal Protection Clause, Chicago may not maintain that other picketing disrupts the school unless that picketing is clearly more disruptive than the picketing Chicago already permits. If peaceful labor picketing is permitted, there is no justification for prohibiting all nonlabor picketing, both peaceful and nonpeaceful. "Peaceful" nonlabor picketing, however the term "peaceful" is defined, is obviously no more disruptive than "peaceful" labor picketing. But Chicago's ordinance permits the latter and prohibits the former. Such unequal treatment is exactly what was condemned in *Niemotko*.

Similarly, we reject the city's argument that, although it permits peaceful labor picketing, it may prohibit all nonlabor picketing because, as a class, nonlabor picketing is more prone to produce violence than labor picketing. Predictions about imminent disruption from picketing involve judgments appropriately made on an individualized basis, not by means of broad classifications, especially those based on subject matter. Freedom of expression, and its intersection with the guarantee of equal protection, would rest on a soft foundation indeed if government could distinguish among picketers on such a wholesale and categorical basis. . . .

The Equal Protection Clause requires that statutes affecting First Amendment interests be narrowly tailored to their legitimate objectives. . . . Given what Chicago tolerates from labor picketing, the excesses of some nonlabor picketing may not be controlled by a broad ordinance prohibiting both peaceful and violent picketing. Such excesses "can be controlled by narrowly drawn statutes," *Saia v. New York*, 334 U.S. 558 (1948), focusing on the abuses and dealing evenhandedly with picketing regardless of subject matter. . . . Far from being tailored to a substantial governmental interest, the discrimination among pickets is based on the content of their expression. Therefore, under the Equal Protection Clause, it may not stand.

Mr. Justice Blackmun and Mr. Justice Rehnquist concur in the result.

Mr. Chief Justice Burger, concurring.

I join the Court's opinion but with the reservation that some of the language used in the discussion of the First Amendment could, if read out of context, be misleading. Numerous holdings of this Court attest to the fact that the First Amendment does not literally mean that we "are guaranteed the right to express any thought, free from government censorship." This statement is subject to some qualifications, as for example those of *Roth v. United States* [Chapter 2]; *Chaplinsky v. New Hampshire* [Chapter 2]. *See also New York Times Co. v. Sullivan* [Chapter 2].

———

Note: "Above All Else . . .": The Mosley Principle

1. The opinion of the Court in *Mosley* states emphatically that "above all else, the First Amendment means that government has no power to restrict expression because of its message, its ideas, its *subject matter*, or its *content*." (Emphasis added.) Chief Justice Burger suggests in his brief concurring opinion that this statement cannot be taken literally. Is he correct? If so, what does the Court mean?

2. In *Simon & Schuster, Inc. v. Members of New York State Crime Victims Board*, 502 U.S. 105 (1991), the Court unanimously struck down New York's "Son of Sam" law. The law required that income received by an accused or convicted criminal from works describing his crime had to be made available to the victims of the crime and the criminal's other creditors. The Court found that the law discriminated on the basis of content. Such discrimination, the Court said, could survive only if the state showed that its regulation was "necessary to serve a compelling state interest and [was] narrowly drawn to achieve that end." Not surprisingly, the state failed to make that showing.

Justice Kennedy, concurring in the judgment, objected to the Court's use of the "compelling interest" test. His opinion offered a more nuanced version of the *Mosley* principle. After quoting the "above all else" language from *Mosley*, he wrote:

> [General statements like the one in *Mosley*] about the government's lack of power to engage in content discrimination reflect a surer basis for protecting speech than does the test used by the Court today.
>
> There are a few legal categories in which content-based regulation has been permitted or at least contemplated. These include obscenity, defamation, incitement, or situations presenting some grave and imminent danger the government has the power to prevent. These are, however, historic and

traditional categories long familiar to the bar.... While it cannot be said with certainty that the foregoing types of expression are or will remain the only ones that are without First Amendment protection, as evidenced by the proscription of some visual depictions of sexual conduct by children, see *New York v. Ferber* (1982) [Chapter 3], the use of these traditional legal categories is preferable to the sort of ad hoc balancing that the Court henceforth must perform in every case if the analysis here used becomes our standard test.

As a practical matter, perhaps we will interpret the compelling interest test in cases involving content regulation so that the results become parallel to the historic categories I have discussed, although an enterprise such as today's tends not to remain pro forma but to take on a life of its own. When we leave open the possibility that various sorts of content regulations are appropriate, we discount the value of our precedents and invite experiments that in fact present clear violations of the First Amendment, as is true in the case before us.

To forgo the compelling interest test in cases involving direct content-based burdens on speech would not, of course, eliminate the need for difficult judgments respecting First Amendment issues. Among the questions we cannot avoid the necessity of deciding are: Whether the restricted expression falls within one of the unprotected categories discussed above; whether some other constitutional right is impaired, see *Nebraska Press Ass'n v. Stuart*, 427 U.S. 539 (1976); whether, in the case of a regulation of activity which combines expressive with nonexpressive elements, the regulation aims at the activity or the expression, compare *United States v. O'Brien* (1968) [Chapter 7], with *Texas v. Johnson* (1989) [Chapter 7]; whether the regulation restricts speech itself or only the time, place, or manner of speech, see *Ward v. Rock Against Racism* (1989) [Chapter 6]; and whether the regulation is in fact content based or content neutral. *See Boos v. Barry*, 485 U.S. 312 (1988) [Chapter 7[. However difficult the lines may be to draw in some cases, here the answer to each of these questions is clear.

Do you think that Justice Kennedy's approach is preferable to the *Simon & Schuster* majority's? Return to this question after reading the next primary case, *Reed v. Town of Gilbert* [*infra* this chapter].

3. In striking contrast to Justice Kennedy's position, Justice Stevens has expressed great skepticism about the *Mosley* dictum. In a lecture delivered in 1992, Justice Stevens criticized efforts to organize First Amendment law "in rigidly defined compartments." He continued:

> Perhaps most striking with regard to abstract categories is the Court's effort to lay down a black-letter rule involving content-based regulation of speech.... Although [the *Mosley* dictum] is often cited as a proposition of law, it is perhaps more accurately described as a goal or an ideal, for the Court's decisions do, in actuality, tolerate quite a bit of content-based regulation....

> Perhaps most interesting is the degree to which some decisions departing from the rule depart also from the spirit animating Justice Marshall's defense

of content-neutrality, which draws, I think, from Justice Jackson's understanding that the First Amendment protects centrally against the imposition of an official orthodoxy. . . .

There are other decisions, however, that depart from the prohibition on content-based regulation without undermining its central goals. They do so by supplementing, if not replacing, the black-letter rule with a sensitivity to fact and context that allows for advancement of the principles underlying the protection of free speech.

John Paul Stevens, *The Freedom of Speech*, 102 YALE L.J. 1293, 1304–05 (1993).

4. Justice Marshall, writing for the Court in *Mosley*, and Justice Kennedy, concurring in *Simon & Schuster*, both state without qualification that, under the First Amendment, "government has no power to restrict expression because of . . . its content." Apart from the familiar case law cited in Chief Justice Burger's concurring opinion in *Mosley*, one other qualification requires mention. As Professor James Weinstein has pointed out, the rule against content discrimination "does not apply across the entire expanse of human utterances." Rather, it "is primarily limited to public discourse — that is, expression on matters of public concern occurring in settings dedicated or essential to public communication, such as books, magazines, films, the Internet, or in 'public forums,' such as the speaker's corner of a park." James Weinstein, *Hate Speech, Viewpoint Neutrality, and the American Concept of Democracy*, *in* THE BOUNDARIES OF FREEDOM OF EXPRESSION & ORDER IN AMERICAN DEMOCRACY 149 (Thomas R. Hensley ed., 2002).

Professor Weinstein suggests that the "public discourse" limitation explains why "perjury, bribery, and solicitation of a crime may be banned because of their content." But recall the proposition associated with *Giboney v. Empire Storage & Ice Co.*, 336 U.S. 490 (1949) [Chapter 3 Note]: freedom of speech does not protect "speech or writing used as an integral part of conduct in violation of a valid criminal statute." Is the *Giboney* principle a particularized application of the "public discourse" limitation? Or is it a separate qualification to the rule against content discrimination?

What other kinds of speech fall outside the domain of "public discourse"? For example, Professor Weinstein suggests that "public discourse" does not embrace false or misleading advertising, instruction in the public school classroom, the administration of justice in the courtroom, or speech by government employees that is disloyal to their superiors. The first of these is dealt with under the "commercial speech" doctrine; the others are treated in later chapters in this book. Consider, as you study the cases, whether the "public discourse" concept is helpful in (a) reconciling the decisions, or (b) reaching sensible results.

———

Note: Speech Near Polling Places

In his concurring opinion in *Simon & Schuster*, Justice Kennedy criticized the use of "the compelling interest test in cases involving direct content-based burdens on speech," but he appeared to acknowledge that application of the test generally resulted in protection of the speech. A few months later, however, the Court upheld a regulation that concededly restricted speech on the basis of its content. The case was *Burson v. Freeman*, 504 U.S. 191 (1992), and it involved a Tennessee statute that prohibited the solicitation of votes and the display or distribution of campaign materials within 100 feet of the entrance to a polling place on Election Day.

There was no opinion for the Court. A plurality opinion by Justice Blackmun applied the "compelling interest" test and found this was the "rare case" in which a law could survive strict scrutiny:

> Here, the State, as recognized administrator of elections, has asserted that the exercise of free speech rights conflicts with another fundamental right, the right to cast a ballot in an election free from the taint of intimidation and fraud. A long history, a substantial consensus, and simple common sense show that some restricted zone around polling places is necessary to protect that fundamental right. Given the conflict between these two rights, we hold that requiring solicitors to stand 100 feet from the entrances to polling places does not constitute an unconstitutional compromise.

Justice Scalia concurred only in the judgment. He said strict scrutiny was not appropriate: "Because restrictions on speech around polling places on election day are as venerable a part of the American tradition as the secret ballot, [the Tennessee law] does not restrict speech in a traditional public forum." Three Justices dissented, agreeing that the "compelling interest" test was applicable but disagreeing that the standard was met. Justice Thomas took no part in the decision of the case.

Justice Kennedy joined the plurality opinion. He acknowledged his skepticism about the "compelling interest" test, but said that the test "may have a legitimate role . . . in sorting out what is and what is not a content-based restriction." He explained:

> In some cases, a censorial justification will not be apparent from the face of a regulation which draws distinctions based on content, and the government will tender a plausible justification unrelated to the suppression of speech or ideas. There the compelling-interest test may be one analytical device to detect, in an objective way, whether the asserted justification is in fact an accurate description of the purpose and effect of the law. . . .

> The [use] of the compelling-interest test is adopted today, not to justify or condemn a category of suppression but to determine the accuracy of the justification the State gives for its law. The outcome of that analysis is that the justification for the speech restriction is to protect another constitutional right. As I noted in *Simon & Schuster*, there is a narrow area in which the First Amendment permits freedom of expression to yield to the extent necessary for the accommodation of another constitutional right. That principle can apply here without danger that the general rule permitting no content restriction will be engulfed by the analysis; for under the statute the State acts to protect the integrity of the polling place where citizens exercise the right to vote. Voting is one of the most fundamental and cherished liberties in our

democratic system of government. The State is not using this justification to suppress legitimate expression.

Is Justice Kennedy's rationale limited to cases in which the state restricts speech "to protect another constitutional right"? Or is it more broadly applicable "to determine the accuracy of the justification the State gives for its law"? If the latter, how much is left of the *Mosley* principle? The next section explores these questions.

B. Defining Content Discrimination

In his separate opinion in *Burson v. Freeman*, Justice Kennedy suggests that the purpose of strict scrutiny is to determine whether a content-based law has a "censorial justification." Three years earlier, in an opinion authored by Justice Kennedy, the Court had gone further, stating in dictum that "[t]he principal inquiry in determining content neutrality . . . is whether the government has adopted a regulation because of disagreement with the message it conveys." *Ward v. Rock Against Racism* (1989) [Chapter 6]. In other words, the *Ward* Court suggested that the content neutrality determination itself turned on the government's purpose in adopting a law. On the other hand, in *Simon & Schuster* the Court unequivocally rejected the proposition that strict scrutiny applies "only when the legislature intends to suppress certain ideas." The result was prolonged confusion and inconsistency regarding the meaning of content discrimination (or conversely, neutrality), both among the lower courts and in the Court's own opinions. The Court sought to resolve the issue in the following case.

Reed v. Town of Gilbert
135 S. Ct. 2218 (2015)

Justice Thomas delivered the opinion of the Court.

The town of Gilbert, Arizona (or Town), has adopted a comprehensive code governing the manner in which people may display outdoor signs. The Sign Code identifies various categories of signs based on the type of information they convey, then subjects each category to different restrictions. One of the categories is "Temporary Directional Signs Relating to a Qualifying Event," loosely defined as signs directing the public to a meeting of a nonprofit group. The Code imposes more stringent restrictions on these signs than it does on signs conveying other messages. We hold that these provisions are content-based regulations of speech that cannot survive strict scrutiny.

I

A

The Sign Code prohibits the display of outdoor signs anywhere within the Town without a permit, but it then exempts 23 categories of signs from that requirement. These exemptions include everything from bazaar signs to flying banners. Three categories of exempt signs are particularly relevant here.

The first is "Ideological Signs." This category includes any "sign communicating a message or ideas for noncommercial purposes that is not a Construction Sign, Directional Sign, Temporary Directional Sign Relating to a Qualifying Event, Political Sign, Garage Sale Sign, or a sign owned or required by a governmental agency." Of the three categories discussed here, the Code treats ideological signs most favorably, allowing them to be up to 20 square feet in area and to be placed in all "zoning districts" without time limits.

The second category is "Political Signs." This includes any "temporary sign designed to influence the outcome of an election called by a public body." The Code treats these signs less favorably than ideological signs. The Code allows the placement of political signs up to 16 square feet on residential property and up to 32 square feet on non-residential property, undeveloped municipal property, and "rights-of-way." These signs may be displayed up to 60 days before a primary election and up to 15 days following a general election.

The third category is "Temporary Directional Signs Relating to a Qualifying Event." This includes any "Temporary Sign intended to direct pedestrians, motorists, and other passersby to a 'qualifying event.'" A "qualifying event" is defined as any "assembly, gathering, activity, or meeting sponsored, arranged, or promoted by a religious, charitable, community service, educational, or other similar non-profit organization." The Code treats temporary directional signs even less favorably than political signs. Temporary directional signs may be no larger than six square feet. They may be placed on private property or on a public right-of-way, but no more than four signs may be placed on a single property at any time. And, they may be displayed no more than 12 hours before the "qualifying event" and no more than 1 hour afterward.

B

Petitioners Good News Community Church (Church) and its pastor, Clyde Reed, wish to advertise the time and location of their Sunday church services. The Church is a small, cash-strapped entity that owns no building, so it holds its services at elementary schools or other locations in or near the Town. In order to inform the public about its services, which are held in a variety of different locations, the Church began placing 15 to 20 temporary signs around the Town, frequently in the public right-of-way abutting the street. The signs typically displayed the Church's name, along with the time and location of the upcoming service. Church members would post the signs early in the day on Saturday and then remove them around midday on Sunday. The display of these signs requires little money and manpower, and thus has proved to be an economical and effective way for the Church to let the community know where its services are being held each week.

This practice caught the attention of the Town's Sign Code compliance manager, who twice cited the Church for violating the Code. [Pastor Reed attempted to reach an accommodation with the Sign Department, but his efforts were unsuccessful. Quite the contrary; the Compliance Manager promised to punish any future violations. Pastor Reed filed suit in Federal District Court. Ultimately the Ninth Circuit, applying the *Ward* test, held that the Code's sign categories were content-neutral because they lacked a censorial motive. It applied a lower level of scrutiny and found no First Amendment violation. The Supreme Court granted certiorari.]

II

A

. . . Under [the First Amendment], a government, including a municipal government vested with state authority, "has no power to restrict expression because of its message, its ideas, its subject matter, or its content." *Police Dept. of Chicago v. Mosley* (1972) [*supra* this chapter]. Content-based laws—those that target speech based on its communicative content—are presumptively unconstitutional and may be justified only if the government proves that they are narrowly tailored to serve compelling state interests. *R.A.V. v. City of St. Paul* (1992) [Chapter 15]; *Simon & Schuster, Inc. v. Members of N.Y. State Crime Victims Bd.* (1991) [*supra* this chapter Note].

Government regulation of speech is content based if a law applies to particular speech because of the topic discussed or the idea or message expressed. *E.g., Sorrell v. IMS Health, Inc.* (2011) [Chapter 3 Note]; *Mosley*. This commonsense meaning of the phrase "content based" requires a court to consider whether a regulation of speech "on its face" draws distinctions based on the message a speaker conveys. *Sorrell*. Some facial distinctions based on a message are obvious, defining regulated speech by particular subject matter, and others are more subtle, defining regulated speech by its function or purpose. Both are distinctions drawn based on the message a speaker conveys, and, therefore, are subject to strict scrutiny.

Our precedents have also recognized a separate and additional category of laws that, though facially content neutral, will be considered content-based regulations of speech: laws that cannot be "justified without reference to the content of the regulated speech," or that were adopted by the government "because of disagreement with the message [the speech] conveys," *Ward v. Rock Against Racism* (1989) [Chapter 6]. Those laws, like those that are content based on their face, must also satisfy strict scrutiny.

B

The Town's Sign Code is content based on its face. It defines "Temporary Directional Signs" on the basis of whether a sign conveys the message of directing the public to church or some other "qualifying event." It defines "Political Signs" on the basis of whether a sign's message is "designed to influence the outcome of an election." And it defines "Ideological Signs" on the basis of whether a sign "communicat[es] a message or ideas" that do not fit within the Code's other categories. It then subjects each of these categories to different restrictions.

The restrictions in the Sign Code that apply to any given sign thus depend entirely on the communicative content of the sign. If a sign informs its reader of the time and place a book club will discuss John Locke's Two Treatises of Government, that sign will be treated differently from a sign expressing the view that one should vote for one of Locke's followers in an upcoming election, and both signs will be treated differently from a sign expressing an ideological view rooted in Locke's theory of government. More to the point, the Church's signs inviting people to attend its worship services are treated differently from signs conveying other types of ideas. On its face, the Sign Code is a content-based regulation of speech. We thus have no need to consider the government's justifications or purposes for enacting the Code to determine whether it is subject to strict scrutiny.

C

In reaching the contrary conclusion, the Court of Appeals offered several theories to explain why the Town's Sign Code should be deemed content neutral. None is persuasive.

1

The Court of Appeals first determined that the Sign Code was content neutral because the Town "did not adopt its regulation of speech [based on] disagree[ment] with the message conveyed," and its justifications for regulating temporary directional signs were "unrelated to the content of the sign." In its brief to this Court, the United States similarly contends that a sign regulation is content neutral — even if it expressly draws distinctions based on the sign's communicative content — if those distinctions can be "justified without reference to the content of the regulated speech." Brief for United States as *Amicus Curiae* (quoting *Ward*).

But this analysis skips the crucial first step in the content-neutrality analysis: determining whether the law is content neutral on its face. A law that is content based on its face is subject to strict scrutiny regardless of the government's benign motive, content-neutral justification, or lack of "animus toward the ideas contained" in the regulated speech. *Cincinnati v. Discovery Network, Inc.* (1993) [Chapter 3 Note]. We have thus made clear that "illicit legislative intent is not the *sine qua non* of a violation of the First Amendment," and a party opposing the government "need adduce 'no evidence of an improper censorial motive.'" *Simon & Schuster.* . . . In other words, an innocuous justification cannot transform a facially content-based law into one that is content neutral.

That is why we have repeatedly considered whether a law is content neutral on its face *before* turning to the law's justification or purpose. *See, e.g., United States v. O'Brien* (1968) [Chapter 7] (noting that the statute "on its face deals with conduct having no connection with speech," but examining whether the "the governmental interest is unrelated to the suppression of free expression"). Because strict scrutiny applies either when a law is content based on its face or when the purpose and justification for the law are content based, a court must evaluate each question before it concludes that the law is content neutral and thus subject to a lower level of scrutiny. . . .

The First Amendment requires no less. Innocent motives do not eliminate the danger of censorship presented by a facially content-based statute, as future government officials may one day wield such statutes to suppress disfavored speech. That is why the First Amendment expressly targets the operation of the laws — i.e., the "abridg[ement] of speech" — rather than merely the motives of those who enacted them. . . .

[One] could easily imagine a Sign Code compliance manager who disliked the Church's substantive teachings deploying the Sign Code to make it more difficult for the Church to inform the public of the location of its services. Accordingly, we have repeatedly "rejected the argument that 'discriminatory . . . treatment is suspect under the First Amendment only when the legislature intends to suppress certain ideas.'" *Discovery Network*. We do so again today.

2

The Court of Appeals next reasoned that the Sign Code was content neutral because it "does not mention any idea or viewpoint, let alone single one out for differential treatment." It reasoned that, for the purpose of the Code provisions, "[i]t makes no difference which candidate is supported, who sponsors the event, or what ideological perspective is asserted." . . .

This analysis conflates two distinct but related limitations that the First Amendment places on government regulation of speech. Government discrimination among viewpoints—or the regulation of speech based on "the specific motivating ideology or the opinion or perspective of the speaker"—is a "more blatant" and "egregious form of content discrimination." *Rosenberger v. Rector and Visitors of Univ. of Va.* (1995) [Chapter 19]. But it is well established that "[t]he First Amendment's hostility to content-based regulation extends not only to restrictions on particular viewpoints, but also to prohibition of public discussion of an entire topic."

Thus, a speech regulation targeted at specific subject matter is content based even if it does not discriminate among viewpoints within that subject matter. For example, a law banning the use of sound trucks for political speech—and only political speech—would be a content-based regulation, even if it imposed no limits on the political viewpoints that could be expressed. *See Discovery Network*. The Town's Sign Code likewise singles out specific subject matter for differential treatment, even if it does not target viewpoints within that subject matter. Ideological messages are given more favorable treatment than messages concerning a political candidate, which are themselves given more favorable treatment than messages announcing an assembly of like-minded individuals. That is a paradigmatic example of content-based discrimination. . . .

III

Because the Town's Sign Code imposes content-based restrictions on speech, those provisions can stand only if they survive strict scrutiny, "which requires the Government to prove that the restriction furthers a compelling interest and is narrowly tailored to achieve that interest." Thus, it is the Town's burden to demonstrate that the Code's differentiation between temporary directional signs and other types of signs, such as political signs and ideological signs, furthers a compelling governmental interest and is narrowly tailored to that end.

The Town cannot do so. It has offered only two governmental interests in support of the distinctions the Sign Code draws: preserving the Town's aesthetic appeal and traffic safety. Assuming for the sake of argument that those are compelling governmental interests, the Code's distinctions fail as hopelessly underinclusive.

Starting with the preservation of aesthetics, temporary directional signs are "no greater an eyesore," *Discovery Network*, than ideological or political ones. Yet the Code allows unlimited proliferation of larger ideological signs while strictly limiting the number, size, and duration of smaller directional ones. The Town cannot claim that placing strict limits on temporary directional signs is necessary to beautify the Town while at the same time allowing unlimited numbers of other types of signs that create the same problem.

The Town similarly has not shown that limiting temporary directional signs is necessary to eliminate threats to traffic safety, but that limiting other types of signs is not. The Town has offered no reason to believe that directional signs pose a greater threat to safety than do ideological or political signs. If anything, a sharply worded ideological sign seems more likely to distract a driver than a sign directing the public to a nearby church meeting.

In light of this underinclusiveness, the Town has not met its burden to prove that its Sign Code is narrowly tailored to further a compelling government interest. Because a "law cannot be regarded as protecting an interest of the highest order, and thus as justifying a restriction on truthful speech, when it leaves appreciable damage to that supposedly vital interest unprohibited," *Republican Party of Minn. v. White*, 536 U.S. 765 (2002), the Sign Code fails strict scrutiny.

IV

Our decision today will not prevent governments from enacting effective sign laws. The Town asserts that an "absolutist" content-neutrality rule would render "virtually all distinctions in sign laws . . . subject to strict scrutiny," but that is not the case. Not "all distinctions" are subject to strict scrutiny, only *content-based* ones are. Laws that are *content neutral* are instead subject to lesser scrutiny.

The Town has ample content-neutral options available to resolve problems with safety and aesthetics. For example, its current Code regulates many aspects of signs that have nothing to do with a sign's message: size, building materials, lighting, moving parts, and portability. And on public property, the Town may go a long way toward entirely forbidding the posting of signs, so long as it does so in an evenhanded, content-neutral manner. Indeed, some lower courts have long held that similar content-based sign laws receive strict scrutiny, but there is no evidence that towns in those jurisdictions have suffered catastrophic effects.

We acknowledge that a city might reasonably view the general regulation of signs as necessary because signs "take up space and may obstruct views, distract motorists, displace alternative uses for land, and pose other problems that legitimately call for regulation." *City of Ladue*. At the same time, the presence of certain signs may be essential, both for vehicles and pedestrians, to guide traffic or to identify hazards and ensure safety. A sign ordinance narrowly tailored to the challenges of protecting the safety of pedestrians, drivers, and passengers—such as warning signs marking hazards on private property, signs directing traffic, or street numbers associated with private houses—well might survive strict scrutiny. The signs at issue in this case, including political and ideological signs and signs for events, are far removed from those purposes. As discussed above, they are facially content based and are neither justified by traditional safety concerns nor narrowly tailored.

* * *

We reverse the judgment of the Court of Appeals and remand the case for proceedings consistent with this opinion.

JUSTICE ALITO, with whom JUSTICE KENNEDY and JUSTICE SOTOMAYOR join, concurring.

I join the opinion of the Court but add a few words of further explanation.

As the Court holds, what we have termed "content-based" laws must satisfy strict scrutiny. Content-based laws merit this protection because they present, albeit sometimes in a subtler form, the same dangers as laws that regulate speech based on viewpoint. Limiting speech based on its "topic" or "subject" favors those who do not want to disturb the status quo. Such regulations may interfere with democratic self-government and the search for truth.

As the Court shows, the regulations at issue in this case are replete with content-based distinctions, and as a result they must satisfy strict scrutiny. This does not mean, however, that municipalities are powerless to enact and enforce reasonable sign regulations. . . .

In addition to regulating signs put up by private actors, government entities may also erect their own signs consistent with the principles that allow governmental speech. *See Pleasant Grove City v. Summum* (2009) [Chapter 13 Note]. They may put up all manner of signs to promote safety, as well as directional signs and signs pointing out historic sites and scenic spots.

Properly understood, today's decision will not prevent cities from regulating signs in a way that fully protects public safety and serves legitimate esthetic objectives.

JUSTICE BREYER, concurring in the judgment.

. . . Like Justice Kagan I believe that categories alone cannot satisfactorily resolve the legal problem before us. The First Amendment requires greater judicial sensitivity both to the Amendment's expressive objectives and to the public's legitimate need for regulation than a simple recitation of categories, such as "content discrimination" and "strict scrutiny," would permit. In my view, the category "content discrimination" is better considered in many contexts, including here, as a rule of thumb, rather than as an automatic "strict scrutiny" trigger, leading to almost certain legal condemnation.

To use content discrimination to trigger strict scrutiny sometimes makes perfect sense. There are cases in which the Court has found content discrimination an unconstitutional method for suppressing a viewpoint. *E.g., Rosenberger v. Rector and Visitors of Univ. of Va.* (1995) [Chapter 19]. And there are cases where the Court has found content discrimination to reveal that rules governing a traditional public forum are, in fact, not a neutral way of fairly managing the forum in the interest of all speakers. *Police Dept. of Chicago v. Mosley* (1972) [*supra* this chapter]. In these types of cases, strict scrutiny is often appropriate, and content discrimination has thus served a useful purpose.

But content discrimination, while helping courts to identify unconstitutional suppression of expression, cannot and should not *always* trigger strict scrutiny. . . . I readily concede . . . that content discrimination, as a conceptual tool, can sometimes reveal weaknesses in the government's rationale for a rule that limits speech. If, for example, a city looks to litter prevention as the rationale for a prohibition against placing newsracks dispensing free advertisements on public property, why does it exempt other newsracks causing similar litter? *Cf. Cincinnati v. Discovery Network, Inc.* (1993) [Chapter 3 Note]. I also concede that, whenever government disfavors one kind of speech, it places that speech at a disadvantage, potentially interfering with the free marketplace of ideas and with an individual's ability to express thoughts and ideas that can help that individual determine the kind of society in which he wishes to live, help shape that society, and help define his place within it.

Nonetheless, in these latter instances to use the presence of content discrimination automatically to trigger strict scrutiny and thereby call into play a strong presumption against constitutionality goes too far. That is because virtually all government activities involve speech, many of which involve the regulation of speech. Regulatory programs almost always require content discrimination. And to hold that such content discrimination triggers strict scrutiny is to write a recipe for judicial management of ordinary government regulatory activity. . . .

I recognize that the Court could escape the problem by watering down the force of the presumption against constitutionality that "strict scrutiny" normally carries with it. But, in my view, doing so will weaken the First Amendment's protection in instances where "strict scrutiny" should apply in full force.

The better approach is to generally treat content discrimination as a strong reason weighing against the constitutionality of a rule where a traditional public forum, or where viewpoint discrimination, is threatened, but elsewhere treat it as a rule of thumb, finding it a helpful, but not determinative legal tool, in an appropriate case, to determine the strength of a justification. I would use content discrimination as a supplement to a more basic analysis, which, tracking most of our First Amendment cases, asks whether the regulation at issue works harm to First Amendment interests that is disproportionate in light of the relevant regulatory objectives. Answering this question requires examining the seriousness of the harm to speech, the importance of the countervailing objectives, the extent to which the law will achieve those objectives, and whether there are other, less restrictive ways of doing so. Admittedly, this approach does not have the simplicity of a mechanical use of categories. But it does permit the government to regulate speech in numerous instances where the voters have authorized the government to regulate and where courts should hesitate to substitute judicial judgment for that of administrators.

Here, regulation of signage along the roadside, for purposes of safety and beautification is at issue. There is no traditional public forum nor do I find any general effort to censor a particular viewpoint. Consequently, the specific regulation at issue does not warrant "strict scrutiny."

Nonetheless, for the reasons that Justice Kagan sets forth, I believe that the Town of Gilbert's regulatory rules violate the First Amendment. I consequently concur in the Court's judgment only.

Justice Kagan, with whom Justice Ginsburg and Justice Breyer join, concurring in the judgment.

Countless cities and towns across America have adopted ordinances regulating the posting of signs, while exempting certain categories of signs based on their subject matter. For example, some municipalities generally prohibit illuminated signs in residential neighborhoods, but lift that ban for signs that identify the address of a home or the name of its owner or occupant. In other municipalities, safety signs such as "Blind Pedestrian Crossing" and "Hidden Driveway" can be posted without a permit, even as other permanent signs require one. Elsewhere, historic site markers — for example, "George Washington Slept Here" — are also exempt from general regulations. And similarly, the federal Highway Beautification Act limits signs along interstate highways unless, for instance, they direct travelers to "scenic and historical attractions" or advertise free coffee.

Given the Court's analysis, many sign ordinances of that kind are now in jeopardy. Says the majority: When laws "single[ ] out specific subject matter," they are "facially content based"; and when they are facially content based, they are automatically subject to strict scrutiny. And although the majority holds out hope that some sign laws with subject-matter exemptions "might survive" that stringent review, the likelihood is that most will be struck down. . . . To clear that high bar, the government must show that a content-based distinction "is necessary to serve a compelling state interest and is narrowly drawn to achieve that end." So on the majority's view, courts would have to determine that a town has a compelling interest in informing passersby where George Washington slept. And likewise, courts would have to find that a town has no other way to prevent hidden-driveway mishaps than by specially treating hidden-driveway signs. (Well-placed speed bumps? Lower speed limits? Or how about just a ban on hidden driveways?) The consequence — unless courts water down strict scrutiny to something unrecognizable — is that our communities will find themselves in an unenviable bind: They will have to either repeal the exemptions that allow for helpful signs on streets and sidewalks, or else lift their sign restrictions altogether and resign themselves to the resulting clutter.

Although the majority insists that applying strict scrutiny to all such ordinances is "essential" to protecting First Amendment freedoms, I find it challenging to understand why that is so. This Court's decisions articulate two important and related reasons for subjecting content-based speech regulations to the most exacting standard of review. The first is "to preserve an uninhibited marketplace of ideas in which truth will ultimately prevail." *McCullen v. Coakley* (2014) [Chapter 6]. The second is to ensure that the government has not regulated speech "based on hostility — or favoritism — towards the underlying message expressed." *R.A.V. v. St. Paul* (1992)

[Chapter 15]. Yet the subject-matter exemptions included in many sign ordinances do not implicate those concerns. Allowing residents, say, to install a light bulb over "name and address" signs but no others does not distort the marketplace of ideas. Nor does that different treatment give rise to an inference of impermissible government motive.

We apply strict scrutiny to facially content-based regulations of speech, in keeping with the rationales just described, when there is any "realistic possibility that official suppression of ideas is afoot." *R.A.V.* That is always the case when the regulation facially differentiates on the basis of viewpoint. *See Rosenberger v. Rector and Visitors of Univ. of Va.* (1995) [Chapter 19]. It is also the case (except in non-public or limited public forums) when a law restricts "discussion of an entire topic" in public debate. . . . Subject-matter regulation, . . . may have the intent or effect of favoring some ideas over others. When that is realistically possible—when the restriction "raises the specter that the Government may effectively drive certain ideas or view-points from the marketplace"—we insist that the law pass the most demanding constitutional test.

But when that is not realistically possible, we may do well to relax our guard so that "entirely reasonable" laws imperiled by strict scrutiny can survive. . . . To do its intended work, of course, the category of content-based regulation triggering strict scrutiny must sweep more broadly than the actual harm; that category exists to create a buffer zone guaranteeing that the government cannot favor or disfavor certain viewpoints. But that buffer zone need not extend forever. We can administer our content-regulation doctrine with a dose of common sense, so as to leave standing laws that in no way implicate its intended function.

And indeed we have done just that: Our cases have been far less rigid than the majority admits in applying strict scrutiny to facially content-based laws—including in cases just like this one. [*See, e.g.,*] *Renton v. Playtime Theatres, Inc.* (1986) [Chapter 7] (applying intermediate scrutiny to a zoning law that facially distinguished among movie theaters based on content because it was "designed to prevent crime, protect the city's retail trade, [and] maintain property values . . . , not to suppress the expression of unpopular views"). And another decision involving a similar law provides an alternative model. In *City of Ladue v. Gilleo* (1994) [Chapter 6], the Court assumed *arguendo* that a sign ordinance's exceptions for address signs, safety signs, and for-sale signs in residential areas did not trigger strict scrutiny. We did not need to, and so did not, decide the level-of-scrutiny question because the law's breadth made it unconstitutional under any standard.

The majority could easily have taken *Ladue*'s tack here. The Town of Gilbert's defense of its sign ordinance—most notably, the law's distinctions between directional signs and others—does not pass strict scrutiny, or intermediate scrutiny, or even the laugh test. The Town, for example, provides no reason at all for prohibiting more than four directional signs on a property while placing no limits on the number of other types of signs. Similarly, the Town offers no coherent justification for restricting the size of directional signs to 6 square feet while allowing other signs to reach 20 square feet. The best the Town could come up with at oral argument was that directional signs "need to be smaller because they need to guide travelers along a route." Why exactly a smaller sign better helps travelers get to where they are going is left a mystery. The absence of any sensible basis for these and other distinctions dooms the Town's ordinance under even the intermediate scrutiny that the Court typically applies to "time, place, or manner" speech regulations. Accordingly, there is no need to decide in this case whether strict scrutiny applies to every sign ordinance in every town across this country containing a subject-matter exemption.

I suspect this Court and others will regret the majority's insistence today on answering that question in the affirmative. As the years go by, courts will discover that thousands of towns have such ordinances, many of them "entirely reasonable." And as the challenges to them mount, courts will have to invalidate one after the other. (This Court may soon find itself a veritable Supreme Board of Sign Review.) And courts will strike down those democratically enacted local laws even though no one—certainly not the majority—has ever explained why the vindication of First Amendment values requires that result. Because I see no reason why such an easy case calls for us to cast a constitutional pall on reasonable regulations quite unlike the law before us, I concur only in the judgment.

Note: A Narrower View of Content Neutrality?

1. As discussed in the Note preceding *Reed*, prior to this decision, lower courts—and even the Justices—were inconsistent regarding the meaning of content discrimination. Does the *Reed* decision resolve this disagreement?

2. In Chapter 7, we examine the "secondary effects doctrine." When you read the cases in that section, consider whether the doctrine is consistent with the Court's analysis in *Reed*.

3. Justice Breyer, in his opinion concurring in the judgment, gives several "examples of speech regulated by government that inevitably involve content discrimination, but where a strong presumption against constitutionality has no place." These include:

- requirements for content that must be included on labels of certain consumer electronics;
- a regulation requiring pilots to ensure that each passenger has been briefed on flight procedures, such as seatbelt fastening;
- a New York statute requiring petting zoos to post a sign at every exit "strongly recommending that persons wash their hands upon exiting the petting zoo area."

Would the Court apply strict scrutiny to requirements such as these? If so, does that lead you to agree with Justice Breyer that a more flexible approach is preferable?

4. The Court insists that its decision "will not prevent governments from enacting effective sign laws." Consider these possibilities, drawn from the concurring opinions of Justice Alito and Justice Kagan:

- A rule that distinguishes between the placement of signs on commercial and residential property. (Would it make a difference which rules are more restrictive?)

- A rule imposing time restrictions on signs announcing a one-time event.

- A rule sharply limiting the number and location of electronic signs with messages that change.

- A rule that generally prohibits illuminated signs in residential neighborhoods, but lifts that ban for signs that identify the address of a home or the name of its owner or occupant.

- A rule that generally requires a permit to post a permanent sign but does not require a permit for "safety signs" such as "Blind Pedestrian Crossing" and "Hidden Driveway."

Would these laws be subject to strict scrutiny? If so, how might the government satisfy that standard?

Problem: Flags on Holidays

The Town of Independence, California, generally imposes strict restrictions on signs or other displays (including flags and pennants) on residential and nonresidential property, by requiring permits for most signs. However, the ordinance recognizes a number of exceptions to the permitting requirement.

One of those exceptions is that a business holding a grand opening or promoting a special sale may display one temporary sign — including a banner not exceeding 50 square feet, or an inflatable sign not exceeding 50 feet in height — for no longer than 30 consecutive days.

Another exception permits residences and businesses to display one additional flag (in addition to those otherwise allowed), up to 12 square feet, for three days before and after Memorial Day, Independence Day, and Veterans Day.

Does either of these exceptions constitute a content-based regulation of speech, under the reasoning of *Reed v. Town of Gilbert*? If so, can the Town satisfy strict scrutiny with respect to either of the exceptions?

Problem: A Panhandling Ordinance

In response to complaints from business owners that aggressive panhandling is deterring shoppers and tourists and from visiting Northfield's downtown area, the City of Northfield adopts an ordinance that prohibits panhandling in Northfield's "downtown historic district." The covered district includes less than two percent of the City's geographic area, but contains most of the City's shopping and entertainment facilities as well as most government buildings (Northfield is the state capital). The ordinance defines panhandling as an oral request for an immediate donation of money.

Suppose that a group of individuals who engage in panhandling in the downtown district sue the City, claiming the ordinance violates the First Amendment. After *Reed v. Town of Gilbert*, should the ordinance be subject to strict scrutiny? If so, can it survive strict scrutiny?

If the current ordinance is unconstitutional, how might Northfield redraft the ordinance to comply with the First Amendment?

C. Applying Strict Scrutiny

Williams-Yulee v. Florida Bar

135 S. Ct. 1656 (2015)

CHIEF JUSTICE ROBERTS delivered the opinion of the Court, except as to Part II.

Our Founders vested authority to appoint federal judges in the President, with the advice and consent of the Senate, and entrusted those judges to hold their offices during good behavior. The Constitution permits States to make a different choice, and most of them have done so. In 39 States, voters elect trial or appellate judges at the polls. In an effort to preserve public confidence in the integrity of their judiciaries, many of those States prohibit judges and judicial candidates from personally soliciting funds for their campaigns. We must decide whether the First Amendment permits such restrictions on speech.

We hold that it does. Judges are not politicians, even when they come to the bench by way of the ballot. And a State's decision to elect its judiciary does not compel it to treat judicial candidates like campaigners for political office. A State may assure its people that judges will apply the law without fear or favor—and without having personally asked anyone for money. We affirm the judgment of the Florida Supreme Court.

I

A

When Florida entered the Union in 1845, its Constitution provided for trial and appellate judges to be elected by the General Assembly. Florida soon followed more than a dozen of its sister States in transferring authority to elect judges to the voting public. . . .

In the early 1970s, four Florida Supreme Court justices resigned from office following corruption scandals. Florida voters responded by amending their Constitution again. Under the system now in place, appellate judges are appointed by the Governor from a list of candidates proposed by a nominating committee—a process known as "merit selection." Then, every six years, voters decide whether to retain incumbent appellate judges for another term. Trial judges are still elected by popular vote, unless the local jurisdiction opts instead for merit selection. FLA. CONST. art. V, § 10.

Amid the corruption scandals of the 1970s, the Florida Supreme Court adopted a new Code of Judicial Conduct. In its present form, the first sentence of Canon 1 reads, "An independent and honorable judiciary is indispensable to justice in our society." Canon 1 instructs judges to observe "high standards of conduct" so that "the integrity and independence of the judiciary may be preserved." Canon 2 directs that a judge "shall act at all times in a manner that promotes public confidence in the integrity and impartiality of the judiciary." Other provisions prohibit judges from lending the prestige of their offices to private interests, engaging in certain business transactions, and personally participating in soliciting funds for nonprofit organizations.

Canon 7C(1) governs fundraising in judicial elections. The Canon, which is based on a provision in the American Bar Association's Model Code of Judicial Conduct, provides:

> A candidate, including an incumbent judge, for a judicial office that is filled by public election between competing candidates shall not personally solicit campaign funds, or solicit attorneys for publicly stated support, but may establish committees of responsible persons to secure and manage the expenditure of funds for the candidate's campaign and to obtain public statements of support for his or her candidacy. Such committees are not prohibited from soliciting campaign contributions and public support from any person or corporation authorized by law. . . .

Like Florida, most other States prohibit judicial candidates from soliciting campaign funds personally, but allow them to raise money through committees. According to the American Bar Association, 30 of the 39 States that elect trial or appellate judges have adopted restrictions similar to Canon 7C(1).

B

Lanell Williams-Yulee, who refers to herself as Yulee, has practiced law in Florida since 1991. In September 2009, she decided to run for a seat on the county court for Hillsborough County, a jurisdiction of about 1.3 million people that includes the city of Tampa. Shortly after filing paperwork to enter the race, Yulee drafted a letter announcing her candidacy. The letter described her experience and desire to "bring fresh ideas and positive solutions to the Judicial bench." The letter then stated:

> An early contribution of $25, $50, $100, $250, or $500, made payable to "Lanell Williams-Yulee Campaign for County Judge," will help raise the initial funds needed to launch the campaign and get our message out to the public. I ask for your support [i]n meeting the primary election fund raiser goals. Thank you in advance for your support.

Yulee signed the letter and mailed it to local voters. She also posted the letter on her campaign Web site. [Yulee lost her election. Later, the Florida Bar filed a complaint against her, claiming that her fundraising letter violated the Florida Code of Judicial Conduct. The Florida Supreme Court sustained the complaint, concluding that her letter did violate Canon 7C(1), and that the Canon was constitutional because it satisfied strict scrutiny.]

II

. . . The parties agree that Canon 7C(1) restricts Yulee's speech on the basis of its content by prohibiting her from soliciting contributions to her election campaign. The parties disagree, however, about the level of scrutiny that should govern our review.

We have applied exacting scrutiny to laws restricting the solicitation of contributions to charity, upholding the speech limitations only if they are narrowly tailored to serve a compelling interest. As we have explained, noncommercial solicitation "is characteristically intertwined with informative and perhaps persuasive speech." Applying a lesser standard of scrutiny to such speech would threaten "the exercise of rights so vital to the maintenance of democratic institutions." *Schneider v. State (Town of Irvington)* (1939) [Chapter 6].

The principles underlying these charitable solicitation cases apply with even greater force here. Before asking for money in her fundraising letter, Yulee explained her fitness for the bench and expressed her vision for the judiciary. Her stated purpose for the solicitation was to get her "message out to the public." As we have long recognized, speech about public issues and the qualifications of candidates for elected office commands the highest level of First Amendment protection. Indeed, in our only prior case concerning speech restrictions on a candidate for judicial office, this Court and both parties assumed that strict scrutiny applied. *Republican Party of Minn. v. White*, 536 U.S. 765 (2002)....

[We] hold today what we assumed in *White*: A State may restrict the speech of a judicial candidate only if the restriction is narrowly tailored to serve a compelling interest.

III

The Florida Bar faces a demanding task in defending Canon 7C(1) against Yulee's First Amendment challenge. We have emphasized that "it is the rare case" in which a State demonstrates that a speech restriction is narrowly tailored to serve a compelling interest. *Burson v. Freeman* [*supra* this chapter Note]. But those cases do arise. *Holder v. Humanitarian Law Project*, 561 U.S. 1 (2010); *cf. Adarand Constructors, Inc. v. Peña*, 515 U.S. 200 (1995) ("we wish to dispel the notion that strict scrutiny is 'strict in theory, but fatal in fact'"). Here, Canon 7C(1) advances the State's compelling interest in preserving public confidence in the integrity of the judiciary, and it does so through means narrowly tailored to avoid unnecessarily abridging speech. This is therefore one of the rare cases in which a speech restriction withstands strict scrutiny.

A

The Florida Supreme Court adopted Canon 7C(1) to promote the State's interests in "protecting the integrity of the judiciary" and "maintaining the public's confidence in an impartial judiciary." The way the Canon advances those interests is intuitive: Judges, charged with exercising strict neutrality and independence, cannot supplicate campaign donors without diminishing public confidence in judicial integrity. This principle dates back at least eight centuries to Magna Carta, which proclaimed, "To no one will we sell, to no one will we refuse or delay, right or justice." Cl. 40 (1215). The same concept underlies the common law judicial oath, which binds a judge to "do right to all manner of people ... without fear or favour, affection or ill-will," and the oath that each of us took to "administer justice without respect to persons, and do equal right to the poor and to the rich." Simply put, Florida and most other States have concluded that the public may lack confidence in a judge's ability to administer justice without fear or favor if he comes to office by asking for favors.

The interest served by Canon 7C(1) has firm support in our precedents. We have recognized the "vital state interest" in safeguarding "public confidence in the fairness and integrity of the nation's elected judges." . . .

The principal dissent observes that bans on judicial candidate solicitation lack a lengthy historical pedigree. We do not dispute that fact, but it has no relevance here. As the precedent cited by the principal dissent demonstrates, a history and tradition of regulation are important factors in determining whether to recognize "new categories of unprotected speech." *Brown v. Entertainment Merchants Assn.* (2011) [Chapter 3]. But nobody argues that solicitation of campaign funds by judicial candidates is a category of unprotected speech. As explained above, the First Amendment fully applies to Yulee's speech. The question is instead whether that Amendment permits the particular regulation of speech at issue here.

The parties devote considerable attention to our cases analyzing campaign finance restrictions in political elections. But a State's interest in preserving public confidence in the integrity of its judiciary extends beyond its interest in preventing the appearance of corruption in legislative and executive elections. As we explained in *White*, States may regulate judicial elections differently than they regulate political elections, because the role of judges differs from the role of politicians. Politicians are expected to be appropriately responsive to the preferences of their supporters. . . . The same is not true of judges. In deciding cases, a judge is not to follow the preferences of his supporters, or provide any special consideration to his campaign donors. . . .

The concept of public confidence in judicial integrity does not easily reduce to precise definition, nor does it lend itself to proof by documentary record. But no one denies that it is genuine and compelling. In short, it is the regrettable but unavoidable appearance that judges who personally ask for money may diminish their integrity that prompted the Supreme Court of Florida and most other States to sever the direct link between judicial candidates and campaign contributors. . . . Moreover, personal solicitation by a judicial candidate "inevitably places the solicited individuals in a position to fear retaliation if they fail to financially support that candidate." Potential litigants then fear that "the integrity of the judicial system has been compromised, forcing them to search for an attorney in part based upon the criteria of which attorneys have made the obligatory contributions." A State's decision to elect its judges does not require it to tolerate these risks. The Florida Bar's interest is compelling.

B

Yulee acknowledges the State's compelling interest in judicial integrity. She argues, however, that the Canon's failure to restrict other speech equally damaging to judicial integrity and its appearance undercuts the Bar's position. In particular, she notes that Canon 7C(1) allows a judge's campaign committee to solicit money, which arguably reduces public confidence in the integrity of the judiciary just as much as a judge's personal solicitation. Yulee also points out that Florida permits judicial candidates to write thank you notes to campaign donors, which ensures that candidates know who contributes and who does not.

It is always somewhat counterintuitive to argue that a law violates the First Amendment by abridging *too little* speech. We have recognized, however, that underinclusiveness can raise "doubts about whether the government is in fact pursuing the interest it invokes, rather than disfavoring a particular speaker or viewpoint." *Brown*. . . . Underinclusiveness can also reveal that a law does not actually advance a compelling interest. For example, a State's decision to prohibit newspapers, but not electronic media, from releasing the names of juvenile defendants suggested that the law did not advance its stated purpose of protecting youth privacy. *Smith v. Daily Mail Publishing Co.*, 443 U.S. 97 (1979).

Although a law's underinclusivity raises a red flag, the First Amendment imposes no freestanding "underinclusiveness limitation." *R.A.V. v. St. Paul* (1992) [Chapter 15]. A State need not address all aspects of a problem in one fell swoop; policymakers may focus on their most pressing concerns. We have accordingly upheld laws — even under strict scrutiny — that conceivably could have restricted even greater amounts of speech in service of their stated interests. *Burson*.

Viewed in light of these principles, Canon 7C(1) raises no fatal underinclusivity concerns. The solicitation ban aims squarely at the conduct most likely to undermine public confidence in the integrity of the judiciary: personal requests for money by judges and judicial candidates. The Canon applies evenhandedly to all judges and judicial candidates, regardless of their viewpoint or chosen means of solicitation. And unlike some laws that we have found impermissibly underinclusive, Canon 7C(1) is not riddled with exceptions. *See City of Ladue v. Gilleo* (1994) [Chapter 6]. Indeed, the Canon contains zero exceptions to its ban on personal solicitation.

Yulee relies heavily on the provision of Canon 7C(1) that allows solicitation by a candidate's campaign committee. But Florida, along with most other States, has reasonably concluded that solicitation by the candidate personally creates a categorically different and more severe risk of undermining public confidence than does solicitation by a campaign committee. The identity of the solicitor matters, as anyone who has encountered a Girl Scout selling cookies outside a grocery store can attest. When the judicial candidate himself asks for money, the stakes are higher for all involved. The candidate has personally invested his time and effort in the fundraising appeal; he has placed his name and reputation behind the request. The solicited individual knows that, and also knows that the solicitor might be in a position to singlehandedly make decisions of great weight: The same person who signed the fundraising letter might one day sign the judgment. This dynamic inevitably creates pressure for the recipient to comply, and it does so in a way that solicitation by a third party does not. Just as inevitably, the personal involvement of the candidate in the solicitation creates the public appearance that the candidate will remember who says yes, and who says no.

In short, personal solicitation by judicial candidates implicates a different problem than solicitation by campaign committees. However similar the two solicitations may be in substance, a State may conclude that they present markedly different appearances to the public. Florida's choice to allow solicitation by campaign committees does not undermine its decision to ban solicitation by judges.

Likewise, allowing judicial candidates to write thank you notes to campaign donors does not detract from the State's interest in preserving public confidence in the integrity of the judiciary. Yulee argues that permitting thank you notes heightens the likelihood of actual bias by ensuring that judicial candidates know who supported their campaigns, and ensuring that the supporter knows that the candidate knows. Maybe so. But the State's compelling interest is implicated most directly by the candidate's personal solicitation itself. A failure to ban thank you notes for contributions not solicited by the candidate does not undercut the Bar's rationale. . . .

The principal dissent also suggests that Canon 7C(1) is underinclusive because Florida does not ban judicial candidates from asking individuals for personal gifts or loans. But Florida law treats a personal "gift" or "loan" as a campaign contribution if the donor makes it "for the purpose of influencing the results of an election," and Florida's Judicial Qualifications Commission has determined that a judicial candidate violates Canon 7C(1) by personally soliciting such a loan. In any event, Florida can ban personal solicitation of campaign funds by judicial candidates without making them obey a comprehensive code to leading an ethical life. Underinclusivity creates a First Amendment concern when the State regulates one aspect of a problem while declining to regulate a different aspect of the problem that affects its stated interest *in a comparable way*. The principal dissent offers no basis to conclude that judicial candidates are in the habit of soliciting personal loans, football tickets, or anything of the sort. Even under strict scrutiny, "[t]he First Amendment does not require States to regulate for problems that do not exist."

Taken to its logical conclusion, the position advanced by Yulee and the principal dissent is that Florida may ban the solicitation of funds by judicial candidates only if the State bans *all* solicitation of funds in judicial elections. The First Amendment does not put a State to that all-or-nothing choice. We will not punish Florida for leaving open more, rather than fewer, avenues of expression, especially when there is no indication that the selective restriction of speech reflects a pretextual motive.

C

After arguing that Canon 7C(1) violates the First Amendment because it restricts too little speech, Yulee argues that the Canon violates the First Amendment because it restricts too much. In her view, the Canon is not narrowly tailored to advance the State's compelling interest through the least restrictive means.

By any measure, Canon 7C(1) restricts a narrow slice of speech. A reader of Justice Kennedy's dissent could be forgiven for concluding that the Court has just upheld a latter-day version of the Alien and Sedition Acts, approving "state censorship" that "locks the First Amendment out," imposes a "gag" on candidates, and inflicts "dead weight" on a "silenced" public debate. But in reality, Canon 7C(1) leaves judicial candidates free to discuss any issue with any person at any time. Candidates can write letters, give speeches, and put up billboards. They can contact potential supporters in person, on the phone, or online. They can promote their campaigns on radio, television, or other media. They cannot say, "Please give me money." They can, however, direct their campaign committees to do so. Whatever else may be said of the Canon, it is surely not a "wildly disproportionate restriction upon speech." *Post* (Scalia, J., dissenting).

Indeed, Yulee concedes—and the principal dissent seems to agree—that Canon 7C(1) is valid in numerous applications. Yulee acknowledges that Florida can prohibit judges from soliciting money from lawyers and litigants appearing before them. In addition, she says the State "might" be able to ban "direct one-to-one solicitation of lawyers and individuals or businesses that could reasonably appear in the court for which the individual is a candidate." She also suggests that the Bar could forbid "in person" solicitation by judicial candidates. But Yulee argues that the Canon cannot constitutionally be applied to her chosen form of solicitation: a letter posted online and distributed via mass mailing. No one, she contends, will lose confidence in the integrity of the judiciary based on personal solicitation to such a broad audience.

This argument misperceives the breadth of the compelling interest that underlies Canon 7C(1). Florida has reasonably determined that personal appeals for money by a judicial candidate inherently create an appearance of impropriety that may cause the public to lose confidence in the integrity of the judiciary. That interest may be implicated to varying degrees in particular contexts, but the interest remains whenever the public perceives the judge personally asking for money.

Moreover, the lines Yulee asks us to draw are unworkable. Even under her theory of the case, a mass mailing would create an appearance of impropriety if addressed to a list of all lawyers and litigants with pending cases. So would a speech soliciting contributions from the 100 most frequently appearing attorneys in the jurisdiction. Yulee says she might accept a ban on one-to-one solicitation, but is the public impression really any different if a judicial candidate tries to buttonhole not one prospective donor but two at a time? Ten? Yulee also agrees that in person solicitation creates a problem. But would the public's concern recede if the request for money came in a phone call or a text message?

We decline to wade into this swamp. The First Amendment requires that Canon 7C(1) be narrowly tailored, not that it be "perfectly tailored." *Burson.* The impossibility of perfect tailoring is especially apparent when the State's compelling interest is as intangible as public confidence in the integrity of the judiciary. . . .

In considering Yulee's tailoring arguments, we are mindful that most States with elected judges have determined that drawing a line between personal solicitation by candidates and solicitation by committees is necessary to preserve public confidence in the integrity of the judiciary. These considered judgments deserve our respect, especially because they reflect sensitive choices by States in an area central to their own governance—how to select those who "sit as their judges."

Finally, Yulee contends that Florida can accomplish its compelling interest through the less restrictive means of recusal rules and campaign contribution limits. We disagree. A rule requiring judges to recuse themselves from every case in which a lawyer or litigant made a campaign contribution would disable many jurisdictions. And a flood of postelection recusal motions could "erode public confidence in judicial impartiality" and thereby exacerbate the very appearance problem the State is trying to solve. Moreover, the rule that Yulee envisions could create a perverse incentive for litigants to make campaign contributions to judges solely as a means to trigger their later recusal—a form of peremptory strike against a judge that would enable transparent forum shopping.

As for campaign contribution limits, Florida already applies them to judicial elections. A State may decide that the threat to public confidence created by personal solicitation exists apart from the amount of money that a judge or judicial candidate seeks. . . .

In sum, because Canon 7C(1) is narrowly tailored to serve a compelling government interest, the First Amendment poses no obstacle to its enforcement in this case. . . .

* * *

The desirability of judicial elections is a question that has sparked disagreement for more than 200 years. . . . It is not our place to resolve this enduring debate. Our limited task is to apply the Constitution to the question presented in this case. Judicial candidates have a First Amendment right to speak in support of their campaigns. States have a compelling interest in preserving public confidence in their judiciaries. When the State adopts a narrowly tailored restriction like the one at issue here, those principles do not conflict. A State's decision to elect judges does not compel it to compromise public confidence in their integrity.

The judgment of the Florida Supreme Court is

Affirmed.

JUSTICE BREYER, concurring.

As I have previously said, I view this Court's doctrine referring to tiers of scrutiny as guidelines informing our approach to the case at hand, not tests to be mechanically applied. *See, e.g., United States v. Alvarez* (2012) (Breyer, J., concurring in judgment) [Chapter 3]. On that understanding, I join the Court's opinion.

JUSTICE GINSBURG, with whom JUSTICE BREYER joins as to Part II, concurring in part and concurring in the judgment.

I

I join the Court's opinion save for Part II. As explained in my dissenting opinion in *White*, I would not apply exacting scrutiny to a State's endeavor sensibly to "differentiate elections for political offices . . . , from elections designed to select those whose office it is to administer justice without respect to persons."

II

I write separately to reiterate the substantial latitude, in my view, States should possess to enact campaign-finance rules geared to judicial elections. "Judges," the Court rightly recognizes, "are not politicians," so "States may regulate judicial elections differently than they regulate political elections." And because "the role of judges differs from the role of politicians," this Court's "precedents applying the First Amendment to political elections [should] have little bearing" on elections to judicial office. . . .

Disproportionate spending to influence court judgments threatens both the appearance and actuality of judicial independence. . . . "A State's decision to elect its judges does not require it to tolerate these risks." . . . States should not be put to the polar choices of either equating judicial elections to political elections, or else abandoning public participation in the selection of judges altogether. Instead, States should have leeway to "balance the constitutional interests in judicial integrity and free expression within the unique setting of an elected judiciary." *White* (Ginsburg, J., dissenting).

JUSTICE SCALIA, with whom JUSTICE THOMAS joins, dissenting.

An ethics canon adopted by the Florida Supreme Court bans a candidate in a judicial election from asking anyone, under any circumstances, for a contribution to his campaign. Faithful application of our precedents would have made short work of this wildly disproportionate restriction upon speech. Intent upon upholding the Canon, however, the Court flattens one settled First Amendment principle after another.

I

The first axiom of the First Amendment is this: As a general rule, the state has no power to ban speech on the basis of its content. One need not equate judges with politicians to see that this principle does not grow weaker merely because the censored speech is a judicial candidate's request for a campaign contribution. Our cases hold that speech enjoys the full protection of the First Amendment unless a widespread and longstanding tradition ratifies its regulation. *Brown v. Entertainment Merchants Association* [Chapter 3]. No such tradition looms here. Georgia became the first State to elect its judges in 1812, and judicial elections had spread to a large majority of the States by the time of the Civil War. *White.* Yet there appears to have been no regulation of judicial candidates' speech throughout the 19th and early 20th centuries. . . .

One likewise need not equate judges with politicians to see that the electoral setting calls for all the more vigilance in ensuring observance of the First Amendment. When a candidate asks someone for a campaign contribution, he tends (as the principal opinion acknowledges) also to talk about his qualifications for office and his views on public issues. This expression lies at the heart of what the First Amendment is meant to protect. In addition, banning candidates from asking for money personally "favors some candidates over others — incumbent judges (who benefit from their current status) over non-judicial candidates, the well-to-do (who may not need to raise any money at all) over lower-income candidates, and the well-connected (who have an army of potential fundraisers) over outsiders." This danger of legislated (or judicially imposed) favoritism is the very reason the First Amendment exists.

Because Canon 7C(1) restricts fully protected speech on the basis of content, it presumptively violates the First Amendment. We may uphold it only if the State meets its burden of showing that the Canon survives strict scrutiny—that is to say, only if it shows that the Canon is narrowly tailored to serve a compelling interest. I do not for a moment question the Court's conclusion that States have different compelling interests when regulating judicial elections than when regulating political ones. Unlike a legislator, a judge must be impartial—without bias for or against any party or attorney who comes before him. I accept for the sake of argument that States have a compelling interest in ensuring that its judges are seen to be impartial. I will likewise assume that a judicial candidate's request to a litigant or attorney presents a danger of coercion that a political candidate's request to a constituent does not. But Canon 7C(1) does not narrowly target concerns about impartiality or its appearance; it applies even when the person asked for a financial contribution has no chance of ever appearing in the candidate's court. And Florida does not invoke concerns about coercion, presumably because the Canon bans solicitations regardless of whether their object is a lawyer, litigant, or other person vulnerable to judicial pressure. So Canon 7C(1) fails exacting scrutiny and infringes the First Amendment. This case should have been just that straightforward.

II

The Court concludes that Florida may prohibit personal solicitations by judicial candidates as a means of preserving "public confidence in the integrity of the judiciary." It purports to reach this destination by applying strict scrutiny, but it would be more accurate to say that it does so by applying the appearance of strict scrutiny.

A

The first sign that mischief is afoot comes when the Court describes Florida's compelling interest. The State must first identify its objective with precision before one can tell whether that interest is compelling and whether the speech restriction narrowly targets it. . . .

[T]he Court today relies on Florida's invocation of an ill-defined interest in "public confidence in judicial integrity." The Court at first suggests that "judicial integrity" involves the "ability to administer justice without fear or favor." As its opinion unfolds, however, today's concept of judicial integrity turns out to be "a mere thing of wax in the hands of the judiciary, which they may twist, and shape into any form they please." 12 THE WORKS OF THOMAS JEFFERSON (P. Ford ed., 1905). When the Court explains how solicitation undermines confidence in judicial integrity, integrity starts to sound like saintliness. It involves independence from any "'*possible* temptation'" that "'*might* lead'" the judge, "even unknowingly," to favor one party. When the Court turns to distinguishing in-person solicitation from solicitation by proxy, the any-possible-temptation standard no longer helps and thus drops out. The critical factors instead become the "pressure" a listener feels during a solicitation and the "appearance that the candidate will remember who says yes, and who says no." But when it comes time to explain Florida's decision to allow candidates to write thank-you notes, the "appearance that the candidate . . . remember[s] who says yes" gets nary a mention. And when the Court confronts Florida's decision to prohibit mass-mailed solicitations, concern about pressure fades away. More outrageous still, the Court at times molds the interest in the perception that judges have integrity into an interest in the perception that judges do not solicit . . . . This is not strict scrutiny; it is sleight of hand.

B

The Court's twistifications have not come to an end; indeed, they are just beginning. In order to uphold Canon 7C(1) under strict scrutiny, Florida must do more than point to a vital public objective brooding overhead. The State must also meet a difficult burden of demonstrating that the speech restriction substantially advances the claimed objective. The State "bears the risk of uncertainty," so "ambiguous proof will not suffice." *Entertainment Merchants Association.* . . .

Neither the Court nor the State identifies the slightest evidence that banning requests for contributions will substantially improve public trust in judges. Nor does common sense make this happy forecast obvious. The concept of judicial integrity "dates back at least eight centuries," and judicial elections in America date back more than two centuries — but rules against personal solicitations date back only to 1972. The peaceful coexistence of judicial elections and personal solicitations for most of our history calls into doubt any claim that allowing personal solicitations would imperil public faith in judges. . . . In the final analysis, Florida comes nowhere near making the convincing demonstration required by our cases that the speech restriction in this case substantially advances its objective.

C

But suppose we play along with the premise that prohibiting solicitations will significantly improve the public reputation of judges. Even then, Florida must show that the ban restricts no more speech than necessary to achieve the objective.

Canon 7C(1) falls miles short of satisfying this requirement. The Court seems to accept Florida's claim that solicitations erode public confidence by creating the perception that judges are selling justice to lawyers and litigants. Yet the Canon prohibits candidates from asking for money from *anybody* — even from someone who is neither lawyer nor litigant, even from someone who (because of recusal rules) cannot possibly appear before the candidate as lawyer or litigant. Yulee thus may not call up an old friend, a cousin, or even her parents to ask for a donation to her campaign. The State has not come up with a plausible explanation of how soliciting someone who has no chance of appearing in the candidate's court will diminish public confidence in judges.

No less important, Canon 7C(1) bans candidates from asking for contributions even in messages that do not target any listener in particular — mass-mailed letters, flyers posted on telephone poles, speeches to large gatherings, and Web sites addressed to the general public. Messages like these do not share the features that lead the Court to pronounce personal solicitations a menace to public confidence in the judiciary. Consider online solicitations. They avoid "the spectacle of lawyers or potential litigants directly handing over money to judicial candidates." People who come across online solicitations do not feel "pressure" to comply with the request. Nor does the candidate's signature on the online solicitation suggest "that the candidate will remember who says yes, and who says no." Yet Canon 7C(1) prohibits these and similar solicitations anyway. This tailoring is as narrow as the Court's scrutiny is strict. . . .

D

Even if Florida could show that banning all personal appeals for campaign funds is necessary to protect public confidence in judicial integrity, the Court must overpower one last sentinel of free speech before it can uphold Canon 7C(1). Among its other functions, the First Amendment is a kind of Equal Protection Clause for ideas. The state ordinarily may not regulate one message because it harms a government interest yet refuse to regulate other messages that impair the interest in a comparable way. . . .

The Court's decision disregards these principles. The Court tells us that "all personal solicitations by judicial candidates create a public appearance that undermines confidence in the integrity of the judiciary." But Canon 7C(1) does not restrict *all* personal solicitations; it restricts only personal solicitations related to campaigns. The part of the Canon challenged here prohibits personal pleas for "campaign funds," and the Canon elsewhere prohibits personal appeals to attorneys for "publicly stated support." So although Canon 7C(1) prevents Yulee from asking a lawyer for a few dollars to help her buy campaign pamphlets, it does not prevent her asking the same lawyer for a personal loan, access to his law firm's luxury suite at the local football stadium, or even a donation to help her fight the Florida Bar's charges. What could possibly justify these distinctions? Surely the Court does not believe that requests for campaign favors erode public confidence in a way that requests for favors unrelated to elections do not. Could anyone say with a straight face that it looks *worse* for a candidate to say "please give my campaign $25" than to say "please give *me* $25"?

Fumbling around for a fig-leaf, the Court says that "the First Amendment imposes no freestanding underinclusiveness limitation." This analysis elides the distinction between selectivity on the basis of content and selectivity on other grounds. Because the First Amendment does not prohibit underinclusiveness as such, lawmakers may target a problem only at certain times or in certain places. Because the First Amendment *does* prohibit content discrimination as such, lawmakers may *not* target a problem only in certain messages. . . .

Even on the Court's own terms, Canon 7C(1) cannot stand. The Court concedes that "underinclusiveness can raise 'doubts about whether the government is in fact pursuing the interest it invokes.'" Canon 7C(1)'s scope suggests that it has nothing to do with the appearances created by judges' asking for money, and everything to do with hostility toward judicial campaigning. How else to explain the Florida Supreme Court's decision to ban *all* personal appeals for campaign funds (even when the solicitee could never appear before the candidate), but to tolerate appeals for other kinds of funds (even when the solicitee will surely appear before the candidate)? It should come as no surprise that the ABA, whose model rules the Florida Supreme Court followed when framing Canon 7C(1), opposes judicial elections—preferring instead a system in which (surprise!) a committee of lawyers proposes candidates from among whom the Governor must make his selection. *See White.*

The Court tries to strike a pose of neutrality between appointment and election of judges, but no one should be deceived. A Court that sees impropriety in a candidate's request for *any* contributions to his election campaign does not much like judicial selection by the people. . . .

⁎ ⁎ ⁎

This Court has not been shy to enforce the First Amendment in recent Terms— even in cases that do not involve election speech. It has accorded robust protection to depictions of animal torture, sale of violent video games to children, and lies about having won military medals. *See United States v. Stevens* (2010) [Chapter 3]; *Entertainment Merchants Association*; *Alvarez*. Who would have thought that the same Court would today exert such heroic efforts to save so plain an abridgement of the freedom of speech? It is no great mystery what is going on here. The judges of this Court, like the judges of the Supreme Court of Florida who promulgated Canon 7C(1), evidently consider the preservation of public respect for the courts a policy objective of the highest order. So it is—but so too are preventing animal torture, protecting the innocence of children, and honoring valiant soldiers. The Court did not relax the Constitution's guarantee of freedom of speech when legislatures pursued those goals; it should not relax the guarantee when the Supreme Court of Florida pursues this one. The First Amendment is not abridged for the benefit of the Brotherhood of the Robe.

I respectfully dissent.

JUSTICE KENNEDY, dissenting.

. . . With all due respect for the Court, it seems fair and necessary to say its decision rests on two premises, neither one correct. One premise is that in certain elections— here an election to choose the best qualified judge—the public lacks the necessary judgment to make an informed choice. Instead, the State must protect voters by altering the usual dynamics of free speech. The other premise is that since judges should be accorded special respect and dignity, their election can be subject to certain content-based rules that would be unacceptable in other elections. In my respectful view neither premise can justify the speech restriction at issue here. Although States have a compelling interest in seeking to ensure the appearance and the reality of an impartial judiciary, it does not follow that the State may alter basic First Amendment principles in pursuing that goal. *See White.* . . .

In addition to narrowing the First Amendment's reach, there is another flaw in the Court's analysis. That is its error in the application of strict scrutiny. The Court's evisceration of that judicial standard now risks long-term harm to what was once the Court's own preferred First Amendment test. As Justice Scalia well explains, the state law at issue fails strict scrutiny for any number of reasons. The candidate who is not wealthy or well connected cannot ask even a close friend or relative for a bit of financial help, despite the lack of any increased risk of partiality and despite the fact that disclosure laws might be enacted to make the solicitation and support public. This law comes nowhere close to being narrowly tailored. And by saying that it survives that vital First Amendment requirement, the Court now writes what is literally a case-book guide to eviscerating strict scrutiny any time the Court encounters speech it dislikes. On these premises, and for the reasons explained in more detail by Justice Scalia, it is necessary for me to file this respectful dissent.

JUSTICE ALITO, dissenting.

I largely agree with what I view as the essential elements of the dissents filed by Justices Scalia and Kennedy. The Florida rule before us regulates speech that is part of the process of selecting those who wield the power of the State. Such speech lies at the heart of the protection provided by the First Amendment. The Florida rule regulates that speech based on content and must therefore satisfy strict scrutiny. This means that it must be narrowly tailored to further a compelling state interest. Florida has a compelling interest in making sure that its courts decide cases impartially and in accordance with the law and that its citizens have no good reason to lack confidence that its courts are performing their proper role. But the Florida rule is not narrowly tailored to serve that interest.

Indeed, this rule is about as narrowly tailored as a burlap bag. It applies to all solicitations made in the name of a candidate for judicial office—including, as was the case here, a mass mailing. It even applies to an ad in a newspaper. It applies to requests for contributions in any amount, and it applies even if the person solicited is not a lawyer, has never had any interest at stake in any case in the court in question, and has no prospect of ever having any interest at stake in any litigation in that court. If this rule can be characterized as narrowly tailored, then narrow tailoring has no meaning, and strict scrutiny, which is essential to the protection of free speech, is seriously impaired. . . .

Note: How Strict Is "Strict"?

1. As all of the opinions in *Williams-Yulee* indicate, the result in that case—upholding a content-based law after subjecting it to strict scrutiny—is extremely rare. In fact, the Court has found strict scrutiny satisfied in only a handful of First Amendment cases since *Mosley* was decided in 1972, the most prominent other example being *Holder v. Humanitarian Law Project*, 561 U.S. 1 (2010), a case implicating national security.

Far more typical is the analysis and result in *Brown v. Entertainment Merchants Association* (2011) [Chapter 3], heavily relied upon in Justice Scalia's *Williams-Yulee* dissent. Recall that the issue in *Entertainment Merchants Association* was the constitutionality of a California law banning the sale of violent video games to minors. After rejecting an argument that violent video games fall into a category of "low value" or unprotected speech, Justice Scalia's opinion for the Court applied strict scrutiny to the law. First, the Court stated that the State had not met its burden of proving that exposure to violent video games harmed children. The Court went on:

> Even taking for granted Dr. Anderson's conclusions [Dr. Anderson was a psychologist whose research the State cited] that violent video games produce some effect on children's feelings of aggression, those effects are both small and indistinguishable from effects produced by other media. In his

testimony in a similar lawsuit, Dr. Anderson admitted that the "effect sizes" of children's exposure to violent video games are "about the same" as that produced by their exposure to violence on television. And he admits that the *same* effects have been found when children watch cartoons starring Bugs Bunny or the Road Runner, or when they play video games like Sonic the Hedgehog that are rated "E" (appropriate for all ages), or even when they "vie[w] a picture of a gun."

Of course, California has (wisely) declined to restrict Saturday morning cartoons, the sale of games rated for young children, or the distribution of pictures of guns. The consequence is that its regulation is wildly underinclusive when judged against its asserted justification, which in our view is alone enough to defeat it. Underinclusiveness raises serious doubts about whether the government is in fact pursuing the interest it invokes, rather than disfavoring a particular speaker or viewpoint. *See City of Ladue v. Gilleo* (1994) [Chapter 6]. Here, California has singled out the purveyors of video games for disfavored treatment — at least when compared to booksellers, cartoonists, and movie producers — and has given no persuasive reason why.

The Act is also seriously underinclusive in another respect — and a respect that renders irrelevant the contentions of the concurrence and the dissents that video games are qualitatively different from other portrayals of violence. The California Legislature is perfectly willing to leave this dangerous, mind-altering material in the hands of children so long as one parent (or even an aunt or uncle) says it's OK. And there are not even any requirements as to how this parental or avuncular relationship is to be verified; apparently the child's or putative parent's, aunt's, or uncle's say-so suffices. That is not how one addresses a serious social problem.

Is it so obvious that the underinclusiveness in *Entertainment Merchants Association* was more severe than the underinclusiveness in *Williams-Yulee*? What about the under-inclusiveness analysis in *Reed v. Town of Gilbert*, which was decided just weeks after *Williams-Yulee*?

2. In his dissent in *Williams-Yulee*, Justice Scalia describes the majority's analysis as "the appearance of strict scrutiny." Do you agree with Justice Scalia that the majority's scrutiny is not "strict" in the sense required by First Amendment doctrine? Consider first his argument that the majority did not define the state's interest with the "precision" the First Amendment requires. In particular, recall his criticism of the majority's conception of the state's interest in "public confidence in judicial integrity" as including concerns about "possible" temptation that "might" lead a judge to favor one party over another. To be sure, his concern here is mainly about the allegedly-shifting character of the interest the Court relies on to uphold the challenged canon. But nevertheless, he criticizes the interest itself, describing it as an interest in judicial "saintliness."

Consider also Justice Scalia's critique of the majority's narrow-tailoring analysis. He criticizes that analysis, arguing that "Florida bears the burden of showing that banning requests for lawful contributions will improve public confidence in judges—not just a little bit, but significantly . . . ." Is it even possible for a state to demonstrate that a rule such as the one challenged in *Williams-Yulee* satisfies that requirement, given the difficulty in demonstrating that such a rule would "improve public confidence in judges—not just a little bit, but significantly"? If you were a judicial ethics official, how would you go about trying to make that showing?

3. Finally, consider *Williams-Yulee* in light of *Reed v. Town of Gilbert* [*supra* this chapter]. Dissenting in *Reed*, Justice Kagan raised the possibility that overly broad application of the strict scrutiny requirement might lead the Court to "water down strict scrutiny to something unrecognizable." Does *Williams-Yulee* represent just such a "watering down"? Do decisions like *Reed* and *Williams-Yulee* support Justice Breyer's long-standing view that what the Court should do in pretty much all cases is to simply ask "whether the regulation at issue works harm to First Amendment interests that is disproportionate in light of the relevant regulatory objectives"? (Justice Breyer adds: "Answering this question requires examining the seriousness of the harm to speech, the importance of the countervailing objectives, the extent to which the law will achieve those objectives, and whether there are other, less restrictive ways of doing so.") How different is that from what the Court actually does?

Problem: Nondisclosure of National Security Letters

A federal statute permits the Federal Bureau of Investigation (FBI) to issue National Security Letters (NSLs) to "wire or electronic communication service providers," including landline and cellular telephone companies, and certain Internet firms. NSLs typically request information about communications by specific individuals or entities, and before issuing an NSL the FBI must certify that the requested information is relevant to an ongoing terrorism or intelligence investigation. Federal law also authorizes the FBI to include in any NSL a requirement that the recipient not disclose that it has received an NSL, if the FBI concludes that such disclosure might cause specific, serious harms.

Suppose that a recipient of an NSL containing a nondisclosure requirement challenges the nondisclosure requirement under the First Amendment. What standard of review should the court apply? And what result under that standard of review?

Chapter 6

Regulating the "Time, Place, and Manner" of Protected Speech

In the first three chapters of this book we saw that the Supreme Court, starting in the aftermath of World War I, developed doctrines that responded to government efforts to regulate speech based on the harm it causes and its purportedly low social value. With respect to some categories of speech, such as fighting words, obscenity, and child pornography, the Court was receptive to regulation. In others, such as subversive speech, libel, violent speech, and commercial speech, it was or eventually became much less receptive. These lines of authority evolved largely independently of one another; thus, one can study the law of obscenity, at least in outline, without delving very deeply into decisions on libel or subversive speech. We also saw that in recent years, the Court generally declined to recognize specific new categories of speech freely subject to regulation.

In the previous chapter, we began examining the primary doctrinal framework applicable to regulations of speech that do not fall within these types of categories. As we saw, when the Court determines that a law regulates speech based on its content, it applies "strict scrutiny" and the law is usually (but not always) struck down. In this chapter we begin to look at how the Court has analyzed laws that do *not* regulate based on content, but rather on other "content-neutral" bases. As we will see, this distinction is sometimes difficult to make and the Justices often disagree over whether a regulation is or is not content-based.

The earliest decisions in this area predate the Court's exposition (starting with *Police Department of Chicago v. Mosley* (1972) (Chapter 5)) of the concept of content discrimination, but rather were decided contemporaneously with the prior cases dealing with subversive speech, fighting words, and obscenity. More recently, the Court has built on these early cases to expound more precise doctrinal "tests" applicable to content-neutral regulations. But the early cases remain highly relevant today, and are cited regularly by the modern Court.

A. Early Development of the Doctrine

Lovell v. City of Griffin

303 U.S. 444 (1938)

[The report of this decision appears in Chapter 4, section A.]

Schneider v. New Jersey

308 U.S. 147 (1939)

Mr. Justice Roberts delivered the opinion of the Court.

Four cases are here, each of which presents the question whether regulations embodied in a municipal ordinance abridge the freedom of speech and of the press secured against state invasion by the Fourteenth Amendment of the Constitution.

[In one of the cases, the appellant was convicted of violating a Los Angeles ordinance that provided in section 28.01:] "No person shall distribute any hand-bill to or among pedestrians along or upon any street, sidewalk or park, or to passengers on any street car, or throw, place or attach any hand-bill in, to or upon any automobile or other vehicle."

[The appellant had distributed handbills to pedestrians on a public sidewalk. The handbills announced a meeting to be held under the auspices of "Friends of Lincoln Brigade" at which speakers would discuss the war in Spain.]

The court below sustained the validity of the ordinance on the ground that experience shows littering of the streets results from the indiscriminate distribution of handbills. It held that the right of free expression is not absolute but subject to reasonable regulation and that the ordinance does not transgress the bounds of reasonableness. *Lovell v. City of Griffin* was distinguished on the ground that the ordinance there in question prohibited distribution anywhere within the city while the one involved forbids distribution in a very limited number of places. [The Wisconsin and Massachusetts courts expressed similar views in upholding ordinances of Milwaukee and Worcester. The New Jersey court upheld an ordinance of the Town of Irvington requiring a license for canvassing or the distribution of circulars.]

The freedom of speech and of the press secured by the First Amendment against abridgment by the United States is similarly secured to all persons by the Fourteenth against abridgment by a state. Although a municipality may enact regulations in the interest of the public safety, health, welfare or convenience, these may not abridge the individual liberties secured by the Constitution to those who wish to speak, write, print or circulate information or opinion.

Municipal authorities, as trustees for the public, have the duty to keep their communities' streets open and available for movement of people and property, the primary purpose to which the streets are dedicated. So long as legislation to this end does not abridge the constitutional liberty of one rightfully upon the street to impart information through speech or the distribution of literature, it may lawfully regulate the conduct of those using the streets. For example, a person could not exercise this liberty by taking his stand in the middle of a crowded street, contrary to traffic regulations, and maintain his position to the stoppage of all traffic; a group of distributors could not insist upon a constitutional right to form a cordon across the street and to allow no pedestrian to pass who did not accept a tendered leaflet; nor does the guarantee of freedom of speech or of the press deprive a municipality of power to enact regulations against throwing literature broadcast in the streets. Prohibition of such conduct would not abridge the constitutional liberty since such activity bears no necessary relationship to the freedom to speak, write, print or distribute information or opinion.

This court has characterized the freedom of speech and that of the press as fundamental personal rights and liberties. . . .

In every case, therefore, where legislative abridgment of the rights is asserted, the courts should be astute to examine the effect of the challenged legislation. Mere legislative preferences or beliefs respecting matters of public convenience may well support regulation directed at other personal activities, but be insufficient to justify such as diminishes the exercise of rights so vital to the maintenance of democratic institutions. And so, as cases arise, the delicate and difficult task falls upon the courts to weigh the circumstances and to appraise the substantiality of the reasons advanced in support of the regulation of the free enjoyment of the rights.

In *Lovell*, this court held void an ordinance which forbade the distribution by hand or otherwise of literature of any kind without written permission from the city manager. . . . The court said that, whatever the motive, the ordinance was bad because it imposed penalties for the distribution of pamphlets, which had become historical weapons in the defense of liberty, by subjecting such distribution to license and censorship; and that the ordinance was void on its face, because it abridged the freedom of the press. Similarly in *Hague v. C.I.O.*, 307 U.S. 496 (1939), an ordinance was held void on its face because it provided for previous administrative censorship of the exercise of the right of speech and assembly in appropriate public places.

The Los Angeles, the Milwaukee, and the Worcester ordinances under review do not purport to license distribution but all of them absolutely prohibit it in the streets and, one of them, in other public places as well.

The motive of the legislation under attack . . . is held by the courts below to be the prevention of littering of the streets and, although the alleged offenders were not charged with themselves scattering paper in the streets, their convictions were sustained upon the theory that distribution by them encouraged or resulted in such littering. We are of opinion that the purpose to keep the streets clean and of good appearance is insufficient to justify an ordinance which prohibits a person rightfully on a public street from handing literature to one willing to receive it. Any burden imposed upon the city authorities in cleaning and caring for the streets as an indirect consequence of such distribution results from the constitutional protection of the freedom of speech and press. This constitutional protection does not deprive a city of all power to prevent street littering. There are obvious methods of preventing littering. Amongst these is the punishment of those who actually throw papers on the streets.

It is argued that the circumstance that in the actual enforcement of the Milwaukee ordinance the distributor is arrested only if those who receive the literature throw it in the streets, renders it valid. But, even as thus construed, the ordinance cannot be enforced without unconstitutionally abridging the liberty of free speech. As we have pointed out, the public convenience in respect of cleanliness of the streets does not justify an exertion of the police power which invades the free communication of information and opinion secured by the Constitution.

It is suggested that the Los Angeles and Worcester ordinances are valid because their operation is limited to streets and alleys and leaves persons free to distribute printed matter in other public places. But, as we have said, the streets are natural and proper places for the dissemination of information and opinion; and one is not to have the exercise of his liberty of expression in appropriate places abridged on the plea that it may be exercised in some other place.

The judgment in each case is reversed and the causes are remanded for further proceedings not inconsistent with this opinion.

MR. JUSTICE MCREYNOLDS is of opinion that the judgment in each case should be affirmed.

————

Note: From Lovell to Schneider

As the Court points out, the ordinance in *Lovell v. City of Griffin* was struck down as a prior restraint because it subjected the distribution of pamphlets to "license and censorship." The ordinances in *Schneider* did not impose licensing requirements; they prohibited the activity altogether. Does the Court say that the earlier precedents govern this case? Or is the Court establishing a new principle of First Amendment law? If the latter, where does the principle come from?

Martin v. City of Struthers
319 U.S. 141 (1943)

DRAFT OPINION*

[*Editor's note.* Three Terms after the decision in *Schneider v. New Jersey*, the Court granted plenary review in *Martin v. City of Struthers*, an appeal that challenged the validity of a canvassing or "doorbell" ordinance. In the Court's initial conference on the case, the Justices voted 5–4 to uphold the validity of the law. The writing of the opinion was assigned to Justice Black, presumably by Justice Roberts, the senior Justice in the majority. (Chief Justice Stone was among the Justices who would have held the law unconstitutional.) Justice Black circulated an opinion that read in part as follows.]

MR. JUSTICE BLACK delivered the opinion of the court.

Advertisements are sometimes circulated to residences by canvassers who summon the householders to his door for the purpose of receiving a leaflet. The question in this case is whether a state, through its municipalities, may constitutionally prohibit this practice when the leaflet distributed advertises a religious meeting.

————

 * The draft opinion can be found in the Felix Frankfurter papers in the Manuscripts Collection of the Harvard Law School Library, Paige Box No. 11 (available in the University Publications of America microfilm collection).

Struthers is a city adjacent to Youngstown, Ohio, whose residents are primarily employed in the iron and steel industry of that area. Approximately forty years ago the following ordinance was adopted in order, we are told by counsel, that employees who then worked on twelve hour shifts might have undisturbed rest:

> It is unlawful for any person distributing handbills, circulars, or other advertisements, to ring the doorbell, sound the doorknocker, or otherwise summon the inmate, or inmates, of any residence to the door for the purpose of receiving such handbills, circulars, or other advertisements, they, or any person with them may be distributing.

The ordinance before us broadly prohibits any advertiser from ringing a doorbell or sounding any other alarm for the purpose of summoning the inmate of a house to his door to receive a circular. The ordinance has not been construed as applying to an invitee. . . .

If the ordinance were directed solely at commercial advertisements, there would be little question of the authority of the community. *Valentine v. Chrestensen*, 316 U.S. 52 (1942) [Chapter 3 Note]. . . .

The right of freedom of speech and press . . . embraces the right to distribute literature, *Lovell v. Griffin*, even at the expense of the minor nuisance to a community of cleaning litter from its streets. *Schneider*. Yet the peace, good order, and comfort of the community may imperatively require regulation of the time, place, and manner of distribution. *Cantwell v. Connecticut* (1940) [Chapter 8]. No one supposes, for example, that a city need permit a man with a communicable disease to distribute leaflets on the street, or that the First Amendment prohibits a state from preventing the distribution of leaflets in a church against the will of the church authorities.

We are faced in the instant case with the necessity of weighing the conflicting interests of the appellant in the civil rights she claims and of the community in the protection of the interests of its citizens. In considering legislation of this sort, which to some extent limits the dissemination of knowledge, we must "be astute to examine the effects of the challenged legislation" and must "weigh the circumstances and . . . appraise the substantiality of the reason advanced in support of the regulation." *Schneider*. Approaching this legislation in the spirit of careful criticism, since it involves an asserted conflict with a basic civil right, we conclude that the ordinance before us is valid. We base our conclusion on the fact that an ordinance of this sort can control conduct leading to substantial social evils which a city may find it necessary to restrain.

Constant callers, whether selling pots or distributing leaflets, may lessen the peaceful enjoyment of a home as much as a neighborhood glue factory or a railroad yard which zoning ordinances may prohibit. That "a man's home is his castle" is no mere sentimental flourish. When a man enters his home after his day's or his night's work, he is entitled to rest, or read, or to enjoy himself with his family and friends. This Court has written feelingly of the significance of a secure and quiet home, and has spoken of the Constitution as protecting against "all invasions on the part of the government and its employees of the sanctity of a man's home and the privacies of life." *Boyd v.*

United States, 116 U.S. 616, 630 (1886). Such decisions stem from an underlying philosophy that a man in his home is entitled to a maximum of privacy and seclusion, a philosophy equally applicable against intrusion by the State or by uninvited canvassers.

An industrial community with many of its citizens sleeping at odd hours may properly feel that it has special need to protect the peace and quiet of residential areas. While the record in this case has not been formally prepared to show the extent of this problem in Struthers, the difficulty of adjustment to shift work is so apparent a social phenomenon that we cannot ignore it. The disorganization of life due to night work has been a subject of comment in the popular press, and several government agencies have given consideration to the problem. We cannot say that the Constitution prevents the State from taking reasonable steps to lessen the effect of so apparent a dislocation of normal life.

It is said that the city may regulate as to time of canvassing, but that if it would prohibit doorbell ringing by canvassers, it must require the householder to placard his home with "No Trespassing" signs, and then punish those who call in violation of the mandate of the placard.

Protection of the homeowner from indiscriminate bell ringing in communities whose inhabitants work around the clock may necessarily amount to complete prohibition. If a substantial number of the citizens of a community are sleeping at all hours, it is impossible to pick hours for canvassing in which the townspeople will not be disturbed. Accept the assumption of multiple work shifts that twelve o'clock noon is someone's midnight, and it is impossible to speak of regulation of time of canvassing as a solution to the disturbance problem. Some cities may, in analyzing the facts of their particular situation, conclude that the canvassing is adequately controlled by restricting it to the daylight hours; we cannot say that the Federal Constitution requires a city to reach this result.

The Constitution does not demand that cities solve the canvassing problem only by adopting a placard ordinance of the type suggested or by inventing some variants of this method. While the National Institute of Municipal Law Officers has begun its tentative consideration of such a proposal, we are not informed of a single community in the United States which has ever adopted such a plan. If a city does not choose to adopt a placard device, the householder who desires canvassers to call retains full freedom to post his own notices welcoming solicitors for advertisers, thus making them invitees.

The ordinance does not appear to be a disguised attempt to suppress constitutionally guaranteed freedom. It does not, as it could not, prohibit appellant's activity in the streets and parks of the community. *Hague.* The ordinance is aimed at all advertisements including the commercial. There is no allegation that it is being enforced in a discriminatory manner.

If we are to support the contention of the appellant, we must conclude that no state may constitutionally forbid uninvited persons to disturb the occupants of houses or apartments by accosting the householder at his door. Our determination, alterable only by constitutional amendment, would bar the state from dealing in a recognized manner with a genuine problem in the control of crime. Like freedom of speech and religion, the protection of peaceful home life occupies a high place in the scale of human values. Its protection is largely the duty of the states, with which we are reluctant to interfere.

We do not intimate that ordinances of this sort are universally desirable. . . . Many—perhaps most—cities will conclude that it is desirable not to pass such sweeping ordinances as this. . . . Each city must decide for itself whether the doorbell ringing problem is sufficiently acute to justify so strenuous a remedy; but the difficulties of determining wide policies make this problem one better solved by States or local boards of aldermen than by courts unfamiliar with local needs. Resulting ordinances will be scrutinized only to insure that regulation either in term or in practice, is not a form of discrimination intended to suppress the free communication of beliefs. [Judgment affirmed.]

FINAL OPINION

[Shortly after circulating the draft opinion, Justice Black changed his mind about the case. (For Justice Frankfurter's explanation of this shift, see H.N. HIRSCH, THE ENIGMA OF FELIX FRANKFURTER 167 (1981).) Chief Justice Stone, now a member of the new majority, assigned the writing of the Court opinion to Justice Black.]

MR. JUSTICE BLACK delivered the opinion of the court.

For centuries it has been a common practice in this and other countries for persons not specifically invited to go from home to home and knock on doors or ring doorbells to communicate ideas to the occupants or to invite them to political, religious, or other kinds of public meetings. Whether such visiting shall be permitted has in general been deemed to depend upon the will of the individual master of each household, and not upon the determination of the community. In the instant case, the City of Struthers, Ohio, has attempted to make this decision for all its inhabitants. The question to be decided is whether the City, consistently with the federal Constitution's guarantee of free speech and press, possesses this power. . . .

The right of freedom of speech and press . . . embraces the right to distribute literature, *Lovell v. Griffin*, and necessarily protects the right to receive it. The privilege may not be withdrawn even if it creates the minor nuisance for a community of cleaning litter from its streets. *Schneider*.**

We are faced in the instant case with the necessity of weighing the conflicting interests of the appellant in the civil rights she claims, as well as the right of the individual householder to determine whether he is willing to receive her message, against the interest of the community which by this ordinance offers to protect the interests of

---

** [*Editor's note.* The remainder of this paragraph is identical to that of the corresponding paragraph of the initial version.]

all of its citizens, whether particular citizens want that protection or not.*** The ordinance does not control anything but the distribution of literature, and in that respect it substitutes the judgment of the community for the judgment of the individual householder. It submits the distributer to criminal punishment for annoying the person on whom he calls, even though the recipient of the literature distributed is in fact glad to receive it. In considering legislation which thus limits the dissemination of knowledge, we must "be astute to examine the effect of the challenged legislation" and must "weigh the circumstances and . . . appraise the substantiality of the reasons advanced in support of the regulation." *Schneider.* . . .

While door to door distributers of literature may be either a nuisance or a blind for criminal activities, they may also be useful members of society engaged in the dissemination of ideas in accordance with the best tradition of free discussion. The widespread use of this method of communication by many groups espousing various causes attests its major importance. . . . Door to door distribution of circulars is essential to the poorly financed causes of little people.

Freedom to distribute information to every citizen wherever he desires to receive it is so clearly vital to the preservation of a free society that, putting aside reasonable police and health regulations of time and manner of distribution, it must be fully preserved. The dangers of distribution can so easily be controlled by traditional legal methods, leaving to each householder the full right to decide whether he will receive strangers as visitors, that stringent prohibition can serve no purpose but that forbidden by the Constitution, the naked restriction of the dissemination of ideas.

Traditionally the American law punishes persons who enter onto the property of another after having been warned by the owner to keep off. . . . We know of no state which, as does the Struthers ordinance in effect, makes a person a criminal trespasser if he enters the property of another for an innocent purpose without an explicit command from the owners to stay away. . . . A city can punish those who call at a home in defiance of the previously expressed will of the occupant and, in addition, can by identification devices control the abuse of the privilege by criminals posing as canvassers. In any case the problem must be worked out by each community for itself with due respect for the constitutional rights of those desiring to distribute literature and those desiring to receive it, as well as those who choose to exclude such distributers from the home. [Judgment reversed.]

[Justice Reed dissented, joined by Justice Roberts and Justice Jackson. Justice Frankfurter joined a separate dissent by Justice Jackson.]

————

Note: Regulating the Manner of Expressive Activity

1. *Martin v. City of Struthers* provides a rare insight into the craft of opinion writing. We see the same Justice first writing an opinion rejecting the First Amendment

---

*** [*Editor's note.* Compare this statement of the interests to be balanced with the statement in the opinion for affirmance. Does the revision perhaps explain Justice Black's shift of position?]

claim, then an opinion upholding the claim. Carefully compare the two opinions. What themes or considerations appear in the later opinion that did not appear in the earlier one? Is the difference only a matter of substance? Compare, for example, the opening paragraphs of the two opinions.

2. How might the development of First Amendment law have been different if Justice Black's initial draft had come down as the opinion of the Court? Consider this question as you read the other cases in this chapter. To what extent do those cases rely or draw on the opinion in *Martin v. Struthers*?

3. Most of the early cases recognizing the power of governments to regulate the time, place, and manner of protected expression did so in dictum. See, for example, the lengthy paragraph near the beginning of the opinion in *Schneider v. New Jersey*. One of the first decisions to actually uphold a law that limited the use of a particular means of communication was *Kovacs v. Cooper*, 336 U.S. 77 (1949). The appellant in that case was convicted of violating a city ordinance that prohibited the use of sound trucks within the city. Although the Justices disagreed as to the scope of the prohibition, the plurality accepted the determination of the state court that the ordinance applied only to "(1) vehicles (2) containing an instrument in the nature of a sound amplifier or any other instrument emitting loud and raucous noises and (3) such vehicle operated or standing upon the public streets, alleys or thoroughfares of the city." On that premise, the plurality held that the ordinance was constitutional. It rejected the plaintiff's reliance on *Martin v. City of Struthers*:

> We do not think that the *Struthers* case requires us to expand this interdiction of legislation to include ordinance against obtaining an audience for the broadcaster's ideas by way of sound trucks with loud and raucous noises on city streets. The unwilling listener is not like the passer-by who may be offered a pamphlet in the street but cannot be made to take it. In his home or on the street he is practically helpless to escape this interference with his privacy by loud speakers except through the protection of the municipality.

> City streets are recognized as a normal place for the exchange of ideas by speech or paper. But this does not mean the freedom is beyond all control. We think it is a permissible exercise of legislative discretion to bar sound trucks with broadcasts of public interest, amplified to a loud and raucous volume, from the public ways of municipalities. On the business streets of cities like Trenton, with its more than 125,000 people, such distractions would be dangerous to traffic at all hours useful for the dissemination of information, and in the residential thoroughfares the quiet and tranquility so desirable for city dwellers would likewise be at the mercy of advocates of particular religious, social or political persuasions. We cannot believe that rights of free speech compel a municipality to allow such mechanical voice amplification on any of its streets. . . .

> That more people may be more easily and cheaply reached by sound trucks, perhaps borrowed without cost from some zealous supporter, is not enough to call forth constitutional protection for what those charged with

public welfare reasonably think is a nuisance when easy means of publicity are open. Section 4 of the ordinance bars sound trucks from broadcasting in a loud and raucous manner on the streets. There is no restriction upon the communication of ideas or discussion of issues by the human voice, by newspapers, by pamphlets, by dodgers. We think that the need for reasonable protection in the homes or business houses from the distracting noises of vehicles equipped with such sound amplifying devices justifies the ordinance.

The decision was by a vote of 5-4. Two Justices concurred only in the judgment because they could not endorse the plurality's attempt to distinguish *Saia v. New York*, 334 U.S. 558 (1948), a case handed down one year earlier holding a loudspeaker ordinance unconstitutional. Justice Black, writing for three of the dissenters, described the new decision as "a dangerous and unjustifiable breach in the constitutional barriers designed to insure freedom of expression." He explained:

> If Trenton can completely bar the streets to the advantageous use of loud speakers, all cities can do the same. In that event preference in the dissemination of ideas is given those who can obtain the support of newspapers, etc., or those who have money enough to buy advertising from newspapers, radios, or moving pictures. . . .
>
> I am aware that the "blare" of this new method of carrying ideas is susceptible of abuse and may under certain circumstances constitute an intolerable nuisance. . . . A city ordinance that reasonably restricts the volume of sound [or] the hours during which an amplifier may be used, [or which bans the use of amplifiers on busy streets in the business area], does not, in my mind, infringe the constitutionally protected area of free speech. It is because this ordinance does none of these things, but is instead an absolute prohibition of all uses of an amplifier on any of the streets of Trenton at any time that I must dissent.

4. As you will see in the next section, the Court now applies a multipart test to evaluate laws regulating the time, place, and manner of protected expression. In reading these cases, consider whether this test is an improvement over the approach taken in the earlier decisions.

B. Applications of the Doctrine

Frisby v. Schultz
487 U.S. 474 (1988)

Justice O'Connor delivered the opinion of the Court.

Brookfield, Wisconsin, has adopted an ordinance that completely bans picketing "before or about" any residence. This case presents a facial First Amendment challenge to that ordinance.

I

Brookfield, Wisconsin, is a residential suburb of Milwaukee with a population of approximately 4,300. The appellees, Sandra C. Schultz and Robert C. Braun, are individuals strongly opposed to abortion and wish to express their views on the subject by picketing on a public street outside the Brookfield residence of a doctor who apparently performs abortions at two clinics in neighboring towns. Appellees and others engaged in precisely that activity, assembling outside the doctor's home on at least six occasions between April 20, 1985, and May 20, 1985, for periods ranging from one to one and a half hours. The size of the group varied from 11 to more than 40. The picketing was generally orderly and peaceful; the town never had occasion to invoke any of its various ordinances prohibiting obstruction of the streets, loud and unnecessary noises, or disorderly conduct. Nonetheless, the picketing generated substantial controversy and numerous complaints.

[In May 1985 the Town Board adopted] the following flat ban on all residential picketing:

> It is unlawful for any person to engage in picketing before or about the
> residence or dwelling of any individual in the Town of Brookfield.

The ordinance itself recites the primary purpose of this ban: "the protection and preservation of the home" through assurance "that members of the community enjoy in their homes and dwellings a feeling of well-being, tranquility, and privacy." . . . The ordinance also evinces a concern for public safety, noting that picketing obstructs and interferes with "the free use of public sidewalks and public ways of travel." . . .

II

[The Town argued that residential streets should be treated as a "nonpublic forum," but the Supreme Court unanimously rejected that position. (For discussion of that concept, see Chapter 8.) Thus, the Court held, "the antipicketing ordinance must be judged against the stringent standards we have established for restrictions on speech in traditional public fora." Under those standards, the state may "enforce regulations of the time, place, and manner of expression which are content-neutral, are narrowly tailored to serve a significant government interest, and leave open ample alternative channels of communication."]

. . . [We] accept the lower courts' conclusion that the Brookfield ordinance is content neutral. Accordingly, we turn to consider whether the ordinance is "narrowly tailored to serve a significant government interest" and whether it "leave[s] open ample alternative channels of communication."

Because the last question is so easily answered, we address it first. Of course, before we are able to assess the available alternatives, we must consider more carefully the reach of the ordinance. The precise scope of the ban is not further described within the text of the ordinance, but in our view the ordinance is readily subject to a narrowing construction that avoids constitutional difficulties. Specifically, the use of the singular form of the words "residence" and "dwelling" suggests that the ordinance is intended to prohibit only picketing focused on, and taking place in front of, a particular residence. . . . This narrow reading is supported by the representations of counsel for the town at oral argument, which indicate that the town takes, and will enforce, a limited view of the "picketing" proscribed by the ordinance. Thus, generally speaking, "picketing would be having the picket proceed on a definite course or route in front of a home." The picket need not be carrying a sign, but in order to fall within the scope of the ordinance the picketing must be directed at a single residence. General marching through residential neighborhoods, or even walking a route in front of an entire block of houses, is not prohibited by this ordinance. Accordingly, we construe the ban to be a limited one; only focused picketing taking place solely in front of a particular residence is prohibited.

So narrowed, the ordinance permits the more general dissemination of a message. As appellants explain, the limited nature of the prohibition makes it virtually self-evident that ample alternatives remain:

> Protestors have not been barred from the residential neighborhoods. They may enter such neighborhoods, alone or in groups, even marching. . . . They may go door-to-door to proselytize their views. They may distribute literature in this manner . . . or through the mails. They may contact residents by telephone, short of harassment.

We readily agree that the ordinance preserves ample alternative channels of communication and thus move on to inquire whether the ordinance serves a significant government interest. We find that such an interest is identified within the text of the ordinance itself: the protection of residential privacy.

"The State's interest in protecting the well-being, tranquility, and privacy of the home is certainly of the highest order in a free and civilized society." *Carey v. Brown*, 447 U.S. 455 (1980). . . . One important aspect of residential privacy is protection of the unwilling listener. Although in many locations, we expect individuals simply to avoid speech they do not want to hear, cf. *Erznoznik v. City of Jacksonville* (1975) [Chapter 3 Note]; *Cohen v. California* (1971) [Chapter 3], the home is different. "That we are often 'captives' outside the sanctuary of the home and subject to objectionable speech . . . does not mean we must be captives everywhere." *Rowan v. United States Post Office Dept.*, 397 U.S. 728, 738 (1970). Instead, a special benefit of the privacy all citizens enjoy within their own walls, which the State may legislate to protect, is an ability to avoid intrusions. Thus, we have repeatedly held that individuals are not required to welcome unwanted speech into their own homes and that the government may protect this freedom. *See, e.g., FCC v. Pacifica Foundation* (1978) [Chapter 3] (offensive radio broadcasts); *Kovacs v. Cooper* (1949) [Note *supra* this chapter] (sound trucks).

This principle is reflected even in prior decisions in which we have invalidated complete bans on expressive activity, including bans operating in residential areas. *See, e.g., Schneider v. State* (handbilling); *Martin v. Struthers* (door-to-door solicitation). In all such cases, we have been careful to acknowledge that unwilling listeners may be protected when within their own homes. . . . We have "never intimated that the visitor could insert a foot in the door and insist on a hearing." There simply is no right to force speech into the home of an unwilling listener.

It remains to be considered, however, whether the Brookfield ordinance is narrowly tailored to protect only unwilling recipients of the communications. A statute is narrowly tailored if it targets and eliminates no more than the exact source of the "evil" it seeks to remedy. *City Council of Los Angeles v. Taxpayers for Vincent*, 466 U.S. 789, 808–10 (1984). A complete ban can be narrowly tailored, but only if each activity within the proscription's scope is an appropriately targeted evil. For example, in *Taxpayers for Vincent* we upheld an ordinance that banned all signs on public property because the interest supporting the regulation, an esthetic interest in avoiding visual clutter and blight, rendered each sign an evil. Complete prohibition was necessary because "the substantive evil—visual blight—[was] not merely a possible byproduct of the activity, but [was] created by the medium of expression itself."

The same is true here. The type of focused picketing prohibited by the Brookfield ordinance is fundamentally different from more generally directed means of communication that may not be completely banned in residential areas. *See, e.g., Schneider* (handbilling); *Martin* (solicitation). In such cases "the flow of information [is not] into . . . household[s], but to the public." *Organization for a Better Austin v. Keefe*, 402 U.S. 415, 420 (1971). Here, in contrast, the picketing is narrowly directed at the household, not the public. The type of picketers banned by the Brookfield ordinance generally do not seek to disseminate a message to the general public, but to intrude upon the targeted resident, and to do so in an especially offensive way. Moreover, even if some such picketers have a broader communicative purpose, their activity nonetheless inherently and offensively intrudes on residential privacy. The devastating effect of targeted picketing on the quiet enjoyment of the home is beyond doubt:

> To those inside . . . the home becomes something less than a home when and while the picketing . . . continue[s]. . . . [The] tensions and pressures may be psychological, not physical, but they are not, for that reason, less inimical to family privacy and truly domestic tranquility. *Carey* (Rehnquist, J., dissenting).

In this case, for example, appellees subjected the doctor and his family to the presence of a relatively large group of protesters on their doorstep in an attempt to force the doctor to cease performing abortions. But the actual size of the group is irrelevant; even a solitary picket can invade residential privacy. *See Carey* (Rehnquist, J., dissenting) ("Whether . . . alone or accompanied by others . . . there are few of us that would feel comfortable knowing that a stranger lurks outside our home"). The offensive and disturbing nature of the form of the communication banned by the Brookfield ordinance thus can scarcely be questioned. . . .

The First Amendment permits the government to prohibit offensive speech as intrusive when the "captive" audience cannot avoid the objectionable speech. The target of the focused picketing banned by the Brookfield ordinance is just such a "captive." The resident is figuratively, and perhaps literally, trapped within the home, and because of the unique and subtle impact of such picketing is left with no ready means of avoiding the unwanted speech. Thus, the "evil" of targeted residential picketing, "the very presence of an unwelcome visitor at the home," *Carey* (Rehnquist, J., dissenting), is "created by the medium of expression itself." Accordingly, the Brookfield ordinance's complete ban of that particular medium of expression is narrowly tailored.

Of course, this case presents only a facial challenge to the ordinance. Particular hypothetical applications of the ordinance—to, for example, a particular resident's use of his or her home as a place of business or public meeting, or to picketers present at a particular home by invitation of the resident—may present somewhat different questions. . . .

Because the picketing prohibited by the Brookfield ordinance is speech directed primarily at those who are presumptively unwilling to receive it, the State has a substantial and justifiable interest in banning it. The nature and scope of this interest make the ban narrowly tailored. The ordinance also leaves open ample alternative channels of communication and is content neutral. Thus, largely because of its narrow scope, the facial challenge to the ordinance must fail. The contrary judgment of the Court of Appeals is reversed.

Justice White, concurring in the judgment. [Omitted.]

Justice Brennan, with whom Justice Marshall joins, dissenting.

. . . Assuming one construes the ordinance as the Court does, I agree that the regulation reserves ample alternative channels of communication. I also agree with the Court that the town has a substantial interest in protecting its residents' right to be left alone in their homes. It is, however, critical to specify the precise scope of this interest. The mere fact that speech takes place in a residential neighborhood does not automatically implicate a residential privacy interest. It is the intrusion of speech into the home or the unduly coercive nature of a particular manner of speech around the home that is subject to more exacting regulation. . . . But so long as the speech remains outside the home and does not unduly coerce the occupant, the government's heightened interest in protecting residential privacy is not implicated.

The foregoing distinction is crucial here because it directly affects the last prong of the time, place, and manner test: whether the ordinance is narrowly tailored to achieve the governmental interest. . . .

Without question there are many aspects of residential picketing that, if unregulated, might easily become intrusive or unduly coercive. Indeed, some of these aspects are illustrated by this very case. As the District Court found, before the ordinance took effect up to 40 sign-carrying, slogan-shouting protesters regularly converged on Dr. Victoria's home and, in addition to protesting, warned young children not to go near the house because Dr. Victoria was a "baby killer." Further, the throng repeatedly trespassed onto the Victorias' property and at least once blocked the exits to their home. Surely it is within the government's power to enact regulations as necessary to prevent such intrusive and coercive abuses. Thus, for example, the government could constitutionally regulate the number of residential picketers, the hours during which a residential picket may take place, or the noise level of such a picket. . . . But to say that picketing may be substantially regulated is not to say that it may be prohibited in its entirety. Once size, time, volume, and the like have been controlled to ensure that the picket is no longer intrusive or coercive, only the speech itself remains, conveyed perhaps by a lone, silent individual, walking back and forth with a sign. Such speech, which no longer implicates the heightened governmental interest in residential privacy, is nevertheless banned by the Brookfield law. Therefore, the ordinance is not narrowly tailored. . . .

. . . [The Court] assumes that the intrusive elements of a residential picket are "inherent." . . . The Court's reference to the *Carey* dissent, its sole support for this assertion, conjures up images of a "lurking" stranger, secreting himself or herself outside a residence like a thief in the night, threatening physical harm. This hardly seems an apt depiction of a solitary picket, especially at midafternoon, whose presence is objectionable because it is notorious. Contrary to the Court's declaration in this regard, it seems far more likely that a picketer who truly desires only to harass those inside a particular residence will find that goal unachievable in the face of a narrowly tailored ordinance substantially limiting, for example, the size, time, and volume of the protest. If, on the other hand, the picketer intends to communicate generally, a carefully crafted ordinance will allow him or her to do so without intruding upon or unduly harassing the resident. Consequently, the discomfort to which the Court must refer is merely that of knowing there is a person outside who disagrees with someone inside. This may indeed be uncomfortable, but it does not implicate the town's interest in residential privacy and therefore does not warrant silencing speech. . . .

JUSTICE STEVENS, dissenting.

"GET WELL CHARLIE—OUR TEAM NEEDS YOU."

In Brookfield, Wisconsin, it is unlawful for a fifth grader to carry such a sign in front of a residence for the period of time necessary to convey its friendly message to its intended audience.

[The Court concludes] that the total ban on residential picketing is "narrowly tailored" to protect "only unwilling recipients of the communications." The plain language of the ordinance, however, applies to communications to willing and indifferent recipients as well as to the unwilling. . . .

. . . My hunch is that the town will probably not enforce its ban against friendly, innocuous, or even brief unfriendly picketing, and that the Court may be right in concluding that its legitimate sweep makes its overbreadth insubstantial. But there are two countervailing considerations that are persuasive to me. The scope of the ordinance gives the town officials far too much discretion in making enforcement decisions; while we sit by and await further developments, potential picketers must act at their peril. Second, it is a simple matter for the town to amend its ordinance and to limit the ban to conduct that unreasonably interferes with the privacy of the home and does not serve a reasonable communicative purpose. . . .

Ward v. Rock Against Racism

491 U.S. 781 (1989)

Justice Kennedy delivered the opinion of the Court.

In the southeast portion of New York City's Central Park, about 10 blocks upward from the park's beginning point at 59th Street, there is an amphitheater and stage structure known as the Naumberg Acoustic Bandshell. The bandshell faces west across the remaining width of the park. In close proximity to the bandshell, and lying within the directional path of its sound, is a grassy open area called the Sheep Meadow. The city has designated the Sheep Meadow as a quiet area for passive recreations like reclining, walking, and reading. Just beyond the park, and also within the potential sound range of the bandshell, are the apartments and residences of Central Park West.

This case arises from the city's attempt to regulate the volume of amplified music at the bandshell so the performances are satisfactory to the audience without intruding upon those who use the Sheep Meadow or live on Central Park West and in its vicinity. The city's regulation requires bandshell performers to use sound-amplification equipment and a sound technician provided by the city. The challenge to this volume control technique comes from the sponsor of a rock concert. The trial court sustained the noise control measures, but the Court of Appeals for the Second Circuit reversed. . . .

[W]e decide the case as one in which the bandshell is a public forum for performances in which the government's right to regulate expression is subject to the protections of the First Amendment. Our cases make clear, however, that even in a public forum the government may impose reasonable restrictions on the time, place, or manner of protected speech, provided the restrictions "are justified without reference to the content of the regulated speech, that they are narrowly tailored to serve a significant governmental interest, and that they leave open ample alternative channels for communication of the information." *Clark v. Community for Creative Non-Violence*, 468 U.S. 288, 293 (1984). We consider these requirements in turn.

A

The principal inquiry in determining content neutrality, in speech cases generally and in time, place, or manner cases in particular, is whether the government has adopted a regulation of speech because of disagreement with the message it conveys. The government's purpose is the controlling consideration. . . . Government regulation of expressive activity is content neutral so long as it is "*justified* without reference to the content of the regulated speech." *Community for Creative Non-Violence* (emphasis added).

The principal justification for the sound-amplification guideline is the city's desire to control noise levels at bandshell events, in order to retain the character of the Sheep Meadow and its more sedate activities, and to avoid undue intrusion into residential areas and other areas of the park. This justification [satisfies] the requirement that time, place, or manner regulations be content neutral. . . .

The Court of Appeals recognized the city's substantial interest in limiting the sound emanating from the bandshell. The court concluded, however, that the city's sound-amplification guideline was not narrowly tailored to further this interest, because "it has not [been] shown . . . that the requirement of the use of the city's sound system and technician was the *least intrusive means* of regulating the volume." (Emphasis added). In the court's judgment, there were several alternative methods of achieving the desired end that would have been less restrictive of respondent's First Amendment rights.

The Court of Appeals erred in sifting through all the available or imagined alternative means of regulating sound volume in order to determine whether the city's solution was "the least intrusive means" of achieving the desired end. This "less-restrictive-alternative analysis . . . has never been a part of the inquiry into the validity of a time, place, and manner regulation." *Regan v. Time, Inc.*, 468 U.S. 641, 657 (1984) (opinion of White, J.). Instead, our cases quite clearly hold that restrictions on the time, place, or manner of protected speech are not invalid "simply because there is some imaginable alternative that might be less burdensome on speech." *United States v. Albertini*, 472 U.S. 675, 689 (1985).

The Court of Appeals apparently drew its least-intrusive-means requirement from *United States v. O'Brien* (1968) [Chapter 7], the case in which we established the standard for judging the validity of restrictions on expressive conduct. The court's reliance was misplaced, however, for we have held that the *O'Brien* test "in the last analysis is little, if any, different from the standard applied to time, place, or manner restrictions." *Community for Creative Non-Violence.* Indeed, in *Community for Creative Non-Violence* we squarely rejected reasoning identical to that of the court below: "We are unmoved by the Court of Appeals' view that the challenged regulation is unnecessary, and hence invalid, because there are less speech-restrictive alternatives that could have satisfied the Government interest in preserving park lands. . . . We do not believe . . . that either *United States v. O'Brien* or the time, place, or manner decisions assign to the judiciary the authority to replace the [parks department] as the manager of the [city's] parks or endow the judiciary with the competence to judge how much protection of park lands is wise and how that level of conservation is to be attained."

Lest any confusion on the point remain, we reaffirm today that a regulation of the time, place, or manner of protected speech must be narrowly tailored to serve the government's legitimate, content-neutral interests but that it need not be the least restrictive or least intrusive means of doing so. Rather, the requirement of narrow tailoring is satisfied "so long as the . . . regulation promotes a substantial government interest that would be achieved less effectively absent the regulation." *Albertini.* To be sure, this standard does not mean that a time, place, or manner regulation may burden substantially more speech than is necessary to further the government's legitimate interests. Government may not regulate expression in such a manner that a substantial portion of the burden on speech does not serve to advance its goals.[7] *See*

---

7. The dissent's attempt to analogize the sound-amplification guideline to a total ban on distribution of handbills is imaginative but misguided. The guideline does not ban all concerts, or even all rock concerts, but instead focuses on the source of the evils the city seeks to eliminate — excessive and

Frisby ("A complete ban can be narrowly tailored but only if each activity within the proscription's scope is an appropriately targeted evil"). So long as the means chosen are not substantially broader than necessary to achieve the government's interest, however, the regulation will not be invalid simply because a court concludes that the government's interest could be adequately served by some less-speech-restrictive alternative. . . .

It is undeniable that the city's substantial interest in limiting sound volume is served in a direct and effective way by the requirement that the city's sound technician control the mixing board during performances. Absent this requirement, the city's interest would have been served less well, as is evidenced by the complaints about excessive volume generated by respondent's past concerts. The alternative regulatory methods hypothesized by the Court of Appeals reflect nothing more than a disagreement with the city over how much control of volume is appropriate or how that level of control is to be achieved. The Court of Appeals erred in failing to defer to the city's reasonable determination that its interest in controlling volume would be best served by requiring bandshell performers to utilize the city's sound technician.

The city's second content-neutral justification for the guideline, that of ensuring "that the sound amplification [is] sufficient to reach all listeners within the defined concertground," also supports the city's choice of regulatory methods. By providing competent sound technicians and adequate amplification equipment, the city eliminated the problems of inexperienced technicians and insufficient sound volume that had plagued some bandshell performers in the past. No doubt this concern is not applicable to respondent's concerts . . . [However,] the regulation's effectiveness must be judged by considering all the varied groups that use the bandshell, and it is valid so long as the city could reasonably have determined that its interests overall would be served less effectively without the sound-amplification guideline than with it. Considering these proffered justifications together, therefore, it is apparent that the guideline directly furthers the city's legitimate governmental interests and that those interests would have been less well served in the absence of the sound-amplification guideline. . . .

C

The final requirement, that the guideline leave open ample alternative channels of communication, is easily met. Indeed, in this respect the guideline is far less restrictive than regulations we have upheld in other cases, for it does not attempt to ban any particular manner or type of expression at a given place or time. Rather, the guideline continues to permit expressive activity in the bandshell, and has no effect on the quantity or content of that expression beyond regulating the extent of amplification. . . .

---

inadequate sound amplification—and eliminates them without at the same time banning or significantly restricting a substantial quantity of speech that does not create the same evils. This is the essence of narrow tailoring. A ban on handbilling, of course, would suppress a great quantity of speech that does not cause the evils that it seeks to eliminate, whether they be fraud, crime, litter, traffic congestion, or noise. *See Martin v. Struthers* (1943) [*supra* this chapter]. For that reason, a complete ban on handbilling would be substantially broader than necessary to achieve the interests justifying it.

The city's sound-amplification guideline is narrowly tailored to serve the substantial and content-neutral governmental interests of avoiding excessive sound volume and providing sufficient amplification within the bandshell concert ground, and the guideline leaves open ample channels of communication. Accordingly, it is valid under the First Amendment as a reasonable regulation of the place and manner of expression. The judgment of the Court of Appeals is reversed.

Justice Blackmun concurs in the result.

Justice Marshall, with whom Justice Brennan and Justice Stevens join, dissenting.

. . . The guidelines indisputably are content-neutral as they apply to all bandshell users irrespective of the message of their music. They also serve government's significant interest in limiting loud noise in public places, by giving the city exclusive control of all sound equipment.

My complaint is with the majority's serious distortion of the narrow tailoring requirement. Our cases have not, as the majority asserts, "clearly" rejected a less-restrictive-alternative test. On the contrary, just last Term, we held that a statute is narrowly tailored only "if it targets and eliminates no more than the exact source of the 'evil' it seeks to remedy." *Frisby v. Schultz* (1988) [*supra* this chapter]. While there is language in a few opinions which, taken out of context, supports the majority's position, in practice, the Court has interpreted the narrow tailoring requirement to mandate an examination of alternative methods of serving the asserted governmental interest and a determination whether the greater efficacy of the challenged regulation outweighs the increased burden it places on protected speech. *See, e.g., Martin v. Struthers; Schneider v. State* (1939) [*supra* this chapter].

The Court's past concern for the extent to which a regulation burdens speech more than would a satisfactory alternative is noticeably absent from today's decision. The majority requires only that government show that its interest cannot be served as effectively without the challenged restriction. It will be enough, therefore, that the challenged regulation advances the government's interest only in the slightest, for any differential burden on speech that results does not enter the calculus. Despite its protestations to the contrary, the majority thus has abandoned the requirement that restrictions on speech be narrowly tailored in any ordinary use of the phrase. Indeed, after today's decision, a city could claim that bans on handbill distribution or on door-to-door solicitation are the most effective means of avoiding littering and fraud, or that a ban on loudspeakers and radios in a public park is the most effective means of avoiding loud noise. . . .

True, the majority states that "[g]overnment may not regulate expression in such a manner that a substantial portion of the burden on speech does not serve to advance its goals." But this means that only those regulations that "engage in the gratuitous inhibition of expression" will be invalidated. Moreover, the majority has robbed courts of the necessary analytic tools to make even this limited inquiry. The Court of Appeals examined "how much control of volume is appropriate [and] how that level of control is to be achieved," but the majority admonishes that court for doing so, stating that it should have "defer[red] to the city's reasonable determination." The majority thus instructs courts to refrain from examining how much speech may be restricted to serve an asserted interest and how that level of restriction is to be achieved. If a court cannot engage in such inquiries, I am at a loss to understand how a court can ascertain whether the government has adopted a regulation that burdens substantially more speech than is necessary.

Had the majority not abandoned the narrow tailoring requirement, the Guidelines could not possibly survive constitutional scrutiny. Government's interest in avoiding loud sounds cannot justify giving government total control over sound equipment, any more than its interest in avoiding litter could justify a ban on handbill distribution. In both cases, government's legitimate goals can be effectively and less intrusively served by directly punishing the evil—the persons responsible for excessive sounds and the persons who litter. Indeed, the city concedes that it has an ordinance generally limiting noise but has chosen not to enforce it.

By holding that the Guidelines are valid time, place, and manner restrictions, notwithstanding the availability of less intrusive but effective means of controlling volume, the majority deprives the narrow tailoring requirement of all meaning.[6] Today, the majority enshrines efficacy but sacrifices free speech.

City of Ladue v. Gilleo
512 U.S. 43 (1994)

Justice Stevens delivered the opinion of the Court.

An ordinance of the City of Ladue prohibits homeowners from displaying any signs on their property except "residence identification" signs, "for sale" signs, and signs warning of safety hazards. The ordinance permits commercial establishments, churches, and nonprofit organizations to erect certain signs that are not allowed at residences. The question presented is whether the ordinance violates a Ladue resident's right to free speech.

I

Respondent Margaret P. Gilleo owns one of the 57 single-family homes in the Willow Hill subdivision of Ladue. [Initially Gilleo placed on her front lawn a 24- by 36-inch sign printed with the words, "Say No to War in the Persian Gulf, Call Congress Now." Later she placed an 8.5- by 11-inch sign in the second story window of her home stating, "For Peace in the Gulf." After the federal district court enjoined enforcement of an earlier version of the ordinance, the Ladue City Council enacted a replacement.] Like its predecessor, the new ordinance contains a general prohibition of "signs" and defines that term broadly. The ordinance prohibits all signs except those that fall within 1 of 10 exemptions. Thus, "residential identification signs" no larger than one square foot are allowed, as are signs advertising "that the property is for sale, lease or exchange" and identifying the owner or agent. Also exempted are signs "for churches, religious institutions, and schools," "commercial signs in commercially zoned or industrial zoned districts," and on-site signs advertising "gasoline filling stations." . . .

Gilleo amended her complaint to challenge the new ordinance, which explicitly prohibits window signs like hers. [The Court of Appeals] held the ordinance invalid as a "content based" regulation because the City treated commercial speech more favorably than noncommercial speech and favored some kinds of noncommercial speech over others. Acknowledging that "Ladue's interests in enacting its ordinance are substantial," the Court of Appeals nevertheless concluded that those interests were "not sufficiently 'compelling' to support a content-based restriction." [We affirm.]

II

While signs are a form of expression protected by the Free Speech Clause, they pose distinctive problems that are subject to municipalities' police powers. Unlike oral speech, signs take up space and may obstruct views, distract motorists, displace alternative uses for land, and pose other problems that legitimately call for regulation. It is common ground that governments may regulate the physical characteristics of signs—just as they can, within reasonable bounds and absent censorial purpose, regulate audible expression in its capacity as noise. However, because regulation of a medium inevitably affects communication itself, it is not surprising that we have had occasion to review the constitutionality of municipal ordinances prohibiting the display of certain outdoor signs.

[The opinion here reviewed three of the Court's precedents. In *Linmark Associates, Inc. v. Willingboro*, 431 U.S. 85 (1977), the Court struck down an ordinance that sought to maintain stable, integrated neighborhoods by prohibiting homeowners from placing "For Sale" or "Sold" signs on their property. In *Metromedia Inc. v. San Diego* (1981), 453 U.S. 490 (1981), the Court struck down an ordinance imposing substantial prohibitions on outdoor advertising displays within the city of San Diego in the interest of traffic safety and esthetics. In *Members of City Council of Los Angeles v. Taxpayers for Vincent*, 466 U.S. 789 (1984), the Court upheld a Los Angeles ordinance that prohibited the posting of signs on public property.]

These decisions identify two analytically distinct grounds for challenging the constitutionality of a municipal ordinance regulating the display of signs. One is that the measure in effect restricts too little speech because its exemptions discriminate on the basis of the signs' messages. Alternatively, such provisions are subject to attack on the ground that they simply prohibit too much protected speech. The City of Ladue contends, first, that the Court of Appeals' reliance on the former rationale was misplaced because the City's regulatory purposes are content neutral, and, second, that those purposes justify the comprehensiveness of the sign prohibition. A comment on the former contention will help explain why we ultimately base our decision on a rejection of the latter.

III

While surprising at first glance, the notion that a regulation of speech may be impermissibly *underinclusive* is firmly grounded in basic First Amendment principles. Thus, an exemption from an otherwise permissible regulation of speech may represent a governmental "attempt to give one side of a debatable public question an advantage in expressing its views to the people." Alternatively, through the combined operation of a general speech restriction and its exemptions, the government might seek to select the "permissible subjects for public debate" and thereby to "control . . . the search for political truth."

The City argues that its sign ordinance implicates neither of these concerns, and that the Court of Appeals therefore erred in demanding a "compelling" justification for the exemptions. The mix of prohibitions and exemptions in the ordinance, Ladue maintains, reflects legitimate differences among the side effects of various kinds of signs. These differences are only adventitiously connected with content, and supply a sufficient justification, unrelated to the City's approval or disapproval of specific messages, for carving out the specified categories from the general ban. Thus, according to the [declaration of purposes] supporting the ordinance, the permitted signs, unlike the prohibited signs, are unlikely to contribute to the dangers of "unlimited proliferation" associated with categories of signs that are not inherently limited in number. . . . Even if we assume the validity of these arguments, the exemptions in Ladue's ordinance nevertheless shed light on the separate question whether the ordinance prohibits too much speech.

Exemptions from an otherwise legitimate regulation of a medium of speech may be noteworthy for a reason quite apart from the risks of viewpoint and content discrimination: They may diminish the credibility of the government's rationale for restricting speech in the first place. *See, e.g., Cincinnati v. Discovery Network, Inc.* (1993) [Chapter 3 Note]. In this case, at the very least, the exemptions from Ladue's ordinance demonstrate that Ladue has concluded that the interest in allowing certain messages to be conveyed by means of residential signs outweighs the City's esthetic interest in eliminating outdoor signs. Ladue has not imposed a flat ban on signs because it has determined that at least some of them are too vital to be banned.

Under the Court of Appeals' content discrimination rationale, the City might theoretically remove the defects in its ordinance by simply repealing all of the exemptions. If, however, the ordinance is also vulnerable because it prohibits too much speech, that solution would not save it. Moreover, if the prohibitions in Ladue's ordinance are impermissible, resting our decision on its exemptions would afford scant relief for respondent Gilleo. . . . Therefore, we first ask whether Ladue may properly *prohibit* Gilleo from displaying her sign, and then, only if necessary, consider the separate question whether it was improper for the City simultaneously to *permit* certain other signs. In examining the propriety of Ladue's near-total prohibition of residential signs, we will assume, *arguendo*, the validity of the City's submission that the various exemptions are free of impermissible content or viewpoint discrimination.

IV

In *Linmark* we held that the city's interest in maintaining a stable, racially integrated neighborhood was not sufficient to support a prohibition of residential "For Sale" signs. . . . Ladue's sign ordinance is supported principally by the City's interest in minimizing the visual clutter associated with signs, an interest that is concededly valid but certainly no more compelling than the interests at stake in *Linmark*. Moreover, whereas the ordinance in *Linmark* applied only to a form of commercial speech, Ladue's ordinance covers even such absolutely pivotal speech as a sign protesting an imminent governmental decision to go to war.

The impact on free communication of Ladue's broad sign prohibition, moreover, is manifestly greater than in *Linmark*. Gilleo and other residents of Ladue are forbidden to display virtually any "sign" on their property. The ordinance defines that term sweepingly. A prohibition is not always invalid merely because it applies to a sizeable category of speech; the sign ban we upheld in *Vincent*, for example, was quite broad. But in *Vincent* we specifically noted that the category of speech in question—signs placed on public property—was not a "uniquely valuable or important mode of communication," and that there was no evidence that "appellees' ability to communicate effectively is threatened by ever-increasing restrictions on expression."

Here, in contrast, Ladue has almost completely foreclosed a venerable means of communication that is both unique and important. It has totally foreclosed that medium to political, religious, or personal messages. Signs that react to a local happening or express a view on a controversial issue both reflect and animate change in the life of a community. Often placed on lawns or in windows, residential signs play an important part in political campaigns, during which they are displayed to signal the resident's support for particular candidates, parties, or causes. They may not afford the same opportunities for conveying complex ideas as do other media, but residential signs have long been an important and distinct medium of expression.

Our prior decisions have voiced particular concern with laws that foreclose an entire medium of expression. Thus, we have held invalid ordinances that completely banned the distribution of pamphlets within the municipality [and] the door-to-door distribution of literature. [The Court cited *Lovell*, *Martin*, and *Schneider*.] Although prohibitions foreclosing entire media may be completely free of content or viewpoint discrimination, the danger they pose to the freedom of speech is readily apparent—by eliminating a common means of speaking, such measures can suppress too much speech.

Ladue contends, however, that its ordinance is a mere regulation of the "time, place, or manner" of speech because residents remain free to convey their desired messages by other means, such as *hand-held* signs, "letters, handbills, flyers, telephone calls, newspaper advertisements, bumper stickers, speeches, and neighborhood or community meetings." However, even regulations that do not foreclose an entire medium of expression, but merely shift the time, place, or manner of its use, must "leave open ample alternative channels for communication." In this case, we are not persuaded that adequate substitutes exist for the important medium of speech that Ladue has closed off.

Displaying a sign from one's own residence often carries a message quite distinct from placing the same sign someplace else, or conveying the same text or picture by other means. Precisely because of their location, such signs provide information about the identity of the "speaker." . . . A sign advocating "Peace in the Gulf" in the front lawn of a retired general or decorated war veteran may provoke a different reaction than the same sign in a 10-year-old child's bedroom window or the same message on a bumper sticker of a passing automobile. An espousal of socialism may carry different implications when displayed on the grounds of a stately mansion than when pasted on a factory wall or an ambulatory sandwich board.

Residential signs are an unusually cheap and convenient form of communication. Especially for persons of modest means or limited mobility, a yard or window sign may have no practical substitute. Even for the affluent, the added costs in money or time of taking out a newspaper advertisement, handing out leaflets on the street, or standing in front of one's house with a hand-held sign may make the difference between participating and not participating in some public debate. Furthermore, a person who puts up a sign at her residence often intends to reach *neighbors*, an audience that could not be reached nearly as well by other means.

Our decision . . . by no means leaves the City powerless to address the ills that may be associated with residential signs. It bears mentioning that individual residents themselves have strong incentives to keep their own property values up and to prevent "visual clutter" in their own yards and neighborhoods — incentives markedly different from those of persons who erect signs on others' land, in others' neighborhoods, or on public property. Residents' self-interest diminishes the danger of the "unlimited" proliferation of residential signs that concerns the City of Ladue. We are confident that more temperate measures could in large part satisfy Ladue's stated regulatory needs without harm to the First Amendment rights of its citizens. As currently framed, however, the ordinance abridges those rights. [Affirmed.]

Justice O'Connor, concurring.

It is unusual for us, when faced with a regulation that on its face draws content distinctions, to "assume, *arguendo*, the validity of the City's submission that the various exemptions are free of impermissible content or viewpoint discrimination." . . . The normal inquiry that our doctrine dictates is, first, to determine whether a regulation is content based or content neutral, and then, based on the answer to that question, to apply the proper level of scrutiny.

Over the years, some cogent criticisms have been leveled at our approach. And it is quite true that regulations are occasionally struck down because of their content-based nature, even though common sense may suggest that they are entirely reasonable. The content distinctions present in this ordinance may, to some, be a good example of this.

But though our rule has flaws, it has substantial merit as well. It is a rule, in an area where fairly precise rules are better than more discretionary and more subjective balancing tests. On a theoretical level, it reflects important insights into the meaning of the free speech principle — for instance, that content-based speech restrictions are especially likely to be improper attempts to value some forms of speech over others, or are particularly susceptible to being used by the government to distort public debate. On a practical level, it has in application generally led to seemingly sensible results. And, perhaps most importantly, no better alternative has yet come to light.

I would have preferred to apply our normal analytical structure in this case, which may well have required us to examine this law with the scrutiny appropriate to content-based regulations. Perhaps this would have forced us to confront some of the difficulties with the existing doctrine; perhaps it would have shown weaknesses in the rule, and led us to modify it to take into account the special factors this case presents. But such reexamination is part of the process by which our rules evolve and improve.

Nonetheless, I join the Court's opinion, because I agree with its conclusion in Part IV that even if the restriction were content neutral, it would still be invalid, and because I do not think Part III casts any doubt on the propriety of our normal content discrimination inquiry.

———————

Note: Foreclosing Particular Modes of Expression

1. In *Gilleo*, the Court states: "Our prior decisions have voiced particular concern with laws that foreclose an entire medium of expression." The Court cites *Lovell*, *Martin*, and *Schneider*. But the Court also acknowledges that in *Taxpayers for Vincent* (1984) the Court upheld an ordinance that prohibited the posting of signs on public property. The challengers in *Taxpayers* sought to place political signs on utility poles. They argued that *Schneider* supported their constitutional claim, but the Court, in an opinion by Justice Stevens, found that the case was distinguishable:

> Taxpayers contend that their interest in supporting Vincent's political campaign, which affords them a constitutional right [under *Schneider*] to distribute brochures and leaflets on the public streets of Los Angeles, provides equal support for their asserted right to post temporary signs on objects adjacent to the streets and sidewalks. They argue that the mere fact that their temporary signs "add somewhat" to the city's visual clutter is entitled to no more weight than the temporary unsightliness of discarded handbills and the additional street-cleaning burden that were insufficient to justify the ordinances reviewed in *Schneider*.

> The rationale of *Schneider* is inapposite in the context of the instant case. . . . The right recognized in *Schneider* is to tender the written material to the passerby who may reject it or accept it, and who thereafter may keep it, dispose of it properly, or incur the risk of punishment if he lets it fall to the ground. . . . In *Schneider*, an antilittering statute could have addressed the substantive evil without prohibiting expressive activity, whereas application of the prophylactic rule actually employed gratuitously infringed upon the right of an individual to communicate directly with a willing listener. Here, the substantive evil—visual blight—is not merely a possible by-product

of the activity, but is created by the medium of expression itself. In contrast to *Schneider*, therefore, the application of the ordinance in this case responds precisely to the substantive problem which legitimately concerns the City. The ordinance curtails no more speech than is necessary to accomplish its purpose.

2. The Court in *Taxpayers* acknowledged that "a restriction on expressive activity may be invalid if the remaining modes of communication are inadequate." But, in the Court's view, the Los Angeles ordinance did not suffer from that defect:

> The Los Angeles ordinance does not affect any individual's freedom to exercise the right to speak and to distribute literature in the same place where the posting of signs on public property is prohibited. To the extent that the posting of signs on public property has advantages over these forms of expression, there is no reason to believe that these same advantages cannot be obtained through other means. To the contrary, the findings of the District Court indicate that there are ample alternative modes of communication in Los Angeles.

The city, in defending the constitutionality of its ordinance, emphasized two alternative modes in particular: posting signs on private property and distributing handbills. Justice Brennan, in his dissenting opinion, said the city had not shown that these were adequate substitutes for posting signs on public property. What sorts of evidence might be relevant to that determination? Or can courts rely on common sense and experience?

Review the *Gilleo* Court's explanation of why the Ladue ordinance did not "leave open ample alternative channels for communication." To what extent would these arguments apply to the ordinance challenged in *Taxpayers for Vincent*?

3. In *Schneider*, *Taxpayers*, and *Gilleo*, the ordinances were found to be (or were assumed to be) content-neutral. Are those holdings (or assumptions) still valid after the Court's decision in *Reed v. Town of Gilbert* (2015) (Chapter 5)?

4. The Court's decision in *Gilleo* strongly suggests that a flat ban on signs on residential property, in order to advance aesthetic interests, would be unconstitutional. On the other hand, in *Taxpayers for Vincent* the Court upheld a flat ban on signs on public property, also justified as advancing aesthetic interests. Is this because aesthetic interests are stronger on public property than in residential neighborhoods? Or is it because individuals have a stronger interest in posting signs on their own property? In either event, why would this be so?

––––––––

Note: Narrow Tailoring and "Underinclusiveness"

In *Frisby* and again in *Ward*, the disagreement within the Court centers on the second prong of the test for "time, place, and manner" regulations: whether the regulation is "narrowly tailored to serve a significant government interest." *City of Ladue v. Gilleo* discusses (but does not rely on) "the notion that a regulation of speech may be impermissibly *underinclusive*." (Emphasis in original.) "Narrow tailoring" and "underinclusiveness" may sound like similar concepts, but they are quite distinct and should not be confused.

Admittedly, the concept of "narrow tailoring" is not easily captured. The *Ward* Court offers several formulations before telling us (in a footnote) that "the essence of narrow tailoring" is that the regulation "focuses on the source of the evils the [government] seeks to eliminate . . . and eliminates them without at the same time banning or significantly restricting a substantial quantity of speech that does not create the same evils." In other words, "narrow tailoring" focuses on the speech that *is* regulated and asks whether some of that speech does not create the evils that the regulation is designed to control. "Underinclusiveness" focuses on speech that is *not* regulated and asks whether the *exemption* impugns an otherwise permissible regulation.

When does an "underinclusiveness" argument come into play? And what is the relation between underinclusiveness and the "time, place, and manner" doctrine? The Court in *Gilleo* sketches two possible roles for an underinclusiveness argument. First, "an exemption from an otherwise permissible regulation of speech" may suggest that a regulation represents an attempt to control the substance of public debate. Although the Court does not make the point as explicitly as one might like, the implication is that the regulation would not be treated as "content neutral" for purposes of the first prong of the *Ward* test.

The second line of argument is somewhat more elusive. The Court says: "Exemptions from an otherwise legitimate regulation of a medium of speech . . . may diminish the credibility of the government's rationale for restricting speech in the first place." In support of this proposition the Court cites *Discovery Network* (1993) (Chapter 3 Note). However, the Court acknowledges that, in *Taxpayers for Vincent*, the Court rejected an argument "that the validity of the city's esthetic interest had been compromised by failing to extend the ban [on outdoor advertising] to private property."

So the question remains: under what circumstances, if any, do exemptions provide a basis for attacking an otherwise permissible regulation of time, place, and manner? Consider the Problem that follows.

———

Problem: Regulating Newsracks

In *City of Lakewood v. Plain Dealer Publishing Co.* (1987) (Chapter 4 Note), the Supreme Court struck down a city ordinance that gave the mayor authority to grant or deny applications for annual newsrack permits. The Court held that the ordinance vested too much discretion in the mayor. The Court did not decide whether "a city may constitutionally prohibit the placement of newsracks on public property." That question thus remains open.

Justice White's dissent outlined "the significant governmental interests of cities — like Lakewood — that are threatened by newsrack placements." He said:

One of these interests . . . is keeping the streets and sidewalks free for the use of all members of the public, and not just the exclusive use of any one entity. But this is not the only concern at issue here. The Court has consistently recognized the important interest that localities have in insuring the safety of persons using city streets and public forums. In this case, testimony at trial detailed a variety of potential safety risks posed by newsboxes, running the gamut from the obvious to the unimaginable. Based on such testimony, the District Court found that newsracks along the streets increase the probability for accidents and injury.

A third concern is the protection of cities' recognized aesthetic interests. Lakewood and countless other American cities have invested substantial sums of money to renovate their urban centers and commercial districts. Increasingly, they find newsracks to be discordant with the surrounding area.

To support his discussion of safety concerns, Justice White added the following footnote:

A city official testifying at trial reported numerous incidents where objects located in the sidewalk areas where appellee wishes to erect its newsboxes — signposts, signal poles, and utility poles — were hit by cars, bicycles, or pedestrians. A vehicle may strike a newsrack on a city sidewalk, injuring its occupants or passersby. Cars may stop so that their drivers can purchase papers from newsracks, increasing the traffic hazards of city driving. Other testimony at trial and exhibits introduced there described newsracks restricting pedestrian traffic, blocking ramps for the handicapped, or being too near fire hydrants. Even a one-on-one encounter with a seemingly benign newsrack has its risks. Indeed, appellee's newspaper reported recently that a man had received a serious electrical shock when he approached a newsrack, apparently resulting from the fact that the bolts used to anchor the newsrack to the ground had penetrated an electrical power line.

(a) Until 1983, Lakewood absolutely prohibited the private placement of *any structure* on public property. Could the city re-enact that ordinance and apply it to newsracks as well as other structures?

(b) Could the city enact an ordinance that prohibited the placement of *newsracks* on public property?

(c) If your answer to both questions is "No," what other regulations would be permissible?

McCullen v. Coakley

134 S. Ct. 2518 (2014)

Chief Justice Roberts delivered the opinion of the Court.

A Massachusetts statute makes it a crime to knowingly stand on a "public way or sidewalk" within 35 feet of an entrance or driveway to any place, other than a hospital, where abortions are performed. Petitioners are individuals who approach and talk to women outside such facilities, attempting to dissuade them from having abortions. The statute prevents petitioners from doing so near the facilities' entrances. The question presented is whether the statute violates the First Amendment.

I

A

In 2000, the Massachusetts Legislature enacted the Massachusetts Reproductive Health Care Facilities Act. The law was designed to address clashes between abortion opponents and advocates of abortion rights that were occurring outside clinics where abortions were performed. The Act established a defined area with an 18-foot radius around the entrances and driveways of such facilities. Anyone could enter that area, but once within it, no one (other than certain exempt individuals) could knowingly approach within six feet of another person—unless that person consented— "for the purpose of passing a leaflet or handbill to, displaying a sign to, or engaging in oral protest, education, or counseling with such other person." A separate provision subjected to criminal punishment anyone who "knowingly obstructs, detains, hinders, impedes or blocks another person's entry to or exit from a reproductive health care facility."

The statute was modeled on a similar Colorado law that this Court had upheld in *Hill v. Colorado* (2000) [Note *infra* this chapter]. Relying on *Hill*, the United States Court of Appeals for the First Circuit sustained the Massachusetts statute against a First Amendment challenge.

By 2007, some Massachusetts legislators and law enforcement officials had come to regard the 2000 statute as inadequate. At legislative hearings, multiple witnesses recounted apparent violations of the law. Massachusetts Attorney General Martha Coakley, for example, testified that protestors violated the statute "on a routine basis." To illustrate this claim, she played a video depicting protestors approaching patients and clinic staff within the buffer zones, ostensibly without the latter individuals' consent. Clinic employees and volunteers also testified that protestors congregated near the doors and in the driveways of the clinics, with the result that prospective patients occasionally retreated from the clinics rather than try to make their way to the clinic entrances or parking lots.

Captain William B. Evans of the Boston Police Department . . . testified that the 18-foot zones were so crowded with protestors that they resembled "a goalie's crease," making it hard to determine whether a protestor had deliberately approached a patient or, if so, whether the patient had consented. . . .

To address these concerns, the Massachusetts Legislature amended the statute in 2007, replacing the six-foot no-approach zones (within the 18-foot area) with a 35-foot fixed buffer zone from which individuals are categorically excluded. The statute now provides:

No person shall knowingly enter or remain on a public way or sidewalk adjacent to a reproductive health care facility within a radius of 35 feet of any portion of an entrance, exit or driveway of a reproductive health care facility or within the area within a rectangle created by extending the outside boundaries of any entrance, exit or driveway of a reproductive health care facility in straight lines to the point where such lines intersect the sideline of the street in front of such entrance, exit or driveway.

A "reproductive health care facility," in turn, is defined as "a place, other than within or upon the grounds of a hospital, where abortions are offered or performed."

The 35-foot buffer zone applies only "during a facility's business hours," and the area must be "clearly marked and posted." In practice, facilities typically mark the zones with painted arcs and posted signs on adjacent sidewalks and streets. A first violation of the statute is punishable by a fine of up to $500, up to three months in prison, or both, while a subsequent offense is punishable by a fine of between $500 and $5,000, up to two and a half years in prison, or both.

The Act exempts four classes of individuals: (1) "persons entering or leaving such facility"; (2) "employees or agents of such facility acting within the scope of their employment"; (3) "law enforcement, ambulance, firefighting, construction, utilities, public works and other municipal agents acting within the scope of their employment"; and (4) "persons using the public sidewalk or street right-of-way adjacent to such facility solely for the purpose of reaching a destination other than such facility." The legislature also retained the separate provision from the 2000 version that proscribes the knowing obstruction of access to a facility.

B

Some of the individuals who stand outside Massachusetts abortion clinics are fairly described as protestors, who express their moral or religious opposition to abortion through signs and chants or, in some cases, more aggressive methods such as face-to-face confrontation. Petitioners take a different tack. They attempt to engage women approaching the clinics in what they call "sidewalk counseling," which involves offering information about alternatives to abortion and help pursuing those options. Petitioner Eleanor McCullen, for instance, will typically initiate a conversation this way: "Good morning, may I give you my literature? Is there anything I can do for you? I'm available if you have any questions." If the woman seems receptive, McCullen will provide additional information. McCullen and the other petitioners consider it essential to maintain a caring demeanor, a calm tone of voice, and direct eye contact during these exchanges. Such interactions, petitioners believe, are a much more effective means of dissuading women from having abortions than confrontational methods such as shouting or brandishing signs, which in petitioners' view tend only to antagonize their intended audience. In unrefuted testimony, petitioners say they have collectively persuaded hundreds of women to forgo abortions.

The buffer zones have displaced petitioners from their previous positions outside the clinics. [For example, McCullen and other petitioners are effectively excluded from a 56-foot-wide expanse of the public sidewalk in front of the Boston clinic.] Petitioners at all three clinics claim that the buffer zones have considerably hampered their counseling efforts. . . .

The second statutory exemption allows clinic employees and agents acting within the scope of their employment to enter the buffer zones. Relying on this exemption, the Boston clinic uses "escorts" to greet women as they approach the clinic, accompanying them through the zones to the clinic entrance. Petitioners claim that the escorts sometimes thwart petitioners' attempts to communicate with patients by blocking petitioners from handing literature to patients, telling patients not to "pay any attention" or "listen to" petitioners, and disparaging petitioners as "crazy."

C

In January 2008, petitioners sued Attorney General Coakley and other Commonwealth officials. They sought to enjoin enforcement of the Act, alleging that it violates the First and Fourteenth Amendments, both on its face and as applied to them. [After two bench trials, the district court rejected all of petitioners' constitutional challenges, and the Court of Appeals for the First Circuit affirmed. The Supreme Court granted certiorari.]

II

By its very terms, the Massachusetts Act regulates access to "public way[s]" and "sidewalk[s]." Such areas occupy a "special position in terms of First Amendment protection" because of their historic role as sites for discussion and debate. [We have labeled these places] "traditional public fora." . . .

It is no accident that public streets and sidewalks have developed as venues for the exchange of ideas. Even today, they remain one of the few places where a speaker can be confident that he is not simply preaching to the choir. With respect to other means of communication, an individual confronted with an uncomfortable message can always turn the page, change the channel, or leave the Web site. Not so on public streets and sidewalks. There, a listener often encounters speech he might otherwise tune out. In light of the First Amendment's purpose "to preserve an uninhibited marketplace of ideas in which truth will ultimately prevail," this aspect of traditional public fora is a virtue, not a vice.

In short, traditional public fora are areas that have historically been open to the public for speech activities. Thus, even though the Act says nothing about speech on its face, there is no doubt — and respondents do not dispute — that it restricts access to traditional public fora and is therefore subject to First Amendment scrutiny.

Consistent with the traditionally open character of public streets and sidewalks, we have held that the government's ability to restrict speech in such locations is "very limited." In particular, the guiding First Amendment principle that the "government has no power to restrict expression because of its message, its ideas, its subject matter, or its content" applies with full force in a traditional public forum. *Police Dept. of Chicago v. Mosley* (1972) [Chapter 5]. . . .

We have, however, afforded the government somewhat wider leeway to regulate features of speech unrelated to its content. "[E]ven in a public forum the government may impose reasonable restrictions on the time, place, or manner of protected speech, provided the restrictions 'are justified without reference to the content of the regulated speech, that they are narrowly tailored to serve a significant governmental interest, and that they leave open ample alternative channels for communication of the information.'" *Ward v. Rock Against Racism* (1989) [*supra* this chapter].

While the parties agree that this test supplies the proper framework for assessing the constitutionality of the Massachusetts Act, they disagree about whether the Act satisfies the test's three requirements.

III

Petitioners contend that the Act is not content neutral for two independent reasons: First, they argue that it discriminates against abortion-related speech because it establishes buffer zones only at clinics that perform abortions. Second, petitioners contend that the Act, by exempting clinic employees and agents, favors one viewpoint about abortion over the other. If either of these arguments is correct, then the Act must satisfy strict scrutiny—that is, it must be the least restrictive means of achieving a compelling state interest. *See United States v. Playboy Entertainment Group, Inc.*, 529 U.S. 803, 813 (2000). Respondents do not argue that the Act can survive this exacting standard. . . .

A

The Act applies only at a "reproductive health care facility," defined as "a place, other than within or upon the grounds of a hospital, where abortions are offered or performed." Given this definition, petitioners argue, "virtually all speech affected by the Act is speech concerning abortion," thus rendering the Act content based.

We disagree. To begin, the Act does not draw content-based distinctions on its face. Contrast *Boos v. Barry* (1988) [Chapter 7] (ordinance prohibiting the display within 500 feet of a foreign embassy of any sign that tends to bring the foreign government into "public odium" or "public disrepute"). The Act would be content based if it required "enforcement authorities" to "examine the content of the message that is conveyed to determine whether" a violation has occurred. But it does not. Whether petitioners violate the Act "depends" not "on what they say," *Holder v. Humanitarian Law Project*, 561 U.S. 1 (2010), but simply on where they say it. Indeed, petitioners can violate the Act merely by standing in a buffer zone, without displaying a sign or uttering a word.

It is true, of course, that by limiting the buffer zones to abortion clinics, the Act has the "inevitable effect" of restricting abortion-related speech more than speech on other subjects. *United States v. O'Brien* (1968) [Chapter 7]. But a facially neutral law does not become content based simply because it may disproportionately affect speech on certain topics. On the contrary, "[a] regulation that serves purposes unrelated to the content of expression is deemed neutral, even if it has an incidental effect on some speakers or messages but not others." *Ward*. The question in such a case is whether the law is "justified without reference to the content of the regulated speech." *Renton v. Playtime Theatres, Inc.* (1986) [Chapter 7].

The Massachusetts Act is. Its stated purpose is to "increase forthwith public safety at reproductive health care facilities." Respondents have articulated similar purposes before this Court — namely, "public safety, patient access to healthcare, and the unobstructed use of public sidewalks and roadways." It is not the case that "[e]very objective indication shows that the provision's primary purpose is to restrict speech that opposes abortion."

We have previously deemed the foregoing concerns to be content neutral. Obstructed access and congested sidewalks are problems no matter what caused them. A group of individuals can obstruct clinic access and clog sidewalks just as much when they loiter as when they protest abortion or counsel patients.

To be clear, the Act would not be content neutral if it were concerned with undesirable effects that arise from "the direct impact of speech on its audience" or "[l]isteners' reactions to speech." *Boos*. If, for example, the speech outside Massachusetts abortion clinics caused offense or made listeners uncomfortable, such offense or discomfort would not give the Commonwealth a content-neutral justification to restrict the speech. All of the problems identified by the Commonwealth here, however, arise irrespective of any listener's reactions. Whether or not a single person reacts to abortion protestors' chants or petitioners' counseling, large crowds outside abortion clinics can still compromise public safety, impede access, and obstruct sidewalks.

Petitioners do not really dispute that the Commonwealth's interests in ensuring safety and preventing obstruction are, as a general matter, content neutral. But petitioners note that these interests "apply outside every building in the State that hosts any activity that might occasion protest or comment," not just abortion clinics. By choosing to pursue these interests only at abortion clinics, petitioners argue, the Massachusetts Legislature evinced a purpose to "single[ ] out for regulation speech about one particular topic: abortion."

We cannot infer such a purpose from the Act's limited scope. The broad reach of a statute can help confirm that it was not enacted to burden a narrower category of disfavored speech. *See* Kagan, *Private Speech, Public Purpose: The Role of Governmental Motive in First Amendment Doctrine*, 63 U. CHI. L. REV. 413, 451–52 (1996). At the same time, however, "States adopt laws to address the problems that confront them. The First Amendment does not require States to regulate for problems that do not exist." *Burson v. Freeman* (1992) [Chapter 5 Note]. The Massachusetts Legislature amended the Act in 2007 in response to a problem that was, in its experience, limited to abortion clinics. There was a record of crowding, obstruction, and even violence outside such clinics. . . . In light of the limited nature of the problem, it was reasonable for the Massachusetts Legislature to enact a limited solution. When selecting among various options for combating a particular problem, legislatures should be encouraged to choose the one that restricts less speech, not more. . . .

B

Petitioners also argue that the Act is content based because it exempts four classes of individuals, one of which comprises "employees or agents of [a reproductive healthcare] facility acting within the scope of their employment." This exemption, petitioners say, favors one side in the abortion debate and thus constitutes viewpoint discrimination—an "egregious form of content discrimination," *Rosenberger v. Rector and Visitors of Univ. of Va.* (1995) [Chapter 19]. In particular, petitioners argue that the exemption allows clinic employees and agents—including the volunteers who "escort" patients arriving at the Boston clinic—to speak inside the buffer zones.

It is of course true that "an exemption from an otherwise permissible regulation of speech may represent a governmental 'attempt to give one side of a debatable public question an advantage in expressing its views to the people.'" *City of Ladue v. Gilleo* (1994) [*supra* this chapter]. At least on the record before us, however, the statutory exemption for clinic employees and agents acting within the scope of their employment does not appear to be such an attempt.

There is nothing inherently suspect about providing some kind of exemption to allow individuals who work at the clinics to enter or remain within the buffer zones. In particular, the exemption cannot be regarded as simply a carve-out for the clinic escorts; it also covers employees such as the maintenance worker shoveling a snowy sidewalk or the security guard patrolling a clinic entrance.

Given the need for an exemption for clinic employees, the "scope of their employment" qualification simply ensures that the exemption is limited to its purpose of allowing the employees to do their jobs. . . . There is no suggestion in the record that any of the clinics authorize their employees to speak about abortion in the buffer zones. The "scope of their employment" limitation thus seems designed to protect against exactly the sort of conduct that petitioners and Justice Scalia fear. . . .

It would be a very different question if it turned out that a clinic authorized escorts to speak about abortion inside the buffer zones. See [concurring opinion of Justice Alito]. In that case, the escorts would not seem to be violating the Act because the speech would be within the scope of their employment. The Act's exemption for clinic employees would then facilitate speech on only one side of the abortion debate—a clear form of viewpoint discrimination that would support an as-applied challenge to the buffer zone at that clinic. But the record before us contains insufficient evidence to show that the exemption operates in this way at any of the clinics, perhaps because the clinics do not want to doom the Act by allowing their employees to speak about abortion within the buffer zones.

We thus conclude that the Act is neither content nor viewpoint based and therefore need not be analyzed under strict scrutiny.

IV

Even though the Act is content neutral, it still must be "narrowly tailored to serve a significant governmental interest." *Ward*. The tailoring requirement does not simply guard against an impermissible desire to censor. The government may attempt to suppress speech not only because it disagrees with the message being expressed, but also for mere convenience. Where certain speech is associated with particular problems, silencing the speech is sometimes the path of least resistance. But by demanding a close fit between ends and means, the tailoring requirement prevents the government from too readily "sacrific[ing] speech for efficiency."

For a content-neutral time, place, or manner regulation to be narrowly tailored, it must not "burden substantially more speech than is necessary to further the government's legitimate interests." *Ward*. Such a regulation, unlike a content-based restriction of speech, "need not be the least restrictive or least intrusive means of " serving the government's interests. *Id.* But the government still "may not regulate expression in such a manner that a substantial portion of the burden on speech does not serve to advance its goals." *Id.*

A

As noted, respondents claim that the Act promotes "public safety, patient access to healthcare, and the unobstructed use of public sidewalks and roadways." Petitioners do not dispute the significance of these interests. . . . The buffer zones clearly serve these interests.

At the same time, the buffer zones impose serious burdens on petitioners' speech. At each of the three Planned Parenthood clinics where petitioners attempt to counsel patients, the zones carve out a significant portion of the adjacent public sidewalks, pushing petitioners well back from the clinics' entrances and driveways. The zones thereby compromise petitioners' ability to initiate the close, personal conversations that they view as essential to "sidewalk counseling."

For example, in uncontradicted testimony, McCullen explained that she often cannot distinguish patients from passersby outside the Boston clinic in time to initiate a conversation before they enter the buffer zone. And even when she does manage to begin a discussion outside the zone, she must stop abruptly at its painted border, which she believes causes her to appear "untrustworthy" or "suspicious." Given these limitations, McCullen is often reduced to raising her voice at patients from outside the zone—a mode of communication sharply at odds with the compassionate message she wishes to convey. Clark gave similar testimony about her experience at the Worcester clinic.

These burdens on petitioners' speech have clearly taken their toll. [For example, Zarrella estimated having about 100 successful interactions over the years before the 2007 amendment, but not a single one since.]

The buffer zones have also made it substantially more difficult for petitioners to distribute literature to arriving patients. [Because] petitioners in Boston cannot readily identify patients before they enter the zone, they often cannot approach them in time to place literature near their hands — the most effective means of getting the patients to accept it. In Worcester and Springfield, the zones have pushed petitioners so far back from the clinics' driveways that they can no longer even attempt to offer literature as drivers turn into the parking lots. In short, the Act operates to deprive petitioners of their two primary methods of communicating with patients.

The Court of Appeals and respondents are wrong to downplay these burdens on petitioners' speech. As the Court of Appeals saw it, the Constitution does not accord "special protection" to close conversations or "handbilling." But while the First Amendment does not guarantee a speaker the right to any particular form of expression, some forms — such as normal conversation and leafletting on a public sidewalk — have historically been more closely associated with the transmission of ideas than others.

In the context of petition campaigns, we have observed that "one-on-one communication" is "the most effective, fundamental, and perhaps economical avenue of political discourse." And "handing out leaflets in the advocacy of a politically controversial viewpoint . . . is the essence of First Amendment expression"; "[n]o form of speech is entitled to greater constitutional protection." *McIntyre v. Ohio Elections Comm'n*, 514 U.S. 334 (1995). When the government makes it more difficult to engage in these modes of communication, it imposes an especially significant First Amendment burden.

Respondents also emphasize that the Act does not prevent petitioners from engaging in various forms of "protest" — such as chanting slogans and displaying signs — outside the buffer zones. That misses the point. Petitioners are not protestors. They seek not merely to express their opposition to abortion, but to inform women of various alternatives and to provide help in pursuing them. Petitioners believe that they can accomplish this objective only through personal, caring, consensual conversations. And for good reason: It is easier to ignore a strained voice or a waving hand than a direct greeting or an outstretched arm. While the record indicates that petitioners have been able to have a number of quiet conversations outside the buffer zones, respondents have not refuted petitioners' testimony that the conversations have been far less frequent and far less successful since the buffer zones were instituted. It is thus no answer to say that petitioners can still be "seen and heard" by women within the buffer zones. If all that the women can see and hear are vociferous opponents of abortion, then the buffer zones have effectively stifled petitioners' message. . . .

B

1

The buffer zones burden substantially more speech than necessary to achieve the Commonwealth's asserted interests. At the outset, we note that the Act is truly exceptional: Respondents and their amici identify no other State with a law that creates fixed buffer zones around abortion clinics. That of course does not mean that the law is invalid. It does, however, raise concern that the Commonwealth has too readily forgone options that could serve its interests just as well, without substantially burdening the kind of speech in which petitioners wish to engage.

That is the case here. The Commonwealth's interests include ensuring public safety outside abortion clinics, preventing harassment and intimidation of patients and clinic staff, and combating deliberate obstruction of clinic entrances. The Act itself contains a separate provision, subsection (e)—unchallenged by petitioners—that prohibits much of this conduct. That provision subjects to criminal punishment "[a]ny person who knowingly obstructs, detains, hinders, impedes or blocks another person's entry to or exit from a reproductive health care facility." If Massachusetts determines that broader prohibitions along the same lines are necessary, it could enact legislation similar to the federal Freedom of Access to Clinic Entrances Act of 1994 (FACE Act), which subjects to both criminal and civil penalties anyone who "by force or threat of force or by physical obstruction, intentionally injures, intimidates or interferes with or attempts to injure, intimidate or interfere with any person because that person is or has been, or in order to intimidate such person or any other person or any class of persons from, obtaining or providing reproductive health services." Some dozen other States have done so. If the Commonwealth is particularly concerned about harassment, it could also consider an ordinance such as the one adopted in New York City that not only prohibits obstructing access to a clinic, but also makes it a crime "to follow and harass another person within 15 feet of the premises of a reproductive health care facility."

The Commonwealth points to a substantial public safety risk created when protestors obstruct driveways leading to the clinics. That is, however, an example of its failure to look to less intrusive means of addressing its concerns. Any such obstruction can readily be addressed through existing local ordinances. *See, e.g.*, Worcester, Mass., Revised Ordinances of 2008 ("No person shall stand, or place any obstruction of any kind, upon any street, sidewalk or crosswalk in such a manner as to obstruct a free passage for travelers thereon").

All of the foregoing measures are, of course, in addition to available generic criminal statutes forbidding assault, breach of the peace, trespass, vandalism, and the like.

In addition, subsection (e) of the Act, the FACE Act, and the New York City anti-harassment ordinance are all enforceable not only through criminal prosecutions but also through public and private civil actions for injunctions and other equitable relief. . . . [Injunctive relief] focuses on the precise individuals and the precise conduct causing a particular problem. The Act, by contrast, categorically excludes non exempt individuals from the buffer zones, unnecessarily sweeping in innocent individuals and their speech.

The Commonwealth also asserts an interest in preventing congestion in front of abortion clinics. According to respondents, even when individuals do not deliberately obstruct access to clinics, they can inadvertently do so simply by gathering in large numbers. But the Commonwealth could address that problem through more targeted means. Some localities, for example, have ordinances that require crowds blocking a clinic entrance to disperse when ordered to do so by the police, and that forbid the individuals to reassemble within a certain distance of the clinic for a certain period. We upheld a similar law forbidding three or more people "to congregate within 500 feet of [a foreign embassy], and refuse to disperse after having been ordered so to do by the police," *Boos*—an order the police could give only when they "reasonably believe[d] that a threat to the security or peace of the embassy [was] present."

And to the extent the Commonwealth argues that even these types of laws are ineffective, it has another problem. The portions of the record that respondents cite to support the anticongestion interest pertain mainly to one place at one time: the Boston Planned Parenthood clinic on Saturday mornings. Respondents point us to no evidence that individuals regularly gather at other clinics, or at other times in Boston, in sufficiently large groups to obstruct access. For a problem shown to arise only once a week in one city at one clinic, creating 35-foot buffer zones at every clinic across the Commonwealth is hardly a narrowly tailored solution.

The point is not that Massachusetts must enact all or even any of the proposed measures discussed above. The point is instead that the Commonwealth has available to it a variety of approaches that appear capable of serving its interests, without excluding individuals from areas historically open for speech and debate.

2

Respondents have but one reply: "We have tried other approaches, but they do not work." . . . We cannot accept that contention. Although respondents claim that Massachusetts "tried other laws already on the books," they identify not a single prosecution brought under those laws within at least the last 17 years. . . . In short, the Commonwealth has not shown that it seriously undertook to address the problem with less intrusive tools readily available to it. Nor has it shown that it considered different methods that other jurisdictions have found effective.

Respondents contend that the alternatives we have discussed suffer from two defects: First, given the "widespread" nature of the problem, it is simply not "practicable" to rely on individual prosecutions and injunctions. But far from being "widespread," the problem appears from the record to be limited principally to the Boston clinic on Saturday mornings. Moreover, by their own account, the police appear perfectly capable of singling out lawbreakers. . . . If Commonwealth officials can compile an extensive record of obstruction and harassment to support their preferred legislation, we do not see why they cannot do the same to support injunctions and prosecutions against those who might deliberately flout the law.

The second supposed defect in the alternatives we have identified is that laws like subsection (e) of the Act and the federal FACE Act require a showing of intentional or deliberate obstruction, intimidation, or harassment, which is often difficult to prove. As Captain Evans predicted in his legislative testimony, fixed buffer zones would "make our job so much easier."

Of course they would. But that is not enough to satisfy the First Amendment. To meet the requirement of narrow tailoring, the government must demonstrate that alternative measures that burden substantially less speech would fail to achieve the government's interests, not simply that the chosen route is easier. A painted line on the sidewalk is easy to enforce, but the prime objective of the First Amendment is not efficiency. In any case, we do not think that showing intentional obstruction is nearly so difficult in this context as respondents suggest. To determine whether a protestor intends to block access to a clinic, a police officer need only order him to move. If he refuses, then there is no question that his continued conduct is knowing or intentional....

Given the vital First Amendment interests at stake, it is not enough for Massachusetts simply to say that other approaches have not worked.[9]

* * *

Petitioners wish to converse with their fellow citizens about an important subject on the public streets and sidewalks—sites that have hosted discussions about the issues of the day throughout history. Respondents assert undeniably significant interests in maintaining public safety on those same streets and sidewalks, as well as in preserving access to adjacent healthcare facilities. But here the Commonwealth has pursued those interests by the extreme step of closing a substantial portion of a traditional public forum to all speakers. It has done so without seriously addressing the problem through alternatives that leave the forum open for its time-honored purposes. The Commonwealth may not do that consistent with the First Amendment.

The judgment of the Court of Appeals for the First Circuit is reversed, and the case is remanded for further proceedings consistent with this opinion.

It is so ordered.

JUSTICE SCALIA, with whom JUSTICE KENNEDY and JUSTICE THOMAS join, concurring in the judgment.

Today's opinion carries forward this Court's practice of giving abortion-rights advocates a pass when it comes to suppressing the free-speech rights of their opponents. There is an entirely separate, abridged edition of the First Amendment applicable to speech against abortion. *See, e.g., Hill v. Colorado* (2000) [Note *infra* this chapter]; *Madsen v. Women's Health Center, Inc.*, 512 U.S. 753 (1994).

The second half of the Court's analysis today, invalidating the law at issue because of inadequate "tailoring," is certainly attractive to those of us who oppose an abortion speech edition of the First Amendment. But think again. This is an opinion that has Something for Everyone, and the more significant portion continues the onward march of abortion-speech-only jurisprudence. That is the first half of the Court's analysis, which concludes that a statute of this sort is not content based and hence not subject to so-called strict scrutiny. The Court reaches out to decide that question unnecessarily—or at least unnecessarily insofar as legal analysis is concerned.

---

9. Because we find that the Act is not narrowly tailored, we need not consider whether the Act leaves open ample alternative channels of communication. Nor need we consider petitioners' overbreadth challenge.

I disagree with the Court's dicta (Part III) and hence see no reason to opine on its holding (Part IV).

I. The Court's Content-Neutrality Discussion Is Unnecessary

The gratuitous portion of today's opinion is Part III, which concludes—in seven pages of the purest dicta—that subsection (b) of the Massachusetts Reproductive Health Care Facilities Act is not specifically directed at speech opposing (or even concerning) abortion and hence need not meet the strict-scrutiny standard applicable to content-based speech regulations. Inasmuch as Part IV holds that the Act is unconstitutional because it does not survive the lesser level of scrutiny associated with content-neutral "time, place, and manner" regulations, there is no principled reason for the majority to decide whether the statute is subject to strict scrutiny. . . .

II. The Statute Is Content Based and Fails Strict Scrutiny

Having eagerly volunteered to take on the level-of-scrutiny question, the Court provides the wrong answer. Petitioners argue for two reasons that subsection (b) articulates a content-based speech restriction—and that we must therefore evaluate it through the lens of strict scrutiny.

A. Application to Abortion Clinics Only

First, petitioners maintain that the Act targets abortion-related—for practical purposes, abortion-opposing—speech because it applies outside abortion clinics only (rather than outside other buildings as well).

Public streets and sidewalks are traditional forums for speech on matters of public concern. . . . Moreover, "the public spaces outside of [abortion-providing] facilities . . . ha[ve] become, by necessity and by virtue of this Court's decisions, a forum of last resort for those who oppose abortion." *Hill* (Scalia, J., dissenting). It blinks reality to say, as the majority does, that a blanket prohibition on the use of streets and sidewalks where speech on only one politically controversial topic is likely to occur—and where that speech can most effectively be communicated— is not content based. Would the Court exempt from strict scrutiny a law banning access to the streets and sidewalks surrounding the site of the Republican National Convention? Or those used annually to commemorate the 1965 Selma-to-Montgomery civil rights marches? Or those outside the Internal Revenue Service? Surely not.

The majority says, correctly enough, that a facially neutral speech restriction escapes strict scrutiny, even when it "may disproportionately affect speech on certain topics," so long as it is "justified without reference to the content of the regulated speech." [But in concluding that the Massachusetts statute is "justified without reference to the content of the regulated speech," the] majority points only to the statute's stated purpose of increasing "public safety" at abortion clinics and to the additional aims articulated by respondents before this Court—namely, protecting "patient access to healthcare . . . and the unobstructed use of public side walks and roadways." Really? Does a statute become "justified without reference to the content of the regulated speech" simply because the statute itself and those defending it in court say that it is?

Every objective indication shows that the provision's primary purpose is to restrict speech that opposes abortion.

I begin, as suggested above, with the fact that the Act burdens only the public spaces outside abortion clinics. One might have expected the majority to defend the statute's peculiar targeting by arguing that those locations regularly face the safety and access problems that it says the Act was designed to solve. But the majority does not make that argument because it would be untrue. As the Court belatedly discovers in Part IV of its opinion, although the statute applies to all abortion clinics in Massachusetts, only one is known to have been beset by the problems that the statute supposedly addresses. The Court uses this striking fact (a smoking gun, so to speak) as a basis for concluding that the law is insufficiently "tailored" to safety and access concerns (Part IV) rather than as a basis for concluding that it is not *directed* to those concerns at all, but to the suppression of antiabortion speech. That is rather like invoking the eight missed human targets of a shooter who has killed one victim to prove, not that he is guilty of attempted mass murder, but that *he has bad aim*.

Whether the statute "restrict[s] more speech than necessary" in light of the problems that it allegedly addresses is, to be sure, relevant to the tailoring component of the First Amendment analysis (the shooter doubtless did have bad aim), but it is also relevant—powerfully relevant—to whether the law is really directed to safety and access concerns or rather to the suppression of a particular type of speech. Showing that a law that suppresses speech on a specific subject is so far-reaching that it applies even when the asserted non-speech-related problems are not present is persuasive evidence that the law is content based. In its zeal to treat abortion-related speech as a special category, the majority distorts not only the First Amendment but also the ordinary logic of probative inferences.

The structure of the Act also indicates that it rests on content-based concerns. The goals of "public safety, patient access to healthcare, and the unobstructed use of public sidewalks and roadways" are already achieved by an earlier-enacted subsection of the statute, which provides criminal penalties for "[a]ny person who knowingly obstructs, detains, hinders, impedes or blocks another person's entry to or exit from a reproductive health care facility." As the majority recognizes, that provision is easy to enforce. Thus, the speech-free zones carved out by subsection (b) add nothing to safety and access; what they achieve, and what they were obviously designed to achieve, is the suppression of speech opposing abortion.

Further contradicting the Court's fanciful defense of the Act is the fact that subsection (b) was enacted as a more easily enforceable substitute for a prior provision. That provision did not exclude people entirely from the restricted areas around abortion clinics; rather, it forbade people in those areas to approach within six feet of another person *without that person's consent* "for the purpose of passing a leaflet or handbill to, displaying a sign to, or engaging in oral protest, education or counseling with such other person." As the majority acknowledges, that provision was "modeled on a . . . Colorado law that this Court had upheld in *Hill*." And in that case, the Court recognized that the statute in question was directed at the suppression of unwelcome speech, vindicating what *Hill* called "[t]he unwilling listener's interest in avoiding unwanted communication." The Court held that interest to be content neutral.

The provision at issue here was indisputably meant to serve the same interest in protecting citizens' supposed right to avoid speech that they would rather not hear. For that reason, we granted a second question for review in this case (though one would not know that from the Court's opinion, which fails to mention it): whether *Hill* should be cut back or cast aside. The majority avoids that question by declaring the Act content neutral on other (entirely unpersuasive) grounds. In concluding that the statute is content based and therefore subject to strict scrutiny, I necessarily conclude that *Hill* should be overruled. Reasons for doing so are set forth in the dissents in that case, and in the abundance of scathing academic commentary describing how *Hill* stands in contradiction to our First Amendment jurisprudence.[4] Protecting people from speech they do not want to hear is not a function that the First Amendment allows the government to undertake in the public streets and sidewalks.

One final thought regarding *Hill*: It can be argued, and it should be argued in the next case, that by stating that "the Act would not be content neutral if it were concerned with undesirable effects that arise from . . . '[l]isteners' reactions to speech,'" and then holding the Act unconstitutional for being insufficiently tailored to safety and access concerns, the Court itself has sub silentio (and perhaps inadvertently) overruled *Hill*. The unavoidable implication of that holding is that protection against unwelcome speech cannot justify restrictions on the use of public streets and sidewalks.

B. Exemption for Abortion-Clinic Employees or Agents

Petitioners contend that the Act targets speech opposing abortion (and thus constitutes a presumptively invalid viewpoint-discriminatory restriction) for another reason as well: It exempts "employees or agents" of an abortion clinic "acting within the scope of their employment." [For discussion of this point, see Justice Alito's opinion concurring in the judgment, *infra*.]

C. Conclusion

In sum, the Act should be reviewed under the strict-scrutiny standard applicable to content-based legislation. . . . Respondents do not even attempt to argue that subsection (b) survives this test. "Suffice it to say that if protecting people from unwelcome communications"—the actual purpose of the provision—"is a compelling state interest, the First Amendment is a dead letter." *Hill* (Scalia, J., dissenting).

III. Narrow Tailoring

Having determined that the Act is content based and does not withstand strict scrutiny, I need not pursue the inquiry conducted in Part IV of the Court's opinion . . . .

---

4. "*Hill* . . . is inexplicable on standard free-speech grounds[,] and . . . it is shameful the Supreme Court would have upheld this piece of legislation on the reasoning that it gave." Constitutional Law Symposium, *Professor Michael W. McConnell's Response*, 28 Pepperdine L. Rev. 747 (2001). "I don't think [*Hill*] was a difficult case. I think it was slam-dunk simple and slam-dunk wrong." *Id.* at 750 (remarks of Laurence Tribe). The list could go on.

[If] I did, I suspect I would agree with the majority that the legislation is not narrowly tailored to advance the interests asserted by respondents. But I prefer not to take part in the assembling of an apparent but specious unanimity. . . .

* * *

The obvious purpose of the challenged portion of the Massachusetts Reproductive Health Care Facilities Act is to "protect" prospective clients of abortion clinics from having to hear abortion-opposing speech on public streets and sidewalks. The provision is thus unconstitutional root and branch and cannot be saved, as the majority suggests, by limiting its application to the single facility that has experienced the safety and access problems to which it is quite obviously not addressed. I concur only in the judgment that the statute is unconstitutional under the First Amendment.

JUSTICE ALITO, concurring in the judgment.

I agree that the Massachusetts statute at issue in this case violates the First Amendment. As the Court recognizes, if the Massachusetts law discriminates on the basis of viewpoint, it is unconstitutional, and I believe the law clearly discriminates on this ground.

The Massachusetts statute generally prohibits any person from entering a buffer zone around an abortion clinic during the clinic's business hours, but the law contains an exemption for "employees or agents of such facility acting within the scope of their employment." Thus, during business hours, individuals who wish to counsel against abortion or to criticize the particular clinic may not do so within the buffer zone. If they engage in such conduct, they commit a crime. By contrast, . . . [a clinic] may direct or authorize an employee or agent, while within the zone, to express favorable views about abortion or the clinic, and if the employee exercises that authority, the employee's conduct is perfectly lawful. In short, petitioners and other critics of a clinic are silenced, while the clinic may authorize its employees to express speech in support of the clinic and its work.

Consider this entirely realistic situation. A woman enters a buffer zone and heads haltingly toward the entrance. A sidewalk counselor, such as petitioners, enters the buffer zone, approaches the woman and says, "If you have doubts about an abortion, let me try to answer any questions you may have. The clinic will not give you good information." At the same time, a clinic employee, as instructed by the management, approaches the same woman and says, "Come inside and we will give you honest answers to all your questions." The sidewalk counselor and the clinic employee expressed opposing viewpoints, but only the first violated the statute. . . .

It is clear on the face of the Massachusetts law that it discriminates based on viewpoint. Speech in favor of the clinic and its work by employees and agents is permitted; speech criticizing the clinic and its work is a crime. This is blatant viewpoint discrimination. . . .

[If] the law were truly content neutral, I would agree with the Court that the law would still be unconstitutional on the ground that it burdens more speech than is necessary to serve the Commonwealth's asserted interests.

————

Note: Restrictions on Anti-Abortion Speech

1. As Justice Scalia notes in his opinion concurring (only) in the judgment, the petitioners in *McCullen* asked the Court to limit or overrule *Hill v. Colorado*, 530 U.S. 703 (2000). There the Court upheld a statute that regulated speech-related conduct within 100 feet of the entrance to any health care facility. The specific section of the statute that was challenged made it unlawful within the regulated areas for any person to "knowingly approach" within eight feet of another person, without that person's consent, "for the purpose of passing a leaflet or handbill to, displaying a sign to, or engaging in oral protest, education, or counseling with such other person." The *Hill* majority found that the statute satisfied all three prongs of the *Ward* test.

Except for a brief reference in Part I (describing the genesis of the Massachusetts statute), the Court's opinion in *McCullen* does not mention *Hill* at all. What is the status of *Hill* today? This Note provides some excerpts to help you answer that question.

2. In *Hill*, the Court found that the Colorado statute was content-neutral. The *Hill* opinion also emphasized "[t]he unwilling listener's interest in avoiding unwanted communication," and implied that the purpose of the Colorado statute was to protect that interest. In *McCullen*, the Court found that the Massachusetts statute also was content-neutral. But the Court cautioned that "the Act would *not* be content neutral if it were concerned with undesirable effects that arise from . . . listeners' reactions to speech." If the statute's purpose was to protect "[t]he unwilling listener's interest in avoiding unwanted communication," would that be content-neutral?

3. In *McCullen*, the Court found that the Massachusetts law was not narrowly tailored. The Court reached the opposite conclusion in *Hill* with respect to the Colorado statute. In reaching its conclusion, the Court explained:

> [Whether] or not the 8-foot interval is the best possible accommodation of the competing interests at stake, we must accord a measure of deference to the judgment of the Colorado Legislature. Once again, it is worth reiterating that only attempts to address unwilling listeners are affected. . . .
>
> The statute seeks to protect those who wish to enter health care facilities, many of whom may be under special physical or emotional stress, from close physical approaches by demonstrators. In doing so, the statute takes a prophylactic approach; it forbids all unwelcome demonstrators to come closer than eight feet. We recognize that by doing so, it will sometimes inhibit a demonstrator whose approach in fact would have proved harmless. But the statute's prophylactic aspect is justified by the great difficulty of protecting, say, a pregnant woman from physical harassment with legal rules that focus exclusively on the individual impact of each instance of behavior, demanding in each case an accurate characterization (as harassing or not harassing) of each individual movement within the 8-foot boundary. Such individualized

characterization of each individual movement is often difficult to make accurately. A bright-line prophylactic rule may be the best way to provide protection, and, at the same time, by offering clear guidance and avoiding subjectivity, to protect speech itself.

Does the *McCullen* opinion "accord a measure of deference to the judgment of the [Massachusetts] legislature" in determining whether the 35-foot buffer zone is narrowly tailored? Is a "prophylactic rule" consistent with *McCullen*'s approach to the "narrow tailoring" prong?

4. The Court, in a footnote near the end of the *McCullen* opinion, says that because the Massachusetts statute is not narrowly tailored, there is no need to consider whether the law leaves open ample alternative channels of communication. But look at Part IV-A of the Court's opinion. Is the question really open?

In *Hill*, the Court did consider this prong and found it was satisfied:

> With respect to oral statements, the [8-foot separation between the speaker and the audience] certainly can make it more difficult for a speaker to be heard, particularly if the level of background noise is high and other speakers are competing for the pedestrian's attention. Notably, the statute places no limitation on the number of speakers or the noise level, including the use of amplification equipment, although we have upheld such restrictions in past cases.

> The burden on the ability to distribute handbills is more serious because it seems possible that an 8-foot interval could hinder the ability of a leafletter to deliver handbills to some unwilling recipients. The statute does not, however, prevent a leafletter from simply standing near the path of oncoming pedestrians and proffering his or her material, which the pedestrians can easily accept. And, as in all leafletting situations, pedestrians continue to be free to decline the tender. . . .

> [The] 8-foot restriction on an unwanted physical approach leaves ample room to communicate a message through speech. Signs, pictures, and voice itself can cross an 8-foot gap with ease. If the clinics in Colorado resemble those in [a prior case], demonstrators with leaflets might easily stand on the sidewalk at entrances (without blocking the entrance) and, without physically approaching those who are entering the clinic, peacefully hand them leaflets as they pass by.

Is this assessment consistent with the analysis in Part IV-A of the Court's opinion in *McCullen*?

5. In *McCullen*, the Court rejected the argument that the challenged statute was content-based because it only restricted speech near abortion clinics, and so would inevitably have the effect of primarily restricting antiabortion speech. It said that any such effect was "incidental" and so not fatal. Do you agree? What is the difference between the statute in *McCullen* and a hypothetical statute, posited by Justice Scalia in dissent, banning access to the streets and sidewalks surrounding the site of the Republican National Convention? Should the latter be deemed content-neutral? What if the enacting government argued that the restrictions were motivated by security concerns, and not hostility to any particular message?

Problem: Buffer or Bubble?

In 2005, the City of Pittsburgh enacted an ordinance that established two different kinds of zones—"buffer zones" and "bubble zones"—around hospitals, medical offices, and clinics. The "buffer zone" extended "15 feet from any entrance to the hospital or health care facility." The ordinance provided that, within the buffer zone, no person shall "knowingly congregate, patrol, picket or demonstrate." The "bubble zone" encompassed "the public way or sidewalk area within a radius of 100 feet from any entrance door to a hospital and/or medical office/clinic." Within this 100-foot zone, the ordinance provided that "no person shall knowingly approach another person within eight feet of such person, unless such other person consents, for the purpose of passing a leaflet or handbill to, displaying a sign to, or engaging in oral protest, education or counseling with such other person." The "bubble zone" provision in the ordinance was virtually identical to the one in the Colorado statute found facially valid in *Hill.*

Mary Kathryn Brown, a registered nurse and "sidewalk counsellor," challenged the ordinance under the First Amendment. The Third Circuit held that "in tandem the buffer and bubble zones [were] inadequately tailored, but either of them individually would be facially valid." *Brown v. City of Pittsburgh*, 586 F.3d 263 (3d Cir. 2009). In response to the Court of Appeals decision, the City jettisoned the bubble zone but retained the 15-foot buffer zone.

You are the counsel to the Mayor of Pittsburgh, who voted for the law as a city councilman in 2005. The mayor asks you, "Is our ordinance still valid after *McCullen*? Would we be on surer ground in abandoning the buffer zone and reinstating the bubble ordinance instead?"

How would you answer the mayor's question?

Problem: Picketing of Religious Activities

For more than a year, picketers have been demonstrating outside the First Presbyterian Church of Lewiston. The picketers believe that abortion is wrong, and they object to the appointment of William Moreau, M.D., a physician who performs abortions, as a deacon and elder in the church. After Church leaders and members of the congregation complained about the demonstrations, the Lewiston City Council held a hearing. It heard testimony by both protesters and members of the Church. Following extensive discussion and redrafting, the Lewiston City Council passed an ordinance that provides in relevant part:

(a) It shall be deemed an unlawful disturbance of the peace for any person intentionally or knowingly to engage in focused picketing of a scheduled religious activity at any time within the period from one-half hour before to one-half hour after the scheduled activity, at any place (1) on the religious organization's exterior premises, including its parking lots; or (2) on the portion of the right of way including any sidewalk on the same side of the street and adjoining the boundary of the religious premises, including its parking lots; or (3) on the portion of the right of way adjoining the boundary of the religious premises which is a street or roadway including any median within such street or roadway.

(b) For purposes of this ordinance, the term "focused picketing" shall mean the act of one or more persons stationing herself, himself or themselves outside religious premises on the exterior grounds, or on the sidewalks, streets or other part of the right of way in the immediate vicinity of religious premises, or moving in a repeated manner past or around religious premises, while displaying a banner, placard, sign, or other demonstrative material as a part of their expressive conduct. The term "focused picketing" shall not include distribution of leaflets or literature.

Four of the protesters have now brought suit in federal district court challenging the enforcement of the ordinance on First Amendment grounds. The plaintiffs are four individuals who have engaged in protests and demonstrations on the public sidewalk that adjoins the church, carrying signs which read, "William Moreau, Abortionist and Elder," "1 Corinthians 5:13," "Dr. Moreau is Unfit to be an Elder," "Jesus Loves the Little Children," and "Life." Other protesters (not the plaintiffs) have demonstrated near the church with other kinds of signs, including graphic representations of aborted fetuses.

At the hearing on the ordinance, many church members testified that the picketing outside their church had become disruptive and was preventing them from peaceably attending church. An associate pastor at the church testified that "five to six foot images of decapitations and mutilations are held in parishioners' faces, placed against their family vehicles, and directed at them at a close range. Statements about fetuses being murdered, killed, and butchered by a member of their church [Dr. Moreau] are shouted at them as they enter the church building."

Members of the First Presbyterian congregation testified that their families, and especially young children, have undergone emotional distress because of the picketing. Several churchgoers testified that their children experienced nightmares, frequent crying, and a negative shift in attitude towards church in general. Psychologists testified that the children of First Presbyterian were the most vulnerable to the picketers' signs and shouting.

In some instances, members have taken dramatic measures to avoid the demonstrators. According to one church member, "Our six year old niece was forced to ride on the floorboard of her car for protection while arriving for the service." While some have done their best to circumvent the demonstrations, some have left the church because of the picketing.

The City Council referred to, and quoted from, this testimony in a "statement of legislative findings and intent" that accompanied the ordinance. The statement explains that the purpose of the ordinance is to "preserve the peace at religious premises." It also says that the purpose is to "forbid demonstrations that disrupt religious activities or hinder reasonable access to them, especially by families with young children, while respecting First Amendment rights of protesters."

How should the First Amendment challenge be resolved?

Chapter 7

Expressive Conduct and Secondary Effects

In the previous two chapters, we have seen how the modern Supreme Court has built its free speech doctrine around a distinction between "content-based" versus "content-neutral" regulations. In this chapter, we examine some further implications of this distinction. First, we examine how the content discrimination framework plays out when the activity being regulated is a combination of speech and conduct and the government claims it is regulating the conduct. Then, we look at a series of cases in which the Justices seem to have blurred the distinction between content-based and content-neutral regulation. Finally, we see how these two concepts can occasionally overlap or collide.

A. Expressive Conduct

United States v. O'Brien

391 U.S. 367 (1968)

Mr. Chief Justice Warren delivered the opinion of the Court.

On the morning of March 31, 1966, David Paul O'Brien and three companions burned their Selective Service registration certificates on the steps of the South Boston Courthouse. A sizable crowd, including several agents of the Federal Bureau of Investigation, witnessed the event. Immediately after the burning, members of the crowd began attacking O'Brien and his companions. An FBI agent ushered O'Brien to safety inside the courthouse. After he was advised of his right to counsel and to silence, O'Brien stated to FBI agents that he had burned his registration certificate because of his beliefs, knowing that he was violating federal law. He produced the charred remains of the certificate, which, with his consent, were photographed.

For this act, O'Brien was indicted, tried, convicted, and sentenced in the United States District Court for the District of Massachusetts. He did not contest the fact that he had burned the certificate. He stated in argument to the jury that he burned the certificate publicly to influence others to adopt his antiwar beliefs, as he put it, "so that other people would reevaluate their positions with Selective Service, with the armed forces, and reevaluate their place in the culture of today, to hopefully consider my position."

The indictment upon which he was tried charged that he "willfully and knowingly did mutilate, destroy, and change by burning . . . [his] Registration Certificate" [in violation of Section 462(b) of the Universal Military Training and Service Act of 1948.] Section 462(b)(3), one of six numbered subdivisions of § 462(b), was amended by Congress in 1965 (adding the words italicized below), so that at the time O'Brien burned his certificate an offense was committed by any person, "who forges, alters, *knowingly destroys, knowingly mutilates*, or in any manner changes any such certificate. . . ." (Italics supplied.) [The Court of Appeals for the First Circuit held the 1965 Amendment unconstitutional as a law abridging freedom of speech.] We hold that the 1965 Amendment is constitutional both as enacted and as applied. . . .

I.

When a male reaches the age of 18, he is required by the Universal Military Training and Service Act to register with a local draft board. He is assigned a Selective Service number, and within five days he is issued a registration certificate. Subsequently [he] is assigned a classification denoting his eligibility for induction. [Both the registration and classification certificates are small white cards, approximately 2 by 3 inches.]

Congress demonstrated its concern that certificates issued by the Selective Service System might be abused well before the 1965 Amendment here challenged. . . . Under [the 1948 Act itself], it was unlawful (1) to transfer a certificate to aid a person in making false identification; (2) to possess a certificate not duly issued with the intent of using it for false identification; (3) to forge, alter, "or in any manner" change a certificate or any notation validly inscribed thereon; (4) to photograph or make an imitation of a certificate for the purpose of false identification; and (5) to possess a counterfeited or altered certificate. In addition, . . . regulations of the Selective Service System required registrants to keep both their registration and classification certificates in their personal possession at all times. And § 12(b)(6) of the Act made knowing violation of any provision of the Act or rules and regulations promulgated pursuant thereto a felony.

. . . We note at the outset that the 1965 Amendment [quoted above] plainly does not abridge free speech on its face, and we do not understand O'Brien to argue otherwise. Amended § 12(b)(3) on its face deals with conduct having no connection with speech. It prohibits the knowing destruction of certificates issued by the Selective Service System, and there is nothing necessarily expressive about such conduct. The Amendment does not distinguish between public and private destruction, and it does not punish only destruction engaged in for the purpose of expressing views. . . .

O'Brien nonetheless argues that the 1965 Amendment is unconstitutional in its application to him, and is unconstitutional as enacted because what he calls the "purpose" of Congress was "to suppress freedom of speech." We consider these arguments separately.

II.

O'Brien first argues that the 1965 Amendment is unconstitutional as applied to him because his act of burning his registration certificate was protected "symbolic speech" within the First Amendment. His argument is that the freedom of expression which the First Amendment guarantees includes all modes of "communication of ideas by conduct," and that his conduct is within this definition because he did it in "demonstration against the war and against the draft."

We cannot accept the view that an apparently limitless variety of conduct can be labeled "speech" whenever the person engaging in the conduct intends thereby to express an idea. However, even on the assumption that the alleged communicative element in O'Brien's conduct is sufficient to bring into play the First Amendment, it does not necessarily follow that the destruction of a registration certificate is constitutionally protected activity. This Court has held that when "speech" and "nonspeech" elements are combined in the same course of conduct, a sufficiently important governmental interest in regulating the nonspeech element can justify incidental limitations on First Amendment freedoms. To characterize the quality of the governmental interest which must appear, the Court has employed a variety of descriptive terms: compelling; substantial; subordinating; paramount; cogent; strong. Whatever imprecision inheres in these terms, we think it clear that a government regulation is sufficiently justified if it is within the constitutional power of the Government; if it furthers an important or substantial governmental interest; if the governmental interest is unrelated to the suppression of free expression; and if the incidental restriction on alleged First Amendment freedoms is no greater than is essential to the furtherance of that interest. We find that the [1965 Amendment] meets all of these requirements, and consequently that O'Brien can be constitutionally convicted for violating it. . . .

[O'Brien] essentially adopts the position that [Selective Service] certificates are so many pieces of paper designed to notify registrants of their registration or classification, to be retained or tossed in the wastebasket according to the convenience or taste of the registrant. Once the registrant has received notification, according to this view, there is no reason for him to retain the certificates. O'Brien notes that most of the information on a registration certificate serves no notification purpose at all; the registrant hardly needs to be told his address and physical characteristics. We agree that the registration certificate contains much information of which the registrant needs no notification. This circumstance, however, does not lead to the conclusion that the certificate serves no purpose, but that, like the classification certificate, it serves purposes in addition to initial notification. Many of these purposes would be defeated by the certificates' destruction or mutilation. Among these are:

1. The registration certificate serves as proof that the individual described thereon has registered for the draft. The classification certificate shows the eligibility classification of a named but undescribed individual. Voluntarily displaying the two certificates is an easy and painless way for a young man to dispel a question as to whether he might be delinquent in his Selective Service obligations. Correspondingly, the availability of the certificates for such display relieves the Selective Service System of the administrative burden it would otherwise have in verifying the registration and classification of all suspected delinquents. Further, since both certificates are in the nature of "receipts" attesting that the registrant has done what the law requires, it is in the

interest of the just and efficient administration of the system that they be continually available, in the event, for example, of a mix-up in the registrant's file. Additionally, in a time of national crisis, reasonable availability to each registrant of the two small cards assures a rapid and uncomplicated means for determining his fitness for immediate induction, no matter how distant in our mobile society he may be from his local board.

2. The information supplied on the certificates facilitates communication between registrants and local boards, simplifying the system and benefiting all concerned. To begin with, each certificate bears the address of the registrant's local board, an item unlikely to be committed to memory. Further, each card bears the registrant's Selective Service number, and a registrant who has his number readily available so that he can communicate it to his local board when he supplies or requests information can make simpler the board's task in locating his file. Finally, a registrant's inquiry, particularly through a local board other than his own, concerning his eligibility status is frequently answerable simply on the basis of his classification certificate; whereas, if the certificate were not reasonably available and the registrant were uncertain of his classification, the task of answering his questions would be considerably complicated.

3. Both certificates carry continual reminders that the registrant must notify his local board of any change of address, and other specified changes in his status. The smooth functioning of the system requires that local boards be continually aware of the status and whereabouts of registrants, and the destruction of certificates deprives the system of a potentially useful notice device.

4. The regulatory scheme involving Selective Service certificates includes clearly valid prohibitions against the alteration, forgery, or similar deceptive misuse of certificates. The destruction or mutilation of certificates obviously increases the difficulty of detecting and tracing abuses such as these. Further, a mutilated certificate might itself be used for deceptive purposes.

The many functions performed by Selective Service certificates establish beyond doubt that Congress has a legitimate and substantial interest in preventing their wanton and unrestrained destruction and assuring their continuing availability by punishing people who knowingly and wilfully destroy or mutilate them. And we are unpersuaded that the pre-existence of the nonpossession regulations in any way negates this interest. . . .

Equally important, a comparison of the regulations with the 1965 Amendment indicates that they protect overlapping but not identical governmental interests, and that they reach somewhat different classes of wrongdoers. The gravamen of the offense defined by the statute is the deliberate rendering of certificates unavailable for the various purposes which they may serve. Whether registrants keep their certificates in their personal possession at all times, as required by the regulations, is of no particular concern under the 1965 Amendment, as long as they do not mutilate or destroy the certificates so as to render them unavailable. Although as we note below we are not concerned here with the nonpossession regulations, it is not inappropriate to observe that the essential elements of nonpossession are not identical with those of mutilation or destruction. Finally, the 1965 Amendment, like § 12(b) which it amended, is concerned with abuses involving any issued Selective Service certificates, not only with the registrant's own certificates. The knowing destruction or mutilation of someone else's certificates would therefore violate the statute but not the nonpossession regulations.

We think it apparent that the continuing availability to each registrant of his Selective Service certificates substantially furthers the smooth and proper functioning of the system that Congress has established to raise armies. . . . [T]he Government has a substantial interest in assuring the continuing availability of issued Selective Service certificates.

It is equally clear that the 1965 Amendment specifically protects this substantial governmental interest. We perceive no alternative means that would more precisely and narrowly assure the continuing availability of issued Selective Service certificates than a law which prohibits their wilful mutilation or destruction. The 1965 Amendment prohibits such conduct and does nothing more. In other words, both the governmental interest and the operation of the 1965 Amendment are limited to the noncommunicative aspect of O'Brien's conduct. The governmental interest and the scope of the 1965 Amendment are limited to preventing harm to the smooth and efficient functioning of the Selective Service System. When O'Brien deliberately rendered unavailable his registration certificate, he wilfully frustrated this governmental interest. For this noncommunicative impact of his conduct, and for nothing else, he was convicted. . . .

In conclusion, we find that because of the Government's substantial interest in assuring the continuing availability of issued Selective Service certificates, because amended § 462(b) is an appropriately narrow means of protecting this interest and condemns only the independent noncommunicative impact of conduct within its reach, and because the noncommunicative impact of O'Brien's act of burning his registration certificate frustrated the Government's interest, a sufficient governmental interest has been shown to justify O'Brien's conviction.

III.

O'Brien finally argues that the 1965 Amendment is unconstitutional as enacted because what he calls the "purpose" of Congress was "to suppress freedom of speech." We reject this argument because under settled principles the purpose of Congress, as O'Brien uses that term, is not a basis for declaring this legislation unconstitutional.

It is a familiar principle of constitutional law that this Court will not strike down an otherwise constitutional statute on the basis of an alleged illicit legislative motive. . . . Inquiries into congressional motives or purposes are a hazardous matter. When the issue is simply the interpretation of legislation, the Court will look to statements by legislators for guidance as to the purpose of the legislature, because the benefit to sound decision-making in this circumstance is thought sufficient to risk the possibility of misreading Congress' purpose. It is entirely a different matter when we are asked to void a statute that is, under well-settled criteria, constitutional on its face, on the basis of what fewer than a handful of Congressmen said about it. What motivates one legislator to make a speech about a statute is not necessarily what motivates scores of others to enact it, and the stakes are sufficiently high for us to eschew guesswork. We decline to void essentially on the ground that it is unwise legislation which Congress had the undoubted power to enact and which could be reenacted in its exact form if the same or another legislator made a "wiser" speech about it. . . .

We think it not amiss, in passing, to comment upon O'Brien's legislative-purpose argument. There was little floor debate on this legislation in either House. Only Senator Thurmond commented on its substantive features in the Senate. After his brief statement, and without any additional substantive comments, the bill, H.R. 10306, passed the Senate. In the House debate only two Congressmen addressed themselves to the Amendment—Congressmen Rivers and Bray. The bill was passed after their statements without any further debate by a vote of 393 to 1. It is principally on the basis of the statements by these three Congressmen that O'Brien makes his congressional "purpose" argument. We note that if we were to examine legislative purpose in the instant case, we would be obliged to consider not only these statements but also the more authoritative reports of the Senate and House Armed Services Committees. The portions of those reports explaining the purpose of the Amendment are reproduced in the Appendix in their entirety [omitted here]. While both reports make clear a concern with the "defiant" destruction of so-called "draft cards" and with "open" encouragement to others to destroy their cards, both reports also indicate that this concern stemmed from an apprehension that unrestrained destruction of cards would disrupt the smooth functioning of the Selective Service System.

IV.

[The 1965 Amendment] is constitutional as enacted and as applied . . . Accordingly, we vacate the judgment of the Court of Appeals, and reinstate the judgment and sentence of the District Court. . . .

Mr. Justice Marshall took no part in the consideration or decision of these cases.

Mr. Justice Harlan, concurring.

. . . I wish to make explicit my understanding that [the Court's decision] does not foreclose consideration of First Amendment claims in those rare instances when an "incidental" restriction upon expression, imposed by a regulation which furthers an "important or substantial" governmental interest and satisfies the Court's other criteria, in practice has the effect of entirely preventing a "speaker" from reaching a significant audience with whom he could not otherwise lawfully communicate. This is not such a case, since O'Brien manifestly could have conveyed his message in many ways other than by burning his draft card.

Mr. Justice Douglas, dissenting.

. . . The underlying and basic problem in this case [is] whether conscription is permissible in the absence of a declaration of war. That question has not been briefed nor was it presented in oral argument; but it is, I submit, a question upon which the litigants and the country are entitled to a ruling. . . .

Note: "Symbolic Speech" and the Tinker Case

Less than a year after *O'Brien*, the Court decided the case of *Tinker v. Des Moines Independent School District* (1969) (Chapter 12). In *Tinker*, two high school students wore black armbands to school to publicize their objections to the hostilities in Vietnam and their support for a truce. Both students were suspended from school until they would come back without their armbands.

The Supreme Court held that the suspension violated the First Amendment rights of the students. On the question of whether the wearing of armbands is protected by the First Amendment, the entire discussion was as follows:

> The District Court recognized that the wearing of an armband for the purpose of expressing certain views is the type of symbolic act that is within the Free Speech Clause of the First Amendment. As we shall discuss, the wearing of armbands in the circumstances of this case was entirely divorced from actually or potentially disruptive conduct by those participating in it. It was closely akin to "pure speech" which, we have repeatedly held, is entitled to comprehensive protection under the First Amendment.

Justice Black dissented strongly from the Court's holding, but he was willing to assume that "the conduct of wearing armbands for the purpose of conveying political ideas is protected by the First Amendment." He made no mention of *O'Brien*, nor did the Court. Was the case relevant? Why was the wearing of armbands by the Des Moines students "closely akin to 'pure speech,'" while *O'Brien*'s burning of his draft card barely qualified for First Amendment consideration?

Note: "Incidental" Burdens on Expression

1. In *O'Brien*, the Court appears to set forth a test for situations where "'speech' and 'nonspeech' elements are combined in the same course of conduct," and a government regulation imposes "incidental" burdens on First Amendment freedoms. How broadly is this test to be applied? For example, suppose that a television news reporter, on his way to the scene of a breaking story of great importance, drives 80 mph in a 55-mph zone and fails to stop at several red lights. Would the state have to satisfy the *O'Brien* standard in order to prosecute him for violating its traffic laws?

2. In *Arcara v. Cloud Books, Inc.*, 478 U.S. 697 (1986), a New York State statute authorized a one-year closure of premises found to be used as a place for prostitution or lewdness. An undercover investigation revealed that illicit sexual activities were taking place on the premises of an adult bookstore and that the management of the store was fully aware of these activities. Based on the findings of the investigation, the county attorney applied for a court order closing the bookstore for one year in accordance with the state statute. The New York Court of Appeals held that the case was governed by *O'Brien* and that the closure remedy failed the fourth part of the *O'Brien* test.

The Supreme Court reversed. Chief Justice Burger, in his last First Amendment opinion, wrote for a six-Justice majority. He said:

> The New York Court of Appeals held that the *O'Brien* test for permissible governmental regulation was applicable to this case because the closure order sought by petitioner would also impose an incidental burden upon respondents' bookselling activities. That court ignored a crucial distinction between the circumstances presented in *O'Brien* and the circumstances of this case: unlike the symbolic draft card burning in *O'Brien*, the sexual activity carried on in this case manifests absolutely no element of protected expression. . . .
>
> It is true that the closure order in this case would require respondents to move their bookselling business to another location. Yet we have not traditionally subjected every criminal and civil sanction imposed through legal process to "least restrictive means" scrutiny simply because each particular remedy will have some effect on the First Amendment activities of those subject to sanction. Rather, we have subjected such restrictions to scrutiny only where it was conduct with a significant expressive element that drew the legal remedy in the first place, as in *O'Brien*, or where a statute based on a nonexpressive activity has the inevitable effect of singling out those engaged in expressive activity, as in *Minneapolis Star & Tribune Co. v. Minnesota Comm'r of Revenue*, 460 U.S. 575 (1983) [Chapter 14]. This case involves neither situation, and we conclude the First Amendment is not implicated by the enforcement of a public health regulation of general application against the physical premises in which respondents happen to sell books.
>
> The New York Court of Appeals thus misread *O'Brien*, which has no relevance to a statute directed at imposing sanctions on nonexpressive activity. . . . Bookselling in an establishment used for prostitution does not confer First Amendment coverage to defeat a valid statute aimed at penalizing and terminating illegal uses of premises.

3. The Court in *Arcara* describes *O'Brien* as a case in which "it was conduct with a significant expressive element that drew the legal remedy in the first place." Is that the way the Court in *O'Brien* viewed the statute under which the defendant was convicted? Compare the treatment of *O'Brien* in *Texas v. Johnson*, the next principal case.

4. On remand, the New York Court of Appeals reinstated its prior holding, but this time it relied on the state constitution. The court explained:

> [Under the state constitution, the] crucial factor in determining whether State action affects freedom of expression is the impact of the action on the protected activity and not the nature of the activity which prompted the government to act. The test, in traditional terms, is not who is aimed at but who is hit.

If this "impact" test is met, the state must "prove that . . . it has chosen a course no broader than necessary to accomplish its purpose." *People ex rel. Arcara v. Cloud Books, Inc.*, 503 N.E.2d 492 (N.Y. 1986). But the court also emphasized that constitutional guarantees are implicated only when the impact on protected activity is "substantial" (albeit "incidental") rather than "slight."

How much more speech-protective is the New York court's approach than the one taken by the United States Supreme Court? Reconsider this question as you read the other cases in this chapter.

Texas v. Johnson

491 U.S. 397 (1989)

Justice Brennan delivered the opinion of the Court.

After publicly burning an American flag as a means of political protest, Gregory Lee Johnson was convicted of desecrating a flag in violation of Texas law. This case presents the question whether his conviction is consistent with the First Amendment. We hold that it is not.

I

While the Republican National Convention was taking place in Dallas in 1984, respondent Johnson participated in a political demonstration dubbed the "Republican War Chest Tour." As explained in literature distributed by the demonstrators and in speeches made by them, the purpose of this event was to protest the policies of the Reagan administration and of certain Dallas-based corporations. The demonstrators marched through the Dallas streets, chanting political slogans and stopping at several corporate locations to stage "die-ins" intended to dramatize the consequences of nuclear war. On several occasions they spray-painted the walls of buildings and overturned potted plants, but Johnson himself took no part in such activities. He did, however, accept an American flag handed to him by a fellow protestor who had taken it from a flag pole outside one of the targeted buildings.

The demonstration ended in front of Dallas City Hall, where Johnson unfurled the American flag, doused it with kerosene, and set it on fire. While the flag burned, the protestors chanted, "America, the red, white, and blue, we spit on you." After the demonstrators dispersed, a witness to the flag burning collected the flag's remains and buried them in his backyard. No one was physically injured or threatened with injury, though several witnesses testified that they had been seriously offended by the flag burning.

Of the approximately 100 demonstrators, Johnson alone was charged with a crime. The only criminal offense with which he was charged was the desecration of a venerated object in violation of Tex. Penal Code Ann. § 42.09(a)(3) (1989).[1] After a trial, he was convicted, sentenced to one year in prison, and fined $2,000. [The Texas

---

1. Tex. Penal Code Ann. § 42.09 (1989) provides . . . : "§ 42.09. Desecration of Venerated Object. (a) A person commits an offense if he intentionally or knowingly desecrates: (1) a public monument; (2) a place of worship or burial; or (3) a state or national flag. (b) For purposes of this section, 'desecrate' means deface, damage, or otherwise physically mistreat in a way that the actor knows will seriously offend one or more persons likely to observe or discover his action."

Court of Criminal Appeals] reversed, holding that the State could not, consistent with the First Amendment, punish Johnson for burning the flag in these circumstances. . . .

II

Johnson was convicted of flag desecration for burning the flag rather than for uttering insulting words. This fact somewhat complicates our consideration of his conviction under the First Amendment. We must first determine whether Johnson's burning of the flag constituted expressive conduct, permitting him to invoke the First Amendment in challenging his conviction. *See, e.g., Spence v. Washington*, 418 U.S. 405 (1974). If his conduct was expressive, we next decide whether the State's regulation is related to the suppression of free expression. *See, e.g., United States v. O'Brien* (1968) [*supra* this chapter]. If the State's regulation is not related to expression, then the less stringent standard we announced in *O'Brien* for regulations of noncommunicative conduct controls. If it is, then we are outside of *O'Brien*'s test, and we must ask whether this interest justifies Johnson's conviction under a more demanding standard.[3] A third possibility is that the State's asserted interest is simply not implicated on these facts, and in that event the interest drops out of the picture.

The First Amendment literally forbids the abridgment only of "speech," but we have long recognized that its protection does not end at the spoken or written word. While we have rejected "the view that an apparently limitless variety of conduct can be labeled 'speech' whenever the person engaging in the conduct intends thereby to express an idea," *O'Brien*, we have acknowledged that conduct may be "sufficiently imbued with elements of communication to fall within the scope of the First and Fourteenth Amendments," *Spence*.

In deciding whether particular conduct possesses sufficient communicative elements to bring the First Amendment into play, we have asked whether "[a]n intent to convey a particularized message was present, and [whether] the likelihood was great that the message would be understood by those who viewed it." Hence, we have recognized the expressive nature of students' wearing of black armbands to protest American military involvement in Vietnam, *Tinker v. Des Moines Independent School District* [Note *supra* this chapter]; of a sit-in by blacks in a "whites only" area to protest segregation, *Brown v. Louisiana*, 383 U.S. 131, 141–42 (1966); of the wearing of American military uniforms in a dramatic presentation criticizing American

---

3. Although Johnson has raised a facial challenge to Texas' flag-desecration statute, we choose to resolve this case on the basis of his claim that the statute as applied to him violates the First Amendment. Section 42.09 regulates only physical conduct with respect to the flag, not the written or spoken word, and although one violates the statute only if one "knows" that one's physical treatment of the flag "will seriously offend one or more persons likely to observe or discover his action," this fact does not necessarily mean that the statute applies only to expressive conduct protected by the First Amendment. A tired person might, for example, drag a flag through the mud, knowing that this conduct is likely to offend others, and yet have no thought of expressing any idea; neither the language nor the Texas courts' interpretations of the statute precludes the possibility that such a person would be prosecuted for flag desecration. Because the prosecution of a person who had not engaged in expressive conduct would pose a different case, and because this case may be disposed of on narrower grounds, we address only Johnson's claim that § 42.09 as applied to political expression like his violates the First Amendment.

involvement in Vietnam, *Schacht v. United States*, 398 U.S. 58 (1970); and of picketing about a wide variety of causes.

Especially pertinent to this case are our decisions recognizing the communicative nature of conduct relating to flags. Attaching a peace sign to the flag, *Spence*; refusing to salute the flag, *West Virginia Board of Education v. Barnette* (1943) [Chapter 9]; and displaying a red flag, *Stromberg v. California*, 283 U.S. 359 (1931), we have held, all may find shelter under the First Amendment. That we have had little difficulty identifying an expressive element in conduct relating to flags should not be surprising. The very purpose of a national flag is to serve as a symbol of our country. . . .

We have not automatically concluded, however, that any action taken with respect to our flag is expressive. Instead, in characterizing such action for First Amendment purposes, we have considered the context in which it occurred. In *Spence*, for example, we emphasized that Spence's taping of a peace sign to his flag was "roughly simultaneous with and concededly triggered by the Cambodian incursion and the Kent State tragedy." The State of Washington had conceded, in fact, that Spence's conduct was a form of communication, and we stated that "the State's concession is inevitable on this record."

The State of Texas conceded for purposes of its oral argument in this case that Johnson's conduct was expressive conduct, and this concession seems to us as prudent as was Washington's in *Spence*. . . . At his trial, Johnson explained his reasons for burning the flag as follows: "The American Flag was burned as Ronald Reagan was being renominated as President. And a more powerful statement of symbolic speech, whether you agree with it or not, couldn't have been made at that time. It's quite a [juxtaposition]. We had new patriotism and no patriotism." In these circumstances, Johnson's burning of the flag was conduct "sufficiently imbued with elements of communication" to implicate the First Amendment.

III

The government generally has a freer hand in restricting expressive conduct than it has in restricting the written or spoken word. It may not, however, proscribe particular conduct *because* it has expressive elements. . . . It is [not simply] the verbal or nonverbal nature of the expression, but the governmental interest at stake, that helps to determine whether a restriction on that expression is valid.

Thus, although we have recognized that where "'speech' and 'nonspeech' elements are combined in the same course of conduct, a sufficiently important governmental interest in regulating the nonspeech element can justify incidental limitations on First Amendment freedoms," we have limited the applicability of *O'Brien*'s relatively lenient standard to those cases in which "the governmental interest is unrelated to the suppression of free expression." In stating, moreover, that *O'Brien*'s test "in the last analysis is little, if any, different from the standard applied to time, place, or manner restrictions," we have highlighted the requirement that the governmental interest in question be unconnected to expression in order to come under *O'Brien*'s less demanding rule.

In order to decide whether *O'Brien*'s test applies here, therefore, we must decide whether Texas has asserted an interest in support of Johnson's conviction that is unrelated to the suppression of expression. If we find that an interest asserted by the State is simply not implicated on the facts before us, we need not ask whether *O'Brien*'s test applies. The State offers two separate interests to justify this conviction: preventing breaches of the peace and preserving the flag as a symbol of nationhood and national unity. We hold that the first interest is not implicated on this record and that the second is related to the suppression of expression.

A

Texas claims that its interest in preventing breaches of the peace justifies Johnson's conviction for flag desecration. However, no disturbance of the peace actually occurred or threatened to occur because of Johnson's burning of the flag. . . . The only evidence offered by the State at trial to show the reaction to Johnson's actions was the testimony of several persons who had been seriously offended by the flag burning.

The State's position, therefore, amounts to a claim that an audience that takes serious offense at particular expression is necessarily likely to disturb the peace and that the expression may be prohibited on this basis. Our precedents do not countenance such a presumption. On the contrary, they recognize that a principal "function of free speech under our system of government is to invite dispute. It may indeed best serve its high purpose when it induces a condition of unrest, creates dissatisfaction with conditions as they are, or even stirs people to anger." *Terminiello v. Chicago*, 337 U.S. 1 (1949) [Chapter 8]. . . .

Thus, we have not permitted the government to assume that every expression of a provocative idea will incite a riot, but have instead required careful consideration of the actual circumstances surrounding such expression, asking whether the expression "is directed to inciting or producing imminent lawless action and is likely to incite or produce such action." *Brandenburg v. Ohio* (1969) [Chapter 1]. To accept Texas' arguments that it need only demonstrate "the potential for a breach of the peace," and that every flag burning necessarily possesses that potential, would be to eviscerate our holding in *Brandenburg*. This we decline to do.

Nor does Johnson's expressive conduct fall within that small class of "fighting words" that are "likely to provoke the average person to retaliation, and thereby cause a breach of the peace." *Chaplinsky v. New Hampshire* (1942) [Chapter 2]. No reasonable onlooker would have regarded Johnson's generalized expression of dissatisfaction with the policies of the Federal Government as a direct personal insult or an invitation to exchange fisticuffs.

We thus conclude that the State's interest in maintaining order is not implicated on these facts. The State need not worry that our holding will disable it from preserving the peace. We do not suggest that the First Amendment forbids a State to prevent "imminent lawless action." *Brandenburg*. And, in fact, Texas already has a statute specifically prohibiting breaches of the peace, which tends to confirm that Texas need not punish this flag desecration in order to keep the peace.

B

The State also asserts an interest in preserving the flag as a symbol of nationhood and national unity. In *Spence*, we acknowledged that the government's interest in preserving the flag's special symbolic value "is directly related to expression in the context of activity" such as affixing a peace symbol to a flag. We are equally persuaded that this interest is related to expression in the case of Johnson's burning of the flag. The State, apparently, is concerned that such conduct will lead people to believe either that the flag does not stand for nationhood and national unity, but instead reflects other, less positive concepts, or that the concepts reflected in the flag do not in fact exist, that is, that we do not enjoy unity as a Nation. These concerns blossom only when a person's treatment of the flag communicates some message, and thus are related "to the suppression of free expression" within the meaning of *O'Brien*. We are thus outside of *O'Brien*'s test altogether.

IV

It remains to consider whether the State's interest in preserving the flag as a symbol of nationhood and national unity justifies Johnson's conviction.

As in *Spence*, "[w]e are confronted with a case of prosecution for the expression of an idea through activity," and "[a]ccordingly, we must examine with particular care the interests advanced by [petitioner] to support its prosecution." Johnson was not, we add, prosecuted for the expression of just any idea; he was prosecuted for his expression of dissatisfaction with the policies of this country, expression situated at the core of our First Amendment values. . . .

Moreover, Johnson was prosecuted because he knew that his politically charged expression would cause "serious offense." . . . The Texas law [is] not aimed at protecting the physical integrity of the flag in all circumstances, but is designed instead to protect it only against impairments that would cause serious offense to others. [*See* footnote 1.] Texas concedes as much . . . .

Whether Johnson's treatment of the flag violated Texas law thus depended on the likely communicative impact of his expressive conduct. Our decision in *Boos v. Barry* (1988) [*infra* this chapter] tells us that this restriction on Johnson's expression is content based. [In *Boos*,] we held that "[t]he emotive impact of speech on its audience is not a 'secondary effect'" unrelated to the content of the expression itself.

According to the principles announced in *Boos*, Johnson's political expression was restricted because of the content of the message he conveyed. We must therefore subject the State's asserted interest in preserving the special symbolic character of the flag to "the most exacting scrutiny." *Boos*.

Texas argues that its interest in preserving the flag as a symbol of nationhood and national unity survives this close analysis. Quoting extensively from the writings of this Court chronicling the flag's historic and symbolic role in our society, the State emphasizes the "'special place'" reserved for the flag in our Nation. The State's argument is not that it has an interest simply in maintaining the flag as a symbol of something, no matter what it symbolizes; indeed, if that were the State's position, it would be difficult to see how that interest is endangered by highly symbolic conduct such as Johnson's. Rather, the State's claim is that it has an interest in preserving the flag as a symbol of nationhood and national unity, a symbol with a determinate range of meanings. According to Texas, if one physically treats the flag in a way that would tend to cast doubt on either the idea that nationhood and national unity are the flag's referents or that national unity actually exists, the message conveyed thereby is a harmful one and therefore may be prohibited.

If there is a bedrock principle underlying the First Amendment, it is that the government may not prohibit the expression of an idea simply because society finds the idea itself offensive or disagreeable. *See, e.g., Hustler Magazine v. Falwell* (1988) [Chapter 2 Note]; . . . .

We have not recognized an exception to this principle even where our flag has been involved. In *Street v. New York*, 394 U.S. 576 (1969), we held that a State may not criminally punish a person for uttering words critical of the flag. . . .

In [*Barnette*], Justice Jackson described one of our society's defining principles in words deserving of their frequent repetition: "If there is any fixed star in our constitutional constellation, it is that no official, high or petty, can prescribe what shall be orthodox in politics, nationalism, religion, or other matters of opinion or force citizens to confess by word or act their faith therein." In *Spence*, we held that the same interest asserted by Texas here was insufficient to support a criminal conviction under a flag-misuse statute for the taping of a peace sign to an American flag. . . .

In short, nothing in our precedents suggests that a State may foster its own view of the flag by prohibiting expressive conduct relating to it. To bring its argument outside our precedents, Texas attempts to convince us that even if its interest in preserving the flag's symbolic role does not allow it to prohibit words or some expressive conduct critical of the flag, it does permit it to forbid the outright destruction of the flag. The State's argument cannot depend here on the distinction between written or spoken words and nonverbal conduct. That distinction, we have shown, is of no moment where the nonverbal conduct is expressive, as it is here, and where the regulation of that conduct is related to expression, as it is here. In addition, both *Barnette* and *Spence* involved expressive conduct, not only verbal communication, and both found that conduct protected.

Texas' focus on the precise nature of Johnson's expression, moreover, misses the point of our prior decisions: their enduring lesson, that the government may not prohibit expression simply because it disagrees with its message, is not dependent on the particular mode in which one chooses to express an idea. If we were to hold that a State may forbid flag burning wherever it is likely to endanger the flag's symbolic role, but allow it wherever burning a flag promotes that role—as where, for example, a person ceremoniously burns a dirty flag—we would be saying that when it comes to impairing the flag's physical integrity, the flag itself may be used as a symbol—as a substitute for the written or spoken word or a "short cut from mind to mind"—only in one direction. We would be permitting a State to "prescribe what shall be orthodox" by saying that one may burn the flag to convey one's attitude toward it and its referents only if one does not endanger the flag's representation of nationhood and national unity.

We never before have held that the Government may ensure that a symbol be used to express only one view of that symbol or its referents. Indeed, in *Schacht v. United States*, we invalidated a federal statute permitting an actor portraying a member of one of our armed forces to "'wear the uniform of that armed force if the portrayal does not tend to discredit that armed force.'" This proviso, we held, "which leaves Americans free to praise the war in Vietnam but can send persons like Schacht to prison for opposing it, cannot survive in a country which has the First Amendment."

We perceive no basis on which to hold that the principle underlying our decision in *Schacht* does not apply to this case. To conclude that the government may permit designated symbols to be used to communicate only a limited set of messages would be to enter territory having no discernible or defensible boundaries. Could the government, on this theory, prohibit the burning of state flags? Of copies of the Presidential seal? Of the Constitution? In evaluating these choices under the First Amendment, how would we decide which symbols were sufficiently special to warrant this unique status? To do so, we would be forced to consult our own political preferences, and impose them on the citizenry, in the very way that the First Amendment forbids us to do.

There is, moreover, no indication—either in the text of the Constitution or in our cases interpreting it—that a separate juridical category exists for the American flag alone. Indeed, we would not be surprised to learn that the persons who framed our Constitution and wrote the Amendment that we now construe were not known for their reverence for the Union Jack. The First Amendment does not guarantee that other concepts virtually sacred to our Nation as a whole—such as the principle that discrimination on the basis of race is odious and destructive—will go unquestioned in the marketplace of ideas. *See Brandenburg*. We decline, therefore, to create for the flag an exception to the joust of principles protected by the First Amendment.

It is not the State's ends, but its means, to which we object. . . . We reject the suggestion, urged at oral argument by counsel for Johnson, that the government lacks "any state interest whatsoever" in regulating the manner in which the flag may be displayed. Congress has, for example, enacted precatory regulations describing the proper treatment of the flag, and we cast no doubt on the legitimacy of its interest in making such recommendations. . . .

The way to preserve the flag's special role is not to punish those who feel differently about these matters. It is to persuade them that they are wrong. . . . And, precisely because it is our flag that is involved, one's response to the flag burner may exploit the uniquely persuasive power of the flag itself. We can imagine no more appropriate response to burning a flag than waving one's own, no better way to counter a flag burner's message than by saluting the flag that burns, no surer means of preserving the dignity even of the flag that burned than by—as one witness here did—according its remains a respectful burial. We do not consecrate the flag by punishing its desecration, for in doing so we dilute the freedom that this cherished emblem represents. . . . [Affirmed.]

JUSTICE KENNEDY, concurring. [Omitted.]

CHIEF JUSTICE REHNQUIST, with whom JUSTICE WHITE and JUSTICE O'CONNOR join, dissenting.

In holding this Texas statute unconstitutional, the Court ignores Justice Holmes' familiar aphorism that "a page of history is worth a volume of logic." For more than 200 years, the American flag has occupied a unique position as the symbol of our Nation, a uniqueness that justifies a governmental prohibition against flag burning in the way respondent Johnson did here.

[The Chief Justice here traced the role of the flag from the American Revolution through the Civil War.]

One of the great stories of the Civil War is told in John Greenleaf Whittier's poem, Barbara Frietchie: [The Chief Justice here set forth the poem in its entirety, including the line, "'Shoot, if you must, this old gray head, But spare your country's flag,' she said."]

The American flag, then, throughout more than 200 years of our history, has come to be the visible symbol embodying our Nation. . . . The flag is not simply another "idea" or "point of view" competing for recognition in the marketplace of ideas. Millions and millions of Americans regard it with an almost mystical reverence regardless of what sort of social, political, or philosophical beliefs they may have. . . .

But the Court insists that the Texas statute prohibiting the public burning of the American flag infringes on respondent Johnson's freedom of expression. Such freedom, of course, is not absolute. [The Chief Justice here quoted the familiar language from *Chaplinsky*.] Here it may equally well be said that the public burning of the American flag by Johnson was no essential part of any exposition of ideas, and at the same time it had a tendency to incite a breach of the peace. . . .

The Court could not, and did not, say that Chaplinsky's utterances were not expressive phrases — they clearly and succinctly conveyed an extremely low opinion of the addressee. The same may be said of Johnson's public burning of the flag in this case; it obviously did convey Johnson's bitter dislike of his country. But his act, like Chaplinsky's provocative words, conveyed nothing that could not have been conveyed and was not conveyed just as forcefully in a dozen different ways. As with "fighting words," so with flag burning, for purposes of the First Amendment: It is "no essential part of any exposition of ideas, and [is] of such slight social value as a step to truth that any benefit that may be derived from [it] is clearly outweighed" by the public interest in avoiding a probable breach of the peace. . . .

. . . Far from being a case of "one picture being worth a thousand words," flag burning is the equivalent of an inarticulate grunt or roar that, it seems fair to say, is most likely to be indulged in not to express any particular idea, but to antagonize others. . . . The Texas statute deprived Johnson of only one rather inarticulate symbolic form of protest—a form of protest that was profoundly offensive to many—and left him with a full panoply of other symbols and every conceivable form of verbal expression to express his deep disapproval of national policy. Thus, in no way can it be said that Texas is punishing him because his hearers—or any other group of people—were profoundly opposed to the message that he sought to convey. Such opposition is no proper basis for restricting speech or expression under the First Amendment. It was Johnson's use of this particular symbol, and not the idea that he sought to convey by it or by his many other expressions, for which he was punished. . . .

Justice Stevens, dissenting.

. . . Even if flag burning could be considered just another species of symbolic speech under the logical application of the rules that the Court has developed in its interpretation of the First Amendment in other contexts, this case has an intangible dimension that makes those rules inapplicable.

A country's flag is a symbol of more than "nationhood and national unity." It also signifies the ideas that characterize the society that has chosen that emblem as well as the special history that has animated the growth and power of those ideas. . . . The value of the flag as a symbol cannot be measured. . . . The creation of a federal right to post bulletin boards and graffiti on the Washington Monument might enlarge the market for free expression, but at a cost I would not pay. Similarly, in my considered judgment, sanctioning the public desecration of the flag will tarnish its value—both for those who cherish the ideas for which it waves and for those who desire to don the robes of martyrdom by burning it. That tarnish is not justified by the trivial burden on free expression occasioned by requiring that an available, alternative mode of expression—including uttering words critical of the flag, see *Street v. New York*, 394 U.S. 576 (1969)—be employed.

It is appropriate to emphasize certain propositions that are not implicated by this case. The statutory prohibition of flag desecration does not "prescribe what shall be orthodox in politics, nationalism, religion, or other matters of opinion or force citizens to confess by word or act their faith therein." *Barnette*. The statute does not compel any conduct or any profession of respect for any idea or any symbol.

Nor does the statute violate "the government's paramount obligation of neutrality in its regulation of protected communication." The content of respondent's message has no relevance whatsoever to the case. The concept of "desecration" does not turn on the substance of the message the actor intends to convey, but rather on whether those who view the act will take serious offense. Accordingly, one intending to convey a message of respect for the flag by burning it in a public square might nonetheless be guilty of desecration if he knows that others—perhaps simply because they misperceive the intended message—will be seriously offended. . . . [This] case has nothing to do with "disagreeable ideas." It involves disagreeable conduct that, in my opinion, diminishes the value of an important national asset.

The Court is therefore quite wrong in blandly asserting that respondent "was prosecuted for his expression of dissatisfaction with the policies of this country, expression situated at the core of our First Amendment values." Respondent was prosecuted because of the method he chose to express his dissatisfaction with those policies. Had he chosen to spray-paint—or perhaps convey with a motion picture projector—his message of dissatisfaction on the facade of the Lincoln Memorial, there would be no question about the power of the Government to prohibit his means of expression. The prohibition would be supported by the legitimate interest in preserving the quality of an important national asset. Though the asset at stake in this case is intangible, given its unique value, the same interest supports a prohibition on the desecration of the American flag.

The Court suggests that a prohibition against flag desecration is not content neutral because this form of symbolic speech is only used by persons who are critical of the flag or the ideas it represents. In making this suggestion the Court does not pause to consider the far-reaching consequences of its introduction of disparate-impact analysis into our First Amendment jurisprudence. It seems obvious that a prohibition against the desecration of a gravesite is content neutral even if it denies some protesters the right to make a symbolic statement by extinguishing the flame in Arlington Cemetery where John F. Kennedy is buried while permitting others to salute the flame by bowing their heads. . . . In such a case, as in a flag burning case, the prohibition against desecration has absolutely nothing to do with the content of the message that the symbolic speech is intended to convey.

———

Note: Flag Burning as Protected Speech

1. *United States v. O'Brien* is a leading precedent on "symbolic speech," and burning a flag appears to be a quintessential example of symbolic speech. But in *Texas v. Johnson* the Court tells us that *O'Brien* does not furnish the governing rule. Why not?

2. If *O'Brien* does not furnish the rule of decision, what does? Can you articulate a major premise that underlies the majority opinion?

3. Chief Justice Rehnquist, in dissent, says that flag burning is "the equivalent of an inarticulate grunt or roar"—conduct that "is most likely to be indulged in not to express any particular idea, but to antagonize others." Does the latter purpose necessarily exclude the former?

———

Problem: A New Flag Protection Act

The Supreme Court's decision in *Texas v. Johnson* aroused great controversy. Within four months, Congress passed the Flag Protection Act of 1989. The Act provides in relevant part:

> (a)(1) Whoever knowingly mutilates, defaces, physically defiles, burns, maintains on the floor or ground, or tramples upon any flag of the United States shall be fined under this title or imprisoned for not more than one year, or both.

(2) This subsection does not prohibit any conduct consisting of the disposal of a flag when it has become worn or soiled.

(b) As used in this section, the term "flag of the United States" means any flag of the United States, or any part thereof, made of any substance, of any size, in a form that is commonly displayed.

Can the statute be distinguished from the Texas statute struck down in *Johnson*? *See United States v. Eichman*, 496 U.S. 310 (1990) (prosecution for violating the Act by knowingly setting fire to several United States flags on the steps of the United States Capitol while protesting various aspects of the government's domestic and foreign policy).

B. "Secondary Effects" as a Basis for Regulation

City of Renton v. Playtime Theatres, Inc.

475 U.S. 41 (1986)

Justice Rehnquist delivered the opinion of the Court.

This case involves a constitutional challenge to a zoning ordinance, enacted by appellant city of Renton, Washington, that prohibits adult motion picture theaters from locating within 1,000 feet of any residential zone, single- or multiple-family dwelling, church, park, or school. . . .

In May 1980, the Mayor of Renton, a city of approximately 32,000 people located just south of Seattle, suggested to the Renton City Council that it consider the advisability of enacting zoning legislation dealing with adult entertainment uses. No such uses existed in the city at that time. Upon the Mayor's suggestion, the City Council referred the matter to the city's Planning and Development Committee. The Committee held public hearings, reviewed the experiences of Seattle and other cities, and received a report from the City Attorney's Office advising as to developments in other cities. . . .

In April 1981, acting on the basis of the Planning and Development Committee's recommendation, the City Council enacted Ordinance No. 3526. The ordinance prohibited any "adult motion picture theater" from locating within 1,000 feet of any residential zone, single- or multiple-family dwelling, church, or park, and within one mile of any school. The term "adult motion picture theater" was defined as "[a]n enclosed building used for presenting motion picture films, video cassettes, cable television, or any other such visual media, distinguished or characteri[zed] by an emphasis on matter depicting, describing or relating to 'specified sexual activities' or 'specified anatomical areas' . . . for observation by patrons therein."

In early 1982, respondents acquired two existing theaters in downtown Renton, with the intention of using them to exhibit feature-length adult films. The theaters were located within the area proscribed by Ordinance No. 3526. At about the same time, respondents filed [a lawsuit challenging the ordinance on First and Fourteenth Amendment grounds]. While the federal action was pending, the City Council amended the ordinance in several respects, adding a statement of reasons for its enactment and reducing the minimum distance from any school to 1,000 feet. . . .

In our view, the resolution of this case is largely dictated by our decision in *Young v. American Mini Theatres, Inc.*, 427 U.S. 50 (1976). There, although five Members of the Court did not agree on a single rationale for the decision, we held that the city of Detroit's zoning ordinance, which prohibited locating an adult theater within 1,000 feet of any two other "regulated uses" or within 500 feet of any residential zone, did not violate the First and Fourteenth Amendments. The Renton ordinance, like the one in *American Mini Theatres*, does not ban adult theaters altogether, but merely provides that such theaters may not be located within 1,000 feet of any residential zone, single- or multiple-family dwelling, church, park, or school. The ordinance is therefore properly analyzed as a form of time, place, and manner regulation.

Describing the ordinance as a time, place, and manner regulation is, of course, only the first step in our inquiry. This Court has long held that regulations enacted for the purpose of restraining speech on the basis of its content presumptively violate the First Amendment. On the other hand, so-called "content-neutral" time, place, and manner regulations are acceptable so long as they are designed to serve a substantial governmental interest and do not unreasonably limit alternative avenues of communication.

At first glance, the Renton ordinance, like the ordinance in *American Mini Theatres*, does not appear to fit neatly into either the "content-based" or the "content-neutral" category. To be sure, the ordinance treats theaters that specialize in adult films differently from other kinds of theaters. Nevertheless, as the District Court concluded, the Renton ordinance is aimed not at the *content* of the films shown at "adult motion picture theatres," but rather at the *secondary effects* of such theaters on the surrounding community. The District Court found that the City Council's "*predominate* concerns" were with the secondary effects of adult theaters, and not with the content of adult films themselves. (Emphasis added). But the Court of Appeals [held] that this was not enough to sustain the ordinance. According to the Court of Appeals, if "*a motivating factor*" in enacting the ordinance was to restrict respondents' exercise of First Amendment rights the ordinance would be invalid, apparently no matter how small a part this motivating factor may have played in the City Council's decision. (Emphasis in original). This view of the law was rejected in *United States v. O'Brien* [*supra* this chapter], the very case that the Court of Appeals said it was applying:

> It is a familiar principle of constitutional law that this Court will not strike down an otherwise constitutional statute on the basis of an alleged illicit legislative motive. . . . What motivates one legislator to make a speech about a statute is not necessarily what motivates scores of others to enact it, and the stakes are sufficiently high for us to eschew guesswork.

The District Court's finding as to "predominate" intent, left undisturbed by the Court of Appeals, is more than adequate to establish that the city's pursuit of its zoning interests here was unrelated to the suppression of free expression. The ordinance by its terms is designed to prevent crime, protect the city's retail trade, maintain property values, and generally "protec[t] and preserv[e] the quality of [the city's] neighborhoods, commercial districts, and the quality of urban life," not to suppress the expression of unpopular views. As Justice Powell observed in *American Mini Theatres*, "[i]f [the city] had been concerned with restricting the message purveyed by adult theaters, it would have tried to close them or restrict their number rather than circumscribe their choice as to location."

In short, the Renton ordinance is completely consistent with our definition of "content-neutral" speech regulations as those that "are *justified* without reference to the content of the regulated speech." *Virginia Pharmacy Board v. Virginia Citizens Consumer Council, Inc.* (1976) [Chapter 3] (emphasis added). The ordinance does not contravene the fundamental principle that underlies our concern about "content-based" speech regulations: that "government may not grant the use of a forum to people whose views it finds acceptable, but deny use to those wishing to express less favored or more controversial views." *Mosley*.

It was with this understanding in mind that, in *American Mini Theatres*, a majority of this Court decided that, at least with respect to businesses that purvey sexually explicit materials, zoning ordinances designed to combat the undesirable secondary effects of such businesses are to be reviewed under the standards applicable to "content-neutral" time, place, and manner regulations. Justice Stevens, writing for the plurality, concluded that the city of Detroit was entitled to draw a distinction between adult theaters and other kinds of theaters "without violating the government's paramount obligation of neutrality in its regulation of protected communication," noting that "[i]t is th[e] secondary effect which these zoning ordinances attempt to avoid, not the dissemination of 'offensive' speech," *id.* at 71 n.34. Justice Powell, in concurrence, elaborated:

> [The] dissent misconceives the issue in this case by insisting that it involves an impermissible time, place, and manner restriction based on the content of expression. It involves nothing of the kind. We have here merely a decision by the city to treat certain movie theaters differently because they have markedly different effects upon their surroundings. . . . Moreover, even if this were a case involving a special governmental response to the content of one type of movie, it is possible that the result would be supported by a line of cases recognizing that the government can tailor its reaction to different types of speech according to the degree to which its special and overriding interests are implicated.

The appropriate inquiry in this case, then, is whether the Renton ordinance is designed to serve a substantial governmental interest and allows for reasonable alternative avenues of communication. It is clear that the ordinance meets such a standard. As a majority of this Court recognized in *American Mini Theatres*, a city's "interest in attempting to preserve the quality of urban life is one that must be accorded high respect." Exactly the same vital governmental interests are at stake here.

The Court of Appeals ruled, however, that because the Renton ordinance was enacted without the benefit of studies specifically relating to "the particular problems or needs of Renton," the city's justifications for the ordinance were "conclusory and speculative." We think the Court of Appeals imposed on the city an unnecessarily rigid burden of proof. The record in this case reveals that Renton relied heavily on the experience of, and studies produced by, the city of Seattle. In Seattle, as in Renton, the adult theater zoning ordinance was aimed at preventing the secondary effects caused by the presence of even one such theater in a given neighborhood. The opinion of the Supreme Court of Washington in *Northend Cinema* [was] before the Renton City Council when it enacted the ordinance in question here.

. . . [In that case the trial court] "heard expert testimony on the adverse effects of the presence of adult motion picture theaters on neighborhood children and community improvement efforts. The court's detailed findings, which include a finding that the location of adult theaters has a harmful effect on the area and contribute to neighborhood blight, are supported by substantial evidence in the record." . . .

We hold that Renton was entitled to rely on the experiences of Seattle and other cities, and in particular on the "detailed findings" summarized in the Washington Supreme Court's *Northend Cinema* opinion, in enacting its adult theater zoning ordinance. The First Amendment does not require a city, before enacting such an ordinance, to conduct new studies or produce evidence independent of that already generated by other cities, so long as whatever evidence the city relies upon is reasonably believed to be relevant to the problem that the city addresses. That was the case here. Nor is our holding affected by the fact that Seattle ultimately chose a different method of adult theater zoning than that chosen by Renton, since Seattle's choice of a different remedy to combat the secondary effects of adult theaters does not call into question either Seattle's identification of those secondary effects or the relevance of Seattle's experience to Renton.

We also find no constitutional defect in the method chosen by Renton to further its substantial interests. Cities may regulate adult theaters by dispersing them, as in Detroit, or by effectively concentrating them, as in Renton. . . . Moreover, the Renton ordinance is "narrowly tailored" to affect only that category of theaters shown to produce the unwanted secondary effects, thus avoiding the flaw that proved fatal to the regulations [in] *Erznoznik v. City of Jacksonville*, 422 U.S. 205 (1975) [Chapter 3 Note].

Respondents contend that the Renton ordinance is "under-inclusive," in that it fails to regulate other kinds of adult businesses that are likely to produce secondary effects similar to those produced by adult theaters. On this record the contention must fail. There is no evidence that, at the time the Renton ordinance was enacted, any other adult business was located in, or was contemplating moving into, Renton. . . . That Renton chose first to address the potential problems created by one particular kind of adult business in no way suggests that the city has "singled out" adult theaters for discriminatory treatment. We simply have no basis on this record for assuming that Renton will not, in the future, amend its ordinance to include other kinds of adult businesses that have been shown to produce the same kinds of secondary effects as adult theaters. *See Williamson v. Lee Optical Co.*, 348 U.S. 483, 488–89 (1955).

Finally, turning to the question whether the Renton ordinance allows for reasonable alternative avenues of communication, we note that the ordinance leaves some 520 acres, or more than five percent of the entire land area of Renton, open to use as adult theater sites. . . . Respondents argue, however, that some of the land in question is already occupied by existing businesses, that "practically none" of the undeveloped land is currently for sale or lease, and that in general there are no "commercially viable" adult theater sites within the 520 acres left open by the Renton ordinance. The Court of Appeals accepted these arguments, concluded that the 520 acres was not truly "available" land, and therefore held that the Renton ordinance "would result in a substantial restriction" on speech.

We disagree with both the reasoning and the conclusion of the Court of Appeals. That respondents must fend for themselves in the real estate market, on an equal footing with other prospective purchasers and lessees, does not give rise to a First Amendment violation. And although we have cautioned against the enactment of zoning regulations that have "the effect of suppressing, or greatly restricting access to, lawful speech," we have never suggested that the First Amendment compels the Government to ensure that adult theaters, or any other kinds of speech-related businesses for that matter, will be able to obtain sites at bargain prices. In our view, the First Amendment requires only that Renton refrain from effectively denying respondents a reasonable opportunity to open and operate an adult theater within the city, and the ordinance before us easily meets this requirement.

. . . The judgment of the Court of Appeals is therefore [reversed].

Justice Blackmun concurs in the result.

Justice Brennan with whom Justice Marshall joins, dissenting.

Renton's zoning ordinance selectively imposes limitations on the location of a movie theater based exclusively on the content of the films shown there. The constitutionality of the ordinance is therefore not correctly analyzed under standards applied to content-neutral time, place, and manner restrictions. But even assuming that the ordinance may fairly be characterized as content neutral, it is plainly unconstitutional under the standards established by the decisions of this Court. Although the Court's analysis is limited to cases involving "businesses that purvey sexually explicit materials," and thus does not affect our holdings in cases involving state regulation of other kinds of speech, I dissent.

. . . The Court asserts that the ordinance is "aimed not at the *content* of the films shown at 'adult motion picture theatres,' but rather at the *secondary effects* of such theaters on the surrounding community" (emphasis in original), and thus is simply a time, place, and manner regulation. This analysis is misguided.

The fact that adult movie theaters may cause harmful "secondary" land-use effects may arguably give Renton a compelling reason to regulate such establishments; it does not mean, however, that such regulations are content neutral. . . . In this case, both the language of the ordinance and its dubious legislative history belie the

Court's conclusion that "the city's pursuit of its zoning interests here was unrelated to the suppression of free expression." . . .

Prior to [an amendment adopted after this lawsuit was commenced], there was no indication that the ordinance was designed to address any "secondary effects" a single adult theater might create. In addition to the suspiciously coincidental timing of the amendment, many of the City Council's "findings" do not relate to legitimate land-use concerns. As the Court of Appeals observed, "[b]oth the magistrate and the district court recognized that many of the stated reasons for the ordinance were no more than expressions of dislike for the subject matter."[3] . . .

Some of the "findings" added by the City Council do relate to supposed "secondary effects" associated with adult movie theaters. However, the Court cannot, as it does, merely accept these post hoc statements at face value. . . . The Court allows Renton to conceal its illicit motives [by] reliance on the fact that other communities adopted similar restrictions. The Court's approach largely immunizes such measures from judicial scrutiny, since a municipality can readily find other municipal ordinances to rely upon, thus always retrospectively justifying special zoning regulations for adult theaters. Rather than speculate about Renton's motives for adopting such measures, our cases require the conclusion that the ordinance, like any other content-based restriction on speech, is constitutional "only if the [city] can show that [it] is a precisely drawn means of serving a compelling [governmental] interest." . . .

Applying this standard to the facts of this case, the ordinance is patently unconstitutional. Renton has not shown that locating adult movie theaters in proximity to its churches, schools, parks, and residences will necessarily result in undesirable "secondary effects," or that these problems could not be effectively addressed by less intrusive restrictions. . . .

––––––––––

Note: Origins of the "Secondary Effects" Doctrine

1. The Court in *Renton* agrees with the district court that the city ordinance was not aimed at the content of the films shown at adult motion picture theaters, but at the *secondary effects* of such theaters on the surrounding community. Therefore, the Court holds, the regulation should be reviewed under the relatively undemanding standard applied to "content-neutral" time, place, and manner regulations.

––––––––––

3. For example, "finding" number 2 states that

[l]ocation of adult entertainment land uses on the main commercial thoroughfares of the City gives an impression of legitimacy to, and causes a loss of sensitivity to the adverse effect of pornography upon children, established family relations, respect for marital relationship and for the sanctity of marriage relations of others, and the concept of non-aggressive, consensual sexual relations.

"Finding" number 6 states that

[l]ocation of adult land uses in close proximity to residential uses, churches, parks, and other public facilities, and schools, will cause a degradation of the community standard of morality. Pornographic material has a degrading effect upon the relationship between spouses.

The Court tells us that the latter point was "decided" in *American Mini Theatres*. But the matter is not quite that simple. The phrase itself was used only in the plurality opinion authored by Justice Stevens. Moreover, the reference was by no means at the heart of the plurality's reasoning. It appears only in a footnote. In text, the plurality said:

> [Few] of us would march our sons and daughters off to war to preserve the citizen's right to see "Specified Sexual Activities" exhibited in the theaters of our choice. Even though the First Amendment protects communication in this area from total suppression, we hold that the State may legitimately use the content of these materials as the basis for placing them in a different classification from other motion pictures.

The plurality thus acknowledged that the Detroit ordinance treated speech differently on the basis of content, but took the position that the particular distinction was acceptable. The footnote quoted in *Renton* addressed the question "whether the line drawn by [the city ordinances was] justified by the city's interest in preserving the character of its neighborhoods." However, Justice Powell's concurring opinion explicitly disavowed "the holding [and] supporting discussion that nonobscene, erotic materials may be treated differently under First Amendment principles from other forms of protected expression."

In this light, it is hardly surprising that *Renton*, not *American Mini Theatres*, is viewed as the foundation case for the "secondary effects" doctrine.

2. In response to the argument that Renton "singled out" adult theaters for discriminatory treatment, the Court cites the 1955 decision in *Williamson v. Lee Optical Co.* That case is widely viewed as signaling the Court's "abdication" of any judicial role in examining the rationality of economic legislation. *See* Robert G. McCloskey, *Economic Due Process and the Supreme Court: An Exhumation and Reburial*, 1962 SUP. CT. REV. 34. Is the Court suggesting that as long as a regulation is *justified* without reference to content, the regulation should be tested by the standards the Court applies to economic regulation under the due process and equal protection clauses? Would that be a sound approach?

Boos v. Barry
485 U.S. 312 (1988)

JUSTICE O'CONNOR delivered the opinion of the Court, except as to Part II-A.

The question presented in this case is whether a provision of the District of Columbia Code, § 22-1115, violates the First Amendment. This section prohibits the display of any sign within 500 feet of a foreign embassy if that sign tends to bring that foreign government into "public odium" or "public disrepute." It also prohibits any congregation of three or more persons within 500 feet of a foreign embassy.

I

Petitioners are three individuals who wish to carry signs critical of the Governments of the Soviet Union and Nicaragua on the public sidewalks within 500 feet of the embassies of those Governments in Washington, D.C. Petitioners Bridget M. Brooker and Michael Boos, for example, wish to display signs stating "RELEASE SAKHAROV" and "SOLIDARITY" in front of the Soviet Embassy. Petitioner J. Michael Waller wishes to display a sign reading "STOP THE KILLING" within 500 feet of the Nicaraguan Embassy. All of the petitioners also wish to congregate with two or more other persons within 500 feet of official foreign buildings.

Asserting that D.C. CODE § 22-1115 (1981) prohibited them from engaging in these expressive activities, [petitioners] brought a facial First Amendment challenge to that provision in the District Court for the District of Columbia. . . .

Congress enacted § 22-1115 in 1938, pursuant to its authority under Article I, § 8, cl. 10, of the Constitution to "define and punish . . . Offenses against the Law of Nations." The first portion of [the] statute, the "display" clause, applies to signs tending to bring a foreign government into public odium or public disrepute, such as signs critical of a foreign government or its policies. The display clause applies only to the display of signs, not to the spoken word. The second portion of the statute, the "congregation" clause, addresses a different concern. It prohibits congregation, which District of Columbia common law defines as an assemblage of three or more people. Both of these prohibitions generally operate within a 500-foot zone surrounding embassies or consulates owned by foreign governments, but the statute also can extend to other buildings if foreign officials are inside for some official purpose.

[The Court of Appeals upheld both clauses.] We . . . reverse the Court of Appeals' conclusion as to the display clause, but affirm as to the congregation clause.

II

A

Analysis of the display clause must begin with several important features of that provision. First, the display clause operates at the core of the First Amendment by prohibiting petitioners from engaging in classically political speech. . . .

Second, the display clause bars such speech on public streets and sidewalks, traditional public fora that "time out of mind, have been used for purposes of assembly, communicating thoughts between citizens, and discussing public questions." *Hague v. CIO* (1939) (Roberts, J.) [Chapter 8]. In such places, which occupy a "special position in terms of First Amendment protection," the government's ability to restrict expressive activity "is very limited."

Third, § 22-1115 is content-based. Whether individuals may picket in front of a foreign embassy depends entirely upon whether their picket signs are critical of the foreign government or not. One category of speech has been completely prohibited within 500 feet of embassies. Other categories of speech, however, such as favorable speech about a foreign government or speech concerning a labor dispute with a foreign government, are permitted. [Nevertheless, both respondents and the United States now contend] that the statute is not content-based because the government is not itself selecting between viewpoints; the permissible message on a picket sign is determined solely by the policies of a foreign government.

We reject this contention, although we agree the provision is not viewpoint-based. The display clause determines which viewpoint is acceptable in a neutral fashion by looking to the policies of foreign governments. While this prevents the display clause from being directly viewpoint-based, a label with potential First Amendment ramifications of its own, it does not render the statute content neutral. Rather, we have held that a regulation that "does not favor either side of a political controversy" is nonetheless impermissible because the "First Amendment's hostility to content-based regulation extends . . . to prohibition of public discussion of an entire topic." *Consolidated Edison Co. v. Public Service Comm'n*, 447 U.S. 530 (1980). Here the government has determined that an entire category of speech — signs or displays critical of foreign governments — is not to be permitted.

We most recently considered the definition of a content-neutral statute in *Renton v. Playtime Theatres, Inc.* [*supra* this chapter]. Drawing on prior decisions, we described "'content-neutral' speech restrictions as those that 'are *justified* without reference to the content of the regulated speech.'" The regulation at issue in *Renton* described prohibited speech by reference to the type of movie theater involved, treating "theaters that specialize in adult films differently from other kinds of theaters." But while the regulation in *Renton* applied only to a particular category of speech, its justification had nothing to do with that speech. The content of the films being shown inside the theaters was irrelevant and was not the target of the regulation. Instead, the ordinance was aimed at the "*secondary effects* of such theaters in the surrounding community" (emphasis in original), effects that are almost unique to theaters featuring sexually explicit films, i.e., prevention of crime, maintenance of property values, and protection of residential neighborhoods. In short, the ordinance in *Renton* did not aim at the suppression of free expression.

Respondents attempt to bring the display clause within *Renton* by arguing that here too the real concern is a secondary effect, namely, our international law obligation to shield diplomats from speech that offends their dignity. We think this misreads *Renton*. We spoke in that decision only of secondary effects of speech, referring to regulations that apply to a particular category of speech because the regulatory targets happen to be associated with that type of speech. So long as the justifications for regulation have nothing to do with content, i.e., the desire to suppress crime has nothing to do with the actual films being shown inside adult movie theaters, we concluded that the regulation was properly analyzed as content neutral.

Regulations that focus on the direct impact of speech on its audience present a different situation. Listeners' reactions to speech are not the type of "secondary effects" we referred to in *Renton*. To take an example factually close to *Renton*, if the ordinance there was justified by the city's desire to prevent the psychological damage it felt was associated with viewing adult movies, then analysis of the measure as a content-based statute would have been appropriate. The hypothetical regulation targets the direct impact of a particular category of speech, not a secondary feature that happens to be associated with that type of speech.

416 · 7 · EXPRESSIVE CONDUCT AND SECONDARY EFFECTS

416   7 · EXPRESSIVE CONDUCT AND SECONDARY EFFECTS

Applying these principles to the case at hand leads readily to the conclusion that the display clause is content-based. The clause is justified only by reference to the content of speech. Respondents and the United States do not point to the "secondary effects" of picket signs in front of embassies. They do not point to congestion, to interference with ingress or egress, to visual clutter, or to the need to protect the security of embassies. Rather, they rely on the need to protect the dignity of foreign diplomatic personnel by shielding them from speech that is critical of their governments. This justification focuses only on the content of the speech and the direct impact that speech has on its listeners. The emotive impact of speech on its audience is not a "secondary effect." Because the display clause regulates speech due to its potential primary impact, we conclude it must be considered content-based.

B

Our cases indicate that as a content-based restriction on political speech in a public forum, § 22-1115 must be subjected to the most exacting scrutiny. Thus, we have required the State to show that the "regulation is necessary to serve a compelling state interest and that it is narrowly drawn to achieve that end."

We first consider whether the display clause serves a compelling governmental interest in protecting the dignity of foreign diplomatic personnel. . . .

. . . Even if we assume that international law recognizes a dignity interest and that it should be considered sufficiently "compelling" to support a content-based restriction on speech, we conclude that § 22-1115 is not narrowly tailored to serve that interest.

[The Court compared § 22-1115 with 18 U.S.C. § 112, which subjects to criminal punishment willful acts or attempts to "intimidate, coerce, threaten, or harass a foreign official or an official guest or obstruct a foreign official in the performance of his duties."] . . . Relying on congressional judgment in this delicate area, we conclude that the availability of alternatives such as § 112 amply demonstrates that the display clause is not crafted with sufficient precision to withstand First Amendment scrutiny.

[Discussion of the congregation clause is omitted.]

JUSTICE KENNEDY took no part in the consideration or decision of this case.

JUSTICE BRENNAN, with whom JUSTICE MARSHALL joins, concurring in part and concurring in the judgment.

I join all but Part II-A of Justice O'Connor's opinion. I also join Part II-A to the extent it concludes that even under the analysis set forth in *Renton v. Playtime Theatres, Inc.*, the display clause constitutes a content-based restriction on speech that merits strict scrutiny. Whatever "secondary effects" means, I agree that it cannot include listeners' reactions to speech. I write separately, however, to register my continued disagreement with the proposition that an otherwise content-based restriction on speech can be recast as "content neutral" if the restriction "aims" at "secondary effects" of the speech, and to object to Justice O'Connor's assumption that the *Renton* analysis applies not only outside the context of businesses purveying sexually explicit materials but even to political speech.

The dangers and difficulties posed by the *Renton* analysis are extensive. Although in this case it is easy enough to determine that the display clause does not aim at a "secondary effect" of speech, future litigants are unlikely to be so bold or so forthright as to defend a restriction on speech with the argument that the restriction aims to protect listeners from the indignity of hearing speech that criticizes them. Rather, they are likely to defend content-based restrictions by pointing, as Justice O'Connor suggests, to secondary effects like "congestion, . . . visual clutter, or . . . security. . . ." But such secondary effects offer countless excuses for content-based suppression of political speech. No doubt a plausible argument could be made that the political gatherings of some parties are more likely than others to attract large crowds causing congestion, that picketing for certain causes is more likely than other picketing to cause visual clutter, or that speakers delivering a particular message are more likely than others to attract an unruly audience. Our traditional analysis rejects such a priori categorical judgments based on the content of speech, *Police Department of Chicago v. Mosley* (1972) [Chapter 5], requiring governments to regulate based on actual congestion, visual clutter, or violence rather than based on predictions that speech with a certain content will induce those effects. . . .

. . . [The *Renton* analysis] plunges courts into the morass of legislative motive, a notoriously hazardous and indeterminate inquiry, particularly where, as under the *Renton* approach, the posited purpose flies in the face of plain statutory language. *See, e.g., O'Brien.* [But the root problem is that the *Renton* analysis] relies on the dubious proposition that a statute which on its face discriminates based on the content of speech aims not at content but at some secondary effect that does not itself affect the operation of the statute. . . . Although an inquiry into motive is sometimes a useful supplement, the best protection against governmental attempts to squelch opposition has never lain in our ability to assess the purity of legislative motive but rather in the requirement that the government act through content-neutral means that restrict expression the government favors as well as expression it disfavors. . . .

Until today, the *Renton* analysis, however unwise, had at least never been applied to political speech. *Renton* itself seemed to confine its application to "businesses that purvey sexually explicit materials." . . . True, today's application of the *Renton* analysis to political speech is dictum. . . . It is nonetheless ominous dictum, for it could set the Court on a road that will lead to the evisceration of First Amendment freedoms. . . .

CHIEF JUSTICE REHNQUIST, with whom JUSTICES WHITE and BLACKMUN join, concurring in part and dissenting in part. [The dissenters argued that § 22-1115 was necessary to serve the "compelling interest at stake."]

City of Los Angeles v. Alameda Books, Inc.
535 U.S. 425 (2002)

JUSTICE O'CONNOR announced the judgment of the Court and delivered an opinion, in which THE CHIEF JUSTICE, JUSTICE SCALIA, and JUSTICE THOMAS join.

Los Angeles Municipal Code § 12.70(C) (1983), as amended, prohibits "the establishment or maintenance of more than one adult entertainment business in the same building, structure or portion thereof." [The Court of Appeals for the Ninth Circuit held the Los Angeles prohibition invalid under *Renton v. Playtime Theatres, Inc.* (1986) (*supra* this chapter), and its precedents interpreting that case.] We reverse and remand. The city of Los Angeles may reasonably rely on a study it conducted some years before enacting the present version of § 12.70(C) to demonstrate that its ban on multiple-use adult establishments serves its interest in reducing crime.

I

In 1977, the city of Los Angeles conducted a comprehensive study of adult establishments and concluded that concentrations of adult businesses are associated with higher rates of prostitution, robbery, assaults, and thefts in surrounding communities. Accordingly, [in 1978] the city enacted an ordinance prohibiting the establishment, substantial enlargement, or transfer of ownership of an adult arcade, bookstore, cabaret, motel, theater, or massage parlor or a place for sexual encounters within 1,000 feet of another such enterprise or within 500 feet of any religious institution, school, or public park. [Later, the city realized that its method of calculating distances created a loophole permitting the concentration of multiple adult enterprises in a single structure.]

Concerned that allowing an adult-oriented department store to replace a strip of adult establishments could defeat the goal of the original ordinance, the city council amended § 12.70(C) by adding a prohibition on "the establishment or maintenance of more than one adult entertainment business in the same building, structure or portion thereof."

[Alameda Books, Inc., operated both as an adult bookstore and an adult arcade in violation of the city's adult zoning regulations. An adult arcade is an operation where, "for any form of consideration," five or fewer patrons together may view films or videocassettes that emphasize the depiction of specified sexual activities. The Court of Appeals for the Ninth Circuit held that the challenged ordinance was invalid under *Renton*.] We granted certiorari to clarify the standard for determining whether an ordinance serves a substantial government interest under *Renton*.

II

The Court of Appeals [held] that, even if the Los Angeles ordinance were content neutral, the city had failed to demonstrate, as required by the third step of the *Renton* analysis, that its prohibition on multiple-use adult establishments was designed to serve its substantial interest in reducing crime. The Court of Appeals noted that the primary evidence relied upon by Los Angeles to demonstrate a link between combination adult businesses and harmful secondary effects was the 1977 study conducted by the city's planning department. . . . The Court of Appeals found that the 1977 study did not reasonably support the inference that a concentration of adult operations within a single adult establishment produced greater levels of criminal activity because the study focused on the effect that a concentration of establishments—not a concentration of operations within a single establishment—had on crime rates.

The Court of Appeals pointed out that the study treated combination adult bookstore/arcades as single establishments and did not study the effect of any separate-standing adult bookstore or arcade.

The Court of Appeals misunderstood the implications of the 1977 study. While the study reveals that areas with high concentrations of adult establishments are associated with high crime rates, areas with high concentrations of adult establishments are also areas with high concentrations of adult operations, albeit each in separate establishments. It was therefore consistent with the findings of the 1977 study, and thus reasonable, for Los Angeles to suppose that a concentration of adult establishments is correlated with high crime rates because a concentration of operations in one locale draws, for example, a greater concentration of adult consumers to the neighborhood, and a high density of such consumers either attracts or generates criminal activity. The assumption behind this theory is that having a number of adult operations in one single adult establishment draws the same dense foot traffic as having a number of distinct adult establishments in close proximity, much as minimalls and department stores similarly attract the crowds of consumers. Under this view, it is rational for the city to infer that reducing the concentration of adult operations in a neighborhood, whether within separate establishments or in one large establishment, will reduce crime rates.

Neither the Court of Appeals, nor respondents, nor the dissent provides any reason to question the city's theory. In particular, they do not offer a competing theory, let alone data, that explains why the elevated crime rates in neighborhoods with a concentration of adult establishments can be attributed entirely to the presence of permanent walls between, and separate entrances to, each individual adult operation. While the city certainly bears the burden of providing evidence that supports a link between concentrations of adult operations and asserted secondary effects, it does not bear the burden of providing evidence that rules out every theory for the link between concentrations of adult establishments that is inconsistent with its own. . . .

In *Renton*, [we held] that a municipality may rely on any evidence that is "reasonably believed to be relevant" for demonstrating a connection between speech and a substantial, independent government interest. This is not to say that a municipality can get away with shoddy data or reasoning. The municipality's evidence must fairly support the municipality's rationale for its ordinance. If plaintiffs fail to cast direct doubt on this rationale, either by demonstrating that the municipality's evidence does not support its rationale or by furnishing evidence that disputes the municipality's factual findings, the municipality meets the standard set forth in *Renton*. [We conclude that the city, at this very early stage of the litigation,] has complied with the evidentiary requirement in *Renton*.

Justice Souter faults the city for relying on the 1977 study not because the study fails to support the city's theory that adult department stores, like adult minimalls, attract customers and thus crime, but because the city does not demonstrate that freestanding single-use adult establishments reduce crime. In effect, Justice Souter asks the city to demonstrate, not merely by appeal to common sense, but also with empirical data, that its ordinance will successfully lower crime. Our cases have never required that municipalities make such a showing, certainly not without actual and convincing evidence from plaintiffs to the contrary. Such a requirement would go too far in undermining our settled position that municipalities must be given a "'reasonable opportunity to experiment with solutions'" to address the secondary effects of protected speech.

. . . *Renton* requires that municipal ordinances receive only intermediate scrutiny if they are content neutral. There is less reason to be concerned that municipalities will use these ordinances to discriminate against unpopular speech.

Justice Souter would have us rethink this balance, and indeed the entire *Renton* framework. In *Renton*, the Court distinguished the inquiry into whether a municipal ordinance is content neutral from the inquiry into whether it is "designed to serve a substantial government interest and do not unreasonably limit alternative avenues of communication." . . . Only at [the second] stage did *Renton* contemplate that courts would examine evidence concerning regulated speech and secondary effects. Justice Souter would either merge these two inquiries or move the evidentiary analysis into the inquiry on content neutrality, and raise the evidentiary bar that a municipality must pass. His logic is that verifying that the ordinance actually reduces the secondary effects asserted would ensure that zoning regulations are not merely content-based regulations in disguise.

We think this proposal unwise. . . . [There] is no evidence suggesting that courts have difficulty determining whether municipal ordinances are motivated primarily by the content of adult speech or by its secondary effects without looking to evidence connecting such speech to the asserted secondary effects. . . . [Also,] Justice Souter does not clarify the sort of evidence upon which municipalities may rely to meet the evidentiary burden he would require. It is easy to say that courts must demand evidence when "common experiences" or "common assumptions" are incorrect, but it is difficult for courts to know ahead of time whether that condition is met. . . .

III

Before concluding, it should be noted that respondents argue, as an alternative basis to sustain the Court of Appeals' judgment, that the Los Angeles ordinance is not a typical zoning regulation. Rather, respondents explain, the prohibition on multiuse adult establishments is effectively a ban on adult video arcades because no such business exists independently of an adult bookstore. Respondents request that the Court hold that the Los Angeles ordinance is not a time, place, and manner regulation, and that the Court subject the ordinance to strict scrutiny. This also appears to be the theme of Justice Kennedy's concurrence. He contends that "[a] city may not assert that it will reduce secondary effects by reducing speech in the same proportion." We consider that unobjectionable proposition as simply a reformulation of the requirement that an ordinance warrants intermediate scrutiny only if it is a time, place, and manner regulation and not a ban. The Court of Appeals held, however, that the city's prohibition on the combination of adult bookstores and arcades is not a ban and respondents did not petition for review of that determination.

Accordingly, we reverse the Court of Appeals' judgment granting summary judgment to respondents and remand the case for further proceedings.

JUSTICE SCALIA, concurring.

I join the plurality opinion because I think it represents a correct application of our jurisprudence concerning regulation of the "secondary effects" of pornographic speech. As I have said elsewhere, however, in a case such as this our First Amendment traditions make "secondary effects" analysis quite unnecessary. The Constitution does not prevent those communities that wish to do so from regulating, or indeed entirely suppressing, the business of pandering sex.

JUSTICE KENNEDY, concurring in the judgment.

Speech can produce tangible consequences. It can change minds. It can prompt actions. These primary effects signify the power and the necessity of free speech. Speech can also cause secondary effects, however, unrelated to the impact of the speech on its audience. A newspaper factory may cause pollution, and a billboard may obstruct a view. These secondary consequences are not always immune from regulation by zoning laws even though they are produced by speech.

Municipal governments know that high concentrations of adult businesses can damage the value and the integrity of a neighborhood. The damage is measurable; it is all too real. The law does not require a city to ignore these consequences if it uses its zoning power in a reasonable way to ameliorate them without suppressing speech. . . .

The question in this case is whether Los Angeles can seek to reduce these tangible, adverse consequences by separating adult speech businesses from one another—even two businesses that have always been under the same roof. In my view our precedents may allow the city to impose its regulation in the exercise of the zoning authority. The city is not, at least, to be foreclosed by summary judgment, so I concur in the judgment.

This separate statement seems to me necessary, however, for two reasons. First, *Renton* described a similar ordinance as "content neutral," and I agree with the dissent that the designation is imprecise. Second, in my view, the plurality's application of *Renton* might constitute a subtle expansion, with which I do not concur.

I

In *Renton*, the Court determined that while the material inside adult bookstores and movie theaters is speech, the consequent sordidness outside is not. The challenge is to correct the latter while leaving the former, as far as possible, untouched. If a city can decrease the crime and blight associated with certain speech by the traditional exercise of its zoning power, and at the same time leave the quantity and accessibility of the speech substantially undiminished, there is no First Amendment objection. This is so even if the measure identifies the problem outside by reference to the speech inside—that is, even if the measure is in that sense content based.

On the other hand, a city may not regulate the secondary effects of speech by suppressing the speech itself. . . . The purpose and effect of a zoning ordinance must be to reduce secondary effects and not to reduce speech.

A zoning measure can be consistent with the First Amendment if it is likely to cause a significant decrease in secondary effects and a trivial decrease in the quantity of speech. It is well documented that multiple adult businesses in close proximity may change the character of a neighborhood for the worse. Those same businesses spread across the city may not have the same deleterious effects. At least in theory, a dispersal ordinance causes these businesses to separate rather than to close, so negative externalities are diminished but speech is not. . . .

The ordinance at issue in this case is not limited to expressive activities. It also extends, for example, to massage parlors, which the city has found to cause similar secondary effects. This ordinance, moreover, is just one part of an elaborate web of land-use regulations in Los Angeles, all of which are intended to promote the social value of the land as a whole without suppressing some activities or favoring others. All this further suggests that the ordinance is more in the nature of a typical land-use restriction and less in the nature of a law suppressing speech.

For these reasons, the ordinance is not so suspect that we must employ the usual rigorous analysis that content-based laws demand in other instances. The ordinance may be a covert attack on speech, but we should not presume it to be so. In the language of our First Amendment doctrine it calls for intermediate and not strict scrutiny, as we held in *Renton*.

II

In *Renton*, . . . the Court designated the restriction "content neutral." The Court appeared to recognize, however, that the designation was something of a fiction, which, perhaps, is why it kept the phrase in quotes. After all, whether a statute is content neutral or content based is something that can be determined on the face of it; if the statute describes speech by content then it is content based. And the ordinance in *Renton* "treated theaters that specialize in adult films differently from other kinds of theaters." The fiction that this sort of ordinance is content neutral—or "content neutral"—is perhaps more confusing than helpful, as Justice Souter demonstrates. . . . These ordinances are content based and we should call them so.

Nevertheless, for the reasons discussed above, the central holding of *Renton* is sound: A zoning restriction that is designed to decrease secondary effects and not speech should be subject to intermediate rather than strict scrutiny. Generally, the government has no power to restrict speech based on content, but there are exceptions to the rule. *See Simon & Schuster* (Kennedy, J., concurring in judgment) [Chapter 5 Note]. And zoning regulations do not automatically raise the specter of impermissible content discrimination, even if they are content based, because they have a prima facie legitimate purpose: to limit the negative externalities of land use. . . . The zoning context provides a built-in legitimate rationale, which rebuts the usual presumption that content-based restrictions are unconstitutional. For this reason, we apply intermediate rather than strict scrutiny.

III

The narrow question presented in this case is whether the ordinance at issue is invalid "because the city did not study the negative effects of such combinations of adult businesses, but rather relied on judicially approved statutory precedent from other jurisdictions." This question is actually two questions. First, what proposition does a city need to advance in order to sustain a secondary-effects ordinance? Second, how much evidence is required to support the proposition? The plurality skips to the second question and gives the correct answer; but in my view more attention must be given to the first.

At the outset, we must identify the claim a city must make in order to justify a content-based zoning ordinance. As discussed above, a city must advance some basis to show that its regulation has the purpose and effect of suppressing secondary effects, while leaving the quantity and accessibility of speech substantially intact. The ordinance may identify the speech based on content, but only as a shorthand for identifying the secondary effects outside. A city may not assert that it will reduce secondary effects by reducing speech in the same proportion. On this point, I agree with Justice Souter. . . .

. . . The plurality's analysis does not address how speech will fare under the city's ordinance. . . . It is no trick to reduce secondary effects by reducing speech or its audience; but a city may not attack secondary effects indirectly by attacking speech.

The analysis requires a few more steps. If two adult businesses are under the same roof, an ordinance requiring them to separate will have one of two results: One business will either move elsewhere or close. The city's premise cannot be the latter. It is true that cutting adult speech in half would probably reduce secondary effects proportionately. But again, a promised proportional reduction does not suffice. Content-based taxes could achieve that, yet these are impermissible.

The premise, therefore, must be that businesses—even those that have always been under one roof—will for the most part disperse rather than shut down. True, this premise has its own conundrum. As Justice Souter writes, "the city . . . claims no interest in the proliferation of adult businesses." The claim, therefore, must be that this ordinance will cause two businesses to split rather than one to close, that the quantity of speech will be substantially undiminished, and that total secondary effects will be significantly reduced. This must be the rationale of a dispersal statute.

Only after identifying the proposition to be proved can we ask the second part of the question presented: is there sufficient evidence to support the proposition? As to this, we have consistently held that a city must have latitude to experiment, at least at the outset, and that very little evidence is required. . . . In this case the proposition to be shown is supported by a single study and common experience. The city's study shows a correlation between the concentration of adult establishments and crime. Two or more adult businesses in close proximity seem to attract a critical mass of unsavory characters and the crime rate may increase as a result. The city, therefore, sought to disperse these businesses. This original ordinance is not challenged here, and we may assume that it is constitutional.

If we assume that the study supports the original ordinance, then most of the necessary analysis follows. We may posit that two adult stores next door to each other attract 100 patrons per day. The two businesses split apart might attract 49 patrons each. (Two patrons, perhaps, will be discouraged by the inconvenience of the separation—a relatively small cost to speech.) On the other hand, the reduction in secondary effects might be dramatic, because secondary effects may require a critical mass. Depending on the economics of vice, 100 potential customers/victims might attract a coterie of thieves, prostitutes, and other ne'er-do-wells; yet 49 might attract none at all. If so, a dispersal ordinance would cause a great reduction in secondary effects at very small cost to speech. Indeed, the very absence of secondary effects might increase the audience for the speech; perhaps for every two people who are discouraged by the inconvenience of two-stop shopping, another two are encouraged by hospitable surroundings. In that case, secondary effects might be eliminated at no cost to speech whatsoever, and both the city and the speaker will have their interests well served.

Only one small step remains to justify the ordinance at issue in this case. The city may next infer—from its study and from its own experience—that two adult businesses under the same roof are no better than two next door. . . . If the city's first ordinance was justified, therefore, then the second is too. Dispersing two adult businesses under one roof is reasonably likely to cause a substantial reduction in secondary effects while reducing speech very little.

IV

These propositions are well established in common experience and in zoning policies that we have already examined, and for these reasons this ordinance is not invalid on its face. If these assumptions can be proved unsound at trial, then the ordinance might not withstand intermediate scrutiny. The ordinance does, however, survive the summary judgment motion that the Court of Appeals ordered granted in this case.

JUSTICE SOUTER, with whom JUSTICE STEVENS and JUSTICE GINSBURG join, and with whom JUSTICE BREYER joins as to Part II, dissenting. . . .

From a policy of dispersing adult establishments, the city [has] moved to a policy of dividing them in two. . . . [The insufficiency of the evidence supporting the breakup policy] bears emphasis and is the principal reason that I respectfully dissent from the Court's judgment today.

I

This ordinance stands or falls on the results of what our cases speak of as intermediate scrutiny, generally contrasted with the demanding standard applied under the First Amendment to a content-based regulation of expression. The variants of middle-tier tests cover a grab-bag of restrictive statutes, with a corresponding variety of justifications. . . . It is worth being clear [on] how close to a content basis adult business zoning can get, and why the application of a middle-tier standard to zoning regulation of adult bookstores calls for particular care. . . .

The comparatively softer intermediate scrutiny is reserved for regulations justified by something other than content of the message, such as a straightforward restriction going only to the time, place, or manner of speech or other expression. . . . [One] middle-tier variety is zoning restriction as a means of responding to the "secondary effects" of adult businesses, principally crime and declining property values in the neighborhood.

Although this type of land-use restriction has even been called a variety of time, place, or manner regulation, equating a secondary-effects zoning regulation with a mere regulation of time, place, or manner jumps over an important difference between them. A restriction on loudspeakers has no obvious relationship to the substance of what is broadcast, while a zoning regulation of businesses in adult expression just as obviously does. And while it may be true that an adult business is burdened only because of its secondary effects, it is clearly burdened only if its expressive products have adult content. Thus, the Court has recognized that this kind of regulation, though called content neutral, occupies a kind of limbo between full-blown, content-based restrictions and regulations that apply without any reference to the substance of what is said.

It would in fact make sense to give this kind of zoning regulation a First Amendment label of its own, and if we called it content correlated, we would not only describe it for what it is, but keep alert to a risk of content-based regulation that it poses. The risk lies in the fact that when a law applies selectively only to speech of particular content, the more precisely the content is identified, the greater is the opportunity for government censorship. Adult speech refers not merely to sexually explicit content, but to speech reflecting a favorable view of being explicit about sex and a favorable view of the practices it depicts; a restriction on adult content is thus also a restriction turning on a particular viewpoint, of which the government may disapprove.

This risk of viewpoint discrimination is subject to a relatively simple safeguard, however. If combating secondary effects of property devaluation and crime is truly the reason for the regulation, it is possible to show by empirical evidence that the effects exist, that they are caused by the expressive activity subject to the zoning, and that the zoning can be expected either to ameliorate them or to enhance the capacity of the government to combat them (say, by concentrating them in one area), without suppressing the expressive activity itself. This capacity of zoning regulation to address the practical problems without eliminating the speech is, after all, the only possible excuse for speaking of secondary-effects zoning as akin to time, place, or manner regulations.

In examining claims that there are causal relationships between adult businesses and an increase in secondary effects (distinct from disagreement), and between zoning and the mitigation of the effects, stress needs to be placed on the empirical character of the demonstration available. The weaker the demonstration of facts distinct from disapproval of the "adult" viewpoint, the greater the likelihood that nothing more than condemnation of the viewpoint drives the regulation.

Equal stress should be placed on the point that requiring empirical justification of claims about property value or crime is not demanding anything Herculean. Increased crime, like prostitution and muggings, and declining property values in areas surrounding adult businesses, are all readily observable, often to the untrained eye and certainly to the police officer and urban planner. These harms can be shown by police reports, crime statistics, and studies of market value, all of which are within a municipality's capacity or available from the distilled experiences of comparable communities. . . .

The lesson is that the lesser scrutiny applied to content-correlated zoning restrictions is no excuse for a government's failure to provide a factual demonstration for claims it makes about secondary effects; on the contrary, this is what demands the demonstration. In this case, however, the government has not shown that bookstores containing viewing booths, isolated from other adult establishments, increase crime or produce other negative secondary effects in surrounding neighborhoods, and we are thus left without substantial justification for viewing the city's First Amendment restriction as content correlated but not simply content based. By the same token, the city has failed to show any causal relationship between the breakup policy and elimination or regulation of secondary effects.

II

. . . [The city] apparently assumes that a bookstore selling videos and providing viewing booths produces secondary effects of crime, and more crime than would result from having a single store without booths in one part of town and a video arcade in another. But the city neither says this in so many words nor proffers any evidence to support even the simple proposition that an otherwise lawfully located adult bookstore combined with video booths will produce any criminal effects. The Los Angeles study treats such combined stores as one, and draws no general conclusion that individual stores spread apart from other adult establishments (as under the basic Los Angeles ordinance) are associated with any degree of criminal activity above the general norm; nor has the city called the Court's attention to any other empirical study, or even anecdotal police evidence, that supports the city's assumption. In fact, if the Los Angeles study sheds any light whatever on the city's position, it is the light of skepticism, for we may fairly suspect that the study said nothing about the secondary effects of freestanding stores because no effects were observed. The reasonable supposition, then, is that splitting some of them up will have no consequence for secondary effects whatever.

The inescapable point is that the city does not even claim that the 1977 study provides any support for its assumption. . . . And even if splitting viewing booths from the bookstores that continue to sell videos were to turn some customers away (or send them in search of video arcades in other neighborhoods), it is nothing but speculation to think that marginally lower traffic to one store would have any measurable effect on the neighborhood, let alone an effect on associated crime that has never been shown to exist in the first place. . . .

. . . Whereas *Young v. American Mini Theatres* (1976) [Note *supra* this chapter] and *Renton* gave cities the choice between two strategies when each was causally related to the city's interest, the plurality today gives Los Angeles a right to "experiment" with a First Amendment restriction in response to a problem of increased crime that the city has never even shown to be associated with combined bookstore-arcades standing alone. But the government's freedom of experimentation cannot displace its burden under the intermediate scrutiny standard to show that the restriction on speech is no greater than essential to realizing an important objective, in this case policing crime. Since we cannot make even a best guess that the city's breakup policy will have any effect on crime or law enforcement, we are a very far cry from any assurance against covert content-based regulation.

And concern with content-based regulation targeting a viewpoint is right to the point here, as witness a fact that involves no guesswork. If we take the city's breakup policy at its face, enforcing it will mean that in every case two establishments will operate instead of the traditional one. Since the city presumably does not wish merely to multiply adult establishments, it makes sense to ask what offsetting gain the city may obtain from its new breakup policy. The answer may lie in the fact that two establishments in place of one will entail two business overheads in place of one: two monthly rents, two electricity bills, two payrolls. Every month business will be more expensive than it used to be, perhaps even twice as much. That sounds like a good strategy for driving out expressive adult businesses. It sounds, in other words, like a policy of content-based regulation.

I respectfully dissent.

———

Note: Continuing Controversy over "Secondary Effects"

1. Although then-Justice Rehnquist was able to muster a solid majority for his opinion in *City of Renton*, Justice O'Connor gains only a plurality for her application of the "secondary effects" doctrine in *Alameda Books*. What aspects of the doctrine continue to have majority support?

2. Justice Kennedy stakes out his own position, and in the course of doing so, he provides a comprehensive exposition of the doctrine and its rationale. He concedes that ordinances like those of Renton and Los Angeles "are content based," but he agrees with the plurality that intermediate rather than strict scrutiny is appropriate. Is he persuasive on this point?

3. Justice Souter suggests a new label for "this kind of zoning regulation": *content-correlated.* Is the new terminology helpful? How does Justice Souter's version of "intermediate scrutiny" differ from that of the plurality?

4. Justice Souter calls attention to the "variants of middle-tier tests," and he identifies three. One is the *Ward* standard for regulation of "time, place, and manner." A second is *O'Brien.* The third is the "secondary effects" test. Justice Souter adds (in a footnote):

Because *Renton* called its secondary-effects ordinance a mere time, place, or manner restriction and thereby glossed over the role of content in secondary-effects zoning, I believe the soft focus of its statement of the middle-tier test should be rejected in favor of [the *O'Brien* formulation]. *O'Brien* is a closer relative of secondary-effects zoning than mere time, place, or manner regulations.

What makes *Renton*'s statement of the middle-tier test "softer" than the *O'Brien* formulation? Are there really three different middle-tier tests?

5. In his separate opinion in *Boos v. Barry* (*supra* this chapter), Justice Brennan objected to the "secondary effects" analysis on the grounds that it "plunges courts into the morass of legislative motive." Whatever the merits of this objection, Justice Brennan appears to be correct that the "secondary effects" doctrine does require an inquiry into legislative motive. The Court's most recent "secondary effects" case, *Alameda Books*, was decided in 2002. Since then, however, in *Reed v. Town of Gilbert* (2015) (Chapter 5), the Court has held that a law is content-based, and subject to strict scrutiny, *either* if it is facially content-based or if is motivated by hostility to the content of speech. The *Reed* Court made clear that a facially content-based law is subject to strict scrutiny regardless of benign legislative motive. After *Reed*, is there any principled way in which the Court can adhere to the secondary effects doctrine? Put differently, is there a difference between a facially content-based regulation adopted without apparent censorial motives (which *Reed* condemns) and a facially content-based regulation directed at tangible, real-world harms associated with the regulated speech (which the "secondary effects" doctrine appears to permit)?

Problem: Limiting the Hours of Adult Businesses

The legislature of the State of New Harmony has passed a law that requires all sexually oriented businesses to close "between the hours of 1:00 a.m. and 8:00 a.m. on Monday through Saturday and between the hours of 1:00 a.m. and 12:00 noon on Sunday." A sexually oriented business is an "adult arcade, adult bookstore or video store, adult cabaret, adult motion picture theater, adult theater, escort agency or nude model studio. . . ."

Owners and operator of sexually oriented businesses in New Harmony have brought suit in federal court alleging that the law violates the First Amendment. The plaintiffs include nude-dancer clubs, X-rated video arcades and sellers of sexually related magazines and paraphernalia. They seek a preliminary injunction against enforcement of the law.

The parties have stipulated that sexually oriented businesses draw a substantial amount of their patronage in the evening and late night hours. Several of the businesses who are plaintiffs in this litigation were open 24 hours a day prior to the enactment of the law.

The parties have also stipulated to the materials that were in the legislative record at the time the law was enacted. This record consisted of testimonial evidence from several individuals, as well as some limited documentary evidence with respect to the need for restricting sexually oriented businesses' hours of operation. The following is representative of the material in the record:

(a) Two individuals who worked for mixed-use real estate parks located in the largest city of New Harmony testified that nearby sexually oriented businesses were disruptive of their attempts to attract new employers to the parks, and that prospective employers expressed concern for their employees who worked night-shifts.

(b) The executive director of a civic organization in the largest city of New Harmony testified that approximately 15 studies had been conducted concerning the negative secondary effects associated with sexually oriented businesses. Those studies documented increased crime, prostitution, public sexual indecency and health risks associated with HIV and AIDS transmission.

(c) Supporters of the legislation submitted a letter discussing the acute problems associated with sexually oriented businesses as documented in a report from the Denver (Colorado) Metropolitan Police Department, which concluded that sexually oriented businesses "disproportionately deplete police time and resources during the overnight hours." The report itself was not presented to the New Harmony legislature.

In support of their request for a preliminary injunction, the plaintiffs rely heavily on Justice Kennedy's concurring opinion in *Alameda Books*. They remind the court of the established rule for Supreme Court cases decided by plurality opinion: "When a fragmented Court decides a case and no single rationale explaining the result enjoys the assent of five Justices, the holding of the Court may be viewed as that position taken by those Members who concurred in the judgment on the narrowest grounds." (The quotation is from *Marks v. United States*, 430 U.S. 188 (1976).)

Should the district court grant the preliminary injunction?

C. Expression and Conduct: Untangling the Doctrines

In *United States v. O'Brien*, the Court said that when "speech" and "nonspeech" elements are combined in the same course of conduct, a sufficiently important governmental interest in regulating the "nonspeech" element can justify "*incidental*" limitations on expression. In *City of Renton* and its progeny, the Court holds that a regulation applicable only to a particular category of speech is properly analyzed as content-neutral if the regulation is aimed at the "*secondary effects*" of the speech — i.e., targets that "happen to be associated with that type of speech."

What is the relationship between *O'Brien* and the "secondary effects" doctrine? Are they alternative modes of analysis for a particular class of cases? Or do they apply in different situations? The Justices debated those questions in *City of Erie v. Pap's A.M.*, but without a majority opinion.

City of Erie v. Pap's A.M.
529 U.S. 277 (2000)

Justice O'Connor announced the judgment of the Court and delivered the opinion of the Court with respect to Parts I and II, and an opinion with respect to Parts III and IV, in which The Chief Justice, Justice Kennedy, and Justice Breyer join.

[The city council for the city of Erie, Pennsylvania, enacted Ordinance 75-1994, a public indecency ordinance that makes it a summary offense to knowingly or intentionally appear in public in a "state of nudity." Respondent Pap's A.M. (hereinafter Pap's) operated an establishment in Erie known as "Kandyland" that featured totally nude erotic dancing performed by women. To comply with the ordinance, these dancers must wear, at a minimum, "pasties" and a "G-string." Pap's filed a complaint seeking declaratory relief and a permanent injunction against the enforcement of the ordinance.]

The Pennsylvania Supreme Court, although noting that this Court in *Barnes v. Glen Theatre, Inc.*, 501 U.S. 560 (1991), had upheld an Indiana ordinance that was "strikingly similar" to Erie's, found that the public nudity sections of the ordinance violated respondent's right to freedom of expression under the United States Constitution. . . . We hold that Erie's ordinance is a content-neutral regulation that satisfies the four-part test of *United States v. O'Brien* (1968) [*supra* this chapter]. Accordingly, we reverse the decision of the Pennsylvania Supreme Court and remand for the consideration of any remaining issues.

III

Being "in a state of nudity" is not an inherently expressive condition. As we explained in *Barnes*, however, nude dancing of the type at issue here is expressive conduct, although we think that it falls only within the outer ambit of the First Amendment's protection.

To determine what level of scrutiny applies to the ordinance at issue here, we must decide "whether the State's regulation is related to the suppression of expression." *Texas v. Johnson* [*supra* this chapter]; *see also O'Brien*. If the governmental purpose in enacting the regulation is unrelated to the suppression of expression, then the regulation need only satisfy the "less stringent" standard from *O'Brien* for evaluating restrictions on symbolic speech. If the government interest is related to the content of the expression, however, then the regulation falls outside the scope of the *O'Brien* test and must be justified under a more demanding standard.

In *Barnes*, we analyzed an almost identical statute, holding that Indiana's public nudity ban did not violate the First Amendment, although no five Members of the Court agreed on a single rationale for that conclusion. We now clarify that government restrictions on public nudity such as the ordinance at issue here should be evaluated under the framework set forth in *O'Brien* for content-neutral restrictions on symbolic speech.

The city of Erie argues that the ordinance is a content-neutral restriction that is reviewable under *O'Brien* because the ordinance bans conduct, not speech; specifically, public nudity. Respondent counters that the ordinance targets nude dancing and, as such, is aimed specifically at suppressing expression, making the ordinance a content-based restriction that must be subjected to strict scrutiny.

The ordinance here, like the statute in *Barnes*, is on its face a general prohibition on public nudity. By its terms, the ordinance regulates conduct alone. It does not target nudity that contains an erotic message; rather, it bans all public nudity, regardless of whether that nudity is accompanied by expressive activity. And like the statute in *Barnes*, the Erie ordinance replaces and updates provisions of an "Indecency and Immorality" ordinance that has been on the books since 1866, predating the prevalence of nude dancing establishments such as Kandyland.

Respondent and Justice Stevens contend nonetheless that the ordinance is related to the suppression of expression because language in the ordinance's preamble suggests that its actual purpose is to prohibit erotic dancing of the type performed at Kandyland. . . . In the preamble to the ordinance, the city council stated that it was adopting the regulation

> for the purpose of limiting a recent increase in nude live entertainment within the City, which activity adversely impacts and threatens to impact on the public health, safety and welfare by providing an atmosphere conducive to violence, sexual harassment, public intoxication, prostitution, the spread of sexually transmitted diseases and other deleterious effects. . . .

As Justice Souter noted in *Barnes*, "on its face, the governmental interest in combating prostitution and other criminal activity is not at all inherently related to expression." In that sense, this case is similar to *O'Brien*. [In *O'Brien*], the Government regulation prohibiting the destruction of draft cards was aimed at maintaining the integrity of the Selective Service System and not at suppressing the message of draft resistance that O'Brien sought to convey by burning his draft card. So too here, the ordinance prohibiting public nudity is aimed at combating crime and other negative secondary effects caused by the presence of adult entertainment establishments like Kandyland and not at suppressing the erotic message conveyed by this type of nude dancing. . . .

Although the Pennsylvania Supreme Court acknowledged that one goal of the ordinance was to combat the negative secondary effects associated with nude dancing establishments, the court concluded that the ordinance was nevertheless content based, relying on Justice White's position in dissent in *Barnes* for the proposition that a ban of this type *necessarily* has the purpose of suppressing the erotic message of the dance. . . . That is, the Pennsylvania court adopted the dissent's view in *Barnes* that "since the State permits the dancers to perform if they wear pasties and G-strings but forbids nude dancing, it is precisely because of the distinctive, expressive content of the nude dancing performances at issue in this case that the State seeks to apply the statutory prohibition." A majority of the Court rejected that view in *Barnes*, and we do so again here.

Respondent's argument that the ordinance is "aimed" at suppressing expression through a ban on nude dancing—an argument that respondent supports by pointing to statements by the city attorney that the public nudity ban was not intended to apply to "legitimate" theater productions—is really an argument that the city council also had an illicit motive in enacting the ordinance. As we have said before, however, this Court will not strike down an otherwise constitutional statute on the basis of an alleged illicit motive....

Justice Stevens argues that the ordinance enacts a complete ban on expression. We respectfully disagree with that characterization. The public nudity ban certainly has the effect of limiting one particular means of expressing the kind of erotic message being disseminated at Kandyland. But simply to define what is being banned as the "message" is to assume the conclusion. We did not analyze the regulation in *O'Brien* as having enacted a total ban on expression. Instead, the Court recognized that the regulation against destroying one's draft card was justified by the Government's interest in preventing the harmful "secondary effects" of that conduct (disruption to the Selective Service System), even though that regulation may have some incidental effect on the expressive element of the conduct. Because this justification was unrelated to the suppression of O'Brien's antiwar message, the regulation was content neutral. Although there may be cases in which banning the means of expression so interferes with the message that it essentially bans the message, that is not the case here.

Even if we had not already rejected the view that a ban on public nudity is necessarily related to the suppression of the erotic message of nude dancing, we would do so now because the premise of such a view is flawed. The State's interest in preventing harmful secondary effects is not related to the suppression of expression. In trying to control the secondary effects of nude dancing, the ordinance seeks to deter crime and the other deleterious effects caused by the presence of such an establishment in the neighborhood. *See Renton*....

Similarly, even if Erie's public nudity ban has some minimal effect on the erotic message by muting that portion of the expression that occurs when the last stitch is dropped, the dancers at Kandyland and other such establishments are free to perform wearing pasties and G-strings. Any effect on the overall expression is *de minimis*.... If States are to be able to regulate secondary effects, then *de minimis* intrusions on expression such as those at issue here cannot be sufficient to render the ordinance content based....

This case is, in fact, similar to *O'Brien* [and] *Ward v. Rock Against Racism* (1989) [Chapter 6]. The justification for the government regulation in each case prevents harmful "secondary" effects that are unrelated to the suppression of expression. *See, e.g., Ward* (noting that "the principal justification for the sound-amplification guideline is the city's desire to control noise levels at bandshell events, in order to retain the character of [the adjacent] Sheep Meadow and its more sedate activities," and citing *City of Renton v. Playtime Theatres, Inc.* (1986) [*supra* this chapter] for the proposition that "[a] regulation that serves purposes unrelated to the content of expression is deemed neutral, even if it has an incidental effect on some speakers or messages but not others"). While the doctrinal theories behind "incidental burdens" and "secondary effects" are, of course, not identical, there is nothing objectionable about a city passing a general ordinance to ban public nudity (even though such a ban may place incidental burdens on some protected speech) and at the same time recognizing that one specific occurrence of public nudity—nude erotic dancing—is particularly problematic because it produces harmful secondary effects.

Justice Stevens claims that today we "for the first time" extend *Renton*'s secondary effects doctrine to justify restrictions other than the location of a commercial enterprise. Our reliance on *Renton* to justify other restrictions is not new, however. In *Ward*, the Court relied on *Renton* to evaluate restrictions on sound amplification at an outdoor bandshell, rejecting the dissent's contention that *Renton* was inapplicable. . . . Moreover, Erie's ordinance does not effect a "total ban" on protected expression.

. . . Here, Erie's ordinance is on its face a content-neutral restriction on conduct. Even if the city thought that nude dancing at clubs like Kandyland constituted a particularly problematic instance of public nudity, the regulation is still properly evaluated as a content-neutral restriction because the interest in combating the secondary effects associated with those clubs is unrelated to the suppression of the erotic message conveyed by nude dancing. . . . The ordinance [is] therefore valid if it satisfies the four-factor test from *O'Brien* for evaluating restrictions on symbolic speech.

IV

Applying that standard here, we conclude that Erie's ordinance is justified under *O'Brien*. The first factor of the *O'Brien* test is whether the government regulation is within the constitutional power of the government to enact. Here, Erie's efforts to protect public health and safety are clearly within the city's police powers. The second factor is whether the regulation furthers an important or substantial government interest. The asserted interests of regulating conduct through a public nudity ban and of combating the harmful secondary effects associated with nude dancing are undeniably important. And in terms of demonstrating that such secondary effects pose a threat, the city need not "conduct new studies or produce evidence independent of that already generated by other cities" to demonstrate the problem of secondary effects, "so long as whatever evidence the city relies upon is reasonably believed to be relevant to the problem that the city addresses." Because the nude dancing at Kandyland is of the same character as the adult entertainment at issue in *Renton* [and prior cases], it was reasonable for Erie to conclude that such nude dancing was likely to produce the same secondary effects. . . . In fact, Erie expressly relied on *Barnes* and its discussion of secondary effects, including its reference to *Renton* and *American Mini Theatres*. . . . Regardless of whether Justice Souter now wishes to disavow his opinion in *Barnes* on this point, the evidentiary standard described in *Renton* controls here, and Erie meets that standard.

In any event, Erie also relied on its own findings. The preamble to the ordinance states that "the Council of the City of Erie *has, at various times over more than a century, expressed its findings* that certain lewd, immoral activities carried on in public places for profit are highly detrimental to the public health, safety and welfare, and lead to the debasement of both women and men, promote violence, public intoxication, prostitution and other serious criminal activity." The city council members, familiar with commercial downtown Erie, are the individuals who would likely have had first-hand knowledge of what took place at and around nude dancing establishments in Erie, and can make particularized, expert judgments about the resulting harmful secondary effects. . . . Here, Kandyland has had ample opportunity to contest the council's findings about secondary effects — before the council itself, throughout the state proceedings, and before this Court. Yet to this day, Kandyland has never challenged the city council's findings or cast any specific doubt on the validity of those findings. Instead, it has simply asserted that the council's evidentiary proof was lacking. . . .

Finally, it is worth repeating that Erie's ordinance is on its face a content neutral restriction that regulates conduct, not First Amendment expression. And the government should have sufficient leeway to justify such a law based on secondary effects. On this point, *O'Brien* is especially instructive. . . . There was no study documenting instances of draft card mutilation or the actual effect of such mutilation on the Government's asserted efficiency interests. But the Court permitted Congress to take official notice, as it were, that draft card destruction would jeopardize the system. . . .

Justice Souter, however, would require Erie to develop a specific evidentiary record supporting its ordinance. . . . Justice Souter conflates two distinct concepts under *O'Brien*: whether there is a substantial government interest and whether the regulation furthers that interest. As to the government interest, i.e., whether the threatened harm is real, the city council relied on this Court's opinions detailing the harmful secondary effects caused by establishments like Kandyland, as well as on its own experiences in Erie. . . .

As to the second point — whether the regulation furthers the government interest — it is evident that, since crime and other public health and safety problems are caused by the presence of nude dancing establishments like Kandyland, a ban on such nude dancing would further Erie's interest in preventing such secondary effects. To be sure, requiring dancers to wear pasties and G-strings may not greatly reduce these secondary effects, but *O'Brien* requires only that the regulation further the interest in combating such effects. . . . It also may be true that a pasties and G-string requirement would not be as effective as, for example, a requirement that the dancers be fully clothed, but the city must balance its efforts to address the problem with the requirement that the restriction be no greater than necessary to further the city's interest.

The ordinance also satisfies *O'Brien*'s third factor, that the government interest is unrelated to the suppression of free expression, as discussed *supra*. The fourth and final *O'Brien* factor — that the restriction is no greater than is essential to the furtherance of the government interest — is satisfied as well. The ordinance regulates conduct, and any incidental impact on the expressive element of nude dancing is *de minimis*. The requirement that dancers wear pasties and G-strings is a minimal restriction in furtherance of the asserted government interests, and the restriction leaves ample capacity to convey the dancer's erotic message. Justice Souter points out that zoning is an alternative means of addressing this problem. It is far from clear, however, that zoning imposes less of a burden on expression than the minimal requirement implemented here. In any event, since this is a content-neutral restriction, least restrictive means analysis is not required. *See Ward.*

We hold, therefore, that Erie's ordinance is a content-neutral regulation that is valid under *O'Brien*. Accordingly, the judgment of the Pennsylvania Supreme Court is reversed, and the case is remanded for further proceedings not inconsistent with this opinion.

Justice Scalia, with whom Justice Thomas joins, concurring in the judgment.

. . . I agree that the decision of the Pennsylvania Supreme Court must be reversed, but disagree with the mode of analysis the Court has applied.

The city of Erie self-consciously modeled its ordinance on the public nudity statute we upheld against constitutional challenge in *Barnes*, calculating (one would have supposed reasonably) that the courts of Pennsylvania would consider themselves bound by our judgment on a question of federal constitutional law. In *Barnes*, I voted to uphold the challenged Indiana statute "not because it survives some lower level of First Amendment scrutiny, but because, as a general law regulating conduct and not specifically directed at expression, it is not subject to First Amendment scrutiny at all." Erie's ordinance, too, by its terms prohibits not merely nude dancing, but the act — irrespective of whether it is engaged in for expressive purposes — of going nude in public. The facts that a preamble to the ordinance explains that its purpose, in part, is to "limit a recent increase in nude live entertainment," that city councilmembers in supporting the ordinance commented to that effect, and that the ordinance includes in the definition of nudity the exposure of devices simulating that condition, neither make the law any less general in its reach nor demonstrate that what the municipal authorities *really* find objectionable is expression rather than public nakedness. As far as appears (and as seems overwhelmingly likely), the preamble, the councilmembers' comments, and the chosen definition of the prohibited conduct simply reflect the fact that Erie had recently been having a public nudity problem not with streakers, sunbathers or hot-dog vendors, but with lap dancers.

There is no basis for the contention that the ordinance does not apply to nudity in theatrical productions such as Equus or Hair. Its text contains no such limitation. It was stipulated in the trial court that no effort was made to enforce the ordinance against a production of Equus involving nudity that was being staged in Erie at the time the ordinance became effective. . . . [But one] instance of nonenforcement — against a play already in production that prosecutorial discretion might reasonably have "grandfathered" — does not render this ordinance discriminatory on its face. . . .

Moreover, even were I to conclude that the city of Erie had specifically singled out the activity of nude dancing, I still would not find that this regulation violated the First Amendment unless I could be persuaded (as on this record I cannot) that it was the communicative character of nude dancing that prompted the ban. When conduct other than speech itself is regulated, it is my view that the First Amendment is violated only "where the government prohibits conduct precisely because of its communicative attributes." Here, even if one hypothesizes that the city's object was to suppress only nude dancing, that would not establish an intent to suppress what (if anything) nude dancing communicates. I do not feel the need, as the Court does, to identify some "secondary effects" associated with nude dancing that the city could properly seek to eliminate. (I am highly skeptical, to tell the truth, that the addition of pasties and g-strings will at all reduce the tendency of establishments such as Kandyland to attract crime and prostitution, and hence to foster sexually transmitted disease.) The traditional power of government to foster good morals (*bonos mores*), and the acceptability of the traditional judgment (if Erie wishes to endorse it) that nude public dancing *itself* is immoral, have not been repealed by the First Amendment.

Justice Souter, concurring in part and dissenting in part.

[I agree] with the analytical approach that the plurality employs in deciding this case. Erie's stated interest in combating the secondary effects associated with nude dancing establishments is an interest unrelated to the suppression of expression under *O'Brien*, and the city's regulation is thus properly considered under the *O'Brien* standards. I do not believe, however, that the current record allows us to say that the city has made a sufficient evidentiary showing to sustain its regulation, and I would therefore [remand] the case for further proceedings. . . .

[Intermediate] scrutiny requires a regulating government to make some demonstration of an evidentiary basis for the harm it claims to flow from the expressive activity, and for the alleviation expected from the restriction imposed. That evidentiary basis may be borrowed from the records made by other governments if the experience elsewhere is germane to the measure under consideration and actually relied upon. . . .

By these standards, the record before us today is deficient in its failure to reveal any evidence on which Erie may have relied, either for the seriousness of the threatened harm or for the efficacy of its chosen remedy. The plurality does the best it can with the materials to hand, but the pickings are slim. . . . [T]he city council's closest approach to an evidentiary record on secondary effects and their causes was the statement of one councilor, during the debate over the ordinance, who spoke of increases in sex crimes in a way that might be construed as a reference to secondary effects. But that reference came at the end of a litany of concerns ("free condoms in schools, drive-by shootings, abortions, suicide machines" and declining student achievement test scores) that do not seem to be secondary effects of nude dancing. Nor does the invocation of *Barnes v. Glen Theatre, Inc.*, in one paragraph of the preamble to Erie's ordinance suffice. The plurality opinion in *Barnes* made no mention of evidentiary showings at all. . . .

There is one point, however, on which an evidentiary record is not quite so hard to find, but it hurts, not helps, the city. The final *O'Brien* requirement is that the incidental speech restriction be shown to be no greater than essential to achieve the government's legitimate purpose. To deal with this issue, we have to ask what basis there is to think that the city would be unsuccessful in countering any secondary effects by the significantly lesser restriction of zoning to control the location of nude dancing, thus allowing for efficient law enforcement, restricting effects on property values, and limiting exposure of the public. The record shows that for 23 years there has been a zoning ordinance on the books to regulate the location of establishments like Kandyland, but the city has not enforced it. . . . Even on the plurality's view of the evidentiary burden, this hurdle to the application of *O'Brien* requires an evidentiary response. . . .

Careful readers, and not just those on the Erie City Council, will of course realize that my partial dissent rests on a demand for an evidentiary basis that I failed to make when I concurred in *Barnes*. I should have demanded the evidence then, too, and my mistake calls to mind Justice Jackson's foolproof explanation of a lapse of his own, when he quoted Samuel Johnson, "'Ignorance, sir, ignorance.'" *McGrath v. Kristensen*, 340 U.S. 162, 178 (1950) (concurring opinion). I may not be less ignorant of nude dancing than I was nine years ago, but after many subsequent occasions to think further about the needs of the First Amendment, I have come to believe that a government must toe the mark more carefully than I first insisted. I hope it is enlightenment on my part, and acceptable even if a little late.

JUSTICE STEVENS, with whom JUSTICE GINSBURG joins, dissenting.

Far more important than the question whether nude dancing is entitled to the protection of the First Amendment are the dramatic changes in legal doctrine that the Court endorses today. Until now, the "secondary effects" of commercial enterprises featuring indecent entertainment have justified only the regulation of their location. For the first time, the Court has now held that such effects may justify the total suppression of protected speech. Indeed, the plurality opinion concludes that admittedly trivial advancements of a State's interests may provide the basis for censorship. The Court's commendable attempt to replace the fractured decision in *Barnes v. Glen Theatre, Inc.*, with a single coherent rationale is strikingly unsuccessful; it is supported neither by precedent nor by persuasive reasoning.

I

. . . [Nude dancing] receives First Amendment protection, even if that protection lies only in the "outer ambit" of that Amendment. Erie's ordinance, therefore, burdens a message protected by the First Amendment. If one assumes that the same erotic message is conveyed by nude dancers as by those wearing miniscule costumes, one means of expressing that message is banned; if one assumes that the messages are different, one of those messages is banned. In either event, the ordinance is a total ban.

The Court relies on the so-called "secondary effects" test to defend the ordinance. The present use of that rationale, however, finds no support whatsoever in our precedents. Never before have we approved the use of that doctrine to justify a total ban on protected First Amendment expression. On the contrary, we have been quite clear that the doctrine would not support that end. . . .

. . . [In] both *Renton* and *Young v. American Mini Theatres* (1976) [Note *supra* this chapter], the zoning ordinances were analyzed as mere "time, place, and manner" regulations. Because time, place, and manner regulations must "leave open ample alternative channels for communication of information," a total ban would necessarily fail that test. . . .

The reason we have limited our secondary effects cases to zoning and declined to extend their reasoning to total bans is clear and straightforward: A dispersal that simply limits the places where speech may occur is a minimal imposition whereas a total ban is the most exacting of restrictions. The State's interest in fighting presumed secondary effects is sufficiently strong to justify the former, but far too weak to support the latter, more severe burden. Yet it is perfectly clear that in the present case—to use Justice Powell's metaphor in *American Mini Theatres*—the city of Erie has totally silenced a message the dancers at Kandyland want to convey. . . .

The Court's use of the secondary effects rationale to permit a total ban has grave implications for basic free speech principles. Ordinarily, laws regulating the primary effects of speech, i.e., the intended persuasive effects caused by the speech, are presumptively invalid. Under today's opinion, a State may totally ban speech based on its secondary effects—which are defined as those effects that "happen to be associated" with speech, *Boos v. Barry* (1988) [*supra* this chapter]—yet the regulation is not presumptively invalid. Because the category of effects that "happen to be associated" with speech includes the narrower subset of effects caused by speech, today's holding has the effect of swallowing whole a most fundamental principle of First Amendment jurisprudence.

II

The Court's mishandling of our secondary effects cases is not limited to its approval of a total ban. It compounds that error by dramatically reducing the degree to which the State's interest must be furthered by the restriction imposed on speech, and by ignoring the critical difference between secondary effects caused by speech and the incidental effects on speech that may be caused by a regulation of conduct.

In what can most delicately be characterized as an enormous understatement, the plurality concedes that "requiring dancers to wear pasties and G-strings may not greatly reduce these secondary effects." To believe that the mandatory addition of pasties and a G-string will have *any* kind of noticeable impact on secondary effects requires nothing short of a titanic surrender to the implausible. . . . Nevertheless, the plurality concludes that the "less stringent" test announced in *United States v. O'Brien* "requires only that the regulation further the interest in combating such effects." It is one thing to say, however, that *O'Brien* is more lenient than the "more demanding standard" we have imposed in cases such as *Texas v. Johnson*. It is quite another to say that the test can be satisfied by nothing more than the mere possibility of *de minimis* effects on the neighborhood.

The Court is also mistaken in equating our secondary effects cases with the "incidental burdens" doctrine applied in cases such as *O'Brien*; and it aggravates the error by invoking the latter line of cases to support its assertion that Erie's ordinance is unrelated to speech. The incidental burdens doctrine applies when "'speech' and 'nonspeech' elements are combined in the same course of conduct," and the government's interest in regulating the latter justifies incidental burdens on the former. Secondary effects, on the other hand, are indirect consequences of protected speech and may justify regulation of the places where that speech may occur. When a State enacts a regulation, it might focus on the secondary effects of speech as its aim, or it might concentrate on nonspeech related concerns, having no thoughts at all with respect to how its regulation will affect speech—and only later, when the regulation is found to burden speech, justify the imposition as an unintended incidental consequence. But those interests are not the same, and the Court cannot ignore their differences and insist that both aims are equally unrelated to speech simply because Erie might have "recognized" that it could possibly have had either aim in mind. . . .

Of course, the line between governmental interests aimed at conduct and unrelated to speech, on the one hand, and interests arising out of the effects of the speech, on the other, may be somewhat imprecise in some cases. In this case, however, we need not wrestle with any such difficulty because Erie has expressly justified its ordinance with reference to secondary effects. Indeed, if Erie's concern with the effects of the message were unrelated to the message itself, it is strange that the only means used to combat those effects is the suppression of the message. For these reasons, the Court's argument that "this case is similar to *O'Brien*," is quite wrong . . . . The Court cannot have its cake and eat it too—either Erie's ordinance was not aimed at speech and the Court may attempt to justify the regulation under the incidental burdens test, or Erie has aimed its law at the secondary effects of speech, and the Court can try to justify the law under that doctrine. But it cannot conflate the two with the expectation that Erie's interests aimed at secondary effects will be rendered unrelated to speech by virtue of this doctrinal polyglot.

Correct analysis of the issue in this case should begin with the proposition that nude dancing is a species of expressive conduct that is protected by the First Amendment. As Chief Judge Posner has observed, nude dancing fits well within a broad, cultural tradition recognized as expressive in nature and entitled to First Amendment protection. The nudity of the dancer is both a component of the protected expression and the specific target of the ordinance. It is pure sophistry to reason from the premise that the regulation of the nudity component of nude dancing is unrelated to the message conveyed by nude dancers. Indeed, both the text of the ordinance and the reasoning in the Court's opinion make it pellucidly clear that the city of Erie has prohibited nude dancing "*precisely because of its communicative attributes.*" *Barnes* (Scalia, J., occurring in judgment) (emphasis in original).

III

The censorial purpose of Erie's ordinance precludes reliance on the judgment in *Barnes* as sufficient support for the Court's holding today. . . . As presented to us, the ordinance is deliberately targeted at Kandyland's type of nude dancing (to the exclusion of plays like Equus), in terms of both its applicable scope and the city's enforcement.

This narrow aim is confirmed by the expressed views of the Erie City Councilmembers who voted for the ordinance. The four city councilmembers who approved the measure (of the six total councilmembers) each stated his or her view that the ordinance was aimed specifically at nude adult entertainment, and not at more mainstream forms of entertainment that include total nudity, nor even at nudity in general. . . . Given that the Court has not even tried to defend the ordinance's total ban on the ground that its censorship of protected speech might be justified by an overriding state interest, it should conclude that the ordinance is patently invalid. . . .

———

Note: Expressive Conduct, Secondary Effects, and Incidental Burdens

1. As the absence of a majority opinion in *Pap's A.M.* indicates, cases involving "expressive conduct" have proved very difficult for the Court. Certainly we cannot assume that Justices who support a First Amendment claim in one context will do so when a different claim is presented. For example, Justice Scalia and Justice Kennedy agreed with the decision in *Texas v. Johnson* that the First Amendment protects flag burning, but they also agreed with the decisions holding that nude dancing is *not* protected. Justice Stevens and Justice White dissented in *Texas v. Johnson*, but they also dissented in the nude dancing cases.

Can you articulate a theory of the First Amendment that would invalidate a law against nude dancing but allow prosecution for the public burning of an American flag as part of a protest against government policy?

2. In *Barnes v. Glen Theatre, Inc.*, 501 U.S. 560 (1991), the predecessor case to *Pap's A.M.*, Justice Scalia explained his position:

The First Amendment explicitly protects "the freedom of speech [and] of the press"—oral and written speech—not "expressive conduct." When any law restricts speech, even for a purpose that has nothing to do with the suppression of communication (for instance, to reduce noise, see *Saia v. New York*, 334 U.S. 558 (1948), to regulate election campaigns, see *Buckley v. Valeo*, 424 U.S. 1 (1976) [Chapter 11], or to prevent littering, see *Schneider v. State*, 308 U.S. 147 (1939) [Chapter 6]), we insist that it meet the high, First-Amendment standard of justification. But virtually *every* law restricts conduct, and virtually *any* prohibited conduct can be performed for an expressive purpose—if only expressive of the fact that the actor disagrees with the prohibition. *See, e.g., Florida Free Beaches, Inc. v. Miami*, 734 F.2d 608 (CA11 1984) (nude sunbathers challenging public indecency law claimed their "message" was that nudity is not indecent). It cannot reasonably be demanded, therefore, that every restriction of expression incidentally produced by a general law regulating conduct pass normal First Amendment scrutiny, or even—as some of our cases have suggested, *see, e.g., United States v. O'Brien*—that it be justified by an "important or substantial" government interest. Nor do our holdings require such justification: We have never invalidated the application of a general law simply because the conduct that it reached was being engaged in for expressive purposes and the government could not demonstrate a sufficiently important state interest.

This is not to say that the First Amendment affords no protection to expressive conduct. Where the government prohibits conduct *precisely because of its communicative attributes*, we hold the regulation unconstitutional. *See, e.g., Texas v. Johnson* (burning flag); *Spence v. Washington* (defacing flag); *Tinker v. Des Moines Independent Community School Dist.* (1969) [Chapter 12] (wearing black arm bands); *Brown v. Louisiana*, 383 U.S. 131 (1966) (participating in silent sit-in); *Stromberg v. California*, 283 U.S. 359 (1931) (flying a red flag). In each of the foregoing cases, we explicitly found that suppressing communication was the object of the regulation of conduct. Where that has not been the case, however—where suppression of communicative use of the conduct was merely the incidental effect of forbidding the conduct for other reasons—we have allowed the regulation to stand. [E.g.,] *O'Brien* (law banning destruction of draft card upheld in application against card burning to protest war); *Clark v. Community for Creative Non-Violence*, 468 U.S. 288 (1984) (rule barring sleeping in parks upheld in application against persons engaging in such conduct to dramatize plight of homeless).

In a footnote, Justice Scalia added:

It is easy to conclude that conduct has been forbidden because of its communicative attributes when the conduct in question is what the Court has called "inherently expressive," and what I would prefer to call "conventionally expressive"—such as flying a red flag. I mean by that phrase (as I assume the Court means by "inherently expressive") conduct that is normally engaged in for the purpose of communicating an idea, or perhaps an emotion, to someone else. I am not sure whether dancing fits that description. But even if it does, this law is directed against nudity, not dancing. Nudity is *not* normally engaged in for the purpose of communicating an idea or an emotion.

Do you agree that the crucial question should be whether the government is prohibiting conduct "precisely because of its communicative attributes"? How does a court make that determination? Consider the Problems that follow.

3. Justice Stevens, dissenting in *Pap's A.M.*, criticizes the plurality for equating "secondary effects" with "incidental burdens." Is this an accurate characterization of the opinion? The plurality acknowledges (in Part III of the opinion) that the two "doctrinal theories" are "not identical." Under the plurality's view, what is the relation between the two doctrines?

4. Drawing on the record, Justice Stevens insists that the Erie ordinance "is deliberately targeted at Kandyland's type of nude dancing." Does the plurality dispute this proposition? Or does the plurality concede it and nevertheless find that this kind of "targeting" does not render the ordinance unconstitutional?

———————

Problem: Nudity "for Entertainment Purposes"

The State Legislature has enacted a law that provides as follows: "It shall be unlawful for any business establishment or any private club to show or allow to be shown for entertainment purposes the human male or female genitals, pubic area, or buttocks with less than a fully opaque covering, or the showing of the female breast with less than a fully opaque covering of any portion thereof below the top of the nipple, or the depiction of covered male genitals in a discernibly turgid state."

(a) Assume first that no legislative findings accompany the prohibition. Is the statute constitutional?

(b) Now assume that the prohibition is part of an enactment that includes the following introductory language:

The Legislature finds and declares:

That in order to protect children from exposure to obscenity, prevent assaults on the sensibilities of unwilling adults by the purveyor of obscene material, and suppress the proliferation of "adult-only video stores," "adult bookstores," "adult movie houses," and "adult-only entertainment," the sale and dissemination of obscene material should be regulated without impinging on the First Amendment rights of free speech by erecting barriers to the open display of erotic and lascivious material.

That the premises in which a violation of this Act occurs should be declared a public nuisance.

(c) Now assume that the introductory language is as follows.

The Legislature finds and declares:

That there is substantial evidence, including numerous studies, reports, and findings on the potential harmful effect of adult entertainment uses made by numerous cities, experts, city planners, etc., which document that such uses adversely affect property values, cause an increase in crime, encourage businesses to move elsewhere, and contribute to neighborhood blight.

That it is necessary, expedient and in the best interest of the citizenry to regulate the operation and location of adult entertainment establishments for the purpose of stemming a potential increase in the criminal activities and disturbances of the peace and good order of the community, maintaining property values, preventing injuries to residential neighborhoods and commercial districts, and protecting and preserving the quality of life in this State.

————

Problem: An "Affirmative Action Bake Sale"

The College Republican Club at West Fremont State University has announced plans for a "bake sale" designed to protest affirmative action policies at the University. Using the model of similar activities at other campuses, the organization plans to sell cookies at different prices depending on the customer's race and sex. As the group explains in a leaflet that will be handed out at the table:

> The purpose of this bake sale is to spark debate about affirmative action policies, not to raise revenue. We have therefore priced the cookies according to the same categories that West Fremont State University uses in its admission application. Black, Latino and American Indian females will be charged 25 cents for a cookie, while their male counterparts will be charged 50 cents. White females will be charged a dollar. White males will be charged two dollars. Asian males and females will also be charged two dollars a cookie.

Upon learning of the organization's plan, the Dean of Students sent the following message to the organization's president:

> My office has been informed that the College Republicans are planning a Bake Sale in Village Square next Friday where lower prices for baked goods will be charged to non-white, non-male purchasers as a commentary about Affirmative Action Laws. Please be aware that, even if you plan to charge less to minority and female customers (as it was described to me), this action violates the University's discrimination statement found on page one of the Academic Catalogue of West Fremont State University for the current academic year:
>
> > West Fremont State University subscribes to the principles of equal opportunity and affirmative action and does not discriminate against any individual on the basis of age, color, disability, gender, national origin, race, religion, sexual orientation, or veteran status.
> >
> > This policy is applicable to all members of the WFSU Community, including students and student clubs.
>
> For this reason, I strongly urge the College Republicans to either charge one price to all or to halt the event entirely. Violating University rules can and will result in charges being filed against the College Republicans through the Charter and Rules Committee of the Student Government Association and against individual members of the group through the Student Conduct Code.
>
> I suggest, if you wish to debate or comment on the issue of affirmative action, your group should choose a different method—one that does not run contrary to University policies.

Upon receiving this message, the president of the College Republicans asks you: "Our bake sale is protected by the First Amendment. Isn't it"?

Is it? How would the question be analyzed?

Chapter 8

Speech on Government Property and the Public Forum Doctrine

In *Commonwealth v. Davis*, 39 N.E. 113 (Mass. 1895), the defendant spoke on Boston Common without a permit. He was convicted of violating an ordinance that required a permit for conducting various activities on any of the public grounds of the city. In an opinion by Justice Holmes, the Supreme Judicial Court of Massachusetts affirmed the conviction. Said Justice Holmes: "For the legislature absolutely or conditionally to forbid public speaking in a highway or public park is no more an infringement of rights of a member of the public than for the owner of a private house to forbid it in the house."

Plainly, that is not the law today. Under the First Amendment, as interpreted by the Supreme Court, "a member of the public" does have a right to use public property to communicate ideas. But the Court has also emphasized that the First Amendment "does not forbid a State to control the use of its own property for its own lawful nondiscriminatory purpose."

What are the limitations on government power to regulate expressive activities on public property? What interests may the government invoke, and what kinds of regulations are permissible? Those questions are explored in this chapter.

A. Foundations of the Doctrine

Hague v. Committee for Industrial Organization

307 U.S. 496 (1939)

[*Editor's note*: In this case the lower courts found that officials of Jersey City, New Jersey, acting in reliance on a city ordinance, had prevented the plaintiffs from distributing leaflets in the city and from holding meetings in public places. The lower courts issued an injunction against enforcement of the ordinance, and the Supreme Court affirmed. There was no majority opinion.]

MR. JUSTICE ROBERTS delivered an opinion in which MR. JUSTICE BLACK concurred:

[The city officials contend that] the city's ownership of streets and parks is as absolute as one's ownership of his home, with consequent power altogether to exclude citizens from the use thereof. . . . [In support of this argument the city officials] rely upon *Davis v. Massachusetts*, 167 U.S. 43 (1897). There it appeared that, pursuant to

445

enabling legislation, the city of Boston adopted an ordinance prohibiting anyone from speaking, discharging fire arms, selling goods, or maintaining any booth for public amusement on any of the public grounds of the city except under a permit from the Mayor. Davis spoke on Boston Common without a permit and without applying to the Mayor for one. [Davis was convicted under the ordinance, and the United States Supreme Court affirmed.]

The ordinance there in question . . . was not directed solely at the exercise of the right of speech and assembly, but was addressed as well to other activities, not in the nature of civil rights, which doubtless might be regulated or prohibited as respects their enjoyment in parks. . . .

We have no occasion to determine whether, on the facts disclosed, the *Davis* case was rightly decided, but we cannot agree that it rules the instant case. Wherever the title of streets and parks may rest, they have immemorially been held in trust for the use of the public and, time out of mind, have been used for purposes of assembly, communicating thoughts between citizens, and discussing public questions. Such use of the streets and public places has, from ancient times, been a part of the privileges, immunities, rights, and liberties of citizens. The privilege of a citizen of the United States to use the streets and parks for communication of views on national questions may be regulated in the interest of all; it is not absolute, but relative, and must be exercised in subordination to the general comfort and convenience, and in consonance with peace and good order; but it must not, in the guise of regulation, be abridged or denied.

We think the court below was right in holding the ordinance . . . void upon its face. *Lovell v. Griffin* (1938) [Chapter 4]. It does not make comfort or convenience in the use of streets or parks the standard of official action. It enables the Director of Safety to refuse a permit on his mere opinion that such refusal will prevent "riots, disturbances or disorderly assemblage." It can thus, as the record discloses, be made the instrument of arbitrary suppression of free expression of views on national affairs for the prohibition of all speaking will undoubtedly "prevent" such eventualities. But uncontrolled official suppression of the privilege cannot be made a substitute for the duty to maintain order in connection with the exercise of the right.

Mr. Justice Stone [joined by Mr. Justice Reed]:

. . . I think respondents' right to maintain [their suit] does not depend on their citizenship and cannot rightly be made to turn on the existence or non-existence of a purpose to disseminate information about the National Labor Relations Act. It is enough that petitioners have prevented respondents from holding meetings and disseminating information whether for the organization of labor unions or for any other lawful purpose. [Justice Stone did not discuss the issue considered in the part of Justice Roberts' opinion set forth above, nor did he offer any view on the continuing vitality of *Davis v. Massachusetts*, 167 U.S. 43 (1897).]

Mr. Chief Justice Hughes, concurring:

With respect to the merits I agree with the opinion of Mr. Justice Roberts and in the affirmance of the judgment as modified. . . .

MR. JUSTICE MCREYNOLDS, dissenting [omitted].

MR. JUSTICE BUTLER, dissenting:

I am of opinion that the challenged ordinance is not void on its face; that in principle it does not differ from the Boston ordinance, as applied and upheld by this Court, speaking through Mr. Justice White, in *Davis v. Massachusetts*, 167 U.S. 43, affirming the Supreme Judicial Court of Massachusetts, speaking through Mr. Justice Holmes, in *Commonwealth v. Davis*, 162 Mass. 510, 39 N.E. 113, and that the decree of the Circuit Court of Appeals should be reversed.

MR. JUSTICE FRANKFURTER and MR. JUSTICE DOUGLAS took no part in the consideration or decision of the case.

Schneider v. New Jersey
308 U.S. 147 (1939)

[The report of this decision appears in Chapter 6, section A.]

Cantwell v. Connecticut
310 U.S. 296 (1940)

MR. JUSTICE ROBERTS delivered the opinion of the Court.

Newton Cantwell and his two sons, Jesse and Russell, members of a group known as Jehovah's Witnesses, and claiming to be ordained ministers, were arrested in New Haven, Connecticut, and each was charged by information in five counts, with statutory and common law offenses. [Jesse Cantwell was convicted of the common law offense of inciting a breach of the peace. The state supreme court affirmed.]

. . . The facts which were held to support the conviction of Jesse Cantwell on the fifth count were that he stopped two men in the street, asked, and received, permission to play a phonograph record, and played the record "Enemies," which attacked the religion and church of the two men, who were Catholics. Both were incensed by the contents of the record and were tempted to strike Cantwell unless he went away. On being told to be on his way he left their presence. There was no evidence that he was personally offensive or entered into any argument with those he interviewed.

The [state] court held that the charge was not assault or breach of the peace or threats on Cantwell's part, but invoking or inciting others to breach of the peace, and that the facts supported the conviction of that offense. . . . We must determine whether the alleged protection of the State's interest [in peace and good order] has been pressed, in this instance, to a point where it has come into fatal collision with the overriding interest protected by the [First Amendment].

Conviction on the fifth count was not pursuant to a statute evincing a legislative judgment that street discussion of religious affairs, because of its tendency to provoke disorder, should be regulated, or a judgment that the playing of a phonograph on the streets should in the interest of comfort or privacy be limited or prevented. Violation of an Act exhibiting such a legislative judgment and narrowly drawn to prevent the supposed evil, would pose a question differing from that we must here answer. Compare *Gitlow v. New York* (1925) [Chapter 1]. Such a declaration of the State's policy would weigh heavily in any challenge of the law as infringing constitutional limitations. Here, however, the judgment is based on a common law concept of the most general and undefined nature. . . .

. . . No one would have the hardihood to suggest that the principle of freedom of speech sanctions incitement to riot or that religious liberty connotes the privilege to exhort others to physical attack upon those belonging to another sect. When clear and present danger of riot, disorder, interference with traffic upon the public streets, or other immediate threat to public safety, peace, or order, appears, the power of the State to prevent or punish is obvious. Equally obvious is it that a State may not unduly suppress free communication of views, religious or other, under the guise of conserving desirable conditions. Here we have a situation analogous to a conviction under a statute sweeping in a great variety of conduct under a general and indefinite characterization, and leaving to the executive and judicial branches too wide a discretion in its application.

Having these considerations in mind, we note that Jesse Cantwell, on April 26, 1938, was upon a public street, where he had a right to be, and where he had a right peacefully to impart his views to others. There is no showing that his deportment was noisy, truculent, overbearing or offensive. He requested of two pedestrians permission to play to them a phonograph record. The permission was granted. It is not claimed that he intended to insult or affront the hearers by playing the record. It is plain that he wished only to interest them in his propaganda. The sound of the phonograph is not shown to have disturbed residents of the street, to have drawn a crowd, or to have impeded traffic. Thus far he had invaded no right or interest of the public or of the men accosted.

The record played by Cantwell embodies a general attack on all organized religious systems as instruments of Satan and injurious to man; it then singles out the Roman Catholic Church for strictures couched in terms which naturally would offend not only persons of that persuasion, but all others who respect the honestly held religious faith of their fellows. The hearers were in fact highly offended. One of them said he felt like hitting Cantwell and the other that he was tempted to throw Cantwell off the street. The one who testified he felt like hitting Cantwell said, in answer to the question "Did you do anything else or have any other reaction?" "No, sir, because he said he would take the victrola and he went." The other witness testified that he told Cantwell he had better get off the street before something happened to him and that was the end of the matter as Cantwell picked up his books and walked up the street.

Cantwell's conduct, in the view of the court below, considered apart from the effect of his communication upon his hearers, did not amount to a breach of the peace. One may, however, be guilty of the offense if he commit acts or make statements likely to provoke violence and disturbance of good order, even though no such eventuality be intended. . . . Resort to epithets or personal abuse is not in any proper sense communication of information or opinion safeguarded by the Constitution, and its punishment as a criminal act would raise no question under that instrument.

We find in the instant case no assault or threatening of bodily harm, no truculent bearing, no intentional discourtesy, no personal abuse. On the contrary, we find only an effort to persuade a willing listener to buy a book or to contribute money in the interest of what Cantwell, however misguided others may think him, conceived to be true religion. . . .

Although the contents of the record not unnaturally aroused animosity, we think that, in the absence of a statute narrowly drawn to define and punish specific conduct as constituting a clear and present danger to a substantial interest of the State, the petitioner's communication, considered in the light of the constitutional guarantees, raised no such clear and present menace to public peace and order as to render him liable to conviction of the common law offense in question.

The judgment affirming the [conviction is reversed].

———

Note: The Significance of Cantwell

1. In an omitted portion of the opinion, the Court reversed the convictions of all three defendants under a state statute that restricted solicitation. Although the Court cited *Schneider v. New Jersey* (Chapter 6) and *Near v. Minnesota* (Chapter 4), that part of the holding was grounded in the Free Exercise clause.

2. We have already encountered *Cantwell* as a predecessor of *Chaplinsky*. *See* Chapter 2. *Cantwell* has also been important in the development of the public forum doctrine, as later cases in this chapter demonstrate.

3. In *Cantwell*, the Court emphasizes "the absence of a statute narrowly drawn to define and punish specific conduct as constituting a clear and present danger to a substantial interest of the State." Could Cantwell have been prosecuted under the statute invoked in *Chaplinsky*?

4. Both *Lovell v. Griffin* and *Hague v. CIO* were on the books at the time *Cantwell* was argued and decided, and it is hard to understand why the Court did not cite either case. (Note that the statement that "Jesse Cantwell . . . was upon a public street, . . . where he had a right peacefully to impart his view to others," would have been a logical point at which to cite *Hague*.)

Cox v. New Hampshire
312 U.S. 569 (1941)

Mr. Chief Justice Hughes delivered the opinion of the Court.

Appellants are five "Jehovah's Witnesses" who, with sixty-three others of the same persuasion, were convicted in the municipal court of Manchester, New Hampshire, for violation of a state statute prohibiting a "parade or procession" upon a public street without a special license. [The State Supreme Court affirmed the convictions.]

The [uncontested] facts are these: The sixty-eight defendants and twenty other persons met at a hall in the City of Manchester on the evening of Saturday, July 8, 1939, "for the purpose of engaging in an information march." The company was divided into four or five groups, each with about fifteen to twenty persons. Each group then proceeded to a different part of the business district of the city and there "would line up in single-file formation and then proceed to march along the sidewalk, 'single-file,' that is, following one another." Each of the defendants carried a small staff with a sign reading "Religion is a Snare and a Racket" and on the reverse "Serve God and Christ the King." Some of the marchers carried placards bearing the statement "Fascism or Freedom. Hear Judge Rutherford and Face the Facts." The marchers also handed out printed leaflets announcing a meeting to be held at a later time in the hall from which they had started, where a talk on government would be given to the public free of charge. Defendants did not apply for a permit and none was issued.

. . . [The state court] thus summarizes the effect of the march: "Manchester had a population of over 75,000 in 1930, and there was testimony that on Saturday nights in an hour's time 26,000 persons passed one of the intersections where the defendants marched. The marchers interfered with the normal sidewalk travel, but no technical breach of the peace occurred. The march was a prearranged affair, and no permit for it was sought, although the defendants understood that under the statute one was required." . . .

[The appellants] were not prosecuted for distributing leaflets, or for conveying information by placards or otherwise, or for issuing invitations to a public meeting, or for holding a public meeting, or for maintaining or expressing religious beliefs. Their right to do any one of these things apart from engaging in a "parade or procession" upon a public street is not here involved and the question of the validity of a statute addressed to any other sort of conduct than that complained of is not before us.

There appears to be no ground for challenging the ruling of the state court that appellants were in fact engaged in a parade or procession upon the public streets. . . .

Civil liberties, as guaranteed by the Constitution, imply the existence of an organized society maintaining public order without which liberty itself would be lost in the excesses of unrestrained abuses. The authority of a municipality to impose regulations in order to assure the safety and convenience of the people in the use of public highways has never been regarded as inconsistent with civil liberties but rather as one of the means of safeguarding the good order upon which they ultimately depend. The control of travel on the streets of cities is the most familiar illustration of this recognition of social need. Where a restriction of the use of highways in that relation is designed to promote the public convenience in the interest of all, it cannot be disregarded by the attempted exercise of some civil right which in other circumstances would be entitled to protection. One would not be justified in ignoring the familiar red traffic light because he [sought] by that means to direct public attention to an announcement of his opinions. As regulation of the use of the streets for parades and processions is a traditional exercise of control by local government, the question in a particular case is whether that control is exerted so as not to deny or unwarrantedly abridge the right of assembly and the opportunities for the communication of thought and the discussion of public questions immemorially associated with resort to public places. [The Court here cited *Lovell v. Griffin, Hague v. CIO, Schneider,* and *Cantwell.*]

In the instant case, we are aided by the opinion of the Supreme Court of the State which construed the statute and defined the limitations of the authority conferred for the granting of licenses for parades and processions. Recognizing the importance of the civil liberties invoked by appellants, the court thought it significant . . . that the regulation with respect to parades and processions was applicable only "to organized formations of persons using the highways"; and that "the defendants, separately, or collectively in groups not constituting a parade or procession," were "under no contemplation of the Act." . . .

It was with this view of the limited objective of the statute that the state court considered and defined the duty of the licensing authority and the rights of the appellants to a license for their parade, with regard only to considerations of time, place and manner so as to conserve the public convenience. The obvious advantage of requiring application for a permit was noted as giving the public authorities notice in advance so as to afford opportunity for proper policing. And the court further observed that, in fixing time and place, the license served "to prevent confusion by overlapping parades or processions, to secure convenient use of the streets by other travelers, and to minimize the risk of disorder." But the court held that the licensing board was not vested with arbitrary power or an unfettered discretion; that its discretion must be exercised with "uniformity of method of treatment upon the facts of each application, free from improper or inappropriate considerations and from unfair discrimination"; that a "systematic, consistent and just order of treatment, with reference to the convenience of public use of the highways, is the statutory mandate." . . .

If a municipality has authority to control the use of its public streets for parades or processions, as it undoubtedly has, it cannot be denied authority to give consideration, without unfair discrimination, to time, place and manner in relation to the other proper uses of the streets. We find it impossible to say that the limited authority conferred by the licensing provisions of the statute in question as thus construed by the state court contravened any constitutional right.

There remains the question of license fees which, as the court said, had a permissible range from $300 to a nominal amount. The court construed the Act as requiring "a reasonable fixing of the amount of the fee." "The charge," said the court, "for a circus parade or a celebration procession of length, each drawing crowds of observers, would take into account the greater public expense of policing the spectacle, compared with the slight expense of a less expansive and attractive parade or procession, to which the charge would be adjusted." . . . There is nothing contrary to the Constitution in the charge of a fee limited to the purpose stated. The suggestion that a flat fee should have been charged fails to take account of the difficulty of framing a fair schedule to meet all circumstances, and we perceive no constitutional ground for denying to local governments that flexibility of adjustment of fees which in the light of varying conditions would tend to conserve rather than impair the liberty sought.

There is no evidence that the statute has been administered otherwise than in the fair and non-discriminatory manner which the state court has construed it to require.

The decisions upon which appellants rely are not applicable. In *Lovell v. Griffin*, the ordinance prohibited the distribution of literature of any kind at any time, at any place, and in any manner without a permit from the city manager, thus striking at the very foundation of the freedom of the press by subjecting it to license and censorship. In *Hague v. CIO*, the ordinance . . . enabled the local official absolutely to refuse a permit on his mere opinion that such refusal would prevent "riots, disturbances or disorderly assemblage." The ordinance thus created, as the record disclosed, an instrument of arbitrary suppression of opinions on public questions. . . . In *Schneider v. State*, the ordinance was directed at canvassing and banned unlicensed communication of any views, or the advocacy of any cause, from door to door, subject only to the power of a police officer to determine as a censor what literature might be distributed and who might distribute it. . . .

Nor is any question of peaceful picketing here involved. The statute, as the state court said, is not aimed at any restraint of freedom of speech, and there is no basis for an assumption that it would be applied so as to prevent peaceful picketing as described in the cases cited.

[Judgment affirmed.]

———————

Note: The Law Established by the Foundational Cases

In the space of three years, the Supreme Court established the foundation of the "public forum" doctrine: streets and parks are to be made available "for purposes of assembly, communicating thoughts between citizens, and discussing public questions." But the decisions also raised questions about the scope and application of the doctrine.

First, the Court made clear that governments retain authority to regulate the "time, place and manner" of expressive activity in public places. What kinds of interests may the government invoke in support of regulation, and how are those interests to be weighed against their effect on expressive activity? We considered this question in Chapter 6.

Second, the Court said in *Cantwell* that governments could limit expressive activity in response to "clear and present danger of riot, disorder, interference with traffic upon the public streets, or other immediate threat to public safety, peace, or order." How much leeway does this give to law enforcement officials on the scene, particularly when the threat of disorder comes from those who oppose the speaker's views? That question is considered in section B.

Third, the *Cox* decision found no constitutional infirmity in a municipality's charging a license fee for holding a parade or procession on city streets. The Court emphasized the benefits of "flexibility of adjustment of fees." But how much flexibility does the Constitution allow? That question is considered in *Forsyth County v. Nationalist Movement*, also included in section B.

Finally, language in some of the early opinions refers not simply to "streets and parks," but to "public places." What other kinds of places or facilities might the government be required to open up to expressive activity? We consider that question in section C.

Note, too, that six decades after *Hague v. CIO*, the Court recognized that although a public park is a "traditional public forum," some forms of expression in public parks are "government speech" and "not subject to scrutiny under the Free Speech Clause" at all. This development is examined in Chapter 13.

————

B. Mass Demonstrations and the Problem of the "Hostile Audience"

In dictum in *Cantwell*, the Supreme Court said that when speech creates a "clear and present danger of riot, disorder, interference with traffic upon the public streets, or other immediate threat to public safety, peace, or order," "the power of the State to *prevent or punish* is obvious." (Emphasis added.) The context of the case implied that state action to "prevent or punish" would be permissible even if the threat to order came not from the speaker's followers (as in *Hess* and *Claiborne Hardware, see* Chapter 1), but from the conduct of persons who oppose the speaker's views. But if this is so, it appears to allow a "hostile audience" to silence an unpopular speaker. The effect is to create a "heckler's veto." The problem of the "hostile audience" has proved to be a difficult one, particularly in the context of mass demonstrations. We look first at the state's power "to punish," then at its power "to prevent."

Terminiello v. Chicago
337 U.S. 1 (1949)

Mr. Justice Douglas delivered the opinion of the Court.

Petitioner after jury trial was found guilty of disorderly conduct in violation of a city ordinance of Chicago and fined. The case grew out of an address he delivered in an auditorium in Chicago under the auspices of the Christian Veterans of America. The meeting commanded considerable public attention. The auditorium was filled to capacity with over eight hundred persons present. Others were turned away. Outside of the auditorium a crowd of about one thousand persons gathered to protest against the meeting. A cordon of policemen was assigned to the meeting to maintain order; but they were not able to prevent several disturbances. The crowd outside was angry and turbulent.

Petitioner in his speech condemned the conduct of the crowd outside and vigorously, if not viciously, criticized various political and racial groups whose activities he denounced as inimical to the nation's welfare.

The trial court charged that "breach of the peace" consists of any "misbehavior which violates the public peace and decorum"; and that the "misbehavior may constitute a breach of the peace if it stirs the public to anger, invites dispute, brings about a condition of unrest, or creates a disturbance, or if it molests the inhabitants in the enjoyment of peace and quiet by arousing alarm." Petitioner did not take exception to that instruction. But he maintained at all times that the ordinance as applied to his conduct violated his right of free speech under the Federal Constitution. The judgment of conviction was affirmed by the [state courts]. . . .

The argument here has been focused on the issue of whether the content of petitioner's speech was composed of derisive, fighting words, which carried it outside the scope of the constitutional guarantees. See *Chaplinsky v. New Hampshire* (1942) [Chapter 2]; *Cantwell v. Connecticut* (1940) [*supra* this chapter]. We do not reach that question, for there is a preliminary question that is dispositive of the case.

As we have noted, the statutory words "breach of the peace" were defined in instructions to the jury to include speech which "stirs the public to anger, invites dispute, brings about a condition or unrest, or creates a disturbance . . . ." That construction of the ordinance is a ruling on a question of state law that is as binding on us as though the precise words had been written into the ordinance.

The vitality of civil and political institutions in our society depends on free discussion. . . .

Accordingly a function of free speech under our system of government is to invite dispute. It may indeed best serve its high purpose when it induces a condition of unrest, creates dissatisfaction with conditions as they are, or even stirs people to anger. Speech is often provocative and challenging. It may strike at prejudices and preconceptions and have profound unsettling effects as it presses for acceptance of an idea. That is why freedom of speech, though not absolute, *Chaplinsky*, is nevertheless protected against censorship or punishment, unless shown likely to produce a clear and present danger of a serious substantive evil that rises far above public inconvenience, annoyance, or unrest. . . .

The ordinance as construed by the trial court seriously invaded this province. It permitted conviction of petitioner if his speech stirred people to anger, invited public dispute, or brought about a condition of unrest. A conviction resting on any of those grounds may not stand. [Reversed.]

Mr. Justice Jackson, dissenting.

The Court reverses this conviction by reiterating generalized approbations of freedom of speech with which, in the abstract, no one will disagree. Doubts as to their applicability are lulled by avoidance of more than passing reference to the circumstances of Terminiello's speech and judging it as if he had spoken to persons as dispassionate as empty benches, or like a modern Demosthenes practicing his Philippics on a lonely seashore.

But the local court that tried Terminiello was not indulging in theory. It was dealing with a riot and with a speech that provoked a hostile mob and incited a friendly one, and threatened violence between the two. When the trial judge instructed the jury that it might find Terminiello guilty of inducing a breach of the peace if his behavior stirred the public to anger, invited dispute, brought about unrest, created a disturbance or molested peace and quiet by arousing alarm, he was not speaking of these as harmless or abstract conditions. He was addressing his words to the concrete behavior and specific consequences disclosed by the evidence. He was saying to the jury, in effect, that if this particular speech added fuel to the situation already so inflamed as to threaten to get beyond police control, it could be punished as inducing a breach of peace. . . .

An old proverb warns us to take heed lest we "walk into a well from looking at the stars." To show why I think the Court is in some danger of doing just that, I must bring these deliberations down to earth by a long recital of facts. [Most of Justice Jackson's lengthy account is omitted.]

The court below [heard evidence] that the crowd reached an estimated number of 1,500. Picket lines obstructed and interfered with access to the building. The crowd constituted "a surging, howling mob hurling epithets" at those who would enter and "tried to tear their clothes off." One young woman's coat was torn off and she had to be assisted into the meeting by policemen. Those inside the hall could hear the loud noises and hear those on the outside yell, "Fascists," "Hitlers!" and curse words like "damn Fascists." Bricks were thrown through the windowpanes before and during the speaking. About 28 windows were broken. The street was black with people on both sides for at least a block either way; bottles, stink bombs and brickbats were thrown. Police were unable to control the mob, which kept breaking the windows at the meeting hall, drowning out the speaker's voice at times and breaking in through the back door of the auditorium. About 17 of the group outside were arrested by the police.

Knowing of this environment, Terminiello made a long speech, from the stenographic record of which I omit relatively innocuous passages and add emphasis of what seems especially provocative. [The extracts quoted by Justice Jackson fill five and a half pages in the United States Reports. Here is a tiny sampling.]

[Father Terminiello:] "Now, I am going to whisper my greetings to you, Fellow Christians. I will interpret it. I said, 'Fellow *Christians*,' and I suppose there are *some of the scum got in by mistake*, so I want to tell a story about *the scum*: . . . .

". . . They want to picket our meetings. They don't want us to picket their meetings. It is the same kind of tolerance, if we said there was a bedbug in bed, 'We don't care for you,' or if we looked under the bed and found a snake and said, 'I am going to be tolerant and leave the snake there.' We will not be tolerant of that mob out there. We are not going to be tolerant any longer. . . .

"So, my friends, since we spent much time tonight trying to quiet the howling mob, I am going to bring my thoughts to a conclusion, and the conclusion is this. We must all be like the Apostles before the coming of the Holy Ghost. We must not lock ourselves in an upper room for fear of the Jews. I speak of the Communistic Zionistic

Jew, and those are not American Jews. We don't want them here; we want them to go back where they came from."

. . . Evidence showed that [the speech] stirred the audience not only to cheer and applaud but to expressions of immediate anger, unrest and alarm. One called the speaker a "God damned liar" and was taken out by the police. Another said that "Jews, niggers and Catholics would have to be gotten rid of." One response was, "Yes, the Jews are all killers, murderers. If we don't kill them first, they will kill us." The anti-Jewish stories elicited exclamations of "Oh!" and "Isn't that terrible!" and shouts of "Yes, send the Jews back to Russia," "Kill the Jews," "Dirty kikes," and much more of ugly tenor. This is the specific and concrete kind of anger, unrest and alarm, coupled with that of the mob outside, that the trial court charged the jury might find to be a breach of peace induced by Terminiello. It is difficult to believe that this Court is speaking of the same occasion, but it is the only one involved in this litigation.

. . . I am unable to see the local authorities have transgressed the Federal Constitution. Illinois imposed no prior censorship or suppression upon Terminiello. On the contrary, its sufferance and protection was all that enabled him to speak. It does not appear that the motive in punishing him is to silence the ideology he expressed as offensive to the State's policy or as untrue, or has any purpose of controlling his thought or its peaceful communication to others. . . .

Rioting is a substantive evil, which I take it no one will deny that the State and the City have the right and the duty to prevent and punish. . . . In this case the evidence proves beyond dispute that danger of rioting and violence in response to the speech was clear, present and immediate. . . . Only recently this Court held that a state could punish as a breach of the peace use of epithets such as "damned racketeer" and "damned fascists," addressed to only one person, an official, because likely to provoke the average person to retaliation. But these are mild in comparison to the epithets "slimy scum," "snakes," "bedbugs," and the like, which Terminiello hurled at an already inflamed mob of his adversaries. [Justice Jackson quoted from *Chaplinsky* and *Cantwell*.]

How this present decision, denying state power to punish civilly one who precipitated a public riot involving hundreds of fanatic fighters in a most violent melee, can be squared with those unanimous statements of law, is incomprehensible to me. . . .

[F]reedom of speech exists only under law and not independently of it. . . . Terminiello's theoretical right to speak free from interference would have no reality if Chicago should withdraw its officers to some other section of the city, or if the men assigned to the task should look the other way when the crowd threatens Terminiello. Can society by expected to keep these men at Terminiello's service if it has nothing to say of his behavior which may force them into dangerous action?

. . . [Many] speeches, such as that of Terminiello, may be legally permissible but may nevertheless in some surrounding, be a menace to peace and order. When conditions show the speaker that this is the case, as it did here, there certainly comes a point beyond which he cannot indulge in provocations to violence without being answerable to society.

. . . [The] police have to deal with men as they are. The crowd mind is never tolerant of any idea which does not conform to its herd opinion. . . . [B]oth radical and reactionary mobs endanger liberty as well as order. The authorities must control them and they are entitled to place some checks upon those whose behavior or speech calls such mobs into being. . . .

. . . The choice is not between order and liberty. It is between liberty with order and anarchy without either. There is danger that, if the Court does not temper its doctrinaire logic with a little practical wisdom, it will convert the constitutional Bill of Rights into a suicide pact.

MR. JUSTICE BURTON joins in this opinion. [CHIEF JUSTICE VINSON and JUSTICE FRANKFURTER dissented in separate opinions.]

Note: Hostile Audiences and Provocative Speakers

1. Two years after *Terminiello*, the Court considered another case involving a speaker whose remarks aroused a hostile reaction. In *Feiner v. New York*, 340 U.S. 315 (1951), the defendant was convicted of disorderly conduct. The prosecution arose out of the following facts, as recounted by the Supreme Court.

Feiner addressed an open-air meeting on a street corner in the city of Syracuse. Although the purpose of his speech was to urge his listeners to attend a meeting to be held that night at a hotel, in its course he made derogatory remarks concerning President Truman, the American Legion, the Mayor of Syracuse, and other local political officials. The police received a telephone complaint concerning the meeting. When they arrived at the street corner, they found a crowd of about 75 or 80 people filling the sidewalk and spreading out into the street. The crowd was restless, and there was some pushing, shoving, and milling around. Some of the onlookers made remarks to the police about their inability to handle the crowd, and at least one threatened violence if the police did not act. There were others who appeared to be favoring Feiner's arguments.

Because of the feelings and reactions the officers observed in the crowd both for and against the speaker, the police finally "stepped in to prevent it from resulting in a fight." One of the officers asked Feiner to stop talking, but he did not do so. During all this time, the crowd was pressing closer around Feiner and the officer. Finally, the officer told Feiner he was under arrest and ordered him to get down from the box, reaching up to grab him. Feiner was convicted of disorderly conduct.

On a 6-3 vote, the Supreme Court found no First Amendment violation. Chief Justice Vinson, writing for the Court, explained:

The courts below recognized petitioner's right to hold a street meeting at this locality, to make use of loud-speaking equipment in giving his speech, and to make derogatory remarks concerning public officials and the American Legion. They found that the officers in making the arrest were motivated solely by a proper concern for the preservation of order and protection of the general welfare, and that there was no evidence which could lend color to a claim that the acts of the police were a cover for suppression of petitioner's views and opinions. Petitioner was thus neither arrested nor convicted for the making or the content of his speech. Rather, it was the reaction which it actually engendered. . . .

We are well aware that the ordinary murmurings and objections of a hostile audience cannot be allowed to silence a speaker, and are also mindful of the possible danger of giving overzealous police officials complete discretion to break up otherwise lawful public meetings. . . . But we are not faced here with such a situation. It is one thing to say that the police cannot be used as an instrument for the suppression of unpopular views, and another to say that, when as here the speaker passes the bounds of argument or persuasion and undertakes incitement to riot, they are powerless to prevent a breach of the peace. . . . The findings of the state courts as to the existing situation and the imminence of greater disorder coupled with petitioner's deliberate defiance of the police officers convince us that we should not reverse this conviction in the name of free speech.

Justice Black, in dissent, first argued that the Court should have examined the trial evidence more closely. He continued:

[Even] assuming that the "facts" did indicate a critical situation, I reject the implication of the Court's opinion that the police had no obligation to protect petitioner's constitutional right to talk. The police of course have power to prevent breaches of the peace. But if, in the name of preserving order, they ever can interfere with a lawful public speaker, they first must make all reasonable efforts to protect him. *Cf. Hague v. CIO* (1939); *Terminiello v. Chicago* (1949). Here the policemen did not even pretend to try to protect petitioner. According to the officers' testimony, the crowd was restless but there is no showing of any attempt to quiet it; pedestrians were forced to walk into the street, but there was no effort to clear a path on the sidewalk; one person threatened to assault petitioner but the officers did nothing to discourage this when even a word might have sufficed. Their duty was to protect petitioner's right to talk, even to the extent of arresting the man who threatened to interfere. Instead, they shirked that duty and acted only to suppress the right to speak.

Finally, I cannot agree with the Court's statement that petitioner's disregard of the policeman's unexplained request amounted to such "deliberate defiance" as would justify an arrest or conviction for disorderly conduct. On the contrary, I think that the policeman's action was a "deliberate defiance" of ordinary official duty as well as of the constitutional right of free speech. For at least where time allows, courtesy and explanation of commands are basic elements of good official conduct in a democratic society.

2. A decade after *Feiner*, the South Carolina Supreme Court relied on that decision in affirming almost 200 breach-of-the-peace convictions growing out of a civil rights demonstration at the South Carolina State House grounds. The case was *Edwards v.*

South Carolina, 372 U.S. 229 (1963). The South Carolina court recounted the facts in a way that made the case sound like a replay of *Feiner* on a larger scale:

> The parade was conducted upon the State House grounds for approximately forty-five minutes. It was not until the appellants and the crowd, attracted by their activities, were impeding vehicular and pedestrian traffic upon the adjacent streets and sidewalks that the officers intervened in the interest of public order to stop the activities of the appellants at the time and place. [The appellants] were given fifteen minutes in which to disperse. The orders of the police officers under all of the facts and circumstances were reasonable and motivated solely by a proper concern for the preservation of order and prevention of further interference with traffic upon the public streets and sidewalks. The appellants not only refused to heed and obey the reasonable orders of the police, but engaged in a fifteen minute noisy demonstration in defiance of such orders.

The United States Supreme Court, after making its own "independent examination of the whole record," came to a different conclusion:

> The circumstances in this case reflect an exercise of [basic] constitutional rights in their most pristine and classic form. The petitioners . . . peaceably assembled at the site of the State Government and there peaceably expressed their grievances "to the citizens of South Carolina, along with the Legislative Bodies of South Carolina." Not until they were told by police officials that they must disperse on pain of arrest did they do more. Even then, they but sang patriotic and religious songs after one of their leaders had delivered a "religious harangue." There was no violence or threat of violence on their part, or on the part of any member of the crowd watching them. Police protection was "ample."
>
> This, therefore, was a far cry from the situation in *Feiner*, where two policemen were faced with a crowd which was "pushing, shoving and milling around," where at least one member of the crowd "threatened violence if the police did not act," where "the crowd was pressing closer around petitioner and the officer," and where "the speaker passes the bounds of argument or persuasion and undertakes incitement to riot." And the record is barren of any evidence of "fighting words." See *Chaplinsky*. . . .
>
> The Fourteenth Amendment does not permit a State to make criminal the peaceful expression of unpopular views. *Terminiello*. As in the *Terminiello* case, the courts of South Carolina have defined a criminal offense so as to permit conviction of the petitioners if their speech "stirred people to anger, invited public dispute, or brought about a condition of unrest. A conviction resting on any of those grounds may not stand."

Justice Stewart wrote for eight members of the Court. Only Justice Clark dissented. He said:

> [In] *Feiner*, we upheld a conviction for breach of the peace in a situation no more dangerous than that found here. . . . Here 200 youthful Negro

demonstrators were being aroused to a "fever pitch" before a crowd of some 300 people who undoubtedly were hostile. Perhaps their speech was not so animated but in this setting their actions, their placards reading "You may jail our bodies but not our souls" and their chanting of "I Shall Not Be Moved," accompanied by stamping feet and clapping hands, created a much greater danger of riot and disorder. It is my belief that anyone conversant with the almost spontaneous combustion in some Southern communities in such a situation will agree that the City Manager's action may well have averted a major catastrophe.

3. Justice Frankfurter joined the Court's opinion in *Feiner*, but he also wrote a concurring opinion. He said: "It is not a constitutional principle that, in acting to preserve order, the police must proceed against the crowd, whatever its size and temper, and not against the speaker." The Court has neither endorsed nor rejected that proposition. Is the proposition sound? What might explain the Court's reluctance to lay down a clear rule?

4. *Terminiello, Feiner*, and *Edwards* all involved criminal prosecutions in the aftermath of a speech or demonstration that generated a hostile response. Suppose local officials know in advance that an unpopular group plans to hold a rally or demonstration. The *Cantwell* dictum spoke approvingly of "the power of the State to *prevent*" immediate threats "to public safety, peace, or order." When and how may that power be exercised? We turn now to that question.

Forsyth County v. Nationalist Movement

505 U.S. 123 (1992)

Justice Blackmun delivered the opinion of the Court.

In this case, with its emotional overtones, we must decide whether the free speech guarantees of the First and Fourteenth Amendments are violated by an assembly and parade ordinance that permits a government administrator to vary the fee for assembling or parading to reflect the estimated cost of maintaining public order.

I

Petitioner Forsyth County is a primarily rural Georgia county approximately 30 miles northeast of Atlanta. It has had a troubled racial history. In 1912, in one month, its entire African-American population, over 1,000 citizens, was driven systematically from the county in the wake of the rape and murder of a white woman and the lynching of her accused assailant. Seventy-five years later, in 1987, the county population remained 99% white.

Spurred by this history, Hosea Williams, an Atlanta city councilman and civil rights personality, proposed a Forsyth County "March Against Fear and Intimidation" for January 17, 1987. Approximately 90 civil rights demonstrators attempted to parade in Cumming, the county seat. The marchers were met by members of the Forsyth County Defense League (an independent affiliate of respondent, The Nationalist Movement), of the Ku Klux Klan, and other Cumming residents. In all, some 400 counterdemonstrators lined the parade route, shouting racial slurs. Eventually, the counterdemonstrators, dramatically outnumbering police officers, forced the parade to a premature halt by throwing rocks and beer bottles.

Williams planned a return march the following weekend. It developed into the largest civil rights demonstration in the South since the 1960's. . . . The demonstration cost over $670,000 in police protection, of which Forsyth County apparently paid a small portion.

"As a direct result" of these two demonstrations, the Forsyth County Board of Commissioners enacted Ordinance 34. . . . The board of commissioners justified the ordinance by explaining that "the cost of necessary and reasonable protection of persons participating in or observing . . . parades, assemblies, demonstrations, road closings and other related activities exceeds the usual and normal cost of law enforcement for which those participating should be held accountable and responsible." [As amended, Ordinance 34 provides] that every permit applicant "'shall pay in advance for such permit, for the use of the County, a sum not more than $1,000.00 for each day such parade, procession, or open air public meeting shall take place.'" In addition, the county administrator was empowered to "'adjust the amount to be paid in order to meet the expense incident to the administration of the Ordinance and to the maintenance of public order in the matter licensed.'"

In January 1989, respondent The Nationalist Movement proposed to demonstrate in opposition to the federal holiday commemorating the birthday of Martin Luther King, Jr. In Forsyth County, the Movement sought to "conduct a rally and speeches for one and a half to two hours" on the courthouse steps on a Saturday afternoon. The county imposed a $100 fee. The fee did not include any calculation for expenses incurred by law enforcement authorities, but was based on 10 hours of the county administrator's time in issuing the permit. . . .

The Movement did not pay the fee and did not hold the rally. [Instead, it instituted this action requesting an injunction prohibiting Forsyth County from interfering with the Movement's plans. The District Court denied relief, but the Court of Appeals for the Eleventh Circuit reversed. The Court of Appeals held: "An ordinance which charges more than a nominal fee for using public forums for public issue speech, violates the First Amendment."] We granted certiorari to resolve a conflict among the Courts of Appeals concerning the constitutionality of charging a fee for a speaker in a public forum.

II

Respondent mounts a facial challenge to the Forsyth County ordinance. It is well established that in the area of freedom of expression an overbroad regulation may be subject to facial review and invalidation, even though its application in the case under consideration may be constitutionally unobjectionable. . . .

A

Respondent contends that the county ordinance is facially invalid because it does not prescribe adequate standards for the administrator to apply when he sets a permit fee. . . . In evaluating [this] challenge, we must consider the county's authoritative constructions of the ordinance, including its own implementation and interpretation of it. In the present litigation, the county has made clear how it interprets and implements the ordinance. The ordinance can apply to any activity on public property—from parades, to street corner speeches, to bike races—and the fee assessed may reflect the county's police and administrative costs. Whether or not, in any given instance, the fee would include any or all of the county's administrative and security expenses is decided by the county administrator.

In this case, according to testimony at the District Court hearing, the administrator based the fee on his own judgment of what would be reasonable. . . . The administrator also explained that the county had imposed a fee pursuant to a permit on two prior occasions. The year before, the administrator had assessed a fee of $100 for a permit for the Movement. . . . The administrator also once charged bike-race organizers $25 to hold a race on county roads . . . .

Based on the county's implementation and construction of the ordinance, it simply cannot be said that there are any "narrowly drawn, reasonable and definite standards" guiding the hand of the Forsyth County administrator. . . . There are no articulated standards either in the ordinance or in the county's established practice. . . . Nothing in the law or its application prevents the official from encouraging some views and discouraging others through the arbitrary application of fees.[10] The First Amendment prohibits the vesting of such unbridled discretion in a government official.

B

The Forsyth County ordinance contains more than the possibility of censorship through uncontrolled discretion. As construed by the county, the ordinance often requires that the fee be based on the content of the speech.

The county envisions that the administrator, in appropriate instances, will assess a fee to cover "the cost of necessary and reasonable protection of persons participating in or observing said . . . activity." In order to assess accurately the cost of security for parade participants, the administrator "'must necessarily examine the content of the message that is conveyed,'" estimate the response of others to that content, and judge the number of police necessary to meet that response. The fee assessed will depend on the administrator's measure of the amount of hostility likely to be created by the speech based on its content. Those wishing to express views unpopular with bottle throwers, for example, may have to pay more for their permit.

Although petitioner agrees that the cost of policing relates to content, it contends that the ordinance is content neutral because it is aimed only at a secondary effect—the cost of maintaining public order. It is clear, however, that, in this case, it cannot be said that the fee's justification "'has nothing to do with content.'"

---

10. The District Court's finding that in this instance the Forsyth County administrator applied legitimate, content-neutral criteria, even if correct, is irrelevant to this facial challenge. Facial attacks on the discretion granted a decisionmaker are not dependent on the facts surrounding any particular permit decision. See *Lakewood v. Plain Dealer Publishing Co.* (1988) [Chapter 4 Note]. . . .

The costs to which petitioner refers are those associated with the public's reaction to the speech. Listeners' reaction to speech is not a content-neutral basis for regulation. *Boos v. Barry* (1988) [Chapter 7]. Speech cannot be financially burdened, any more than it can be punished or banned, simply because it might offend a hostile mob.[12]

In this Court, petitioner specifically urges reversal because the lower court has "taken away the right of local government to obtain reimbursement for administration and *policing costs which are incurred in protecting those using government property for expression.*" (Emphasis added). When directly faced with the Court of Appeals' concern about "the enhanced cost associated with policing expressive activity which would generate potentially violent reactions," petitioner responded not by arguing that it did not intend to charge for police protection, but that such a charge was permissible because the ordinance provided a cap. At no point, in any level of proceedings, has petitioner intimated that it did not construe the ordinance consistent with its language permitting fees to be charged for the cost of police protection from hostile crowds. We find no disputed interpretation of the ordinance necessitating a remand.

. . . The county offers only one justification for this ordinance: raising revenue for police services. While this undoubtedly is an important government responsibility, it does not justify a content-based permit fee.

Petitioner insists that its ordinance cannot be unconstitutionally content based because it contains much of the same language as did the state statute upheld in *Cox v. New Hampshire* (1941) [*supra* this chapter]. Although the Supreme Court of New Hampshire had interpreted the statute at issue in *Cox* to authorize the municipality to charge a permit fee for the "maintenance of public order," no fee was actually assessed. Nothing in this Court's opinion suggests that the statute, as interpreted by the New Hampshire Supreme Court, called for charging a premium in the case of a controversial political message delivered before a hostile audience. In light of the Court's subsequent First Amendment jurisprudence, we do not read *Cox* to permit such a premium.

C

Petitioner, as well as the Court of Appeals and the District Court, all rely on the maximum allowable fee as the touchstone of constitutionality. Petitioner contends that the $1,000 cap on the fee ensures that the ordinance will not result in content-based discrimination. The ordinance was found unconstitutional by the Court of Appeals

---

12. The dissent prefers a remand because there are no lower court findings on the question whether the county plans to base parade fees on hostile crowds. We disagree. A remand is unnecessary because there is no question that petitioner intends the ordinance to recoup costs that are related to listeners' reaction to the speech. Petitioner readily admits it did not charge for police protection for the 4th of July parades, although they were substantial parades, which required the closing of streets and drew large crowds. Petitioner imposed a fee only when it became necessary to provide security for parade participants from angry crowds opposing their message. The ordinance itself makes plain that the costs at issue are those needed for "necessary and reasonable protection of persons participating in or observing" the speech. Repayment for police protection is the "most important" purpose underlying the ordinance.

because the $1,000 cap was not sufficiently low to be "nominal." Neither the $1,000 cap on the fee charged, nor even some lower nominal cap, could save the ordinance because in this context, the level of the fee is irrelevant. A tax based on the content of speech does not become more constitutional because it is a small tax.

The lower courts derived their requirement that the permit fee be "nominal" from a sentence in the opinion in *Murdock v. Pennsylvania*, 319 U.S. 105 (1943). In *Murdock*, the Court invalidated a flat license fee levied on distributors of religious literature. In distinguishing the case from *Cox*, where the Court upheld a permit fee, the Court stated: "And the fee is not a nominal one, imposed as a regulatory measure and calculated to defray the expense of protecting those on the streets and at home against the abuses of solicitors." This sentence does not mean that an invalid fee can be saved if it is nominal, or that only nominal charges are constitutionally permissible. It reflects merely one distinction between the facts in *Murdock* and those in *Cox*.

The tax at issue in *Murdock* was invalid because it was unrelated to any legitimate state interest, not because it was of a particular size. Similarly, the provision of the Forsyth County ordinance relating to fees is invalid because it unconstitutionally ties the amount of the fee to the content of the speech and lacks adequate procedural safeguards; no limit on such a fee can remedy these constitutional violations.

The judgment of the Court of Appeals is affirmed.

CHIEF JUSTICE REHNQUIST, with whom JUSTICE WHITE, JUSTICE SCALIA, and JUSTICE THOMAS join, dissenting.

We granted certiorari in this case to consider the following question:

Whether the provisions of the First Amendment to the United States Constitution limit the amount of a license fee assessed pursuant to the provisions of a county parade ordinance to a nominal sum or whether the amount of the license fee may take into account the actual expense incident to the administration of the ordinance and the maintenance of public order in the matter licensed, up to the sum of $1,000.00 per day of the activity.

. . . I believe that the decision in *Cox* squarely controls the disposition of [this question,] and I therefore would explicitly hold that the Constitution does not limit a parade license fee to a nominal amount.

Instead of deciding the particular question on which we granted certiorari, the Court concludes that the county ordinance is facially unconstitutional because it places too much discretion in the hands of the county administrator and forces parade participants to pay for the cost of controlling those who might oppose their speech. [Because the lower courts did not pass on these issues,] I would not decide at this point whether the ordinance fails for lack of adequate standards to guide discretion or for incorporation of a "heckler's veto," but would instead remand the case to the lower courts to initially consider these issues.

The Court first finds fault with the alleged standardless discretion possessed by the county administrator. The mere fact that the permit fees differed in amount does not invalidate the ordinance, however, as our decision in *Cox* clearly allows a governmental entity to adopt an adjustable permit fee scheme. It is true that the Constitution does not permit a system in which the county administrator may vary fees at his pleasure, but there has been no lower court finding that that is what this fledgling ordinance creates. . . .

The Court's second reason for invalidating the ordinance is its belief that any fee imposed will be based in part on the cost of security necessary to control those who *oppose* the message endorsed by those marching in a parade. . . . But there have been no lower court findings on the question whether or not the county plans to base parade fees on anticipated hostile crowds. It has not done so in any of the instances where it has so far imposed fees. And it most certainly did not do so in this case. The Court's analysis on this issue rests on an assumption that the county will interpret the phrase "maintenance of public order" to support the imposition of fees based on opposition crowds. There is nothing in the record to support this assumption, however, and I would remand for a hearing on this question.

————

Note: Fees and Permits for Demonstrations on Public Property

1. In *Cox v. New Hampshire*, the Court said that there was "nothing contrary to the Constitution" in charging different fees that "take into account the greater public expense of policing" parades that draw "crowds of observers." Does *Forsyth County* overrule *Cox* on that point?

2. The Court in *Forsyth County* holds that a fee is unconstitutional if the amount assessed depends on "the administrator's measure of the amount of hostility likely to be created by the speech based on its content." Does the dissent disagree with that proposition?

3. After *Forsyth County*, are governments limited to charging flat fees for the use of public property? If not, what variables may the government take into account? For example, could the city charge a higher fee for demonstrations organized by nonresidents than for those organized by residents? Or based on the size of the anticipated crowd?

4. When the Ku Klux Klan held a rally in a large eastern city a few years ago, a city council member pointed out that if residents of the city want to use a city park for a picnic, they must pay a fee and cover the costs of cleanup. He asked: why should the city have to bear the cost of the services it provides (traffic control, crowd management, cleanup, etc.) when an organization like the Klan uses city property for its rally? How would you answer that question?

5. After *Forsyth County*, what options does a city have when faced with an upcoming demonstration by a group whose rallies have often generated disorder in the past? Can the city impose conditions on the granting of a permit for the use of public property? If so, what kinds of conditions would be permissible? For example, could the city require groups seeking to use a city park to pay a security deposit "equal to the estimated cost of policing, cleaning up, and restoring the park upon the conclusion of the applicant's use or activity"?

6. In the late 1970s, the National Socialist Party of America (NSPA) announced its intention to march in the village of Skokie, Illinois. Members of the NSPA wear uniforms reminiscent of those worn by members of the German Nazi Party during the Third Reich, and they display swastikas both on their uniforms and on a red, white, and black flag they frequently carry. Skokie had a large Jewish population, including as many as several thousand survivors of the Nazi holocaust in Europe before and during World War II.

Village officials denied the NSPA a permit for its march, but the Seventh Circuit held that the denial was unconstitutional. The opinion acknowledged that, in light of the NSPA's views "and the historical associations they would bring with them to Skokie, many people would find their demonstration extremely mentally and emotionally disturbing." The court also expressed "the suspicion that such a result may be relished by" the NPSA. Nevertheless, after scrutinizing Skokie's arguments for disallowing the march, the court found that none of them carried the day. *Smith v. Collin*, 578 F.2d 1197 (7th Cir. 1978).

Suppose the court were to find, in a case like *Collin*, that the would-be marchers had no interest in persuading others to their views; rather, they "relished" the prospect of tormenting Holocaust survivors and their relatives. Would that be a basis for upholding the denial of a permit?

———

Problem: Klan Rally and Counter-Rally

The Ku Klux Klan has scheduled a "grievance rally" in downtown Memphis, Tennessee, on the steps of the county courthouse next Saturday. No permit was required, but the Klan notified city officials of their plans a few weeks ago. Upon learning of the Klan's intention, an opposition group obtained a permit to hold a "Unity" rally on the same day in Jefferson Park, which is across the street from the courthouse. Both rallies are scheduled to start at 2 p.m. and to finish no later than 4 p.m. The police have predicted that between 20 to 50 people will attend the Klan rally. How many will attend the Unity rally is uncertain, but the number is expected to be much larger.

Given the obvious conflicting messages of the two groups, the police suspect the possibility of violence and have developed a Public Safety Plan.

The primary mechanism for keeping the peace is to separate the Klan rally and the Unity rally. To do this, the police will establish a "restricted area" covering several blocks in downtown Memphis. This restricted area will be made up of two inner perimeters and an outer perimeter. The inner perimeters will encompass the rally sites; the outer perimeter will serve as a protective zone around the inner perimeters.

Under the Plan, no automobiles will be allowed into the inner perimeters. Pedestrians wanting to attend either rally will be required to pass through a magnetometer that will detect prohibited weapons like knives and guns. Attendees will also be forbidden to carry "sticks, flag or banner poles, bottles, nuts or bolts, rolled coins, rocks, bricks, cans and any other item that if thrown, could cause injury." Otherwise, no one will be denied entry to either rally. People going to the rallies may carry banners and signs, so long as they are not attached to a stick or pole.

The police plan to use temporary fences to keep the rallies separate. There will be a corridor 30 feet wide between the two rally sites. The police have designed a maze of fencing that will force visitors to choose the rally they wanted to attend and then guide them toward that rally. If a person wants to attend the other rally, he or she would have to leave the "restricted area" altogether, come back to the general entrance and once again go through the magnetometer. There will be no direct route between the two rallies.

Only scheduled speakers will be allowed to make a speech in the restricted area. In addition, there will be a police-enforced buffer zone between Klan speakers and the attendees at the Klan rally. Thus, attendees will not be allowed to commingle with the Klan speakers. No such buffer zone will separate attendees and speakers at the Unity rally.

The organizers of the Klan rally have filed suit in federal district seeking a temporary restraining order against certain elements of the Plan. These include the buffer zone within the Klan rally perimeter and the use of the magnetometer.

Some citizens of Memphis have intervened to challenge other elements of the Plan. They allege that their First Amendment rights will be violated by the separation of the two rallies; they allege, without contradiction, that persons attending one rally will not be able to see or hear the proceedings at the other rally. They also challenge the prohibition against speaking at the Klan rally by anyone other than the scheduled speakers.

Is the city's Plan constitutional? How might it be improved to serve both the interest in free speech and the interest in public order?

C. Access to Nontraditional Forums and Facilities

In *Hague v. CIO*, Justice Roberts articulated a right to use "streets and parks" for expressive purposes. Other language in the opinion suggested that the right might extend to other "public places." How far beyond "streets and parks" would the *Hague* dictum be taken? That question first came before the Court in cases arising out of civil rights protests. Today it is a major issue in First Amendment litigation.

————

Note: Competing Approaches to Speech on Public Property

1. In *Edwards v. South Carolina* (1963) (Note *supra* this chapter), the Supreme Court reversed breach-of-the-peace convictions arising out of a civil rights demonstration at the South Carolina State House grounds. The Court said that the defendants' conduct reflected "an exercise of [basic] constitutional rights in their most pristine and classic form." Three years later, in *Adderley v. Florida*, 385 U.S. 39 (1966), another group of civil rights demonstrators invoked *Edwards* in asking the Supreme Court to reverse their convictions for "trespass with a malicious and mischievous intent" upon the premises of the county jail in violation of the Florida trespass statute. But the Court, in an opinion by Justice Black, held that *Edwards* was not controlling. Justice Black wrote:

> The *Edwards* case, like this one, did come up when a number of persons demonstrated on public property against their State's segregation policies. They also sang hymns and danced, as did the demonstrators in this case. But here the analogies to this case end. In *Edwards*, the demonstrators went to the South Carolina State Capital grounds to protest. In this case they went to the jail. Traditionally, state capitol grounds are open to the public. Jails, built for security purposes, are not. . . .

> The [county] sheriff, as jail custodian, had power, as the state courts have here held, to direct that this large crowd of people get off the grounds. There is not a shred of evidence in this record that this power was exercised, or that its exercise was sanctioned by the lower courts, because the sheriff objected to what was being sung or said by the demonstrators or because he disagreed with the objectives of their protest. The record reveals that he objected only to their presence on that part of the jail grounds reserved for jail uses. There is no evidence at all that on any other occasion had similarly large groups of the public been permitted to gather on this portion of the jail grounds for any purpose. . . .

> The State, no less than a private owner of property, has power to preserve the property under its control for the use to which it is lawfully dedicated. For this reason there is no merit to the petitioners' argument that they had a constitutional right to stay on the property, over the jail custodian's objections, because this "area chosen for the peaceful civil rights demonstration was not only 'reasonable' but also particularly appropriate . . . ." Such an argument has as its major unarticulated premise the assumption that people who want to propagandize protests or views have a constitutional right to do so whenever and however and wherever they please. That concept of constitutional law was vigorously and forthrightly rejected in two [earlier cases]. We reject it again. The United States Constitution does not forbid a State to control the use of its own property for its own lawful nondiscriminatory purpose.

Four Justices dissented in an opinion by Justice Douglas. Justice Douglas wrote:

> The jailhouse, like an executive mansion, a legislative chamber, a courthouse, or the statehouse itself (*Edwards v. South Carolina*) is one of the seats of governments, whether it be the Tower of London, the Bastille, or a small county jail. And when it houses political prisoners or those who many think are unjustly held, it is an obvious center for protest. . . . Those who do not control television and radio, those who cannot afford to advertise in newspapers or circulate elaborate pamphlets may have only a more limited type of access to public officials. Their methods should not be condemned as tactics of obstruction and harassment as long as the assembly and petition are peaceable, as these were.

2. In some of its language, the *Adderley* opinion seemed to return to the position articulated by Justice Holmes in *Davis v. Massachusetts* (quoted in the Introduction to this chapter) and endorsed by the dissent in *Hague*: "For the legislature absolutely or conditionally to forbid public speaking in a highway or public park is no more an infringement of the rights of a member of the public than for the owner of a private house to forbid it in his house." However, six years later, the Court sounded a very different note.

In *Grayned v. City of Rockford*, 408 U.S. 104 (1972), the Court considered a case arising out of a demonstration in front of a high school in Rockford, Illinois. The defendant was convicted under the city's "antinoise" ordinance, which provided in relevant part:

> No person, while on public or private grounds adjacent to any building in which a school or any class thereof is in session, shall willfully make or assist in the making of any noise or diversion which disturbs or tends to disturb the peace or good order of such school session or class thereof.

The defendant argued that the ordinance was unconstitutional on its face because it unduly interfered with First and Fourteenth Amendment rights to picket on a public sidewalk near a school. The Supreme Court rejected that argument, but the opinion by Justice Marshall articulated a general approach that emphasized the First Amendment interests involved:

> The right to use a public place for expressive activity may be restricted only for weighty reasons.... The crucial question is whether the manner of expression is basically incompatible with the normal activity of a particular place at a particular time. Our cases make clear that in assessing the reasonableness of a regulation, we must weigh heavily the fact that communication is involved; the regulation must be narrowly tailored to further the State's legitimate interest.

One might expect that after stating the test in this way the Court would reverse the conviction, but it did not. Rather, the Court found that Rockford's ordinance was not "an unconstitutional regulation of activity around a school." The Court said:

> Rockford's antinoise ordinance ... is narrowly tailored to further Rockford's compelling interest in having an undisrupted school session conducive to the students' learning, and does not unnecessarily interfere with First Amendment rights. Far from having an impermissibly broad prophylactic ordinance, Rockford punishes only conduct which disrupts or is about to disrupt normal school activities. That decision is made, as it should be, on an individualized basis, given the particular fact situation. Peaceful picketing which does not interfere with the ordinary functioning of the school is permitted. And the ordinance gives no license to punish anyone because of what he is saying....
>
> In *Cox v. Louisiana*, 379 U.S. 559 (1965), this Court indicated that, because of the special nature of the place, persons could be constitutionally prohibited from picketing "in or near" a courthouse "with the intent of interfering with,

obstructing, or impeding administration of justice." Likewise, in *Cameron v. Johnson*, 390 U.S. 611 (1968), we upheld a statute prohibiting picketing "in such a manner as to obstruct or unreasonably interfere with free ingress or egress to and from any . . . county . . . courthouses." As in those two cases, Rockford's modest restriction on some peaceful picketing represents a considered and specific legislative judgment that some kinds of expressive activity should be restricted at a particular time and place, here in order to protect the schools. Such a reasonable regulation is not inconsistent with the First and Fourteenth Amendments. The antinoise ordinance is not invalid on its face.

The Court also rejected the defendant's argument that the ordinance was impermissibly vague. For that part of the opinion, see Chapter 4.

3. *Adderley* suggested a categorical approach to First Amendment claims of a right to use public property for expressive purposes: "Traditionally, state capitol grounds are open to the public. Jails, built for security purposes, are not." *Grayned* articulated a seemingly more nuanced view: "The crucial question is whether the manner of expression is basically incompatible with the normal activity of *a particular place at a particular time*." (Emphasis added.) Which approach is preferable? Consider that question as you read the Justices' opinions in the cases that follow.

4. *Adderley* and *Grayned* both involved demonstrations in a publicly owned place — in particular, the grounds of a government building. Two years after *Grayned*, the Court confronted a claim of access to a very different kind of public property.

Lehman v. City of Shaker Heights
418 U.S. 298 (1974)

Mr. Justice Blackmun announced the judgment of the Court and an opinion, in which The Chief Justice [Burger], Mr. Justice White, and Mr. Justice Rehnquist join.

This case presents the question whether a city which operates a public rapid transit system and sells advertising space for car cards on its vehicles is required by the First and Fourteenth Amendments to accept paid political advertising on behalf of a candidate for public office.

In 1970, petitioner Harry J. Lehman was a candidate for the office of State Representative to the Ohio General Assembly for District 56. The district includes the city of Shaker Heights. On July 3, 1970, petitioner sought to promote his candidacy by purchasing car card space on the Shaker Heights Rapid Transit System for the months of August, September, and October. The general election was scheduled for November 3. Petitioner's proposed copy contained his picture and read:

"HARRY J. LEHMAN IS OLD-FASHIONED!

ABOUT HONESTY, INTEGRITY AND GOOD GOVERNMENT

"State Representative—District 56 [X] Harry J. Lehman."

. . . [When petitioner applied for space, he was informed] that, although space was then available, the management agreement with the city did not permit political advertising. The system, however, accepted ads from cigarette companies, banks, savings and loan associations, liquor companies, retail and service establishments, churches, and civic and public-service oriented groups. There was uncontradicted testimony at the trial that during the 26 years of public operation, the Shaker Heights system, pursuant to city council action, had not accepted or permitted any political or public issue advertising on its vehicles.

When petitioner did not succeed in his effort to have his copy accepted, he sought declaratory and injunctive relief in the state courts of Ohio without success. . . .

It is urged that the car cards here constitute a public forum protected by the First Amendment, and that there is a guarantee of nondiscriminatory access to such publicly owned and controlled areas of communication "regardless of the primary purpose for which the area is dedicated."

We disagree. . . . "The streetcar audience is a captive audience. It is there as a matter of necessity, not of choice." *Public Utilities Comm'n v. Pollak*, 343 U.S. 451, 468 (1952) (Douglas, J., dissenting). In such situations, "[the] legislature may recognize degrees of evil and adapt its legislation accordingly." *Packer Corp. v. Utah*, 285 U.S. 105 (1932).

These situations are different from the traditional settings where First Amendment values inalterably prevail. Lord Dunedin, in *M'Ara v. Magistrates of Edinburgh*, (1913) Sess. Cas. 1059, 1073–74, said: "[The] truth is that open spaces and public places differ very much in their character, and before you could say whether a certain thing could be done in a certain place you would have to know the history of the particular place." Although American constitutional jurisprudence, in the light of the First Amendment, has been jealous to preserve access to public places for purposes of free speech, the nature of the forum and the conflicting interests involved have remained important in determining the degree of protection afforded by the Amendment to the speech in question.

Here, we have no open spaces, no meeting hall, park, street corner, or other public thoroughfare. Instead, the city is engaged in commerce. It must provide rapid, convenient, pleasant, and inexpensive service to the commuters of Shaker Heights. The car card space, although incidental to the provision of public transportation, is a part of the commercial venture. In much the same way that a newspaper or periodical, or even a radio or television station, need not accept every proffer of advertising from the general public, a city transit system has discretion to develop and make reasonable choices concerning the type of advertising that may be displayed in its vehicles. . . .

Because state action exists, however, the policies and practices governing access to the transit system's advertising space must not be arbitrary, capricious, or invidious. Here, the city has decided that "[purveyors] of goods and services saleable in commerce may purchase advertising space on an equal basis, whether they be house builders or butchers." This decision is little different from deciding to impose a 10-, 25-, or

35-cent fare, or from changing schedules or the location of bus stops. Revenue earned from long-term commercial advertising could be jeopardized by a requirement that short-term candidacy or issue-oriented advertisements be displayed on car cards. Users would be subjected to the blare of political propaganda. There could be lurking doubts about favoritism, and sticky administrative problems might arise in parceling out limited space to eager politicians. In these circumstances, the managerial decision to limit car card space to innocuous and less controversial commercial and service oriented advertising does not rise to the dignity of a First Amendment violation. Were we to hold to the contrary, display cases in public hospitals, libraries, office buildings, military compounds, and other public facilities immediately would become Hyde Parks open to every would-be pamphleteer and politician. This the Constitution does not require.

No First Amendment forum is here to be found. The city consciously has limited access to its transit system advertising space in order to minimize chances of abuse, the appearance of favoritism, and the risk of imposing upon a captive audience. These are reasonable legislative objectives advanced by the city in a proprietary capacity. In these circumstances, there is no First or Fourteenth Amendment violation.

Mr. Justice Douglas, concurring in the judgment.

. . . [A] streetcar or bus is plainly not a park or sidewalk or other meeting place for discussion, any more than is a highway. It is only a way to get to work or back home. The fact that it is owned and operated by the city does not without more make it a forum. . . .

In asking us to force the system to accept his message as a vindication of his constitutional rights, the petitioner overlooks the constitutional rights of the commuters. While petitioner clearly has a right to express his views to those who wish to listen, he has no right to force his message upon an audience incapable of declining to receive it. In my view the right of the commuters to be free from forced intrusions on their privacy precludes the city from transforming its vehicles of public transportation into forums for the dissemination of ideas upon this captive audience.

Buses are not recreational vehicles used for Sunday chautauquas as a public park might be used on holidays for such a purpose; they are a practical necessity for millions in our urban centers. I have already stated this view in my dissent in *Public Utilities Comm'n v. Pollak*, 343 U.S. 451, 469, involving the challenge by some passengers to the practice of broadcasting radio programs over loudspeakers in buses and streetcars: "One who tunes in on an offensive program at home can turn it off or tune in another station, as he wishes. One who hears disquieting or unpleasant programs in public places, such as restaurants, can get up and leave. But the man on the streetcar has no choice but to sit and listen, or perhaps to sit and to try *not* to listen." There is no difference when the message is visual, not auricular. In each the viewer or listener is captive. . . .

Since I do not believe that petitioner has any constitutional right to spread his message before this captive audience, I concur in the Court's judgment.

Mr. Justice Brennan, with whom Mr. Justice Stewart, Mr. Justice Marshall, and Mr. Justice Powell join, dissenting.

. . . By accepting commercial and public service advertising, the city effectively waived any argument that advertising in its transit cars is incompatible with the rapid transit system's primary function of providing transportation. A forum for communication was voluntarily established when the city installed the physical facilities for the advertisements and . . . created the necessary administrative machinery for regulating access to that forum.

Once a public forum for communication has been established, both free speech and equal protection principles prohibit discrimination based solely upon subject matter or content. *See, e.g., Police Department of Chicago v. Mosley* (1972) [Chapter 5]. That the discrimination is among entire classes of ideas, rather than among points of view within a particular class, does not render it any less odious. Subject matter or content censorship in any form is forbidden. . . .

The Court's special vigilance is triggered in this case because of the city's undisputed ban against political advertising in its transit cars. Commercial and public service advertisements are routinely accepted for display, while political messages are absolutely prohibited. . . . For instance, a commercial advertisement peddling snowmobiles would be accepted, while a counter-advertisement calling upon the public to support legislation controlling the environmental destruction and noise pollution caused by snowmobiles would be rejected. . . .

The city contends that its ban against political advertising is bottomed upon its solicitous regard for "captive riders" of the rapid transit system, who are "forced to endure the advertising thrust upon [them]." . . . Whatever merit the city's argument might have in other contexts, it has a hollow ring in the present case, where the city has voluntarily opened its rapid transit system as a forum for communication. In that circumstance, the occasional appearance of provocative speech should be expected. . . .

. . . This is not a case where an unwilling or unsuspecting rapid transit rider is powerless to avoid messages he deems unsettling. The advertisements accepted by the city and Metromedia are not broadcast over loudspeakers in the transit cars. . . . Should passengers chance to glance at advertisements they find offensive, they can "effectively avoid further bombardment of their sensibilities simply by averting their eyes." *Cohen v. California* (1971) [Chapter 3]. Surely that minor inconvenience is a small price to pay for the continued preservation of so precious a liberty as free speech.

The city's remaining justification is equally unpersuasive. The city argues that acceptance of "political advertisements in the cars of the Shaker Heights rapid transit, would suggest, on the one hand, some political favoritism is being granted to candidates who advertise, or, on the other hand, that the candidate so advertised is being supported or promoted by the government of the City." [But "the] endorsement of an opinion expressed in an advertisement on a motor coach is no more attributable to the transit district than the view of a speaker in a public park is to the city administration or the tenets of an organization using school property for meetings is to the local school board." . . .

Note: Lehman *and the* Perry *Synthesis*

1. The plurality in *Lehman* quotes with approval from an opinion by Lord Dunedin in a 1913 case in a Scottish court. Is that a plausible source of insight into the appropriate interpretation of the First Amendment to the United States Constitution?

2. *Lehman* was one of many cases in the 1970s and early 1980s in which the Court considered whether the government was obliged to grant access to public property for expressive activity. For the most part, the claims were rejected. Among the array of decisions, one stands out because the Court self-consciously sought to synthesize its precedents addressing such claims. This was *Perry Education Association v. Perry Local Educators' Association*, 460 U.S. 37 (1983). Justice White, writing for the Court, divided public property into three categories, with different First Amendment rules for each category. The opinion explained:

> The existence of a right of access to public property and the standard by which limitations upon such a right must be evaluated differ depending on the character of the property at issue.

> In places which by long tradition or by government fiat have been devoted to assembly and debate, the rights of the state to limit expressive activity are sharply circumscribed. At one end of the spectrum are streets and parks which "have immemorially been held in trust for the use of the public, and, time out of mind, have been used for purposes of assembly, communicating thoughts between citizens, and discussing public questions." *Hague v. CIO* (1939) [*supra* this chapter]. In these quintessential public forums, the government may not prohibit all communicative activity. For the state to enforce a content-based exclusion it must show that its regulation is necessary to serve a compelling state interest and that it is narrowly drawn to achieve that end. The state may also enforce regulations of the time, place, and manner of expression which are content-neutral, are narrowly tailored to serve a significant government interest, and leave open ample alternative channels of communication.

> A second category consists of public property which the state has opened for use by the public as a place for expressive activity. The Constitution forbids a state to enforce certain exclusions from a forum generally open to the public even if it was not required to create the forum in the first place. Although a state is not required to indefinitely retain the open character of the facility, as long as it does so it is bound by the same standards as apply in a traditional public forum. Reasonable time, place and manner regulations are permissible, and a content-based prohibition must be narrowly drawn to effectuate a compelling state interest.

> Public property which is not by tradition or designation a forum for public communication is governed by different standards. . . . In addition to time, place, and manner regulations, the state may reserve the forum for its

intended purposes, communicative or otherwise, as long as the regulation on speech is reasonable and not an effort to suppress expression merely because public officials oppose the speaker's view.

3. The Court's first category — the "quintessential" public forum — encompasses places which "*immemorially . . .* have been used" for expressive purposes. (Emphasis added.) The Court lists "streets and parks"; other decisions have made clear that the category also includes public sidewalks. The Court has emphasized, too, that streets and sidewalks do not lose their status as traditional public forums simply because they run through residential neighborhoods. *See, e.g., Frisby v. Schultz* (1988) (Chapter 6).

Beyond this, however, the category is not readily subject to expansion. Thus, in the litigated cases, plaintiffs argue that various types of government property fall with the Court's second category. But what does it mean to say that "the state has opened [property] for use by the public as a place for expressive activity"? Will any allowance of use by the public satisfy this standard? *Perry* made clear that the answer is "no." Rather, the Court distinguishes between "indiscriminate use" and "selective use."

Perry itself involved the inter-school mail system in a public school district. Under the district's collective bargaining agreement, access was granted to the union that represented the teachers, but not to other unions. A rival union, the Perry Local Educators' Association (PLEA), brought suit seeking access to the mail system. PLEA argued that because the district had allowed "periodic use of the system by private non-school connected groups," the system had become a limited public forum. The Supreme Court disagreed:

> If by policy or by practice the Perry School District has opened its mail system for indiscriminate use by the general public, then [the rival union] could justifiably argue a public forum has been created. This, however, is not the case. . . . Permission to use the system to communicate with teachers must be secured from the individual building principal. There is no court finding or evidence in the record which demonstrates that this permission has been granted as a matter of course to all who seek to distribute material. We can only conclude that the schools do allow some outside organizations such as the YMCA, Cub Scouts, and other civic and church organizations to use the facilities. This type of selective access does not transform government property into a public forum.

4. The Court in *Perry* went on to give governments a second line of defense against claims of access to property that is not a traditional forum:

> [Even] if we assume that by granting access to the Cub Scouts, YMCAs, and parochial schools, the school district has created a "limited" public forum, the constitutional right of access would in any event extend only to other entities of similar character. While the school mail facilities thus might be a forum generally open for use by the Girl Scouts, the local boys' club and other organizations that engage in activities of interest and educational relevance to students, they would not as a consequence be open to an

organization such as PLEA, which is concerned with the terms and conditions of teacher employment.

Cornelius v. NAACP Legal Defense and Educational Fund, Inc.
473 U.S. 788 (1985)

JUSTICE O'CONNOR delivered the opinion of the Court.

This case requires us to decide whether the Federal Government violates the First Amendment when it excludes legal defense and political advocacy organizations from participation in the Combined Federal Campaign (CFC or Campaign), a charity drive aimed at federal employees. . . .

I

The CFC is an annual charitable fundraising drive conducted in the federal workplace during working hours largely through the voluntary efforts of federal employees. At all times relevant to this litigation, participating organizations confined their fundraising activities to a 30-word statement submitted by them for inclusion in the Campaign literature. Volunteer federal employees distribute to their co-workers literature describing the Campaign and the participants along with pledge cards. . . . Contributions may take the form of either a payroll deduction or a lump-sum payment made to a designated agency or to the general Campaign fund. Undesignated contributions are distributed on the local level by a private umbrella organization to certain participating organizations. Designated funds are paid directly to the specified recipient. Through the CFC, the Government employees contribute in excess of $100 million to charitable organizations each year. . . .

Respondents in this case are the NAACP Legal Defense and Educational Fund, Inc., the Sierra Club Legal Defense Fund, [and other similar groups]. Each of the respondents attempts to influence public policy through one or more of the following means: political activity, advocacy, lobbying, or litigation on behalf of others. . . .

[After prior lawsuits,] President Reagan took several steps to restore the CFC to what he determined to be its original purpose. . . . [An Executive Order specified that the] CFC was designed to lessen the Government's burden in meeting human health and welfare needs by providing a convenient, nondisruptive channel for federal employees to contribute to nonpartisan agencies that directly serve those needs. The Order limited participation to "voluntary, charitable, health and welfare agencies that provide or support direct health and welfare services to individuals or their families," and specifically excluded those "[agencies] that seek to influence the outcomes of elections or the determination of public policy through political activity or advocacy, lobbying, or litigation on behalf of parties other than themselves."

Respondents brought this action challenging their threatened exclusion under the new Executive Order. The Court of Appeals held that the Government restrictions were not reasonable and therefore failed even the least exacting scrutiny. . . .

II

The issue presented is whether respondents have a First Amendment right to solicit contributions that was violated by their exclusion from the CFC. To resolve this issue we must first decide whether solicitation in the context of the CFC is speech protected by the First Amendment, for, if it is not, we need go no further. Assuming that such solicitation is protected speech, we must identify the nature of the forum, because the extent to which the Government may limit access depends on whether the forum is public or nonpublic. Finally, we must assess whether the justifications for exclusion from the relevant forum satisfy the requisite standard. Applying this analysis, we find that respondents' solicitation is protected speech occurring in the context of a nonpublic forum and that the Government's reasons for excluding respondents from the CFC appear, at least facially, to satisfy the reasonableness standard. We express no opinion on the question whether petitioner's explanation is merely a pretext for viewpoint discrimination. Accordingly, we reverse and remand for further proceedings consistent with this opinion.

A

Charitable solicitation of funds has been recognized by this Court as a form of protected speech. *Village of Schaumburg v. Citizens for a Better Environment*, 444 U.S. 620 (1980).... [The 30-word written statements] in the CFC literature directly advance the speaker's interest in informing readers about its existence and its goals. [These statements implicate] interests protected by the First Amendment.

B

The conclusion that the solicitation which occurs in the CFC is protected speech merely begins our inquiry. Even protected speech is not equally permissible in all places and at all times. Nothing in the Constitution requires the Government freely to grant access to all who wish to exercise their right to free speech on every type of Government property without regard to the nature of the property or to the disruption that might be caused by the speaker's activities. Recognizing that the Government, "no less than a private owner of property, has power to preserve the property under its control for the use to which it is lawfully dedicated," *Greer v. Spock*, 424 U.S. 828, 836 (1976), the Court has adopted a forum analysis as a means of determining when the Government's interest in limiting the use of its property to its intended purpose outweighs the interest of those wishing to use the property for other purposes. . . .

To determine whether the First Amendment permits the Government to exclude respondents from the CFC, we must first decide whether the forum consists of the federal workplace, as petitioner contends, or the CFC, as respondents maintain. Having defined the relevant forum, we must then determine whether it is public or nonpublic in nature.

Petitioner contends that a First Amendment forum necessarily consists of tangible government property. [However, we] agree with respondents that the relevant forum for our purposes is the CFC. Although petitioner is correct that as an initial matter a speaker must seek access to public property or to private property dedicated to public use to evoke First Amendment concerns, forum analysis is not completed merely by identifying the government property at issue. Rather, in defining the forum we have focused on the access sought by the speaker. When speakers seek general access to public property, the forum encompasses that property. *See, e.g., Greer v. Spock, supra.* In cases in which limited access is sought, our cases have taken a more tailored approach to ascertaining the perimeters of a forum within the confines of the government property. For example, *Perry Education Association v. Perry Local Educators' Association* (1983) [Note *supra* this chapter] examined the access sought by the speaker and defined the forum as a school's internal mail system and the teachers' mailboxes, notwithstanding that an "internal mail system" lacks a physical situs. Similarly, in *Lehman v. City of Shaker Heights* (1974) [*supra* this chapter], where petitioners sought to compel the city to permit political advertising on city-owned buses, the Court treated the advertising spaces on the buses as the forum.

Here, as in *Perry*, respondents seek access to a particular means of communication. Consistent with the approach taken in prior cases, we find that the CFC, rather than the federal workplace, is the forum. This conclusion does not mean, however, that the Court will ignore the special nature and function of the federal workplace in evaluating the limits that may be imposed on an organization's right to participate in the CFC. See *Perry*.

Having identified the forum as the CFC, we must decide whether it is nonpublic or public in nature. Most relevant in this regard, of course, is *Perry*. There the Court identified three types of fora: the traditional public forum, the public forum created by government designation, and the nonpublic forum. Traditional public fora are those places which "by long tradition or by government fiat have been devoted to assembly and debate." Public streets and parks fall into this category. In addition to traditional public fora, a public forum may be created by government designation of a place or channel of communication for use by the public at large for assembly and speech, for use by certain speakers, or for the discussion of certain subjects. Of course, the government "is not required to indefinitely retain the open character of the facility."

The government does not create a public forum by inaction or by permitting limited discourse, but only by intentionally opening a nontraditional forum for public discourse. Accordingly, the Court has looked to the policy and practice of the government to ascertain whether it intended to designate a place not traditionally open to assembly and debate as a public forum. The Court has also examined the nature of the property and its compatibility with expressive activity to discern the government's intent. For example, in *Widmar v. Vincent*, 454 U.S. 263 (1981), we found that a state university that had an express policy of making its meeting facilities available to registered student groups had created a public forum for their use. . . . Additionally, we noted that a university campus, at least as to its students, possesses many of the characteristics of a traditional public forum. . . . Similarly, the Court found a public forum where a municipal auditorium and a city-leased theater were designed for and dedicated to expressive activities. *Southeastern Promotions, Ltd. v. Conrad*, 420 U.S. 546 (1975).

Not every instrumentality used for communication, however, is a traditional public forum or a public forum by designation. [The Court cited, *inter alia, Perry Education Assn.* and *Lehman v. City of Shaker Heights.*] In cases where the principal function of the property would be disrupted by expressive activity, the Court is particularly reluctant to hold that the government intended to designate a public forum. Accordingly, we have held that military reservations, *Greer v. Spock*, 424 U.S. 828 (1976), and jailhouse grounds, *Adderley v. Florida* (1966) [*supra* this chapter Note], do not constitute public fora.

Here the parties agree that neither the CFC nor the federal workplace is a traditional public forum. Respondents argue, however, that the Government created a limited public forum for use by all charitable organizations to solicit funds from federal employees. Petitioner contends, and we agree, that neither its practice nor its policy is consistent with an intent to designate the CFC as a public forum open to all tax-exempt organizations. In 1980, an estimated 850,000 organizations qualified for tax-exempt status. In contrast, only 237 organizations participated in the 1981 CFC of the National Capital Area. The Government's consistent policy has been to limit participation in the CFC to "appropriate" voluntary agencies and to require agencies seeking admission to obtain permission from federal and local Campaign officials. Although the record does not show how many organizations have been denied permission throughout the 24-year history of the CFC, there is no evidence suggesting that the granting of the requisite permission is merely ministerial. The Civil Service Commission and, after 1978, the Office of Personnel Management developed extensive admission criteria to limit access to the Campaign to those organizations considered appropriate. Such selective access, unsupported by evidence of a purposeful designation for public use, does not create a public forum.

Nor does the history of the CFC support a finding that the Government was motivated by an affirmative desire to provide an open forum for charitable solicitation in the federal workplace when it began the Campaign. The historical background indicates that the Campaign was designed to minimize the disruption to the workplace that had resulted from unlimited ad hoc solicitation activities by *lessening* the amount of expressive activity occurring on federal property. Indeed, the OPM stringently limited expression to the 30-word statement included in the Campaign literature. The decision of the Government to limit access to the CFC is not dispositive in itself; instead, it is relevant for what it suggests about the Government's intent in creating the forum. The Government did not create the CFC for purposes of providing a forum for expressive activity. That such activity occurs in the context of the forum created does not imply that the forum thereby becomes a public forum for First Amendment purposes.

An examination of the nature of the Government property involved strengthens the conclusion that the CFC is a nonpublic forum. The federal workplace, like any place of employment, exists to accomplish the business of the employer. It follows that the Government has the right to exercise control over access to the federal workplace in order to avoid interruptions to the performance of the duties of its employees. In light of the Government policy in creating the CFC and its practice in limiting access, we conclude that the CFC is a nonpublic forum.

C

Control over access to a nonpublic forum can be based on subject matter and speaker identity so long as the distinctions drawn are reasonable in light of the purpose served by the forum and are viewpoint neutral. *Perry Education Assn.* Although a speaker may be excluded from a nonpublic forum if he wishes to address a topic not encompassed within the purpose of the forum, see *Lehman*, or if he is not a member of the class of speakers for whose especial benefit the forum was created, see *Perry Education Assn.*, the government violates the First Amendment when it denies access to a speaker solely to suppress the point of view he espouses on an otherwise includible subject. The Court of Appeals found it unnecessary to resolve whether the government's denial of access to respondents was viewpoint based, because it determined that respondents' exclusion was unreasonable in light of the purpose served by the CFC. . . .

[The Court of Appeals agreed with respondents that] the reasonableness standard is satisfied only when there is some basic incompatibility between the communication at issue and the principal activity occurring on the Government property. . . . [This conclusion] fails to reflect the nature of a nonpublic forum. The Government's decision to restrict access to a nonpublic forum need only be *reasonable*; it need not be the most reasonable or the only reasonable limitation. In contrast to a public forum, a finding of strict incompatibility between the nature of the speech or the identity of the speaker and the functioning of the nonpublic forum is not mandated. *Cf. Perry Education Assn.; Lehman.* Even if some incompatibility with general expressive activity were required, the CFC would meet the requirement because it would be administratively unmanageable if access could not be curtailed in a reasonable manner. Nor is there a requirement that the restriction be narrowly tailored or that the Government's interest be compelling. The First Amendment does not demand unrestricted access to a nonpublic forum merely because use of that forum may be the most efficient means of delivering the speaker's message. Rarely will a nonpublic forum provide the only means of contact with a particular audience. Here, as in *Perry Education Assn.*, the speakers have access to alternative channels, including direct mail and in-person solicitation outside the workplace, to solicit contributions from federal employees.

The reasonableness of the Government's restriction of access to a nonpublic forum must be assessed in the light of the purpose of the forum and all the surrounding circumstances. Here the President could reasonably conclude that a dollar directly spent on providing food or shelter to the needy is more beneficial than a dollar spent on litigation that might or might not result in aid to the needy. Moreover, avoiding the appearance of political favoritism is a valid justification for limiting speech in a nonpublic forum. [See] *Lehman.* In furthering this interest, the Government is not bound by decisions of other executive agencies made in other contexts. Thus, respondents' tax status, while perhaps relevant, does not determine the reasonableness of the Government's conclusion that participation by such agencies in the CFC will create the appearance of favoritism.

The Court of Appeals' rejection of the Government's interest in avoiding controversy that would disrupt the workplace and adversely affect the Campaign is inconsistent with our prior cases. In *Perry Education Assn.*, we noted that "exclusion of the rival union may reasonably be considered a means of insuring labor peace within the schools." Similarly, the exclusion of respondents may reasonably be considered a means of "insuring peace" in the federal workplace. Inasmuch as the Court of Appeals rejected this reason for lack of conclusive proof of an actual effect on the workplace, it ignored the teachings of this Court that the Government need not wait until havoc is wreaked to restrict access to a nonpublic forum.

Finally, the record amply supports an inference that respondents' participation in the CFC jeopardized the success of the Campaign. OPM submitted a number of letters from federal employees and managers, as well as from Chairmen of local Federal Coordinating Committees and Members of Congress expressing concern about the inclusion of groups termed "political" or "nontraditional" in the CFC. . . . Thus, the record adequately supported petitioner's position that respondents' continued participation in the Campaign would be detrimental to the Campaign and disruptive of the federal workplace. Although the avoidance of controversy is not a valid ground for restricting speech in a public forum, a nonpublic forum by definition is not dedicated to general debate or the free exchange of ideas. The First Amendment does not forbid a viewpoint-neutral exclusion of speakers who would disrupt a nonpublic forum and hinder its effectiveness for its intended purpose.

D

On this record, the Government's posited justifications for denying respondents access to the CFC appear to be reasonable in light of the purpose of the CFC. The existence of reasonable grounds for limiting access to a nonpublic forum, however, will not save a regulation that is in reality a facade for viewpoint-based discrimination. . . .

Petitioner argues that a decision to exclude all advocacy groups, regardless of political or philosophical orientation, is by definition viewpoint neutral. Exclusion of groups advocating the use of litigation is not viewpoint-based, petitioner asserts, because litigation is a means of promoting a viewpoint, not a viewpoint in itself. While we accept the validity and reasonableness of the justifications offered by petitioner for excluding advocacy groups from the CFC, those justifications cannot save an exclusion that is in fact based on the desire to suppress a particular point of view.

Petitioner contends that controversial groups must be eliminated from the CFC to avoid disruption and ensure the success of the Campaign. As noted *supra*, we agree that these are facially neutral and valid justifications for exclusion from the nonpublic forum created by the CFC. Nonetheless, the purported concern to avoid controversy excited by particular groups may conceal a bias against the viewpoint advanced by the excluded speakers. In addition, petitioner maintains that limiting CFC participation to organizations that provide direct health and welfare services to needy persons is necessary to achieve the goals of the CFC as set forth in Executive Order 12404. Although this concern is also sufficient to provide reasonable grounds for excluding certain groups from the CFC, respondents offered some evidence to cast doubt on its genuineness. Organizations that do not provide direct health and welfare services, such as the World Wildlife Fund, the Wilderness Society, and the United States Olympic Committee, have been permitted to participate in the CFC.

Although there is no requirement that regulations limiting access to a nonpublic forum must be precisely tailored, the issue whether the Government excluded respondents because it disagreed with their viewpoints was neither decided below nor fully briefed before this Court. We decline to decide in the first instance whether the exclusion of respondents was impermissibly motivated by a desire to suppress a particular point of view. Respondents are free to pursue this contention on remand.

III

We conclude that the Government does not violate the First Amendment when it limits participation in the CFC in order to minimize disruption to the federal workplace, to ensure the success of the fundraising effort, or to avoid the appearance of political favoritism without regard to the viewpoint of the excluded groups. Accordingly, we reverse the judgment of the Court of Appeals that the exclusion of respondents was unreasonable, and we remand this case for further proceedings consistent with this opinion.

JUSTICE MARSHALL took no part in the consideration or decision of this case. JUSTICE POWELL took no part in the decision of this case.

JUSTICE BLACKMUN, with whom JUSTICE BRENNAN joins, dissenting.

I agree with the Court that the Combined Federal Campaign (CFC) is not a traditional public forum. [However, I cannot accept] the Court's circular reasoning that the CFC is not a limited public forum because the Government intended to limit the forum to a particular class of speakers. Nor can I agree with the Court's conclusion that distinctions the Government makes between speakers in defining the limits of a forum need not be narrowly tailored and necessary to achieve a compelling governmental interest. Finally, I would hold that the exclusion of the several respondents from the CFC was, on its face, viewpoint-based discrimination. Accordingly, I dissent.

I

[Justice Blackmun reviewed the origins and development of the public forum doctrine. He concluded:] [The] public forum, limited-public-forum, and nonpublic forum categories are but analytical shorthand for the principles that have guided the Court's decisions regarding claims to access to public property for expressive activity. . . . [The] fact that the Government "owns" the property to which a citizen seeks access for expressive activity does not dispose of the First Amendment claim; it requires that we balance the First Amendment interests of those who seek access for expressive activity against the interests of the other users of the property and the interests served by reserving the property for its intended uses. The Court's analysis forsakes that balancing, and abandons the compatibility test that always has served as a threshold indicator of the proper balance.

B

Not only does the Court err in labeling the CFC a nonpublic forum without first engaging in a compatibility inquiry, but it errs as well in reasoning that the CFC is not a limited public forum because the Government permitted only "limited discourse," rather than "intentionally opening" the CFC for "public discourse." That reasoning is at odds with the cases in which the Court has found public property to be a limited public forum. Just as the Government's "consistent policy has been to limit participation in the CFC to 'appropriate' voluntary agencies and to require agencies seeking admission to obtain permission" from the relevant officials, the theater in *Southeastern Promotions, Ltd.*, limited the use of its facilities to "clean, healthful entertainment which will make for the upbuilding of a better citizenship" and required productions wishing to use the theater to obtain permission of the relevant officials. Under the Court's reasoning, therefore, the theater in *Southeastern Promotions* would not have been a limited public forum. Similarly, the university meeting rooms in *Widmar v. Vincent*, despite the Court's disclaimer, would not have been a limited public forum by the Court's reasoning, because the University had a policy of "selective access" whereby only registered nonreligious student groups, not religious student groups or the public at large, were allowed to meet in the rooms....

C

The Court's analysis empties the limited-public-forum concept of meaning and collapses the three categories of public forum, limited public forum, and nonpublic forum into two. The Court makes it *virtually* impossible to prove that a forum restricted to a particular class of speakers is a limited public forum. If the Government does not create a limited public forum unless it intends to provide an "open forum" for expressive activity, and if the exclusion of some speakers is evidence that the Government did not intend to create such a forum, no speaker challenging denial of access will ever be able to prove that the forum is a limited public forum. The very fact that the Government denied access to the speaker indicates that the Government did not intend to provide an open forum for expressive activity, and under the Court's analysis that fact alone would demonstrate that the forum is not a limited public forum.

Further, the Court today explicitly redefines a limited public forum as a place which the Government intentionally opens "for public discourse." But traditional public forums are "places which by long tradition or *by government fiat* have been devoted to assembly and debate." *Perry* (emphasis added). I fail to see how the Court's new definition of limited public forums distinguishes them from public forums.

II

A

The Court's strained efforts to avoid recognizing that the CFC is a limited public forum obscure the real issue in this case: what constraint does the First Amendment impose upon the Government's efforts to define the boundaries of a limited public forum?. . . .

The Court has said that access to a limited public forum extends only to "other entities of similar character." *Perry*. It never has indicated, however, that the First Amendment imposes no limits on the government's power to define which speakers are of "similar character" to those already allowed access. Obviously, if the government's ability to define the boundaries of a limited public forum is unconstrained, the limited-public-forum concept is meaningless. Under that reasoning, the defendants in *Widmar v. Vincent* would have been allowed to define the University's meeting places as limited to speakers of similar character to "nonreligious" groups; and the defendants in *Southeastern Promotions, Ltd. v. Conrad* would have been allowed to define their theater as limited to plays of similar character to "clean, healthful entertainment". . . .

. . . As noted, the government's acquiescence in the use of property for expressive activity indicates that at least some expressive activity is compatible with the intended uses of the public property. . . . If the government draws the line at a point which excludes speech that would be compatible with the intended uses of the property, [then] the government must explain how its exclusion of compatible speech is necessary to serve, and is narrowly tailored to serve, some compelling governmental interest other than preserving the property for its intended uses.

B

[Here Justice Blackmun argued that "petitioner's justifications for excluding respondents neither reserve the CFC for expressive activity compatible with the property nor serve any other compelling governmental interest."]

The Court [states] that "avoiding the appearance of political favoritism is a valid justification for limiting speech in a nonpublic forum." The Court, however, flatly has rejected that justification in the context of limited public forums. *Widmar v. Vincent*. In addition, petitioner's proffered justification again fails to explain why respondents are excluded when other groups, such as the National Right to Life Educational Trust Fund and Planned Parenthood, at least one of which the Government presumably would wish to avoid the appearance of supporting, are allowed to participate. And petitioner offers no explanation why a simple disclaimer in the brochure would not suffice to achieve the Government's interest in avoiding the appearance of support. . . .

III

Even if I were to agree with the Court's determination that the CFC is a nonpublic forum, or even if I thought that the Government's exclusion of respondents from the CFC was necessary and narrowly tailored to serve a compelling governmental interest, I still would disagree with the Court's disposition, because I think the eligibility criteria, which exclude charities that "seek to influence . . . the determination of public policy," is [sic] on its face viewpoint based. Petitioner contends that the criteria are viewpoint neutral because they apply equally to all "advocacy" groups regardless of their "political or philosophical leanings." The relevant comparison, however, is not between the individual organizations that make up the group excluded, but between those organizations allowed access to the CFC and those denied such access.

By devoting its resources to a particular activity, a charity expresses a view about the manner in which charitable goals can best be achieved. . . . [Respondents] obviously think that the best way to achieve [their goals] is by changing social policy, creating new rights for various groups in society, or enforcing existing rights through litigation, lobbying, and political activism. That view cannot be communicated through the CFC, according to the Government's eligibility criteria. Instead, Government employees may hear only from those charities that think that charitable goals can best be achieved within the confines of existing social policy and the status quo. The distinction is blatantly viewpoint based, so I see no reason to remand for a determination of whether the eligibility criteria are a "facade" for viewpoint-based discrimination.

I would affirm the judgment of the Court of Appeals.

Justice Stevens, dissenting.

. . . [My] study of the case has persuaded me that the Court of Appeals correctly affirmed the entry of summary judgment in favor of respondents. . . .

[Largely] for the reasons that Justice Blackmun has set forth in Parts II-B and III of his opinion, the arguments advanced in support of the exclusion are so plainly without merit that they actually lend support to an inference of bias.

International Society for Krishna Consciousness, Inc. v. Lee

505 U.S. 672 (1992)

Chief Justice Rehnquist delivered the opinion of the Court.

In this case we consider whether an airport terminal operated by a public authority is a public forum and whether a regulation prohibiting solicitation in the interior of an airport terminal violates the First Amendment.

. . . Petitioner International Society for Krishna Consciousness, Inc. (ISKCON), is a not-for-profit religious corporation whose members perform a ritual known as *sankirtan*. The ritual consists of "going into public places, disseminating religious literature and soliciting funds to support the religion." The primary purpose of this ritual is raising funds for the movement.

Respondent Walter Lee [was] the police superintendent of the Port Authority of New York and New Jersey and was charged with enforcing the regulation at issue. The Port Authority owns and operates three major airports in the greater New York City area: John F. Kennedy International Airport (Kennedy), La Guardia Airport (La Guardia), and Newark International Airport (Newark). The three airports collectively form one of the world's busiest metropolitan airport complexes. They serve approximately 8% of this country's domestic airline market and more than 50% of the trans-Atlantic market. By decade's end they are expected to serve at least 110 million passengers annually.

The airports are funded by user fees and operated to make a regulated profit. Most space at the three airports is leased to commercial airlines, which bear primary responsibility for the leasehold. The Port Authority retains control over unleased portions, including [the terminals]. The terminals are generally accessible to the general public and contain various commercial establishments such as restaurants, snack stands, bars, newsstands, and stores of various types. Virtually all who visit the terminals do so for purposes related to air travel. These visitors principally include passengers, those meeting or seeing off passengers, flight crews, and terminal employees.

The Port Authority has adopted a regulation forbidding within the terminals the repetitive solicitation of money or distribution of literature. The regulation states:

1. The following conduct is prohibited within the interior areas of buildings or structures at an air terminal if conducted by a person to or with passers-by in a continuous or repetitive manner:

    (a) The sale or distribution of any merchandise, including but not limited to jewelry, food stuffs, candles, flowers, badges and clothing.

    (b) The sale or distribution of flyers, brochures, pamphlets, books or any other printed or written material.

    (c) The solicitation and receipt of funds.

The regulation governs only the terminals; the Port Authority permits solicitation and distribution on the sidewalks outside the terminal buildings. The regulation effectively prohibits ISKCON from performing *sankirtan* in the terminals.

[The Court of Appeals, relying on the Supreme Court's decision in *United States v. Kokinda*, 497 U.S. 720 (1990), concluded that the terminals are not public fora. As a result, the restrictions were required only to satisfy a standard of reasonableness. The Court of Appeals then concluded that, if presented with the issue, this Court would find that the ban on solicitation was reasonable, but the ban on distribution was not. Both sides sought certiorari.] We granted both petitions to resolve whether airport terminals are public fora, a question on which the Circuits have split . . . .[3]

It is uncontested that the solicitation at issue in this case is a form of speech protected under the First Amendment. But it is also well settled that the government need not permit all forms of speech on property that it owns and controls. Where the government is acting as a proprietor, managing its internal operations, rather than acting as lawmaker with the power to regulate or license, its action will not be subjected to the heightened review to which its actions as a lawmaker may be subject. *Kokinda* (plurality opinion). Thus, we have upheld a ban on political advertisements in city-operated transit vehicles, *Lehman*, even though the city permitted other types of advertising on those vehicles. Similarly, we have permitted a school district to limit access to an internal mail system used to communicate with teachers employed by the district. *Perry*.

---

3. We deal here only with petitioners' claim regarding the permissibility of solicitation. Respondent's cross-petition concerning the leafletting ban is disposed of in the companion case, *Lee v. International Soc. for Krishna Consciousness, Inc.* [*infra* this chapter].

These cases reflect, either implicitly or explicitly, a "forum based" approach for assessing restrictions that the government seeks to place on the use of its property. *Cornelius v. NAACP Legal Defense & Ed. Fund, Inc.* (1985) [*supra* this chapter]. Under this approach, regulation of speech on government property that has traditionally been available for public expression is subject to the highest scrutiny. Such regulations survive only if they are narrowly drawn to achieve a compelling state interest. *Perry*. The second category of public property is the designated public forum, whether of a limited or unlimited character—property that the State has opened for expressive activity by part or all of the public. Regulation of such property is subject to the same limitations as that governing a traditional public forum. Finally, there is all remaining public property. Limitations on expressive activity conducted on this last category of property must survive only a much more limited review. The challenged regulation need only be reasonable, as long as the regulation is not an effort to suppress the speaker's activity due to disagreement with the speaker's view.

The parties do not disagree that this is the proper framework. Rather, they disagree whether the airport terminals are public fora or nonpublic fora. They also disagree whether the regulation survives the "reasonableness" review governing nonpublic fora, should that prove the appropriate category. Like the Court of Appeals, we conclude that the terminals are nonpublic fora and that the regulation reasonably limits solicitation.

The suggestion that the government has a high burden in justifying speech restrictions relating to traditional public fora made its first appearance in *Hague v. CIO* (1939) [*supra* this chapter] .... Our recent cases provide additional guidance on the characteristics of a public forum. In *Cornelius* we noted that a traditional public forum is property that has as "a principal purpose ... the free exchange of ideas." Moreover, consistent with the notion that the government—like other property owners—"has power to preserve the property under its control for the use to which it is lawfully dedicated," the government does not create a public forum by inaction. Nor is a public forum created "whenever members of the public are permitted freely to visit a place owned or operated by the Government." The decision to create a public forum must instead be made "by intentionally opening a nontraditional forum for public discourse." Finally, we have recognized that the location of property also has bearing because separation from acknowledged public areas may serve to indicate that the separated property is a special enclave, subject to greater restriction. *United States v. Grace*, 461 U.S. 171 (1983).

These precedents foreclose the conclusion that airport terminals are public fora. ... [Given] the lateness with which the modern air terminal has made its appearance, it hardly qualifies for the description of having "immemorially ... time out of mind" been held in the public trust and used for purposes of expressive activity. Moreover, even within the rather short history of air transport, it is only "in recent years [that] it has become a common practice for various religious and nonprofit organizations to use commercial airports as a forum for the distribution of literature, the solicitation of funds, the proselytizing of new members, and other similar activities." 45 Fed. Reg. 35314 (1980). Thus, the tradition of airport activity does not demonstrate that airports have historically been made available for speech activity. Nor can we say that these particular terminals, or airport terminals generally, have been intentionally opened by their operators to such activity; the frequent and continuing litigation evidencing the operators' objections belies any such claim. . . .

Petitioners attempt to circumvent the history and practice governing airport activity by pointing our attention to the variety of speech activity that they claim historically occurred at various "transportation nodes" such as rail stations, bus stations, wharves, and Ellis Island. Even if we were inclined to accept petitioners' historical account, . . . we think that such evidence is of little import for two reasons. First, much of the evidence is irrelevant to *public* fora analysis, because sites such as bus and rail terminals traditionally have had *private* ownership. . . .

Second, the relevant unit for our inquiry is an airport, not "transportation nodes" generally. . . . To make a category of "transportation nodes" [would] unjustifiably elide what may prove to be critical differences of which we should rightfully take account. The "security magnet," for example, is an airport commonplace that lacks a counterpart in bus terminals and train stations. . . .

The differences among such facilities are unsurprising [since] airports are commercial establishments funded by users fees and designed to make a regulated profit, and where nearly all who visit do so for some travel related purpose. As commercial enterprises, airports must provide services attractive to the marketplace. In light of this, it cannot fairly be said that an airport terminal has as a principal purpose promoting "the free exchange of ideas." *Cornelius.* . . . Even if we look beyond the intent of the Port Authority to the manner in which the terminals have been operated, the terminals have never been dedicated (except under the threat of court order) to expression in the form sought to be exercised here: i.e., the solicitation of contributions and the distribution of literature.

. . . Although many airports have expanded their function beyond merely contributing to efficient air travel, few have included among their purposes the designation of a forum for solicitation and distribution activities. Thus, we think that neither by tradition nor purpose can the terminals be described as satisfying the standards we have previously set out for identifying a public forum.

The restrictions here challenged, therefore, need only satisfy a requirement of reasonableness. We reiterate what we stated in [the *Kokinda* plurality opinion, quoting *Cornelius*]: The restriction "need only be *reasonable*; it need not be the most reasonable or the only reasonable limitation." We have no doubt that under this standard the prohibition on solicitation passes muster.

We have on many prior occasions noted the disruptive effect that solicitation may have on business. "Solicitation requires action by those who would respond: The individual solicited must decide whether or not to contribute (which itself might involve reading the solicitor's literature or hearing his pitch), and then, having decided to do so, reach for a wallet, search it for money, write a check, or produce a credit card." Passengers who wish to avoid the solicitor may have to alter their paths, slowing both themselves and those around them. The result is that the normal flow of traffic is impeded. This is especially so in an airport, where "air travelers, who are often weighted down by cumbersome baggage . . . may be hurrying to catch a plane or to arrange ground transportation." Delays may be particularly costly in this setting, as a flight missed by only a few minutes can result in hours worth of subsequent inconvenience.

In addition, face-to-face solicitation presents risks of duress that are an appropriate target of regulation. The skillful, and unprincipled, solicitor can target the most vulnerable, including those accompanying children or those suffering physical impairment and who cannot easily avoid the solicitation. The unsavory solicitor can also commit fraud through concealment of his affiliation or through deliberate efforts to shortchange those who agree to purchase. Compounding this problem is the fact that, in an airport, the targets of such activity frequently are on tight schedules. This in turn makes such visitors unlikely to stop and formally complain to airport authorities. As a result, the airport faces considerable difficulty in achieving its legitimate interest in monitoring solicitation activity to assure that travelers are not interfered with unduly.

The Port Authority has concluded that its interest in monitoring the activities can best be accomplished by limiting solicitation and distribution to the sidewalk areas outside the terminals. This sidewalk area is frequented by an overwhelming percentage of airport users. Thus the resulting access of those who would solicit the general public is quite complete. In turn we think it would be odd to conclude that the Port Authority's terminal regulation is unreasonable despite the Port Authority having otherwise assured access to an area universally traveled.

The inconveniences to passengers and the burdens on Port Authority officials flowing from solicitation activity may seem small, but viewed against the fact that "pedestrian congestion is one of the greatest problems facing the three terminals," the Port Authority could reasonably worry that even such incremental effects would prove quite disruptive. Moreover, "the justification for the Rule should not be measured by the disorder that would result from granting an exemption solely to ISKCON." For if ISKCON is given access, so too must other groups. "Obviously, there would be a much larger threat to the State's interest in crowd control if all other religious, nonreligious, and noncommercial organizations could likewise move freely." As a result, we conclude that the solicitation ban is reasonable.

For the foregoing reasons, the judgment of the Court of Appeals sustaining the ban on solicitation in Port Authority terminals is affirmed.

JUSTICE O'CONNOR, concurring in No. 91-155 [*ISKCON v. Lee*] and concurring in the judgment in No. 91-339 [*Lee v. ISKCON*].

. . . I concur in the Court's opinion in *ISKCON v. Lee* and agree that publicly owned airports are not public fora. . . . That airports are not public fora, however, does not mean that the government can restrict speech in whatever way it likes. . . . [We] have consistently stated that restrictions on speech in nonpublic fora are valid only if they are "reasonable" and "not an effort to suppress expression merely because public officials oppose the speaker's view." . . .

"The reasonableness of the Government's restriction [on speech in a nonpublic forum] must be assessed in light of the purpose of the forum and all the surrounding circumstances." *Cornelius.* "Consideration of a forum's special attributes is relevant to the constitutionality of a regulation since the significance of the governmental interest must be assessed in light of the characteristic nature and function of the particular forum involved." *Kokinda.* In this case, the "special attributes" and "surrounding circumstances" of the airports operated by the Port Authority are determinative. Not only has the Port Authority chosen *not* to limit access to the airports under its control, it has created a huge complex open to travelers and nontravelers alike. The airports house restaurants, cafeterias, snack bars, coffee shops, cocktail lounges, post offices, banks, telegraph offices, clothing shops, drug stores, food stores, nurseries, barber shops, currency exchanges, art exhibits, commercial advertising displays, bookstores, newsstands, dental offices, and private clubs. The International Arrivals Building at JFK Airport even has two branches of Bloomingdale's.

We have said that a restriction on speech in a nonpublic forum is "reasonable" when it is "consistent with the [government's] legitimate interest in 'preserving the property . . . for the use to which it is lawfully dedicated.'" *Perry Education Association v. Perry Local Educators' Association* (1983) [Note *supra* this chapter]. Ordinarily, this inquiry is relatively straightforward, because we have almost always been confronted with cases where the fora at issue were discrete, single-purpose facilities. *See, e.g., Kokinda* (dedicated sidewalk between parking lot and post office); *Cornelius* (literature for charity drive); *City Council of Los Angeles v. Taxpayers for Vincent,* 466 U.S. 789 (1984) [Chapter 6 Note] (utility poles); *Perry* (interschool mail system); *Adderley* (curtilage of jailhouse). The Port Authority urges that this case is no different and contends that it, too, has dedicated its airports to a single purpose—facilitating air travel—and that the speech it seeks to prohibit is not consistent with that purpose. But the wide range of activities promoted by the Port Authority is no more directly related to facilitating air travel than are the types of activities in which ISKCON wishes to engage. In my view, the Port Authority is operating a shopping mall as well as an airport. The reasonableness inquiry, therefore, is not whether the restrictions on speech are "consistent with . . . preserving the property" for air travel, *Perry,* but whether they are reasonably related to maintaining the multipurpose environment that the Port Authority has deliberately created.

Applying that standard, I agree with the Court in *ISKCON v. Lee* that the ban on solicitation is reasonable. Face-to-face solicitation is incompatible with the airport's functioning in a way that the other, permitted activities are not. [Justice O'Connor's arguments here echoed those of the Court.]

In my view, however, the regulation banning leafletting—or, in the Port Authority's words, the "continuous or repetitive . . . distribution of . . . printed or written material"—cannot be upheld as reasonable on this record. . . . [We] have expressly noted that leafletting does not entail the same kinds of problems presented by face-to-face solicitation. Specifically, "one need not ponder the contents of a leaflet or pamphlet in order mechanically to take it out of someone's hand . . . . 'The distribution of literature does not require that the recipient stop in order to receive the message the speaker wishes to convey; instead the recipient is free to read the message at a later time.'" With the possible exception of avoiding litter, see *Schneider v. State* (1939) [Chapter 6], it is difficult to point to any problems intrinsic to the act of leafletting that would make it naturally incompatible with a large, multipurpose forum such as those at issue here. . . .

Of course, it is still open for the Port Authority to promulgate regulations of the time, place, and manner of leafletting which are "content-neutral, are narrowly tailored to serve a significant government interest, and leave open ample alternative channels of communication." For example, during the many years that this litigation has been in progress, the Port Authority has not banned *sankirtan* completely from JFK International Airport, but has restricted it to a relatively uncongested part of the airport terminals, the same part that houses the airport chapel. In my view, that regulation meets the standards we have applied to time, place, and manner restrictions of protected expression.

I would affirm the judgment of the Court of Appeals in both *ISKCON v. Lee* and *Lee v. ISKCON*.

Justice Kennedy, with whom Justice Blackmun, Justice Stevens, and Justice Souter join as to Part I, concurring in the judgments.*

While I concur in the judgments affirming in these cases, my analysis differs in substantial respects from that of the Court. In my view the airport corridors and shopping areas outside of the passenger security zones, areas operated by the Port Authority, are public forums, and speech in those places is entitled to protection against all government regulation inconsistent with public forum principles. The Port Authority's blanket prohibition on the distribution or sale of literature cannot meet those stringent standards, and I agree it is invalid under the First and Fourteenth Amendments. The Port Authority's rule disallowing in-person solicitation of money for immediate payment, however, is in my view a narrow and valid regulation of the time, place, and manner of protected speech in this forum, or else is a valid regulation of the non-speech element of expressive conduct. I would sustain the Port Authority's ban on solicitation and receipt of funds.

I

An earlier opinion expressed my concern that "if our public forum jurisprudence is to retain vitality, we must recognize that certain objective characteristics of Government property and its customary use by the public may control" the status of the property. *Kokinda* (Kennedy, J., concurring in judgment). The cases before us do not heed that principle. Our public forum doctrine ought not to be a jurisprudence of categories rather than ideas or convert what was once an analysis protective of expression into one which grants the government authority to restrict speech by fiat. I believe that the Court's public forum analysis in these cases is inconsistent with the values underlying the Speech and Press Clauses of the First Amendment.

---

* [This opinion applies also to No. 91-339, *Lee v. ISKCON*].

Our public forum analysis has its origins in Justice Roberts' rather sweeping dictum in *Hague*. The doctrine was not stated with much precision or elaboration, though, until our more recent decisions in *Perry* and *Cornelius*. These cases describe a three-part analysis to designate government-owned property as either a traditional public forum, a designated public forum, or a nonpublic forum. . . . Under this categorical view the application of public forum analysis to airport terminals seems easy. Airports are of course public spaces of recent vintage, and so there can be no time-honored tradition associated with airports of permitting free speech. And because governments have often attempted to restrict speech within airports, it follows *a fortiori* under the Court's analysis that they cannot be so-called "designated" forums. So, the Court concludes, airports must be nonpublic forums, subject to minimal First Amendment protection.

This analysis is flawed at its very beginning. It leaves the government with almost unlimited authority to restrict speech on its property by doing nothing more than articulating a non-speech-related purpose for the area, and it leaves almost no scope for the development of new public forums absent the rare approval of the government. The Court's error lies in its conclusion that the public forum status of public property depends on the government's defined purpose for the property, or on an explicit decision by the government to dedicate the property to expressive activity. In my view, the inquiry must be an objective one, based on the actual, physical characteristics and uses of the property. The fact that in our public forum cases we discuss and analyze these precise characteristics tends to support my position.

The First Amendment is a limitation on government, not a grant of power. Its design is to prevent the government from controlling speech. Yet under the Court's view the authority of the government to control speech on its property is paramount, for in almost all cases the critical step in the Court's analysis is a classification of the property that turns on the government's own definition or decision, unconstrained by an independent duty to respect the speech its citizens can voice there. The Court acknowledges as much, by reintroducing today into our First Amendment law a strict doctrinal line between the proprietary and regulatory functions of government which I thought had been abandoned long ago.

The Court's approach is contrary to the underlying purposes of the public forum doctrine. The liberties protected by our doctrine derive from the Assembly, as well as the Speech and Press Clauses of the First Amendment, and are essential to a functioning democracy. Public places are of necessity the locus for discussion of public issues, as well as protest against arbitrary government action. At the heart of our jurisprudence lies the principle that in a free nation citizens must have the right to gather and speak with other persons in public places. The recognition that certain government-owned property is a public forum provides open notice to citizens that their freedoms may be exercised there without fear of a censorial government, adding tangible reinforcement to the idea that we are a free people. . . .

The Court's analysis rests on an inaccurate view of history. The notion that traditional public forums are properties that have public discourse as their principal purpose is a most doubtful fiction. The types of property that we have recognized as the quintessential public forums are streets, parks, and sidewalks. It would seem apparent that the principal purpose of streets and sidewalks, like airports, is to facilitate transportation, not public discourse, ... Similarly, the purpose for the creation of public parks may be as much for beauty and open space as for discourse. Thus under the Court's analysis, even the quintessential public forums would appear to lack the necessary elements of what the Court defines as a public forum.

The effect of the Court's narrow view of the first category of public forums is compounded by its description of the second purported category, the so-called "designated" forum. The requirements for such a designation are so stringent that I cannot be certain whether the category has any content left at all. In any event, it seems evident that under the Court's analysis today few, if any, types of property other than those already recognized as public forums will be accorded that status.

The Court's answer to these objections appears to be a recourse to history as justifying its recognition of streets, parks, and sidewalks, but apparently no other types of government property, as traditional public forums. . . . In my view the policies underlying the doctrine cannot be given effect unless we recognize that open, public spaces and thoroughfares that are suitable for discourse may be public forums, whatever their historical pedigree and without concern for a precise classification of the property. There is support in our precedents for such a view. See *Lehman* (plurality opinion); *Hague* (speaking of "streets and public places" as forums). Without this recognition our forum doctrine retains no relevance in times of fast-changing technology and increasing insularity. In a country where most citizens travel by automobile, and parks all too often become locales for crime rather than social intercourse, our failure to recognize the possibility that new types of government property may be appropriate forums for speech will lead to a serious curtailment of our expressive activity.

One of the places left in our mobile society that is suitable for discourse is a metropolitan airport. It is of particular importance to recognize that such spaces are public forums because in these days an airport is one of the few government-owned spaces where many persons have extensive contact with other members of the public. Given that private spaces of similar character are not subject to the dictates of the First Amendment, see *Hudgens v. NLRB* (1976) [*infra* this chapter Note], it is critical that we preserve these areas for protected speech. . . .

. . . If the objective, physical characteristics of the property at issue and the actual public access and uses that have been permitted by the government indicate that expressive activity would be appropriate and compatible with those uses, the property is a public forum. The most important considerations in this analysis are whether the property shares physical similarities with more traditional public forums, whether the government has permitted or acquiesced in broad public access to the property, and whether expressive activity would tend to interfere in a significant way with the uses to which the government has as a factual matter dedicated the property. In conducting the last inquiry, courts must consider the consistency of those uses with expressive activities in general, rather than the specific sort of speech at issue in the case before it; otherwise the analysis would be one not of classification but rather of case-by-case balancing, and would provide little guidance to the State regarding its discretion to regulate speech. Courts must also consider the availability of reasonable time, place, and manner restrictions in undertaking this compatibility analysis. The possibility of some theoretical inconsistency between expressive activities and the property's uses should not bar a finding of a public forum, if those inconsistencies can be avoided through simple and permitted regulations.

The second category of the Court's jurisprudence, the so-called designated forum, provides little, if any, additional protection for speech. Where government property does not satisfy the criteria of a public forum, the government retains the power to dedicate the property for speech, whether for all expressive activity or for limited purposes only. I do not quarrel with the fact that speech must often be restricted on property of this kind to retain the purpose for which it has been designated. And I recognize that when property has been designated for a particular expressive use, the government may choose to eliminate that designation. But this increases the need to protect speech in other places, where discourse may occur free of such restrictions. . . .

Under this analysis, it is evident that the public spaces of the Port Authority's airports are public forums. First, the District Court made detailed findings regarding the physical similarities between the Port Authority's airports and public streets. These findings show that the public spaces in the airports are broad, public thoroughfares full of people and lined with stores and other commercial activities. . . .

Second, the airport areas involved here are open to the public without restriction. . . . And while most people who come to the Port Authority's airports do so for a reason related to air travel, [this] does not distinguish an airport from streets or sidewalks, which most people use for travel. Further, the group visiting the airports encompasses a vast portion of the public: In 1986 the Authority's three airports served over 78 million passengers. It is the very breadth and extent of the public's use of airports that makes it imperative to protect speech rights there. . . .

Third, and perhaps most important, it is apparent from the record, and from the recent history of airports, that when adequate time, place, and manner regulations are in place, expressive activity is quite compatible with the uses of major airports. The Port Authority's primary argument to the contrary is that the problem of congestion in its airports' corridors makes expressive activity inconsistent with the airports' primary purpose, which is to facilitate air travel. The First Amendment is often inconvenient. But that is beside the point. Inconvenience does not absolve the government of its obligation to tolerate speech. . . .

The Authority has for many years permitted expressive activities by petitioners and others, without any apparent interference with its ability to meet its transportation purposes. . . . And, in fact, expressive activity has been a commonplace feature of our Nation's major airports for many years, in part because of the wide consensus among the Courts of Appeals, prior to the decision in these cases, that the public spaces of airports are public forums. [The] logical consequence of the Port Authority's congestion argument is that the crowded streets and sidewalks of major cities cannot be public forums. These problems have been dealt with in the past, and in other settings, through proper time, place, and manner restrictions; and the Port Authority does not make any showing that similar regulations would not be effective in its airports. The Port Authority makes a half-hearted argument that the special security concerns associated with airports suggest they are not public forums; but this position is belied by the unlimited public access the Authority allows to its airports. . . .

The danger of allowing the government to suppress speech is shown in the cases now before us. A grant of plenary power allows the government to tilt the dialog heard by the public, to exclude many, more marginal, voices. The first challenged Port Authority regulation establishes a flat prohibition on "the sale or distribution of flyers, brochures, pamphlets, books or any other printed or written material," if conducted within the airport terminal, "in a continuous or repetitive manner." We have long recognized that the right to distribute flyers and literature lies at the heart of the liberties guaranteed by the Speech and Press Clauses of the First Amendment. [The Port Authority's regulation] is not drawn in narrow terms, and it does not leave open ample alternative channels for communication. The Port Authority's concerns with the problem of congestion can be addressed through narrow restrictions on the time and place of expressive activity. I would strike down the regulation as an unconstitutional restriction of speech.

II

It is my view, however, that the Port Authority's ban on the "solicitation and receipt of funds" within its airport terminals should be upheld under the standards applicable to speech regulations in public forums. The regulation may be upheld as either a reasonable time, place, and manner restriction, or as a regulation directed at the nonspeech element of expressive conduct. The two standards have considerable overlap in a case like this one. . . .

I am in full agreement with the statement of the Court that solicitation is a form of protected speech. If the Port Authority's solicitation regulation prohibited all speech that requested the contribution of funds, I would conclude that it was a direct, content-based restriction of speech in clear violation of the First Amendment. The Authority's regulation does not prohibit all solicitation, however; it prohibits the "solicitation and receipt of funds." I do not understand this regulation to prohibit all speech that solicits funds. It reaches only personal solicitations for immediate payment of money. Otherwise, the "receipt of funds" phrase would be written out of the provision. The regulation does not cover, for example, the distribution of preaddressed envelopes along with a plea to contribute money to the distributor or his organization. As I understand the restriction it is directed only at the physical exchange of money, which is an element of conduct interwoven with otherwise expressive solicitation. In other words, the regulation permits expression that solicits funds, but limits the manner of that expression to forms other than the immediate receipt of money.

So viewed, I believe the Port Authority's rule survives our test for speech restrictions in the public forum. In-person solicitation of funds, when combined with immediate receipt of that money, creates a risk of fraud and duress that is well recognized, and that is different in kind from other forms of expression or conduct. Travelers who are unfamiliar with the airport, perhaps even unfamiliar with this country, its customs, and its language, are an easy prey for the money solicitor. I agree in full with the Court's discussion of these dangers in *ISKCON v. Lee*.

Because the Port Authority's solicitation ban is directed at these abusive practices and not at any particular message, idea, or form of speech, the regulation is a content-neutral rule serving a significant government interest. . . . The government cannot, of course, prohibit speech for the sole reason that it is concerned the speech may be fraudulent. But the Port Authority's regulation does not do this. It recognizes that the risk of fraud and duress is intensified by particular conduct, the immediate exchange of money; and it addresses only that conduct. . . . The regulation does not burden any broader category of speech or expressive conduct than is the source of the evil sought to be avoided. And in fact, the regulation is even more narrow because it only prohibits such behavior if conducted in a continuous or repetitive manner. . . .

I have little difficulty in deciding that the Port Authority has left open ample alternative channels for the communication of the message which is an aspect of solicitation. . . . Requests for money continue to be permitted, and in the course of requesting money solicitors may explain their cause, or the purposes of their organization, without violating the regulation. It is only if the solicitor accepts immediate payment that a violation occurs. Thus the solicitor can continue to disseminate his message, for example, by distributing preaddressed envelopes in which potential contributors may mail their donations.

Much of what I have said about the solicitation of funds may seem to apply to the sale of literature, but the differences between the two activities are of sufficient significance to require they be distinguished for constitutional purposes. The Port Authority's flat ban on the distribution or sale of printed material must, in my view, fall in its entirety. . . . For one [thing], the government interest in regulating the sales of literature is not as powerful as in the case of solicitation. The danger of a fraud arising from such sales is much more limited than from pure solicitation, because in the case of a sale the nature of the exchange tends to be clearer to both parties. Also, the Port Authority's sale regulation is not as narrowly drawn as the solicitation rule, since it does not specify the receipt of money as a critical element of a violation. And perhaps most important, the flat ban on sales of literature leaves open fewer alternative channels of communication than the Port Authority's more limited prohibition on the solicitation and receipt of funds. Given the practicalities and ad hoc nature of much expressive activity in the public forum, sales of literature must be completed in one transaction to be workable. . . .

Against all of this must be balanced the great need, recognized by our precedents, to give the sale of literature full First Amendment protection. . . . One of the primary purposes of the public forum is to provide persons who lack access to more sophisticated media the opportunity to speak. A prohibition on sales forecloses that opportunity for the very persons who need it most. And while the same arguments might be made regarding solicitation of funds, the answer is that the Port Authority has not prohibited all solicitation, but only a narrow class of conduct associated with a particular manner of solicitation.

For these reasons I agree that the Court of Appeals should be affirmed in full in finding the Port Authority's ban on the distribution or sale of literature unconstitutional, but upholding the prohibition on solicitation and immediate receipt of funds.

JUSTICE SOUTER, with whom JUSTICE BLACKMUN and JUSTICE STEVENS join, concurring in the judgment in *Lee v. ISKCON*, and dissenting in *ISKCON v. Lee*.

I join in Part I of Justice Kennedy's opinion and the judgment of affirmance in *Lee v. ISKCON* . . . . The designation of a given piece of public property as a traditional public forum must not merely state a conclusion that the property falls within a static category including streets, parks, sidewalks, and perhaps not much more, but must represent a conclusion that the property is no different in principle from such examples. . . . [The] enquiry may and must relate to the particular property at issue and not necessarily to the "precise classification of the property." . . . One can imagine a public airport of a size or design or need for extraordinary security that would render expressive activity incompatible with its normal use. But that would be no reason to conclude that one of the more usual variety of metropolitan airports is not a public forum.

I also agree with Justice Kennedy's statement of the public forum principle: We should classify as a public forum any piece of public property that is "suitable for discourse" in its physical character, where expressive activity is "compatible" with the use to which it has actually been put. *See also Grayned v. City of Rockford* (1972) [*supra* this chapter Note]. Applying this test, I have no difficulty concluding that the unleased public areas at airports like the metropolitan New York airports at issue in these cases are public forums.

From the Court's conclusion in *ISKCON v. Lee*, however, sustaining the total ban on solicitation of money for immediate payment, I respectfully dissent. . . . Even if I assume, *arguendo*, that the ban on the petitioners' activity at issue here is both content neutral and merely a restriction on the manner of communication, the regulation must be struck down for its failure to satisfy the requirements of narrow tailoring to further a significant state interest and availability of "ample alternative channels for communication."

As Justice Kennedy's opinion indicates, respondent comes closest to justifying the restriction as one furthering the government's interest in preventing coercion and fraud.* The claim to be preventing coercion is weak to start with. While a solicitor can be insistent a pedestrian on the street or airport concourse can simply walk away or walk on. . . .

———————————

  * Respondent also attempts to justify his regulation on the alternative basis of "interference with air travelers," referring in particular to problems of "annoyance" and "congestion." The First Amendment inevitably requires people to put up with annoyance and uninvited persuasion. . . . While there may, of course, be congested locations where solicitation could severely compromise the efficient flow of pedestrians, the proper response would be to tailor the restrictions to those choke points.

As for fraud, our cases do not provide government with plenary authority to ban solicitation just because it could be fraudulent. . . . The evidence of fraudulent conduct here is virtually nonexistent. . . .

Even assuming a governmental interest adequate to justify some regulation, the present ban would fall when subjected to the requirement of narrow tailoring. . . .

Finally, I do not think the Port Authority's solicitation ban leaves open the "ample" channels of communication required of a valid content-neutral time, place, and manner restriction. A distribution of preaddressed envelopes is unlikely to be much of an alternative. The practical reality of the regulation, which this Court can never ignore, is that it shuts off a uniquely powerful avenue of communication for organizations like the International Society for Krishna Consciousness, and may, in effect, completely prohibit unpopular and poorly funded groups from receiving funds in response to protected solicitation.

Lee v. International Society for Krishna Consciousness Inc.
505 U.S. 830 (1992)

Per Curiam.

For the reasons expressed in the opinions of Justice O'Connor, Justice Kennedy, and Justice Souter in *ISKCON v. Lee*, the judgment of the Court of Appeals holding that the ban on distribution of literature in the Port Authority airport terminals is invalid under the First Amendment is affirmed.

Chief Justice Rehnquist, with whom Justice White, Justice Scalia, and Justice Thomas join, dissenting.

Leafletting presents risks of congestion similar to those posed by solicitation. It presents, in addition, some risks unique to leafletting. And of course, as with solicitation, these risks must be evaluated against a backdrop of the substantial congestion problem facing the Port Authority and with an eye to the cumulative impact that will result if all groups are permitted terminal access. Viewed in this light, I conclude that the distribution ban, no less than the solicitation ban, is reasonable. I therefore dissent from the Court's holding striking the distribution ban.

I will not trouble to repeat in detail all that has been stated in *ISKCON v. Lee*, describing the risks and burdens flowing to travelers and the Port Authority from permitting solicitation in airport terminals. Suffice it to say that the risks and burdens posed by leafletting are quite similar to those posed by solicitation. The weary, harried, or hurried traveler may have no less desire and need to avoid the delays generated by having literature foisted upon him than he does to avoid delays from a financial solicitation. And while a busy passenger perhaps may succeed in fending off a leafletter with minimal disruption to himself by agreeing simply to take the proffered material, this does not completely ameliorate the dangers of congestion flowing from such leafletting. Others may choose not simply to accept the material but also to stop and engage the leafletter in debate, obstructing those who follow. Moreover, those who accept material may often simply drop it on the floor once out of the leafletter's range, creating an eyesore, a safety hazard, and additional cleanup work for airport staff.

In addition, a differential ban that permits leafletting but prohibits solicitation, while giving the impression of permitting the Port Authority at least half of what it seeks, may in fact prove for the Port Authority to be a much more Pyrrhic victory. Under the regime that is today sustained, the Port Authority is obliged to permit leafletting. But monitoring leafletting activity in order to ensure that it is *only* leafletting that occurs, and not also soliciting, may prove little less burdensome than the monitoring that would be required if solicitation were permitted. At a minimum, therefore, I think it remains open whether at some future date the Port Authority may be able to reimpose a complete ban, having developed evidence that enforcement of a differential ban is overly burdensome. Until now it has had no reason or means to do this, since it is only today that such a requirement has been announced.

———

Note: Competing Views of the Public Forum

1. Three decades after Justice Marshall's expansive dictum in *Grayned*, the Court remained deeply divided over the standard for evaluating regulations that limit expressive activity on government property other than streets, parks, and sidewalks. In the *ISKCON* cases, a bare majority adhered to the tripartite classification approach first articulated in *Perry*. Justice O'Connor agreed with this approach, but in applying the "reasonableness" test, she was more willing to second-guess the government both as to the purpose of the property and as to the asserted justification for the regulation.

Justice Kennedy found the Court's analysis to be "flawed at its very beginning." He repudiated a "jurisprudence of categories" and instead suggested an approach that is reminiscent of the *Grayned* dictum: "If the objective, physical characteristics of the property at issue and the actual public access and uses that have been permitted by the government indicate that expressive activity would be appropriate and compatible with those uses, the property is a public forum."

How significant is the difference in approach? Justice Kennedy, after all, reached the same result on the solicitation ban as did Chief Justice Rehnquist, who applied the tripartite classification scheme. Meanwhile, three Justices who endorsed Justice Kennedy's approach disagreed with his resolution of the solicitation issue.

2. Justice Kennedy argues that the forum doctrine must be flexible in order to combat the "increasing insularity" of modern life. Do you agree that people are more "insular" than they were in decades past? If so, is this a consideration the Court should take into account in shaping First Amendment doctrine? Note that the *ISKCON* cases were decided in 1992, before the explosive growth of the World Wide Web. What are the implications for the public forum doctrine of the fact that most public discourse has now migrated onto privately-owned electronic platforms? The Court recently touched on, but did not resolve, these questions in *Packingham v. North Carolina* (2017) (Chapter 15).

3. Justice Kennedy also argues: "Inconvenience does not absolve the government of its obligation to tolerate speech." Is he referring only to the effect on the airport, or also to the effect on travelers? Chief Justice Rehnquist, dissenting from the decision to strike down the ban on leafletting, emphasizes the "risks and burdens" for "the weary, harried, or hurried traveler." Does Justice Kennedy adequately consider the traveler's interests? Are they relevant?

4. Justice Kennedy believes that if the Port Authority's solicitation regulation prohibited all speech that requested the contribution of funds, it would be a "direct, content-based restriction of speech in clear violation of the First Amendment." Do you agree? Would a ban on aggressive panhandling on city sidewalks and streets be constitutional?

————

Note: Rosenberger *and Viewpoint Discrimination*

In his separate opinion in *ISKCON*, Justice Kennedy—echoing Justice Blackmun's dissent in *Cornelius*—said of the second *Perry* category, "The requirements [for recognizing government property as a "designated forum"] are so stringent that I cannot be certain whether the category has any content left at all." Only three years after *ISKCON*, Justice Kennedy, writing for the Court, made clear that the middle category does have "content"—and indeed bite.

The case was *Rosenberger v. Rector and Visitors of University of Virginia*, 515 U.S. 819 (1995). The University of Virginia (a state institution) had established a Student Activities Fund (SAF) that was authorized to pay outside contractors for expenses incurred by student groups for activities that were "related to the educational purpose of the University." The SAF refused to pay the printing costs of a student magazine called Wide Awake: A Christian Perspective at the University of Virginia. The sole reason for the refusal was that paper was a "religious activity" within the meaning of SAF's guidelines. A "religious activity" was defined as any activity that "primarily promotes or manifests a particular belief in or about a deity or an ultimate reality." Religious activities were not eligible for funding.

The principal issue in *Rosenberger* was whether a grant from the SAF to pay Wide Awake's printing expenses would violate the Establishment Clause. (For that aspect of the opinion, see Chapter 17.) However, before reaching that issue, the Court addressed the question whether, apart from the Establishment Clause, the limit on funding violated the free speech rights of the students who published Wide Awake. The Court held that it did.

The opinion made no mention of the tripartite classification established by *Perry* and *Cornelius*. However, the Court apparently assumed that the University had created a limited public forum. Justice Kennedy wrote:

> The necessities of confining a forum to the limited and legitimate purposes for which it was created may justify the State in reserving it for certain groups or for the discussion of certain topics. *See, e.g., Cornelius; Perry*. Once it has opened a limited forum, however, the State must respect the lawful boundaries

it has itself set. The State may not exclude speech where its distinction is not "reasonable in light of the purpose served by the forum," *Cornelius*, nor may it discriminate against speech on the basis of its viewpoint. Thus, in determining whether the State is acting to preserve the limits of the forum it has created so that the exclusion of a class of speech is legitimate, we have observed a distinction between, on the one hand, content discrimination, which may be permissible if it preserves the purposes of that limited forum, and, on the other hand, viewpoint discrimination, which is presumed impermissible when directed against speech otherwise within the forum's limitations. See *Perry*.

The SAF is a forum more in a metaphysical than in a spatial or geographic sense, but the same principles are applicable. *See, e.g., Perry* (forum analysis of a school mail system); *Cornelius* (forum analysis of charitable contribution program).

The University . . . insists that this case does not present that issue because the Guidelines draw lines based on content, not viewpoint. [We acknowledge that] the distinction is not a precise one. . . . We conclude, nonetheless, [that] viewpoint discrimination is the proper way to interpret the University's objections to Wide Awake. By the very terms of the SAF prohibition, the University does not exclude religion as a subject matter but selects for disfavored treatment those student journalistic efforts with religious editorial viewpoints. Religion may be a vast area of inquiry, but it also provides, as it did here, a specific premise, a perspective, a standpoint from which a variety of subjects may be discussed and considered. The prohibited perspective, not the general subject matter, resulted in the refusal to make third-party payments, for the subjects discussed were otherwise within the approved category of publications.

Four Justices dissented in an opinion by Justice Souter. They found no viewpoint discrimination and argued that the Court departed from precedent:

The Court's . . . holding amounts to a significant reformulation of our viewpoint discrimination precedents and will significantly expand access to limited-access forums. See *Greer v. Spock*, 424 U.S. 828 (1976) (upholding regulation prohibiting political speeches on military base); *Cornelius* (exclusion from fundraising drive of political activity or advocacy groups is facially viewpoint neutral despite inclusion of charitable, health, and welfare agencies); *Perry* (ability of teachers' bargaining representative to use internal school mail system does not require that access be provided to "any other citizen's group or community organization with a message for school personnel"); *Lehman* (exclusion of political messages from forum permissible despite ability of nonpolitical speakers to use the forum).

The dissent appears to argue that under the majority's approach, cases like *Cornelius* and *Lehman* would come out the other way because they would be held to involve viewpoint discrimination. Do you agree?

———

Note: *"Limited" and "Designated" Forums*

1. In *Perry*, the Court said that the government could create a forum "by designation"; the Court also used the term "limited public forum." Were these alternative labels for the same category, or was the Court describing two distinct categories? Footnote 7 (which followed the text describing the second category) added to the confusion by stating: "A public forum may be created for a limited purpose such as use by certain groups . . . or for the discussion of certain subjects."

In *ISKCON v. Lee*, the Court referred to the second *Perry* category as "the designated public forum, whether of a limited or unlimited character — property that the State has opened for expressive activity by part or all of the public." Justice Kennedy in his concurring opinion referred to "the so-called designated forum." But in his opinion for the Court in *Rosenberger* he referred to "a limited forum."

2. Not surprisingly, lawyers and lower courts have continued to struggle with the Court's categories. For example, in *Child Evangelism Fellowship of Md., Inc. v. Montgomery County Public Schools*, 457 F.3d 376 (4th Cir. 2006), the court said:

> Although the [Supreme] Court has never squarely addressed the difference between a designated public forum and a limited public forum, its most recent opinions suggest that there indeed is a distinction. In a limited public forum, the government creates a channel for a specific or limited type of expression where one did not previously exist. In such a forum, "the State may be justified in reserving [its forum] for certain groups or for the discussion of certain topics," subject only to the limitation that its actions must be viewpoint neutral and reasonable. *Good News Club v. Milford Cent. Sch.* (2001) [Chapter 19], (quoting *Rosenberger*). In a designated public forum, by contrast, the government makes public property (that would not otherwise qualify as a traditional public forum) generally accessible to all speakers. In such a forum, regulations on speech are "subject to the same limitations as that governing a traditional public forum" — namely, strict scrutiny. *ISKCON*.

The court acknowledged, however, that other courts interpreted the precedents differently: "[M]any of our sister circuits have held that a limited public forum, a forum opened only to certain speakers or for discussion of certain subjects, is in fact a *subset* of the larger category of designated public forums specifically opened by the government for use by all speakers." (Emphasis added.)

Not all circuits fall into one camp or the other. The Ninth Circuit, for example, has said:

> There is also a fourth category, the limited public forum, which is a partially designated public forum. [As stated in an earlier case, the government] is not left with only the two options of maintaining a non-public forum or creating a designated public forum; if the government chooses to open a non-public forum, the First Amendment allows the government to open the non-public forum for limited purposes. The limited public forum is a

sub-category of a designated public forum that refers to a type of nonpublic forum that the government has intentionally opened to certain groups or to certain topics.

OSU Student Alliance v. Ray, 699 F.3d 1053, 1062 (9th Cir. 2012). But can the "limited public forum" be both a fourth category and a subcategory of the third category?

Consider the Problems below. How would they be analyzed under the categorical approach? Would it be preferable to return to the approach of *Grayned* and its "incompatibility" test?

————

Problem: Display of Controversial Art

A few years ago, the City of Arkham remodeled a former school building and converted it into a new city hall. In an effort to decorate the bare walls of the new space, Gary Winters, the City Manager, decided to institute an experimental program whereby local artists would be invited to display their work in the newly remodeled building. Because Winters did not want city employees to devote time and energy administering this program, he sought assistance from the Arkham Arts Council ("the Arts Council"), a private entity that promoted the arts.

Winters' primary contact at the Arts Council was its director, Barbara Mansfield. Winters and Mansfield agreed that the Arts Council would locate the art and administer the program in exchange for a $500 quarterly fee.

From the start, Winters made clear to Mansfield that Arkham wanted to avoid controversy. He instructed her that, in selecting art for the program, work of a "questionable nature" should not be displayed.

Shortly after announcing the project, Mansfield sent a letter to artists inviting submissions for display. Consistent with Arkham's concerns, the letter warned of the need to avoid controversial subject matter.

The first exhibit ran from February through April of last year; the second ran from September through November. There is no evidence that either Arkham or the Arts Council screened the artwork before its display in these two exhibits. Although some individuals criticized a few pieces, there is no evidence that Arkham or the Arts Council prevented the display of any work or that they removed any work from display in response to public complaints. Some works depicted nudity, but these were very abstract and did not cause any genuine controversy.

Among the artists invited to participate in the third exhibit were Martha Lilith and Hilary Betts. Lilith submitted prints showing a naked couple in varied scenes. Betts submitted a sculpture titled "To the Democrats, Republicans, and Bipartisans," which depicted a woman's bare buttocks "mooning" the viewer.

Lilith's prints were never displayed. After Lilith delivered her prints, but prior to their hanging, Mansfield examined them and determined that some were potentially controversial or political because the couple was depicted nude in public, and public nudity is illegal in Arkham. Over the next few days she showed the prints to several City Hall employees in order to get their opinions. The employees found some of the prints "offensive" and "sexually suggestive." In view of these assessments, Mansfield decided not to display any of the prints. She wrote a letter to Lilith informing her of the decision. The letter stated in part:

> We firmly believe that this program should remain out of the political realm. Displaying art which could be misconstrued by activists as "sexual" or "prurient," will make the decision whether to maintain the program a political one, thereby endangering the entire program.

Betts' sculpture was displayed, but soon after the display went up Mansfield received complaints about the work. Some viewed the sculpture as depicting the woman in a "sexual position" or as depicting a "sexual act"; others simply thought it "offensive and disgusting," or "derogatory to women." After discussing the matter with Winters, Mansfield ordered the Arts Council to remove the sculpture from the display case. Mansfield sent Betts a letter similar to the one sent to Lilith.

Lilith and Betts have sued the city, claiming a violation of their First Amendment rights. Is the claim meritorious? What more might you need to know?

———

Problem: Flags and Banners on Highway Overpasses

Since September 11, 2001, it has become a common practice for private individuals to hang American flags from highway overpasses. One place where the flag has been displayed is the Ramsey Road overpass on Interstate 11, just inside the New Harmony state border.

George Cramer is a citizen of New Harmony who opposes American policy in Afghanistan. A few weeks ago, Cramer hung a banner adjacent to the American flag on the Ramsey Road overpass. His banner read, "Afghanistan — At What Cost?" Personnel from the New Harmony Department of Transportation (DOT) removed the banner. When Cramer protested, they informed him that they were acting in accordance with DOT policy.

DOT policy is set forth in a policy statement adopted in 1995. Under that policy, persons who wish to display a sign on a New Harmony highway overpass must obtain a permit to do so. Even then, permits are available only for signs designating turnoffs for special events. Persons wishing to display any other message are prohibited from using the highway overpass to do so. Notwithstanding this policy, DOT does not prohibit the display of American flags, nor does it impose a permitting process for their display. DOT justifies its policy on safety grounds; it believes that messages, irrespective of their content, will be distracting to motorists, especially on freeways, where the speed limit is 70 mph. The American flag is not distracting, DOT believes, because it is so familiar.

Cramer has brought suit against DOT in federal district court seeking an injunction against DOT's policy of exempting American flags from permit requirements but requiring permits for, or prohibiting altogether, the display of all other expressive signs and banners. How should the claim be analyzed, and how should the court rule?

D. Speech on Private Property

In the preceding sections, we considered the question: under what circumstances must the government allow speech or other expressive activity on property that it owns? We now ask: When must the *private* owner of property allow access to persons who wish to engage in expressive activity?

At first blush, it might seem that the answer is: Never. After all, the First Amendment applies only to the Federal Government, and the Fourteenth Amendment applies only to action of the "state." The "state action" doctrine would thus seem to negate any possible claim of a right to engage in expressive activity on another person's private property. However, thanks to a Supreme Court decision handed down in 1946, the matter is not quite so simple.

————

Note: The Marsh *Decision*

In *Marsh v. Alabama*, 326 U.S. 501 (1946), the Court considered "whether a State, consistently with the First and Fourteenth Amendments, can impose criminal punishment on a person who undertakes to distribute religious literature on the premises of a company-owned town contrary to the wishes of the town's management." The Court's opinion, by Justice Black, began by describing the town:

> The town, a suburb of Mobile, Alabama, known as Chickasaw, is owned by the Gulf Shipbuilding Corporation. Except for that it has all the characteristics of any other American town. The property consists of residential buildings, streets, a system of sewers, a sewage disposal plant and a "business block" on which business places are situated. A deputy of the Mobile County Sheriff, paid by the company, serves as the town's policeman. Merchants and service establishments have rented the stores and business places on the business block and the United States uses one of the places as a post office from which six carriers deliver mail to the people of Chickasaw and the adjacent area.
>
> The town and the surrounding neighborhood, which can not be distinguished from the Gulf property by anyone not familiar with the property lines, are thickly settled, and according to all indications the residents use the business block as their regular shopping center. To do so, they now, as they have for many years, make use of a company-owned paved street and sidewalk located alongside the store fronts in order to enter and leave the stores and the post office. Intersecting company-owned roads at each end of the business block lead into a four-lane public highway which runs parallel to the business block at a distance of thirty feet. There is nothing to stop

highway traffic from coming onto the business block and upon arrival a traveler may make free use of the facilities available there.

In short the town and its shopping district are accessible to and freely used by the public in general and there is nothing to distinguish them from any other town and shopping center except the fact that the title to the property belongs to a private corporation.

Grace Marsh, a Jehovah's Witness, stood near the post office and undertook to distribute religious literature. She was warned that she could not distribute the literature without a permit and was told that no permit would be issued to her. When she was asked to leave the sidewalk and the town, she declined. She was convicted under a state law making it a crime to enter or remain on the premises of another after having been warned not to do so. The state courts rejected her First Amendment claim, but the Supreme Court reversed. Writing for a 5–3 majority, Justice Black said:

We do not agree that the corporation's property interests settle the question. . . . Ownership does not always mean absolute dominion. The more an owner, for his advantage, opens up his property for use by the public in general, the more do his rights become circumscribed by the statutory and constitutional rights of those who use it. Thus, the owners of privately held bridges, ferries, turnpikes and railroads may not operate them as freely as a farmer does his farm. Since these facilities are built and operated primarily to benefit the public and since their operation is essentially a public function, it is subject to state regulation. . . .

Whether a corporation or a municipality owns or possesses the town the public in either case has an identical interest in the functioning of the community in such manner that the channels of communication remain free. As [already] stated, the town of Chickasaw does not function differently from any other town. The managers appointed by the corporation cannot curtail the liberty of press and religion of these people consistently with the purposes of the Constitutional guarantees, and a state statute, as the one here involved, which enforces such action by criminally punishing those who attempt to distribute religious literature clearly violates the First and Fourteenth Amendments to the Constitution.

———

Note: The Shopping Center Cases

1. By the time the Court decided *Marsh*, the "company town" was a disappearing institution. However, before long, a new kind of economic enterprise presented a similar legal question. This was the shopping center. In *Amalgamated Food Employees Union v. Logan Valley Plaza, Inc.*, 391 U.S. 308 (1968), a union invoked *Marsh* to support its claim that under the First Amendment it was entitled to engage in peaceful picketing within the confines of a privately owned shopping center near Altoona,

Pennsylvania. The Pennsylvania courts rejected the claim, but the Supreme Court reversed. The Court said:

> The similarities between the business block in *Marsh* and the shopping center in the present case are striking. The perimeter of Logan Valley Mall is a little less than 1.1 miles. Inside the mall were situated, at the time of trial, two substantial commercial enterprises with numerous others soon to follow. Immediately adjacent to the mall are two roads, one of which is a heavily traveled state highway and from both of which lead entrances directly into the mall. Adjoining the buildings in the middle of the mall are sidewalks for the use of pedestrians going to and from their cars and from building to building. In the parking areas, roadways for the use of vehicular traffic entering and leaving the mall are clearly marked out. The general public has unrestricted access to the mall property. The shopping center here is clearly the functional equivalent of the business district of Chickasaw involved in *Marsh.* . . .
>
> We see no reason why access to a business district in a company town for the purpose of exercising First Amendment rights should be constitutionally required, while access for the same purpose to property functioning as a business district should be limited simply because the property surrounding the "business district" is not under the same ownership.

Justice Black — the author of *Marsh* — dissented. He insisted that the majority's reasoning "completely misreads *Marsh* and begs the question." He explained:

> *Marsh* was never intended to apply to this kind of situation. . . . The question is, Under what circumstances can private property be treated as though it were public? The answer that *Marsh* gives is when that property has taken on *all* the attributes of a town, i.e., "residential buildings, streets, a system of sewers, a sewage disposal plant and a 'business block' on which business places are situated."

2. Four years after *Logan Valley*, the Court decided another shopping center case, *Lloyd Corp., Ltd. v. Tanner*, 407 U.S. 551 (1972). According to the Court, the case presented a question "reserved by" the decision in *Logan Valley*, "the right of a privately owned shopping center to prohibit the distribution of handbills on its property when the handbilling is unrelated to the shopping center's operations." The Court distinguished *Logan Valley* on that basis and found that the handbilling was not protected by the First Amendment. Four Justices — the four remaining members of the *Logan Valley* majority — dissented. They insisted that there was "no valid distinction between [*Logan Valley*] and this [case]."

3. Finally, in *Hudgens v. NLRB*, 424 U.S. 507 (1976), the Court reexamined its precedents and concluded that "the rationale of *Logan Valley* did not survive the Court's decision in the *Lloyd* case." The Court quoted at length from *Lloyd*:

> The basic issue in this case is whether respondents, in the exercise of asserted First Amendment rights, may distribute handbills on Lloyd's private

property contrary to its wishes and contrary to a policy enforced against all handbilling. In addressing this issue, it must be remembered that the First and Fourteenth Amendments safeguard the rights of free speech and assembly by limitations on state action, not on action by the owner of private property used nondiscriminatorily for private purposes only. . . .

Respondents [contend] that the property of a large shopping center is "open to the public," serves the same purposes as a "business district" of a municipality, and therefore has been dedicated to certain types of public use. . . .

The argument reaches too far. The Constitution by no means requires such an attenuated doctrine of dedication of private property to public use. The closest decision in theory, *Marsh v. Alabama*, involved the assumption by a private enterprise of all of the attributes of a state-created municipality and the exercise by that enterprise of semiofficial municipal functions as a delegate of the State. In effect, the owner of the company town was performing the full spectrum of municipal powers and stood in the shoes of the State. In the instant case where is no comparable assumption or exercise of municipal functions or power. . . .

We hold that there has been no such dedication of Lloyd's privately owned and operated shopping center to public use as to entitle respondents to exercise therein the asserted First Amendment rights.

The *Hudgens* opinion added:

If a large self-contained shopping center is the functional equivalent of a municipality, as *Logan Valley* held, then the First and Fourteenth Amendments would not permit control of speech within such a center to depend upon the speech's content. . . . It conversely follows, therefore, that if the respondents in the *Lloyd* case did not have a First Amendment right to enter that shopping center distribute handbills concerning Vietnam, then the pickets in the present case did not have a First Amendment right to enter this shopping center for the purpose of advertising their strike against the Butler Shoe Co.

We conclude, in short, that under the present state of the law the constitutional guarantee of free expression has no part to play in a case such as this.

4. The Court in *Hudgens* did not repudiate *Marsh*. But does *Marsh* have any applicability beyond the "company town"? Consider the Problem that follows.

5. Some state courts have held that the state constitution protects speech and petitioning in shopping centers even when the centers are privately owned. Does this rule of state law violate the free-speech rights of the shopping center owner under federal law? The Supreme Court has addressed this question in only one case. In *PruneYard Shopping Center v. Robins*, 447 U.S. 74 (1980), the Court unanimously rejected the shopping center owner's claims under the First Amendment as well its claims of interference with property rights. (For a brief discussion, see Chapter 9.)

Chapter 9

Compelled Expression

A. Compelled Speech

While the First Amendment speaks of laws abridging the freedom of "speech," the Supreme Court has long held that freedom of speech includes the right *not* to speak. As you read the following cases, consider what goal of free speech is served by recognizing a correlative right not to speak, and how far the right not to speak must be taken in order to serve that goal.

West Virginia State Board of Education v. Barnette
319 U.S. 624 (1943)

[*Editor's note.* In *Minersville School District v. Gobitis*, 310 U.S. 586 (1940), a local Board of Education required both teachers and pupils to salute the flag of the United States as part of a daily school exercise. Lillian Gobitis, aged twelve, and her brother William, aged ten, were expelled from school for refusing to participate in the ceremony. Their refusal was based on their religious convictions as members of the Jehovah's Witnesses. The Supreme Court, in an opinion by Justice Frankfurter, held that the compulsory flag salute did not violate the children's federal constitutional rights. Only Justice Stone dissented.]

MR. JUSTICE JACKSON delivered the opinion of the Court.

Following the decision by this Court on June 3, 1940, in *Minersville School District v. Gobitis*, the West Virginia legislature amended its statutes to require all schools therein to conduct courses of instruction in history, civics, and in the Constitutions of the United States and of the State "for the purpose of teaching, fostering and perpetuating the ideals, principles and spirit of Americanism, and increasing the knowledge of the organization and machinery of the government." Appellant Board of Education was directed, with advice of the State Superintendent of Schools, to "prescribe the courses of study covering these subjects" for public schools. The Act made it the duty of private, parochial and denominational schools to prescribe courses of study "similar to those required for the public schools."

The Board of Education on January 9, 1942, adopted a resolution containing recitals taken largely from the Court's *Gobitis* opinion and ordering that the salute to the flag become "a regular part of the program of activities in the public schools," that all teachers and pupils "shall be required to participate in the salute honoring the Nation represented by the Flag; provided, however, that refusal to salute the Flag be regarded as an act of insubordination, and shall be dealt with accordingly." . . .

Appellees, citizens of the United States and of West Virginia, brought suit in the United States District Court for themselves and others similarly situated asking its injunction to restrain enforcement of these laws and regulations against Jehovah's Witnesses. The Witnesses are an unincorporated body teaching that the obligation imposed by law of God is superior to that of laws enacted by temporal government. Their religious beliefs include a literal version of Exodus, Chapter 20, verses 4 and 5, which says: "Thou shalt not make unto thee any graven image, or any likeness of anything that is in heaven above, or that is in the earth beneath, or that is in the water under the earth; thou shalt not bow down thyself to them nor serve them." They consider that the flag is an "image" within this command. For this reason they refuse to salute it.

Children of this faith have been expelled from school and are threatened with exclusion for no other cause. Officials threaten to send them to reformatories maintained for criminally inclined juveniles. Parents of such children have been prosecuted and are threatened with prosecutions for causing delinquency.

The Board of Education moved to dismiss the complaint setting forth these facts and alleging that the law and regulations are an unconstitutional denial of religious freedom, and of freedom of speech, and are invalid under the "due process" and "equal protection" clauses of the Fourteenth Amendment to the Federal Constitution. The cause was submitted on the pleadings to a District Court of three judges. It restrained enforcement as to the plaintiffs and those of that class. The Board of Education brought the case here by direct appeal. . . .

As the present Chief Justice said in dissent in the *Gobitis* case, the State may "require teaching by instruction and study of all in our history and in the structure and organization of our government, including the guaranties of civil liberty which tend to inspire patriotism and love of country." Here, however, we are dealing with a compulsion of students to declare a belief. They are not merely made acquainted with the flag salute so that they may be informed as to what it is or even what it means. The issue here is whether this slow and easily neglected route to aroused loyalties constitutionally may be short-cut by substituting a compulsory salute and slogan. This issue is not prejudiced by the Court's previous holding that where a State, without compelling attendance, extends college facilities to pupils who voluntarily enroll, it may prescribe military training as part of the course without offense to the Constitution. *Hamilton v. Regents*, 293 U.S. 245 (1934). It was held that those who take advantage of its opportunities may not on ground of conscience refuse compliance with such conditions. In the present case attendance is not optional. . . .

There is no doubt that, in connection with the pledges, the flag salute is a form of utterance. Symbolism is a primitive but effective way of communicating ideas. The use of an emblem or flag to symbolize some system, idea, institution, or personality, is a short cut from mind to mind. . . .

It is also to be noted that the compulsory flag salute and pledge requires affirmation of a belief and an attitude of mind. It is not clear whether the regulation contemplates that pupils forego any contrary convictions of their own and become unwilling converts to the prescribed ceremony or whether it will be acceptable if they simulate assent by words without belief and by a gesture barren of meaning. It is now a commonplace that censorship or suppression of expression of opinion is tolerated by our Constitution only when the expression presents a clear and present danger of action of a kind the State is empowered to prevent and punish. It would seem that involuntary affirmation could be commanded only on even more immediate and urgent grounds than silence. But here the power of compulsion is invoked without any allegation that remaining passive during a flag salute ritual creates a clear and present danger that would justify an effort even to muffle expression. To sustain the compulsory flag salute we are required to say that a Bill of Rights which guards the individual's right to speak his own mind, left it open to public authorities to compel him to utter what is not in his mind. . . .

1. It was said [in *Gobitis*] that the flag-salute controversy confronted the Court with "the problem which Lincoln cast in memorable dilemma: 'Must a government of necessity be too *strong* for the liberties of its people, or too *weak* to maintain its own existence?'" and that the answer must be in favor of strength.

We think these issues may be examined free of pressure or restraint growing out of such considerations.

It may be doubted whether Mr. Lincoln would have thought that the strength of government to maintain itself would be impressively vindicated by our confirming power of the state to expel a handful of children from school. Such oversimplification, so handy in political debate, often lacks the precision necessary to postulates of judicial reasoning. If validly applied to this problem, the utterance cited would resolve every issue of power in favor of those in authority and would require us to override every liberty thought to weaken or delay execution of their policies. . . .

2. It was also considered in the *Gobitis* case that functions of educational officers in States, counties and school districts were such that to interfere with their authority "would in effect make us the school board for the country." . . .

Such Boards are numerous and their territorial jurisdiction often small. But small and local authority may feel less sense of responsibility to the Constitution, and agencies of publicity may be less vigilant in calling it to account. The action of Congress in making flag observance voluntary and respecting the conscience of the objector in a matter so vital as raising the Army contrasts sharply with these local regulations in matters relatively trivial to the welfare of the nation. There are village tyrants as well as village Hampdens, but none who acts under color of law is beyond reach of the Constitution.

3. The *Gobitis* opinion reasoned that this is a field "where courts possess no marked and certainly no controlling competence," that it is committed to the legislatures as well as the courts to guard cherished liberties and that it is constitutionally appropriate to "fight out the wise use of legislative authority in the forum of public opinion and before legislative assemblies rather than to transfer such a contest to the judicial arena," since all the "effective means of inducing political changes are left free."

The very purpose of a Bill of Rights was to withdraw certain subjects from the vicissitudes of political controversy, to place them beyond the reach of majorities and officials and to establish them as legal principles to be applied by the courts. One's right to life, liberty, and property, to free speech, a free press, freedom of worship and assembly, and other fundamental rights may not be submitted to vote; they depend on the outcome of no elections.

In weighing arguments of the parties it is important to distinguish between the due process clause of the Fourteenth Amendment as an instrument for transmitting the principles of the First Amendment and those cases in which it is applied for its own sake. The test of legislation which collides with the Fourteenth Amendment, because it also collides with the principles of the First, is much more definite than the test when only the Fourteenth is involved. Much of the vagueness of the due process clause disappears when the specific prohibitions of the First become its standard. The right of a State to regulate, for example, a public utility may well include, so far as the due process test is concerned, power to impose all of the restrictions which a legislature may have a "rational basis" for adopting. But freedoms of speech and of press, of assembly, and of worship may not be infringed on such slender grounds. They are susceptible of restriction only to prevent grave and immediate danger to interests which the state may lawfully protect. It is important to note that while it is the Fourteenth Amendment which bears directly upon the State it is the more specific limiting principles of the First Amendment that finally govern this case.

Nor does our duty to apply the Bill of Rights to assertions of official authority depend upon our possession of marked competence in the field where the invasion of rights occurs. True, the task of translating the majestic generalities of the Bill of Rights, conceived as part of the pattern of liberal government in the eighteenth century, into concrete restraints on officials dealing with the problems of the twentieth century, is one to disturb self-confidence. These principles grew in soil which also produced a philosophy that the individual was the center of society, that his liberty was attainable through mere absence of governmental restraints, and that government should be entrusted with few controls and only the mildest supervision over men's affairs. We must transplant these rights to a soil in which the *laissez-faire* concept or principle of non-interference has withered at least as to economic affairs, and social advancements are increasingly sought through closer integration of society and through expanded and strengthened governmental controls. These changed conditions often deprive precedents of reliability and cast us more than we would choose upon our own judgment. But we act in these matters not by authority of our competence but by force of our commissions. We cannot, because of modest estimates of our competence in such specialties as public education, withhold the judgment that history authenticates as the function of this Court when liberty is infringed.

4. Lastly, and this is the very heart of the *Gobitis* opinion, it reasons that "National unity is the basis of national security," that the authorities have "the right to select appropriate means for its attainment," and hence reaches the conclusion that such

compulsory measures toward "national unity" are constitutional. Upon the verity of this assumption depends our answer in this case.

National unity as an end which officials may foster by persuasion and example is not in question. The problem is whether under our Constitution compulsion as here employed is a permissible means for its achievement.

Struggles to coerce uniformity of sentiment in support of some end thought essential to their time and country have been waged by many good as well as by evil men. Nationalism is a relatively recent phenomenon but at other times and places the ends have been racial or territorial security, support of a dynasty or regime, and particular plans for saving souls. As first and moderate methods to attain unity have failed, those bent on its accomplishment must resort to an ever-increasing severity. As governmental pressure toward unity becomes greater, so strife becomes more bitter as to whose unity it shall be. Probably no deeper division of our people could proceed from any provocation than from finding it necessary to choose what doctrine and whose program public educational officials shall compel youth to unite in embracing. Ultimate futility of such attempts to compel coherence is the lesson of every such effort from the Roman drive to stamp out Christianity as a disturber of its pagan unity, the Inquisition, as a means to religious and dynastic unity, the Siberian exiles as a means to Russian unity, down to the fast failing efforts of our present totalitarian enemies. Those who begin coercive elimination of dissent soon find themselves exterminating dissenters. Compulsory unification of opinion achieves only the unanimity of the graveyard.

It seems trite but necessary to say that the First Amendment to our Constitution was designed to avoid these ends by avoiding these beginnings. There is no mysticism in the American concept of the State or of the nature or origin of its authority. We set up government by consent of the governed, and the Bill of Rights denies those in power any legal opportunity to coerce that consent. Authority here is to be controlled by public opinion, not public opinion by authority.

The case is made difficult not because the principles of its decision are obscure but because the flag involved is our own. Nevertheless, we apply the limitations of the Constitution with no fear that freedom to be intellectually and spiritually diverse or even contrary will disintegrate the social organization. To believe that patriotism will not flourish if patriotic ceremonies are voluntary and spontaneous instead of a compulsory routine is to make an unflattering estimate of the appeal of our institutions to free minds. We can have intellectual individualism and the rich cultural diversities that we owe to exceptional minds only at the price of occasional eccentricity and abnormal attitudes. When they are so harmless to others or to the State as those we deal with here, the price is not too great. But freedom to differ is not limited to things that do not matter much. That would be a mere shadow of freedom. The test of its substance is the right to differ as to things that touch the heart of the existing order.

If there is any fixed star in our constitutional constellation, it is that no official, high or petty, can prescribe what shall be orthodox in politics, nationalism, religion, or other matters of opinion or force citizens to confess by word or act their faith therein. If there are any circumstances which permit an exception, they do not now occur to us.

We think the action of the local authorities in compelling the flag salute and pledge transcends constitutional limitations on their power and invades the sphere of intellect and spirit which it is the purpose of the First Amendment to our Constitution to reserve from all official control.

The decision of this Court in *Minersville School District v. Gobitis* and the holdings of those few *per curiam* decisions which preceded and foreshadowed it are overruled, and the judgment enjoining enforcement of the West Virginia Regulation is

Affirmed.

Mr. Justice Roberts and Mr. Justice Reed adhere to the views expressed by the Court in *Minersville School District v. Gobitis*, and are of the opinion that the judgment below should be reversed.

Mr. Justice Black and Mr. Justice Douglas, concurring.

We are substantially in agreement with the opinion just read, but since we originally joined with the Court in the *Gobitis* case, it is appropriate that we make a brief statement of reasons for our change of view.

Reluctance to make the Federal Constitution a rigid bar against state regulation of conduct thought inimical to the public welfare was the controlling influence which moved us to consent to the *Gobitis* decision. Long reflection convinced us that although the principle is sound, its application in the particular case was wrong. We believe that the statute before us fails to accord full scope to the freedom of religion secured to the appellees by the First and Fourteenth Amendments.

The statute requires the appellees to participate in a ceremony aimed at inculcating respect for the flag and for this country. The Jehovah's Witnesses, without any desire to show disrespect for either the flag or the country, interpret the Bible as commanding, at the risk of God's displeasure, that they not go through the form of a pledge of allegiance to any flag. The devoutness of their belief is evidenced by their willingness to suffer persecution and punishment, rather than make the pledge.

No well-ordered society can leave to the individuals an absolute right to make final decisions, unassailable by the State, as to everything they will or will not do. The First Amendment does not go so far. Religious faiths, honestly held, do not free individuals from responsibility to conduct themselves obediently to laws which are either imperatively necessary to protect society as a whole from grave and pressingly imminent dangers or which, without any general prohibition, merely regulate time, place or manner of religious activity. Decision as to the constitutionality of particular laws which strike at the substance of religious tenets and practices must be made by this Court. The duty is a solemn one, and in meeting it we cannot say that a failure, because of religious scruples, to assume a particular physical position and to repeat the words of a patriotic formula creates a grave danger to the nation. Such a statutory exaction is a form of test oath, and the test oath has always been abhorrent in the United States. . . .

Mr. Justice Murphy, concurring.

I agree with the opinion of the Court and join in it. . . .

I am unable to agree that the benefits that may accrue to society from the compulsory flag salute are sufficiently definite and tangible to justify the invasion of freedom and privacy that it entailed or to compensate for a restraint on the freedom of the individual to be vocal or silent according to his conscience or personal inclination. The trenchant words in the preamble to the Virginia Statute for Religious Freedom remain unanswerable: ". . . all attempts to influence [the mind] by temporal punishment, or burthens, or by civil incapacitations, tend only to beget habits of hypocrisy and meanness. . . ." Any spark of love for country which may be generated in a child or his associates by forcing him to make what is to him an empty gesture and recite words wrung from him contrary to his religious beliefs is overshadowed by the desirability of preserving freedom of conscience to the full. It is in that freedom and the example of persuasion, not in force and compulsion, that the real unity of America lies.

Mr. Justice Frankfurter, dissenting.

One who belongs to the most vilified and persecuted minority in history is not likely to be insensible to the freedoms guaranteed by our Constitution. Were my purely personal attitude relevant I should whole-heartedly associate myself with the general libertarian views in the Court's opinion, representing as they do the thought and action of a lifetime. But as judges we are neither Jew nor Gentile, neither Catholic nor agnostic. We owe equal attachment to the Constitution and are equally bound by our judicial obligations whether we derive our citizenship from the earliest or the latest immigrants to these shores. As a member of this Court I am not justified in writing my private notions of policy into the Constitution, no matter how deeply I may cherish them or how mischievous I may deem their disregard. . . . Most unwillingly, therefore, I must differ from my brethren with regard to legislation like this. I cannot bring my mind to believe that the "liberty" secured by the Due Process Clause gives this Court authority to deny to the State of West Virginia the attainment of that which we all recognize as a legitimate legislative end, namely, the promotion of good citizenship, by employment of the means here chosen. . . .

Conscientious scruples, all would admit, cannot stand against every legislative compulsion to do positive acts in conflict with such scruples. We have been told that such compulsions override religious scruples only as to major concerns of the state. But the determination of what is major and what is minor itself raises questions of policy. For the way in which men equally guided by reason appraise importance goes to the very heart of policy. Judges should be very diffident in setting their judgment against that of a state in determining what is and what is not a major concern, what means are appropriate to proper ends, and what is the total social cost in striking the balance of imponderables. . . .

The essence of the religious freedom guaranteed by our Constitution is therefore this: no religion shall either receive the state's support or incur its hostility. Religion is outside the sphere of political government. This does not mean that all matters on which religious organizations or beliefs may pronounce are outside the sphere of government. Were this so, instead of the separation of church and state, there would be the subordination of the state on any matter deemed within the sovereignty of the religious conscience. . . . The validity of secular laws cannot be measured by their conformity to religious doctrines. It is only in a theocratic state that ecclesiastical doctrines measure legal right or wrong.

An act compelling profession of allegiance to a religion, no matter how subtly or tenuously promoted, is bad. But an act promoting good citizenship and national allegiance is within the domain of governmental authority and is therefore to be judged by the same considerations of power and of constitutionality as those involved in the many claims of immunity from civil obedience because of religious scruples. . . .

The subjection of dissidents to the general requirement of saluting the flag, as a measure conducive to the training of children in good citizenship, is very far from being the first instance of exacting obedience to general laws that have offended deep religious scruples. Compulsory vaccination, see *Jacobson v. Massachusetts*, 197 U.S. 11 (1905), food inspection regulations, see *Shapiro v. Lyle*, 30 F.2d 971 (D. Wash. 1929), the obligation to bear arms, see *Hamilton v. Regents*, 293 U.S. 245 (1934), testimonial duties, see *Stansbury v. Marks*, 2 Dall. 213 (1793), compulsory medical treatment, see *People v. Vogelgesang*, 221 N.Y. 290 (1917) — these are but illustrations of conduct that has often been compelled in the enforcement of legislation of general applicability even though the religious consciences of particular individuals rebelled at the exaction. . . .

The right of West Virginia to utilize the flag salute as part of its educational process is denied because, so it is argued, it cannot be justified as a means of meeting a "clear and present danger" to national unity. In passing it deserves to be noted that the four cases which unanimously sustained the power of states to utilize such an educational measure arose and were all decided before the present World War. But to measure the state's power to make such regulations as are here resisted by the imminence of national danger is wholly to misconceive the origin and purpose of the concept of "clear and present danger." To apply such a test is for the Court to assume, however unwittingly, a legislative responsibility that does not belong to it. To talk about "clear and present danger" as the touchstone of allowable educational policy by the states whenever school curricula may impinge upon the boundaries of individual conscience, is to take a felicitous phrase out of the context of the particular situation where it arose and for which it was adapted.

Mr. Justice Holmes used the phrase "clear and present danger" in a case involving mere speech as a means by which alone to accomplish sedition in time of war. By that phrase he meant merely to indicate that, in view of the protection given to utterance by the First Amendment, in order that mere utterance may not be proscribed, "the words used are used in such circumstances and are of such a nature as to create a clear and present danger that they will bring about the substantive evils that Congress has a right to prevent." *Schenck v. United States* (1919) [*supra* Chapter 1]. The "substantive evils" about which he was speaking were inducement of insubordination in the military and naval forces of the United States and obstruction of enlistment while the country was at war. He was not enunciating a formal rule that there can be no restriction upon speech and, still less, no compulsion where conscience balks, unless imminent danger would thereby be wrought "to our institutions or our government."

The flag salute exercise has no kinship whatever to the oath tests so odious in history. For the oath test was one of the instruments for suppressing heretical beliefs. Saluting the flag suppresses no belief nor curbs it. Children and their parents may believe what they please, avow their belief and practice it. It is not even remotely suggested that the requirement for saluting the flag involves the slightest restriction against the fullest opportunity on the part both of the children and of their parents to disavow as publicly as they choose to do so the meaning that others attach to the gesture of salute. All channels of affirmative free expression are open to both children and parents. Had we before us any act of the state putting the slightest curbs upon such free expression, I should not lag behind any member of this Court in striking down such an invasion of the right to freedom of thought and freedom of speech protected by the Constitution. . . .

———

Note: Barnette *and Its Implications*

1. The two concurring opinions, joined by three Justices, take the position that the compulsory flag salute infringes on the plaintiffs' freedom of religion. Is the Free Exercise Clause the basis of the Court's opinion? To what extent, if any, does that opinion rely on the fact that the plaintiffs' objection to the salute is based on their religious beliefs?

2. On what basis does the Court conclude that the Constitution protects against government action that commands "involuntary affirmation" of belief? Is it the text of the First Amendment? Precedent? (Note: The opinion as reported above includes all of the Court's case citations.) The intent of the Framers? Or something else?

———

Problem: A State University Pledge

It is not unusual for colleges and universities to require students to "pledge" to adhere to specified principles and responsibilities. Suppose that a state university's pledge includes the following:

> As a member of the social community, I will respect individual differences and the rights of all others. I understand that bias on the basis of gender, handicapped status, national origin, race, religious belief, or sexual orientation, whether expressed in word or action, is repugnant.

The student must "acknowledge that breaking my word and failing to keep faith with this statement can lead to sanctions, which can end at separation from [the] University."

Under *Barnette*, is this "pledge" permissible? Consider also *Wooley v. Maynard*, the next principal case.

Wooley v. Maynard

430 U.S. 705 (1977)

Mr. Chief Justice Burger delivered the opinion of the Court.

The issue on appeal is whether the State of New Hampshire may constitutionally enforce criminal sanctions against persons who cover the motto "Live Free or Die" on passenger vehicle license plates because that motto is repugnant to their moral and religious beliefs.

Since 1969, New Hampshire has required that noncommercial vehicles bear license plates embossed with the state motto, "Live Free or Die." Another New Hampshire statute makes it a misdemeanor "knowingly [to obscure] . . . the figures or letters on any number plate." The term "letters" in this section has been interpreted by the State's highest court to include the state motto.

Appellees George Maynard and his wife Maxine are followers of the Jehovah's Witnesses faith. The Maynards consider the New Hampshire State motto to be repugnant to their moral, religious, and political beliefs, and therefore assert it objectionable to disseminate this message by displaying it on their automobiles. Pursuant to these beliefs, the Maynards began early in 1974 to cover up the motto on their license plates. . . .

On March 4, 1975, appellees brought the present action. . . . On March 11, 1975, the single District Judge issued a temporary restraining order against further arrests and prosecutions of the Maynards. . . . Following a hearing on the merits, the District Court entered an order enjoining the State "from arresting and prosecuting [the Maynards] at any time in the future for covering over that portion of their license plates that contains the motto 'Live Free or Die.'" We noted probable jurisdiction of the appeal. . . .

(4)

The District Court held that, by covering up the state motto "Live Free or Die" on his automobile license plate, Mr. Maynard was engaging in symbolic speech, and that "New Hampshire's interest in the enforcement of its defacement statute is not sufficient to justify the restriction on [appellee's] constitutionally protected expression." We find it unnecessary to pass on the "symbolic speech" issue, since we find more appropriate First Amendment grounds to affirm the judgment of the District Court. We turn instead to what, in our view, is the essence of appellees' objection to the requirement that they display the motto "Live Free or Die" on their automobile license plates. This is succinctly summarized in the statement made by Mr. Maynard in his affidavit filed with the District Court:

> I refuse to be coerced by the State into advertising a slogan which I find morally, ethically, religiously and politically abhorrent.

We are thus faced with the question of whether the State may constitutionally require an individual to participate in the dissemination of an ideological message by displaying it on his private property in a manner and for the express purpose that it be observed and read by the public. We hold that the State may not do so.

A

We begin with the proposition that the right of freedom of thought protected by the First Amendment against state action includes both the right to speak freely and the right to refrain from speaking at all. *See West Virginia Bd. of Ed. v. Barnette* (1943). A system which secures the right to proselytize religious, political, and ideological causes must also guarantee the concomitant right to decline to foster such concepts. The right to speak and the right to refrain from speaking are complementary components of the broader concept of "individual freedom of mind." . . .

The Court in *Barnette* was faced with a state statute which required public school students to participate in daily public ceremonies by honoring the flag both with words and traditional salute gestures. In overruling its prior decision in *Minersville District v. Gobitis*, 310 U.S. 586 (1940), the Court held that "a ceremony so touching matters of opinion and political attitude may [not] be imposed upon the individual by official authority under powers committed to any political organization under our Constitution." Compelling the affirmative act of a flag salute involved a more serious infringement upon personal liberties than the passive act of carrying the state motto on a license plate, but the difference is essentially one of degree. Here, as in *Barnette*, we are faced with a state measure which forces an individual, as part of his daily life—indeed constantly while his automobile is in public view—to be an instrument for fostering public adherence to an ideological point of view he finds unacceptable. In doing so, the State "invades the sphere of intellect and spirit which it is the purpose of the First Amendment to our Constitution to reserve from all official control." *Barnette*.

New Hampshire's statute in effect requires that appellees use their private property as a "mobile billboard" for the State's ideological message—or suffer a penalty, as Maynard already has. As a condition to driving an automobile—a virtual necessity for most Americans—the Maynards must display "Live Free or Die" to hundreds of people each day. The fact that most individuals agree with the thrust of New Hampshire's motto is not the test; most Americans also find the flag salute acceptable. The First Amendment protects the right of individuals to hold a point of view different from the majority, and to refuse to foster, in the way New Hampshire commands, an idea they find morally objectionable.

B

Identifying the Maynards' interests as implicating First Amendment protections does not end our inquiry however. We must also determine whether the State's countervailing interest is sufficiently compelling to justify requiring appellees to display the state motto on their license plates. *See, e.g., United States v. O'Brien* (1968) [*supra* Chapter 7]. The two interests advanced by the State are that display of the motto (1) facilitates the identification of passenger vehicles, and (2) promotes appreciation of history, individualism, and state pride.

The State first points out that passenger vehicles, but not commercial, trailer, or other vehicles are required to display the state motto. Thus, the argument proceeds, officers of the law are more easily able to determine whether passenger vehicles are carrying the proper plates. However, the record here reveals that New Hampshire passenger license plates normally consist of a specific configuration of letters and numbers, which makes them readily distinguishable from other types of plates, even without reference to the state motto. Even were we to credit the State's reasons, and "even though the governmental purpose be legitimate and substantial, that purpose cannot be pursued by means that broadly stifle fundamental personal liberties when the end can be more narrowly achieved. The breadth of legislative abridgment must be viewed in the light of less drastic means for achieving the same basic purpose." *Shelton v. Tucker*, 364 U.S. 479 (1960).

The State's second claimed interest is not ideologically neutral. The State is seeking to communicate to others an official view as to proper appreciation of history, state pride, and individualism. Of course, the State may legitimately pursue such interests in any number of ways. However, where the State's interest is to disseminate an ideology, no matter how acceptable to some, such interest cannot outweigh an individual's First Amendment right to avoid becoming the courier for such message.

We conclude that the State of New Hampshire may not require appellees to display the state motto upon their vehicle license plates; and, accordingly, we affirm the judgment of the District Court.

Mr. Justice White, with whom Mr. Justice Blackmun and Mr. Justice Rehnquist join in part, dissenting in part. [Omitted.]

Mr. Justice Rehnquist, with whom Mr. Justice Blackmun joins, dissenting.

. . . I not only agree with the Court's implicit recognition that there is no protected "symbolic speech" in this case, but I think that that conclusion goes far to undermine the Court's ultimate holding that there is an element of protected expression here. The State has not forced appellees to "say" anything; and it has not forced them to communicate ideas with nonverbal actions reasonably likened to "speech," such as wearing a lapel button promoting a political candidate or waving a flag as a symbolic gesture. The State has simply required that *all* noncommercial automobiles bear license tags with the state motto, "Live Free or Die." Appellees have not been forced to affirm or reject that motto; they are simply required by the State, under its police power, to carry a state auto license tag for identification and registration purposes.

In Part 4-A, the Court relies almost solely on *Barnette*. The Court cites *Barnette* for the proposition that there is a constitutional right, in some cases, to "refrain from speaking." What the Court does not demonstrate is that there is any "speech" or "speaking" in the context of this case. . . . The issue, unconfronted by the Court, is whether appellees, in displaying, as they are required to do, state license tags, the format of which is known to all as having been prescribed by the State, would be considered to be advocating political or ideological views.

The Court recognizes, as it must, that this case substantially differs from *Barnette*, in which schoolchildren were forced to recite the pledge of allegiance while giving the flag salute. However, the Court states "the difference is essentially one of degree." But having recognized the rather obvious differences between these two cases, the Court does not explain why the same result should obtain. The Court suggests that the test is whether the individual is forced "to be an instrument for fostering public adherence to an ideological point of view he finds unacceptable." But, once again, these are merely conclusory words, barren of analysis. For example, were New Hampshire to erect a multitude of billboards, each proclaiming "Live Free or Die," and tax all citizens for the cost of erection and maintenance, clearly the message would be "fostered" by the individual citizen-taxpayers and just as clearly those individuals would be "instruments" in that communication. Certainly, however, that case would not fall within the ambit of *Barnette*. In that case, as in this case, there is no *affirmation* of belief. For First Amendment principles to be implicated, the State must place the citizen in the position of either apparently or actually "asserting as true" the message. This was the focus of *Barnette*, and clearly distinguishes this case from that one.

. . . As found by the New Hampshire Supreme Court in [an earlier case], there is nothing in state law which precludes appellees from displaying their disagreement with the state motto as long as the methods used do not obscure the license plates. Thus appellees could place on their bumper a conspicuous bumper sticker explaining in no uncertain terms that they do not profess the motto "Live Free or Die" and that they violently disagree with the connotations of that motto. Since any implication that they affirm the motto can be so easily displaced, I cannot agree that the state statutory system for motor vehicle identification and tourist promotion may be invalidated under the fiction that appellees are unconstitutionally forced to affirm, or profess belief in, the state motto.

The logic of the Court's opinion leads to startling, and I believe totally unacceptable, results. For example, the mottoes "In God We Trust" and "E Pluribus Unum" appear on the coin and currency of the United States. I cannot imagine that the statutes proscribing defacement of United States currency impinge upon the First Amendment rights of an atheist. The fact that an atheist carries and uses United States currency does not, in any meaningful sense, convey any affirmation of belief on his part in the motto "In God We Trust." Similarly, there is no affirmation of belief involved in the display of state license tags upon the private automobiles involved here.

I would reverse the judgment of the District Court.

———

Note: The Barnette Principle

1. What is the First Amendment principle underlying *Barnette* and *Wooley*? Is it that coercing private speech closes down Holmes' marketplace of ideas? Or is that argument untenable because the coerced speaker can always utter his or her own thoughts anyway?

Or is it the theory that coerced speech impairs people's ability to govern themselves? Does the ability of the coerced speaker to retract or even attack the coerced statement negate that argument?

Recall the comment by Professor Dworkin quoted in Chapter 1: "freedom of speech is valuable, not just in virtue of the consequences it has, but because it is an essential and 'constitutive' feature of a just political society that government treat all its adult members . . . as responsible moral agents." Does this premise explain the Court's holding that a requirement of "involuntary affirmation" violates the First Amendment?

2. If everyone knows that certain expression—such as the pledge in *Barnette* or the motto in *Wooley*—is compelled by government, does that mean that listeners will discount its significance, or at least will not attribute that belief to the speaker? If so, does that undercut the First Amendment claim?

In *PruneYard Shopping Center v. Robins*, 447 U.S. 74 (1980), the Court considered the First Amendment implications of a state-court ruling that required shopping center owners to open their property to expressive activity by individuals. In *PruneYard*, high school students had set up a table in the corner of the shopping center's central courtyard and solicited signatures for a petition to be sent to the President and Congress opposing a particular United Nations resolution. A security guard informed them that their activity violated the center's policy against visitors or tenants engaging in any publicly expressive activity unrelated to the center's commercial purposes. The students left, and later filed suit in state court, alleging a violation of their free speech rights under the California Constitution. The state supreme court concluded that the state constitution's free speech provision protected the students' right to solicit signatures at the shopping center. The shopping center owner appealed to the U.S. Supreme Court. He argued that the state court's interpretation of the state constitutional provision violated his First Amendment rights by compelling him, as he put it, "to use his property as a forum for the speech of others." The Court rejected the owner's argument. It distinguished *Wooley* as follows:

> Most important, the shopping center by choice of its owner is not limited to the personal use of appellants. It is instead a business establishment that is open to the public to come and go as they please. The views expressed by members of the public in passing out pamphlets or seeking signatures for a petition thus will not likely be identified with those of the owner. Second, no specific message is dictated by the State to be displayed on appellants' property. There consequently is no danger of governmental discrimination for or against a particular message. Finally, as far as appears here appellants can expressly disavow any connection with the message by simply posting signs in the area where the speakers or handbillers stand. Such signs, for example, could disclaim any sponsorship of the message and could explain that the persons are communicating their own messages by virtue of state law.

Does the compelled and impersonal nature of the display in *Wooley* satisfy the first of *PruneYard*'s observations? Does the ability to post a bumper sticker disagreeing with the motto satisfy the third?

Reverse the perspective and consider the issue from the point of view of the would-be private speaker. After *Wooley*, would a New Hampshire resident who disagrees with "Live Free or Die" feel additional pressure to exercise his right to request a non-offending license plate, exactly because the existence of that option means that displaying the motto implies agreement with it? If so, does this suggest that compelling display of the motto makes it constitutionally inoffensive?

3. One effect of coercing private parties to speak is the damage it does to the individual's own sense of self, as the individual's own expressive capabilities are, in a sense, commandeered by the government for its own ends. This more personal model of the value of freedom for coerced speech fits neatly within *Wooley*'s admonition that government may not make individuals into "mobile billboards" for the government's message, and even more so within *Barnette*'s statement that compelled expression "invades the sphere of intellect and spirit." But this theory raises difficult questions about what types of coerced expression causes this sort of personal harm. Consider the Problems that follow. Consider also how this theory impacts First Amendment issues arising out of compelled subsidization of speech. This latter issue is treated in the *Abood* case and the materials that follow it.

Problem: Navajo Spiritualism on License Plates?

The State of Monroe has a large Navajo population. For several years, the State's standard license plate has depicted a scene of a young male Navajo dressed in traditional garb, kneeling on one knee, shooting an arrow into the sky. Tom Fredericks, a devout Christian, citizen of Monroe, and newly licensed motorist, believes the scene to be based on a famous sculpture entitled "Spirit Warrior," which depicts the story of a mythical Navajo warrior who shot a sacred arrow into the sky in order to beseech the gods to bring rain and end a long drought. When Fredericks buys his first car and visits the State's Department of Motor Vehicles to obtain license plates, he inquires whether he can legally cover up the depiction on the standard plate. Upon being advised that Monroe law forbids "the concealment of any portion of a motor vehicle's license plate or registration tag," Fredericks sues, alleging that the State is compelling him to endorse a religious message with which he disagrees.

Does Fredericks have a good claim under *Barnette* and *Wooley*?

———

Note: "Trivializing" Barnette?

Not every compelled utterance constitutes a violation of the *Barnette* principle. Consider *Rumsfeld v. Forum for Academic and Institutional Rights (FAIR)*, 547 U.S. 47 (2006). In *FAIR* a group of law schools mounted a First Amendment-based challenge to the Solomon Amendment, a federal law that requires educational institutions receiving federal funds to give military recruiters access to universities' career services facilities "that is at least equal in quality and scope to the access . . . that is provided to any other employer." The law schools protested having to make their career service facilities available to military recruiters, who violated the schools' policies against providing such facilities to employers that discriminate on the basis of sexual orientation. The schools argued that the law violated their First Amendment rights by, as the appellate court put it, compelling them "to speak the Government's message."

On an 8-0 vote (Justice Alito not participating), the Supreme Court held that the federal law would not violate the First Amendment even if it took the form of a direct mandate rather than a funding condition; it thus rejected the claim that the funding condition was unconstitutional. The Court, speaking through Chief Justice Roberts, conceded that under the law, if a school spoke in regard to other recruiters—for example, by "send[ing] emails or post[ing] notices on bulletin boards on an employer's behalf"—then it would have to do the same for military recruiters. It noted: "As FAIR points out, these compelled statements of fact ('The U.S. Army recruiter will meet interested students in Room 123 at 11 a.m.'), like compelled statements of opinion, are subject to First Amendment scrutiny." The Court continued:

> This sort of recruiting assistance, however, is a far cry from the compelled speech in *Barnette* and *Wooley*. The Solomon Amendment, unlike the laws at issue in those cases, does not dictate the content of the speech at all, which is only "compelled" if, and to the extent, the school provides such speech for other recruiters. There is nothing in this case approaching a Government-mandated pledge or motto that the school must endorse.

> The compelled speech to which the law schools point is plainly incidental to the Solomon Amendment's regulation of conduct, and "it has never been deemed an abridgement of freedom of speech or press to make a course of conduct illegal merely because the conduct was in part initiated, evidenced, or carried out by means of language, either spoken, written, or printed." *Giboney v. Empire Storage & Ice Co.*, 336 U.S. 490 (1949) [Note *supra* Chapter 3]. Congress, for example, can prohibit employers from discriminating in hiring on the basis of race. The fact that this will require an employer to take down a sign reading "White Applicants Only" hardly means that the law should be analyzed as one regulating the employer's speech rather than conduct. Compelling a law school that sends scheduling e-mails for other recruiters to send one for a military recruiter is simply not the same as forcing a student to pledge allegiance, or forcing a Jehovah's Witness to display the motto "Live Free or Die," and it trivializes the freedom protected in *Barnette* and *Wooley* to suggest that it is.

What characteristics of the compelled speech in *FAIR* make it, in the Court's view, "a far cry" from the compelled speech in *Barnette* and *Wooley*?

————

Problem: The Wedding Photographer and the Gay Couple

Same-sex marriages are legal in Massachusetts. Bobby Bennett, a gay man in Boston preparing for his wedding, hires Angie Adams, a photographer. The photographer agrees to all the terms, which include Angie posing Bobby and his spouse in a traditional marriage pose and selecting an appropriate backdrop. Angie's performance of these functions is crucial to the reason Bobby hired her, as he has seen Angie's wedding photography and believes that it captures exactly what he wants his wedding pictures to convey. However, when Angie learns that the planned marriage is between two men, she refuses to work. She claims that to photograph the men as a wedding couple would force her to communicate an impression that the two men were a married couple, in contradiction to both her political opposition to gay marriage and her religious view that two people of the same sex can never be truly "married."

Massachusetts has a public accommodations law, which has been applied by the state courts to commercial photographers such as Angie, that bans discrimination on the basis of race, gender, and sexual orientation. The state sues Angie, alleging a violation of that law. Does Angie have a First Amendment claim against application of the law to her under these circumstances?

Assume now that Angie is not a wedding photographer, but a wedding singer. Does that change your analysis?

———

Note: Speech, Coercion, and Meaning

1. The first set of Problems above deals with the straightforward question whether government can compel individuals to speak certain words. More subtle questions also exist. One difficulty is whether it is in fact speech that is being coerced. Consider a prison guard who refuses to wear the American flag shoulder patch prescribed for his uniform, declaring that such displays trivialize the flag in ways he finds deeply offensive. Do *Barnette* and *Wooley* require a finding in his favor? Or can the cases be distinguished on the ground that wearing a flag patch does not necessarily convey any message at all?

Consider other possible circumstances in which the state may argue that its requirement simply does not involve expression. For example, what if, rather than placing "Live Free or Die" on its license plates, New Hampshire designed its license plates to include an American flag? What about a picture of a patriot who was well known for having preferred death to living under oppression? Recall that the opinion in *Wooley* conceded that the coerced pledge in *Barnette* was "a more serious infringement on personal liberties" than the coerced display of a state motto on a license plate, but concluded that the difference was "essentially one of degree." How close to the facts of *Barnette* and *Wooley* does one have to get before coerced expression comes within their rule? Does coerced speech have to be verbal before it can be considered speech?

2. Indeed, can words themselves become so anodyne that they do not convey any meaning? What about coinage? We all carry around coins that say "In God We Trust." Does United States currency violate *Wooley*? In *Wooley* the Court acknowledged that its analysis could be taken as supporting this argument, but sidestepped it by saying, in a footnote, that currency "differs in significant respects from an automobile, which is readily associated with its operator. Currency is generally carried in a purse or pocket, and need not be displayed to the public. The bearer of currency is thus not required to publicly advertise the national motto." Do you find this distinction persuasive?

Cases considering Establishment Clause challenges to official references to God have suggested that purely ceremonial references to God in government-prescribed oaths should not be construed as conveying approval of religion. *See, e.g., Marsh v. Chambers*, 463 U.S. 783 (1983) (upholding the practice of opening a legislative session with a prayer); *United States v. Oliver*, 363 F.2d 15 (7th Cir. 1966) (upholding the requirement that jurors swear "so help me God"). Thus, some words do seem to be empty of meaning. In light of that fact, should the *Wooley* Court have given more consideration to the possibility that the phrase "Live Free or Die" on a license plate is similarly empty?

B. Compelled Subsidy

Barnette and *Wooley* deal with government attempts to coerce individuals into *expressing* messages favored by the government. This section deals with attempts by government to coerce individuals to *subsidize* expression with which they disagree. Note that the expression in *Abood* is expression by another private party — in particular, a labor union. In other cases, the dispute centers on whether the expression is in fact private or governmental. This latter line of cases is discussed briefly in a Note at the end of this chapter as well as in Chapter 13. As you read the materials that follow, consider the degree to which the doctrinal analysis derived from *Barnette* and *Wooley* shifts to accommodate the different values at stake in cases of compelled subsidization of private speech. Is the First Amendment harm also different?

Abood v. Detroit Board of Education
431 U.S. 209 (1977)

Mr. Justice Stewart delivered the opinion of the Court.

The State of Michigan has enacted legislation authorizing a system for union representation of local governmental employees. A union and a local government employer are specifically permitted to agree to an "agency shop" arrangement, whereby every employee represented by a union even though not a union member must pay to the union, as a condition of employment, a service fee equal in amount to union dues. The issue before us is whether this arrangement violates the constitutional rights of government employees who object to public-sector unions as such or to various union activities financed by the compulsory service fees.

I

[As part of the labor contract between the Detroit Federation of Teachers and the Board of Education, all teachers who were employed by the Board but were not union members had to pay the union a service charge equal to a member's union dues. Teachers who did not belong to the union sued, alleging that that provision violated their freedom of association. The plaintiffs alleged that they opposed collective bargaining in public employment, and that the union engaged in various political and economic activities that the plaintiffs opposed, and in which the plaintiffs, as non-members, would have no voice. The trial court granted summary judgment to the Board of

Education, and the plaintiffs appealed. The state appellate court upheld the facial validity of the agency shop clause.]

II

A

... To compel employees financially to support their collective-bargaining representative has an impact upon their First Amendment interests. An employee may very well have ideological objections to a wide variety of activities undertaken by the union in its role as exclusive representative. His moral or religious views about the desirability of abortion may not square with the union's policy in negotiating a medical benefits plan. One individual might disagree with a union policy of negotiating limits on the right to strike, believing that to be the road to serfdom for the working class, while another might have economic or political objections to unionism itself. An employee might object to the union's wage policy because it violates guidelines designed to limit inflation, or might object to the union's seeking a clause in the collective-bargaining agreement proscribing racial discrimination.

The examples could be multiplied. To be required to help finance the union as a collective-bargaining agent might well be thought, therefore, to interfere in some way with an employee's freedom to associate for the advancement of ideas, or to refrain from doing so, as he sees fit. But the judgment clearly made in *Railway Employes' Dept. v. Hanson*, 351 U.S. 225 (1956), and *Machinists v. Street*, 367 U.S. 740 (1961), is that such interference as exists is constitutionally justified by the legislative assessment of the important contribution of the union shop to the system of labor relations established by Congress. "The furtherance of the common cause leaves some leeway for the leadership of the group. As long as they act to promote the cause which justified bringing the group together, the individual cannot withdraw his financial support merely because he disagrees with the group's strategy. If that were allowed, we would be reversing the *Hanson* case, *sub silentio.*" *Street* (Douglas, J., concurring). . . .

C

Because the Michigan Court of Appeals ruled that state law "sanctions the use of nonunion members' fees for purposes other than collective bargaining," and because the complaints allege that such expenditures were made, this case presents constitutional issues not decided in *Hanson* or *Street.* . . .

Our decisions establish with unmistakable clarity that the freedom of an individual to associate for the purpose of advancing beliefs and ideas is protected by the First and Fourteenth Amendments. E.g., *NAACP v. Alabama* (1958) [*infra* Chapter 10]. Equally clear is the proposition that a government may not require an individual to relinquish rights guaranteed him by the First Amendment as a condition of public employment. E.g., *Elrod v. Burns*, 427 U.S. 347 (1976) [Note *infra* Chapter 12]. The appellants argue that they fall within the protection of these cases because they have been prohibited, not from actively associating, but rather from refusing to associate. They specifically argue that they may constitutionally prevent the Union's spending a part of their required service fees to contribute to political candidates and to express political views unrelated to its duties as exclusive bargaining representative. We have concluded that this argument is a meritorious one.

One of the principles underlying the Court's decision in *Buckley v. Valeo* (1976) [*infra* Chapter 11] was that contributing to an organization for the purpose of spreading a political message is protected by the First Amendment. Because "[m]aking a contribution . . . enables like-minded persons to pool their resources in furtherance of common political goals," the Court reasoned that limitations upon the freedom to contribute "implicate fundamental First Amendment interests."

The fact that the appellants are compelled to make, rather than prohibited from making, contributions for political purposes works no less an infringement of their constitutional rights. For at the heart of the First Amendment is the notion that an individual should be free to believe as he will, and that in a free society one's beliefs should be shaped by his mind and his conscience rather than coerced by the State. E.g., *Elrod*. And the freedom of belief is no incidental or secondary aspect of the First Amendment's protections:

> If there is any fixed star in our constitutional constellation, it is that no official, high or petty, can prescribe what shall be orthodox in politics, nationalism, religion, or other matters of opinion or force citizens to confess by word or act their faith therein. *West Virginia Bd. of Ed. v. Barnette* [*supra* this chapter].

These principles prohibit a State from compelling any individual to affirm his belief in God, *Torcaso v. Watkins*, 367 U.S. 488 (1961) [*infra* Chapter 19], or to associate with a political party, *Elrod*, as a condition of retaining public employment. They are no less applicable to the case at bar, and they thus prohibit the appellees from requiring any of the appellants to contribute to the support of an ideological cause he may oppose as a condition of holding a job as a public school teacher.

We do not hold that a union cannot constitutionally spend funds for the expression of political views, on behalf of political candidates, or toward the advancement of other ideological causes not germane to its duties as collective-bargaining representative. Rather, the Constitution requires only that such expenditures be financed from charges, dues, or assessments paid by employees who do not object to advancing those ideas and who are not coerced into doing so against their will by the threat of loss of governmental employment.

There will, of course, be difficult problems in drawing lines between collective-bargaining activities, for which contributions may be compelled, and ideological activities unrelated to collective bargaining, for which such compulsion is prohibited. . . . We have no occasion in this case, however, to try to define such a dividing line. The case comes to us after a judgment on the pleadings, and there is no evidentiary record of any kind. The allegations in the complaints are general ones, and the parties have neither briefed nor argued the question of what specific Union activities in the present context properly fall under the definition of collective bargaining. . . . All that we decide is that the general allegations in the complaints, if proved, establish a cause of action under the First and Fourteenth Amendments. . . .

The judgment is vacated, and the case is remanded for further proceedings not inconsistent with this opinion.

Mr. Justice Rehnquist, concurring. [Omitted.]

Mr. Justice Stevens, concurring. [Omitted.]

Mr. Justice Powell, with whom The Chief Justice [Burger] and Mr. Justice Blackmun join, concurring in the judgment. . . .

II

The Court today holds that compelling an employee to finance a union's "ideological activities unrelated to collective bargaining" violates the First Amendment regardless of any asserted governmental justification. But the Court also decides that compelling an employee to finance any union activity that may be "related" in some way to collective bargaining is permissible under the First Amendment because such compulsion is "relevant or appropriate" to asserted governmental interests. And the Court places the burden of litigation on the individual. In order to vindicate his First Amendment rights in a union shop, the individual employee apparently must declare his opposition to the union and initiate a proceeding to determine what part of the union's budget has been allocated to activities that are both "ideological" and "unrelated to collective bargaining."

I can agree neither with the Court's rigid two-tiered analysis under the First Amendment, nor with the burden it places on the individual. Under First Amendment principles that have become settled . . . it is now clear, first, that *any* withholding of financial support for a public-sector union is within the protection of the First Amendment; and, second, that the State should bear the burden of proving that any union dues or fees that it requires of nonunion employees are needed to serve paramount governmental interests. . . .

B

"Neither the right to associate nor the right to participate in political activities is absolute. . . ." This is particularly true in the field of public employment, where "the State has interests as an employer in regulating the speech of its employees that differ significantly from those it possesses in connection with regulation of the speech of the citizenry in general." *Pickering v. Board of Education*, 391 U.S. 563 (1968) [Note *infra* Chapter 12]. Nevertheless, even in public employment, "a significant impairment of First Amendment rights must survive exacting scrutiny." *Elrod.* . . .

The justifications offered by the Detroit Board of Education must be tested under this settled standard of review. . . .

. . . I would adhere to established First Amendment principles and require the State to come forward and demonstrate, as to each union expenditure for which it would exact support from minority employees, that the compelled contribution is necessary to serve overriding governmental objectives. This placement of the burden of litigation, not the Court's, gives appropriate protection to First Amendment rights without sacrificing ends of government that may be deemed important.

————

Note: Unease with Abood

In the years after *Abood*, the Court has decided a number of cases that sought to apply *Abood*'s distinction between collective bargaining activities (for which contributions could be compelled from dissenting nonmembers of the union) and ideological activities (for which contributions from such persons could not be compelled). In more recent years, however, members of the Court have questioned *Abood* itself and argued that even compelled exactions for collective bargaining activities were unconstitutional in the public employee context.

1. In *Knox v. Service Employees International*, 567 U.S. 298 (2012), the Court considered non-members' challenge to a union's procedures for collecting supplemental fees to engage in political activities. Seven Justices agreed that at least some of those procedures violated the dissenters' First Amendment rights, although Justice Alito's opinion for the Court spoke for only five Justices. In that opinion he said the following about the constitutionality of agency shop fees under the First Amendment:

> Closely related to compelled speech and compelled association is compelled funding of the speech of other private speakers or groups. *See Abood*. In *United States v. United Foods, Inc.* (2001) [Note *infra* this chapter], we considered the constitutionality of a state scheme that compelled such funding. . . . We made it clear that compulsory subsidies for private speech are subject to exacting First Amendment scrutiny and cannot be sustained unless two criteria are met. First, there must be a comprehensive regulatory scheme involving a "mandated association" among those who are required to pay the subsidy. Such situations are exceedingly rare because, as we have stated elsewhere, mandatory associations are permissible only when they serve a "compelling state interes[t] . . . that cannot be achieved through means significantly less restrictive of associational freedoms." *Roberts* [*supra* this chapter]. Second, even in the rare case where a mandatory association can be justified, compulsory fees can be levied only insofar as they are a "necessary incident" of the "larger regulatory purpose which justified the required association." . . .
>
> When a State establishes an "agency shop" that exacts compulsory union fees as a condition of public employment, "[t]he dissenting employee is forced to support financially an organization with whose principles and demands he may disagree." Because a public-sector union takes many positions during collective bargaining that have powerful political and civic consequences, the compulsory fees constitute a form of compelled speech and association that imposes a "significant impingement on First Amendment rights." Our cases to date have tolerated this "impingement," and we do not revisit today whether the Court's former cases have given adequate recognition to the critical First Amendment rights at stake.

"The primary purpose" of permitting unions to collect fees from nonmem-bers, we have said, is "to prevent nonmembers from free-riding on the union's efforts, sharing the employment benefits obtained by the union's col-lective bargaining without sharing the costs incurred." Such free-rider argu-ments, however, are generally insufficient to overcome First Amendment objections. Consider the following examples:

> If a community association engages in a clean-up campaign or opposes encroachments by industrial development, no one suggests that all resi-dents or property owners who benefit be required to contribute. If a parent-teacher association raises money for the school library, assessments are not levied on all parents. If an association of university professors has as a major function bringing pressure on universities to observe standards of tenure and academic freedom, most professors would consider it an outrage to be required to join. If a medical association lobbies against reg-ulation of fees, not all doctors who share in the benefits share in the costs.[2]

Acceptance of the free-rider argument as a justification for compelling non-members to pay a portion of union dues represents something of an anomaly— one that we have found to be justified by the interest in furthering "labor peace." But it is an anomaly nevertheless.

2. Justice Sotomayor, joined by Justice Ginsburg, concurred in the majority's result, rejecting as constitutionally inadequate the procedures used by the union to collect funds from nonmembers for ideological activities. But she criticized the majority's decision to question *Abood* more fundamentally, arguing that the parties had not briefed that broader question. Justice Breyer, joined by Justice Kagan, dis-sented. He concluded that the union's procedures for collecting such funds were con-stitutional. But he agreed with Justice Sotomayor's critique of what he and Justice Sotomayor both described as the majority's reaching out to analyze larger First Amendment questions about unions' constitutional right to compel payments from nonmembers.

———

Note: Applying Abood *Beyond the Union Context*

Abood held that the First Amendment allowed government to compel non-union members to pay the union charges related to the union's collective-bargaining activi-ties. As explained in *Abood*, this conceded "interference" with employees' First Amendment rights "is constitutionally justified by the legislative assessment of the important contributions of the union shop to the system of labor relations estab-lished by Congress." As exemplified by a series of cases involving exactions from agri-cultural producers for the purpose of paying for the advertising of farm produce, the Court has encountered some degree of difficulty in considering how far to extend its approval of such speech exactions beyond the context of the closed union shop.

———

2. Summers, Book Review, *Sheldon Leader, Freedom of Association: A Study in Labor Law and Political Theory*, 16 COMPARATIVE LABOR L.J. 262, 268 (1995).

1. In the first of these cases, *Glickman v. Wileman Brothers & Elliott*, 521 U.S. 457 (1997), the Court upheld a U.S. Department of Agriculture-run advertising program promoting California tree fruits, funded by assessments on growers of those fruits. The Court, in an opinion by Justice Stevens speaking for five Justices, began its analysis as follows:

> In answering [the compelled subsidy] question we stress the importance of the statutory context in which it arises. California nectarines and peaches are marketed pursuant to detailed marketing orders that have displaced many aspects of independent business activity that characterize other portions of the economy in which competition is fully protected by the antitrust laws. The business entities that are compelled to fund the generic advertising at issue in this litigation do so as a part of a broader collective enterprise in which their freedom to act independently is already constrained by the regulatory scheme. It is in this context that we consider whether we should review the assessments used to fund collective advertising, together with other collective activities, under the standard appropriate for the review of economic regulation or under a heightened standard appropriate for the review of First Amendment issues.

At the start of the next section of the Court's opinion, the Court continued:

> Three characteristics of the regulatory scheme at issue distinguish it from laws that we have found to abridge the freedom of speech protected by the First Amendment. First, the marketing orders impose no restraint on the freedom of any producer to communicate any message to any audience.[12] Second, they do not compel any person to engage in any actual or symbolic speech.[13] Third, they do not compel the producers to endorse or to finance any political or ideological views.[14] ... Thus, none of our First Amendment jurisprudence provides any support for the suggestion that the promotional regulations should be scrutinized under a different standard from that applicable to the other anticompetitive features of the marketing orders. ...

> Although this regulatory scheme may not compel speech as recognized by our case law, it does compel financial contributions that are used to fund advertising. ... However, ... *Abood* merely recognized a First Amendment interest in not being compelled to contribute to an organization whose expressive activities conflict with one's "freedom of belief." *Abood*. ...

---

12. This fact distinguishes the limits on commercial speech at issue in *Central Hudson Gas & Elec. Corp. v. Public Serv. Comm'n of N.Y.* (1980) [*supra* Chapter 3], *Virginia State Bd. of Pharmacy v. Virginia Citizens Consumer Council, Inc.* (1976) [*supra* Chapter 3], and *44 Liquormart, Inc. v. Rhode Island*, 517 U.S. 484 (1996).

13. This fact distinguishes the compelled speech in *Barnette* [and] *Wooley,* and the compelled association in *Hurley v. Irish-American Gay, Lesbian and Bisexual Group of Boston, Inc.*, 515 U.S. 557 (1995) [Note *infra* Chapter 10].

14. This fact distinguishes cases like ... *Abood.*

Here, however, requiring respondents to pay the assessments cannot be said to engender any crisis of conscience. None of the advertising in this record promotes any particular message other than encouraging consumers to buy California tree fruit. Neither the fact that respondents may prefer to foster that message independently in order to promote and distinguish their own products, nor the fact that they think more or less money should be spent fostering it, makes this case comparable to those in which an objection rested on political or ideological disagreement with the content of the message. . . .

Justice Souter, writing for himself, Chief Justice Rehnquist and Justice Scalia, dissented. He summarized his disagreement as follows:

The legitimacy of governmental regulation does not validate coerced subsidies for speech that the government cannot show to be reasonably necessary to implement the regulation, and the very reasons for recognizing that commercial speech falls within the scope of First Amendment protection likewise justifies the protection of those who object to subsidizing it against their will. I therefore conclude that forced payment for commercial speech should be subject to the same level of judicial scrutiny as any restriction on communications in that category. Because I believe that the advertising scheme here fails that test, I respectfully dissent.

Justice Thomas also joined Justice Souter's dissent except to the extent it applied the less speech-protective test for commercial speech regulation set forth in *Central Hudson Gas & Elec. Corp. v. Public Serv. Comm'n of N.Y.* (1980) [*supra* Chapter 3]. He wrote a separate dissent, joined by Justice Scalia, to make clear his view that commercial speech should receive the same protection as other speech, and to "note [his] disagreement with the majority's conclusion that coerced funding of advertising by others does not involve 'speech' at all and does not even raise a First Amendment 'issue.'"

2. Three years later, the Court distinguished *Glickman* in *United States v. United Foods*, 533 U.S. 405 (2001). At issue in *United Foods* was a government program assessing fees to mushroom growers to fund a generic advertising campaign for mushrooms. The Court, in an opinion by Justice Kennedy speaking for six Justices, struck down the compelled assessment. Early in his analysis he confronted *Glickman*:

In the Government's view the assessment in this case is permitted by *Glickman* because it is similar in important respects. It imposes no restraint on the freedom of an objecting party to communicate its own message; the program does not compel an objecting party . . . itself to express views it disfavors; and the mandated scheme does not compel the expression of political or ideological views. These points were noted in *Glickman* in the context of a different type of regulatory scheme and are not controlling of the outcome. The program sustained in *Glickman* differs from the one under review in a most fundamental respect. In *Glickman* the mandated assessments for speech were ancillary to a more comprehensive program restricting marketing autonomy. Here, for all practical purposes, the advertising itself, far from being ancillary, is the principal object of the regulatory scheme. . . .

The features of the marketing scheme found important in *Glickman* are not present in the case now before us. . . . [Almost] all of the funds collected under the mandatory assessments are for one purpose: generic advertising. . . .

The Government claims that, despite the lack of cooperative marketing, the *Abood* rule protecting against compelled assessments for some speech is inapplicable. We did say in *Glickman* that *Abood* "recognized a First Amendment interest in not being compelled to contribute to an organization whose expressive activities conflict with one's 'freedom of belief.'" *Glickman* (quoting *Abood*). We take further instruction, however, from *Abood*'s statement that speech need not be characterized as political before it receives First Amendment protection. *Abood*. A proper application of the rule in *Abood* requires us to invalidate the instant statutory scheme. . . .

Justice Stevens, the author of *Glickman*, joined the majority and also wrote a separate concurrence. He read *Glickman* as permitting a compelled subsidy "when it is ancillary, or 'germane,' to a valid cooperative endeavor." He understood *United Foods* to raise "the open question whether such compulsion is constitutional when nothing more than commercial advertising is at stake," an imposition that, "like a naked restraint on speech itself, seems quite different to me." Justice Thomas also joined the majority and wrote a separate concurrence, in his case to reiterate his view that "paying money for the purposes of advertising involves speech."

Justice Breyer, joined by Justice Ginsburg and in part by Justice O'Connor, dissented. He found it "difficult to understand why the presence or absence of price and output regulations could make a critical First Amendment difference." He argued that there was no necessary connection between the compelled advertising assessments and the price and production restrictions in *Glickman*. By contrast, he said, the advertising in *United Foods* related directly to the program's underlying goal of expanding the market for mushrooms. He distinguished *Abood* by noting that the funded activities in this case, "like identical activities in *Glickman*, do *not* involve [the] kind of expression [in *Abood*]. In *Glickman* we described the messages at issue as incapable of 'engender[ing] any crisis of conscience' and the producers' objections as 'trivial.' *Glickman*. The messages here are indistinguishable. . . ." He continued: "Neither does this case resemble either *Barnette* or *Wooley*. . . . In *Glickman* we found *Barnette* and *Wooley* . . . clearly inapplicable to compelled financial support of generic advertising."

3. In the third case of this series, *Johanns v. Livestock Mktg Ass'n*, 544 U.S. 550 (2005), the Court concluded that the compelled speech, which generically promoted beef, was that of the government. The question of when challenged speech is in fact speech by the government itself, rather than private speech coerced by the government, is considered in Chapter 13.

4. The next chapter takes up the First Amendment issues raised by government regulations that affect individuals when they associate to express themselves. As you read that material, consider whether the First Amendment should distinguish between compelled association in the literal sense—i.e., forcing people to accept certain types of individuals into their expressive group—and compelled association as discussed in *Abood*—i.e., forcing people to join together and to provide financial support for speech with which they disagree. Is there a difference in terms of First Amendment harms between a worker forced to subsidize union speech with which he disagrees, and a member of a political or activist group being forced to accept non-adherents into the organization?

————

Problem: Satirical Anti-Tobacco Advertising

California collects a special excise tax on the distribution of tobacco products, with the proceeds used to fund anti-smoking advertisements. The advertisements are hard-hitting; one of them features children playing in a large pile of cigarettes, with a narrator saying the following: "We market to your kids. We have to. Our adult customers keep dying. That's right, we're Big Tobacco."

On these facts, would a tobacco company have a First Amendment claim that it was being unconstitutionally compelled to subsidize speech with which it disagreed?

Chapter 10

Freedom of Association

In addition to protecting individuals' speech rights, the First Amendment has also been interpreted to protect individuals when they seek to associate in order to engage in expression.

NAACP v. Alabama

357 U.S. 449 (1958)

MR. JUSTICE HARLAN delivered the opinion of the Court.

We review from the standpoint of its validity under the Federal Constitution a judgment of civil contempt entered against petitioner, the National Association for the Advancement of Colored People, in the courts of Alabama. The question presented is whether Alabama, consistently with the Due Process Clause of the Fourteenth Amendment, can compel petitioner to reveal to the State's Attorney General the names and addresses of all its Alabama members and agents, without regard to their positions or functions in the Association. The judgment of contempt was based upon petitioner's refusal to comply fully with a court order requiring in part the production of membership lists. Petitioner's claim is that the order, in the circumstances shown by this record, violated rights assured to petitioner and its members under the Constitution.

Alabama has a statute similar to those of many other States which requires a foreign corporation, except as exempted, to qualify before doing business by filing its corporate charter with the Secretary of State and designating a place of business and an agent to receive service of process. . . .

In 1956 the Attorney General of Alabama brought an equity suit in the State Circuit Court, Montgomery County, to enjoin the Association from conducting further activities within, and to oust it from, the State. . . . On the day the complaint was filed, the Circuit Court issued ex parte an order restraining the Association, pendente lite, from engaging in further activities within the State and forbidding it to take any steps to qualify itself to do business therein.

Petitioner demurred to the allegations of the bill and moved to dissolve the restraining order. It contended that its activities did not subject it to the qualification requirements of the statute and that in any event what the State sought to accomplish by its suit would violate rights to freedom of speech and assembly guaranteed under the Fourteenth Amendment to the Constitution of the United States. Before the date set for a hearing on this motion, the State moved for the production of a large number of the Association's records and papers, including bank statements, leases, deeds, and records containing the names and addresses of all Alabama "members" and "agents" of the Association. It alleged that all such documents were necessary for adequate preparation for the hearing, in view of petitioner's denial of the conduct of intrastate business within the meaning of the qualification statute. Over petitioner's objections, the court ordered the production of a substantial part of the requested records, including the membership lists, and postponed the hearing on the restraining order to a date later than the time ordered for production. . . .

The State Supreme Court thereafter twice dismissed petitions for certiorari. . . . We granted certiorari because of the importance of the constitutional questions presented. . . .

III.

We thus reach petitioner's claim that the production order in the state litigation trespasses upon fundamental freedoms protected by the Due Process Clause of the Fourteenth Amendment. Petitioner argues that in view of the facts and circumstances shown in the record, the effect of compelled disclosure of the membership lists will be to abridge the rights of its rank-and-file members to engage in lawful association in support of their common beliefs. It contends that governmental action which, although not directly suppressing association, nevertheless carries this consequence, can be justified only upon some overriding valid interest of the State.

Effective advocacy of both public and private points of view, particularly controversial ones, is undeniably enhanced by group association, as this Court has more than once recognized by remarking upon the close nexus between the freedoms of speech and assembly. [E.g.] *De Jonge v. Oregon*, 299 U.S. 353 (1937) [Note *supra* Chapter 1]. It is beyond debate that freedom to engage in association for the advancement of beliefs and ideas is an inseparable aspect of the "liberty" assured by the Due Process Clause of the Fourteenth Amendment, which embraces freedom of speech. *See, e.g., Gitlow v. New York* (1925) [*supra* Chapter 1]; *Palko v. Connecticut*, 302 U.S. 319 (1937); *Cantwell v. Connecticut*, 310 U.S. 296 (1940) [*supra* Chapter 8]. Of course, it is immaterial whether the beliefs sought to be advanced by association pertain to political, economic, religious or cultural matters, and state action which may have the effect of curtailing the freedom to associate is subject to the closest scrutiny.

The fact that Alabama, so far as is relevant to the validity of the contempt judgment presently under review, has taken no direct action to restrict the right of petitioner's members to associate freely does not end inquiry into the effect of the production order. In the domain of these indispensable liberties, whether of speech, press, or association, the decisions of this Court recognize that abridgement of such rights, even though unintended, may inevitably follow from varied forms of governmental action. . . .

It is hardly a novel perception that compelled disclosure of affiliation with groups engaged in advocacy may constitute [an] effective . . . restraint on freedom of association. . . . This Court has recognized the vital relationship between freedom to associate and privacy in one's associations. When referring to the varied forms of governmental action which might interfere with freedom of assembly, it said: "A requirement that adherents of particular religious faiths or political parties wear identifying arm-bands, for example, is obviously of this nature." Compelled disclosure of membership in an organization engaged in advocacy of particular beliefs is of the same order. Inviolability of privacy in group association may in many circumstances be indispensable to preservation of freedom of association, particularly where a group espouses dissident beliefs.

We think that the production order, in the respects here drawn in question, must be regarded as entailing the likelihood of a substantial restraint upon the exercise by petitioner's members of their right to freedom of association. Petitioner has made an uncontroverted showing that on past occasions revelation of the identity of its rank-and-file members has exposed these members to economic reprisal, loss of employment, threat of physical coercion, and other manifestations of public hostility. Under these circumstances, we think it apparent that compelled disclosure of petitioner's Alabama membership is likely to affect adversely the ability of petitioner and its members to pursue their collective effort to foster beliefs which they admittedly have the right to advocate, in that it may induce members to withdraw from the Association and dissuade others from joining it because of fear of exposure of their beliefs shown through their associations and of the consequences of this exposure.

It is not sufficient to answer, as the State does here, that whatever repressive effect compulsory disclosure of names of petitioner's members may have upon participation by Alabama citizens in petitioner's activities follows not from *state* action but from *private* community pressures. The crucial factor is the interplay of governmental and private action, for it is only after the initial exertion of state power represented by the production order that private action takes hold.

We turn to the final question whether Alabama has demonstrated an interest in obtaining the disclosures it seeks from petitioner which is sufficient to justify the deterrent effect which we have concluded these disclosures may well have on the free exercise by petitioner's members of their constitutionally protected right of association. See [e.g.] *Schneider v. State* (1939) [*supra* Chapter 6]. Such a "* * * subordinating interest of the State must be compelling." *Sweezy v. New Hampshire*, 354 U.S. 234 (1957) (concurring opinion). . . .

Whether there was "justification" in this instance turns solely on the substantiality of Alabama's interest in obtaining the membership lists. . . . The exclusive purpose was to determine whether petitioner was conducting intrastate business in violation of the Alabama foreign corporation registration statute, and the membership lists were expected to help resolve this question. The issues in the litigation commenced by Alabama by its bill in equity were whether the character of petitioner and its activities in Alabama had been such as to make petitioner subject to the registration statute, and whether the extent of petitioner's activities without qualifying suggested its permanent ouster from the State. Without intimating the slightest view upon the merits of these issues, we are unable to perceive that the disclosure of the names of petitioner's rank-and-file members has a substantial bearing on either of them. . . .

We hold that the immunity from state scrutiny of membership lists which the Association claims on behalf of its members is here so related to the right of the members to pursue their lawful private interests privately and to associate freely with others in so doing as to come within the protection of the Fourteenth Amendment. And we conclude that Alabama has fallen short of showing a controlling justification for the deterrent effect on the free enjoyment of the right to associate which disclosure of membership lists is likely to have. Accordingly, the judgment of civil contempt and the $100,000 fine which resulted from petitioner's refusal to comply with the production order in this respect must fall. . . .

Reversed.

———

Note: NAACP *and Beyond*

1. Note the Court's comparison of Alabama's membership disclosure requirement with government requirements that members of particular groups wear armbands. This evocative comparison, coming less than 15 years after the defeat of Nazi Germany and in light of the situation facing civil rights activists in the South in the 1950s, suggests the stakes in *NAACP.*

2. As the following cases illustrate, in the decades after *NAACP* the focus of the right to associate shifted to government attempts to enforce non-discrimination laws on organizations. As you read subsequent cases, ask yourself whether the stakes are different when government seeks to force associations to admit individuals they would prefer to exclude. If they are different, should the strict scrutiny established in *NAACP* be the standard?

Roberts v. United States Jaycees
468 U.S. 609 (1984)

Justice Brennan delivered the opinion of the Court.

This case requires us to address a conflict between a State's efforts to eliminate gender-based discrimination against its citizens and the constitutional freedom of association asserted by members of a private organization. In the decision under review, the Court of Appeals for the Eighth Circuit concluded that, by requiring the United States Jaycees to admit women as full voting members, the Minnesota Human Rights Act violates the First and Fourteenth Amendment rights of the organization's members. We noted probable jurisdiction, and now reverse.

I

A

The United States Jaycees (Jaycees), founded in 1920 as the Junior Chamber of Commerce, is a nonprofit membership corporation, incorporated in Missouri with national headquarters in Tulsa, Okla. The objective of the Jaycees, as set out in its bylaws, is to pursue

> such educational and charitable purposes as will promote and foster the growth and development of young men's civic organizations in the United States, designed to inculcate in the individual membership of such organization a spirit of genuine Americanism and civic interest, and as a supplementary education institution to provide them with opportunity for personal development and achievement and an avenue for intelligent participation by young men in the affairs of their community, state and nation, and to develop true friendship and understanding among young men of all nations. . . .

B

In 1974 and 1975, respectively, the Minneapolis and St. Paul chapters of the Jaycees began admitting women as regular members. Currently, the memberships and boards of directors of both chapters include a substantial proportion of women. As a result, the two chapters have been in violation of the national organization's bylaws for about 10 years. . . .

In December 1978, the president of the national organization advised both chapters that a motion to revoke their charters would be considered at a forthcoming meeting of the national board of directors in Tulsa. Shortly after receiving this notification, members of both chapters filed charges of discrimination with the Minnesota Department of Human Rights. The complaints alleged that the exclusion of women from full membership required by the national organization's bylaws violated the Minnesota Human Rights Act (Act), which provides in part:

It is an unfair discriminatory practice:

> To deny any person the full and equal enjoyment of the goods, services, facilities, privileges, advantages, and accommodations of a place of public accommodation because of race, color, creed, religion, disability, national origin or sex. . . .

After an investigation, the Commissioner of the Minnesota Department of Human Rights found probable cause to believe that the sanctions imposed on the local chapters by the national organization violated the statute and ordered that an evidentiary hearing be held before a state hearing examiner. Before that hearing took place, however, the national organization brought suit against various state officials, appellants here, in the United States District Court for the District of Minnesota, seeking declaratory and injunctive relief to prevent enforcement of the Act. The complaint alleged that, by requiring the organization to accept women as regular members, application of the Act would violate the male members' constitutional rights of free speech and association. . . .

. . . The federal suit then proceeded to trial, after which the District Court entered judgment in favor of the state officials. On appeal, a divided Court of Appeals for the Eighth Circuit reversed. . . .

II

Our decisions have referred to constitutionally protected "freedom of association" in two distinct senses. In one line of decisions, the Court has concluded that choices to enter into and maintain certain intimate human relationships must be secured against undue intrusion by the State because of the role of such relationships in safeguarding the individual freedom that is central to our constitutional scheme. In this respect, freedom of association receives protection as a fundamental element of personal liberty. In another set of decisions, the Court has recognized a right to associate for the purpose of engaging in those activities protected by the First Amendment — speech, assembly, petition for the redress of grievances, and the exercise of religion. The Constitution guarantees freedom of association of this kind as an indispensable means of preserving other individual liberties. . . .

A

[The Court first considered the Jaycees' claim to a right of intimate association. The Court recognized that individual liberty requires the protection of certain kinds of highly personal relationships, citing *Pierce v. Society of Sisters*, 268 U.S. 510 (1925), and *Meyer v. Nebraska*, 262 U.S. 390 (1923). The Court stated that the determination whether an association is sufficiently intimate to qualify for this protection requires consideration of the association's size, purpose, policies, selectivity, and congeniality. It concluded that the Jaycees, as a large group with a non-selective admission process, whose activities closely involved non-members, did not satisfy these criteria.]

B

An individual's freedom to speak, to worship, and to petition the government for the redress of grievances could not be vigorously protected from interference by the State unless a correlative freedom to engage in group effort toward those ends were not also guaranteed. According protection to collective effort on behalf of shared goals is especially important in preserving political and cultural diversity and in shielding dissident expression from suppression by the majority. *See, e.g., Griswold v. Connecticut*, 381 U.S. 479 (1965); *NAACP v. Alabama* (1958) [*supra* this chapter]. Consequently, we have long understood as implicit in the right to engage in activities protected by the First Amendment a corresponding right to associate with others in pursuit of a wide variety of political, social, economic, educational, religious, and cultural ends. *See, e.g., NAACP v. Claiborne Hardware* (1982) [*supra* Chapter 1]; *Abood v. Detroit Board of Education* (1977) [*supra* Chapter 9]. In view of the various protected activities in which the Jaycees engages, that right is plainly implicated in this case. . . .

. . . There can be no clearer example of an intrusion into the internal structure or affairs of an association than a regulation that forces the group to accept members it does not desire. Such a regulation may impair the ability of the original members to express only those views that brought them together. Freedom of association therefore plainly presupposes a freedom not to associate. *See Abood*.

The right to associate for expressive purposes is not, however, absolute. Infringements on that right may be justified by regulations adopted to serve compelling state interests, unrelated to the suppression of ideas, that cannot be achieved through means significantly less restrictive of associational freedoms. *E.g., Buckley v. Valeo* (1976) [*infra* Chapter 11]. We are persuaded that Minnesota's compelling interest in eradicating discrimination against its female citizens justifies the impact that application of the statute to the Jaycees may have on the male members' associational freedoms.

On its face, the Minnesota Act does not aim at the suppression of speech, does not distinguish between prohibited and permitted activity on the basis of viewpoint, and does not license enforcement authorities to administer the statute on the basis of such constitutionally impermissible criteria. Nor does the Jaycees contend that the Act has been applied in this case for the purpose of hampering the organization's ability to express its views. Instead, as the Minnesota Supreme Court explained, the Act reflects the State's strong historical commitment to eliminating discrimination and assuring its citizens equal access to publicly available goods and services. That goal, which is unrelated to the suppression of expression, plainly serves compelling state interests of the highest order. . . .

In applying the Act to the Jaycees, the State has advanced those interests through the least restrictive means of achieving its ends. Indeed, the Jaycees has failed to demonstrate that the Act imposes any serious burdens on the male members' freedom of expressive association. . . . To be sure, as the Court of Appeals noted, a "not insubstantial part" of the Jaycees' activities constitutes protected expression on political, economic, cultural, and social affairs. . . . There is, however, no basis in the record for concluding that admission of women as full voting members will impede the organization's ability to engage in these protected activities or to disseminate its preferred views. The Act requires no change in the Jaycees' creed of promoting the interests of young men, and it imposes no restrictions on the organization's ability to exclude individuals with ideologies or philosophies different from those of its existing members. Moreover, the Jaycees already invites women to share the group's views and philosophy and to participate in much of its training and community activities. Accordingly, any claim that admission of women as full voting members will impair a symbolic message conveyed by the very fact that women are not permitted to vote is attenuated at best.

While acknowledging that "the specific content of most of the resolutions adopted over the years by the Jaycees has nothing to do with sex," the Court of Appeals nonetheless entertained the hypothesis that women members might have a different view or agenda with respect to these matters so that, if they are allowed to vote, "some change in the Jaycees' philosophical cast can reasonably be expected." It is similarly arguable that, insofar as the Jaycees is organized to promote the views of young men whatever those views happen to be, admission of women as voting members will change the message communicated by the group's speech because of the gender-based assumptions of the audience. Neither supposition, however, is supported by the record. In claiming that women might have a different attitude about such issues as the federal budget, school prayer, voting rights, and foreign relations, or that the organization's public positions would have a different effect if the group were not "a purely young men's association," the Jaycees relies solely on unsupported generalizations about the relative interests and perspectives of men and women. Although such generalizations may or may not have a statistical basis in fact with respect to particular positions adopted by the Jaycees, we have repeatedly condemned legal decisionmaking that relies uncritically on such assumptions. *See, e.g., Palmore v. Sidoti*, 466 U.S. 429 (1984); *Heckler v. Mathews*, 465 U.S. 728 (1984). In the absence of a showing far more substantial than that attempted by the Jaycees, we decline to indulge in the sexual stereotyping that underlies appellee's contention that, by allowing women to vote, application of the Minnesota Act will change the content or impact of the organization's speech.

In any event, even if enforcement of the Act causes some incidental abridgment of the Jaycees' protected speech, that effect is no greater than is necessary to accomplish the State's legitimate purposes. As we have explained, acts of invidious discrimination in the distribution of publicly available goods, services, and other advantages cause unique evils that government has a compelling interest to prevent—wholly apart from the point of view such conduct may transmit. Accordingly, like violence or other types of potentially expressive activities that produce special harms distinct from their communicative impact, such practices are entitled to no constitutional protection. *Runyon v. McCrary*, 427 U.S. 160 (1976). In prohibiting such practices, the Minnesota Act therefore "responds precisely to the substantive problem which legitimately concerns" the State and abridges no more speech or associational freedom than is necessary to accomplish that purpose. *See City Council of Los Angeles v. Taxpayers for Vincent*, 466 U.S. 789 (1984)....

IV

The judgment of the Court of Appeals is *reversed.*

JUSTICE REHNQUIST concurs in the judgment.

THE CHIEF JUSTICE and JUSTICE BLACKMUN took no part in the decision of this case.

JUSTICE O'CONNOR, concurring in part and concurring in the judgment.

... With respect to Part II-A of the Court's opinion, I agree with the Court that the Jaycees cannot claim a right of association deriving from this Court's cases concerning "marriage, procreation, contraception, family relationships, and child rearing and education."...

I part company with the Court over its First Amendment analysis in Part II-B of its opinion. I agree with the Court that application of the Minnesota law to the Jaycees does not contravene the First Amendment, but I reach that conclusion for reasons distinct from those offered by the Court. I believe the Court has adopted a test that unadvisedly casts doubt on the power of States to pursue the profoundly important goal of ensuring nondiscriminatory access to commercial opportunities in our society. At the same time, the Court has adopted an approach to the general problem presented by this case that accords insufficient protection to expressive associations and places inappropriate burdens on groups claiming the protection of the First Amendment.

I

The Court analyzes Minnesota's attempt to regulate the Jaycees' membership using a test that I find both overprotective of activities undeserving of constitutional shelter and underprotective of important First Amendment concerns. The Court declares that the Jaycees' right of association depends on the organization's making a "substantial" showing that the admission of unwelcome members "will change the message communicated by the group's speech." I am not sure what showing the Court thinks would satisfy its requirement of proof of a membership-message connection, but whatever it means, the focus on such a connection is objectionable.

Imposing such a requirement, especially in the context of the balancing-of-interests test articulated by the Court, raises the possibility that certain commercial associations, by engaging occasionally in certain kinds of expressive activities, might improperly gain protection for discrimination. The Court's focus raises other problems as well. How are we to analyze the First Amendment associational claims of an organization that invokes its right, settled by the Court in *NAACP*, to protect the privacy of its membership? And would the Court's analysis of this case be different if, for example, the Jaycees membership had a steady history of opposing public issues thought (by the Court) to be favored by women? It might seem easy to conclude, in the latter case, that the admission of women to the Jaycees' ranks would affect the content of the organization's message, but I do not believe that should change the outcome of this case. Whether an association is or is not constitutionally protected in the selection of its membership should not depend on what the association says or why its members say it.

The Court's readiness to inquire into the connection between membership and message reveals a more fundamental flaw in its analysis. The Court pursues this inquiry as part of its mechanical application of a "compelling interest" test, under which the Court weighs the interests of the State of Minnesota in ending gender discrimination against the Jaycees' First Amendment right of association. The Court entirely neglects to establish at the threshold that the Jaycees is an association whose activities or purposes should engage the strong protections that the First Amendment extends to expressive associations.

On the one hand, an association engaged exclusively in protected expression enjoys First Amendment protection of both the content of its message and the choice of its members. Protection of the message itself is judged by the same standards as protection of speech by an individual. Protection of the association's right to define its membership derives from the recognition that the formation of an expressive association is the creation of a voice, and the selection of members is the definition of that voice.... A ban on specific group voices on public affairs violates the most basic guarantee of the First Amendment—that citizens, not the government, control the content of public discussion.

On the other hand, there is only minimal constitutional protection of the freedom of *commercial* association. There are, of course, some constitutional protections of commercial speech — speech intended and used to promote a commercial transaction with the speaker. But the State is free to impose any rational regulation on the commercial transaction itself. The Constitution does not guarantee a right to choose employees, customers, suppliers, or those with whom one engages in simple commercial transactions, without restraint from the State. A shopkeeper has no constitutional right to deal only with persons of one sex. . . .

Many associations cannot readily be described as purely expressive or purely commercial. No association is likely ever to be exclusively engaged in expressive activities, if only because it will collect dues from its members or purchase printing materials or rent lecture halls or serve coffee and cakes at its meetings. And innumerable commercial associations also engage in some incidental protected speech or advocacy. The standard for deciding just how much of an association's involvement in commercial activity is enough to suspend the association's First Amendment right to control its membership cannot, therefore, be articulated with simple precision. Clearly the standard must accept the reality that even the most expressive of associations is likely to touch, in some way or other, matters of commerce. The standard must nevertheless give substance to the ideal of complete protection for purely expressive association, even while it readily permits state regulation of commercial affairs.

In my view, an association should be characterized as commercial, and therefore subject to rationally related state regulation of its membership and other associational activities, when, and only when, the association's activities are not predominantly of the type protected by the First Amendment. It is only when the association is predominantly engaged in protected expression that state regulation of its membership will necessarily affect, change, dilute, or silence one collective voice that would otherwise be heard. An association must choose its market. Once it enters the marketplace of commerce in any substantial degree it loses the complete control over its membership that it would otherwise enjoy if it confined its affairs to the marketplace of ideas.

Determining whether an association's activity is predominantly protected expression will often be difficult, if only because a broad range of activities can be expressive. It is easy enough to identify expressive words or conduct that are strident, contentious, or divisive, but protected expression may also take the form of quiet persuasion, inculcation of traditional values, instruction of the young, and community service. *Cf. Pierce v. Society of Sisters*, 268 U.S. 510 (1925); *Meyer v. Nebraska*, 262 U.S. 390 (1923). The purposes of an association, and the purposes of its members in adhering to it, are doubtless relevant in determining whether the association is primarily engaged in protected expression. Lawyering to advance social goals may be speech, but ordinary commercial law practice is not. A group boycott or refusal to deal for political purposes may be speech, though a similar boycott for purposes of maintaining a cartel is not. Even the training of outdoor survival skills or participation in community service might become expressive when the activity is intended to develop good morals, reverence, patriotism, and a desire for self-improvement.

The considerations that may enter into the determination of when a particular association of persons is predominantly engaged in expression are therefore fluid and somewhat uncertain. . . .

II

Minnesota's attempt to regulate the membership of the Jaycees chapters operating in that State presents a relatively easy case for application of the expressive-commercial dichotomy. Both the Minnesota Supreme Court and the United States District Court, which expressly adopted the state court's findings, made findings of fact concerning the commercial nature of the Jaycees' activities. . . .

There is no reason to question the accuracy of this characterization. Notwithstanding its protected expressive activities, the Jaycees—otherwise known as the Junior Chamber of Commerce—is, first and foremost, an organization that, at both the national and local levels, promotes and practices the art of solicitation and management. . . .

Recruitment and selling are commercial activities, even when conducted for training rather than for profit. The "not insubstantial" volume of protected Jaycees activity found by the Court of Appeals is simply not enough to preclude state regulation of the Jaycees' commercial activities. The State of Minnesota has a legitimate interest in ensuring nondiscriminatory access to the commercial opportunity presented by membership in the Jaycees. The members of the Jaycees may not claim constitutional immunity from Minnesota's antidiscrimination law by seeking to exercise their First Amendment rights through this commercial organization.

For these reasons, I agree with the Court that the Jaycees' First Amendment challenge to the application of Minnesota's public accommodations law is meritless. I therefore concur in Parts I and III of the Court's opinion and in the judgment.

———

Note: Competing Approaches to Freedom of Association

1. In *Roberts*, Justice Brennan inquires into the degree to which the government-compelled association will actually affect the group's speech. By contrast, Justice O'Connor inquires into whether the group was formed for expressive purposes. What does this difference suggest about what each Justice values in expressive association?

2. Putting theory aside, what practical workability issues arise under each of these approaches? Consider Justice Brennan's approach. How easy is it for a court to determine how forced inclusion of a particular group will affect that group's speech? Is the difficulty compounded in situations where the group's expression is not completely consistent or coherent? In such situations, does a court have to give the group the benefit of the doubt when it claims that the compelled association will affect its expression? If not, then is a court forced into a situation where it has to distill the association's "real" message and then determine how the compelled association will affect it? Reconsider these questions after reading *Dale*, the next principal case.

3. Is Justice O'Connor's approach any easier to apply? She concedes that few associations are exclusively commercial or expressive, and ultimately concludes that First Amendment protections should be withheld only when the particular group's activities "are not predominantly of the type protected by the First Amendment." Is this question any easier to answer than the question of whether compelled association will affect the group's speech? Is a court's investigation of Justice O'Connor's question more or less intrusive on the values protected by the right of association? Keep these questions in mind as you read the rest of the material in this chapter.

4. In *Board of Directors of Rotary International v. Rotary Club of Duarte*, 481 U.S. 537 (1987), the Court applied the majority approach in *Roberts* to uphold application of California's public accommodations law to the Rotary Club, which excluded women as members. Justice Powell noted that "as a matter of policy, Rotary Clubs do not take positions on public questions, including political or international issues." He continued:

> To be sure, Rotary Clubs engage in a variety of commendable service activities that are protected by the First Amendment. But [the California public accommodations law] does not require the clubs to abandon or alter any of these activities. It does not require them to abandon their basic goals of humanitarian service. . . . Nor does it require them to abandon [the gender-neutral aspects of the process by which Rotary Clubs chose their members].

He concluded that "even if [the California law] does work some slight infringement on Rotary members' right of expressive association, that infringement is justified because it serves the State's compelling interest in eliminating discrimination against women."

One stated goal of Rotary's selection process is to ensure, in the club's own words, "that each Rotary Club includes a representative of every worthy and recognized business, professional, or institutional activity in the community." At the end of the paragraph excerpted above in block quotation, Justice Powell added that "by opening membership to leading business and professional women in the community, Rotary Clubs are likely to obtain a more representative cross section of community leaders with a broadened capacity for service." Was it appropriate for the Court to make that statement?

———

Problem: The New Age Coalition and the Fundamentalist

The New Age Coalition (NAC) is an Oregon group that espouses a hazy vision of non-materialism, self-sufficiency, and environmental sustainability. Its members have joined together to espouse and discuss these views; although their potluck dinners and camping trips often seem to be nothing more than social gatherings, their literature and by-laws claim that through such activities they explore and reinforce their creed of living simply, communally, and with minimum use of natural resources. The NAC's by-laws speak of "Mother Earth" and Native American spirit gods as guiding forces behind their philosophy, even though its actual public statements address public policy issues such as environmental policy without reference to such theologies. Indeed, those statements almost invariably constitute nothing more than signing amicus briefs in environmental law cases and writing policy-based (rather than philosophically based) letters to government officials on behalf of environmental initiatives.

Ralph Paulson is a fundamentalist Christian who believes that Jesus was the first environmentalist, and that in the Old Testament God gave humans dominion over the earth with the direction to tread lightly and be good stewards of the land. He seeks to join the NAC, but is rejected because on his application form he answers the question, "Why do you want to join the NAC?" by citing his theological views. When he finds out he is rejected, he sues under the Oregon public accommodations law, which prohibits discrimination in public accommodations on the basis of religion, among other criteria. The NAC defends based on its First Amendment right of association. Will it win? What other facts would you want to know before you decide?

———

Note: Hurley v. Irish-American Gay, Lesbian and Bisexual Group of Boston

1. In *Hurley v. Irish-American Gay, Lesbian and Bisexual Group of Boston*, 515 U.S. 557 (1995), GLIB, a group representing gay, lesbian and bisexual Irish-Americans, applied to march as a contingent in Boston's privately run St. Patrick's Day parade. The organizers of the parade denied the application and the group sued, relying on the Massachusetts public accommodations law. The Massachusetts courts ruled in GLIB's favor, but the Supreme Court unanimously reversed. In an opinion by Justice Souter, the Court held that the state court mandate violated the organizers' First Amendment right to exclude "a group imparting a message the organizers do not wish to convey."

The Court began by noting that parades are inherently expressive and thus protected by the First Amendment. It then noted that the organizers disclaimed any intention to exclude from the parade gays and lesbians as such, but only as a particular contingent marching under its own banner. Thus, the Court described the Massachusetts public accommodations law as in this case compelling access not to an organization per se, but to the organization's expression, and remarked that this presented a "peculiar" application of the law.

Next, the Court stated that the organizers' decisions about which groups could march in the parade constituted the organizers' speech:

> . . . Rather like a composer, the Council [the group organizing the parade] selects the expressive units of the parade from potential participants, and though the score may not produce a particularized message, each contingent's expression in the Council's eyes comports with what merits celebration on that day. . . . Although GLIB's point (like the Council's) is not wholly articulate, a contingent marching behind the organization's banner would at least bear witness to the fact that some Irish are gay, lesbian, or bisexual, and the

presence of the organized marchers would suggest their view that people of their sexual orientations have as much claim to unqualified social acceptance as heterosexuals. . . . The parade's organizers may not believe these facts about Irish sexuality to be so, or they may . . . have some other reason to keep GLIB's message out of the parade. But whatever the reason, it boils down to the choice of a speaker not to propound a particular point of view, and that choice is presumed to lie beyond the government's power to control.

Finally, the Court rejected GLIB's argument that the parade was simply a neutral conduit for the marchers' expression. It contrasted the parade with cable television, reasoning that while the public might assume that the network programs presented on cable television did not reflect the cable company's own views, the public normally understands a parade to reflect the expressive choices of its organizers.

2. What explains the different results in *Hurley* and *Roberts*? Is it simply that forced acceptance of GLIB's entry into the Boston parade would affect the parade organizers' speech in a way not true of forced acceptance of women into the Jaycees? Consider Justice Souter's statement about the likely message communicated by GLIB's presence in the parade. Is there a fundamental difference about a group seeking access to a parade and a group seeking access to an organization that engages in expression?

3. In *Hurley*, GLIB argued that the parade was simply a conduit for the speech of the marchers and that therefore inclusion of GLIB in the parade would not affect the speech of the parade organizers. The Court rejected that argument by citing the likelihood that parade viewers would think that the organizers had in fact endorsed GLIB's views. Consider the Court's argument in the context of *Wooley v. Maynard* (*supra* Chapter 9). If everyone in New Hampshire knew that state law required "Live Free or Die" to appear on license plates, does *Hurley*'s approach mean that *Wooley* was wrongly decided?

Boy Scouts of America v. Dale

530 U.S. 640 (2000)

CHIEF JUSTICE REHNQUIST delivered the opinion of the Court.

Petitioners are the Boy Scouts of America and the Monmouth Council, a division of the Boy Scouts of America (collectively, Boy Scouts). The Boy Scouts is a private, not-for-profit organization engaged in instilling its system of values in young people. The Boy Scouts asserts that homosexual conduct is inconsistent with the values it seeks to instill. Respondent is James Dale, a former Eagle Scout whose adult membership in the Boy Scouts was revoked when the Boy Scouts learned that he is an avowed homosexual and gay rights activist. The New Jersey Supreme Court held that New Jersey's public accommodations law requires that the Boy Scouts readmit Dale. This case presents the question whether applying New Jersey's public accommodations law in this way violates the Boy Scouts' First Amendment right of expressive association. We hold that it does.

I

James Dale entered Scouting in 1978 at the age of eight by joining Monmouth Council's Cub Scout Pack 142. Dale became a Boy Scout in 1981 and remained a Scout until he turned 18. By all accounts, Dale was an exemplary Scout. In 1988, he achieved the rank of Eagle Scout, one of Scouting's highest honors.

Dale applied for adult membership in the Boy Scouts in 1989. The Boy Scouts approved his application for the position of assistant scoutmaster of Troop 73. Around the same time, Dale left home to attend Rutgers University. After arriving at Rutgers, Dale first acknowledged to himself and others that he is gay. He quickly became involved with, and eventually became the copresident of, the Rutgers University Lesbian/Gay Alliance. In 1990, Dale attended a seminar addressing the psychological and health needs of lesbian and gay teenagers. A newspaper covering the event interviewed Dale about his advocacy of homosexual teenagers' need for gay role models. In early July 1990, the newspaper published the interview and Dale's photograph over a caption identifying him as the copresident of the Lesbian/Gay Alliance.

Later that month, Dale received a letter from Monmouth Council Executive James Kay revoking his adult membership. Dale wrote to Kay requesting the reason for Monmouth Council's decision. Kay responded by letter that the Boy Scouts "specifically forbid membership to homosexuals."

In 1992, Dale filed a complaint against the Boy Scouts in the New Jersey Superior Court. The complaint alleged that the Boy Scouts had violated New Jersey's public accommodations statute and its common law by revoking Dale's membership based solely on his sexual orientation. . . . [The New Jersey Supreme Court allowed Dale to proceed with his claim under the public accommodations statute, rejecting the Boy Scouts' arguments under the Federal Constitution.]

We granted the Boy Scouts' petition for certiorari to determine whether the application of New Jersey's public accommodations law violated the First Amendment.

II

In *Roberts v. United States Jaycees* (1984) [*supra* this chapter], we observed that "implicit in the right to engage in activities protected by the First Amendment" is "a corresponding right to associate with others in pursuit of a wide variety of political, social, economic, educational, religious, and cultural ends." . . .

The forced inclusion of an unwanted person in a group infringes the group's freedom of expressive association if the presence of that person affects in a significant way the group's ability to advocate public or private viewpoints. *New York State Club Ass'n, Inc. v. City of New York*, 487 U.S. 1 (1988). But the freedom of expressive association, like many freedoms, is not absolute. We have held that the freedom could be overridden "by regulations adopted to serve compelling state interests, unrelated to the suppression of ideas, that cannot be achieved through means significantly less restrictive of associational freedoms." *Roberts*.

To determine whether a group is protected by the First Amendment's expressive associational right, we must determine whether the group engages in "expressive association." The First Amendment's protection of expressive association is not reserved for advocacy groups. But to come within its ambit, a group must engage in some form of expression, whether it be public or private.

Because this is a First Amendment case where the ultimate conclusions of law are virtually inseparable from findings of fact, we are obligated to independently review the factual record to ensure that the state court's judgment does not unlawfully intrude on free expression. See *Hurley* [Note *supra* this chapter]. The record reveals the following. The Boy Scouts is a private, nonprofit organization. According to its mission statement:

> It is the mission of the Boy Scouts of America to serve others by helping to instill values in young people and, in other ways, to prepare them to make ethical choices over their lifetime in achieving their full potential.

> The values we strive to instill are based on those found in the Scout Oath and Law:

Scout Oath

On my honor I will do my best

To do my duty to God and my country

and to obey the Scout Law;

To help other people at all times;

To keep myself physically strong,

mentally awake, and morally straight.

Scout Law

A Scout is:

Trustworthy	Obedient
Loyal	Cheerful
Helpful	Thrifty
Friendly	Brave
Courteous	Clean
Kind	Reverent.

Thus, the general mission of the Boy Scouts is clear: "[T]o instill values in young people." . . .

Given that the Boy Scouts engages in expressive activity, we must determine whether the forced inclusion of Dale as an assistant scoutmaster would significantly affect the Boy Scouts' ability to advocate public or private viewpoints. This inquiry necessarily requires us first to explore, to a limited extent, the nature of the Boy Scouts' view of homosexuality.

The values the Boy Scouts seeks to instill are "based on" those listed in the Scout Oath and Law. . . . The Boy Scouts asserts that homosexual conduct is inconsistent with the values embodied in the Scout Oath and Law, particularly with the values represented by the terms "morally straight" and "clean." . . .

The New Jersey Supreme Court analyzed the Boy Scouts' beliefs and found that the "exclusion of members solely on the basis of their sexual orientation is inconsistent with Boy Scouts' commitment to a diverse and 'representative' membership . . . [and] contradicts Boy Scouts' overarching objective to reach 'all eligible youth.'" The court concluded that the exclusion of members like Dale "appears antithetical to the organization's goals and philosophy." But our cases reject this sort of inquiry; it is not the role of the courts to reject a group's expressed values because they disagree with those values or find them internally inconsistent. *See Democratic Party of United States v. Wisconsin ex rel. LaFollette*, 450 U.S. 107 (1981) ("[A]s is true of all expressions of First Amendment freedoms, the courts may not interfere on the ground that they view a particular expression as unwise or irrational.").

The Boy Scouts asserts that it "teach[es] that homosexual conduct is not morally straight," Brief for Petitioners 39, and that it does "not want to promote homosexual conduct as a legitimate form of behavior," Reply Brief for Petitioners 5. We accept the Boy Scouts' assertion. We need not inquire further to determine the nature of the Boy Scouts' expression with respect to homosexuality. But because the record before us contains written evidence of the Boy Scouts' viewpoint, we look to it as instructive, if only on the question of the sincerity of the professed beliefs.

A 1978 position statement to the Boy Scouts' Executive Committee, signed by Downing B. Jenks, the President of the Boy Scouts, and Harvey L. Price, the Chief Scout Executive, expresses the Boy Scouts' "official position" with regard to "homosexuality and Scouting":

> "Q. May an individual who openly declares himself to be a homosexual be a volunteer Scout leader?

> "A. No. The Boy Scouts of America is a private, membership organization and leadership therein is a privilege and not a right. We do not believe that homosexuality and leadership in Scouting are appropriate. We will continue to select only those who in our judgment meet our standards and qualifications for leadership."

Thus, at least as of 1978—the year James Dale entered Scouting—the official position of the Boy Scouts was that avowed homosexuals were not to be Scout leaders.

A position statement promulgated by the Boy Scouts in 1991 (after Dale's membership was revoked but before this litigation was filed) also supports its current view:

> We believe that homosexual conduct is inconsistent with the requirement in the Scout Oath that a Scout be morally straight and in the Scout Law that a Scout be clean in word and deed, and that homosexuals do not provide a desirable role model for Scouts.

This position statement was redrafted numerous times but its core message remained consistent. . . .

We must then determine whether Dale's presence as an assistant scoutmaster would significantly burden the Boy Scouts' desire to not "promote homosexual conduct as a legitimate form of behavior." Reply Brief for Petitioners 5. As we give deference to an association's assertions regarding the nature of its expression, we must also give deference to an association's view of what would impair its expression. *See, e.g., LaFollette* (considering whether a Wisconsin law burdened the National Party's associational rights and stating that "a State, or a court, may not constitutionally substitute its own judgment for that of the Party"). That is not to say that an expressive association can erect a shield against antidiscrimination laws simply by asserting that mere acceptance of a member from a particular group would impair its message. But here Dale, by his own admission, is one of a group of gay Scouts who have "become leaders in their community and are open and honest about their sexual orientation." Dale was the copresident of a gay and lesbian organization at college and remains a gay rights activist. Dale's presence in the Boy Scouts would, at the very least, force the organization to send a message, both to the youth members and the world, that the Boy Scouts accepts homosexual conduct as a legitimate form of behavior.

Hurley is illustrative on this point. . . . We noted that the parade organizers did not wish to exclude the GLIB members because of their sexual orientations, but because they wanted to march behind a GLIB banner. We observed:

> [A] contingent marching behind the organization's banner would at least bear witness to the fact that some Irish are gay, lesbian, or bisexual, and the presence of the organized marchers would suggest their view that people of their sexual orientations have as much claim to unqualified social acceptance as heterosexuals. . . . The parade's organizers may not believe these facts about Irish sexuality to be so, or they may object to unqualified social acceptance of gays and lesbians or have some other reason for wishing to keep GLIB's message out of the parade. But whatever the reason, it boils down to the choice of a speaker not to propound a particular point of view, and that choice is presumed to lie beyond the government's power to control.

Here, we have found that the Boy Scouts believes that homosexual conduct is inconsistent with the values it seeks to instill in its youth members; it will not "promote homosexual conduct as a legitimate form of behavior." Reply Brief for Petitioners 5. As the presence of GLIB in Boston's St. Patrick's Day parade would have interfered with the parade organizers' choice not to propound a particular point of view, the presence of Dale as an assistant scoutmaster would just as surely interfere with the Boy Scouts' choice not to propound a point of view contrary to its beliefs.

The New Jersey Supreme Court determined that the Boy Scouts' ability to disseminate its message was not significantly affected by the forced inclusion of Dale as an assistant scoutmaster because of the following findings:

> Boy Scout members do not associate for the purpose of disseminating the belief that homosexuality is immoral; Boy Scouts discourages its leaders from disseminating *any* views on sexual issues; and Boy Scouts includes sponsors and members who subscribe to different views in respect of homosexuality.

We disagree with the New Jersey Supreme Court's conclusion drawn from these findings.

First, associations do not have to associate for the "purpose" of disseminating a certain message in order to be entitled to the protections of the First Amendment. An association must merely engage in expressive activity that could be impaired in order to be entitled to protection. For example, the purpose of the St. Patrick's Day parade in *Hurley* was not to espouse any views about sexual orientation, but we held that the parade organizers had a right to exclude certain participants nonetheless.

Second, even if the Boy Scouts discourages Scout leaders from disseminating views on sexual issues — a fact that the Boy Scouts disputes with contrary evidence — the First Amendment protects the Boy Scouts' method of expression. If the Boy Scouts wishes Scout leaders to avoid questions of sexuality and teach only by example, this fact does not negate the sincerity of its belief discussed above.

Third, the First Amendment simply does not require that every member of a group agree on every issue in order for the group's policy to be "expressive association." The Boy Scouts takes an official position with respect to homosexual conduct, and that is sufficient for First Amendment purposes. . . . The fact that the organization does not trumpet its views from the housetops, or that it tolerates dissent within its ranks, does not mean that its views receive no First Amendment protection.

Having determined that the Boy Scouts is an expressive association and that the forced inclusion of Dale would significantly affect its expression, we inquire whether the application of New Jersey's public accommodations law to require that the Boy Scouts accept Dale as an assistant scoutmaster runs afoul of the Scouts' freedom of expressive association. We conclude that it does.

State public accommodations laws were originally enacted to prevent discrimination in traditional places of public accommodation — like inns and trains. . . . As the definition of "public accommodation" has expanded from clearly commercial entities, such as restaurants, bars, and hotels, to membership organizations such as the Boy Scouts, the potential for conflict between state public accommodations laws and the First Amendment rights of organizations has increased.

We recognized in cases such as *Roberts* and *Board of Directors of Rotary Int'l v. Rotary Club of Duarte*, 481 U.S. 537 (1987) [Note this chapter], that States have a compelling interest in eliminating discrimination against women in public accommodations. But in each of these cases we went on to conclude that the enforcement of these statutes would not materially interfere with the ideas that the organization sought to express. . . .

In *Hurley*, we applied traditional First Amendment analysis to hold that the application of the Massachusetts public accommodations law to a parade violated the First Amendment rights of the parade organizers. Although we did not explicitly deem the parade in *Hurley* an expressive association, the analysis we applied there is similar to the analysis we apply here. We have already concluded that a state requirement that the Boy Scouts retain Dale as an assistant scoutmaster would significantly burden the organization's right to oppose or disfavor homosexual conduct. The state interests embodied in New Jersey's public accommodations law do not justify such a severe intrusion on the Boy Scouts' rights to freedom of expressive association. That being the case, we hold that the First Amendment prohibits the State from imposing such a requirement through the application of its public accommodations law. . . .

The judgment of the New Jersey Supreme Court is reversed, and the case is remanded for further proceedings not inconsistent with this opinion.

Justice Stevens, with whom Justice Souter, Justice Ginsburg, and Justice Breyer join, dissenting.

. . . The majority holds that New Jersey's law violates BSA's right to associate and its right to free speech. But that law does not "impos[e] any serious burdens" on BSA's "collective effort on behalf of [its] shared goals," *Roberts*, nor does it force BSA to communicate any message that it does not wish to endorse. New Jersey's law, therefore, abridges no constitutional right of BSA.

I

. . . [In] this case, BSA contends that it teaches the young boys who are Scouts that homosexuality is immoral. Consequently, it argues, it would violate its right to associate to force it to admit homosexuals as members, as doing so would be at odds with its own shared goals and values. This contention, quite plainly, requires us to look at what, exactly, are the values that BSA actually teaches.

BSA's mission statement reads as follows: "It is the mission of the Boy Scouts of America to serve others by helping to instill values in young people and, in other ways, to prepare them to make ethical choices over their lifetime in achieving their full potential." . . . BSA describes itself as having a "representative membership," which it defines as "boy membership [that] reflects proportionately the characteristics of the boy population of its service area." In particular, the group emphasizes that "[n]either the charter nor the bylaws of the Boy Scouts of America permits the exclusion of any boy." . . .

To bolster its claim that its shared goals include teaching that homosexuality is wrong, BSA directs our attention to two terms appearing in the Scout Oath and Law. The first is the phrase "morally straight," which appears in the Oath ("On my honor I will do my best . . . To keep myself . . . morally straight"); the second term is the word "clean," which appears in a list of 12 characteristics together constituting the Scout Law.

The Boy Scout Handbook defines "morally straight," as such:

"To be a person of strong character, guide your life with honesty, purity, and justice. Respect and defend the rights of all people. Your relationships with others should be honest and open. Be clean in your speech and actions, and faithful in your religious beliefs. The values you follow as a Scout will help you become virtuous and self-reliant."

The Scoutmaster Handbook emphasizes these points about being "morally straight":

"In any consideration of moral fitness, a key word has to be 'courage.' A boy's courage to do what his head and his heart tell him is right. And the courage to refuse to do what his heart and his head say is wrong. Moral fitness, like emotional fitness, will clearly present opportunities for wise guidance by an alert Scoutmaster."

As for the term "clean," the Boy Scout Handbook offers the following:

"A Scout is CLEAN. *A Scout keeps his body and mind fit and clean. He chooses the company of those who live by these same ideals. He helps keep his home and community clean.* . . .

"Swear words, profanity, and dirty stories are weapons that ridicule other people and hurt their feelings. The same is true of racial slurs and jokes making fun of ethnic groups or people with physical or mental limitations. A Scout knows there is no kindness or honor in such mean-spirited behavior. He avoids it in his own words and deeds. He defends those who are targets of insults."

It is plain as the light of day that neither one of these principles — "morally straight" and "clean" — says the slightest thing about homosexuality. Indeed, neither term in the Boy Scouts' Law and Oath expresses any position whatsoever on sexual matters.

BSA's published guidance on that topic underscores this point. Scouts, for example, are directed to receive their sex education at home or in school, but not from the organization. . . . Moreover, Scoutmasters are specifically directed to steer curious adolescents to other sources of information. . . .

In light of BSA's self-proclaimed ecumenism, furthermore, it is even more difficult to discern any shared goals or common moral stance on homosexuality. Insofar as religious matters are concerned, BSA's bylaws state that it is "absolutely nonsectarian in its attitude toward . . . religious training." . . . Because a number of religious groups do not view homosexuality as immoral or wrong and reject discrimination against homosexuals, it is exceedingly difficult to believe that BSA nonetheless adopts a single particular religious or moral philosophy when it comes to sexual orientation. This is especially so in light of the fact that Scouts are advised to seek guidance on sexual matters from their religious leaders (and Scoutmasters are told to refer Scouts to them); BSA surely is aware that some religions do not teach that homosexuality is wrong. . . .

III

BSA's claim finds no support in our cases. . . . In fact, until today, we have never once found a claimed right to associate in the selection of members to prevail in the face of a State's antidiscrimination law. To the contrary, we have squarely held that a

State's antidiscrimination law does not violate a group's right to associate simply because the law conflicts with that group's exclusionary membership policy.

In *Roberts*, we addressed just such a conflict. . . . We found the State's purpose of eliminating discrimination is a compelling state interest that is unrelated to the suppression of ideas. We also held that Minnesota's law is the least restrictive means of achieving that interest. The Jaycees had "failed to demonstrate that the Act imposes any serious burdens on the male members' freedom of expressive association." . . .

We took a similar approach in *Rotary Club of Duarte*. . . .

Several principles are made perfectly clear by *Jaycees* and *Rotary Club*. First, to prevail on a claim of expressive association in the face of a State's antidiscrimination law, it is not enough simply to engage in *some kind* of expressive activity. Both the Jaycees and the Rotary Club engaged in expressive activity protected by the First Amendment, yet that fact was not dispositive. Second, it is not enough to adopt an openly avowed exclusionary membership policy. Both the Jaycees and the Rotary Club did that as well. Third, it is not sufficient merely to articulate *some* connection between the group's expressive activities and its exclusionary policy. The Rotary Club, for example, justified its male-only membership policy by pointing to the "'aspect of fellowship . . . that is enjoyed by the [exclusively] male membership'" and by claiming that only with an exclusively male membership could it "operate effectively" in foreign countries.

Rather, in *Jaycees*, we asked whether Minnesota's Human Rights Law requiring the admission of women "impose[d] any *serious burdens*" on the group's "collective effort on behalf of [its] *shared goals*." Notwithstanding the group's obvious publicly stated exclusionary policy, we did not view the inclusion of women as a "serious burden" on the Jaycees' ability to engage in the protected speech of its choice. [*See, e.g.,*] *NAACP v. Alabama* (1958) [*supra* this chapter] (asking whether law "entail[ed] the likelihood of a substantial restraint upon the exercise by petitioner's members of their right to freedom of association" and whether law is "likely to affect adversely the ability of petitioner and its members to pursue their collective effort to foster beliefs"). . . . The relevant question is whether the mere inclusion of the person at issue would "impose any serious burden," "affect in any significant way," or be "a substantial restraint upon" the organization's "shared goals," "basic goals," or "collective effort to foster beliefs." Accordingly, it is necessary to examine what, exactly, are BSA's shared goals and the degree to which its expressive activities would be burdened, affected, or restrained by including homosexuals.

The evidence before this Court makes it exceptionally clear that BSA has, at most, simply adopted an exclusionary membership policy and has no shared goal of disapproving of homosexuality. BSA's mission statement and federal charter say nothing on the matter; its official membership policy is silent; its Scout Oath and Law—and accompanying definitions—are devoid of any view on the topic; its guidance for Scouts and Scoutmasters on sexuality declare that such matters are "not construed to be Scouting's proper area," but are the province of a Scout's parents and pastor; and

BSA's posture respecting religion tolerates a wide variety of views on the issue of homosexuality. Moreover, there is simply no evidence that BSA otherwise teaches anything in this area, or that it instructs Scouts on matters involving homosexuality in ways not conveyed in the Boy Scout or Scoutmaster Handbooks. In short, Boy Scouts of America is simply silent on homosexuality. There is no shared goal or collective effort to foster a belief about homosexuality at all—let alone one that is significantly burdened by admitting homosexuals.

As in *Jaycees*, there is "no basis in the record for concluding that admission of [homosexuals] will impede the [Boy Scouts'] ability to engage in [its] protected activities or to disseminate its preferred views" and New Jersey's law "requires no change in [BSA's] creed." . . . BSA's temporary, though ultimately abandoned, view that homosexuality is incompatible with being "morally straight" and "clean" is a far cry from the clear, unequivocal statement necessary to prevail on its claim. Despite the solitary sentences in the 1991 and 1992 policies, the group continued to disclaim any single religious or moral position as a general matter and actively eschewed teaching any lesson on sexuality. It also continued to define "morally straight" and "clean" in the Boy Scout and Scoutmaster Handbooks without any reference to homosexuality. As noted earlier, nothing in our cases suggests that a group can prevail on a right to expressive association if it, effectively, speaks out of both sides of its mouth. A State's antidiscrimination law does not impose a "serious burden" or a "substantial restraint" upon the group's "shared goals" if the group itself is unable to identify its own stance with any clarity.

IV

The majority pretermits this entire analysis. It finds that BSA in fact "teach[es] that homosexual conduct is not morally straight." This conclusion, remarkably, rests entirely on statements in BSA's briefs. Moreover, the majority insists that we must "give deference to an association's assertions regarding the nature of its expression" and "[w]e must also give deference to an association's view of what would impair its expression." So long as the record "contains written evidence" to support a group's bare assertion, "we need not inquire further." Once the organization "asserts" that it engages in particular expression, "[w]e cannot doubt" the truth of that assertion.

This is an astounding view of the law. I am unaware of any previous instance in which our analysis of the scope of a constitutional right was determined by looking at what a litigant asserts in his or her brief and inquiring no further. It is even more astonishing in the First Amendment area, because, as the majority itself acknowledges, "we are obligated to independently review the factual record." It is an odd form of independent review that consists of deferring entirely to whatever a litigant claims. But the majority insists that our inquiry must be "limited," because "it is not the role of the courts to reject a group's expressed values because they disagree with those values or find them internally inconsistent."

But nothing in our cases calls for this Court to do any such thing. An organization can adopt the message of its choice, and it is not this Court's place to disagree with it. But we must inquire whether the group is, in fact, expressing a message (whatever it may be) and whether that message (if one is expressed) is significantly affected by a State's antidiscrimination law. More critically, that inquiry requires our *independent* analysis, rather than deference to a group's litigating posture. Reflection on the subject dictates that such an inquiry is required.

Surely there are instances in which an organization that truly aims to foster a belief at odds with the purposes of a State's antidiscrimination laws will have a First Amendment right to association that precludes forced compliance with those laws. But that right is not a freedom to discriminate at will, nor is it a right to maintain an exclusionary membership policy simply out of fear of what the public reaction would be if the group's membership were opened up. It is an implicit right designed to protect the enumerated rights of the First Amendment, not a license to act on any discriminatory impulse. To prevail in asserting a right of expressive association as a defense to a charge of violating an antidiscrimination law, the organization must at least show it has adopted and advocated an unequivocal position inconsistent with a position advocated or epitomized by the person whom the organization seeks to exclude. If this Court were to defer to whatever position an organization is prepared to assert in its briefs, there would be no way to mark the proper boundary between genuine exercises of the right to associate, on the one hand, and sham claims that are simply attempts to insulate nonexpressive private discrimination, on the other hand. Shielding a litigant's claim from judicial scrutiny would, in turn, render civil rights legislation a nullity, and turn this important constitutional right into a farce. Accordingly, the Court's prescription of total deference will not do. . . .

There is, of course, a valid concern that a court's independent review may run the risk of paying too little heed to an organization's sincerely held views. But unless one is prepared to turn the right to associate into a free pass out of antidiscrimination laws, an independent inquiry is a necessity. Though the group must show that its expressive activities will be substantially burdened by the State's law, if that law truly has a significant effect on a group's speech, even the subtle speaker will be able to identify that impact.

In this case, no such concern is warranted. It is entirely clear that BSA in fact expresses no clear, unequivocal message burdened by New Jersey's law.

V

Even if BSA's right to associate argument fails, it nonetheless might have a First Amendment right to refrain from including debate and dialogue about homosexuality as part of its mission to instill values in Scouts. It can, for example, advise Scouts who are entering adulthood and have questions about sex to talk "with your parents, religious leaders, teachers, or Scoutmaster," and, in turn, it can direct Scoutmasters who are asked such questions "not undertake to instruct Scouts, in any formalized manner, in the subject of sex and family life" because "it is not construed to be Scouting's proper area." Dale's right to advocate certain beliefs in a public forum or in a private debate does not include a right to advocate these ideas when he is working as a Scoutmaster. And BSA cannot be compelled to include a message about homosexuality among the values it actually chooses to teach its Scouts, if it would prefer to remain silent on that subject.

In *West Virginia Bd. of Ed. v. Barnette* (1943) [*supra* Chapter 9], we recognized that the government may not "requir[e] affirmation of a belief and an attitude of mind," nor "force an American citizen publicly to profess any statement of belief," even if doing so does not require the person to "forego any contrary convictions of their own." "[O]ne important manifestation of the principle of free speech is that one who chooses to speak may also decide 'what not to say.'" Though the majority mistakenly treats this statement as going to the right to associate, it actually refers to a free speech claim. As with the right to associate claim, though, the court is obligated to engage in an independent inquiry into whether the mere inclusion of homosexuals would actually force BSA to proclaim a message it does not want to send. . . .

The majority . . . contends that Dale's mere presence among the Boy Scouts will itself force the group to convey a message about homosexuality—even if Dale has no intention of doing so. The majority holds that "[t]he presence of an avowed homosexual and gay rights activist in an assistant scoutmaster's uniform sends a distinc[t] . . . message," and, accordingly, BSA is entitled to exclude that message. In particular, "Dale's presence in the Boy Scouts would, at the very least, force the organization to send a message, both to the youth members and the world, that the Boy Scouts accepts homosexual conduct as a legitimate form of behavior."

The majority's argument relies exclusively on *Hurley* [Note *supra* this chapter]. . . . Though *Hurley* has a superficial similarity to the present case, a close inspection reveals a wide gulf between that case and the one before us today.

First, it was critical to our analysis that GLIB was actually conveying a message by participating in the parade—otherwise, the parade organizers could hardly claim that they were being forced to include any unwanted message at all. . . . Indeed, we expressly distinguished between the members of GLIB, who marched as a unit to express their views about their own sexual orientation, on the one hand, and homosexuals who might participate as individuals in the parade without intending to express anything about their sexuality by doing so.

Second, we found it relevant that GLIB's message "would likely be perceived" as the parade organizers' own speech. . . .

Dale's inclusion in the Boy Scouts is nothing like the case in *Hurley*. His participation sends no cognizable message to the Scouts or to the world. Unlike GLIB, Dale did not carry a banner or a sign; he did not distribute any factsheet; and he expressed no intent to send any message. If there is any kind of message being sent, then, it is by the mere act of joining the Boy Scouts. Such an act does not constitute an instance of symbolic speech under the First Amendment.

It is true, of course, that some acts are so imbued with symbolic meaning that they qualify as "speech" under the First Amendment. *See United States v. O'Brien* (1968) [*supra* Chapter 7]. At the same time, however, "[w]e cannot accept the view that an apparently limitless variety of conduct can be labeled 'speech' whenever the person engaging in the conduct intends thereby to express an idea." *O'Brien*. Though participating in the Scouts could itself conceivably send a message on some level, it is not the kind of act that we have recognized as speech. *See Dallas v. Stanglin*, 490 U.S. 19 (1989). Indeed, if merely joining a group did constitute symbolic speech; and such speech were attributable to the group being joined; and that group has the right to exclude that speech (and hence, the right to exclude that person from joining), then the right of free speech effectively becomes a limitless right to exclude for every organization, whether or not it engages in *any* expressive activities. That cannot be, and never has been, the law.

The only apparent explanation for the majority's holding, then, is that homosexuals are simply so different from the rest of society that their presence alone—unlike any other individual's—should be singled out for special First Amendment treatment. Under the majority's reasoning, an openly gay male is irreversibly affixed with the label "homosexual." That label, even though unseen, communicates a message that permits his exclusion wherever he goes. His openness is the sole and sufficient justification for his ostracism. Though unintended, reliance on such a justification is tantamount to a constitutionally prescribed symbol of inferiority. As counsel for BSA remarked, Dale "put a banner around his neck when he . . . got himself into the newspaper. . . . He created a reputation. . . . He can't take that banner off. He put it on himself and, indeed, he has continued to put it on himself."

Another difference between this case and *Hurley* lies in the fact that *Hurley* involved the parade organizers' claim to determine the content of the message they wish to give at a particular time and place. The standards governing such a claim are simply different from the standards that govern BSA's claim of a right of expressive association. Generally, a private person or a private organization has a right to refuse to broadcast a message with which it disagrees, and a right to refuse to contradict or garble its own specific statement at any given place or time by including the messages of others. An expressive association claim, however, normally involves the avowal and advocacy of a consistent position on some issue over time. This is why a different kind of scrutiny must be given to an expressive association claim, lest the right of expressive association simply turn into a right to discriminate whenever some group can think of an expressive object that would seem to be inconsistent with the admission of some person as a member or at odds with the appointment of a person to a leadership position in the group.

Furthermore, it is not likely that BSA would be understood to send any message, either to Scouts or to the world, simply by admitting someone as a member. . . . In 1992 over one million adults were active BSA members. The notion that an organization of that size and enormous prestige implicitly endorses the views that each of those adults may express in a non-Scouting context is simply mind boggling. Indeed, in this case there is no evidence that the young Scouts in Dale's troop, or members of their families, were even aware of his sexual orientation, either before or after his public statements at Rutgers University. It is equally farfetched to assert that Dale's open declaration of his homosexuality, reported in a local newspaper, will effectively force BSA to send a message to anyone simply because it allows Dale to be an Assistant Scoutmaster. For an Olympic gold medal winner or a Wimbledon tennis champion, being "openly gay" perhaps communicates a message — for example, that openness about one's sexual orientation is more virtuous than concealment; that a homosexual person can be a capable and virtuous person who should be judged like anyone else; and that homosexuality is not immoral — but it certainly does not follow that they necessarily send a message on behalf of the organizations that sponsor the activities in which they excel. . . .

JUSTICE SOUTER, with whom JUSTICE GINSBURG and JUSTICE BREYER join, dissenting. [Omitted.]

———

Note: Dale *and the Precedents*

1. How does *Dale* fit with *Roberts* and *Hurley*? In *Roberts,* the Jaycees claimed that inclusion of women would affect their message because women might take different positions on issues the Jaycees speak on. In *Hurley,* Justice Souter notes that the Boston parade organizers disclaimed any intent to exclude gays in their capacity as gay people; rather, they sought to exclude them to the extent they sought to march under a particular banner and thus alter the parade's speech. How does the Boy Scouts' claim differ from these claims? Note in particular Chief Justice Rehnquist's statement in *Dale* (in the last substantive paragraph of the excerpt of his opinion) that, while the Court "did not explicitly deem the parade in *Hurley* an expressive association, the analysis we applied there is similar to the analysis we apply here." This statement reflects a reading of *Hurley* as a compelled speech, rather than a compelled association case. (This reading is buttressed by the fact that Justice Stevens discusses *Hurley* in Part V of his dissent, which focuses on compelled speech.) Nevertheless, the majority describes the analysis in both cases as "similar." Is it?

2. How carefully should a court review an organization's claim that compelled admission of a certain person or type of person would alter that speech? Leaving aside the *Dale* dissent's argument that deferential review would give organizations a "free pass" out of anti-discrimination laws, does the answer to this question turn on the theory you adopt about the value of speech? In particular, if a court defers to the organization's own views, does that suggest a more speaker-oriented view of the First Amendment, as opposed to an approach that focuses on the social value of having a variety of views present in the marketplace of ideas? By contrast, if a court makes its own decisions about whether forced association will impair a group's expression, does that suggest a focus on the social value of free speech, with the court determining whether forced inclusion will change the type of expression offered in the marketplace?

Regardless of your answer to this question, recall now the dissent's "free pass" argument. How important a factor should that argument be? At the end of the day, does *Dale* turn on the fact that the majority believes the state to have a less compelling interest in eradicating sexual orientation discrimination than discrimination based, for example, on gender?

————

Note: Status and Message

1. When does an individual's status inevitably communicate a message? Should a group of whites that espouses racial segregation be able to exclude a black nationalist who also favors racial segregation, on the theory that the very admission of the black person would dilute the group's message? If so, how far should that theory extend? In this example, compelled admission of the black applicant would explicitly conflict with the very message the organization was trying to send. Can status communicate other messages, too? Consider an organization that advocates the view that women should take only traditionally feminine roles in society. Does the organization have a First Amendment right to exclude women, on the ground that their very admission would dilute its message?

2. Does the communicative impact of a person's status depend in part on whether that status is obvious to the general public, or to the recipients of the group's speech? For example, assume that Dale had not disclosed his sexual orientation to a newspaper, and that the Scouts had learned about it only in his written application to be a scoutmaster. If Dale had promised to keep his sexual orientation private, not just to the scouts and scoutmasters, but to the public at large, would he have an argument that the Scouts' expression would not be affected by his taking the role of Scoutmaster? Would the Scouts have an argument that his mere presence as a gay man, even if that status was known only to those who had seen his application, would alter the internal processes by which the Scouts decided on their expression about homosexuality?

————

Problem: Exclusion from a Gay Softball League

Over the last 30 years, amateur sports organizations have become a fixture in the gay and lesbian community. In particular, gay softball leagues have sprung up all over the country. Many of them have had to face the question whether to allow heterosexuals to participate.

The Elm City Gay Softball Association ("Association") is one such organization. The relevant parts of its by-laws appear below:

Preamble

. . . The Association exists to promote a sense of pride and self-worth among members of the Elm City LGBT community. Too often, LGBT people associate sports with childhood experiences of ridicule, humiliation and exclusion. The Association seeks to provide opportunities for LGBT people to experience the camaraderie and confidence-building provided by participation in sports, in an environment that is welcoming, non-judgmental and non-threatening. It also believes that the example of LGBT people excelling in sports provides positive role models for the rest of the LGBT community, breaks down stereotypes about LGBT people in the broader Elm City community, and promotes social and civil equality. . . .

Non-Discrimination

. . . The Association does not wish to discriminate based on sexual orientation or any other invidious basis. However, in order to accomplish the goals set forth in the Preamble, the Association must ensure that every team in the league is predominantly comprised of LGBT players. For this reason, no team in the Association may have more than two players on the roster who self-identify as heterosexual. The Association reserves the right to conduct a discrete, respectful inquiry whenever it obtains probable cause to believe that a team is violating this rule. . . .

Last April the managers of each team in the league submitted their rosters for the annual summer season. Upon reviewing the rosters of the other teams, the manager of the Rangers filed a formal challenge to the roster of another team, the Bruins. In support of his challenge, the manager, a photographer, asserted that he had been the wedding photographer at the opposite-sex weddings of three men who appeared on the Bruins' roster. Upon investigating, the league upheld the challenge, and ordered the Bruins to drop one of the three men. The Bruins manager asked if any of the men would voluntarily resign from the team. When none of them did, the Bruins manager dropped one of them, Sam Sidley, based on a random selection.

The State of Nutmeg, where Elm City is located, has a law prohibiting any "public accommodation" from discriminating "on the basis of race, national origin, sex, religion, or sexual orientation." Sidley sues the Association under that law, alleging that he was discriminated against because he is heterosexual. Assume that the Association is a "public accommodation" under the state law. Does it nonetheless have a good First Amendment defense?

Chapter 11

Campaign Finance

A. Foundational Principles
Buckley v. Valeo
424 U.S. 1 (1976)

Per Curiam.

These appeals present constitutional challenges to the key provisions of the Federal Election Campaign Act of 1971 (Act), and related provisions of the Internal Revenue Code of 1954, all as amended in 1974.

. . . The statutes at issue summarized in broad terms, contain the following provisions: (a) individual political contributions are limited to $1,000 to any single candidate per election, with an overall annual limitation of $25,000 by any contributor; independent expenditures by individuals and groups "relative to a clearly identified candidate" are limited to $1,000 a year; campaign spending by candidates for various federal offices and spending for national conventions by political parties are subject to prescribed limits; (b) contributions and expenditures above certain threshold levels must be reported and publicly disclosed; (c) a system for public funding of Presidential campaign activities is established by Subtitle H of the Internal Revenue Code; and (d) a Federal Election Commission is established to administer and enforce the legislation. . . .

[The District Court transferred the case to the Court of Appeals for consideration of the constitutional issues raised by the suit, as provided for by the statute. The Court of Appeals rejected most of the plaintiffs' constitutional arguments and sustained the legislation in large part.]

I. CONTRIBUTION AND EXPENDITURE LIMITATIONS

The intricate statutory scheme adopted by Congress to regulate federal election campaigns includes restrictions on political contributions and expenditures that apply broadly to all phases of and all participants in the election process. The major contribution and expenditure limitations in the Act prohibit individuals from contributing more than $25,000 in a single year or more than $1,000 to any single candidate for an election campaign and from spending more than $1,000 a year "relative to a clearly identified candidate." Other provisions restrict a candidate's use of personal and family resources in his campaign and limit the overall amount that can be spent by a candidate in campaigning for federal office. . . .

A. General Principles

The Act's contribution and expenditure limitations operate in an area of the most fundamental First Amendment activities. Discussion of public issues and debate on the qualifications of candidates are integral to the operation of the system of government established by our Constitution. The First Amendment affords the broadest protection to such political expression in order "to assure [the] unfettered interchange of ideas for the bringing about of political and social changes desired by the people." *Roth v. United States* (1957) [Chapter 2].... This no more than reflects our "profound national commitment to the principle that debate on public issues should be uninhibited, robust, and wide-open," *New York Times Co. v. Sullivan* (1964) [Chapter 2]....

The First Amendment protects political association as well as political expression. The constitutional right of association explicated in *NAACP v. Alabama* (1958) [Chapter 10] stemmed from the Court's recognition that "[e]ffective advocacy of both public and private points of view, particularly controversial ones, is undeniably enhanced by group association." Subsequent decisions have made clear that the First and Fourteenth Amendments guarantee "freedom to associate with others for the common advancement of political beliefs and ideas," a freedom that encompasses "[t]he right to associate with the political party of one's choice." *Kusper v. Pontikes*, 414 U.S. 51 (1973).

It is with these principles in mind that we consider the primary contentions of the parties with respect to the Act's limitations upon the giving and spending of money in political campaigns. Those conflicting contentions could not more sharply define the basic issues before us. Appellees contend that what the Act regulates is conduct, and that its effect on speech and association is incidental at most. Appellants respond that contributions and expenditures are at the very core of political speech, and that the Act's limitations thus constitute restraints on First Amendment liberty that are both gross and direct.

In upholding the constitutional validity of the Act's contribution and expenditure provisions on the ground that those provisions should be viewed as regulating conduct, not speech, the Court of Appeals relied upon *United States v. O'Brien* (1968) [Chapter 8]. The *O'Brien* case involved a defendant's claim that the First Amendment prohibited his prosecution for burning his draft card because his act was "symbolic speech" engaged in as a "demonstration against the war and against the draft." On the assumption that "the alleged communicative element in O'Brien's conduct [was] sufficient to bring into play the First Amendment," the Court sustained the conviction because it found "a sufficiently important governmental interest in regulating the non-speech element" that was "unrelated to the suppression of free expression" and that had an "incidental restriction on alleged First Amendment freedoms ... no greater than [was] essential to the furtherance of that interest." The Court expressly emphasized that *O'Brien* was not a case "where the alleged governmental interest in regulating conduct arises in some measure because the communication allegedly integral to the conduct is itself thought to be harmful."

We cannot share the view that the present Act's contribution and expenditure limitations are comparable to the restrictions on conduct upheld in *O'Brien*. The expenditure of money simply cannot be equated with such conduct as destruction of a draft card. Some forms of communication made possible by the giving and spending of money involve speech alone, some involve conduct primarily, and some involve a combination of the two. Yet this Court has never suggested that the dependence of a communication on the expenditure of money operates itself to introduce a nonspeech element or to reduce the exacting scrutiny required by the First Amendment. [*E.g.*] *New York Times Co. v. Sullivan*. For example, in *Cox v. Louisiana*, 379 U.S. 559 (1965), the Court contrasted picketing and parading with a newspaper comment and a telegram by a citizen to a public official. The parading and picketing activities were said to constitute conduct "intertwined with expression and association," whereas the newspaper comment and the telegram were described as a "pure form of expression" involving "free speech alone" rather than "expression mixed with particular conduct."

Even if the categorization of the expenditure of money as conduct were accepted, the limitations challenged here would not meet the *O'Brien* test because the governmental interests advanced in support of the Act involve "suppressing communication." The interests served by the Act include restricting the voices of people and interest groups who have money to spend and reducing the overall scope of federal election campaigns. Although the Act does not focus on the ideas expressed by persons or groups subject to its regulations, it is aimed in part at equalizing the relative ability of all voters to affect electoral outcomes by placing a ceiling on expenditures for political expression by citizens and groups. Unlike *O'Brien*, where the Selective Service System's administrative interest in the preservation of draft cards was wholly unrelated to their use as a means of communication, it is beyond dispute that the interest in regulating the alleged "conduct" of giving or spending money "arises in some measure because the communication allegedly integral to the conduct is itself thought to be harmful."

Nor can the Act's contribution and expenditure limitations be sustained, as some of the parties suggest, by reference to the constitutional principles reflected in such decisions as *Cox v. Louisiana*, 379 U.S. 559 (1965); *Adderley v. Florida* (1966) [Chapter 9 Note]; and *Kovacs v. Cooper* (1949) [Chapter 7 Note]. Those cases stand for the proposition that the government may adopt reasonable time, place, and manner regulations, which do not discriminate among speakers or ideas, in order to further an important governmental interest unrelated to the restriction of communication. *See Erznoznik v. City of Jacksonville* (1975) [Chapter 3 Note]. In contrast to *O'Brien*, where the method of expression was held to be subject to prohibition, *Cox*, *Adderley*, and *Kovacs* involved place or manner restrictions on legitimate modes of expression — picketing, parading, demonstrating, and using a soundtruck. The critical difference between this case and those time, place, and manner cases is that the present Act's contribution and expenditure limitations impose direct quantity restrictions on political communication and association by persons, groups, candidates, and political parties in addition to any reasonable time, place, and manner regulations otherwise imposed.

A restriction on the amount of money a person or group can spend on political communication during a campaign necessarily reduces the quantity of expression by restricting the number of issues discussed, the depth of their exploration, and the size of the audience reached. This is because virtually every means of communicating ideas in today's mass society requires the expenditure of money. . . . The electorate's increasing dependence on television, radio, and other mass media for news and information has made these expensive modes of communication indispensable instruments of effective political speech.

The expenditure limitations contained in the Act represent substantial rather than merely theoretical restraints on the quantity and diversity of political speech. The $1,000 ceiling on spending "relative to a clearly identified candidate" would appear to exclude all citizens and groups except candidates, political parties, and the institutional press from any significant use of the most effective modes of communication. . . .

By contrast with a limitation upon expenditures for political expression, a limitation upon the amount that any one person or group may contribute to a candidate or political committee entails only a marginal restriction upon the contributor's ability to engage in free communication. A contribution serves as a general expression of support for the candidate and his views, but does not communicate the underlying basis for the support. The quantity of communication by the contributor does not increase perceptibly with the size of his contribution, since the expression rests solely on the undifferentiated, symbolic act of contributing. At most, the size of the contribution provides a very rough index of the intensity of the contributor's support for the candidate. A limitation on the amount of money a person may give to a candidate or campaign organization thus involves little direct restraint on his political communication, for it permits the symbolic expression of support evidenced by a contribution but does not in any way infringe the contributor's freedom to discuss candidates and issues. While contributions may result in political expression if spent by a candidate or an association to present views to the voters, the transformation of contributions into political debate involves speech by someone other than the contributor.

Given the important role of contributions in financing political campaigns, contribution restrictions could have a severe impact on political dialogue if the limitations prevented candidates and political committees from amassing the resources necessary for effective advocacy. There is no indication, however, that the contribution limitations imposed by the Act would have any dramatic adverse effect on the funding of campaigns and political associations. The overall effect of the Act's contribution ceilings is merely to require candidates and political committees to raise funds from a greater number of persons and to compel people who would otherwise contribute amounts greater than the statutory limits to expend such funds on direct political expression, rather than to reduce the total amount of money potentially available to promote political expression.

The Act's contribution and expenditure limitations also impinge on protected associational freedoms. Making a contribution, like joining a political party, serves to affiliate a person with a candidate. In addition, it enables like-minded persons to pool their resources in furtherance of common political goals. The Act's contribution ceilings thus limit one important means of associating with a candidate or committee, but leave the contributor free to become a member of any political association and to assist personally in the association's efforts on behalf of candidates. And the Act's contribution limitations permit associations and candidates to aggregate large sums of money to promote effective advocacy. By contrast, the Act's $1,000 limitation on independent expenditures "relative to a clearly identified candidate" precludes most associations from effectively amplifying the voice of their adherents, the original basis for the recognition of First Amendment protection of the freedom of association. *See NAACP v. Alabama*. The Act's constraints on the ability of independent associations and candidate campaign organizations to expend resources on political expression "is simultaneously an interference with the freedom of [their] adherents," *Sweezy v. New Hampshire*, 354 U.S. 234 (1957) (plurality opinion).

In sum, although the Act's contribution and expenditure limitations both implicate fundamental First Amendment interests, its expenditure ceilings impose significantly more severe restrictions on protected freedoms of political expression and association than do its limitations on financial contributions.

B. Contribution Limitations

1. The $1,000 Limitation on Contributions by Individuals and Groups to Candidates and Authorized Campaign Committees

Section 608(b) provides, with certain limited exceptions, that "no person shall make contributions to any candidate with respect to any election for Federal office which, in the aggregate, exceed $1,000." The statute defines "person" broadly to include "an individual, partnership, committee, association, corporation, or any other organization or group of persons." . . .

(a)

As the general discussion in Part I-A indicated, the primary First Amendment problem raised by the Act's contribution limitations is their restriction of one aspect of the contributor's freedom of political association. The Court's decisions involving associational freedoms establish that the right of association is a "basic constitutional freedom," *Kusper v. Pontikes*, 414 U.S. 51 (1973), that is "closely allied to freedom of speech and a right which, like free speech, lies at the foundation of a free society." *Shelton v. Tucker*, 364 U.S. 479 (1960). *See, e.g., NAACP v. Alabama*. In view of the fundamental nature of the right to associate, governmental "action which may have the effect of curtailing the freedom to associate is subject to the closest scrutiny." *NAACP v. Alabama*. Yet, it is clear that "[n]either the right to associate nor the right to participate in political activities is absolute." *CSC v. Letter Carriers*, 413 U.S. 548 (1973). Even a "'significant interference' with protected rights of political association" may be sustained if the State demonstrates a sufficiently important interest and employs means closely drawn to avoid unnecessary abridgment of associational freedoms. [E.g.] *Cousins v. Wigoda*, 419 U.S. 477 (1975).

Appellees argue that the Act's restrictions on large campaign contributions are justified by three governmental interests. According to the parties and amici, the primary interest served by the limitations and, indeed, by the Act as a whole, is the prevention of corruption and the appearance of corruption spawned by the real or imagined coercive influence of large financial contributions on candidates' positions and on their actions if elected to office. Two "ancillary" interests underlying the Act are also allegedly furthered by the $1,000 limits on contributions. First, the limits serve to mute the voices of affluent persons and groups in the election process and thereby to equalize the relative ability of all citizens to affect the outcome of elections. Second, it is argued, the ceilings may to some extent act as a brake on the skyrocketing cost of political campaigns and thereby serve to open the political system more widely to candidates without access to sources of large amounts of money.

It is unnecessary to look beyond the Act's primary purpose to limit the actuality and appearance of corruption resulting from large individual financial contributions in order to find a constitutionally sufficient justification for the $1,000 contribution limitation. Under a system of private financing of elections, a candidate lacking immense personal or family wealth must depend on financial contributions from others to provide the resources necessary to conduct a successful campaign. . . . To the extent that large contributions are given to secure a political quid pro quo from current and potential office holders, the integrity of our system of representative democracy is undermined. Although the scope of such pernicious practices can never be reliably ascertained, the deeply disturbing examples surfacing after the 1972 election demonstrate that the problem is not an illusory one.

Of almost equal concern as the danger of actual quid pro quo arrangements is the impact of the appearance of corruption stemming from public awareness of the opportunities for abuse inherent in a regime of large individual financial contributions. In *CSC v. Letter Carriers*, the Court found that the danger to "fair and effective government" posed by partisan political conduct on the part of federal employees charged with administering the law was a sufficiently important concern to justify broad restrictions on the employees' right of partisan political association. Here, as there, Congress could legitimately conclude that the avoidance of the appearance of improper influence "is also critical . . . if confidence in the system of representative Government is not to be eroded to a disastrous extent."

Appellants contend that the contribution limitations must be invalidated because bribery laws and narrowly drawn disclosure requirements constitute a less restrictive means of dealing with "proven and suspected quid pro quo arrangements." But laws making criminal the giving and taking of bribes deal with only the most blatant and specific attempts of those with money to influence governmental action. And [Congress] was surely entitled to conclude that disclosure was only a partial measure, and that contribution ceilings were a necessary legislative concomitant to deal with the reality or appearance of corruption inherent in a system permitting unlimited financial contributions, even when the identities of the contributors and the amounts of their contributions are fully disclosed.

The Act's $1,000 contribution limitation focuses precisely on the problem of large campaign contributions — the narrow aspect of political association where the actuality and potential for corruption have been identified — while leaving persons free to engage in independent political expression, to associate actively through volunteering their services, and to assist to a limited but nonetheless substantial extent in supporting candidates and committees with financial resources. Significantly, the Act's contribution limitations in themselves do not undermine to any material degree the potential for robust and effective discussion of candidates and campaign issues by individual citizens, associations, the institutional press, candidates, and political parties. . . .

We find that, under the rigorous standard of review established by our prior decisions, the weighty interests served by restricting the size of financial contributions to political candidates are sufficient to justify the limited effect upon First Amendment freedoms caused by the $1,000 contribution ceiling. . . .

4. The $25,000 Limitation on Total Contributions During any Calendar Year

In addition to the $1,000 limitation on the nonexempt contributions that an individual may make to a particular candidate for any single election, the Act contains an overall $25,000 limitation on total contributions by an individual during any calendar year. . . . The overall $25,000 ceiling does impose an ultimate restriction upon the number of candidates and committees with which an individual may associate himself by means of financial support. But this quite modest restraint upon protected political activity serves to prevent evasion of the $1,000 contribution limitation by a person who might otherwise contribute massive amounts of money to a particular candidate through the use of unearmarked contributions to political committees likely to contribute to that candidate, or huge contributions to the candidate's political party. The limited, additional restriction on associational freedom imposed by the overall ceiling is thus no more than a corollary of the basic individual contribution limitation that we have found to be constitutionally valid.

C. Expenditure Limitations

The Act's expenditure ceilings impose direct and substantial restraints on the quantity of political speech. The most drastic of the limitations restricts individuals and groups, including political parties that fail to place a candidate on the ballot, to an expenditure of $1,000 "relative to a clearly identified candidate during a calendar year." Other expenditure ceilings limit spending by candidates, their campaigns, and political parties in connection with election campaigns. It is clear that a primary effect of these expenditure limitations is to restrict the quantity of campaign speech by individuals, groups, and candidates. The restrictions, while neutral as to the ideas expressed, limit political expression "at the core of our electoral process and of the First Amendment freedoms." *Williams v. Rhodes*, 393 U.S. 23 (1968).

1. The $1,000 Limitation on Expenditures "Relative to a Clearly Identified Candidate"

Section 608(e)(1) provides that "[n]o person may make any expenditure . . . relative to a clearly identified candidate during a calendar year which, when added to all other expenditures made by such person during the year advocating the election or defeat of such candidate, exceeds $1,000." The plain effect of § 608(e)(1) is to prohibit all individuals, who are neither candidates nor owners of institutional press facilities, and all groups, except political parties and campaign organizations, from voicing their views "relative to a clearly identified candidate" through means that entail aggregate expenditures of more than $1,000 during a calendar year. The provision, for example, would make it a federal criminal offense for a person or association to place a single one-quarter page advertisement "relative to a clearly identified candidate" in a major metropolitan newspaper.

[In order to save the statute from possible unconstitutional vagueness, the Court construed the phrase "relative to a clearly identified candidate" to require that in order to come within the statute's restrictions, the advertisements contain "explicit words of advocacy of election or defeat of a candidate."]

We turn then to the basic First Amendment question — whether § 608(e)(1), even as thus narrowly and explicitly construed, impermissibly burdens the constitutional right of free expression. . . .

The discussion in Part I-A explains why the Act's expenditure limitations impose far greater restraints on the freedom of speech and association than do its contribution limitations. The markedly greater burden on basic freedoms caused by § 608(e)(1) thus cannot be sustained simply by invoking the interest in maximizing the effectiveness of the less intrusive contribution limitations. Rather, the constitutionality of § 608(e)(1) turns on whether the governmental interests advanced in its support satisfy the exacting scrutiny applicable to limitations on core First Amendment rights of political expression.

We find that the governmental interest in preventing corruption and the appearance of corruption is inadequate to justify § 608(e)(1)'s ceiling on independent expenditures. First, assuming, arguendo, that large independent expenditures pose the same dangers of actual or apparent quid pro quo arrangements as do large contributions, § 608(e)(1) does not provide an answer that sufficiently relates to the elimination of those dangers. Unlike the contribution limitations' total ban on the giving of large amounts of money to candidates, § 608(e)(1) prevents only some large expenditures. So long as persons and groups eschew expenditures that in express terms advocate the election or defeat of a clearly identified candidate, they are free to spend as much as they want to promote the candidate and his views. The exacting interpretation of the statutory language necessary to avoid unconstitutional vagueness thus undermines the limitation's effectiveness as a loophole-closing provision by facilitating circumvention by those seeking to exert improper influence upon a candidate or office-holder. . . .

Second, quite apart from the shortcomings of § 608(e)(1) in preventing any abuses generated by large independent expenditures, the independent advocacy restricted by the provision does not presently appear to pose dangers of real or apparent corruption comparable to those identified with large campaign contributions. The parties defending § 608(e)(1) contend that it is necessary to prevent would-be contributors from avoiding the contribution limitations by the simple expedient of paying directly for media advertisements or for other portions of the candidate's campaign activities. They argue that expenditures controlled by or coordinated with the candidate and his campaign might well have virtually the same value to the candidate as a contribution and would pose similar dangers of abuse. Yet such controlled or coordinated expenditures are treated as contributions rather than expenditures under the Act. Section 608(b)'s contribution ceilings rather than § 608(e)(1)'s independent expenditure limitation prevent attempts to circumvent the Act through prearranged or coordinated expenditures amounting to disguised contributions. By contrast, § 608(e)(1) limits expenditures for express advocacy of candidates made totally independently of the candidate and his campaign. Unlike contributions, such independent expenditures may well provide little assistance to the candidate's campaign and indeed may prove counterproductive. The absence of prearrangement and coordination of an expenditure with the candidate or his agent not only undermines the value of the expenditure to the candidate, but also alleviates the danger that expenditures will be given as a quid pro quo for improper commitments from the candidate. Rather than preventing circumvention of the contribution limitations, § 608(e)(1) severely restricts all independent advocacy despite its substantially diminished potential for abuse.

While the independent expenditure ceiling thus fails to serve any substantial governmental interest in stemming the reality or appearance of corruption in the electoral process, it heavily burdens core First Amendment expression. . . .

It is argued, however, that the ancillary governmental interest in equalizing the relative ability of individuals and groups to influence the outcome of elections serves to justify the limitation on express advocacy of the election or defeat of candidates imposed by § 608(e)(1)'s expenditure ceiling. But the concept that government may restrict the speech of some elements of our society in order to enhance the relative voice of others is wholly foreign to the First Amendment, which was designed "to secure 'the widest possible dissemination of information from diverse and antagonistic sources,'" and "'to assure unfettered interchange of ideas for the bringing about of political and social changes desired by the people.'" *New York Times Co. v. Sullivan*, quoting *Roth*. The First Amendment's protection against governmental abridgment of free expression cannot properly be made to depend on a person's financial ability to engage in public discussion.

The Court's decisions in *Mills v. Alabama*, 384 U.S. 214 (1966), and *Miami Herald Publishing Co. v. Tornillo*, 418 U.S. 241 (1974) [Chapter 10 Note], held that legislative restrictions on advocacy of the election or defeat of political candidates are wholly at odds with the guarantees of the First Amendment. In *Mills*, the Court addressed the question whether "a State, consistently with the United States Constitution, can make it a crime for the editor of a daily newspaper to write and publish an editorial *on election day* urging people to vote a certain way on issues submitted to them." We held that "no test of reasonableness can save [such] a state law from invalidation as a violation of the First Amendment." Yet the prohibition of election day-editorials invalidated in *Mills* is clearly a lesser intrusion on constitutional freedom than a $1,000 limitation on the amount of money any person or association can spend *during an entire election year* in advocating the election or defeat of a candidate for public office. More recently in *Tornillo*, the Court held that Florida could not constitutionally require a newspaper to make space available for a political candidate to reply to its criticism. Yet under the Florida statute, every newspaper was free to criticize any candidate as much as it pleased so long as it undertook the modest burden of printing his reply. The legislative restraint involved in *Tornillo* thus also pales in comparison to the limitations imposed by §608(e)(1).

For the reasons stated, we conclude that §608(e)(1)'s independent expenditure limitation is unconstitutional under the First Amendment.

2. Limitation on Expenditures by Candidates from Personal or Family Resources

The Act also sets limits on expenditures by a candidate "from his personal funds, or the personal funds of his immediate family, in connection with his campaigns during any calendar year." §608(a)(1). These ceilings vary from $50,000 for Presidential or Vice Presidential candidates to $35,000 for senatorial candidates, and $25,000 for most candidates for the House of Representatives.

The ceiling on personal expenditures by candidates on their own behalf, like the limitations on independent expenditures contained in §608(e)(1), imposes a substantial restraint on the ability of persons to engage in protected First Amendment expression. The candidate, no less than any other person, has a First Amendment right to engage in the discussion of public issues and vigorously and tirelessly to advocate his own election and the election of other candidates. Indeed, it is of particular importance that candidates have the unfettered opportunity to make their views known so that the electorate may intelligently evaluate the candidates' personal qualities and their positions on vital public issues before choosing among them on election day. . . .

The primary governmental interest served by the Act—the prevention of actual and apparent corruption of the political process—does not support the limitation on the candidate's expenditure of his own personal funds. As the Court of Appeals concluded: "Manifestly, the core problem of avoiding undisclosed and undue influence on candidates from outside interests has lesser application when the monies involved come from the candidate himself or from his immediate family." . . .

The ancillary interest in equalizing the relative financial resources of candidates competing for elective office, therefore, provides the sole relevant rationale for §608(a)'s expenditure ceiling. That interest is clearly not sufficient to justify the provision's infringement of fundamental First Amendment rights. First, the limitation may fail to promote financial equality among candidates. A candidate who spends less of his personal resources on his campaign may nonetheless outspend his rival as a result of more successful fundraising efforts. . . . Second, and more fundamentally, the First Amendment simply cannot tolerate § 608(a)'s restriction upon the freedom of a candidate to speak without legislative limit on behalf of his own candidacy. We therefore hold that § 608(a)'s restriction on a candidate's personal expenditures is unconstitutional.

3. Limitations on Campaign Expenditures

Section 608(c) places limitations on overall campaign expenditures by candidates seeking nomination for election and election to federal office. Presidential candidates may spend $10,000,000 in seeking nomination for office and an additional $20,000,000 in the general election campaign. The ceiling on senatorial campaigns is pegged to the size of the voting-age population of the State with minimum dollar amounts applicable to campaigns in States with small populations. . . . These ceilings are to be adjusted upwards at the beginning of each calendar year by the average percentage rise in the consumer price index for the 12 preceding months.

No governmental interest that has been suggested is sufficient to justify the restriction on the quantity of political expression imposed by § 608(c)'s campaign expenditure limitations. The major evil associated with rapidly increasing campaign expenditures is the danger of candidate dependence on large contributions. The interest in alleviating the corrupting influence of large contributions is served by the Act's contribution limitations and disclosure provisions rather than by § 608(c)'s campaign expenditure ceilings. The Court of Appeals' assertion that the expenditure restrictions are necessary to reduce the incentive to circumvent direct contribution limits is not persuasive. There is no indication that the substantial criminal penalties for violating the contribution ceilings combined with the political repercussion of such violations will be insufficient to police the contribution provisions. . . . Moreover, as the Court of Appeals noted, the Act permits an officeholder or successful candidate to retain contributions in excess of the expenditure ceiling and to use these funds for "any other lawful purpose." This provision undercuts whatever marginal role the expenditure limitations might otherwise play in enforcing the contribution ceilings.

The interest in equalizing the financial resources of candidates competing for federal office is no more convincing a justification for restricting the scope of federal election campaigns. Given the limitation on the size of outside contributions, the financial resources available to a candidate's campaign, like the number of volunteers recruited, will normally vary with the size and intensity of the candidate's support. There is nothing invidious, improper, or unhealthy in permitting such funds to be spent to carry the candidate's message to the electorate. . . .

The campaign expenditure ceilings appear to be designed primarily to serve the governmental interests in reducing the allegedly skyrocketing costs of political campaigns. . . . [T]he mere growth in the cost of federal election campaigns in and of itself provides no basis for governmental restrictions on the quantity of campaign spending and the resulting limitation on the scope of federal campaigns. . . . In the free society ordained by our Constitution it is not the government, but the people individually as citizens and candidates and collectively as associations and political committees who must retain control over the quantity and range of debate on public issues in a political campaign. . . .

II. REPORTING AND DISCLOSURE REQUIREMENTS

Unlike the limitations on contributions and expenditures imposed by 18 U.S.C. § 608, the disclosure requirements of the Act, 2 U.S.C. § 431 *et seq.*, are not challenged by appellants as *per se* unconstitutional restrictions on the exercise of First Amendment freedoms of speech and association. . . . The particular requirements embodied in the Act are attacked as overbroad—both in their application to minor-party and independent candidates and in their extension to contributions as small as $11 or $101. Appellants also challenge the provision for disclosure by those who make independent contributions and expenditures, § 434(e). The Court of Appeals found no constitutional infirmities in the provisions challenged here. We affirm the determination on overbreadth and hold that § 434(e), if narrowly construed, also is within constitutional bounds. . . .

The Act presently under review replaced all prior disclosure laws. Its primary disclosure provisions impose reporting obligations on "political committees" and candidates. . . .

Each political committee is required to register with the Commission and to keep detailed records of both contributions and expenditures. These records must include the name and address of everyone making a contribution in excess of $10, along with the date and amount of the contribution. If a person's contributions aggregate more than $100, his occupation and principal place of business are also to be included. . . .

Each committee and each candidate also is required to file quarterly reports. The reports are to contain detailed financial information, including the full name, mailing address, occupation, and principal place of business of each person who has contributed over $100 in a calendar year, as well as the amount and date of the contributions. They are to be made available by the Commission "for public inspection and copying." . . .

A. General Principles

Unlike the overall limitations on contributions and expenditures, the disclosure requirements impose no ceiling on campaign-related activities. But we have repeatedly found that compelled disclosure, in itself, can seriously infringe on privacy of association and belief guaranteed by the First Amendment. E.g., *Bates v. Little Rock*, 361 U.S. 516 (1960); *NAACP v. Alabama* (1958) [*supra* Chapter 10].

We long have recognized that significant encroachments on First Amendment rights of the sort that compelled disclosure imposes cannot be justified by a mere showing of some legitimate governmental interest. Since *NAACP v. Alabama* we have required that the subordinating interests of the State must survive exacting scrutiny. We also have insisted that there be a "relevant correlation" or "substantial relation" between the governmental interest and the information required to be disclosed. This type of scrutiny is necessary even if any deterrent effect on the exercise of First Amendment rights arises, not through direct government action, but indirectly as an unintended but inevitable result of the government's conduct in requiring disclosure. *NAACP v. Alabama.* . . .

The strict test established by *NAACP v. Alabama* is necessary because compelled disclosure has the potential for substantially infringing the exercise of First Amendment rights. But we have acknowledged that there are governmental interests sufficiently important to outweigh the possibility of infringement, particularly when the "free functioning of our national institutions" is involved. *Communist Party v. Subversive Activities Control Bd.*, 367 U.S. 1 (1961).

The governmental interests sought to be vindicated by the disclosure requirements are of this magnitude. They fall into three categories. First, disclosure provides the electorate with information "as to where political campaign money comes from and how it is spent by the candidate" in order to aid the voters in evaluating those who seek federal office. . . .

Second, disclosure requirements deter actual corruption and avoid the appearance of corruption by exposing large contributions and expenditures to the light of publicity. . . . In enacting these requirements [Congress] may have been mindful of Mr. Justice Brandeis' advice:

> Publicity is justly commended as a remedy for social and industrial diseases. Sunlight is said to be the best of disinfectants; electric light the most efficient policeman.

Third, and not least significant, recordkeeping, reporting, and disclosure requirements are an essential means of gathering the data necessary to detect violations of the contribution limitations described above.

The disclosure requirements, as a general matter, directly serve substantial governmental interests. In determining whether these interests are sufficient to justify the requirements we must look to the extent of the burden that they place on individual rights.

It is undoubtedly true that public disclosure of contributions to candidates and political parties will deter some individuals who otherwise might contribute. In some instances, disclosure may even expose contributors to harassment or retaliation. These are not insignificant burdens on individual rights, and they must be weighed carefully against the interests which Congress has sought to promote by this legislation. In this process, we note and agree with appellants' concession that disclosure requirements certainly in most applications appear to be the least restrictive means of curbing the evils of campaign ignorance and corruption that Congress found to exist. Appellants argue, however, that the balance tips against disclosure when it is required of contributors to certain parties and candidates. We turn now to this contention.

B. Application to Minor Parties and Independents

Appellants contend that the Act's requirements are overbroad insofar as they apply to contributions to minor parties and independent candidates because the governmental interest in this information is minimal and the danger of significant infringement on First Amendment rights is greatly increased.

1. Requisite Factual Showing

In *NAACP v. Alabama* the organization had "made an uncontroverted showing that on past occasions revelation of the identity of its rank-and-file members [had] exposed these members to economic reprisal, loss of employment, threat of physical coercion, and other manifestations of public hostility," and the State was unable to show that the disclosure it sought had a "substantial bearing" on the issues it sought to clarify. Under those circumstances, the Court held that "whatever interest the State may have in disclosure has not been shown to be sufficient to overcome petitioner's constitutional objections." . . .

There could well be a case, similar to [that] before the Court in *NAACP v. Alabama* . . . , where the threat to the exercise of First Amendment rights is so serious and the state interest furthered by disclosure so insubstantial that the Act's requirements cannot be constitutionally applied. But no appellant in this case has tendered record evidence of the sort proffered in *NAACP v. Alabama*. . . . On this record, the substantial public interest in disclosure identified by the legislative history of this Act outweighs the harm generally alleged. . . .

C. Section 434(e)

Section 434(e) requires "[e]very person (other than a political committee or candidate) who makes contributions or expenditures" aggregating over $100 in a calendar year "other than by contribution to a political committee or candidate" to file a statement with the Commission. Unlike the other disclosure provisions, this section does not seek the contribution list of any association. Instead, it requires direct disclosure of what an individual or group contributes or spends.

In considering this provision we must apply the same strict standard of scrutiny, for the right of associational privacy developed in *NAACP v. Alabama* derives from the rights of the organization's members to advocate their personal points of view in the most effective way. *NAACP*. . . .

[In order to obviate concerns that this provision was unconstitutionally vague, the Court construed it to impose reporting requirements only when the contributions are "earmarked for political purposes or authorized or requested by a candidate or his agent, to some person other than a candidate or political committee," and when the contributor makes "expenditures for communications that expressly advocate the election or defeat of a clearly identified candidate."]

Unlike 18 U.S.C. § 608(e)(1), § 434(e), as construed, bears a sufficient relationship to a substantial governmental interest. As narrowed, § 434(e), like § 608(e)(1), does not reach all partisan discussion for it only requires disclosure of those expenditures that expressly advocate a particular election result. This might have been fatal if the only purpose of §434(e) were to stem corruption or its appearance by closing a loophole in the general disclosure requirements. But the disclosure provisions, including §434(e), serve another, informational interest, and even as construed §434(e) increases the fund of information concerning those who support the candidates. . . .

Mr. Justice Stevens took no part in the consideration or decision of these cases.

Mr. Chief Justice Burger, concurring in part and dissenting in part. . . .

I agree fully with that part of the Court's opinion that holds unconstitutional the limitations the Act puts on campaign expenditures which "place substantial and direct restrictions on the ability of candidates, citizens, and associations to engage in protected political expression, restrictions that the First Amendment cannot tolerate." Yet when it approves similarly stringent limitations on contributions, the Court ignores the reasons it finds so persuasive in the context of expenditures. For me contributions and expenditures are two sides of the same First Amendment coin.

By limiting campaign contributions, the Act restricts the amount of money that will be spent on political activity and does so directly. . . . Limiting contributions, as a practical matter, will limit expenditures and will put an effective ceiling on the amount of political activity and debate that the Government will permit to take place. . . .

The Court attempts to separate the two communicative aspects of political contributions—the "moral" support that the gift itself conveys, which the Court suggests is the same whether the gift is $10 or $10,000, and the fact that money translates into communication. The Court dismisses the effect of the limitations on the second aspect of contributions: "[T]he transformation of contributions into political debate involves speech by someone other than the contributor." On this premise that contribution limitations restrict only the speech of "someone other than the contributor" rests the Court's justification for treating contributions differently from expenditures. The premise is demonstrably flawed; the contribution limitations will, in specific instances, limit exactly the same political activity that the expenditure ceilings limit, and at least one of the "expenditure" limitations the Court finds objectionable operates precisely like the "contribution" limitations.

The Court's attempt to distinguish the communication inherent in political *contributions* from the speech aspects of political *expenditures* simply "will not wash." We do little but engage in word games unless we recognize that people—candidates and contributors—spend money on political activity because they wish to communicate ideas, and their constitutional interest in doing so is precisely the same whether they or someone else utters the words.

The Court attempts to make the Act seem less restrictive by casting the problem as one that goes to freedom of association rather than freedom of speech. I have long thought freedom of association and freedom of expression were two peas from the same pod. . . .

At any rate, the contribution limits are a far more severe restriction on First Amendment activity than the sort of "chilling" legislation for which the Court has shown such extraordinary concern in the past. *See, e.g., Cohen v. California* (1971) [Chapter 3]; *see also* cases reviewed in *Miller v. California* (1973) [Chapter 2]. If such restraints can be justified at all, they must be justified by the very strongest of state interests. With this much the Court clearly agrees; the Court even goes so far as to note that legislation cutting into these important interests must employ "means closely drawn to avoid unnecessary abridgment of associational freedoms."

After a bow to the "weighty interests" Congress meant to serve, the Court then forsakes this analysis in one sentence: "Congress was surely entitled to conclude that disclosure was only a partial measure, and that contribution ceilings were a necessary legislative concomitant to deal with the reality or appearance of corruption . . . ." In striking down the limitations on campaign expenditures, the Court relies in part on its conclusion that other means—namely, disclosure and contribution ceilings—will adequately serve the statute's aim. It is not clear why the same analysis is not also appropriate in weighing the need for contribution ceilings in addition to disclosure requirements. Congress may well be entitled to conclude that disclosure was a "partial measure," but I had not thought until today that Congress could enact its conclusions in the First Amendment area into laws immune from the most searching review by this Court. . . .

Mr. Justice White, concurring in part and dissenting in part.

. . . I agree with the Court's conclusion and much of its opinion with respect to sustaining the disclosure provisions. I am also in agreement with the Court's judgment upholding the limitations on contributions. I dissent, however, from the Court's view that the expenditure limitations of [FECA] violate the First Amendment.

Concededly, neither the limitations on contributions nor those on expenditures directly or indirectly purport to control the content of political speech by candidates or by their supporters or detractors. What the Act regulates is giving and spending money, acts that have First Amendment significance not because they are themselves communicative with respect to the qualifications of the candidate, but because money may be used to defray the expenses of speaking or otherwise communicating about the merits or demerits of federal candidates for election. . . .

It would make little sense to me, and apparently made none to Congress, to limit the amounts an individual may give to a candidate or spend with his approval but fail to limit the amounts that could be spent on his behalf. Yet the Court permits the former while striking down the latter limitation. No more than $1,000 may be given to a candidate or spent at his request or with his approval or cooperation; but otherwise, apparently, a contributor is to be constitutionally protected in spending unlimited amounts of money in support of his chosen candidate or candidates. . . . For constitutional purposes it is difficult to see the difference between the two situations. I would take the word of those who know that limiting independent expenditures is essential to prevent transparent and widespread evasion of the contribution limits. . . .

In the first place, expenditure ceilings reinforce the contribution limits and help eradicate the hazard of corruption. . . . Without limits on total expenditures, campaign costs will inevitably and endlessly escalate. Pressure to raise funds will constantly build and with it the temptation to resort in "emergencies" to those sources of large sums, who, history shows, are sufficiently confident of not being caught to risk flouting contribution limits. Congress would save the candidate from this predicament by establishing a reasonable ceiling on all candidates. . . .

Besides backing up the contribution provisions . . . expenditure limits have their own potential for preventing the corruption of federal elections themselves. . . . One would be blind to history to deny that unlimited money tempts people to spend it on whatever money can buy to influence an election. On the assumption that financing illegal activities is low on the campaign organization's priority list, the expenditure limits could play a substantial role in preventing unethical practices. There just would not be enough of "that kind of money" to go around. . . .

It is also important to restore and maintain public confidence in federal elections. It is critical to obviate or dispel the impression that federal elections are purely and simply a function of money, that federal offices are bought and sold or that political races are reserved for those who have the facility and the stomach for doing whatever it takes to bring together those interests, groups, and individuals that can raise or contribute large fortunes in order to prevail at the polls.

The ceiling on candidate expenditures represents the considered judgment of Congress that elections are to be decided among candidates none of whom has overpowering advantage by reason of a huge campaign war chest. At least so long as the ceiling placed upon the candidates is not plainly too low, elections are not to turn on the difference in the amounts of money that candidates have to spend. This seems an acceptable purpose and the means chosen a common-sense way to achieve it. . . .

I also disagree with the Court's judgment that §608(a), which limits the amount of money that a candidate or his family may spend on his campaign, violates the Constitution. Although it is true that this provision does not promote any interest in preventing the corruption of candidates, the provision does, nevertheless, serve salutary purposes related to the integrity of federal campaigns. By limiting the importance of personal wealth, §608(a) helps to assure that only individuals with a modicum of support from others will be viable candidates. This in turn would tend to discourage any notion that the outcome of elections is primarily a function of money. Similarly, §608(a) tends to equalize access to the political arena, encouraging the less wealthy, unable to bankroll their own campaigns, to run for political office. . . .

Mr. Justice Marshall, concurring in part and dissenting in part.

I join in all of the Court's opinion except Part I-C-2, which deals with 18 U.S.C. §608(a). That section limits the amount a candidate may spend from his personal funds, or family funds under his control, in connection with his campaigns during any calendar year. The Court invalidates §608(a) as violative of the candidate's First Amendment rights. . . . I disagree. . . .

The Court views "[t]he ancillary interest in equalizing the relative financial resources of candidates" as the relevant rationale for § 608(a), and deems that interest insufficient to justify § 608(a). In my view the interest is more precisely the interest in promoting the reality and appearance of equal access to the political arena. Our ballot-access decisions serve as a reminder of the importance of the general interest in promoting equal access among potential candidates. *See, e.g., Lubin v. Panish*, 415 U.S. 709 (1974); *Bullock v. Carter*, 405 U.S. 134 (1972). While admittedly those cases dealt with barriers to entry different from those we consider here, the barriers to which § 608(a) is directed are formidable ones, and the interest in removing them substantial.

One of the points on which all Members of the Court agree is that money is essential for effective communication in a political campaign. It would appear to follow that the candidate with a substantial personal fortune at his disposal is off to a significant "headstart." . . . And even if the advantage can be overcome, the perception that personal wealth wins elections may not only discourage potential candidates without significant personal wealth from entering the political arena, but also undermine public confidence in the integrity of the electoral process.

The concern that candidacy for public office not become, or appear to become, the exclusive province of the wealthy assumes heightened significance when one considers the impact of § 608(b), which the Court today upholds. That provision prohibits contributions from individuals and groups to candidates in excess of $1,000, and contributions from political committees in excess of $5,000. While the limitations on contributions are neutral in the sense that all candidates are foreclosed from accepting large contributions, there can be no question that large contributions generally mean more to the candidate without a substantial personal fortune to spend on his campaign. Large contributions are the less wealthy candidate's only hope of countering the wealthy candidate's immediate access to substantial sums of money. With that option removed, the less wealthy candidate is without the means to match the large initial expenditures of money of which the wealthy candidate is capable. In short, the limitations on contributions put a premium on a candidate's personal wealth.

In view of § 608(b)'s limitations on contributions, then, § 608(a) emerges not simply as a device to reduce the natural advantage of the wealthy candidate, but as a provision providing some symmetry to a regulatory scheme that otherwise enhances the natural advantage of the wealthy. Regardless of whether the goal of equalizing access would justify a legislative limit on personal candidate expenditures standing by itself, I think it clear that that goal justifies § 608(a)'s limits when they are considered in conjunction with the remainder of the Act. I therefore respectfully dissent from the Court's invalidation of § 608(a).

In addition to § 608(a), § 608(c), which limits overall candidate expenditures in a campaign, also provides a check on the advantage of the wealthy candidate. But we today invalidate that section, which unlike § 608(a) imposes a flat prohibition on candidate expenditures above a certain level, and which is less tailored to the interest in equalizing access than § 608(a). The effect of invalidating both § 608(c) and § 608(a) is to enable the wealthy candidate to spend his personal resources without limit, while his less wealthy opponent is forced to make do with whatever amount he can accumulate through relatively small contributions.

MR. JUSTICE BLACKMUN, concurring in part and dissenting in part.

I am not persuaded that the Court makes, or indeed is able to make, a principled constitutional distinction between the contribution limitations, on the one hand, and the expenditure limitations on the other, that are involved here. I therefore do not join Part I-B of the Court's opinion or those portions of Part I-A that are consistent with Part I-B. As to those, I dissent. . . .

I do join the remainder of the Court's opinion . . . .

MR. JUSTICE REHNQUIST, concurring in part and dissenting in part. [Omitted.]

Note: Buckley *and Its Progeny*

1. *Buckley v. Valeo* was decided by only eight justices; Justice Stevens did not take his seat on the Court until after oral argument. Five justices agreed that the restrictions on expenditures in FECA violated the First Amendment but that the restrictions on contributions were constitutional. Three Justices rejected the distinction between the two types of regulations. Justice White would have upheld the restrictions on expenditures as well as the restrictions on contributions; Chief Justice Burger and Justice Blackmun would have ruled that both were unconstitutional.

2. *Buckley* is sometimes viewed as resting on the proposition that "money is speech." The Court does not say that, but it does say (in Part I-A) that "virtually every means of communicating ideas in today's mass society requires the expenditure of money." A quarter of a century later, Justice Stevens—who, as noted above, took no part in *Buckley*— articulated a different view. In a concurring opinion in *Nixon v. Shrink Missouri Government PAC*, 528 U.S. 377 (2000), he suggested that the protection of property and liberty interests, not First Amendment interests, adequately explained *Buckley*'s invalidation of limits on campaign expenditures. Justice Stevens stated: "Money is property; it is not speech."

Is this a preferable way of analyzing campaign finance regulation? Consider this question as you study the issues raised by the materials presented in the rest of this chapter.

3. Far from resolving the constitutionality of campaign finance regulation, *Buckley* was only an early round in a long and continuing series of battles over campaign finance regulation and the First Amendment. Those battles involved a large number of issues, many of which are too intricate for a general book on First Amendment law. The remainder of this chapter focuses on three basic issues: corporate and union political speech rights, requirements that funders of political speech disclose their identities, and government attempts to prevent circumvention of the contribution limits upheld in *Buckley*.

B. Corporate and Union Political Speech

Note: Corporate and Union Speech, Electoral Integrity, and the First Amendment

1. *Buckley*'s expenditure/contribution distinction is probably the deepest faultline at the intersection of campaign finance and the First Amendment. Until recently, however, attention has focused on a second issue that proved to be even more controversial: the speech rights of corporations and unions. Between 1978 and 2003, the Court decided a series of cases considering this issue, which set the stage for the Court's decision in *Citizens United v. Federal Election Commission*, 558 U.S. 310 (2010), which is excerpted after this extended note, and in which the justices debated the meaning of these cases.

Bellotti: Two years after *Buckley*, the Court decided *First National Bank of Boston v. Bellotti*, 435 U.S. 765 (1978). In *Bellotti*, a five-justice majority struck down a law that severely limited corporations' ability to make contributions or expenditures "for the purpose of . . . influencing or affecting the vote on any question submitted to the voters, other than one materially affecting any of the property, business or assets of the corporation." As explained by Justice Powell, who wrote for the majority, the state defended his law by asserting both its "interest in sustaining the active role of the individual citizen in the electoral process and thereby preventing diminution of the citizen's confidence in government," and its interest in protecting the rights of shareholders "whose views differ from those expressed by management on behalf of the corporation."

Justice Powell began his consideration of these interests by distinguishing the case before the Court from one involving "partisan candidate elections." He observed that "[h]owever weighty [the state's] interests may be in the context of partisan candidate elections, they are either not implicated in this case or are not served at all, or in other than a random matter." In a footnote appended to this sentence (footnote 26 of the opinion), he elaborated on the referendum/election distinction, writing that federal and state laws restricting or prohibiting corporate spending on elections were motivated by an "overriding concern" with "the problem of corruption of elected officials through the creation of political debts." He continued: "The case before us presents no comparable problem, and our consideration of a corporation's right to speak on issues of general public interest implies no comparable right in the quite different context of participation in a political campaign for election to public office. Congress might well be able to demonstrate the existence of a danger of real or apparent corruption in independent expenditures by corporations to influence candidate elections. *Cf. Buckley*."

Turning to the state's first interest, Justice Powell conceded that if the state had provided "record or legislative evidence that corporate advocacy threatened imminently to undermine democratic processes . . . those arguments would merit our consideration." But he concluded that "there has been no showing that the relative voice of corporations has been overwhelming or even significant in influencing referenda in

Massachusetts." He also rejected the state's shareholder-protection interest, noting that it was both under-inclusive and over-inclusive, given that, for example, the law did not regulate corporate lobbying in defiance of shareholder wishes, but regulated referendum spending even when shareholders unanimously approved. Chief Justice Burger joined the Court's opinion and wrote a separate concurrence to emphasize that the state law would allow restrictions on press entities doing business through the corporate form.

Justice White, joined by Justices Brennan and Marshall, dissented. He observed that corporate speech was divorced from the individual self-expression that animates much of the concern for free speech rights. He also noted that restrictions on speech leave natural persons "free to communicate their thoughts" individually. He also argued that corporate speech threatened "the role of the First Amendment as a guarantor of a free marketplace of ideas," reasoning in a manner that other justices later adopted:

> Ordinarily, the expenditure of funds to promote political causes may be assumed to bear some relation to the fervency with which they are held. Corporate political expression, however, is not only divorced from the convictions of individual corporate shareholders, but also, because of the ease with which corporations are permitted to accumulate capital, bears no relation to the conviction with which the ideas expressed are held by the communicator.

Justice White also endorsed the state's shareholder protection rationale. He found roughly analogous the Court's recognition, a term earlier in *Abood v. Detroit Board of Education* (*supra* Chapter 9), of the legitimacy of non-union members' First Amendment objections to subsidizing unions' political speech through closed-shop arrangements.

Writing only for himself, Justice Rehnquist wrote a more far-reaching dissent, questioning whether corporations, as state-created entities "with the blessings of perpetual life and limited liability," should enjoy free speech rights at all.

NRWC: Four years after *Bellotti*, in *Federal Election Commission v. National Right to Work Committee*, 459 U.S. 197 (1982) (*NRWC*), the Court unanimously upheld a federal law requiring corporations wishing to engage in electoral contributions or expenditures to do so only via a segregated fund, for which contributions could be solicited only from "members" of the corporation. Writing for all the justices, Justice Rehnquist found the law justified by two government purposes: first, "to ensure that substantial aggregations of wealth amassed by the special advantages which go with the corporate form of organization should not be converted into political 'war chests,' which could be used to incur political debts," and, second, "to protect the individuals who have paid money into a corporation or union for purposes other than the support of candidates from having that money used to support political candidates to who they may be opposed." He distinguished *Bellotti* by citing footnote 26 of that case, discussed above.

MCFL: In *Federal Election Commission v. Massachusetts Citizens for Life*, 479 U.S. 238 (1986) (*MCFL*), the Court considered the problem of political participation by non-profit, ideological corporations. *MCFL* involved a federal law that allows corporations and unions to fund electoral advocacy only if funded from segregated funds fed through voluntary contributions. Citing, among other cases, *NRWC*, Justice Brennan, writing for a five-justice majority, acknowledged that the Court had recognized the government's interest in regulating political uses of wealth earned by utilization of the corporate form. He also concluded that "[d]irect corporate spending on political activity raises the prospect that resources amassed in the economic marketplace may be used to provide an unfair advantage in the political marketplace."

Nevertheless, the five-justice majority struck down application of the statute to the organization in that case. According to Justice Brennan, the non-profit, ideological nature of the corporation in question did not pose threats to those interests. He wrote: "MCFL was formed to disseminate ideas, not to amass capital. The resources it has available are not a function of its success in the economic marketplace, but its popularity in the political marketplace."

Justice O'Connor joined most of Justice Brennan's opinion, including the parts described above. Chief Justice Rehnquist, joined by Justices White, Blackmun, and Stevens, dissented. They would have upheld application of the law to MCFL, deferring to congressional judgments about the kinds of political activity that raise the risk of corruption or its appearance.

Austin: Four years later, in *Austin v. Michigan Chamber of Commerce*, 494 U.S. 652 (1990), the Court upheld a Michigan law similar to the federal law at issue in *MCFL*, but involving a different type of plaintiff — a corporation (the Chamber of Commerce) that was formed for reasons that went beyond political expression, whose members joined for economic rather than ideological reasons, and that admitted for-profit corporations as members.

Applying strict scrutiny, a six-justice majority upheld the Michigan law. Writing for the Court, Justice Marshall concluded that the law targeted corruption — not classic, *quid pro quo* corruption, but what he described as "the corrosive and distorting effects of immense aggregations of wealth that are accumulated with the help of the corporate form and that have little or no correlation to the public's support for the corporation's political ideas." He also found that the law was "sufficiently narrowly tailored to achieve" this interest, because it allowed corporations to make political expenditures through segregated funds.

Justice Brennan, the author of *MCFL*, joined the majority but also wrote separately to emphasize the difference between the corporations at issue in those two cases, and also to note the shareholder protection rationale for the law. Justice Stevens also joined the majority and wrote separately to argue that combating the reality or appearance of corruption sufficed to justify limits on both corporate contributions and independent expenditures.

Justice Scalia dissented, attacking the majority's understanding of corruption as an "illiberal free-speech principle of 'one man, one minute,'" which had been "proposed and soundly rejected in *Buckley*." Justice Kennedy, joined by Justices O'Connor and

Scalia, also dissented. He conceded that language in *MCFL* supported the majority's analysis, but argued that the result contravened the fundamental principle of that case, that non-profit corporations enjoy full First Amendment protection when speaking about electoral candidates and elections.

The aftermath of Austin: *Austin*'s approval of restrictions on corporate electoral expenditures led corporations to spend large amounts of money on so-called "issue ads." Issue ads are ads that do not expressly advocate the election or defeat of a candidate, but instead advocate a particular position on an issue and criticize or praise a candidate's stand on that issue. For example, such an ad might call for increased military spending, note that Candidate X opposed such an increase, and implore viewers to "call Candidate X and ask him why he refuses to protect America." Recall that as early as *Buckley* the Court (in Part I-C-1 of its opinion) construed the expenditure limitations imposed by the challenged law to apply only to funds used for communications that contain "explicit words of advocacy or defeat of a candidate." *MCFL* adopted a similar limiting construction on of the federal statutory prohibition on use of general corporate or union funds for electoral expenditures. In combination, then, *MCFL* and *Austin* upheld limits on corporate expenditures on electoral advocacy, but interpreted the relevant statutes to define such advocacy in a restricted way that exempted issue ads. This combination allowed corporations and unions to fund "issue ads." In a 2003 case the Court noted an estimate that corporations and unions spent hundreds of millions of dollars on issue ads during the 2000 election cycle.

After several years of deliberations, in 2002 Congress enacted an omnibus campaign finance regulation statute, the Bipartisan Campaign Reform Act ("BCRA"). Among (many) other things, in Section 203 BCRA regulated issue ads, which it called "electioneering communications" and defined as any broadcast communication that "refers to a clearly identified candidate for Federal office" and airs either 60 days before a general election or 30 days before a primary. Corporations and unions funding such communications could do so only out of segregated funds or PACs they establish.

McConnell: In *McConnell v. Federal Election Commission*, 540 U.S. 93 (2003), a five-justice majority upheld this provision of BCRA. Speaking through a joint opinion of Justices Stevens and O'Connor, the Court stated that "[s]ince our decision in *Buckley*, Congress's power to prohibit corporations and unions from using funds in their treasuries to finance advertisements expressly advocating the election or defeat of candidates in federal elections has been firmly embedded in our law." The Court identified the plaintiffs' claim as one that issue ads were not the functional equivalent of the express advocacy whose regulation was well-established as constitutional. It credited congressional testimony from campaign professionals that the most effective advocacy was often indirect rather than taking the form of explicit appeals to vote for or against a particular candidate. It also observed that the vast majority of such ads ran in the 60 days immediately preceding a federal election.

Four justices (Rehnquist, Scalia, Kennedy, and Thomas) dissented from this part of *McConnell*, and among them authored three separate opinions addressing this part of BCRA. Among other things, those opinions called for the overruling of *Austin*, without which they maintained nothing was left supporting Section 203, and criticized the general idea that corporate speech could be abridged.

2. Can you discern any themes in these cases? Do the cases upholding regulation of corporate and union speech make a persuasive case for restricting the political speech that is at the core of the First Amendment? Are these cases' discussions of corruption consistent with *Buckley*?

Citizens United v. Federal Election Commission

558 U.S. 310 (2010)

Justice Kennedy delivered the opinion of the Court.

Federal law prohibits corporations and unions from using their general treasury funds to make independent expenditures for speech defined as an "electioneering communication" or for speech expressly advocating the election or defeat of a candidate. 2 U.S.C. § 441b. Limits on electioneering communications were upheld in *McConnell v. Federal Election Comm'n* (2003). The holding of *McConnell* rested to a large extent on an earlier case, *Austin v. Michigan Chamber of Commerce* (1990). *Austin* had held that political speech may be banned based on the speaker's corporate identity.

In this case we are asked to reconsider *Austin* and, in effect, *McConnell*. It has been noted that "*Austin* was a significant departure from ancient First Amendment principles," *Federal Election Comm'n v. Wisconsin Right to Life, Inc.*, 551 U.S. 449 (2007) (*WRTL II*) (Scalia, J., concurring in part and concurring in judgment). We agree with that conclusion and hold that *stare decisis* does not compel the continued acceptance of *Austin*. The Government may regulate corporate political speech through disclaimer and disclosure requirements, but it may not suppress that speech altogether. We turn to the case now before us.

I

A

Citizens United is a nonprofit corporation. It . . . has an annual budget of about $12 million. Most of its funds are from donations by individuals; but, in addition, it accepts a small portion of its funds from for-profit corporations.

In January 2008, Citizens United released a film entitled *Hillary: The Movie*. We refer to the film as *Hillary*. It is a 90-minute documentary about then-Senator Hillary Clinton, who was a candidate in the Democratic Party's 2008 Presidential primary elections. *Hillary* mentions Senator Clinton by name and depicts interviews with political commentators and other persons, most of them quite critical of Senator Clinton. *Hillary* was released in theaters and on DVD, but Citizens United wanted to increase distribution by making it available through video-on-demand. . . .

To implement the proposal, Citizens United was prepared to pay for the video-on-demand; and to promote the film, it produced two 10-second ads and one 30-second ad for *Hillary*. Each ad includes a short (and, in our view, pejorative) statement about Senator Clinton, followed by the name of the movie and the movie's Website address.

Citizens United desired to promote the video-on-demand offering by running advertisements on broadcast and cable television.

B

Before the Bipartisan Campaign Reform Act of 2002 (BCRA), federal law prohibited—and still does prohibit—corporations and unions from using general treasury funds to make direct contributions to candidates or independent expenditures that expressly advocate the election or defeat of a candidate, through any form of media, in connection with certain qualified federal elections. BCRA § 203 amended § 441b to prohibit any "electioneering communication" as well. An electioneering communication is defined as "any broadcast, cable, or satellite communication" that "refers to a clearly identified candidate for Federal office" and is made within 30 days of a primary or 60 days of a general election. . . . Corporations and unions are barred from using their general treasury funds for express advocacy or electioneering communications. They may establish, however, a "separate segregated fund" (known as a political action committee, or PAC) for these purposes. The moneys received by the segregated fund are limited to donations from stockholders and employees of the corporation or, in the case of unions, members of the union.

C

Citizens United wanted to make *Hillary* available through video-on-demand within 30 days of the 2008 primary elections. It feared, however, that both the film and the ads would be covered by § 441b's ban on corporate-funded independent expenditures, thus subjecting the corporation to civil and criminal penalties under § 437g. In December 2007, Citizens United sought declaratory and injunctive relief against the FEC. It argued that (1) § 441b is unconstitutional as applied to *Hillary;* and (2) BCRA's disclaimer and disclosure requirements, BCRA §§ 201 and 311, are unconstitutional as applied to *Hillary* and to the three ads for the movie.

The District Court denied Citizens United's motion for a preliminary injunction, and then granted the FEC's motion for summary judgment . . . . We noted probable jurisdiction.

II

Before considering whether *Austin* should be overruled, we first address whether Citizens United's claim that § 441b cannot be applied to *Hillary* may be resolved on other, narrower grounds. [The Court considered, and rejected, the possibility that it rule for Citizens United on a narrower ground. First, the Court ruled that *Hillary* was an "electioneering communication" as that term is used in BCRA, rejecting Citizens United's argument that video-on-demand distribution did not count as the public distribution of communications regulated by BCRA. It next held that *Hillary* had to be understood as express advocacy, and thus subject to BCRA's limits on corporate speech.]

III

 . . . The law before us is an outright ban, backed by criminal sanctions. Section 441b makes it a felony for all corporations—including nonprofit advocacy corporations—either to expressly advocate the election or defeat of candidates or to broadcast electioneering communications within 30 days of a primary election and 60 days of a general election. Thus, the following acts would all be felonies under § 441b: The Sierra Club runs an ad, within the crucial phase of 60 days before the general election, that exhorts the public to disapprove of a Congressman who favors logging in national forests; the National Rifle Association publishes a book urging the public to vote for the challenger because the incumbent U.S. Senator supports a handgun ban; and the American Civil Liberties Union creates a Web site telling the public to vote for a Presidential candidate in light of that candidate's defense of free speech. These prohibitions are classic examples of censorship.

Section 441b is a ban on corporate speech notwithstanding the fact that a PAC created by a corporation can still speak. A PAC is a separate association from the corporation. So the PAC exemption from § 441b's expenditure ban does not allow corporations to speak. . . .

Section 441b's prohibition on corporate independent expenditures is thus a ban on speech. As a "restriction on the amount of money a person or group can spend on political communication during a campaign," that statute "necessarily reduces the quantity of expression by restricting the number of issues discussed, the depth of their exploration, and the size of the audience reached." *Buckley v. Valeo* (1976) [*supra* this chapter]. Were the Court to uphold these restrictions, the Government could repress speech by silencing certain voices at any of the various points in the speech process. If § 441b applied to individuals, no one would believe that it is merely a time, place, or manner restriction on speech. Its purpose and effect are to silence entities whose voices the Government deems to be suspect.

Speech is an essential mechanism of democracy, for it is the means to hold officials accountable to the people. . . . The First Amendment "has its fullest and most urgent application to speech uttered during a campaign for political office."

For these reasons, political speech must prevail against laws that would suppress it, whether by design or inadvertence. Laws that burden political speech are "subject to strict scrutiny," which requires the Government to prove that the restriction "furthers a compelling interest and is narrowly tailored to achieve that interest." . . .

Premised on mistrust of governmental power, the First Amendment stands against attempts to disfavor certain subjects or viewpoints. Prohibited, too, are restrictions distinguishing among different speakers, allowing speech by some but not others. *See First Nat. Bank of Boston v. Bellotti*, 435 U.S. 765 (1978) [Note *supra* this chapter]. As instruments to censor, these categories are interrelated: Speech restrictions based on the identity of the speaker are all too often simply a means to control content. . . .

The Court has upheld a narrow class of speech restrictions that operate to the disadvantage of certain persons, but these rulings were based on an interest in allowing governmental entities to perform their functions. *See, e.g., Bethel School Dist. No. 403 v. Fraser*, 478 U.S. 675 (1986) [Note *supra* Chapter 12] (protecting the "function of public school education"). The corporate independent expenditures at issue in this case, however, would not interfere with governmental functions, so these cases are inapposite. These precedents stand only for the proposition that there are certain governmental functions that cannot operate without some restrictions on particular kinds of speech. By contrast, it is inherent in the nature of the political process that voters must be free to obtain information from diverse sources in order to determine how to cast their votes. At least before *Austin*, the Court had not allowed the exclusion of a class of speakers from the general public dialogue.

A

1

The Court has recognized that First Amendment protection extends to corporations. *Bellotti* (citing *Linmark Associates, Inc. v. Willingboro*, 431 U.S. 85 (1977)); *Time, Inc. v. Firestone*, 424 U.S. 448 (1976) [Note *supra* Chapter 2]; *Southeastern Promotions, Ltd. v. Conrad*, 420 U.S. 546 (1975); *Miami Herald Publishing Co. v. Tornillo*, 418 U.S. 241 (1974); *New York Times Co. v. United States* (1971) (*per curiam*) [*supra* Chapter 4]; *Time, Inc. v. Hill*, 385 U.S. 374 (1967); *New York Times Co. v. Sullivan* (1964) [*supra* Chapter 2]); *see, e.g., Turner Broadcasting System v. FCC*, 512 U.S. 622 (1994); *Simon & Schuster, Inc. v. Members of New York State Crime Victims Board*, 502 U.S. 105 (1991) [Note *supra* Chapter 5]; *Sable Communications of Cal., Inc. v. FCC*, 492 U.S. 115 (1989); *Florida Star v. B.J.F.*, 491 U.S. 524 (1989); *Philadelphia Newspapers, Inc. v. Hepps*, 475 U.S. 767 (1986); *Young v. American Mini Theatres, Inc.*, 427 U.S. 50 (1976); *Gertz v. Robert Welch, Inc.* (1974) [*supra* Chapter 2].

This protection has been extended by explicit holdings to the context of political speech. *See, e.g., Grosjean v. American Press Co.*, 297 U.S. 233 (1936). Under the rationale of these precedents, political speech does not lose First Amendment protection "simply because its source is a corporation." *Bellotti*. The Court has thus rejected the argument that political speech of corporations or other associations should be treated differently under the First Amendment simply because such associations are not "natural persons."

At least since the latter part of the 19th century, the laws of some States and of the United States imposed a ban on corporate direct contributions to candidates. Yet not until 1947 did Congress first prohibit independent expenditures by corporations and labor unions . . . . In passing this Act Congress overrode the veto of President Truman, who warned that the expenditure ban was a "dangerous intrusion on free speech."

For almost three decades thereafter, the Court did not reach the question whether restrictions on corporate and union expenditures are constitutional. The question was in the background of *United States v. CIO*, 335 U.S. 106 (1948). There, a labor union endorsed a congressional candidate in its weekly periodical. The Court stated that "the gravest doubt would arise in our minds as to [the federal expenditure prohibition's] constitutionality" if it were construed to suppress that writing. The Court engaged in statutory interpretation and found the statute did not cover the publication. Four Justices, however, said they would reach the constitutional question and invalidate the Labor Management Relations Act's expenditure ban. The concurrence explained that any "undue influence" generated by a speaker's "large expenditures" was outweighed "by the loss for democratic processes resulting from the restrictions upon free and full public discussion."

In *United States v. Automobile Workers*, 352 U.S. 567 (1957), the Court again encountered the independent expenditure ban. After holding only that a union television broadcast that endorsed candidates was covered by the statute, the Court "[r]efus[ed] to anticipate constitutional questions" and remanded for the trial to proceed. Three Justices dissented, arguing that the Court should have reached the constitutional question and that the ban on independent expenditures was unconstitutional. . . . The dissent concluded that deeming a particular group "too powerful" was not a "justificatio[n] for withholding First Amendment rights from any group—labor or corporate." . . .

Later, in *Pipefitters v. United States*, 407 U.S. 385 (1972), the Court reversed a conviction for expenditure of union funds for political speech—again without reaching the constitutional question. The Court would not resolve that question for another four years.

2

In *Buckley*, the Court addressed various challenges to the Federal Election Campaign Act of 1971 (FECA) as amended in 1974. These amendments created 18 U.S.C. § 608(e), an independent expenditure ban separate from § 610 that applied to individuals as well as corporations and labor unions.

Before addressing the constitutionality of § 608(e)'s independent expenditure ban, *Buckley* first upheld § 608(b), FECA's limits on direct contributions to candidates. . . . This followed from the Court's concern that large contributions could be given "to secure a political *quid pro quo*."

The *Buckley* Court explained that the potential for *quid pro quo* corruption distinguished direct contributions to candidates from independent expenditures. The Court emphasized that "the independent expenditure ceiling . . . fails to serve any substantial governmental interest in stemming the reality or appearance of corruption in the electoral process," because "[t]he absence of prearrangement and coordination . . . alleviates the danger that expenditures will be given as a *quid pro quo* for improper commitments from the candidate." *Buckley* invalidated § 608(e)'s restrictions on independent expenditures, with only one Justice dissenting.

Buckley did not consider § 610's separate ban on corporate and union independent expenditures, the prohibition that had also been in the background in *CIO, Automobile Workers*, and *Pipefitters*. Had § 610 been challenged in the wake of *Buckley*, however, it could not have been squared with the reasoning and analysis of that precedent. The expenditure ban invalidated in *Buckley*, § 608(e), applied to corporations and unions, and some of the prevailing plaintiffs in *Buckley* were corporations. The *Buckley* Court did not invoke the First Amendment's overbreadth doctrine to suggest that § 608(e)'s expenditure ban would have been constitutional if it had applied only to corporations and not to individuals. *Buckley* cited with approval the *Automobile Workers* dissent, which argued that § 610 was unconstitutional.

Notwithstanding this precedent, Congress recodified § 610's corporate and union expenditure ban at 2 U.S.C. § 441b four months after *Buckley* was decided. Section 441b is the independent expenditure restriction challenged here.

Less than two years after *Buckley*, *Bellotti* reaffirmed the First Amendment principle that the Government cannot restrict political speech based on the speaker's corporate identity. *Bellotti* could not have been clearer when it struck down a state-law prohibition on corporate independent expenditures related to referenda issues:

> We thus find no support in the First . . . Amendment, or in the decisions of this Court, for the proposition that speech that otherwise would be within the protection of the First Amendment loses that protection simply because its source is a corporation that cannot prove, to the satisfaction of a court, a material effect on its business or property. . . . [That proposition] amounts to an impermissible legislative prohibition of speech based on the identity of the interests that spokesmen may represent in public debate over controversial issues and a requirement that the speaker have a sufficiently great interest in the subject to justify communication.

> ＊ ＊ ＊

> In the realm of protected speech, the legislature is constitutionally disqualified from dictating the subjects about which persons may speak and the speakers who may address a public issue.

It is important to note that the reasoning and holding of *Bellotti* did not rest on the existence of a viewpoint-discriminatory statute. It rested on the principle that the Government lacks the power to ban corporations from speaking.

Bellotti did not address the constitutionality of the State's ban on corporate independent expenditures to support candidates. In our view, however, that restriction would have been unconstitutional under *Bellotti*'s central principle: that the First Amendment does not allow political speech restrictions based on a speaker's corporate identity.

3

Thus the law stood until *Austin*. . . . To bypass *Buckley* and *Bellotti*, the *Austin* Court identified a new governmental interest in limiting political speech: an antidistortion interest. *Austin* found a compelling governmental interest in preventing "the corrosive and distorting effects of immense aggregations of wealth that are accumulated with the help of the corporate form and that have little or no correlation to the public's support for the corporation's political ideas."

B

The Court is thus confronted with conflicting lines of precedent: a pre-*Austin* line that forbids restrictions on political speech based on the speaker's corporate identity and a post-*Austin* line that permits them. No case before *Austin* had held that Congress could prohibit independent expenditures for political speech based on the speaker's corporate identity. . . .

In its defense of the corporate-speech restrictions in § 441b, the Government notes the antidistortion rationale on which *Austin* and its progeny rest in part, yet it all but abandons reliance upon it. It argues instead that two other compelling interests support *Austin*'s holding that corporate expenditure restrictions are constitutional: an anticorruption interest, see *Austin* (Stevens, J., concurring), and a shareholder-protection interest, see *Austin* (Brennan, J., concurring). We consider the three points in turn.

1

As for *Austin*'s antidistortion rationale, the Government does little to defend it. And with good reason, for the rationale cannot support § 441b. . . .

Austin interferes with the "open marketplace" of ideas protected by the First Amendment. It permits the Government to ban the political speech of millions of associations of citizens. Most of these are small corporations without large amounts of wealth. This fact belies the Government's argument that the statute is justified on the ground that it prevents the "distorting effects of immense aggregations of wealth." It is not even aimed at amassed wealth. . . .

2

. . . For the most part relinquishing the antidistortion rationale, the Government falls back on the argument that corporate political speech can be banned in order to prevent corruption or its appearance. In *Buckley*, the Court found this interest "sufficiently important" to allow limits on contributions but did not extend that reasoning to expenditure limits. . . .

A single footnote in *Bellotti* purported to leave open the possibility that corporate independent expenditures could be shown to cause corruption. *Bellotti* n.26 . . . . [We] now conclude that independent expenditures, including those made by corporations, do not give rise to corruption or the appearance of corruption. Dicta in *Bellotti*'s footnote suggested that "a corporation's right to speak on issues of general public interest implies no comparable right in the quite different context of participation in a political campaign for election to public office." Citing the portion of *Buckley* that invalidated the federal independent expenditure ban and a law review student comment, *Bellotti* surmised that "Congress might well be able to demonstrate the existence of a danger of real or apparent corruption in independent expenditures by corporations to influence candidate elections." *Bellotti* n.26. *Buckley*, however, struck down a ban on independent expenditures to support candidates that covered corporations, and explained that "the distinction between discussion of issues and candidates and advocacy of election or defeat of candidates may often dissolve in practical application." *Bellotti*'s dictum is thus supported only by a law review student comment, which misinterpreted *Buckley*.

Seizing on this aside in *Bellotti*'s footnote, the Court in *FEC v. National Right to Work Committee* (1982) [Note *supra* this chapter] did say there is a "sufficient" governmental interest in "ensur[ing] that substantial aggregations of wealth amassed" by corporations would not "be used to incur political debts from legislators who are aided by the contributions." *NRWC* (citing *Automobile Workers*). *NRWC* decided no more than that a restriction on a corporation's ability to solicit funds for its segregated PAC, which made direct contributions to candidates, did not violate the First Amendment. *NRWC* thus involved contribution limits, which, unlike limits on independent expenditures, have been an accepted means to prevent *quid pro quo* corruption. Citizens United has not made direct contributions to candidates, and it has not suggested that the Court should reconsider whether contribution limits should be subjected to rigorous First Amendment scrutiny.

When *Buckley* identified a sufficiently important governmental interest in preventing corruption or the appearance of corruption, that interest was limited to *quid pro quo* corruption. The fact that speakers may have influence over or access to elected officials does not mean that these officials are corrupt:

> Favoritism and influence are not . . . avoidable in representative politics. It is in the nature of an elected representative to favor certain policies, and, by necessary corollary, to favor the voters and contributors who support those policies. It is well understood that a substantial and legitimate reason, if not the only reason, to cast a vote for, or to make a contribution to, one candidate over another is that the candidate will respond by producing those political outcomes the supporter favors. Democracy is premised on responsiveness.

McConnell (opinion of Kennedy, J.).

Reliance on a "generic favoritism or influence theory . . . is at odds with standard First Amendment analyses because it is unbounded and susceptible to no limiting principle."

The appearance of influence or access, furthermore, will not cause the electorate to lose faith in our democracy. . . . The fact that a corporation, or any other speaker, is willing to spend money to try to persuade voters presupposes that the people have the ultimate influence over elected officials. This is inconsistent with any suggestion that the electorate will refuse "to take part in democratic governance" because of additional political speech made by a corporation or any other speaker. *McConnell*. . . .

The *McConnell* record was "over 100,000 pages" long, yet it "does not have any direct examples of votes being exchanged for . . . expenditures." This confirms *Buckley*'s reasoning that independent expenditures do not lead to, or create the appearance of, *quid pro quo* corruption. In fact, there is only scant evidence that independent expenditures even ingratiate. Ingratiation and access, in any event, are not corruption. The BCRA record establishes that certain donations to political parties, called "soft money," were made to gain access to elected officials. This case, however, is about independent expenditures, not soft money. When Congress finds that a problem exists, we must give that finding due deference; but Congress may not choose an unconstitutional remedy. If elected officials succumb to improper influences from independent expenditures; if they surrender their best judgment; and if they put expediency before principle, then surely there is cause for concern. We must give weight to attempts by Congress to seek to dispel either the appearance or the reality of these influences. The remedies enacted by law, however, must comply with the First Amendment; and, it is our law and our tradition that more speech, not less, is the governing rule. . . .

3

The Government contends further that corporate independent expenditures can be limited because of its interest in protecting dissenting shareholders from being compelled to fund corporate political speech. This asserted interest, like *Austin*'s antidistortion rationale, would allow the Government to ban the political speech even of media corporations. . . . The First Amendment does not allow that power. There is, furthermore, little evidence of abuse that cannot be corrected by shareholders "through the procedures of corporate democracy." *Bellotti*. . . .

D

Austin is overruled, so it provides no basis for allowing the Government to limit corporate independent expenditures. As the Government appears to concede, overruling *Austin* "effectively invalidate[s] not only BCRA Section 203, but also 2 U.S.C. 441b's prohibition on the use of corporate treasury funds for express advocacy." Section 441b's restrictions on corporate independent expenditures are therefore invalid and cannot be applied to *Hillary*.

Given our conclusion we are further required to overrule the part of *McConnell* that upheld BCRA § 203's extension of § 441b's restrictions on corporate independent expenditures. The *McConnell* Court relied on the antidistortion interest recognized in *Austin* to uphold a greater restriction on speech than the restriction upheld in *Austin*, and we have found this interest unconvincing and insufficient. This part of *McConnell* is now overruled. . . .

IV

[In part IV of the opinion the Court, now joined by the four partial dissenters but not by Justice Thomas, upheld BCRA's disclosure provisions. This part of the opinion is discussed in a Note, *infra*.]

V

When word concerning the plot of the movie *Mr. Smith Goes to Washington* reached the circles of Government, some officials sought, by persuasion, to discourage its distribution. Under *Austin*, though, officials could have done more than discourage its distribution—they could have banned the film. After all, it, like *Hillary*, was speech funded by a corporation that was critical of Members of Congress. *Mr. Smith Goes to Washington* may be fiction and caricature; but fiction and caricature can be a powerful force. . . .

Some members of the public might consider *Hillary* to be insightful and instructive; some might find it to be neither high art nor a fair discussion on how to set the Nation's course; still others simply might suspend judgment on these points but decide to think more about issues and candidates. Those choices and assessments, however, are not for the Government to make. "The First Amendment underwrites the freedom to experiment and to create in the realm of thought and speech. Citizens must be free to use new forms, and new forums, for the expression of ideas. The civic discourse belongs to the people, and the Government may not prescribe the means used to conduct it."

The judgment of the District Court is reversed with respect to the constitutionality of 2 U.S.C. § 441b's restrictions on corporate independent expenditures. The judgment is affirmed with respect to BCRA's disclaimer and disclosure requirements. The case is remanded for further proceedings consistent with this opinion. . . .

CHIEF JUSTICE ROBERTS, with whom JUSTICE ALITO joins, concurring. [Omitted.]

JUSTICE SCALIA, with whom JUSTICE ALITO joins, and with whom JUSTICE THOMAS joins in part, concurring.

I join the opinion of the Court.[1]

I write separately to address Justice Stevens' discussion of *"Original Understandings"* . . . . This section of the dissent purports to show that today's decision is not supported by the original understanding of the First Amendment. The dissent attempts this demonstration, however, in splendid isolation from the text of the First Amendment. It never shows why "the freedom of speech" that was the right of Englishmen did not include the freedom to speak in association with other individuals, including association in the corporate form. . . .

JUSTICE STEVENS, with whom JUSTICE GINSBURG, JUSTICE BREYER, and JUSTICE SOTOMAYOR join, concurring in part and dissenting in part.

The real issue in this case concerns how, not if, the appellant may finance its electioneering. Citizens United is a wealthy nonprofit corporation that runs a political action committee (PAC) with millions of dollars in assets. Under the Bipartisan Campaign Reform Act of 2002 (BCRA), it could have used those assets to televise and promote *Hillary: The Movie* wherever and whenever it wanted to. It also could have spent unrestricted sums to broadcast *Hillary* at any time other than the 30 days before the last primary election. Neither Citizens United's nor any other corporation's speech has been "banned." All that the parties dispute is whether Citizens United had a right to use the funds in its general treasury to pay for broadcasts during the 30-day period. The notion that the First Amendment dictates an affirmative answer to that question is, in my judgment, profoundly misguided. Even more misguided is the notion that the Court must rewrite the law relating to campaign expenditures by *for-profit* corporations and unions to decide this case.

The basic premise underlying the Court's ruling is its iteration, and constant reiteration, of the proposition that the First Amendment bars regulatory distinctions based on a speaker's identity, including its "identity" as a corporation. While that glittering generality has rhetorical appeal, it is not a correct statement of the law. . . .

The majority's approach to corporate electioneering marks a dramatic break from our past. Congress has placed special limitations on campaign spending by corporations ever since the passage of the Tillman Act in 1907. We have unanimously

---

1. Justice Thomas does not join Part IV of the Court's opinion.

concluded that this "reflects a permissible assessment of the dangers posed by those entities to the electoral process," *FEC v. National Right to Work Comm.*, 459 U.S. 197 (1982) (*NRWC*) [Note *supra* this chapter], and have accepted the "legislative judgment that the special characteristics of the corporate structure require particularly careful regulation." The Court today rejects a century of history when it treats the distinction between corporate and individual campaign spending as an invidious novelty born of *Austin v. Michigan Chamber of Commerce.* Relying largely on individual dissenting opinions, the majority blazes through our precedents . . . .

. . . Although I concur in the Court's decision to sustain BCRA's disclosure provisions and join Part IV of its opinion, I emphatically dissent from its principal holding. . . .

III

The novelty of the Court's procedural dereliction and its approach to *stare decisis* is matched by the novelty of its ruling on the merits. The ruling rests on several premises. First, the Court claims that *Austin* and *McConnell* have "banned" corporate speech. Second, it claims that the First Amendment precludes regulatory distinctions based on speaker identity, including the speaker's identity as a corporation. Third, it claims that *Austin* and *McConnell* were radical outliers in our First Amendment tradition and our campaign finance jurisprudence. Each of these claims is wrong.

The So-Called "Ban"

Pervading the Court's analysis is the ominous image of a "categorical ba[n]" on corporate speech. . . . This characterization is highly misleading, and needs to be corrected.

In fact it already has been. Our cases have repeatedly pointed out that, "[c]ontrary to the [majority's] critical assumptions," the statutes upheld in *Austin* and *McConnell* do "not impose an *absolute* ban on all forms of corporate political spending." For starters, both statutes provide exemptions for PACs, separate segregated funds established by a corporation for political purposes. "The ability to form and administer separate segregated funds," we observed in *McConnell*, "has provided corporations and unions with a constitutionally sufficient opportunity to engage in express advocacy. That has been this Court's unanimous view." . . .

The laws upheld in *Austin* and *McConnell* leave open many additional avenues for corporations' political speech. . . .

At the time Citizens United brought this lawsuit, the only types of speech that could be regulated under § 203 were: (1) broadcast, cable, or satellite communications; (2) capable of reaching at least 50,000 persons in the relevant electorate; (3) made within 30 days of a primary or 60 days of a general federal election; (4) by a labor union or a non-*MCFL*, nonmedia corporation; (5) paid for with general treasury funds; and (6) "susceptible of no reasonable interpretation other than as an appeal to vote for or against a specific candidate." The category of communications meeting all of these criteria is not trivial, but the notion that corporate political speech has been "suppress[ed] . . . altogether," that corporations have been "exclu[ded] . . . from the general public dialogue," or that a work of fiction such as *Mr. Smith Goes to Washington* might be covered is nonsense. . . .

Identity-Based Distinctions

The second pillar of the Court's opinion is its assertion that "the Government cannot restrict political speech based on the speaker's . . . identity." . . . Like its paeans to unfettered discourse, the Court's denunciation of identity-based distinctions may have rhetorical appeal but it obscures reality.

. . . The First Amendment provides that "Congress shall make no law . . . abridging the freedom of speech, or of the press." Apart perhaps from measures designed to protect the press, that text might seem to permit no distinctions of any kind. Yet in a variety of contexts, we have held that speech can be regulated differentially on account of the speaker's identity, when identity is understood in categorical or institutional terms. The Government routinely places special restrictions on the speech rights of students, prisoners, members of the Armed Forces, foreigners, and its own employees. When such restrictions are justified by a legitimate governmental interest, they do not necessarily raise constitutional problems.[46] . . .

. . . It is fair to say that our First Amendment doctrine has "frowned on" certain identity-based distinctions, particularly those that may reflect invidious discrimination or preferential treatment of a politically powerful group. But it is simply incorrect to suggest that we have prohibited all legislative distinctions based on identity or content. Not even close.

The election context is distinctive in many ways, and the Court, of course, is right that the First Amendment closely guards political speech. But in this context, too, the authority of legislatures to enact viewpoint-neutral regulations based on content and identity is well settled. We have, for example, . . . consistently approved laws that bar Government employees, but not others, from contributing to or participating in political activities. . . .

In short, the Court dramatically overstates its critique of identity-based distinctions, without ever explaining why corporate identity demands the same treatment as individual identity. Only the most wooden approach to the First Amendment could justify the unprecedented line it seeks to draw.

Our First Amendment Tradition

A third fulcrum of the Court's opinion is the idea that *Austin* and *McConnell* are radical outliers, "aberration[s]" in our First Amendment tradition. The Court has it exactly backwards. It is today's holding that is the radical departure from what had been settled First Amendment law. To see why, it is useful to take a long view.

---

46. The majority states that the cases just cited are "inapposite" because they "stand only for the proposition that there are certain governmental functions that cannot operate without some restrictions on particular kinds of speech." The majority's creative suggestion that these cases stand only for that one proposition is quite implausible. In any event, the proposition lies at the heart of this case, as Congress and half the state legislatures have concluded, over many decades, that their core functions of administering elections and passing legislation cannot operate effectively without some narrow restrictions on corporate electioneering paid for by general treasury funds.

1. *Original Understandings*

Let us start from the beginning. The Court invokes "ancient First Amendment principles" and original understandings to defend today's ruling, yet it makes only a perfunctory attempt to ground its analysis in the principles or understandings of those who drafted and ratified the Amendment. Perhaps this is because there is not a scintilla of evidence to support the notion that anyone believed it would preclude regulatory distinctions based on the corporate form. To the extent that the Framers' views are discernible and relevant to the disposition of this case, they would appear to cut strongly against the majority's position.

This is not only because the Framers and their contemporaries conceived of speech more narrowly than we now think of it, but also because they held very different views about the nature of the First Amendment right and the role of corporations in society. . . .

2. *Legislative and Judicial Interpretation*

A century of more recent history puts to rest any notion that today's ruling is faithful to our First Amendment tradition. At the federal level, the express distinction between corporate and individual political spending on elections stretches back to 1907, when Congress passed the Tillman Act, banning all corporate contributions to candidates. . . .

Over the years, the limitations on corporate political spending have been modified in a number of ways, as Congress responded to changes in the American economy and political practices that threatened to displace the commonweal. . . . The Taft-Hartley Act of 1947 is of special significance for this case. In that Act passed more than 60 years ago, Congress extended the prohibition on corporate support of candidates to cover not only direct contributions, but independent expenditures as well. The bar on contributions "was being so narrowly construed" that corporations were easily able to defeat the purposes of the Act by supporting candidates through other means.

Our colleagues emphasize that in two cases from the middle of the 20th century, several Justices wrote separately to criticize the expenditure restriction as applied to unions, even though the Court declined to pass on its constitutionality. Two features of these cases are of far greater relevance. First, those Justices were writing separately; which is to say, their position failed to command a majority. Prior to today, this was a fact we found significant in evaluating precedents. Second, each case in this line expressed support for the principle that corporate and union political speech financed with PAC funds, collected voluntarily from the organization's stockholders or members, receives greater protection than speech financed with general treasury funds.

This principle was carried forward when Congress enacted comprehensive campaign finance reform in the Federal Election Campaign Act of 1971 (FECA), which retained the restriction on using general treasury funds for contributions and expenditures. . . .

By the time Congress passed FECA in 1971, the bar on corporate contributions and expenditures had become such an accepted part of federal campaign finance regulation that when a large number of plaintiffs, including several nonprofit corporations, challenged virtually every aspect of the Act in *Buckley v. Valeo* (1976), no one even bothered to argue that the bar as such was unconstitutional. *Buckley* famously (or infamously) distinguished direct contributions from independent expenditures, but its silence on corporations only reinforced the understanding that corporate expenditures could be treated differently from individual expenditures. . . .

The corporate/individual distinction was not questioned by the Court's disposition, in 1986, of a challenge to the expenditure restriction as applied to a distinctive type of nonprofit corporation. In *Federal Election Comm'n v. Massachusetts Citizens for Life, Inc.*, 479 U.S. 238 (1986) (*MCFL*) [Note *supra* this chapter], we stated again "that 'the special characteristics of the corporate structure require particularly careful regulation'" (quoting *NRWC*), and again we acknowledged that the Government has a legitimate interest in "regulat[ing] the substantial aggregations of wealth amassed by the special advantages which go with the corporate form." Those aggregations can distort the "free trade in ideas" crucial to candidate elections at the expense of members or shareholders who may disagree with the object of the expenditures. What the Court held by a 5-to-4 vote was that a limited class of corporations must be allowed to use their general treasury funds for independent expenditures, because Congress' interests in protecting shareholders and "restrict[ing] the influence of political war chests funneled through the corporate form" did not apply to corporations that were structurally insulated from those concerns.

It is worth remembering for present purposes that the four *MCFL* dissenters, led by Chief Justice Rehnquist, thought the Court was carrying the First Amendment *too far*. They would have recognized congressional authority to bar general treasury electioneering expenditures even by this class of nonprofits . . . . Not a single Justice suggested that regulation of corporate political speech could be no more stringent than of speech by an individual.

Four years later, in *Austin*, we considered whether corporations falling outside the *MCFL* exception could be barred from using general treasury funds to make independent expenditures in support of, or in opposition to, candidates. We held they could be. . . . In light of the corrupting effects such spending might have on the political process, we permitted the State of Michigan to limit corporate expenditures on candidate elections to corporations' PACs, which rely on voluntary contributions and thus "reflect actual public support for the political ideals espoused by corporations." . . .

In the 20 years since *Austin*, we have reaffirmed its holding and rationale a number of times, most importantly in *McConnell*, where we upheld the provision challenged here, § 203 of BCRA. Congress crafted § 203 in response to a problem created by *Buckley*. . . . After *Buckley*, corporations and unions figured out how to circumvent the limits on express advocacy by using sham "issue ads" that "eschewed the use of magic words" but nonetheless "advocate[d] the election or defeat of clearly identified federal candidates." . . . Congress passed § 203 to address this circumvention, prohibiting corporations and unions from using general treasury funds for electioneering communications that "refe[r] to a clearly identified candidate," whether or not those communications use the magic words.

When we asked in *McConnell* "whether a compelling governmental interest justifie[d]" §203, we found the question "easily answered": "We have repeatedly sustained legislation aimed at the corrosive and distorting effects of immense aggregations of wealth that are accumulated with the help of the corporate form and that have little or no correlation to the public's support for the corporation's political ideas." . . .

3. Buckley *and* Bellotti

Against this extensive background of congressional regulation of corporate campaign spending, and our repeated affirmation of this regulation as constitutionally sound, the majority dismisses *Austin* as "a significant departure from ancient First Amendment principles." How does the majority attempt to justify this claim? Selected passages from two cases, *Buckley* and *First Nat. Bank of Boston v. Bellotti* (1978), do all of the work. In the Court's view, *Buckley* and *Bellotti* decisively rejected the possibility of distinguishing corporations from natural persons in the 1970's; it just so happens that in every single case in which the Court has reviewed campaign finance legislation in the decades since, the majority failed to grasp this truth. The Federal Congress and dozens of state legislatures, we now know, have been similarly deluded.

The majority emphasizes *Buckley*'s statement that "[t]he concept that government may restrict the speech of some elements of our society in order to enhance the relative voice of others is wholly foreign to the First Amendment." . . . It is not apparent why this is relevant to the case before us. The majority suggests that *Austin* rests on the foreign concept of speech equalization, but we made it clear in *Austin* (as in several cases before and since) that a restriction on the way corporations spend their money is no mere exercise in disfavoring the voice of some elements of our society in preference to others. Indeed, we *expressly* ruled that the compelling interest supporting Michigan's statute was not one of "equaliz[ing] the relative influence of speakers on elections," but rather the need to confront the distinctive corrupting potential of corporate electoral advocacy financed by general treasury dollars. . . .

The case on which the majority places even greater weight than *Buckley*, however, is *Bellotti*, claiming it "could not have been clearer" that *Bellotti*'s holding forbade distinctions between corporate and individual expenditures like the one at issue here. The Court's reliance is odd. The only thing about *Bellotti* that could not be clearer is that it declined to adopt the majority's position. *Bellotti* ruled, in an explicit limitation on the scope of its holding, that "our consideration of a corporation's right to speak on issues of general public interest implies no comparable right in the quite different context of participation in a political campaign for election to public office." *Bellotti* n.26. *Bellotti*, in other words, did not touch the question presented in *Austin* and *McConnell*, and the opinion squarely disavowed the proposition for which the majority cites it.

The majority attempts to explain away the distinction *Bellotti* drew—between general corporate speech and campaign speech intended to promote or prevent the election of specific candidates for office—as inconsistent with the rest of the opinion and with *Buckley*. Yet the basis for this distinction is perfectly coherent: The anticorruption interests that animate regulations of corporate participation in candidate elections, the "importance" of which "has never been doubted," do not apply equally to regulations of corporate participation in referenda. . . . The majority likewise overlooks the fact that, over the past 30 years, our cases have repeatedly recognized the candidate/issue distinction. The Court's critique of *Bellotti*'s footnote 26 puts it in the strange position of trying to elevate *Bellotti* to canonical status, while simultaneously disparaging a critical piece of its analysis as unsupported and irreconcilable with *Buckley*. *Bellotti*, apparently, is both the font of all wisdom and internally incoherent. . . .

The majority grasps a quotational straw from *Bellotti*, that speech does not fall entirely outside the protection of the First Amendment merely because it comes from a corporation. Of course not, but no one suggests the contrary and neither *Austin* nor *McConnell* held otherwise. They held that even though the expenditures at issue were subject to First Amendment scrutiny, the restrictions on those expenditures were justified by a compelling state interest. We acknowledged in *Bellotti* that numerous "interests of the highest importance" can justify campaign finance regulation. But we found no evidence that these interests were served by the Massachusetts law. We left open the possibility that our decision might have been different if there had been "record or legislative findings that corporate advocacy threatened imminently to undermine democratic processes, thereby denigrating rather than serving First Amendment interests."

Austin and *McConnell*, then, sit perfectly well with *Bellotti*. . . . The difference between the cases is not that *Austin* and *McConnell* rejected First Amendment protection for corporations whereas *Bellotti* accepted it. The difference is that the statute at issue in *Bellotti* smacked of viewpoint discrimination, targeted one class of corporations, and provided no PAC option; and the State has a greater interest in regulating independent corporate expenditures on candidate elections than on referenda, because in a functioning democracy the public must have faith that its representatives owe their positions to the people, not to the corporations with the deepest pockets. . . .

IV

. . . The majority recognizes that *Austin* and *McConnell* may be defended on anticorruption, antidistortion, and shareholder protection rationales. It badly errs both in explaining the nature of these rationales, which overlap and complement each other, and in applying them to the case at hand. . . . [Justice Stevens restated, explained, and defended *Austin* and *McConnell*'s analyses of these arguments.]

————

Problem: Corporate Contributions to an Independent Spender

Citizens for a Fantastic Economy ("CFE"), based in Chicago, is an association whose sole purpose is to make independent expenditures promoting political candidates who espouse CFE's views about sound government policy on the economy. Consolidated

Megacorp, a leading American business corporation, wishes to contribute $5,000,000 to CFE. Illinois law prohibits for-profit corporations from contributing more than $10,000 to "any person, association, corporation or other entity whose primary purpose is to advocate the election or defeat of political candidates." Is the Illinois law valid?

Would the result be different if CFE made both independent expenditures and contributions? In answering this question, assume that Illinois law prohibits any person from contributing more than $10,000 to a candidate during an election cycle.

Problem: A State Response to Citizens United?

The State of New Hope has traditionally had some of the nation's strictest campaign finance regulations. After *Citizens United*, the state legislature considered what room it still had to limit independent expenditures by corporations and unions. After much consideration, it enacted the following law:

New Hope Revised Statutes 10-14-389:

> a. An entity, other than an individual, shall not make an independent expenditure of over $750 advocating the defeat or election of a candidate for office in New Hope, or disburse funds from its treasury to pay for, in whole or in part, any such independent expenditure made by another person unless a majority of the entity's board of directors, executive council, or similar organizational leadership body authorizes such expenditure or disbursement. Such authorization must occur in the same calendar year in which the independent expenditure or disbursement is incurred.

> b. Such authorization shall expressly provide whether the board of directors, executive council, or similar organizational leadership body authorizes one or more independent expenditures that expressly advocate the nomination or election of a candidate or passage of a ballot issue or authorizes one or more independent expenditures that expressly advocate the defeat of a candidate or ballot issue.

Amalgamated Corporation, a large corporation headquartered in New Hope, sues to challenge the new law, alleging that it imposes restrictions on political speech that are inconsistent with *Citizens United*. What arguments could it make? How would a court analyze them?

C. Disclosure Requirements

Note: Disclosure Requirements and the First Amendment

1. *Buckley v. Valeo* upheld the disclosure requirements the plaintiffs in that case had challenged, even though the Court recognized the risk that such compelled disclosure could possibly chill protected associational activity. To account for that risk,

Buckley authorized future as-applied challenges to such requirements, when plaintiffs, unlike those in *Buckley*, could demonstrate that disclosure of their particular political associational activity would expose them to threats or harassment. Cases since *Buckley* have continued to adhere to these principles.

2. In *McConnell*, the Court upheld BCRA's reporting and disclosure requirements. Eight justices, speaking through two separate opinions, upheld its expansion of FEC reporting requirements to include those who spend more than $10,000 to fund electioneering activities. (Three of these justices dissented on a minor reporting provision.) These eight justices agreed that the reporting requirements were justified by the government interest in providing voters with more information. Just as in *Buckley*, the *McConnell* plaintiffs failed to show that their particular situation was such that disclosing their electoral activity put them at risk for threats or harassment from others.

The same eight justices, now speaking through Chief Justice Rehnquist, also upheld BCRA's requirement that so-called "issue ads" identify the source of their funding. He wrote: "We think BCRA § 311's inclusion of electioneering communications in [the preexisting] disclosure regime bears a sufficient relationship to the important governmental interest of 'shed[ding] the light of publicity' on campaign financing. *Buckley*." Only Justice Thomas dissented from these parts of *McConnell*.

3. In *Citizens United*, the Court upheld BCRA's disclosure requirements, enacted as BCRA §§ 201 and 311, as applied to the Citizens United group and its *Hillary* movie and ads for the movie. Section 311 requires, among other things, that the communication state the name of the party responsible for the ad and that it was not authorized by any candidate. It also requires that the communication display the name and address (or website) of the responsible party. Section 201 requires that parties spending more than $10,000 on electioneering communications within a calendar year file a disclosure statement with the FEC, including the person responsible for the expenditure, the amount spent, and the names of large contributors.

Writing for eight Justices, Justice Kennedy noted that, in the past, "[t]he Court has subjected [disclosure] requirements to 'exacting scrutiny,' which requires a 'substantial relation' between the disclosure statement and a 'sufficiently important' governmental interest." *Citizens United* (quoting *Buckley v. Valeo*). Again quoting *Buckley*, he described the government interest in disclosure as the "interest in 'provid[ing] the electorate with information' about the sources of election-related spending." He noted that the *McConnell* Court, in upholding the facial validity of these provisions, had found "evidence in the record that independent groups were running election-related advertisements while hiding behind dubious and misleading names." He then noted both *Buckley*'s and *McConnell*'s caveat that "as-applied challenges [to such requirements] would be available if a group could show a 'reasonable probability' that disclosure of its contributors' names 'will subject them to threats, harassment, or reprisals from either Government officials or private parties.'" *Citizens United* (quoting *McConnell* and *Buckley*).

Applying these principles, the Court upheld the requirements as applied to both the ads for *Hillary* and the movie itself, observing that "disclosure is a less restrictive alternative to more comprehensive regulation." The Court also concluded that Citizens United had "offered no evidence" that its members might face threats or reprisals if they were forced to disclose their identities. Justice Stevens and the four dissenters from the rest of Justice Kennedy's opinion joined his analysis of the disclosure provisions.

Justice Thomas, who had joined the rest of the Court's opinion, dissented from the part of the opinion upholding these provisions. Justice Thomas described "the right of anonymous speech" as one whose infringement was not justified by "the simple interest in providing voters with additional relevant information." He discussed events in California during and after the campaign over Proposition 8 (the 2008 California voter initiative that sought to reverse a state court decision in favor of same-sex marriage rights), where supporters and opponents received threats when their identities and addresses were disclosed as part of mandatory disclosure requirements for those contributing to initiative campaigns. He dismissed the possibility of an as-applied challenge to BCRA's disclosure requirements, arguing that speech would be chilled by the prospect of disclosure (and the possible threats that might ensue), "long before a plaintiff could prevail on an as-applied challenge." Quoting Justice Kennedy's analysis of the disclosure provisions, he noted: "now more than ever, [the disclosure provisions] will chill protected speech because — as California voters can attest — 'the advent of the Internet' enables 'prompt disclosure of expenditures,' which 'provide[s]' political opponents 'with the information needed' to intimidate and retaliate against their foes."

4. The same term as *Citizens United*, the Court decided a different, but related, type of campaign expression disclosure case. In *Doe v. Reed*, 561 U.S. 186 (2010), the Court rejected a challenge to a Washington State law mandating disclosure of public records, as that law generally applied to disclosure of the names and addresses of citizens who signed petitions seeking to place certain laws up for review in referenda. The plaintiffs in this case had signed petitions seeking to put up for a referendum a law expanding the rights of same-sex couples. As the case reached the Court, however, it concerned the general applicability of the public records law to mandate disclosure of the names and addresses of any person who signed any referendum petition.

Thus posed, the Court rejected the plaintiffs' claim that the disclosure statute violated their right to political expression. Writing for six Justices, Chief Justice Roberts cited *Buckley* and *Citizens United* for the proposition that application of disclosure statutes to the electoral context requires a court to apply "exacting scrutiny." Quoting both of those cases, he explained that that standard "requires a substantial relation between the disclosure requirement and a sufficiently important government interest."

The state had offered as justifications both the preservation of the integrity of the electoral process, "by combatting fraud . . . and fostering government transparency," and, second, "providing information to the electorate about who supports the petition." Chief Justice Roberts found the first of these justifications to be adequate, and thus did not reach the second. He rejected the argument that internal checks within the government adequately ensured the integrity of the process, noting the potential for bureaucratic mistakes that could be identified by public disclosure. He also rejected the argument that the government interest did not "reflect the seriousness of the actual burden" the disclosure requirement imposed on First Amendment rights. He noted the posture of the case, which concerned not just signatories to a controversial petition who might suffer reprisals if their identities were disclosed, but all signatories to all petitions. Examining such burdens more generally, the Chief Justice described them as "modest." However, he noted that the plaintiffs had also alleged that the disclosure law was invalid as applied to the signatories to this particular petition. Because the lower courts had not passed on that more particularized claim, the Court did not reach it, instead remanding for lower courts to consider it.

Several justices wrote separately. Justice Alito concurred. While he agreed with the Court's resolution of the claim before it, he insisted that a more particularized challenge to a disclosure law could protect signatories' First Amendment rights only if "(1) speakers can obtain the exemption sufficiently far in advance to avoid chilling protected speech and (2) the showing necessary to obtain the exemption is not overly burdensome." In light of those considerations, he concluded that the plaintiffs had "a strong argument" on their more particularized claim. Justice Sotomayor, joined by Justices Stevens and Ginsburg, also concurred, affirming the validity of the state's justifications for the disclosure and describing as "minimal" the burden public disclosure imposed "on speech and associational rights." She therefore concluded that "any party attempting to challenge particular applications of the State's regulations will bear a heavy burden." Justice Stevens, joined by Justice Breyer, concurred in part and concurred in the judgment. He concluded that the law "does not substantially burden any individual's expression," since it was "not a regulation of pure speech," and has only a "minimal" effect on speech. Commenting on the claim not decided by the Court, he observed that it was "unlikely" that the plaintiffs would be able to show that application of the law to their signatures on this particular petition would subject them to burdens that amounted to an unconstitutional restriction of their First Amendment rights. Justice Scalia concurred in the judgment to repeat his long-standing view that the First Amendment did not protect anonymity "in the performance of an act with governmental effect." Justice Thomas alone dissented. He would have subjected application of the law to any petition signers to strict scrutiny. He found that standard not to have been met in this case, as the state could have ensured the integrity of its electoral process in other less speech-restrictive ways. He also concluded that the Court had previously rejected the second of the state's justifications.

5. Tying together the two parts of his opinion (striking down the spending restrictions but upholding the disclosure requirements), Justice Kennedy in *Citizens United* made the following observations about the campaign finance system that emerged after that case:

> A campaign finance system that pairs corporate independent expenditures with effective disclosure has not existed before today. It must be noted, furthermore, that many of Congress' findings in passing BCRA were premised

on a system without adequate disclosure. With the advent of the Internet, prompt disclosure of expenditures can provide shareholders and citizens with the information needed to hold corporations and elected officials accountable for their positions and supporters. . . . The First Amendment protects political speech; and disclosure permits citizens and shareholders to react to the speech of corporate entities in a proper way. This transparency enables the electorate to make informed decisions and give proper weight to different speakers and messages.

In this passage Justice Kennedy summarizes the regulatory regime that he believes reflects a correct interpretation of the First Amendment. The Court's decision that same term in *Reed* reinforced the foundation for this regime. In the passage above Justice Kennedy implies that this regime—combining freedom of corporate and union speech with disclosure requirements—is also sound policy. Do you agree? Is your answer influenced by the fact that today the Internet makes it possible to combine disclosed political speech with other available data to create a detailed profile of who is engaging in what types of political speech? Does greater online access to such information, and thus the fuller realization of the potential for more effective disclosure, render a disclosure regime more effective in vindicating legitimate government interests and thus more likely constitutional? Or does such a regime "provide[] political opponents with the information needed to intimidate and retaliate against their foes," as Justice Thomas warned in *Reed*? Justice Brandeis, in a famous phrase about disclosure and transparency in government, once commented that "sunlight is said to be the best of disinfectants." Does that change when the disinfectant has extra-strength?

D. Circumvention of Contribution Limits and *Buckley*'s Limits

Note: The Anti-Circumvention Idea

1. Recall that *Buckley* upheld limits on direct contributions to electoral candidates as a legitimate way for government to prevent either the reality or the appearance of corruption. In *Buckley* itself the Court also recognized the potential for evasion of constitutionally acceptable contribution limits via what it described as "massive . . . contributions to political committees likely to contribute to [the original contributor's preferred] candidate, or huge contributions to the candidate's political party." The legislative response, upheld in *Buckley*, was an overall cap on a single individual's federal election contributions in a given year. In the years after *Buckley*, the Court considered the constitutionality of other limitations devised by legislatures to thwart evasion of valid contribution limits. In 2014 it re-examined *Buckley*'s upholding of such an aggregate cap.

2. In *California Medical Ass'n v. FEC*, 453 U.S. 182 (1981), the Court upheld a law that limited the contributions that could be made to political action committees that in turn contributed to federal candidates. Writing for a plurality of four Justices,

Justice Marshall reasoned that such limits helped prevent circumvention of direct contribution caps, since without them an individual could contribute unlimited amounts to a PAC, which could then forward them to a candidate. He wrote that "[t]hese concerns prompted Congress to enact [the provision at issue], and it is clear that this provision is an appropriate means by which Congress could seek to protect the integrity of the contribution restrictions upheld by the Court in *Buckley*."

Justice Blackmun concurred only in the judgment. He subjected the contribution restriction to a "rigorous standard of review," but nonetheless endorsed Justice Marshall's anti-circumvention rationale for upholding the law. Four justices did not reach the merits of the issue.

3. Another aspect of the attempted circumvention of contribution limitations involves political parties. In the years after *Buckley*, national and state political parties became important fundraisers for the large, unregulated contributions (also known as "soft money") that could no longer be made to candidates themselves. The Court in *McConnell* reported that between 1984 and 2000, soft money rose from 5% of total spending by the two major parties ($21.6 million) to 42% ($498 million). *McConnell* also noted that a 1998 Senate investigation revealed that political parties promised special access to lawmakers in return for soft money contributions.

In response, BCRA (the 2002 statute largely upheld in *McConnell* and partly struck down in *Citizens United*), attempted to limit contributions to parties. Section 323(a) of BCRA provides that "national committee[s] of a political party . . . may not solicit, receive, or direct to another person a contribution, donation, or transfer of funds or any other thing of value, or spend any funds, that are not subject to the limitations, prohibitions, and reporting requirements of this Act." The *McConnell* opinion remarked, "[i]n short, § 323(a) takes national parties out of the soft-money business."

In explaining why § 323(a) is constitutional, the *McConnell* majority stated that contributions to parties carry with them the possibility of corruption, or its appearance, since parties allocate these funds to particular candidates—often the same candidates who brought the contributions into the party. Section 323(a) was thus designed to prevent national political party organizations from becoming conduits for unregulated contributions to a candidate, and thus again evading the direct contribution limits.

Note: McCutcheon *and the Limits of the Anti-Circumvention Rationale*

1. The Court's willingness to accept anti-circumvention rationales for more indirect limitations on campaign contributions came to a halt in 2014 when the Court decided *McCutcheon v. Federal Election Commission*, 134 S. Ct. 1434 (2014). *McCutcheon* involved the interaction of two federal law limits on contributions: the so-called "base" limit, which specified how much an individual could contribute to a particular candidate, and the "aggregate" limit (discussed in Item 1 of the previous note), which specified the total amount an individual could give to all federal candidates in a given election cycle. In *McCutcheon*, an individual reached the aggregate limit after contributing to a variety of federal candidates in amounts that complied with the base limit. He then alleged that he wished to contribute to additional federal candidates, but was unconstitutionally prevented from doing so by the aggregate limit. The lower court rejected his First Amendment challenge to the aggregate limit, concluding, in the words of the Supreme Court, that the aggregate limit "prevented evasion of the base limits."

2. The Supreme Court reversed. Writing for four justices of a five-justice majority, Chief Justice Roberts noted that *Buckley* had, "in one paragraph of its 139-page opinion," evaluated and upheld the aggregate limit. (That paragraph appears in Part I(B)(4) of the *Buckley* opinion, and is included in the *Buckley* excerpt in this chapter.) The Court declined to follow *Buckley*'s decision upholding of that limit. It noted that in intervening years federal law had imposed "more targeted anticircumvention measures," which, according to the Chief Justice, made "the indiscriminate aggregate limits . . . appear particularly heavy-handed." He observed that Congress had made a considered judgment that a contribution to a particular candidate that was less than the base limit did not risk corruption or its appearance; thus, he concluded no anti-corruption rationale existed for an aggregate limit that effectively prevented a person who had contributed to other candidates from giving any money at all to additional candidates. In particular, he rejected the argument that an individual's heavy spending on a party's candidates, spread out over many such candidates, risked the kind of corruption *Buckley* recognized as a legitimate target of regulation. He wrote:

> Spending large sums of money in connection with elections, but not in connection with an effort to control the exercise of an officeholder's official duties, does not give rise to . . . *quid pro quo* corruption. Nor does the possibility that an individual who spends large sums may garner "influence over or access to" elected officials or political parties.

Importantly, he also wrote the following:

> A final point: It is worth keeping in mind that the *base limits* themselves are a prophylactic measure. As we have explained, "restrictions on direct contributions are preventative, because few if any contributions to candidates will involve *quid pro quo* arrangements." *Citizens United.* The aggregate limits are then layered on top, ostensibly to prevent circumvention of the base limits. This "prophylaxis-upon-prophylaxis approach" requires that we be particularly diligent in scrutinizing the law's fit.

Justice Thomas concurred only in the judgment, to express his continuing rejection of *Buckley*'s contribution/expenditure distinction, and to call for *Buckley* to be overruled.

3. Justice Breyer, joined by Justices Ginsburg, Sotomayor, and Kagan, dissented. He argued that the plurality had adopted an inappropriately narrow understanding of corruption. In Justice Breyer's view, the First Amendment allowed the creation of "a public opinion that can and will influence elected representatives." He argued that "[c]orruption breaks the constitutionally necessary 'chain of communication' between the people and their representatives." In his view, corruption included the reality and perception that large contributors enjoyed "privileged access to and pernicious influence upon elected representatives." He also argued that, even on the plurality's own terms, large aggregate contributions to a party's candidates could find their way from candidate to candidate, thus circumventing the base limit.

4. Leave aside the intricate questions about how easy or difficult it is for a contribution to candidate X to be funneled to candidate Y of the same party — in other words, leave aside the empirical question of how necessary the aggregate limit is in order to prevent circumvention of the base limit. Consider instead how deferential the Court should be to congressional determinations about such matters. On the one hand, surely members of Congress know better than most of us how the system works, and how corruption can enter into it. On the other hand, those same members surely have a self-interest in creating a system that works to their advantage, even if it means shutting off political expression. Where is the proper balance on the deference question?

Consider also an even more fundamental question: what is the proper understanding of the type of corruption that justifies contribution limits? Chief Justice Roberts insists that only classic, *quid pro quo* corruption should count. Justice Breyer argues for a broader understanding of corruption. Which side has more support in the caselaw? Even more generally, which understanding of corruption *should* govern? For example, is the privileged access to elected officials enjoyed by large contributors (and independent spenders) the very definition of corruption, or is it simply the very definition of democracy, in which office-holders respond most readily to their most faithful (and fervent) supporters? Does your answer to this question depend on your conception of democratic politics? If so, does the correct First Amendment answer to this question also depend on one's political philosophy?

As you consider these final questions, think about what Chief Justice Roberts wrote in the penultimate substantive paragraph of his majority opinion in *McCutcheon*:

> For the past 40 years, our campaign finance jurisprudence has focused on the need to preserve authority for the Government to combat corruption, without at the same time compromising the political responsiveness at the heart of the democratic process, or allowing the Government to favor some participants in that process over others. As Edmund Burke explained in his famous speech to the electors of Bristol, a representative owes constituents the exercise of his "mature judgment," but judgment informed by "the strictest union, the closest correspondence, and the most unreserved communication with his constituents." The Speeches of the Right Hon. Edmund Burke 129–30 (J. Burke ed. 1867). Constituents have the right to support candidates who share their views and concerns. Representatives are not to follow constituent orders, but can be expected to be cognizant of and responsive to those concerns. Such responsiveness is key to the very concept of self-governance through elected officials.

To what extent do limits on campaign contributions—including the aggregate limits at issue in *McCutcheon*—"compromis[e] the political responsiveness at the heart of the democratic process"? In particular, to what extent do such limits impair constituents' right "to support candidates who share their views and concerns," and representatives' ability "to be cognizant of and responsive to [constituents'] concerns"? In other words, to what extent are campaign contributions speech that constituents make and to which representatives can be expected to be responsive in a well-functioning democracy?

Chapter 12

Beyond Regulation: The Government as Employer and Educator

A. First Amendment Rights of Government Employees

Plainly, under the First Amendment, the state could not punish a citizen for expressing the view that the state's Emergency Management Agency is woefully unprepared to meet the next large-scale natural disaster. But suppose the citizen is an employee of the agency, and she expresses her view in an internal memorandum that she circulates to her fellow employees. Does the First Amendment protect her from discharge or discipline if her supervisor concludes that circulation of the memorandum violated agency policy and undermined office relationships? That is a very different question, as the first case in this section makes clear.

Connick v. Myers
461 U.S. 138 (1983)

JUSTICE WHITE delivered the opinion of the Court.

In *Pickering v. Board of Education*, 391 U.S. 563 (1968), we stated that a public employee does not relinquish First Amendment rights to comment on matters of public interest by virtue of government employment. We also recognized that the State's interests as an employer in regulating the speech of its employees "differ significantly from those it possesses in connection with regulation of the speech of the citizenry in general." The problem, we thought, was arriving "at a balance between the interests of the [employee], as a citizen, in commenting upon matters of public concern and the interest of the State, as an employer, in promoting the efficiency of the public services it performs through its employees." We return to this problem today and consider whether the First and Fourteenth Amendments prevent the discharge of a state employee for circulating a questionnaire concerning internal office affairs.

I

The respondent, Sheila Myers, was employed as an Assistant District Attorney in New Orleans for five and a half years. She served at the pleasure of petitioner Harry

Connick, the District Attorney for Orleans Parish. During this period Myers competently performed her responsibilities of trying criminal cases.

In the early part of October, 1980, Myers was informed that she would be transferred to prosecute cases in a different section of the criminal court. [Myers was strongly opposed to the proposed transfer. She expressed her view to several of her supervisors, including Connick and Dennis Waldron, one of the first assistant district attorneys. When Waldron suggested that her concerns were not shared by others in the office, she informed him that she would do some research on the matter.]

That night Myers prepared a questionnaire soliciting the views of her fellow staff members concerning office transfer policy, office morale, the need for a grievance committee, the level of confidence in supervisors, and whether employees felt pressured to work in political campaigns. Early the following morning, Myers typed and copied the questionnaire. She also met with Connick, who urged her to accept the transfer. She said she would "consider" it. Connick then left the office. Myers then distributed the questionnaire to 15 assistant district attorneys. Shortly after noon, Waldron learned that Myers was distributing the survey. He immediately phoned Connick and informed him that Myers was creating a "mini-insurrection" within the office. Connick returned to the office and told Myers that she was being terminated because of her refusal to accept the transfer. She was also told that her distribution of the questionnaire was considered an act of insubordination. Connick particularly objected to the question which inquired whether employees "had confidence in and would rely on the word" of various superiors in the office, and to a question concerning pressure to work in political campaigns which he felt would be damaging if discovered by the press.

Myers filed suit under 42 U.S.C. § 1983, contending that her employment was wrongfully terminated because she had exercised her constitutionally-protected right of free speech. The District Court agreed, ordered Myers reinstated, and awarded back-pay, damages, and attorney's fees. [The Fifth Circuit affirmed.]

II

For at least 15 years, it has been settled that a state cannot condition public employment on a basis that infringes the employee's constitutionally protected interest in freedom of expression. *Keyishian v. Board of Regents*, 385 U.S. 589 (1967); *Pickering v. Board of Education*, 391 U.S. 563 (1968); *Branti v. Finkel*, 445 U.S. 507 (1980). Our task, as we defined it in *Pickering*, is to seek "a balance between the interests of the [employee], as a citizen, in commenting upon matters of public concern and the interest of the State, as an employer, in promoting the efficiency of the public services it performs through its employees." The District Court, and thus the Court of Appeals as well, misapplied our decision in *Pickering* and consequently, in our view, erred in striking the balance for respondent.

A

The District Court got off on the wrong foot in this case by initially finding that, "[t]aken as a whole, the issues presented in the questionnaire relate to the effective functioning of the District Attorney's Office and are matters of public importance and concern." Connick contends at the outset that no balancing of interests is required in this case because Myers' questionnaire concerned only internal office matters and that such speech is not upon a matter of "public concern," as the term was used in *Pickering*. Although we do not agree that Myers' communication in this case was wholly without First Amendment protection, there is much force to Connick's submission. The repeated emphasis in *Pickering* on the right of a public employee "as a citizen, in commenting upon matters of public concern," was not accidental. This language, reiterated in all of *Pickering*'s progeny, reflects both the historical evolvement of the rights of public employees, and the common sense realization that government offices could not function if every employment decision became a constitutional matter.[5]

For most of this century, the unchallenged dogma was that a public employee had no right to object to conditions placed upon the terms of employment — including those which restricted the exercise of constitutional rights. The classic formulation of this position was Justice Holmes', who, when sitting on the Supreme Judicial Court of Massachusetts, observed: "A policeman may have a constitutional right to talk politics, but he has no constitutional right to be a policeman." *McAuliffe v. Mayor of New Bedford*, 155 Mass. 216, 220, 29 N.E. 517, 517 (1892). For many years, Holmes' epigram expressed this Court's law. [E.g.,] *Adler v. Board of Education*, 342 U.S. 485 (1952); *Garner v. Board of Public Works*, 341 U.S. 716 (1951); *United Public Workers v. Mitchell*, 330 U.S. 75 (1947).

The Court cast new light on the matter in a series of cases arising from the widespread efforts in the 1950s and early 1960s to require public employees, particularly teachers, to swear oaths of loyalty to the state and reveal the groups with which they associated. In *Wieman v. Updegraff*, 344 U.S. 183 (1952), the Court held that a State could not require its employees to establish their loyalty by extracting an oath denying past affiliation with Communists. In *Cafeteria Workers v. McElroy*, 367 U.S. 886 (1961), the Court recognized that the government could not deny employment because of previous membership in a particular party. By the time *Sherbert v. Verner*, 374 U.S. 398 (1963), was decided, it was already "too late in the day to doubt that the liberties of religion and expression may be infringed by the denial of or placing of conditions upon a benefit or privilege." It was therefore no surprise when in *Keyishian v. Board of Regents*, 385 U.S. 589 (1967), the Court invalidated New York statutes barring employment on the basis of membership in "subversive" organizations, observing that the theory that public employment which may be denied altogether may be subjected to any conditions, regardless of how unreasonable, had been uniformly rejected.

In all of these cases, the precedents in which *Pickering* is rooted, the invalidated statutes and actions sought to suppress the rights of public employees to participate in public affairs. The issue was whether government employees could be prevented

---

5. The question of whether expression is of a kind that is of legitimate concern to the public is also the standard in determining whether a common-law action for invasion of privacy is present. See RESTATEMENT (SECOND) OF TORTS § 652D. *See also Cox Broadcasting Co. v. Cohn*, 420 U.S. 469 (1975) (action for invasion of privacy cannot be maintained when the subject-matter of the publicity is matter of public record); *Time, Inc. v. Hill*, 385 U.S. 374 (1967).

or "chilled" by the fear of discharge from joining political parties and other associations that certain public officials might find "subversive." The explanation for the Constitution's special concern with threats to the right of citizens to participate in political affairs is no mystery. The First Amendment "was fashioned to assure unfettered interchange of ideas for the bringing about of political and social changes desired by the people." *Roth v. United States* (1957) [*supra* Chapter 2]. Accordingly, the Court has frequently reaffirmed that speech on public issues occupies the "highest rung of the hierarchy of First Amendment values," and is entitled to special protection. *NAACP v. Claiborne Hardware Co.* (1982) [*supra* Chapter 1].

Pickering v. Board of Education followed from this understanding of the First Amendment. In *Pickering*, the Court held impermissible under the First Amendment the dismissal of a high school teacher for openly criticizing the Board of Education on its allocation of school funds between athletics and education and its methods of informing taxpayers about the need for additional revenue. Pickering's subject was "a matter of legitimate public concern" upon which "free and open debate is vital to informed decision-making by the electorate."

Our cases following *Pickering* also involved safeguarding speech on matters of public concern. The controversy in *Perry v. Sindermann*, 408 U.S. 593 (1972), arose from the failure to rehire a teacher in the state college system who had testified before committees of the Texas legislature and had become involved in public disagreement over whether the college should be elevated to four-year status—a change opposed by the Regents. In *Mt. Healthy City Board of Ed. v. Doyle*, 429 U.S. 274 (1977), a public school teacher was not rehired because, allegedly, he had relayed to a radio station the substance of a memorandum relating to teacher dress and appearance that the school principal had circulated to various teachers. The memorandum was apparently prompted by the view of some in the administration that there was a relationship between teacher appearance and public support for bond issues, and indeed, the radio station promptly announced the adoption of the dress code as a news item. Most recently, in *Givhan v. Western Line Consolidated School District*, 439 U.S. 410 (1979), we held that First Amendment protection applies when a public employee arranges to communicate privately with his employer rather than to express his views publicly. Although the subject-matter of Mrs. Givhan's statements were not the issue before the Court, it is clear that her statements concerning the school district's allegedly racially discriminatory policies involved a matter of public concern.

Pickering, its antecedents and progeny, lead us to conclude that if Myers' questionnaire cannot be fairly characterized as constituting speech on a matter of public concern, it is unnecessary for us to scrutinize the reasons for her discharge. When employee expression cannot be fairly considered as relating to any matter of political, social, or other concern to the community, government officials should enjoy wide latitude in managing their offices, without intrusive oversight by the judiciary in the name of the First Amendment. Perhaps the government employer's dismissal of the worker may not be fair, but ordinary dismissals from government service which violate no fixed tenure or applicable statute or regulation are not subject to judicial review even if the reasons for the dismissal are alleged to be mistaken or unreasonable.

We do not suggest, however, that Myers' speech, even if not touching upon a matter of public concern, is totally beyond the protection of the First Amendment. . . . For example, an employee's false criticism of his employer on grounds not of public concern may be cause for his discharge but would be entitled to the same protection in a libel action accorded an identical statement made by a man on the street. We hold only that when a public employee speaks not as a citizen upon matters of public concern, but instead as an employee upon matters only of personal interest, absent the most unusual circumstances, a federal court is not the appropriate forum in which to review the wisdom of a personnel decision taken by a public agency allegedly in reaction to the employee's behavior. Our responsibility is to ensure that citizens are not deprived of fundamental rights by virtue of working for the government; this does not require a grant of immunity for employee grievances not afforded by the First Amendment to those who do not work for the state.

Whether an employee's speech addresses a matter of public concern must be determined by the content, form, and context of a given statement, as revealed by the whole record. In this case, with but one exception, the questions posed by Myers to her coworkers do not fall under the rubric of matters of "public concern." We view the questions pertaining to the confidence and trust that Myers' coworkers possess in various supervisors, the level of office morale, and the need for a grievance committee as mere extensions of Myers' dispute over her transfer to another section of the criminal court. Unlike the dissent, we do not believe these questions are of public import in evaluating the performance of the District Attorney as an elected official. Myers did not seek to inform the public that the District Attorney's office was not discharging its governmental responsibilities in the investigation and prosecution of criminal cases. Nor did Myers seek to bring to light actual or potential wrongdoing or breach of public trust on the part of Connick and others. Indeed, the questionnaire, if released to the public, would convey no information at all other than the fact that a single employee is upset with the status quo.

While discipline and morale in the workplace are related to an agency's efficient performance of its duties, the focus of Myers' questions is not to evaluate the performance of the office but rather to gather ammunition for another round of controversy with her superiors. These questions reflect one employee's dissatisfaction with a transfer and an attempt to turn that displeasure into a cause celebre.

To presume that all matters which transpire within a government office are of public concern would mean that virtually every remark—and certainly every criticism directed at a public official—would plant the seed of a constitutional case. While as a matter of good judgment, public officials should be receptive to constructive criticism offered by their employees, the First Amendment does not require a public office to be run as a roundtable for employee complaints over internal office affairs.

One question in Myers' questionnaire, however, does touch upon a matter of public concern. Question 11 inquires if assistant district attorneys "ever feel pressured to work in political campaigns on behalf of office supported candidates." We have recently noted that official pressure upon employees to work for political candidates not of the worker's own choice constitutes a coercion of belief in violation of fundamental constitutional rights. *Branti v. Finkel*, 445 U.S. 507 (1980); *Elrod v. Burns*, 427 U.S. 347 (1976). In addition, there is a demonstrated interest in this country that government service should depend upon meritorious performance rather than political service. Given this history, we believe it apparent that the issue of whether assistant district attorneys are pressured to work in political campaigns is a matter of interest to the community upon which it is essential that public employees be able to speak out freely without fear of retaliatory dismissal.

B

Because one of the questions in Myers' survey touched upon a matter of public concern and contributed to her discharge, we must determine whether Connick was justified in discharging Myers. Here the District Court again erred in imposing an unduly onerous burden on the state to justify Myers' discharge. The District Court viewed the issue of whether Myers' speech was upon a matter of "public concern" as a threshold inquiry, after which it became the government's burden to "clearly demonstrate" that the speech involved "substantially interfered" with official responsibilities. Yet *Pickering* unmistakably states, and respondent agrees, that the state's burden in justifying a particular discharge varies depending upon the nature of the employee's expression. Although such particularized balancing is difficult, the courts must reach the most appropriate possible balance of the competing interests.

C

The *Pickering* balance requires full consideration of the government's interest in the effective and efficient fulfillment of its responsibilities to the public. One hundred years ago, the Court noted the government's legitimate purpose in "promot[ing] efficiency and integrity in the discharge of official duties, and to maintain proper discipline in the public service." *Ex parte Curtis*, 106 U.S. 371 (1882). As Justice Powell explained in his separate opinion in *Arnett v. Kennedy*, 416 U.S. 134 (1974): "To this end, the Government, as an employer, must have wide discretion and control over the management of its personnel and internal affairs. This includes the prerogative to remove employees whose conduct hinders efficient operation and to do so with dispatch. Prolonged retention of a disruptive or otherwise unsatisfactory employee can adversely affect discipline and morale in the work place, foster disharmony, and ultimately impair the efficiency of an office or agency."

We agree with the District Court that there is no demonstration here that the questionnaire impeded Myers' ability to perform her responsibilities. The District Court was also correct to recognize that "it is important to the efficient and successful operation of the District Attorney's office for Assistants to maintain close working relationships with their superiors." Connick's judgment, and apparently also that of his first assistant Dennis Waldron, who characterized Myers' actions as causing a "mini-insurrection," was that Myers' questionnaire was an act of insubordination which interfered with working relationships. When close working relationships are essential to fulfilling public responsibilities, a wide degree of deference to the employer's judgment is appropriate. Furthermore, we do not see the necessity for an employer to allow events to unfold to the extent that the disruption of the office and the destruction of working relationships is manifest before taking action. We caution that a stronger showing may be necessary if the employee's speech more substantially involved matters of public concern. . . .

Also relevant is the manner, time, and place in which the questionnaire was distributed. As noted in *Givhan*, "Private expression . . . may in some situations bring additional factors to the *Pickering* calculus. When a government employee personally confronts his immediate superior, the employing agency's institutional efficiency may be threatened not only by the content of the employee's message but also by the manner, time, and place in which it is delivered." Here the questionnaire was prepared, and distributed at the office; the manner of distribution required not only Myers to leave her work but for others to do the same in order that the questionnaire be completed. Although some latitude in when official work is performed is to be allowed when professional employees are involved, and Myers did not violate announced office policy, the fact that Myers, unlike Pickering, exercised her rights to speech at the office supports Connick's fears that the functioning of his office was endangered.

Finally, the context in which the dispute arose is also significant. This is not a case where an employee, out of purely academic interest, circulated a questionnaire so as to obtain useful research. Myers acknowledges that it is no coincidence that the questionnaire followed upon the heels of the transfer notice. When employee speech concerning office policy arises from an employment dispute concerning the very application of that policy to the speaker, additional weight must be given to the supervisor's view that the employee has threatened the authority of the employer to run the office. . . .

III

Myers' questionnaire touched upon matters of public concern in only a most limited sense; her survey, in our view, is most accurately characterized as an employee grievance concerning internal office policy. The limited First Amendment interest involved here does not require that Connick tolerate action which he reasonably believed would disrupt the office, undermine his authority, and destroy close working relationships. Myers' discharge therefore did not offend the First Amendment. We reiterate, however, the caveat we expressed in *Pickering*: "Because of the enormous variety of fact situations in which critical statements by . . . public employees may be thought by their superiors . . . to furnish grounds for dismissal, we do not deem it either appropriate or feasible to lay down a general standard against which all such statements may be judged."

Our holding today is grounded in our long-standing recognition that the First Amendment's primary aim is the full protection of speech upon issues of public concern, as well as the practical realities involved in the administration of a government office. Although today the balance is struck for the government, this is no defeat for the First Amendment. For it would indeed be a Pyrrhic victory for the great principles of free expression if the Amendment's safeguarding of a public employee's right, as a citizen, to participate in discussions concerning public affairs were confused with the attempt to constitutionalize the employee grievance that we see presented here. The judgment of the Court of Appeals is *reversed*.

JUSTICE BRENNAN, with whom JUSTICE MARSHALL, JUSTICE BLACKMUN, and JUSTICE STEVENS join, dissenting.

. . . It is hornbook law [that] speech about "the manner in which government is operated or should be operated" is an essential part of the communications necessary for self-governance the protection of which was a central purpose of the First Amendment. *Mills v. Alabama*, 384 U.S. 214, 218 (1966). Because the questionnaire addressed such matters and its distribution did not adversely affect the operations of the District Attorney's Office or interfere with Myers' working relationship with her fellow employees, I dissent. . . .

The Court's decision today is flawed in three respects. First, the Court distorts the balancing analysis required under *Pickering* by suggesting that one factor, the context in which a statement is made, is to be weighed twice — first in determining whether an employee's speech addresses a matter of public concern and then in deciding whether the statement adversely affected the government's interest as an employer. Second, in concluding that the effect of respondent's personnel policies on employee morale and the work performance of the District Attorney's Office is not a matter of public concern, the Court impermissibly narrows the class of subjects on which public employees may speak out without fear of retaliatory dismissal. Third, the Court misapplies the *Pickering* balancing test in holding that Myers could constitutionally be dismissed for circulating a questionnaire addressed to at least one subject that was "a matter of interest to the community," in the absence of evidence that her conduct disrupted the efficient functioning of the District Attorney's Office. . . .

The standard announced by the Court suggests that the manner and context in which a statement is made must be weighed on both sides of the *Pickering* balance. It is beyond dispute that how and where a public employee expresses his views are relevant in the second half of the *Pickering* inquiry — determining whether the employee's speech adversely affects the government's interests as an employer. . . . But the fact that a public employee has chosen to express his views in private has nothing whatsoever to do with the first half of the *Pickering* calculus — whether those views relate to a matter of public concern. . . .

. . . I would hold that Myers' questionnaire addressed matters of public concern because it discussed subjects that could reasonably be expected to be of interest to persons seeking to develop informed opinions about the manner in which the Orleans Parish District Attorney, an elected official charged with managing a vital governmental agency, discharges his responsibilities. The questionnaire sought primarily to obtain information about the impact of the recent transfers on morale in the District Attorney's Office. It is beyond doubt that personnel decisions that adversely affect discipline and morale may ultimately impair an agency's efficient performance of its duties. Because I believe the First Amendment protects the right of public employees to discuss such matters so that the public may be better informed about how their elected officials fulfill their responsibilities, I would affirm the District

Court's conclusion that the questionnaire related to matters of public importance and concern.

The Court's adoption of a far narrower conception of what subjects are of public concern seems prompted by its fears that a broader view "would mean that virtually every remark—and certainly every criticism directed at a public official—would plant the seed of a constitutional case." Obviously, not every remark directed at a public official by a public employee is protected by the First Amendment. . . . [But the] proper means to ensure that the courts are not swamped with routine employee grievances mischaracterized as First Amendment cases is not to restrict artificially the concept of "public concern," but to require that adequate weight be given to the public's important interests in the efficient performance of governmental functions and in preserving employee discipline and harmony sufficient to achieve that end.

The Court's decision today inevitably will deter public employees from making critical statements about the manner in which government agencies are operated for fear that doing so will provoke their dismissal. As a result, the public will be deprived of valuable information with which to evaluate the performance of elected officials. Because protecting the dissemination of such information is an essential function of the First Amendment, I dissent.

———

Note: Pickering *and Its Progeny*

1. Justice White's opinion for the Court in *Connick v. Myers* presents a good brief summary of the evolution of the law governing the First Amendment rights of government employees. As Justice White explains, for most of the twentieth century the dominant view was the one expressed by Justice Holmes while sitting on the Massachusetts Supreme Judicial Court: "A policeman may have a constitutional right to talk politics, but he has no constitutional right to be a policeman."

The Court moved away from that position in a series of decisions starting in the 1950s. But those early cases, arising out of government efforts to uncover "subversive" activities, hardly suggested a broad protection for speech by government employees. The turning point (at least in retrospect) came toward the end of the Warren Court in *Pickering v. Board of Education*, 391 U.S. 563 (1968).

What is the scope of the right protected under *Pickering* and its progeny? *Connick* holds that to prevail on a *Pickering* claim, the government employee must satisfy two tests. The threshold question is whether the employee's speech "addresses a matter of public concern." If the answer is "no," the First Amendment provides no protection from discharge or discipline. But even if the answer is "yes," the court must balance the First Amendment interests against "the government's interest in the effective and efficient fulfillment of its responsibilities to the public."

2. Two decades after *Connick*, the Court identified a second "line of cases" delineating the First Amendment rights of government employees. In *City of San Diego v. Roe*, 543 U.S. 77 (2004) (per curiam), the Court explained:

The Court has recognized the right of employees to speak on matters of public concern, typically matters concerning government policies that are of interest to the public at large, a subject on which public employees are uniquely qualified to comment. *See Connick*; *Pickering*. Outside of this category, the Court has held that when government employees speak or write on their own time on topics unrelated to their employment, the speech can have First Amendment protection, absent some governmental justification "far stronger than mere speculation" in regulating it.

The Court cited only one case as exemplifying the second "category." This was *United States v. National Treasury Employees Union*, 513 U.S. 454 (1995) (*NTEU*). The question in *NTEU* "was whether the Federal Government could impose certain monetary limitations on outside earnings from speaking or writing on a class of federal employees." The Court held that the regulation was unconstitutional. As explained in the *Roe* opinion:

> In *NTEU* it was established that the speech was unrelated to the employment and had no effect on the mission and purpose of the employer. . . . The Court held that, within the particular classification of employment, the Government had shown no justification for the outside salary limitations. The First Amendment right of the employees sufficed to invalidate the restrictions on the outside earnings for such activities. The Court noted that throughout history public employees who undertook to write or to speak in their spare time had made substantial contributions to literature and art, and observed that none of the speech at issue "even arguably [had] any adverse impact" on the employer.

What kinds of claims fall within the *NTEU* "line of cases"? Consider the Problem that follows.

———

Problem: An Activist Clerk

Three years ago, Walter Johnson was hired as a full-time clerk in the records section of the Calhoun City Police Department. His duties involved the filing of both public and confidential records. He also registered firearms and fingerprinted persons seeking employment. Johnson performed his duties in exemplary fashion. He was courteous, conscientious, and got along well with his fellow records section employees. He was largely unsupervised during the working day.

In recent months a series of police-involved shootings have roiled Calhoun City. The shootings have all involved African-Americans who the police claimed were either fleeing from a serious crime or threatening a police officer with a deadly weapon. Despite those explanations, local civil rights groups have staged marches, demanding an independent investigation of the shootings.

Johnson is a member of the local chapter of Black Lives Matter (BLM), one of the groups that have coordinated the marches. During the most recent and largest march, the BLM presence was highly visible, with many marchers marching behind a BLM banner. Those marchers carried signs with different messages, including "We Demand Respect" and "Investigate Police Shootings," but also including more incendiary ones such as "Remove Killer Cops" and "The Police Are the Enemy."

Johnson marched with the BLM contingent during that most recent march. While he did not carry any signs, he did wear a T-shirt that read "I Stand With Black Lives Matter." A local television station carried footage of the march on its news program that evening, and Johnson appeared onscreen for several seconds, with the more incendiary signs noted above clearly visible around him. Several civilian employees of the Police Department, as well as several police officers and the police chief herself, saw the broadcast.

The next day the Records Office was abuzz with nervous conversation about Johnson. Two of the police officers who saw the broadcast tell the police chief that they are uncomfortable with Johnson working in the office; one of them announces that he will have no dealings with Johnson. The police chief calls Johnson in and asks for his assurance that he will not participate in further marches or that, if he does, he not associate himself with BLM or its local chapter. When he refuses to provide that assurance, the police chief fires him, explaining that his presence in the office under such circumstances would be highly disruptive.

Johnson sues, alleging that he was unconstitutionally fired for his speech. Is the claim meritorious? Why or why not?

Garcetti v. Ceballos

547 U.S. 410 (2006)

JUSTICE KENNEDY delivered the opinion of the Court.

It is well settled that "a State cannot condition public employment on a basis that infringes the employee's constitutionally protected interest in freedom of expression." *Connick v. Myers*, 461 U.S. 138, 142 (1983). The question presented by the instant case is whether the First Amendment protects a government employee from discipline based on speech made pursuant to the employee's official duties.

I

Respondent Richard Ceballos has been employed since 1989 as a deputy district attorney for the Los Angeles County District Attorney's Office. During the period relevant to this case, Ceballos was a calendar deputy in the office's Pomona branch, and in this capacity he exercised certain supervisory responsibilities over other lawyers. In February 2000, a defense attorney contacted Ceballos about a pending criminal case. The defense attorney said there were inaccuracies in an affidavit used to obtain a critical search warrant. The attorney informed Ceballos that he had filed a motion to traverse, or challenge, the warrant, but he also wanted Ceballos to review the case. According to Ceballos, it was not unusual for defense attorneys to ask calendar deputies to investigate aspects of pending cases.

After examining the affidavit and visiting the location it described, Ceballos determined the affidavit contained serious misrepresentations. The affidavit called a long driveway what Ceballos thought should have been referred to as a separate roadway. Ceballos also questioned the affidavit's statement that tire tracks led from a stripped-down truck to the premises covered by the warrant. His doubts arose from his conclusion that the roadway's composition in some places made it difficult or impossible to leave visible tire tracks.

Ceballos spoke on the telephone to the warrant affiant, a deputy sheriff from the Los Angeles County Sheriff's Department, but he did not receive a satisfactory explanation for the perceived inaccuracies. He relayed his findings to his supervisors, petitioners Carol Najera and Frank Sundstedt, and followed up by preparing a disposition memorandum. The memo explained Ceballos' concerns and recommended dismissal of the case. On March 2, 2000, Ceballos submitted the memo to Sundstedt for his review. A few days later, Ceballos presented Sundstedt with another memo, this one describing a second telephone conversation between Ceballos and the warrant affiant.

Based on Ceballos' statements, a meeting was held to discuss the affidavit. . . . The meeting allegedly became heated, with one lieutenant sharply criticizing Ceballos for his handling of the case.

Despite Ceballos' concerns, Sundstedt decided to proceed with the prosecution, pending disposition of the defense motion to traverse. The trial court held a hearing on the motion. Ceballos was called by the defense and recounted his observations about the affidavit, but the trial court rejected the challenge to the warrant.

Ceballos claims that in the aftermath of these events he was subjected to a series of retaliatory employment actions. The actions included reassignment from his calendar deputy position to a trial deputy position, transfer to another courthouse, and denial of a promotion. Ceballos initiated an employment grievance, but the grievance was denied based on a finding that he had not suffered any retaliation. Unsatisfied, Ceballos sued in [federal district court, asserting a claim under 42 U.S.C. § 1983]. He alleged petitioners violated the First and Fourteenth Amendments by retaliating against him based on his memo of March 2.

[The District Court granted the defendants' motion for summary judgment. The court noted that Ceballos wrote his memo pursuant to his employment duties, and it concluded that he was not entitled to First Amendment protection for the memo's contents.]

The Court of Appeals for the Ninth Circuit reversed. . . . [The court] determined that Ceballos' memo, which recited what he thought to be governmental misconduct, was "inherently a matter of public concern." The court did not, however, consider whether the speech was made in Ceballos' capacity as a citizen. Rather, it relied on Circuit precedent rejecting the idea that "a public employee's speech is deprived of First Amendment protection whenever those views are expressed, to government workers or others, pursuant to an employment responsibility."

Having concluded that Ceballos' memo satisfied the public-concern requirement, the Court of Appeals proceeded to balance Ceballos' interest in his speech against his supervisors' interest in responding to it. The court struck the balance in Ceballos' favor, noting that petitioners "failed even to suggest disruption or inefficiency in the workings of the District Attorney's Office" as a result of the memo. . . .

We granted certiorari, and we now reverse.

II

[The Court has held that] the First Amendment protects a public employee's right, in certain circumstances, to speak as a citizen addressing matters of public concern.

Pickering provides a useful starting point in explaining the Court's doctrine. There the relevant speech was a teacher's letter to a local newspaper addressing issues including the funding policies of his school board. . . .

Pickering and the cases decided in its wake identify two inquiries to guide interpretation of the constitutional protections accorded to public employee speech. The first requires determining whether the employee spoke as a citizen on a matter of public concern. If the answer is no, the employee has no First Amendment cause of action based on his or her employer's reaction to the speech. *See Connick.* If the answer is yes, then the possibility of a First Amendment claim arises. The question becomes whether the relevant government entity had an adequate justification for treating the employee differently from any other member of the general public. *See Pickering.* This consideration reflects the importance of the relationship between the speaker's expressions and employment. A government entity has broader discretion to restrict speech when it acts in its role as employer, but the restrictions it imposes must be directed at speech that has some potential to affect the entity's operations.

To be sure, conducting these inquiries sometimes has proved difficult. This is the necessary product of "the enormous variety of fact situations in which critical statements by teachers and other public employees may be thought by their superiors . . . to furnish grounds for dismissal." *Pickering.* The Court's overarching objectives, though, are evident.

When a citizen enters government service, the citizen by necessity must accept certain limitations on his or her freedom. Government employers, like private employers, need a significant degree of control over their employees' words and actions; without it, there would be little chance for the efficient provision of public services. Public employees, moreover, often occupy trusted positions in society. When they speak out, they can express views that contravene governmental policies or impair the proper performance of governmental functions.

At the same time, the Court has recognized that a citizen who works for the government is nonetheless a citizen. The First Amendment limits the ability of a public employer to leverage the employment relationship to restrict, incidentally or intentionally, the liberties employees enjoy in their capacities as private citizens. So long as employees are speaking as citizens about matters of public concern, they must face only those speech restrictions that are necessary for their employers to operate efficiently and effectively.

The Court's employee-speech jurisprudence protects, of course, the constitutional rights of public employees. Yet the First Amendment interests at stake extend beyond the individual speaker. The Court has acknowledged the importance of promoting the public's interest in receiving the well-informed views of government employees engaging in civic discussion. *Pickering* again provides an instructive example. The Court characterized its holding as rejecting the attempt of school administrators to "limi[t] teachers' opportunities to contribute to public debate." It also noted that teachers are "the members of a community most likely to have informed and definite opinions" about school expenditures. The Court's approach acknowledged the necessity for informed, vibrant dialogue in a democratic society. It suggested, in addition, that widespread costs may arise when dialogue is repressed. The Court's more recent cases have expressed similar concerns. . . .

The Court's decisions, then, have sought both to promote the individual and societal interests that are served when employees speak as citizens on matters of public concern and to respect the needs of government employers attempting to perform their important public functions. Underlying our cases has been the premise that while the First Amendment invests public employees with certain rights, it does not empower them to "constitutionalize the employee grievance." *Connick.*

III

With these principles in mind we turn to the instant case. Respondent Ceballos believed the affidavit used to obtain a search warrant contained serious misrepresentations. He conveyed his opinion and recommendation in a memo to his supervisor. That Ceballos expressed his views inside his office, rather than publicly, is not dispositive. Employees in some cases may receive First Amendment protection for expressions made at work. *See, e.g., Givhan v. Western Line Consol. School Dist.*, 439 U.S. 410, 414 (1979). Many citizens do much of their talking inside their respective workplaces, and it would not serve the goal of treating public employees like "any member of the general public," *Pickering*, to hold that all speech within the office is automatically exposed to restriction.

The memo concerned the subject matter of Ceballos' employment, but this, too, is nondispositive. The First Amendment protects some expressions related to the speaker's job. *See, e.g., Pickering; Givhan.* As the Court noted in *Pickering*: "Teachers are, as a class, the members of a community most likely to have informed and definite opinions as to how funds allotted to the operation of the schools should be spent. Accordingly, it is essential that they be able to speak out freely on such questions without fear of retaliatory dismissal." The same is true of many other categories of public employees.

The controlling factor in Ceballos' case is that his expressions were made pursuant to his duties as a calendar deputy. That consideration—the fact that Ceballos spoke as a prosecutor fulfilling a responsibility to advise his supervisor about how best to proceed with a pending case—distinguishes Ceballos' case from those in which the First Amendment provides protection against discipline. We hold that when public employees make statements pursuant to their official duties, the employees are not speaking as citizens for First Amendment purposes, and the Constitution does not insulate their communications from employer discipline.

Ceballos wrote his disposition memo because that is part of what he, as a calendar deputy, was employed to do. It is immaterial whether he experienced some personal gratification from writing the memo; his First Amendment rights do not depend on his job satisfaction. The significant point is that the memo was written pursuant to Ceballos' official duties. Restricting speech that owes its existence to a public employee's professional responsibilities does not infringe any liberties the employee might have enjoyed as a private citizen. It simply reflects the exercise of employer control over what the employer itself has commissioned or created. *Cf. Rosenberger v. Rector and Visitors of Univ. of Va.*, 515 U.S. 819, 833 (1995) [Note *supra* Chapter 8] ("[W]hen the government appropriates public funds to promote a particular policy of its own it is entitled to say what it wishes"). Contrast, for example, the expressions made by the speaker in *Pickering*, whose letter to the newspaper had no official significance and bore similarities to letters submitted by numerous citizens every day.

Ceballos did not act as a citizen when he went about conducting his daily professional activities, such as supervising attorneys, investigating charges, and preparing filings. In the same way he did not speak as a citizen by writing a memo that addressed the proper disposition of a pending criminal case. When he went to work and performed the tasks he was paid to perform, Ceballos acted as a government employee. The fact that his duties sometimes required him to speak or write does not mean his supervisors were prohibited from evaluating his performance.

This result is consistent with our precedents' attention to the potential societal value of employee speech. Refusing to recognize First Amendment claims based on government employees' work product does not prevent them from participating in public debate. The employees retain the prospect of constitutional protection for their contributions to the civic discourse. This prospect of protection, however, does not invest them with a right to perform their jobs however they see fit.

Our holding likewise is supported by the emphasis of our precedents on affording government employers sufficient discretion to manage their operations. Employers have heightened interests in controlling speech made by an employee in his or her professional capacity. Official communications have official consequences, creating a need for substantive consistency and clarity. Supervisors must ensure that their employees' official communications are accurate, demonstrate sound judgment, and promote the employer's mission. Ceballos' memo is illustrative. It demanded the attention of his supervisors and led to a heated meeting with employees from the sheriff's department. If Ceballos' superiors thought his memo was inflammatory or misguided, they had the authority to take proper corrective action.

Ceballos' proposed contrary rule, adopted by the Court of Appeals, would commit state and federal courts to a new, permanent, and intrusive role, mandating judicial oversight of communications between and among government employees and their superiors in the course of official business. This displacement of managerial discretion by judicial supervision finds no support in our precedents. When an employee speaks as a citizen addressing a matter of public concern, the First Amendment requires a delicate balancing of the competing interests surrounding the speech and its consequences. When, however, the employee is simply performing his or her job duties, there is no warrant for a similar degree of scrutiny. To hold otherwise would be to demand permanent judicial intervention in the conduct of governmental operations to a degree inconsistent with sound principles of federalism and the separation of powers.

The Court of Appeals based its holding in part on what it perceived as a doctrinal anomaly. The court suggested it would be inconsistent to compel public employers to tolerate certain employee speech made publicly but not speech made pursuant to an employee's assigned duties. This objection misconceives the theoretical under-pinnings of our decisions. Employees who make public statements outside the course of performing their official duties retain some possibility of First Amendment pro-tection because that is the kind of activity engaged in by citizens who do not work for the government. The same goes for writing a letter to a local newspaper, see *Pickering*, or discussing politics with a co-worker, see *Rankin*. When a public employee speaks pursuant to employment responsibilities, however, there is no relevant analogue to speech by citizens who are not government employees.

The Court of Appeals' concern also is unfounded as a practical matter. The per-ceived anomaly, it should be noted, is limited in scope: It relates only to the expres-sions an employee makes pursuant to his or her official responsibilities, not to statements or complaints (such as those at issue in cases like *Pickering* and *Connick*) that are made outside the duties of employment. If, moreover, a government employer is troubled by the perceived anomaly, it has the means at hand to avoid it. A public employer that wishes to encourage its employees to voice concerns privately retains the option of instituting internal policies and procedures that are receptive to employee criticism. Giving employees an internal forum for their speech will discourage them from concluding that the safest avenue of expression is to state their views in public.

Proper application of our precedents thus leads to the conclusion that the First Amendment does not prohibit managerial discipline based on an employee's expres-sions made pursuant to official responsibilities. Because Ceballos' memo falls into this category, his allegation of unconstitutional retaliation must fail.

Two final points warrant mentioning. First, as indicated above, the parties in this case do not dispute that Ceballos wrote his disposition memo pursuant to his employ-ment duties. We thus have no occasion to articulate a comprehensive framework for defining the scope of an employee's duties in cases where there is room for serious debate. We reject, however, the suggestion that employers can restrict employees' rights by creating excessively broad job descriptions. *See post*, n.2 (Souter, J., dissenting). The proper inquiry is a practical one. Formal job descriptions often bear little resemblance to the duties an employee actually is expected to perform, and the listing of a given task in an employee's written job description is neither necessary nor sufficient to dem-onstrate that conducting the task is within the scope of the employee's professional duties for First Amendment purposes.

Second, Justice Souter suggests today's decision may have important ramifications for academic freedom, at least as a constitutional value. There is some argument that expression related to academic scholarship or classroom instruction implicates additional constitutional interests that are not fully accounted for by this Court's customary employee-speech jurisprudence. We need not, and for that reason do not, decide whether the analysis we conduct today would apply in the same manner to a case involving speech related to scholarship or teaching.

IV

Exposing governmental inefficiency and misconduct is a matter of considerable significance. As the Court noted in *Connick*, public employers should, "as a matter of good judgment," be "receptive to constructive criticism offered by their employees." The dictates of sound judgment are reinforced by the powerful network of legislative enactments—such as whistle-blower protection laws and labor codes—available to those who seek to expose wrongdoing. Cases involving government attorneys implicate additional safeguards in the form of, for example, rules of conduct and constitutional obligations apart from the First Amendment. These imperatives, as well as obligations arising from any other applicable constitutional provisions and mandates of the criminal and civil laws, protect employees and provide checks on supervisors who would order unlawful or otherwise inappropriate actions.

We reject, however, the notion that the First Amendment shields from discipline the expressions employees make pursuant to their professional duties. Our precedents do not support the existence of a constitutional cause of action behind every statement a public employee makes in the course of doing his or her job.

The judgment of the Court of Appeals is reversed, and the case is remanded for proceedings consistent with this opinion.

JUSTICE STEVENS, dissenting.

The proper answer to the question "whether the First Amendment protects a government employee from discipline based on speech made pursuant to the employee's official duties" is "Sometimes," not "Never." . . .

The notion that there is a categorical difference between speaking as a citizen and speaking in the course of one's employment is quite wrong. . . . [In] *Givhan v. Western Line Consol. School Dist.*, 439 U.S. 410 (1979), [we] had no difficulty recognizing that the First Amendment applied when Bessie Givhan, an English teacher, raised concerns about the school's racist employment practices to the principal. Our silence as to whether or not her speech was made pursuant to her job duties demonstrates that the point was immaterial. That is equally true today, for it is senseless to let constitutional protection for exactly the same words hinge on whether they fall within a job description. Moreover, it seems perverse to fashion a new rule that provides employees with an incentive to voice their concerns publicly before talking frankly to their superiors. . . .

JUSTICE SOUTER, with whom JUSTICE STEVENS and JUSTICE GINSBURG join, dissenting.

. . . I would hold that private and public interests in addressing official wrongdoing and threats to health and safety can outweigh the government's stake in the efficient implementation of policy, and when they do public employees who speak on these matters in the course of their duties should be eligible to claim First Amendment protection.

I

Open speech by a private citizen on a matter of public importance lies at the heart of expression subject to protection by the First Amendment. At the other extreme, a statement by a government employee complaining about nothing beyond treatment under personnel rules raises no greater claim to constitutional protection against retaliatory response than the remarks of a private employee. *See Connick.* In between these points lies a public employee's speech unwelcome to the government but on a significant public issue. Such an employee speaking as a citizen, that is, with a citizen's interest, is protected from reprisal unless the statements are too damaging to the government's capacity to conduct public business to be justified by any individual or public benefit thought to flow from the statements. *Pickering.* Entitlement to protection is thus not absolute. . . .

The reason that protection of employee speech is qualified is that it can distract co-workers and supervisors from their tasks at hand and thwart the implementation of legitimate policy, the risks of which grow greater the closer the employee's speech gets to commenting on his own workplace and responsibilities. It is one thing for an office clerk to say there is waste in government and quite another to charge that his own department pays full-time salaries to part-time workers. Even so, we have regarded eligibility for protection by *Pickering* balancing as the proper approach when an employee speaks critically about the administration of his own government employer. In *Givhan v. Western Line Consol. School Dist.*, 439 U.S. 410 (1979), we followed *Pickering* when a teacher was fired for complaining to a superior about the racial composition of the school's administrative, cafeteria, and library staffs. . . .

The difference between a case like *Givhan* and this one is that the subject of Ceballos's speech fell within the scope of his job responsibilities, whereas choosing personnel was not what the teacher was hired to do. The effect of the majority's constitutional line between these two cases, then, is that a *Givhan* schoolteacher is protected when complaining to the principal about hiring policy, but a school personnel officer would not be if he protested that the principal disapproved of hiring minority job applicants. This is an odd place to draw a distinction,[1] and while necessary judicial linedrawing sometimes looks arbitrary, any distinction obliges a court to justify its choice. Here, there is no adequate justification for the majority's line categorically denying *Pickering* protection to any speech uttered "pursuant to . . . official duties."

As all agree, the qualified speech protection embodied in *Pickering* balancing resolves the tension between individual and public interests in the speech, on the one hand, and the government's interest in operating efficiently without distraction or embarrassment by talkative or headline-grabbing employees. The need for a balance

---

1. It seems stranger still in light of the majority's concession of some First Amendment protection when a public employee repeats statements made pursuant to his duties but in a separate, public forum or in a letter to a newspaper.

hardly disappears when an employee speaks on matters his job requires him to address; rather, it seems obvious that the individual and public value of such speech is no less, and may well be greater, when the employee speaks pursuant to his duties in addressing a subject he knows intimately for the very reason that it falls within his duties.[2] ...

... Would anyone deny that a prosecutor like Richard Ceballos may claim the interest of any citizen in speaking out against a rogue law enforcement officer, simply because his job requires him to express a judgment about the officer's performance? (But the majority says the First Amendment gives Ceballos no protection, even if his judgment in this case was sound and appropriately expressed.) ...

Nor is there any reason to raise the counterintuitive question whether the public interest in hearing informed employees evaporates when they speak as required on some subject at the core of their jobs. ... Nothing [accountable] on the individual and public side of the *Pickering* balance changes when an employee speaks "pursuant" to public duties. On the side of the government employer, however, something is different, and to this extent, I agree with the majority of the Court. The majority is rightly concerned that the employee who speaks out on matters subject to comment in doing his own work has the greater leverage to create office uproars and fracture the government's authority to set policy to be carried out coherently through the ranks. ... Up to a point, then, the majority makes good points: government needs civility in the workplace, consistency in policy, and honesty and competence in public service.

But why do the majority's concerns, which we all share, require categorical exclusion of First Amendment protection against any official retaliation for things said on the job? Is it not possible to respect the unchallenged individual and public interests in the speech through a *Pickering* balance without drawing the strange line I mentioned before? ...

Two reasons in particular make me think an adjustment using the basic *Pickering* balancing scheme is perfectly feasible here. First, the extent of the government's legitimate authority over subjects of speech required by a public job can be recognized in advance by setting in effect a minimum heft for comments with any claim to outweigh it. Thus, the risks to the government are great enough for us to hold from the outset that an employee commenting on subjects in the course of duties should not prevail on balance unless he speaks on a matter of unusual importance and satisfies high standards of responsibility in the way he does it. ... [Only] comment on official dishonesty, deliberately unconstitutional action, other serious wrongdoing, or threats to health and safety can weigh out in an employee's favor. If promulgation of this standard should fail to discourage meritless [civil rights] actions before they get filed, the standard itself would sift them out at the summary-judgment stage.

---

2. I do not say the value of speech "pursuant to ... duties" will always be greater, because I am pessimistic enough to expect that one response to the Court's holding will be moves by government employers to expand stated job descriptions to include more official duties and so exclude even some currently protectable speech from First Amendment purview. ...

My second reason for adapting *Pickering* to the circumstances at hand is the experience in Circuits that have recognized claims like Ceballos's here. First Amendment protection less circumscribed than what I would recognize has been available in the Ninth Circuit for over 17 years, and neither there nor in other Circuits that accept claims like this one has there been a debilitating flood of litigation. There has indeed been some: as represented by Ceballos's lawyer at oral argument, each year over the last five years, approximately 70 cases in the different Courts of Appeals and approximately 100 in the various District Courts. But even these figures reflect a readiness to litigate that might well have been cooled by my view about the importance required before *Pickering* treatment is in order.

For that matter, the majority's position comes with no guarantee against factbound litigation over whether a public employee's statements were made "pursuant to . . . official duties." In fact, the majority invites such litigation by describing the enquiry as a "practical one," apparently based on the totality of employment circumstances. Are prosecutors' discretionary statements about cases addressed to the press on the courthouse steps made "pursuant to their official duties"? Are government nuclear scientists' complaints to their supervisors about a colleague's improper handling of radioactive materials made "pursuant" to duties?

II

The majority seeks support in two lines of argument extraneous to *Pickering* doctrine. The one turns on a fallacious reading of cases on government speech, the other on a mistaken assessment of protection available under whistle-blower statutes.

A

The majority accepts the fallacy propounded by the county petitioners and the Federal Government as *amicus* that any statement made within the scope of public employment is (or should be treated as) the government's own speech, and should thus be differentiated as a matter of law from the personal statements the First Amendment protects. . . . [The Court's description of the] ostensible domain beyond the pale of the First Amendment is spacious enough to include even the teaching of a public university professor, and I have to hope that today's majority does not mean to imperil First Amendment protection of academic freedom in public colleges and universities, whose teachers necessarily speak and write "pursuant to official duties."

B

The majority's second argument for its disputed limitation of *Pickering* doctrine is that the First Amendment has little or no work to do here owing to an assertedly comprehensive complement of state and national statutes protecting government whistle-blowers from vindictive bosses. [But] the majority's counsel to rest easy fails on its own terms.

To begin with, speech addressing official wrongdoing may well fall outside protected whistle-blowing, defined in the classic sense of exposing an official's fault to a third party or to the public; the teacher in *Givhan*, for example, who raised the issue of unconstitutional hiring bias, would not have qualified as that sort of whistle-blower, for she was fired after a private conversation with the school principal. In any event, the combined variants of statutory whistle-blower definitions and protections add up to a patchwork, not a showing that worries may be remitted to legislatures for relief. . . .

JUSTICE BREYER, dissenting.

This case asks whether the First Amendment protects public employees when they engage in speech that both (1) involves matters of public concern and (2) takes place in the ordinary course of performing the duties of a government job. I write separately to explain why I cannot fully accept either the Court's or Justice Souter's answer to the question presented.

I

I begin with what I believe is common ground:

[Where] a government employee speaks "as an employee upon matters only of personal interest," the First Amendment does not offer protection. *Connick*. Where the employee speaks "as a citizen . . . upon matters of public concern," the First Amendment offers protection but only where the speech survives a screening test. *Pickering*. That test, called, in legal shorthand, "*Pickering* balancing," requires a judge to "balance . . . the interests" of the employee "in commenting upon matters of public concern and the interest of the State, as an employer, in promoting the efficiency of the public services it performs through its employees."

Our prior cases do not decide what screening test a judge should apply in the circumstances before us, namely when the government employee both speaks upon a matter of public concern and does so in the course of his ordinary duties as a government employee.

II

The majority answers the question by holding that "when public employees make statements pursuant to their official duties, the employees are not speaking as citizens for First Amendment purposes, and the Constitution does not insulate their communications from employer discipline." In a word, the majority says, "never." That word, in my view, is too absolute.

Like the majority, I understand the need to "afford government employers sufficient discretion to manage their operations." And I agree that the Constitution does not seek to "displace . . . managerial discretion by judicial supervision." Nonetheless, there may well be circumstances with special demand for constitutional protection of the speech at issue, where governmental justifications may be limited, and where administrable standards seem readily available — to the point where the majority's fears of department management by lawsuit are misplaced. In such an instance, I believe that courts should apply the *Pickering* standard, even though the government employee speaks upon matters of public concern in the course of his ordinary duties.

This is such a case. The respondent, a government lawyer, complained of retaliation, in part, on the basis of speech contained in his disposition memorandum that he says fell within the scope of his obligations under *Brady v. Maryland*, 373 U.S. 83 (1963).

The facts present two special circumstances that together justify First Amendment review.

First, the speech at issue is professional speech — the speech of a lawyer. Such speech is subject to independent regulation by canons of the profession. Those canons provide an obligation to speak in certain instances. And where that is so, the government's own interest in forbidding that speech is diminished. . . .

Second, the Constitution itself here imposes speech obligations upon the government's professional employee. A prosecutor has a constitutional obligation to learn of, to preserve, and to communicate with the defense about exculpatory and impeachment evidence in the government's possession. So, for example, might a prison doctor have a similar constitutionally related professional obligation to communicate with superiors about seriously unsafe or unsanitary conditions in the cellblock. There may well be other examples.

Where professional and special constitutional obligations are both present, the need to protect the employee's speech is augmented, the need for broad government authority to control that speech is likely diminished, and administrable standards are quite likely available. Hence, I would find that the Constitution mandates special protection of employee speech in such circumstances. Thus I would apply the *Pickering* balancing test here.

III

While I agree with much of Justice Souter's analysis, I believe that the constitutional standard he enunciates fails to give sufficient weight to the serious managerial and administrative concerns that the majority describes. . . . There are . . . far too many issues of public concern, even if defined as "matters of unusual importance," for the screen to screen out very much. Government administration typically involves matters of public concern. This aspect of Justice Souter's "adjustment" of "the basic *Pickering* balancing scheme" . . . gives no extra weight to the government's augmented need to direct speech that is an ordinary part of the employee's job-related duties.

Moreover, the speech of vast numbers of public employees deals with wrongdoing, health, safety, and honesty: for example, police officers, firefighters, environmental protection agents, building inspectors, hospital workers, bank regulators, and so on. Indeed, this categorization could encompass speech by an employee performing almost any public function, except perhaps setting electricity rates. Nor do these categories bear any obvious relation to the constitutional importance of protecting the job-related speech at issue.

The underlying problem with this breadth of coverage is that the standard (despite predictions that the government is likely to *prevail* in the balance unless the speech concerns "official dishonesty, deliberately unconstitutional action, other serious wrongdoing, or threats to health and safety"), does not avoid the judicial need to *undertake the balance* in the first place. And this form of judicial activity — the ability of a dissatisfied employee to file a complaint, engage in discovery, and insist that the court undertake a balancing of interests—itself may interfere unreasonably with both the managerial function (the ability of the employer to control the way in which an employee performs his basic job) and with the use of other grievance-resolution mechanisms, such as arbitration, civil service review boards, and whistle-blower remedies, for which employees and employers may have bargained or which legislatures may have enacted.

At the same time, the list of categories substantially overlaps areas where the law already provides nonconstitutional protection through whistle-blower statutes and the like. That overlap diminishes the need for a constitutional forum and also means that adoption of the test would authorize federal Constitution-based legal actions that threaten to upset the legislatively struck (or administratively struck) balance that those statutes (or administrative procedures) embody.

IV

I conclude that the First Amendment sometimes does authorize judicial actions based upon a government employee's speech that both (1) involves a matter of public concern and also (2) takes place in the course of ordinary job-related duties. But it does so only in the presence of augmented need for constitutional protection and diminished risk of undue judicial interference with governmental management of the public's affairs. In my view, these conditions are met in this case and *Pickering* balancing is consequently appropriate.

With respect, I dissent.

————

Note: The Implications of Garcetti

1. Justice Souter, in dissent, emphasizes that the public interest in hearing speech by public employees remains high when the employees "speak as required on some subject at the core of their jobs." Does the majority take issue with that proposition?

2. The Court acknowledges that government employees "in some cases may receive First Amendment protection for expressions made at work." The Court cites *Givhan v. Western Line Consol. School District*, a 1979 decision summarized in Justice Stevens's dissent. Does the Court adequately explain why Givhan's speech was protected, but Ceballos's is not?

3. Justice Breyer stakes out a middle ground between the Court's position and that of Justice Souter. Does his proposed standard provide a better balance? Is it more workable than Justice Souter's?

4. The Court, responding to a concern expressed by Justice Souter, declines to decide "whether the analysis we conduct today would apply in the same manner to a case involving speech related to scholarship or teaching." Should it? If not, how should it be modified?

————

Problem: The Outspoken University Administrator

Rachel Rogers is the assistant director of student housing at State University. The student housing office, where she works, administers the dormitories at the University. Recently the University announced a new policy of excluding unmarried couples from the school's "family" dormitories. In response, Rogers wrote an op-ed for the local newspaper calling upon the University to change its policy. The op-ed said that the University did not follow its normal procedures when promulgating the policy; it also contended the new rule reinforces what Rogers called "a climate of conformity on campus that is antithetical to the university's mission of free inquiry."

The op-ed generated a great deal of controversy in the student housing department. Different administrators took sides on the question of whether unmarried couples should be housed together. In fact, the controversy led to what the head of the department later called a "mini-insurrection" in the office. Ultimately, after several sometimes raucous staff meetings, calm was restored. The op-ed also generated much public discussion of the issue and even some speeches by members of the state legislature supporting the university rule.

Can the university constitutionally suspend Rogers for the op-ed?

––––––––

Note: Testimony as Part of an Employee's "Ordinary" Work Responsibilities

In *Lane v. Franks*, 134 S. Ct. 2369 (2014), the Court considered how broadly *Garcetti* should be read, in the context of a firing precipitated by the fired employee's testimony before a grand jury and a court.

Lane involved Edward Lane, an administrator of a community program in Alabama. After an audit revealed that Suzanne Schmitz, a state representative who was on the program's payroll, was not reporting to work, he confronted Schmitz and eventually fired her. That termination attracted attention, including from federal law enforcement authorities, who began an investigation into Schmitz's employment with the program. Later, Lane testified before a grand jury about his decision to fire Schmitz, and eventually the grand jury indicted Schmitz on federal fraud charges. He also testified at both of her trials, the second of which led to her conviction. Meanwhile, the program continued to suffer financial shortfalls. When Lane recommended to Franks, the head of the program, that there be layoffs, Franks fired Lane. Lane sued. The district court and Court of Appeals both ruled in Franks' favor. Both courts relied on *Garcetti* to conclude that Lane's testimony constituted speech as an employee rather than a citizen, since he had learned of Schmitz's conduct as part of his official duties.

The Supreme Court unanimously reversed. Writing for all nine justices, Justice Sotomayor began her analysis by describing "the question presented: whether the First Amendment protects a public employee who provides truthful sworn testimony, compelled by subpoena, outside the scope of his ordinary job responsibilities." She appended to that sentence a footnote that read, in its entirety, as follows:

It is undisputed that Lane's ordinary job responsibilities did not include testifying in court proceedings. For that reason, Lane asked the Court to decide only whether truthful sworn testimony that is not part of an employee's ordinary job responsibilities is citizen speech on a matter of public concern. We accordingly need not address in this case whether truthful sworn testimony would constitute citizen speech under *Garcetti* when given as part of a public employee's ordinary job duties, and express no opinion on the matter today.

Justice Sotomayor rejected the Court of Appeals' analysis, concluding that it had "read *Garcetti* far too broadly" in holding that Lane spoke as an employee rather than as a citizen when he testified, and thus had no First Amendment right to speak as he did. She observed that, under *Garcetti*, "the mere fact that a citizen's speech concerns information acquired by virtue of his public employment does not transform that speech into employee—rather than citizen—speech." She continued in the next sentence, "[t]he critical question under *Garcetti* is whether the speech at issue is itself ordinarily within the scope of an employee's duties, not whether it merely concerns those duties." In concluding that Lane's testimony constituted speech in his capacity as a citizen, she observed that "[i]t bears emphasis that our precedents dating back to *Pickering* have recognized that speech by public employees on subject matter related to their employment holds special value precisely because those employees gain knowledge of matters of public concern through their employment."

After concluding that Lane spoke as a citizen, Justice Sotomayor then wrote that his testimony, about "corruption in a public program and misuse of state funds," involved a matter of public concern. Turning to the other side of the *Pickering* balance, she concluded that "the employer's side of the *Pickering* scale is entirely empty," given the truthfulness of his testimony and the lack of any other government interest in punishing the speech.

Justice Thomas, joined by Justices Scalia and Alito, concurred to emphasize and approve of the Court's refusal to decide the question about the First Amendment rights of a government employee who testifies "in the course of his ordinary job responsibilities."

Problem: The Police Chief Versus the Mayor

Gilbert Godfrey, the Chief of Police of Monticello City, Jefferson, was suspicious. The mayor of Monticello City, Kelsey Kramden, was reporting unusually large expenses on his city-issue gasoline account, which was administered by the police department. When a subordinate notified Godfrey of the mayor's large charges, Godfrey ordered his subordinates to monitor the mayor's account. When that monitoring revealed further suspicious charges, Godfrey went outside his normal reporting channels and contacted the office of the Jefferson State Auditor to report his concern that Kramden was using his city-issued gasoline card for personal business. Those reports led to the Auditor's office to investigate, and ultimately to order the mayor to reimburse the city for his unauthorized charges. Soon after the Auditor informed the mayor that he was under investigation, the mayor fired Godfrey.

Godfrey sues Kramden, alleging that his firing was retaliation for his exercise of his First Amendment rights. What result, under *Lane v. Franks*? Is there any other information about the case you might need in order to answer that question?

Note: Patronage Dismissals

1. One of the precedents cited in *Connick v. Myers* is *Elrod v. Burns*, 427 U.S. 347 (1976). *Elrod* proved to be the progenitor of another line of cases on the First Amendment rights of public employees. In *Elrod*, the Court (with only a plurality opinion) held that the practice of "patronage dismissals" is unconstitutional. Four years later, in *Branti v. Finkel*, 445 U.S. 507 (1980), a majority endorsed the proposition (as stated in a later case) that "the First Amendment forbids government officials to discharge or threaten to discharge public employees solely for not being supporters of the political party in power, unless party affiliation is an appropriate requirement for the position involved."

The quoted language is from *Rutan v. Republican Party of Illinois*, 497 U.S. 62 (1990). There the Court held that the rule of *Elrod* and *Branti* extends also to "promotion, transfer, recall, and hiring decisions involving low-level public employees." Dissenting in *Rutan*, Justice Scalia argued that patronage dismissals had a long history in American government, and for that reason were constitutional. He also argued that they served important government interests:

> As Justice Powell discussed at length in his *Elrod* dissent, patronage stabilizes political parties and prevents excessive political fragmentation — both of which are results in which States have a strong governmental interest. . . . Patronage, moreover, has been a powerful means of achieving the social and political integration of excluded groups. . . .
>
> I do not deny that the patronage system influences or redirects, perhaps to a substantial degree, individual political expression and political association. But like the many generations of Americans that have preceded us, I do not consider that a significant impairment of free speech or free association.

2. Note that under the *Elrod-Branti* line of cases, public employee plaintiffs can prevail solely by showing that they were discharged "because they were not affiliated with or sponsored by" the party in power. The government's only defense is that "party affiliation is an appropriate requirement for the position involved." In contrast, a *Pickering* claim requires the twofold showing described in *Connick*, including a balancing of the First Amendment interest with the government interest. Why should a public employee's choice of party affiliation receive greater protection than speech on matters of public concern?

B. The First Amendment in the Public Schools

In *Brown v. Board of Education*, 347 U.S. 483 (1954), Chief Justice Warren famously wrote: "Today, education is perhaps the most important function of state and local governments." Not surprisingly, there is probably no setting that has given rise to a greater volume—or variety—of free-speech controversies than the public school. Some of the litigation is brought by teachers asserting rights that they share with other public employees. (*See* section A.) In other cases, parents challenge curricular decisions by teachers or school boards. The public school has also generated a unique body of law delineating the free-speech rights of students. That body of law is the focus of this section.

Tinker v. Des Moines Independent School District
393 U.S. 503 (1969)

Mr. Justice Fortas delivered the opinion of the Court.

Petitioner John F. Tinker, 15 years old, and petitioner Christopher Eckhardt, 16 years old, attended high schools in Des Moines, Iowa. Petitioner Mary Beth Tinker, John's sister, was a 13-year-old student in junior high school.

[In December 1965, a group of adults and students in Des Moines determined to publicize their objections to the hostilities in Vietnam and their support for a truce by wearing black armbands during the holiday season. The principals of the Des Moines schools became aware of the plan and adopted a policy that any student wearing an armband to school would be asked to remove it. Upon refusal the student would be suspended until he or she returned without the armband. Petitioners were aware of the regulation that the school authorities adopted.]

On December 16, Mary Beth and Christopher wore black armbands to their schools. John Tinker wore his armband the next day. They were all sent home and suspended from school until they would come back without their armbands. They did not return to school until after the planned period for wearing armbands had expired—that is, until after New Year's Day.

[The students sued in federal court seeking an injunction restraining the school officials from imposing discipline. After an evidentiary hearing the District Court dismissed the complaint. The court expressly declined to follow the Fifth Circuit's holding in a similar case that the wearing of symbols like the armbands cannot be prohibited unless it "materially and substantially interfere[s] with the requirements of appropriate discipline in the operation of the school." *Burnside v. Byars*, 363 F.2d 744, 749 (1966).[1] The Eighth Circuit, sitting en banc, affirmed by an equally divided court.]

---

1. In *Burnside*, the Fifth Circuit ordered that high school authorities be enjoined from enforcing a regulation forbidding students to wear "freedom buttons." It is instructive that in *Blackwell v. Issaquena County Board of Education*, 363 F.2d 749 (1966), the same panel on the same day reached the opposite result on different facts. It declined to enjoin enforcement of such a regulation in another

I.

The District Court recognized that the wearing of an armband for the purpose of expressing certain views is the type of symbolic act that is within the Free Speech Clause of the First Amendment. As we shall discuss, the wearing of armbands in the circumstances of this case was entirely divorced from actually or potentially disruptive conduct by those participating in it. It was closely akin to "pure speech" which, we have repeatedly held, is entitled to comprehensive protection under the First Amendment.

First Amendment rights, applied in light of the special characteristics of the school environment, are available to teachers and students. It can hardly be argued that either students or teachers shed their constitutional rights to freedom of speech or expression at the schoolhouse gate. This has been the unmistakable holding of this Court for almost 50 years. In *Meyer v. Nebraska*, 262 U.S. 390 (1923), this Court, in [an opinion] by Mr. Justice McReynolds, held that the Due Process Clause of the Fourteenth Amendment prevents States from forbidding the teaching of a foreign language to young students. Statutes to this effect, the Court held, unconstitutionally interfere with the liberty of teacher, student, and parent.

. . . On the other hand, the Court has repeatedly emphasized the need for affirming the comprehensive authority of the States and of school officials, consistent with fundamental constitutional safeguards, to prescribe and control conduct in the schools. Our problem lies in the area where students in the exercise of First Amendment rights collide with the rules of the school authorities.

II.

The problem posed by the present case does not relate to regulation of the length of skirts or the type of clothing, to hair style, or deportment. It does not concern aggressive, disruptive action or even group demonstrations. Our problem involves direct, primary First Amendment rights akin to "pure speech."

The school officials banned and sought to punish petitioners for a silent, passive expression of opinion, unaccompanied by any disorder or disturbance on the part of petitioners. There is here no evidence whatever of petitioners' interference, actual or nascent, with the schools' work or of collision with the rights of other students to be secure and to be let alone. Accordingly, this case does not concern speech or action that intrudes upon the work of the schools or the rights of other students.

Only a few of the 18,000 students in the school system wore the black armbands. Only five students were suspended for wearing them. There is no indication that the work of the schools or any class was disrupted. Outside the classrooms, a few students made hostile remarks to the children wearing armbands, but there were no threats or acts of violence on school premises.

_____
high school where the students wearing freedom buttons harassed students who did not wear them and created much disturbance.

The District Court concluded that the action of the school authorities was reasonable because it was based upon their fear of a disturbance from the wearing of the armbands. But, in our system, undifferentiated fear or apprehension of disturbance is not enough to overcome the right to freedom of expression. Any departure from absolute regimentation may cause trouble. Any variation from the majority's opinion may inspire fear. Any word spoken, in class, in the lunchroom, or on the campus, that deviates from the views of another person may start an argument or cause a disturbance. But our Constitution says we must take this risk, *Terminiello v. Chicago* (1949) [*supra* Chapter 8]; and our history says that it is this sort of hazardous freedom—this kind of openness—that is the basis of our national strength and of the independence and vigor of Americans who grow up and live in this relatively permissive, often disputatious, society.

In order for the State in the person of school officials to justify prohibition of a particular expression of opinion, it must be able to show that its action was caused by something more than a mere desire to avoid the discomfort and unpleasantness that always accompany an unpopular viewpoint. Certainly where there is no finding and no showing that engaging in the forbidden conduct would "materially and substantially interfere with the requirements of appropriate discipline in the operation of the school," the prohibition cannot be sustained. *Burnside v. Byars.*

In the present case, the District Court made no such finding, and our independent examination of the record fails to yield evidence that the school authorities had reason to anticipate that the wearing of the armbands would substantially interfere with the work of the school or impinge upon the rights of other students. . . . On the contrary, the action of the school authorities appears to have been based upon an urgent wish to avoid the controversy which might result from the expression, even by the silent symbol of armbands, of opposition to this Nation's part in the conflagration in Vietnam. . . .

It is also relevant that the school authorities did not purport to prohibit the wearing of all symbols of political or controversial significance. The record shows that students in some of the schools wore buttons relating to national political campaigns, and some even wore the Iron Cross, traditionally a symbol of Nazism. The order prohibiting the wearing of armbands did not extend to these. Instead, a particular symbol—black armbands worn to exhibit opposition to this Nation's involvement in Vietnam—was singled out for prohibition. Clearly, the prohibition of expression of one particular opinion, at least without evidence that it is necessary to avoid material and substantial interference with schoolwork or discipline, is not constitutionally permissible.

In our system, state-operated schools may not be enclaves of totalitarianism. School officials do not possess absolute authority over their students. Students in school as well as out of school are "persons" under our Constitution. They are possessed of fundamental rights which the State must respect, just as they themselves must respect their obligations to the State. In our system, students may not be regarded as closed-circuit recipients of only that which the State chooses to communicate. They may not be confined to the expression of those sentiments that are officially approved. In the absence of a specific showing of constitutionally valid reasons to regulate their speech, students are entitled to freedom of expression of their views. . . .

. . . The principal use to which the schools are dedicated is to accommodate students during prescribed hours for the purpose of certain types of activities. Among those activities is personal intercommunication among the students. This is not only an inevitable part of the process of attending school; it is also an important part of the educational process. A student's rights, therefore, do not embrace merely the classroom hours. When he is in the cafeteria, or on the playing field, or on the campus during the authorized hours, he may express his opinions, even on controversial subjects like the conflict in Vietnam, if he does so without "materially and substantially interfer[ing] with the requirements of appropriate discipline in the operation of the school" and without colliding with the rights of others. But conduct by the student, in class or out of it, which for any reason — whether it stems from time, place, or type of behavior — materially disrupts classwork or involves substantial disorder or invasion of the rights of others is, of course, not immunized by the constitutional guarantee of freedom of speech. *Cf. Blackwell v. Issaquena County Board of Education* [footnote 1] . . .

As we have discussed, the record does not demonstrate any facts which might reasonably have led school authorities to forecast substantial disruption of or material interference with school activities, and no disturbances or disorders on the school premises in fact occurred. These petitioners . . . neither interrupted school activities nor sought to intrude in the school affairs or the lives of others. They caused discussion outside of the classrooms, but no interference with work and no disorder. In the circumstances, our Constitution does not permit officials of the State to deny their form of expression. [Reversed.]

Mr. Justice Stewart, concurring.

Although I agree with much of what is said in the Court's opinion, and with its judgment in this case, I cannot share the Court's uncritical assumption that, school discipline aside, the First Amendment rights of children are co-extensive with those of adults. Indeed, I had thought the Court decided otherwise just last Term in *Ginsberg v. New York*, 390 U.S. 629 (1968). I continue to hold the view I expressed in that case: "[A] State may permissibly determine that, at least in some precisely delineated areas, a child — like someone in a captive audience — is not possessed of that full capacity for individual choice which is the presupposition of First Amendment guarantees."

Mr. Justice White, concurring. [Omitted.]

Mr. Justice Black, dissenting.

The Court's holding in this case ushers in what I deem to be an entirely new era in which the power to control pupils by the elected "officials of state supported public schools" in the United States is in ultimate effect transferred to the Supreme Court. . . .

Assuming that the Court is correct in holding that the conduct of wearing arm-bands for the purpose of conveying political ideas is protected by the First Amendment, *cf.*, *e.g.*, *Giboney v. Empire Storage & Ice Co.*, 336 U.S. 490 (1949) [Note *supra* Chapter 2], the crucial remaining questions are whether students and teachers may use the schools at their whim as a platform for the exercise of free speech— "symbolic" or "pure"—and whether the courts will allocate to themselves the func-tion of deciding how the pupils' school day will be spent. While I have always believed that under the First and Fourteenth Amendments neither the State nor the Federal Government has any authority to regulate or censor the content of speech, I have never believed that any person has a right to give speeches or engage in demonstra-tions where he pleased and when he pleases. This Court has already rejected such a notion. . . .

While the record does not show that any of these armband students shouted, used profane language, or were violent in any manner, detailed testimony by some of them shows their armbands caused comments, warnings by other students, the poking of fun at them, and a warning by an older football player that other, nonprotesting stu-dents had better let them alone. There is also evidence that a teacher of mathematics had his lesson period practically "wrecked" chiefly by disputes with Mary Beth Tinker, who wore her armband for her "demonstration." Even a casual reading of the record shows that this armband did divert students' minds from their regular lessons, and that talk, comments, etc., made John Tinker "self-conscious" in attending school with his armband. While the absence of obscene remarks or boisterous and loud disorder per-haps justifies the Court's statement that the few armband students did not actually "disrupt" the classwork, I think the record overwhelmingly shows that the armbands did exactly what the elected school officials and principals foresaw they would, that is, took the students' minds off their classwork and diverted them to thoughts about the highly emotional subject of the Vietnam war. . . .

[I deny] that it has been the "unmistakable holding of this Court for almost 50 years" that "students" and "teachers" take with them into the "schoolhouse gate" constitu-tional rights to "freedom of speech or expression." Even *Meyer* did not hold that. It makes no reference to "symbolic speech" at all; what it did was to strike down as "unreasonable" and therefore unconstitutional a Nebraska law barring the teaching of the German language before the children reached the eighth grade. One can well agree with Mr. Justice Holmes and Mr. Justice Sutherland, as I do, that such a law was no more unreasonable than it would be to bar the teaching of Latin and Greek to pupils who have not reached the eighth grade. . . .

Mr. Justice Harlan, dissenting.

I certainly agree that state public school authorities in the discharge of their responsibilities are not wholly exempt from the requirements of the Fourteenth Amendment respecting the freedoms of expression and association. At the same time I am reluctant to believe that there is any disagreement between the majority and myself on the proposition that school officials should be accorded the widest authority in maintaining discipline and good order in their institutions. To translate that proposition into a workable constitutional rule, I would, in cases like this, cast upon those complaining the burden of showing that a particular school measure was motivated by other than legitimate school concerns—for example, a desire to prohibit the expression of an unpopular point of view, while permitting expression of the dominant opinion.

Finding nothing in this record which impugns the good faith of respondents in promulgating the armband regulation, I would affirm the judgment below.

————

Note: The Implications of Tinker

1. The extracts from Justice Black's dissent constitute only a small portion of a lengthy (and very angry) opinion. Why did Justice Black, usually a vigorous defender of First Amendment rights, resist so strongly the claim in *Tinker*?

2. Justice Fortas' invocation of *Meyer v. Nebraska* is somewhat disingenuous, is it not? Certainly nothing could have been more calculated to arouse the opposition of Justice Black. See, for example, Justice Black's dissent in *Griswold v. Connecticut*, 381 U.S. 479 (1965).

3. In rejecting the school district's arguments based on "undifferentiated fear or apprehension of disturbance," the Court cites *Terminiello v. Chicago* (1949) (*supra* Chapter 8), a criminal prosecution. Is the Court suggesting that students can be disciplined for expressive activity only when a criminal prosecution would be constitutionally permissible? Would that be a sensible standard?

4. The Court repeatedly cites the Fifth Circuit decision in *Burnside v. Byars*, 363 F.2d 744 (5th Cir. 1966), which required a showing that the student activity "materially and substantially interfere[d] with the requirements of appropriate discipline." Consider what happens to that standard in the later decisions on the First Amendment rights of public school students.

————

Note: From Tinker to the "Bong Hits" Case

1. Like *New York Times v. Sullivan* (*supra* Chapter 2), the *Tinker* decision created a new area of First Amendment litigation. But in contrast to the constitutionalization of libel law, the Court made no immediate effort to clarify or refine the particulars of the newly announced constitutional doctrine. On the contrary, for more than 15 years the Court left the development of the law entirely to the lower courts. Not until 1986 did the Court again speak to the constitutional rights of public school students. Another decision followed two years later—after which the Court again remained silent, this time for almost two decades.

2. The first of the post-*Tinker* cases was *Bethel School District No. 403 v. Fraser*, 478 U.S. 675 (1986). In *Fraser*, a high school student was disciplined for delivering a "sexually explicit" speech at a school assembly. The speech—nominating a fellow student for student elective office—was as follows:

> I know a man who is firm—he's firm in his pants, he's firm in his shirt, his character is firm—but most . . . of all, his belief in you, the students of Bethel, is firm.
>
> Jeff Kuhlman is a man who takes his point and pounds it in. If necessary, he'll take an issue and nail it to the wall. He doesn't attack things in spurts—he drives hard, pushing and pushing until finally—he succeeds.
>
> Jeff is a man who will go to the very end—even the climax, for each and every one of you.
>
> So vote for Jeff for A.S.B. vice-president—he'll never come between you and the best our high school can be.

The lower court held that the imposition of discipline violated Fraser's First Amendment rights, but the Supreme Court reversed in an opinion by Chief Justice Burger. The opinion distinguished *Tinker* in the following language:

> Unlike the sanctions imposed on the students wearing armbands in *Tinker*, the penalties imposed in this case were unrelated to any political viewpoint. The First Amendment does not prevent the school officials from determining that to permit a vulgar and lewd speech such as [Fraser's] would undermine the school's basic educational mission. A high school assembly or classroom is no place for a sexually explicit monologue directed towards an unsuspecting audience of teenage students. Accordingly, it was perfectly appropriate for the school to disassociate itself to make the point to the pupils that vulgar speech and lewd conduct is wholly inconsistent with the "fundamental values" of public school education. Justice Black, dissenting in *Tinker*, made a point that is especially relevant in this case: "I wish therefore, . . . to disclaim any purpose . . . to hold that the Federal Constitution compels the teachers, parents, and elected school officials to surrender control of the American public school system to public school students."

Two aspects of the *Fraser* opinion were noteworthy. First, as seen in the extract above, the Court quoted from the *dissent* in *Tinker* and said that Justice Black's point was "especially relevant in this case." Second, the Court conspicuously did *not* say that *Tinker* was distinguishable because Fraser's speech did cause disruption.

Five Justices joined Chief Justice Burger's opinion. Justice Brennan concurred only in the judgment. In his separate opinion, he disputed the Court's characterization of Fraser's remarks as "vulgar" and "lewd." Rather, he emphasized "the discretion school officials have . . . to prevent disruption of school educational activities." He said: "[The] Court holds that under certain circumstances, high school students may properly be reprimanded for giving a speech at a high school assembly which school officials conclude disrupted the school's educational mission." Justice Blackmun concurred in the judgment without opinion. Justice Marshall and Justice Stevens dissented.

3. Two years after *Fraser*, the Court decided *Hazelwood School District v. Kuhlmeier*, 484 U.S. 260 (1988). The plaintiffs were three former students of a public high school, Hazelwood East, who had been staff members of Spectrum, the school newspaper.

They contended that the school principal violated their First Amendment rights by requiring the deletion of two articles from the May 13, 1983, issue of Spectrum. One of the articles described three Hazelwood East students' experiences with pregnancy; the other discussed the impact of divorce on students at the school.

The Court first considered whether Spectrum "may appropriately be characterized as a forum for public expression." The Court found that school officials "reserve[d] the forum for its intended purpos[e]," as a supervised learning experience for journalism students. The opinion continued:

> The question whether the First Amendment requires a school to tolerate particular student speech — the question that we addressed in *Tinker* — is different from the question whether the First Amendment requires a school affirmatively to promote particular student speech. The former question addresses educators' ability to silence a student's personal expression that happens to occur on the school premises. The latter question concerns educators' authority over school-sponsored publications, theatrical productions, and other expressive activities that students, parents, and members of the public might reasonably perceive to bear the imprimatur of the school. These activities may fairly be characterized as part of the school curriculum, whether or not they occur in a traditional classroom setting, so long as they are supervised by faculty members and designed to impart particular knowledge or skills to student participants and audiences.

> Educators are entitled to exercise greater control over this second form of student expression to assure that participants learn whatever lessons the activity is designed to teach, that readers or listeners are not exposed to material that may be inappropriate for their level of maturity, and that the views of the individual speaker are not erroneously attributed to the school. Hence, a school may in its capacity as publisher of a school newspaper or producer of a school play "disassociate itself," *Fraser*, not only from speech that would "substantially interfere with [its] work . . . or impinge upon the rights of other students," *Tinker*, but also from speech that is, for example, ungrammatical, poorly written, inadequately researched, biased or prejudiced, vulgar or profane, or unsuitable for immature audiences. A school must be able to set high standards for the student speech that is disseminated under its auspices — standards that may be higher than those demanded by some newspaper publishers or theatrical producers in the "real" world — and may refuse to disseminate student speech that does not meet those standards.

> In addition, a school must be able to take into account the emotional maturity of the intended audience in determining whether to disseminate student speech on potentially sensitive topics, which might range from the existence of Santa Claus in an elementary school setting to the particulars of teenage sexual activity in a high school setting. A school must also retain the authority to refuse to sponsor student speech that might reasonably be perceived to advocate drug or alcohol use, irresponsible sex, or conduct

otherwise inconsistent with "the shared values of a civilized social order," *Fraser*, or to associate the school with any position other than neutrality on matters of political controversy. . . .

Accordingly, we conclude that the standard articulated in *Tinker* for determining when a school may punish student expression need not also be the standard for determining when a school may refuse to lend its name and resources to the dissemination of student expression. Instead, we hold that educators do not offend the First Amendment by exercising editorial control over the style and content of student speech in school-sponsored expressive activities so long as their actions are reasonably related to legitimate pedagogical concerns.

. . . It is only when the decision to censor a school-sponsored publication, theatrical production, or other vehicle of student expression has no valid educational purpose that the First Amendment is so "directly and sharply implicate[d]," as to require judicial intervention to protect students' constitutional rights.

The Court then found that the principal had acted reasonably in requiring the deletion of the two contested articles.

Justice Brennan, joined by Justice Marshall and Justice Blackmun, dissented. He invoked both precedent and policy. On precedent, he said:

The Court today . . . erects a taxonomy of school censorship, concluding that *Tinker* applies to one category and not another. On the one hand is censorship "to silence a student's personal expression that happens to occur on the school premises." On the other hand is censorship of expression that arises in the context of "school-sponsored . . . expressive activities that students, parents, and members of the public might reasonably perceive to bear the imprimatur of the school."

The Court does not, for it cannot, purport to discern from our precedents the distinction it creates. One could, I suppose, readily characterize the students' symbolic speech in *Tinker* as "personal expression that happens to [have] occur[red] on school premises," although *Tinker* did not even hint that the personal nature of the speech was of any (much less dispositive) relevance. But that same description could not by any stretch of the imagination fit Fraser's speech. . . . [If] ever a forum for student expression was "school-sponsored," Fraser's was.

Justice Brennan quoted from the *Fraser* opinion: "The assembly [at which Fraser delivered his nominating speech] was part of a *school-sponsored* educational program in self-government." (Emphasis added by Justice Brennan.)

The dissent continued:

Even if we were writing on a clean slate, I would reject the Court's rationale for abandoning *Tinker* in this case. The Court offers no more than an obscure tangle of three excuses to afford educators "greater control" over school-sponsored speech than the *Tinker* test would permit: the public educator's prerogative to control curriculum; the pedagogical interest in shielding the high school audience from objectionable viewpoints and sensitive topics; and the school's need to dissociate itself from student expression. None of the excuses, once disentangled, supports the distinction that the Court draws. *Tinker* fully addresses the first concern; the second is illegitimate; and the third is readily achievable through less oppressive means.

4. How far did *Fraser* and *Kuhlmeier* cut into the *Tinker* holding? For nearly two decades, the Supreme Court turned down every opportunity to answer that question. The Court ended its silence in 2007 in a case that received widespread public attention.

Morse v. Frederick

551 U.S. 393 (2007)

CHIEF JUSTICE ROBERTS delivered the opinion of the Court.

At a school-sanctioned and school-supervised event, a high school principal saw some of her students unfurl a large banner conveying a message she reasonably regarded as promoting illegal drug use. Consistent with established school policy prohibiting such messages at school events, the principal directed the students to take down the banner. One student—among those who had brought the banner to the event—refused to do so. The principal confiscated the banner and later suspended the student. The Ninth Circuit held that the principal's actions violated the First Amendment, and that the student could sue the principal for damages.

Our cases make clear that students do not "shed their constitutional rights to freedom of speech or expression at the schoolhouse gate." *Tinker*. At the same time, we have held that "the constitutional rights of students in public school are not automatically coextensive with the rights of adults in other settings," *Fraser*, 478 U.S. 675 (1986), and that the rights of students "must be 'applied in light of the special characteristics of the school environment.'" *Hazelwood School Dist. v. Kuhlmeier* (quoting *Tinker*). Consistent with these principles, we hold that schools may take steps to safeguard those entrusted to their care from speech that can reasonably be regarded as encouraging illegal drug use. We conclude that the school officials in this case did not violate the First Amendment by confiscating the pro-drug banner and suspending the student responsible for it.

I

On January 24, 2002, the Olympic Torch Relay passed through Juneau, Alaska, on its way to the winter games in Salt Lake City, Utah. The torchbearers were to proceed along a street in front of Juneau-Douglas High School (JDHS) while school was in session. Petitioner Deborah Morse, the school principal, decided to permit staff and students to participate in the Torch Relay as an approved social event or class trip.

Students were allowed to leave class to observe the relay from either side of the street. Teachers and administrative officials monitored the students' actions.

Respondent Joseph Frederick, a JDHS senior, was late to school that day. When he arrived, he joined his friends (all but one of whom were JDHS students) across the street from the school to watch the event. Not all the students waited patiently. Some became rambunctious, throwing plastic cola bottles and snowballs and scuffling with their classmates. As the torchbearers and camera crews passed by, Frederick and his friends unfurled a 14-foot banner bearing the phrase: "BONG HiTS 4 JESUS." The large banner was easily readable by the students on the other side of the street.

Principal Morse immediately crossed the street and demanded that the banner be taken down. Everyone but Frederick complied. Morse confiscated the banner and told Frederick to report to her office, where she suspended him for 10 days. Morse later explained that she told Frederick to take the banner down because she thought it encouraged illegal drug use, in violation of established school policy. Juneau School Board Policy No. 5520 states: "The Board specifically prohibits any assembly or public expression that . . . advocates the use of substances that are illegal to minors. . . ."

Frederick administratively appealed his suspension, but the Juneau School District Superintendent upheld it, limiting it to time served (8 days). In a memorandum setting forth his reasons, the superintendent determined that Frederick had displayed his banner "in the midst of his fellow students, during school hours, at a school-sanctioned activity." He further explained that Frederick "was not disciplined because the principal of the school 'disagreed' with his message, but because his speech appeared to advocate the use of illegal drugs."

The superintendent continued:

> The common-sense understanding of the phrase "bong hits" is that it is a reference to a means of smoking marijuana. Given [Frederick's] inability or unwillingness to express any other credible meaning for the phrase, I can only agree with the principal and countless others who saw the banner as advocating the use of illegal drugs. [Frederick's] speech was not political. He was not advocating the legalization of marijuana or promoting a religious belief. He was displaying a fairly silly message promoting illegal drug usage in the midst of a school activity, for the benefit of television cameras covering the Torch Relay. [Frederick's] speech was potentially disruptive to the event and clearly disruptive of and inconsistent with the school's educational mission to educate students about the dangers of illegal drugs and to discourage their use.

Relying on our decision in *Fraser*, the superintendent concluded that the principal's actions were permissible because Frederick's banner was "speech or action that intrudes upon the work of the schools." The Juneau School District Board of Education upheld the suspension.

Frederick then filed suit under 42 U.S.C. § 1983, alleging that the school board and Morse had violated his First Amendment rights. [The district court ruled for the school board, but the Ninth Circuit reversed.] The court [concluded] that Frederick's right to display his banner was so "clearly established" that a reasonable principal in Morse's position would have understood that her actions were unconstitutional, and that Morse was therefore not entitled to qualified immunity.

We granted certiorari on two questions: whether Frederick had a First Amendment right to wield his banner, and, if so, whether that right was so clearly established that the principal may be held liable for damages. We resolve the first question against Frederick, and therefore have no occasion to reach the second.

II

At the outset, we reject Frederick's argument that this is not a school speech case — as has every other authority to address the question. . . . [We] agree with the superintendent that Frederick cannot "stand in the midst of his fellow students, during school hours, at a school-sanctioned activity and claim he is not at school." There is some uncertainty at the outer boundaries as to when courts should apply school-speech precedents, see *Porter v. Ascension Parish School Bd.*, 393 F.3d 608, 615 n.22 (5th Cir. 2004), but not on these facts.

III

The message on Frederick's banner is cryptic. It is no doubt offensive to some, perhaps amusing to others. To still others, it probably means nothing at all. Frederick himself claimed "that the words were just nonsense meant to attract television cameras." But Principal Morse thought the banner would be interpreted by those viewing it as promoting illegal drug use, and that interpretation is plainly a reasonable one. . . .

At least two interpretations of the words on the banner demonstrate that the sign advocated the use of illegal drugs. First, the phrase could be interpreted as an imperative: "[Take] bong hits . . ." — a message equivalent, as Morse explained in her declaration, to "smoke marijuana" or "use an illegal drug." Alternatively, the phrase could be viewed as celebrating drug use — "bong hits [are a good thing]," or "[we take] bong hits" — and we discern no meaningful distinction between celebrating illegal drug use in the midst of fellow students and outright advocacy or promotion. . . .

The dissent mentions Frederick's "credible and uncontradicted explanation for the message — he just wanted to get on television." But that is a description of Frederick's *motive* for displaying the banner; it is not an interpretation of what the banner says. The *way* Frederick was going to fulfill his ambition of appearing on television was by unfurling a pro-drug banner at a school event, in the presence of teachers and fellow students.

Elsewhere in its opinion, the dissent emphasizes the importance of political speech and the need to foster "national debate about a serious issue," as if to suggest that the banner is political speech. But not even Frederick argues that the banner conveys any sort of political or religious message. Contrary to the dissent's suggestion, this is plainly not a case about political debate over the criminalization of drug use or possession.

IV

The question thus becomes whether a principal may, consistent with the First Amendment, restrict student speech at a school event, when that speech is reasonably viewed as promoting illegal drug use. We hold that she may.

In *Tinker*, this Court . . . held that student expression may not be suppressed unless school officials reasonably conclude that it will "materially and substantially disrupt the work and discipline of the school." The essential facts of *Tinker* are quite stark, implicating concerns at the heart of the First Amendment. The students sought to engage in political speech, using the armbands to express their "disapproval of the Vietnam hostilities and their advocacy of a truce, to make their views known, and, by their example, to influence others to adopt them." . . . The only interest the Court discerned underlying the school's actions was the "mere desire to avoid the discomfort and unpleasantness that always accompany an unpopular viewpoint," or "an urgent wish to avoid the controversy which might result from the expression." That interest was not enough to justify banning "a silent, passive expression of opinion, unaccompanied by any disorder or disturbance."

This Court's next student speech case was *Fraser*. . . . The mode of analysis employed in *Fraser* is not entirely clear. . . . We need not resolve [the] debate to decide this case. For present purposes, it is enough to distill from *Fraser* two basic principles. First, *Fraser*'s holding demonstrates that "the constitutional rights of students in public school are not automatically coextensive with the rights of adults in other settings." Had Fraser delivered the same speech in a public forum outside the school context, it would have been protected. *See Cohen v. California* (1971) [*supra* Chapter 3]. In school, however, Fraser's First Amendment rights were circumscribed "in light of the special characteristics of the school environment." *Tinker*. Second, *Fraser* established that the mode of analysis set forth in *Tinker* is not absolute. Whatever approach *Fraser* employed, it certainly did not conduct the "substantial disruption" analysis prescribed by *Tinker*.

Our most recent student speech case [is] *Kuhlmeier*. . . . *Kuhlmeier* does not control this case because no one would reasonably believe that Frederick's banner bore the school's imprimatur. The case is nevertheless instructive because it confirms both principles cited above. . . . [Like] *Fraser*, it confirms that the rule of *Tinker* is not the only basis for restricting student speech.

Drawing on the principles applied in our student speech cases, we have held in the Fourth Amendment context that "while children assuredly do not 'shed their constitutional rights . . . at the schoolhouse gate,' . . . the nature of those rights is what is appropriate for children in school." *Vernonia School Dist. 47J v. Acton*, 515 U.S. 646 (1995) (quoting *Tinker*). . . .

Even more to the point, these cases also recognize that deterring drug use by schoolchildren is an "important—indeed, perhaps compelling" interest. Drug abuse can cause severe and permanent damage to the health and well-being of young people. . . .

Congress has declared that part of a school's job is educating students about the dangers of illegal drug use. It has provided billions of dollars to support state and local drug-prevention programs, and required that schools receiving federal funds under the Safe and Drug-Free Schools and Communities Act of 1994 certify that their drug prevention programs "convey a clear and consistent message that . . . the illegal use of drugs [is] wrong and harmful."

Thousands of school boards throughout the country—including JDHS—have adopted policies aimed at effectuating this message. Those school boards know that peer pressure is perhaps "the single most important factor leading schoolchildren to take drugs," and that students are more likely to use drugs when the norms in school appear to tolerate such behavior. Student speech celebrating illegal drug use at a school event, in the presence of school administrators and teachers, thus poses a particular challenge for school officials working to protect those entrusted to their care from the dangers of drug abuse.

The "special characteristics of the school environment," *Tinker*, and the governmental interest in stopping student drug abuse—reflected in the policies of Congress and myriad school boards, including JDHS—allow schools to restrict student expression that they reasonably regard as promoting illegal drug use. *Tinker* warned that schools may not prohibit student speech because of "undifferentiated fear or apprehension of disturbance" or "a mere desire to avoid the discomfort and unpleasantness that always accompany an unpopular viewpoint." The danger here is far more serious and palpable. The particular concern to prevent student drug abuse at issue here, embodied in established school policy, extends well beyond an abstract desire to avoid controversy.

Petitioners urge us to adopt the broader rule that Frederick's speech is proscribable because it is plainly "offensive" as that term is used in *Fraser*. We think this stretches *Fraser* too far; that case should not be read to encompass any speech that could fit under some definition of "offensive." After all, much political and religious speech might be perceived as offensive to some. The concern here is not that Frederick's speech was offensive, but that it was reasonably viewed as promoting illegal drug use.

Although accusing this decision of doing "serious violence to the First Amendment" by authorizing "viewpoint discrimination," the dissent concludes that "it might well be appropriate to tolerate some targeted viewpoint discrimination in this unique setting." Nor do we understand the dissent to take the position that schools are required to tolerate student advocacy of illegal drug use at school events, even if that advocacy falls short of inviting "imminent" lawless action. And even the dissent recognizes that the issues here are close enough that the principal should not be held liable in damages, but should instead enjoy qualified immunity for her actions. Stripped of rhetorical flourishes, then, the debate between the dissent and this opinion is less about constitutional first principles than about whether Frederick's banner constitutes promotion of illegal drug use. We have explained our view that it does. The dissent's contrary view on that relatively narrow question hardly justifies sounding the First Amendment bugle.

* * *

School principals have a difficult job, and a vitally important one. When Frederick suddenly and unexpectedly unfurled his banner, Morse had to decide to act — or not act — on the spot. It was reasonable for her to conclude that the banner promoted illegal drug use — in violation of established school policy — and that failing to act would send a powerful message to the students in her charge, including Frederick, about how serious the school was about the dangers of illegal drug use. The First Amendment does not require schools to tolerate at school events student expression that contributes to those dangers.

The judgment of the United States Court of Appeals for the Ninth Circuit is reversed, and the case is remanded for further proceedings consistent with this opinion.

JUSTICE THOMAS, concurring.

[Justice Thomas joined the opinion of the Court, but he also wrote a concurring opinion arguing at length that "the standard set forth in *Tinker* is without basis in the Constitution" and that *Tinker* should be overruled when the opportunity arises. In his view, "the history of public education suggest that the First Amendment, as originally understood, does not protect student speech in public schools."]

JUSTICE ALITO, with whom JUSTICE KENNEDY joins, concurring.

I join the opinion of the Court on the understanding that (a) it goes no further than to hold that a public school may restrict speech that a reasonable observer would interpret as advocating illegal drug use and (b) it provides no support for any restriction of speech that can plausibly be interpreted as commenting on any political or social issue, including speech on issues such as "the wisdom of the war on drugs or of legalizing marijuana for medicinal use." . . .

The Court is [correct] in noting that *Tinker*, which permits the regulation of student speech that threatens a concrete and "substantial disruption," does not set out the only ground on which in-school student speech may be regulated by state actors in a way that would not be constitutional in other settings.

But I do not read the opinion to mean that there are necessarily any grounds for such regulation that are not already recognized in the holdings of this Court. In addition to *Tinker*, the decision in the present case allows the restriction of speech advocating illegal drug use; *Fraser* permits the regulation of speech that is delivered in a lewd or vulgar manner as part of a middle school program; and *Kuhlmeier* allows a school to regulate what is in essence the school's own speech, that is, articles that appear in a publication that is an official school organ. I join the opinion of the Court on the understanding that the opinion does not hold that the special characteristics of the public schools necessarily justify any other speech restrictions.

The opinion of the Court does not endorse the broad argument advanced by petitioners and the United States that the First Amendment permits public school officials to censor any student speech that interferes with a school's "educational mission." This argument can easily be manipulated in dangerous ways, and I would reject it before such abuse occurs. The "educational mission" of the public schools is defined by the elected and appointed public officials with authority over the schools and by the school administrators and faculty. As a result, some public schools have defined their educational missions as including the inculcation of whatever political and social views are held by the members of these groups.

During the *Tinker* era, a public school could have defined its educational mission to include solidarity with our soldiers and their families and thus could have attempted to outlaw the wearing of black armbands on the ground that they undermined this mission. Alternatively, a school could have defined its educational mission to include the promotion of world peace and could have sought to ban the wearing of buttons expressing support for the troops on the ground that the buttons signified approval of war. The "educational mission" argument would give public school authorities a license to suppress speech on political and social issues based on disagreement with the viewpoint expressed. The argument, therefore, strikes at the very heart of the First Amendment.

The public schools are invaluable and beneficent institutions, but they are, after all, organs of the State. . . . Most parents, realistically, have no choice but to send their children to a public school and little ability to influence what occurs in the school. . . .

For these reasons, any argument for altering the usual free speech rules in the public schools cannot rest on a theory of delegation but must instead be based on some special characteristic of the school setting. The special characteristic that is relevant in this case is the threat to the physical safety of students. School attendance can expose students to threats to their physical safety that they would not otherwise face. . . . Students may be compelled on a daily basis to spend time at close quarters with other students who may do them harm. Experience shows that schools can be places of special danger.

In most settings, the First Amendment strongly limits the government's ability to suppress speech on the ground that it presents a threat of violence. *See Brandenburg v. Ohio* [*supra* Chapter 1]. But due to the special features of the school environment, school officials must have greater authority to intervene before speech leads to violence. And, in most cases, *Tinker*'s "substantial disruption" standard permits school officials to step in before actual violence erupts.

Speech advocating illegal drug use poses a threat to student safety that is just as serious, if not always as immediately obvious. As we have recognized in the past and as the opinion of the Court today details, illegal drug use presents a grave and in many ways unique threat to the physical safety of students. I therefore conclude that the public schools may ban speech advocating illegal drug use. But I regard such regulation as standing at the far reaches of what the First Amendment permits. I join the opinion of the Court with the understanding that the opinion does not endorse any further extension.

Justice Breyer, concurring in the judgment in part and dissenting in part.

[Justice Breyer argued that the Court did not have to resolve "the fractious underlying constitutional question"; rather, it should hold that "[q]ualified immunity applies here and entitles Principal Morse to judgment on Frederick's monetary damages claim because she did not clearly violate the law during her confrontation with the student."]

JUSTICE STEVENS, with whom JUSTICE SOUTER and JUSTICE GINSBURG join, dissenting.

I

. . . I agree with the Court that the principal should not be held liable for pulling down Frederick's banner. I would hold, however, that the school's interest in protecting its students from exposure to speech "reasonably regarded as promoting illegal drug use" cannot justify disciplining Frederick for his attempt to make an ambiguous statement to a television audience simply because it contained an oblique reference to drugs. The First Amendment demands more, indeed, much more. . . .

In my judgment, the First Amendment protects student speech if the message itself neither violates a permissible rule nor expressly advocates conduct that is illegal and harmful to students. This nonsense banner does neither, and the Court does serious violence to the First Amendment in upholding—indeed, lauding—a school's decision to punish Frederick for expressing a view with which it disagreed. . . .

Two cardinal First Amendment principles animate both the Court's opinion in *Tinker* and Justice Harlan's dissent. First, censorship based on the content of speech, particularly censorship that depends on the viewpoint of the speaker, is subject to the most rigorous burden of justification. . . .

Second, punishing someone for advocating illegal conduct is constitutional only when the advocacy is likely to provoke the harm that the government seeks to avoid. *See Brandenburg v. Ohio.*

However necessary it may be to modify those principles in the school setting, *Tinker* affirmed their continuing vitality. . . .

Yet today the Court fashions a test that trivializes the two cardinal principles upon which *Tinker* rests. The Court's test invites stark viewpoint discrimination. In this case, for example, the principal has unabashedly acknowledged that she disciplined Frederick because she disagreed with the pro-drug viewpoint she ascribed to the message on the banner. . . .

It is also perfectly clear that "promoting illegal drug use" comes nowhere close to proscribable "incitement to imminent lawless action." *Brandenburg.*

II

The Court rejects outright these twin foundations of *Tinker* because, in its view, the unusual importance of protecting children from the scourge of drugs supports a ban on all speech in the school environment that promotes drug use. Whether or not such a rule is sensible as a matter of policy, carving out pro-drug speech for uniquely harsh treatment finds no support in our case law and is inimical to the values protected by the First Amendment.

I will nevertheless assume for the sake of argument that the school's concededly powerful interest in protecting its students adequately supports its restriction on "any assembly or public expression that . . . advocates the use of substances that are illegal to minors. . . ." [And] it is possible that our rigid imminence requirement ought to be relaxed at schools.

But it is one thing to restrict speech that *advocates* drug use. It is another thing entirely to prohibit an obscure message with a drug theme that a third party subjectively — and not very reasonably — thinks is tantamount to express advocacy. . . .

On occasion, the Court suggests it is deferring to the principal's "reasonable" judgment that Frederick's sign qualified as drug advocacy. At other times, the Court seems to say that *it* thinks the banner's message constitutes express advocacy. Either way, its approach is indefensible.

To the extent the Court defers to the principal's ostensibly reasonable judgment, it abdicates its constitutional responsibility. The beliefs of third parties, reasonable or otherwise, have never dictated which messages amount to proscribable advocacy. . . .

To the extent the Court independently finds that "BONG HiTS 4 JESUS" *objectively* amounts to the advocacy of illegal drug use — in other words, that it can *most* reasonably be interpreted as such — that conclusion practically refutes itself. This is a nonsense message, not advocacy. . . . Frederick's credible and uncontradicted explanation for the message — he just wanted to get on television — is also relevant because a speaker who does not intend to persuade his audience can hardly be said to be advocating anything. . . . The notion that the message on this banner would actually persuade either the average student or even the dumbest one to change his or her behavior is most implausible. That the Court believes such a silly message can be proscribed as advocacy underscores the novelty of its position, and suggests that the principle it articulates has no stopping point. . . .

Among other things, the Court's ham-handed, categorical approach is deaf to the constitutional imperative to permit unfettered debate, even among high-school students, about the wisdom of the war on drugs or of legalizing marijuana for medicinal use. If Frederick's stupid reference to marijuana can in the Court's view justify censorship, then high school students everywhere could be forgiven for zipping their mouths about drugs at school lest some "reasonable" observer censor and then punish them for promoting drugs.

Consider, too, that the school district's rule draws no distinction between alcohol and marijuana, but applies evenhandedly to all "substances that are illegal to minors." . . . While I find it hard to believe the Court would support punishing Frederick for flying a "WINE SiPS 4 JESUS" banner — which could quite reasonably be construed either as a protected religious message or as a pro-alcohol message — the breathtaking sweep of its opinion suggests it would. . . .

———

Note: The Implications of Morse v. Frederick

1. Both the Court and Justice Alito in his concurring opinion (joined by Justice Kennedy) seek to portray the holding as a narrow one. Justice Alito goes so far as to say that the regulation in this case stands "at the far reaches of what the First Amendment permits." But Justice Breyer, in dissent, objects that "while the holding is theoretically limited to speech promoting the use of illegal drugs, it could in fact authorize further viewpoint-based restrictions." Is Justice Breyer's assessment persuasive? Consider these examples from his opinion:

> (a) Student messages that encourage the underage consumption of alcohol.

> (b) "A conversation during the lunch period where one student suggests that glaucoma sufferers should smoke marijuana to relieve the pain."

> (c) "Deprecating commentary about an antidrug film shown in school."

> (d) "Drug messages mixed with other, more expressly political, content." For example, suppose that Frederick's banner had read "LEGALIZE BONG HiTS."

2. Justice Alito, in his concurring opinion, lists the grounds for regulation of student speech "recognized in the holdings of this Court." He summarizes the four cases and expresses his understanding that "the opinion does not hold that the special characteristics of the public schools necessarily justify any other speech restrictions." Does that mean that the four decisions define all of the grounds on which public schools may restrict student speech?

3. Many litigated cases have involved messages or images on T-shirts worn by students at school. Consider this example: A school dress code prohibits all images of weapons on clothing. A student arrives at school wearing a National Rifle Association T-shirt that depicts three black silhouettes of men holding firearms superimposed on the letters "NRA" positioned above the phrase "SHOOTING SPORTS CAMP." The principal asks him to change shirts, saying that the image conflicts with the school's message that "Guns and Schools Don't Mix." Permissible?

4. According to the Court, the holding of *Tinker* is that "student expression may not be suppressed unless school officials reasonably conclude that it will 'materially and substantially disrupt the work and discipline of the school.'" Justice Alito, in his concurring opinion, refers to "substantial disruption" as the standard endorsed by *Tinker*. But at several points in the *Tinker* opinion the Court also specifies "invasion of the rights of others" as a permissible ground for restricting student speech.

After *Morse v. Frederick*, does the First Amendment permit school officials to regulate student expression out of concern that the expression impinges on the rights of others? Consider the Problems below.

5. The Court acknowledges "uncertainty at the outer boundaries as to when courts should apply school-speech precedents." On that point the Court cites a footnote in a Fifth Circuit case, *Porter v. Ascension Parish School Bd.*, 393 F.3d 608 (5th Cir. 2004).

The question in *Porter* was "whether officials within the [school district] responded appropriately in removing [a student] from [high school] and requiring him to enroll in an alternative school for a sketch depicting a violent siege on the [high school] that he had drawn two years earlier, and was accidentally taken to school by his younger brother." The Fifth Circuit said:

> We are aware of the difficulties posed by state regulation of student speech that takes place off-campus and is later brought on-campus either by the communicating student or others to whom the message was communicated. Refusing to differentiate between student speech taking place on-campus and speech taking place off-campus, a number of courts have applied the test in *Tinker* when analyzing off-campus speech brought onto the school campus.

However, the Fifth Circuit panel found that the case before it was "outside the scope of these precedents." The accompanying text explained:

> Given the unique facts of the present case, we decline to find that Adam's drawing constitutes student speech on the school premises. Adam's drawing was completed in his home, stored for two years, and never intended by him to be brought to campus. He took no action that would increase the chances that his drawing would find its way to school; he simply stored it in a closet where it remained until, by chance, it was unwittingly taken to Galvez Middle School by his brother. This is not exactly speech on campus or even speech directed at the campus.

Does *Morse* shed any light on how these cases should be analyzed? Consider the "Trolling on a Blog" Problem below.

———

Problem: Career Guidance and Student Protest

Bayport High School scheduled a mandatory assembly for sophomores and juniors on the topic, "how to get a job." The assembly program was designed in cooperation with QuickBurger, a large fast-food chain. Students were given free meal coupons if they filled out job applications. The mock applications were collected, and a three-person panel (composed of a QuickBurger representative, a teacher, and a student) critiqued some of them.

As part of the hour-long assembly, students watched a 15-minute video produced by QuickBurger that dramatized "good" and "bad" ways of interviewing for a job. After the showing of the video, Barbara Bates, the QuickBurger representative, asked if she could have volunteers to engage in mock job interviews. Jim Stark, a sophomore, raised his hand. Bates asked Stark to tell her about himself. Stark said, "I hate large corporations like QuickBurger." Bates said, "That won't get you a job at QuickBurger." Stark said, "Good. I don't want to work for a company that falsely advertises its products as being vegetarian to vegetarians and Hindus." Stark was alluding to a recent controversy over QuickBurger's allegedly cooking its French fries in beef fat.

Before Stark could say more, he was told to hand over the microphone and go straight to the principal's office. The program continued, with other students taking the part of job applicants.

The principal told Stark: "This was a program to help students to start their careers. You have made a mockery of it. You also humiliated Ms. Bates. I want you to write an apology to Ms. Bates and to your fellow students, and I want you to read the apology over the public address system." The principal threatened to impose discipline if Stark did not make the requested apologies.

Stark asked for time to consider, and the principal gave him 24 hours. Stark has consulted you. He says, "I was just exercising my First Amendment rights. I can't be disciplined for that, can I?"

How would you advise Stark?

————

Problem: A Controversial T-Shirt

In conjunction with the National Day of Silence held throughout the United States, Langston Hughes High School, a public high school, permitted a student group called the Gay-Straight Alliance to hold a "Day of Silence" at the school. The purpose of the "Day of Silence" was "to encourage tolerance and respect for those of a different sexual orientation." Participating students wore duct tape over their mouths to symbolize "the silencing effect of intolerance upon gays and lesbians"; these students would not speak in class except through a designated representative. Some students wore black T-shirts that said "National Day of Silence," with a purple square and a yellow equal sign in the middle. The Gay-Straight Alliance, with the permission of the school, also put up several posters promoting awareness of harassment on the basis of sexual orientation.

On the morning of the "Day of Silence," Todd Jones, an 11th grade student, wore a T-shirt to school with the words "I WILL NOT ACCEPT WHAT GOD HAS CON-DEMNED" hand-printed on the front. Hand-printed on the back was: "HOMO-SEXUALITY IS SHAMEFUL—ROMANS 1:27." Jones' second period teacher noticed Jones' shirt and observed "several students off-task talking about it." The teacher explained to Jones that he believed that the shirt was "inflammatory," that it violated the school's dress code, and that it "created a negative and hostile learning environment for others." When Jones refused to remove his shirt and asked to speak to an administrator, the teacher gave him a dress code violation card to take to the front office.

When Jones arrived at the front office, he met with the principal, who told him that the "Day of Silence" was "not about the school promoting homosexuality" but rather it was a student activity "trying to raise other students' awareness regarding tolerance in their judgment of others." The principal also explained to Jones that it was not right for students to be addressed in such a derogatory manner. He cited the school's dress code, which prohibits "clothing and accessories (including backpacks and T-shirts) that promote or portray violence or hate behavior including derogatory connotations directed toward sexual identity." He called Jones' attention to a "background statement" accompanying the dress code. According to this document, "many studies have found that attacks on students on the basis of their sexual orientation are harmful not only to the students' health and welfare, but also to their educational performance and their ultimate potential for success in life."

The principal proposed some alternatives to wearing the shirt, all of which Jones turned down. Jones was suspended for the rest of the day and was not allowed to attend class.

Jones has brought suit in federal district court seeking nominal damages for the suspension and an injunction against enforcement of the dress code provision cited by the principal. He relies on the First Amendment. Is the claim meritorious?

————

Problem: Trolling on a Blog

Jack Weisenheimer, a 9th grader at Elmhurst High School, was angry. Last week, the principal of Elmhurst, Chester Elliott, canceled a school dance in response to several unrelated incidents of student misconduct during the current semester.

Jack took to social media to express his anger. While at home that Saturday evening, he logged onto his personal blog, "justanelmhursthighdude," and vented his rage at Principal Elliott. In a series of posts Jack called him "Principal Idiot," "a lousy principal who ought to be FIRED," "a big, ugly, leaking douchebag," and "Chester, Chester, the child molester." His last post concluded, "If Elliott is so afraid of students acting up, maybe we should REALLY act up! You KNOW he'd pee his pants!!!"

Jack's rant got noticed. Several of Jack's classmates read his blog that weekend, and over the course of Sunday some of them met, spoke with, or chatted online with other classmates and either showed them or directed them to Jack's posts. Several parents of Elmhurst students also read the posts, when they stumbled onto Jack's blog by doing an Internet search for "Elmhurst High" in order to find the school's website for other purposes.

By Monday morning most of the 9th grade class had read Jack's posts, some of them while they were on campus as they were surfing the web on their cell phones before classes started. That morning a teacher also accessed the site as she searched for "Elmhurst High" from a classroom computer in preparation for teaching a lesson on website design. There was much hallway talk about the posts, and the 9th grade math assembly that afternoon became impossible to control as the assembled students broke out into laughter and hooting when Principal Elliott attempted to address them. Two students who had been molested as children collapsed in tears when a few students started chanting "Chester, Chester, child molester!" When teachers at the assembly asked students about the cause of the commotion, several of them used their phones to show Jack's posts to the teachers.

At the end of the day, Jack was called into the principal's office. He admitted that he posted the rant, but insisted that "I only wanted to blow off steam with my friends who read my blog." When asked if he knew who reads his blog, he shrugged. "Not really. Just my friends, I guess. I dunno. I mean, who else would care?"

Can the school discipline Jack consistent with the First Amendment?

Chapter 13

Beyond Regulation: Whose Message Is It?

When the government regulates activities in the private sector, the Free Speech Clause of the First Amendment applies in full force. In contrast, when the government itself is the speaker, the Clause has no application. But the line between private speech and government speech is not always easy to draw. For example, when the government provides funds to private entities, it may be enlisting their help to convey its own message — or it may be fostering expressive activities by the recipients of the funds. In this chapter we explore the First Amendment issues that arise when the government's role is ambiguous or debatable.

A. Paying the Piper — and Calling the Tune?

Rust v. Sullivan

500 U.S. 173 (1991)

CHIEF JUSTICE REHNQUIST delivered the opinion of the Court.

These cases concern a facial challenge to Department of Health and Human Services (HHS) regulations which limit the ability of Title X fund recipients to engage in abortion-related activities. The United States Court of Appeals for the Second Circuit upheld the regulations, finding them to be a permissible construction of the statute as well as consistent with the First and Fifth Amendments to the Constitution. . . . We affirm.

I

In 1970, Congress enacted Title X of the Public Health Service Act (Act), which provides federal funding for family-planning services. The Act authorizes the Secretary to "make grants to and enter into contracts with public or nonprofit private entities to assist in the establishment and operation of voluntary family planning projects which shall offer a broad range of acceptable and effective family planning methods and services." Grants and contracts under Title X must "be made in accordance with such regulations as the Secretary may promulgate." Section 1008 of the Act, however, provides that "none of the funds appropriated under this subchapter shall be used in programs where abortion is a method of family planning." That restriction was intended to ensure that Title X funds would "be used only to support preventive family planning services, population research, infertility services, and other related medical, informational, and educational activities."

In 1988, the Secretary promulgated new regulations designed to provide "'clear and operational guidance' to grantees about how to preserve the distinction between Title X programs and abortion as a method of family planning." . . .

The regulations attach three principal conditions on the grant of federal funds for Title X projects. First, the regulations specify that a "Title X project may not provide counseling concerning the use of abortion as a method of family planning or provide referral for abortion as a method of family planning." Because Title X is limited to preconceptional services, the program does not furnish services related to childbirth. Only in the context of a referral out of the Title X program is a pregnant woman given transitional information. Title X projects must refer every pregnant client "for appropriate prenatal and/or social services by furnishing a list of available providers that promote the welfare of mother and unborn child." The list may not be used indirectly to encourage or promote abortion, "such as by weighing the list of referrals in favor of health care providers which perform abortions, by including on the list of referral providers health care providers whose principal business is the provision of abortions, by excluding available providers who do not provide abortions, or by 'steering' clients to providers who offer abortion as a method of family planning." The Title X project is expressly prohibited from referring a pregnant woman to an abortion provider, even upon specific request. One permissible response to such an inquiry is that "the project does not consider abortion an appropriate method of family planning and therefore does not counsel or refer for abortion."

Second, the regulations broadly prohibit a Title X project from engaging in activities that "encourage, promote or advocate abortion as a method of family planning." Forbidden activities include lobbying for legislation that would increase the availability of abortion as a method of family planning, developing or disseminating materials advocating abortion as a method of family planning, providing speakers to promote abortion as a method of family planning, using legal action to make abortion available in any way as a method of family planning, and paying dues to any group that advocates abortion as a method of family planning as a substantial part of its activities.

Third, the regulations require that Title X projects be organized so that they are "physically and financially separate" from prohibited abortion activities. To be deemed physically and financially separate, "a Title X project must have an objective integrity and independence from prohibited activities. Mere bookkeeping separation of Title X funds from other monies is not sufficient." . . .

Petitioners are Title X grantees and doctors who supervise Title X funds suing on behalf of themselves and their patients. Respondent is the Secretary of HHS. [The plaintiffs challenged the regulations on the grounds that they were not authorized by Title X and that they violated the First and Fifth Amendment rights of Title X clients and the First Amendment rights of Title X health providers. The District Court rejected the challenges and the Second Circuit affirmed.]

II

We begin by pointing out the posture of the cases before us. Petitioners are challenging the *facial* validity of the regulations. Thus, we are concerned only with the question whether, on their face, the regulations are both authorized by the Act and can be construed in such a manner that they can be applied to a set of individuals without infringing upon constitutionally protected rights. . . .

We turn first to petitioners' contention that the regulations exceed the Secretary's authority under Title X and are arbitrary and capricious. [The Court rejected the argument.]

III

Petitioners contend that the regulations violate the First Amendment by impermissibly discriminating based on viewpoint because they prohibit "all discussion about abortion as a lawful option—including counseling, referral, and the provision of neutral and accurate information about ending a pregnancy—while compelling the clinic or counselor to provide information that promotes continuing a pregnancy to term." They assert that the regulations violate the "free speech rights of private health care organizations that receive Title X funds, of their staff, and of their patients" by impermissibly imposing "viewpoint-discriminatory conditions on government subsidies" and thus "penalize speech funded with non-Title X monies." . . . Relying on *Regan v. Taxation with Representation of Wash.*, 461 U.S. 540 (1983), . . . petitioners also assert that while the Government may place certain conditions on the receipt of federal subsidies, it may not "discriminate invidiously in its subsidies in such a way as to 'aim at the suppression of dangerous ideas.'"

There is no question but that the statutory prohibition contained in § 1008 is constitutional. The Government can, without violating the Constitution, selectively fund a program to encourage certain activities it believes to be in the public interest, without at the same time funding an alternative program which seeks to deal with the problem in another way. In so doing, the Government has not discriminated on the basis of viewpoint; it has merely chosen to fund one activity to the exclusion of the other. "[A] legislature's decision not to subsidize the exercise of a fundamental right does not infringe the right." *Regan* . . .

The challenged regulations implement the statutory prohibition by prohibiting counseling, referral, and the provision of information regarding abortion as a method of family planning. They are designed to ensure that the limits of the federal program are observed. The Title X program is designed not for prenatal care, but to encourage family planning. A doctor who wished to offer prenatal care to a project patient who became pregnant could properly be prohibited from doing so because such service is outside the scope of the federally funded program. The regulations prohibiting abortion counseling and referral are of the same ilk . . . . This is not a case of the Government "suppressing a dangerous idea," but of a prohibition on a project grantee or its employees from engaging in activities outside of the project's scope.

To hold that the Government unconstitutionally discriminates on the basis of viewpoint when it chooses to fund a program dedicated to advance certain permissible goals, because the program in advancing those goals necessarily discourages alternative goals, would render numerous Government programs constitutionally suspect. When Congress established a National Endowment for Democracy to encourage other countries to adopt democratic principles, it was not constitutionally required to fund a program to encourage competing lines of political philosophy such as communism and fascism. . . . Within far broader limits than petitioners are willing to concede, when the Government appropriates public funds to establish a program it is entitled to define the limits of that program. . . .

Petitioners also contend that the restrictions on the subsidization of abortion-related speech contained in the regulations are impermissible because they condition the receipt of a benefit, in these cases Title X funding, on the relinquishment of a constitutional right, the right to engage in abortion advocacy and counseling. [Petitioners] argue that "even though the government may deny [a] . . . benefit for any number of reasons, there are some reasons upon which the government may not rely. It may not deny a benefit to a person on a basis that infringes his constitutionally protected interests—especially, his interest in freedom of speech."

[Here, however,] the Government is not denying a benefit to anyone, but is instead simply insisting that public funds be spent for the purposes for which they were authorized. The Secretary's regulations do not force the Title X grantee to give up abortion-related speech; they merely require that the grantee keep such activities separate and distinct from Title X activities. Title X expressly distinguishes between a Title X *grantee* and a Title X *project*. The grantee, which normally is a health-care organization, may receive funds from a variety of sources for a variety of purposes. The grantee receives Title X funds, however, for the specific and limited purpose of establishing and operating a Title X project. The regulations govern the scope of the Title X *project's* activities, and leave the grantee unfettered in its other activities. The Title X *grantee* can continue to perform abortions, provide abortion-related services, and engage in abortion advocacy; it simply is required to conduct those activities through programs that are separate and independent from the project that receives Title X funds.

In contrast, our "unconstitutional conditions" cases involve situations in which the Government has placed a condition on the *recipient* of the subsidy rather than on a particular program or service, thus effectively prohibiting the recipient from engaging in the protected conduct outside the scope of the federally funded program. In *FCC v. League of Women Voters of Cal.*, 468 U.S. 364 (1984), we invalidated a federal law providing that noncommercial television and radio stations that receive federal grants may not "engage in editorializing." Under that law, a recipient of federal funds was "barred absolutely from all editorializing" because it "is not able to segregate its activities according to the source of its funding" and thus "has no way of limiting the use of its federal funds to all noneditorializing activities." . . . We expressly recognized, however, that were Congress to permit the recipient stations to "establish 'affiliate'

to provide.[2] By refusing to fund those family-planning projects that advocate abortion *because* they advocate abortion, the Government plainly has targeted a particular viewpoint. The majority's reliance on the fact that the regulations pertain solely to funding decisions simply begs the question. Clearly, there are some bases upon which government may not rest its decision to fund or not to fund. For example, the Members of the majority surely would agree that government may not base its decision to support an activity upon considerations of race. As demonstrated above, our cases make clear that ideological viewpoint is a similarly repugnant ground upon which to base funding decisions.

The majority's reliance upon *Regan* in this connection is also misplaced. That case stands for the proposition that government has no obligation to subsidize a private party's efforts to petition the legislature regarding its views. Thus, if the challenged regulations were confined to nonideological limitations upon the use of Title X funds for lobbying activities, there would exist no violation of the First Amendment. The advocacy regulations at issue here, however, are not limited to lobbying but extend to all speech having the effect of encouraging, promoting, or advocating abortion as a method of family planning. Thus, in addition to their impermissible focus upon the viewpoint of regulated speech, the provisions intrude upon a wide range of communicative conduct, including the very words spoken to a woman by her physician. By manipulating the content of the doctor-patient dialogue, the regulations upheld today force each of the petitioners "to be an instrument for fostering public adherence to an ideological point of view [he or she] finds unacceptable." *Wooley v. Maynard* (1977) [*supra* Chapter 9]. This type of intrusive, ideologically based regulation of speech goes far beyond the narrow lobbying limitations approved in *Regan* and cannot be justified simply because it is a condition upon the receipt of a governmental benefit.[3]

The Court concludes that the challenged regulations do not violate the First Amendment rights of Title X staff members because any limitation of the employees' freedom of expression is simply a consequence of their decision to accept employment at a federally funded project. But it has never been sufficient to justify an otherwise unconstitutional condition upon public employment that the employee may escape the condition by relinquishing his or her job. . . .

---

2. In addition to requiring referral for prenatal care and adoption services, the regulations permit general health services such as physical examinations, screening for breast cancer, treatment of gynecological problems, and treatment for sexually transmitted diseases. None of the latter are strictly preventive, preconceptional services.

3. The majority attempts to obscure the breadth of its decision through its curious contention that "the Title X program regulations do not significantly impinge upon the doctor-patient relationship." That the doctor-patient relationship is substantially burdened by a rule prohibiting the dissemination by the physician of pertinent medical information is beyond serious dispute. This burden is undiminished by the fact that the relationship at issue here is not an "all-encompassing" one. A woman seeking the services of a Title X clinic has every reason to expect, as do we all, that her physician will not withhold relevant information regarding the very purpose of her visit. To suggest otherwise is to engage in uninformed fantasy. . . .

The majority attempts to circumvent this principle by emphasizing that Title X physicians and counselors "remain free . . . to pursue abortion-related activities when they are not acting under the auspices of the Title X project." . . . Under the majority's reasoning, the First Amendment could be read to tolerate *any* governmental restriction upon an employee's speech so long as that restriction is limited to the funded workplace. This is a dangerous proposition, and one the Court has rightly rejected in the past. . . . At the least, such conditions require courts to balance the speaker's interest in the message against those of government in preventing its dissemination.

In the cases at bar, the speaker's interest in the communication is both clear and vital. In addressing the family-planning needs of their clients, the physicians and counselors who staff Title X projects seek to provide them with the full range of information and options regarding their health and reproductive freedom. . . . When a client becomes pregnant, the full range of therapeutic alternatives includes the abortion option, and Title X counselors' interest in providing this information is compelling.

The Government's articulated interest in distorting the doctor-patient dialogue — ensuring that federal funds are not spent for a purpose outside the scope of the program — falls far short of that necessary to justify the suppression of truthful information and professional medical opinion regarding constitutionally protected conduct. Moreover, the offending regulation is not narrowly tailored to serve this interest. For example, the governmental interest at stake could be served by imposing rigorous bookkeeping standards to ensure financial separation or adopting content-neutral rules for the balanced dissemination of family-planning and health information. By failing to balance or even to consider the free speech interests claimed by Title X physicians against the Government's asserted interest in suppressing the speech, the Court falters in its duty to implement the protection that the First Amendment clearly provides for this important message.

Finally, it is of no small significance that the speech the Secretary would suppress is truthful information regarding constitutionally protected conduct of vital importance to the listener. One can imagine no legitimate governmental interest that might be served by suppressing such information. . . .

Justice Stevens, dissenting. [Omitted.]

Justice O'Connor, dissenting.

. . . In these cases, we need only tell the Secretary that his regulations are not a reasonable interpretation of the statute; we need not tell Congress that it cannot pass such legislation.

———

Note: Rust *and* Rosenberger

1. Justice Blackmun, dissenting in *Rust*, says, "Until today, the Court has never upheld viewpoint-based suppression of speech simply because that suppression was a condition upon the acceptance of public funds."

Does the Court agree that the regulation is one that suppresses speech? Does the Court agree that the government has discriminated on the basis of viewpoint? Who has the better of the argument?

2. How helpful is precedent in resolving the First Amendment issue in *Rust*? For example, the dissent challenges the majority's "reliance" on *Regan v. Taxation with Representation*. Is *Regan* central to the Court's analysis? (Note that *Regan* is discussed extensively in *Agency for International Development*, the next principal case.)

3. In *Rosenberger v. Rector and Visitors of University of Virginia*, 515 U.S. 819 (1995) [Note *supra* Chapter 8], the university refused to fund a student magazine that promoted religious views. The university, relying in part on *Rust*, argued that content-based funding decisions are both inevitable and lawful. The Court rejected the argument:

> [When] the State is the speaker, it may make content-based choices. When the University determines the content of the education it provides, it is the University speaking, and we have permitted the government to regulate the content of what is or is not expressed when it is the speaker or when it enlists private entities to convey its own message. In the same vein, in *Rust*, we upheld the government's prohibition on abortion-related advice applicable to recipients of federal funds for family planning counseling. There, the government did not create a program to encourage private speech but instead used private speakers to transmit specific information pertaining to its own program. We recognized that when the government appropriates public funds to promote a particular policy of its own it is entitled to say what it wishes. When the government disburses public funds to private entities to convey a governmental message, it may take legitimate and appropriate steps to ensure that its message is neither garbled nor distorted by the grantee.
>
> It does not follow, however, . . . that viewpoint-based restrictions are proper when the University does not itself speak or subsidize transmittal of a message it favors but instead expends funds to encourage a diversity of views from private speakers.

When does the government convey its own message, and when does the government create a program "to encourage a diversity of views from private speakers"? Are there other circumstances in which *Rosenberger*, not *Rust*, is the governing precedent? The Court has confronted these issues in several settings, including funding for legal services, as discussed in the next Note.

Note: Government Funding of Legal Services

1. The Legal Services Corporation (LSC) was established by Congress in 1974. It is a District of Columbia nonprofit corporation whose mission is to distribute funds appropriated by Congress to eligible local grantee organizations "for the purpose of providing financial support for legal assistance in noncriminal proceedings or matters to persons financially unable to afford legal assistance."

Congress has imposed various restrictions on the use of LSC funds. For example, recipients may not advocate or oppose ballot measures and may not attempt to influence the passage or defeat of any legislation. Starting in 1996, Congress also prohibited recipients from initiating legal representation "involving an effort to reform a Federal or State welfare system." As interpreted by the LSC and by the Government, the restriction prevented an attorney from arguing to a court in a welfare case that a state statute conflicted with a federal statute or that either a state or federal statute by its terms or in its application violated the United States Constitution. The prohibition applied to all of the activities of an LSC grantee, including those paid for by non-LSC funds.

In *Legal Services Corp. v. Velazquez*, 531 U.S. 533 (2001), the restriction was challenged under the First Amendment. The United States and the LSC relied on *Rust v. Sullivan* in arguing that the restriction was constitutional, but the Supreme Court disagreed. In a 5-4 decision, the Court held that the funding condition was invalid. Justice Kennedy wrote the Court's opinion. He said:

> The Court in *Rust* did not place explicit reliance on the rationale that the counseling activities of the doctors under Title X amounted to governmental speech; when interpreting the holding in later cases, however, we have explained *Rust* on this understanding. We have said that viewpoint-based funding decisions can be sustained in instances in which the government is itself the speaker, see *Board of Regents of Univ. of Wis. System v. Southworth*, 529 U.S. 217 (2000), or instances, like *Rust*, in which the government "used private speakers to transmit information pertaining to its own program." *Rosenberger*. As we said in *Rosenberger*, "when the government disburses public funds to private entities to convey a governmental message, it may take legitimate and appropriate steps to ensure that its message is neither garbled nor distorted by the grantee." The latitude which may exist for restrictions on speech where the government's own message is being delivered flows in part from our observation that, "when the government speaks, for instance to promote its own policies or to advance a particular idea, it is, in the end, accountable to the electorate and the political process for its advocacy. If the citizenry objects, newly elected officials later could espouse some different or contrary position." *Southworth*.

> Neither the latitude for government speech nor its rationale applies to subsidies for private speech in every instance, however. As we have pointed out, "it does not follow . . . that viewpoint-based restrictions are proper when the [government] does not itself speak or subsidize transmittal of a message it favors but instead expends funds to encourage a diversity of views from private speakers." *Rosenberger*.

> Although the LSC program differs from the program at issue in *Rosenberger* in that its purpose is not to "encourage a diversity of views," the salient point is that, like the program in *Rosenberger*, the LSC program was designed to facilitate private speech, not to promote a governmental message.

Congress funded LSC grantees to provide attorneys to represent the interests of indigent clients. In the specific context of § 504(a)(16) suits for benefits, an LSC-funded attorney speaks on the behalf of the client in a claim against the government for welfare benefits. The lawyer is not the government's speaker. The attorney defending the decision to deny benefits will deliver the government's message in the litigation. The LSC lawyer, however, speaks on the behalf of his or her private, indigent client.

The Government has designed this program to use the legal profession and the established Judiciary of the States and the Federal Government to accomplish its end of assisting welfare claimants in determination or receipt of their benefits. The advice from the attorney to the client and the advocacy by the attorney to the courts cannot be classified as governmental speech even under a generous understanding of the concept. In this vital respect this suit is distinguishable from *Rust*.

The Court concluded:

There can be little doubt that the LSC Act funds constitutionally protected expression; and in the context of this statute there is no programmatic message of the kind recognized in *Rust* and which sufficed there to allow the Government to specify the advice deemed necessary for its legitimate objectives. This serves to distinguish § 504(a)(16) from any of the Title X program restrictions upheld in *Rust*, and to place it beyond any congressional funding condition approved in the past by this Court.

2. Four Justices dissented in an opinion by Justice Scalia. The dissent insisted that *Rust* was "on all fours with the present case." Justice Scalia wrote:

[In *Rust* we explained] that "the Government can, without violating the Constitution, selectively fund a program to encourage certain activities it believes to be in the public interest, without at the same time funding an alternative program which seeks to deal with the problem another way." This was not, we said, the type of "discrimination on the basis of viewpoint" that triggers strict scrutiny, because the "'decision not to subsidize the exercise of a fundamental right does not infringe the right.'"

The same is true here. The LSC Act, like the scheme in *Rust*, does not create a public forum. Far from encouraging a diversity of views, it has always, as the Court accurately states, "placed restrictions on its use of funds." Nor does § 504(a)(16) discriminate on the basis of viewpoint, since it funds neither challenges to nor defenses of existing welfare law. The provision simply declines to subsidize a certain class of litigation, and under *Rust* that decision "does not infringe the right" to bring such litigation. The Court's repeated claims that § 504(a)(16) "restricts" and "prohibits" speech, and "insulates" laws from judicial review, are simply baseless. No litigant who, in the absence of LSC funding, would bring a suit challenging existing welfare law is deterred from doing so by § 504(a)(16). *Rust* thus controls these cases and compels the conclusion that § 504(a)(16) is constitutional.

The Court contends that *Rust* is different because the program at issue subsidized government speech, while the LSC funds private speech. This is so unpersuasive it hardly needs response. If the private doctors' confidential advice to their patients at issue in *Rust* constituted "government speech," it is hard to imagine what subsidized speech would not be government speech. Moreover, the majority's contention that the subsidized speech in these cases is not government speech because the lawyers have a professional obligation to represent the interests of their clients founders on the reality that the doctors in *Rust* had a professional obligation to serve the interests of their patients . . . . Even respondents agree that "the true speaker in *Rust* was not the government, but a doctor."

3. The Court says that *Velazquez* is distinguishable from *Rust* because the speech in question "cannot be classified as governmental speech even under a generous understanding of the concept." But did *Rust* rest on the premise that the doctors were speaking for the government?

————

Agency for International Development v. Alliance for Open Society International, Inc.

570 U.S. 205 (2013)

CHIEF JUSTICE ROBERTS delivered the opinion of the Court.

The United States Leadership Against HIV/AIDS, Tuberculosis, and Malaria Act of 2003 (Leadership Act) outlined a comprehensive strategy to combat the spread of HIV/AIDS around the world. As part of that strategy, Congress authorized the appropriation of billions of dollars to fund efforts by nongovernmental organizations to assist in the fight. The Act imposes two related conditions on that funding: First, no funds made available by the Act "may be used to promote or advocate the legalization or practice of prostitution or sex trafficking." § 7631(e). And second, no funds may be used by an organization "that does not have a policy explicitly opposing prostitution and sex trafficking." § 7631(f). This case concerns the second of these conditions, referred to as the Policy Requirement. The question is whether that funding condition violates a recipient's First Amendment rights.

I

Congress passed the Leadership Act in 2003 after finding that HIV/AIDS had "assumed pandemic proportions, spreading from the most severely affected regions, sub-Saharan Africa and the Caribbean, to all corners of the world, and leaving an unprecedented path of death and devastation." . . . The disease not only directly endangered those infected, but also increased the potential for social and political instability and economic devastation, posing a security issue for the entire international community.

In the Leadership Act, Congress directed the President to establish a "comprehensive, integrated" strategy to combat HIV/AIDS around the world. . . .

The Act "make[s] the reduction of HIV/AIDS behavioral risks a priority of all prevention efforts." The Act's approach to reducing behavioral risks is multifaceted. The President's strategy for addressing such risks must, for example, promote abstinence, encourage monogamy, increase the availability of condoms, promote voluntary counseling and treatment for drug users, and, as relevant here, "educat[e] men and boys about the risks of procuring sex commercially" as well as "promote alternative livelihoods, safety, and social reintegration strategies for commercial sex workers." Congress found that the "sex industry, the trafficking of individuals into such industry, and sexual violence" were factors in the spread of the HIV/AIDS epidemic, and determined that "it should be the policy of the United States to eradicate" prostitution and "other sexual victimization."

The United States has enlisted the assistance of nongovernmental organizations to help achieve the many goals of the program. . . . Since 2003, Congress has authorized the appropriation of billions of dollars for funding these organizations' fight against HIV/AIDS around the world.

Those funds, however, come with two conditions: First, no funds made available to carry out the Leadership Act "may be used to promote or advocate the legalization or practice of prostitution or sex trafficking." § 7631(e). Second, [with exceptions not relevant here], no funds made available may "provide assistance to any group or organization that does not have a policy explicitly opposing prostitution and sex trafficking." § 7631(f). It is this second condition—the Policy Requirement—that is at issue here.

The Department of Health and Human Services (HHS) and the United States Agency for International Development (USAID) are the federal agencies primarily responsible for overseeing implementation of the Leadership Act. To enforce the Policy Requirement, the agencies have directed that the recipient of any funding under the Act agree in the award document that it is opposed to "prostitution and sex trafficking because of the psychological and physical risks they pose for women, men, and children."

II

Respondents are a group of domestic organizations engaged in combating HIV/AIDS overseas. In addition to substantial private funding, they receive billions annually in financial assistance from the United States, including under the Leadership Act. Their work includes programs aimed at limiting injection drug use in Uzbekistan, Tajikistan, and Kyrgyzstan, preventing mother-to-child HIV transmission in Kenya, and promoting safer sex practices in India. Respondents fear that adopting a policy explicitly opposing prostitution may alienate certain host governments, and may diminish the effectiveness of some of their programs by making it more difficult to work with prostitutes in the fight against HIV/AIDS. They are also concerned that the Policy Requirement may require them to censor their privately funded discussions in publications, at conferences, and in other forums about how best to prevent the spread of HIV/AIDS among prostitutes.

[Respondents sued HHS and USAID, arguing that the Government's implementation of the Policy Requirement violated their First Amendment rights. In the course of the litigation, HHS and USAID issued guidelines on how recipients of Leadership Act funds could retain funding while working with affiliated organizations not bound by the Policy Requirement. (These "affiliate guidelines" are discussed in Part III-D of the opinion.) The Second Circuit held that the Policy Requirement, as implemented by the agencies (including the affiliate guidelines), "falls well beyond what the Supreme Court . . . ha[s] upheld as permissible funding conditions." The Supreme Court granted the Government's petition for certiorari.]

III

The Policy Requirement mandates that recipients of Leadership Act funds explicitly agree with the Government's policy to oppose prostitution and sex trafficking. It is, however, a basic First Amendment principle that "freedom of speech prohibits the government from telling people what they must say." *Rumsfeld v. Forum for Academic and Institutional Rights, Inc. (FAIR)*, 547 U.S. 47 (2006) [Note *supra* Chapter 9] (citing *West Virginia Bd. of Ed. v. Barnette* (1943) [*supra* Chapter 9], and *Wooley v. Maynard* (1977) [*supra* Chapter 9]). "At the heart of the First Amendment lies the principle that each person should decide for himself or herself the ideas and beliefs deserving of expression, consideration, and adherence." *Turner Broadcasting System, Inc. v. FCC*, 512 U.S. 622 (1994). Were it enacted as a direct regulation of speech, the Policy Requirement would plainly violate the First Amendment. The question is whether the Government may nonetheless impose that requirement as a condition on the receipt of federal funds.

A

The Spending Clause of the Federal Constitution . . . provides Congress broad discretion to tax and spend for the "general Welfare," including by funding particular state or private programs or activities. That power includes the authority to impose limits on the use of such funds to ensure they are used in the manner Congress intends. *Rust v. Sullivan* (1991) [*supra* this chapter].

As a general matter, if a party objects to a condition on the receipt of federal funding, its recourse is to decline the funds. This remains true when the objection is that a condition may affect the recipient's exercise of its First Amendment rights. *See, e.g., Regan v. Taxation With Representation of Wash.*, 461 U.S. 540 (1983) (dismissing "the notion that First Amendment rights are somehow not fully realized unless they are subsidized by the State").

At the same time, however, we have held that the Government "may not deny a benefit to a person on a basis that infringes his constitutionally protected . . . freedom of speech even if he has no entitlement to that benefit." *FAIR*. In some cases, a funding condition can result in an unconstitutional burden on First Amendment rights.

The dissent thinks that can only be true when the condition is not relevant to the objectives of the program (although it has its doubts about that), or when the condition is actually coercive, in the sense of an offer that cannot be refused. Our precedents, however, are not so limited. In the present context, the relevant distinction that has emerged from our cases is between conditions that define the limits of the government spending program — those that specify the activities Congress wants to subsidize — and conditions that seek to leverage funding to regulate speech outside the contours of the program itself. The line is hardly clear, in part because the definition of a particular program can always be manipulated to subsume the challenged condition. We have held, however, that "Congress cannot recast a condition on funding as a mere definition of its program in every case, lest the First Amendment be reduced to a simple semantic exercise." *Legal Services Corporation v. Velazquez,* 531 U.S. 533 (2001) [Note *supra* this chapter].

A comparison of two cases helps illustrate the distinction: In *Regan v. Taxation With Representation of Washington*, the Court upheld a requirement that nonprofit organizations seeking tax-exempt status under 26 U.S.C. § 501(c)(3) not engage in substantial efforts to influence legislation. The tax-exempt status, we explained, "ha[d] much the same effect as a cash grant to the organization." And by limiting § 501(c)(3) status to organizations that did not attempt to influence legislation, Congress had merely "chose[n] not to subsidize lobbying." In rejecting the nonprofit's First Amendment claim, the Court highlighted — in the text of its opinion — the fact that the condition did not prohibit that organization from lobbying Congress altogether. By returning to a "dual structure" it had used in the past — separately incorporating as a § 501(c)(3) organization and § 501(c)(4) organization — the nonprofit could continue to claim § 501(c)(3) status for its nonlobbying activities, while attempting to influence legislation in its § 501(c)(4) capacity with separate funds. Maintaining such a structure, the Court noted, was not "unduly burdensome." The condition thus did not deny the organization a government benefit "on account of its intention to lobby."

In *FCC v. League of Women Voters of California*, by contrast, the Court struck down a condition on federal financial assistance to noncommercial broadcast television and radio stations that prohibited all editorializing, including with private funds. 468 U.S. 364 (1984). Even a station receiving only one percent of its overall budget from the Federal Government, the Court explained, was "barred absolutely from all editorializing." Unlike the situation in *Regan*, the law provided no way for a station to limit its use of federal funds to noneditorializing activities, while using private funds "to make known its views on matters of public importance." The prohibition thus went beyond ensuring that federal funds not be used to subsidize "public broadcasting station editorials," and instead leveraged the federal funding to regulate the stations' speech outside the scope of the program.

Our decision in *Rust v. Sullivan* elaborated on the approach reflected in *Regan* and *League of Women Voters*. In *Rust*, we considered Title X of the Public Health Service Act, a Spending Clause program that issued grants to nonprofit health-care organizations "to assist in the establishment and operation of voluntary family planning projects [to] offer a broad range of acceptable and effective family planning methods and services." The organizations received funds from a variety of sources other than the Federal Government for a variety of purposes. The Act, however, prohibited the

Title X federal funds from being "used in programs where abortion is a method of family planning." To enforce this provision, HHS regulations barred Title X projects from advocating abortion as a method of family planning, and required grantees to ensure that their Title X projects were "'physically and financially separate'" from their other projects that engaged in the prohibited activities. A group of Title X funding recipients brought suit, claiming the regulations imposed an unconstitutional condition on their First Amendment rights. We rejected their claim.

We explained that Congress can, without offending the Constitution, selectively fund certain programs to address an issue of public concern, without funding alternative ways of addressing the same problem. In Title X, Congress had defined the federal program to encourage only particular family planning methods. The challenged regulations were simply "designed to ensure that the limits of the federal program are observed," and "that public funds [are] spent for the purposes for which they were authorized."

In making this determination, the Court stressed that "Title X expressly distinguishes between a Title X *grantee* and a Title X *project*." The regulations governed only the scope of the grantee's Title X projects, leaving it "unfettered in its other activities." "The Title X *grantee* can continue to . . . engage in abortion advocacy; it simply is required to conduct those activities through programs that are separate and independent from the project that receives Title X funds." Because the regulations did not "prohibit[] the recipient from engaging in the protected conduct outside the scope of the federally funded program," they did not run afoul of the First Amendment.

B

As noted, the distinction drawn in these cases—between conditions that define the federal program and those that reach outside it—is not always self-evident. . . . Here, however, we are confident that the Policy Requirement falls on the unconstitutional side of the line.

To begin, it is important to recall that the Leadership Act has two conditions relevant here. The first—unchallenged in this litigation—prohibits Leadership Act funds from being used "to promote or advocate the legalization or practice of prostitution or sex trafficking." The Government concedes that § 7631(e) by itself ensures that federal funds will not be used for the prohibited purposes.

The Policy Requirement therefore must be doing something more—and it is. The dissent views the Requirement as simply a selection criterion by which the Government identifies organizations "who believe in its ideas to carry them to fruition." As an initial matter, whatever purpose the Policy Requirement serves in selecting funding recipients, its effects go beyond selection. The Policy Requirement is an ongoing condition on recipients' speech and activities, a ground for terminating a grant after selection is complete.

In any event, as the Government acknowledges, it is not simply seeking organizations that oppose prostitution. Rather, it explains, "Congress has expressed its purpose 'to eradicate' prostitution and sex trafficking, and it wants recipients *to adopt* a similar stance." (Emphasis added.) This case is not about the Government's ability to enlist the assistance of those with whom it already agrees. It is about compelling a grant recipient to adopt a particular belief as a condition of funding.

By demanding that funding recipients adopt—as their own—the Government's view on an issue of public concern, the condition by its very nature affects "protected conduct outside the scope of the federally funded program." *Rust*. A recipient cannot avow the belief dictated by the Policy Requirement when spending Leadership Act funds, and then turn around and assert a contrary belief, or claim neutrality, when participating in activities on its own time and dime. By requiring recipients to profess a specific belief, the Policy Requirement goes beyond defining the limits of the federally funded program to defining the recipient.

The Government contends that the affiliate guidelines, established while this litigation was pending, save the program. Under those guidelines, funding recipients are permitted to work with affiliated organizations that do not abide by the condition, as long as the recipients retain "objective integrity and independence" from the unfettered affiliates. The Government suggests the guidelines alleviate any unconstitutional burden on the respondents' First Amendment rights by allowing them to either: (1) accept Leadership Act funding and comply with Policy Requirement, but establish affiliates to communicate contrary views on prostitution; or (2) decline funding themselves (thus remaining free to express their own views or remain neutral), while creating affiliates whose sole purpose is to receive and administer Leadership Act funds, thereby "cabin[ing] the effects" of the Policy Requirement within the scope of the federal program.

Neither approach is sufficient. When we have noted the importance of affiliates in this context, it has been because they allow an organization bound by a funding condition to exercise its First Amendment rights outside the scope of the federal program. *See Rust*. Affiliates cannot serve that purpose when the condition is that a funding recipient espouse a specific belief as its own. If the affiliate is distinct from the recipient, the arrangement does not afford a means for the *recipient* to express *its* beliefs. If the affiliate is more clearly identified with the recipient, the recipient can express those beliefs only at the price of evident hypocrisy. . . .

The Government suggests that the Policy Requirement is necessary because, without it, the grant of federal funds could free a recipient's private funds "to be used to promote prostitution or sex trafficking." That argument assumes that federal funding will simply supplant private funding, rather than pay for new programs or expand existing ones. The Government offers no support for that assumption as a general matter, or any reason to believe it is true here. And if the Government's argument were correct, *League of Women Voters* would have come out differently, and much of the reasoning of *Regan* and *Rust* would have been beside the point.

The Government cites but one case to support that argument, *Holder v. Humanitarian Law Project*, 561 U.S. 1 (2010). That case concerned the quite different context of a ban on providing material support to terrorist organizations, where the record indicated that support for those organizations' nonviolent operations was funneled to support their violent activities.

Pressing its argument further, the Government contends that "if organizations awarded federal funds to implement Leadership Act programs could at the same time promote or affirmatively condone prostitution or sex trafficking, whether using public *or private* funds, it would undermine the government's program and confuse its message opposing prostitution and sex trafficking." But the Policy Requirement goes beyond preventing recipients from using private funds in a way that would undermine the federal program. It requires them to pledge allegiance to the Government's policy of eradicating prostitution. As to that, we cannot improve upon what Justice Jackson wrote for the Court 70 years ago: "If there is any fixed star in our constitutional constellation, it is that no official, high or petty, can prescribe what shall be orthodox in politics, nationalism, religion, or other matters of opinion or force citizens to confess by word or act their faith therein." *Barnette*.

The Policy Requirement compels as a condition of federal funding the affirmation of a belief that by its nature cannot be confined within the scope of the Government program. In so doing, it violates the First Amendment and cannot be sustained. The judgment of the Court of Appeals is affirmed.

Justice Kagan took no part in the consideration or decision of this case.

Justice Scalia, with whom Justice Thomas joins, dissenting.

The Leadership Act provides that "any group or organization that does not have a policy explicitly opposing prostitution and sex trafficking" may not receive funds appropriated under the Act. This Policy Requirement is nothing more than a means of selecting suitable agents to implement the Government's chosen strategy to eradicate HIV/AIDS. That is perfectly permissible under the Constitution.

The First Amendment does not mandate a viewpoint-neutral government. Government must choose between rival ideas and adopt some as its own: competition over cartels, solar energy over coal, weapon development over disarmament, and so forth. Moreover, the government may enlist the assistance of those who believe in its ideas to carry them to fruition; and it need not enlist for that purpose those who oppose or do not support the ideas. That seems to me a matter of the most common common sense. For example: One of the purposes of America's foreign-aid programs is the fostering of good will towards this country. If the organization Hamas — reputed to have an efficient system for delivering welfare — were excluded from a program for the distribution of U.S. food assistance, no one could reasonably object. . . . A federal program to encourage healthy eating habits need not be administered by the American Gourmet Society, which has nothing against healthy food but does not insist upon it.

The argument is that this commonsense principle will enable the government to discriminate against, and injure, points of view to which it is opposed. Of course the Constitution does not prohibit government spending that discriminates against, and injures, points of view to which the government is opposed; every government program which takes a position on a controversial issue does that. Anti-smoking programs injure cigar aficionados, programs encouraging sexual abstinence injure free-love advocates, etc. The constitutional prohibition at issue here is not a prohibition against discriminating against or injuring opposing points of view, but the First Amendment's prohibition against the coercing of speech. I am frankly dubious that a condition for eligibility to participate in a minor federal program such as this one runs afoul of that prohibition even when the condition is irrelevant to the goals of the program. Not every disadvantage is a coercion.

But that is not the issue before us here. Here the views that the Government demands an applicant forswear—or that the Government insists an applicant favor—are relevant to the program in question. The program is valid only if the Government is entitled to disfavor the opposing view (here, advocacy of or toleration of prostitution). And if the program can disfavor it, so can the selection of those who are to administer the program. There is no risk that this principle will enable the Government to discriminate arbitrarily against positions it disfavors. It would not, for example, permit the Government to exclude from bidding on defense contracts anyone who refuses to abjure prostitution. But here a central part of the Government's HIV/AIDS strategy is the suppression of prostitution, by which HIV is transmitted. It is entirely reasonable to admit to participation in the program only those who believe in that goal.

According to the Court, however, this transgresses a constitutional line between conditions that operate *inside* a spending program and those that control speech *outside* of it. I am at a loss to explain what this central pillar of the Court's opinion—this distinction that the Court itself admits is "hardly clear" and "not always self-evident"—has to do with the First Amendment. The distinction was alluded to, to be sure, in *Rust v. Sullivan*, but not as (what the Court now makes it) an invariable requirement for First Amendment validity. That the pro-abortion speech prohibition was limited to "inside the program" speech was relevant in *Rust* because the program itself was not an anti-abortion program. The Government remained neutral on that controversial issue, but did not wish abortion to be promoted within its family-planning-services program. The statutory objective could not be impaired, in other words, by "outside the program" pro-abortion speech. The purpose of the limitation was to prevent Government funding from providing the *means* of pro-abortion propaganda, which the Government did not wish (and had no constitutional obligation) to provide. The situation here is vastly different. Elimination of prostitution *is* an objective of the HIV/AIDS program, and *any* promotion of prostitution—whether made inside or outside the program—*does* harm the program.

Of course the most obvious manner in which the admission to a program of an ideological opponent can frustrate the purpose of the program is by freeing up the opponent's funds for use in its ideological opposition. To use the Hamas example again: Subsidizing that organization's provision of social services enables the money that it would otherwise use for that purpose to be used, instead, for anti-American propaganda. Perhaps that problem does not exist in this case since the respondents do not affirmatively promote prostitution. But the Court's analysis categorically rejects that justification for ideological requirements in *all* cases, demanding "record indica[tion]" that "federal funding will simply supplant private funding, rather than pay for new programs." This seems to me quite naive. Money is fungible. The economic reality is that when NGOs can conduct their AIDS work on the Government's dime, they can expend greater resources on policies that undercut the Leadership Act. The Government need not establish by record evidence that this will happen. To make it a valid consideration in determining participation in federal programs, it suffices that this is a real and obvious risk.

None of the cases the Court cites for its holding provide support. I have already discussed *Rust*. As for *Regan v. Taxation With Representation of Wash.*, 461 U.S. 540 (1983), that case *upheld* rather than invalidated a prohibition against lobbying as a condition of receiving 26 U.S.C. § 501(c)(3) tax-exempt status. . . . As for *FCC v. League of Women Voters of Cal.*, 468 U.S. 364 (1984), the ban on editorializing at issue there was disallowed precisely because it did not further a relevant, permissible policy of the Federal Communications Act — and indeed was simply incompatible with the Act's "affirmativ[e] encourage[ment]" of the "vigorous expression of controversial opinions" by licensed broadcasters.

The Court makes a head-fake at the unconstitutional conditions doctrine, but that doctrine is of no help. There is no case of ours in which a condition that is relevant to a statute's valid purpose and that is not in itself unconstitutional (*e.g.*, a religious-affiliation condition that violates the Establishment Clause) has been held to violate the doctrine. Moreover, as I suggested earlier, the contention that the condition here "coerces" respondents' speech is on its face implausible. Those organizations that wish to take a different tack with respect to prostitution "are as unconstrained now as they were before the enactment of [the Leadership Act]." As the Court acknowledges, "[a]s a general matter, if a party objects to a condition on the receipt of federal funding, its recourse is to decline the funds," and to draw on its own coffers.

The majority cannot credibly say that this speech condition is coercive, so it does not. It pussyfoots around the lack of coercion by invalidating the Leadership Act for "*requiring* recipients to profess a specific belief" and "*demanding* that funding recipients adopt — as their own — the Government's view on an issue of public concern." (Emphasis mine.) But like King Cnut's commanding of the tides, here the Government's "requiring" and "demanding" have no coercive effect. In the end, and in the circumstances of this case, "compell[ing] *as a condition* of federal funding the affirmation of a belief" (emphasis mine) is no compulsion at all. It is the reasonable price of admission to a limited government-spending program that each organization remains free to accept or reject. Section 7631(f) "defin[es] the recipient" only to the extent he decides that it is in his interest to be so defined.

Ideological-commitment requirements such as the one here are quite rare; but making the choice between competing applicants on relevant ideological grounds is undoubtedly quite common. As far as the Constitution is concerned, it is quite impossible to distinguish between the two. If the government cannot demand a relevant ideological commitment as a condition of application, neither can it distinguish between applicants on a relevant ideological ground. And that is the real evil of today's opinion. One can expect, in the future, frequent challenges to the denial of government funding for relevant ideological reasons.

The Court's opinion contains stirring quotations from cases like *West Virginia Bd. of Ed. v. Barnette* (1943) [*supra* Chapter 9]. They serve only to distract attention from the elephant in the room: that the Government is not forcing *anyone* to say *anything*. What Congress has done here—requiring an ideological commitment relevant to the Government task at hand—is approved by the Constitution itself. Americans need not support the Constitution; they may be Communists or anarchists. But "[t]he Senators and Representatives . . . , and the Members of the several State Legislatures, and all executive and judicial Officers, both of the United States and of the several States, shall be bound by Oath or Affirmation, to support [the] Constitution." U.S. Const., Art. VI, cl. 3. The Framers saw the wisdom of imposing affirmative ideological commitments prerequisite to assisting in the government's work. And so should we.

Note: "Inside" the Program—or "Outside"?

1. Chief Justice Roberts begins his analysis by saying that if Congress had enacted the Policy Requirement "as a direct regulation of speech," it "would plainly violate the First Amendment." Does the dissent take issue with that proposition?

2. The Court says that to determine whether a funding condition imposes an unconstitutional burden, "the relevant distinction that has emerged from our cases is between conditions that define the limits of the government spending program—those that specify the activities Congress wants to subsidize—and conditions that seek to leverage funding to regulate speech outside the contours of the program itself." The former are permissible; the latter are not. The dissent insists that this distinction—"between conditions that operate inside a spending program and those that control speech outside of it"—is irrelevant to the First Amendment. Reread the precedents, particularly *Rust*. Who has the better of this argument?

3. In *Holder v. Humanitarian Law Project*, 561 U.S. 1 (2010) *(HLP)*, also written by the Chief Justice, the Court agreed with the Government that ostensibly peaceful aid to foreign terrorist organizations could be prohibited, in part because "[m]oney is fungible," and material support meant to promote peaceable, lawful conduct "frees up other resources within the organization that may be put to violent ends." The Government made a similar argument here, but the Court rejects it, saying that in *HLP* "the record indicated that support for those organizations' nonviolent operations was funneled to support their violent activities." Is this distinction persuasive? (Note that the dissent here echoes the Court's observation in *HLP* that "[m]oney is fungible.")

The dissent appeals to "economic reality," saying that "when NGOs can conduct their AIDS work on the Government's dime, they can expend greater resources on policies that undercut the Leadership Act." Suppose that the Government showed that this was in fact happening. Would that change the result? Or is the dissent persuasive in saying that the risk of such displacement is "real and obvious," so that evidence is not needed?

4. In *Rosenberger, Velazquez*, and now in *Agency for International Development*, the Court has distinguished *Rust v. Sullivan*. How much is left of the ruling in *Rust*? Consider also the *Summum* case in section B.

B. When Is the Government the Speaker?

Note: The Government Speech Doctrine

1. "A government entity . . . is entitled to say what it wishes, and to select the views that it wants to express. . . . Indeed, it is not easy to imagine how government could function if it lacked this freedom." Justice Alito wrote these words in *Pleasant Grove City v. Summum*, 555 U.S. 460 (2009). There is a great deal of common sense in his statement: after all, "it is not easy to imagine how government could function" if, for example, it could not urge citizens to vote or enlist in the armed forces, and its regulatory powers would be severely hampered if, for example, it could not urge people to quit smoking or take public transportation, or if it had to provide equal time to anti-voting and pro-smoking messages.

Despite the logic underlying the concept of government speech, if left uncabined it offers great potential for restricting *private* speech. Government interacts with private speakers in all kinds of nuanced ways. If any connection between government and a speaker suffices to convert otherwise private speech into government speech, then much speech will be subject to a governmental veto or, conversely, government compulsion. Working out the boundaries of this common sense, yet potentially broad, limitation on the First Amendment constitutes a difficult challenge for courts.

2. Despite its underlying logic, the government speech doctrine *per se* is of relatively recent vintage. While earlier cases had adverted to the basic idea, the Supreme Court did not explicitly acknowledge that doctrine until 2005. In that year, the Court decided *Johanns v. Livestock Marketing Association*, 544 U.S. 550 (2005). *Johanns* considered a claim that a federal agricultural marketing program promoting beef consumption violated the First Amendment because it taxed beef producers to pay for the pro-beef messages. The objecting producers claimed that the tax violated the First Amendment because it forced them to subsidize a generic pro-beef message crafted by an industry committee created by federal law, when they preferred to speak more specifically in favor of Americans consuming high-quality beef products. Their claims rested on two cases decided within the previous decade where the Court had considered similar challenges to forced subsidization of agricultural marketing messages. Those cases — *Glickman v. Wileman Brothers and Elliot*, 521 U.S. 457 (1997), and *United States v. United Foods*, 533 U.S. 405 (2001) — are discussed in Chapter 9. Those earlier opinions did not discuss the government speech issue.

In *Johanns*, a six-justice majority rejected the plaintiffs' argument, concluding that the beef marketing speech was government speech, rather than private speech whose subsidization was coerced by the government. Writing for five of those justices, Justice

Scalia concluded that Congress's general specification of the beef promotion program, and the Secretary of Agriculture's approval "of every word used in every [beef] promotional campaign" distinguished the case from those in which private parties were compelled to subsidize the speech of other private parties. Rather, Justice Scalia concluded that those characteristics of the program rendered the speech that of the government.

Justice Scalia also rejected the argument that the targeted nature of the assessment, as one taxing only beef producers rather than the taxpaying public in general, heightened the First Amendment problem. The plaintiffs argued that the targeted character of the assessment shifted accountability for the message away from the government and toward the committee of beef producers that worked with the Secretary of Agriculture to develop the message. They also argued that this targeted assessment, and the ads' tagline that the ads were paid for by "America's Beef Producers," led the public to attribute the ads' speech to the plaintiffs rather than the government. As to the first point, Justice Scalia found no constitutionally significant difference in the method by which the ad campaign was funded. As to the second, he recognized the possibility that misattribution could raise a valid First Amendment claim. But he noted that such a fact-intensive argument was inconsistent with the plaintiffs' facial attack on the beef marketing program.

3. Justices Thomas and Breyer both joined the majority opinion, and each wrote a short separate concurrence. Justice Ginsburg concurred only in the judgment, repeating her view from the earlier marketing cases that such programs were valid as economic regulations.

Justice Souter, joined by Justices Stevens and Kennedy, dissented. He observed that the government speech doctrine was "relatively new, and correspondingly imprecise." He noted, though, that it was common ground in earlier cases that "the First Amendment interest in avoiding forced subsidies is served, though not necessarily satisfied, by the political process as a check on what government chooses to say." On this theory, "[d]emocracy . . . ensures that government is not untouchable when its speech rubs against the First Amendment interests of those who object to supporting it: if enough voters disagree with what government says, the next election will cancel the message."

Justice Souter also argued that the targeted nature of the assessment made people like the plaintiffs "suffer a more acute limitation on their presumptive autonomy as speakers to decide what to say and what to pay for others to say." In such a case, he argued, courts should give particularly close scrutiny to the political process checks on the government speech. In *Johanns*, he found those checks wanting, because there was no requirement that the ads identify the government as the source of the message.

Justice Kennedy joined Justice Souter's dissent, but wrote a short separate dissent to reserve "the difficult First Amendment questions that would arise if the government were to target a discrete group of citizens to pay even for speech that the government does embrace as publicly as it speaks."

4. Four years later, the Court unanimously found that the speech at issue in a First Amendment case was that of the government, but remained divided in its approach to the government speech issue. *Pleasant Grove City v. Summum*, 555 U.S. 460 (2009), involved the request by a religious group to place in a city park a large, permanent stone monument stating its religious precepts. (At the time of that request, a large stone rendering of the Ten Commandments had been present in the park for over three decades, and the park contained several non-religious monuments.) When the city declined the request, the religious group sued, contending that its private speech (the monument) was being unconstitutionally excluded from a traditional public forum (the park).

The Court unanimously rejected that argument, and concluded that the city's acceptance of some monuments but not others constituted government speech. Writing for eight justices, Justice Alito wrote that "[t]here may be situations in which it is difficult to tell whether a government entity is speaking on its own behalf or is providing a forum for private speech, but this case does not present a situation. Permanent monuments displayed on public property typically represent government speech." In support of this statement, Justice Alito noted the tradition of governments using monuments to express messages, and concluded that the perception that it was the government that was thus speaking did not change when the government accepted a privately-funded donated monument. He also noted that in accepting such donated monuments, governments generally, and the City of Pleasant Grove in particular, had exercised selectivity, rather than accepting all such donations.

Justice Alito then rejected Summum's suggestion that, in order for the speech to be considered government speech, the city be required to adopt a formal resolution embracing "the message" conveyed by a given monument. He noted that the messages of monuments often change over time and that viewers at any one time often receive different messages from a monument.

In explaining why the public forum doctrine did not apply to this case, Justice Alito noted that, unlike with orators, pamphleteers, and other traditional speakers, the government could simply not accommodate every speaker who wished to speak by placing a permanent monument in a park. Finally, he rejected Summum's suggestion that this latter problem could be solved by requiring cities to make acceptance decisions based on content- and viewpoint-neutral criteria. In rejecting that suggestion, he observed that, for example, such a rule would have mandated that New York City's acceptance of the Statue of Liberty from France be matched by its willingness to accept a "Statue of Autocracy" from Tsarist Russia or Imperial Germany.

5. Justice Stevens, joined by Justice Ginsburg, wrote to state his view that, despite the Court's reasoning (which he endorsed), "our decisions relying on the recently minted government speech doctrine to uphold government action have been few and . . . of doubtful merit." Justice Breyer also wrote a separate concurrence to argue for understanding the government speech doctrine as "a rule of thumb, not a rigid category." He argued that the proper inquiry was "whether a government action burdens speech disproportionately in light of the action's tendency to further a

legitimate government objective." He found that the plaintiffs had not met that requirement. Justice Scalia, joined by Justice Thomas, concurred to argue that, despite the City's adoption of a Ten Commandments monument as its own speech, and its rejection of a monument to Summum, it should not be understood as having violated the Establishment Clause.

6. Only Justice Souter declined to join Justice Alito's opinion. While he agreed with the ruling in the city's favor, he expressed hesitation with the idea that "public monuments are government speech categorically." He counseled caution over broad statements deeming particular types of statements as government speech, worrying that the "recently minted" government speech doctrine "will affect existing doctrine in ways not explored." In particular, he agreed with Justice Scalia that this case was "litigated by the parties with one eye on the Establishment Clause." He then worried that broad statements about the applicability of the government speech doctrine to monuments might entice governments that accept such monuments to accept other additional religious monuments in order to blunt an Establishment Clause attack. In turn, such ambivalent "chatter" might cast doubt on the government's original government speech rationale.

7. Consider the themes from the Court's early encounters with the government speech doctrine. First, what role does political accountability play? Of course, as a general matter it is a good thing when government is accountable through the democratic process. But why does accountability matter, particularly in the government speech context? In addition, what do you think of Justice Souter's argument that the targeted nature of the assessment in *Johanns* affects such accountability and thus, the strength of the plaintiffs' First Amendment claim?

What role does public perception play in this doctrine? Recall that in *Johanns* Justice Scalia was willing to countenance a First Amendment claim by the plaintiffs if in fact there was evidence that the beef ads were being (mis)attributed to them rather than to the government. Similarly, in *Summum* Justice Alito observed that "because property owners typically do not permit the construction of [monuments that communicate messages the owner dislikes] on their land, persons who observe donated monuments routinely—and reasonably—interpret them as conveying some message on the property owner's behalf." Why should viewer perceptions matter to the question of who is speaking? Recall *Wooley v. Maynard* from Chapter 9. Presumably, nobody who saw the Wooleys' car would think that the Wooleys necessarily agreed with the "Live Free or Die" message on the license plate. Was *Wooley* therefore a case of government speech, with the result that the case was wrongly decided? Reconsider that question after you read *Walker v. Sons of Confederate Veterans*, which appears later in this chapter.

Finally, and relatedly, consider the question of government consistency. In his *Johanns* dissent, Justice Souter notes that, if the pro-beef message at issue in that case really was the government's speech, then the federal government had been speaking quite inconsistently, given its dietary guidelines that all-but explicitly discourage increased beef consumption. Is message inconsistency an argument against finding particular speech to be that of the government? Why should that be? Private parties get to say inconsistent things and still claim the protection of the First Amendment. Is there something different about government?

Walker v. Texas Division, Sons of Confederate Veterans, Inc.
135 S. Ct. 2239 (2015)

Justice Breyer delivered the opinion of the Court.

Texas offers automobile owners a choice between ordinary and specialty license plates. Those who want the State to issue a particular specialty plate may propose a plate design, comprising a slogan, a graphic, or (most commonly) both. If the Texas Department of Motor Vehicles Board approves the design, the State will make it available for display on vehicles registered in Texas.

In this case, the Texas Division of the Sons of Confederate Veterans proposed a specialty license plate design featuring a Confederate battle flag. The Board rejected the proposal. We must decide whether that rejection violated the Constitution's free speech guarantees. We conclude that it did not.

I

A

Texas law requires all motor vehicles operating on the State's roads to display valid license plates. And Texas makes available several kinds of plates. Drivers may choose to display the State's general-issue license plates. Each of these plates contains the word "Texas," a license plate number, a silhouette of the State, a graphic of the Lone Star, and the slogan "The Lone Star State." In the alternative, drivers may choose from an assortment of specialty license plates. Each of these plates contains the word "Texas," a license plate number, and one of a selection of designs prepared by the State. Finally, Texas law provides for personalized plates (also known as vanity plates). Pursuant to the personalization program, a vehicle owner may request a particular alphanumeric pattern for use as a plate number, such as "BOB" or "TEXPL8."

Here we are concerned only with the second category of plates, namely specialty license plates, not with the personalization program. Texas offers vehicle owners a variety of specialty plates, generally for an annual fee. And Texas selects the designs for specialty plates through three distinct processes.

First, the state legislature may specifically call for the development of a specialty license plate. The legislature has enacted statutes authorizing, for example, plates that say "Keep Texas Beautiful" and "Mothers Against Drunk Driving," plates that "honor" the Texas citrus industry, and plates that feature an image of the World Trade Center towers and the words "Fight Terrorism."

Second, the Board may approve a specialty plate design proposal that a state-designated private vendor has created at the request of an individual or organization. Among the plates created through the private-vendor process are plates promoting the "Keller Indians" and plates with the slogan "Get it Sold with RE/MAX."

Third, the Board "may create new specialty license plates on its own initiative or on receipt of an application from a" nonprofit entity seeking to sponsor a specialty plate. A nonprofit must include in its application "a draft design of the specialty license plate." And Texas law vests in the Board authority to approve or to disapprove an application. The relevant statute says that the Board "may refuse to create a new specialty license plate" for a number of reasons, for example "if the design might be offensive to any member of the public . . . or for any other reason established by rule." Specialty plates that the Board has sanctioned through this process include plates featuring the words "The Gator Nation," together with the Florida Gators logo, and plates featuring the logo of Rotary International and the words "SERVICE ABOVE SELF."

B

In 2009, the Sons of Confederate Veterans, Texas Division (a nonprofit entity), applied to sponsor a specialty license plate through this last-mentioned process. SCV's application included a draft plate design. *See* Appendix, *infra*. At the bottom of the proposed plate were the words "SONS OF CONFEDERATE VETERANS." At the side was the organization's logo, a square Confederate battle flag framed by the words "Sons of Confederate Veterans 1896." A faint Confederate battle flag appeared in the background on the lower portion of the plate. Additionally, in the middle of the plate was the license plate number, and at the top was the State's name and silhouette. . . .

The Board invited public comment on its website and at an open meeting. After considering the responses, including a number of letters sent by elected officials who opposed the proposal, the Board voted unanimously against issuing the plate. The Board explained that it had found "it necessary to deny th[e] plate design application, specifically the confederate flag portion of the design, because public comments ha[d] shown that many members of the general public find the design offensive, and because such comments are reasonable." The Board added "that a significant portion of the public associate the confederate flag with organizations advocating expressions of hate directed toward people or groups that is demeaning to those people or groups."

In 2012, SCV and two of its officers (collectively SCV) brought this lawsuit against the chairman and members of the Board (collectively Board). [The Fifth Circuit held that Texas's specialty license plate designs are private speech and that the Board, in refusing to approve SCV's design, engaged in constitutionally forbidden viewpoint discrimination.]

We granted the Board's petition for certiorari, and we now reverse.

II

When government speaks, it is not barred by the Free Speech Clause from determining the content of what it says. *Pleasant Grove City v. Summum*, 555 U.S. 460 (2009) [Note *supra* this chapter]. That freedom in part reflects the fact that it is the democratic electoral process that first and foremost provides a check on government speech. Thus, government statements (and government actions and programs that take the form of speech) do not normally trigger the First Amendment rules designed to protect the marketplace of ideas. *See Johanns v. Livestock Marketing Assn.*, 544 U.S. 550 (2005) [Note *supra* this chapter]. Instead, the Free Speech Clause helps produce informed opinions among members of the public, who are then able to influence the choices of a government that, through words and deeds, will reflect its electoral mandate.

Were the Free Speech Clause interpreted otherwise, government would not work. How could a city government create a successful recycling program if officials, when writing householders asking them to recycle cans and bottles, had to include in the letter a long plea from the local trash disposal enterprise demanding the contrary? How could a state government effectively develop programs designed to encourage and provide vaccinations, if officials also had to voice the perspective of those who oppose this type of immunization? . . .

That is not to say that a government's ability to express itself is without restriction. Constitutional and statutory provisions outside of the Free Speech Clause may limit government speech. *Summum*. And the Free Speech Clause itself may constrain the government's speech if, for example, the government seeks to compel private persons to convey the government's speech. But, as a general matter, when the government speaks it is entitled to promote a program, to espouse a policy, or to take a position. In doing so, it represents its citizens and it carries out its duties on their behalf.

III

In our view, specialty license plates issued pursuant to Texas's statutory scheme convey government speech. Our reasoning rests primarily on our analysis in *Summum*, a recent case that presented a similar problem. We conclude here, as we did there, that our precedents regarding government speech (and not our precedents regarding forums for private speech) provide the appropriate framework through which to approach the case.

A

In *Summum*, we considered a religious organization's request to erect in a 2.5-acre city park a monument setting forth the organization's religious tenets. In the park were 15 other permanent displays. At least 11 of these—including a wishing well, a September 11 monument, a historic granary, the city's first fire station, and a Ten Commandments monument—had been donated to the city by private entities. The religious organization argued that the Free Speech Clause required the city to display the organization's proposed monument because, by accepting a broad range of permanent exhibitions at the park, the city had created a forum for private speech in the form of monuments.

This Court rejected the organization's argument. We held that the city had not "provided a forum for private speech" with respect to monuments. Rather, the city, even when "accepting a privately donated monument and placing it on city property," had "engaged in expressive conduct." The speech at issue, this Court decided, was "best viewed as a form of government speech" and "therefore [was] not subject to scrutiny under the Free Speech Clause."

We based our conclusion on several factors. First, history shows that "[g]overnments have long used monuments to speak to the public." Thus, we observed that "[w]hen a government entity arranges for the construction of a monument, it does so because it wishes to convey some thought or instill some feeling in those who see the structure."

Second, we noted that it "is not common for property owners to open up their property for the installation of permanent monuments that convey a message with which they do not wish to be associated." As a result, "persons who observe donated monuments routinely—and reasonably—interpret them as conveying some message on the property owner's behalf." And "observers" of such monuments, as a consequence, ordinarily "appreciate the identity of the speaker."

Third, we found relevant the fact that the city maintained control over the selection of monuments. We thought it "fair to say that throughout our Nation's history, the general government practice with respect to donated monuments has been one of selective receptivity." And we observed that the city government in *Summum* "'effectively controlled' the messages sent by the monuments in the [p]ark by exercising 'final approval authority' over their selection."

In light of these and a few other relevant considerations, the Court concluded that the expression at issue was government speech. And, in reaching that conclusion, the Court rejected the premise that the involvement of private parties in designing the monuments was sufficient to prevent the government from controlling which monuments it placed in its own public park.

B

Our analysis in *Summum* leads us to the conclusion that here, too, government speech is at issue. First, the history of license plates shows that, insofar as license plates have conveyed more than state names and vehicle identification numbers, they long have communicated messages from the States. In 1917, Arizona became the first State to display a graphic on its plates. . . .

In 1928, Idaho became the first State to include a slogan on its plates. . . . States have used license plate slogans to urge action, to promote tourism, and to tout local industries.

Texas, too, has selected various messages to communicate through its license plate designs. . . . [The] Texas Legislature has specifically authorized specialty plate designs stating, among other things, "Read to Succeed," "Houston Livestock Show and Rodeo," "Texans Conquer Cancer," and "Girl Scouts." This kind of state speech has appeared on Texas plates for decades.

Second, Texas license plate designs "are often closely identified in the public mind with the [State]." *Summum*. Each Texas license plate is a government article serving the governmental purposes of vehicle registration and identification. The governmental nature of the plates is clear from their faces: The State places the name "TEXAS" in large letters at the top of every plate. Moreover, the State requires Texas vehicle owners to display license plates, and every Texas license plate is issued by the State.

Texas also owns the designs on its license plates, including the designs that Texas adopts on the basis of proposals made by private individuals and organizations. And Texas dictates the manner in which drivers may dispose of unused plates.

Texas license plates are, essentially, government IDs. And issuers of ID "typically do not permit" the placement on their IDs of "message[s] with which they do not wish to be associated." *Summum*. Consequently, "persons who observe" designs on IDs "routinely — and reasonably — interpret them as conveying some message on the [issuer's] behalf." *Ibid.*

Indeed, a person who displays a message on a Texas license plate likely intends to convey to the public that the State has endorsed that message. If not, the individual could simply display the message in question in larger letters on a bumper sticker right next to the plate. But the individual prefers a license plate design to the purely private speech expressed through bumper stickers. That may well be because Texas's license plate designs convey government agreement with the message displayed.

Third, Texas maintains direct control over the messages conveyed on its specialty plates. . . . And the Board and its predecessor have actively exercised this authority. Texas asserts, and SCV concedes, that the State has rejected at least a dozen proposed designs. Accordingly, like the city government in *Summum*, Texas "has 'effectively controlled' the messages [conveyed] by exercising 'final approval authority' over their selection."

This final approval authority allows Texas to choose how to present itself and its constituency. Thus, Texas offers plates celebrating the many educational institutions attended by its citizens. But it need not issue plates deriding schooling. Texas offers plates that pay tribute to the Texas citrus industry. But it need not issue plates praising Florida's oranges as far better. And Texas offers plates that say "Fight Terrorism." But it need not issue plates promoting al Qaeda.

These considerations, taken together, convince us that the specialty plates here in question are similar enough to the monuments in *Summum* to call for the same result. That is not to say that every element of our discussion in *Summum* is relevant here. For instance, in *Summum* we emphasized that monuments were "permanent" and we observed that "public parks can accommodate only a limited number of permanent monuments." . . . Here, a State could theoretically offer a much larger number of license plate designs, and those designs need not be available for time immemorial.

But those characteristics of the speech at issue in *Summum* were particularly important because the government speech at issue occurred in public parks, which are traditional public forums for "the delivery of speeches and the holding of marches and demonstrations" by private citizens. By contrast, license plates are not traditional public forums for private speech.

And other features of the designs on Texas's specialty license plates indicate that the message conveyed by those designs is conveyed on behalf of the government. Texas, through its Board, selects each design featured on the State's specialty license plates. Texas presents these designs on government-mandated, government-controlled, and government-issued IDs that have traditionally been used as a medium for government speech. And it places the designs directly below the large letters identifying "TEXAS" as the issuer of the IDs. "The [designs] that are accepted, therefore, are meant to convey and have the effect of conveying a government message, and they thus constitute government speech." . . .

C

[In this part of his opinion, Justice Breyer considered, and rejected, the argument that Texas had created a forum for private speech with its specialty license plate program.]

IV

Our determination that Texas's specialty license plate designs are government speech does not mean that the designs do not also implicate the free speech rights of private persons. We have acknowledged that drivers who display a State's selected license plate designs convey the messages communicated through those designs. *See Wooley v. Maynard* (1977) [*supra* Chapter 9] (observing that a vehicle "is readily associated with its operator" and that drivers displaying license plates "use their private property as a 'mobile billboard' for the State's ideological message"). And we have recognized that the First Amendment stringently limits a State's authority to compel a private party to express a view with which the private party disagrees. But here, compelled private speech is not at issue. And just as Texas cannot require SCV to convey "the State's ideological message," SCV cannot force Texas to include a Confederate battle flag on its specialty license plates.

* * *

For the reasons stated, we hold that Texas's specialty license plate designs constitute government speech and that Texas was consequently entitled to refuse to issue plates featuring SCV's proposed design. Accordingly, the judgment of the United States Court of Appeals for the Fifth Circuit is

Reversed.

Justice Alito, with whom The Chief Justice, Justice Scalia, and Justice Kennedy join, dissenting.

The Court's decision passes off private speech as government speech and, in doing so, establishes a precedent that threatens private speech that government finds displeasing. Under our First Amendment cases, the distinction between government speech and private speech is critical. The First Amendment "does not regulate government speech," and therefore when government speaks, it is free "to select the views that it wants to express." *Summum.* By contrast, "in the realm of private speech or expression, government regulation may not favor one speaker over another." *Rosenberger.*

Unfortunately, the Court's decision categorizes private speech as government speech and thus strips it of all First Amendment protection. The Court holds that all the privately created messages on the many specialty plates issued by the State of Texas

APPENDIX

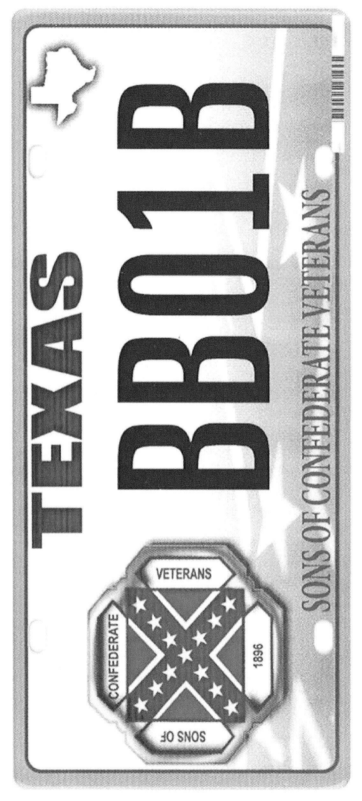

Proposed License Plate Design. App. to Pet. for Cert. 191a.

convey a government message rather than the message of the motorist displaying the plate. Can this possibly be correct?

Here is a test. Suppose you sat by the side of a Texas highway and studied the license plates on the vehicles passing by. You would see, in addition to the standard Texas plates, an impressive array of specialty plates. (There are now more than 350 varieties.) You would likely observe plates that honor numerous colleges and universities. You might see plates bearing the name of a high school, a fraternity or sorority, the Masons, the Knights of Columbus, the Daughters of the American Revolution, a realty company, a favorite soft drink, a favorite burger restaurant, and a favorite NASCAR driver.

As you sat there watching these plates speed by, would you really think that the sentiments reflected in these specialty plates are the views of the State of Texas and not those of the owners of the cars? If a car with a plate that says "Rather Be Golfing" passed by at 8:30 a.m. on a Monday morning, would you think: "This is the official policy of the State—better to golf than to work?" If you did your viewing at the start of the college football season and you saw Texas plates with the names of the University of Texas's out-of-state competitors in upcoming games—Notre Dame, Oklahoma State, the University of Oklahoma, Kansas State, Iowa State—would you assume that the State of Texas was officially (and perhaps treasonously) rooting for the Longhorns' opponents? And when a car zipped by with a plate that reads "NASCAR—24 Jeff Gordon," would you think that Gordon (born in California, raised in Indiana, resides in North Carolina) is the official favorite of the State government?

The Court says that all of these messages are government speech. It is essential that government be able to express its own viewpoint, the Court reminds us, because otherwise, how would it promote its programs, like recycling and vaccinations? So when Texas issues a "Rather Be Golfing" plate, but not a "Rather Be Playing Tennis" or "Rather Be Bowling" plate, it is furthering a state policy to promote golf but not tennis or bowling. And when Texas allows motorists to obtain a Notre Dame license plate but not a University of Southern California plate, it is taking sides in that long-time rivalry.

This capacious understanding of government speech takes a large and painful bite out of the First Amendment. Specialty plates may seem innocuous. They make motorists happy, and they put money in a State's coffers. But the precedent this case sets is dangerous. While all license plates unquestionably contain *some* government speech (*e.g.*, the name of the State and the numbers and/or letters identifying the vehicle), the State of Texas has converted the remaining space on its specialty plates into little mobile billboards on which motorists can display their own messages. And what Texas did here was to reject one of the messages that members of a private group wanted to post on some of these little billboards because the State thought that many of its citizens would find the message offensive. That is blatant viewpoint discrimination.

If the State can do this with its little mobile billboards, could it do the same with big, stationary billboards? Suppose that a State erected electronic billboards along its highways. Suppose that the State posted some government messages on these billboards and then, to raise money, allowed private entities and individuals to purchase the right to post their own messages. And suppose that the State allowed only those messages that it liked or found not too controversial. Would that be constitutional?

What if a state college or university did the same thing with a similar billboard or a campus bulletin board or dorm list serve? What if it allowed private messages that are consistent with prevailing views on campus but banned those that disturbed some students or faculty?

Can there be any doubt that these examples of viewpoint discrimination would violate the First Amendment? I hope not, but the future uses of today's precedent remain to be seen.

I

A

Specialty plates like those involved in this case are a recent development. . . . Once the idea of specialty plates took hold, the number of varieties quickly multiplied, and today, we are told, Texas motorists can choose from more than 350 messages, including many designs proposed by nonprofit groups or by individuals and for-profit businesses through the State's third-party vendor. Drivers can select plates advertising organizations and causes. . . . There are plates for fraternities and sororities and for in-state schools. . . . An even larger number of schools from out-of-state are honored. . . . There are political slogans, like "Come and Take It" and "Don't Tread on Me," and plates promoting the citrus industry and the "Cotton Boll." Commercial businesses can have specialty plates, too. There are plates advertising Remax ("Get It Sold with Remax"), Dr. Pepper ("Always One of a Kind"), and Mighty Fine Burgers.

B

[When the Motor Vehicles Board met to consider SCV's application,] many opponents of the plate turned out to voice objections. The Board then voted unanimously against approval and issued an order stating:

> The Board has considered the information and finds it necessary to deny this plate design application, specifically the confederate flag portion of the design, because public comments have shown that many members of the general public find the design offensive, and because such comments are reasonable. The Board finds that a significant portion of the public associate the confederate flag with organizations advocating expressions of hate directed toward people or groups that is demeaning to those people or groups.

The Board also saw "a compelling public interest in protecting a conspicuous mechanism for identification, such as a license plate, from degrading into a possible public safety issue." And it thought that the public interest required rejection of the plate design because the controversy surrounding the plate was so great that "the design could distract or disturb some drivers to the point of being unreasonably dangerous."

At the same meeting, the Board approved a Buffalo Soldiers plate design by a 5-to-3 vote. Proceeds from fees paid by motorists who select that plate benefit the Buffalo Soldier National Museum in Houston, which is "dedicated primarily to preserving the legacy and honor of the African American soldier." "Buffalo Soldiers" is a nickname that was originally given to black soldiers in the Army's 10th Cavalry Regiment, which was formed after the Civil War, and the name was later used to describe other black soldiers. The original Buffalo Soldiers fought with distinction in the Indian Wars, but the "Buffalo Soldiers" plate was opposed by some Native Americans. One leader commented that he felt "'the same way about the Buffalo Soldiers'" as African-Americans felt about the Confederate flag. "When we see the U.S. Cavalry uniform," he explained, "we are forced to relive an American holocaust."

II

A

Relying almost entirely on one precedent—*Summum*—the Court holds that messages that private groups succeed in placing on Texas license plates are government messages. The Court badly misunderstands *Summum*.

In *Summum*, [we] held that the monuments represented government speech, and we identified several important factors that led to this conclusion. . . . These characteristics, which rendered public monuments government speech in *Summum*, are not present in Texas's specialty plate program.

B

1

I begin with history. As we said in *Summum*, governments have used monuments since time immemorial to express important government messages, and there is no history of governments giving equal space to those wishing to express dissenting views. [For example, when] the United States accepted the Third French Republic's gift of the Statue of Liberty in 1877, Congress, it seems safe to say, would not have welcomed a gift of a Statue of Authoritarianism if one had been offered by another country. . . . Governments have always used public monuments to express a government message, and members of the public understand this.

The history of messages on license plates is quite different. After the beginning of motor vehicle registration in 1917, more than 70 years passed before the proliferation of specialty plates in Texas. It was not until the 1990's that motorists were allowed to choose from among 10 messages, such as "Read to Succeed" and "Keep Texas Beautiful."

Up to this point, the words on the Texas plates can be considered government speech. The messages were created by the State, and they plausibly promoted state programs. But when, at some point within the last 20 years or so, the State began to allow private entities to secure plates conveying their own messages, Texas crossed the line.

The contrast between the history of public monuments, which have been used to convey government messages for centuries, and the Texas license plate program could not be starker. . . .

The words and symbols on plates of this sort were and are government speech, but plates that are essentially commissioned by private entities (at a cost that exceeds $8,000) and that express a message chosen by those entities are very different—and quite new. Unlike in *Summum*, history here does not suggest that the messages at issue are government speech.

2

The Texas specialty plate program also does not exhibit the "selective receptivity" present in *Summum*. To the contrary, Texas's program is not selective by design. The Board's chairman, who is charged with approving designs, explained that the program's purpose is "to encourage private plates" in order to "generate additional revenue for the state." And most of the time, the Board "base[s] [its] decisions on rules that primarily deal with reflectivity and readability." . . .

. . . [The] picture here is different from that in *Summum*. Texas does not take care to approve only those proposed plates that convey messages that the State supports. Instead, it proclaims that it is open to all private messages—except those, like the SCV plate, that would offend some who viewed them.

The Court believes that messages on privately created plates are government speech because motorists want a seal of state approval for their messages and therefore prefer plates over bumper stickers. This is dangerous reasoning. There is a big difference between government speech (that is, speech by the government in furtherance of its programs) and governmental blessing (or condemnation) of private speech. Many private speakers in a forum would welcome a sign of government approval. But in the realm of private speech, government regulation may not favor one viewpoint over another. *Rosenberger*.

3

A final factor that was important in *Summum* was space. A park can accommodate only so many permanent monuments. Often large and made of stone, monuments can last for centuries and are difficult to move. License plates, on the other hand, are small, light, mobile, and designed to last for only a relatively brief time. The only absolute limit on the number of specialty plates that a State could issue is the number of registered vehicles. The variety of available plates is limitless, too. Today Texas offers more than 350 varieties. In 10 years, might it be 3,500?

In sum, the Texas specialty plate program has none of the factors that were critical in *Summum*, and the Texas program exhibits a very important characteristic that was missing in that case: Individuals who want to display a Texas specialty plate, instead of the standard plate, must pay an increased annual registration fee. How many groups or individuals would clamor to pay $8,000 (the cost of the deposit required to create a new plate) in order to broadcast the government's message as opposed to their own? . . . The fees Texas collects pay for much more than merely the administration of the program.

States have not adopted specialty license plate programs like Texas's because they are now bursting with things they want to say on their license plates. Those programs were adopted because they bring in money. Texas makes public the revenue totals generated by its specialty plate program, and it is apparent that the program brings in many millions of dollars every year.

Texas has space available on millions of little mobile billboards. And Texas, in effect, sells that space to those who wish to use it to express a personal message — provided only that the message does not express a viewpoint that the State finds unacceptable. That is not government speech; it is the regulation of private speech.

III

What Texas has done by selling space on its license plates is to create what we have called a limited public forum. It has allowed state property (i.e., motor vehicle license plates) to be used by private speakers according to rules that the State prescribes. Under the First Amendment, however, those rules cannot discriminate on the basis of viewpoint. But that is exactly what Texas did here. The Board rejected Texas SCV's design, "specifically the confederate flag portion of the design, because public comments have shown that many members of the general public find the design offensive, and because such comments are reasonable." These statements indisputably demonstrate that the Board denied Texas SCV's design because of its viewpoint. . . .

The Board's decision cannot be saved by its suggestion that the plate, if allowed, "could distract or disturb some drivers to the point of being unreasonably dangerous." This rationale cannot withstand strict scrutiny. Other States allow specialty plates with the Confederate Battle Flag, and Texas has not pointed to evidence that these plates have led to incidents of road rage or accidents. Texas does not ban bumper stickers bearing the image of the Confederate battle flag. Nor does it ban any of the many other bumper stickers that convey political messages and other messages that are capable of exciting the ire of those who loathe the ideas they express.

* * *

Messages that are proposed by private parties and placed on Texas specialty plates are private speech, not government speech. Texas cannot forbid private speech based on its viewpoint. That is what it did here. Because the Court approves this violation of the First Amendment, I respectfully dissent.

Note: Expanding the Government Speech Doctrine

1. In *Summum*, Justice Stevens and Justice Souter characterized the government speech doctrine as "recently minted," and Justice Souter said "it would do well for us to go slow in setting its bounds." Does the Court in *Walker* heed that counsel?

2. The Court does not respond to Justice Alito's "test": sitting by the side of a Texas highway and studying the license plates on the vehicles passing by, would the observer think that the sentiments expressed on the special plates are the views of the state of Texas? Does this mean that the Court rejects the "reasonable observer" approach suggested by Justice Souter in *Summum*?

3. Consider the hypotheticals posed by Justice Alito:

> Suppose that a State erected electronic billboards along its highways. Suppose that the State posted some government messages on these billboards and then, to raise money, allowed private entities and individuals to purchase the right to post their own messages. And suppose that the State allowed only those messages that it liked or found not too controversial.

> What if a state college or university did the same thing with a similar billboard or a campus bulletin board or dorm list serve? What if it allowed private messages that are consistent with prevailing views on campus but banned those that disturbed some students or faculty?

Can these hypotheticals be distinguished from *Walker*? Or would the Court say that in these instances also the First Amendment would not be violated?

4. Consider the Problems at the end of this chapter. How would these be analyzed under *Walker*?

5. The Court says that "just as Texas cannot require SCV to convey 'the State's ideological message,' SCV cannot force Texas to include a Confederate battle flag on its specialty license plates." Is the Court saying that Texas has a First Amendment right not to speak? If so, where does the right come from?

Matal v. Tam

137 S. Ct. 1744 (2017)

[This case is excerpted in Chapter 15. As part of your reading for this chapter, read the introduction and Parts I–III (A) of the majority opinion.]

————

Problem: "Enhanced Underwriting" by the Ku Klux Klan

KNOQ is a not-for-profit public broadcast radio station located on the campus of the University of West Fremont (UWF). KNOQ is owned and operated by The Trustees of the University of New Fremont, a public corporation established under state law and licensed by the Federal Communications Commission (FCC) to run the station.

To help fund the station, KNOQ operates an "enhanced underwriting" program within its sales division. Pursuant to federal law, the station acknowledges on air any individual or group source of funding for a particular broadcast matter. Contributors of such funds are referred to as "donors" or "underwriters." Although federal law forbids noncommercial educational FM broadcasters like KNOQ from broadcasting "advertisements," public broadcasters are permitted to "enhance" or expand the scope of donor or underwriter acknowledgments by including (1) logograms or slogans which identify the underwriter but do not promote it, (2) location information on the donor, (3) value neutral descriptions of the underwriter's product line or service, and (4) donor brand names, trade names, and product or service listings. Typically, the announcement is a 15-second message, drafted by the underwriter or KNOQ staff. All scripts are reviewed and edited by station management to ensure compliance with federal law and regulations as well as KNOQ underwriting guidelines, because UWF (as the licensee of KNOQ) is ultimately liable for all transmissions. Here are two representative messages that have been broadcast on KNOQ:

- "Local funding for Mobil Masterpiece Theater is provided in part by a grant from Sprint. Life should be simpler, less complicated. That's the thinking behind everything Sprint has been doing. It all makes sense. Sprint."

- "KNOQ broadcast operations are funded in part by Blessed Spirit University. Professionals with master's degrees working in business, education, health care, and other careers, are earning Ph.Ds in Leadership Studies on weekends. Applications and information for the fall semester are available on the web at leadershipstudies.org."

The general manager of the station designates the percentage of total air time available for underwriting spots as well as the amount of underwriting time allotted to particular programs. She accepts donor funds from, and approves accompanying messages of, approximately 30 underwriters per week. Bennett does not generally examine the philosophy or policies of each potential donor. Nonetheless, over the last 10 years, she has rejected financial support from several potential underwriters, including a group called "Ultimate Fighting Championships" and an establishment known to be "a house of ill repute."

Gerald Cone, the state coordinator for the West Fremont branch of the Ku Klux Klan (KKK), wrote to the station requesting the opportunity for the West Fremont KKK to sponsor four segments of NPR's news show "All Things Considered." He submitted the following message to be read as an underwriting acknowledgment:

> The Knights of the Ku Klux Klan, a White Christian organization, standing up for rights and values of White Christian America since 1865. For more information, please contact the Knights of the Ku Klux Klan, at P.O. Box . . . Let your voice be heard!

The station manager contacted her supervisor, who contacted the chancellor of the university. The chancellor instructed the manager to reject the KKK's proposed underwriting gift. The chancellor explained that the station was legally required to acknowledge donors on the air, and he anticipated that an acknowledgement of the West Fremont KKK as an underwriter would result in a significant loss of revenue to the University. It would jeopardize future gifts from black and other minority donors, and would lead some students to leave the University, resulting in revenue loss. He emphasized that these business and economic reasons, not the views of the West Fremont KKK, were the basis for his decision.

The KKK has brought suit seeking injunctive relief, asserting that the University and its officials violated its First Amendment rights by refusing Cone's request for program underwriting. The University has moved for summary judgment, asserting that the enhanced underwriting program is not a forum for speech and does not implicate the First Amendment.

How should the court rule?

————

Problem: Exclusion from a State's Adopt-a-Highway Program

The State of New Harmony, like many other states, has an "Adopt-A-Highway" (AAH) program. Participants in the AAH program agree to collect litter along a specific portion of highway at least twice every six months and, in return, the New Harmony Highways and Transportation Commission (the State) installs signs bearing the name of the adopter at both ends of the adopted section.

Unit 103 of the Knights of the Ku Klux Klan, the New Harmony chapter of the national Ku Klux Klan, applied to participate in the program. The State notified Unit 103 that its application was denied because it did not meet the AAH program's eligibility requirements that were set forth in state regulations. One of these requirements limits the class of organizations eligible to participate in the program to those "for whom state or federal courts have not taken judicial notice of a history of violence."

The State has not denied any other application on this basis, but it cites the Supreme Court's opinion in *Virginia v. Black*, 538 U.S. 343 (2003) (Note *infra* Chapter 15) in support of its denial of the KKK application. (In *Black*, the Court noted the history of the national KKK's use of racial intimidation and violence.) The State acknowledges that the *Black* case did not involve Unit 103 of the KKK, but it notes that Unit 103 has chosen to adopt a name similar to that used by others who have had judicial notice taken of a history of violence.

The State argues further that even if the exclusion would be improper in a regulatory setting, the only speech that the AAH program implicates is that of the government itself. In the State's view, the government "speaks" by composing and erecting the signs identifying the adopter, while the adopter itself engages in no protected speech by participating in the program, and thus the exclusion of Unit 103 pursuant to the regulation could not have abridged its freedom of speech.

Is the exclusion permissible under the First Amendment?

Chapter 14

Freedom of the Press

The First Amendment states, in part, that "Congress shall make no law . . . abridging the freedom of speech, *or of the press. . . .*" (Emphasis added.) The distinct references to "freedom of speech" and freedom "of the press" raise difficult questions. Justice Potter Stewart once said, "If the Free Press guarantee meant no more than freedom of expression, it would be a constitutional redundancy."* But if the Free Press Clause is not a "constitutional redundancy," what does it add to the Free Speech Clause?

There are more specific questions as well. Does freedom of the press simply mean freedom from prior restraints on publishing? Does it give the press a right not to be singled out for worse treatment than that accorded other institutions? Does it require that all members of the press be treated equally, i.e., that there be no discrimination in favor of some members of the press at the expense of others? At the farthest extreme, does it provide the press with special rights or immunities not granted to the general public? The cases in this chapter consider these problems. As you read these cases, consider what role the various Justices explicitly or implicitly assign to the press, and thus to press freedom, in our system.

Note: What Is "The Press," Anyway?

This chapter proceeds for the most part as if it is clear which persons and institutions the Court is referring to when it speaks of "the freedom . . . of the press." But it is not. Part of this ambiguity stems from the fact that the Speech Clause, which protects all speakers, including reporters and other journalists, has been interpreted so expansively that there has been little need to consider whether "the press," however defined, merits unique protections. For example, the seminal case on First Amendment protection against libel liability, *New York Times v. Sullivan* (1964) (*supra* Chapter 2), expressed its holding in terms of both the freedom of speech and the press. Indeed, the cases with which this chapter ends—involving access to criminal proceedings—treat the press's rights as equivalent to those enjoyed by the public via the Speech Clause. In other cases—including all the major Press Clause cases presented in this chapter—the plaintiff would undeniably be considered a member of the press, even under the narrowest definition.

This is not to say that the Court has never commented on the definitional question. Perhaps most famously, in *Branzburg v. Hayes*, 408 U.S. 665 (1972) (*infra* this chapter), the Court rejected a claim that the Press Clause bestowed a qualified

---

* Potter Stewart, *"Or of the Press,"* 26 Hastings L.J. 631 (1975).

privilege on reporters to refuse to testify before grand juries. Justice White, writing for the five-justice majority, wrote that "liberty of the press is the right of the lonely pamphleteer who uses carbon paper or a mimeograph just as much as of the large metropolitan publisher who utilizes the latest photocomposition methods." He continued, "Freedom of the press is a fundamental personal right which is not confined to newspapers and periodicals. . . . The press in its historic connotation comprehends every sort of publication which affords a vehicle of information and opinion."

At times, individual justices have expressed potentially different views. Most famously, Justice Potter Stewart (who dissented in *Branzburg*), argued that "the Free Press Clause extends protection to an institution. The publishing business is, in short, the only organized private business that is given explicit constitutional protection." Potter Stewart, *"Or of the Press,"* 26 HASTINGS L. REV. 631 (1975).

Consider the implications of these two viewpoints in light of the Court's resolution of the press freedom cases you will read in this chapter. What difficulties do the Court's analyses raise for one or the other of these conclusions? Do those difficulties suggest a particular answer to the "what is the press?" question? In particular, consider the implications of a broad definition for modern technology. If, as *Branzburg* suggests, the "press" refers to technology used to create materials for mass dissemination, what does that mean in the age of the Internet and social media? Are websites such as the Drudge Report and the Huffington Post the press? Or is everyone the press when, for example, they post on Facebook? If the answer to these last two questions is yes, then what does that imply for special privileges for the press? If the answer is no, how are we to draw lines?

A. Singling Out the Press

Grosjean v. American Press Co.

297 U.S. 233 (1936)

MR. JUSTICE SUTHERLAND delivered the opinion of the Court.

This suit was brought by appellees, nine publishers of newspapers in the State of Louisiana, to enjoin the enforcement against them of the provisions of § 1 of the act of the legislature of Louisiana known as Act No. 23, passed and approved July 12, 1934, as follows:

> That every person, firm, association, or corporation, domestic or foreign, engaged in the business of selling, or making any charge for, advertising or for advertisements, whether printed or published, or to be printed or published, in any newspaper, magazine, periodical or publication whatever having a circulation of more than 20,000 copies per week, or displayed and exhibited, or to be displayed and exhibited by means of moving pictures, in the State of Louisiana, shall, in addition to all other taxes and licenses levied and assessed in this State, pay a license tax for the privilege of engaging in

such business in this State of two per cent. (2%) of the gross receipts of such business.

The nine publishers who brought the suit publish thirteen newspapers; and these thirteen publications are the only ones within the State of Louisiana having each a circulation of more than 20,000 copies per week, although the lower court finds there are four other daily newspapers each having a circulation of "slightly less than 20,000 copies per week" which are in competition with those published by appellees both as to circulation and as to advertising. In addition, there are 120 weekly newspapers published in the state, also in competition, to a greater or less degree, with the newspapers of appellees. The revenue derived from appellees' newspapers comes almost entirely from regular subscribers or purchasers thereof and from payments received for the insertion of advertisements therein. . . .

The lower court entered a decree for appellees and granted a permanent injunction. . . .

Third. The validity of the act is assailed as violating the Federal Constitution in two particulars—(1) that it abridges the freedom of the press in contravention of the due process clause contained in § 1 of the Fourteenth Amendment; (2) that it denies appellees the equal protection of the laws in contravention of the same Amendment.

1. The first point presents a question of the utmost gravity and importance; for, if well made, it goes to the heart of the natural right of the members of an organized society, united for their common good, to impart and acquire information about their common interests. . . .

The tax imposed is designated a "license tax for the privilege of engaging in such business"—that is to say, the business of selling, or making any charge for, advertising. As applied to appellees, it is a tax of two per cent. on the gross receipts derived from advertisements carried in their newspapers when, and only when, the newspapers of each enjoy a circulation of more than 20,000 copies per week. It thus operates as a restraint in a double sense. First, its effect is to curtail the amount of revenue realized from advertising, and, second, its direct tendency is to restrict circulation. This is plain enough when we consider that, if it were increased to a high degree, as it could be if valid, it well might result in destroying both advertising and circulation.

A determination of the question whether the tax is valid in respect of the point now under review, requires an examination of the history and circumstances which antedated and attended the adoption of the abridgement clause of the First Amendment, since that clause expresses one of those "fundamental principles of liberty and justice which lie at the base of all our civil and political institutions" (*Hebert v. Louisiana*, 272 U.S. 312 (1926)), and, as such, is embodied in the concept "due process of law" (*Twining v. New Jersey*, 211 U.S. 78 (1908)), and, therefore, protected against hostile state invasion by the due process clause of the Fourteenth Amendment. The history is a long one; but for present purposes it may be greatly abbreviated.

For more than a century prior to the adoption of the amendment—and, indeed, for many years thereafter—history discloses a persistent effort on the part of the

British government to prevent or abridge the free expression of any opinion which seemed to criticize or exhibit in an unfavorable light, however truly, the agencies and operations of the government. The struggle between the proponents of measures to that end and those who asserted the right of free expression was continuous and unceasing. As early as 1644, John Milton, in an "Appeal for the Liberty of Unlicensed Printing," assailed an act of Parliament which had just been passed providing for censorship of the press previous to publication. He vigorously defended the right of every man to make public his honest views "without previous censure"; and declared the impossibility of finding any man base enough to accept the office of censor and at the same time good enough to be allowed to perform its duties. Collett, History of the Taxes on Knowledge. The act expired by its own terms in 1695. It was never renewed; and the liberty of the press thus became, as pointed out by Wickwar (*The Struggle for the Freedom of the Press*), merely "a right or liberty to publish *without* a license what formerly could be published only *with* one." But mere exemption from previous censorship was soon recognized as too narrow a view of the liberty of the press.

In 1712, in response to a message from Queen Anne, Parliament imposed a tax upon all newspapers and upon advertisements. That the main purpose of these taxes was to suppress the publication of comments and criticisms objectionable to the Crown does not admit of doubt. Stewart, *Lennox and the Taxes on Knowledge*, 15 Scottish Historical Review 322–27. There followed more than a century of resistance to, and evasion of, the taxes, and of agitation for their repeal. In the article last referred to, which was written in 1918, it was pointed out that these taxes constituted one of the factors that aroused the American colonists to protest against taxation for the purposes of the home government; and that the revolution really began when, in 1765, that government sent stamps for newspaper duties to the American colonies.

These duties were quite commonly characterized as "taxes on knowledge," a phrase used for the purpose of describing the effect of the exactions and at the same time condemning them. That the taxes had, and were intended to have, the effect of curtailing the circulation of newspapers, and particularly the cheaper ones whose readers were generally found among the masses of the people, went almost without question, even on the part of those who defended the act. May (Constitutional History of England), after discussing the control by "previous censure," says: ". . . a new restraint was devised in the form of a stamp duty on newspapers and advertisements,—avowedly for the purpose of repressing libels. This policy, being found effectual in limiting the circulation of cheap papers, was improved upon in the two following reigns, and continued in high esteem until our own time." Collett says, "Any man who carried on printing or publishing for a livelihood was actually at the mercy of the Commissioners of Stamps, when they chose to exert their powers."

Citations of similar import might be multiplied many times; but the foregoing is enough to demonstrate beyond peradventure that in the adoption of the English newspaper stamp tax and the tax on advertisements, revenue was of subordinate concern;

and that the dominant and controlling aim was to prevent, or curtail the opportunity for, the acquisition of knowledge by the people in respect of their governmental affairs. It is idle to suppose that so many of the best men of England would for a century of time have waged, as they did, stubborn and often precarious warfare against these taxes if a mere matter of taxation had been involved. The aim of the struggle was not to relieve taxpayers from a burden, but to establish and preserve the right of the English people to full information in respect of the doings or misdoings of their government. Upon the correctness of this conclusion the very characterization of the exactions as "taxes on knowledge" sheds a flood of corroborative light. In the ultimate, an informed and enlightened public opinion was the thing at stake; for, as Erskine, in his great speech in defense of Paine, has said, "The liberty of opinion keeps governments themselves in due subjection to their duties." *Erskine's Speeches*.

In 1785, only four years before Congress had proposed the First Amendment, the Massachusetts legislature, following the English example, imposed a stamp tax on all newspapers and magazines. The following year an advertisement tax was imposed. Both taxes met with such violent opposition that the former was repealed in 1786, and the latter in 1788. Duniway, *Freedom of the Press in Massachusetts*.

The framers of the First Amendment were familiar with the English struggle, which then had continued for nearly eighty years and was destined to go on for another sixty-five years, at the end of which time it culminated in a lasting abandonment of the obnoxious taxes. The framers were likewise familiar with the then recent Massachusetts episode; and while that occurrence did much to bring about the adoption of the amendment, the predominant influence must have come from the English experience. It is impossible to concede that by the words "freedom of the press" the framers of the amendment intended to adopt merely the narrow view then reflected by the law of England that such freedom consisted only in immunity from previous censorship; for this abuse had then permanently disappeared from English practice. It is equally impossible to believe that it was not intended to bring within the reach of these words such modes of restraint as were embodied in the two forms of taxation already described. Such belief must be rejected in the face of the then well known purpose of the exactions and the general adverse sentiment of the colonies in respect of them. Undoubtedly, the range of a constitutional provision phrased in terms of the common law sometimes may be fixed by recourse to the applicable rules of that law. But the doctrine which justifies such recourse, like other canons of construction, must yield to more compelling reasons whenever they exist. And, obviously, it is subject to the qualification that the common law rule invoked shall be one not rejected by our ancestors as unsuited to their civil or political conditions. [E.g.] *Powell v. Alabama*, 287 U.S. 45 (1932).

In the light of all that has now been said, it is evident that the restricted rules of the English law in respect of the freedom of the press in force when the Constitution was adopted were never accepted by the American colonists, and that by the First Amendment it was meant to preclude the national government, and by the Fourteenth Amendment to preclude the states, from adopting any form of previous restraint upon printed publications, or their circulation, including that which had theretofore been effected by these two well-known and odious methods.

This court had occasion in *Near v. Minnesota* (1931) [*supra* Chapter 4] to discuss at some length the subject in its general aspect. The conclusion there stated is that the object of the constitutional provisions was to prevent previous restraints on publication; and the court was careful not to limit the protection of the right to any particular way of abridging it. Liberty of the press within the meaning of the constitutional provision, it was broadly said, meant "principally although not exclusively, immunity from previous restraints or from censorship."

Judge Cooley has laid down the test to be applied—"The evils to be prevented were not the censorship of the press merely, but any action of the government by means of which it might prevent such free and general discussion of public matters as seems absolutely essential to prepare the people for an intelligent exercise of their rights as citizens." 2 Cooley's Constitutional Limitations.

It is not intended by anything we have said to suggest that the owners of newspapers are immune from any of the ordinary forms of taxation for support of the government. But this is not an ordinary form of tax, but one single in kind, with a long history of hostile misuse against the freedom of the press.

The predominant purpose of the grant of immunity here invoked was to preserve an untrammeled press as a vital source of public information. The newspapers, magazines and other journals of the country, it is safe to say, have shed and continue to shed, more light on the public and business affairs of the nation than any other instrumentality of publicity; and since informed public opinion is the most potent of all restraints upon misgovernment, the suppression or abridgement of the publicity afforded by a free press cannot be regarded otherwise than with grave concern. The tax here involved is bad not because it takes money from the pockets of the appellees. If that were all, a wholly different question would be presented. It is bad because, in the light of its history and of its present setting, it is seen to be a deliberate and calculated device in the guise of a tax to limit the circulation of information to which the public is entitled in virtue of the constitutional guaranties. A free press stands as one of the great interpreters between the government and the people. To allow it to be fettered is to fetter ourselves.

In view of the persistent search for new subjects of taxation, it is not without significance that, with the single exception of the Louisiana statute, so far as we can discover, no state during the one hundred fifty years of our national existence has undertaken to impose a tax like that now in question.

The form in which the tax is imposed is in itself suspicious. It is not measured or limited by the volume of advertisements. It is measured alone by the extent of the circulation of the publication in which the advertisements are carried, with the plain purpose of penalizing the publishers and curtailing the circulation of a selected group of newspapers.

2. Having reached the conclusion that the act imposing the tax in question is unconstitutional under the due process of law clause because it abridges the freedom of the press, we deem it unnecessary to consider the further ground assigned that it also constitutes a denial of the equal protection of the laws.

Decree affirmed.

————

Note: Grosjean *and the Free-Press Clause*

1. Does the opinion in *Grosjean* help to answer the question posed at the start of this chapter: what is the distinct function of the Free Press Clause? Justice Stewart, in the article quoted in the introduction to this chapter, suggested that "the Free Press guarantee is, in essence, a *structural* provision of the Constitution." He said that the primary purpose of the constitutional guarantee was "to create a fourth institution outside the Government as an additional check on the three official branches." Does the opinion in *Grosjean* support this interpretation?

2. Justice Sutherland, the author of the *Grosjean* opinion, is remembered primarily as one of the "Four Horsemen" who repeatedly voted to strike down economic and social legislation in the 1920s and 1930s. Does the *Grosjean* opinion suggest that his jurisprudence was animated by a broader concern about unchecked governmental power? Note that Justice Sutherland also wrote the Court's opinion in *Powell v. Alabama*, 287 U.S. 45 (1932) (cited in *Grosjean*), the first case recognizing a right to counsel in a state criminal prosecution.

Minneapolis Star v. Minnesota Commissioner of Revenue
460 U.S. 575 (1983)

JUSTICE O'CONNOR delivered the opinion of the Court.

This case presents the question of a State's power to impose a special tax on the press and, by enacting exemptions, to limit its effect to only a few newspapers.

I

Since 1967, Minnesota has imposed a sales tax on most sales of goods for a price in excess of a nominal sum. In general, the tax applies only to retail sales. An exemption for industrial and agricultural users shields from the tax sales of components to be used in the production of goods that will themselves be sold at retail. As part of this general system of taxation and in support of the sales tax, Minnesota also enacted a tax on the "privilege of using, storing or consuming in Minnesota tangible personal property." This use tax applies to any nonexempt tangible personal property unless the sales tax was paid on the sales price. Like the classic use tax, this use tax protects the State's sales tax by eliminating the residents' incentive to travel to States with lower sales taxes to buy goods rather than buying them in Minnesota.

The appellant, Minneapolis Star and Tribune Company "Star Tribune," is the publisher of a morning newspaper and an evening newspaper in Minneapolis. From

1967 until 1971, it enjoyed an exemption from the sales and use tax provided by Minnesota for periodic publications. In 1971, however, while leaving the exemption from the sales tax in place, the legislature amended the scheme to impose a "use tax" on the cost of paper and ink products consumed in the production of a publication. Ink and paper used in publications became the only items subject to the use tax that were components of goods to be sold at retail. In 1974, the legislature again amended the statute, this time to exempt the first $100,000 worth of ink and paper consumed by a publication in any calendar year, in effect giving each publication an annual tax credit of $4,000. Publications remained exempt from the sales tax.

After the enactment of the $100,000 exemption, 11 publishers, producing 14 of the 388 paid circulation newspapers in the State, incurred a tax liability in 1974. Star Tribune was one of the 11, and, of the $893,355 collected, it paid $608,634, or roughly two-thirds of the total revenue raised by the tax. . . .

Star Tribune instituted this action to seek a refund of the use taxes it paid from January 1, 1974 to May 31, 1975. It challenged the imposition of the use tax on ink and paper used in publications as a violation of the guarantees of freedom of the press and equal protection in the First and Fourteenth Amendments. The Minnesota Supreme Court upheld the tax against the federal constitutional challenge. We noted probable jurisdiction, and we now reverse.

II

Star Tribune argues that we must strike this tax on the authority of *Grosjean v. American Press Co., Inc.* (1936) [*supra* this chapter]. Although there are similarities between the two cases, we agree with the State that *Grosjean* is not controlling.

In *Grosjean*, the State of Louisiana imposed a license tax of 2% of the gross receipts from the sale of advertising on all newspapers with a weekly circulation above 20,000. Out of at least 124 publishers in the State, only 13 were subject to the tax. After noting that the tax was "single in kind" and that keying the tax to circulation curtailed the flow of information, this Court held the tax invalid as an abridgment of the freedom of the press. Both the brief and the argument of the publishers in this Court emphasized the events leading up to the tax and the contemporary political climate in Louisiana. All but one of the large papers subject to the tax had "ganged up" on Senator Huey Long, and a circular distributed by Long and the governor to each member of the state legislature described "lying newspapers" as conducting "a vicious campaign" and the tax as "a tax on lying, 2c [*sic*] a lie." Although the Court's opinion did not describe this history, it stated, "The tax is bad because, in the light of its history and of its present setting, it is seen to be a deliberate and calculated device in the guise of a tax to limit the circulation of information," an explanation that suggests that the motivation of the legislature may have been significant. . . .

Our subsequent cases have not been consistent in their reading of *Grosjean* on this point. Compare *United States v. O'Brien* (1968) [*supra* Chapter 7] (stating that legislative purpose was irrelevant in *Grosjean*) with *Houchins v. KQED, Inc.*, 438 U.S. 1 (1978) (plurality opinion) [*infra* Note this chapter] (suggesting that purpose was relevant in

Grosjean); *Pittsburgh Press Co. v. Pittsburgh Commission on Human Relations*, 413 U.S. 376 (1973) (same). Commentators have generally viewed *Grosjean* as dependent on the improper censorial goals of the legislature. We think that the result in *Grosjean* may have been attributable in part to the perception on the part of the Court that the state imposed the tax with an intent to penalize a selected group of newspapers. In the case currently before us, however, there is no legislative history and no indication, apart from the structure of the tax itself, of any impermissible or censorial motive on the part of the legislature. We cannot resolve the case by simple citation to *Grosjean.* Instead, we must analyze the problem anew under the general principles of the First Amendment.

III

Clearly, the First Amendment does not prohibit all regulation of the press. It is beyond dispute that the States and the Federal Government can subject newspapers to generally applicable economic regulations without creating constitutional problems. *See, e.g., Breard v. Alexandria*, 341 U.S. 622 (1951) (prohibition of door-to-door solicitation); *Oklahoma Press Publishing Co. v. Walling*, 327 U.S. 186 (1946) (Fair Labor Standards Act); *Mabee v. White Plains Pub. Co.*, 327 U.S. 178 (1946) (same); *Associated Press v. United States*, 326 U.S. 1 (1945) (antitrust laws); *see also Branzburg v. Hayes* (1972) [*infra* this chapter] (enforcement of subpoenas). Minnesota, however, has not chosen to apply its general sales and use tax to newspapers. Instead, it has created a special tax that applies only to certain publications protected by the First Amendment. Although the State argues now that the tax on paper and ink is part of the general scheme of taxation, the use tax provision is facially discriminatory, singling out publications for treatment that is, to our knowledge, unique in Minnesota tax law.

Minnesota's treatment of publications differs from that of other enterprises in at least two important respects: it imposes a use tax that does not serve the function of protecting the sales tax, and it taxes an intermediate transaction rather than the ultimate retail sale. A use tax ordinarily serves to complement the sales tax by eliminating the incentive to make major purchases in States with lower sales taxes; it requires the resident who shops out-of-state to pay a use tax equal to the sales tax savings. Minnesota designed its overall use tax scheme to serve this function. . . . Thus, in general, items exempt from the sales tax are not subject to the use tax, for, in the event of a sales tax exemption, there is no "complementary function" for a use tax to serve. But the use tax on ink and paper serves no such complementary function; it applies to all uses, whether or not the taxpayer purchased the ink and paper in-state, and it applies to items exempt from the sales tax.

Further, the ordinary rule in Minnesota, as discussed above, is to tax only the ultimate, or retail, sale rather than the use of components like ink and paper. . . . Publishers, however, are taxed on their purchase of components, even though they will eventually sell their publications at retail.

By creating this special use tax, which, to our knowledge, is without parallel in the State's tax scheme, Minnesota has singled out the press for special treatment. We then must determine whether the First Amendment permits such special taxation. A tax that burdens rights protected by the First Amendment cannot stand unless the burden is necessary to achieve an overriding governmental interest. *See, e.g., United States v. Lee*, 455 U.S. 252 (1982). Any tax that the press must pay, of course, imposes some "burden." But, as we have observed, this Court has long upheld economic regulation of the press. The cases approving such economic regulation, however, emphasized the general applicability of the challenged regulation to all businesses, *e.g., Oklahoma Press Publishing Co. v. Walling*, suggesting that a regulation that singled out the press might place a heavier burden of justification on the State, and we now conclude that the special problems created by differential treatment do indeed impose such a burden.

There is substantial evidence that differential taxation of the press would have troubled the Framers of the First Amendment. . . . When the Constitution was proposed without an explicit guarantee of freedom of the press, the Antifederalists objected. Proponents of the Constitution, relying on the principle of enumerated powers, responded that such a guarantee was unnecessary because the Constitution granted Congress no power to control the press. The remarks of Richard Henry Lee are typical of the rejoinders of the Antifederalists:

> I confess I do not see in what cases the congress can, with any pretence of right, make a law to suppress the freedom of the press; though I am not clear, that congress is restrained from laying any duties whatever on printing, and from laying duties particularly heavy on certain pieces printed. R. Lee, *Observation Leading to a Fair Examination of the System of Government, Letter IV, reprinted in* 1 B. Schwartz, The Bill of Rights: A Documentary History (1971).

The fears of the Antifederalists were well-founded. A power to tax differentially, as opposed to a power to tax generally, gives a government a powerful weapon against the taxpayer selected. When the State imposes a generally applicable tax, there is little cause for concern. We need not fear that a government will destroy a selected group of taxpayers by burdensome taxation if it must impose the same burden on the rest of its constituency. See *Railway Express Agency v. New York*, 336 U.S. 106 (1949) (Jackson, J., concurring). When the State singles out the press, though, the political constraints that prevent a legislature from passing crippling taxes of general applicability are weakened, and the threat of burdensome taxes becomes acute. That threat can operate as effectively as a censor to check critical comment by the press, undercutting the basic assumption of our political system that the press will often serve as an important restraint on government. . . .

Further, differential treatment, unless justified by some special characteristic of the press, suggests that the goal of the regulation is not unrelated to suppression of expression, and such a goal is presumptively unconstitutional. *See, e.g., Police Department of the City of Chicago v. Mosley* (1972) [*supra* Chapter 5]. Differential taxation of the press, then, places such a burden on the interests protected by the First Amendment that we cannot countenance such treatment unless the State asserts a counterbalancing interest of compelling importance that it cannot achieve without differential taxation.

IV

The main interest asserted by Minnesota in this case is the raising of revenue. Of course that interest is critical to any government. Standing alone, however, it cannot justify the special treatment of the press, for an alternative means of achieving the same interest without raising concerns under the First Amendment is clearly available: the State could raise the revenue by taxing businesses generally, avoiding the censorial threat implicit in a tax that singles out the press.

Addressing the concern with differential treatment, Minnesota invites us to look beyond the form of the tax to its substance. The tax is, according to the State, merely a substitute for the sales tax, which, as a generally applicable tax, would be constitutional as applied to the press. There are two fatal flaws in this reasoning. First, the State has offered no explanation of why it chose to use a substitute for the sales tax rather than the sales tax itself. The court below speculated that the State might have been concerned that collection of a tax on such small transactions would be impractical. That suggestion is unpersuasive, for sales of other low-priced goods are not exempt. . . .

Further, even assuming that the legislature did have valid reasons for substituting another tax for the sales tax, we are not persuaded that this tax does serve as a substitute. The State asserts that this scheme actually *favors* the press over other businesses, because the same rate of tax is applied, but, for the press, the rate applies to the cost of components rather than to the sales price. We would be hesitant to fashion a rule that automatically allowed the State to single out the press for a different method of taxation as long as the effective burden was no different from that on other taxpayers or the burden on the press was lighter than that on other businesses. One reason for this reluctance is that the very selection of the press for special treatment threatens the press not only with the current *differential* treatment, but with the possibility of subsequent differentially *more burdensome* treatment. Thus, even without actually imposing an extra burden on the press, the government might be able to achieve censorial effects, for "the threat of sanctions may deter the exercise of First Amendment rights almost as potently as the actual application of sanctions." *NAACP v. Button*, 371 U.S. 415 (1963).

A second reason to avoid the proposed rule is that courts as institutions are poorly equipped to evaluate with precision the relative burdens of various methods of taxation. . . . In sum, the possibility of error inherent in the proposed rule poses too great a threat to concerns at the heart of the First Amendment, and we cannot tolerate that possibility. . . .

V

Minnesota's ink and paper tax violates the First Amendment not only because it singles out the press, but also because it targets a small group of newspapers. The effect of the $100,000 exemption enacted in 1974 is that only a handful of publishers pay any tax at all, and even fewer pay any significant amount of tax. . . . Whatever the motive of the legislature in this case, we think that recognizing a power in the State not only to single out the press but also to tailor the tax so that it singles out a few members of the press presents such a potential for abuse that no interest suggested by Minnesota can justify the scheme. . . .

VI

We need not and do not impugn the motives of the Minnesota legislature in passing the ink and paper tax. Illicit legislative intent is not the *sine qua non* of a violation of the First Amendment. See [e.g.] *NAACP v. Alabama* (1958) [*supra* Chapter 10]. We have long recognized that even regulations aimed at proper governmental concerns can restrict unduly the exercise of rights protected by the First Amendment. *E.g., Schneider v. State* (1939) [*supra* Chapter 6]. A tax that singles out the press, or that targets individual publications within the press, places a heavy burden on the State to justify its action. Since Minnesota has offered no satisfactory justification for its tax on the use of ink and paper, the tax violates the First Amendment. . . .

JUSTICE WHITE, concurring in part and dissenting in part.

[Justice White concurred in Part V of the Court's opinion and in the result. He described the case as "not difficult" because the $100,000 exemption from the tax limited its burden to only a few newspapers. However, he expressed doubt about the Court's professed inability to determine when even seemingly favorable tax treatment of the press would in fact burden it, and thus did not join in that part of the Court's analysis.]

JUSTICE REHNQUIST, dissenting.

Today we learn from the Court that a State runs afoul of the First Amendment proscription of laws "abridging the freedom of speech, or of the press" where the State structures its taxing system to the advantage of newspapers. . . . Not until the Court's decision in this case, nearly two centuries after adoption of the First Amendment, has it been read to prohibit activities which in no way diminish or curtail the freedoms it protects. . . .

The record reveals that in 1974 the Minneapolis Star & Tribune had an average daily circulation of 489,345 copies. Using the price we were informed of at argument of 25¢ per copy, gross sales revenue for the year would be $38,168,910. The Sunday circulation for 1974 was 640,756; even assuming that it did not sell for more than the daily paper, gross sales revenue for the year would be at least $8,329,828. Thus, total sales revenues in 1974 would be $46,498,738. Had a 4% sales tax been imposed, the Minneapolis Star & Tribune would have been liable for $1,859,950 in 1974. . . .

The record further indicates that the Minneapolis Star & Tribune paid $608,634 in use taxes in 1974. We need no expert testimony from modern day Euclids or Einsteins to determine that the [amount] paid in use taxes is significantly less burdensome than the [amount] that could have been levied by a sales tax. *A fortiori*, the Minnesota taxing scheme which singles out newspapers for "differential treatment" has benefited, not burdened, the "freedom of speech, [and] of the press."

Ignoring these calculations, the Court concludes that "differential treatment" alone in Minnesota's sales and use tax scheme requires that the statutes be found "presumptively unconstitutional" and declared invalid "unless the State asserts a counterbalancing interest of compelling importance that it cannot achieve without differential taxation." The "differential treatment" standard that the Court has conjured up is unprecedented and unwarranted. To my knowledge this Court has never subjected governmental action to the most stringent constitutional review solely on the basis of "differential treatment" of particular groups. The case relied on by the Court, *Police Department of the City of Chicago v. Mosley* (1972) [*supra* Chapter 5], certainly does not stand for this proposition. In *Mosley* all picketing except "peaceful picketing" was prohibited within a particular public area. Thus, "differential treatment" was not the key to the Court's decision; rather the essential fact was that unless a person was considered a "peaceful picketer" his speech through this form of expression would be totally abridged within the area. . . .

Where the State devises classifications that infringe on the fundamental guarantees protected by the Constitution the Court has demanded more of the State in justifying its action. But there is no *infringement*, and thus the Court has never required more, unless the State's classifications *significantly burden* these specially protected rights . . . . To state it in terms of the freedoms at issue here, no First Amendment issue is raised unless First Amendment rights have been infringed; for if there has been no infringement, then there has been no "abridgment" of those guarantees. See *Branzburg.*

Today the Court departs from this rule, refusing to look at the record and determine whether the classifications in the Minnesota use and sales tax statutes significantly burden the First Amendment rights of petitioner and its fellow newspapers. . . .

Wisely not relying solely on its inability to weigh the burdens of the Minnesota tax scheme, the Court also says that even if the resultant burden on the press is lighter than on others

> the very selection of the press for special treatment threatens the press not only with the current *differential* treatment, but with the possibility of subsequent differentially *more burdensome* treatment. Thus, even without actually imposing an extra burden on the press, the government might be able to achieve censorial effects, for "the threat of sanctions may deter [the] exercise of [First Amendment] rights almost as potently as the actual application of sanctions."

Surely the Court does not mean what it seems to say. The Court should be well aware from its discussion of *Grosjean* that this Court is quite capable of dealing with changes in state taxing laws which are intended to penalize newspapers. . . .

The State is required to show that its taxing scheme is rational. But in this case that showing can be made easily. . . . Must everyone buying a paper put 26¢ in the vending machine rather than 25¢; or should the price of a paper be raised to 30¢, giving the paper 4¢ more profit; or should the price be kept at 25¢ with the paper absorbing the tax? . . . The reasonable alternative Minnesota chose was to impose the use tax on ink and paper. . . .

The Court finds in very summary fashion that the exemption newspapers receive for the first $100,000 of ink and paper used also violates the First Amendment because the result is that only a few of the newspapers actually pay a use tax. I cannot agree. As explained by the Minnesota Supreme Court, the exemption is in effect a $4,000 credit which benefits all newspapers. Minneapolis Star & Tribune was benefited to the amount of $16,000 in the two years in question; $4,000 each year for its morning paper and $4,000 each year for its evening paper. Absent any improper motive on the part of the Minnesota legislature in drawing the limits of this exemption, it cannot be construed as violating the First Amendment. See *Oklahoma Press Publishing Co. v. Walling*, 327 U.S. 186 (1946). The Minnesota Supreme Court specifically found that the exemption was not a "deliberate and calculated device" designed with an illicit purpose. There is nothing in the record which would cast doubt on this conclusion. . . .

————

Note: Grosjean *and* Minneapolis Star

1. The Court in *Minneapolis Star* says that "the result in *Grosjean* may have been attributable in part to the perception on the part of the Court that the state imposed the tax with an intent to penalize a selected group of newspapers." Certainly the language quoted from *Grosjean* supports that interpretation. But consider the *Grosjean* opinion's detailed account of the origins of the Press Clause. Does that account support such a narrow reading of *Grosjean*?

2. What does the Court's reasoning in *Minneapolis Star* suggest about the protection the First Amendment accords the press? In particular, consider the Court's rejection of Minnesota's argument that the tax actually favors the press. What does the Court's response suggest about the kinds of risks inherent whenever the government treats the press differently, regardless of whether that differential burdens or favors the press? Consider the fact that the Court could have struck down the Minnesota tax on the more limited ground that the $100,000 exemption limited its effect to only a few papers; recall that Justice White concurred in the result on that ground alone. What does it say about the Court's concern about differential taxation that it rested its result on both grounds, rather than simply on the narrower one?

————

Note: Discrimination among Media Categories

1. Recall that in *Minneapolis Star* the Court identified two constitutional flaws in the Minnesota tax statute: it singled out the press for differential treatment, and it also discriminated within the category of the press by distinguishing between large publishers and smaller ones. In two subsequent cases the Court elaborated on these rules.

2. In *Arkansas Writers' Project v. Ragland*, 481 U.S. 221 (1987), the Court, by a 7-2 vote, struck down an Arkansas tax scheme that exempted from the state's sales tax the proceeds from the sale of newspapers and "religious, professional, trade and sports journals and/or publications." Other types of magazines, including general interest magazines, were required to pay the tax. Writing for six Justices, Justice Marshall concluded that the statute suffered from the second type of discrimination identified in *Minneapolis Star*. He first noted that these two types of discrimination "can be established even where, as here, there is no evidence of an improper censorial motive." He explained that "[t]his is because selective taxation of the press — either singling out the press as a whole or targeting individual members of the press — poses a particular danger of abuse by the State." He then applied these principles to the Arkansas tax:

> On the facts of this case, the fundamental question is not whether the tax singles out the press as a whole, but whether it targets a small group within the press. While we indicated in *Minneapolis Star* that a genuinely nondiscriminatory tax on the receipts of newspapers would be constitutionally permissible, the Arkansas sales tax cannot be characterized as nondiscriminatory, because it is not evenly applied to all magazines. . . . Because the Arkansas sales tax scheme treats some magazines less favorably than others, it suffers from the second type of discrimination identified in *Minneapolis Star*.
>
> Indeed, this case involves a more disturbing use of selective taxation than *Minneapolis Star*, because the basis on which Arkansas differentiates between magazines is particularly repugnant to First Amendment principles: a magazine's tax status depends entirely on its *content*.

Because of that content-based distinction the Court applied strict scrutiny. It rejected Arkansas' justifications for the distinction, including revenue generation and promotion of "fledgling" publishers, holding that the content-based distinction was not sufficiently narrowly tailored to serve them. Given its ruling, the Court reserved judgment on whether the larger distinction between newspapers and magazines could survive First Amendment scrutiny.

Justice Stevens concurred in the result, although he rejected the majority's more absolutist statements about government's lack of power to restrict expression because of its content. Justice Scalia, joined by Justice Rehnquist (the sole dissenter in *Minneapolis Star*), dissented. Justice Scalia argued that denial of a tax exemption, as in this case and *Minneapolis Star*, is not the same as regulation, because government is not constitutionally required to subsidize or grant tax exemptions on a nondiscriminatory basis. According to Justice Scalia, the failure to subsidize, unlike the imposition of regulations, does not have a significant coercive effect.

3. Four years later, in *Leathers v. Medlock*, 499 U.S. 439 (1991), the Court held that a different Arkansas sales tax distinction did not violate the First Amendment. At issue in *Leathers* was the state's exemption from its sales tax of newspapers, magazines and satellite television services, combined with its failure to exempt cable television services. Writing for a seven-Justice majority, Justice O'Connor distinguished the case from *Arkansas Writers'* and *Minneapolis Star*. She concluded that the tax did not single out cable television in a meaningful way, since a long list of non-media businesses were also taxed in the same amount as cable. She also noted that the tax affected approximately 100 cable systems in Arkansas, in contrast to the very small numbers of speakers affected by the differential taxes in the earlier cases. Justice O'Connor summarized the significance of these facts as follows:

> The danger from a tax scheme that targets a small number of speakers is the danger of censorship; a tax on a small number of speakers runs the risk of affecting only a limited range of views. The risk is similar to that from content-based regulation: It will distort the market for ideas. . . . There is no comparable danger from a tax on the services provided by a large number of cable operators offering a wide variety of programming throughout the State.

Justice O'Connor also noted that the Arkansas tax was not content-based.

Justice O'Connor then turned to the claim that the Arkansas tax discriminated between different press media. The plaintiff argued that this "intermedia" discrimination violated the First Amendment whether or not there was any intent to suppress speech. In response, Justice O'Connor cited *Regan v. Taxation with Representation of Washington*, 461 U.S. 540 (1983), a case in which the Court upheld differential government tax exemptions for lobbying groups that sought to speak on different issues. The Court also cited *Mabee v. White Plains Publishing Co.*, 327 U.S. 178 (1946) and *Oklahoma Press Publishing Co. v. Walling*, 327 U.S. 186 (1946) (both of which were also cited in *Minneapolis Star*). In those cases the Court upheld exemptions under the Fair Labor Standards Act for small newspapers. Justice O'Connor then synthesized these precedents:

> Taken together, *Regan*, *Mabee* and *Oklahoma Press* establish that differential taxation of speakers, even members of the press, does not implicate the First Amendment unless the tax is directed at, or presents the danger of suppressing, particular ideas. That was the case in *Grosjean*, *Minneapolis Star* and *Arkansas Writers'*, but it is not the case here. The Arkansas Legislature has chosen simply to exclude or exempt certain media from a generally applicable tax. Nothing about that choice has ever suggested an interest in censoring the expressive activities of cable television. Nor does anything in this record indicate that Arkansas' broad-based, content-neutral sales tax is likely to stifle the free exchange of ideas.

Justice Marshall, the author of *Arkansas Writers'*, dissented in an opinion joined by Justice Blackmun. Justice Marshall summarized the relevant precedent as follows:

> Our decisions on selective taxation establish a nondiscrimination principle for like-situated members of the press. Under this principle, "differential treatment, unless justified by some special characteristic of the press, . . . is presumptively unconstitutional," and must be struck down "unless the State asserts a counterbalancing interest of compelling importance that it cannot achieve without differential taxation." *Minneapolis Star*.
>
> The nondiscrimination principle is an instance of government's First Amendment obligation not to interfere with the press as an institution. As the Court explained in *Grosjean*, the purpose of the Free Press Clause "was to preserve an untrammeled press as a vital source of public information."

Reviewing both the historical abuses associated with England's infamous "taxes on knowledge" and the debates surrounding ratification of the Constitution, see *Grosjean*; *Minneapolis Star*, our decisions have recognized that the Framers viewed selective taxation as a distinctively potent "means of abridging the freedom of the press."

After recognizing the novelty of the intermedia discrimination issue left open in *Arkansas Writers'*, Justice Marshall applied his understanding of the precedent to that issue:

> Because cable competes with members of the print and electronic media in the larger information market, the power to discriminate between these media triggers the central concern underlying the nondiscrimination principle: the risk of covert censorship. The nondiscrimination principle protects the press from censorship prophylactically, condemning any selective-taxation scheme that presents "the *potential* for abuse by the State," *Minneapolis Star*, independent of any actual "evidence of an improper censorial motive," *Arkansas Writers'*. The power to discriminate among like-situated media presents such a risk.

Justice Marshall concluded that the state offered no compelling interest in favor of such discrimination.

———

Problem: Restrictions on College Newspapers

In order to halt what the legislature sees as the creeping commercialization of universities, the State of Lincoln has enacted a law prohibiting student-run university organizations from accepting commercial sponsorships from business entities. Thus, for example, a student organization cannot have an event sponsored by a local business. The statute defines "commercial sponsorship" to include the placement of advertising in student-run school newspapers, regardless of the content of the ad.

The *Lincoln State Voice*, the student-run newspaper for Lincoln State University, sues the state, alleging that, as applied to it, the state law violates the Press Clause. What arguments could it make? What counterarguments could the state make? What else would you want to know before evaluating the newspaper's claim?

Problem: Save the Newspapers!

As the public has become more and more accustomed to obtaining its news through online sites such as blogs, traditional newspapers have experienced a steep decline in their circulations, and thus, crucially, the rates they can charge for advertising. (Historically, advertisers have supplied upwards of 80% of newspaper revenues.) While most newspapers now also have online editions that feature additional advertising, the competitive market for Internet advertising means that they are unable to charge enough for advertising on their online sites to offset their revenue declines in their print publications.

Newspapers' weakened market position has led to great concern about independent, original newsgathering in the United States. Many experts and observers argue that blogs and other Internet news sites are merely "aggregators" of news developed elsewhere—that is, they simply hyperlink to stories on other websites. Thus, these commentators do not believe that these sources are long-term substitutes for traditional media outlets, which are usually the only ones that employ teams of reporters and maintain physical presences ("bureaus") across the nation and around the world. The worrisome prediction is that newsgathering will suffer irremediably.

This state of affairs has led some to call for governmental regulatory action. Among various possible responses that have been floated are the following:

1. An exemption from federal antitrust laws that would allow newspapers to demand, as a group acting together, payment every time a blog links to a newspaper story. Ordinarily, such a united negotiating position would violate federal antitrust laws; this proposal would specifically exempt newspapers from those laws for this limited purpose.

2. A direct tax on all commercial blogs (that is, blogs that sell advertising), based on the number of times per year they link to a newspaper article.

3. A tax on Internet Service Provider (ISP) services. (ISPs are the companies which provide access to the Internet—for example, telephone and cable television companies.) The proceeds of this tax on ISP services would be paid as a direct subsidy to newspapers. The theory behind this proposal is that the tax is an implicit and indirect tax on Internet users who (presumably) patronize the Internet news sites that are harming newspapers.

What constitutional issues would these government actions raise?

B. Claims of Exemption from Generally Applicable Laws

Branzburg v. Hayes

408 U.S. 665 (1972)

Opinion of the Court by Mr. Justice White, announced by The Chief Justice.

The issue in these cases is whether requiring newsmen to appear and testify before state or federal grand juries abridges the freedom of speech and press guaranteed by the First Amendment. We hold that it does not.

[Branzburg, Pappas, and Caldwell, reporters working in different parts of the country, witnessed allegedly illegal activity through the agreement of the alleged perpetrators. When grand juries investigated that activity, they subpoenaed the reporters to testify. The reporters refused, citing the First Amendment rights of the free press. The lower courts reached conflicting answers on the question of reporters' First Amendment rights not to appear before grand juries.]

II

Petitioners Branzburg and Pappas and respondent Caldwell press First Amendment claims that may be simply put: that to gather news it is often necessary to agree either not to identify the source of information published or to publish only part of the facts revealed, or both; that if the reporter is nevertheless forced to reveal these confidences to a grand jury, the source so identified and other confidential sources of other reporters will be measurably deterred from furnishing publishable information, all to the detriment of the free flow of information protected by the First Amendment. Although the newsmen in these cases do not claim an absolute privilege against official interrogation in all circumstances, they assert that the reporter should not be forced either to appear or to testify before a grand jury or at trial until and unless sufficient grounds are shown for believing that the reporter possesses information relevant to a crime the grand jury is investigating, that the information the reporter has is unavailable from other sources, and that the need for the information is sufficiently compelling to override the claimed invasion of First Amendment interests occasioned by the disclosure. Principally relied upon are prior cases emphasizing the importance of the First Amendment guarantees to individual development and to our system of representative government,[17] decisions requiring that official action with adverse impact on First Amendment rights be justified by a public interest that is "compelling" or "paramount,"[18] and those precedents establishing the principle that justifiable governmental goals may not be achieved by unduly broad means having an unnecessary impact on protected rights of speech, press, or association.[19] The heart of the claim is that the burden on news gathering resulting from compelling reporters to disclose confidential information outweighs any public interest in obtaining the information.

We do not question the significance of free speech, press, or assembly to the country's welfare. Nor is it suggested that news gathering does not qualify for First Amendment protection; without some protection for seeking out the news, freedom of the press could be eviscerated. But these cases involve no intrusions upon speech or assembly, no prior restraint or restriction on what the press may publish, and no express or implied command that the press publish what it prefers to withhold. No exaction or tax for the privilege of publishing, and no penalty, civil or criminal, related to the content of published material is at issue here. The use of confidential sources by the press is not forbidden or restricted; reporters remain free to seek news from any source by means within the law. No attempt is made to require the press to publish its sources of information or indiscriminately to disclose them on request.

17. [E.g.] *Curtis Publishing Co. v. Butts*, 388 U.S. 130 (1967) (opinion of Harlan, J.); *New York Times Co. v. Sullivan* (1964) [*supra* Chapter 2]; *Grosjean v. American Press Co.* (1936) [*supra* this chapter]; *Near v. Minnesota* (1931) [*supra* Chapter 4].

18. *NAACP v. Button*, 371 U.S. 415 (1963); *Thomas v. Collins*, 323 U.S. 516 (1945); *DeGregory v. Attorney General of New Hampshire*, 388 U.S. 825 (1966); *Bates v. Little Rock*, 361 U.S. 516 (1960); *Schneider v. State* (1939) [*supra* Chapter 6]; *NAACP v. Alabama* (1958) [*supra* Chapter 10].

19. *Freedman v. Maryland*, 380 U.S. 51 (1965) [Note *supra* Chapter 4]; *NAACP v. Alabama*, 377 U.S. 288 (1964); *Martin v. City of Struthers* (1943) [*supra* Chapter 6]; *Elfbrandt v. Russell*, 384 U.S. 11 (1966).

The sole issue before us is the obligation of reporters to respond to grand jury subpoenas as other citizens do and to answer questions relevant to an investigation into the commission of crime. Citizens generally are not constitutionally immune from grand jury subpoenas; and neither the First Amendment nor any other constitutional provision protects the average citizen from disclosing to a grand jury information that he has received in confidence. The claim is, however, that reporters are exempt from these obligations because if forced to respond to subpoenas and identify their sources or disclose other confidences, their informants will refuse or be reluctant to furnish newsworthy information in the future. This asserted burden on news gathering is said to make compelled testimony from newsmen constitutionally suspect and to require a privileged position for them.

It is clear that the First Amendment does not invalidate every incidental burdening of the press that may result from the enforcement of civil or criminal statutes of general applicability. Under prior cases, otherwise valid laws serving substantial public interests may be enforced against the press as against others, despite the possible burden that may be imposed. The Court has emphasized that "the publisher of a newspaper has no special immunity from the application of general laws. He has no special privilege to invade the rights and liberties of others." *Associated Press v. NLRB*, 301 U.S. 103 (1937). It was there held that the Associated Press, a news-gathering and disseminating organization, was not exempt from the requirements of the National Labor Relations Act. The holding was reaffirmed in *Oklahoma Press Publishing Co. v. Walling*, 327 U.S. 186 (1946), where the Court rejected the claim that applying the Fair Labor Standards Act to a newspaper publishing business would abridge the freedom of the press guaranteed by the First Amendment. *See also Mabee v. White Plains Publishing Co.*, 327 U.S. 178 (1946). *Associated Press v. United States*, 326 U.S. 1 (1945), similarly overruled assertions that the First Amendment precluded application of the Sherman Act to a news-gathering and disseminating organization. Likewise, a newspaper may be subjected to nondiscriminatory forms of general taxation. *Grosjean v. American Press Co.* (1936) [*supra* this chapter].

The prevailing view is that the press is not free to publish with impunity everything and anything it desires to publish. Although it may deter or regulate what is said or published, the press may not circulate knowing or reckless falsehoods damaging to private reputation without subjecting itself to liability for damages, including punitive damages, or even criminal prosecution. See [e.g.] *New York Times Co. v. Sullivan* (1964) [*supra* Chapter 2]. . . .

It has generally been held that the First Amendment does not guarantee the press a constitutional right of special access to information not available to the public generally. *Zemel v. Rusk*, 381 U.S. 1 (1965); *New York Times Co. v. United States*, 403 U.S. 713 (1971) (Stewart, J., concurring) [*supra* Chapter 4]. In *Zemel v. Rusk*, for example, the Court sustained the Government's refusal to validate passports to Cuba even though that restriction "render[ed] less than wholly free the flow of information concerning that country." The ban on travel was held constitutional, for "the right to speak and publish does not carry with it the unrestrained right to gather information."

Despite the fact that news gathering may be hampered, the press is regularly excluded from grand jury proceedings, our own conferences, the meetings of other official bodies gathered in executive session, and the meetings of private organizations. Newsmen have no constitutional right of access to the scenes of crime or disaster when the general public is excluded, and they may be prohibited from attending or publishing information about trials if such restrictions are necessary to assure a defendant a fair trial before an impartial tribunal. In *Sheppard v. Maxwell*, 384 U.S. 333 (1966), for example, the Court reversed a state court conviction where the trial court failed to adopt "stricter rules governing the use of the courtroom by newsmen, as Sheppard's counsel requested." . . .

It is thus not surprising that the great weight of authority is that newsmen are not exempt from the normal duty of appearing before a grand jury and answering questions relevant to a criminal investigation. At common law, courts consistently refused to recognize the existence of any privilege authorizing a newsman to refuse to reveal confidential information to a grand jury. *See, e.g.*, *Ex parte Lawrence*, 116 Cal. 298 (1897); *Plunkett v. Hamilton*, 136 Ga. 72 (1911); *Brewster v. Boston Herald-Traveler Corp.*, 20 F.R.D. 416 (Mass. 1957). In 1958, a news gatherer asserted for the first time that the First Amendment exempted confidential information from public disclosure pursuant to a subpoena issued in a civil suit, *Garland v. Torre*, 259 F.2d 545 (CA2) (1958), but the claim was denied, and this argument has been almost uniformly rejected since then, although there are occasional dicta that, in circumstances not presented here, a newsman might be excused. . . .

A number of States have provided newsmen a statutory privilege of varying breadth, but the majority have not done so, and none has been provided by federal statute. Until now the only testimonial privilege for unofficial witnesses that is rooted in the Federal Constitution is the Fifth Amendment privilege against compelled self-incrimination. We are asked to create another by interpreting the First Amendment to grant newsmen a testimonial privilege that other citizens do not enjoy. This we decline to do. Fair and effective law enforcement aimed at providing security for the person and property of the individual is a fundamental function of government, and the grand jury plays an important, constitutionally mandated role in this process. On the records now before us, we perceive no basis for holding that the public interest in law enforcement and in ensuring effective grand jury proceedings is insufficient to override the consequential, but uncertain, burden on news gathering that is said to result from insisting that reporters, like other citizens, respond to relevant questions put to them in the course of a valid grand jury investigation or criminal trial. . . .

The argument that the flow of news will be diminished by compelling reporters to aid the grand jury in a criminal investigation is not irrational, nor are the records before us silent on the matter. But we remain unclear how often and to what extent informers are actually deterred from furnishing information when newsmen are forced to testify before a grand jury. . . .

Accepting the fact, however, that an undetermined number of informants not themselves implicated in crime will nevertheless, for whatever reason, refuse to talk to newsmen if they fear identification by a reporter in an official investigation, we cannot accept the argument that the public interest in possible future news about crime from undisclosed, unverified sources must take precedence over the public interest in pursuing and prosecuting those crimes reported to the press by informants and in thus deterring the commission of such crimes in the future.

We note first that the privilege claimed is that of the reporter, not the informant, and that if the authorities independently identify the informant, neither his own reluctance to testify nor the objection of the newsman would shield him from grand jury inquiry, whatever the impact on the flow of news or on his future usefulness as a secret source of information. More important, it is obvious that agreements to conceal information relevant to commission of crime have very little to recommend them from the standpoint of public policy. . . .

We are admonished that refusal to provide a First Amendment reporter's privilege will undermine the freedom of the press to collect and disseminate news. But this is not the lesson history teaches us. As noted previously, the common law recognized no such privilege, and the constitutional argument was not even asserted until 1958. From the beginning of our country the press has operated without constitutional protection for press informants, and the press has flourished. . . .

The argument for such a constitutional privilege rests heavily on those cases holding that the infringement of protected First Amendment rights must be no broader than necessary to achieve a permissible governmental purpose, see cases cited at n.19, *supra*. We do not deal, however, with a governmental institution that has abused its proper function, as a legislative committee does when it "expose[s] for the sake of exposure." Nothing in the record indicates that these grand juries were "prob[ing] at will and without relation to existing need." Nor did the grand juries attempt to invade protected First Amendment rights by forcing wholesale disclosure of names and organizational affiliations for a purpose that was not germane to the determination of whether crime has been committed, *cf. NAACP v. Alabama* (1958) [*supra* Chapter 10]; *NAACP v. Button*, 371 U.S. 415 (1963); *Bates v. Little Rock*, 361 U.S. 516 (1960), and the characteristic secrecy of grand jury proceedings is a further protection against the undue invasion of such rights. The investigative power of the grand jury is necessarily broad if its public responsibility is to be adequately discharged.

The requirements of those cases, see n.18, *supra*, which hold that a State's interest must be "compelling" or "paramount" to justify even an indirect burden on First Amendment rights, are also met here. As we have indicated, the investigation of crime by the grand jury implements a fundamental governmental role of securing the safety of the person and property of the citizen, and it appears to us that calling reporters to give testimony in the manner and for the reasons that other citizens are called "bears a reasonable relationship to the achievement of the governmental purpose asserted as its justification." *Bates v. Little Rock*. If the test is that the government "convincingly show a substantial relation between the information sought and a subject of overriding and compelling state interest," *Gibson v. Florida Legislative Investigation Committee*, 372 U.S. 539 (1963), it is quite apparent (1) that the State has the necessary interest [in prosecuting the types of crimes witnessed by the reporters in these cases]; and (2) that, based on the stories Branzburg and Caldwell wrote and Pappas' admitted conduct, the grand jury called these reporters as they would others—because it was likely that they could supply information to help the government determine whether illegal conduct had occurred and, if it had, whether there was sufficient evidence to return an indictment.

Similar considerations dispose of the reporters' claims that preliminary to requiring their grand jury appearance, the State must show that a crime has been committed and that they possess relevant information not available from other sources, for only the grand jury itself can make this determination. The role of the grand jury as an important instrument of effective law enforcement necessarily includes an investigatory function with respect to determining whether a crime has been committed and who committed it. . . . We see no reason to hold that these reporters, any more than other citizens, should be excused from furnishing information that may help the grand jury in arriving at its initial determinations.

The privilege claimed here is conditional, not absolute; given the suggested preliminary showings and compelling need, the reporter would be required to testify. . . . If newsmen's confidential sources are as sensitive as they are claimed to be, the prospect of being unmasked whenever a judge determines the situation justifies it is hardly a satisfactory solution to the problem. For them, it would appear that only an absolute privilege would suffice.

We are unwilling to embark the judiciary on a long and difficult journey to such an uncertain destination. The administration of a constitutional newsman's privilege would present practical and conceptual difficulties of a high order. Sooner or later, it would be necessary to define those categories of newsmen who qualified for the privilege, a questionable procedure in light of the traditional doctrine that liberty of the press is the right of the lonely pamphleteer who uses carbon paper or a mimeograph just as much as of the large metropolitan publisher who utilizes the latest photocomposition methods. Freedom of the press is a "fundamental personal right" which "is not confined to newspapers and periodicals. It necessarily embraces pamphlets and leaflets. . . . The press in its historic connotation comprehends every sort of publication which affords a vehicle of information and opinion." *Lovell v. Griffin* (1938) [*supra* Chapter 4]. . . . Almost any author may quite accurately assert that he is contributing to the flow of information to the public, that he relies on confidential sources of information, and that these sources will be silenced if he is forced to make disclosures before a grand jury.

In each instance where a reporter is subpoenaed to testify, the courts would also be embroiled in preliminary factual and legal determinations with respect to whether the proper predicate had been laid for the reporter's appearance: Is there probable cause to believe a crime has been committed? Is it likely that the reporter has useful information gained in confidence? Could the grand jury obtain the information elsewhere? Is the official interest sufficient to outweigh the claimed privilege? . . .

Finally, as we have earlier indicated, news gathering is not without its First Amendment protections, and grand jury investigations if instituted or conducted other than in good faith, would pose wholly different issues for resolution under the First Amendment. . . .

Mr. Justice Powell, concurring.

I add this brief statement to emphasize what seems to me to be the limited nature of the Court's holding. The Court does not hold that newsmen, subpoenaed to testify before a grand jury, are without constitutional rights with respect to the gathering of news or in safeguarding their sources. Certainly, we do not hold, as suggested in Mr. Justice Stewart's dissenting opinion, that state and federal authorities are free to "annex" the news media as "an investigative arm of government." The solicitude repeatedly shown by this Court for First Amendment freedoms should be sufficient assurance against any such effort, even if one seriously believed that the media — properly free and untrammeled in the fullest sense of these terms — were not able to protect themselves.

As indicated in the concluding portion of the opinion, the Court states that no harassment of newsmen will be tolerated. If a newsman believes that the grand jury investigation is not being conducted in good faith he is not without remedy. Indeed, if the newsman is called upon to give information bearing only a remote and tenuous relationship to the subject of the investigation, or if he has some other reason to believe that his testimony implicates confidential source relationships without a legitimate need of law enforcement, he will have access to the court on a motion to quash and an appropriate protective order may be entered. The asserted claim to privilege should be judged on its facts by the striking of a proper balance between freedom of the press and the obligation of all citizens to give relevant testimony with respect to criminal conduct. The balance of these vital constitutional and societal interests on a case-by-case basis accords with the tried and traditional way of adjudicating such questions.

In short, the courts will be available to newsmen under circumstances where legitimate First Amendment interests require protection.

Mr. Justice Douglas, dissenting . . . [Omitted.]

Mr. Justice Stewart, with whom Mr. Justice Brennan and Mr. Justice Marshall join, dissenting.

The Court's crabbed view of the First Amendment reflects a disturbing insensitivity to the critical role of an independent press in our society. The question whether a reporter has a constitutional right to a confidential relationship with his source is of first impression here, but the principles that should guide our decision are as basic as any to be found in the Constitution. While Mr. Justice Powell's enigmatic concurring opinion gives some hope of a more flexible view in the future, the Court in these cases holds that a newsman has no First Amendment right to protect his sources when called before a grand jury. The Court thus invites state and federal authorities to undermine the historic independence of the press by attempting to annex the journalistic profession as an investigative arm of government. Not only will this decision impair performance of the press' constitutionally protected functions, but it will, I am convinced, in the long run harm rather than help the administration of justice. I respectfully dissent.

I

The reporter's constitutional right to a confidential relationship with his source stems from the broad societal interest in a full and free flow of information to the public. It is this basic concern that underlies the Constitution's protection of a free press, *Grosjean v. American Press Co.* (1936) [*supra* this chapter]; *New York Times Co. v. Sullivan* (1964) [*supra* Chapter 2], because the guarantee is "not for the benefit of the press so much as for the benefit of all of us." . . .

In keeping with this tradition, we have held that the right to publish is central to the First Amendment and basic to the existence of constitutional democracy. *Grosjean*; *New York Times*.

A corollary of the right to publish must be the right to gather news. The full flow of information to the public protected by the free-press guarantee would be severely curtailed if no protection whatever were afforded to the process by which news is assembled and disseminated. We have, therefore, recognized that there is a right to publish without prior governmental approval, *Near v. Minnesota* (1931) [*supra* Chapter 4]; *New York Times Co. v. United States* (1971) [*supra* Chapter 4], a right to distribute information, *see, e.g., Lovell v. Griffin* (1938) [*supra* Chapter 4]; *Marsh v. Alabama*, 326 U.S. 501 (1946); *Martin v. City of Struthers* (1943) [*supra* Chapter 6]; *Grosjean*, and a right to receive printed matter, *Lamont v. Postmaster General*, 381 U.S. 301 (1965).

No less important to the news dissemination process is the gathering of information. News must not be unnecessarily cut off at its source, for without freedom to acquire information the right to publish would be impermissibly compromised. Accordingly, a right to gather news, of some dimensions, must exist. *Zemel v. Rusk*, 381 U.S. 1 (1965).[4] . . .

The right to gather news implies, in turn, a right to a confidential relationship between a reporter and his source. This proposition follows as a matter of simple logic once three factual predicates are recognized: (1) newsmen require informants to gather news; (2) confidentiality—the promise or understanding that names or certain aspects of communications will be kept off the record—is essential to the creation and maintenance of a news-gathering relationship with informants; and (3) an unbridled subpoena power—the absence of a constitutional right protecting, in *any* way, a confidential relationship from compulsory process—will either deter sources from divulging information or deter reporters from gathering and publishing information.

---

4. In *Zemel v. Rusk* we held that the Secretary of State's denial of a passport for travel to Cuba did not violate a citizen's First Amendment rights. The rule was justified by the "weightiest considerations of national security" and we concluded that the "right to speak and publish does not carry with it the *unrestrained* right to gather information." The necessary implication is that some right to gather information does exist.

It is obvious that informants are necessary to the news-gathering process as we know it today. If it is to perform its constitutional mission, the press must do far more than merely print public statements or publish prepared handouts. Familiarity with the people and circumstances involved in the myriad background activities that result in the final product called "news" is vital to complete and responsible journalism, unless the press is to be a captive mouthpiece of "newsmakers."

It is equally obvious that the promise of confidentiality may be a necessary prerequisite to a productive relationship between a newsman and his informants. An office-holder may fear his superior; a member of the bureaucracy, his associates; a dissident, the scorn of majority opinion. All may have information valuable to the public discourse, yet each may be willing to relate that information only in confidence to a reporter whom he trusts, either because of excessive caution or because of a reasonable fear of reprisals or censure for unorthodox views. The First Amendment concern must not be with the motives of any particular news source, but rather with the conditions in which informants of all shades of the spectrum may make information available through the press to the public.

The impairment of the flow of news cannot, of course, be proved with scientific precision, as the Court seems to demand. . . . But we have never before demanded that First Amendment rights rest on elaborate empirical studies demonstrating beyond any conceivable doubt that deterrent effects exist; we have never before required proof of the exact number of people potentially affected by governmental action, who would actually be dissuaded from engaging in First Amendment activity.

Rather, on the basis of common sense and available information, we have asked, often implicitly, (1) whether there was a rational connection between the cause (the governmental action) and the effect (the deterrence or impairment of First Amendment activity), and (2) whether the effect would occur with some regularity, i.e., would not be *de minimis*. And, in making this determination, we have shown a special solicitude towards the "indispensable liberties" protected by the First Amendment, for "freedoms such as these are protected not only against heavy-handed frontal attack, but also from being stifled by more subtle governmental interference." Once this threshold inquiry has been satisfied, we have then examined the competing interests in determining whether there is an unconstitutional infringement of First Amendment freedoms. . . .

Thus, we cannot escape the conclusion that when neither the reporter nor his source can rely on the shield of confidentiality against unrestrained use of the grand jury's subpoena power, valuable information will not be published and the public dialogue will inevitably be impoverished.

II

Posed against the First Amendment's protection of the newsman's confidential relationships in these cases is society's interest in the use of the grand jury to administer justice fairly and effectively. . . .

Yet the longstanding rule making every person's evidence available to the grand jury is not absolute. . . . So it was that in *Blair v. United States*, 250 U.S. 273 (1919), after recognizing that the right against compulsory self-incrimination prohibited certain inquiries, the Court noted that "some confidential matters are shielded from considerations of policy, and perhaps in other cases for *special reasons* a witness may be excused from telling all that he knows." . . .

Such an interest must surely be the First Amendment protection of a confidential relationship that I have discussed above in Part I. . . .

In striking the proper balance between the public interest in the efficient administration of justice and the First Amendment guarantee of the fullest flow of information, we must begin with the basic proposition that because of their "delicate and vulnerable" nature, and their transcendent importance for the just functioning of our society, First Amendment rights require special safeguards.

A

. . . The established method of "carefully" circumscribing investigative powers is to place a heavy burden of justification on government officials when First Amendment rights are impaired. The decisions of this Court have "consistently held that only a compelling state interest in the regulation of a subject within the State's constitutional power to regulate can justify limiting First Amendment freedoms." *NAACP v. Button*, 371 U.S. 415 (1963). And "it is an essential prerequisite to the validity of an investigation which intrudes into the area of constitutionally protected rights of speech, press, association and petition that the State convincingly *show a substantial relation between the information sought and a subject of overriding and compelling state interest.*" *Gibson v. Florida Legislative Investigation Committee*, 372 U.S. 539 (1963) (emphasis supplied). *See also NAACP v. Alabama* (1958) [*supra* Chapter 10]; *Sweezy v. New Hampshire*, 354 U.S. 234 (1957).

Governmental officials must, therefore, demonstrate that the information sought is *clearly* relevant to a *precisely* defined subject of governmental inquiry. *Sweezy*. They must demonstrate that it is reasonable to think the witness in question has that information. *Sweezy*; *Gibson*. And they must show that there is not any means of obtaining the information less destructive of First Amendment liberties. [E.g.,] *Shelton v. Tucker*, 364 U.S. 479 (1960). . . .

Accordingly, when a reporter is asked to appear before a grand jury and reveal confidences, I would hold that the government must (1) show that there is probable cause to believe that the newsman has information that is clearly relevant to a specific probable violation of law; (2) demonstrate that the information sought cannot be obtained by alternative means less destructive of First Amendment rights; and (3) demonstrate a compelling and overriding interest in the information. . . .

B

. . . The error in the Court's absolute rejection of First Amendment interests in these cases seems to me to be most profound. . . . People entrusted with law enforcement responsibility, no less than private citizens, need general information relating to controversial social problems. Obviously, press reports have great value to government, even when the newsman cannot be compelled to testify before a grand jury. The sad paradox of the Court's position is that when a grand jury may exercise an unbridled subpoena power, and sources involved in sensitive matters become fearful of disclosing information, the newsman will not only cease to be a useful grand jury witness; he will cease to investigate and publish information about issues of public import. I cannot subscribe to such an anomalous result, for, in my view, the interests protected by the First Amendment are not antagonistic to the administration of justice. Rather, they can, in the long run, only be complementary, and for that reason must be given great "breathing space." ...

———

Note: Justice Powell's "Enigmatic" Concurrence

1. Justice Powell's concurrence in *Branzburg* has played the role of a classic swing vote, pulling the lower courts away from the majority's seemingly clear rule rejecting a journalist's testimonial privilege and toward the balancing test embraced by Justice Stewart's dissent. As a result, lower courts have provided strikingly different answers to the question whether a journalist has a First Amendment privilege to avoid testifying before a grand jury. (*See* the Note that follows.) But the Supreme Court has steadfastly declined to resolve the disagreement. For example, in 2005, the Court denied review in a high-profile case arising out of a Special Counsel's investigation. The case involved reporters for *Time Magazine* and *The New York Times* who refused to give evidence in response to grand jury subpoenas issued in connection with an investigation of whether White House officials disclosed to reporters the name of an undercover CIA operative, in violation of federal law. *In re Grand Jury Subpoena, Judith Miller*, 397 F.3d 964 (D.C. Cir.), *cert. denied sub nom. Miller v. United States*, 545 U.S. 1150 (2005).

2. How should a lower court deal with a situation where a five-member majority includes one Justice who also writes separately to articulate a vague position somewhere between the majority's analysis and the dissent's? In cases where there is only a plurality opinion, the standard rule is that "the holding of the Court may be viewed as that position taken by those Members who concurred in the judgments on the narrowest grounds." *Marks v. United States*, 430 U.S. 188, 193 (1977). But the opinion in *Branzburg* was a majority, not a plurality, opinion. Consider what Justice Scalia stated (albeit in a dissenting opinion) about a situation where a fifth Justice both joins an opinion (that thereby becomes a majority opinion) and writes a separate concurrence. In such a case:

> [The majority] opinion is *not* a majority opinion except to the extent that it accords with [the concurring Justice's] views. What he writes is not a "gloss," but the least common denominator. To be sure, the separate writing cannot add to what the majority opinion holds, binding the other four

Justices to what they have not said; but it can assuredly narrow what the majority opinion holds, by explaining the more limited interpretation adopted by a necessary member of that majority.

McKoy v. North Carolina, 494 U.S. 433 (1990) (Scalia, J., dissenting).

Ultimately, rejection of the particular privilege claims made in *Branzburg* should probably be seen as resting on Justice Powell's less absolutist approach. This, in turn, makes the lower courts' confusion, discussed below, more understandable. Indeed, Justice Stewart, author of the principal dissent in *Branzburg*, once wrote (perhaps self-servingly) that in *Branzburg* the Court had rejected claims of journalistic testimonial privileges "by a vote of five to four, or . . . perhaps by a vote of four and a half to four and a half." Potter Stewart, *Or of the Press*, 26 Hastings L.J. 631, 635 (1975).

3. Justice Powell continued to hold the middle ground on the issue of journalistic privilege. Six years after *Branzburg*, in *Zurcher v. Stanford Daily*, 436 U.S. 547 (1978), he again provided the crucial fifth vote for rejecting a journalist's claim to special exemptions. The issue in *Zurcher* was whether law enforcement could search a newspaper's files based only on a search warrant, or whether the Fourth Amendment required a subpoena.

As in *Branzburg*, Justice Powell joined a five-justice majority opinion authored by Justice White rejecting the journalists' claim. And, as in *Branzburg*, Justice Powell concurred and added language suggesting a narrower reading of the resulting loss for the press: "This is not to say that a warrant which would be sufficient to support the search of an apartment or an automobile necessarily would be reasonable in supporting the search of a newspaper office. . . . While there is no justification for the establishment of a separate Fourth Amendment procedure for the press, a magistrate asked to issue a warrant for the search of press offices can and should take cognizance of the independent values protected by the First Amendment—such as those highlighted by Mr. Justice Stewart [in the dissenting opinion]—when he weighs such factors."

4. Consider the following postscript to *Branzburg*. In 2007 a researcher looking through Justice Powell's official papers found the Justice's handwritten conference notes in the companion case to *Branzburg*. His notes state as follows (underscoring, misspelling, and abbreviations in the original):

> My vote turned on my conclusion—after hearing arguments of counsel and re-reading principal briefs—that we should not establish a **constitutional** privilege. If we did this, the problems that would flow from it would be difficult to foresee: e.g., applying a privilege of **const. dimensions** to grand jurys, petite juries, congressional committees, etc. And who are "newsmen"—how to define?
>
> I will make clear in an opinion—unless the Court's opinion is clear—that there is a **privilege** analogous to an evidentiary one, which courts should recognize + apply on case by case to protect confidential information.

The Casebook reprints Justice Powell's *Branzburg* concurrence in its entirety. How does his concurrence differ from his notes? How, if at all, might the law have developed differently if his opinion had precisely tracked these notes?

———

Note: Journalists' Privilege in the Lower Courts

1. Lower courts have read *Branzburg* in different ways. While agreeing that *Branzburg* rejects an absolute journalists' privilege, some state and lower federal courts have read the *Branzburg* majority through the lens of Justice Powell's fifth-vote concurrence to mandate a case-by-case balancing test between press freedom and the public's obligation to give testimony with respect to criminal conduct. *See, e.g., In re Letellier*, 578 A.2d 722 (Me. 1990). Others have taken the position that after *Branzburg* there is no journalists' privilege. *See, e.g., In re Grand Jury Proceedings*, 810 F.2d 580 (6th Cir. 1987); *In re Bridge*, 295 A.2d 3 (N.J. Super. 1972).

2. Some courts have also found a journalists' privilege in state constitutional provisions guaranteeing press freedom. *See, e.g., State v. Siel*, 444 A.2d 499 (N.H. 1982). A court's citation of a state constitution's free press guarantee is complicated, at least somewhat, by the question of whether a state constitution's press freedom provision is best interpreted as having the identical meaning as the First Amendment's Press Clause, or whether the state provision should be interpreted as having independent meaning. For example, in *Zelenka v. State*, 266 N.W.2d 279 (Wis. 1978), the court noted that before *Branzburg* the Wisconsin Supreme Court had construed the First Amendment to include a journalist's privilege. In *Zelenka* the court read *Branzburg* to bestow at least a qualified privilege, but noted that it could just as easily reaffirm its earlier holding purely on the Wisconsin Constitution's free press guarantee. At least one court has adopted Justice Stewart's analysis in *Branzburg* for purposes of both the First Amendment and the state's constitutional provision guaranteeing freedom of the press. *See Matter of Contempt of Court of Wright*, 700 P.2d 40 (Idaho 1985).

3. Other courts have crafted a common-law privilege. *See, e.g., State v. Rinaldo*, 689 P.2d 392 (Wash. 1984). In creating such privileges, courts explicitly consider competing policy concerns. For example, in *Rinaldo*, the Washington Supreme Court required that four conditions be met before finding a journalist's privilege in a criminal case: (1) the communication must have originated in confidence that it would not be disclosed; (2) confidentiality was essential to the maintenance of the relation between the parties; (3) the relation was one "which in the opinion of the community ought to be sedulously fostered"; and (4) the injury to that relation that would flow from disclosure was greater than the benefit, including the defendant's right to a fair trial, to be gained from unfettered access to relevant information. Other courts have promulgated rules of evidence that provide protections to reporters. *See, e.g.,* N.M. R. Evid. 11-514.

4. Courts have often drawn distinctions between civil actions and criminal actions, applying a more journalist-protective standard in civil cases. Thus, in *Rinaldo* (the

Washington State case discussed above), the court explained that a common-law privilege in criminal cases poses more difficulties than a civil litigation privilege, given the importance of the defendant's right to a fair trial; nevertheless, it adopted the privilege. In *Siel*, the New Hampshire state constitution provided a qualified journalistic privilege in civil cases; the state supreme court extended that privilege to criminal cases as well, but characterized the privilege as "more tenuous" in criminal cases because of the importance of the defendant's right to a fair trial. For an example of a federal court recognizing a First Amendment-based privilege in a civil case, see *Zerilli v. Smith*, 656 F.2d 705 (D.C. Cir. 1981) (noting the absence, in civil cases, of the public's interest in effective law enforcement that would militate against a privilege).

————

Note: Legislative and Executive Responses to the Shield Issue

1. Many states have dispensed with the need for judicial action by enacting statutes creating a journalist's privilege. At the time of the *Branzburg* opinion 17 states had enacted journalist shield laws of one type or another. By 2017, 40 states and the District of Columbia had such laws. The protection provided by these statutes varies widely: for example, some protect only information about the source's identity, while others privilege all information growing out of the confidential relationship. The laws also vary on the showing needed to overcome the privilege, with some statutes making the privilege absolute. Shield laws even distinguish as between the types of publications for which journalists may claim privilege. *See, e.g.*, *Price v. Time, Inc.*, 416 F.3d 1327 (11th Cir. 2005) (holding that Alabama's shield statute privilege applies only to newspaper — not magazine — reporters).

2. In the immediate aftermath of *Branzburg*, Congress considered, but failed to adopt, a federal statutory privilege. However, in 1975, Congress enacted the Federal Rules of Evidence, including Rule 501, which provides that privileges in federal cases "shall be governed by the principles of the common law as they may be interpreted by the courts of the United States in the light of reason and experience." Some courts have interpreted Rule 501 to provide for a journalistic privilege in a grand jury proceeding. *See, e.g.*, *In re Grand Jury Subpoena of Williams*, 766 F. Supp. 358 (W.D. Pa. 1991); *but see In re Grand Jury Subpoena, Judith Miller*, 397 F.3d 964 (D.C. Cir. 2005) (Sentelle, J., concurring) (finding the argument for a common law privilege to be foreclosed by *Branzburg*).

3. Recall the prior Note's discussion of the distinction between criminal and civil litigation privileges in state common law. Whether federal courts applying a Rule 501-based privilege could draw a similar distinction is unclear. Federal Rule of Evidence 1101(c) expressly provides that "[t]he rule with respect to privileges applies at *all stages of all actions*, cases and proceedings." (Emphasis added.)

4. The executive branch has also been active in this area. Even before *Branzburg*, in 1970, the Justice Department had issued guidelines limiting the federal government's use of reporters to gain information. These guidelines have remained in effect since then. *See* 28 C.F.R. § 50.10.

5. What are the benefits and drawbacks of these varying forms of protecting journalists? Is this a matter that is best handled through common-law adjudication or by legislation? State-by-state, or nationally? Or should the Supreme Court have adopted, as a matter of First Amendment law, a test such as the one quoted in the previous Note from the Washington State Supreme Court opinion?

Note: Branzburg *and Access to Prisons*

1. "Jails, built for security purposes, are not [open to the public]." So said the Court in *Adderley v. Florida*, 385 U.S. 39 (1966) (Note *supra* Chapter 8). But might members of the press have a right of access to jails and prisons for the purpose of gathering news? The Court considered this question in three cases in the 1970s. In all three cases the Court rejected the First Amendment claim.

In two cases handed down on the same day in 1974, *Pell v. Procunier*, 417 U.S. 817 (1974), and *Saxbe v. Washington Post*, 417 U.S. 843 (1974), the newspapers argued that the First Amendment grants the press special rights to enter prisons and interview prisoners whom they specifically name and request to interview. *Pell* involved a challenge to a California prison regulation, and *Saxbe* a federal regulation, both of which prohibited the press from obtaining access to identified prisoners for pre-arranged interviews, but both of which provided the press some degree of access to prisons. Both the federal and state regulations gave the press somewhat more access to prisons than that enjoyed by the general public. For example, under both regulations reporters visiting a prison could spontaneously ask questions of inmates they encountered and could interview randomly selected groups of inmates.

In both cases, Justice Stewart, writing for a five-Justice majority, relied on *Branzburg* as well as on *Zemel v. Rusk*, 381 U.S. 1 (1965), to hold that the First Amendment does not confer upon the press rights to special access or immunities not granted to other individuals. However, Justice Stewart, who authored the dissent in *Branzburg*, wrote the following in *Pell*, seeming to qualify a broad reading of *Branzburg*:

> It is one thing to say that a journalist is free to seek out sources of information not available to members of the general public, that he is entitled to some constitutional protection of the confidentiality of such sources, *cf. Branzburg*, and that government cannot restrain the publication of news emanating from such sources. *Cf. New York Times Co. v. United States* (1971) [*supra* Chapter 4]. It is quite another thing to suggest that the Constitution imposes upon government the affirmative duty to make available to journalists sources of information not available to members of the public generally.

Justice Powell, dissenting in *Saxbe* for himself and Justices Brennan and Marshall, argued that government should be required to cite more than discretionary authority and administrative convenience before being able to ban inmate interviews. As support for the view that the First Amendment requires a stronger government justification before reporters could be denied access to the inmates they wished to interview, Justice Powell cited *Branzburg*'s statement that "news gathering is not without its First Amendment protections," his own concurrence in that case, and the important societal role played by the press when investigating government action. In *Pell*, Justice Powell dissented for himself only, relying on his *Saxbe* dissent. In an opinion addressing both *Saxbe* and *Pell*, Justice Douglas dissented separately, arguing that valid penological interests did not justify an absolute ban on press access. Justices Brennan and Marshall joined Justice Douglas's opinion.

2. The Court reached a still more equivocal result in *Houchins v. KQED, Inc.*, 438 U.S. 1 (1978). A public television station requested access to a local jail where poor conditions had been reported, was turned down, and then sued. After the suit was commenced, the sheriff began a limited program of conducting public tours of the jail. Members of the press were invited on the same terms that were offered to the public, including no photography and no opportunity to question inmates encountered during the tour. The district court issued a preliminary injunction requiring the sheriff to allow the media access to the prison, including allowing photography and inmate interviews, all subject to the sheriff retaining the right to deny access when required by inmate tension and other special circumstances.

In a fractured decision with only seven Justices participating, the Supreme Court reversed the grant of the preliminary injunction. Writing for himself and Justices White and Rehnquist, Chief Justice Burger discussed *Grosjean* and relied on *Branzburg*, *Pell* and *Saxbe* for the proposition that the press does not enjoy special privileges beyond those enjoyed by the public:

> *Grosjean* . . . emphasized the importance of informed public opinion and the traditional role of a free press as a source of public information. But an analysis . . . reveals that the Court was concerned with the freedom of the media to *communicate* information once it is obtained; [not] that the Constitution *compels* the government to provide the media with information or access to it on demand. . . .
>
> *Branzburg* offers even less support for the respondents' position. Its observation, in dictum, that "news gathering is not without its First Amendment protections" in no sense implied a constitutional right of access to news sources. That observation must be read in context; it was in response to the contention that forcing a reporter to disclose to the grand jury information received in confidence would violate the First Amendment by deterring news sources from communicating information. There is an undoubted right to gather news "from any source by means within the law," *Branzburg*, but that affords no basis for the claim that the First Amendment compels others—private persons or governments—to supply information. . . .
>
> *Pell* and *Saxbe* also assumed that there is no constitutional right of access. . . . In those cases the Court declared, explicitly and without reservation, that the media have "no constitutional right of access to prisons or

their inmates beyond that afforded the general public," *Pell*, and on that premise the Court sustained prison regulations that prevented media interviews with inmates. . . .

Justice Stewart provided the crucial fourth vote to reverse the injunction, but wrote a more limited opinion. He agreed that the press does not enjoy special rights of access, but argued that, given the press's unique role in informing the public, equal access for the press requires special terms for its visits:

> That the First Amendment speaks separately of freedom of speech and freedom of the press is no constitutional accident, but an acknowledgement of the critical role played by the press in American society. The Constitution requires sensitivity to that role, and to the special needs of the press in performing it effectively. . . . In short, terms of access that are reasonably imposed on individual members of the public may, if they impede effective reporting without sufficient justification, be unreasonable as applied to journalists who are there to convey to the general public what the visitors see.

In particular, Justice Stewart concluded that the First Amendment requires that the press be able to photograph and record sights and sounds, even if such photography and recording are prohibited to members of the general public. However, he also concluded that under his equal access principle the press does not have a right to access areas of the prison closed to the general public, or to interview inmates when such interviewing opportunities are denied to non-press visitors.

Justice Stevens, joined by Justices Brennan and Powell, dissented. Justice Stevens distinguished *Pell* and *Saxbe* by noting that in those cases the government had afforded at least some public access to the prisons, whereas, at least when the current case was filed, the government had denied all public access. Thus, he argued that the case was not about whether the press enjoys equal access, but whether the public, including the press, enjoys any access at all to an important government function where there is no overriding need for confidentiality.

Chapter 15

Testing the Boundaries of Doctrine

A. "Hate Speech"

Unlike obscenity or fighting words, "hate speech" is not a juridical category. There is no doctrine of "hate speech." The phrase itself appears in only one Supreme Court opinion, and that is a concurring opinion—the concurring opinion by Justice White in *R.A.V. v. City of St. Paul*, the first case in this section. Justice White asserted that the Court's decision "legitimates hate speech as a form of public discussion."

What kinds of expression might be encompassed by the term "hate speech"? Should the Supreme Court recognize "hate speech" as a new category of unprotected expression? If not, how should the Court analyze laws like those in *R.A.V.* and *Virginia v. Black?*

———

Note: Beauharnais *and "Group Libel"*

1. In *Beauharnais v. Illinois*, 343 U.S. 250 (1952) (*supra* Chapter 2), the Court upheld the constitutionality of the Illinois "group libel" law. Reread that case, and consider these excerpts from the dissent of Justice Jackson:

> I agree with the Court that a State has power to bring classes "of any race, color, creed, or religion" within the protection of its libel laws, if indeed traditional forms do not already accomplish it. But I am equally clear that in doing so it is essential to our concept of ordered liberty that the State also protect the accused by those safeguards the necessity for which is verified by legal history. . . .

> Punishment of printed words, based on their tendency either to cause breach of the peace or injury to persons or groups, in my opinion, is justifiable only if the prosecution survives the "clear and present danger" test. It is the most just and workable standard yet evolved for determining criminality of words whose injurious or inciting tendencies are not demonstrated by the event but are ascribed to them on the basis or probabilities. . . .

> One of the merits of the clear and present danger test is that the triers of fact would take into account the realities of race relations and any smouldering fires to be fanned into holocausts. Such consideration might well warrant a conviction here when it would not in another and different environment.

> Group libel statutes represent a commendable desire to reduce sinister abuses of our freedoms of expression — abuses which I have had occasion to learn can tear apart a society, brutalize its dominant elements, and persecute, even to extermination, its minorities. While laws or prosecutions might not alleviate racial or sectarian hatreds and may even invest scoundrels with a specious martyrdom, I should be loath to foreclose the States from a considerable latitude of experimentation in this field.

Would this be a preferable approach to the doctrines applied in *R.A.V.* and *Virginia v. Black*?

2. Justice Jackson notes that he "had occasion to learn" that "sinister abuses of our freedoms of expression" can lead to the persecution, "even to extermination, [of] minorities." He is referring to his experience as chief American prosecutor at the war crime trials of Nazi leaders in Germany after World War II.

Justice Jackson's point is not entirely clear, but he seems to be suggesting that "sinister abuses of our freedoms of expression" could have evil consequences for the United States as they did for Germany in the 1930s. Assuming that his analysis of developments in Germany is correct, can we be confident, more than half a century later, that he was wrong about its implications for this country?

R.A.V. v. City of St. Paul

505 U.S. 377 (1992)

JUSTICE SCALIA delivered the opinion of the Court.

In the predawn hours of June 21, 1990, petitioner and several other teenagers allegedly assembled a crudely made cross by taping together broken chair legs. They then allegedly burned the cross inside the fenced yard of a black family that lived across the street from the house where petitioner was staying. Although this conduct could have been punished under any of a number of laws, one of the two provisions under which respondent city of St. Paul chose to charge petitioner (then a juvenile) was the St. Paul Bias-Motivated Crime Ordinance, which provides:

> Whoever places on public or private property a symbol, object, appellation, characterization or graffiti, including, but not limited to, a burning cross or Nazi swastika, which one knows or has reasonable grounds to know arouses anger, alarm or resentment in others on the basis of race, color, creed, religion or gender commits disorderly conduct and shall be guilty of a misdemeanor.

Petitioner moved to dismiss this count on the ground that the St. Paul ordinance was substantially overbroad and impermissibly content based and therefore facially invalid under the First Amendment. The trial court granted this motion, but the Minnesota Supreme Court reversed. That court rejected petitioner's overbreadth claim because, as construed in prior Minnesota cases, the modifying phrase "arouses anger, alarm or resentment in others" limited the reach of the ordinance to conduct that amounts to "fighting words," i.e., "conduct that itself inflicts injury or tends to incite immediate violence . . . ," and therefore the ordinance reached only expression "that the first amendment does not protect." The court also concluded that the ordinance was not impermissibly content based because, in its view, "the ordinance is a narrowly tailored means toward accomplishing the compelling governmental interest in protecting the community against biasmotivated threats to public safety and order." We granted certiorari.

I

In construing the St. Paul ordinance, we are bound by the construction given to it by the Minnesota court. Accordingly, we accept the Minnesota Supreme Court's authoritative statement that the ordinance reaches only those expressions that constitute "fighting words" within the meaning of *Chaplinsky v. New Hampshire* (1942) [*supra* Chapter 2]. Petitioner and his *amici* urge us to modify the scope of the *Chaplinsky* formulation, thereby invalidating the ordinance as "substantially overbroad," *Broadrick v. Oklahoma*, 413 U.S. 601 (1973). We find it unnecessary to consider this issue. Assuming, *arguendo*, that all of the expression reached by the ordinance is proscribable under the "fighting words" doctrine, we nonetheless conclude that the ordinance is facially unconstitutional in that it prohibits otherwise permitted speech solely on the basis of the subjects the speech addresses.

The First Amendment generally prevents government from proscribing speech or even expressive conduct, *see, e.g., Texas v. Johnson* (1989) [*supra* Chapter 7], because of disapproval of the ideas expressed. Content-based regulations are presumptively invalid. [E.g.,] *Police Dept. of Chicago v. Mosley* (1972) [*supra* Chapter 5]. From 1791 to the present, however, our society, like other free but civilized societies, has permitted restrictions upon the content of speech in a few limited areas, which are "of such slight social value as a step to truth that any benefit that may be derived from them is clearly outweighed by the social interest in order and morality." *Chaplinsky*. We have recognized that "the freedom of speech" referred to by the First Amendment does not include a freedom to disregard these traditional limitations. *See, e.g., Roth v. United States* (1957) (obscenity); *Beauharnais v. Illinois* (1952) (defamation); *Chaplinsky v. New Hampshire* ("fighting words"). Our decisions since the 1960's have narrowed the scope of the traditional categorical exceptions for defamation and for obscenity, but a limited categorical approach has remained an important part of our First Amendment jurisprudence.

We have sometimes said that these categories of expression are "not within the area of constitutionally protected speech," *Roth, Beauharnais, Chaplinsky,* or that the "protection of the First Amendment does not extend" to them, *Bose Corp. v. Consumers Union of United States, Inc.*, 466 U.S. 485 (1984); *Sable Communications of Cal., Inc. v. FCC*, 492 U.S. 115 (1989). Such statements must be taken in context, however, and are no more literally true than is the occasionally repeated shorthand characterizing obscenity "as not being speech at all." What they mean is that these areas of speech can, consistently with the First Amendment, be regulated *because of their constitutionally proscribable content* (obscenity, defamation, etc.)—not that they are categories of speech entirely invisible to the Constitution, so that they may be made the vehicles for content discrimination unrelated to their distinctively proscribable content. Thus, the government may proscribe libel; but it may not make the further content discrimination of proscribing *only* libel critical of the government. We recently acknowledged this distinction in *Ferber v. New York* (1982) [*supra* Chapter 3], where, in upholding New York's child pornography law, we expressly recognized that there was no "question here of censoring a particular literary theme. . . ."

Our cases surely do not establish the proposition [asserted by Justice White] that the First Amendment imposes no obstacle whatsoever to regulation of particular instances of such proscribable expression, so that the government "may regulate [them] freely." That would mean that a city council could enact an ordinance prohibiting only those legally obscene works that contain criticism of the city government or, indeed, that do not include endorsement of the city government. Such a simplistic, all-or-nothing-at-all approach to First Amendment protection is at odds with common sense and with our jurisprudence as well.[4] It is not true that "fighting words" have at most a "*de minimis*" expressive content, or that their content is *in all respects* "worthless and undeserving of constitutional protection"; sometimes they are quite expressive indeed. We have not said that they constitute "*no* part of the expression of ideas," but only that they constitute "no *essential* part of any exposition of ideas." *Chaplinsky* (emphasis added).

The proposition that a particular instance of speech can be proscribable on the basis of one feature (*e.g.*, obscenity) but not on the basis of another (*e.g.*, opposition to the city government) is commonplace and has found application in many contexts. We have long held, for example, that nonverbal expressive activity can be banned because of the action it entails, but not because of the ideas it expresses—so that burning a flag in violation of an ordinance against outdoor fires could be punishable, whereas burning a flag in violation of an ordinance against dishonoring the flag is not. *See*

---

4. Justice White concedes that a city council cannot prohibit only those legally obscene works that contain criticism of the city government, but asserts that to be the consequence, not of the First Amendment, but of the Equal Protection Clause. Such content-based discrimination would not, he asserts, "be rationally related to a legitimate government interest." But of course the only *reason* that government interest is not a "legitimate" one is that it violates the First Amendment. This Court itself has occasionally fused the First Amendment into the Equal Protection Clause in this fashion, but at least with the acknowledgment (which Justice White cannot afford to make) that the First Amendment underlies its analysis. See *Police Dept. of Chicago v. Mosley* (1972) [*supra* Chapter 5] (ordinance prohibiting only nonlabor picketing violated the Equal Protection Clause because there was no "appropriate governmental interest" supporting the distinction inasmuch as "the First Amendment means that government has no power to restrict expression because of its message, its ideas, its subject matter, or its content").

Justice Stevens seeks to avoid the point by dismissing the notion of obscene antigovernment speech as "fantastical," apparently believing that any reference to politics prevents a finding of obscenity. Unfortunately for the purveyors of obscenity, that is obviously false. A shockingly hardcore pornographic movie that contains a model sporting a political tattoo can be found, "*taken as a whole,* [to] lac[k] serious literary, artistic, political, or scientific value," *Miller v. California*, 413 U.S. 15 (1973) (emphasis added). Anyway, it is easy enough to come up with other illustrations of a content-based restriction upon "unprotected speech" that is obviously invalid: the anti-government libel illustration mentioned earlier, for one. And of course the concept of racist fighting words is, unfortunately, anything but a "highly speculative hypothetica[l]."

Johnson. See also Barnes v. Glen Theatre, Inc., 501 U.S. 560 (1991) [Note *supra* Chapter 7] [and] *United States v. O'Brien* (1968) [*supra* Chapter 7]. Similarly, we have upheld reasonable "time, place, or manner" restrictions, but only if they are "justified without reference to the content of the regulated speech." *Ward v. Rock Against Racism* (1989) [*supra* Chapter 6]. And just as the power to proscribe particular speech on the basis of a noncontent element (*e.g.*, noise) does not entail the power to proscribe the same speech on the basis of a content element; so also, the power to proscribe it on the basis of one content element (*e.g.*, obscenity) does not entail the power to proscribe it on the basis of *other* content elements.

In other words, the exclusion of "fighting words" from the scope of the First Amendment simply means that, for purposes of that Amendment, the unprotected features of the words are, despite their verbal character, essentially a "nonspeech" element of communication. Fighting words are thus analogous to a noisy sound truck: Each is, as Justice Frankfurter recognized, a "mode of speech"; both can be used to convey an idea; but neither has, in and of itself, a claim upon the First Amendment. As with the sound truck, however, so also with fighting words: The government may not regulate use based on hostility — or favoritism — towards the underlying message expressed. Compare *Frisby v. Schultz* (1988) (upholding, against facial challenge, a content-neutral ban on targeted residential picketing) [*supra* Chapter 6], with *Carey v. Brown*, 447 U.S. 455 (1980) (invalidating a ban on residential picketing that exempted labor picketing).

The concurrences describe us as setting forth a new First Amendment principle that prohibition of constitutionally proscribable speech cannot be "underinclusiv[e]," a First Amendment "absolutism" whereby "[w]ithin a particular 'proscribable' category of expression, . . . a government must either proscribe *all speech* or no speech at all." That easy target is of the concurrences' own invention. In our view, the First Amendment imposes not an "underinclusiveness" limitation but a "content discrimination" limitation upon a State's prohibition of proscribable speech. There is no problem whatever, for example, with a State's prohibiting obscenity (and other forms of proscribable expression) only in certain media or markets, for although that prohibition would be "underinclusive," it would not discriminate on the basis of content. *See, e.g., Sable Communications* (upholding 47 U.S.C. § 223(b)(1), which prohibits obscene *telephone* communications).

Even the prohibition against content discrimination that we assert the First Amendment requires is not absolute. It applies differently in the context of proscribable speech than in the area of fully protected speech. The rationale of the general prohibition, after all, is that content discrimination "raises the specter that the Government may effectively drive certain ideas or viewpoints from the marketplace." *Simon & Schuster, Inc. v. Members of N.Y. State Crime Victims Bd.*, 502 U.S. 105 (1991) [Note *supra* Chapter 5]. But content discrimination among various instances of a class of proscribable speech often does not pose this threat.

When the basis for the content discrimination consists entirely of the very reason the entire class of speech at issue is proscribable, no significant danger of idea or viewpoint discrimination exists. Such a reason, having been adjudged neutral enough to support exclusion of the entire class of speech from First Amendment protection, is also neutral enough to form the basis of distinction within the class. To illustrate: A State might choose to prohibit only that obscenity which is the most patently offensive *in its prurience* — i.e., that which involves the most lascivious displays of sexual activity. But it may not prohibit, for example, only that obscenity which includes offensive *political* messages. And the Federal Government can criminalize only those threats of violence that are directed against the President, see 18 U.S.C. §871 — since the reasons why threats of violence are outside the First Amendment (protecting individuals from the fear of violence, from the disruption that fear engenders, and from the possibility that the threatened violence will occur) have special force when applied to the person of the President. *See Watts v. United States*, 394 U.S. 705 (1969) [Note *supra* Chapter 1]. But the Federal Government may not criminalize only those threats against the President that mention his policy on aid to inner cities. And to take a final example (one mentioned by Justice Stevens), a State may choose to regulate price advertising in one industry but not in others, because the risk of fraud (one of the characteristics of commercial speech that justifies depriving it of full First Amendment protection). But a State may not prohibit only that commercial advertising that depicts men in a demeaning fashion.

Another valid basis for according differential treatment to even a content-defined subclass of proscribable speech is that the subclass happens to be associated with particular "secondary effects" of the speech, so that the regulation is "*justified* without reference to the content of the . . . speech." *Renton v. Playtime Theatres, Inc.* (1986) [*supra* Chapter 7]. A State could, for example, permit all obscene live performances except those involving minors. Moreover, since words can in some circumstances violate laws directed not against speech but against conduct (a law against treason, for example, is violated by telling the enemy the Nation's defense secrets), a particular content-based subcategory of a proscribable class of speech can be swept up incidentally within the reach of a statute directed at conduct rather than speech. Thus, for example, sexually derogatory "fighting words," among other words, may produce a violation of Title VII's general prohibition against sexual discrimination in employment practices. Where the government does not target conduct on the basis of its expressive content, acts are not shielded from regulation merely because they express a discriminatory idea or philosophy.

These bases for distinction refute the proposition that the selectivity of the restriction is "even arguably 'conditioned upon the sovereign's agreement with what a speaker may intend to say.'" *Metromedia, Inc. v. San Diego*, 453 U.S. 490 (1981) (Stevens, J., dissenting in part). There may be other such bases as well. Indeed, to validate such selectivity (where totally proscribable speech is at issue) it may not even be necessary to identify any particular "neutral" basis, so long as the nature of the content discrimination is such that there is no realistic possibility that official suppression of ideas is afoot. (We cannot think of any First Amendment interest that would stand in the way of a State's prohibiting only those obscene motion pictures with blue-eyed actresses.) Save for that limitation, the regulation of "fighting words," like the regulation of noisy speech, may address some offensive instances and leave other, equally offensive, instances alone. *See Posadas de Puerto Rico*, 478 U.S. 328 (1986).

II

Applying these principles to the St. Paul ordinance, we conclude that, even as narrowly construed by the Minnesota Supreme Court, the ordinance is facially unconstitutional. Although the phrase in the ordinance, "arouses anger, alarm or resentment in others," has been limited by the Minnesota Supreme Court's construction to reach only those symbols or displays that amount to "fighting words," the remaining, unmodified terms make clear that the ordinance applies only to "fighting words" that insult, or provoke violence, "on the basis of race, color, creed, religion or gender." Displays containing abusive invective, no matter how vicious or severe, are permissible unless they are addressed to one of the specified disfavored topics. Those who wish to use "fighting words" in connection with other ideas—to express hostility, for example, on the basis of political affiliation, union membership, or homosexuality—are not covered. The First Amendment does not permit St. Paul to impose special prohibitions on those speakers who express views on disfavored subjects. *See Simon & Schuster.*

In its practical operation, moreover, the ordinance goes even beyond mere content discrimination, to actual viewpoint discrimination. Displays containing some words—odious racial epithets, for example—would be prohibited to proponents of all views. But "fighting words" that do not themselves invoke race, color, creed, religion, or gender—aspersions upon a person's mother, for example—would seemingly be usable *ad libitum* in the placards of those arguing *in favor* of racial, color, etc., tolerance and equality, but could not be used by those speakers' opponents. One could hold up a sign saying, for example, that all "anti-Catholic bigots" are misbegotten; but not that all "papists" are, for that would insult and provoke violence "on the basis of religion." St. Paul has no such authority to license one side of a debate to fight freestyle, while requiring the other to follow Marquis of Queensberry rules.

What we have here, it must be emphasized, is not a prohibition of fighting words that are directed at certain persons or groups (which would be *facially* valid if it met the requirements of the Equal Protection Clause); but rather, a prohibition of fighting words that contain (as the Minnesota Supreme Court repeatedly emphasized) messages of "bias-motivated" hatred and in particular, as applied to this case, messages "based on virulent notions of racial supremacy." One must wholeheartedly agree with the Minnesota Supreme Court that "[i]t is the responsibility, even the obligation, of diverse communities to confront such notions in whatever form they appear," but the manner of that confrontation cannot consist of selective limitations upon speech. St. Paul's brief asserts that a general "fighting words" law would not meet the city's needs because only a content-specific measure can communicate to minority groups that the "group hatred" aspect of such speech "is not condoned by the majority." The point of the First Amendment is that majority preferences must be expressed in some fashion other than silencing speech on the basis of its content.

Despite the fact that the Minnesota Supreme Court and St. Paul acknowledge that the ordinance is directed at expression of group hatred, Justice Stevens suggests that this "fundamentally misreads" the ordinance. It is directed, he claims, not to speech of a particular content, but to particular "injur[ies]" that are "qualitatively different" from other injuries.

This is wordplay. What makes the anger, fear, sense of dishonor, etc., produced by violation of this ordinance distinct from the anger, fear, sense of dishonor, etc., produced by other fighting words is nothing other than the fact that it is caused by a distinctive idea, conveyed by a distinctive message. The First Amendment cannot be evaded that easily. It is obvious that the symbols which will arouse "anger, alarm or resentment in others on the basis of race, color, creed, religion or gender" are those symbols that communicate a message of hostility based on one of these characteristics. St. Paul concedes in its brief that the ordinance applies only to "racial, religious, or gender-specific symbols" such as "a burning cross, Nazi swastika or other instrumentality of like import." St. Paul argued in the Juvenile Court that "[t]he burning of a cross does express a message and it is, in fact, the content of that message which the St. Paul Ordinance attempts to legislate."

The content-based discrimination reflected in the St. Paul ordinance comes within neither any of the specific exceptions to the First Amendment prohibition we discussed earlier nor a more general exception for content discrimination that does not threaten censorship of ideas. It assuredly does not fall within the exception for content discrimination based on the very reasons why the particular class of speech at issue (here, fighting words) is proscribable. As explained earlier, the reason why fighting words are categorically excluded from the protection of the First Amendment is not that their content communicates any particular idea, but that their content embodies a particularly intolerable (and socially unnecessary) *mode* of expressing *whatever* idea the speaker wishes to convey. St. Paul has not singled out an especially offensive mode of expression—it has not, for example, selected for prohibition only those fighting words that communicate ideas in a threatening (as opposed to a merely obnoxious) manner. Rather, it has proscribed fighting words of whatever manner that communicate messages of racial, gender, or religious intolerance. Selectivity of this sort creates the possibility that the city is seeking to handicap the expression of particular ideas. That possibility would alone be enough to render the ordinance presumptively invalid, but St. Paul's comments and concessions in this case elevate the possibility to a certainty.

St. Paul argues that the ordinance comes within another of the specific exceptions we mentioned, the one that allows content discrimination aimed only at the "secondary effects" of the speech, see *City of Renton v. Playtime Theatres, Inc.* (1986) [*supra* Chapter 7]. According to St. Paul, the ordinance is intended, "not to impact on [*sic*] the right of free expression of the accused," but rather to "protect against the victimization of a person or persons who are particularly vulnerable because of their membership in a group that historically has been discriminated against." Even assuming that an ordinance that completely proscribes, rather than merely regulates, a specified category of speech can ever be considered to be directed only to the secondary effects of such speech, it is clear that the St. Paul ordinance is not directed to secondary effects within the meaning of *Renton*. As we said in *Boos v. Barry* (1988) [*supra* Chapter 7], "Listeners' reactions to speech are not the type of 'secondary effects' we referred to in *Renton*." "The emotive impact of speech on its audience is not a 'secondary effect.'"

It hardly needs discussion that the ordinance does not fall within some more general exception permitting *all* selectivity that for any reason is beyond the suspicion of official suppression of ideas. The statements of St. Paul in this very case afford ample basis for, if not full confirmation of, that suspicion.

Finally, St. Paul and its *amici* defend the conclusion of the Minnesota Supreme Court that, even if the ordinance regulates expression based on hostility towards its protected ideological content, this discrimination is nonetheless justified because it is narrowly tailored to serve compelling state interests. Specifically, they assert that the ordinance helps to ensure the basic human rights of members of groups that have historically been subjected to discrimination, including the right of such group members to live in peace where they wish. We do not doubt that these interests are compelling, and that the ordinance can be said to promote them. But the "danger of censorship" presented by a facially content-based statute requires that that weapon be employed only where it is "*necessary* to serve the asserted [compelling] interest." The existence of adequate content-neutral alternatives thus "undercut[s] significantly" any defense of such a statute, *Boos v. Barry*, casting considerable doubt on the government's protestations that "the asserted justification is in fact an accurate description of the purpose and effect of the law."

The dispositive question in this case, therefore, is whether content discrimination is reasonably necessary to achieve St. Paul's compelling interests; it plainly is not. An ordinance not limited to the favored topics, for example, would have precisely the same beneficial effect. In fact the only interest distinctively served by the content limitation is that of displaying the city council's special hostility towards the particular biases thus singled out. That is precisely what the First Amendment forbids. The politicians of St. Paul are entitled to express that hostility—but not through the means of imposing unique limitations upon speakers who (however benightedly) disagree.

* * *

Let there be no mistake about our belief that burning a cross in someone's front yard is reprehensible. But St. Paul has sufficient means at its disposal to prevent such behavior without adding the First Amendment to the fire.

The judgment of the Minnesota Supreme Court is reversed, and the case is remanded for proceedings not inconsistent with this opinion.

JUSTICE WHITE, with whom JUSTICE BLACKMUN and JUSTICE O'CONNOR join, and with whom JUSTICE STEVENS joins except as to Part I-A, concurring in the judgment.

I agree with the majority that the judgment of the Minnesota Supreme Court should be reversed. However, our agreement ends there.

This case could easily be decided within the contours of established First Amendment law by holding, as petitioner argues, that the St. Paul ordinance is fatally overbroad because it criminalizes not only unprotected expression but expression protected by the First Amendment. *See* Part II, *infra*. Instead, . . . the Court holds the ordinance facially unconstitutional on a ground [that] requires serious departures from the teaching of prior cases. . . .

I

A

This Court's decisions have plainly stated that expression falling within certain limited categories so lacks the values the First Amendment was designed to protect that the Constitution affords no protection to that expression. *Chaplinsky v. New Hampshire* (1942) [*supra* Chapter 2] made the point in the clearest possible terms. . . .

Today, however, the Court announces that earlier Courts did not mean their repeated statements that certain categories of expression are "not within the area of constitutionally protected speech." . . . To the contrary, those statements meant precisely what they said. . . .

In its decision today, [the] majority holds that the First Amendment protects those narrow categories of expression long held to be undeserving of First Amendment protection—at least to the extent that lawmakers may not regulate some fighting words more strictly than others because of their content. The Court announces that such content-based distinctions violate the First Amendment because "[t]he government may not regulate use based on hostility—or favoritism—towards the underlying message expressed." Should the government want to criminalize certain fighting words, the Court now requires it to criminalize all fighting words.

To borrow a phrase: "Such a simplistic, all-or-nothing-at-all approach to First Amendment protection is at odds with common sense and with our jurisprudence as well." It is inconsistent to hold that the government may proscribe an entire category of speech because the content of that speech is evil, but that the government may not treat a subset of that category differently without violating the First Amendment; the content of the subset is by definition worthless and undeserving of constitutional protection. . . .

Any contribution of [the Court's] holding to First Amendment jurisprudence is surely a negative one, since it necessarily signals that expressions of violence, such as the message of intimidation and racial hatred conveyed by burning a cross on someone's lawn, are of sufficient value to outweigh the social interest in order and morality that has traditionally placed such fighting words outside the First Amendment.[4]

---

4. This does not suggest, of course, that cross burning is always unprotected. Burning a cross at a political rally would almost certainly be protected expression. *Cf. Brandenburg v. Ohio*, 395 U.S. 444 (1969). But in such a context, the cross burning could not be characterized as a "direct personal insult or an invitation to exchange fisticuffs," *Texas v. Johnson*, 491 U.S. 397 (1989), to which the fighting words doctrine, see Part II, *infra*, applies.

Indeed, by characterizing fighting words as a form of "debate," the majority legitimates hate speech as a form of public discussion. . . .

B

In a second break with precedent, the Court refuses to sustain the ordinance even though it would survive under the strict scrutiny applicable to other protected expression. Assuming, *arguendo*, that the St. Paul ordinance is a content-based regulation of protected expression, it nevertheless would pass First Amendment review under settled law upon a showing that the regulation "'is necessary to serve a compelling state interest and is narrowly drawn to achieve that end.'" *Simon & Schuster, Inc.* . . . The Court expressly concedes that [the city's] interest is compelling and is promoted by the ordinance. [However, under] the majority's view, a narrowly drawn, content-based ordinance could never pass constitutional muster if the object of that legislation could be accomplished by banning a wider category of speech. This appears to be a general renunciation of strict scrutiny review, a fundamental tool of First Amendment analysis.[5] . . .

As with its rejection of the Court's categorical analysis, the majority offers no reasoned basis for discarding our firmly established strict scrutiny analysis at this time. The majority appears to believe that its doctrinal revisionism is necessary to prevent our elected lawmakers from prohibiting libel against members of one political party but not another and from enacting similarly preposterous laws. The majority is misguided.

Although the First Amendment does not apply to categories of unprotected speech, such as fighting words, the Equal Protection Clause requires that the regulation of unprotected speech be rationally related to a legitimate government interest. A defamation statute that drew distinctions on the basis of political affiliation or "an ordinance prohibiting only those legally obscene works that contain criticism of the city government" would unquestionably fail rational-basis review.[9]

---

5. The majority relies on *Boos v. Barry*, 485 U.S. 312 (1988), in arguing that the availability of content-neutral alternatives "'undercut[s] significantly'" a claim that content-based legislation is "'*necessary* to serve the asserted [compelling] interest.'" *Boos* does not support the majority's analysis. In *Boos*, Congress already had decided that the challenged legislation was not necessary, and the Court pointedly deferred to this choice. St. Paul lawmakers have made no such legislative choice.

Moreover, in *Boos*, the Court held that the challenged statute was not narrowly tailored because a less restrictive alternative was available. But the Court's analysis today turns *Boos* inside-out by substituting the majority's policy judgment that a *more* restrictive alternative could adequately serve the compelling need identified by St. Paul lawmakers. The result would be: (a) a statute that was not tailored to fit the need identified by the government; and (b) a greater restriction on fighting words, even though the Court clearly believes that fighting words have protected expressive content.

9. The majority is mistaken in stating that a ban on obscene works critical of government would fail equal protection review only because the ban would violate the First Amendment. While decisions such as *Police Dep't of Chicago v. Mosley*, 408 U.S. 92 (1972), recognize that First Amendment principles may be relevant to an equal protection claim challenging distinctions that impact on protected expression, there is no basis for linking First and Fourteenth Amendment analysis in a case involving unprotected expression. Certainly, one need not resort to First Amendment principles to

Turning to the St. Paul ordinance and assuming, *arguendo*, as the majority does, that the ordinance is not constitutionally overbroad (but see Part II, *infra*), there is no question that it would pass equal protection review. The ordinance proscribes a subset of "fighting words," those that injure "on the basis of race, color, creed, religion or gender." This selective regulation reflects the city's judgment that harms based on race, color, creed, religion, or gender are more pressing public concerns than the harms caused by other fighting words. In light of our Nation's long and painful experience with discrimination, this determination is plainly reasonable. Indeed, as the majority concedes, the interest is compelling.

C

The Court has patched up its argument with an apparently nonexhaustive list of ad hoc exceptions, in what can be viewed either as an attempt to confine the effects of its decision to the facts of this case, or as an effort to anticipate some of the questions that will arise from its radical revision of First Amendment law.

For instance, if the majority were to give general application to the rule on which it decides this case, today's decision would call into question the constitutionality of the statute making it illegal to threaten the life of the President. . . .

To save the statute, the majority has engrafted the following exception onto its newly announced First Amendment rule: Content-based distinctions may be drawn within an unprotected category of speech if the basis for the distinctions is "the very reason the entire class of speech at issue is proscribable." Thus, the argument goes, the statute making it illegal to threaten the life of the President is constitutional, "since the reasons why threats of violence are outside the First Amendment (protecting individuals from the fear of violence, from the disruption that fear engenders, and from the possibility that the threatened violence will occur) have special force when applied to the person of the President."

The exception swallows the majority's rule. Certainly, it should apply to the St. Paul ordinance, since "the reasons why [fighting words] are outside the First Amendment . . . have special force when applied to [groups that have historically been subjected to discrimination]." . . .

As its second exception, the Court posits that certain content-based regulations will survive under the new regime if the regulated subclass "happens to be associated with particular 'secondary effects' of the speech . . . ," which the majority treats as encompassing instances in which "words can . . . violate laws directed not against speech but against conduct. . . ." Again, there is a simple explanation for the Court's eagerness to craft an exception to its new First Amendment rule: Under the general rule the Court applies in this case, Title VII hostile work environment claims would suddenly be unconstitutional. . . .

As to the third exception to the Court's theory for deciding this case, the majority concocts a catchall exclusion to protect against unforeseen problems, a concern

---

conclude that the sort of improbable legislation the majority hypothesizes is based on senseless distinctions.

that is heightened here given the lack of briefing on the majority's decisional theory. This final exception would apply in cases in which "there is no realistic possibility that official suppression of ideas is afoot." As I have demonstrated, this case does not concern the official suppression of ideas. The majority discards this notion out of hand....

II

Although I disagree with the Court's analysis, I do agree with its conclusion: The St. Paul ordinance is unconstitutional. However, I would decide the case on over-breadth grounds.... Although the ordinance as construed reaches categories of speech that are constitutionally unprotected, it also criminalizes a substantial amount of expression that—however repugnant—is shielded by the First Amendment....

In construing the St. Paul ordinance, the Minnesota Supreme Court drew upon the definition of fighting words that appears in *Chaplinsky* —words "which by their very utterance inflict injury or tend to incite an immediate breach of the peace." However, the Minnesota court was far from clear in identifying the "injur[ies]" inflicted by the expression that St. Paul sought to regulate. Indeed, the Minnesota court emphasized (tracking the language of the ordinance) that "the ordinance censors only those displays that one knows or should know will create anger, alarm or resentment based on racial, ethnic, gender or religious bias." I therefore understand the court to have ruled that St. Paul may constitutionally prohibit expression that "by its very utterance" causes "anger, alarm or resentment."

Our fighting words cases have made clear, however, that such generalized reactions are not sufficient to strip expression of its constitutional protection. The mere fact that expressive activity causes hurt feelings, offense, or resentment does not render the expression unprotected. [E.g.] *Hustler Magazine, Inc. v. Falwell*, 485 U.S. 46 (1988) [Note *supra* Chapter 2]; *Cohen v. California* (1971) [*supra* Chapter 3]; *Terminiello v. Chicago* (1949) [*supra* Chapter 8]....

Although the [St. Paul] ordinance reaches conduct that is unprotected, it also makes criminal expressive conduct that causes only hurt feelings, offense, or resentment, and is protected by the First Amendment. The ordinance is therefore fatally overbroad and invalid on its face.

III

Today, the Court has disregarded two established principles of First Amendment law without providing a coherent replacement theory. Its decision is an arid, doctrinaire interpretation, driven by the frequently irresistible impulse of judges to tinker with the First Amendment. The decision is mischievous at best and will surely confuse the lower courts. I join the judgment, but not the folly of the opinion.

JUSTICE BLACKMUN, concurring in the judgment....

I see no First Amendment values that are compromised by a law that prohibits hoodlums from driving minorities out of their homes by burning crosses on their lawns, but I see great harm in preventing the people of Saint Paul from specifically punishing the race-based fighting words that so prejudice their community.

I concur in the judgment, however, because I agree with Justice White that this particular ordinance reaches beyond fighting words to speech protected by the First Amendment.

JUSTICE STEVENS, with whom JUSTICE WHITE and JUSTICE BLACKMUN join as to Part I, concurring in the judgment.

Conduct that creates special risks or causes special harms may be prohibited by special rules. . . . Threatening someone because of her race or religious beliefs may cause particularly severe trauma or touch off a riot, and threatening a high public official may cause substantial social disruption; such threats may be punished more severely than threats against someone based on, say, his support of a particular athletic team. There are legitimate, reasonable, and neutral justifications for such special rules.

This case involves the constitutionality of one such ordinance. Because the regulated conduct has some communicative content — a message of racial, religious, or gender hostility — the ordinance raises two quite different First Amendment questions. Is the ordinance "overbroad" because it prohibits too much speech? If not, is it "underbroad" because it does not prohibit enough speech? . . .

[While] I agree that the St. Paul ordinance is unconstitutionally overbroad for the reasons stated in Part II of Justice White's opinion, I write separately to suggest how the allure of absolute principles has skewed the analysis of both the majority and Justice White's opinions.

I

. . . As an initial matter, the Court's revision of the categorical approach [taken in past cases] seems to me something of an adventure in a doctrinal wonderland, for the concept of "obscene anti-government" speech is fantastical. The category of the obscene is very narrow; to be obscene, expression must be found by the trier of fact to "appea[l] to the prurient interest, . . . depic[t] or describ[e], in a patently offensive way, sexual conduct, [and], taken as a whole, *lac[k] serious literary, artistic, political, or scientific value.*" *Miller v. California* (1973) (emphasis added) [*supra* Chapter 2]. "Obscene antigovernment" speech, then, is a contradiction in terms: If expression is antigovernment, it does not "lac[k] serious . . . political . . . value" and cannot be obscene.

The Court attempts to bolster its argument by likening its novel analysis to that applied to restrictions on the time, place, or manner of expression or on expressive conduct. It is true that loud speech in favor of the Republican Party can be regulated because it is loud, but not because it is pro-Republican; and it is true that the public burning of the American flag can be regulated because it involves public burning and not because it involves the flag. But these analogies are inapposite. In each of these examples, the two elements (*e.g.,* loudness and pro-Republican orientation) can coexist; in the case of "obscene antigovernment" speech, however, the presence of one element ("obscenity") by definition means the absence of the other. To my mind, it is unwise and unsound to craft a new doctrine based on such highly speculative hypotheticals.

I am, however, even more troubled by the second step of the Court's analysis—namely, its conclusion that the St. Paul ordinance is an unconstitutional contentbased regulation of speech. . . .

. . . Contrary to the broad dicta in *Mosley* and elsewhere, our decisions demonstrate that content-based distinctions, far from being presumptively invalid, are an inevitable and indispensable aspect of a coherent understanding of the First Amendment.

This is true at every level of First Amendment law. In broadest terms, our entire First Amendment jurisprudence creates a regime based on the content of speech. [For example,] "the line between permissible advocacy and impermissible incitation to crime or violence depends, not merely on the setting in which the speech occurs, but also on exactly what the speaker had to say." Likewise, whether speech falls within one of the categories of "unprotected" or "proscribable" expression is determined, in part, by its content. . . .

. . . [It] is impossible to reconcile the Court's analysis of the St. Paul ordinance with its recognition that "a prohibition of fighting words that are directed at certain persons or groups . . . would be facially valid." A selective proscription of unprotected expression designed to protect "certain persons or groups" (for example, a law proscribing threats directed at the elderly) would be constitutional if it were based on a legitimate determination that the harm created by the regulated expression differs from that created by the unregulated expression (that is, if the elderly are more severely injured by threats than are the nonelderly). Such selective protection is no different from a law prohibiting minors (and only minors) from obtaining obscene publications. *See Ginsberg v. New York*, 390 U.S. 629 (1968).

St. Paul has determined—reasonably in my judgment—that fighting-word injuries "based on race, color, creed, religion or gender" are qualitatively different and more severe than fighting-word injuries based on other characteristics. Whether the selective proscription of proscribable speech is defined by the protected target ("certain persons or groups") or the basis of the harm (injuries "based on race, color, creed, religion or gender") makes no constitutional difference: What matters is whether the legislature's selection is based on a legitimate, neutral, and reasonable distinction. . . .

II

Although I agree with much of Justice White's analysis, I do not join Part I-A of his opinion because I have reservations about the "categorical approach" to the First Amendment. . . .

[The] categorical approach does not take seriously the importance of *context*. The meaning of any expression and the legitimacy of its regulation can only be determined in context. Whether, for example, a picture or a sentence is obscene cannot be judged in the abstract, but rather only in the context of its setting, its use, and its audience. . . .

III

As the foregoing suggests, I disagree with both the Court's and part of Justice White's analysis of the constitutionality of the St. Paul ordinance. Unlike the Court, I do not believe that all content-based regulations are equally infirm and presumptively invalid; unlike Justice White, I do not believe that fighting words are wholly unprotected by the First Amendment. To the contrary, I believe our decisions establish a more complex and subtle analysis, one that considers the content and context of the regulated speech, and the nature and scope of the restriction on speech. Applying this analysis and assuming, *arguendo*, (as the Court does) that the St. Paul ordinance is not overbroad, I conclude that such a selective, subject-matter regulation on proscribable speech is constitutional. . . .

. . . Looking to the content and character of the regulated activity, two things are clear. First, by hypothesis the ordinance bars only low-value speech, namely, fighting words. . . . Second, the ordinance regulates "expressive conduct [rather] than . . . the written or spoken word." *Texas v. Johnson.* . . .

Fighting words are not words that merely cause offense; fighting words must be directed at individuals so as to "by their very utterance inflict injury." By hypothesis, then, the St. Paul ordinance restricts speech in confrontational and potentially violent situations. The case at hand is illustrative. The cross burning in this case — directed as it was to a single African-American family trapped in their home — was nothing more than a crude form of physical intimidation. That this cross burning sends a message of racial hostility does not automatically endow it with complete constitutional protection.

Significantly, the St. Paul ordinance regulates speech not on the basis of its subject matter or the viewpoint expressed, but rather on the basis of the *harm* the speech causes. In this regard, the Court fundamentally misreads the St. Paul ordinance. . . . Contrary to the Court's suggestion, the ordinance regulates only a subcategory of expression that causes *injuries based on* "race, color, creed, religion or gender," not a subcategory that involves *discussions* that concern those characteristics.[9] . . .

Moreover, even if the St. Paul ordinance did regulate fighting words based on its subject matter, such a regulation would, in my opinion, be constitutional. . . . As we have long recognized, subject-matter regulations generally do not raise the same

---

9. The Court contends that this distinction is "wordplay," reasoning that "[w]hat makes [the harms caused by race-based threats] distinct from [the harms] produced by other fighting words is . . . the fact that [the former are] caused by a *distinctive idea*." In this way, the Court concludes that regulating speech based on the injury it causes is no different from regulating speech based on its subject matter. This analysis fundamentally miscomprehends the role of "race, color, creed, religion [and] gender" in contemporary American society. One need look no further than the recent social unrest in the Nation's cities to see that race-based threats may cause more harm to society and to individuals than other threats. Just as the statute prohibiting threats against the President is justifiable because of the place of the President in our social and political order, so a statute prohibiting race-based threats is justifiable because of the place of race in our social and political order. Although it is regrettable that race occupies such a place and is so incendiary an issue, until the Nation matures beyond that condition, laws such as St. Paul's ordinance will remain reasonable and justifiable.

concerns of government censorship and the distortion of public discourse presented by viewpoint regulations. . . .

Contrary to the suggestion of the majority, the St. Paul ordinance does *not* regulate expression based on viewpoint. . . . In a battle between advocates of tolerance and advocates of intolerance, the ordinance does not prevent either side from hurling fighting words at the other on the basis of their conflicting ideas, but it does bar *both* sides from hurling such words on the basis of the target's "race, color, creed, religion or gender."

Finally, it is noteworthy that the St. Paul ordinance is, as construed by the Court today, quite narrow. The St. Paul ordinance does not ban all "hate speech," nor does it ban, say, all cross burnings or all swastika displays. Rather it only bans a subcategory of the already narrow category of fighting words. Such a limited ordinance leaves open and protected a vast range of expression on the subjects of racial, religious, and gender equality. As construed by the Court today, the ordinance certainly does not "'rais[e] the specter that the Government may effectively drive certain ideas or viewpoints from the marketplace.'" Petitioner is free to burn a cross to announce a rally or to express his views about racial supremacy, he may do so on private property or public land, at day or at night, so long as the burning is not so threatening and so directed at an individual as to "by its very [execution] inflict injury." Such a limited proscription scarcely offends the First Amendment.

In sum, the St. Paul ordinance (as construed by the Court) regulates expressive activity that is wholly proscribable and does so not on the basis of viewpoint, but rather in recognition of the different harms caused by such activity. Taken together, these several considerations persuade me that the St. Paul ordinance is not an unconstitutional content-based regulation of speech. Thus, were the ordinance not overbroad, I would vote to uphold it.

Note: The Implications of R.A.V.

1. The opinions in *R.A.V.* may set some sort of record for the number and variety of Supreme Court cases cited and quoted by the justices. Virtually all of those cases are included in this Casebook. Examine the use of precedent by the opinions in *R.A.V.* Do any of the cited cases provide substantial support for a disputed proposition put forth as a step in any justice's argument?

2. Justice White, in dissent, asserts that the Court's analysis "disregard[s] . . . established principles of First Amendment law." The Court responds, in a footnote:

> [Justice White] cites not a single case (and we are aware of none) that even involved, much less considered and resolved, the issue of content discrimination through regulation of "unprotected" speech—though we plainly recognized that as an issue in *Ferber*. It is of course contrary to all traditions of our jurisprudence to consider the law on this point conclusively resolved by broad language in cases where the issue was not presented or even envisioned.

Who has the better of this argument?

3. The justices disagree not only over the import of the Court's precedents, but also over the operation of the St. Paul ordinance. The majority insists that the ordinance discriminates on the basis of both content and viewpoint. Justice Stevens is equally insistent that "the St. Paul ordinance regulates speech not on the basis of its subject matter or the viewpoint expressed, but rather on the basis of the *harm* the speech causes." Which characterization is more persuasive?

4. In an omitted footnote (note 7) in *R.A.V.*, the majority opinion dismisses the possibility that the St. Paul ordinance could survive as a regulation of "that subclass of fighting words which is most likely to provoke a violent response." As an initial matter, the Court says it is "unlikely" that the ordinance could be so described. (Do you agree?) But the main reason the Court gives for rejecting this potential argument is this:

> The only reason why such expressive conduct would be especially corre-lated with violence is that it conveys a particularly odious message; because the "chain of causation" thus *necessarily* "run[s] through the persuasive effect of the expressive component" of the conduct, it is clear that the St. Paul ordi-nance regulates on the basis of the "primary" effect of the speech—*i.e.*, its persuasive (or repellant) force. (Emphasis in original.)

What distinction is Justice Scalia trying to draw here? Is it possible, in reality, to deter-mine whether certain expressive conduct, e.g., burning a cross to express racial hatred, is likely to cause a violent reaction because of the idea underlying it (e.g., rac-ism), rather than because the idea is one that is often expressed in constitutionally unprotected ways, such as violence? If Justice Scalia is ultimately trying to disentan-gle the persuasive and visceral effects of speech, do you think he has succeeded? Keep this question in mind as you read the note discussing *Virginia v. Black*, which follows after the note below, and observe how the justices try to understand the meaning of cross burning.

5. In 1978, Justice Blackmun commented that "*Beauharnais* has never been over-ruled or formally limited in any way." *Smith v. Collin*, 436 U.S. 953 (1978) (dissent-ing opinion). But none of the dissenters in *R.A.V.* (including Justice Blackmun) place reliance on *Beauharnais*. Does this suggest that *Beauharnais* is no longer good law?

6. Under California law, it is a misdemeanor to file "any allegation of misconduct against any peace officer . . . knowing the allegation to be false." Is this statute vulner-able to constitutional challenge under the rationale of *R.A.V.*?

———

Note: A Penalty Enhancement Statute

One of the first cases to consider the implications of *R.A.V.* was *Wisconsin v. Mitchell*, 508 U.S. 476 (1993). The case involved a Wisconsin statute that enhances the maximum penalty for an offense whenever the defendant "intentionally selects the person against whom the crime . . . is committed . . . because of the race, religion, color, disability, sexual orientation, national origin or ancestry of that person." The Court described the facts as follows:

> On the evening of October 7, 1989, a group of young black men and boys, including Mitchell, gathered at an apartment complex in Kenosha, Wisconsin. Several members of the group discussed a scene from the motion picture "Mississippi Burning," in which a white man beat a young black boy who was praying. The group moved outside and Mitchell asked them: "Do you all feel hyped up to move on some white people?" Shortly thereafter, a young white boy approached the group on the opposite side of the street where they were standing. As the boy walked by, Mitchell said: "You all want to fuck somebody up? There goes a white boy; go get him." Mitchell counted to three and pointed in the boy's direction. The group ran toward the boy, beat him severely, and stole his tennis shoes. The boy was rendered unconscious and remained in a coma for four days.

Mitchell was convicted of aggravated battery after a jury trial. That offense ordinarily carries a maximum sentence of two years' imprisonment. However, the jury found that Mitchell had intentionally selected his victim because of the boy's race. Based on that finding, the trial court invoked the penalty enhancement statute and sentenced Mitchell to four years' imprisonment for the aggravated battery.

The Wisconsin Supreme Court held that the penalty enhancement statute "violates the First Amendment directly by punishing what the legislature has deemed to be offensive thought." Although the court recognized that "the St. Paul ordinance invalidated in *R.A.V.* is clearly distinguishable from the hate crimes statute in that it regulates fighting words rather than merely the actor's biased motive," the court found that the analysis in *R.A.V.* "lends support to our conclusion that the Wisconsin legislature cannot criminalize bigoted thought with which it disagrees."

The Supreme Court reversed in a unanimous opinion by Chief Justice Rehnquist. The Court's discussion of *R.A.V.* was brief. The Court said:

> That case involved a First Amendment challenge to a municipal ordinance prohibiting the use of "'fighting words' that insult, or provoke violence, 'on the basis of race, color, creed, religion or gender.'" Because the ordinance only proscribed a class of "fighting words" deemed particularly offensive by the city—i.e., those "that contain . . . messages of 'bias-motivated' hatred," we held that it violated the rule against content-based discrimination. But whereas the ordinance struck down in *R.A.V.* was explicitly directed at expression (i.e., "speech" or "messages"), the statute in this case is aimed at conduct unprotected by the First Amendment.

> Moreover, the Wisconsin statute singles out for enhancement bias-inspired conduct because this conduct is thought to inflict greater individual and societal harm. For example, according to the State and its amici, bias-motivated crimes are more likely to provoke retaliatory crimes, inflict distinct emotional harms on their victims, and incite community unrest. The State's desire to

redress these perceived harms provides an adequate explanation for its penalty-enhancement provision over and above mere disagreement with offenders' beliefs or biases.

Is this an adequate basis on which to distinguish *R.A.V.*? Is there a better argument to explain why *R.A.V.* is not controlling? Or was the Wisconsin court correct in saying that in enacting the penalty enhancement statute, the Wisconsin legislature had attempted to "criminalize bigoted thought with which it disagrees"?

———

Note: Cross Burning Redux

1. Despite *Mitchell*, after *R.A.V.* one might think that laws singling out cross-burning for criminalization would be on tenuous constitutional ground. But a decade after those two cases, a majority of the Court suggested otherwise.

Virginia v. Black, 538 U.S. 343 (2003), considered a Virginia law that provides in part:

> It shall be unlawful for any person or persons, with the intent of intimidating any person or groups of persons, to burn, or cause to be burned, a cross on the property of another, a highway or other public place. Any person who shall violate any provision of this section shall be guilty of a Class 6 felony.

Black arose out of three cross burning convictions stemming from two separate incidents. In one, an individual (Black) was arrested and convicted for leading a rally in which a cross was burned. In another, two individuals (Elliott and O'Mara) were convicted for attempting to burn a cross on the yard of Elliott's African-American neighbor. On appeal, the Virginia Supreme Court struck down the law, concluding that it discriminated on the basis of content and viewpoint, and thus violated the First Amendment as construed in *R.A.V.*

2. The Supreme Court disagreed. Writing for five justices, Justice O'Connor began by describing the history of cross burning in the United States. She observed that in the United States such conduct was "inextricably intertwined with the history of the Ku Klux Klan." She concluded that review by stating that "while burning a cross does not inevitably convey a message of intimidation, often the cross burner intends that the recipient of the message fear for their lives. And when a cross burning is used to intimidate, few if any messages are more powerful."

Distinguishing *R.A.V.*, she explained that that case concerned a law that prohibited expressive conduct that was intended to "arouse anger, alarm, or resentment" on particular, identified, content-based grounds, such as race and gender. By contrast, Virginia's ban on cross burning with the intent to intimidate applied regardless of the content or the viewpoint of the intimidating message. She wrote:

> The First Amendment permits Virginia to outlaw cross burnings done with the intent to intimidate because burning a cross is a particularly virulent form of intimidation. Instead of prohibiting all intimidating messages, Virginia may choose to regulate this subset of intimidating messages in light of cross

burning's long and pernicious history as a signal of impending violence. Thus, just as a State may regulate only that obscenity which is the most obscene due to its prurient content, so too may a State choose to prohibit only those forms of intimidation that are most likely to inspire fear of bodily harm. A ban on cross burning carried out with the intent to intimidate is fully consistent with our holding in *R.A.V.* and is proscribable under the First Amendment.

Nevertheless, the Court reversed Black's conviction and remanded Elliott's and O'Mara's cases for new trials. As the Court explained, the problem lay with a second provision of the statute, which stated that "Any such burning of a cross shall be prima facie evidence of an intent to intimidate a person or group of persons." The trial court in Black's case instructed the jury that "[t]he burning of a cross, by itself, is sufficient evidence from which you may infer the required intent." Writing now only for four justices, she concluded that this second provision, as interpreted by the trial court in Black's case, rendered the statute overbroad, since it would allow conviction of defendants who had burned crosses even when the cross burning was a component of political expression, but who declined to put on a defense (and thus did not present evidence contesting the "intent to intimidate" element). She remanded Elliott's and O'Mara's cases for a new trial and for the state courts to consider a more limited interpretation of the prima facie provision.

3. Justice Stevens joined Justice O'Connor's opinion, and explained that his decision rested on his and Justice White's opinions in *R.A.V.*, which struck down the St. Paul ordinance on a more limited rationale. Justice Scalia, the author of the majority opinion in *R.A.V.*, provided the fifth vote for the Court's analysis upholding the cross burning provision itself, but he dissented from its overbreadth analysis. He argued that individuals who were convicted for politically motivated cross burning, who failed to put on a defense, and who thus were convicted, could appeal their sentences on a case-by-case basis. He also argued that the provision had less effect in leading to guilty verdicts than Justice O'Connor suggested.

4. Justice Souter, joined by Justices Kennedy and Ginsburg, concurred in the judgment in part and dissented in part. He disputed whether the cross burning statute was equivalent to the examples *R.A.V.* had provided of laws that prohibited a subset of a category of unprotected speech that was defined by reference to the very reason that more general category was unprotected—for example, a law that banned the most prurient obscenity. He thus described the Court's analysis as a move toward a more "pragmatic" understanding of the *R.A.V.* principle on which Justice O'Connor relied. But, quoting *R.A.V.*, he expressed more concern that "no content-based statute should survive even under a pragmatic recasting of *R.A.V.* without a high probability that no 'official suppression of ideas is afoot.'" He saw a risk of such suppression in this case, because he concluded that in close cases the prima facie provision might push juries toward conviction. He wrote: "As I see the likely significance of the evidence provision, its primary effect is to skew jury deliberations toward conviction in cases where the evidence of intent to intimidate is relatively weak and arguably consistent with a solely ideological reason for burning."

5. Justice Thomas dissented only for himself. He concluded that cross burning is unprotected by the First Amendment, because it constitutes conduct rather than expression, given its long association with violent intimidation. He observed that Virginia's cross burning prohibition was originally enacted in the 1950s, and concluded that "[i]t strains credulity to suggest that a state legislature that adopted a litany of segregationist laws self-contradictorily intended to squelch the segregationist message." But even assuming that cross burning was speech, he argued that the statutory presumption did not have the effect the plurality said it did. He also argued that in other First Amendment areas, such as child pornography, protected speech that is mistaken for unprotected speech is often prosecuted without triggering any First Amendment concerns.

Note: Cross Burning and the First Amendment

1. Justice Thomas, dissenting in *Black*, argues that the Virginia statute does not implicate the First Amendment at all because it "prohibits only conduct, not expression." Is this argument sound? Is it consistent with *Texas v. Johnson* (1989) (*supra* Chapter 7)?

2. How much of an inroad on *R.A.V.* does *Virginia v. Black* make? Does the "particular virulence exception," as construed by the majority, swallow the *R.A.V.* Court's rule against content-based discrimination?

3. Justice Souter, also dissenting in *Black* but on a very different ground from Justice Thomas, suggests that the majority's decision may be viewed as "a slight modification of *R.A.V.*'s third exception, which allows content-based discrimination within a proscribable category when its 'nature' is such 'that there is no realistic possibility that official suppression of ideas is a-foot.'" If that is the Court's assessment, is it persuasive?

Justice Thomas points out that at the same time the Virginia legislature enacted the cross-burning statute, it was also adopting "a litany of segregationist laws." He argues that it "strains credulity" to suggest that such a legislature "self-contradictorily intended to squelch the segregationist message." Do you agree? In response, Justice Souter suggests that the legislature might have viewed "dramatic, public espousal of [white supremacy] as a civic embarrassment." Does that refute Justice Thomas's argument?

4. The Court states (at the end of Part III): "A ban on cross burning carried out with the intent to intimidate is fully consistent with our holding in *R.A.V.* and is proscribable under the First Amendment." Recall the facts of *Brandenburg v. Ohio* (1969) (*supra* Chapter 1). On those facts, would the Court uphold a conviction under a cross-burning statute similar to Virginia's (but without the prima facie evidence provision)?

B. Government Programs and Offensive Speech
Matal v. Tam
137 S. Ct. 1744 (2017)

JUSTICE ALITO announced the judgment of the Court and delivered the opinion of the Court with respect to Parts I, II, and III-A, and an opinion with respect to Parts III-B, III-C, and IV, in which the CHIEF JUSTICE, JUSTICE THOMAS, and JUSTICE BREYER join.

This case concerns a dance-rock band's application for federal trademark registration of the band's name, "The Slants." "Slants" is a derogatory term for persons of Asian descent, and members of the band are Asian-Americans. But the band members believe that by taking that slur as the name of their group, they will help to "reclaim" the term and drain its denigrating force.

The Patent and Trademark Office (PTO) denied the application based on a provision of federal law prohibiting the registration of trademarks that may "disparage . . . or bring . . . into contemp[t] or disrepute" any "persons, living or dead." 15 U.S.C. § 1052(a). We now hold that this provision violates the Free Speech Clause of the First Amendment. It offends a bedrock First Amendment principle: Speech may not be banned on the ground that it expresses ideas that offend.

I

A

"The principle underlying trademark protection is that distinctive marks—words, names, symbols, and the like—can help distinguish a particular artisan's goods from those of others." A trademark "designate[s] the goods as the product of a particular trader" and "protect[s] his good will against the sale of another's product as his." It helps consumers identify goods and services that they wish to purchase, as well as those they want to avoid.

"[F]ederal law does not create trademarks." Trademarks and their precursors have ancient origins, and trademarks were protected at common law and in equity at the time of the founding of our country. For most of the 19th century, trademark protection was the province of the States. Eventually, Congress stepped in to provide a degree of national uniformity, passing the first federal legislation protecting trademarks in 1870. The foundation of current federal trademark law is the Lanham Act, enacted in 1946. By that time, trademark had expanded far beyond phrases that do no more than identify a good or service. Then, as now, trademarks often consisted of catchy phrases that convey a message.

Under the Lanham Act, trademarks that are "used in commerce" may be placed on the "principal register," that is, they may be federally registered . . . . There are now more than two million marks that have active federal certificates of registration . . . .

B

Without federal registration, a valid trademark may still be used in commerce. And an unregistered trademark can be enforced against would-be infringers in several ways . . . . Federal registration, however, "confers important legal rights and benefits on trademark owners who register their marks." . . .

C

The Lanham Act contains provisions that bar certain trademarks from the principal register. For example, a trademark cannot be registered if it is "merely descriptive or deceptively misdescriptive" of goods, or if it is so similar to an already registered trademark or trade name that it is "likely . . . to cause confusion, or to cause mistake, or to deceive."

At issue in this case is one such provision, which we will call "the disparagement clause." This provision prohibits the registration of a trademark "which may disparage . . . persons, living or dead, institutions, beliefs, or national symbols, or bring them into contempt, or disrepute." This clause appeared in the original Lanham Act and has remained the same to this day.

When deciding whether a trademark is disparaging, an examiner at the PTO generally applies a "two-part test." The examiner first considers "the likely meaning of the matter in question, taking into account not only dictionary definitions, but also the relationship of the matter to the other elements in the mark, the nature of the goods or services, and the manner in which the mark is used in the marketplace in connection with the goods or services." "If that meaning is found to refer to identifiable persons, institutions, beliefs or national symbols," the examiner moves to the second step, asking "whether that meaning may be disparaging to a substantial composite of the referenced group." If the examiner finds that a "substantial composite, although not necessarily a majority, of the referenced group would find the proposed mark . . . to be disparaging in the context of contemporary attitudes," a prima facie case of disparagement is made out, and the burden shifts to the applicant to prove that the trademark is not disparaging. What is more, the PTO has specified that "[t]he fact that an applicant may be a member of that group or has good intentions underlying its use of a term does not obviate the fact that a substantial composite of the referenced group would find the term objectionable."

D

Simon Tam is the lead singer of "The Slants." He chose this moniker in order to "reclaim" and "take ownership" of stereotypes about people of Asian ethnicity. The group "draws inspiration for its lyrics from childhood slurs and mocking nursery rhymes" and has given its albums names such as "The Yellow Album" and "Slanted Eyes, Slanted Hearts."

Tam sought federal registration of "THE SLANTS," on the principal register, but an examining attorney at the PTO rejected the request, applying the PTO's two-part framework and finding that "there is . . . a substantial composite of persons who find the term in the applied-for mark offensive." The examining attorney relied in part on the fact that "numerous dictionaries define 'slants' or 'slant-eyes' as a derogatory or offensive term." The examining attorney also relied on a finding that "the band's name has been found offensive numerous times"—citing a performance that was canceled because of the band's moniker and the fact that "several bloggers and commenters to articles on the band have indicated that they find the term and the applied-for mark offensive."

Tam contested the denial of registration before the examining attorney and before the PTO's Trademark Trial and Appeal Board (TTAB) but to no avail. Eventually, he took the case to federal court, where the en banc Federal Circuit ultimately found the disparagement clause facially unconstitutional under the First Amendment's Free Speech Clause. . . .

The Government filed a petition for certiorari, which we granted in order to decide whether the disparagement clause "is facially invalid under the Free Speech Clause of the First Amendment."

II

Before reaching the question whether the disparagement clause violates the First Amendment, we consider Tam's argument that the clause does not reach marks that disparage racial or ethnic groups. The clause prohibits the registration of marks that disparage "persons," and Tam claims that the term "persons" "includes only natural and juristic persons," not "non-juristic entities such as racial and ethnic groups." [The Court rejected this argument.]

III

Because the disparagement clause applies to marks that disparage the members of a racial or ethnic group, we must decide whether the clause violates the Free Speech Clause of the First Amendment. And at the outset, we must consider three arguments that would either eliminate any First Amendment protection or result in highly permissive rational-basis review. Specifically, the Government contends (1) that trademarks are government speech, not private speech, (2) that trademarks are a form of government subsidy, and (3) that the constitutionality of the disparagement clause should be tested under a new "government-program" doctrine. We address each of these arguments below.

A

The First Amendment prohibits Congress and other government entities and actors from "abridging the freedom of speech"; the First Amendment does not say that Congress and other government entities must abridge their own ability to speak freely. And our cases recognize that "[t]he Free Speech Clause . . . does not regulate government speech." *Pleasant Grove City v. Summum*, 555 U.S. 460 (2009) [Note *supra* Chapter 13]; *see Johanns v. Livestock Marketing Assn.*, 544 U.S. 550 (2005) [Note *supra* Chapter 13] ("[T]he Government's own speech . . . is exempt from First Amendment scrutiny").

As we have said, "it is not easy to imagine how government could function" if it were subject to the restrictions that the First Amendment imposes on private speech. *Summum; see Walker v. Texas Div., Sons of Confederate Veterans, Inc.* (2015) [*supra* Chapter 13]. "'[T]he First Amendment forbids the government to regulate speech in ways that favor some viewpoints or ideas at the expense of others,'" but imposing a requirement of viewpoint-neutrality on government speech would be paralyzing. When a government entity embarks on a course of action, it necessarily takes a particular viewpoint and rejects others. The Free Speech Clause does not require government to maintain viewpoint neutrality when its officers and employees speak about that venture.

Here is a simple example. During the Second World War, the Federal Government produced and distributed millions of posters to promote the war effort. There were posters urging enlistment, the purchase of war bonds, and the conservation of scarce resources. These posters expressed a viewpoint, but the First Amendment did not demand that the Government balance the message of these posters by producing and distributing posters encouraging Americans to refrain from engaging in these activities.

But while the government-speech doctrine is important—indeed, essential—it is a doctrine that is susceptible to dangerous misuse. If private speech could be passed off as government speech by simply affixing a government seal of approval, government could silence or muffle the expression of disfavored viewpoints. For this reason, we must exercise great caution before extending our government-speech precedents.

At issue here is the content of trademarks that are registered by the PTO, an arm of the Federal Government. The Federal Government does not dream up these marks, and it does not edit marks submitted for registration. Except as required by the statute involved here, an examiner may not reject a mark based on the viewpoint that it appears to express. Thus, unless that section is thought to apply, an examiner does not inquire whether any viewpoint conveyed by a mark is consistent with Government policy or whether any such viewpoint is consistent with that expressed by other marks already on the principal register. Instead, if the mark meets the Lanham Act's viewpoint-neutral requirements, registration is mandatory. . . .

In light of all this, it is far-fetched to suggest that the content of a registered mark is government speech. If the federal registration of a trademark makes the mark government speech, the Federal Government is babbling prodigiously and incoherently. It is saying many unseemly things. It is expressing contradictory views.[9] It is unashamedly endorsing a vast array of commercial products and services. And it is providing Delphic advice to the consuming public. . . .

The PTO has made it clear that registration does not constitute approval of a mark. *See In re Old Glory Condom Corp.*, 26 USPQ 2d 1216 (TTAB 1993) ("[I]ssuance of a trademark registration . . . is not a government imprimatur"). And it is unlikely that

---

9. Compare "Abolish Abortion," Registration No. 4,935,774 (Apr. 12, 2016), with "I Stand With Planned Parenthood," Registration No. 5,073,573 (Nov. 1, 2016); compare "Capitalism Is Not Moral, Not Fair, Not Freedom," Registration No. 4,696,419 (Mar. 3, 2015), with "Capitalism Ensuring Innovation," Registration No. 3,966,092 (May 24, 2011); compare "Global Warming Is Good," Registration No. 4,776,235 (July 21, 2015), with "A Solution to Global Warming," Registration No. 3,875,271 (Nov. 10, 2010).

more than a tiny fraction of the public has any idea what federal registration of a trademark means.

None of our government speech cases even remotely supports the idea that registered trademarks are government speech. In *Johanns,* we considered advertisements promoting the sale of beef products. A federal statute called for the creation of a program of paid advertising "'to advance the image and desirability of beef and beef products.'" Congress and the Secretary of Agriculture provided guidelines for the content of the ads, Department of Agriculture officials attended the meetings at which the content of specific ads was discussed, and the Secretary could edit or reject any proposed ad. Noting that "[t]he message set out in the beef promotions [was] from beginning to end the message established by the Federal Government," we held that the ads were government speech. The Government's involvement in the creation of these beef ads bears no resemblance to anything that occurs when a trademark is registered.

Our decision in *Summum* is similarly far afield. A small city park contained 15 monuments. Eleven had been donated by private groups, and one of these displayed the Ten Commandments. A religious group claimed that the city, by accepting donated monuments, had created a limited public forum for private speech and was therefore obligated to place in the park a monument expressing the group's religious beliefs.

Holding that the monuments in the park represented government speech, we cited many factors. Governments have used monuments to speak to the public since ancient times; parks have traditionally been selective in accepting and displaying donated monuments; parks would be overrun if they were obligated to accept all monuments offered by private groups; "[p]ublic parks are often closely identified in the public mind with the government unit that owns the land"; and "[t]he monuments that are accepted . . . are meant to convey and have the effect of conveying a government message."

Trademarks share none of these characteristics. Trademarks have not traditionally been used to convey a Government message. With the exception of the enforcement of 15 U.S.C. § 1052(a), the viewpoint expressed by a mark has not played a role in the decision whether to place it on the principal register. And there is no evidence that the public associates the contents of trademarks with the Federal Government.

This brings us to the case on which the Government relies most heavily, *Walker,* which likely marks the outer bounds of the government-speech doctrine. Holding that the messages on Texas specialty license plates are government speech, the *Walker* Court cited three factors distilled from *Summum.* First, license plates have long been used by the States to convey state messages. Second, license plates "are often closely identified in the public mind" with the State, since they are manufactured and owned by the State, generally designed by the State, and serve as a form of "government ID." Third, Texas "maintain[ed] direct control over the messages conveyed on its specialty plates." As explained above, none of these factors are present in this case.

In sum, the federal registration of trademarks is vastly different from the beef ads in *Johanns,* the monuments in *Summum,* and even the specialty license plates in *Walker.*

Holding that the registration of a trademark converts the mark into government speech would constitute a huge and dangerous extension of the government-speech doctrine. For if the registration of trademarks constituted government speech, other systems of government registration could easily be characterized in the same way. . . .

Trademarks are private, not government, speech.

B

We next address the Government's argument that this case is governed by cases in which this Court has upheld the constitutionality of government programs that subsidized speech expressing a particular viewpoint. These cases implicate a notoriously tricky question of constitutional law. "[W]e have held that the Government 'may not deny a benefit to a person on a basis that infringes his constitutionally protected . . . freedom of speech even if he has no entitlement to that benefit.'" *Agency for Int'l Development v. Alliance for Open Society Int'l, Inc.* (2013) [*supra* Chapter 13]. But at the same time, government is not required to subsidize activities that it does not wish to promote. Determining which of these principles applies in a particular case "is not always self-evident," *id.*, but no difficult question is presented here.

Unlike the present case, the decisions on which the Government relies all involved cash subsidies or their equivalent. In *Rust v. Sullivan* (1991) [*supra* Chapter 13], a federal law provided funds to private parties for family planning services. In *National Endowment for Arts v. Finley*, 524 U.S. 569 (1998), cash grants were awarded to artists. And federal funding for public libraries was at issue in *United States v. American Library Assn., Inc.*, 539 U.S. 194 (2003). In other cases, we have regarded tax benefits as comparable to cash subsidies.

The federal registration of a trademark is nothing like the programs at issue in these cases. The PTO does not pay money to parties seeking registration of a mark. Quite the contrary is true: An applicant for registration must pay the PTO a filing fee of $225–$600. . . .

The Government responds that registration provides valuable non-monetary benefits that "are directly traceable to the resources devoted by the federal government to examining, publishing, and issuing certificates of registration for those marks." But just about every government service requires the expenditure of government funds. This is true of services that benefit everyone, like police and fire protection, as well as services that are utilized by only some, *e.g.*, the adjudication of private lawsuits and the use of public parks and highways. . . .

Cases like *Rust* and *Finley* are not instructive in analyzing the constitutionality of restrictions on speech imposed in connection with such services.

C

Finally, the Government urges us to sustain the disparagement clause under a new doctrine that would apply to "government-program" cases. For the most part, this argument simply merges our government-speech cases and the previously discussed subsidy cases in an attempt to construct a broader doctrine that can be applied to the registration of trademarks. The only new element in this construct consists of two cases involving a public employer's collection of union dues from its employees. But those cases occupy a special area of First Amendment case law, and they are far removed from the registration of trademarks. . . .

Potentially more analogous are cases in which a unit of government creates a limited public forum for private speech. *See, e.g., Rosenberger v. Rector and Visitors of Univ. of Va.*, 515 U.S. 819 (1995) [Note *supra* Chapter 8]. When government creates such a forum, in either a literal or "metaphysical" sense, see *Rosenberger*, some content- and speaker-based restrictions may be allowed. However, even in such cases, what we have termed "viewpoint discrimination" is forbidden.

Our cases use the term "viewpoint" discrimination in a broad sense, see *ibid.*, and in that sense, the disparagement clause discriminates on the bases of "viewpoint." To be sure, the clause evenhandedly prohibits disparagement of all groups. It applies equally to marks that damn Democrats and Republicans, capitalists and socialists, and those arrayed on both sides of every possible issue. It denies registration to any mark that is offensive to a substantial percentage of the members of any group. But in the sense relevant here, that is viewpoint discrimination: Giving offense is a viewpoint.

We have said time and again that "the public expression of ideas may not be prohibited merely because the ideas are themselves offensive to some of their hearers."

For this reason, the disparagement clause cannot be saved by analyzing it as a type of government program in which some content- and speaker-based restrictions are permitted.

IV

Having concluded that the disparagement clause cannot be sustained under our government-speech or subsidy cases or under the Government's proposed "government-program" doctrine, we must confront a dispute between the parties on the question whether trademarks are commercial speech and are thus subject to the relaxed scrutiny outlined in *Central Hudson Gas & Elec. Corp. v. Public Serv. Comm'n of N.Y.* (1980) [*supra* Chapter 3]. The Government and *amici* supporting its position argue that all trademarks are commercial speech. They note that the central purposes of trademarks are commercial and that federal law regulates trademarks to promote fair and orderly interstate commerce. Tam and his *amici*, on the other hand, contend that many, if not all, trademarks have an expressive component. In other words, these trademarks do not simply identify the source of a product or service but go on to say something more, either about the product or service or some broader issue. The trademark in this case illustrates this point. The name "The Slants" not only identifies the band but expresses a view about social issues.

We need not resolve this debate between the parties because the disparagement clause cannot withstand even *Central Hudson* review. Under *Central Hudson*, a restriction of speech must serve "a substantial interest," and it must be "narrowly drawn." This means, among other things, that "[t]he regulatory technique may extend only as far as the interest it serves." The disparagement clause fails this requirement.

It is claimed that the disparagement clause serves two interests. The first is phrased in a variety of ways in the briefs. Echoing language in one of the opinions below, the Government asserts an interest in preventing "'underrepresented groups'" from being "'bombarded with demeaning messages in commercial advertising.'" An *amicus* supporting the Government refers to "encouraging racial tolerance and protecting the privacy and welfare of individuals." But no matter how the point is phrased, its unmistakable thrust is this: The Government has an interest in preventing speech expressing ideas that offend. And, as we have explained, that idea strikes at the heart of the First Amendment. Speech that demeans on the basis of race, ethnicity, gender, religion, age, disability, or any other similar ground is hateful; but the proudest boast of our free speech jurisprudence is that we protect the freedom to express "the thought that we hate." *United States v. Schwimmer* (1929) (Holmes, J., dissenting) [*supra* Chapter 1].

The second interest asserted is protecting the orderly flow of commerce. Commerce, we are told, is disrupted by trademarks that "involv[e] disparagement of race, gender, ethnicity, national origin, religion, sexual orientation, and similar demographic classification." Such trademarks are analogized to discriminatory conduct, which has been recognized to have an adverse effect on commerce.

A simple answer to this argument is that the disparagement clause is not "narrowly drawn" to drive out trademarks that support invidious discrimination. The clause reaches any trademark that disparages *any person, group, or institution*. It applies to trademarks like the following: "Down with racists," "Down with sexists," "Down with homophobes." It is not an anti-discrimination clause; it is a happy-talk clause. In this way, it goes much further than is necessary to serve the interest asserted.

The clause is far too broad in other ways as well. The clause protects every person living or dead as well as every institution. Is it conceivable that commerce would be disrupted by a trademark saying: "James Buchanan was a disastrous president" or "Slavery is an evil institution"?

There is also a deeper problem with the argument that commercial speech may be cleansed of any expression likely to cause offense. The commercial market is well stocked with merchandise that disparages prominent figures and groups, and the line between commercial and non-commercial speech is not always clear, as this case illustrates. If affixing the commercial label permits the suppression of any speech that may lead to political or social "volatility," free speech would be endangered.

* * *

For these reasons, we hold that the disparagement clause violates the Free Speech Clause of the First Amendment. The judgment of the Federal Circuit is affirmed.

JUSTICE GORSUCH took no part in the consideration or decision of this case.

JUSTICE KENNEDY, with whom JUSTICE GINSBURG, JUSTICE SOTOMAYOR, and JUSTICE KAGAN join, concurring in part and concurring in the judgment.

The Patent and Trademark Office (PTO) has denied the substantial benefits of federal trademark registration to the mark THE SLANTS. The PTO did so under the mandate of the disparagement clause in 15 U.S.C. § 1052(a), which prohibits the registration of marks that may "disparage . . . or bring . . . into contemp[t] or disrepute" any "persons, living or dead, institutions, beliefs, or national symbols."

As the Court is correct to hold, § 1052(a) constitutes viewpoint discrimination — a form of speech suppression so potent that it must be subject to rigorous constitutional scrutiny. The Government's action and the statute on which it is based cannot survive this scrutiny.

The Court is correct in its judgment, and I join Parts I, II, and III-A of its opinion. This separate writing explains in greater detail why the First Amendment's protections against viewpoint discrimination apply to the trademark here. It submits further that the viewpoint discrimination rationale renders unnecessary any extended treatment of other questions raised by the parties.

I

Those few categories of speech that the government can regulate or punish — for instance, fraud, defamation, or incitement — are well established within our constitutional tradition. *See United States v. Stevens* (2010) [*supra* Chapter 3]. Aside from these and a few other narrow exceptions, it is a fundamental principle of the First Amendment that the government may not punish or suppress speech based on disapproval of the ideas or perspectives the speech conveys. *See Rosenberger*.

The First Amendment guards against laws "targeted at specific subject matter," a form of speech suppression known as content based discrimination. *Reed v. Town of Gilbert* (2015) [*supra* Chapter 5]. This category includes a subtype of laws that go further, aimed at the suppression of "particular views . . . on a subject." *Rosenberger*. A law found to discriminate based on viewpoint is an "egregious form of content discrimination," which is "presumptively unconstitutional." *Id.*

At its most basic, the test for viewpoint discrimination is whether — within the relevant subject category — the government has singled out a subset of messages for disfavor based on the views expressed. In the instant case, the disparagement clause the Government now seeks to implement and enforce identifies the relevant subject as "persons, living or dead, institutions, beliefs, or national symbols." 15 U.S.C. § 1052(a). Within that category, an applicant may register a positive or benign mark but not a derogatory one. The law thus reflects the Government's disapproval of a subset of messages it finds offensive. This is the essence of viewpoint discrimination.

The Government disputes this conclusion. It argues, to begin with, that the law is viewpoint neutral because it applies in equal measure to any trademark that demeans or offends. This misses the point. A subject that is first defined by content and then regulated or censored by mandating only one sort of comment is not viewpoint neutral. To prohibit all sides from criticizing their opponents makes a law more viewpoint based, not less so. The logic of the Government's rule is that a law would be viewpoint neutral even if it provided that public officials could be praised but not condemned. The First Amendment's viewpoint neutrality principle protects more than the right to identify with a particular side. It protects the right to create and present arguments for particular positions in particular ways, as the speaker chooses. By mandating positivity, the law here might silence dissent and distort the marketplace of ideas.

The Government next suggests that the statute is viewpoint neutral because the disparagement clause applies to trademarks regardless of the applicant's personal views or reasons for using the mark. Instead, registration is denied based on the expected reaction of the applicant's audience. In this way, the argument goes, it cannot be said that Government is acting with hostility toward a particular point of view. For example, the Government does not dispute that respondent seeks to use his mark in a positive way. Indeed, respondent endeavors to use The Slants to supplant a racial epithet, using new insights, musical talents, and wry humor to make it a badge of pride. Respondent's application was denied not because the Government thought his object was to demean or offend but because the Government thought his trademark would have that effect on at least some Asian-Americans.

The Government may not insulate a law from charges of viewpoint discrimination by tying censorship to the reaction of the speaker's audience. The Court has suggested that viewpoint discrimination occurs when the government intends to suppress a speaker's beliefs, *Reed*, but viewpoint discrimination need not take that form in every instance. The danger of viewpoint discrimination is that the government is attempting to remove certain ideas or perspectives from a broader debate. That danger is all the greater if the ideas or perspectives are ones a particular audience might think offensive, at least at first hearing. An initial reaction may prompt further reflection, leading to a more reasoned, more tolerant position.

Indeed, a speech burden based on audience reactions is simply government hostility and intervention in a different guise. The speech is targeted, after all, based on the government's disapproval of the speaker's choice of message. And it is the government itself that is attempting in this case to decide whether the relevant audience would find the speech offensive. For reasons like these, the Court's cases have long prohibited the government from justifying a First Amendment burden by pointing to the offensiveness of the speech to be suppressed.

The Government's argument in defense of the statute assumes that respondent's mark is a negative comment. In addressing that argument on its own terms, this opinion is not intended to imply that the Government's interpretation is accurate. From respondent's submissions, it is evident he would disagree that his mark means what the Government says it does. The trademark will have the effect, respondent urges, of reclaiming an offensive term for the positive purpose of celebrating all that Asian-Americans can and do contribute to our diverse Nation. While thoughtful persons can agree or disagree with this approach, the dissonance between the trademark's potential to teach and the Government's insistence on its own, opposite, and negative interpretation confirms the constitutional vice of the statute.

II

The parties dispute whether trademarks are commercial speech and whether trademark registration should be considered a federal subsidy. The former issue may turn on whether certain commercial concerns for the protection of trademarks might, as a general matter, be the basis for regulation. However that issue is resolved, the viewpoint based discrimination at issue here necessarily invokes heightened scrutiny.

"Commercial speech is no exception," the Court has explained, to the principle that the First Amendment "requires heightened scrutiny whenever the government creates a regulation of speech because of disagreement with the message it conveys." *Sorrell v. IMS Health Inc.*, 564 U.S. 552 (2011) [Note *supra* Chapter 3]. Unlike content based discrimination, discrimination based on viewpoint, including a regulation that targets speech for its offensiveness, remains of serious concern in the commercial context.

To the extent trademarks qualify as commercial speech, they are an example of why that term or category does not serve as a blanket exemption from the First Amendment's requirement of viewpoint neutrality. Justice Holmes' reference to the "free trade in ideas" and the "power of . . . thought to get itself accepted in the competition of the market," *Abrams v. United States* (1919) (dissenting opinion) [*supra* Chapter 1], was a metaphor. In the realm of trademarks, the metaphorical marketplace of ideas becomes a tangible, powerful reality. Here that real marketplace exists as a matter of state law and our common-law tradition, quite without regard to the Federal Government. These marks make up part of the expression of everyday life, as with the names of entertainment groups, broadcast networks, designer clothing, newspapers, automobiles, candy bars, toys, and so on. . . . To permit viewpoint discrimination in this context is to permit Government censorship. . . .

It is telling that the Court's precedents have recognized just one narrow situation in which viewpoint discrimination is permissible: where the government itself is speaking or recruiting others to communicate a message on its behalf. The exception is necessary to allow the government to stake out positions and pursue policies. But it is also narrow, to prevent the government from claiming that every government program is exempt from the First Amendment. These cases have identified a number of factors that, if present, suggest the government is speaking on its own behalf; but none are present here.

There may be situations where private speakers are selected for a government program to assist the government in advancing a particular message. That is not this case either. The central purpose of trademark registration is to facilitate source identification. To serve that broad purpose, the Government has provided the benefits of federal registration to millions of marks identifying every type of product and cause. Registered trademarks do so by means of a wide diversity of words, symbols, and messages. Whether a mark is disparaging bears no plausible relation to that goal. While defining the purpose and scope of a federal program for these purposes can be complex, see, *e.g.*, *Agency for Int'l Development*, our cases are clear that viewpoint discrimination is not permitted where, as here, the Government "expends funds to encourage a diversity of views from private speakers."

* * *

A law that can be directed against speech found offensive to some portion of the public can be turned against minority and dissenting views to the detriment of all. The First Amendment does not entrust that power to the government's benevolence. Instead, our reliance must be on the substantial safeguards of free and open discussion in a democratic society.

For these reasons, I join the Court's opinion in part and concur in the judgment.

Justice Thomas, concurring in part and concurring in the judgment. [Omitted.]

Note: The Implications of Matal

1. *Matal* illustrates an important fact: government action — here, the registering of trademarks under federal trademark law — can be understood in vastly different ways, with different implications for First Amendment analysis. As *Matal* vividly demonstrates, First Amendment problems — like legal problems more generally — often do not come wrapped in doctrinally neat packages.

2. Consider the Court's government speech analysis. The Court strongly suggests that *Walker v. Sons of Confederate Veterans* marks the outer boundary of the government speech doctrine. On the one hand, this suggestion might not be surprising, since it was written by Justice Alito, who wrote the dissent in *Walker*. But note also that this part of the opinion was unanimous (except for Justice Gorsuch, who had not yet joined the Court when the case was argued). What does *Matal* suggest about the current state of the government speech doctrine?

3. Recall Chapter 8's discussion of the Court's analysis of content- and viewpoint-based laws. Does either of the excerpted *Matal* opinions add to the law governing the definition of viewpoint neutrality?

4. The plurality states: "Giving offense is a viewpoint" and that the disparagement clause "is a happy-talk clause." But the plurality makes no mention of *R.A.V. v. City of St. Paul* (*supra* this chapter). Was that case relevant? The concurring opinion cites *Reed v. Town of Gilbert* (*supra* Chapter 5), but the plurality does not. Do those cases shed light on the issue raised by *Matal*?

C. The Internet as the New Public Square?

Packingham v. North Carolina

137 S. Ct. 1730 (2017)

Justice Kennedy delivered the opinion of the Court.

In 2008, North Carolina enacted a statute making it a felony for a registered sex offender to gain access to a number of websites, including commonplace social media websites like Facebook and Twitter. The question presented is whether that law is permissible under the First Amendment's Free Speech Clause, applicable to the States under the Due Process Clause of the Fourteenth Amendment.

I

A

North Carolina law makes it a felony for a registered sex offender "to access a commercial social networking Web site where the sex offender knows that the site permits minor children to become members or to create or maintain personal Web pages." N.C. Gen. Stat. Ann. § 14-202.5. A "commercial social networking Web site" is defined as a website that meets four criteria. First, it "[i]s operated by a person who derives revenue from membership fees, advertising, or other sources related to the operation of the Web site." Second, it "[f]acilitates the social introduction between two or more persons for the purposes of friendship, meeting other persons, or information exchanges." Third, it "[a]llows users to create Web pages or personal profiles that contain information such as the name or nickname of the user, photographs placed on the personal Web page by the user, other personal information about the user, and links to other personal Web pages on the commercial social networking Web site of friends or associates of the user that may be accessed by other users or visitors to the Web site." And fourth, it "[p]rovides users or visitors . . . mechanisms to communicate with other users, such as a message board, chat room, electronic mail, or instant messenger."

The statute includes two express exemptions. The statutory bar does not extend to websites that "[p]rovid[e] only one of the following discrete services: photo-sharing, electronic mail, instant messenger, or chat room or message board platform." The law also does not encompass websites that have as their "primary purpose the facilitation of commercial transactions involving goods or services between [their] members or visitors."

According to sources cited to the Court, § 14-202.5 applies to about 20,000 people in North Carolina and the State has prosecuted over 1,000 people for violating it.

B

In 2002, petitioner Lester Gerard Packingham—then a 21-year-old college student—had sex with a 13-year-old girl. He pleaded guilty to taking indecent liberties with a child. Because this crime qualifies as "an offense against a minor," petitioner was required to register as a sex offender—a status that can endure for 30 years or more. As a registered sex offender, petitioner was barred under § 14–202.5 from gaining access to commercial social networking sites.

In 2010, a state court dismissed a traffic ticket against petitioner. In response, he logged on to Facebook.com and posted the following statement on his personal profile:

> "Man God is Good! How about I got so much favor they dismissed the ticket before court even started? No fine, no court cost, no nothing spent. . . . Praise be to GOD, WOW! Thanks JESUS!" . . . .

Petitioner was indicted by a grand jury for violating § 14-202.5. The trial court denied his motion to dismiss the indictment on the grounds that the charge against him violated the First Amendment. Petitioner was ultimately convicted and given a suspended prison sentence. At no point during trial or sentencing did the State allege that petitioner contacted a minor — or committed any other illicit act — on the Internet.

Petitioner appealed to the Court of Appeals of North Carolina. That court struck down § 14-202.5 on First Amendment grounds, explaining that the law is not narrowly tailored to serve the State's legitimate interest in protecting minors from sexual abuse. . . . The North Carolina Supreme Court reversed, concluding that the law is "constitutional in all respects." Among other things, the court explained that the law is "carefully tailored . . . to prohibit registered sex offenders from accessing only those Web sites that allow them the opportunity to gather information about minors." The court also held that the law leaves open adequate alternative means of communication because it permits petitioner to gain access to websites that the court believed perform the "same or similar" functions as social media, such as the Paula Deen Network and the website for the local NBC affiliate. . . .

II

A fundamental principle of the First Amendment is that all persons have access to places where they can speak and listen, and then, after reflection, speak and listen once more. The Court has sought to protect the right to speak in this spatial context. A basic rule, for example, is that a street or a park is a quintessential forum for the exercise of First Amendment rights. *See Ward v. Rock Against Racism* (1989) [*supra* Chapter 6]. Even in the modern era, these places are still essential venues for public gatherings to celebrate some views, to protest others, or simply to learn and inquire.

While in the past there may have been difficulty in identifying the most important places (in a spatial sense) for the exchange of views, today the answer is clear. It is cyberspace — the "vast democratic forums of the Internet" in general, *Reno v. American Civil Liberties Union*, 521 U.S. 844 (1997), and social media in particular. Seven in ten American adults use at least one Internet social networking service. One of the most popular of these sites is Facebook, the site used by petitioner leading to his conviction in this case. According to sources cited to the Court in this case, Facebook has 1.79 billion active users. This is about three times the population of North America.

Social media offers "relatively unlimited, low-cost capacity for communication of all kinds." *Reno.* On Facebook, for example, users can debate religion and politics with their friends and neighbors or share vacation photos. On LinkedIn, users can look for work, advertise for employees, or review tips on entrepreneurship. And on Twitter, users can petition their elected representatives and otherwise engage with them in a direct manner. Indeed, Governors in all 50 States and almost every Member of Congress have set up accounts for this purpose. In short, social media users employ these websites to engage in a wide array of protected First Amendment activity on topics "as diverse as human thought." *Reno.*

The nature of a revolution in thought can be that, in its early stages, even its participants may be unaware of it. And when awareness comes, they still may be unable to know or foresee where its changes lead. . . . While we now may be coming to the realization that the Cyber Age is a revolution of historic proportions, we cannot appreciate yet its full dimensions and vast potential to alter how we think, express ourselves, and define who we want to be. The forces and directions of the Internet are so new, so protean, and so far reaching that courts must be conscious that what they say today might be obsolete tomorrow.

This case is one of the first this Court has taken to address the relationship between the First Amendment and the modern Internet. As a result, the Court must exercise extreme caution before suggesting that the First Amendment provides scant protection for access to vast networks in that medium.

III

This background informs the analysis of the North Carolina statute at issue. Even making the assumption that the statute is content neutral and thus subject to intermediate scrutiny, the provision cannot stand. In order to survive intermediate scrutiny, a law must be "narrowly tailored to serve a significant governmental interest." *McCullen v. Coakley* (2014) [*supra* Chapter 6]. In other words, the law must not "burden substantially more speech than is necessary to further the government's legitimate interests." *Id.*

For centuries now, inventions heralded as advances in human progress have been exploited by the criminal mind. New technologies, all too soon, can become instruments used to commit serious crimes. The railroad is one example, see M. CRICHTON, THE GREAT TRAIN ROBBERY at xv (1975), and the telephone another. So it will be with the Internet and social media.

There is also no doubt that, as this Court has recognized, "[t]he sexual abuse of a child is a most serious crime and an act repugnant to the moral instincts of a decent people." *Ashcroft v. Free Speech Coalition* (2002) [*supra* Chapter 3]. And it is clear that a legislature "may pass valid laws to protect children" and other victims of sexual assault "from abuse." *See id.*; *accord New York v. Ferber* (1982) [*supra* Chapter 3]. The government, of course, need not simply stand by and allow these evils to occur. But the assertion of a valid governmental interest "cannot, in every context, be insulated from all constitutional protections." *Stanley v. Georgia* (1969) [*supra* Chapter 2].

It is necessary to make two assumptions to resolve this case. First, given the broad wording of the North Carolina statute at issue, it might well bar access not only to commonplace social media websites but also to websites as varied as Amazon.com, Washingtonpost.com, and Webmd.com. The Court need not decide the precise scope of the statute. It is enough to assume that the law applies (as the State concedes it does) to social networking sites "as commonly understood"—that is, websites like Facebook, LinkedIn, and Twitter.

Second, this opinion should not be interpreted as barring a State from enacting more specific laws than the one at issue. Specific criminal acts are not protected speech even if speech is the means for their commission. *See Brandenburg v. Ohio* (1969) [*supra* Chapter 1]. Though the issue is not before the Court, it can be assumed that the First Amendment permits a State to enact specific, narrowly tailored laws that prohibit a sex offender from engaging in conduct that often presages a sexual crime, like contacting a minor or using a website to gather information about a minor. . . .

Even with these assumptions about the scope of the law and the State's interest, the statute here enacts a prohibition unprecedented in the scope of First Amendment speech it burdens. Social media allows users to gain access to information and communicate with one another about it on any subject that might come to mind. By prohibiting sex offenders from using those websites, North Carolina with one broad stroke bars access to what for many are the principal sources for knowing current events, checking ads for employment, speaking and listening in the modern public square, and otherwise exploring the vast realms of human thought and knowledge. These websites can provide perhaps the most powerful mechanisms available to a private citizen to make his or her voice heard. They allow a person with an Internet connection to "become a town crier with a voice that resonates farther than it could from any soapbox." *Reno*.

In sum, to foreclose access to social media altogether is to prevent the user from engaging in the legitimate exercise of First Amendment rights. It is unsettling to suggest that only a limited set of websites can be used even by persons who have completed their sentences. Even convicted criminals—and in some instances especially convicted criminals—might receive legitimate benefits from these means for access to the world of ideas, in particular if they seek to reform and to pursue lawful and rewarding lives.

IV

The primary response from the State is that the law must be this broad to serve its preventative purpose of keeping convicted sex offenders away from vulnerable victims. The State has not, however, met its burden to show that this sweeping law is necessary or legitimate to serve that purpose. *See McCullen*. . . .

* * *

It is well established that, as a general rule, the Government "may not suppress lawful speech as the means to suppress unlawful speech." *Ashcroft v. Free Speech Coalition* [*supra* Chapter 3]. That is what North Carolina has done here. Its law must be held invalid.

The judgment of the North Carolina Supreme Court is reversed, and the case is remanded for further proceedings not inconsistent with this opinion.

JUSTICE GORSUCH took no part in the consideration or decision of this case.

ALITO, J., with whom THE CHIEF JUSTICE and JUSTICE THOMAS join, concurring in the judgment.

The North Carolina statute at issue in this case was enacted to serve an interest of "surpassing importance." *New York v. Ferber* (1982) [*supra* Chapter 3]—but it has a staggering reach. It makes it a felony for a registered sex offender simply to visit a vast array of websites, including many that appear to provide no realistic opportunity for communications that could facilitate the abuse of children. Because of the law's extraordinary breadth, I agree with the Court that it violates the Free Speech Clause of the First Amendment.

I cannot join the opinion of the Court, however, because of its undisciplined dicta. The Court is unable to resist musings that seem to equate the entirety of the internet with public streets and parks. And this language is bound to be interpreted by some to mean that the States are largely powerless to restrict even the most dangerous sexual predators from visiting any internet sites, including, for example, teenage dating sites and sites designed to permit minors to discuss personal problems with their peers. I am troubled by the implications of the Court's unnecessary rhetoric.

I

A

. . . Packingham and the State debate the analytical framework that governs this case. The State argues that the law in question is content neutral and merely regulates a "place" (i.e., the internet) where convicted sex offenders may wish to engage in speech. Therefore, according to the State, the standard applicable to "time, place, or manner" restrictions should apply. *See Ward v. Rock Against Racism* (1989) [*supra* Chapter 6]. Packingham responds that the challenged statute is "unlike any law this Court has considered as a time, place, or manner restriction," and he advocates a more demanding standard of review.

Like the Court, I find it unnecessary to resolve this dispute because the law in question cannot satisfy the standard applicable to a content-neutral regulation of the place where speech may occur.

B

A content-neutral "time, place, or manner" restriction must serve a "legitimate" government interest, *Ward*, and the North Carolina law easily satisfies this requirement. As we have frequently noted, "[t]he prevention of sexual exploitation and abuse of children constitutes a government objective of surpassing importance." *Ferber* . . . .

Repeat sex offenders pose an especially grave risk to children. "When convicted sex offenders reenter society, they are much more likely than any other type of offender to be rearrested for a new rape or sexual assault."

The State's interest in protecting children from recidivist sex offenders plainly applies to internet use. Several factors make the internet a powerful tool for the would-be child abuser. First, children often use the internet in a way that gives offenders easy access to their personal information—by, for example, communicating with strangers and allowing sites to disclose their location. Second, the internet provides previously unavailable ways of communicating with, stalking, and ultimately abusing children. An abuser can create a false profile that misrepresents the abuser's age and gender. The abuser can lure the minor into engaging in sexual conversations, sending explicit photos, or even meeting in person. And an abuser can use a child's location posts on the internet to determine the pattern of the child's day-to-day activities—and even the child's location at a given moment. Such uses of the internet are already well documented, both in research and in reported decisions.

Because protecting children from abuse is a compelling state interest and sex offenders can (and do) use the internet to engage in such abuse, it is legitimate and entirely reasonable for States to try to stop abuse from occurring before it happens.

C

1

It is not enough, however, that the law before us is designed to serve a compelling state interest; it also must not "burden substantially more speech than is necessary to further the government's legitimate interests." *Ward*; *see also McCullen v. Coakley* (2014) [*supra* Chapter 6]. The North Carolina law fails this requirement.

A straightforward reading of the text of § 14-202.5 compels the conclusion that it prohibits sex offenders from accessing an enormous number of websites. The law defines a "commercial social networking Web site" as one with four characteristics. First, the website must be "operated by a person who derives revenue from membership fees, advertising, or other sources related to the operation of the Web site." Due to the prevalence of advertising on websites of all types, this requirement does little to limit the statute's reach.

Second, the website must "[f]acilitat[e] the social introduction between two or more persons for the purposes of friendship, meeting other persons, or information exchanges." The term "social introduction" easily encompasses any casual exchange, and the term "information exchanges" seems to apply to any site that provides an opportunity for a visitor to post a statement or comment that may be read by other visitors. Today, a great many websites include this feature.

Third, a website must "[a]llo[w] users to create Web pages or personal profiles that contain information *such as* the name or nickname of the user, photographs placed on the personal Web page by the user, other personal information about the user, and links to other personal Web pages on the commercial social networking Web site of friends or associates of the user that may be accessed by other users or visitors to the Web site." This definition covers websites that allow users to create anything that can be called a "personal profile," i.e., a short description of the user. Contrary to the argument of the State, everything that follows the phrase "such as" is an illustration of features that a covered website or personal profile may (but need not) include.

Fourth, in order to fit within the statute, a website must "[p]rovid[e] users or visitors . . . mechanisms to communicate with other users, *such as* a message board, chat room, electronic mail, or instant messenger." This requirement seems to demand no more than that a website allow back-and-forth comments between users. And since a comment function is undoubtedly a "mechanis[m] to communicate with other users," it appears to follow that any website with such a function satisfies this requirement.

2

The fatal problem for § 14-202.5 is that its wide sweep precludes access to a large number of websites that are most unlikely to facilitate the commission of a sex crime against a child. A handful of examples illustrates this point.

Take, for example, the popular retail website Amazon.com, which allows minors to use its services and meets all four requirements of § 14–202.5's definition of a commercial social networking website. . . . Many news websites are also covered by this definition. For example, the Washington Post's website gives minors access and satisfies the four elements that define a commercial social networking website. . . . Or consider WebMD — a website that contains health-related resources, from tools that help users find a doctor to information on preventative care and the symptoms associated with particular medical problems. WebMD, too, allows children on the site. And it exhibits the four hallmarks of a "commercial social networking" website. . . .

As these examples illustrate, the North Carolina law has a very broad reach and covers websites that are ill suited for use in stalking or abusing children. The focus of the discussion on these sites — shopping, news, health — does not provide a convenient jumping off point for conversations that may lead to abuse. In addition, the social exchanges facilitated by these websites occur in the open, and this reduces the possibility of a child being secretly lured into an abusive situation. These websites also give sex offenders little opportunity to gather personal details about a child; the information that can be listed in a profile is limited, and the profiles are brief. What is more, none of these websites make it easy to determine a child's precise location at a given moment. For example, they do not permit photo streams (at most, a child could upload a single profile photograph), and they do not include up-to-the minute location services. Such websites would provide essentially no aid to a would-be child abuser.

Placing this set of websites categorically off limits from registered sex offenders prohibits them from receiving or engaging in speech that the First Amendment protects and does not appreciably advance the State's goal of protecting children from recidivist sex offenders. I am therefore compelled to conclude that, while the law before us addresses a critical problem, it sweeps far too broadly to satisfy the demands of the Free Speech Clause.[15]

II

While I thus agree with the Court that the particular law at issue in this case violates the First Amendment, I am troubled by the Court's loose rhetoric. After noting that "a street or a park is a quintessential forum for the exercise of First Amendment rights," the Court states that "cyberspace" and "social media in particular" are now "the most important places (in a spatial sense) for the exchange of views." The Court declines to explain what this means with respect to free speech law, and the Court holds no more than that the North Carolina law fails the test for content-neutral "time,

---

15. I express no view on whether a law that does not reach the sort of sites discussed above would satisfy the First Amendment. Until such a law is before us, it is premature to address that question.

place, and manner" restrictions. But if the entirety of the internet or even just "social media" sites are the 21st century equivalent of public streets and parks, then States may have little ability to restrict the sites that may be visited by even the most dangerous sex offenders. May a State preclude an adult previously convicted of molesting children from visiting a dating site for teenagers? Or a site where minors communicate with each other about personal problems? The Court should be more attentive to the implications of its rhetoric for, contrary to the Court's suggestion, there are important differences between cyberspace and the physical world.

I will mention a few that are relevant to internet use by sex offenders. First, it is easier for parents to monitor the physical locations that their children visit and the individuals with whom they speak in person than it is to monitor their internet use. Second, if a sex offender is seen approaching children or loitering in a place frequented by children, this conduct may be observed by parents, teachers, or others. Third, the internet offers an unprecedented degree of anonymity and easily permits a would-be molester to assume a false identity.

The Court is correct that we should be cautious in applying our free speech precedents to the internet. Cyberspace is different from the physical world, and if it is true, as the Court believes, that "we cannot appreciate yet" the "full dimensions and vast potential" of "the Cyber Age," we should proceed circumspectly, taking one step at a time. It is regrettable that the Court has not heeded its own admonition of caution.

Note: The Internet as the New Public Forum?

1. After discussing traditional public forums, Justice Kennedy's majority opinion states that "[w]hile in the past there may have been difficulty in identifying the most important place (in a spatial sense) for the exchange of views, today the answer is clear. It is cyberspace. . . ." Does this mean that the Court intends to apply the entire public forum doctrine to the Internet? What are the differences between the Internet and traditional public forums such as streets and parks? What implications should those differences have for First Amendment doctrine?

2. Both Justice Kennedy and Justice Alito agree that, given the novelty of the Internet, the Court should "exercise extreme caution" or "be cautious" in deciding how to apply existing First Amendment precedents to the Internet. Yet their need for caution drives them in opposite directions regarding how to apply the First Amendment to the Internet. What are the differences between them? And where do they stem from?

3. Justice Alito, in his opinion concurring in the judgment, emphasizes that the North Carolina statute is not narrowly tailored because it reaches websites such as Amazon.com, the Washington Post, and Web MD, which are not easily misused by child molesters. Therefore, he refuses to decide whether a more tailored law, which reached only true social media sites such as Facebook and Twitter, would be constitutional. But is it so clear that the North Carolina statute *does* cover sites such as Amazon and the Washington Post? After all, in common parlance few would describe those sites as "social networking" sites.

4. The majority and the concurrence in *Packingham* obviously have very different views of the relationship between technology and First Amendment protections. The majority sees the power of the Internet as a cause for celebration, while the concurrence sees it as a cause for caution. Who is right?

Problem: Net Neutrality

Over the last several years, concerns have grown that Internet Service Providers ("ISPs"), such as Verizon, Comcast, and Time-Warner Cable, have imposed restrictions on the speed with which some online content can be accessed by end users. Complaints have been raised that ISPs have imposed these restrictions in order to drive traffic to the ISP's own websites (for example, an ISP's own news website), or to allow the ISP to extract payments from website owners as a condition of receiving favorable end-user access.

In response to these complaints, the Federal Communications Commission ("FCC") is considering promulgating administrative regulations colloquially known as "net neutrality" rules. Boiled down, those regulations would mandate that ISPs not discriminate between different websites with regard to the ease with which an end user can access a given site.

As an FCC lawyer, you are given two tasks. First, you are asked to identify the factual conclusions that the agency would need to make in order to buttress the agency's argument that its rules not only survive First Amendment scrutiny but do not even implicate the First Amendment. Second, you are asked to suggest limitations on the types of ISPs subject to the net neutrality requirement that would help ensure that a court concludes that the regulations in fact do not implicate the First Amendment.

As part of your assignment, you are given the following pieces of information.

- Some ISPs produce their own content, in addition to simply transmitting the content of other websites. For example, Time-Warner Cable provides its own news websites.

- Some ISPs feature filtering software that blocks certain content (*e.g.*, sexually oriented websites).

- The record developed by the agency reveals that the technology of modern broadband communications is such that there are no technological limits to the amount of content an ISP can transmit over its network.

What factual conclusions about ISPs and end users would help immunize the proposed regulation from First Amendment scrutiny? What limitations to the scope of that regulation would help accomplish the same task?

Problem: Posts on a Commissioner's Facebook Page

When Julie Johnson was elected to the Board of Commissioners of San Fernando County, she set up a new Facebook page that she called "San Fernando Commissioner Johnson." In the "about" section of the page's profile, she wrote that "This page is for constructive, civil communications (comments, questions, and suggestions) between

San Fernando Commissioner Julie Johnson and her constituents regarding any aspect of San Fernando County government. Commissioner Johnson invites all constituents to participate!"

Dave Dengel, one of Johnson's constituents, is deeply dissatisfied with the San Fernando County government, and he makes his displeasure clear on Johnson's Facebook page described above. In a series of comments, he accuses the commissioners of "covering up for corrupt administrators," "feathering their own beds," and "misusing County tax dollars," and asks "Commissioner Johnson, why won't you come clean about all the dirt you're spreading around San Fernando County Hall?" Several of his posts identify particular administrators and commissioners by name (including but not limited to Johnson) as among those engaging in the misconduct he alleges.

After Dengel posts these messages, Commissioner Johnson blocks Dengel from posting on the page. (Blocking prevents the blocked user from posting on or privately communicating with the page, but the user remains able to view and share contact from that page.) After she blocks him, she posts the following statement on the page: "This is just a reminder that this page is designed for CONSTRUCTIVE and CIVIL comments. Let's work together to make this page a forum that works for everyone!"

Upon trying to post to Johnson's page and receiving a message from Facebook that the creator of that page has blocked him from posting, Dengel sues, alleging that Johnson has violated his right to free speech. Assume that Johnson's conduct constitutes "state action"—that is, assume that the First Amendment applies. What result?

Suppose instead that Johnson blocks Dengel from posting, then posts the statement noted above ("This is just a reminder that this page is designed for CONSTRUCTIVE and CIVIL comments. Let's work together to make this page a forum that works for everyone!"), and then posts a lengthy policy that defines "constructive" and "civil" so as to exclude "profanity, personal attacks, and unsubstantiated rumor or innuendo." Does that change the result?

Suppose instead that Johnson responds to Dengel's posts by simply turning off the comments feature of her page for everyone, making it a vehicle only for one-way communication from her to anyone who follows her. Does that change the result?

Part Two

Freedom of Religion

Chapter 16

The History and Purposes of the Religion Clauses

The First Amendment to the Constitution of the United States contains two provisions that deal with religion. The "Establishment Clause" and the "Free Exercise Clause"—known together as the Religion Clauses—provide: "Congress shall make no law respecting an establishment of religion or prohibiting the free exercise thereof." The Religion Clauses have generated an enormous amount of litigation challenging governmental actions that in some way affect religious institutions or practices. Typically, a governmental action that is viewed as benefiting religion is challenged under the Establishment Clause; a governmental action that burdens or disfavors religion gives rise to a "free exercise" claim. This litigation has in turn produced a body of precedent that is as controversial and complex as any in constitutional law. Many issues have been settled, but to a surprising degree, there is a continuing debate over some of the most basic questions. In the chapters that follow, we will consider the law of the Religion Clauses—each clause individually, then the two clauses together.

This chapter takes an historical view of the Religion Clauses through the eyes and minds of the Justices who have sought to understand the history of the clauses in order to interpret them true to their origins and purposes. That history is contested, however; different Justices have examined the history of the framing of the Bill of Rights to reach different conclusions about the purposes behind the clauses. Their differing understandings of history yield different constitutional analyses with distinct emphases which, in turn, lead the Justices to reach different conclusions on the same facts. To understand the arguments and doctrines, one has to appreciate this underlying debate. This debate over origins and purposes is not limited to so-called "originalists." Indeed, when it comes to the Religion Clauses, all the Justices agree that the lessons of history are critical—even when they cannot agree on what those lessons reveal. The Religion Clauses ultimately must be reconciled with our past and our present. The following opinions sample the ongoing interpretative debate among the Justices over the history and purposes of the Religion Clauses.

A. The Debate over the Original Understanding

Consider the following three opinions *seriatim*. First, Justice Black articulates the Jeffersonian "wall of separation" exegesis on the history of the Religion Clauses.

Second, Justice Rehnquist offers his critique of Black and Jefferson in favor of a non-preferentialist approach among religions that would allow government to favor religion over irreligion — which he insists is what the framers really intended. Third, Justice Souter joins issue with Justice Rehnquist to reassert the historical case for maintaining a high and impregnable "wall of separation" between church and state.

Who has the better arguments from history? Which approach is best for our contemporary times? What explains the disagreements among the Justices? Are they relying on different sources of meaning? Are they relying on different views among the Framers? Are they bringing their own different views to the process of interpretation?

Everson v. Board of Education

330 U.S. 1 (1947)

[A New Jersey statute authorized local school districts to pay for the transportation of children to and from school, and the township's board of education authorized reimbursement to parents for bus transportation. A taxpayer brought suit to challenge the reimbursements to parents of children who rode public transportation to attend Catholic parochial schools. In a 5 to 4 decision, the Court upheld the reimbursement. The case will be considered in the next chapter. Here is the historical analysis from Justice Black's majority opinion.]

MR. JUSTICE BLACK delivered the opinion of the Court.

. . . The First Amendment, as made applicable to the states by the Fourteenth, commands that a state "shall make no law respecting an establishment of religion, or prohibiting the free exercise thereof. . . ." These words of the First Amendment reflected in the minds of early Americans a vivid mental picture of conditions and practices which they fervently wished to stamp out in order to preserve liberty for themselves and for their posterity. Doubtless their goal has not been entirely reached; but so far has the Nation moved toward it that the expression "law respecting an establishment of religion," probably does not so vividly remind present-day Americans of the evils, fears, and political problems that caused that expression to be written into our Bill of Rights. Whether this New Jersey law is one respecting an "establishment of religion" requires an understanding of the meaning of that language, particularly with respect to the imposition of taxes. [Therefore,] it is not inappropriate briefly to review the background and environment of the period in which that constitutional language was fashioned and adopted.

A large proportion of the early settlers of this country came here from Europe to escape the bondage of laws which compelled them to support and attend government favored churches. The centuries immediately before and contemporaneous with the colonization of America had been filled with turmoil, civil strife, and persecutions, generated in large part by established sects determined to maintain their absolute political and religious supremacy. With the power of government supporting them, at various times and places, Catholics had persecuted Protestants, Protestants had persecuted Catholics, Protestant sects had persecuted other Protestant sects, Catholics of one shade of belief had persecuted Catholics of another shade of belief, and all of these had from time to time persecuted Jews. In efforts to force loyalty to whatever religious group happened to be on top and in league with the government of a particular time and place, men and women had been fined, cast in jail, cruelly tortured, and killed. Among the offenses for which these punishments had been inflicted were such things as speaking disrespectfully of the views of ministers of government-established churches, nonattendance at those churches, expressions of non-belief in their doctrines, and failure to pay taxes and tithes to support them.

These practices of the old world were transplanted to and began to thrive in the soil of the new America. The very charters granted by the English Crown . . . authorized these individuals and companies to erect religious establishments which all, whether believers or non-believers, would be required to support and attend. An exercise of this authority was accompanied by a repetition of many of the old-world practices and persecutions. Catholics found themselves hounded and proscribed because of their faith; Quakers who followed their conscience went to jail; Baptists were peculiarly obnoxious to certain dominant Protestant sects; men and women of varied faiths who happened to be in a minority in a particular locality were persecuted because they steadfastly persisted in worshipping God only as their own consciences dictated. And all of these dissenters were compelled to pay tithes and taxes to support government-sponsored churches whose ministers preached inflammatory sermons designed to strengthen and consolidate the established faith by generating a burning hatred against dissenters.

These practices became so commonplace as to shock the freedom-loving colonials into a feeling of abhorrence. The imposition of taxes to pay ministers' salaries and to build and maintain churches and church property aroused their indignation. It was these feelings which found expression in the First Amendment. No one locality and no one group throughout the Colonies can rightly be given entire credit for having aroused the sentiment that culminated in adoption of the Bill of Rights' provisions embracing religious liberty. But Virginia, where the established church had achieved a dominant influence in political affairs and where many excesses attracted wide public attention, provided a great stimulus and able leadership for the movement. The people there, as elsewhere, reached the conviction that individual religious liberty could be achieved best under a government which was stripped of all power to tax, to support, or otherwise to assist any or all religions, or to interfere with the beliefs of any religious individual or group.

The movement toward this end reached its dramatic climax in Virginia in 1785–86 when the Virginia legislative body was about to renew Virginia's tax levy for the support of the established church. Thomas Jefferson and James Madison led the fight against this tax. Madison wrote his great Memorial and Remonstrance against the law. In it, he eloquently argued that a true religion did not need the support of law; that no person, either believer or non-believer, should be taxed to support a religious institution of any kind; that the best interest of a society required that the minds of men always be wholly free; and that cruel persecutions were the inevitable result of government-established religions. Madison's Remonstrance received strong support throughout Virginia, and the Assembly postponed consideration of the proposed tax measure until its next session. When the proposal came up for consideration at that session, it not only died in committee, but the Assembly enacted the famous "Virginia Bill for Religious Liberty" originally written by Thomas Jefferson. The preamble to that Bill stated among other things that

> Almighty God hath created the mind free; that all attempts to influence it by temporal punishments, or burthens, or by civil incapacitations, tend only to beget habits of hypocrisy and meanness, and are a departure from the plan of the Holy author of our religion, who being Lord both of body and mind, yet chose not to propagate it by coercions on either . . . ; that to compel a man to furnish contributions of money for the propagation of opinions which he disbelieves, is sinful and tyrannical; that even the forcing him to support this or that teacher of his own religious persuasion, is depriving him of the comfortable liberty of giving his contributions to the particular pastor, whose morals he would make his pattern. . . .

And the statute itself enacted

> That no man shall be compelled to frequent or support any religious worship, place, or ministry whatsoever, nor shall be enforced, restrained, molested, or burthened in his body or goods, nor shall otherwise suffer on account of his religious opinions or belief. . . .

[The] First Amendment, in the drafting and adoption of which Madison and Jefferson played such leading roles, had the same objective and were intended to provide the same protection against governmental intrusion on religious liberty as the Virginia statute. Prior to the adoption of the Fourteenth Amendment, the First Amendment did not apply as a restraint against the states. Most of them did soon provide similar constitutional protections for religious liberty. But some states persisted for about half a century in imposing restraints upon the free exercise of religion and in discriminating against particular religious groups. . . .

The "establishment of religion" clause of the First Amendment means at least this: Neither a state nor the Federal Government can set up a church. Neither can pass laws which aid one religion, aid all religions, or prefer one religion over another. Neither can force nor influence a person to go to or to remain away from church against his will or force him to profess a belief or disbelief in any religion. No person can be punished for entertaining or professing religious beliefs or disbeliefs, for church attendance or non-attendance. No tax in any amount, large or small, can be levied to support any religious activities or institutions, whatever they may be called, or whatever form they may adopt to teach or practice religion. Neither a state nor the Federal Government can, openly or secretly, participate in the affairs of any religious organizations or groups and vice versa. In the words of Jefferson, the clause against establishment of religion by law was intended to erect "a wall of separation between church and State." *Reynolds v. United States* (1878) [Chapter 18]. . . .

Wallace v. Jaffree
472 U.S. 38 (1985)

[In a 5 to 4 decision, the Court held that a state law authorizing a one-minute period of silence in all public schools "for meditation or voluntary prayer" violated the Establishment Clause. The case will be considered in the next chapter. Here is the historical analysis from then–Justice Rehnquist's dissenting opinion.]

JUSTICE REHNQUIST, dissenting.

Thirty-eight years ago this Court, in *Everson v. Board of Education* (1947) [*supra* this chapter], summarized its exegesis of Establishment Clause doctrine thus: "In the words of Jefferson, the clause against establishment of religion by law was intended to erect 'a wall of separation between church and State.' *Reynolds v. United States* (1878) [Chapter 18]."

This language from *Reynolds*, a case involving the Free Exercise Clause of the First Amendment rather than the Establishment Clause, quoted from Thomas Jefferson's letter to the Danbury Baptist Association. . . . It is impossible to build sound constitutional doctrine upon a mistaken understanding of constitutional history, but unfortunately the Establishment Clause has been expressly freighted with Jefferson's misleading metaphor for nearly 40 years. Thomas Jefferson was of course in France at the time the constitutional Amendments known as the Bill of Rights were passed by Congress and ratified by the States. His letter to the Danbury Baptist Association was a short note of courtesy, written 14 years after the Amendments were passed by Congress. He would seem to any detached observer as a less than ideal source of contemporary history as to the meaning of the Religion Clauses of the First Amendment.

Jefferson's fellow Virginian, James Madison, with whom he was joined in the battle for the enactment of the Virginia Statute of Religious Liberty of 1786, did play as large a part as anyone in the drafting of the Bill of Rights. He . . . was present in the United States, and he was a leading Member of the First Congress. But when we turn to the record of the proceedings in the First Congress leading up to the adoption of the Establishment Clause of the Constitution, including Madison's significant contributions thereto, we see a far different picture of its purpose than the highly simplified "wall of separation between church and State."

During the debates in the Thirteen Colonies over ratification of the Constitution, one of the arguments frequently used by opponents of ratification was that without a Bill of Rights guaranteeing individual liberty the new general Government carried with it a potential for tyranny. The typical response to this argument on the part of those who favored ratification was that the general Government established by the Constitution had only delegated powers, and that these delegated powers were so limited that the Government would have no occasion to violate individual liberties. This response satisfied some, but not others, and of the 11 Colonies which ratified the Constitution by early 1789, 5 proposed one or another amendments guaranteeing individual liberty. Three — New Hampshire, New York, and Virginia — included in one form or another a declaration of religious freedom. . . .

On June 8, 1789, James Madison's . . . remarks in urging the House to adopt his drafts of the proposed amendments were less those of a dedicated advocate of the wisdom of such measures than those of a prudent statesman seeking the enactment of measures sought by a number of his fellow citizens which could surely do no harm and might do a great deal of good. . . . The language Madison proposed for what ultimately became the Religion Clauses of the First Amendment was this: "The civil rights of none shall be abridged on account of religious belief or worship, nor shall any national religion be established, nor shall the full and equal rights of conscience be in any manner, or on any pretext, infringed."

On the same day that Madison proposed them, the amendments which formed the basis for the Bill of Rights were referred by the House to a Committee of the Whole, and after several weeks' delay were then referred to a Select Committee consisting of Madison and 10 others. The Committee revised Madison's proposal regarding the establishment of religion to read: "[N]o religion shall be established by law, nor shall the equal rights of conscience be infringed." The Committee's proposed revisions were debated in the House on August 15, 1789. The entire debate on the Religion Clauses is contained in two full columns of the "Annals," and does not seem particularly illuminating. . . .

Madison . . . said that "he apprehended the meaning of the words to be, that Congress should not establish a religion, and enforce the legal observation of it by law, nor compel men to worship God in any manner contrary to their conscience." He said that some of the state conventions had thought that Congress might rely on the Necessary and Proper Clause to infringe the rights of conscience or to establish a national religion, and "to prevent these effects he presumed the amendment was intended, and he thought it as well expressed as the nature of the language would admit."

Representative Benjamin Huntington . . . hoped that "the amendment would be made in such a way as to secure the rights of conscience, and a free exercise of the rights of religion, but not to patronise those who professed no religion at all."

Madison responded that the insertion of the word "national" before the word "religion" in the Committee version should satisfy the minds of those who had criticized the language. . . . Representative Samuel Livermore expressed himself as dissatisfied with Madison's proposed amendment, and thought it would be better if the Committee language were altered to read that "Congress shall make no laws touching religion, or infringing the rights of conscience."

Representative Gerry spoke in opposition to the use of the word "national" because of strong feelings expressed during the ratification debates that a federal government, not a national government, was created by the Constitution. Madison thereby withdrew his proposal. . . . The question was taken on Representative Livermore's motion, which passed by a vote of 31 for and 20 against.

The following week, without any apparent debate, the House voted to alter the language of the Religion Clauses to read "Congress shall make no law establishing religion, or to prevent the free exercise thereof, or to infringe the rights of conscience."

The floor debates in the Senate were secret, and therefore not reported in the Annals. The Senate on September 3, 1789, considered several different forms of the Religion Amendment, and reported this language back to the House: "Congress shall make no law establishing articles of faith or a mode of worship, or prohibiting the free exercise of religion."

The House refused to accept the Senate's changes in the Bill of Rights and asked for a conference; the version which emerged from the conference was that which ultimately found its way into the Constitution as a part of the First Amendment. "Congress shall make no law respecting an establishment of religion, or prohibiting the free exercise thereof." The House and the Senate both accepted this language on successive days, and the Amendment was proposed in this form.

. . . James Madison was undoubtedly the most important architect among the Members of the House of the Amendments which became the Bill of Rights, but it was James Madison speaking as an advocate of sensible legislative compromise, not as an advocate of incorporating the Virginia Statute of Religious Liberty into the United States Constitution. During the ratification debate in the Virginia Convention, Madison had actually opposed the idea of any Bill of Rights. His sponsorship of the Amendments in the House was obviously not that of a zealous believer in the necessity of the Religion Clauses, but of one who felt it might do some good, could do no harm, and would satisfy those who had ratified the Constitution on the condition that Congress propose a Bill of Rights. . . .

It seems indisputable from these glimpses of Madison's thinking, as reflected by actions on the floor of the House in 1789, that he saw the Amendment as designed to prohibit the establishment of a national religion, and perhaps to prevent discrimination among sects. He did not see it as requiring neutrality on the part of government between religion and irreligion. . . .

None of the other Members of Congress who spoke during the . . . debate expressed the slightest indication that they thought the language before them . . . or the evil to be aimed at, would require that the Government be absolutely neutral as between religion and irreligion. The evil to be aimed at, so far as those who spoke were concerned, appears to have been the establishment of a national church, and perhaps the preference of one religious sect over another; but it was definitely not concerned about whether the Government might aid all religions evenhandedly. . . . [One] would have to say that the First Amendment Establishment Clause should be read no more broadly than to prevent the establishment of a national religion or the governmental preference of one religious sect over another.

The actions of the First Congress, which reenacted the Northwest Ordinance for the governance of the Northwest Territory in 1789, confirm the view that Congress did not mean that the Government should be neutral between religion and irreligion. The House of Representatives took up the Northwest Ordinance on the same day as Madison introduced his proposed amendments which became the Bill of Rights. . . . The Northwest Ordinance . . . provided that "[r]eligion, morality, and knowledge, being necessary to good government and the happiness of mankind, schools and the means of education shall forever be encouraged." Land grants for schools in the Northwest Territory were not limited to public schools. . . .

On the day after the House of Representatives voted to adopt the form of the First Amendment Religion Clauses which was ultimately proposed and ratified, Representative Elias Boudinot proposed a resolution asking President George Washington to issue a Thanksgiving Day Proclamation. . . . Washington responded to the Joint Resolution . . . that the President "recommend to the people of the United States a day of public thanksgiving and prayer, to be observed by acknowledging with grateful hearts the many and signal favors of Almighty God, especially by affording them an opportunity peaceably to establish a form of government for their safety and happiness." . . .

George Washington, John Adams, and James Madison all issued Thanksgiving Proclamations; Thomas Jefferson did not, saying:

> Fasting and prayer are religious exercises; the enjoining them an act of discipline. Every religious society has a right to determine for itself the times for these exercises, and the objects proper for them, according to their own particular tenets; and this right can never be safer than in their own hands, where the Constitution has deposited it.

As the United States moved from the 18th into the 19th century, Congress appropriated time and again public moneys in support of sectarian Indian education carried on by religious organizations. . . . This history shows the fallacy of the notion found in *Everson* that "no tax in any amount" may be levied for religious activities in any form. . . . [Here Justice Rehnquist quoted extensively from the two leading nineteenth-century treatises on the Constitution written by Justice Joseph Story and Professor Thomas Cooley.]

It would seem from this evidence that the Establishment Clause of the First Amendment had acquired a well-accepted meaning: it forbade establishment of a national religion, and forbade preference among religious sects or denominations. Indeed, the first American dictionary defined the word "establishment" as "the act of establishing, founding, ratifying or ordaining," such as in "[t]he episcopal form of religion, so called, in England." 1 N. WEBSTER, AMERICAN DICTIONARY OF THE ENGLISH LANGUAGE (1st ed. 1828). The Establishment Clause did not require government neutrality between religion and irreligion nor did it prohibit the Federal Government from providing nondiscriminatory aid to religion. There is simply no historical foundation for the proposition that the Framers intended to build the "wall of separation" that was constitutionalized in *Everson*. . . .

Whether due to its lack of historical support or its practical unworkability, the *Everson* "wall" has proved all but useless as a guide to sound constitutional adjudication. It illustrates only too well the wisdom of Benjamin Cardozo's observation that "[m]etaphors in law are to be narrowly watched, for starting as devices to liberate thought, they end often by enslaving it." But the greatest injury of the "wall" notion is its mischievous diversion of judges from the actual intentions of the drafters of the

Bill of Rights. . . . [No] amount of repetition of historical errors in judicial opinions can make the errors true. The "wall of separation between church and State" is a metaphor based on bad history, a metaphor which has proved useless as a guide to judging. It should be frankly and explicitly abandoned. . . .

Lee v. Weisman

505 U.S. 577 (1992)

[In a 5 to 4 decision, the Court held that inviting a member of the clergy to offer a prayer at an official public school graduation ceremony violated the Establishment Clause. The case will be considered in the next chapter. Here is the historical analysis from Justice Souter's concurring opinion.]

JUSTICE SOUTER, with whom JUSTICE STEVENS and JUSTICE O'CONNOR join, concurring.

. . . Forty-five years ago, this Court announced a basic principle of constitutional law from which it has not strayed: the Establishment Clause forbids not only state practices that "aid one religion . . . or prefer one religion over another," but also those that "aid all religions." *Everson v. Board of Ed.* (1947) [*supra* this chapter]. Today we reaffirm that principle. . . . [We] hold true to a line of precedent from which there is no adequate historical case to depart. . . .

Some have challenged this precedent by reading the Establishment Clause to permit "nonpreferential" state promotion of religion. The challengers argue that, as originally understood by the Framers, "[t]he Establishment Clause did not require government neutrality between religion and irreligion nor did it prohibit the Federal Government from providing nondiscriminatory aid to religion." *Wallace v. Jaffree* (1985) (Rehnquist, J., dissenting) [*supra* this chapter]. While a case has been made for this position, it is not so convincing as to warrant reconsideration of our settled law; indeed, I find in the history of the Clause's textual development a more powerful argument supporting the Court's jurisprudence following *Everson*.

When James Madison arrived at the First Congress with a series of proposals to amend the National Constitution, one of the provisions read that "[t]he civil rights of none shall be abridged on account of religious belief or worship, nor shall any national religion be established, nor shall the full and equal rights of conscience be in any manner, or on any pretext, infringed." Madison's language did not last long. It was sent to a Select Committee of the House, which, without explanation, changed it to read that "no religion shall be established by law, nor shall the equal rights of conscience be infringed." Thence the proposal went to the Committee of the Whole, which was in turn dissatisfied with the Select Committee's language and adopted an alternative proposed by Samuel Livermore of New Hampshire: "Congress shall make no laws touching religion, or infringing the rights of conscience." Livermore's proposal would have forbidden laws having anything to do with religion and was thus not only far broader than Madison's version, but broader even than the scope of the Establishment Clause as we now understand it.

The House rewrote the amendment once more before sending it to the Senate, this time adopting, without recorded debate, language derived from a proposal by Fisher Ames of Massachusetts: "Congress shall make no law establishing Religion, or prohibiting the free exercise thereof, nor shall the rights of conscience be infringed." . . . [The] House rejected the Select Committee's version, which arguably ensured only that "no religion" enjoyed an official preference over others, and deliberately chose instead a prohibition extending to laws establishing "religion" in general.

The sequence of the Senate's treatment of this House proposal, and the House's response to the Senate, confirm that the Framers meant the Establishment Clause's prohibition to encompass nonpreferential aid to religion. In September 1789, the Senate considered a number of provisions that would have permitted such aid, and ultimately it adopted one of them. First, it briefly entertained this language: "Congress shall make no law establishing One Religious Sect or Society in preference to others, nor shall the rights of conscience be infringed." After rejecting two minor amendments to that proposal, the Senate dropped it altogether and chose a provision identical to the House's proposal, but without the clause protecting the "rights of conscience." With no record of the Senate debates, we cannot know what prompted these changes, but the record does tell us that, six days later, the Senate went half circle and adopted its narrowest language yet: "Congress shall make no law establishing articles of faith or a mode of worship, or prohibiting the free exercise of religion." The Senate sent this proposal to the House along with its versions of the other constitutional amendments proposed.

Though it accepted much of the Senate's work on the Bill of Rights, the House rejected the Senate's version of the Establishment Clause and called for a joint conference committee, to which the Senate agreed. The House conferees ultimately won out, persuading the Senate to accept this as the final text of the Religion Clauses: "Congress shall make no law respecting an establishment of religion, or prohibiting the free exercise thereof." What is remarkable is that, unlike the earliest House drafts or the final Senate proposal, the prevailing language is not limited to laws respecting an establishment of "a religion," "a national religion," "one religious sect," or specific "articles of faith."[2] The Framers repeatedly considered and deliberately rejected such narrow language and instead extended their prohibition to state support for "religion" in general.

Implicit in their choice is the distinction between preferential and nonpreferential establishments, which the weight of evidence suggests the Framers appreciated. Of particular note, the Framers were vividly familiar with efforts in the Colonies and,

---

2. Some commentators have suggested that by targeting laws respecting "an" establishment of religion, the Framers adopted the very nonpreferentialist position whose much clearer articulation they repeatedly rejected. Yet the indefinite article before the word "establishment" is better seen as evidence that the Clause forbids any kind of establishment, including a nonpreferential one. If the Framers had wished, for some reason, to use the indefinite term to achieve a narrow meaning for the Clause, they could far more aptly have placed it before the word "religion." See Laycock, *"Nonpreferential" Aid to Religion: A False Claim About Original Intent*, 27 WM. & MARY L. REV. 875 (1986).

later, the States to impose general, nondenominational assessments and other incidents of ostensibly ecumenical establishments. The Virginia statute for religious freedom, written by Jefferson and sponsored by Madison, captured the separationist response to such measures. Condemning all establishments, however nonpreferentialist, the statute broadly guaranteed that "no man shall be compelled to frequent or support any religious worship, place, or ministry whatsoever," including his own. Forcing a citizen to support even his own church would, among other things, deny "the ministry those temporary rewards, which proceeding from an approbation of their personal conduct, are an additional incitement to earnest and unremitting labours for the instruction of mankind." In general, Madison later added, "religion & Govt. will both exist in greater purity, the less they are mixed together." *Letter from J. Madison to E. Livingston* (July 10, 1822).

What we thus know of the Framers' experience underscores the observation of one prominent commentator, that confining the Establishment Clause to a prohibition on preferential aid "requires a premise that the Framers were extraordinarily bad drafters—that they believed one thing but adopted language that said something substantially different, and that they did so after repeatedly attending to the choice of language." Laycock, *"Nonpreferential" Aid*. We must presume, since there is no conclusive evidence to the contrary, that the Framers embraced the significance of their textual judgment. Thus, on balance, history neither contradicts nor warrants reconsideration of the settled principle that the Establishment Clause forbids support for religion in general no less than support for one religion or some. . . .

Like the provisions about "due" process and "unreasonable" searches and seizures, the constitutional language forbidding laws "respecting an establishment of religion" is not pellucid. But virtually everyone acknowledges that the Clause bans more than formal establishments of religion in the traditional sense, that is, massive state support for religion through, among other means, comprehensive schemes of taxation. This much follows from the Framers' explicit rejection of simpler provisions prohibiting either the establishment of a religion or laws "establishing religion" in favor of the broader ban on laws "respecting an establishment of religion." . . .

Petitioners [defending the nondenominational but theistic prayers recited at the public high school graduation] argue from the political setting in which the Establishment Clause was framed, and from the Framers' own political practices following ratification, that government may constitutionally endorse religion so long as it does not coerce religious conformity. The setting and the practices warrant canvassing, but while they yield some evidence for petitioners' argument, they do not reveal the degree of consensus in early constitutional thought that would raise a threat to *stare decisis* by challenging the presumption that the Establishment Clause adds something to the Free Exercise Clause that follows it.

The Framers adopted the Religion Clauses in response to a long tradition of coercive state support for religion, particularly in the form of tax assessments, but their special antipathy to religious coercion did not exhaust their hostility to the features and incidents of establishment. Indeed, Jefferson and Madison opposed any political appropriation of religion, and, even when challenging the hated assessments, they did not always temper their rhetoric with distinctions between coercive and noncoercive state action. When, for example, Madison criticized Virginia's general assessment bill, he invoked principles antithetical to all state efforts to promote religion. An assessment, he wrote, is improper not simply because it forces people to donate "three pence" to religion, but, more broadly, because "it is itself a signal of persecution. It degrades from the equal rank of Citizens all those whose opinions in Religion do not bend to those of the Legislative authority." J. MADISON, MEMORIAL AND REMONSTRANCE AGAINST RELIGIOUS ASSESSMENTS (1785). Madison saw that, even without the tax collector's participation, an official endorsement of religion can impair religious liberty.

Petitioners contend that because the early Presidents included religious messages in their inaugural and Thanksgiving Day addresses, the Framers could not have meant the Establishment Clause to forbid noncoercive state endorsement of religion. The argument ignores the fact, however, that Americans today find such proclamations less controversial than did the founding generation, whose published thoughts on the matter belie petitioners' claim. President Jefferson, for example, steadfastly refused to issue Thanksgiving proclamations of any kind, in part because he thought they violated the Religion Clauses. *Letter from Thomas Jefferson to Rev. S. Miller* (Jan. 23, 1808). In explaining his views to the Reverend Samuel Miller, Jefferson effectively anticipated, and rejected, petitioners' position:

> It is only proposed that I should *recommend*, not prescribe a day of fasting & prayer. That is, that I should *indirectly* assume to the U.S. an authority over religious exercises which the Constitution has directly precluded from them. It must be meant too that this recommendation is to carry some authority, and to be sanctioned by some penalty on those who disregard it; not indeed of fine and imprisonment, but of some degree of proscription perhaps in public opinion.

By condemning such noncoercive state practices that, in "recommending" the majority faith, demean religious dissenters "in public opinion," Jefferson necessarily condemned what, in modern terms, we call official endorsement of religion. He accordingly construed the Establishment Clause to forbid not simply state coercion, but also state endorsement, of religious belief and observance. And if he opposed impersonal Presidential addresses for inflicting "proscription in public opinion," all the more would he have condemned less diffuse expressions of official endorsement.

During his first three years in office, James Madison also refused to call for days of thanksgiving and prayer, though later, amid the political turmoil of the War of 1812, he did so on four separate occasions. Upon retirement, in an essay condemning as an unconstitutional "establishment" the use of public money to support congressional and military chaplains, he concluded that "[r]eligious proclamations by the Executive recommending thanksgivings & fasts are shoots from the same root with the legislative acts reviewed. Altho' recommendations only, they imply a religious agency, making no part of the trust delegated to political rulers." Explaining that "[t]he members of a Govt . . . can in no sense, be regarded as possessing an advisory trust from their Constituents in their religious capacities," he further observed that the state necessarily freights all of its religious messages with political ones: "the idea of policy [is] associated with religion, whatever be the mode or the occasion, when a function of the latter is assumed by those in power."

Madison's failure to keep pace with his principles in the face of congressional pressure cannot erase the principles. He admitted to backsliding, and explained that he had made the content of his wartime proclamations inconsequential enough to mitigate much of their impropriety. While his writings suggest mild variations in his interpretation of the Establishment Clause, Madison was no different in that respect from the rest of his political generation. That he expressed so much doubt about the constitutionality of religious proclamations, however, suggests a brand of separationism stronger even than that embodied in our traditional jurisprudence. . . .

To be sure, the leaders of the young Republic engaged in some of the practices that separationists like Jefferson and Madison criticized. The First Congress did hire institutional chaplains, and Presidents Washington and Adams unapologetically marked days of "'public thanksgiving and prayer.'" Yet in the face of the separationist dissent, those practices prove, at best, that the Framers simply did not share a common understanding of the Establishment Clause, and, at worst, that they, like other politicians, could raise constitutional ideals one day and turn their backs on them the next. . . . If the early Congress's political actions were determinative, and not merely relevant, evidence of constitutional meaning, we would have to gut our current First Amendment doctrine. . . .

While we may be unable to know for certain what the Framers meant by the Clause, we do know that, around the time of its ratification, a respectable body of opinion supported a considerably broader reading than petitioners urge upon us. This consistency with the textual considerations is enough to preclude fundamentally reexamining our settled law. . . .

B. History and Tradition

In companion cases decided the same day, two different five-to-four majorities held that the display of the Ten Commandments in the McCreary County, Kentucky, courthouse violated the Establishment Clause but the display of the Ten Commandments on the grounds of the Texas state capitol was constitutional. Among the nine Justices, only Justice Breyer saw a constitutional distinction between the two cases. The cases will be considered in the next chapter. Here Justice Scalia and Justice Stevens square off in a debate over the history and tradition of religious invocations and observances by the government. In his dissent, Justice Scalia argues that the courthouse display should have been allowed. In his dissent, Justice Stevens argues that the state capitol display should not have been allowed.

Who has the better argument based on history and tradition? What should be the significance for constitutional law of the role and influence religion has played in the civic life of our nation?

McCreary County v. ACLU
545 U.S. 844 (2005)

JUSTICE SCALIA, dissenting.

. . . On September 11, 2001 I was attending in Rome, Italy, an international conference of judges and lawyers, principally from Europe and the United States. That night and the next morning virtually all of the participants watched, in their hotel rooms, the address to the Nation by the President of the United States concerning the murderous attacks upon the Twin Towers and the Pentagon, in which thousands of Americans had been killed. The address ended, as Presidential addresses often do, with the prayer "God bless America." The next afternoon I was approached by one of the judges from a European country, who, after extending his profound condolences for my country's loss, sadly observed "How I wish that the Head of State of my country, at a similar time of national tragedy and distress, could conclude his address 'God bless _____.' It is of course absolutely forbidden."

That is one model of the relationship between church and state—a model spread across Europe by the armies of Napoleon, and reflected in the Constitution of France, which begins "France is [a] . . . secular . . . Republic." Religion is to be strictly excluded from the public forum. This is not, and never was, the model adopted by America. George Washington added to the form of Presidential oath prescribed by Art. II, § 1, cl. 8, of the Constitution, the concluding words "so help me God." The Supreme Court under John Marshall opened its sessions with the prayer, "God save the United States and this Honorable Court." The First Congress instituted the practice of beginning its legislative sessions with a prayer. The same week that Congress submitted the Establishment Clause as part of the Bill of Rights for ratification by the States, it enacted legislation providing for paid chaplains in the House and Senate. The day after the First Amendment was proposed, the same Congress that had proposed it requested the President to proclaim "a day of public thanksgiving and prayer" [and] President Washington offered the first Thanksgiving Proclamation shortly thereafter. . . . And of course the First Amendment itself accords religion (and no other manner of belief) special constitutional protection.

These actions of our First President and Congress and the Marshall Court were not idiosyncratic; they reflected the beliefs of the period. Those who wrote the Constitution believed that morality was essential to the well-being of society and that encouragement of religion was the best way to foster morality. President Washington opened [and closed] his Presidency with a prayer. President John Adams wrote to the Massachusetts Militia, "Our Constitution was made only for a moral and religious people. It is wholly inadequate to the government of any other." Thomas Jefferson concluded his second inaugural address by inviting his audience to pray [for wisdom and guidance]. James Madison, in his first inaugural address, likewise placed his confidence "in the guardianship and guidance of that Almighty Being. . . ."

Nor have the views of our people on this matter significantly changed. Presidents continue to conclude the Presidential oath with the words "so help me God." Our legislatures, state and national, continue to open their sessions with prayer led by official chaplains. The sessions of this Court continue to open with the prayer "God save the United States and this Honorable Court." Invocation of the Almighty by our public figures, at all levels of government, remains commonplace. Our coinage bears the motto "IN GOD WE TRUST." And our Pledge of Allegiance contains the acknowledgment that we are a Nation "under God." As one of our Supreme Court opinions rightly observed, "We are a religious people whose institutions presuppose a Supreme Being." *Zorach v. Clauson*, 343 U.S. 306 (1952).

With all of this reality (and much more) staring it in the face, how can the Court possibly assert that "'the First Amendment mandates governmental neutrality between . . . religion and nonreligion,'" and that "manifesting a purpose to favor . . . adherence to religion generally," is unconstitutional? Who says so? Surely not the words of the Constitution. Surely not the history and traditions that reflect our society's constant understanding of those words. Surely not even the current sense of our society, recently reflected in an Act of Congress adopted unanimously by the Senate and with only 5 nays in the House of Representatives, criticizing a Court of Appeals opinion that had held "under God" in the Pledge of Allegiance unconstitutional. Nothing stands behind the Court's assertion that governmental affirmation of the society's belief in God is unconstitutional except the Court's own say-so, citing as support only the unsubstantiated say-so of earlier Courts going back no farther than the mid-20th century. And it is, moreover, a thoroughly discredited say-so. It is discredited, to begin with, because a majority of the Justices on the current Court (including at least one member of today's majority) have, in separate opinions, repudiated the brain-spun "*Lemon* test" that embodies the supposed principle of neutrality between religion and irreligion. [The "*Lemon* test" is discussed in Chapter 17.] And it is discredited because the Court has not had the courage (or the foolhardiness) to apply the neutrality principle consistently.

What distinguishes the rule of law from the dictatorship of a shifting Supreme Court majority is the absolutely indispensable requirement that judicial opinions be grounded in consistently applied principle. That is what prevents judges from ruling now this way, now that—thumbs up or thumbs down—as their personal preferences dictate. Today's opinion forthrightly (or actually, somewhat less than forthrightly) admits that it does not rest upon consistently applied principle. In a revealing footnote the Court acknowledges that the "Establishment Clause doctrine" it purports to be applying "lacks the comfort of categorical absolutes." What the Court means by this lovely euphemism is that sometimes the Court chooses to decide cases on the principle that government cannot favor religion, and sometimes it does not. The footnote goes on to say that "in special instances we have found good reason" to dispense with the principle, but "no such reasons present themselves here." It does not identify all of those "special instances," much less identify the "good reason" for their existence.

I have cataloged elsewhere the variety of circumstances in which this Court—even after its embrace of *Lemon*'s stated prohibition of such behavior—has approved government action "undertaken with the specific intention of improving the position of religion," *Edwards v. Aguillard* (1987) [Chapter 17] (Scalia, J., dissenting). Suffice it to say here that when the government relieves churches from the obligation to pay property taxes, when it allows students to absent themselves from public school to take religious classes, and when it exempts religious organizations from generally applicable prohibitions of religious discrimination, it surely means to bestow a benefit on religious practice—but we have approved it. Indeed, we have even approved (post-*Lemon*) government-led prayer to God. In *Marsh v. Chambers* (1983), the Court upheld the Nebraska State Legislature's practice of paying a chaplain to lead it in prayer at the opening of legislative sessions. . . .

The only "good reason" for ignoring the neutrality principle set forth in any of these cases was the antiquity of the practice at issue. That would be a good reason for finding the neutrality principle a mistaken interpretation of the Constitution, but it is hardly a good reason for letting an unconstitutional practice continue. . . . What, then, could be the genuine "good reason" for occasionally ignoring the neutrality principle? I suggest it is the instinct for self-preservation, and the recognition that the Court, which "has no influence over either the sword or the purse," *The Federalist No. 78*, cannot go too far down the road of an enforced neutrality that contradicts both historical fact and current practice without losing all that sustains it: the willingness of the people to accept its interpretation of the Constitution as definitive, in preference to the contrary interpretation of the democratically elected branches.

Besides appealing to the demonstrably false principle that the government cannot favor religion over irreligion, today's opinion suggests that the posting of the Ten Commandments violates the principle that the government cannot favor one religion over another. That is indeed a valid principle where public aid or assistance to religion is concerned or where the free exercise of religion is at issue, but it necessarily applies in a more limited sense to public acknowledgment of the Creator. If religion in the public forum had to be entirely nondenominational, there could be no religion in the public forum at all. One cannot say the word "God," or "the Almighty," one cannot offer public supplication or thanksgiving, without contradicting the beliefs of some people that there are many gods, or that God or the gods pay no attention to human affairs. With respect to public acknowledgment of religious belief, it is entirely clear from our Nation's historical practices that the Establishment Clause permits this disregard of polytheists and believers in unconcerned deities, just as it permits the disregard of devout atheists. The Thanksgiving Proclamation issued by George Washington at the instance of the First Congress was scrupulously nondenominational—but it was monotheistic. In *Marsh v. Chambers*, we said that the fact the particular prayers offered in the Nebraska Legislature were "in the

Judeo-Christian tradition," posed no additional problem, because "there is no indication that the prayer opportunity has been exploited to proselytize or advance any one, or to disparage any other, faith or belief."

Historical practices thus demonstrate that there is a distance between the acknowledgment of a single Creator and the establishment of a religion. . . . The three most popular religions in the United States, Christianity, Judaism, and Islam — which combined account for 97.7% of all believers — are monotheistic. All of them, moreover (Islam included), believe that the Ten Commandments were given by God to Moses, and are divine prescriptions for a virtuous life. Publicly honoring the Ten Commandments is thus indistinguishable, insofar as discriminating against other religions is concerned, from publicly honoring God. Both practices are recognized across such a broad and diverse range of the population — from Christians to Muslims — that they cannot be reasonably understood as a government endorsement of a particular religious viewpoint.

A few remarks are necessary in response to the criticism of this dissent by the Court, as well as Justice Stevens' criticism in the related case of *Van Orden v. Perry*. Justice Stevens' writing is largely devoted to an attack upon a straw man. "Reliance on early religious proclamations and statements made by the Founders is . . . problematic," he says, "because those views were not espoused at the Constitutional Convention in 1787 nor enshrined in the Constitution's text." But I have not relied upon (as he and the Court in this case do) mere "proclamations and statements" of the Founders. I have relied primarily upon official acts and official proclamations of the United States or of the component branches of its Government. . . . The only mere "proclamations and statements" of the Founders I have relied upon were statements of Founders who occupied federal office, and spoke in at least a quasi-official capacity. . . . The Court and Justice Stevens, by contrast, appeal to no official or even quasi-official action in support of their view of the Establishment Clause. . . .

It is no answer for Justice Stevens to say that the understanding that these official and quasi-official actions reflect was not "enshrined in the Constitution's text." The Establishment Clause, upon which Justice Stevens would rely, was enshrined in the Constitution's text, and these official actions show what it meant. There were doubtless some who thought it should have a broader meaning, but those views were plainly rejected. Justice Stevens says that reliance on these actions is "bound to paint a misleading picture," but it is hard to see why. What is more probative of the meaning of the Establishment Clause than the actions of the very Congress that proposed it, and of the first President charged with observing it?

Justice Stevens also appeals to the undoubted fact that some in the founding generation thought that the Religion Clauses of the First Amendment should have a narrower meaning, protecting only the Christian religion or perhaps only Protestantism. I am at a loss to see how this helps his case, except by providing a cloud of obfuscating smoke. (Since most thought the Clause permitted government invocation of monotheism, and some others thought it permitted government invocation of Christianity, he proposes that it be construed not to permit any government invocation of religion at all.) At any rate, those narrower views of the Establishment Clause were as clearly rejected as the more expansive ones. . . .

Justice Stevens argues that original meaning should not be the touchstone anyway, but that we should rather "expound the meaning of constitutional provisions with one eye towards our Nation's history and the other fixed on its democratic aspirations." This is not the place to debate the merits of the "living Constitution". . . . Even assuming, however, that the meaning of the Constitution ought to change according to "democratic aspirations," why are those aspirations to be found in Justices' notions of what the Establishment Clause ought to mean, rather than in the democratically adopted dispositions of our current society? [Numerous] provisions of our laws and numerous continuing practices of our people demonstrate that the government's invocation of God (and hence the government's invocation of the Ten Commandments) is unobjectionable—including a statute enacted by Congress almost unanimously less than three years ago, stating that "under God" in the Pledge of Allegiance is constitutional. To ignore all this is not to give effect to "democratic aspirations" but to frustrate them.

Finally, I must respond to Justice Stevens' assertion that I would "marginalize the belief systems of more than 7 million Americans" who adhere to religions that are not monotheistic. Surely that is a gross exaggeration. The beliefs of those citizens are entirely protected by the Free Exercise Clause, and by those aspects of the Establishment Clause that do not relate to government acknowledgment of the Creator. Invocation of God despite their beliefs is permitted not because nonmonotheistic religions cease to be religions recognized by the religion clauses of the First Amendment, but because governmental invocation of God is not an establishment. Justice Stevens fails to recognize that in the context of public acknowledgments of God there are legitimate competing interests: On the one hand, the interest of that minority in not feeling "excluded"; but on the other, the interest of the overwhelming majority of religious believers in being able to give God thanks and supplication as a people, and with respect to our national endeavors. Our national tradition has resolved that conflict in favor of the majority. It is not for this Court to change a disposition that accounts, many Americans think, for the phenomenon remarked upon in a quotation attributed to various authors, including Bismarck, but which I prefer to associate with Charles de Gaulle: "God watches over little children, drunkards, and the United States of America." . . .

Van Orden v. Perry

545 U.S. 677 (2005)

JUSTICE STEVENS, dissenting.

. . . The plurality [in allowing the Texas display] relies heavily on the fact that our Republic was founded, and has been governed since its nascence, by leaders who spoke then (and speak still) in plainly religious rhetoric. . . . Further, the plurality emphatically endorses the seemingly timeless recognition that our "institutions presuppose a

Supreme Being." Many of the submissions made to this Court by the parties and *amici*, in accord with the plurality's opinion, have relied on the ubiquity of references to God throughout our history.

The speeches and rhetoric characteristic of the founding era, however, do not answer the question before us. . . . Our leaders, when delivering public addresses, often express their blessings simultaneously in the service of God and their constituents. Thus, when public officials deliver public speeches, we recognize that their words are not exclusively a transmission from the government because those oratories have embedded within them the inherently personal views of the speaker as an individual member of the polity. . . . [Although] Thanksgiving Day proclamations and inaugural speeches undoubtedly seem official, in most circumstances they will not constitute the sort of governmental endorsement of religion at which the separation of church and state is aimed.

The plurality's reliance on early religious statements and proclamations made by the Founders is also problematic because those views were not espoused at the Constitutional Convention in 1787 nor enshrined in the Constitution's text. Thus, the presentation of these religious statements as a unified historical narrative is bound to paint a misleading picture. It does so here. . . .

. . . Not insignificant numbers of colonists came to this country with memories of religious persecution by monarchs on the other side of the Atlantic. Others experienced religious intolerance at the hands of colonial Puritans, who regrettably failed to practice the tolerance that some of their contemporaries preached. The Chief Justice and Justice Scalia ignore the separationist impulses—in accord with the principle of "neutrality"—that these individuals brought to the debates surrounding the adoption of the Establishment Clause.

Ardent separationists aside, there is another critical nuance lost in the plurality's portrayal of history. Simply put, many of the Founders who are often cited as authoritative expositors of the Constitution's original meaning understood the Establishment Clause to stand for a narrower proposition than the plurality, for whatever reason, is willing to accept. Namely, many of the Framers understood the word "religion" in the Establishment Clause to encompass only the various sects of Christianity. The evidence is compelling. Along these lines, for nearly a century after the Founding, many accepted the idea that America was not just a religious nation, but "a Christian nation." The original understanding of the type of "religion" that qualified for constitutional protection under the Establishment Clause likely did not include those followers of Judaism and Islam who are among the preferred "monotheistic" religions Justice Scalia has embraced in his *McCreary County* opinion. . . . [The] history of the Establishment Clause's original meaning just as strongly supports a preference for Christianity as it does a preference for monotheism. . . . Justice Scalia's inclusion of Judaism and Islam is a laudable act of religious tolerance, but it is one that is unmoored from the Constitution's history and text, and moreover one that is patently arbitrary in its inclusion of some, but exclusion of other (e.g., Buddhism), widely practiced non-Christian religions. Given the original understanding of the men who championed our

"Christian nation"—men who had no cause to view anti-Semitism or contempt for atheists as problems worthy of civic concern—one must ask whether Justice Scalia "has not had the courage (or the foolhardiness) to apply [his originalism] principle consistently." *McCreary County* (Scalia, J., dissenting) [*supra* this chapter]....

It is our duty, therefore, to interpret the First Amendment's command that "Congress shall make no law respecting an establishment of religion" not by merely asking what those words meant to observers at the time of the founding, but instead by deriving from the Clause's text and history the broad principles that remain valid today.... To reason from the broad principles contained in the Constitution does not, as Justice Scalia suggests, require us to abandon our heritage in favor of unprincipled expressions of personal preference. The task of applying the broad principles that the Framers wrote into the text of the First Amendment is, in any event, no more a matter of personal preference than is one's selection between two (or more) sides in a heated historical debate. We serve our constitutional mandate by expounding the meaning of constitutional provisions with one eye towards our Nation's history and the other fixed on its democratic aspirations.

The principle that guides my analysis is neutrality. The basis for that principle is firmly rooted in our Nation's history and our Constitution's text. I recognize that the requirement that government must remain neutral between religion and irreligion would have seemed foreign to some of the Framers.... Fortunately, we are not bound by the Framers' expectations—we are bound by the legal principles they enshrined in our Constitution.... [The] government must remain neutral between valid systems of belief. As religious pluralism has expanded, so has our acceptance of what constitutes valid belief systems. The evil of discriminating today against atheists, "polytheists [and] believers in unconcerned deities," *McCreary County*, (Scalia, J., dissenting), is in my view a direct descendent of the evil of discriminating among Christian sects. The Establishment Clause thus forbids it....

———

Problem: Ceremonial Deism

The year is 2096. Due to radically altered immigration and birth patterns over the past century, Muslims now comprise seventy percent of the American population, while Christians and Jews comprise only twenty-five percent collectively. Elementary school students in most public school systems begin each day with the Pledge of Allegiance in which they dutifully recite that America is one nation "under Allah"; our national currency—both coins and paper—contains the inscription codified as our national motto, "In Allah We Trust"; witnesses in court proceedings and public officials are sworn in by government officials asking them to place one hand on the Koran and to conclude "so help me Allah"; presidential addresses are laced with appeals to Allah; federal and state legislative proceedings begin with a formal prayer typically delivered by a Muslim chaplain in which supplications to Allah are unabashed; state and federal judicial proceedings—including proceedings before the

United States Supreme Court—begin with the invocation "Allah save this Honorable Court"; and, pursuant to federal and state law, only Muslim holy days are officially celebrated as national holidays.

Surely this scenario could not be squared with the First Amendment to the United States Constitution. Surely any court addressing these practices would conclude that the federal and state governments behind them have impermissibly sought to "establish" the religion of Islam. Right? Not necessarily. To date, every court that has analyzed these types of governmental appeals to the deity, albeit in Christian or Judeo-Christian form rather than Muslim form, has assumed as axiomatic that they do not encroach upon the Establishment Clause of the First Amendment.

Steven B. Epstein, *Rethinking the Constitutionality of Ceremonial Deism*, 96 COLUM. L. REV. 2083, 2084–85 (1996).* What is your reaction to Professor Epstein's provocative move to replace what is perhaps the "familiar" with the "unfamiliar"—replacing Judeo-Christian references with Islamic references? How would Justice Scalia and Justice Stevens react to this scenario?

Note: The Incorporation Doctrine

1. To be totally accurate, this Casebook might be titled "First and Fourteenth Amendment Law." In cases involving the Government of the United States, the Supreme Court is interpreting and applying the First Amendment proper, but in cases challenging actions by state and local governments, strictly speaking, it is the Fourteenth Amendment that is in play. This is an application of the Incorporation Doctrine.

2. In *Permoli v. New Orleans*, 44 U.S. (3 How.) 589, 609 (1845), the Supreme Court stated matter-of-factly: "The Constitution makes no provision for protecting the citizens of the respective states in their religious liberties; this is left to the state constitutions and laws: nor is there any inhibition imposed by the Constitution of the United States in this respect on the states." Indeed, this was the accepted original understanding of the entire Bill of Rights. *See Barron v. Baltimore*, 32 U.S. (7 Pet.) 243 (1833) (Marshall, C.J.).

3. The adoption of the Fourteenth Amendment (1868) and its interpretation changed that understanding. The Due Process Clause of the Fourteenth Amendment guarantees individual liberty against state action. Over a long line of cases, the Justices debated amongst themselves whether the Fourteenth Amendment effected a "total incorporation" of all the provisions in the Bill of Rights or a "selective incorporation" of the most fundamental provisions. *See Adamson v. California*, 332 U.S. 46 (1947). Clause-by-clause, almost all of the individual rights in the first eight amendments were applied to the states. The modern test to determine whether a guarantee in the Bill of Rights also applies to the states through the Due Process

---

Clause is whether the right is "fundamental to the American scheme of justice." *Duncan v. Louisiana*, 391 U.S. 145, 149 (1968). Applying this test, the Supreme Court has incorporated all of the rights in the First Amendment. *Cantwell v. Connecticut*, 310 U.S. 296 (1940) (free exercise); *Everson v. Bd. of Educ.*, 330 U.S. 1 (1947) (establishment); *Gitlow v. New York*, 268 U.S. 652 (1925) (speech and press); *De Jonge v. Oregon*, 299 U.S. 353 (1937) (assembly and petition). *Cf. NAACP v. Alabama ex rel. Patterson*, 357 U.S. 449 (1958) (nontextual right of association). Indeed, the doctrine of incorporation has become such a constitutional commonplace that even venerable Supreme Court Justices, like Homer, occasionally nod by mistakenly referring to a state case as a "First Amendment case." *See, e.g., Texas v. Johnson*, 491 U.S. 397, 399 (1989) (Brennan, J., majority opinion).

4. Justice Scalia and Justice Thomas have raised the question whether the Establishment Clause ought to have been incorporated and applied to the states as a matter of original intent. *See, e.g., Zelman v. Simmons-Harris*, 536 U.S. 639, 677–80 (2002) (Thomas, J., concurring); *Lee v. Weisman*, 505 U.S. 577, 641 (1992) (Scalia, J., dissenting). But long-standing precedent is to the contrary. *See School District of Abington Township v. Schempp*, 374 U.S. 203, 230–61 (1963) (Brennan, J., concurring) (offering the traditional justification for incorporation that the Establishment Clause is a fundamental right).

C. Values

In a famous passage, admired by some and mocked by others, Justices O'Connor, Kennedy, and Souter once described matters of ultimate human concern: "At the heart of liberty is the right to define one's own concept of existence, of meaning, of the universe, and of the mystery of human life." *Planned Parenthood v. Casey*, 505 U.S. 833, 851 (1992). Believers use religion to understand and answer that existential mystery.

What are the theoretical and philosophical justifications for the Religion Clauses? What First Amendment values are protected by the Establishment Clause and the Free Exercise Clause? Why does the Constitution treat religion as a fundamental matter of individual conscience? What makes religious beliefs constitutionally special and different from other beliefs?

In the following checklist, Professor Marshall identifies several alternative, sometimes competing values and makes a connection with the "marketplace of ideas" or "discovery of truth" justification for the First Amendment introduced in Chapter 1. As you read and reflect on the cases in these last four chapters on Freedom of Religion, keep in mind these values and consider whether the Justices are advancing these purposes in their opinions. (In Chapter 19, we will return to the explicit question of how to define religion, the constitutional object of the two clauses.)

William P. Marshall
Truth and the Religion Clauses
43 DePaul L. Rev. 243, 244–56 and 260–68 (1994)*

There is little agreement as to what values underlie the Religion Clauses of the First Amendment. The issue, nevertheless, is critical. A jurisprudence that is not based upon an understanding of the values involved is likely to be perceived as shallow, inconsistent, and nonpersuasive. . . .

The question of what values underlie the Religion Clauses has spawned a number of different responses and it is useful to briefly survey the rationales that have been advanced.

Pluralism. Both the free exercise and nonestablishment mandates have been justified as instrumental in promoting religious pluralism. The value of pluralism in turn has been posited as serving a variety of interests. First, pluralism provides a set of mediating institutions that "act as a critical buffer between the individual and the power of the state" and serve to aid individuals in reaching a balance between protecting their individual interests and promoting the public good. In this manner pluralism works as a check on government. In the presence of a multiplicity of divergent groups with constantly shifting alliances, the government will not be beholden to any one prominent interest and is therefore less likely to threaten any one group. Second, pluralism arguably promotes civic virtue. It imbues a sense of community obligation and virtue into the mind of the citizen-believer that is necessary to maintain a system of self-government. Third, pluralism reinforces a diversity within the fabric of society that enriches the lives of all citizens.

Equal Protection. The Religion Clauses have also been explained as codifying a concern for the protection of minority rights similar to that provided by the Equal Protection Clause. It has been argued that religious minorities require special protections from majoritarian discrimination and illegitimate government regulation because of their relative political powerlessness and their histories of persecution. The establishment prohibition against the dominance of one religious group, and the free exercise prohibition against laws which single out religious practice or belief for adverse treatment, potentially further this equal protection concern.

Lessening Divisiveness. Lessening divisiveness is another of the values advanced as underlying the Establishment Clause. History and current events have established all too well that political divisions along religious lines can be particularly acrimonious and tumultuous. Removing the government from religious issues and removing religious issues from the government have been posited as necessary to avoid conflicts between religious groups and between church and state.

Promoting Self-Identity. The protection of religious liberty through the mandates of the Religion Clauses has also been justified as critical to promoting self-identity. According to this theory, religious affiliation reflects a fundamental bonding between

---

* Copyright DePaul Law Review. Reprinted with permission.

the religious adherent and her religious beliefs and religious community. As one commentator has written, "Religious beliefs form a central part of a person's belief structure, his inner self. They define a person's very being—his sense of who he is, why he exists, and how he should relate to the world around him. A person's religious beliefs cannot meaningfully be separated from the person himself; they are who he is." Therefore, allowing the government to interfere with an adherent's religious beliefs would be impermissible because it would attack the individual's fundamental self.

Protecting Conscience. Concern with the rights of conscience is another justification offered for protecting religious liberty. The liberal state, it is argued, may take no position on what is right and good but, rather, must respect the moral and ethical principles of the individual. It is the individual's conscience and not the state that serves as the "moral sovereign" over the individual. The individual's conscience must therefore be protected from government interference which can question or destroy the perceived integrity and validity of the creed or faith to which a person adheres.

Reducing the Risk of Civil Disobedience. Another value offered as underlying the constitutional commitment to religious liberty, particularly through the creation of free exercise exemptions from neutral laws, is the reduction of the risk of civil disobedience. When the laws of the state conflict with religious duties, the believer must choose between obeying her government's laws or following her religious obligations. In the absence of an accommodation for the religious belief, the believer may be forced to violate the government's law for the sake of maintaining the integrity of her beliefs.

Eliminating Special Suffering. Related to the civil disobedience rationale is the value of eliminating special suffering. A believer who chooses not to disobey the civil law may experience special suffering if forced to violate her religious principles. A free exercise exemption from a civil law alleviates the special suffering the adherent might feel if forced to choose between her religious beliefs and legal norms.

The Nonalienation of Citizens. A concern with the nonalienation of citizens has also been suggested as a justification underlying the Establishment Clause. This justification focuses on the supposed harms suffered by those who perceive that the government has been captured by opposing religious interests. Unlike the civil disobedience or special suffering justifications, however, the nonalienation rationale is concerned with an alienated or offended individual's potential withdrawal from political participation.

Voluntarism. Still another proffered justification for the Religion Clauses is religious voluntarism. Religious voluntarism asserts "that both religion and society will be strengthened if spiritual and ideological claims seek recognition on the basis of their intrinsic merit." Voluntarism presumes that the value in protecting religious liberty lies in the protection of the individual's right to choose her belief rather than the individual's right to be bound by her belief. As the Court stated in *Wallace v. Jaffree* [Chapter 17], "Religious beliefs worthy of respect are the product of free and voluntary choice by the faithful. . . ."

The "Religious Justification." [In a recent article a commentator] suggested that there is a "religious justification" which underlies the constitutional commitment to religious freedom. [The] religious justification has two components. The first, the priority claim, asserts the precedence of religious obligations over temporal concerns. The second, the voluntariness claim, contends that "religious goods or duties by their nature entail freedom of choice." However, unlike the voluntarism value just discussed, which is based on the value of freedom of choice, this voluntariness claim is based upon the assertion that compelled religion is impossible. . . .

[*The Search for Truth as an Additional Justification for the Religion Clauses.*] As even a superficial perusal of this list indicates, the values posited as justifications for the Religion Clauses are disparate and wide-ranging. Nevertheless, there is consistency in at least one respect. With the exception of voluntarism, all of the purported values present a similar conception of religion; religion is seen as seminal, authoritative, and absolutist both in the mind of the individual and in the definition of her religious community. It is viewed as a product of external obligation rather than as a product of individual choice. For example, the pluralism and antidivisiveness rationales depend upon the existence of religious communities of settled definition. It is only because a religious community has definable boundaries that—on the positive side—it is able to serve as a mediating structure (in furtherance of the pluralism value), or—on the negative side—that it has sufficient identity and allegiance over its members to allow it to become a politically divisive force.

Similarly, the self-identity rationale emphasizes religion as a deeply-rooted, authoritative, and fixed structure in the mind of the believer. It is for this reason, after all, that religion is so central to the believer's sense of self. Indeed, to reference a number of the proffered values, it is only because her religious beliefs are fixed and authoritative that: (1) the religious believer's conscience might be compromised; (2) her risk of civil disobedience might be increased; (3) her suffering might be made acute; or (4) her alienation might be effectuated by offending governmental action.

To be fair, the preceding analysis suffers from some over-generalization. The value of pluralism, for example, does not totally depend upon the existence of static religious communities. It acknowledges that the religious believer may at times freely choose her religious community rather than be bound to a particular community solely on account of a religious obligation. The pluralism model also recognizes that religious communities may themselves be dynamic and may change their specific ideology and doctrine. Similarly, the self-identity value does not wholly depend upon a bonding of the believer to her religious belief. It acknowledges a positive value in the promotion of self-identity through the individual's freedom to choose her religious belief and religious identity.

Nevertheless, there is no question that the literature discussing these justifications (again excepting voluntarism) views religion more as a source of obligation and authority than as a source of freedom. Indeed, many of the writings explicitly contend that religion is entitled to special constitutional concern precisely because of the purported authority that it holds over its adherents.

Of course, depicting religion as inveterate and absolutist does not mean that it is unworthy of constitutional attention. To the contrary, many of the values previously discussed are persuasive in demonstrating the need for both establishment and free exercise protections. But there are substantial difficulties in maintaining a jurisprudence which primarily emphasizes this side of religion. First, reliance on the absolutist side of religion makes it susceptible to the criticism that it is undemocratic or unduly authoritarian. As such, this view of religion plays into the argument that religion should be properly excluded from the public debate.

Moreover, in a broader sense, the absolutist conception highlights those aspects of religion that have historically proved troublesome. By emphasizing authority, intransigence, and allegiance to a particular doctrine, this conception of religion focuses on those aspects of religion which have worked to divide humanity rather than those that have brought it together. While there may be value in maintaining a society with competing religious communities, as some theorists have argued, there is, assuredly, also value in the realization that there is a universal religious concern common to the human condition.

Similarly, the absolutist model works to undercut principles of tolerance. By protecting that aspect of religion which lays claim to "Truth" or "Right," these theories promote the sort of religious fervor that leads to intolerance. As has been noted, the logical conclusion of the belief that one has discovered truth is an attempt to impose that truth on others. The quieting of the absolutist claim, on the other hand, reinforces tolerance for competing ideas (even if one does not accept them on their merits) because it suggests to the believer that her own certainty is not something beyond question.

There is also a historical objection to the absolutist model. I do not want to overstate the historical case, but it is at least interesting to note that predicating the value of the Religion Clauses on an absolutist conception of religion runs counter to at least one strain of constitutional history. While the views of the Framers regarding religion were diverse, those who were influenced by natural law or Deism, such as Thomas Jefferson, found absolutist forms of religion repugnant. To these thinkers, religion was not valuable because of its affixation to dogma. Instead, the natural law philosophers and Deists encouraged people to move beyond the dogmatic preachings of their chosen religion and to ask questions in pursuit of transcendental truth. Merely accepting the teachings of any sect did not accomplish this goal. Thomas Jefferson's comment in this regard, therefore, is especially revealing: "I have never allowed myself to meditate a specific creed."

Still another problem with the absolutist view is that it makes for a troubled jurisprudence. Constitutional law is rights-based and premised on notions of individual freedom and choice. It is difficult, if not impossible, to meaningfully integrate absolutist theories into a liberal constitutional model.

Finally, and perhaps most importantly, viewing religion only as inveterate and absolutist is incomplete. It omits another aspect of religion — the focus of religion on the individual's search for beliefs rather than the believer's adherence to set groups or principles. Religion may be searching, self-challenging, and not rigidly tied to prefixed dogma or mores. In this type of religious belief, religious meaning does not stem from adherence to one set of beliefs or mores; rather it stems from the search for religious meaning and investigation into the seminal questions of "What is meaning?" and "What is truth?" . . .

Although it has long been associated with freedom of speech, the search for truth has not been thought of as a value underlying freedom of religion. The claim that the truth justification applies to both freedoms, however, has substantial support. After all, the constitutional commitment to freedom of religion is contained alongside the commitment to freedom of speech in a single amendment. Moreover, freedom of religion and freedom of speech have similar goals and purposes and share a common history. . . .

But there is an even more fundamental argument than history or text which supports why truth is properly thought of as a value underlying the Religion Clauses. Religion is more than a form of community bonding or an element of self-definition. At its center, it asks if there is a spiritual reality which defines human existence and if there are metaphysical principles which provide insight into what is meaning, what is purpose, and what is good. Indeed, the question of God is very much a question of metaphysical truth. Structuring a Religion Clause jurisprudence without concern for these most fundamental religious inquiries seems at best shallow and non-persuasive. . . .

The existing jurisprudence regarding the values underlying the Religion Clauses is one-sided. It focuses only on an absolutist model that views religion more as a source of human obligation than as a source of human freedom. At the same time, this jurisprudence fails to account for the relationship that exists between speech and religious freedoms, and the common questions which those freedoms pursue. The search for truth may not be the only value underlying the Religion Clauses, but it is one that helps make sense out of a troubled jurisprudence, one that creates a unifying understanding of the First Amendment, and one that provides an understanding of the meaning of freedom of religion.

Chapter 17

The Establishment Clause

The Establishment Clause reads: "Congress shall make no law respecting an establishment of religion." As we learned in Chapter 16, this Clause applies to the states as well. Everyone agrees that, under the Establishment Clause, neither the national government nor the states may designate an official church or prescribe oaths of belief in a religious faith or oblige persons to attend any church or extract religious tithes from taxpayers.

The word "respecting" is also understood to prohibit lesser measures short of an actual establishment of an official religion. Just what lesser measures are prohibited, however, has been the subject of considerable dispute among the Justices. In this chapter we will examine cases dealing with the five principal areas of litigation: financial aid to religion, prayer in public schools, school curriculum, religious displays in public places, and legislative prayer.

A. Financial Aid to Religion

It has long been a proposition of constitutional law that parents enjoy a fundamental liberty to control the upbringing and education of their children. In 1925, the Supreme Court struck down a state law that in effect had outlawed private and parochial schooling by making public education compulsory. *Pierce v. Society of Sisters*, 268 U.S. 510 (1925). Government support for religious education, however, raises serious and difficult issues for the Establishment Clause.

[1] Basic Principles

Everson v. Board of Education
330 U.S. 1 (1947)

Mr. Justice Black delivered the opinion of the Court.

[A New Jersey statute authorized local districts to pay the actual costs of transportation of elementary and secondary school children to and from school. The Township board of education authorized reimbursements to parents for transportation of their children on regular buses operated by the public transportation system. Some of these payments went to parents of children attending Catholic parochial schools which provided their students, in addition to secular education, regular religious instruction conforming to the religious tenets and modes of worship of the Catholic Faith.

The plaintiff, a district taxpayer, sued in state court and challenged the reimbursement to the parochial school students. The state trial court struck down the reimbursement provisions, but on appeal the New Jersey Court of Errors and Appeals reversed, holding that the statute and the reimbursement were valid under the state and federal constitutions. The plaintiff appealed to the Supreme Court.]

. . . Whether this New Jersey law is one respecting the "establishment of religion" requires an understanding of the meaning of that language, particularly with respect to the imposition of taxes. [*See* historical excerpts in Chapter 16, section A.]

. . . In recent years, so far as the provision against the establishment of a religion is concerned, the question has most frequently arisen in connection with proposed state aid to church schools and efforts to carry on religious teachings in the public schools in accordance with the tenets of a particular sect. Some churches have either sought or accepted state financial support for their schools. Here again the efforts to obtain state aid or acceptance of it have not been limited to any one particular faith. . . .

The "establishment of religion" clause of the First Amendment means at least this: Neither a state nor the Federal Government can set up a church. Neither can pass laws which aid one religion, aid all religions, or prefer one religion over another. Neither can force nor influence a person to go to or to remain away from church against his will or force him to profess a belief or disbelief in any religion. No person can be punished for entertaining or professing religious beliefs or disbeliefs, for church attendance or non-attendance. No tax in any amount, large or small, can be levied to support any religious activities or institutions, whatever they may be called, or whatever form they may adopt to teach or practice religion. Neither a state nor the Federal Government can, openly or secretly, participate in the affairs of any religious organizations or groups and vice versa. In the words of Jefferson, the clause against establishment of religion by law was intended to erect "a wall of separation between Church and State." *Reynolds v. United States* (1878) [Chapter 19].

. . . New Jersey cannot consistently with the "establishment of religion" clause of the First Amendment contribute tax-raised funds to the support of an institution which teaches the tenets and faith of any church. On the other hand, other language of the amendment commands that New Jersey cannot hamper its citizens in the free exercise of their own religion. Consequently, it cannot exclude individual Catholics, Lutherans, Mohammedans, Baptists, Jews, Methodists, Non-believers, Presbyterians, or the members of any other faith, because of their faith, or lack of it, from receiving the benefits of public welfare legislation. While we do not mean to intimate that a state could not provide transportation only to children attending public schools, we must be careful, in protecting the citizens of New Jersey against state-established churches, to be sure that we do not inadvertently prohibit New Jersey from extending its general State law benefits to all its citizens without regard to their religious belief.

Measured by these standards, we cannot say that the First Amendment prohibits New Jersey from spending tax-raised funds to pay the bus fares of parochial school pupils as a part of a general program under which it pays the fares of pupils attending public and other schools. It is undoubtedly true that children are helped to get to church schools. There is even a possibility that some of the children might not be sent to the church schools if the parents were compelled to pay their children's bus fares. . . . [But parents might also] refuse to risk their children to the serious danger of traffic accidents going to and from parochial schools, the approaches to which were not protected by policemen. Similarly, parents might be reluctant to permit their children to attend schools which the state had cut off from such general government services as ordinary police and fire protection, connections for sewage disposal, public highways and sidewalks. Of course, cutting off church schools from these services . . . would make it far more difficult for the schools to operate. But such is obviously not the purpose of the First Amendment. That Amendment requires the state to be a neutral in its relations with groups of religious believers and non-believers; it does not require the state to be their adversary. State power is no more to be used so as to handicap religions, than it is to favor them.

This Court has said that parents may, in the discharge of their duty under state compulsory education laws, send their children to a religious rather than a public school if the school meets the secular educational requirements which the state has power to impose. It appears that these parochial schools meet New Jersey's requirements. The State contributes no money to the schools. It does not support them. Its legislation . . . does no more than provide a general program to help parents get their children, regardless of their religion, safely and expeditiously to and from accredited schools.

The First Amendment has erected a wall between church and state. That wall must be kept high and impregnable. We could not approve the slightest breach. New Jersey has not breached it here.

Affirmed.

Mr. Justice Jackson, dissenting.

. . . What the Township does, and what the taxpayer complains of, is at stated intervals to reimburse parents for the fares paid, provided the children attend either public schools or Catholic Church schools. This expenditure of tax funds has no possible effect on the child's safety or expedition in transit. As passengers on the public busses they travel as fast and no faster, and are as safe and no safer, since their parents are reimbursed as before. . . .

A policeman protects a Catholic, of course — but not because he is a Catholic; it is because he is a man and a member of our society. The fireman protects the Church school — but not because it is a Church school; it is because it is property, part of the assets of our society. . . . To consider the converse of the Court's reasoning will best disclose its fallacy. That there is no parallel between police and fire protection and this plan of reimbursement is apparent from the incongruity of the limitation of this Act if applied to police and fire service. Could we sustain an Act that said police shall protect pupils on the way to or from public schools and Catholic schools but not while going to and coming from other schools, and firemen shall extinguish a blaze in public or Catholic school buildings but shall not put out a blaze in Protestant Church schools or private schools operated for profit? That is the true analogy to the case we have before us and I should think it pretty plain that such a scheme would not be valid. . . .

MR. JUSTICE RUTLEDGE, with whom MR. JUSTICE FRANKFURTER, MR. JUSTICE JACKSON and MR. JUSTICE BURTON agree, dissenting.

. . . Neither so high nor so impregnable today as yesterday is the wall raised between church and state by . . . the First Amendment. . . .

Not simply an established church, but any law respecting an establishment of religion is forbidden. The Amendment was broadly but not loosely phrased. . . . The Amendment's purpose was not to strike merely at the official establishment of a single sect, creed or religion, outlawing only a formal relation such as had prevailed in England and some of the colonies. Necessarily it was to uproot all such relationships. But the object was broader than separating church and state in this narrow sense. It was to create a complete and permanent separation of the spheres of religious activity and civil authority by comprehensively forbidding every form of public aid or support for religion. . . .

Does New Jersey's action furnish support for religion by use of the taxing power? Certainly it does, if the test remains . . . that money taken by taxation from one is not to be used or given to support another's religious training or belief, or indeed one's own. . . .

The funds used here were raised by taxation. . . . Here parents pay money to send their children to parochial schools and funds raised by taxation are used to reimburse them. This not only helps the children to get to school and the parents to send them. It aids them in a substantial way to get the very thing which they are sent to the particular school to secure, namely, religious training and teaching.

Believers of all faiths, and others who do not express their feeling toward ultimate issues of existence in any creedal form, pay the New Jersey tax. . . . Each thus contributes to "the propagation of opinions which he disbelieves" in so far as their religions differ, as do others who accept no creed without regard to those differences. Each thus pays taxes also to support the teaching of his own religion, an exaction equally forbidden since it denies "the comfortable liberty" of giving one's contribution to the particular agency of instruction he approves. . . .

If the fact alone be determinative that religious schools are engaged in education, thus promoting the general and individual welfare, together with the legislature's decision that the payment of public moneys for their aid makes their work a public function, then I can see no possible basis . . . for the state's refusal to make full appropriation for support of private, religious schools, just as is done for public instruction. . . . Our constitutional policy is exactly the opposite. . . .

. . . Public money devoted to payment of religious costs, educational or other, brings the quest for more. It brings too the struggle of sect against sect for the larger share or for any. . . . The end of such strife cannot be other than to destroy the cherished liberty. The dominating group will achieve the dominant benefit; or all will embroil the state in their dissensions. . . .

This is not therefore just a little case over bus fares. . . . The realm of religious training and belief remains, as the Amendment made it, the kingdom of the individual man and his God. It should be kept inviolately private, not "entangled . . . in precedents" or confounded with what legislatures legitimately may take over into the public domain.

No one conscious of religious values can be unsympathetic toward the burden which our constitutional separation puts on parents who desire religious instruction mixed with secular for their children. They pay taxes for others' children's education, at the same time the added cost of instruction for their own. Nor can one happily see benefits denied to children which others receive, because in conscience they or their parents for them desire a different kind of training others do not demand. . . . But that is a constitutional necessity, because we have staked the very existence of our country on the faith that complete separation between the state and religion is best for the state and best for religion. . . .

The judgment should be reversed.

————

Note: Two Competing Principles — "No Aid" and "Equal Aid"

Justice Black's majority opinion proclaims a strong separation-of-church-and-state rhetoric, yet the decision ultimately upholds the New Jersey law authorizing the reimbursement. He invokes the "no aid" principle:

> No tax in any amount, large or small, can be levied to support any religious activities or institutions, whatever they may be called, or whatever form they may adopt to teach or practice religion.

This principle protects citizens from being forced to support churches at the same time it protects churches from becoming dependent on government. Justice Black also invokes the "equal aid" principle:

> [The state] cannot exclude individual Catholics, Lutherans, Mohammedans, Baptists, Jews, Methodists, Non-believers, Presbyterians, or the members of any other faith, *because of their faith, or lack of it*, from receiving the benefits of public welfare legislation.

This principle guarantees equality among religions as well as equality between religious and secular interests; it prohibits both discrimination in favor of religion and discrimination against religion.

In 18th-century establishments, taxes were levied and earmarked exclusively to support a particular denomination or all denominations. These two principles could be harmonized to strike down such laws. Modern Establishment Clause cases, however, present state policies that equally fund religious and secular programs, and therefore these two principles are in opposition. In *Everson*, for example, the state reimbursed bus fares to attend public schools and parochial schools. So the Court was faced with a choice between the "no aid" principle—to deny Catholic parents the public welfare benefit—and the "equal aid" principle—to allow the reimbursement for all parents whether they chose to send their children to public or parochial school. The majority and the dissenters chose differently between these two principles.

In the rest of the cases in this Section, consider how the two principles of "no aid" and "equal aid" ought to apply and observe how the Court attempts to reconcile them. *See generally* Douglas Laycock, *Theology Scholarships, the Pledge of Allegiance, and Religious Liberty: Avoiding the Extremes but Missing the Liberty*, 118 Harv. L. Rev. 155, 162–67 (2004).

[2] The *Lemon* Test as Modified

Lemon v. Kurtzman

403 U.S. 602 (1971)

Mr. Chief Justice Burger delivered the opinion of the Court.

These two appeals raise questions as to Pennsylvania and Rhode Island statutes providing state aid to church-related elementary and secondary schools. Both statutes are challenged as violative of the Establishment and Free Exercise Clauses of the First Amendment and the Due Process Clause of the Fourteenth Amendment. . . . We hold that both statutes are unconstitutional. . . .

I

[The Rhode Island Salary Supplement Act appropriated salary supplements up to 15% for teachers of secular subjects in nonpublic elementary schools to be paid directly to the teacher, so long as the teacher's salary plus state supplement did not exceed the maximum paid to teachers in the state's public schools. Recipients were required to be state-certified in their subject and could use only teaching materials used in the public schools. Approximately 25% of the state's students attended nonpublic schools; approximately 95% of these pupils attended Roman Catholic parochial schools. All the teachers who applied for the supplement were employed by Catholic schools. A three-judge District Court held the Act violated the Establishment Clause.]

[The Pennsylvania Nonpublic Elementary and Secondary Education Act authorized the State to directly reimburse nonpublic schools solely for their actual expenditures for teachers' salaries, textbooks, and instructional materials. A school seeking reimbursement had to maintain prescribed accounting records, subject to state audit, that identified the "separate" cost of the "secular educational service." Reimbursement was limited to courses "presented in the curricula of the public schools." It was further limited "solely" to courses in the following "secular" subjects: mathematics, modern foreign languages, physical science, and physical education. Textbooks and instructional materials included in the program had to be approved by the state Superintendent of Public Instruction. The statute expressly prohibited reimbursement for any course that contained "any subject matter expressing religious teaching, or the morals or forms of worship of any sect." Some $5 million had been expended annually under the Act. The State had contracted with some 1,181 nonpublic elementary and secondary schools with a student population of some 535,215 pupils — more than 20% of the total number of students in the State. More than 96% of these pupils attended church-related schools, and most of these schools were affiliated with the Roman Catholic Church. A three-judge District Court dismissed the complaint.]

II

[We] must draw lines with reference to the three main evils against which the Establishment Clause was intended to afford protection: "sponsorship, financial support, and active involvement of the sovereign in religious activity." *Walz v. Tax Commission*, 397 U.S. 664 (1970). Every analysis in this area must begin with consideration of the cumulative criteria developed by the Court over many years. Three such tests may be gleaned from our cases. First, the statute must have a secular legislative purpose; second, its principal or primary effect must be one that neither advances nor inhibits religion; finally, the statute must not foster "an excessive government entanglement with religion."

[With respect to the inquiry into legislative purpose,] the statutes themselves clearly state that they are intended to enhance the quality of the secular education in all schools covered by the compulsory attendance laws. There is no reason to believe the legislatures meant anything else. A State always has a legitimate concern for maintaining minimum standards in all schools it allows to operate. . . .

The two legislatures [have]. . . . sought to create statutory restrictions designed to guarantee the separation between secular and religious educational functions and to ensure that State financial aid supports only the former. . . . We need not decide whether these legislative precautions restrict the principal or primary effect of the programs to the point where they do not offend the Religion Clauses, for we conclude that the cumulative impact of the entire relationship arising under the statutes in each State involves excessive entanglement between government and religion. . . .

III

In order to determine whether the government entanglement with religion is excessive, we must examine the character and purposes of the institutions that are benefited, the nature of the aid that the State provides, and the resulting relationship between the government and the religious authority. . . . Here we find that both statutes foster an impermissible degree of entanglement.

(a) Rhode Island program

. . . [Parochial] schools involve substantial religious activity and purpose. . . . The dangers and corresponding entanglements are enhanced by the particular form of aid that the Rhode Island Act provides. Our decisions . . . have permitted the States to provide church-related schools with secular, neutral, or nonideological services, facilities, or materials. Bus transportation, school lunches, public health services, and secular textbooks supplied in common to all students were not thought to offend the Establishment Clause. . . .

. . . We cannot, however, refuse here to recognize that teachers have a substantially different ideological character from books. In terms of potential for involving some aspect of faith or morals in secular subjects, a textbook's content is ascertainable, but a teacher's handling of a subject is not. We cannot ignore the danger that a teacher under religious control and discipline poses to the separation of the religious from the purely secular aspects of . . . education. . . .

We need not and do not assume that teachers in parochial schools will be guilty of bad faith or any conscious design to evade the limitations imposed by the statute and the First Amendment. We simply recognize that a dedicated religious person, teaching in a school affiliated with his or her faith and operated to inculcate its tenets, will inevitably experience great difficulty in remaining religiously neutral. Doctrines and faith are not inculcated or advanced by neutrals. With the best of intentions such a teacher would find it hard to make a total separation between secular teaching and religious doctrine. . . .

. . . The State must be certain, given the Religion Clauses, that subsidized teachers do not inculcate religion—indeed the State here has undertaken to do so. To ensure that no trespass occurs, the State has therefore carefully conditioned its aid with pervasive restrictions. . . . A comprehensive, discriminating, and continuing state surveillance will inevitably be required to ensure that these restrictions are obeyed and the First Amendment otherwise respected. . . . These prophylactic contacts will involve excessive and enduring entanglement between state and church. . . .

(b) Pennsylvania program

The Pennsylvania statute also provides state aid to church-related schools for teachers' salaries. . . .

[The] very restrictions and surveillance necessary to ensure that teachers play a strictly non-ideological role give rise to entanglements between church and state. The Pennsylvania statute, like that of Rhode Island, fosters this kind of relationship. . . . The Pennsylvania statute, moreover, has the further defect of providing state financial aid directly to the church-related schools. . . . The history of government grants of a continuing cash subsidy indicates that such programs have almost always been accompanied by varying measures of control and surveillance. . . . In particular the government's post-audit power to inspect and evaluate a church-related school's financial records and to determine which expenditures are religious and which are secular creates an intimate and continuing relationship between church and state.

IV

A broader base of entanglement of yet a different character is presented by the divisive political potential of these state programs. In a community where such a large number of pupils are served by church-related schools, it can be assumed that state assistance will entail considerable political activity. Partisans of parochial schools, understandably concerned with rising costs and sincerely dedicated to both the religious and secular educational missions of their schools, will inevitably champion this cause and promote political action to achieve their goals. Those who oppose state aid, whether for constitutional, religious, or fiscal reasons, will inevitably respond and employ all of the usual political campaign techniques to prevail. Candidates will be forced to declare and voters to choose. It would be unrealistic to ignore the fact that many people confronted with issues of this kind will find their votes aligned with their faith.

. . . [Political] division along religious lines was one of the principal evils against which the First Amendment was intended to protect. The potential divisiveness of such conflict is a threat to the normal political process. . . . It conflicts with our whole history and tradition to permit questions of the Religion Clauses to assume such importance in our legislatures and in our elections. . . . The potential for political divisiveness related to religious belief and practice is aggravated in these two statutory programs by the need for continuing annual appropriations and the likelihood of larger and larger demands as costs and populations grow. . . .

V

Finally, nothing we have said can be construed to disparage the role of church-related elementary and secondary schools in our national life. Their contribution has been and is enormous. Nor do we ignore their economic plight in a period of rising costs and expanding need. Taxpayers generally have been spared vast sums by the maintenance of these educational institutions by religious organizations, largely by the gifts of faithful adherents.

The merit and benefits of these schools, however, are not the issue before us in these cases. The sole question is whether state aid to these schools can be squared with the dictates of the Religion Clauses. Under our system the choice has been made that government is to be entirely excluded from the area of religious instruction and churches excluded from the affairs of government. The Constitution decrees that religion must be a private matter for the individual, the family, and the institutions of private choice, and that while some involvement and entanglement are inevitable, lines must be drawn.

The judgment of the Rhode Island District Court . . . is affirmed. The judgment of the Pennsylvania District Court . . . is reversed, and the case is remanded for further proceedings consistent with this opinion.

Mr. Justice Douglas, whom Mr. Justice Black joins, concurring.

Public financial support of parochial schools puts those schools under disabilities with which they were not previously burdened. . . . Under these laws there will be vast governmental suppression, surveillance, or meddling in church affairs. . . . The constitutional mandate can in part be carried out by censoring the curricula. What is palpably a sectarian course can be marked for deletion. But the problem only starts there. Sectarian instruction, in which, of course, a State may not indulge, can take place in a course on Shakespeare or in one on mathematics. . . .

It is well known that everything taught in most parochial schools is taught with the ultimate goal of religious education in mind. . . . One can imagine what a religious zealot, as contrasted to a civil libertarian, can do with the Reformation or with the

Inquisition. Much history can be given the gloss of a particular religion. I would think that policing these grants to detect sectarian instruction would be insufferable to religious partisans and would breed division and dissension between church and state. . . .

If the government closed its eyes to the manner in which these grants are actually used it would be allowing public funds to promote sectarian education. If it did not close its eyes but undertook the surveillance needed, it would, I fear, intermeddle in parochial affairs in a way that would breed only rancor and dissension. . . .

. . . A history class, a literature class, or a science class in a parochial school is not a separate institute; it is part of the organic whole which the State subsidizes. . . . What the taxpayers give for salaries of those who teach only the humanities or science without any trace of proselytizing enables the school to use all of its own funds for religious training. [We] would be blind to realities if we let "sophisticated bookkeeping" sanction "almost total subsidy of a religious institution by assigning the bulk of the institution's expenses to 'secular' activities." And sophisticated attempts to avoid the Constitution are just as invalid as simple-minded ones. . . .

Mr. Justice Brennan [concurring].

We have sustained the reimbursement of parents for bus fares of students under a scheme applicable to both public and nonpublic schools, *Everson v. Board of Education* (1947) [*supra* this chapter]. We have also sustained the loan of textbooks in secular subjects to students of both public and nonpublic schools, *Board of Education v. Allen*, 392 U.S. 236 (1968).

The statutory schemes before us, however, have features not present in either the *Everson* or *Allen* schemes. For example, the reimbursement or the loan of books ended government involvement in *Everson* and *Allen*. In contrast each of the schemes here exacts a promise in some form that the subsidy will not be used to finance courses in religious subjects—promises that must be and are policed to assure compliance. . . . [The] Rhode Island and Pennsylvania subsidies are restricted to nonpublic schools, and for practical purposes to Roman Catholic parochial schools. . . .

. . . [These] statutes require "too close a proximity" of government to the subsidized sectarian institutions and in my view create real dangers of "the secularization of a creed." The Rhode Island statute requires Roman Catholic teachers to surrender their right to teach religion courses and to promise not to "inject" religious teaching into their secular courses. . . . Both the Rhode Island and Pennsylvania statutes prescribe extensive standardization of the content of secular courses, and of the teaching materials and textbooks to be used in teaching the courses. And the regulations to implement those requirements necessarily require policing of instruction in the schools. The picture of state inspectors prowling the halls of parochial schools and auditing classroom instruction surely raises more than an imagined specter of governmental "secularization of a creed." . . .

Policing the content of courses, the specific textbooks used, and indeed the words of teachers is far different from the legitimate policing carried on under state compulsory attendance laws or laws regulating minimum levels of educational achievement. Government's legitimate interest in ensuring certain minimum skill levels and the acquisition of certain knowledge does not carry with it power to prescribe what shall *not* be taught, or what methods of instruction shall be used, or what opinions the teacher may offer in the course of teaching. . . .

Pennsylvania [and] Rhode Island . . . argue strenuously that the government monies in [these] cases are not "general subsidies of religious activities" because they are paid specifically and solely for the secular education that the sectarian institutions provide. . . .

. . . The present cases, however, involve direct subsidies of tax monies to the schools themselves and we cannot blink the fact that the secular education those schools provide goes hand in hand with the religious mission that is the only reason for the schools' existence. Within the institution, the two are inextricably intertwined. . . .

The common ingredient of the three prongs of the test set forth at the outset of this opinion is whether the statutes involve government in the "essentially religious activities" of religious institutions. My analysis of the operation, purposes, and effects of these statutes leads me inescapably to [that] conclusion. . . .

Mr. Justice White. . . . [Opinion concurring in part and dissenting in part omitted.]

———

Note: The Lemon *Test*

1. The *Lemon* test formally prohibits any government action that *advances* religion as well as any government action that *inhibits* religion. Does not every government action toward religion necessarily do one or the other? Not surprisingly, the doctrine has been characterized by inconsistency and discontent. Critics have complained that the Court selectively follows it in some cases and ignores it in others and that different Justices apply it differently in the same cases, often resulting in fractured plurality rulings based on incomprehensible distinctions. Several of the Justices have expressed their exasperation with the doctrine, but no alternative test has garnered the support of a majority.

2. The next case tweaks the three-part test, but maintains the basic analysis. Notice how the concepts of secular purpose, primary effect, and excessive entanglement weave through the opinions in the rest of this chapter, despite the persistent critique of several of the Justices. Is the Court moving toward some grand unified theory of the Establishment Clause? Or in the direction of an under-theorized *ad hoc* approach? What would a grand unified theory look like?

Agostini v. Felton

521 U.S. 203 (1997)

Justice O'Connor delivered the opinion of the Court.

In *Aguilar v. Felton*, 473 U.S. 402 (1985), this Court held that the Establishment Clause . . . barred the city of New York from sending public school teachers into parochial schools to provide remedial education to disadvantaged children. . . . On remand, the District Court . . . entered a permanent injunction reflecting our ruling. Twelve years later, petitioners . . . seek relief from its operation. Petitioners maintain that *Aguilar* cannot be squared with our intervening Establishment Clause jurisprudence and ask that we explicitly recognize what our more recent cases already dictate: *Aguilar* is no longer good law. We agree. . . .

In 1965, Congress enacted Title I of the Elementary and Secondary Education Act of 1965 to "provid[e] full educational opportunity to every child regardless of economic background." Toward that end, Title I channels federal funds, through the States, to "local educational agencies" (LEA's). The LEA's spend these funds to provide remedial education, guidance, and job counseling to eligible students. An eligible student is one (i) who resides within the attendance boundaries of a public school located in a low-income area; and (ii) who is failing, or is at risk of failing, the State's student performance standards. Title I funds must be made available to *all* eligible children, regardless of whether they attend public schools, and the services provided to children attending private schools must be "equitable in comparison to services and other benefits for public school children."

. . . Title I services may be provided only to those private school students eligible for aid, and cannot be used to provide services on a "school-wide" basis. In addition, the LEA must retain complete control over Title I funds; retain title to all materials used to provide Title I services; and provide those services through public employees or other persons independent of the private school and any religious institution. The Title I services themselves must be "secular, neutral, and nonideological," and must "supplement, and in no case supplant, the level of services" already provided by the private school.

Petitioner Board of Education of the City of New York (Board), an LEA, first applied for Title I funds in 1966. . . . Approximately 10% of the total number of students eligible for Title I services are private school students. Recognizing that more than 90% of the private schools . . . are sectarian, the Board initially arranged to transport children to public schools for after-school Title I instruction. But this enterprise was largely unsuccessful. Attendance was poor, teachers and children were tired, and parents were concerned for the safety of their children. The Board then moved the after-school instruction onto private school campuses. . . . during school hours. [Only] public employees could serve as Title I instructors and counselors. Assignments to private schools were made on a voluntary basis and without regard to the religious affiliation of the employee or the wishes of the private school. [A] large majority of Title I teachers worked in nonpublic schools with religious affiliations different from their own. . . .

Before any public employee could provide Title I instruction at a private school, she would be given a detailed set of written and oral instructions. . . . [The teachers were] told that (i) they were employees of the Board and accountable only to their public school supervisors; (ii) they had exclusive responsibility for selecting students . . . and could teach only those children who met the eligibility criteria . . . ;

(iii) their materials and equipment would be used only in the Title I program; (iv) they could not engage in team teaching or other cooperative instructional activities with private school teachers; and (v) they could not introduce any religious matter into their teaching or become involved in any way with the religious activities of the private schools. All religious symbols were to be removed from classrooms used for Title I services. Title I teachers [were permitted] to consult with a student's regular classroom teacher to assess the student's particular needs and progress, but [they were admonished] to limit those consultations to mutual professional concerns regarding the student's education. To ensure compliance . . . a publicly employed field supervisor [made] at least one unannounced visit to each teacher's classroom every month.

In 1978, six federal taxpayers . . . sued the Board in the District Court [seeking] declaratory and injunctive relief, claiming that the Board's Title I program violated the Establishment Clause. [Parents] of a number of parochial school students who were receiving Title I services [intervened]. The District Court granted summary judgment for the Board, but the Court of Appeals . . . reversed. . . . In a 5-to-4 decision, this Court affirmed on the ground that the Board's Title I program necessitated an "excessive entanglement of church and state. . . ." On remand, the District Court permanently enjoined the Board "from using public funds for any plan or program under [Title I] to the extent that it requires, authorizes or permits public school teachers and guidance counselors to provide teaching and counseling services on the premises of sectarian schools. . . ."

The Board, like other LEA's across the United States, modified its Title I program [by] providing instruction at public school sites, at leased sites, and in mobile instructional units (essentially vans converted into classrooms) parked near the sectarian school. The Board also offered computer-aided instruction, which could be provided "on premises" because it did not require public employees to be physically present on the premises of a religious school.

It is not disputed that the additional costs of complying with *Aguilar*'s mandate are significant. Since the 1986–1987 school year, the Board has spent over $100 million providing computer-aided instruction, leasing sites and mobile instructional units, and transporting students to those sites. . . . These "*Aguilar* costs" . . . reduce the amount of Title I money an LEA has available for remedial education, and LEA's have had to cut back on the number of students who receive Title I benefits. . . .

[In 1995, petitioners—the Board and a new group of parents of parochial school students entitled to Title I services—filed motions in the District Court seeking relief from the permanent injunction under Fed. R. Civ. P. 60(b)(5) because the decisional law had changed to make legal what the injunction was designed to prevent. The District Court denied the motion and the court of appeals affirmed.] We granted certiorari and now reverse.

In order to evaluate whether *Aguilar* has been eroded by our subsequent Establishment Clause cases, it is necessary to understand the rationale upon which *Aguilar*, as well as its companion case, *School Dist. of Grand Rapids v. Ball*, 473 U.S. 373 (1985), rested.

In *Ball*, the [school] district's Shared Time program, the one most analogous to Title I, provided remedial and "enrichment" classes, at public expense, to students attending nonpublic schools. The classes were taught during regular school hours by publicly employed teachers, using materials purchased with public funds, on the premises of nonpublic schools. The . . . courses were in subjects designed to supplement the "core curriculum" of the nonpublic schools. Of the 41 nonpublic schools eligible for the program, 40 were "'pervasively sectarian'". . . .

The Court conducted its analysis by applying the three-part test set forth in *Lemon v. Kurtzman* (1971) [*supra* this chapter]. The Court acknowledged that the Shared Time program served a purely secular purpose, thereby satisfying the first part of the so-called *Lemon* test. Nevertheless, it ultimately concluded that the program had the impermissible effect of advancing religion. . . .

[The] Court's conclusion that the Shared Time program in *Ball* had the impermissible effect of advancing religion rested on three assumptions: (i) any public employee who works on the premises of a religious school is presumed to inculcate religion in her work; (ii) the presence of public employees on private school premises creates a symbolic union between church and state; and (iii) any and all public aid that directly aids the educational function of religious schools impermissibly finances religious indoctrination, even if the aid reaches such schools as a consequence of private decisionmaking. Additionally, in *Aguilar* there was a fourth assumption: that [the] Title I program necessitated an excessive government entanglement with religion because public employees who teach on the premises of religious schools must be closely monitored to ensure that they do not inculcate religion.

Our more recent cases have undermined the assumptions upon which *Ball* and *Aguilar* relied. [We] continue to ask whether the government acted with the purpose of advancing or inhibiting religion, and the nature of that inquiry has remained largely unchanged. Likewise, we continue to explore whether the aid has the "effect" of advancing or inhibiting religion. What has changed since we decided *Ball* and *Aguilar* is our understanding of the criteria used to assess whether aid to religion has an impermissible effect.

Our cases subsequent to *Aguilar* [have] modified in two significant respects the approach we use to assess indoctrination. First, we have abandoned the presumption . . . that the placement of public employees on parochial school grounds inevitably results in the impermissible effect of state-sponsored indoctrination or constitutes a symbolic union between government and religion. In *Zobrest v. Catalina Foothills School Dist.*, 509 U.S. 1 (1993), we examined whether [it] was constitutional [for] a deaf student . . . to bring his state-employed sign-language interpreter with him to his Roman Catholic high school. We held that this was permissible. . . . We refused to presume that a publicly employed interpreter would be pressured by the pervasively sectarian surroundings to inculcate religion. . . . [We] assumed instead that the interpreter would dutifully discharge her responsibilities as a full-time public employee and comply with the ethical guidelines of her profession by accurately translating what was said. . . .

Second, we have departed from the rule . . . that all government aid that directly assists the educational function of religious schools is invalid. In *Witters v. Washington Dept. of Servs. for Blind*, 474 U.S. 481 (1986), we held that the Establishment Clause did not bar a State from issuing a vocational tuition grant to a blind person who wished to use the grant to attend a Christian college and become a pastor, missionary, or youth director. . . . The grants were disbursed directly to students, who then used the money to pay for tuition at the educational institution of their choice. [Any] money that ultimately went to religious institutions did so "only as a result of the genuinely independent and private choices of" individuals. . . .

[Under] current law, . . . New York City's Title I program in *Aguilar* will not, as a matter of law, be deemed to have the effect of advancing religion through indoctrination. . . . First, there is no reason to presume that, simply because she enters a parochial school classroom, a full-time public employee such as a Title I teacher will depart from her assigned duties and instructions and embark on religious indoctrination. . . . Certainly, no evidence has ever shown that any New York City Title I instructor teaching on parochial school premises attempted to inculcate religion in students. Thus, [we] reject respondents' remarkable argument that we must presume Title I instructors to be "uncontrollable and sometimes very unprofessional."

[We also repudiate the] assumption that the presence of Title I teachers in parochial school classrooms will, without more, create the impression of a "symbolic union" between church and state. . . . We do not see any perceptible (let alone dispositive) difference in the degree of symbolic union between a student receiving remedial instruction in a classroom on his sectarian school's campus and one receiving instruction in a van parked just at the school's curbside. . . .

Nor under current law can we conclude that a program placing full-time public employees on parochial campuses to provide Title I instruction would impermissibly finance religious indoctrination. [Aid is made] available only to eligible recipients. That aid is provided to students at whatever school they choose to attend. . . . Title I services are by law supplemental to the regular curricula. These services do not, therefore, "reliev[e] sectarian schools of costs they otherwise would have borne in educating their students."

. . . While it is true that individual students may not directly apply for Title I services, it does not follow from this premise that those services are distributed "directly to the religious schools." In fact, they are not. No Title I funds ever reach the coffers of religious schools, and Title I services may not be provided to religious schools on a school wide basis. Title I funds are instead distributed to a *public* agency (an LEA) that dispenses services directly to the eligible students within its boundaries, no matter where they choose to attend school. . . . We are also not persuaded that Title I services supplant the remedial instruction and guidance counseling already provided in New York City's sectarian schools. . . .

What is most fatal to the argument that New York City's Title I program directly subsidizes religion is that it applies with equal force when those services are provided off campus, and *Aguilar* implied that providing the services off campus is entirely consistent with the Establishment Clause. . . . Because the [economic] incentive is the same either way, we find no logical basis upon which to conclude that Title I services are an impermissible subsidy of religion when offered on campus, but not when offered off campus. Accordingly, contrary to our conclusion in *Aguilar*, placing full-time employees on parochial school campuses does not as a matter of law have the impermissible effect of advancing religion through indoctrination.

. . . A number of our Establishment Clause cases have found that the criteria used for identifying beneficiaries . . . might themselves have the effect of advancing religion by creating a financial incentive to undertake religious indoctrination. This incentive is not present, however, where the aid is allocated on the basis of neutral, secular criteria that neither favor nor disfavor religion, and is made available to both religious and secular beneficiaries on a nondiscriminatory basis. Under such circumstances, the aid is less likely to have the effect of advancing religion. . . .

[It] is clear that Title I services are allocated on the basis of criteria that neither favor nor disfavor religion. The services are available to all children who meet the Act's eligibility requirements, no matter what their religious beliefs or where they go to school. The Board's program does not, therefore, give aid recipients any incentive to modify their religious beliefs or practices in order to obtain those services.

We turn now to *Aguilar*'s conclusion that New York City's Title I program resulted in an excessive entanglement between church and state. Whether a government aid program results in such an entanglement has consistently been an aspect of our Establishment Clause analysis. We have considered entanglement both in the course of assessing whether an aid program has an impermissible effect of advancing religion, and as a factor separate and apart from "effect." Regardless of how we have characterized the issue, however, the factors we use to assess whether an entanglement is "excessive" are similar to the factors we use to examine "effect." . . . Thus, it is simplest to recognize why entanglement is significant and treat it . . . as an aspect of the inquiry into a statute's effect.

Not all entanglements, of course, have the effect of advancing or inhibiting religion. Interaction between church and state is inevitable, and we have always tolerated some level of involvement between the two. Entanglement must be "excessive" before it runs afoul of the Establishment Clause.

. . . [The] Court's finding of "excessive" entanglement in *Aguilar* rested on three grounds: (i) the program would require "pervasive monitoring by public authorities" to ensure that Title I employees did not inculcate religion; (ii) the program required "administrative cooperation" between the Board and parochial schools; and (iii) the program might increase the dangers of "political divisiveness." Under our current understanding of the Establishment Clause, the last two considerations are insufficient by themselves to create an "excessive" entanglement. They are present no matter where Title I services are offered. . . . Further, the assumption underlying the first consideration has been undermined. . . . [We] no longer presume that public employees will inculcate religion simply because they happen to be in a sectarian environment. Since we have abandoned the assumption that properly instructed public employees will fail to discharge their duties faithfully, we must also discard the assumption that *pervasive* monitoring of Title I teachers is required. There is no suggestion in the record before us that unannounced monthly visits of public supervisors are insufficient to prevent or to detect inculcation of religion by public employees. . . .

To summarize, New York City's Title I program does not run afoul of any of three primary criteria we currently use to evaluate whether government aid has the effect of advancing religion: It does not result in governmental indoctrination; define its recipients by reference to religion; or create an excessive entanglement. We therefore hold that a federally funded program providing supplemental, remedial instruction to disadvantaged children on a neutral basis is not invalid under the Establishment Clause when such instruction is given on the premises of sectarian schools by government employees pursuant to a program containing safeguards such as those present here. . . .

The doctrine of *stare decisis* does not preclude us from recognizing the change in our law. . . . [Our] Establishment Clause jurisprudence has changed significantly. . . . We therefore overrule *Ball* and *Aguilar* to the extent those decisions are inconsistent with our current understanding of the Establishment Clause. . . .

For these reasons, we reverse the judgment of the Court of Appeals and remand the cases to the District Court with instructions to vacate its . . . 1985 order.

JUSTICE SOUTER, with whom JUSTICE STEVENS and JUSTICE GINSBURG join, and with whom JUSTICE BREYER joins as to Part II, dissenting.

I

. . . I believe *Aguilar* was a correct and sensible decision. . . . The State is forbidden to subsidize religion directly and is just as surely forbidden to act in any way that could reasonably be viewed as religious endorsement. . . .

These principles were violated by the programs at issue in *Aguilar* and *Ball*, as a consequence of several significant features common to both Title I, as implemented in New York City before *Aguilar*, and the Grand Rapids Shared Time program. . . .

What [was] significant in *Aguilar* and *Ball* about the placement of state-paid teachers into the physical and social settings of the religious schools was not only the consequent temptation of some of those teachers to reflect the schools' religious missions in the rhetoric of their instruction, with a resulting need for monitoring and the certainty of entanglement. What was so remarkable was that the schemes in issue assumed a teaching responsibility indistinguishable from the responsibility of the schools themselves. The obligation of primary and secondary schools to teach reading necessarily extends to teaching those who are having a hard time at it, and the same is true of math. Calling some classes remedial does not distinguish their subjects from the schools' basic subjects, however inadequately the schools may have been addressing them.

What was true of the Title I scheme as struck down in *Aguilar* will be just as true when New York reverts to the old practices with the Court's approval after today. There is simply no line that can be drawn between the instruction paid for at taxpayers' expense and the instruction in any subject that is not identified as formally religious. . . .

II

In *Zobrest*, the Court did indeed recognize that the Establishment Clause lays down no absolute bar to placing public employees in a sectarian school, but the rejection of such a *per se* rule was hinged expressly on the nature of the employee's job, sign-language interpretation (or signing) and the circumscribed role of the signer. . . . The signer could thus be seen as more like a hearing aid than a teacher, and the signing could not be understood as an opportunity to inject religious content in what was supposed to be secular instruction. *Zobrest* accordingly holds only that in these limited circumstances . . . the employee's presence in the sectarian school does not violate the Establishment Clause. . . .

The Court next claims that *Ball* rested on the assumption that "any and all public aid that directly aids the educational function of religious schools impermissibly finances religious indoctrination, even if the aid reaches such schools as a consequence of private decisionmaking." . . . *Ball* did not establish that "any and all" such aid to religious schools necessarily violates the Establishment Clause. It held that the Shared Time program subsidized the religious functions of the parochial schools by taking over a significant portion of their responsibility for teaching secular subjects. The Court noted that it had "never accepted the mere possibility of subsidization . . . as sufficient to invalidate an aid program," and instead enquired whether the effect of the proffered aid was "'direct and substantial'" (and, so, unconstitutional) or merely "indirect and incidental" (and, so, permissible), emphasizing that the question "'is one of degree.'" . . .

In sum, nothing since *Ball* and *Aguilar* and before this litigation has eroded the distinction between "direct and substantial" and "indirect and incidental." That principled line is being breached only here and now. . . .

Justice Ginsburg, with whom Justice Stevens, Justice Souter, and Justice Breyer join, dissenting. [Omitted.]

Mitchell v. Helms
530 U.S. 793 (2000)

Justice Thomas announced the judgment of the Court and delivered an opinion, in which The Chief Justice, Justice Scalia, and Justice Kennedy join.

[Chapter 2 of the Education Consolidation and Improvement Act of 1981 is a closely related statute to the Elementary and Secondary Education Act of 1965 that the Court considered and upheld in the preceding case of *Agostini v. Felton* (1997). Chapter 2 channels federal funds to public school districts via state educational agencies to implement programs to assist elementary and secondary students enrolled in public and private nonprofit schools. Participating private schools receive aid based on the number of children consistent with aid provided public schools. Chapter 2 funds only supplement and may not supplant funds from non-Federal sources.

Several restrictions apply to aid to private schools. Most significantly, the services, materials, and equipment provided must be "secular, neutral, and non-ideological." Private schools may not acquire control of Chapter 2 funds or title to Chapter 2 materials, equipment, or property. The private school submits an application detailing the items and how it will use them; the state agency, if it approves the application, purchases the items from the school's allocation, and lends them to that school.

In Jefferson Parish, as in Louisiana as a whole, private schools have primarily used their allocations for nonrecurring expenses, usually materials and equipment. In 1986–1987, 44% of the money budgeted for private schools in Jefferson Parish was spent by the state agency acquiring library and media materials, and 48% for instructional equipment. Among the materials and equipment provided have been library books, computers, and computer software, and also slide and movie projectors, overhead projectors, television sets, tape recorders, VCR's, projection screens, laboratory equipment, maps, globes, filmstrips, slides, and cassette recordings. In an average year, about 30% of Chapter 2 funds spent in Jefferson Parish are allocated for private schools. For 1986–1987, 46 private schools participated: "34 were Roman Catholic; 7 were otherwise religiously affiliated; and 5 were not religiously affiliated."

Respondents filed suit in 1985, alleging that Chapter 2 violated the Establishment Clause. There followed 15 years of tortuous litigation back and forth between the District Court and the Court of Appeals. The District Court at first enjoined participation by sectarian schools in Chapter 2, but subsequently, after years had passed, the District Court upheld Chapter 2 on post-judgment motions, relying on its understanding of the direction of the more recent cases. The Fifth Circuit acknowledged the inconsistency and tension in Supreme Court precedents but determined that *Meek v. Pittenger*, 421 U.S. 349 (1975) and *Wolman v. Walter*, 433 U.S. 229 (1977) required that Chapter 2 be invalidated.]

II

. . . In *Agostini*, [we] brought some clarity to our case law, by overruling [anomalous] precedents [and] by consolidating some of our previously disparate considerations under a revised test. Whereas in *Lemon v. Kurtzman* (1971) [*supra* this chapter] we had considered whether a statute (1) has a secular purpose, (2) has a primary effect of advancing or inhibiting religion, or (3) creates an excessive entanglement between government and religion, in *Agostini* we modified *Lemon* for purposes of evaluating aid to schools and examined only the first and second factors. We acknowledged that our cases discussing excessive entanglement had applied many of the same considerations as had our cases discussing primary effect, and we therefore recast *Lemon*'s entanglement inquiry as simply one criterion relevant to determining a statute's effect. We also acknowledged that our cases had pared somewhat the factors that could justify a finding of excessive entanglement. We then set out revised criteria for determining the effect of a statute:

> To summarize, New York City's Title I program does not run afoul of any of three primary criteria we currently use to evaluate whether government aid has the effect of advancing religion: It does not result in governmental

indoctrination; define its recipients by reference to religion; or create an excessive entanglement.

In this case, our inquiry under *Agostini*'s purpose and effect test is a narrow one. Because respondents do not challenge the District Court's holding that Chapter 2 has a secular purpose, and because the Fifth Circuit also did not question that holding, we will consider only Chapter 2's effect. Further, in determining that effect, we will consider only the first two *Agostini* criteria, since neither respondents nor the Fifth Circuit has questioned the District Court's holding that Chapter 2 does not create an excessive entanglement. Considering Chapter 2 in light of our more recent case law, we conclude that it neither results in religious indoctrination by the government nor defines its recipients by reference to religion. We therefore hold that Chapter 2 is not a "law respecting an establishment of religion." In so holding, we acknowledge [that *Meek v. Pittenger* (1975) and *Wolman v. Walter* (1977), in which we struck down programs that provided many of the same sorts of materials and equipment as does Chapter 2] are anomalies in our case law. We therefore conclude that they are no longer good law.

[The] question whether governmental aid to religious schools results in governmental indoctrination is ultimately a question whether any religious indoctrination that occurs in those schools could reasonably be attributed to governmental action. We have also indicated that the answer to the question of indoctrination will resolve the question whether a program of educational aid "subsidizes" religion, as our religion cases use that term.

In distinguishing between indoctrination that is attributable to the State and indoctrination that is not, we have consistently turned to the principle of neutrality, upholding aid that is offered to a broad range of groups or persons without regard to their religion. If the religious, irreligious, and areligious are all alike eligible for governmental aid, no one would conclude that any indoctrination that any particular recipient conducts has been done at the behest of the government. For attribution of indoctrination is a relative question. If the government is offering assistance to recipients who provide, so to speak, a broad range of indoctrination, the government itself is not thought responsible for any particular indoctrination. To put the point differently, if the government, seeking to further some legitimate secular purpose, offers aid on the same terms, without regard to religion, to all who adequately further that purpose, then it is fair to say that any aid going to a religious recipient only has the effect of furthering that secular purpose. . . .

Agostini's second primary criterion . . . requires a court to consider whether an aid program "define[s] its recipients by reference to religion." [This] second criterion looks to the same set of facts as does our focus, under the first criterion, on neutrality, but the second criterion uses those facts to answer a somewhat different question—whether the criteria for allocating the aid "creat[e] a financial incentive to undertake religious indoctrination." In *Agostini* we set out the following [rule]: "This incentive is not present, however, where the aid is allocated on the basis of neutral, secular criteria that neither favor nor disfavor religion, and is made available to both religious and secular beneficiaries on a nondiscriminatory basis. Under such circumstances, the aid is less likely to have the effect of advancing religion." . . . [Simply] because an aid program offers private schools, and thus religious schools, a benefit that they did not previously receive does not mean that the program, by reducing the cost of securing a religious education, creates, under *Agostini*'s second criterion, an "incentive" for parents to choose such an education for their children. For *any* aid will have some such effect. . . .

Although some of our earlier cases did emphasize the distinction between direct and indirect aid, the purpose of this distinction was merely to prevent "subsidization" of religion. [Our] more recent cases address this purpose not through the direct/indirect distinction but rather through the principle of private choice, as incorporated in the first *Agostini* criterion (i.e., whether any indoctrination could be attributed to the government). If aid to schools, even "direct aid," is neutrally available and, before reaching or benefiting any religious school, first passes through the hands (literally or figuratively) of numerous private citizens who are free to direct the aid elsewhere, the government has not provided any "support of religion." Although the presence of private choice is easier to see when aid literally passes through the hands of individuals — which is why we have mentioned directness in the same breath with private choice — there is no reason why the Establishment Clause requires such a form.

Indeed, *Agostini* expressly rejected the absolute line that respondents would have us draw. . . . Whether one chooses to label [a] program "direct" or "indirect" is a rather arbitrary choice, one that does not further the constitutional analysis. Of course, we have seen "special Establishment Clause dangers" when *money* is given to religious schools or entities directly rather than indirectly. But direct payments of money are not at issue in this case, and we refuse to allow a "special" case to create a rule for all cases.

Respondents also contend that the Establishment Clause requires that aid to religious schools not be impermissibly religious in nature or be divertible to religious use. We agree with the first part of this argument but not the second. Respondents' "no divertibility" rule is inconsistent with our more recent case law and is unworkable. So long as the governmental aid is not itself "unsuitable for use in the public schools because of religious content," and eligibility for aid is determined in a constitutionally permissible manner, any use of that aid to indoctrinate cannot be attributed to the government and is thus not of constitutional concern. . . .

The issue is not divertibility of aid but rather whether the aid itself has an impermissible content. Where the aid would be suitable for use in a public school, it is also suitable for use in any private school. Similarly, the prohibition against the government providing impermissible content resolves the Establishment Clause concerns that exist if aid is actually diverted to religious uses. . . . [Just] as a government interpreter does not herself inculcate a religious message — even when she is conveying one — so also a government computer or overhead projector does not itself inculcate a religious message, even when it is conveying one. In *Agostini* itself, we approved the provision of public employees to teach secular remedial classes in private schools partly because we concluded that there was no reason to suspect that indoctrinating content would be part of such governmental aid. . . .

A concern for divertibility, as opposed to improper content, is misplaced not only because it fails to explain why the sort of aid that we have allowed is permissible, but also because it is boundless—enveloping all aid, no matter how trivial—and thus has only the most attenuated (if any) link to any realistic concern for preventing an "establishment of religion." Presumably, for example, government-provided lecterns, chalk, crayons, pens, paper, and paintbrushes would have to be excluded from religious schools under respondents' proposed rule. But we fail to see how indoctrination by means of (i.e., diversion of) such aid could be attributed to the government. In fact, the risk of improper attribution is less when the aid *lacks* content, for there is no risk (as there is with books) of the government inadvertently providing improper content. Finally, *any* aid, with or without content, is "divertible" in the sense that it allows schools to "divert" resources. Yet we have "'not accepted the recurrent argument that all aid is forbidden because aid to one aspect of an institution frees it to spend its other resources on religious ends.'"

It is perhaps conceivable that courts could take upon themselves the task of distinguishing among the myriad kinds of possible aid based on the ease of diverting each kind. But it escapes us how a court might coherently draw any such line. It not only is far more workable, but also is actually related to real concerns about preventing advancement of religion by government, simply to require that a program of aid to schools not provide improper content and that it determine eligibility and allocate the aid on a permissible basis. . . .

III

Applying the two relevant *Agostini* criteria, we see no basis for concluding that Jefferson Parish's Chapter 2 program "has the effect of advancing religion." Chapter 2 does not result in governmental indoctrination, because it determines eligibility for aid neutrally, allocates that aid based on the private choices of the parents of schoolchildren, and does not provide aid that has an impermissible content. Nor does Chapter 2 define its recipients by reference to religion.

Taking the second criterion first, it is clear that Chapter 2 aid "is allocated on the basis of neutral, secular criteria that neither favor nor disfavor religion, and is made available to both religious and secular beneficiaries on a nondiscriminatory basis." Aid is allocated based on enrollment. . . . The allocation criteria therefore create no improper incentive. . . .

Chapter 2 also satisfies the first *Agostini* criterion. The program makes a broad array of schools eligible for aid without regard to their religious affiliations or lack thereof. We therefore have no difficulty concluding that Chapter 2 is neutral with regard to religion. Chapter 2 aid also [reaches] participating schools only "as a consequence of private decisionmaking." Private decisionmaking controls because of the per capita allocation scheme, and those decisions are independent because of the program's neutrality. It is the students and their parents—not the government—who, through their choice of school, determine who receives Chapter 2 funds. The aid follows the child.

Because Chapter 2 aid is provided pursuant to private choices, it is not problematic that one could fairly describe Chapter 2 as providing "direct" aid. The materials and equipment provided under Chapter 2 are presumably used from time to time by entire classes rather than by individual students (although individual students are likely the chief consumers of library books and, perhaps, of computers and computer software), and students themselves do not need to apply for Chapter 2 aid in order for their schools to receive it, but [these] traits are not constitutionally significant or meaningful. Nor [is] it of constitutional significance that the schools themselves, rather than the students, are the bailees of the Chapter 2 aid. The ultimate beneficiaries of Chapter 2 aid are the students who attend the schools that receive that aid, and this is so regardless of whether individual students lug computers to school each day or, as Jefferson Parish has more sensibly provided, the schools receive the computers. . . .

Finally, Chapter 2 satisfies the first *Agostini* criterion because it does not provide to religious schools aid that has an impermissible content. The statute explicitly bars anything of the sort, providing that all Chapter 2 aid for the benefit of children in private schools shall be "secular, neutral, and nonideological," and the record indicates that the Louisiana SEA and the Jefferson Parish LEA have faithfully enforced this requirement insofar as relevant to this case. The chief aid at issue is computers, computer software, and library books. The computers presumably have no pre-existing content, or at least none that would be impermissible for use in public schools. . . .

[Chapter 2] satisfies both the first and second primary criteria of *Agostini*. It therefore does not have the effect of advancing religion. For the same reason, Chapter 2 also "cannot reasonably be viewed as an endorsement of religion." Accordingly, we hold that Chapter 2 is not a law respecting an establishment of religion. Jefferson Parish need not exclude religious schools from its Chapter 2 program. To the extent that *Meek* and *Wolman* conflict with this holding, we overrule them. . . .

The judgment of the Fifth Circuit is reversed.

Justice O'Connor, with whom Justice Breyer joins, concurring in the judgment.

. . . I [agree that *Agostini v. Felton* (1997) (*supra* this chapter) controls] the constitutional inquiry respecting Title II presented here, and requires the reversal of the Court of Appeals' judgment that the program is unconstitutional as applied in Jefferson Parish, Louisiana. To the extent our decisions in *Meek v. Pittenger* and *Wolman v. Walter* are inconsistent with the Court's judgment today, I agree that those decisions should be overruled. I therefore concur in the judgment.

I

I write separately because, in my view, the plurality announces a rule of unprecedented breadth for the evaluation of Establishment Clause challenges to government school aid programs. Reduced to its essentials, the plurality's rule states that government aid to religious schools does not have the effect of advancing religion so long as the aid is offered on a neutral basis and the aid is secular in content. The plurality also rejects the distinction between direct and indirect aid, and holds that the actual diversion of secular aid by a religious school to the advancement of its religious mission is permissible. . . .

[Neutrality] is an important reason for upholding government-aid programs against Establishment Clause challenges. . . . Nevertheless, we have never held that a government-aid program passes constitutional muster *solely* because of the neutral criteria it employs as a basis for distributing aid. . . .

I also disagree with the plurality's conclusion that actual diversion of government aid to religious indoctrination is consistent with the Establishment Clause. . . . [We] have long been concerned that secular government aid not be diverted to the advancement of religion. . . .

. . . I do not believe that we should treat a per-capita-aid program the same as [a true private-choice program]. . . . First, when the government provides aid directly to the student beneficiary, that student can attend a religious school and yet retain control over whether the secular government aid will be applied toward the religious education. The fact that aid flows to the religious school and is used for the advancement of religion is therefore *wholly* dependent on the student's private decision. . . .

Second, I believe the distinction between a per capita school aid program and a true private-choice program is significant for purposes of endorsement. In terms of public perception, a government program of direct aid to religious schools based on the number of students attending each school differs meaningfully from the government distributing aid directly to individual students who, in turn, decide to use the aid at the same religious schools. In the former example, if the religious school uses the aid to inculcate religion in its students, it is reasonable to say that the government has communicated a message of endorsement. Because the religious indoctrination is supported by government assistance, the reasonable observer would naturally perceive the aid program as government support for the advancement of religion. . . . In contrast, when government aid supports a school's religious mission only because of independent decisions made by numerous individuals to guide their secular aid to that school, "[n]o reasonable observer is likely to draw from the facts . . . an inference that the State itself is endorsing a religious practice or belief." Rather, endorsement of the religious message is reasonably attributed to the individuals who select the path of the aid.

Finally, the distinction between a per-capita-aid program and a true private-choice program is important when considering aid that consists of direct monetary subsidies. . . . If, as the plurality contends, a per-capita-aid program is identical in relevant constitutional respects to a true private-choice program, then there is no reason that, under the plurality's reasoning, the government should be precluded from providing direct money payments to religious organizations (including churches) based on the number of persons belonging to each organization. And, because actual diversion is permissible under the plurality's holding, the participating religious organizations (including churches) could use that aid to support religious indoctrination. . . .

In its logic — as well as its specific advisory language — the plurality opinion fore-shadows the approval of direct monetary subsidies to religious organizations, even when they use the money to advance their religious objectives.

. . . *Agostini* represents our most recent attempt to devise a general framework for approaching questions concerning neutral school aid programs. *Agostini* also concerned an Establishment Clause challenge to a school aid program closely related to the one at issue here. For these reasons, as well as my disagreement with the plurality's approach, I would decide today's case by applying the criteria set forth in *Agostini.* . . .

III

Respondents insist that [the] presumption that religious schools will use instructional materials and equipment to inculcate religion is sound because such materials and equipment [are] reasonably divertible to religious uses. For example, no matter what secular criteria the government employs in selecting a film projector to lend to a religious school, school officials can always divert that projector to religious instruction. Respondents therefore claim that the Establishment Clause prohibits the government from giving or lending aid to religious schools when that aid is reasonably divertible to religious uses. Justice Souter also states that the divertibility of secular government aid is an important consideration under the Establishment Clause, although he apparently would not ascribe it the constitutionally determinative status that respondents do.

I would reject respondents' proposed divertibility rule. First, respondents cite no precedent of this Court that would require it. . . . Justice Souter's attempt to defend the divertibility rationale as a viable distinction in our Establishment Clause jurisprudence fares no better. For Justice Souter, secular school aid presents constitutional problems not only when it is actually diverted to religious ends, but also when it simply has the capacity for, or presents the possibility of, such diversion. . . .

[Even apart from precedent, I] would still reject [the divertibility rationale urged by respondents and Justice Souter] for a more fundamental reason. Stated simply, the theory does not provide a logical distinction between the lending of textbooks and the lending of instructional materials and equipment. An educator can use virtually any instructional tool, whether it has ascertainable content or not, to teach a religious message. . . . In today's case, for example, we are asked to draw a constitutional distinction between lending a textbook and lending a library book. . . . Regardless of whether [Justice Souter's] explanation is even correct (for a student surely could be given a religious assignment in connection with a textbook too), it is hardly a distinction on which constitutional law should turn. Moreover, if the mere ability of a teacher to devise a religious lesson involving the secular aid in question suffices to hold the provision of that aid unconstitutional, it is difficult to discern any limiting principle to the divertibility rule. For example, even a publicly financed lunch would apparently be unconstitutional under a divertibility rationale because religious school officials conceivably could use the lunch to lead the students in a blessing over the bread. . . .

IV

Because divertibility fails to explain the distinction our cases have drawn between textbooks and instructional materials and equipment, there remains the question of which of the two irreconcilable strands of our Establishment Clause jurisprudence we should now follow. Between the two, I would adhere to the rule that we have applied in the context of textbook lending programs: To establish a First Amendment violation, plaintiffs must prove that the aid in question actually is, or has been, used for religious purposes. . . .

V

Respondents, the plurality, and Justice Souter all appear to proceed from the premise that, so long as actual diversion presents a constitutional problem, the government must have a failsafe mechanism capable of detecting *any* instance of diversion. We rejected that very assumption, however, in *Agostini*. . . .

I [believe] that it is entirely proper to presume that these school officials will act in good faith. That presumption is especially appropriate in this case, since there is no proof that religious school officials have breached their schools' assurances or failed to tell government officials the truth. The evidence proffered by respondents, and relied on by the plurality and Justice Souter, concerning actual diversion of Chapter 2 aid in Jefferson Parish is *de minimis*. . . .

I know of no case in which we have declared an entire aid program unconstitutional on Establishment Clause grounds solely because of violations on the minuscule scale of those at issue here. . . . While extensive violations might require a remedy along the lines asked for by respondents, no such evidence has been presented here. . . .

[As] in *Agostini*, the Chapter 2 aid is allocated on the basis of neutral, secular criteria; the aid must be supplementary and cannot supplant non-Federal funds; no Chapter 2 funds ever reach the coffers of religious schools; the aid must be secular; any evidence of actual diversion is *de minimis*; and the program includes adequate safeguards. Regardless of whether these factors are constitutional requirements, they are surely sufficient to find that the program at issue here does not have the impermissible effect of advancing religion. . . .

JUSTICE SOUTER, with whom JUSTICE STEVENS and JUSTICE GINSBURG join, dissenting.

. . . In all the years of its effort, the Court has isolated no single test of constitutional sufficiency, and the question in every case addresses the substantive principle of no aid: what reasons are there to characterize this benefit as aid to the sectarian school in discharging its religious mission? Particular factual circumstances control, and the answer is a matter of judgment.

[It] is not just that a majority today mistakes the significance of facts that have led to conclusions of unconstitutionality in earlier cases, though I believe the Court commits error in failing to recognize the divertibility of funds to the service of religious objectives. What is more important is the view revealed in the plurality opinion, which espouses a new conception of neutrality as a practically sufficient test of constitutionality that would, if adopted by the Court, eliminate enquiry into a law's effects. The plurality position breaks fundamentally with Establishment Clause principle, and with the methodology painstakingly worked out in support of it. . . .

II

. . . [We have used the term "neutrality"] in at least three ways in our cases. . . . "Neutrality" has been employed as a term to describe the requisite state of government equipoise between the forbidden encouragement and discouragement of religion; to characterize a benefit or aid as secular; and to indicate evenhandedness in distributing it. . . . In sum, "neutrality" originally entered this field of jurisprudence as a conclusory term, a label for the required relationship between the government and religion as a state of equipoise between government as ally and government as adversary. Reexamining *Everson*'s paradigm cases to derive a prescriptive guideline, we first determined that "neutral" aid was secular, nonideological, or unrelated to religious education. Our subsequent reexamination, [most] recently in *Agostini*, recast neutrality as a concept of "evenhandedness." . . .

[I]f we looked no further than evenhandedness, and failed to ask what activities the aid might support, or in fact did support, religious schools could be blessed with government funding as massive as expenditures made for the benefit of their public school counterparts, and religious missions would thrive on public money. This is why the consideration of less than universal neutrality has never been recognized as dispositive and has always been teamed with attention to other facts bearing on the substantive prohibition of support for a school's religious objective.

At least three main lines of enquiry addressed particularly to school aid have emerged to complement evenhandedness neutrality. First, we have noted that two types of aid recipients heighten Establishment Clause concern: pervasively religious schools and primary and secondary religious schools. Second, we have identified two important characteristics of the method of distributing aid: directness or indirectness of distribution and distribution by genuinely independent choice. Third, we have found relevance in at least five characteristics of the aid itself: its religious content; its cash form; its divertibility or actually diversion to religious support; its supplantation of traditional items of religious school expense; and its substantiality. . . .

[We] have long held government aid invalid when circumstances would allow its diversion to religious education. The risk of diversion is obviously high when aid in the form of government funds makes its way into the coffers of religious organizations, and so from the start we have understood the Constitution to bar outright money grants of aid to religion. . . .

Divertibility is not, of course, a characteristic of cash alone, and when examining provisions for ostensibly secular supplies we have considered their susceptibility to the service of religious ends. . . . [Our] cases have recognized the distinction, adopted by statute in the Chapter 2 legislation, between aid that merely supplements and aid that supplants expenditures for offerings at religious schools, the latter being barred.

Although we have never adopted the position that any benefit that flows to a religious school is impermissible because it frees up resources for the school to engage in religious indoctrination, from our first decision holding it permissible to provide textbooks for religious schools we have repeatedly explained the unconstitutionality of aid that supplants an item of the school's traditional expense.... [We] have recognized what is obvious (however imprecise), in holding "substantial" amounts of aid to be unconstitutional whether or not a plaintiff can show that it supplants a specific item of expense a religious school would have borne....

This stretch of doctrinal history leaves one point clear beyond peradventure: [we] have consistently understood the Establishment Clause to impose a substantive prohibition against public aid to religion and, hence, to the religious mission of sectarian schools. Evenhandedness neutrality is one, nondispositive pointer toward an intent and (to a lesser degree) probable effect on the permissible side of the line between forbidden aid and general public welfare benefit. Other pointers are facts about the religious mission and education level of benefited schools and their pupils, the pathway by which a benefit travels from public treasury to educational effect, the form and content of the aid, its adaptability to religious ends, and its effects on school budgets. The object of all enquiries into such matters is the same whatever the particular circumstances: is the benefit intended to aid in providing the religious element of the education and is it likely to do so? ...

III

... As a break with consistent doctrine the plurality's new criterion is unequaled in the history of Establishment Clause interpretation. Simple on its face, it appears to take evenhandedness neutrality and in practical terms promote it to a single and sufficient test for the establishment constitutionality of school aid. Even on its own terms, its errors are manifold, and attention to at least three of its mistaken assumptions will show the degree to which the plurality's proposal would replace the principle of no aid with a formula for generous religious support.

First, the plurality treats an external observer's attribution of religious support to the government as the sole impermissible effect of a government aid scheme.... Under the plurality's rule of neutrality, if a program met the first part of the *Lemon* enquiry, by declining to define a program's recipients by religion, it would automatically satisfy the second, in supposedly having no impermissible effect of aiding religion. Second, the plurality apparently assumes as a fact that equal amounts of aid to religious and nonreligious schools will have exclusively secular and equal effects, on both external perception and on incentives to attend different schools. But there is no reason to believe that this will be the case; the effects of same-terms aid may not be confined to the secular sphere at all.... Third, the plurality assumes that per capita distribution rules safeguard the same principles as independent, private choices. But that is clearly not so.... Not the least of the significant differences between per capita aid and aid individually determined and directed is the right and genuine opportunity of the recipient to choose not to give the aid. To hold otherwise would be to license the government to donate funds to churches based on the number of their members, on the patent fiction of independent private choice. . . . Under the plurality's regime, little would be left of the right of conscience against compelled support for religion; the more massive the aid the more potent would be the influence of the government on the teaching mission; the more generous the support, the more divisive would be the resentments of those resisting religious support, and those religions without school systems ready to claim their fair share.

. . . The facts most obviously relevant to the Chapter 2 scheme in Jefferson Parish are those showing divertibility and actual diversion in the circumstance of pervasively sectarian religious schools. The type of aid, the structure of the program, and the lack of effective safeguards clearly demonstrate the divertibility of the aid. While little is known about its use, owing to the anemic enforcement system in the parish, even the thin record before us reveals that actual diversion occurred.

The aid that the government provided was highly susceptible to unconstitutional use. Much of the equipment provided under Chapter 2 was not of the type provided for individual students, but included "slide projectors, movie projectors, overhead projectors, television sets, tape recorders, projection screens, maps, globes, filmstrips, cassettes, computers," and computer software and peripherals, as well as library books and materials. The videocassette players, overhead projectors, and other instructional aids were of the sort that we have found can easily be used by religious teachers for religious purposes. The same was true of the computers, which were as readily employable for religious teaching as the other equipment, and presumably as immune to any countervailing safeguard. Although library books, like textbooks, have fixed content, religious teachers can assign secular library books for religious critique, and books for libraries may be religious, as any divinity school library would demonstrate. The sheer number and variety of books that could be and were ordered gave ample opportunity for such diversion.

The divertibility thus inherent in the forms of Chapter 2 aid was enhanced by the structure of the program in Jefferson Parish. Requests for specific items under Chapter 2 came not from secular officials, but from officials of the religious schools (and even parents of religious school pupils). The sectarian schools decided what they wanted and often ordered the supplies to be forwarded directly to themselves. It was easy to select whatever instructional materials and library books the schools wanted, just as it was easy to employ computers for the support of the religious content of the curriculum infused with religious instruction. . . . Such precautionary features as there were in the Jefferson Parish scheme were grossly inadequate to counter the threat. To be sure, the disbursement of the aid was subject to statutory admonitions against diversion and was supposedly subject to a variety of safeguards. But the provisions for onsite monitoring visits, labeling of government property, and government oversight cannot be accepted as sufficient in the face of record evidence that the safeguard provisions proved to be empty phrases in Jefferson Parish. . . .

The risk of immediate diversion of Chapter 2 benefits had its complement in the risk of future diversion, against which the Jefferson Parish program had absolutely no protection. By statute all purchases with Chapter 2 aid were to remain the property of the United States, merely being "lent" to the recipient nonpublic schools. In actuality, however, the record indicates that nothing in the Jefferson Parish program stood in the way of giving the Chapter 2 property outright to the religious schools when it became older. . . . Providing such governmental aid without effective safeguards against future diversion itself offends the Establishment Clause, and even without evidence of actual diversion, our cases have repeatedly held that a "substantial risk" of it suffices to invalidate a government aid program on establishment grounds. A substantial risk of diversion in this case was more than clear, as the plurality has conceded. . . . But the record here goes beyond risk, to instances of actual diversion. What one would expect from such paltry efforts at monitoring and enforcement naturally resulted, and the record strongly suggests that other, undocumented diversions probably occurred as well. . . .

IV

The plurality would break with the law. The majority misapplies it. That misapplication is, however, the only consolation in the case, which reaches an erroneous result but does not stage a doctrinal coup. But there is no mistaking the abandonment of doctrine that would occur if the plurality were to become a majority. It is beyond question that the plurality's notion of evenhandedness neutrality as a practical guarantee of the validity of aid to sectarian schools would be the end of the principle of no aid to the schools' religious mission. . . . To the plurality there is nothing wrong with aiding a school's religious mission; the only question is whether religious teaching obtains its tax support under a formally evenhanded criterion of distribution. The principle of no aid to religious teaching has no independent significance. [In] rejecting the principle of no aid to a school's religious mission the plurality is attacking the most fundamental assumption underlying the Establishment Clause, that government can in fact operate with neutrality in its relation to religion. I believe that it can, and so respectfully dissent.

[3] School Vouchers

The previous three cases dealt with government aid to religious schools. The next case deals with aid to students at religious schools or to their parents. Should the different identity of the object of the aid—the religious school versus the student attending the religious school—make a constitutional difference?

Zelman v. Simmons-Harris
536 U.S. 639 (2002)

CHIEF JUSTICE REHNQUIST delivered the opinion of the Court.

The State of Ohio has established a pilot program designed to provide educational choices to families with children who reside in the Cleveland City School District. The question presented is whether this program offends the Establishment Clause of the United States Constitution. We hold that it does not.

There are more than 75,000 children enrolled in the Cleveland City School District. The majority of these children are from low-income and minority families. Few of these families enjoy the means to send their children to any school other than an inner-city public school. For more than a generation, however, Cleveland's public schools have been among the worst performing public schools in the Nation. In 1995, a Federal District Court declared a "crisis of magnitude" and placed the entire Cleveland school district under state control. . . . The district had failed to meet any of the 18 state standards for minimal acceptable performance. . . .

It is against this backdrop that Ohio enacted, among other initiatives, its Pilot Project Scholarship Program. The program provides financial assistance to families in any Ohio school district that is or has been "under federal court order requiring supervision and operational management of the district by the state superintendent." Cleveland is the only Ohio school district to fall within that category.

The program provides two basic kinds of assistance to parents of children in a covered district. First, the program provides tuition aid for students in kindergarten through third grade, expanding each year through eighth grade, to attend a participating public or private school of their parent's choosing. Second, the program provides tutorial aid for students who choose to remain enrolled in public school.

The tuition aid portion of the program is designed to provide educational choices to parents who reside in a covered district. Any private school, whether religious or nonreligious, may participate in the program and accept program students so long as the school is located within the boundaries of a covered district and meets statewide educational standards. Participating private schools must agree not to discriminate on the basis of race, religion, or ethnic background, or to "advocate or foster unlawful behavior or teach hatred of any person or group on the basis of race, ethnicity, national origin, or religion." Any public school located in a school district adjacent to the covered district may also participate in the program. Adjacent public schools are eligible to receive a $2,250 tuition grant for each program student accepted in addition to the full amount of per-pupil state funding attributable to each additional student. . . .

Tuition aid is distributed to parents according to financial need. Families with incomes below 200% of the poverty line are given priority and are eligible to receive 90% of private school tuition up to $2,250. For these lowest income families, participating private schools may not charge a parental copayment greater than $250. For all other families, the program pays 75% of tuition costs, up to $1,875, with no copayment cap. These families receive tuition aid only if the number of available scholarships exceeds the number of low-income children who choose to participate. Where tuition aid is spent depends solely upon where parents who receive tuition aid choose to enroll their child. If parents choose a private school, checks are made payable to the parents who then endorse the checks over to the chosen school. The tutorial aid portion of the program provides tutorial assistance through grants to any student in a covered district who chooses to remain in public school. . . .

The program has been in operation within the Cleveland City School District since the 1996–1997 school year. In the 1999–2000 school year, 56 private schools participated in the program, 46 (or 82%) of which had a religious affiliation. None of the public schools in districts adjacent to Cleveland have elected to participate. More than 3,700 students participated in the scholarship program, most of whom (96%) enrolled in religiously affiliated schools. Sixty percent of these students were from families at or below the poverty line. In the 1998–1999 school year, approximately 1,400 Cleveland public school students received tutorial aid. This number was expected to double during the 1999–2000 school year. The program is part of a broader undertaking by the State to enhance the educational options of Cleveland's schoolchildren in response to the 1995 takeover. That undertaking includes programs governing community and magnet schools.

[In 1999, respondents filed this action in District Court, seeking to enjoin the program on the ground that it violated the Establishment Clause. The District Court issued a preliminary injunction barring further implementation of the program, which we stayed pending review by the Court of Appeals. The District Court eventually granted a summary judgment for respondents. The Court of Appeals affirmed, finding that the program had the "primary effect" of advancing religion, but stayed its mandate pending disposition in this Court.] We granted certiorari, and now reverse the Court of Appeals.

The Establishment Clause of the First Amendment, applied to the States through the Fourteenth Amendment, prevents a State from enacting laws that have the "purpose" or "effect" of advancing or inhibiting religion. *Agostini v. Felton* (1997) [*supra* this chapter]. There is no dispute that the program challenged here was enacted for the valid secular purpose of providing educational assistance to poor children in a demonstrably failing public school system. Thus, the question presented is whether the Ohio program nonetheless has the forbidden "effect" of advancing or inhibiting religion.

To answer that question, our decisions have drawn a consistent distinction between government programs that provide aid directly to religious schools, and programs of true private choice, in which government aid reaches religious schools only as a result of the genuine and independent choices of private individuals. While our jurisprudence with respect to the constitutionality of direct aid programs has "changed significantly" over the past two decades, *Agostini*, our jurisprudence with respect to true private choice programs has remained consistent and unbroken. Three times we have confronted Establishment Clause challenges to neutral government programs that provide aid directly to a broad class of individuals, who, in turn, direct the aid to religious schools or institutions of their own choosing. Three times we have rejected such challenges.

In *Mueller v. Allen*, 463 U.S. 388 (1983), we rejected an Establishment Clause challenge to a Minnesota program authorizing tax deductions for various educational expenses, including private school tuition costs, even though the great majority of the program's beneficiaries (96%) were parents of children in religious schools. . . . In

Witters v. Washington Dept. Servs. for Blind, 474 U.S. 481 (1986), we used identical reasoning to reject an Establishment Clause challenge to a vocational scholarship program that provided tuition aid to a student studying at a religious institution to become a pastor. . . . Finally, in *Zobrest v. Catalina Foothills School Dist.*, 509 U.S. 1 (1993), we applied *Mueller* and *Witters* to reject an Establishment Clause challenge to a federal program that permitted sign-language interpreters to assist deaf children enrolled in religious schools. . . .

Mueller, *Witters*, and *Zobrest* thus make clear that where a government aid program is neutral with respect to religion, and provides assistance directly to a broad class of citizens who, in turn, direct government aid to religious schools wholly as a result of their own genuine and independent private choice, the program is not readily subject to challenge under the Establishment Clause. A program that shares these features permits government aid to reach religious institutions only by way of the deliberate choices of numerous individual recipients. The incidental advancement of a religious mission, or the perceived endorsement of a religious message, is reasonably attributable to the individual recipient, not to the government, whose role ends with the disbursement of benefits. . . .

We believe that the program challenged here is a program of true private choice, consistent with *Mueller*, *Witters*, and *Zobrest*, and thus constitutional.

As was true in those cases, the Ohio program is neutral in all respects toward religion. It is part of a general and multifaceted undertaking by the State of Ohio to provide educational opportunities to the children of a failed school district. It confers educational assistance directly to a broad class of individuals defined without reference to religion, i.e., any parent of a school-age child who resides in the Cleveland City School District. The program permits the participation of *all* schools within the district, religious or nonreligious. Adjacent public schools also may participate and have a financial incentive to do so. Program benefits are available to participating families on neutral terms, with no reference to religion. The only preference stated anywhere in the program is a preference for low-income families, who receive greater assistance and are given priority for admission at participating schools.

. . . The program here in fact creates financial *dis*incentives for religious schools, with private schools receiving only half the government assistance given to community schools and one-third the assistance given to magnet schools. Adjacent public schools, should any choose to accept program students, are also eligible to receive two to three times the state funding of a private religious school. Families too have a financial disincentive to choose a private religious school over other schools. Parents that choose to participate in the scholarship program and then to enroll their children in a private school (religious or nonreligious) must copay a portion of the school's tuition. Families that choose a community school, magnet school, or traditional public school pay nothing. Although such features of the program are not necessary to its constitutionality, they clearly dispel the claim that the program "creates . . . financial incentive[s] for parents to choose a sectarian school."

Respondents suggest that . . . the program creates a "public perception that the State is endorsing religious practices and beliefs." But we have repeatedly recognized that no reasonable observer would think a neutral program of private choice, where state aid reaches religious schools solely as a result of the numerous independent decisions of private individuals, carries with it the *imprimatur* of government endorsement. . . . Any objective observer familiar with the full history and context of the Ohio program would reasonably view it as one aspect of a broader undertaking to assist poor children in failed schools, not as an endorsement of religious schooling in general.

. . . Cleveland schoolchildren enjoy a range of educational choices: They may remain in public school as before, remain in public school with publicly funded tutoring aid, obtain a scholarship and choose a religious school, obtain a scholarship and choose a nonreligious private school, enroll in a community school, or enroll in a magnet school. That 46 of the 56 private schools now participating in the program are religious schools does not condemn it as a violation of the Establishment Clause. The Establishment Clause question is whether Ohio is coercing parents into sending their children to religious schools, and that question must be answered by evaluating *all* options Ohio provides Cleveland schoolchildren, only one of which is to obtain a program scholarship and then choose a religious school.

Justice Souter speculates that because more private religious schools currently participate in the program, the program itself must somehow discourage the participation of private nonreligious schools. But Cleveland's preponderance of religiously affiliated private schools certainly did not arise as a result of the program; it is a phenomenon common to many American cities. Indeed, by all accounts the program has captured a remarkable cross-section of private schools, religious and nonreligious. It is true that 82% of Cleveland's participating private schools are religious schools, but it is also true that 81% of private schools in Ohio are religious schools. . . .

Respondents and Justice Souter claim that even if we do not focus on the number of participating schools that are religious schools, we should attach constitutional significance to the fact that 96% of scholarship recipients have enrolled in religious schools. . . . The constitutionality of a neutral educational aid program simply does not turn on whether and why, in a particular area, at a particular time, most private schools are run by religious organizations, or most recipients choose to use the aid at a religious school. . . . This point is aptly illustrated here. The 96% figure upon which respondents and Justice Souter rely discounts entirely (1) the more than 1,900 Cleveland children enrolled in alternative community schools, (2) the more than 13,000 children enrolled in alternative magnet schools, and (3) the more than 1,400 children enrolled in traditional public schools with tutorial assistance. Including some or all of these children in the denominator of children enrolled in nontraditional schools during the 1999–2000 school year drops the percentage enrolled in religious schools from 96% to under 20%. . . .

In sum, the Ohio program is entirely neutral with respect to religion. It provides benefits directly to a wide spectrum of individuals, defined only by financial need and residence in a particular school district. It permits such individuals to exercise genuine choice among options public and private, secular and religious. The program is therefore a program of true private choice. In keeping with an unbroken line of decisions rejecting challenges to similar programs, we hold that the program does not offend the Establishment Clause.

The judgment of the Court of Appeals is *reversed*.

Justice O'Connor, concurring.

. . . These cases are different from prior indirect aid cases in part because a significant portion of the funds appropriated for the voucher program reach religious schools without restrictions on the use of these funds. The share of public resources that reach religious schools is not, however, as significant as respondents suggest. Data from the 1999–2000 school year indicate that 82 percent of schools participating in the voucher program were religious and that 96 percent of participating students enrolled in religious schools, but these data are incomplete. These statistics do not take into account all of the reasonable educational choices that may be available to students in Cleveland public schools. When one considers the option to attend community schools, the percentage of students enrolled in religious schools falls to 62.1 percent. If magnet schools are included in the mix, this percentage falls to 16.5 percent.

Even these numbers do not paint a complete picture. . . . Even if one assumes that all voucher students came from low-income families and that each voucher student used up the entire $2,250 voucher, at most $8.2 million of public funds flowed to religious schools under the voucher program in 1999–2000. Although just over one-half as many students attended community schools as religious private schools on the state fisc, the State spent over $1 million more—$9.4 million—on students in community schools than on students in religious private schools because per-pupil aid to community schools is more than double the per-pupil aid to private schools under the voucher program. Moreover, the amount spent on religious private schools is minor compared to the $114.8 million the State spent on students in the Cleveland magnet schools.

Although $8.2 million is no small sum, it pales in comparison to the amount of funds that federal, state, and local governments already provide religious institutions. Religious organizations may qualify for exemptions from the federal corporate income tax; the corporate income tax in many States; and property taxes in all 50 States; and clergy qualify for a federal tax break on income used for housing expenses. In addition, the Federal Government provides individuals, corporations, trusts, and estates a tax deduction for charitable contributions to qualified religious groups. Finally, the Federal Government and certain state governments provide tax credits for educational expenses, many of which are spent on education at religious schools. Most of these tax policies are well established, yet confer a significant relative benefit on religious institutions. The state property tax exemptions for religious institutions alone amount to very large sums annually. . . .

These tax exemptions, which have "much the same effect as [cash grants] . . . of the amount of tax [avoided]," are just part of the picture. Federal dollars also reach religiously affiliated organizations through public health programs such as Medicare and Medicaid, through educational programs such as the Pell Grant program and the G.I. Bill of Rights, and through childcare programs such as the Child Care and Development Block Grant Program.... These programs are well-established parts of our social welfare system, and can be quite substantial. A significant portion of the funds appropriated for these programs reach religiously affiliated institutions, typically without restrictions on its subsequent use....

Against this background, the support that the Cleveland voucher program provides religious institutions is neither substantial nor atypical of existing government programs. While this observation is not intended to justify the Cleveland voucher program under the Establishment Clause, it places in broader perspective [the dissenters'] alarmist claims about implications of the Cleveland program and the Court's decision in these cases.

Nor does today's decision signal a major departure from this Court's prior Establishment Clause jurisprudence. A central tool in our analysis of cases in this area has been the *Lemon* test. As originally formulated, a statute passed this test only if it had "a secular legislative purpose," if its "principal or primary effect" was one that "neither advance[d] nor inhibit[ed] religion," and if it did "not foster an excessive government entanglement with religion." *Lemon v. Kurtzman* (1971) [*supra* this chapter]. In *Agostini v. Felton* (1997) [*supra* this chapter], we folded the entanglement inquiry into the primary effect inquiry. This made sense because both inquiries rely on the same evidence, and the degree of entanglement has implications for whether a statute advances or inhibits religion. The test today is basically the same as that set forth in *School Dist. of Abington Township v. Schempp* (1963) [*infra* this chapter], more than 40 years ago.

The Court's opinion in these cases focuses on a narrow question related to the *Lemon* test: how to apply the primary effects prong in indirect aid cases? Specifically, it clarifies the basic inquiry when trying to determine whether a program that distributes aid to beneficiaries, rather than directly to service providers, has the primary effect of advancing or inhibiting religion.... Courts are instructed to consider two factors: first, whether the program administers aid in a neutral fashion, without differentiation based on the religious status of beneficiaries or providers of services; second, and more importantly, whether beneficiaries of indirect aid have a genuine choice among religious and nonreligious organizations when determining the organization to which they will direct that aid. If the answer to either query is "no," the program should be struck down under the Establishment Clause.... What the Court clarifies in these cases is that the Establishment Clause also requires that state aid flowing to religious organizations through the hands of beneficiaries must do so only at the direction of those beneficiaries....

There is little question in my mind that the Cleveland voucher program is neutral as between religious schools and nonreligious schools.... I do not agree that the nonreligious schools have failed to provide Cleveland parents reasonable alternatives to religious schools in the voucher program.... The District Court record demonstrates that nonreligious schools were able to compete effectively with Catholic and other religious schools in the Cleveland voucher program. The best evidence of this is that many parents with vouchers selected nonreligious private schools over religious alternatives and an even larger number of parents send their children to community and magnet schools rather than seeking vouchers at all. . . .

In my view the more significant finding in these cases is that Cleveland parents who use vouchers to send their children to religious private schools do so as a result of true private choice. . . . I find the Court's answer to the question whether parents of students eligible for vouchers have a genuine choice between religious and nonreligious schools persuasive. In looking at the voucher program, all the choices available to potential beneficiaries of the government program should be considered. . . . Considering all the educational options available to parents whose children are eligible for vouchers, including community and magnet schools, the Court finds that parents in the Cleveland schools have an array of nonreligious options. . . .

Based on the reasoning in the Court's opinion, which is consistent with the realities of the Cleveland educational system, I am persuaded that the Cleveland voucher program affords parents of eligible children genuine nonreligious options and is consistent with the Establishment Clause.

JUSTICE THOMAS, concurring. [Omitted.]

JUSTICE STEVENS, dissenting.

. . . I am convinced that the Court's decision is profoundly misguided. Admittedly, in reaching that conclusion I have been influenced by my understanding of the impact of religious strife on the decisions of our forebears to migrate to this continent, and on the decisions of neighbors in the Balkans, Northern Ireland, and the Middle East to mistrust one another. Whenever we remove a brick from the wall that was designed to separate religion and government, we increase the risk of religious strife and weaken the foundation of our democracy. . . .

JUSTICE SOUTER, with whom JUSTICE STEVENS, JUSTICE GINSBURG, and JUSTICE BREYER join, dissenting.

The Court's majority holds that the Establishment Clause is no bar to Ohio's payment of tuition at private religious elementary and middle schools under a scheme that systematically provides tax money to support the schools' religious missions. . . . The applicability of the Establishment Clause to public funding of benefits to religious schools was settled in *Everson v. Board of Educ.* (1947) [*supra* this chapter], which inaugurated the modern era of establishment doctrine. The Court stated the principle in words from which there was no dissent: "No tax in any amount, large or small, can be levied to support any religious activities or institutions, whatever they may be called, or whatever form they may adopt to teach or practice religion." The Court has never in so many words repudiated this statement, let alone, in so many words, overruled *Everson.*

Today, however, the majority holds that the Establishment Clause is not offended by Ohio's Pilot Project Scholarship Program, under which students may be eligible to receive . . . tuition vouchers transferable to religious schools. In the city of Cleveland the overwhelming proportion of large appropriations for voucher money must be spent on religious schools if it is to be spent at all, and will be spent in amounts that cover almost all of tuition. The money will thus pay for eligible students' instruction not only in secular subjects but in religion as well, in schools that can fairly be characterized as founded to teach religious doctrine and to imbue teaching in all subjects with a religious dimension. Public tax money will pay at a systemic level for teaching the covenant with Israel and Mosaic law in Jewish schools, the primacy of the Apostle Peter and the Papacy in Catholic schools, the truth of reformed Christianity in Protestant schools, and the revelation to the Prophet in Muslim schools, to speak only of major religious groupings in the Republic.

How can a Court consistently leave *Everson* on the books and approve the Ohio vouchers? The answer is that it cannot. It is only by ignoring *Everson* that the majority can claim to rest on traditional law in its invocation of neutral aid provisions and private choice to sanction the Ohio law. It is, moreover, only by ignoring the meaning of neutrality and private choice themselves that the majority can even pretend to rest today's decision on those criteria. . . .

I

[It] seems fair to say that it was not until today that substantiality of aid has clearly been rejected as irrelevant by a majority of this Court, just as it has not been until today that a majority, not a plurality, has held purely formal criteria to suffice for scrutinizing aid that ends up in the coffers of religious schools. Today's cases are notable for their stark illustration of the inadequacy of the majority's chosen formal analysis.

II

Although it has taken half a century since *Everson* to reach the majority's twin standards of neutrality and free choice, the facts show that, in the majority's hands, even these criteria cannot convincingly legitimize the Ohio scheme.

Consider first the criterion of neutrality. . . . In order to apply the neutrality test, [it] makes sense to focus on a category of aid that may be directed to religious as well as secular schools, and ask whether the scheme favors a religious direction. Here, one would ask whether the voucher provisions, allowing for as much as $2,250 toward private school tuition (or a grant to a public school in an adjacent district), were written in a way that skewed the scheme toward benefiting religious schools.

This, however, is not what the majority asks. The majority looks not to the provisions for tuition vouchers, but to every provision for educational opportunity. . . . The majority then finds confirmation that "participation of *all* schools" satisfies neutrality by noting that the better part of total state educational expenditure goes to public schools, thus showing there is no favor of religion. The illogic is patent. If regular, public schools (which can get no voucher payments) "participate" in a voucher scheme with schools that can, and public expenditure is still predominantly on public schools, then the majority's reasoning would find neutrality in a scheme of vouchers available for private tuition in districts with no secular private schools at all. "Neutrality" as the majority employs the term is, literally, verbal and nothing more. . . .

The majority addresses the issue of choice the same way it addresses neutrality, by asking whether recipients or potential recipients of voucher aid have a choice of public schools among secular alternatives to religious schools. Again, however, the majority asks the wrong question and misapplies the criterion. The majority has confused choice in spending scholarships with choice from the entire menu of possible educational placements, most of them open to anyone willing to attend a public school. . . . The majority's view that all educational choices are comparable for purposes of choice thus ignores the whole point of the choice test: it is a criterion for deciding whether indirect aid to a religious school is legitimate because it passes through private hands that can spend or use the aid in a secular school. The question is whether the private hand is genuinely free to send the money in either a secular direction or a religious one. . . . When the choice test is transformed from where to spend the money to where to go to school, it is cut loose from its very purpose. . . .

If, contrary to the majority, we ask the right question about genuine choice to use the vouchers, the answer shows that something is influencing choices in a way that aims the money in a religious direction: of 56 private schools in the district participating in the voucher program (only 53 of which accepted voucher students in 1999–2000), 46 of them are religious; 96.6% of all voucher recipients go to religious schools, only 3.4% to nonreligious ones. Unfortunately for the majority position, there is no explanation for this that suggests the religious direction results simply from free choices by parents. . . . Evidence shows, however, that almost two out of three families using vouchers to send their children to religious schools did not embrace the religion of those schools. The families made it clear they had not chosen the schools because they wished their children to be proselytized in a religion not their own, or in any religion, but because of educational opportunity. . . .

There is, in any case, no way to interpret the 96.6% of current voucher money going to religious schools as reflecting a free and genuine choice by the families that apply for vouchers. . . . For the overwhelming number of children in the voucher scheme, the only alternative to the public schools is religious. And it is entirely irrelevant that the State did not deliberately design the network of private schools for the sake of channeling money into religious institutions. The criterion is one of genuinely free choice on the part of the private individuals who choose, and a Hobson's choice is not a choice, whatever the reason for being Hobsonian.

III

. . . [Even] if I assumed *arguendo* that the majority's formal criteria were satisfied on the facts, today's conclusion would be profoundly at odds with the Constitution. . . . The scale of the aid to religious schools approved today is unprecedented, both in the number of dollars and in the proportion of systemic school expenditure supported. . . . The Cleveland voucher program has cost Ohio taxpayers $33 million since its implementation in 1996 ($28 million in voucher payments, $5 million in administrative costs), and its cost was expected to exceed $8 million in the 2001–2002 school year.

These tax-raised funds are on top of the textbooks, reading and math tutors, laboratory equipment, and the like that Ohio provides to private schools, worth roughly $600 per child. The gross amounts of public money contributed are symptomatic of the scope of what the taxpayers' money buys for a broad class of religious-school students. In paying for practically the full amount of tuition for thousands of qualifying students, the scholarships purchase everything that tuition purchases, be it instruction in math or indoctrination in faith. The . . . majority makes no pretense that substantial amounts of tax money are not systematically underwriting religious practice and indoctrination.

It is virtually superfluous to point out that every objective underlying the prohibition of religious establishment is betrayed by this scheme, . . . the first being respect for freedom of conscience. . . . Madison thought it violated by any "'authority which can force a citizen to contribute three pence . . . of his property for the support of any . . . establishment.'" *Memorial and Remonstrance.* . . . Madison's objection to three pence has simply been lost in the majority's formalism.

As for the second objective, to save religion from its own corruption, . . . [the] risk is already being realized. In Ohio, for example, a condition of receiving government money under the program is that participating religious schools may not "discriminate on the basis of . . . religion," which means the school may not give admission preferences to children who are members of the patron faith; children of a parish are generally consigned to the same admission lotteries as non-believers. . . . Indeed, a separate condition that "[t]he school . . . not . . . teach hatred of any person or group on the basis of . . . religion," could be understood (or subsequently broadened) to prohibit religions from teaching traditionally legitimate articles of faith as to the error, sinfulness, or ignorance of others, if they want government money for their schools. For perspective on this foot-in-the-door of religious regulation, it is well to remember that the money has barely begun to flow. Prior examples of aid, whether grants through individuals or in-kind assistance, were never significant enough to alter the basic fiscal structure of religious schools; state aid was welcome, but not indispensable. . . .

When government aid goes up, so does reliance on it; the only thing likely to go down is [religious] independence. . . . A day will come when religious schools will learn what political leverage can do, just as Ohio's politicians are now getting a lesson in the leverage exercised by religion. Increased voucher spending is not, however, the sole portent of growing regulation of religious practice in the school, for state mandates to moderate religious teaching may well be the most obvious response to the third concern behind the ban on establishment, its inextricable link with social conflict. As appropriations for religious subsidy rise, competition for the money will tap sectarian religion's capacity for discord. . . .

. . . Religious teaching at taxpayer expense simply cannot be cordoned from taxpayer politics, and every major religion currently espouses social positions that provoke intense opposition. Not all taxpaying Protestant citizens, for example, will be content to underwrite the teaching of the Roman Catholic Church condemning the death penalty. Nor will all of America's Muslims acquiesce in paying for the endorsement of the religious Zionism taught in many religious Jewish schools, which combines "a nationalistic sentiment" in support of Israel with a "deeply religious" element. Nor will every secular taxpayer be content to support Muslim views on differential treatment of the sexes, or, for that matter, to fund the espousal of a wife's obligation of obedience to her husband, presumably taught in any schools adopting the articles of faith of the Southern Baptist Convention. Views like these, and innumerable others, have been safe in the sectarian pulpits and classrooms of this Nation not only because the Free Exercise Clause protects them directly, but because the ban on supporting religious establishment has protected free exercise, by keeping it relatively private. With the arrival of vouchers in religious schools, that privacy will go, and along with it will go confidence that religious disagreement will stay moderate.

If the divisiveness permitted by today's majority is to be avoided in the short term, it will be avoided only by action of the political branches at the state and national levels. Legislatures not driven to desperation by the problems of public education may be able to see the threat in vouchers negotiable in sectarian schools. Perhaps even cities with problems like Cleveland's will perceive the danger, now that they know a federal court will not save them from it.

My own course as a judge on the Court cannot, however, simply be to hope that the political branches will save us from the consequences of the majority's decision. *Everson*'s statement is still the touchstone of sound law, even though the reality is that in the matter of educational aid the Establishment Clause has largely been read away. True, the majority has not approved vouchers for religious schools alone, or aid earmarked for religious instruction. But no scheme so clumsy will ever get before us, and in the cases that we may see, like these, the Establishment Clause is largely silenced. I do not have the option to leave it silent, and I hope that a future Court will reconsider today's dramatic departure from basic Establishment Clause principle.

JUSTICE BREYER, with whom JUSTICE STEVENS and JUSTICE SOUTER join, dissenting.

I join Justice Souter's opinion, and I agree substantially with Justice Stevens. I write separately, however, to emphasize the risk that publicly financed voucher programs pose in terms of religiously based social conflict. I do so because I believe that the Establishment Clause concern for protecting the Nation's social fabric from religious conflict poses an overriding obstacle to the implementation of this well-intentioned school voucher program. And by explaining the nature of the concern, I hope to demonstrate why, in my view, "parental choice" cannot significantly alleviate the constitutional problem. . . .

I

[The] Court's 20th-century Establishment Clause cases—both those limiting the practice of religion in public schools and those limiting the public funding of private religious education—focused directly upon social conflict, potentially created when government becomes involved in religious education. . . .

When it decided these 20th-century Establishment Clause cases, the Court did not deny that an earlier American society might have found a less clear-cut church/state separation compatible with social tranquility. Indeed, historians point out that during the early years of the Republic, American schools—including the first public schools—were Protestant in character. Their students recited Protestant prayers, read the King James version of the Bible, and learned Protestant religious ideals. . . .

The 20th-century Court was fully aware, however, that immigration and growth had changed American society dramatically since its early years. By 1850, 1.6 million Catholics lived in America, and by 1900 that number rose to 12 million. There were similar percentage increases in the Jewish population. Not surprisingly, with this increase in numbers, members of non-Protestant religions, particularly Catholics, began to resist the Protestant domination of the public schools. [By] the mid-19th century religious conflict over matters such as Bible reading "grew intense," as Catholics resisted and Protestants fought back to preserve their domination. . . .

The 20th-century Court was also aware that political efforts to right the wrong of discrimination against religious minorities in primary education had failed; in fact they had exacerbated religious conflict. Catholics sought equal government support for the education of their children in the form of aid for private Catholic schools. But the "Protestant position" on this matter, scholars report, "was that public schools must be 'nonsectarian' (which was usually understood to allow Bible reading and other Protestant observances) and public money must not support 'sectarian' schools (which in practical terms meant Catholic)." . . .

These historical circumstances suggest that the Court, applying the Establishment Clause through the Fourteenth Amendment to 20th-century American society, faced an interpretive dilemma that was in part practical. The Court . . . understood the Establishment Clause to prohibit (among other things) any favoritism. Yet *how* did the Clause achieve that objective? Did it simply require the government to give each religion an equal chance to introduce religion into the primary schools—a kind of "equal opportunity" approach to the interpretation of the Establishment Clause? Or, did that Clause avoid government favoritism of some religions by insisting upon "separation"—that the government achieve equal treatment by removing itself from the business of providing religious education for children? This interpretive choice arose in respect both to religious activities in public schools and government aid to private education.

In both areas the Court concluded that the Establishment Clause required "separation," in part because an "equal opportunity" approach was not workable. . . . The upshot is the development of constitutional doctrine that reads the Establishment Clause as avoiding religious strife, *not* by providing every religion with an *equal opportunity* (say, to secure state funding or to pray in the public schools), but by drawing fairly clear lines of *separation* between church and state—at least where the heartland of religious belief, such as primary religious education, is at issue.

II

The principle underlying these cases—avoiding religiously based social conflict—remains of great concern. As religiously diverse as America had become when the

Court decided its major 20th-century Establishment Clause cases, we are exponentially more diverse today. America boasts more than 55 different religious groups and subgroups with a significant number of members. Major religions include, among others, Protestants, Catholics, Jews, Muslims, Buddhists, Hindus, and Sikhs. And several of these major religions contain different subsidiary sects with different religious beliefs. . . .

Under these modern-day circumstances, how is the "equal opportunity" principle to work—without risking the "struggle of sect against sect" . . . ? School voucher programs finance the religious education of the young. And, if widely adopted, they may well provide billions of dollars that will do so. Why will different religions not become concerned about, and seek to influence, the criteria used to channel this money to religious schools? Why will they not want to examine the implementation of the programs that provide this money—to determine, for example, whether implementation has biased a program toward or against particular sects, or whether recipient religious schools are adequately fulfilling a program's criteria? If so, just how is the State to resolve the resulting controversies without provoking legitimate fears of the kinds of religious favoritism that, in so religiously diverse a Nation, threaten social dissension?

Consider the voucher program here at issue. That program insists that the religious school accept students of all religions. Does that criterion treat fairly groups whose religion forbids them to do so? The program also insists that no participating school "advocate or foster unlawful behavior or teach hatred of any person or group on the basis of race, ethnicity, national origin, or religion." And it requires the State to "revoke the registration of any school if, after a hearing, the superintendent determines that the school is in violation" of the program's rules. As one *amicus* argues, "it is difficult to imagine a more divisive activity" than the appointment of state officials as referees to determine whether a particular religious doctrine "teaches hatred or advocates lawlessness."

How are state officials to adjudicate claims that one religion or another is advocating, for example, civil disobedience in response to unjust laws, the use of illegal drugs in a religious ceremony, or resort to force to call attention to what it views as an immoral social practice? What kind of public hearing will there be in response to claims that one religion or another is continuing to teach a view of history that casts members of other religions in the worst possible light? How will the public react to government funding for schools that take controversial religious positions on topics that are of current popular interest—say, the conflict in the Middle East or the war on terrorism? Yet any major funding program for primary religious education will require criteria. And the selection of those criteria, as well as their application, inevitably pose problems that are divisive. Efforts to respond to these problems not only will seriously entangle church and state, but also will promote division among religious groups, as one group or another fears (often legitimately) that it will receive unfair treatment at the hands of the government. . . .

In a society as religiously diverse as ours, the Court has recognized that we must rely on the Religion Clauses of the First Amendment to protect against religious strife, particularly when what is at issue is an area as central to religious belief as the shaping, through primary education, of the next generation's minds and spirits.

III

I concede that the Establishment Clause currently permits States to channel various forms of assistance to religious schools, for example, transportation costs for students, computers, and secular texts. States now certify the nonsectarian educational content of religious school education. Yet the consequence has not been great turmoil.

School voucher programs differ, however, in both *kind* and *degree* from aid programs upheld in the past. They differ in *kind* because they direct financing to a core function of the church: the teaching of religious truths to young children. For that reason the constitutional demand for "separation" is of particular constitutional concern. . . .

Vouchers also differ in *degree*. The aid programs recently upheld by the Court involved limited amounts of aid to religion. But the majority's analysis here appears to permit a considerable shift of taxpayer dollars from public secular schools to private religious schools. That fact, combined with the use to which these dollars will be put, exacerbates the conflict problem. State aid that takes the form of peripheral secular items, with prohibitions against diversion of funds to religious teaching, holds significantly less potential for social division. . . .

I do not believe that the "parental choice" aspect of the voucher program sufficiently offsets the concerns I have mentioned. Parental choice cannot help the taxpayer who does not want to finance the religious education of children. It will not always help the parent who may see little real choice between inadequate nonsectarian public education and adequate education at a school whose religious teachings are contrary to his own. It will not satisfy religious minorities unable to participate because they are too few in number to support the creation of their own private schools. It will not satisfy groups whose religious beliefs preclude them from participating in a government-sponsored program, and who may well feel ignored as government funds primarily support the education of children in the doctrines of the dominant religions. And it does little to ameliorate the entanglement problems or the related problems of social division. . . . Consequently, the fact that the parent may choose which school can cash the government's voucher check does not alleviate the Establishment Clause concerns associated with voucher programs.

The Court, in effect, turns the clock back. It adopts, under the name of "neutrality," an interpretation of the Establishment Clause that this Court rejected more than half a century ago. In its view, the parental choice that offers each religious group a kind of equal opportunity to secure government funding overcomes the Establishment Clause concern for social concord. An earlier Court found that "equal opportunity" principle insufficient; it read the Clause as insisting upon greater separation of church and state, at least in respect to primary education. In a society composed of many different religious creeds, I fear that this present departure from the Court's earlier understanding risks creating a form of religiously based conflict potentially harmful to the Nation's social fabric. Because I believe the Establishment Clause was written in part to avoid this kind of conflict . . . I respectfully dissent.

———

Problem: Faith-Based Social Service Providers

When a convicted criminal is placed on probation and then commits a violation of the terms of his probation, his probation officer may offer him, as an alternative to going to prison, enrollment in one of several approved halfway houses. The probation officer may recommend a particular halfway house, but the probationer is free to choose any state-approved halfway house with which the state has a contract to reimburse on a *per capita* basis for room and board, counseling, and other rehabilitative services.

One of the state-approved halfway houses, Faith Works, which focuses on employment training, drug and alcohol addiction, and parenting responsibility, has a distinctly religious theme: it encourages the probationer to establish a personal relationship with Jesus Christ to mediate his efforts to rehabilitate himself. Probation officers who recommend Faith Works are required to offer the probationer a secular alternative placement as well. And while Faith Works will accept clients who are not Christian, the probation service will not recommend Faith Works to a probationer who does not identify himself as a Christian.

The Religious Freedom Foundation brought suit to enjoin the state from funding Faith Works, alleging that such funding is an unconstitutional establishment of religion. How should the district court rule and why?

B. School Prayer

In the preceding Section, we examined the Establishment Clause as a limitation on government programs that provide financial aid to private religious schools and their students. Now we turn to the other side of the coin: governmental policies that bring—or appear to bring—religion into the state-funded and state-administered public schools. Profound concerns for Establishment Clause values are raised when school officials impose an obligation of formal prayer on students attending public schools under compulsory education laws.

Engel v. Vitale
370 U.S. 421 (1962)

MR. JUSTICE BLACK delivered the opinion of the Court.

The respondent Board of Education of Union Free School District No. 9, New Hyde Park, New York, acting in its official capacity under state law, directed the School District's principal to cause the following prayer to be said aloud by each class in the presence of a teacher at the beginning of each school day:

> Almighty God, we acknowledge our dependence upon Thee, and we beg
> Thy blessings upon us, our parents, our teachers and our Country.

This daily procedure was adopted on the recommendation of the State Board of Regents, a governmental agency created by the State Constitution to which the New York Legislature has granted broad supervisory, executive, and legislative powers over the State's public school system. These state officials composed the prayer which they recommended and published as a part of their "Statement on Moral and Spiritual Training in the Schools," saying: "We believe that this Statement will be subscribed to by all men and women of good will, and we call upon all of them to aid in giving life to our program."

Shortly after the practice of reciting the Regents' prayer was adopted by the School District, the parents of ten pupils brought this action in a New York State Court insisting that use of this official prayer in the public schools was contrary to the beliefs, religions, or religious practices of both themselves and their children. . . . The New York Court of Appeals [sustained] an order of the lower state courts which had upheld the power of New York to use the Regents' prayer as a part of the daily procedures of its public schools so long as the schools did not compel any pupil to join in the prayer over his or his parents' objection. . . .

We think that by using its public school system to encourage recitation of the Regents' prayer, the State of New York has adopted a practice wholly inconsistent with the Establishment Clause. There can, of course, be no doubt that New York's program of daily classroom invocation of God's blessings as prescribed in the Regents' prayer is a religious activity. It is a solemn avowal of divine faith and supplication for the blessings of the Almighty. . . .

. . . [We] think that the constitutional prohibition against laws respecting an establishment of religion must at least mean that in this country it is no part of the business of government to compose official prayers for any group of the American people to recite as a part of a religious program carried on by government.

It is a matter of history that this very practice of establishing governmentally composed prayers for religious services was one of the reasons which caused many of our early colonists to leave England and seek religious freedom in America. . . . It is an unfortunate fact of history that when some of the very groups which had most strenuously opposed the established Church of England found themselves sufficiently in control of colonial governments in this country to write their own prayers into law, they passed laws making their own religion the official religion of their respective colonies. . . . By the time of the adoption of the Constitution, our history shows that there was a widespread awareness among many Americans of the dangers of a union of Church and State. These people knew, some of them from bitter personal experience, that one of the greatest dangers to the freedom of the individual to worship in his own way lay in the Government's placing its official stamp of approval upon one particular kind of prayer or one particular form of religious services. They knew the anguish, hardship and bitter strife that could come when zealous religious groups struggled with one another to obtain the Government's stamp of approval. . . .

The First Amendment was added to the Constitution to stand as a guarantee that neither the power nor the prestige of the Federal Government would be used to control, support or influence the kinds of prayer the American people can say — that the people's religions must not be subjected to the pressures of government for change each time a new political administration is elected to office. Under that Amendment's prohibition against governmental establishment of religion, as reinforced by the provisions of the Fourteenth Amendment, government in this country, be it state or federal, is without power to prescribe by law any particular form of prayer which is to be used as an official prayer in carrying on any program of governmentally sponsored religious activity.

There can be no doubt that New York's state prayer program officially establishes the religious beliefs embodied in the Regents' prayer. . . . Neither the fact that the prayer may be denominationally neutral nor the fact that its observance on the part of the students is voluntary can serve to free it from the limitations of the Establishment Clause. . . . The Establishment Clause [does] not depend upon any showing of direct governmental compulsion and is violated by the enactment of laws which establish an official religion whether those laws operate directly to coerce nonobserving individuals or not. . . . When the power, prestige and financial support of government is placed behind a particular religious belief, the indirect coercive pressure upon religious minorities to conform to the prevailing officially approved religion is plain. But the purposes underlying the Establishment Clause go much further than that. Its first and most immediate purpose rested on the belief that a union of government and religion tends to destroy government and to degrade religion. The history of governmentally established religion, both in England and in this country, showed that whenever government had allied itself with one particular form of religion, the inevitable result had been that it had incurred the hatred, disrespect and even contempt of those who held contrary beliefs. That same history showed that many people had lost their respect for any religion that had relied upon the support of government to spread its faith. The Establishment Clause thus stands as an expression of principle on the part of the Founders of our Constitution that religion is too personal, too sacred, too holy, to permit its "unhallowed perversion" by a civil magistrate.

Another purpose of the Establishment Clause rested upon an awareness of the historical fact that governmentally established religions and religious persecutions go hand in hand. . . . It was in large part to get completely away from [religious] persecution that the Founders brought into being our Nation, our Constitution, and our Bill of Rights with its prohibition against any governmental establishment of religion. The New York laws officially prescribing the Regents' prayer are inconsistent both with the purposes of the Establishment Clause and with the Establishment Clause itself.

It has been argued that to apply the Constitution in such a way as to prohibit state laws respecting an establishment of religious services in public schools is to indicate a hostility toward religion or toward prayer. Nothing, of course, could be more wrong. The history of man is inseparable from the history of religion. And perhaps it is not too much to say that since the beginning of that history many people have devoutly believed that "More things are wrought by prayer than this world dreams of." . . . And there were men of this same faith in the power of prayer who led the fight for adoption of our Constitution and also for our Bill of Rights with the very guarantees of religious freedom that forbid the sort of governmental activity which New York has attempted here. . . . It is neither sacrilegious nor antireligious to say that each separate government in this country should stay out of the business of writing or sanctioning official prayers and leave that purely religious function to the people themselves and to those the people choose to look to for religious guidance.

It is true that New York's establishment of its Regents' prayer as an officially approved religious doctrine of that State does not amount to a total establishment of one particular religious sect to the exclusion of all others—that, indeed, the governmental endorsement of that prayer seems relatively insignificant when compared to the governmental encroachments upon religion which were commonplace 200 years ago. To those who may subscribe to the view that because the Regents' official prayer is so brief and general there can be no danger to religious freedom in its governmental establishment, however, it may be appropriate to say in the words of James Madison, the author of the First Amendment [in his *Memorial and Remonstrance against Religious Assessments*]:

> It is proper to take alarm at the first experiment on our liberties. . . . Who does not see that the same authority which can establish Christianity, in exclusion of all other Religions, may establish with the same ease any particular sect of Christians, in exclusion of all other Sects? That the same authority which can force a citizen to contribute three pence only of his property for the support of any one establishment, may force him to conform to any other establishment in all cases whatsoever?

Reversed and remanded.

Mr. Justice Frankfurter took no part in the decision of this case.

Mr. Justice White took no part in the consideration or decision of this case.

Mr. Justice Douglas, concurring.

The question presented by this case is [an] extremely narrow one. It is whether New York oversteps the bounds when it finances a religious exercise. . . . [I] cannot say that to authorize this prayer is to establish a religion in the strictly historic meaning of those words. A religion is not established in the usual sense merely by letting those who choose to do so say the prayer that the public school teacher leads. Yet once government finances a religious exercise it inserts a divisive influence into our communities. The New York Court said that the prayer given does not conform to all of the tenets of the Jewish, Unitarian, and Ethical Culture groups. One of the petitioners is an agnostic. . . .

The First Amendment leaves the Government in a position not of hostility to religion but of neutrality. The philosophy is that the atheist or agnostic—the nonbeliever—is entitled to go his own way. The philosophy is that if government interferes in matters spiritual, it will be a divisive force. The First Amendment teaches that a government neutral in the field of religion better serves all religious interests.

Mr. Justice Stewart, dissenting.

. . . With all respect, I think the Court has misapplied a great constitutional principle. I cannot see how an "official religion" is established by letting those who want to say a prayer say it. On the contrary, I think that to deny the wish of these school children to join in reciting this prayer is to deny them the opportunity of sharing in the spiritual heritage of our Nation.

The Court's historical review [throws] no light for me on the issue before us in this case. . . . Moreover, I think that the Court's task, in this as in all areas of constitutional adjudication, is not responsibly aided by the uncritical invocation of metaphors like the "wall of separation," a phrase nowhere to be found in the Constitution. What is relevant to the issue here is not the history of an established church in sixteenth century England or in eighteenth century America, but the history of the religious traditions of our people, reflected in countless practices of the institutions and officials of our government.

At the opening of each day's Session of this Court we stand, while one of our officials invokes the protection of God. Since the days of John Marshall our Crier has said, "God save the United States and this Honorable Court." Both the Senate and the House of Representatives open their daily Sessions with prayer. Each of our Presidents, from George Washington to John F. Kennedy, has upon assuming his Office asked the protection and help of God. The Court today says that the state and federal governments are without constitutional power to prescribe any particular form of words to be recited by any group of the American people on any subject touching religion. . . .

Countless similar examples could be listed, but there is no need to belabor the obvious. It was all summed up by this Court just ten years ago in a single sentence: "We are a religious people whose institutions presuppose a Supreme Being." *Zorach v. Clauson*, 343 U.S. 306 (1952).

I do not believe that this Court, or the Congress, or the President has by the actions and practices I have mentioned established an "official religion" in violation of the Constitution. And I do not believe the State of New York has done so in this case. What each has done has been to recognize and to follow the deeply entrenched and highly cherished spiritual traditions of our Nation. . . .

I dissent.

School District of Abington Township v. Schempp
374 U.S. 203 (1963)

Mr. Justice Clark delivered the opinion of the Court.

. . . These companion cases present [issues under the Establishment Clause] in the context of state action requiring that schools begin each day with readings from the Bible. . . . In light of the history of the First Amendment and of our cases interpreting and applying its requirements, we hold that the practices at issue and the laws requiring them are unconstitutional under the Establishment Clause, as applied to the States through the Fourteenth Amendment.

[*The Facts in Each Case*: No. 142. A 1959 Pennsylvania statute requires that "at least ten verses from the Holy Bible shall be read, without comment, at the opening of each public school on each school day. Any child shall be excused from such Bible reading, or attending such Bible reading, upon the written request of his parent or guardian." Suit was brought by the Schempp family, the parents and their two children, who were practicing Unitarians and whose personal religious beliefs were regularly contradicted by the selected readings. At trial, expert testimony gave detailed and elaborate explanations of marked differences in various versions of the Bible between Jews and Christians and among different denominations of Christians. A three-judge U.S. District Court enjoined the school district from conducting the readings and the recitation of the Lord's Prayer. The school officials appealed to this Court.

No. 119. In 1905, the Board of School Commissioners of Baltimore City adopted a rule pursuant to a Maryland statute providing for the holding of opening exercises in the schools of the city, consisting primarily of the "reading, without comment, of a chapter in the Holy Bible and/or the use of the Lord's Prayer." The petitioners, Madalyn Murray and her son, William J. Murray III, both professed atheists, challenged the statute and the practice under the First and Fourteenth Amendments. The state trial court, recognizing that the respondent-school officials' demurrer admitted all facts well-pleaded, sustained the policy. The Maryland Court of Appeals affirmed.] We granted certiorari.

Applying the Establishment Clause principles to the cases at bar we find that the States are requiring the selection and reading at the opening of the school day of verses from the Holy Bible and the recitation of the Lord's Prayer by the students in unison. These exercises are prescribed as part of the curricular activities of students who are required by law to attend school. They are held in the school buildings under the supervision and with the participation of teachers employed in those schools. . . . The trial court in [the Pennsylvania case] has found that such an opening exercise is a religious ceremony and was intended by the State to be so. We agree with the trial court's finding as to the religious character of the exercises. Given that finding, the exercises and the law requiring them are in violation of the Establishment Clause.

There is no such specific finding as to the religious character of the exercises in [the Baltimore case], and the State contends [as does Pennsylvania] that the program is an effort to extend its benefits to all public school children without regard to their religious belief. Included within its secular purposes, it says, are the promotion of moral values, the contradiction to the materialistic trends of our times, the perpetuation of our institutions and the teaching of literature. The case came up on demurrer, of course, to a petition which alleged that the uniform practice under the rule had been to read from the King James version of the Bible and that the exercise was sectarian. The short answer, therefore, is that the religious character of the exercise was admitted by the State. But even if its purpose is not strictly religious, it is sought to be accomplished through readings, without comment, from the Bible. Surely the place of the Bible as an instrument of religion cannot be gainsaid, and the State's recognition of the pervading religious character of the ceremony is evident from the rule's specific permission of the alternative use of the Catholic Douay version as well as the recent amendment permitting nonattendance at the exercises. None of these factors is consistent with the contention that the Bible is here used either as an instrument for nonreligious moral inspiration or as a reference for the teaching of secular subjects.

The conclusion follows that in both cases the laws require religious exercises and such exercises are being conducted in direct violation of the rights of the appellees and petitioners. Nor are these required exercises mitigated by the fact that individual students may absent themselves upon parental request, for that fact furnishes no defense to a claim of unconstitutionality under the Establishment Clause. Further, it is no defense to urge that the religious practices here may be relatively minor encroachments on the First Amendment. The breach of neutrality that is today a trickling stream may all too soon become a raging torrent and, in the words of Madison, "it is proper to take alarm at the first experiment on our liberties." *Memorial and Remonstrance Against Religious Assessments.*

It is insisted that unless these religious exercises are permitted a "religion of secularism" is established in the schools. We agree of course that the State may not establish a "religion of secularism" in the sense of affirmatively opposing or showing hostility to religion, thus "preferring those who believe in no religion over those who do believe." *Zorach v. Clauson* (1952). We do not agree, however, that this decision in any sense has that effect. In addition, it might well be said that one's education is not complete without a study of comparative religion or the history of religion and its relationship to the advancement of civilization. It certainly may be said that the Bible is worthy of study for its literary and historic qualities. Nothing we have said here indicates that such study of the Bible or of religion, when presented objectively as part of a secular program of education, may not be effected consistently with the First Amendment. But the exercises here do not fall into those categories. They are religious exercises, required by the States in violation of the command of the First Amendment that the Government maintain strict neutrality, neither aiding nor opposing religion.

Finally, we cannot accept that the concept of neutrality, which does not permit a State to require a religious exercise even with the consent of the majority of those affected, collides with the majority's right to free exercise of religion. While the Free Exercise Clause clearly prohibits the use of state action to deny the rights of free exercise to *anyone*, it has never meant that a majority could use the machinery of the State to practice its beliefs. . . .

. . . [We] affirm the judgment in [the Pennsylvania case]. In [the Baltimore case], the judgment is reversed and the cause remanded to the Maryland Court of Appeals for further proceedings consistent with this opinion.

Mr. Justice Douglas, concurring.

[These] regimes violate the Establishment Clause in two different ways. In each case the State is conducting a religious exercise; and, as the Court holds, that cannot be done without violating the "neutrality" required of the State by the balance of power between individual, church and state that has been struck by the First Amendment. But the Establishment Clause is not limited to precluding the State itself from conducting religious exercises. It also forbids the State to employ its facilities or funds in a way that gives any church, or all churches, greater strength in our society than it would have by relying on its members alone. Thus, the present regimes must fall under that clause for the additional reason that public funds, though small in amount, are being used to promote a religious exercise. Through the mechanism of the State, all of the people are being required to finance a religious exercise that only some of the people want and that violates the sensibilities of others. . . .

Mr. Justice Brennan, concurring.

. . . The reasons we gave only last Term in *Engel v. Vitale* (1962) [*supra* this chapter], for finding in the New York Regents' prayer an impermissible establishment of religion, compel the same judgment of the practices at bar. The involvement of the secular with the religious is no less intimate here; and it is constitutionally irrelevant that the State has not composed the material for the inspirational exercises presently involved. . . .

The religious nature of the exercises here challenged seems plain. Unless *Engel v. Vitale* is to be overruled, or we are to engage in wholly disingenuous distinction, we cannot sustain these practices. Daily recital of the Lord's Prayer and the reading of passages of Scripture are quite as clearly breaches of the command of the Establishment Clause as was the daily use of the rather bland Regents' Prayer in the New York public schools. Indeed, I would suppose that, if anything, the Lord's Prayer and the Holy Bible are more clearly sectarian, and the present violations of the First Amendment consequently more serious. . . .

. . . The secular purposes which devotional exercises are said to serve fall into two categories—those which depend upon an immediately religious experience shared by the participating children; and those which appear sufficiently divorced from the religious content of the devotional material that they can be served equally by nonreligious materials. With respect to the first objective, much has been written about the moral and spiritual values of infusing some religious influence or instruction into the public school classroom. To the extent that only religious materials will serve this purpose, it seems to me that the purpose as well as the means is so plainly religious that the exercise is necessarily forbidden by the Establishment Clause. . . .

The second justification assumes that religious exercises at the start of the school day may directly serve solely secular ends—for example, by fostering harmony and tolerance among the pupils, enhancing the authority of the teacher, and inspiring better discipline. To the extent that such benefits result not from the content of the readings and recitation, but simply from the holding of such a solemn exercise at the opening assembly or the first class of the day, it would seem that less sensitive materials might equally well serve the same purpose. . . . It has not been shown that readings from the speeches and messages of great Americans, for example, or from the documents of our heritage of liberty, daily recitation of the Pledge of Allegiance, or even the observance of a moment of reverent silence at the opening of class, may not adequately serve the solely secular purposes of the devotional activities without jeopardizing either the religious liberties of any members of the community or the proper degree of separation between the spheres of religion and government. Such substitutes would, I think, be unsatisfactory or inadequate only to the extent that the present activities do in fact serve religious goals. While I do not question the judgment of experienced educators that the challenged practices may well achieve valuable secular ends, it seems to me that the State acts unconstitutionally if it either sets about to attain even indirectly religious ends by religious means, or if it uses religious means to serve secular ends where secular means would suffice. . . .

[It] is argued that the particular practices involved in the two cases before us are unobjectionable because they prefer no particular sect or sects at the expense of others. Both the Baltimore and [Pennsylvania] procedures permit, for example, the reading of any of several versions of the Bible, and this flexibility is said to ensure neutrality sufficiently to avoid the constitutional prohibition. One answer, which might be dispositive, is that any version of the Bible is inherently sectarian, else there would be no need to offer a system of rotation or alternation of versions in the first place, that is, to allow different sectarian versions to be used on different days. The sectarian character of the Holy Bible has been at the core of the whole controversy over religious practices in the public schools throughout its long and often bitter history. . . . The argument contains, however, a more basic flaw. There are persons in every community—often deeply devout—to whom any version of the Judaeo-Christian Bible is offensive. There are others whose reverence for the Holy Scriptures demands private study or reflection and to whom public reading or recitation is sacrilegious. . . .

It has been suggested that a tentative solution to these problems may lie in the fashioning of a "common core" of theology tolerable to all creeds but preferential to none. [But] "[h]istory is not encouraging to" those who hope to fashion a "common denominator of religion detached from its manifestation in any organized church." Thus, the notion of a "common core" litany or supplication offends many deeply devout worshippers who do not find clearly sectarian practices objectionable. . . . Moreover, even if the Establishment Clause were oblivious to nonsectarian religious practices, I think it quite likely that the "common core" approach would be sufficiently objectionable to many groups to be foreclosed by the prohibitions of the Free Exercise Clause. . . .

Mr. Justice Goldberg, with whom Mr. Justice Harlan joins, concurring. [Omitted.]

Mr. Justice Stewart, dissenting.

It might [be] argued that parents who want their children exposed to religious influences can adequately fulfill that wish off school property and outside school time.

With all its surface persuasiveness, however, this argument seriously misconceives the basic constitutional justification for permitting the exercises at issue in these cases. For a compulsory state educational system so structures a child's life that if religious exercises are held to be an impermissible activity in schools, religion is placed at an artificial and state-created disadvantage. Viewed in this light, permission of such exercises for those who want them is necessary if the schools are truly to be neutral in the matter of religion. And a refusal to permit religious exercises thus is seen, not as the realization of state neutrality, but rather as the establishment of a religion of secularism, or at the least, as government support of the beliefs of those who think that religious exercises should be conducted only in private. . . .

The dangers both to government and to religion inherent in official support of instruction in the tenets of various religious sects are absent in the present cases, which involve only a reading from the Bible unaccompanied by comments which might otherwise constitute instruction. Indeed, since, from all that appears in either record, any teacher who does not wish to do so is free not to participate, it cannot even be contended that some infinitesimal part of the salaries paid by the State are made contingent upon the performance of a religious function. . . .

The governmental neutrality which the First and Fourteenth Amendments require in the cases before us, in other words, is the extension of evenhanded treatment to all who believe, doubt, or disbelieve — a refusal on the part of the State to weight the scales of private choice. In these cases, therefore, what is involved is not state action based on impermissible categories, but rather an attempt by the State to accommodate those differences which the existence in our society of a variety of religious beliefs makes inevitable. The Constitution requires that such efforts be struck down only if they are proven to entail the use of the secular authority of government to coerce a preference among such beliefs.

. . . [Religious] exercises are not constitutionally invalid if they simply reflect differences which exist in the society from which the school draws its pupils. They become constitutionally invalid only if their administration places the sanction of secular authority behind one or more particular religious or irreligious beliefs.

What our Constitution indispensably protects is the freedom of each of us, be he Jew or Agnostic, Christian or Atheist, Buddhist or Freethinker, to believe or disbelieve, to worship or not worship, to pray or keep silent, according to his own conscience, uncoerced and unrestrained by government. It is conceivable that these school boards, or even all school boards, might eventually find it impossible to administer a system of religious exercises during school hours in such a way as to meet this constitutional standard — in such a way as completely to free from any kind of official coercion those who do not affirmatively want to participate. But I think we must not assume that school boards so lack the qualities of inventiveness and good will as to make impossible the achievement of that goal. I would remand both cases for further hearings.

Wallace v. Jaffree

472 U.S. 38 (1985)

Justice Stevens delivered the opinion of the Court.

[Earlier stages of this litigation involved the constitutionality of three Alabama statutes: (1) § 16-1-20, enacted in 1978, which authorized a 1-minute period of silence in all public schools "for meditation"; (2) § 16-1-20.1, enacted in 1981, which authorized a period of silence "for meditation or voluntary prayer"; and (3) § 16-1-20.2, enacted in 1982, which authorized teachers to lead "willing students" in a prescribed prayer to "Almighty God . . . the Creator and Supreme Judge of the world."

At the preliminary-injunction stage of this case, the District Court held that §§ 16-1-20.1 and 16-1-20.2 were both invalid, but held that there was "nothing wrong" with § 16-1-20. The Court of Appeals agreed with the District Court's interpretation of the unconstitutional purpose of § 16-1-20.1 and § 16-1-20.2, and held them both unconstitutional. The Court of Appeals' holding with respect to § 16-1-20.2 was affirmed. *Wallace v. Jaffree*, 466 U.S. 924 (1984). Moreover, appellees have not questioned the holding that § 16-1-20 is valid. Thus, the narrow question for decision is whether § 16-1-20.1 is a law respecting the establishment of religion within the meaning of the First Amendment. It provides:

> At the commencement of the first class of each day in all grades in all public schools the teacher in charge of the room in which each class is held may announce that a period of silence not to exceed one minute in duration shall be observed for meditation or voluntary prayer, and during any such period no other activities shall be engaged in.]

When the Court has been called upon to construe the breadth of the Establishment Clause, it has examined the criteria developed. . . . [in] *Lemon v. Kurtzman* (1971) [*supra* this chapter]. . . .

It is the first of these three criteria that is most plainly implicated by this case. . . . [The] First Amendment requires that a statute must be invalidated if it is entirely motivated by a purpose to advance religion.

In applying the purpose test, it is appropriate to ask "whether government's actual purpose is to endorse or disapprove of religion." In this case, the answer to that question is dispositive. For the record not only provides us with an unambiguous affirmative answer, but it also reveals that the enactment of § 16-1-20.1 was not motivated by any clearly secular purpose — indeed, the statute had *no* secular purpose.

The sponsor of the bill that became § 16-1-20.1, Senator Donald Holmes, inserted into the legislative record — apparently without dissent — a statement indicating that the legislation was an "effort to return voluntary prayer" to the public schools. Later Senator Holmes confirmed this purpose before the District Court. In response to the question whether he had any purpose for the legislation other than returning voluntary prayer to public schools, he stated: "No, I did not have no other purpose in mind." The State did not present evidence of *any* secular purpose.

The unrebutted evidence of legislative intent contained in the legislative record and in the testimony of the sponsor of § 16-1-20.1 is confirmed by a consideration of the relationship between this statute and the two other measures that were considered in this case. . . . The wholly religious character of the later enactment is plainly evident from its text. . . . [The] earlier statute refers only to "meditation" whereas § 16-1-20.1 refers to "meditation or voluntary prayer." . . . [The] only significant textual difference is the addition of the words "or voluntary prayer."

The legislative intent to return prayer to the public schools is, of course, quite different from merely protecting every student's right to engage in voluntary prayer during an appropriate moment of silence during the school day. The 1978 statute already protected that right, containing nothing that prevented any student from engaging in voluntary prayer during a silent minute of meditation. Appellants have not identified any secular purpose that was not fully served by § 16-1-20 before the enactment of § 16-1-20.1 [in 1981]. Thus, only two conclusions are consistent with the text of § 16-1-20.1: (1) the statute was enacted to convey a message of state endorsement and promotion of prayer; or (2) the statute was enacted for no purpose. No one suggests that the statute was nothing but a meaningless or irrational act.

We must, therefore, conclude that the Alabama Legislature intended to change existing law. . . . The legislature enacted § 16-1-20.1, despite the existence of § 16-1-20 for the sole purpose of expressing the State's endorsement of prayer activities for one minute at the beginning of each school day. The addition of "or voluntary prayer" indicates that the State intended to characterize prayer as a favored practice. Such an endorsement is not consistent with the established principle that the government must pursue a course of complete neutrality toward religion.

The importance of that principle does not permit us to treat this as an inconsequential case involving nothing more than a few words of symbolic speech on behalf of the political majority. . . . [The fact] that § 16-1-20.1 was intended to convey a message of state approval of prayer activities in the public schools make[s] it unnecessary, and indeed inappropriate, to evaluate the practical significance of the addition of the words "or voluntary prayer" to the statute. . . . [We] conclude that § 16-1-20.1 violates the First Amendment.

The judgment of the Court of Appeals is affirmed.

JUSTICE POWELL, concurring. [Omitted.]

JUSTICE O'CONNOR, concurring in the judgment.

Nothing in the United States Constitution as interpreted by this Court or in the laws of the State of Alabama prohibits public school students from voluntarily praying at any time before, during, or after the school day. Alabama has facilitated voluntary silent prayers of students who are so inclined by enacting ALA. CODE § 16-1-20, which provides a moment of silence [in] schools each day. The parties to these proceedings concede the validity of this enactment. . . .

Twenty-five states permit or require public school teachers to have students observe a moment of silence in their classrooms. A few statutes provide that the moment of silence is for the purpose of meditation alone. The typical statute, however, calls for a moment of silence at the beginning of the school day during which students may meditate, pray, or reflect on the activities of the day. . . .

A state-sponsored moment of silence in the public schools is different from state-sponsored vocal prayer or Bible reading. First, a moment of silence is not inherently religious. Silence, unlike prayer or Bible reading, need not be associated with a religious exercise. Second, a pupil who participates in a moment of silence need not compromise his or her beliefs. During a moment of silence, a student who objects to prayer is left to his or her own thoughts, and is not compelled to listen to the prayers or thoughts of others. For these simple reasons, a moment of silence statute does not stand or fall under the Establishment Clause according to how the Court regards vocal prayer or Bible reading. . . . It is difficult to discern a serious threat to religious liberty from a room of silent, thoughtful schoolchildren.

By mandating a moment of silence, a State does not necessarily endorse any activity that might occur during the period. Even if a statute specifies that a student may choose to pray silently during a quiet moment, the State has not thereby encouraged prayer over other specified alternatives. Nonetheless, it is also possible that a moment of silence statute, either as drafted or as actually implemented, could effectively favor the child who prays over the child who does not. . . . The crucial question is whether the State has conveyed or attempted to convey the message that children should use the moment of silence for prayer. This question cannot be answered in the abstract, but instead requires courts to examine the history, language, and administration of a particular statute to determine whether it operates as an endorsement of religion.

. . . [The] inquiry into the purpose of the legislature in enacting a moment of silence law should be deferential and limited. . . . If a legislature expresses a plausible secular purpose for a moment of silence statute in either the text or the legislative history, or if the statute disclaims an intent to encourage prayer over alternatives during a moment of silence, then courts should generally defer to that stated intent. . . . Since there is arguably a secular pedagogical value to a moment of silence in public schools, courts should find an improper purpose behind such a statute only if the statute on its face, in its official legislative history, or in its interpretation by a responsible administrative agency suggests it has the primary purpose of endorsing prayer. . . .

In finding that the purpose of § 16-1-20.1 is to endorse voluntary prayer during a moment of silence, the Court relies on testimony elicited from [the sponsor] State Senator Donald G. Holmes during a preliminary injunction hearing. . . . I would give little, if any, weight to this sort of evidence of legislative intent. Nevertheless, the text of the statute in light of its official legislative history leaves little doubt that the purpose of this statute corresponds to the purpose expressed by Senator Holmes at the preliminary injunction hearing. . . .

The Court does not hold that the Establishment Clause is so hostile to religion that it precludes the States from affording schoolchildren an opportunity for voluntary silent prayer. To the contrary, the moment of silence statutes of many States should satisfy the Establishment Clause standard we have here applied. The Court holds only that Alabama has intentionally crossed the line between creating a quiet moment during which those so inclined may pray, and affirmatively endorsing the particular religious practice of prayer. . . . In my view, the judgment of the Court of Appeals must be affirmed.

CHIEF JUSTICE BURGER, dissenting.

. . . It makes no sense to say that Alabama has "endorsed prayer" by merely enacting a new statute "to specify expressly that voluntary prayer is *one* of the authorized activities during a moment of silence." To suggest that a moment-of-silence statute that includes the word "prayer" unconstitutionally endorses religion, while one that simply provides for a moment of silence does not, manifests not neutrality but hostility toward religion. [Hostility] toward any religion or toward all religions is as much forbidden by the Constitution as is an official establishment of religion. The Alabama Legislature has no more "endorsed" religion than a state or the Congress does when it provides for legislative chaplains, or than this Court does when it opens each session with an invocation to God. . . .

The notion that the Alabama statute is a step toward creating an established church borders on [the] ridiculous. The statute does not remotely threaten religious liberty; it affirmatively furthers the values of religious freedom and tolerance. . . . Without pressuring those who do not wish to pray, the statute simply creates an opportunity to think, to plan, or to pray if one wishes. . . . It accommodates the purely private, voluntary religious choices of the individual pupils who wish to pray while at the same time creating a time for nonreligious reflection for those who do not choose to pray. The statute also provides a meaningful opportunity for schoolchildren to appreciate the absolute constitutional right of each individual to worship and believe as the individual wishes. The statute "endorses" only the view that the religious observances of others should be tolerated and, where possible, accommodated. . . .

JUSTICE WHITE, dissenting.

. . . As I read the filed opinions, a majority of the Court would approve statutes that provided for a moment of silence but did not mention prayer. But if a student asked whether he could pray during that moment, it is difficult to believe that the teacher could not answer in the affirmative. If that is the case, I would not invalidate a statute that at the outset provided the legislative answer to the question "May I pray?" This is so even if the Alabama statute is infirm, which I do not believe it is, because of its peculiar legislative history. . . .

JUSTICE REHNQUIST, dissenting. [This dissent questioned the historical basis for the Supreme Court's Establishment Clause doctrine. *See* Chapter 16, section A.]

Lee v. Weisman

505 U.S. 577 (1992)

Justice Kennedy delivered the opinion of the Court.

[It has been the long-standing policy of the Providence, Rhode Island public schools to permit principals to invite members of the clergy to give invocations and benedictions at middle school and high school graduations. Many, but not all, of the principals elected to include prayers. Acting for himself and his 14-year-old daughter Deborah, Daniel Weisman, objected to any prayers at her middle school graduation, but to no avail. The school principal, petitioner Robert E. Lee, invited a rabbi to deliver prayers at the graduation exercises for Deborah's class. School officials provide invited clergy with a pamphlet entitled "Guidelines for Civic Occasions," prepared by the National Conference of Christians and Jews. The Guidelines recommend that public prayers at nonsectarian civic ceremonies be composed with "inclusiveness and sensitivity" though they acknowledge that "prayer of any kind may be inappropriate on some civic occasions."]

The school board (and the United States as *amicus curiae*) argue that these relatively short prayers and others like them at other graduation exercises are of profound meaning to many students and parents throughout this country who consider that due respect and acknowledgment for divine guidance and for the deepest spiritual aspirations of our people ought to be expressed at an event as important in life as a graduation. We assume this to be so in addressing the difficult case now before us, for the significance of the prayers lies also at the heart of Daniel and Deborah Weisman's case.

[Four days before the ceremony, Daniel Weisman, in his individual capacity as a Providence taxpayer and as next friend of Deborah, sought a temporary restraining order in the U.S. District Court to prohibit school officials from including an invocation or benediction in the graduation ceremony. The court denied the motion for lack of adequate time to consider it. Deborah and her family attended the graduation, where the prayers were recited. In July 1989, Daniel Weisman filed an amended complaint seeking a permanent injunction barring petitioners, various officials of the Providence public schools, from inviting the clergy to deliver invocations and benedictions at future graduations, including Deborah's own high school graduation.

The case was submitted on stipulated facts. The District Court held that petitioners' practice of including invocations and benedictions in public school graduations violated the Establishment Clause, and it enjoined petitioners from continuing the practice. On appeal, a divided panel of the U.S. Court of Appeals for the First Circuit affirmed.] We granted certiorari and now affirm.

. . . [The] Constitution guarantees that government may not coerce anyone to support or participate in religion or its exercise, or otherwise act in a way which "establishes a [state] religion or religious faith, or tends to do so." The State's involvement in the school prayers challenged today violates these central principles. That involvement is as troubling as it is undenied. A school official, the principal, decided that an invocation and a benediction should be given; this is a choice attributable to the State, and from a constitutional perspective it is as if a state statute decreed that the prayers must occur. The principal chose the religious participant, here a rabbi, and that choice is also attributable to the State. The [potential] for divisiveness over the choice of a particular member of the clergy to conduct the ceremony is apparent.

Divisiveness, of course, can attend any state decision respecting religions, and neither its existence nor its potential necessarily invalidates the State's attempts to accommodate religion in all cases. The potential for divisiveness is of particular relevance here though, because it centers around an overt religious exercise in a secondary school environment [where] subtle coercive pressures exist and where the student had no real alternative which would have allowed her to avoid the fact or appearance of participation.

The State's role did not end with the decision to include a prayer and with the choice of a clergyman. Principal Lee provided Rabbi Gutterman with a copy of the "Guidelines for Civic Occasions," and advised him that his prayers should be nonsectarian. Through these means the principal directed and controlled the content of the prayers. Even if the only sanction for ignoring the instructions were that the rabbi would not be invited back, we think no religious representative who valued his or her continued reputation and effectiveness in the community would incur the State's displeasure in this regard. It is a cornerstone principle of our Establishment Clause jurisprudence that "it is no part of the business of government to compose official prayers for any group of the American people to recite as a part of a religious program carried on by government," *Engel v. Vitale* (1962) [*supra* this chapter], and that is what the school officials attempted to do.

Petitioners argue [that] the directions for the content of the prayers were a good-faith attempt by the school to ensure that the sectarianism which is so often the flashpoint for religious animosity be removed from the graduation ceremony.... The question is not the good faith of the school in attempting to make the prayer acceptable to most persons, but the legitimacy of its undertaking that enterprise at all....

We are asked to recognize the existence of a practice of nonsectarian prayer, prayer within [what] is known as the Judeo-Christian tradition, prayer which is more acceptable than one which, for example, makes explicit references to the God of Israel, or to Jesus Christ, or to a patron saint. There may be some support, as an empirical observation, [for the proposition that] there has emerged in this country a civic religion, one which is tolerated when sectarian exercises are not.... But though the First Amendment does not allow the government to stifle prayers which aspire to these ends, neither does it permit the government to undertake that task for itself.

The First Amendment's Religion Clauses mean that religious beliefs and religious expression are too precious to be either proscribed or prescribed by the State. The design of the Constitution is that preservation and transmission of religious beliefs and worship is a responsibility and a choice committed to the private sphere.... [while] concern must be given to define the protection granted to an objector or a dissenting nonbeliever, these same Clauses exist to protect religion from government interference....

These concerns have particular application in the case of school officials, whose effort to monitor prayer will be perceived by the students as inducing a participation they might otherwise reject. Though the efforts of the school officials in this case to find common ground appear to have been a good-faith attempt to recognize the common aspects of religions and not the divisive ones, our precedents do not permit school officials to assist in composing prayers as an incident to a formal exercise for their students. *Engel v. Vitale*. . . . The suggestion that government may establish an official or civic religion as a means of avoiding the establishment of a religion with more specific creeds strikes us as a contradiction that cannot be accepted. . . .

. . . It is argued that our constitutional vision of a free society requires confidence in our own ability to accept or reject ideas of which we do not approve, and that prayer at a high school graduation does nothing more than offer a choice. . . . This argument [overlooks] a fundamental dynamic of the Constitution. . . . [If] citizens are subjected to state-sponsored religious exercises, the State disavows its own duty to guard and respect that sphere of inviolable conscience and belief which is the mark of a free people. . . .

. . . [There] are heightened concerns with protecting freedom of conscience from subtle coercive pressure in the elementary and secondary public schools. Our decisions in *Engel v. Vitale* (1962) [*supra* this chapter], and *School Dist. of Abington Township v. Schempp* (1963) [*supra* this chapter], recognize, among other things, that prayer exercises in public schools carry a particular risk of indirect coercion. . . . The undeniable fact is that the school district's supervision and control of a high school graduation ceremony places public pressure, as well as peer pressure, on attending students to stand as a group or, at least, maintain respectful silence during the invocation and benediction. This pressure, though subtle and indirect, can be as real as any overt compulsion. . . . The injury caused by the government's action, and the reason why Daniel and Deborah Weisman object to it, is that the State, in a school setting, in effect required participation in a religious exercise. . . .

There was a stipulation in the District Court that attendance at graduation and promotional ceremonies is voluntary. Petitioners and the United States, as *amicus*, [argue] that the option of not attending the graduation excuses any inducement or coercion in the ceremony itself. The argument lacks all persuasion. Law reaches past formalism. And to say a teenage student has a real choice not to attend her high school graduation is formalistic in the extreme. . . . Everyone knows that in our society and in our culture high school graduation is one of life's most significant occasions. A school rule which excuses attendance is beside the point. . . .

. . . [The school district argues] that the prayers are an essential part of these ceremonies because for many persons an occasion of this significance lacks meaning if there is no recognition, however brief, that human achievements cannot be understood apart from their spiritual essence. . . . [This argument] fails to acknowledge that what for many of Deborah's classmates and their parents was a spiritual imperative was for Daniel and Deborah Weisman religious conformance compelled by the State. While in some societies the wishes of the majority might prevail, the Establishment

Clause [forbids] the State to exact religious conformity from a student as the price of attending her own high school graduation. . . .

. . . At a high school graduation, teachers and principals must and do retain a high degree of control over the precise contents of the program, the speeches, the timing, the movements, the dress, and the decorum of the students. In this atmosphere the state-imposed character of an invocation and benediction by clergy selected by the school combine to make the prayer a state-sanctioned religious exercise in which the student was left with no alternative but to submit. . . .

. . . The sole question presented is whether a religious exercise may be conducted at a graduation ceremony in circumstances where, as we have found, young graduates who object are induced to conform. No holding by this Court suggests that a school can persuade or compel a student to participate in a religious exercise. That is being done here, and it is forbidden by the Establishment Clause. . . .

Affirmed.

JUSTICE BLACKMUN, with whom JUSTICE STEVENS and JUSTICE O'CONNOR join, concurring.

. . . [When] the government "composes official prayers," selects the member of the clergy to deliver the prayer, has the prayer delivered at a public school event that is planned, supervised, and given by school officials, and pressures students to attend and participate in the prayer, there can be no doubt that the government is advancing and promoting religion. . . .

. . . The Court holds that the graduation prayer is unconstitutional because the State "in effect required participation in a religious exercise." Although our precedents make clear that proof of government coercion is not necessary to prove an Establishment Clause violation, it is sufficient. Government pressure to participate in a religious activity is an obvious indication that the government is endorsing or promoting religion.

But it is not enough that the government restrain from compelling religious practices: It must not engage in them either. . . . The mixing of government and religion can be a threat to free government, even if no one is forced to participate. When the government puts its *imprimatur* on a particular religion, it conveys a message of exclusion to all those who do not adhere to the favored beliefs. A government cannot be premised on the belief that all persons are created equal when it asserts that God prefers some. . . .

JUSTICE SOUTER, with whom JUSTICE STEVENS and JUSTICE O'CONNOR join, concurring.

[Justice Souter canvassed the history and purposes of the religion clauses and reaffirmed the principle of strict separation of Church and State. *See* Chapter 16, section A.]

Some [read] the Establishment Clause to permit "nonpreferential" state promotion of religion. . . . In many contexts, including this one, nonpreferentialism requires some distinction between "sectarian" religious practices and those that would be, by some measure, ecumenical enough to pass Establishment Clause muster. Simply by requiring the enquiry, nonpreferentialists invite the courts to engage in comparative theology. I can hardly imagine a subject less amenable to the competence of the federal judiciary, or more deliberately to be avoided where possible. . . . Nor does it solve the problem to say that the State should promote a "diversity" of religious views; that position would necessarily compel the government and, inevitably, the courts to make wholly inappropriate judgments about the number of religions the State should sponsor and the relative frequency with which it should sponsor each. . . .

Religious students cannot complain that omitting prayers from their graduation ceremony would, in any realistic sense, "burden" their spiritual callings. To be sure, many of them invest this rite of passage with spiritual significance, but they may express their religious feelings about it before and after the ceremony. They may even organize a privately sponsored baccalaureate if they desire the company of likeminded students. Because they accordingly have no need for the machinery of the State to affirm their beliefs, the government's sponsorship of prayer at the graduation ceremony is most reasonably understood as an official endorsement of religion and, in this instance, of theistic religion. One may fairly say [that] the government brought prayer into the ceremony "precisely because some people want a symbolic affirmation that government approves and endorses their religion, and because many of the people who want this affirmation place little or no value on the costs to religious minorities." . . . When public school officials, armed with the State's authority, convey an endorsement of religion to their students, they strike near the core of the Establishment Clause. However "ceremonial" their messages may be, they are flatly unconstitutional.

JUSTICE SCALIA, with whom THE CHIEF JUSTICE, JUSTICE WHITE, and JUSTICE THOMAS join, dissenting.

. . . In holding that the Establishment Clause prohibits invocations and benedictions at public school graduation ceremonies, the Court—with nary a mention that it is doing so—lays waste a tradition that is as old as public school graduation ceremonies themselves, and that is a component of an even more longstanding American tradition of nonsectarian prayer to God at public celebrations generally. . . . The history and tradition of our Nation are replete with public ceremonies featuring prayers of thanksgiving and petition. . . . In addition to this general tradition of prayer at public ceremonies, there exists a more specific tradition of invocations and benedictions at public school graduation exercises. . . .

The Court presumably would separate graduation invocations and benedictions from other instances of public "preservation and transmission of religious beliefs" on the ground that they involve "psychological coercion." A few citations of "research in psychology" that have no particular bearing upon the precise issue here cannot disguise the fact that the Court has gone beyond the realm where judges know what they are doing. The Court's argument that state officials have "coerced" students to take part in the invocation and benediction at graduation ceremonies is [incoherent]. . . .

[The Court] does not say . . . that students are psychologically coerced to bow their heads, place their hands in a Dürer-like prayer position, pay attention to the prayers, utter "Amen," or in fact pray. . . . It claims only that students are psychologically coerced "to stand . . . *or*, at least, maintain respectful silence." (Emphasis added.) Both halves of this disjunctive (*both* of which must amount to the fact or appearance of participation in prayer if the Court's analysis is to survive on its own terms) merit particular attention.

. . . The Court's notion that a student who simply *sits* in "respectful silence" during the invocation and benediction (when all others are standing) has somehow joined — or would somehow be perceived as having joined — in the prayers is nothing short of ludicrous. . . . But let us assume the very worst, that the nonparticipating graduate is "subtly coerced" . . . to stand! . . . Even that half of the disjunctive does not remotely establish a "participation" (or an "appearance of participation") in a religious exercise. The Court acknowledges that "in our culture standing . . . can signify adherence to a view or simple respect for the views of others." (Much more often the latter than the former, I think, except perhaps in the proverbial town meeting, where one votes by standing.) But if it is a permissible inference that one who is standing is doing so simply out of respect for the prayers of others that are in progress, then how can it possibly be said that a "reasonable dissenter . . . could believe that the group exercise signified her own participation or approval"? Quite obviously, it cannot. [Maintaining] respect for the religious observances of others is a fundamental civic virtue that government (including the public schools) can and should cultivate. . . .

[The] Court itself has not given careful consideration to its test of psychological coercion. For if it had, how could it observe, with no hint of concern or disapproval, that students stood for the Pledge of Allegiance, which immediately preceded Rabbi Gutterman's invocation? The government can, of course, no more coerce political orthodoxy than religious orthodoxy. . . .

I also find it odd that the Court concludes that high school graduates may not be subjected to this supposed psychological coercion, yet refrains from addressing whether "mature adults" may. [The] reason graduation from high school is regarded as so significant an event is that it is generally associated with transition from adolescence to young adulthood. Many graduating seniors, of course, are old enough to vote. Why, then, does the Court treat them as though they were first-graders? . . . The deeper flaw in the Court's opinion does not lie in its wrong answer to the question whether there was state-induced "peer-pressure" coercion; it lies, rather, in the Court's making violation of the Establishment Clause hinge on such a precious question. The coercion that was a hallmark of historical establishments of religion was coercion of religious orthodoxy and of financial support *by force of law and threat of penalty.* . . .

The reader has been told much in this case about the personal interest of Mr. Weisman and his daughter, and very little about the personal interests on the other side. They are not inconsequential. Church and state would not be such a difficult subject if religion were, as the Court apparently thinks it to be, some purely personal avocation that can be indulged entirely in secret, like pornography, in the privacy of one's room. For most believers it is not that, and has never been. Religious men and women of almost all denominations have felt it necessary to acknowledge and beseech the blessing of God as a people, and not just as individuals. . . . One can believe in the effectiveness of such public worship, or one can deprecate and deride it. But the longstanding American tradition of prayer at official ceremonies displays with unmistakable clarity that the Establishment Clause does not forbid the government to accommodate it. . . .

[The] Founders of our Republic knew the fearsome potential of sectarian religious belief to generate civil dissension and civil strife. And they also knew that nothing, absolutely nothing, is so inclined to foster among religious believers of various faiths a toleration—no, an affection—for one another than voluntarily joining in prayer together, to the God whom they all worship and seek. Needless to say, no one should be compelled to do that, but it is a shame to deprive our public culture of the opportunity, and indeed the encouragement, for people to do it voluntarily. The Baptist or Catholic who heard and joined in the simple and inspiring prayers of Rabbi Gutterman on this official and patriotic occasion was inoculated from religious bigotry and prejudice in a manner that cannot be replicated. To deprive our society of that important unifying mechanism, in order to spare the nonbeliever what seems to me the minimal inconvenience of standing or even sitting in respectful nonparticipation, is as senseless in policy as it is unsupported in law. . . .

———

Problem: Drafting a Moment-of-Silence Policy

Suppose you are the attorney for the local public school board and the board wants to adopt a constitutionally valid moment-of-silence policy. What would the official policy have to say? The board also asks you to draft an explanatory statement which will be printed on little cards—like the *Miranda* warning cards the police use—and distributed to homeroom teachers to read to their students to mark a daily 90-second moment of silence at the start of the school day.

C. School Curriculum

Conflicts between religion and science in the public school curriculum can raise profound constitutional issues for the separation of church and state. Under the Establishment Clause, the government is competent to teach science but incompetent to preach religion. How can public schools teach about the origins of life and the nature of the Universe when scientific paradigms and religious dogmas collide?

Edwards v. Aguillard
482 U.S. 578 (1987)

JUSTICE BRENNAN delivered the opinion of the Court.*

The question for decision is whether Louisiana's "Balanced Treatment for Creation-Science and Evolution-Science in Public School Instruction" Act (Creationism Act) is facially invalid as violative of the Establishment Clause of the First Amendment.

———

* Justice O'Connor joins all but Part II of this opinion.

I

The Creationism Act forbids the teaching of the theory of evolution in public schools unless accompanied by instruction in "creation science." No school is required to teach evolution or creation science. If either is taught, however, the other must also be taught. The theories of evolution and creation science are statutorily defined as "the scientific evidences for [creation or evolution] and inferences from those scientific evidences."

[Appellees, who include parents of children attending Louisiana public schools, Louisiana teachers, and religious leaders, challenged the constitutionality of the Creationism Act in District Court. Appellants, Louisiana officials charged with implementing the Act, defended on the ground that the purpose of the Act is to protect a legitimate secular interest, namely, academic freedom. The District Court granted a motion for summary judgment and held that the Creationism Act violated the Establishment Clause either because it prohibited the teaching of evolution or because it required the teaching of creation science with the purpose of advancing a particular religious doctrine. The Court of Appeals affirmed.] We . . . now affirm.

II

The Court has applied a three-pronged test to determine whether legislation comports with the Establishment Clause. . . . *Lemon v. Kurtzman* (1971) [*supra* this chapter]. State action violates the Establishment Clause if it fails to satisfy any of these prongs. . . .

The Court has been particularly vigilant in monitoring compliance with the Establishment Clause in elementary and secondary schools. Families entrust public schools with the education of their children, but condition their trust on the understanding that the classroom will not purposely be used to advance religious views that may conflict with the private beliefs of the student and his or her family. Students in such institutions are impressionable and their attendance is involuntary. The State exerts great authority and coercive power through mandatory attendance requirements, and because of the students' emulation of teachers as role models and the children's susceptibility to peer pressure. . . . Therefore, in employing the three-pronged *Lemon* test, we must do so mindful of the particular concerns that arise in the context of public elementary and secondary schools. . . .

III

Lemon's first prong focuses on the purpose that animated adoption of the Act. . . . [The] Act's stated purpose is to protect academic freedom. This phrase might [be] understood as referring to enhancing the freedom of teachers to teach what they will. [The] Act was not designed to further that goal. . . . While the Court is normally deferential to a State's articulation of a secular purpose, it is required that the statement of such purpose be sincere and not a sham. . . . It is clear from the legislative history that the purpose of the legislative sponsor [was] to narrow the science curriculum. During the legislative hearings, [he] stated: "My preference would be that neither [creationism nor evolution] be taught." Such a ban on teaching does not promote—indeed, it undermines—the provision of a comprehensive scientific education.

It is equally clear that requiring schools to teach creation science with evolution does not advance academic freedom. The Act does not grant teachers a flexibility that they did not already possess to supplant the present science curriculum with the presentation of theories, besides evolution, about the origin of life. [No] law prohibited Louisiana public school teachers from teaching any scientific theory. . . . The Act provides Louisiana school teachers with no new authority. Thus the stated purpose is not furthered by it. . . .

[The] goal of basic "fairness" is hardly furthered by the Act's discriminatory preference for the teaching of creation science and against the teaching of evolution. While requiring that curriculum guides be developed for creation science, the Act says nothing of comparable guides for evolution. Similarly, resource services are supplied for creation science but not for evolution. Only "creation scientists" can serve on the panel that supplies the resource services. The Act forbids school boards to discriminate against anyone who "chooses to be a creation-scientist" or to teach "creationism," but fails to protect those who choose to teach evolution or any other noncreation science theory, or who refuse to teach creation science.

If the Louisiana Legislature's purpose was solely to maximize the comprehensiveness and effectiveness of science instruction, it would have encouraged the teaching of all scientific theories about the origins of humankind. But under the Act's requirements, teachers who were once free to teach any and all facets of this subject are now unable to do so. Moreover, the Act fails even to ensure that creation science will be taught, but instead requires the teaching of this theory only when the theory of evolution is taught. Thus [the] Act does not serve to protect academic freedom, but has the distinctly different purpose of discrediting "evolution by counterbalancing its teaching at every turn with the teaching of creationism. . . ."

[We] need not be blind in this case to the legislature's preeminent religious purpose in enacting this statute. There is a historic and contemporaneous link between the teachings of certain religious denominations and the teaching of evolution. It was this link that concerned the Court in *Epperson v. Arkansas* (1968), which also involved a facial challenge to a statute regulating the teaching of evolution. In that case, the Court reviewed an Arkansas statute that made it unlawful for an instructor to teach evolution or to use a textbook that referred to this scientific theory. Although the Arkansas antievolution law did not explicitly state its predominant religious purpose, the Court could not ignore that "the statute was a product of the upsurge of 'fundamentalist' religious fervor" that has long viewed this particular scientific theory as contradicting the literal interpretation of the Bible. [The Court evaluated the statute in light of a series of antievolution statutes adopted by state legislatures dating back to the Tennessee statute that was the focus of the celebrated *Scopes* trial in 1925. The Court found the Arkansas statute comparable to this Tennessee "monkey law," since both gave preference to "religious establishments which have as one of their tenets or dogmas the instantaneous creation of man." *Id. quoting Scopes v. State*, 289 S.W. 363, 369 (1927).] After reviewing the history of antievolution statutes, the Court determined that "there can be no doubt that the motivation for the [Arkansas] law was the same [as other antievolution statutes]: to suppress the teaching of a theory which, it was thought, 'denied' the divine creation of man." The Court found that there can be no legitimate state interest in protecting particular religions from scientific views "distasteful to them," and concluded "that the First Amendment does not permit the State to require that teaching and learning must be tailored to the principles or prohibitions of any religious sect or dogma."

These same historic and contemporaneous antagonisms between the teachings of certain religious denominations and the teaching of evolution are present in this case. The preeminent purpose of the Louisiana Legislature was clearly to advance the religious viewpoint that a supernatural being created humankind. The term "creation science" was defined as embracing this particular religious doctrine by those responsible for the passage of the Creationism Act. . . . The legislative history [reveals] that the term "creation science," as contemplated by the legislature that adopted this Act, embodies the religious belief that a supernatural creator was responsible for the creation of humankind.

[The] legislative history documents that the Act's primary purpose was to change the science curriculum of public schools in order to provide persuasive advantage to a particular religious doctrine that rejects the factual basis of evolution in its entirety. The sponsor of the Creationism Act [explained] during the legislative hearings that his disdain for the theory of evolution resulted from the support that evolution supplied to views contrary to his own religious beliefs. According to [the Act's sponsor], the theory of evolution was consonant with the "cardinal principle[s] of religious humanism, secular humanism, theological liberalism, aetheistism [sic]." [He] repeatedly stated that scientific evidence supporting his religious views should be included in the public school curriculum to redress the fact that the theory of evolution incidentally coincided with what he characterized as religious beliefs antithetical to his own. The legislation therefore sought to alter the science curriculum to reflect endorsement of a religious view that is antagonistic to the theory of evolution.

In this case, the purpose of the Creationism Act was to restructure the science curriculum to conform with a particular religious viewpoint. Out of many possible science subjects taught in the public schools, the legislature chose to affect the teaching of the one scientific theory that historically has been opposed by certain religious sects. As in *Epperson*, the legislature passed the Act to give preference to those religious groups which have as one of their tenets the creation of humankind by a divine creator. . . . Similarly, the Creationism Act is designed *either* to promote the theory of creation science which embodies a particular religious tenet by requiring that creation science be taught whenever evolution is taught *or* to prohibit the teaching of a scientific theory disfavored by certain religious sects by forbidding the teaching of evolution when creation science is not also taught. The Establishment Clause, however, "forbids *alike* the preference of a religious doctrine *or* the prohibition of theory which is deemed antagonistic to a particular dogma." Because the primary purpose of the Creationism Act is to advance a particular religious belief, the Act endorses religion in violation of the First Amendment.

We do not imply that a legislature could never require that scientific critiques of prevailing scientific theories be taught. . . . [Teaching] a variety of scientific theories about the origins of humankind to schoolchildren might be validly done with the clear secular intent of enhancing the effectiveness of science instruction. But because the primary purpose of the Creationism Act is to endorse a particular religious doctrine, the Act furthers religion in violation of the Establishment Clause. . . .

V

The Louisiana Creationism Act advances a religious doctrine by requiring either the banishment of the theory of evolution from public school classrooms or the presentation of a religious viewpoint that rejects evolution in its entirety. The Act violates the Establishment Clause [because] it seeks to employ the symbolic and financial support of government to achieve a religious purpose. The judgment of the Court of Appeals therefore is affirmed.

JUSTICE POWELL, with whom JUSTICE O'CONNOR joins, concurring. [Omitted.]

JUSTICE WHITE, concurring in the judgment. [Omitted.]

JUSTICE SCALIA, with whom THE CHIEF JUSTICE joins, dissenting.

. . . This case arrives here in the following posture: The Louisiana Supreme Court has never been given an opportunity to interpret the Balanced Treatment Act, State officials have never attempted to implement it, and it has never been the subject of a full evidentiary hearing. We can only guess at its meaning. We know that it forbids instruction in either "creation-science" or "evolution-science" without instruction in the other, but the parties are sharply divided over what creation science consists of. Appellants insist that it is a collection of educationally valuable scientific data that has been censored from classrooms by an embarrassed scientific establishment. Appellees insist it is not science at all but thinly veiled religious doctrine. Both interpretations of the intended meaning of that phrase find considerable support in the legislative history.

At least at this stage in the litigation, it is plain to me that we must accept appellants' view of what the statute means. To begin with, the statute itself *defines* "creation-science" as "the *scientific evidences* for creation and inferences from those *scientific evidences*." . . . The only evidence in the record of the "received meaning and acceptation" of "creation science" is found in five affidavits filed by appellants. In those affidavits, two scientists, a philosopher, a theologian, and an educator, all of whom claim extensive knowledge of creation science, swear that it is essentially a collection of scientific data supporting the theory that the physical universe and life within it appeared suddenly and have not changed substantially since appearing. At this point, then, we must assume that the Balanced Treatment Act does *not* require the presentation of religious doctrine. . . .

. . . [The] Court holds that the Louisiana Legislature acted without "a secular legislative purpose" and that the Act therefore fails the "purpose" prong of the three-part test set forth in *Lemon v. Kurtzman* (1971) [*supra* this chapter]. . . . I doubt whether that "purpose" requirement of *Lemon* is a proper interpretation of the Constitution; but even if it were, I could not agree with the Court's assessment that the requirement was not satisfied here. . . .

. . . [Regardless] of what "legislative purpose" may mean in other contexts, for the purpose of the *Lemon* test it means the "actual" motives of those responsible for the challenged action. . . . Thus, if those legislators who supported the Balanced Treatment Act *in fact* acted with a "sincere" secular purpose, the Act survives the first component of the *Lemon* test, regardless of whether that purpose is likely to be achieved by the provisions they enacted. Our cases have also confirmed that when the *Lemon* Court referred to "a secular . . . purpose," it meant "*a* secular purpose." . . . Thus, the majority's invalidation of the Balanced Treatment Act is defensible only if the record indicates that the Louisiana Legislature had *no* secular purpose.

It is important to stress that the purpose forbidden by *Lemon* is the purpose to "advance religion." Our cases in no way imply that the Establishment Clause forbids legislators merely to act upon their religious convictions. We surely would not strike down a law providing money to feed the hungry or shelter the homeless if it could be demonstrated that, but for the religious beliefs of the legislators, the funds would not have been approved. Also, political activism by the religiously motivated is part of our heritage. [We] do not presume that the sole purpose of a law is to advance religion merely because it was supported strongly by organized religions or by adherents of particular faiths. . . . Similarly, we will not presume that a law's purpose is to advance religion merely because it "'happens to coincide or harmonize with the tenets of some or all religions,'" or because it benefits religion, even substantially. . . . Thus, the fact that creation science coincides with the beliefs of certain religions, a fact upon which the majority relies heavily, does not itself justify invalidation of the Act. . . .

We have relatively little information upon which to judge the motives of those who supported the Act. About the only direct evidence is the statute itself and transcripts of the seven committee hearings at which it was considered. Unfortunately, several of those hearings were sparsely attended, and the legislators who were present revealed little about their motives. We have no committee reports, no floor debates, no remarks inserted into the legislative history, no statement from the Governor, and no postenactment statements or testimony from the bill's sponsor or any other legislators. Nevertheless, there is ample evidence that the majority is wrong in holding that the Balanced Treatment Act is without secular purpose.

At the outset, it is important to note that the Balanced Treatment Act did not fly through the Louisiana Legislature on wings of fundamentalist religious fervor — which would be unlikely, in any event, since only a small minority of the State's citizens belong to fundamentalist religious denominations. . . . Before summarizing the [legislative history], I wish to make clear that I by no means intend to endorse its accuracy. But my views (and the views of this Court) about creation science and evolution are (or should be) beside the point. Our task is not to judge the debate about teaching the origins of life, but to ascertain what the members of the Louisiana Legislature believed.

The vast majority of them voted to approve a bill which explicitly stated a secular purpose; what is crucial is not their *wisdom* in believing that purpose would be achieved by the bill, but their *sincerity* in believing it would be.

Most of the testimony in support of [the] bill came from the [sponsor] himself and from scientists and educators he presented, many of whom enjoyed academic credentials that may have been regarded as quite impressive by members of the Louisiana Legislature. To a substantial extent, their testimony was devoted to lengthy, and, to the layman, seemingly expert scientific expositions on the origin of life. These scientific lectures touched upon, *inter alia*, biology, paleontology, genetics, astronomy, astrophysics, probability analysis, and biochemistry. The witnesses repeatedly assured committee members that "hundreds and hundreds" of highly respected, internationally renowned scientists believed in creation science and would support their testimony.

[The] witnesses testified essentially as set forth in the following numbered paragraphs:

(1) There are two and only two scientific explanations for the beginning of life—evolution and creation science. . . . Both posit a theory of the origin of life and subject that theory to empirical testing. . . .

(2) The body of scientific evidence supporting creation science is as strong as that supporting evolution. In fact, it may be *stronger*. The evidence for evolution is far less compelling than we have been led to believe. Evolution is not a scientific "fact," since it cannot actually be observed in a laboratory. Rather, evolution is merely a scientific theory or "guess." It is a very bad guess at that. The scientific problems with evolution are so serious that it could accurately be termed a "myth."

(3) Creation science is educationally valuable. Students exposed to it better understand the current state of scientific evidence about the origin of life. Those students even have a better understanding of evolution. Creation science can and should be presented to children without any religious content.

(4) Although creation science is educationally valuable and strictly scientific, it is now being censored from or misrepresented in the public schools. . . . Teachers have been brainwashed by an entrenched scientific establishment composed almost exclusively of scientists to whom evolution is like a "religion." These scientists discriminate against creation scientists so as to prevent evolution's weaknesses from being exposed.

(5) The censorship of creation science has at least two harmful effects. First, it deprives students of knowledge of one of the two scientific explanations for the origin of life and leads them to believe that evolution is proven fact; thus, their education suffers and they are wrongly taught that science has proved their religious beliefs false. Second, it violates the Establishment Clause. The United States Supreme Court has held that secular humanism is a religion. Belief in evolution is a central tenet of that religion. Thus, by censoring creation science and instructing students that evolution is fact, public school teachers are *now* advancing religion in violation of the Establishment Clause.

[The sponsor] repeatedly and vehemently denied that his purpose was to advance a particular religious doctrine. . . . We have no way of knowing, of course, how many legislators believed the testimony of [the sponsor] and his witnesses. But in the absence of evidence to the contrary, we have to assume that many of them did. Given that assumption, the Court today plainly errs in holding that the Louisiana Legislature passed the Balanced Treatment Act for exclusively religious purposes.

Even with nothing more than this legislative history to go on, I think it would be extraordinary to invalidate the Balanced Treatment Act for lack of a valid secular purpose. Striking down a law approved by the democratically elected representatives of the people is no minor matter. . . .

The Court seeks to evade the force of this expression of purpose by stubbornly misinterpreting it, and then finding that the provisions of the Act do not advance that misinterpreted purpose, thereby showing it to be a sham. . . . Had the Court devoted to this central question of the [legislatively] expressed purpose [it] would have discerned quite readily what "academic freedom" meant: *students'* freedom from *indoctrination*. The legislature wanted to ensure that students would be free to decide for themselves how life began, based upon a fair and balanced presentation of the scientific evidence. . . . The legislature did not care *whether* the topic of origins was taught; it simply wished to ensure that *when* the topic was taught, students would receive " 'all of the evidence.' " If one adopts the obviously intended meaning of the statutory term "academic freedom," there is no basis whatever for concluding that the purpose they express is a "sham." To the contrary, the Act pursues that purpose plainly and consistently. It requires that, whenever the subject of origins is covered, evolution be "taught as a theory, rather than as proven scientific fact" and that scientific evidence inconsistent with the theory of evolution (*viz.*, "creation science") be taught as well. . . .

The legislative history gives ample evidence of the sincerity of the Balanced Treatment Act's articulated purpose. . . . It is undoubtedly true that what prompted the legislature to direct its attention to the misrepresentation of evolution in the schools (rather than the inaccurate presentation of other topics) was its awareness of the tension between evolution and the religious beliefs of many children. But even appellees concede that a valid secular purpose is not rendered impermissible simply because its pursuit is prompted by concern for religious sensitivities. . . . Because I believe that the Balanced Treatment Act had a secular purpose, which is all the first component of the *Lemon* test requires, I would reverse the judgment of the Court of Appeals and remand for further consideration.

———

Problem: Intelligent Design

After conducting public hearings, the elected School Board of Darwin, Pennsylvania adopted the following resolution, by a 6-to-3 vote:

> In order to develop a balanced science curriculum, junior high students will be made aware of the gaps/problems in Darwin's theory and of other theories of evolution including, but not limited to, intelligent design. All

teachers are required to read this statement to students in ninth grade biology classes:

> Because Darwin's Theory is a theory, it is still being tested as new evidence is discovered. The Theory is not a fact. Gaps in the Theory exist for which there is no evidence. A theory is defined as a well-tested explanation that unifies a broad range of observations.
>
> Intelligent design is an explanation of the origin of life that differs from Darwin's view. The reference book, OF PANDAS AND PEOPLE, is available in the school library for students to see if they would like to explore this view in an effort to gain an understanding of what intelligent design actually involves. As is true with any theory, students are encouraged to keep an open mind.

The theory of "Intelligent Design" maintains that the structure of life on Earth is far too complex to have evolved from natural selection, challenging a core principle in the theory of evolution first put forward by Charles Darwin's ON THE ORIGIN OF SPECIES in 1859. Instead, as first explained in 1993 in the alternative textbook cited in the School Board's resolution above, intelligent design theory hypothesizes that the intervention of an intelligent agent, rather than unguided matter and random events, better accounts for the existence of the Universe and the complexity of natural phenomena.

What constitutional challenges could be raised against this resolution? How might the School Board defend its resolution? How would a court resolve the dispute?

————

D. Displays in Public Places

Plazas, parks, city halls, town squares, and other government properties are the spaces we all own, the spaces we all share, the spaces within which we encounter each other, believers and nonbelievers alike. Historically, the Supreme Court has struggled to articulate the constitutional etiquette for religious displays in our shared public spaces. The underlying difficulty is that the Establishment Clause creates a paradox: Government "sends a message" whether it permits these displays or bans them. So, what may or must the government do?

County of Allegheny v. Greater Pittsburgh ACLU
492 U.S. 573 (1989)

JUSTICE BLACKMUN announced the judgment of the Court and delivered the opinion of the Court with respect to Parts III-A, IV, and V, an opinion with respect to Parts I and II, in which JUSTICE STEVENS and JUSTICE O'CONNOR join, an opinion with respect to Part III-B, in which JUSTICE STEVENS joins, an opinion with respect to Part VII, in which JUSTICE O'CONNOR joins, and an opinion with respect to Part VI.

This litigation concerns the constitutionality of two recurring holiday displays located on public property in downtown Pittsburgh. The first is a crèche placed on the Grand Staircase of the Allegheny County Courthouse. The second is a Chanukah menorah placed just outside the City-County Building, next to a Christmas tree and a sign saluting liberty. The Court of Appeals for the Third Circuit ruled that each display violates the Establishment Clause of the First Amendment because each has the impermissible effect of endorsing religion. We agree that the crèche display has that unconstitutional effect but reverse the Court of Appeals' judgment regarding the menorah display.

I

The county courthouse is owned by Allegheny County and is its seat of government. It houses the offices of the county commissioners, controller, treasurer, sheriff, and clerk of court. Civil and criminal trials are held there. . . .

Since 1981, the county has permitted [a] Roman Catholic group to display a crèche in the county courthouse during the Christmas holiday season. . . . The crèche includes figures of the infant Jesus, Mary, Joseph, farm animals, shepherds, and wise men, all placed in or before a wooden representation of a manger, which has at its crest an angel bearing a banner that proclaims "*Gloria in Excelsis Deo!*". . . . It had a wooden fence on three sides and bore a plaque stating: "This Display Donated by the Holy Name Society." [The] county placed red and white poinsettia plants around the fence. The county also placed a small evergreen tree, decorated with a red bow, behind each of the two endposts of the fence. These trees stood alongside the manger backdrop and were slightly shorter than it was. The angel [was] at the apex of the crèche display. Altogether, the crèche, the fence, the poinsettias, and the trees occupied a substantial amount of space on the Grand Staircase. No figures of Santa Claus or other decorations appeared on the Grand Staircase. The county uses the crèche as the setting for its annual Christmas-carol program. During the 1986 season, the county invited high school choirs and other musical groups to perform during weekday lunch hours. . . . The county dedicated this program to world peace and to the families of prisoners-of-war and of persons missing in action in Southeast Asia. . . .

The City-County Building is separate and a block removed from the county courthouse and [is] jointly owned by the city of Pittsburgh and Allegheny County. . . . For a number of years, the city has had a large Christmas tree under the middle arch outside the Grant Street entrance. [The] city placed at the foot of the tree a sign bearing the mayor's name and entitled "Salute to Liberty." Beneath the title, the sign stated:

> During this holiday season, the city of Pittsburgh salutes liberty. Let these festive lights remind us that we are the keepers of the flame of liberty and our legacy of freedom.

. . . [The] city placed at the Grant Street entrance to the City-County Building an 18-foot Chanukah menorah of an abstract tree-and-branch design [next] to the city's 45-foot Christmas tree, against one of the columns that supports the arch into which the tree was set. The menorah is owned by Chabad, a Jewish group, but is stored, erected, and removed each year by the city. The tree, the sign, and the menorah were all removed on January 13.

II

[Respondents, the Greater Pittsburgh Chapter of the American Civil Liberties Union and seven local residents, filed suit against the county and the city, seeking permanently to enjoin the county from displaying the crèche in the county courthouse and the city from displaying the menorah in front of the City-County Building. The District Court denied the injunction, relying on *Lynch v. Donnelly*, 465 U.S. 668 (1984). Respondents appealed, and a divided panel of the Court of Appeals reversed. The county, the city, and Chabad each filed a petition for certiorari. The Supreme Court granted all three petitions.]

III

A

... In the course of adjudicating specific cases, this Court has come to understand the Establishment Clause to mean that government may not promote or affiliate itself with any religious doctrine or organization, may not discriminate among persons on the basis of their religious beliefs and practices, may not delegate a governmental power to a religious institution, and may not involve itself too deeply in such an institution's affairs. ... [Under the analysis in *Lemon v. Kurtzman* (1971) (*supra* this chapter)] a statute or practice which touches upon religion, if it is to be permissible under the Establishment Clause, must have a secular purpose; it must neither advance nor inhibit religion in its principal or primary effect; and it must not foster an excessive entanglement with religion. ...

Our subsequent decisions further have refined the definition of governmental action that unconstitutionally advances religion. In recent years, we have paid particularly close attention to whether the challenged governmental practice either has the purpose or effect of "endorsing" religion, a concern that has long had a place in our Establishment Clause jurisprudence. [The] prohibition against governmental endorsement of religion "preclude[s] government from conveying or attempting to convey a message that religion or a particular religious belief is *favored* or *preferred*." Moreover, the term "endorsement" is closely linked to the term "promotion," and this Court long since has held that government "may not . . . promote one religion or religious theory against another or even against the militant opposite." Whether the key word is "endorsement," "favoritism," or "promotion," the essential principle remains the same. The Establishment Clause, at the very least, prohibits government from appearing to take a position on questions of religious belief or from "making adherence to a religion relevant in any way to a person's standing in the political community."

B

We have had occasion in the past to apply Establishment Clause principles to the government's display of objects with religious significance. ... [Close] to the facts of this litigation is *Lynch v. Donnelly*, in which we considered whether the city of Pawtucket, R.I., had violated the Establishment Clause by including a crèche in its annual Christmas display, located in a private park within the downtown shopping district. By a 5-to-4 decision in that difficult case, the Court upheld inclusion of the crèche in the Pawtucket display, holding, *inter alia*, that the inclusion of the crèche did not have the impermissible effect of advancing or promoting religion.

The rationale of the majority opinion in *Lynch* is none too clear. . . . [Justice O'Connor] wrote a concurrence that differs in significant respects from the majority opinion [and] provides a sound analytical framework for evaluating governmental use of religious symbols.

First and foremost, the concurrence squarely rejects any notion that this Court will tolerate some government endorsement of religion. [Any] endorsement of religion [is] "invalid" because it "sends a message to nonadherents that they are outsiders, not full members of the political community, and an accompanying message to adherents that they are insiders, favored members of the political community." Second, the concurrence articulates a method for determining whether the government's use of an object with religious meaning has the effect of endorsing religion. The effect of the display depends upon the message that the government's practice communicates: the question is "what viewers may fairly understand to be the purpose of the display." That inquiry, of necessity, turns upon the context in which the contested object appears: "[A] typical museum setting, though not neutralizing the religious content of a religious painting, negates any message of endorsement of that content." The concurrence thus emphasizes that the constitutionality of the crèche in that case depended upon its "particular physical setting," [and] "must be judged in its unique circumstances to determine whether it endorses religion."

The concurrence applied this mode of analysis to the Pawtucket crèche, seen in the context of that city's holiday celebration as a whole. In addition to the crèche, the city's display contained: a Santa Claus house with a live Santa distributing candy; reindeer pulling Santa's sleigh; a live 40-foot Christmas tree strung with lights; statues of carolers in old-fashioned dress; candy-striped poles; a "talking" wishing well; a large banner proclaiming "SEASONS GREETINGS"; a miniature "village" with several houses and a church; and various "cut-out" figures, including those of a clown, a dancing elephant, a robot, and a teddy bear. The concurrence concluded that both because the crèche is "a traditional symbol" of Christmas, a holiday with strong secular elements, and because the crèche was "displayed along with purely secular symbols," the crèche's setting "changes what viewers may fairly understand to be the purpose of the display" and "negates any message of endorsement" of "the Christian beliefs represented by the crèche."

The four *Lynch* dissenters agreed with the concurrence that the controlling question was "whether Pawtucket ha[d] run afoul of the Establishment Clause by endorsing religion through its display of the crèche." . . . They simply reached a different answer. . . . Thus, despite divergence at the bottom line, the five Justices in concurrence and dissent in *Lynch* agreed upon the relevant constitutional principles: the government's use of religious symbolism is unconstitutional if it has the effect of endorsing religious beliefs, and the effect of the government's use of religious symbolism depends upon its context. . . . Accordingly, our present task is to determine whether the display of the crèche and the menorah, in their respective "particular physical settings," has the effect of endorsing or disapproving religious beliefs.

IV

We turn first to the county's crèche display. There is no doubt, of course, that the crèche itself is capable of communicating a religious message. Indeed, the crèche in this lawsuit uses words, as well as the picture of the Nativity scene, to make its religious meaning unmistakably clear. "Glory to God in the Highest!" says the angel in the crèche — Glory to God because of the birth of Jesus. This praise to God in Christian terms is indisputably religious — indeed sectarian — just as it is when said in the Gospel or in a church service.

[The] effect of a crèche display turns on its setting. Here, unlike in *Lynch*, nothing in the context of the display detracts from the crèche's religious message. The *Lynch* display comprised a series of figures and objects, each group of which had its own focal point. . . . Here, in contrast, the crèche stands alone: it is the single element of the display on the Grand Staircase. . . .

Furthermore, the crèche sits on the Grand Staircase, the "main" and "most beautiful part" of the building that is the seat of county government. No viewer could reasonably think that it occupies this location without the support and approval of the government. Thus, by permitting the "display of the crèche in this particular physical setting," the county sends an unmistakable message that it supports and promotes the Christian praise to God that is the crèche's religious message. The fact that the crèche bears a sign disclosing its ownership by a Roman Catholic organization does not alter this conclusion. On the contrary, the sign simply demonstrates that the government is endorsing the religious message of that organization, rather than communicating a message of its own. . . .

Finally, the county argues that it is sufficient to validate the display of the crèche on the Grand Staircase that the display celebrates Christmas, and Christmas is a national holiday. This argument obviously proves too much. . . . The government may acknowledge Christmas as a cultural phenomenon, but under the First Amendment it may not observe it as a Christian holy day by suggesting that people praise God for the birth of Jesus.

In sum, *Lynch* teaches that government may celebrate Christmas in some manner and form, but not in a way that endorses Christian doctrine. Here, Allegheny County has transgressed this line. It has chosen to celebrate Christmas in a way that has the effect of endorsing a patently Christian message: Glory to God for the birth of Jesus Christ. Under *Lynch*, and the rest of our cases, nothing more is required to demonstrate a violation of the Establishment Clause. The display of the crèche in this context, therefore, must be permanently enjoined.

V

Justice Kennedy and the three Justices who join him would find the display of the crèche consistent with the Establishment Clause. . . . He also asserts that the crèche, even in this setting, poses "no realistic risk" of "represent[ing] an effort to proselytize," having repudiated the Court's endorsement inquiry in favor of a "proselytization" approach. The Court's analysis of the crèche, he contends, "reflects an unjustified hostility toward religion." . . .

. . . However history may affect the constitutionality of nonsectarian references to religion by the government, history cannot legitimate practices that demonstrate the government's allegiance to a particular sect or creed. . . . Whatever else the Establishment Clause may mean (and we have held it to mean no official preference even for religion over nonreligion), it certainly means at the very least that government may not demonstrate a preference for one particular sect or creed (including a preference for Christianity over other religions). . . . Although Justice Kennedy's [accommodationist approach] is predicated on a failure to recognize the bedrock Establishment Clause principle that, regardless of history, government may not demonstrate a preference for a particular faith, even he is forced to acknowledge that some instances of such favoritism are constitutionally intolerable. He concedes also that the term "endorsement" long has been another way of defining a forbidden "preference" for a particular sect, but he would repudiate the Court's endorsement inquiry as a "jurisprudence of minutiae" because it examines the particular contexts in which the government employs religious symbols. [When] all is said and done, Justice Kennedy's effort to abandon the "endorsement" inquiry in favor of his "proselytization" test seems nothing more than an attempt to lower considerably the level of scrutiny in Establishment Clause cases. We choose, however, to adhere to the vigilance the Court has managed to maintain thus far, and to the endorsement inquiry that reflects our vigilance.

Although Justice Kennedy repeatedly accuses the Court of harboring a "latent hostility" or "callous indifference" toward religion, nothing could be further from the truth, and the accusations could be said to be as offensive as they are absurd. Justice Kennedy apparently has misperceived a respect for religious pluralism, a respect commanded by the Constitution, as hostility or indifference to religion. . . .

. . . [The] Constitution mandates that the government remain secular, rather than affiliate itself with religious beliefs or institutions, precisely in order to avoid discriminating among citizens on the basis of their religious faiths. A secular state, it must be remembered, is not the same as an atheistic or antireligious state. A secular state establishes neither atheism nor religion as its official creed. . . . It follows directly from the Constitution's proscription against government affiliation with religious beliefs or institutions that there is no orthodoxy on religious matters in the secular state. . . . For this reason, the claim that prohibiting government from celebrating Christmas as a religious holiday discriminates against Christians in favor of nonadherents must fail. . . .

[Not] all religious celebrations of Christmas located on government property violate the Establishment Clause. It obviously is not unconstitutional, for example, for a group of parishioners from a local church to go caroling through a city park on any Sunday in Advent or for a Christian club at a public university to sing carols during their Christmas meeting. The reason is that activities of this nature do not demonstrate the government's allegiance to, or endorsement of, the Christian faith.

Equally obvious, however, is the proposition that not all proclamations of Christian faith located on government property are permitted by the Establishment Clause just because they occur during the Christmas holiday season. . . . And once the judgment has been made that a particular proclamation of Christian belief, when disseminated from a particular location on government property, has the effect of demonstrating the government's endorsement of Christian faith, then it necessarily follows that the practice must be enjoined to protect the constitutional rights of those citizens who follow some creed other than Christianity. . . .

VI

[The] Chanukah menorah in front of the City-County Building may well present a closer constitutional question. The menorah [is] a religious symbol: it serves to commemorate the miracle of the oil as described in the Talmud. But the menorah's message is not exclusively religious. The menorah is the primary visual symbol for a holiday that, like Christmas, has both religious and secular dimensions.

[The] menorah here stands next to a Christmas tree and a sign saluting liberty. While no challenge has been made here to the display of the tree and the sign, their presence is obviously relevant in determining the effect of the menorah's display. The necessary result of placing a menorah next to a Christmas tree is to create an "overall holiday setting" that represents both Christmas and Chanukah—two holidays, not one. [If] the city celebrates both Christmas and Chanukah as religious holidays, then it violates the Establishment Clause. . . . Conversely, if the city celebrates both Christmas and Chanukah as secular holidays, then its conduct is beyond the reach of the Establishment Clause. Because government may celebrate Christmas as a secular holiday, it follows that government may also acknowledge Chanukah as a secular holiday. . . .

Accordingly, the relevant question for Establishment Clause purposes is whether the combined display of the tree, the sign, and the menorah has the effect of endorsing both Christian and Jewish faiths, or rather simply recognizes that both Christmas and Chanukah are part of the same winter-holiday season, which has attained a secular status in our society. Of the two interpretations of this particular display, the latter seems far more plausible and is also in line with *Lynch*.

The Christmas tree, unlike the menorah, is not itself a religious symbol. Although Christmas trees once carried religious connotations, today they typify the secular celebration of Christmas. Numerous Americans place Christmas trees in their homes without subscribing to Christian religious beliefs, and when the city's tree stands alone in front of the City-County Building, it is not considered an endorsement of

Christian faith. Indeed, [a] Christmas tree was one of the objects that validated the crèche in *Lynch*. The widely accepted view of the Christmas tree as the preeminent secular symbol of the Christmas holiday season serves to emphasize the secular component of the message communicated by other elements of an accompanying holiday display, including the Chanukah menorah.

The tree, moreover, is clearly the predominant element in the city's display. The 45-foot tree occupies the central position beneath the middle archway in front of the Grant Street entrance to the City-County Building; the 18-foot menorah is positioned to one side. Given this configuration, it is much more sensible to interpret the meaning of the menorah in light of the tree, rather than vice versa. In the shadow of the tree, the menorah is readily understood as simply a recognition that Christmas is not the only traditional way of observing the winter-holiday season. In these circumstances, then, the combination of the tree and the menorah communicates, not a simultaneous endorsement of both the Christian and Jewish faiths, but instead, a secular celebration of Christmas coupled with an acknowledgment of Chanukah as a contemporaneous alternative tradition. . . .

The mayor's sign further diminishes the possibility that the tree and the menorah will be interpreted as a dual endorsement of Christianity and Judaism. . . . While no sign can disclaim an overwhelming message of endorsement, an "explanatory plaque" may confirm that in particular contexts the government's association with a religious symbol does not represent the government's sponsorship of religious beliefs. . . .

Given all these considerations, it is not "sufficiently likely" that residents of Pittsburgh will perceive the combined display of the tree, the sign, and the menorah as an "endorsement" or "disapproval . . . of their individual religious choices." While an adjudication of the display's effect must take into account the perspective of one who is neither Christian nor Jewish, as well as of those who adhere to either of these religions, the constitutionality of its effect must also be judged according to the standard of a "reasonable observer." . . . [For] purposes of the Establishment Clause, the city's overall display must be understood as conveying the city's secular recognition of different traditions for celebrating the winter-holiday season. . . .

VII

Lynch v. Donnelly confirms, and in no way repudiates, the longstanding constitutional principle that government may not engage in a practice that has the effect of promoting or endorsing religious beliefs. The display of the crèche in the county courthouse has this unconstitutional effect. The display of the menorah in front of the City-County Building, however, does not have this effect, given its "particular physical setting."

The judgment of the Court of Appeals is affirmed in part and reversed in part, and the cases are remanded for further proceedings.

JUSTICE O'CONNOR, with whom JUSTICE BRENNAN and JUSTICE STEVENS join as to Part II, concurring in part and concurring in the judgment.

I

. . . The constitutionality of the two displays at issue in these cases turns on how we interpret and apply the holding in *Lynch v. Donnelly*, in which we rejected an Establishment Clause challenge to the city of Pawtucket's inclusion of a crèche in its annual Christmas holiday display. . . .

I joined the majority opinion in *Lynch* because, as I read that opinion, it was consistent with the analysis set forth in my separate concurrence, which stressed that "[e]very government practice must be judged in its *unique circumstances* to determine whether it constitutes an endorsement or disapproval of religion." . . . In my concurrence in *Lynch*, I suggested a clarification of our Establishment Clause doctrine to reinforce the concept that the Establishment Clause "prohibits government from making adherence to a religion relevant in any way to a person's standing in the political community." The government violates this prohibition if it endorses or disapproves of religion. . . .

For the reasons stated in Part IV of the Court's opinion in these cases, I agree that the crèche displayed on the Grand Staircase of the Allegheny County Courthouse, the seat of county government, conveys a message to nonadherents of Christianity that they are not full members of the political community, and a corresponding message to Christians that they are favored members of the political community. . . . The Court correctly concludes that placement of the central religious symbol of the Christmas holiday season at the Allegheny County Courthouse has the unconstitutional effect of conveying a government endorsement of Christianity.

II

In his separate opinion, Justice Kennedy asserts that the endorsement test "is flawed in its fundamentals and unworkable in practice." In my view, neither criticism is persuasive. As a theoretical matter, the endorsement test captures the essential command of the Establishment Clause, namely, that government must not make a person's religious beliefs relevant to his or her standing in the political community by conveying a message "that religion or a particular religious belief is favored or preferred." . . . If government is to be neutral in matters of religion, rather than showing either favoritism or disapproval towards citizens based on their personal religious choices, government cannot endorse the religious practices and beliefs of some citizens without sending a clear message to nonadherents that they are outsiders or less than full members of the political community.

An Establishment Clause standard that prohibits only "coercive" practices or overt efforts at government proselytization, but fails to take account of the numerous more subtle ways that government can show favoritism to particular beliefs or convey a message of disapproval to others, would not, in my view, adequately protect the religious liberty or respect the religious diversity of the members of our pluralistic political community. Thus, this Court has never relied on coercion alone as the touchstone of Establishment Clause analysis. . . .

Justice Kennedy submits that the endorsement test is inconsistent with our precedents and traditions because, in his words, if it were "applied without artificial exceptions for historical practice," it would invalidate many traditional practices recognizing the role of religion in our society. This criticism shortchanges both the endorsement test itself and my explanation of the reason why certain longstanding government acknowledgments of religion do not, under that test, convey a message of endorsement. Practices such as legislative prayers or opening Court sessions with "God save the United States and this honorable Court" serve the secular purposes of "solemnizing public occasions" and "expressing confidence in the future." These examples of ceremonial deism do not survive Establishment Clause scrutiny simply by virtue of their historical longevity alone. . . . On the contrary, the "history and ubiquity" of a practice is relevant because it provides part of the context in which a reasonable observer evaluates whether a challenged governmental practice conveys a message of endorsement of religion. It is the combination of the longstanding existence of [such practices], as well as their nonsectarian nature, that leads me to the conclusion that those particular practices, despite their religious roots, do not convey a message of endorsement of particular religious beliefs. . . . The question under endorsement analysis [is] whether a reasonable observer would view such longstanding practices as a disapproval of his or her particular religious choices, in light of the fact that they serve a secular purpose rather than a sectarian one and have largely lost their religious significance over time. . . .

Contrary to Justice Kennedy's assertions, neither the endorsement test nor its application in these cases reflects "an unjustified hostility toward religion." Instead, the endorsement standard recognizes that the religious liberty so precious to the citizens who make up our diverse country is protected, not impeded, when government avoids endorsing religion or favoring particular beliefs over others. Clearly, the government can *acknowledge* the role of religion in our society in numerous ways that do not amount to an endorsement. Moreover, the government can accommodate religion by lifting government-imposed burdens on religion. . . . By repeatedly using the terms "acknowledgment" of religion and "accommodation" of religion interchangeably, however, Justice Kennedy obscures the fact that the displays at issue in these cases were not placed at city hall in order to remove a government-imposed burden on the free exercise of religion. Christians remain free to display their crèches at their homes and churches. Allegheny County has neither placed nor removed a governmental burden on the free exercise of religion but rather [has] conveyed a message of governmental endorsement of Christian beliefs. This the Establishment Clause does not permit.

III

. . . I also conclude that the city of Pittsburgh's combined holiday display of a Chanukah menorah, a Christmas tree, and a sign saluting liberty does not have the effect of conveying an endorsement of religion. . . . In my view, the relevant question for Establishment Clause purposes is whether the city of Pittsburgh's display of the menorah, the religious symbol of a religious holiday, next to a Christmas tree and a sign saluting liberty sends a message of government endorsement of Judaism or whether it sends a message of pluralism and freedom to choose one's own beliefs.

. . . By accompanying its display of a Christmas tree—a secular symbol of the Christmas holiday season—with a salute to liberty, and by adding a religious symbol from a Jewish holiday also celebrated at roughly the same time of year, I conclude that the city did not endorse Judaism or religion in general, but rather conveyed a message of pluralism and freedom of belief during the holiday season. . . . The message of pluralism conveyed by the city's combined holiday display is not a message that endorses religion over nonreligion. Just as government may not favor particular religious beliefs over others, "government may not favor religious belief over disbelief." . . . A reasonable observer would, in my view, appreciate that the combined display is an effort to acknowledge the cultural diversity of our country and to convey tolerance of different choices in matters of religious belief or nonbelief by recognizing that the winter holiday season is celebrated in diverse ways by our citizens. In [the] holiday context, this combined display in its particular physical setting conveys neither an endorsement of Judaism or Christianity nor disapproval of alternative beliefs, and thus does not have the impermissible effect of "mak[ing] religion relevant, in reality or public perception, to status in the political community." *Lynch* (concurring opinion). . . .

In sum, I conclude that the city of Pittsburgh's combined holiday display had neither the purpose nor the effect of endorsing religion, but that Allegheny County's crèche display had such an effect. Accordingly, I join Parts I, II, III-A, IV, V, and VII of the Court's opinion and concur in the judgment.

Justice Brennan, with whom Justice Marshall and Justice Stevens join, concurring in part and dissenting in part.

. . . [I] agree with the Court that Allegheny County's display of a crèche at the county courthouse signals an endorsement of the Christian faith in violation of the Establishment Clause. . . . I cannot agree, however, that the city's display of a 45-foot Christmas tree and an 18-foot Chanukah menorah at the entrance to the building housing the mayor's office shows no favoritism towards Christianity, Judaism, or both. Indeed, I should have thought that the answer as to the first display supplied the answer to the second. . . .

Justice Stevens, with whom Justice Brennan and Justice Marshall join, concurring in part and dissenting in part.

. . . In my opinion the Establishment Clause should be construed to create a strong presumption against the display of religious symbols on public property. There is always a risk that such symbols will offend nonmembers of the faith being advertised as well as adherents who consider the particular advertisement disrespectful. . . .

Application of a strong presumption against the public use of religious symbols scarcely will "require a relentless extirpation of all contact between government and religion," for it will prohibit a display only when its message, evaluated in the context in which it is presented, is nonsecular. . . .

. . . Allegheny County's unambiguous exposition of a sacred symbol inside its court-house promoted Christianity to a degree that violated the Establishment Clause. Accordingly, I concur in the Court's judgment regarding the crèche. . . . I cannot agree with the Court's conclusion that the display at Pittsburgh's City-County Building was constitutional. . . . [The] presence of the Chanukah menorah, unquestionably a religious symbol, gives religious significance to the Christmas tree. The overall display thus manifests governmental approval of the Jewish and Christian religions. [The] message is not sufficiently clear to overcome the strong presumption that the display, respecting two religions to the exclusion of all others, is the very kind of double establishment that the First Amendment was designed to outlaw. I would, therefore, affirm the judgment of the Court of Appeals in its entirety.

JUSTICE KENNEDY, with whom THE CHIEF JUSTICE, JUSTICE WHITE, and JUSTICE SCALIA join, concurring in the judgment in part and dissenting in part.

The majority [opinion's] view of the Establishment Clause reflects an unjusti-fied hostility toward religion, a hostility inconsistent with our history and our precedents. . . . The crèche display is constitutional, and, for the same reasons, the display of [the menorah is] permissible as well. . . .

. . . In permitting the displays on government property of the menorah and the crèche, the city and county sought to do no more than "celebrate the season," and to acknowledge, along with many of their citizens, the historical background and the reli-gious, as well as secular, nature of the Chanukah and Christmas holidays. This inter-est falls well within the tradition of government accommodation and acknowledgment of religion that has marked our history from the beginning. . . .

If government is to participate in its citizens' celebration of a holiday that contains both a secular and a religious component, enforced recognition of only the secular aspect would signify the callous indifference toward religious faith that our cases and traditions do not require; for by commemorating the holiday only as it is celebrated by nonadherents, the government would be refusing to acknowledge the plain fact, and the historical reality, that many of its citizens celebrate its religious aspects as well. Judicial invalidation of government's attempts to recognize the religious under-pinnings of the holiday would signal not neutrality but a pervasive intent to insulate government from all things religious. The Religion Clauses do not require govern-ment to acknowledge these holidays or their religious component; but our strong tra-dition of government accommodation and acknowledgment permits government to do so.

There is no suggestion here that the government's power to coerce has been used to further the interests of Christianity or Judaism in any way. No one was compelled to observe or participate in any religious ceremony or activity. Neither the city nor the county contributed significant amounts of tax money to serve the cause of one religious faith. The crèche and the menorah are purely passive symbols of religious holidays. Passersby who disagree with the message conveyed by these displays are free to ignore them, or even to turn their backs, just as they are free to do when they disagree with any other form of government speech.

There is no realistic risk that the crèche and the menorah represent an effort to proselytize or are otherwise the first step down the road to an establishment of religion. *Lynch* is dispositive of this claim with respect to the crèche, and I find no reason for reaching a different result with respect to the menorah. Both are the traditional symbols of religious holidays that over time have acquired a secular component. . . .

Even if *Lynch* did not control, I would not commit this Court to the test applied by the majority today. The notion that cases arising under the Establishment Clause should be decided by an inquiry into whether a "'reasonable observer'" may "'fairly understand'" government action to "'sen[d] a message to nonadherents that they are outsiders, not full members of the political community,'" is a recent, and in my view most unwelcome, addition to our tangled Establishment Clause jurisprudence. Although a scattering of our cases have used "endorsement" as another word for "preference" or "imprimatur," the endorsement test applied by the majority had its genesis in Justice O'Connor's concurring opinion in *Lynch*. . . . I submit that the endorsement test is flawed in its fundamentals and unworkable in practice. The uncritical adoption of this standard is every bit as troubling as the bizarre result it produces in the cases before us. . . .

In addition to disregarding precedent and historical fact, the majority's approach to government use of religious symbolism threatens to trivialize constitutional adjudication [and] embraces a jurisprudence of minutiae. A reviewing court must consider whether the city has included Santas, talking wishing wells, reindeer, or other secular symbols as "a center of attention separate from the crèche." After determining whether these centers of attention are sufficiently "separate" that each "had their specific visual story to tell," the court must then measure their proximity to the crèche. A community that wishes to construct a constitutional display must also take care to avoid floral frames or other devices that might insulate the crèche from the sanitizing effect of the secular portions of the display. The majority also notes the presence of evergreens near the crèche that are identical to two small evergreens placed near official county signs. After today's decision, municipal greenery must be used with care. . . .

My description of the majority's test, though perhaps uncharitable, is intended to illustrate the inevitable difficulties with its application. This test could provide workable guidance to the lower courts, if ever, only after this Court has decided a long series of holiday display cases, using little more than intuition and a tape measure. Deciding cases on the basis of such an unguided examination of marginalia is irreconcilable with the imperative of applying neutral principles in constitutional adjudication. . . .

The result the Court reaches in these cases is perhaps the clearest illustration of the unwisdom of the endorsement test. . . . If there be such a person as the "reasonable observer," I am quite certain that he or she will take away a salient message from our holding in these cases: the Supreme Court of the United States has concluded that the First Amendment creates classes of religions based on the relative numbers of their adherents. Those religions enjoying the largest following must be consigned to the status of least favored faiths so as to avoid any possible risk of offending members of minority religions. . . .

The suit before us is admittedly a troubling one. It must be conceded that, however neutral the purpose of the city and county, the eager proselytizer may seek to use these symbols for his own ends. The urge to use them to teach or to taunt is always present. It is also true that some devout adherents of Judaism or Christianity may be as offended by the holiday display as are nonbelievers, if not more so. To place these religious symbols in a common hallway or sidewalk, where they may be ignored or even insulted, must be distasteful to many who cherish their meaning.

For these reasons, I might have voted against installation of these particular displays were I a local legislative official. But we have no jurisdiction over matters of taste within the realm of constitutionally permissible discretion. Our role is enforcement of a written Constitution. In my view, the principles of the Establishment Clause and our Nation's historic traditions of diversity and pluralism allow communities to make reasonable judgments respecting the accommodation or acknowledgment of holidays with both cultural and religious aspects. No constitutional violation occurs when they do so by displaying a symbol of the holiday's religious origins.

McCreary County v. ACLU

545 U.S. 844 (2005)

JUSTICE SOUTER delivered the opinion of the Court.

I

[In] 1999, petitioners McCreary County and Pulaski County, Kentucky . . . put up in their respective courthouses large, gold-framed copies of an abridged text of the King James version of the Ten Commandments, including a citation to the Book of *Exodus*. In McCreary County, the placement of the Commandments responded to an order of the county legislative body. . . . In Pulaski County, [the] Commandments were hung in a ceremony presided over by the county Judge-Executive. . . . In each county, the hallway display was "readily visible to . . . county citizens who use the courthouse to conduct their civic business, to obtain or renew driver's licenses and permits, to register cars, to pay local taxes, and to register to vote."

[Respondents] American Civil Liberties Union of Kentucky [and others] sued the Counties in Federal District Court and sought a preliminary injunction against maintaining the displays. . . . [Before] the District Court [responded] to the request for injunction, the legislative body of each County authorized a second, expanded display, by nearly identical resolutions reciting that the Ten Commandments are "the precedent legal code upon which the civil and criminal codes of . . . Kentucky are founded," and stating several grounds for taking that position. . . .

As directed by the resolutions, the Counties expanded the displays of the Ten Commandments in their locations, presumably along with copies of the resolution, which instructed that it, too, be posted. In addition to the first display's large framed copy of the edited King James version of the Commandments, the second included eight other documents in smaller frames, each either having a religious theme or excerpted to highlight a religious element. The documents were the "endowed by their Creator" passage from the Declaration of Independence; the Preamble to the Constitution of Kentucky; the national motto, "In God We Trust"; a page from the Congressional Record of February 2, 1983, proclaiming the Year of the Bible and including a statement of the Ten Commandments; a proclamation by President Abraham Lincoln designating April 30, 1863, a National Day of Prayer and Humiliation; an excerpt from President Lincoln's "Reply to Loyal Colored People of Baltimore upon Presentation of a Bible," reading that "the Bible is the best gift God has ever given to man"; a proclamation by President Reagan marking 1983 the Year of the Bible; and the Mayflower Compact.

[The] District Court entered a preliminary injunction [ordering] that the "display . . . be removed from [each] County Courthouse IMMEDIATELY" and that no county official "erect or cause to be erected similar displays." The court's analysis [followed] the three-part formulation first stated in *Lemon v. Kurtzman* (1971) [*supra* this chapter]. . . . The Counties [then] installed another display in each courthouse, the third within a year. No new resolution authorized this one, nor did the Counties repeal the resolutions that preceded the second. The posting consists of nine framed documents of equal size, one of them setting out the Ten Commandments explicitly identified as the "King James Version" at *Exodus* 20:3–17, and quoted at greater length than before:

> Thou shalt have no other gods before me.
>
> Thou shalt not make unto thee any graven image, or any likeness of any thing that is in heaven above, or that is in the earth beneath, or that is in the water underneath the earth: Thou shalt not bow down thyself to them, nor serve them: for I the LORD thy God am a jealous God, visiting the iniquity of the fathers upon the children unto the third and fourth generation of them that hate me.
>
> Thou shalt not take the name of the LORD thy God in vain: for the LORD will not hold him guiltless that taketh his name in vain.
>
> Remember the sabbath day, to keep it holy.
>
> Honour thy father and thy mother: that thy days may be long upon the land which the LORD thy God giveth thee.
>
> Thou shalt not kill.
>
> Thou shalt not commit adultery.
>
> Thou shalt not steal.
>
> Thou shalt not bear false witness against thy neighbour.
>
> Thou shalt not covet thy neighbour's house, thou shalt not covet thy neighbor's wife, nor his manservant, nor his maidservant, nor his ox, nor his ass, nor anything that is thy neighbour's.

Assembled with the Commandments are framed copies of the Magna Carta, the Declaration of Independence, the Bill of Rights, the lyrics of the Star Spangled Banner, the Mayflower Compact, the National Motto, the Preamble to the Kentucky Constitution, and a picture of Lady Justice. The collection is entitled "The Foundations of American Law and Government Display" and each document comes with a statement about its historical and legal significance. The comment on the Ten Commandments reads:

> The Ten Commandments have profoundly influenced the formation of Western legal thought and the formation of our country. That influence is clearly seen in the Declaration of Independence, which declared that "We hold these truths to be self-evident, that all men are created equal, that they are endowed by their Creator with certain unalienable Rights, that among these are Life, Liberty, and the pursuit of Happiness." The Ten Commandments provide the moral background of the Declaration of Independence and the foundation of our legal tradition.

The ACLU moved to supplement the preliminary injunction to enjoin the Counties' third display, and the Counties responded with several explanations for the new version, including desires "to demonstrate that the Ten Commandments were part of the foundation of American Law and Government" and "to educate the citizens of the county regarding some of the documents that played a significant role in the foundation of our system of law and government." . . . [The] trial court supplemented the injunction, and a divided panel of the Court of Appeals for the Sixth Circuit affirmed. . . . We granted certiorari, and now affirm.

II

Twenty-five years ago in a case prompted by posting the Ten Commandments in Kentucky's public schools, this Court recognized that the Commandments "are undeniably a sacred text in the Jewish and Christian faiths" and held that their display in public classrooms violated the First Amendment's bar against establishment of religion. *Stone v. Graham*, 449 U.S. 39 (1980) (per curiam). *Stone* found a predominantly religious purpose in the government's posting of the Commandments, given their prominence as "'an instrument of religion.'" The Counties ask for a different approach here by arguing that official purpose is unknowable and the search for it inherently vain. In the alternative, the Counties would avoid the District Court's conclusion by having us limit the scope of the purpose inquiry so severely that any trivial rationalization would suffice, under a standard oblivious to the history of religious government action like the progression of exhibits in this case.

Ever since *Lemon v. Kurtzman* (1971) [*supra* this chapter] summarized the three familiar considerations for evaluating Establishment Clause claims, looking to whether government action has "a secular legislative purpose" has been a common, albeit seldom dispositive, element of our cases. . . . The touchstone for our analysis is the principle that the "First Amendment mandates governmental neutrality between religion and religion, and between religion and nonreligion." *Everson v. Board of Ed.* (1947) [*supra* this chapter]; *Wallace v. Jaffree* (1985) [*supra* this chapter]. When the government acts with the ostensible and predominant purpose of advancing religion, it violates that central Establishment Clause value of official religious neutrality, there being no neutrality when the government's ostensible object is to take sides. . . .

Despite the intuitive importance of official purpose to the realization of Establishment Clause values, the Counties ask us to abandon *Lemon*'s purpose test, or at least to truncate any enquiry into purpose here. Their first argument is that the very consideration of purpose is deceptive: according to them, true "purpose" is unknowable, and its search merely an excuse for courts to act selectively and unpredictably in picking out evidence of subjective intent. The assertions are as seismic as they are unconvincing. . . .

[Scrutinizing] purpose does make practical sense [in] Establishment Clause analysis, where an understanding of official objective emerges from readily discoverable fact, without any judicial psychoanalysis of a drafter's heart of hearts. The eyes that look to purpose belong to an "'objective observer,'" one who takes account of the traditional external signs that show up in the "'text, legislative history, and implementation of the statute,'" or comparable official act. There is, then, nothing hinting at an unpredictable or disingenuous exercise when a court enquires into purpose after a claim is raised under the Establishment Clause.

The cases with findings of a predominantly religious purpose point to the straightforward nature of the test. In *Wallace*, for example, we inferred purpose from a change of wording from an earlier statute to a later one, each dealing with prayer in schools. And in *Edwards v. Aguillard* (1987) [*supra* this chapter], we relied on a statute's text and the detailed public comments of its sponsor, when we sought the purpose of a state law requiring creationism to be taught alongside evolution. In other cases, the government action itself bespoke the purpose, as in *School District of Abington Township v. Schemp* (1963) [*supra* this chapter], where the object of required Bible study in public schools was patently religious; in *Stone*, the Court held that the "posting of religious texts on the wall served no . . . educational function," and found that if "the posted copies of the Ten Commandments [were] to have any effect at all, it [would] be to induce the schoolchildren to read, meditate upon, perhaps to venerate and obey, the Commandments." In each case, the government's action was held unconstitutional only because openly available data supported a commonsense conclusion that a religious objective permeated the government's action. Nor is there any indication that the enquiry is rigged in practice to finding a religious purpose dominant every time a case is filed. In the past, the test has not been fatal very often, presumably because government does not generally act unconstitutionally, with the predominant purpose of advancing religion. . . .

After declining the invitation to abandon concern with purpose wholesale, we also have to avoid the Counties' alternative tack of trivializing the enquiry into it. The Counties would read the cases as if the purpose enquiry were so naive that any transparent claim to secularity would satisfy it, and they would cut context out of the enquiry, to the point of ignoring history, no matter what bearing it actually had on the significance of current circumstances. There is no precedent for the Counties' arguments, or reason supporting them.

Lemon said that government action must have "a secular . . . purpose," and after a host of cases it is fair to add that although a legislature's stated reasons will generally get deference, the secular purpose required has to be genuine, not a sham, and not merely secondary to a religious objective. . . .

[We] have not made the purpose test a pushover for any secular claim. . . . [The] Court often does accept governmental statements of purpose, in keeping with the respect owed in the first instance to such official claims. But in those unusual cases where the claim was an apparent sham, or the secular purpose secondary, the unsurprising results have been findings of no adequate secular object, as against a predominantly religious one.

The Counties [also] argue that purpose in a case like this one should be inferred, if at all, only from the latest news about the last in a series of governmental actions, however close they may all be in time and subject. But the world is not made brand new every morning, and the Counties are simply asking us to ignore perfectly probative evidence; they want an absentminded objective observer, not one presumed to be familiar with the history of the government's actions and competent to learn what history has to show. The Counties' position just bucks common sense: reasonable observers have reasonable memories, and our precedents sensibly forbid an observer "to turn a blind eye to the context in which [the] policy arose."

III

[On appeal from a preliminary injunction, we] review the District Court's legal rulings *de novo*, and its ultimate conclusion for abuse of discretion. [The only factor in the preliminary injunction analysis at issue here is the likelihood of the ACLU's success on the merits.]

[Our] only case dealing with the constitutionality of displaying the Commandments [*Stone v. Graham*] recognized that the Commandments are an "instrument of religion" and that, at least on the facts before it, the display of their text could presumptively be understood as meant to advance religion: although state law specifically required their posting in public school classrooms, their isolated exhibition did not leave room even for an argument that secular education explained their being there. But *Stone* did not purport to decide the constitutionality of every possible way the Commandments might be set out by the government, and under the Establishment Clause detail is key. *County of Allegheny v. American Civil Liberties Union* (1989) [*supra* this chapter]. Hence, we look to the record of evidence showing the progression leading up to the third display of the Commandments.

The display rejected in *Stone* had two obvious similarities to the first one in the sequence here: both set out a text of the Commandments as distinct from any traditionally symbolic representation, and each stood alone, not part of an arguably secular display. *Stone* stressed the significance of integrating the Commandments into a secular scheme to forestall the broadcast of an otherwise clearly religious message. . . .

Displaying that text is thus different from a symbolic depiction, like tablets with 10 roman numerals, which could be seen as alluding to a general notion of law, not a sectarian conception of faith. [The] Counties' solo exhibit here did nothing more to counter the sectarian implication than the postings at issue in *Stone*. [At] the ceremony for posting the framed Commandments in Pulaski County, the county executive was accompanied by his pastor, who testified to the certainty of the existence of God. The reasonable observer could only think that the Counties meant to emphasize and celebrate the Commandments' religious message.

This is not to deny that the Commandments have had influence on civil or secular law; a major text of a majority religion is bound to be felt. The point is simply that the original text viewed in its entirety is an unmistakably religious statement dealing with religious obligations and with morality subject to religious sanction. When the government initiates an effort to place this statement alone in public view, a religious object is unmistakable.

Once the Counties were sued, they modified the exhibits [by] forthright and nearly identical [resolutions] listing a series of American historical documents with theistic and Christian references, which were to be posted in order to furnish a setting for displaying the Ten Commandments [without] raising concern about "any Christian or religious references" in them. . . . In this second display, unlike the first, the Commandments were not hung in isolation. . . . Instead, the second version was required to include the statement of the government's purpose expressly set out in the county resolutions, and underscored it by juxtaposing the Commandments to other documents with highlighted references to God as their sole common element. The display's unstinting focus was on religious passages, showing that the Counties were posting the Commandments precisely because of their sectarian content. . . . Together, the display and resolution presented an indisputable, and undisputed, showing of an impermissible purpose. Today, the Counties make no attempt to defend their undeniable objective, but instead hopefully describe version two as "dead and buried." Their refusal to defend the second display is understandable, but the reasonable observer could not forget it.

After the Counties changed lawyers, they mounted a third display, without a new resolution or repeal of the old one. The result was the "Foundations of American Law and Government" exhibit, which placed the Commandments in the company of other documents the Counties thought especially significant in the historical foundation of American government. [The] Counties cited several new purposes for the third version, including a desire "to educate the citizens of the county regarding some of the documents that played a significant role in the foundation of our system of law and government." . . . These new statements of purpose were presented only as a litigating position, there being no further authorizing action by the Counties' governing boards. And although repeal of the earlier county authorizations would not have erased them from the record of evidence bearing on current purpose, the extraordinary resolutions for the second display passed just months earlier were not repealed or otherwise repudiated. [The] sectarian spirit of the common resolution[s] found enhanced expression in the third display, which quoted more of the purely religious language of the Commandments than the first two displays had done. No reasonable observer could swallow the claim that the Counties had cast off the objective so unmistakable in the earlier displays. Nor did the selection of posted material suggest a clear theme that might prevail over evidence of the continuing religious object. . . . [The same observer] would probably suspect that the Counties were simply reaching for any way to keep a religious document on the walls of courthouses constitutionally required to embody religious neutrality.

In holding the preliminary injunction adequately supported by evidence that the Counties' purpose had not changed at the third stage, we do not decide that the Counties' past actions forever taint any effort on their part to deal with the subject matter. We hold only that purpose needs to be taken seriously under the Establishment Clause and needs to be understood in light of context; an implausible claim that governmental purpose has changed should not carry the day in a court of law any more than in a head with common sense. . . .

Nor do we have occasion here to hold that a sacred text can never be integrated constitutionally into a governmental display on the subject of law, or American history. We do not forget, and in this litigation have frequently been reminded, that our own courtroom frieze was deliberately designed in the exercise of governmental authority so as to include the figure of Moses holding tablets exhibiting a portion of the Hebrew text of the later, secularly phrased Commandments; in the company of 17 other lawgivers, most of them secular figures, there is no risk that Moses would strike an observer as evidence that the National Government was violating neutrality in religion. . . .

V

Given the ample support for the District Court's finding of a predominantly religious purpose behind the Counties' third display, we affirm the Sixth Circuit in upholding the preliminary injunction.

JUSTICE O'CONNOR, concurring.

. . . Reasonable minds can disagree about how to apply the Religion Clauses in a given case. But the goal of the Clauses is clear: to carry out the Founders' plan of preserving religious liberty to the fullest extent possible in a pluralistic society. By enforcing the Clauses, we have kept religion a matter for the individual conscience, not for the prosecutor or bureaucrat. At a time when we see around the world the violent consequences of the assumption of religious authority by government, Americans may count themselves fortunate: Our regard for constitutional boundaries has protected us from similar travails, while allowing private religious exercise to flourish. . . . Americans attend their places of worship more often than do citizens of other developed nations, and describe religion as playing an especially important role in their lives. Those who would renegotiate the boundaries between church and state must therefore answer a difficult question: Why would we trade a system that has served us so well for one that has served others so poorly? . . .

When we enforce these restrictions, we do so for the same reason that guided the Framers—respect for religion's special role in society. Our Founders conceived of a Republic receptive to voluntary religious expression, and provided for the possibility of judicial intervention when government action threatens or impedes such expression. Voluntary religious belief and expression may be as threatened when government takes the mantle of religion upon itself as when government directly interferes with private religious practices. When the government associates one set of religious beliefs with the state and identifies nonadherents as outsiders, it encroaches upon the individual's decision about whether and how to worship. . . .

Given the history of this particular display of the Ten Commandments, the Court correctly finds an Establishment Clause violation. The purpose behind the counties' display is relevant because it conveys an unmistakable message of endorsement to the reasonable observer.

It is true that many Americans find the Commandments in accord with their personal beliefs. But we do not count heads before enforcing the First Amendment. Nor can we accept the theory that Americans who do not accept the Commandments' validity are outside the First Amendment's protections. There is no list of approved and disapproved beliefs appended to the First Amendment—and the Amendment's broad terms ("free exercise," "establishment," "religion") do not admit of such a cramped reading. . . . The Religion Clauses [protect] adherents of all religions, as well as those who believe in no religion at all. . . .

JUSTICE SCALIA, with whom THE CHIEF JUSTICE and JUSTICE THOMAS join, and with whom JUSTICE KENNEDY joins as to Parts II and III, dissenting. . . .

II

As bad as the *Lemon* test is, it is worse for the fact that, since its inception, its seemingly simple mandates have been manipulated to fit whatever result the Court aimed to achieve. Today's opinion is no different. In two respects it modifies *Lemon* to ratchet up the Court's hostility to religion. First, the Court justifies inquiry into legislative purpose, not as an end itself, but as a means to ascertain the appearance of the government action to an "'objective observer.'" Because in the Court's view the true danger to be guarded against is that the objective observer would feel like an "outsider" or "not [a] full member of the political community," its inquiry focuses not on the *actual purpose* of government action, but the "purpose apparent from government action." Under this approach, even if a government could show that its actual purpose was not to advance religion, it would presumably violate the Constitution as long as the Court's objective observer would think otherwise. . . .

Second, the Court replaces *Lemon*'s requirement that the government have "*a* secular . . . purpose," with the heightened requirement that the secular purpose "predominate" over any purpose to advance religion. The Court treats this extension as a natural outgrowth of the longstanding requirement that the government's secular purpose not be a sham, but simple logic shows the two to be unrelated. If the government's proffered secular purpose is not genuine, then the government has no secular purpose at all. The new demand that secular purpose predominate contradicts *Lemon*'s more limited requirement, and finds no support in our cases. . . .

I have urged that *Lemon*'s purpose prong be abandoned, because . . . even an *exclusive* purpose to foster or assist religious practice is not necessarily invalidating. But today's extension makes things even worse. By shifting the focus of *Lemon*'s purpose prong from the search for a genuine, secular motivation to the hunt for a predominantly religious purpose, the Court converts what has in the past been a fairly limited inquiry into a rigorous review of the full record. . . .

III

Even accepting the Court's *Lemon*-based premises, the displays at issue here [in their final versions were] constitutional.

To any person who happened to walk down the hallway of the McCreary or Pulaski County Courthouse during the roughly nine months when the Foundations Displays were exhibited, the displays must have seemed unremarkable—if indeed they were noticed at all. The walls of both courthouses were already lined with historical documents and other assorted portraits; each Foundations Display was exhibited in the same format as these other displays and nothing in the record suggests that either County took steps to give it greater prominence.

Entitled "The Foundations of American Law and Government Display," each display consisted of nine equally sized documents. . . . The displays did not emphasize any of the nine documents in any way: The frame holding the Ten Commandments was of the same size and had the same appearance as that which held each of the other documents. Posted with the documents was a plaque, identifying the display, and explaining that it "contains documents that played a significant role in the foundation of our system of law and government." The explanation related to the Ten Commandments [did] not serve to distinguish it from the other documents. . . .

On its face, the Foundations Displays manifested the purely secular purpose that the Counties asserted before the District Court: "to display documents that played a significant role in the foundation of our system of law and government." That the Displays included the Ten Commandments did not transform their apparent secular purpose into one of impermissible advocacy for Judeo-Christian beliefs. . . . [When] the Ten Commandments appear alongside other documents of secular significance in a display devoted to the foundations of American law and government, the context communicates that the Ten Commandments are included, not to teach their binding nature as a religious text, but to show their unique contribution to the development of the legal system. . . .

Acknowledgment of the contribution that religion has made to our Nation's legal and governmental heritage partakes of a centuries-old tradition. . . . Display of the Ten Commandments is well within the mainstream of this practice of acknowledgment. Federal, State, and local governments across the Nation have engaged in such display. The Supreme Court Building itself includes depictions of Moses with the Ten Commandments in the Courtroom and on the east pediment of the building, and symbols of the Ten Commandments "adorn the metal gates lining the north and south sides of the Courtroom as well as the doors leading into the Courtroom." Similar depictions of the Decalogue appear on public buildings and monuments throughout our Nation's Capital. The frequency of these displays testifies to the popular understanding that the Ten Commandments are a foundation of the rule of law, and a symbol of the role that religion played, and continues to play, in our system of government.

Perhaps in recognition of the centrality of the Ten Commandments as a widely recognized symbol of religion in public life, the Court is at pains to dispel the impression that its decision will require governments across the country to sandblast the Ten Commandments from the public square. The constitutional problem, the Court says, is with the Counties' *purpose* in erecting the Foundations Displays, not the displays themselves. . . .

This inconsistency may be explicable in theory, but I suspect that the "objective observer" with whom the Court is so concerned will recognize its absurdity in practice. By virtue of details familiar only to the parties to litigation and their lawyers, McCreary and Pulaski Counties, Kentucky, have been ordered to remove [their displays]. Displays erected in silence (and under the direction of good legal advice) are permissible, while those hung after discussion and debate are deemed unconstitutional. Reduction of the Establishment Clause to such minutiae trivializes the Clause's protection against religious establishment. . . .

. . . In the Court's view, the impermissible motive was apparent from the [first versions of the] displays of the Ten Commandments all by themselves. . . . Surely that cannot be. If, as discussed above, the Commandments have a proper place in our civic history, even placing them by themselves can be civically motivated — especially when they are placed, not in a school (as they were in the *Stone* case upon which the Court places such reliance), but in a courthouse. . . .

The Court has in the past prohibited government actions that "proselytize or advance any one, or . . . disparage any other, faith or belief," or that apply some level of coercion. . . . The passive display of the Ten Commandments, even standing alone, does not begin to do either. . . . Nor is it the case that a solo display of the Ten Commandments advances any one faith. They are assuredly a religious symbol, but they are not so closely associated with a single religious belief that their display can reasonably be understood as preferring one religious sect over another. The Ten Commandments are recognized by Judaism, Christianity, and Islam alike as divinely given.

The Court also points to the Counties' second [version of the] displays, which featured a number of statements in historical documents reflecting a religious influence, and the resolutions that accompanied their erection, as evidence of an impermissible religious purpose. In the Court's view, "the [second] display's unstinting focus . . . on religious passages, shows that the Counties were posting the Commandments precisely because of their sectarian content." No, all it necessarily shows is that the exhibit was meant to focus upon the historic role of religious belief in our national life—which is entirely permissible. And the same can be said of the resolution. To forbid any government focus upon this aspect of our history is to display . . . "untutored devotion to the concept of neutrality," that would commit the Court (and the Nation) to a revisionist agenda of secularization. . . .

In sum: The first displays did not necessarily evidence an intent to further religious practice; nor did the second displays, or the resolutions authorizing them; and there is in any event no basis for attributing whatever intent motivated the first and second displays to the third. [The] Court has identified no evidence of a purpose to advance religion in a way that is inconsistent with our cases. The Court may well be correct in identifying the third displays as the fruit of a desire to display the Ten Commandments, but neither our cases nor our history support its assertion that such a desire renders the fruit poisonous.

. . . I would reverse the judgment of the Court of Appeals.

Van Orden v. Perry

545 U.S. 677 (2005)

CHIEF JUSTICE REHNQUIST announced the judgment of the Court and delivered an opinion, in which JUSTICE SCALIA, JUSTICE KENNEDY, and JUSTICE THOMAS join.

The question here is whether the Establishment Clause of the First Amendment allows the display of a monument inscribed with the Ten Commandments on the Texas State Capitol grounds. We hold that it does.

The 22 acres surrounding the Texas State Capitol contain 17 monuments and 21 historical markers commemorating the "people, ideals, and events that compose Texan identity." [The monuments are: Heroes of the Alamo, Hood's Brigade, Confederate Soldiers, Volunteer Fireman, Terry's Texas Rangers, Texas Cowboy, Spanish-American War, Texas National Guard, Ten Commandments, Tribute to Texas School Children, Texas Pioneer Woman, The Boy Scouts' Statue of Liberty Replica, Pearl Harbor Veterans, Korean War Veterans, Soldiers of World War I, Disabled Veterans, and Texas Peace Officers.]

The monolith challenged here stands 6-feet high and 3-feet wide. It is located to the north of the Capitol building, between the Capitol and the Supreme Court building. Its primary content is the text of the Ten Commandments. An eagle grasping the American flag, an eye inside of a pyramid, and two small tablets with what appears to be an ancient script are carved above the text of the Ten Commandments. Below the text are two Stars of David and the superimposed Greek letters Chi and Rho, which represent Christ. The bottom of the monument bears the inscription "PRESENTED TO THE PEOPLE AND YOUTH OF TEXAS BY THE FRATERNAL ORDER OF EAGLES OF TEXAS 1961."

The legislative record surrounding the State's acceptance of the monument from the Eagles—a national social, civic, and patriotic organization—is limited to legislative journal entries. After the monument was accepted, the State selected a site for the monument based on the recommendation of the state organization responsible for maintaining the Capitol grounds. The Eagles paid the cost of erecting the monument, the dedication of which was presided over by two state legislators.

Petitioner Thomas Van Orden is a native Texan and a resident of Austin. At one time he was a licensed lawyer. . . . Van Orden testified that, since 1995, he has encountered the Ten Commandments monument during his frequent visits to the Capitol grounds [for] the purpose of using the law library in the Supreme Court building. . . .

Forty years after the monument's erection and six years after Van Orden began to encounter the monument frequently, he sued numerous state officials in their official capacities, [seeking] both a declaration that the monument's placement violates the Establishment Clause and an injunction requiring its removal. [The] District Court held that the monument did not contravene the Establishment Clause. . . . The Court of Appeals affirmed. . . . We granted certiorari, and now affirm.

Our cases, Januslike, point in two directions in applying the Establishment Clause. One face looks toward the strong role played by religion and religious traditions throughout our Nation's history. . . . The other face looks toward the principle that governmental intervention in religious matters can itself endanger religious freedom. . . . These two faces are evident in representative cases both upholding and invalidating laws under the Establishment Clause. Over the last 25 years, we have sometimes pointed to *Lemon v. Kurtzman* (1971) [*supra* this chapter], as providing the governing test in Establishment Clause challenges. Yet, just two years after *Lemon* was decided, we noted that the factors identified in *Lemon* serve as "no more than helpful signposts." Many of our recent cases simply have not applied the *Lemon* test. Others have applied it only after concluding that the challenged practice was invalid under a different Establishment Clause test. Whatever may be the fate of the *Lemon* test in the larger scheme of Establishment Clause jurisprudence, we think it not useful in dealing with the sort of passive monument that Texas has erected on its Capitol grounds. Instead, our analysis is driven both by the nature of the monument and by our Nation's history.

As we explained in *Lynch v. Donnelly*, 465 U.S. 668 (1984): "There is an unbroken history of official acknowledgment by all three branches of government of the role of religion in American life from at least 1789." . . . Recognition of the role of God in our Nation's heritage has also been reflected in our decisions. We have acknowledged, for example, that "religion has been closely identified with our history and government," *School Dist. of Abington Township v. Schempp* (1963) [*supra* this chapter], and that "the history of man is inseparable from the history of religion," *Engel v. Vitale* (1962) [*supra* this chapter]. This recognition has led us to hold that the Establishment Clause permits a state legislature to open its daily sessions with a prayer by a chaplain paid by the State. *Marsh v. Chambers*, 463 U.S. 783 (1983). Such a practice, we thought, was "deeply embedded in the history and tradition of this country." . . .

In this case we are faced with a display of the Ten Commandments on government property outside the Texas State Capitol. Such acknowledgments of the role played by the Ten Commandments in our Nation's heritage are common throughout America. We need only look within our own Courtroom. Since 1935, Moses has stood, holding two tablets that reveal portions of the Ten Commandments written in Hebrew, among other lawgivers in the south frieze. Representations of the Ten Commandments adorn the metal gates lining the north and south sides of the Courtroom as well as the doors leading into the Courtroom. Moses also sits on the exterior east facade of the building holding the Ten Commandments tablets.

Similar acknowledgments can be seen throughout a visitor's tour of our Nation's Capital. For example, a large statue of Moses holding the Ten Commandments, alongside a statue of the Apostle Paul, has overlooked the rotunda of the Library of Congress' Jefferson Building since 1897. And the Jefferson Building's Great Reading Room contains a sculpture of a woman beside the Ten Commandments with a quote above her from the Old Testament (*Micah* 6:8). A medallion with two tablets depicting the Ten Commandments decorates the floor of the National Archives. Inside the Department of Justice, a statue entitled "The Spirit of Law" has two tablets representing the Ten Commandments lying at its feet. In front of the Ronald Reagan Building is another sculpture that includes a depiction of the Ten Commandments. So too a 24-foot-tall sculpture, depicting, among other things, the Ten Commandments and a cross, stands outside the federal courthouse that houses both the Court of Appeals and the District Court for the District of Columbia. Moses is also prominently featured in the Chamber of the United States House of Representatives.

Our opinions, like our building, have recognized the role the Decalogue plays in America's heritage. The Executive and Legislative Branches have also acknowledged the historical role of the Ten Commandments. These displays and recognitions of the Ten Commandments bespeak the rich American tradition of religious acknowledgments.

Of course, the Ten Commandments are religious—they were so viewed at their inception and so remain. The monument, therefore, has religious significance. According to Judeo-Christian belief, the Ten Commandments were given to Moses by God on Mt. Sinai. But Moses was a lawgiver as well as a religious leader. And the Ten Commandments have an undeniable historical meaning, as the foregoing examples demonstrate. Simply having religious content or promoting a message consistent with a religious doctrine does not run afoul of the Establishment Clause.

There are, of course, limits to the display of religious messages or symbols. For example, we held unconstitutional a Kentucky statute requiring the posting of the Ten Commandments in every public schoolroom. *Stone v. Graham*, 449 U.S. 39 (1980) (per curiam). In the classroom context, we found that the Kentucky statute had an improper and plainly religious purpose. As evidenced by *Stone*'s almost exclusive reliance upon two of our school prayer cases, (*School Dist. of Abington Township v. Schempp* and *Engel v. Vitale*), it stands as an example of the fact that we have "been particularly vigilant in monitoring compliance with the Establishment Clause in elementary and secondary schools." *Compare Lee v. Weisman* (1992) [*supra* this chapter] (holding unconstitutional a prayer at a secondary school graduation) with *Marsh v. Chambers*, 463 U.S. 783 (1983) (upholding a prayer in the state legislature). . . .

The placement of the Ten Commandments monument on the Texas State Capitol grounds is a far more passive use of those texts than was the case in *Stone*, where the text confronted elementary school students every day. Indeed, Van Orden, the petitioner here, apparently walked by the monument for a number of years before bringing this lawsuit. . . . Texas has treated her Capitol grounds monuments as representing the several strands in the State's political and legal history. The inclusion of the Ten Commandments monument in this group has a dual significance, partaking of both religion and government. We cannot say that Texas' display of this monument violates the Establishment Clause of the First Amendment.

The judgment of the Court of Appeals is *affirmed*.

JUSTICE SCALIA, concurring.

. . . I would prefer to reach the same result by adopting an Establishment Clause jurisprudence that is in accord with our Nation's past and present practices, and that can be consistently applied—the central relevant feature of which is that there is nothing unconstitutional in a State's favoring religion generally, honoring God through public prayer and acknowledgment, or, in a nonproselytizing manner, venerating the Ten Commandments. *See McCreary County v. Am. Civil Liberties Union* (2005) (Scalia, J., dissenting) [*supra* this chapter].

JUSTICE THOMAS, concurring.

. . . There is no question that, based on the original meaning of the Establishment Clause, the Ten Commandments display at issue here is constitutional. In no sense does Texas compel petitioner Van Orden to do anything. The only injury to him is that he takes offense at seeing the monument as he passes it on his way to the Texas Supreme Court Library. He need not stop to read it or even to look at it, let alone to express support for it or adopt the Commandments as guides for his life. The mere presence of the monument along his path involves no coercion and thus does not violate the Establishment Clause. . . .

Much, if not all, of [the inconsistency and incoherency in our decisions] would be avoided if the Court would return to the views of the Framers and adopt coercion as the touchstone for our Establishment Clause inquiry. Every acknowledgment of religion would not give rise to an Establishment Clause claim. Courts would not act as theological commissions, judging the meaning of religious matters. Most important, our precedent would be capable of consistent and coherent application. While the Court correctly rejects the challenge to the Ten Commandments monument on the Texas Capitol grounds, a more fundamental rethinking of our Establishment Clause jurisprudence remains in order.

JUSTICE BREYER, concurring in the judgment.

. . . If the relation between government and religion is one of separation, but not of mutual hostility and suspicion, one will inevitably find difficult borderline cases. And in such cases, I see no test-related substitute for the exercise of legal judgment. That judgment is not a personal judgment. Rather, as in all constitutional cases, it must reflect and remain faithful to the underlying purposes of the Clauses, and it must take account of context and consequences measured in light of those purposes. While the Court's prior tests provide useful guideposts — and might well lead to the same result the Court reaches today — no exact formula can dictate a resolution to such fact-intensive cases.

The case before us is a borderline case. . . . On the one hand, the Commandments' text undeniably has a religious message, invoking, indeed emphasizing, the Deity. On the other hand, focusing on the text of the Commandments alone cannot conclusively resolve this case. Rather, to determine the message that the text here conveys, we must examine how the text is *used*. And that inquiry requires us to consider the context of the display.

In certain contexts, a display of the tablets of the Ten Commandments can convey not simply a religious message but also a secular moral message (about proper standards of social conduct). And in certain contexts, a display of the tablets can also convey a historical message (about a historic relation between those standards and the law) — a fact that helps to explain the display of those tablets in dozens of courthouses throughout the Nation, including the Supreme Court of the United States.

Here the tablets have been used as part of a display that communicates not simply a religious message, but a secular message as well. The circumstances surrounding the display's placement on the capitol grounds and its physical setting suggest that the State itself intended the latter, nonreligious aspects of the tablets' message to predominate. And the monument's 40-year history on the Texas state grounds indicates that that has been its effect.

The group that donated the monument, the Fraternal Order of Eagles, a private civic (and primarily secular) organization, while interested in the religious aspect of the Ten Commandments, sought to highlight the Commandments' role in shaping civic morality as part of that organization's efforts to combat juvenile delinquency. The Eagles' consultation with a committee composed of members of several faiths in order to find a nonsectarian text underscores the group's ethics-based motives. The tablets, as displayed on the monument, prominently acknowledge that the Eagles donated the display, a factor which, though not sufficient, thereby further distances the State itself from the religious aspect of the Commandments' message.

The physical setting of the monument, moreover, suggests little or nothing of the sacred. The monument sits in a large park containing 17 monuments and 21 historical markers, all designed to illustrate the "ideals" of those who settled in Texas and of those who have lived there since that time. The setting does not readily lend itself to meditation or any other religious activity. But it does provide a context of history and moral ideals. It (together with the display's inscription about its origin) communicates to visitors that the State sought to reflect moral principles, illustrating a relation between ethics and law that the State's citizens, historically speaking, have endorsed. That is to say, the context suggests that the State intended the display's moral message—an illustrative message reflecting the historical "ideals" of Texans—to predominate.

If these factors provide a strong, but not conclusive, indication that the Commandments' text on this monument conveys a predominantly secular message, a further factor is determinative here. As far as I can tell, 40 years passed in which the presence of this monument, legally speaking, went unchallenged (until the single legal objection raised by petitioner). . . . Hence, those 40 years suggest more strongly than can any set of formulaic tests that few individuals, whatever their system of beliefs, are likely to have understood the monument as amounting, in any significantly detrimental way, to a government effort to favor a particular religious sect, primarily to promote religion over nonreligion, to "engage in" any "religious practice," to "compel" any "religious practice," or to "work deterrence" of any "religious belief." Those 40 years suggest that the public visiting the capitol grounds has considered the religious aspect of the tablets' message as part of what is a broader moral and historical message reflective of a cultural heritage.

This case, moreover, is distinguishable from instances where the Court has found Ten Commandments displays impermissible. The display is not on the grounds of a public school, where, given the impressionability of the young, government must exercise particular care in separating church and state. This case also differs from *McCreary County*, where the short (and stormy) history of the courthouse Commandments' displays demonstrates the substantially religious objectives of those who mounted them, and the effect of this readily apparent objective upon those who view them. That history there indicates a governmental effort substantially to promote religion, not simply an effort primarily to reflect, historically, the secular impact of a religiously inspired document. . . .

For these reasons, I believe that the Texas display—serving a mixed but primarily nonreligious purpose, not primarily "advancing" or "inhibiting religion," and not creating an "excessive government entanglement with religion,"—might satisfy this Court's more formal Establishment Clause tests. But, as I have said, in reaching the conclusion that the Texas display falls on the permissible side of the constitutional line, I rely less upon a literal application of any particular test than upon consideration of the basic purposes of the First Amendment's Religion Clauses themselves. This display has stood apparently uncontested for nearly two generations. That experience helps us understand that as a practical matter of *degree* this display is unlikely to prove divisive. And this matter of degree is, I believe, critical in a borderline case such as this one.

At the same time, to reach a contrary conclusion here, based primarily upon on the religious nature of the tablets' text would, I fear, lead the law to exhibit a hostility toward religion that has no place in our Establishment Clause traditions. Such a holding might well encourage disputes concerning the removal of longstanding depictions of the Ten Commandments from public buildings across the Nation. And it could thereby create the very kind of religiously based divisiveness that the Establishment Clause seeks to avoid. . . .

In light of these considerations, I cannot agree with today's plurality's analysis. Nor can I agree with Justice Scalia's dissent in *McCreary County*. I do agree with Justice O'Connor's statement of principles in *McCreary County*, though I disagree with her evaluation of the evidence as it bears on the application of those principles to this case. I concur in the judgment of the Court.

JUSTICE STEVENS, with whom JUSTICE GINSBURG joins, dissenting.

. . . Viewed on its face, Texas' display has no purported connection to God's role in the formation of Texas or the founding of our Nation; nor does it provide the reasonable observer with any basis to guess that it was erected to honor any individual or organization. The message transmitted by Texas' chosen display is quite plain: This State endorses the divine code of the "Judeo-Christian" God. . . .

Government's obligation to avoid divisiveness and exclusion in the religious sphere is compelled by the Establishment and Free Exercise Clauses, which together erect a wall of separation between church and state. This metaphorical wall protects [the] first and most fundamental of [principles], one that a majority of this Court today affirms, [that] the Establishment Clause demands religious neutrality—government may not exercise a preference for one religious faith over another. This essential command, however, is not merely a prohibition against the government's differentiation among religious sects. We have repeatedly reaffirmed that neither a State nor the Federal Government "can constitutionally pass laws or impose requirements which aid all religions as against non-believers, and neither can aid those religions based on a belief in the existence of God as against those religions founded on different beliefs." . . .

In restating this principle, I do not discount the importance of avoiding an overly strict interpretation of the metaphor so often used to define the reach of the Establishment Clause. . . . The wall that separates the church from the State does not prohibit the government from acknowledging the religious beliefs and practices of the American people, nor does it require governments to hide works of art or historic memorabilia from public view just because they also have religious significance. This case, however, is not about historic preservation or the mere recognition of religion. . . .

The monolith displayed on Texas Capitol grounds cannot be discounted as a passive acknowledgment of religion, nor can the State's refusal to remove it upon objection be explained as a simple desire to preserve a historic relic. This Nation's resolute commitment to neutrality with respect to religion is flatly inconsistent with the plurality's wholehearted validation of an official state endorsement of the message that there is one, and only one, God.

When the Ten Commandments monument was donated to the State of Texas in 1961, it was not for the purpose of commemorating a noteworthy event in Texas history, signifying the Commandments' influence on the development of secular law, or even denoting the religious beliefs of Texans at that time. To the contrary, the donation was only one of over a hundred largely identical monoliths, and of over a thousand paper replicas, distributed to state and local governments throughout the Nation over the course of several decades. This ambitious project was the work of the Fraternal Order of Eagles. . . .

As the story goes, the program was initiated by [a] Minnesota juvenile court judge and then-Chairman of the Eagles National Commission on Youth Guidance. Inspired by a juvenile offender who had never heard of the Ten Commandments, the judge approached the Minnesota Eagles with the idea of distributing paper copies of the Commandments to be posted in courthouses nationwide. The State's Aerie undertook this project and its popularity spread. When Cecil B. DeMille, who at that time was filming the movie *The Ten Commandments*, heard of the judge's endeavor, he teamed up with the Eagles to produce the type of granite monolith now displayed in front of the Texas Capitol and at courthouse squares, city halls, and public parks throughout the Nation. . . . It is the Eagles' belief that disseminating the message conveyed by the Ten Commandments will help to persuade young men and women to observe civilized standards of behavior, and will lead to more productive lives. Significantly, although the Eagles' organization is nonsectarian, eligibility for membership is premised on a belief in the existence of a "Supreme Being." . . . The desire to combat juvenile delinquency by providing guidance to youths is both admirable and unquestionably secular. But achieving that goal through biblical teachings injects a religious purpose into an otherwise secular endeavor. . . . Though the State of Texas may genuinely wish to combat juvenile delinquency, and may rightly want to honor the Eagles for their efforts, it cannot effectuate these admirable purposes through an explicitly religious medium. . . .

The reason this message stands apart is that the Decalogue is a venerable religious text. As we held 25 years ago, it is beyond dispute that "the Ten Commandments are undeniably a sacred text in the Jewish and Christian faiths." *Stone v. Graham*, 449 U.S. 39 (1981). . . . Moreover, despite the Eagles' best efforts to choose a benign nondenominational text, the Ten Commandments display projects not just a religious, but an inherently sectarian message. There are many distinctive versions of the Decalogue, ascribed to by different religions and even different denominations within a particular faith; to a pious and learned observer, these differences may be of enormous religious significance. In choosing to display this version of the Commandments, Texas tells the observer that the State supports this side of the doctrinal religious debate. The reasonable observer, after all, has no way of knowing that this text was the product of a compromise, or that there is a rationale of any kind for the text's selection. . . .

Even if, however, the message of the monument, despite the inscribed text, fairly could be said to represent the belief system of all Judeo-Christians, it would still run afoul of the Establishment Clause by prescribing a compelled code of conduct from one God, namely a Judeo-Christian God, that is rejected by prominent polytheistic sects, such as Hinduism, as well as nontheistic religions, such as Buddhism. And, at the very least, the text of the Ten Commandments impermissibly commands a preference for religion over irreligion. Any of those bases, in my judgment, would be sufficient to conclude that the message should not be proclaimed by the State of Texas on a permanent monument at the seat of its government.

I do not doubt that some Texans, including those elected to the Texas Legislature, may believe that the statues displayed on the Texas Capitol grounds, including the Ten Commandments monument, reflect the "ideals . . . that compose Texan identity." But Texas, like our entire country, is now a much more diversified community than it was when it became a part of the United States or even when the monument was erected. Today there are many Texans who do not believe in the God whose Commandments are displayed at their seat of government. Many of them worship a different god or no god at all. . . . Recognizing the diversity of religious and secular beliefs held by Texans and by all Americans, it seems beyond peradventure that allowing the seat of government to serve as a stage for the propagation of an unmistakably Judeo-Christian message of piety would have the tendency to make nonmonotheists and nonbelievers "feel like [outsiders] in matters of faith, and [strangers] in the political community." . . .

A reading of the First Amendment dependent on either of the purported original meanings [— either the narrowest interpretation that the clause concerned only Christians or the federalism interpretation that the clause applied only to the national government —] would eviscerate the heart of the Establishment Clause. It would replace Jefferson's "wall of separation" with a perverse wall of exclusion — Christians inside, non-Christians out. It would permit States to construct walls of their own choosing — Baptists inside, Mormons out; Jewish Orthodox inside, Jewish Reform out. A Clause so understood might be faithful to the expectations of some of our Founders, but it is plainly not worthy of a society whose enviable hallmark over the course of two centuries has been the continuing expansion of religious pluralism and tolerance. . . .

It is our duty, therefore, to interpret the First Amendment [not] by merely asking what those words meant to observers at the time of the founding, but instead by deriving from the Clause's text and history the broad principles that remain valid today. . . . The principle that guides my analysis is neutrality. The basis for that principle is firmly rooted in our Nation's history and our Constitution's text. I recognize that the requirement that government must remain neutral between religion and irreligion would have seemed foreign to some of the Framers. . . . [We] are not bound by the Framers' expectations — we are bound by the legal principles they enshrined in our Constitution. [Their] vision that States should not discriminate between Christian sects has as its foundation the principle that government must remain neutral between valid systems of belief. As religious pluralism has expanded, so has our acceptance of what constitutes valid belief systems. The evil of discriminating today against atheists, "polytheists[,] and believers in unconcerned deities," *McCreary County*, (Scalia, J., dissenting) [*supra* this chapter], is in my view a direct descendent of the evil of discriminating among Christian sects. The Establishment Clause thus forbids it and, in turn, forbids Texas from displaying the Ten Commandments monument the plurality so casually affirms. . . .

The disconnect between this Court's approval of Texas's monument and the constitutional prohibition against preferring religion to irreligion cannot be reduced to the exercise of plotting two adjacent locations on a slippery slope. *Cf. ante* (Breyer, J., concurring in judgment). Rather, it is the difference between the shelter of a fortress and exposure to "the winds that would blow" if the wall were allowed to crumble. That wall, however imperfect, remains worth preserving.

I respectfully dissent.

Justice O'Connor, dissenting.

For essentially the reasons given by Justice Souter, as well as the reasons given in my concurrence in *McCreary County v. Am. Civil Liberties Union of Ky.* (2005) [*supra* this chapter], I respectfully dissent.

Justice Souter, with whom Justice Stevens and Justice Ginsburg join, dissenting.

. . . A governmental display of an obviously religious text cannot be squared with neutrality, except in a setting that plausibly indicates that the statement is not placed in view with a predominant purpose on the part of government either to adopt the religious message or to urge its acceptance by others.

Until today, only one of our cases addressed the constitutionality of posting the Ten Commandments, *Stone v. Graham.* A Kentucky statute required posting the Commandments on the walls of public school classrooms, and the Court described the State's purpose (relevant under the tripartite test laid out in *Lemon v. Kurtzman*) as being at odds with the obligation of religious neutrality. . . .

[A] pedestrian happening upon the monument at issue here needs no training in religious doctrine to realize that the statement of the Commandments, quoting God himself, proclaims that the will of the divine being is the source of obligation to obey the rules, including the facially secular ones. In this case, moreover, the text is presented to give particular prominence to the Commandments' first sectarian reference, "I am the Lord thy God." That proclamation is centered on the stone and written in slightly larger letters than the subsequent recitation. To ensure that the religious nature of the monument is clear to even the most casual passerby, the word "Lord" appears in all capital letters (as does the word "am"), so that the most eye-catching segment of the quotation is the declaration "I AM the LORD thy God." What follows, of course, are the rules against other gods, graven images, vain swearing, and Sabbath breaking. And the full text of the fifth Commandment puts forward filial respect as a condition of long life in the land "which the Lord they God giveth thee." These "words . . . make [the] . . . religious meaning unmistakably clear."

To drive the religious point home, and identify the message as religious to any viewer who failed to read the text, the engraved quotation is framed by religious symbols: two tablets with what appears to be ancient script on them, two Stars of David, and the superimposed Greek letters Chi and Rho as the familiar monogram of Christ. Nothing on the monument, in fact, detracts from its religious nature, and the plurality does not suggest otherwise. It would therefore be difficult to miss the point that the government of Texas is telling everyone who sees the monument to live up to a moral code because God requires it, with both code and conception of God being rightly understood as the inheritances specifically of Jews and Christians. . . .

The monument's presentation of the Commandments with religious text emphasized and enhanced stands in contrast to any number of perfectly constitutional depictions of them, the frieze of our own Courtroom providing a good example, where the figure of Moses stands among history's great lawgivers. While Moses holds the tablets of the Commandments showing some Hebrew text, no one looking at the lines of figures in marble relief is likely to see a religious purpose behind the assemblage or take away a religious message from it. Only one other depiction represents a religious leader, and the historical personages are mixed with symbols of moral and intellectual abstractions like Equity and Authority. Since Moses enjoys no especial prominence on the frieze, viewers can readily take him to be there as a lawgiver in the company of other lawgivers; and the viewers may just as naturally see the tablets of the Commandments (showing the later ones, forbidding things like killing and theft, but without the divine preface) as background from which the concept of law emerged, ultimately having a secular influence in the history of the Nation. Government may, of course, constitutionally call attention to this influence, and may post displays or erect monuments recounting this aspect of our history no less than any other, so long as there is a context and that context is historical. Hence, a display of the Commandments accompanied by an exposition of how they have influenced modern law would most likely be constitutionally unobjectionable. . . .

Texas seeks to take advantage of the recognition that visual symbol and written text can manifest a secular purpose in secular company, when it argues that its monument (like Moses in the frieze) is not alone and ought to be viewed as only 1 among 17 placed on the 22 acres surrounding the state capitol. Texas, indeed, says that the Capitol grounds are like a museum for a collection of exhibits, the kind of setting that several Members of the Court have said can render the exhibition of religious artifacts permissible, even though in other circumstances their display would be seen as meant to convey a religious message forbidden to the State. So, for example, the Government of the United States does not violate the Establishment Clause by hanging Giotto's Madonna on the wall of the National Gallery.

But 17 monuments with no common appearance, history, or esthetic role scattered over 22 acres is not a museum, and anyone strolling around the lawn would surely take each memorial on its own terms without any dawning sense that some purpose held the miscellany together more coherently than fortuity and the edge of the grass. One monument expresses admiration for pioneer women. One pays respect to the fighters of World War II. And one quotes the God of Abraham whose command is the sanction for moral law. The themes are individual grit, patriotic courage, and God as the source of Jewish and Christian morality; there is no common denominator. . . .

If the State's museum argument does nothing to blunt the religious message and manifestly religious purpose behind it, neither does the plurality's reliance on generalities culled from cases factually different from this one. In fact, it is not until the end of its opinion that the plurality turns to the relevant precedent of *Stone*, a case actually dealing with a display of the Decalogue. When the plurality finally does confront *Stone*, it tries to avoid the case's obvious applicability by limiting its holding to the classroom setting. . . . [Our] numerous prior discussions of *Stone* have never treated its holding as restricted to the classroom. Nor can the plurality deflect *Stone* by calling the Texas monument "a far more passive use of [the Decalogue]. . . ." Placing a monument on the ground is not more "passive" than hanging a sheet of paper on a wall when both contain the same text to be read by anyone who looks at it. . . .

Finally, [I] do not see a persuasive argument for constitutionality in the plurality's observation that Van Orden's lawsuit comes "forty years after the monument's erection. . . ." It is not that I think the passage of time is necessarily irrelevant in Establishment Clause analysis. [The] State's argument [seems] to be that 40 years without a challenge shows that as a factual matter the religious expression is too tepid to provoke a serious reaction and constitute a violation. Perhaps, but the writer of Exodus chapter 20 was not lukewarm, and other explanations may do better in accounting for the late resort to the courts. Suing a State over religion puts nothing in a plaintiff's pocket and can take a great deal out, and even with volunteer litigators to supply time and energy, the risk of social ostracism can be powerfully deterrent. I doubt that a slow walk to the courthouse, even one that took 40 years, is much evidentiary help in applying the Establishment Clause.

I would reverse the judgment of the Court of Appeals.

———

Note: Justice Breyer's Constitutional Distinctions

In his 2005 book explaining his theory of constitutional interpretation, Justice Breyer offered a rare off-the-bench and remarkably candid explanation of the distinction he made to disapprove the McCreary County courthouse display and to approve the Texas capitol display. His was the controlling vote and he was the only Justice to see a constitutional difference between the two displays. All the others would have decided the two cases the same way—four to allow both displays and four to prohibit both displays. He insisted that his approach was not "subjective." Do you agree?

> [The] constitutional concern [for] the need to avoid "divisiveness based upon religion that promotes social conflict" helped me determine whether the Establishment Clause forbade two public displays of the tablets of the Ten Commandments. . . . [Given] the religious beliefs of most Americans, an absolutist approach that would purge all religious references from the public sphere could well promote the very kind of social conflict that the

Establishment Clause seeks to avoid. Thus, I thought, the Establishment Clause cannot *automatically* forbid every public display of the Ten Commandments, despite the religious nature of its text. Rather, one must examine the context of the *particular* display to see whether, in that context, the tablets convey the kind of government-endorsed religious message that the Establishment Clause forbids.

The history of the Kentucky courthouse display convinced me and the other members of the Court's majority that the display sought to serve its sponsors' primarily religious objectives and that many of its viewers would understand it as reflecting that motivation. But the context of the Texas display differed significantly. A private civic (and primarily secular) organization had placed the tablets on the Capitol grounds as part of the organization's efforts to combat juvenile delinquency. Those grounds contained seventeen other monuments and twenty-one historical markers, none of which conveyed any religious message and all of which sought to illustrate the historical "ideals" of Texans. And the monument had stood for forty years without legal challenge. These circumstances strongly suggested that the public visiting the Capitol grounds had long considered the tablets' religious message as a secondary part of a broader moral and historical message reflecting a cultural heritage — a view of the display consistent with its promoters' basic objective.

It was particularly important that the Texas display stood uncontested for forty years. That fact indicated, as a practical matter of degree, that (unlike the Kentucky display) the Texas display was unlikely to prove socially divisive. Indeed, to require the display's removal itself would encourage disputes over the removal of longstanding depictions of the Ten Commandments from public buildings across the nation, thereby creating the very kind of religiously based divisiveness that the Establishment Clause was designed to prevent. By way of contrast, the short and stormy history of the more contemporary Kentucky display revealed both religious motivation and consequent social controversy. Thus, in the two cases, which I called borderline cases, consideration of the likely consequences — evaluated in light of the purposes or values embodied within the Establishment Clause — helped produce a legal result: The Clause allowed the Texas display, while it forbade the display in Kentucky.

I am not arguing here that I was right in [these] cases. I am arguing that my opinions sought to identify a critical value underlying the Religion Clauses — [the avoidance of social conflict]. They considered how that value applied in modern-day America; they looked for consequences relevant to that value. And they sought to evaluate likely consequences in terms of that value. That is what I mean by an interpretive approach that emphasizes consequences. Under that approach language, precedent, constitutional values, and factual circumstances all constrain judicial subjectivity.*

Problem: Atheists Cross about Highway Memorials

American Atheists, Inc., an organization dedicated to promoting the separation of church and state and litigating on behalf of the civil rights of atheists, has brought a federal lawsuit against the Utah Department of Transportation and the Highway Patrol Association (HPA). The lawsuit challenges the practice of erecting 12-foot high white Latin crosses alongside state highways as memorials to state troopers who have been killed in the line of duty. The name of the deceased trooper and the official insignia of the Utah Highway Patrol are inscribed on each cross. A picture and a short biography of the deceased trooper also are attached to the cross. The crosses are paid for and erected by the HPA, a private non-religious fraternal organization of troopers, with the permission of the family of the deceased trooper. But the crosses are erected on public property and the HPA is required to obtain the permission of the Department of Transportation for each cross installation.

There are 13 crosses currently dotting the state highways, each located as near as possible to the site of the trooper's death, so the crosses are readily visible to drivers and pedestrians traveling throughout the state. The practice of erecting crosses began in 1998 and has continued without public controversy until this lawsuit.

What are the arguments for the plaintiffs and for the defendants? If you were the judge, how would you rule and why?

E. Legislative Prayer

In *Marsh v. Chambers*, 463 U.S. 783 (1983), the Supreme Court upheld a state legislature's practice of employing a religious chaplain whose primary responsibility was to open each legislative day with a prayer. A Presbyterian minister held the position for sixteen years and was paid from state funds. The prayers were characterized as "nonsectarian" and "Judeo-Christian." Chief Justice Burger wrote for the majority that included Justices White, Blackmun, Powell, Rehnquist, and O'Connor; Justices Brennan, Marshall, and Stevens dissented. The majority opinion did not even mention the *Lemon* test. Instead, the majority based its holding on the "unambiguous and unbroken history of more than two hundred years . . . [of] the practice of opening legislative sessions with a prayer." The majority made much of the historical fact that in 1789 both houses of the First Congress—which drafted the First Amendment—began the continuing practice of employing a chaplain to begin their sessions with a

---

* From Active Liberty: Interpreting Our Democratic Constitution by Stephen Breyer, copyright © 2005 by Stephen Breyer. Used by permission of Alfred A. Knopf, a division of Random House, Inc. Any third party use of this material, outside of this publication, is prohibited. Interested parties must apply directly to Random House, Inc. for permission.

prayer. The majority concluded "their actions reveal their intent," that is, "the First Amendment draftsmen . . . saw no real threat to the Establishment Clause arising from a practice of prayer similar to that now challenged."

In the next case, the Court revisited the issue of legislative prayer. All nine of the Justices approved of *Marsh v. Chambers* in principle, but they divided 5 to 4 whether the particular practices of the town's board violated the incorporated Establishment Clause.

Town of Greece v. Galloway

134 S. Ct. 1811 (2014)

JUSTICE KENNEDY delivered the opinion of the Court, except as to Part II-B.*

The Court must decide whether the town of Greece, New York, imposes an impermissible establishment of religion by opening its monthly board meetings with a prayer. It must be concluded, consistent with the Court's opinion in *Marsh v. Chambers*, 463 U.S. 783 (1983), that no violation of the Constitution has been shown.

I

Greece, a town with a population of 94,000, is in upstate New York. For some years, it began its monthly town board meetings with a moment of silence. In 1999, the newly elected town supervisor . . . decided to replicate the prayer practice he had found meaningful while serving in the county legislature. Following the roll call and recitation of the Pledge of Allegiance, [the supervisor] would invite a local clergyman to the front of the room to deliver an invocation. After the prayer, [the supervisor] would thank the minister for serving as the board's "chaplain for the month" and present him with a commemorative plaque. The prayer was intended to place town board members in a solemn and deliberative frame of mind, invoke divine guidance in town affairs, and follow a tradition practiced by Congress and dozens of state legislatures.

The town followed an informal method for selecting prayer givers, all of whom were unpaid volunteers. A town employee would call the congregations listed in a local directory until she found a minister available for that month's meeting. The town eventually compiled a list of willing "board chaplains" who had accepted invitations and agreed to return in the future. The town at no point excluded or denied an opportunity to a would-be prayer giver. Its leaders maintained that a minister or layperson of any persuasion, including an atheist, could give the invocation. But nearly all of the congregations in town were Christian; and from 1999 to 2007, all of the participating ministers were too.

Greece neither reviewed the prayers in advance of the meetings nor provided guidance as to their tone or content, in the belief that exercising any degree of control over the prayers would infringe both the free exercise and speech rights of the

---

* THE CHIEF JUSTICE and JUSTICE ALITO join this opinion in full. JUSTICE SCALIA and JUSTICE THOMAS join this opinion except as to Part II-B.

ministers. The town instead left the guest clergy free to compose their own devotions. The resulting prayers often sounded both civic and religious themes. Typical were invocations that asked the divinity to abide at the meeting and bestow blessings on the community. . . . Some of the ministers spoke in a distinctly Christian idiom; and a minority invoked religious holidays, scripture, or doctrine. . . .

Respondents Susan Galloway and Linda Stephens attended town board meetings to speak about issues of local concern, and they objected that the prayers violated their religious or philosophical views. . . .

Galloway and Stephens brought suit in the United States District Court for the Western District of New York. . . . They did not seek an end to the prayer practice, but rather requested an injunction that would limit the town to "inclusive and ecumenical" prayers that referred only to a "generic God" and would not associate the government with any one faith or belief.

The District Court on summary judgment upheld the prayer practice as consistent with the First Amendment. . . . The District Court also rejected the theory that legislative prayer must be nonsectarian. . . . The Court of Appeals for the Second Circuit reversed. . . . Having granted certiorari to decide whether the town's prayer practice violates the Establishment Clause, the Court now reverses the judgment of the Court of Appeals.

II

In *Marsh v. Chambers*, the Court found no First Amendment violation in the Nebraska Legislature's practice of opening its sessions with a prayer delivered by a chaplain paid from state funds. The decision concluded that legislative prayer, while religious in nature, has long been understood as compatible with the Establishment Clause. As practiced by Congress since the framing of the Constitution, legislative prayer lends gravity to public business, reminds lawmakers to transcend petty differences in pursuit of a higher purpose, and expresses a common aspiration to a just and peaceful society. The Court [considered] this symbolic expression to be a "tolerable acknowledgement of beliefs widely held," rather than a first, treacherous step towards establishment of a state church.

Marsh . . . sustained legislative prayer without subjecting the practice to "any of the formal 'tests' that have traditionally structured" this inquiry. *Id.* (Brennan, J., dissenting). The Court in *Marsh* found those tests unnecessary because history supported the conclusion that legislative invocations are compatible with the Establishment Clause. The First Congress made it an early item of business to appoint and pay official chaplains, and both the House and Senate have maintained the office virtually uninterrupted since that time. When *Marsh* was decided, in 1983, legislative prayer had persisted in the Nebraska Legislature for more than a century, and the majority of the other States also had the same, consistent practice. Although no information has been cited by the parties to indicate how many local legislative bodies open their meetings with prayer, this practice too has historical precedent. "In light of the unambiguous and unbroken history of more than 200 years, there can be no doubt that the practice of opening legislative sessions with a prayer has become part of the fabric of our society." *Marsh.*

Yet *Marsh* must not be understood as permitting a practice that would amount to a constitutional violation if not for its historical foundation. The case teaches instead that the Establishment Clause must be interpreted "by reference to historical practices and understandings." *County of Allegheny v. American Civil Liberties Union, Greater Pittsburgh Chapter* (Kennedy, J., concurring in part and dissenting in part) [*supra* this chapter]. That the First Congress provided for the appointment of chaplains only days after approving language for the First Amendment demonstrates that the Framers considered legislative prayer a benign acknowledgment of religion's role in society. . . . *Marsh* stands for the proposition that it is not necessary to define the precise boundary of the Establishment Clause where history shows that the specific practice is permitted. Any test the Court adopts must acknowledge a practice that was accepted by the Framers and has withstood the critical scrutiny of time and political change. *County of Allegheny* (Kennedy, J.); *see also School Dist. of Abington Township v. Schempp* (Brennan, J., concurring) [*supra* this chapter]. A test that would sweep away what has so long been settled would create new controversy and begin anew the very divisions along religious lines that the Establishment Clause seeks to prevent. *See Van Orden v. Perry* (Breyer, J., concurring) [*supra* this chapter].

The Court's inquiry, then, must be to determine whether the prayer practice in the town of Greece fits within the tradition long followed in Congress and the state legislatures. . . .

A

Respondents maintain that prayer must be nonsectarian, or not identifiable with any one religion; and they fault the town for permitting guest chaplains to deliver prayers that "use overtly Christian terms" or "invoke specifics of Christian theology." A prayer is fitting for the public sphere, in their view, only if it contains the "most general, nonsectarian reference to God," and eschews mention of doctrines associated with any one faith. . . .

An insistence on nonsectarian or ecumenical prayer as a single, fixed standard is not consistent with the tradition of legislative prayer outlined in the Court's cases. The Court found the prayers in *Marsh* consistent with the First Amendment not because they espoused only a generic theism but because our history and tradition have shown that prayer in this limited context could "coexist with the principles of disestablishment and religious freedom." The Congress that drafted the First Amendment would have been accustomed to invocations containing explicitly religious themes of the sort respondents find objectionable. . . . The decidedly Christian nature of these prayers must not be dismissed as the relic of a time when our Nation was less pluralistic than it is today. Congress continues to permit its appointed and visiting chaplains to express themselves in a religious idiom. It acknowledges our growing diversity not by proscribing sectarian content but by welcoming ministers of many creeds. *See, e.g.,* [quoting the *Congressional Record* from 2012–14]: (Dalai Lama: "I am a Buddhist monk—a simple Buddhist monk—so we pray to Buddha and all other Gods"); (Rabbi Joshua

Gruenberg: "Our God and God of our ancestors, Everlasting Spirit of the Universe . . ."); (Satguru Bodhinatha Veylanswami: "Hindu scripture declares, without equivocation, that the highest of high ideals is to never knowingly harm anyone"); (Imam Nayyar Imam: "The final prophet of God, Muhammad, peace be upon him, stated: 'The leaders of a people are a representation of their deeds'"). . . .

Marsh nowhere suggested that the constitutionality of legislative prayer turns on the neutrality of its content. . . . Nor did the Court imply the rule that prayer violates the Establishment Clause any time it is given in the name of a figure deified by only one faith or creed. To the contrary, the [*Marsh* opinion explicitly] instructed that the "content of the prayer is not of concern to judges," provided "there is no indication that the prayer opportunity has been exploited to proselytize or advance any one, or to disparage any other, faith or belief."

To hold that invocations must be nonsectarian would force the legislatures that sponsor prayers and the courts that are asked to decide these cases to act as supervisors and censors of religious speech, a rule that would involve government in religious matters to a far greater degree than is the case under the town's current practice of neither editing or approving prayers in advance nor criticizing their content after the fact. . . .

Respondents argue, in effect, that legislative prayer may be addressed only to a generic God. The law and the Court could not draw this line for each specific prayer or seek to require ministers to set aside their nuanced and deeply personal beliefs for vague and artificial ones. There is doubt, in any event, that consensus might be reached as to what qualifies as generic or nonsectarian. . . . [Even] seemingly general references to God or the Father might alienate nonbelievers or polytheists. *McCreary County v. American Civil Liberties Union of Ky.* (2005) (Scalia, J., dissenting) [*supra* this chapter]. Because it is unlikely that prayer will be inclusive beyond dispute, it would be unwise to adopt what respondents think is the next-best option: permitting those religious words, and only those words, that are acceptable to the majority, even if they will exclude some. The First Amendment is not a majority rule, and government may not seek to define permissible categories of religious speech. Once it invites prayer into the public sphere, government must permit a prayer giver to address his or her own God or gods as conscience dictates, unfettered by what an administrator or judge considers to be nonsectarian.

In rejecting the suggestion that legislative prayer must be nonsectarian, the Court does not imply that no constraints remain on its content. . . . If the course and practice over time shows that the invocations denigrate nonbelievers or religious minorities, threaten damnation, or preach conversion, many present may consider the prayer to fall short of the desire to elevate the purpose of the occasion and to unite lawmakers in their common effort. That circumstance would present a different case than the one presently before the Court.

The tradition reflected in *Marsh* permits chaplains to ask their own God for blessings of peace, justice, and freedom that find appreciation among people of all faiths.

That a prayer is given in the name of Jesus, Allah, or Jehovah, or that it makes passing reference to religious doctrines, does not remove it from that tradition. . . . Prayer that reflects beliefs specific to only some creeds can still serve to solemnize the occasion, so long as the practice over time is not "exploited to proselytize or advance any one, or to disparage any other, faith or belief." *Marsh*.

It [is] possible to discern in the prayers offered to Congress a commonality of theme and tone. While these prayers vary in their degree of religiosity, they often seek peace for the Nation, wisdom for its lawmakers, and justice for its people, values that count as universal and that are embodied not only in religious traditions, but in our founding documents and laws. . . . Our tradition assumes that adult citizens, firm in their own beliefs, can tolerate and perhaps appreciate a ceremonial prayer delivered by a person of a different faith.

The prayers delivered in the town of Greece do not fall outside the tradition this Court has recognized. A number of the prayers did invoke the name of Jesus, the Heavenly Father, or the Holy Spirit, but they also invoked universal themes, as by celebrating the changing of the seasons or calling for a "spirit of cooperation" among town leaders. . . . Absent a pattern of prayers that over time denigrate, proselytize, or betray an impermissible government purpose, a challenge based solely on the content of a prayer will not likely establish a constitutional violation. *Marsh*, indeed, requires an inquiry into the prayer opportunity as a whole, rather than into the contents of a single prayer.

Finally, the Court disagrees with the view taken by the Court of Appeals that the town of Greece contravened the Establishment Clause by inviting a predominantly Christian set of ministers to lead the prayer. The town made reasonable efforts to identify all of the congregations located within its borders and represented that it would welcome a prayer by any minister or layman who wished to give one. That nearly all of the congregations in town turned out to be Christian does not reflect an aversion or bias on the part of town leaders against minority faiths. So long as the town maintains a policy of nondiscrimination, the Constitution does not require it to search beyond its borders for non-Christian prayer givers in an effort to achieve religious balancing. The quest to promote "a 'diversity' of religious views" would require the town "to make wholly inappropriate judgments about the number of religions it should sponsor and the relative frequency with which it should sponsor each," *Lee v. Weisman* (Souter, J., concurring) [*supra* this chapter], a form of government entanglement with religion that is far more troublesome than the current approach.

B

Respondents further seek to distinguish the town's prayer practice from the tradition upheld in *Marsh* on the ground that it coerces participation by nonadherents. They and some *amici* contend that prayer conducted in the intimate setting of a town board meeting differs in fundamental ways from the invocations delivered in Congress and state legislatures, where the public remains segregated from legislative activity and may not address the body except by occasional invitation. Citizens attend town meetings, on the other hand, to accept awards; speak on matters of local importance; and petition the board for action that may affect their economic interests, such as the granting of permits, business licenses, and zoning variances. Respondents argue that the public may feel subtle pressure to participate in prayers that violate their beliefs . . . .

It is an elemental First Amendment principle that government may not coerce its citizens "to support or participate in any religion or its exercise." *County of Allegheny* (Kennedy, J.). On the record in this case the Court is not persuaded that the town of Greece, through the act of offering a brief, solemn, and respectful prayer to open its monthly meetings, compelled its citizens to engage in a religious observance. The inquiry remains a fact-sensitive one that considers both the setting in which the prayer arises and the audience to whom it is directed.

[As] a practice that has long endured, legislative prayer has become part of our heritage and tradition, part of our expressive idiom, similar to the Pledge of Allegiance, inaugural prayer, or the recitation of "God save the United States and this honorable Court" at the opening of this Court's sessions. *See Lynch v. Donnelly* (1984) (O'Connor, J., concurring). It is presumed that the reasonable observer is acquainted with this tradition and understands that its purposes are to lend gravity to public proceedings and to acknowledge the place religion holds in the lives of many private citizens, not to afford government an opportunity to proselytize or force truant constituents into the pews. . . .

The principal audience for these invocations is not, indeed, the public but lawmakers themselves, who may find that a moment of prayer or quiet reflection sets the mind to a higher purpose and thereby eases the task of governing. . . . [Their] purpose is largely to accommodate the spiritual needs of lawmakers and connect them to a tradition dating to the time of the Framers. For members of town boards and commissions, who often serve part-time and as volunteers, ceremonial prayer may also reflect the values they hold as private citizens. . . .

The analysis would be different if town board members directed the public to participate in the prayers, singled out dissidents for opprobrium, or indicated that their decisions might be influenced by a person's acquiescence in the prayer opportunity. No such thing occurred in the town of Greece. Although board members themselves stood, bowed their heads, or made the sign of the cross during the prayer, they at no point solicited similar gestures by the public. Respondents point to several occasions where audience members were asked to rise for the prayer. These requests, however, came not from town leaders but from the guest ministers, who presumably are accustomed to directing their congregations in this way and might have done so thinking the action was inclusive, not coercive. ("Would you bow your heads with me as we invite the Lord's presence here tonight?"; "Would you join me in a moment of prayer?") Respondents suggest that constituents might feel pressure to join the prayers to avoid irritating the officials who would be ruling on their petitions, but this argument has no evidentiary support. . . .

In their declarations in the trial court, respondents stated that the prayers gave them offense and made them feel excluded and disrespected. Offense, however, does not equate to coercion. Adults often encounter speech they find disagreeable; and an Establishment Clause violation is not made out any time a person experiences a sense of affront from the expression of contrary religious views in a legislative forum, especially where, as here, any member of the public is welcome in turn to offer an invocation reflecting his or her own convictions. If circumstances arise in which the pattern and practice of ceremonial, legislative prayer is alleged to be a means to coerce or intimidate others, the objection can be addressed in the regular course. But the showing has not been made here, where the prayers neither chastised dissenters nor attempted lengthy disquisition on religious dogma. Courts remain free to review the pattern of prayers over time to determine whether they comport with the tradition of solemn, respectful prayer approved in *Marsh*, or whether coercion is a real and substantial likelihood. But in the general course legislative bodies do not engage in impermissible coercion merely by exposing constituents to prayer they would rather not hear and in which they need not participate. *See County of Allegheny* (Kennedy, J.).

This case can be distinguished from the conclusions and holding of *Lee v. Weisman* [*supra* this chapter]. There the Court found that, in the context of a graduation where school authorities maintained close supervision over the conduct of the students and the substance of the ceremony, a religious invocation was coercive as to an objecting student. [The] circumstances the Court confronted there are not present in this case and do not control its outcome. Nothing in the record suggests that members of the public are dissuaded from leaving the meeting room during the prayer, arriving late, or even, as happened here, making a later protest. [Board] members and constituents are "free to enter and leave with little comment and for any number of reasons." Should nonbelievers choose to exit the room during a prayer they find distasteful, their absence will not stand out as disrespectful or even noteworthy. And should they remain, their quiet acquiescence will not, in light of our traditions, be interpreted as an agreement with the words or ideas expressed. Neither choice represents an unconstitutional imposition as to mature adults, who "presumably" are "not readily susceptible to religious indoctrination or peer pressure." *Marsh.*

In the town of Greece, the prayer is delivered during the ceremonial portion of the town's meeting. Board members are not engaged in policymaking at this time, but in more general functions, such as swearing in new police officers, inducting high school athletes into the town hall of fame, and presenting proclamations to volunteers, civic groups, and senior citizens. . . . By inviting ministers to serve as chaplain for the month, and welcoming them to the front of the room alongside civic leaders, the town is acknowledging the central place that religion, and religious institutions, hold in the lives of those present. . . . The inclusion of a brief, ceremonial prayer as part of a larger exercise in civic recognition suggests that its purpose and effect are to acknowledge religious leaders and the institutions they represent rather than to exclude or coerce nonbelievers.

Ceremonial prayer is but a recognition that, since this Nation was founded and until the present day, many Americans deem that their own existence must be understood by precepts far beyond the authority of government to alter or define and that willing participation in civic affairs can be consistent with a brief acknowledgment of their belief in a higher power, always with due respect for those who adhere to other beliefs. The prayer in this case has a permissible ceremonial purpose. It is not an unconstitutional establishment of religion.

* * *

The town of Greece does not violate the First Amendment by opening its meetings with prayer that comports with our tradition and does not coerce participation by nonadherents. The judgment of the U.S. Court of Appeals for the Second Circuit is reversed.

It is so ordered.

Justice Alito, with whom Justice Scalia joins, concurring.

I write separately to respond to the principal dissent, which really consists of two very different but intertwined opinions. One is quite narrow; the other is sweeping. I will address both.

I

First, however, since [Justice Kagan's] principal dissent accuses the Court of being blind to the facts of this case, I recount facts that I find particularly salient. [Here Justice Alito gave his own detailed summary of the facts and record.]

II

I turn now to the narrow aspect of the principal dissent, and what we find here is that the principal dissent's objection, in the end, is really quite niggling. According to the principal dissent, the town could have avoided any constitutional problem in either of two ways.

A

First, the principal dissent writes, "if the Town Board had let its chaplains know that they should speak in nonsectarian terms, common to diverse religious groups, then no one would have valid grounds for complaint." . . .

Not only is there no historical support for the proposition that only generic prayer is allowed, but as our country has become more diverse, composing a prayer that is acceptable to all members of the community who hold religious beliefs has become harder and harder. It was one thing to compose a prayer that is acceptable to both Christians and Jews; it is much harder to compose a prayer that is also acceptable to followers of Eastern religions that are now well represented in this country. Many local clergy may find the project daunting, if not impossible, and some may feel that they cannot in good faith deliver such a vague prayer.

In addition, if a town attempts to go beyond simply *recommending* that a guest chaplain deliver a prayer that is broadly acceptable to all members of a particular community (and the groups represented in different communities will vary), the town will inevitably encounter sensitive problems. Must a town screen and, if necessary, edit prayers before they are given? If prescreening is not required, must the town review prayers after they are delivered in order to determine if they were sufficiently generic? And if a guest chaplain crosses the line, what must the town do? Must the chaplain be corrected on the spot? Must the town strike this chaplain (and perhaps his or her house of worship) from the approved list?

B

If a town wants to avoid the problems associated with this first option, the principal dissent argues, it has another choice: It may "invite clergy of many faiths." . . .

If, as the principal dissent appears to concede, such a rotating system would obviate any constitutional problems, then despite all its high rhetoric, the principal dissent's quarrel with the town of Greece really boils down to this: The town's clerical employees did a bad job in compiling the list of potential guest chaplains. For that is really the only difference between what the town did and what the principal dissent is willing to accept. . . .

[When] a municipality like the town of Greece seeks in good faith to emulate the congressional practice on which our holding in *Marsh v. Chambers* was largely based, that municipality should not be held to have violated the Constitution simply because its method of recruiting guest chaplains lacks the demographic exactitude that might be regarded as optimal.

The effect of requiring such exactitude would be to pressure towns to forswear altogether the practice of having a prayer before meetings of the town council. . . . Indeed, the Court of Appeals' opinion in this case advised towns that constitutional difficulties "may well prompt municipalities to pause and think carefully before adopting legislative prayer." But if, as precedent and historic practice make clear (and the principal dissent concedes), prayer before a legislative session is not inherently inconsistent with the First Amendment, then a unit of local government should not be held to have violated the First Amendment simply because its procedure for lining up guest chaplains does not comply in all respects with what might be termed a "best practices" standard.

III

While the principal dissent, in the end, would demand no more than a small modification in the procedure that the town of Greece initially followed, much of the rhetoric in that opinion sweeps more broadly. Indeed, the logical thrust of many of its arguments is that prayer is *never* permissible prior to meetings of local government legislative bodies. . . . Before a session of this sort, the principal dissent argues, any prayer that is not acceptable to all in attendance is out of bounds.

The features of Greece meetings that the principal dissent highlights are by no means unusual. . . . [I] see nothing out of the ordinary about any of the features that the principal dissent notes. Therefore, if prayer is not allowed at meetings with those characteristics, local government legislative bodies, unlike their national and state counterparts, cannot begin their meetings with a prayer. I see no sound basis for drawing such a distinction.

IV

The principal dissent claims to accept the Court's decision in *Marsh v. Chambers* . . . but the principal dissent's acceptance of *Marsh* appears to be predicated on the view that the prayer at issue in that case was little more than a formality to which the legislators paid scant attention. . . .

[What] is important is not so much what happened in Nebraska in the years prior to *Marsh*, but what happened before congressional sessions during the period leading up to the adoption of the First Amendment. By that time, prayer before legislative sessions already had an impressive pedigree, and it is important to recall that history and the events that led to the adoption of the practice. . . .

This Court has often noted that actions taken by the First Congress are presumptively consistent with the Bill of Rights, and this principle has special force when it comes to the interpretation of the Establishment Clause. This Court has always purported to base its Establishment Clause decisions on the original meaning of that provision. Thus, in *Marsh* . . . we relied heavily on the history of prayer before sessions of Congress and held that a state legislature may follow a similar practice. There can be little doubt that the decision in *Marsh* reflected the original understanding of the First Amendment [in] the First Congress [and], the state legislatures that ratified the First Amendment. . . .

V

[Although] I do not suggest that the implication is intentional, I am concerned that at least some readers will take [the dissent's rhetoric and] hypotheticals as a warning that [today's decision will lead] to a country in which religious minorities are denied the equal benefits of citizenship. Nothing could be further from the truth. All that the Court does today is to allow a town to follow a practice that we have previously held is permissible for Congress and state legislatures. . . .

Justice Thomas, with whom Justice Scalia joins as to Part II, concurring in part and concurring in the judgment.

Except for Part II-B, I join the opinion of the Court, which faithfully applies *Marsh v. Chambers*. I write separately to reiterate my view that the Establishment Clause is "best understood as a federalism provision," *Elk Grove Unified School Dist. v. Newdow*, 542 U.S. 1, 50 (2004) (Thomas, J., concurring), and to state my understanding of the proper "coercion" analysis.

I

[Here Justice Thomas reiterated his position that the Establishment Clause ought not be incorporated and applied to the States through the Fourteenth Amendment.]

II

[The] municipal prayers at issue in this case bear no resemblance to the coercive state establishments that existed at the founding. "The coercion that was a hallmark of historical establishments of religion was coercion of religious orthodoxy and of financial support by force of law and threat of penalty." *Lee v. Weisman* (1992) (Scalia, J., dissenting). In a typical case, attendance at the established church was mandatory, and taxes were levied to generate church revenue. Dissenting ministers were barred from preaching, and political participation was limited to members of the established church. . . . [Both] state and local forms of establishment involved "actual legal coercion"—government power [was exercised] in order to exact financial support of the church, compel religious observance, or control religious doctrine.

[At] a minimum, there is no support for the proposition that the framers of the Fourteenth Amendment embraced wholly modern notions that the Establishment Clause is violated whenever the "reasonable observer" feels "subtle pressure," or perceives governmental "endorsement." . . . Moreover, the state constitutional provisions that prohibited religious "compulsion" made clear that the relevant sort of compulsion was legal in nature, of the same type that had characterized founding-era establishments. . . .

Thus, to the extent coercion is relevant to the Establishment Clause analysis, it is actual legal coercion that counts—not the "subtle coercive pressures" allegedly felt by respondents in this case. . . .

JUSTICE BREYER, dissenting.

. . . In my view, the Court of Appeals' conclusion and its reasoning are convincing. Justice Kagan's dissent is consistent with that view, and I join it. I also here emphasize several factors that I believe underlie the conclusion that, on the particular facts of this case, the town's prayer practice violated the Establishment Clause.

First, Greece is a predominantly Christian town, but it is not exclusively so. . . . Yet during the more than 120 monthly meetings at which prayers were delivered during the record period (from 1999 to 2010), only four prayers were delivered by non-Christians. And all of these occurred in 2008, shortly after the plaintiffs began complaining about the town's Christian prayer practice and nearly a decade after that practice had commenced. . . .

Second, the town made no significant effort to inform the area's non-Christian houses of worship about the possibility of delivering an opening prayer. . . .

Third, in this context, the fact that nearly all of the prayers given reflected a single denomination takes on significance. That significance would have been the same had all the prayers been Jewish, or Hindu, or Buddhist, or of any other denomination. The significance is that, in a context where religious minorities exist and where more could easily have been done to include their participation, the town chose to do nothing. . . .

Fourth, the fact that the board meeting audience included citizens with business to conduct also contributes to the importance of making more of an effort to include members of other denominations. It does not, however, automatically change the nature of the meeting from one where an opening prayer is permissible under the Establishment Clause to one where it is not.

Fifth, [the] Constitution does not forbid opening prayers [but] neither does the Constitution forbid efforts to explain to those who give the prayers the nature of the occasion and the audience. . . . The town made no effort to promote [an] inclusive prayer practice here.

[The] question in this case is whether the prayer practice of the town of Greece, by doing too little to reflect the religious diversity of its citizens, did too much, even if unintentionally, to promote the "political division along religious lines" that "was one of the principal evils against which the First Amendment was intended to protect." *Lemon v. Kurtzman* (1971) [*supra* this chapter].

In seeking an answer to that fact-sensitive question, "I see no test-related substitute for the exercise of legal judgment." *Van Orden v. Perry* (2005) (Breyer, J., concurring in judgment) [*supra* this chapter]. Having applied my legal judgment to the relevant facts, I conclude, like Justice Kagan, that the town of Greece failed to make reasonable efforts to include prayer givers of minority faiths, with the result that, although it is a community of several faiths, its prayer givers were almost exclusively persons of a single faith. Under these circumstances, . . . Greece's prayer practice violated the Establishment Clause. I dissent from the Court's decision to the contrary.

JUSTICE KAGAN, with whom JUSTICE GINSBURG, JUSTICE BREYER, and JUSTICE SOTOMAYOR join, dissenting.

[I] respectfully dissent from the Court's opinion because I think the Town of Greece's prayer practices violate [the] norm of religious equality—the breathtakingly generous constitutional idea that our public institutions belong no less to the Buddhist or Hindu than to the Methodist or Episcopalian. I do not contend that principle translates here into a bright separationist line. To the contrary, I agree with the Court's decision in *Marsh v. Chambers* (1983), upholding the Nebraska Legislature's tradition of beginning each session with a chaplain's prayer. And I believe that pluralism and inclusion in a town hall can satisfy the constitutional requirement of neutrality; such a forum need not become a religion-free zone. But still, the Town of Greece should lose this case. . . .

I

[Our] constitutional tradition, from the Declaration of Independence and the first inaugural address of Washington . . . down to the present day, has . . . ruled out of order government-sponsored endorsement of religion . . . where the endorsement is sectarian, in the sense of specifying details upon which men and women who believe in a benevolent, omnipotent Creator and Ruler of the world are known to differ (for example, the divinity of Christ).

Lee v. Weisman (Scalia, J., dissenting) [*supra* this chapter]. *See also County of Allegheny* [*supra* this chapter]. . . .

When a person goes to court, a polling place, or an immigration proceeding—I could go on: to a zoning agency, a parole board hearing, or the DMV—government officials do not engage in sectarian worship, nor do they ask her to do likewise. They all participate in the business of government not as Christians, Jews, Muslims (and more), but only as Americans—none of them different from any other for that civic purpose. Why not, then, at a town meeting?

II

[Under] *Marsh*, legislative prayer has a distinctive constitutional warrant by virtue of tradition. . . . Relying on that "unbroken" national tradition, *Marsh* upheld (I think correctly) the Nebraska Legislature's practice of opening each day with a chaplain's prayer . . . And so I agree with the majority that the issue here is "whether the prayer practice in the Town of Greece fits within the tradition long followed in Congress and the state legislatures."

Where I depart from the majority is in my reply to that question. The town hall here is a kind of hybrid. Greece's Board indeed has legislative functions, as Congress and state assemblies do—and that means some opening prayers are allowed there. But [the] Board's meetings are also occasions for ordinary citizens to engage with and petition their government, often on highly individualized matters. That feature calls for Board members to exercise special care to ensure that the prayers offered are inclusive—that they respect each and every member of the community as an equal citizen.[2] But the Board, and the clergy members it selected, made no such effort. Instead, the prayers given in Greece, addressed directly to the Town's citizenry, were *more* sectarian, and *less* inclusive, than anything this Court sustained in *Marsh*. For those reasons, the prayer in Greece departs from the legislative tradition that the majority takes as its benchmark.

A

Start by comparing two pictures, drawn precisely from reality. The first is of Nebraska's (unicameral) Legislature, as this Court and the state senators themselves described it. The second is of town council meetings in Greece, as revealed in this case's record. [Here Justice Kagan gave her own detailed summary of the facts in the two cases.]

B

Let's count the ways in which these pictures diverge. First, the governmental proceedings at which the prayers occur differ significantly in nature and purpose.

---

2. Because Justice Alito questions this point, it bears repeating. I do not remotely contend that "prayer is not allowed" at participatory meetings of "local government legislative bodies"; nor is that the "logical thrust" of any argument I make. Rather, what I say throughout this opinion is that in this citizen-centered venue, government officials must take steps to ensure—as none of Greece's Board members ever did—that opening prayers are inclusive of different faiths, rather than always identified with a single religion.

The Nebraska Legislature's floor sessions—like those of the U.S. Congress and other state assemblies—are of, by, and for elected lawmakers. Members of the public take no part in those proceedings; any few who attend are spectators only, watching from a high-up visitors' gallery. . . . Greece's town meetings, by contrast, revolve around ordinary members of the community. Each and every aspect of those sessions provides opportunities for Town residents to interact with public officials. . . . [During] the Public Forum, they urge (or oppose) changes in the Board's policies and priorities; and then, in what are essentially adjudicatory hearings they request the Board to grant (or deny) applications for various permits, licenses, and zoning variances. . . .

Second, . . . the prayers in these two settings have different audiences. In the Nebraska Legislature, the chaplain spoke to, and only to, the elected representatives. . . . As several Justices later noted (and the majority today agrees),[3] *Marsh* involved "government officials invoking spiritual inspiration entirely for their own benefit without directing any religious message at the citizens they lead." *Lee v. Weisman* (Souter, J., concurring) [*supra* this chapter].

The very opposite is true in Greece: [the] prayers there are directed squarely at the citizens. Remember that the chaplain of the month stands with his back to the Town Board; his real audience is the group he is facing—the 10 or so members of the public, perhaps including children. And he typically addresses those people . . . as though he is "directing his congregation." . . . Often, he calls on everyone to stand and bow their heads, and he may ask them to recite a common prayer with him. . . . In essence, the chaplain leads, as the first part of a town meeting, a highly intimate (albeit relatively brief) prayer service, with the public serving as his congregation.

And third, the prayers themselves differ in their content and character. *Marsh* characterized the prayers in the Nebraska Legislature as "in the Judeo-Christian tradition." . . . But no one can fairly read the prayers from Greece's Town meetings as anything other than explicitly Christian—constantly and exclusively so. From the time Greece established its prayer practice in 1999 until litigation loomed nine years later, all of its monthly chaplains were Christian clergy. And after a brief spell surrounding the filing of this suit (when a Jewish layman, a Wiccan priestess, and a Baha'i minister appeared at meetings), the Town resumed its practice of inviting only clergy from neighboring Protestant and Catholic churches. About two-thirds of the prayers given over this decade or so invoked "Jesus," "Christ," "Your Son," or "the Holy Spirit"; in the 18 months before the record closed, 85% included those references. Many prayers contained elaborations of Christian doctrine or recitations of scripture. And the prayers usually close with phrases like "in the name of Jesus Christ" or "in the name of Your son."

---

3. For ease of reference and to avoid confusion, I refer to Justice Kennedy's opinion as "the majority." But the language I cite that appears in Part II-B of that opinion is, in fact, only attributable to a plurality of the Court.

[The] monthly chaplains appear almost always to assume that everyone in the room is Christian (and of a kind who has no objection to government-sponsored worship).[4] The Town itself has never urged its chaplains to reach out to members of other faiths, or even to recall that they might be present. And accordingly, few chaplains have made any effort to be inclusive; none has thought even to assure attending members of the public that they need not participate in the prayer session. . . .

C

Those three differences, taken together, remove this case from the protective ambit of *Marsh* and the history on which it relied. . . . And so, contra the majority, Greece's prayers cannot simply ride on the constitutional coattails of the legislative tradition *Marsh* described. The Board's practice must, in its own particulars, meet constitutional requirements.

And the guideposts for addressing that inquiry include [constitutional] principles of religious neutrality. . . . The government (whether federal, state, or local) may not favor, or align itself with, any particular creed. And that is nowhere more true than when officials and citizens come face-to-face in their shared institutions of governance. . . .

To decide how Greece fares on that score, think again about how its prayer practice works, meeting after meeting. . . . Let's say that a Muslim citizen of Greece goes before the Board to share her views on policy or request some permit. Maybe she wants the Board to put up a traffic light at a dangerous intersection; or maybe she needs a zoning variance to build an addition on her home. But just before she gets to say her piece, a minister deputized by the Town asks her to pray "in the name of God's only son Jesus Christ." She must think—it is hardly paranoia, but only the truth—that Christian worship has become entwined with local governance. And now she faces a choice—to pray alongside the majority as one of that group or somehow to register her deeply felt difference. She is a strong person, but that is no easy call—especially given that the room is small and her every action (or inaction) will be noticed. She does not wish to be rude to her neighbors, nor does she wish to aggravate the Board members whom she will soon be trying to persuade. And yet she does not want to acknowledge Christ's divinity, any more than many of her neighbors would want to deny that tenet. So assume she declines to participate with the others in the first act of the meeting—or even, as the majority proposes, that she stands up and leaves the room altogether. At the least, she becomes a different kind of citizen, one who will not join in the religious practice that the Town Board has chosen as reflecting its own and the community's most cherished beliefs. And she thus stands at a remove, based solely on religion, from her fellow citizens and her elected representatives.

---

4. Leaders of several Baptist and other Christian congregations have explained to the Court that "many Christians believe . . . that their freedom of conscience is violated when they are pressured to participate in government prayer, because such acts of worship should only be performed voluntarily." *Amicus Curiae Brief for Baptist Joint Committee for Religious Liberty.*

Everything about that situation, I think, infringes the First Amendment. (And of course, [it] would do so no less if the Town's clergy always used the liturgy of some other religion.) That the Town Board selects, month after month and year after year, prayer givers who will reliably speak in the voice of Christianity, and so places itself behind a single creed. That in offering those sectarian prayers, the Board's chosen clergy members repeatedly call on individuals, prior to participating in local governance, to join in a form of worship that may be at odds with their own beliefs. That the clergy thus put some residents to the unenviable choice of either pretending to pray like the majority or declining to join its communal activity, at the very moment of petitioning their elected leaders. That the practice thus divides the citizenry, creating one class that shares the Board's own evident religious beliefs and another (far smaller) class that does not. And that the practice also alters a dissenting citizen's relationship with her government, making her religious difference salient when she seeks only to engage her elected representatives as would any other citizen.

None of this means that Greece's town hall must be religion- or prayer-free. . . . What the circumstances here demand is the recognition that we are a pluralistic people too. When citizens of all faiths come to speak to each other and their elected representatives in a legislative session, the government must take especial care to ensure that the prayers they hear will seek to include, rather than serve to divide. No more is required—but that much is crucial—to treat every citizen, of whatever religion, as an equal participant in her government.

And contrary to the majority's (and Justice Alito's) view, that is not difficult to do. If the Town Board had let its chaplains know that they should speak in nonsectarian terms, common to diverse religious groups, then no one would have valid grounds for complaint. Priests and ministers, rabbis and imams give such invocations all the time; there is no great mystery to the project. (And providing that guidance would hardly have caused the Board to run afoul of the idea that "the First Amendment is not a majority rule," as the Court (headspinningly) suggests; what does that is the Board's refusal to reach out to members of minority religious groups.) Or if the Board preferred, it might have invited clergy of many faiths to serve as chaplains, as the majority notes that Congress does. When one month a clergy member refers to Jesus, and the next to Allah or Jehovah—as the majority hopefully though counterfactually suggests happened here—the government does not identify itself with one religion or align itself with that faith's citizens, and the effect of even sectarian prayer is transformed. So Greece had multiple ways of incorporating prayer into its town meetings—reflecting all the ways that prayer (as most of us know from daily life) can forge common bonds, rather than divide.

[In] this country, when citizens go before the government, they go not as Christians or Muslims or Jews (or what have you), but just as Americans (or here, as Grecians). That is what it means to be an equal citizen, irrespective of religion. And that is what the Town of Greece precluded by so identifying itself with a single faith.

III

How, then, does the majority go so far astray, allowing the Town of Greece to turn its assemblies for citizens into a forum for Christian prayer? The answer does not lie in first principles: I have no doubt that every member of this Court believes as firmly as I that our institutions of government belong equally to all, regardless of faith. Rather, the error reflects two kinds of blindness. First, the majority misapprehends the facts of this case, as distinct from those characterizing traditional legislative prayer. And second, the majority misjudges the essential meaning of the religious worship in Greece's town hall, along with its capacity to exclude and divide. . . .

And the month in, month out sectarianism the Board chose for its meetings belies the majority's refrain that the prayers in Greece were "ceremonial" in nature. Ceremonial references to the divine surely abound: The majority is right that "the Pledge of Allegiance, inaugural prayer, or the recitation of 'God save the United States and this honorable Court'" each fits the bill. But prayers evoking [for example] "the saving sacrifice of Jesus Christ on the cross" [or] "the life and death, resurrection and ascension of the Savior Jesus Christ"? No. These are statements of profound belief and deep meaning, subscribed to by many, denied by some. They "speak of the depths of one's life, of the source of one's being, of one's ultimate concern, of what one takes seriously without any reservation." PAUL TILLICH, THE SHAKING OF THE FOUNDATIONS 57 (1948). If they (and the central tenets of other religions) ever become mere ceremony, this country will be a fundamentally different — and, I think, poorer — place to live.

But just for that reason, the not-so-implicit message of the majority's opinion — "What's the big deal, anyway?" — is mistaken. The content of Greece's prayers *is* a big deal, to Christians and non-Christians alike. . . . They express beliefs that are fundamental to some, foreign to others — and because that is so they carry the ever-present potential to both exclude and divide. The majority, I think, assesses too lightly the significance of these religious differences, and so fears too little the "religiously based divisiveness that the Establishment Clause seeks to avoid." *Van Orden v. Perry* (Breyer, J., concurring) [*supra* this chapter]. I would treat more seriously the multiplicity of Americans' religious commitments, along with the challenge they can pose to the project — the distinctively American project — of creating one from the many, and governing all as united.

IV

[America's] promise in the First Amendment [is] full and equal membership in the polity for members of every religious group . . . . For me, that remarkable guarantee means at least this much: When the citizens of this country approach their government, they do so only as Americans, not as members of one faith or another. . . . I believe, for all the reasons I have given, that the Town of Greece betrayed that promise. I therefore respectfully dissent from the Court's decision.

Chapter 18

The Free Exercise Clause

Laws "prohibiting the free exercise [of religion]" violate the guarantees of religious liberty in the First and Fourteenth Amendments. The eighteenth-century motivation behind the Free Exercise Clause was to reject the history of religious persecution in the Old World and the colonies. As Justice Jackson famously proclaimed in *West Virginia Bd. of Educ. v. Barnette*, 319 U.S. 624, 642 (1943) (Chapter 9):

> If there is any fixed star in our constitutional constellation, it is that no official, high or petty, can prescribe what shall be orthodox in politics, nationalism, religion, or other matters of opinion or force citizens to confess by word or act their faith therein. If there are any circumstances which permit an exception, they do not now occur to us.

The Supreme Court draws a constitutional distinction between religious belief and religious conduct, a dichotomy that resembles the speech/conduct dichotomy in the realm of freedom of expression. *Freedom of belief* is absolute, the Court has repeatedly proclaimed—but what does that mean? *Freedom of conduct* is not absolute—but what good is having an abstract freedom of belief without the corresponding individual liberty to act upon one's most sacred beliefs? The cases in this chapter consider this classic conflict between the government and the individual: When should the state law prevail over the individual's free will motivated by a sincerely held religious belief, and when should the state law give way?

A. Early Cases

Here again is the paradox of the Free Exercise Clause. Every individual has the inalienable right to accept or reject religious faith, and the government has no say in the matter whatsoever; yet, personal religious beliefs cannot be absolute and always supreme. Majoritarian self-government and the rule of law would be impossible if each individual conscience were allowed to reign as a law unto itself. The next two cases seek to reconcile these conflicting terms in the social contract.

Reynolds v. United States
98 U.S. 145 (1878)

MR. CHIEF JUSTICE WAITE delivered the opinion of the court.

This is an indictment found in the District Court for [the] Territory of Utah, charging George Reynolds with bigamy, in violation of § 5352 of the Revised Statutes, which [provides]: "Every person having a husband or wife living, who marries another, whether married or single, in a Territory, or other place over which the United States have exclusive jurisdiction, is guilty of bigamy, and shall be punished by a fine of not more than $500, and by imprisonment for a term of not more than five years."

. . . On the trial, the plaintiff in error, the accused, proved that at the time of his alleged second marriage he was, and for many years before had been, a member of the Church of Jesus Christ of Latter-Day Saints, commonly called the Mormon Church, and a believer in its doctrines; that it was an accepted doctrine of that church "that it was the duty of male members of said church, circumstances permitting, to practise polygamy; . . . that this duty was enjoined by different books which the members of said church believed to be of divine origin, and among others the Holy Bible, and also that the members of the church believed that the practice of polygamy was directly enjoined upon the male members thereof by the Almighty God, in a revelation to Joseph Smith, the founder and prophet of said church; that the failing or refusing to practise polygamy by such male members of said church, when circumstances would admit, would be punished, and that the penalty for such failure and refusal would be damnation in the life to come." He also proved "that he had received permission from the recognized authorities in said church to enter into polygamous marriage; . . . that Daniel H. Wells, one having authority in said church to perform the marriage ceremony, married the said defendant on or about the time the crime is alleged to have been committed, to some woman by the name of Schofield, and that such marriage ceremony was performed under and pursuant to the doctrines of said church."

Upon this proof he asked the court to instruct the jury that if they found from the evidence that he "was married as charged — if he was married — in pursuance of and in conformity with what he believed at the time to be a religious duty, that the verdict must be 'not guilty.'" This request was refused, and the court did charge "that there must have been a criminal intent, but that if the defendant, under the influence of a religious belief that it was right, — under an inspiration, if you please, that it was right, — deliberately married a second time, having a first wife living, the want of consciousness of evil intent — the want of understanding on his part that he was committing a crime — did not excuse him; but the law inexorably in such case implies the criminal intent."

Upon this charge and refusal to charge the question is raised, whether religious belief can be accepted as a justification of an overt act made criminal by the law of the land. . . . Congress cannot pass a law for the government of the Territories which shall prohibit the free exercise of religion. The first amendment to the Constitution expressly forbids such legislation. . . . The question to be determined is, whether the law now under consideration comes within this prohibition.

The word "religion" is not defined in the Constitution. We must go elsewhere, therefore, to ascertain its meaning, and nowhere more appropriately, we think, than to the history of the times in the midst of which the provision was adopted. The precise point of the inquiry is, what is the religious freedom which has been guaranteed.

[Here the Court recounted the history leading up to the First Amendment and concluded with a quotation from Thomas Jefferson's famous 1802 letter, which, as we saw in Chapter 16, section A, has been the subject of controversy and debate among the Justices.] Mr. Jefferson afterwards, in reply to an address to him by a committee of the Danbury Baptist Association, took occasion to say:

> Believing with you that religion is a matter which lies solely between man and his god; that he owes account to none other for his faith or his worship; that the legislative powers of the government reach actions only, and not opinions,—I contemplate with sovereign reverence that act of the whole American people which declared that their legislature should "make no law respecting an establishment of religion or prohibiting the free exercise thereof," thus building a wall of separation between church and State. Adhering to this expression of the supreme will of the nation in behalf of the rights of conscience, I shall see with sincere satisfaction the progress of those sentiments which tend to restore man to all his natural rights, convinced he has no natural right in opposition to his social duties.

Coming as this does from an acknowledged leader of the advocates of the measure, it may be accepted almost as an authoritative declaration of the scope and effect of the amendment thus secured. Congress was deprived of all legislative power over mere opinion, but was left free to reach actions which were in violation of social duties or subversive of good order.

Polygamy has always been odious among the northern and western nations of Europe, and, until the establishment of the Mormon Church, was almost exclusively a feature of the life of Asiatic and of African people. At common law, the second marriage was always void, and from the earliest history of England polygamy has been treated as an offence against society. . . . From that day to this we think it may safely be said there never has been a time in any State of the Union when polygamy has not been an offence against society, cognizable by the civil courts and punishable with more or less severity.

In the face of all this evidence, it is impossible to believe that the constitutional guaranty of religious freedom was intended to prohibit legislation in respect to this most important feature of social life. Marriage, while from its very nature a sacred obligation, is nevertheless, in most civilized nations, a civil contract, and usually regulated by law. Upon it society may be said to be built, and out of its fruits spring social relations and social obligations and duties, with which government is necessarily required to deal. . . . [There] cannot be a doubt that, unless restricted by some form of constitution, it is within the legitimate scope of the power of every civil government to determine whether polygamy or monogamy shall be the law of social life under its dominion.

In our opinion, the statute immediately under consideration is within the legislative power of Congress. . . . This being so, the only question which remains is, whether those who make polygamy a part of their religion are excepted from the operation of the statute. If they are, then those who do not make polygamy a part of their religious belief may be found guilty and punished, while those who do, must be acquitted and go free. This would be introducing a new element into criminal law. Laws are made for the government of actions, and while they cannot interfere with mere religious belief and opinions, they may with practices. Suppose one believed that human sacrifices were a necessary part of religious worship, would it be seriously contended that the civil government under which he lived could not interfere to prevent a sacrifice? Or if a wife religiously believed it was her duty to burn herself upon the funeral pile of her dead husband, would it be beyond the power of the civil government to prevent her carrying her belief into practice?

So here, as a law of the organization of society under the exclusive dominion of the United States, it is provided that plural marriages shall not be allowed. Can a man excuse his practices to the contrary because of his religious belief? To permit this would be to make the professed doctrines of religious belief superior to the law of the land, and in effect to permit every citizen to become a law unto himself. Government could exist only in name under such circumstances. . . .

The only defence of the accused in this case is his belief that the law ought not to have been enacted. It matters not that his belief was a part of his professed religion: it was still belief, and belief only. . . .

Judgment affirmed.

United States v. Ballard
322 U.S. 78 (1944)

Mr. Justice Douglas delivered the opinion of the Court.

[Respondents were indicted and convicted for using, and conspiring to use, the mails to defraud. The twelve-count indictment charged a scheme to defraud by organizing and promoting the "I Am" movement, forming corporations, distributing and selling literature, and soliciting funds and memberships "by means of false and fraudulent representations, pretenses and promises." The charged false representations covered respondents' alleged religious doctrines or beliefs. They were set forth in detail in the first count, including the following: that Guy W. Ballard, alias Saint Germain, Jesus, George Washington, and Godfre Ray King, had been selected and thereby designated by the alleged "ascertained masters," as a divine messenger; that Guy W. Ballard, and Edna W. Ballard, and Donald Ballard, by reason of their alleged high spiritual attainments and righteous conduct, had been selected as divine messengers through which the words of the alleged "ascended masters," including the alleged Saint Germain, would be communicated to mankind under the teachings of the "I Am" movement; and that Guy W. Ballard, Edna W. Ballard and Donald Ballard had, by reason of supernatural attainments, the power to heal persons of ailments and diseases and to make well persons afflicted with any diseases, injuries, or ailments normally classified as curable and also of diseases which are ordinarily classified by the medical profession as being incurable diseases and had in fact cured hundreds of persons.

Each of these representations enumerated in the indictment was followed by the charge that respondents "well knew" it was false and untrue. The indictment further alleged that respondents made these representations with the intention to cheat, wrong, and defraud their victims in order to obtain money and property from them. The District Court limited the evidence and instructed the jury to consider only the good faith of respondents. The Court of Appeals held that the question of the truth of the representations concerning respondents' religious doctrines or beliefs should have been submitted to the jury. It reversed the judgment of conviction, and granted a new trial.]

. . . [We] do not agree with the Court of Appeals that the truth or verity of respondents' religious doctrines or beliefs should have been submitted to the jury. Whatever this particular indictment might require, the First Amendment precludes such a course, as the United States seems to concede. "The law knows no heresy, and is committed to the support of no dogma, the establishment of no sect." The First Amendment has a dual aspect. It not only "forestalls compulsion by law of the acceptance of any creed or the practice of any form of worship" but also "safeguards the free exercise of the chosen form of religion." *Cantwell v. Connecticut* (1940) [Chapter 8]. "Thus the Amendment embraces two concepts—freedom to believe and freedom to act. The first is absolute but, in the nature of things, the second cannot be." Freedom of thought, which includes freedom of religious belief, is basic in a society of free men. *Board of Education v. Barnette* (1943) [Chapter 9]. It embraces the right to maintain theories of life and of death and of the hereafter which are rank heresy to followers of the orthodox faiths.

Heresy trials are foreign to our Constitution. Men may believe what they cannot prove. They may not be put to the proof of their religious doctrines or beliefs. Religious experiences which are as real as life to some may be incomprehensible to others. Yet the fact that they may be beyond the ken of mortals does not mean that they can be made suspect before the law. Many take their gospel from the New Testament. But it would hardly be supposed that they could be tried before a jury charged with the duty of determining whether those teachings contained false representations. The miracles of the New Testament, the Divinity of Christ, life after death, the power of prayer are deep in the religious convictions of many.

If one could be sent to jail because a jury in a hostile environment found those teachings false, little indeed would be left of religious freedom. The Fathers of the Constitution were not unaware of the varied and extreme views of religious sects, of the violence of disagreement among them, and of the lack of any one religious creed on which all men would agree. They fashioned a charter of government which envisaged the widest possible toleration of conflicting views. Man's relation to his God was made no concern of the state. He was granted the right to worship as he pleased and to answer to no man for the verity of his religious views.

The religious views espoused by respondents might seem incredible, if not preposterous, to most people. But if those doctrines are subject to trial before a jury charged with finding their truth or falsity, then the same can be done with the religious beliefs of any sect. When the triers of fact undertake that task, they enter a forbidden domain. The First Amendment does not select any one group or any one type of religion for preferred treatment. It puts them all in that position. "With man's relations to his Maker and the obligations he may think they impose, and the manner in which an expression shall be made by him of his belief on those subjects, no interference can be permitted, provided always the laws of society, designed to secure its peace and prosperity, and the morals of its people, are not interfered with." So we conclude that the District Court ruled properly when it withheld from the jury all questions concerning the truth or falsity of the religious beliefs or doctrines of respondents. . . .

The judgment is reversed and the cause is remanded to the Court of Appeals for further proceedings in conformity to this opinion.

Reversed.

Mr. Chief Justice Stone, dissenting:

I am not prepared to say that the constitutional guaranty of freedom of religion affords immunity from criminal prosecution for the fraudulent procurement of money by false statements as to one's religious experiences. . . . I cannot say that freedom of thought and worship includes freedom to procure money by making knowingly false statements about one's religious experiences. To go no further, if it were shown that a defendant in this case had asserted as a part of the alleged fraudulent scheme, that he had physically shaken hands with St. Germain in San Francisco on a day named, or that, as the indictment here alleges, by the exertion of his spiritual power he "had in fact cured . . . hundreds of persons afflicted with diseases and ailments," I should not doubt that it would be open to the Government to submit to the jury proof that he had never been in San Francisco and that no such cures had ever been effected. . . .

. . . [The] trial judge withdrew from the consideration of the jury the question whether the alleged religious experiences had in fact occurred, but submitted to the jury the single issue whether [respondents] honestly believed that they had occurred, with the instruction that if the jury did not so find, then it should return a verdict of guilty. On this issue the jury, on ample evidence that respondents were without belief in the statements which they had made to their victims, found a verdict of guilty. The state of one's mind is a fact [capable] of fraudulent misrepresentation. . . . Since the indictment and the evidence support the conviction, it is irrelevant whether the religious experiences alleged did or did not in fact occur or whether that issue could or could not, for constitutional reasons, have been rightly submitted to the jury. Certainly none of respondents' constitutional rights are violated if they are prosecuted for the fraudulent procurement of money by false representations as to their beliefs, religious or otherwise. . . .

On the issue submitted to the jury in this case it properly rendered a verdict of guilty. . . . I think the judgment below should be reversed and that of the District Court reinstated.

Mr. Justice Roberts and Mr. Justice Frankfurter join in this opinion.

Mr. Justice Jackson, dissenting:

I should say the defendants have done just that for which they are indicted. If I might agree to their conviction without creating a precedent, I cheerfully would do so. I can see in their teachings nothing but humbug, untainted by any trace of truth. But that does not dispose of the constitutional question whether misrepresentation of religious experience or belief is prosecutable; it rather emphasizes the danger of such prosecutions. . . .

[As] a matter of either practice or philosophy I do not see how we can separate an issue as to what is believed from considerations as to what is believable. The most convincing proof that one believes his statements is to show that they have been true in his experience. Likewise, that one knowingly falsified is best proved by showing that what he said happened never did happen. How can the Government prove these persons knew something to be false which it cannot prove to be false? . . .

. . . If religious liberty includes, as it must, the right to communicate such experiences to others, it seems to me an impossible task for juries to separate fancied ones from real ones, dreams from happenings, and hallucinations from true clairvoyance. Such experiences, like some tones and colors, have existence for one, but none at all for another. They cannot be verified to the minds of those whose field of consciousness does not include religious insight. When one comes to trial which turns on any aspect of religious belief or representation, unbelievers among his judges are likely not to understand and are almost certain not to believe him.

And then I do not know what degree of skepticism or disbelief in a religious representation amounts to actionable fraud. . . . Belief in what one may demonstrate to the senses is not faith. All schools of religious thought make enormous assumptions, generally on the basis of revelations authenticated by some sign or miracle. The appeal in such matters is to a very different plane of credulity than is invoked by representations of secular fact in commerce. Some who profess belief in the Bible read literally what others read as allegory or metaphor, as they read Aesop's fables. Religious symbolism is even used by some with the same mental reservations one has in teaching of Santa Claus or Uncle Sam or Easter bunnies or dispassionate judges. It is hard in matters so mystical to say how literally one is bound to believe the doctrine he teaches and even more difficult to say how far it is reliance upon a teacher's literal belief which induces followers to give him money.

There appear to be persons—let us hope not many—who find refreshment and courage in the teachings of the "I Am" cult. [However] doubtful it seems to me, it is hard to say that they do not get what they pay for. Scores of sects flourish in this country by teaching what to me are queer notions. It is plain that there is wide variety in American religious taste. The Ballards are not alone in catering to it with a pretty dubious product.

The chief wrong which false prophets do to their following is not financial. The collections aggregate a tempting total, but individual payments are not ruinous. . . . [The] real harm is on the mental and spiritual plane. There are those who hunger and thirst after higher values which they feel wanting in their humdrum lives. They live in mental confusion or moral anarchy and seek vaguely for truth and beauty and moral support. When they are deluded and then disillusioned, cynicism and confusion follow. . . . But that is precisely the thing the Constitution put beyond the reach of the prosecutor, for the price of freedom of religion or of speech or of the press is that we must put up with, and even pay for, a good deal of rubbish.

Prosecutions of this character easily could degenerate into religious persecution. I do not doubt that religious leaders may be convicted of fraud for making false representations on matters other than faith or experience, as for example if one represents that funds are being used to construct a church when in fact they are being used for personal purposes. But that is not this case, which reaches into wholly dangerous ground. When does less than full belief in a professed credo become actionable fraud if one is soliciting gifts or legacies? Such inquiries may discomfort orthodox as well as unconventional religious teachers, for even the most regular of them are sometimes accused of taking their orthodoxy with a grain of salt.

I would dismiss the indictment and have done with this business of judicially examining other people's faiths.

B. Modern Cases

Between 1963 and 1990, the Supreme Court took the approach that a government-imposed burden on a religious practice would be held to violate the Free Exercise Clause unless the government could demonstrate that the law was necessary to serve a compelling purpose—an analysis similar to the familiar strict scrutiny test. The first case in this Section, *Sherbert v. Verner*, describes and applies that mode of analysis. The second case, *Wisconsin v. Yoder*, explores what amounts to a balancing test on facts that the Justices believed were compellingly favorable to the religionists. The third case, *Employment Division v. Smith*, represents a paradigm shift in Free Exercise jurisprudence. If the law burdening the religious exercise is "neutral" and "generally applicable," then the law is presumed to be valid so long as it satisfies lowly rational review. If the law is not "neutral" or "generally applicable"—if it discriminates against religion—then the law must pass a heightened level of scrutiny.

As you read these three decisions, consider which of these two different approaches—the *Sherbert-Yoder* approach or the *Smith* approach—best suits the history and purposes of the Religion Clauses. Which approach is the better constitutional interpretation for the fullest protection of individual conscience? Conduct this thought experiment: apply the *Smith* test to the facts in *Sherbert* and *Yoder*, then apply the *Sherbert* test to the facts in *Smith*. Do the different tests ineluctably lead to different outcomes?

Sherbert v. Verner

374 U.S. 398 (1963)

Mr. Justice Brennan delivered the opinion of the Court.

Appellant, a member of the Seventh-day Adventist Church, was discharged by her South Carolina employer because she would not work on Saturday, the Sabbath Day of her faith.[1] When she was unable to obtain other employment because from conscientious scruples she would not take Saturday work,[2] she filed a claim for unemployment compensation benefits under the South Carolina Unemployment Compensation Act. That law provides that, to be eligible for benefits, a claimant must be "able to work and . . . available for work"; and, further, that a claimant is ineligible for benefits "if . . . he has failed, without good cause . . . to accept available suitable work when offered him by the employment office or the employer. . . ." The appellee Employment Security Commission, in administrative proceedings under the statute, found that appellant's restriction upon her availability for Saturday work brought her within the provision disqualifying for benefits insured workers who fail, without good cause, to accept "suitable work when offered . . . by the employment office or the employer. . . ." The Commission's finding was sustained by the Court of Common Pleas [and] by the South Carolina Supreme Court. . . . We noted probable jurisdiction [and now] reverse. . . .

[Appellant's] conscientious objection to Saturday work constitutes no conduct prompted by religious principles of a kind within the reach of state legislation. If, therefore, the decision of the South Carolina Supreme Court is to withstand appellant's constitutional challenge, it must be either because her disqualification as a beneficiary represents no infringement by the State of her constitutional rights of free exercise, or because any incidental burden on the free exercise of appellant's religion may be justified by a "compelling state interest in the regulation of a subject within the State's constitutional power to regulate." *NAACP v. Button*, 371 U.S. 415 (1963).

We turn first to the question whether the disqualification for benefits imposes any burden on the free exercise of appellant's religion. We think it is clear that it does. In a sense the consequences of such a disqualification to religious principles and practices may be only an indirect result of welfare legislation within the State's general competence to enact; it is true that no criminal sanctions directly compel appellant to work a six-day week. But this is only the beginning, not the end, of our inquiry. . . . Here not only is it apparent that appellant's declared ineligibility for benefits derives solely from the practice of her religion, but the pressure upon her to forego that practice is unmistakable. The ruling forces her to choose between following the precepts of her religion and forfeiting benefits, on the one hand, and abandoning one of the precepts of her religion in order to accept work, on the other hand. Governmental imposition of such a choice puts the same kind of burden upon the free exercise of religion as would a fine imposed against appellant for her Saturday worship.

---

1. Appellant became a member of the Seventh-day Adventist Church in 1957, at a time when her employer, a textile-mill operator, permitted her to work a five-day week. It was not until 1959 that the work week was changed to six days, including Saturday, for all three shifts in the employer's mill. . . .

2. After her discharge, appellant sought employment with three other mills in the Spartanburg area, but found no suitable five-day work available at any of the mills. In filing her claim with the Commission, she expressed a willingness to accept employment at other mills, or even in another industry, so long as Saturday work was not required. . . .

Nor may the South Carolina court's construction of the statute be saved from constitutional infirmity on the ground that unemployment compensation benefits are not appellant's "right" but merely a "privilege." It is too late in the day to doubt that the liberties of religion and expression may be infringed by the denial of or placing of conditions upon a benefit or privilege.... [To] condition the availability of benefits upon this appellant's willingness to violate a cardinal principle of her religious faith effectively penalizes the free exercise of her constitutional liberties.

Significantly South Carolina expressly saves the Sunday worshipper from having to make the kind of choice which we here hold infringes the Sabbatarian's religious liberty. When in times of "national emergency" the textile plants are authorized by the State Commissioner of Labor to operate on Sunday, "no employee shall be required to work on Sunday . . . who is conscientiously opposed to Sunday work; and if any employee should refuse to work on Sunday on account of conscientious . . . objections he or she shall not jeopardize his or her seniority by such refusal or be discriminated against in any other manner." S.C. CODE, § 64-4.... The unconstitutionality of the disqualification of the Sabbatarian is thus compounded by the religious discrimination which South Carolina's general statutory scheme necessarily effects.

We must next consider whether some compelling state interest enforced in the eligibility provisions of the South Carolina statute justifies the substantial infringement of appellant's First Amendment right. It is basic that no showing merely of a rational relationship to some colorable state interest would suffice; in this highly sensitive constitutional area, "only the gravest abuses, endangering paramount interests, give occasion for permissible limitation." *Thomas v. Collins*, 323 U.S. 516 (1945). No such abuse or danger has been advanced in the present case. The appellees suggest no more than a possibility that the filing of fraudulent claims by unscrupulous claimants feigning religious objections to Saturday work might not only dilute the unemployment compensation fund but also hinder the scheduling by employers of necessary Saturday work.... Even if consideration of such evidence is not foreclosed by the prohibition against judicial inquiry into the truth or falsity of religious beliefs, *United States v. Ballard* (1944) [*supra* this chapter], [it] is highly doubtful whether such evidence would be sufficient to warrant a substantial infringement of religious liberties. For even if the possibility of spurious claims did threaten to dilute the fund and disrupt the scheduling of work, it would plainly be incumbent upon the appellees to demonstrate that no alternative forms of regulation would combat such abuses without infringing First Amendment rights.

In these respects, then, the state interest asserted in the present case is wholly dissimilar to the interests which were found to justify the less direct burden upon religious practices in *Braunfeld v. Brown*, 366 U.S. 599 (1961). The Court recognized that the Sunday closing law which that decision sustained undoubtedly served "to make the practice of [the Orthodox Jewish merchants'] . . . religious beliefs more expensive." But the statute was nevertheless saved by a countervailing factor which finds no equivalent in the instant case — a strong state interest in providing one uniform day of rest for all workers. That secular objective could be achieved, the Court found, only by declaring Sunday to be that day of rest. Requiring exemptions for Sabbatarians, while theoretically possible, appeared to present an administrative problem of such magnitude, or to afford the exempted class so great a competitive advantage, that such a requirement would have rendered the entire statutory scheme unworkable. In the present case no such justifications underlie the determination of the state court that appellant's religion makes her ineligible to receive benefits.

In holding as we do, plainly we are not fostering the "establishment" of the Seventh-day Adventist religion in South Carolina, for the extension of unemployment benefits to Sabbatarians in common with Sunday worshippers reflects nothing more than the governmental obligation of neutrality in the face of religious differences, and does not represent that involvement of religious with secular institutions which it is the object of the Establishment Clause to forestall. Nor does the recognition of the appellant's right to unemployment benefits under the state statute serve to abridge any other person's religious liberties. Nor do we [declare] the existence of a constitutional right to unemployment benefits on the part of all persons whose religious convictions are the cause of their unemployment. This is not a case in which an employee's religious convictions serve to make him a nonproductive member of society. . . . Our holding today is only that South Carolina may not constitutionally apply the eligibility provisions so as to constrain a worker to abandon his religious convictions respecting the day of rest. This holding but reaffirms a principle that we announced a decade and a half ago, namely that no State may "exclude individual Catholics, Lutherans, Mohammedans, Baptists, Jews, Methodists, Non-believers, Presbyterians, or the members of any other faith, *because of their faith, or lack of it*, from receiving the benefits of public welfare legislation." *Everson v. Board of Education* (1947) [Chapter 17].

The judgment of the South Carolina Supreme Court is reversed and the case is remanded for further proceedings not inconsistent with this opinion.

Mr. Justice Douglas, concurring.

The case we have for decision seems to me to be of small dimensions, though profoundly important. . . . It seems obvious to me that this law does run afoul of [the free exercise] clause.

Religious scruples of Moslems require them to attend a mosque on Friday and to pray five times daily. Religious scruples of a Sikh require him to carry a regular or a symbolic sword. Religious scruples of a Jehovah's Witness teach him to be a colporteur, going from door to door, from town to town, distributing his religious pamphlets. Religious scruples of a Quaker compel him to refrain from swearing and to affirm instead. Religious scruples of a Buddhist may require him to refrain from partaking of any flesh, even of fish.

The examples could be multiplied, including those of the Seventh-day Adventist whose Sabbath is Saturday. . . . These suffice, however, to show that many people hold beliefs alien to the majority of our society — beliefs that are protected by the First Amendment but which could easily be trod upon under the guise of "police" or "health" regulations reflecting the majority's views.

Some have thought that a majority of a community can, through state action, compel a minority to observe their particular religious scruples so long as the majority's rule can be said to perform some valid secular function. That was the essence of the Court's decision in the Sunday Blue Law Cases (*Braunfeld v. Brown*, 366 U.S. 599 (1961); *McGowan v. Maryland*, 366 U.S. 420 (1961)), a ruling from which I then dissented and still dissent. . . .

The result turns not on the degree of injury, which may indeed be nonexistent by ordinary standards. The harm is the interference with the individual's scruples or conscience—an important area of privacy which the First Amendment fences off from government. The interference here is as plain as it is in Soviet Russia, where a churchgoer is given a second-class citizenship, resulting in harm though perhaps not in measurable damages.

This case is resolvable not in terms of what an individual can demand of government, but solely in terms of what government may not do to an individual in violation of his religious scruples. The fact that government cannot exact from me a surrender of one iota of my religious scruples does not, of course, mean that I can demand of government a sum of money, the better to exercise them. For the Free Exercise Clause is written in terms of what the government cannot do to the individual, not in terms of what the individual can exact from the government. Those considerations, however, are not relevant here. If appellant is otherwise qualified for unemployment benefits, payments will be made to her not as a Seventh-day Adventist, but as an unemployed worker. . . .

MR. JUSTICE STEWART, concurring in the result. [Omitted.]

MR. JUSTICE HARLAN, whom MR. JUSTICE WHITE joins, dissenting.

Today's decision is disturbing both in its rejection of existing precedent and in its implications for the future. . . .

First, despite the Court's protestations to the contrary, the decision necessarily overrules *Braunfeld v. Brown*, which held that it did not offend the "Free Exercise" Clause of the Constitution for a State to forbid a Sabbatarian to do business on Sunday. The secular purpose of the statute before us today is even clearer than that involved in *Braunfeld*. And just as in *Braunfeld*—where exceptions to the Sunday closing laws for Sabbatarians would have been inconsistent with the purpose to achieve a uniform day of rest and would have required case-by-case inquiry into religious beliefs—so here, an exception to the rules of eligibility based on religious convictions would necessitate judicial examination of those convictions and would be at odds with the limited purpose of the statute to smooth out the economy during periods of industrial instability. Finally, the indirect financial burden of the present law is far less than that involved in *Braunfeld*. Forcing a store owner to close his business on Sunday may well have the effect of depriving him of a satisfactory livelihood if his religious convictions require him to close on Saturday as well. Here we are dealing only with temporary benefits, amounting to a fraction of regular weekly wages and running for not more than 22 weeks. Clearly, any differences between this case and *Braunfeld* cut against the present appellant.

Second, the implications of the present decision are far more troublesome than its apparently narrow dimensions would indicate at first glance. The meaning of today's holding [is] that the State must furnish unemployment benefits to one who is unavailable for work if the unavailability stems from the exercise of religious convictions. The State, in other words, must *single out* for financial assistance those whose behavior is religiously motivated, even though it denies such assistance to others whose identical behavior (in this case, inability to work on Saturdays) is not religiously motivated.

It has been suggested that such singling out of religious conduct for special treatment may violate the constitutional limitations on state action. My own view, however, is that at least under the circumstances of this case it would be a permissible accommodation of religion for the State, if it *chose* to do so, to create an exception to its eligibility requirements for persons like the appellant. . . .

[However], I cannot subscribe to the conclusion that the State is constitutionally *compelled* to carve out an exception to its general rule of eligibility in the present case. Those situations in which the Constitution may require special treatment on account of religion are, in my view, few and far between. . . . Such compulsion in the present case is particularly inappropriate in light of the indirect, remote, and insubstantial effect of the decision below on the exercise of appellant's religion and in light of the direct financial assistance to religion that today's decision requires. . . .

Wisconsin v. Yoder

406 U.S. 205 (1972)

Mr. Chief Justice Burger delivered the opinion of the Court.

On petition of the State of Wisconsin, we granted the writ of certiorari in this case to review a decision of the Wisconsin Supreme Court holding that respondents' convictions of violating the State's compulsory school-attendance law were invalid under the Free Exercise Clause. . . . [We] affirm. . . .

Respondents are members of the Old Order Amish religion. . . . Wisconsin's compulsory school-attendance law required them to cause their children to attend public or private school until reaching age 16 but the respondents declined to send their children, ages 14 and 15, to public school after they completed the eighth grade. The children were not enrolled in any private school, or within any recognized exception to the compulsory-attendance law. . . .

On complaint of the school district administrator for the public schools, respondents were charged, tried, and convicted of violating the compulsory-attendance law [and] were fined the sum of $5 each. Respondents defended on the ground that the application of the compulsory-attendance law violated their rights under the First and Fourteenth Amendments. The trial testimony showed that respondents believed, in accordance with the tenets of Old Order Amish communities generally, that their children's attendance at high school, public or private, was contrary to the Amish religion and way of life. They believed that by sending their children to high school, they would not only expose themselves to the danger of the censure of the church community, but, as found by the [trial] court, also endanger their own salvation and that of their children. The State stipulated that respondents' religious beliefs were sincere.

. . . [Respondents] presented as expert witnesses scholars on religion and education whose testimony is uncontradicted. They expressed their opinions on the relationship of the Amish belief concerning school attendance to the more general tenets of their religion, and described the impact that compulsory high school attendance could have on the continued survival of Amish communities. . . . [Old Order Amish] communities today are characterized by a fundamental belief that salvation requires life in a church community separate and apart from the world and worldly influence. This concept of life aloof from the world and its values is central to their faith.

A related feature of Old Order Amish communities is their devotion to a life in harmony with nature and the soil, as exemplified by the simple life of the early Christian era that continued in America during much of our early national life. Amish beliefs require members of the community to make their living by farming or closely related activities. Broadly speaking, the Old Order Amish religion pervades and determines the entire mode of life of its adherents. Their conduct is regulated in great detail by the *Ordnung*, or rules, of the church community. . . .

Amish objection to formal education beyond the eighth grade is firmly grounded in these central religious concepts. They object to the high school, and higher education generally, because the values they teach are in marked variance with Amish values and the Amish way of life; they view secondary school education as an impermissible exposure of their children to a "worldly" influence in conflict with their beliefs. The high school tends to emphasize intellectual and scientific accomplishments, self-distinction, competitiveness, worldly success, and social life with other students. Amish society emphasizes informal learning-through-doing; a life of "goodness," rather than a life of intellect; wisdom, rather than technical knowledge; community welfare, rather than competition; and separation from, rather than integration with, contemporary worldly society.

Formal high school education beyond the eighth grade is contrary to Amish beliefs, not only because it places Amish children in an environment hostile to Amish beliefs with increasing emphasis on competition in class work and sports and with pressure to conform to the styles, manners, and ways of the peer group, but also because it takes them away from their community, physically and emotionally, during the crucial and formative adolescent period of life. During this period, the children must acquire Amish attitudes favoring manual work and self-reliance and the specific skills needed to perform the adult role of an Amish farmer or housewife. They must learn to enjoy physical labor. Once a child has learned basic reading, writing, and elementary mathematics, these traits, skills, and attitudes admittedly fall within the category of those best learned through example and "doing" rather than in a classroom. And, at this time in life, the Amish child must also grow in his faith and his relationship to the Amish community if he is to be prepared to accept the heavy obligations imposed by adult baptism. In short, high school attendance with teachers who are not of the Amish faith — and may even be hostile to it — interposes a serious barrier to the integration of the Amish child into the Amish religious community. . . .

The Amish do not object to elementary education through the first eight grades as a general proposition because they agree that their children must have basic skills in the "three R's" in order to read the Bible, to be good farmers and citizens, and to be able to deal with non-Amish people when necessary in the course of daily affairs. They view such a basic education as acceptable because it does not significantly expose their children to worldly values or interfere with their development in the Amish community during the crucial adolescent period. While Amish accept compulsory elementary education generally, wherever possible they have established their own elementary schools in many respects like the small local schools of the past. In the Amish belief higher learning tends to develop values they reject as influences that alienate man from God.

[One expert] testified that compulsory high school attendance could not only result in great psychological harm to Amish children, because of the conflicts it would produce, but would also [ultimately] result in the destruction of the Old Order Amish church community. . . . [Another] expert witness on education [showed] that the Amish succeed in preparing their high school age children to be productive members of the Amish community. He described their system of learning through doing the skills directly relevant to their adult roles in the Amish community as "ideal" and perhaps superior to ordinary high school education. The evidence also showed that the Amish have an excellent record as law-abiding and generally self-sufficient members of society.

I

There is no doubt as to the power of a State, having a high responsibility for education of its citizens, to impose reasonable regulations for the control and duration of basic education. Providing public schools ranks at the very apex of the function of a State. Yet even this paramount responsibility was [made] to yield [in *Pierce v. Society of Sisters*, 268 U.S. 510 (1925)]. . . . There the Court held that Oregon's statute compelling attendance in a public school from age eight to age 16 unreasonably interfered with the interest of parents in directing the rearing of their offspring, including their education in church-operated schools. As that case suggests, the values of parental direction of the religious upbringing and education of their children in their early and formative years have a high place in our society. Thus, a State's interest in universal education, however highly we rank it, is not totally free from a balancing process when it impinges on fundamental rights and interests, such as those specifically protected by the Free Exercise Clause of the First Amendment, and the traditional interest of parents with respect to the religious upbringing of their children so long as they, in the words of *Pierce*, "prepare [them] for additional obligations."

It follows that in order for Wisconsin to compel school attendance beyond the eighth grade against a claim that such attendance interferes with the practice of a legitimate religious belief, it must appear either that the State does not deny the free exercise of religious belief by its requirement, or that there is a state interest of sufficient magnitude to override the interest claiming protection under the Free Exercise Clause. Long before there was general acknowledgment of the need for universal formal education, the Religion Clauses had specifically and firmly fixed the right to free exercise of religious beliefs. . . . [Only] those interests of the highest order and those not otherwise served can overbalance legitimate claims to the free exercise of religion. We can accept it as settled, therefore, that, however strong the State's interest in universal compulsory education, it is by no means absolute to the exclusion or subordination of all other interests. *E.g., Sherbert v. Verner* (1963) [*supra* this chapter].

II

[We] must be careful to determine whether the Amish religious faith and their mode of life are, as they claim, inseparable and interdependent. A way of life, however virtuous and admirable, may not be interposed as a barrier to reasonable state regulation of education if it is based on purely secular considerations; to have the protection of the Religion Clauses, the claims must be rooted in religious belief. Although a determination of what is a "religious" belief or practice entitled to constitutional protection may present a most delicate question, the very concept of ordered liberty precludes allowing every person to make his own standards on matters of conduct in which society as a whole has important interests.

[The] record in this case abundantly supports the claim that the traditional way of life of the Amish is not merely a matter of personal preference, but one of deep religious conviction, shared by an organized group, and intimately related to daily living. [The] Old Order Amish daily life and religious practice stem from [their] literal interpretation of the Biblical injunction from the Epistle of Paul to the Romans, "be not conformed to this world. . . ." This command is fundamental to the Amish faith. Moreover, for the Old Order Amish, religion is not simply a matter of theocratic belief. As the expert witnesses explained, the Old Order Amish religion pervades and determines virtually their entire way of life, regulating it [in detail] through the strictly enforced rules of the church community.

[Respondents'] religious beliefs and attitude toward life, family, and home have remained constant — perhaps some would say static — in a period of unparalleled progress in human knowledge generally and great changes in education. [Their] religious beliefs and what we would today call "life style" have not altered in fundamentals for centuries. Their way of life in a church-oriented community, separated from the outside world and "worldly" influences, their attachment to nature and the soil, is a way inherently simple and uncomplicated, albeit difficult to preserve against the pressure to conform. Their rejection of telephones, automobiles, radios, and television, their mode of dress, of speech, their habits of manual work do indeed set them apart from much of contemporary society; these customs are both symbolic and practical.

As the society around the Amish has become more populous, urban, industrialized, and complex, particularly in this century, government regulation of human affairs has correspondingly become more detailed and pervasive. The Amish mode of life has thus come into conflict increasingly with requirements of contemporary society exerting a hydraulic insistence on conformity to majoritarian standards. So long as compulsory education laws were confined to eight grades of elementary basic education imparted in a nearby rural schoolhouse, with a large proportion of students of the Amish faith, the Old Order Amish had little basis to fear that school attendance would expose their children to the worldly influence they reject. But modern compulsory secondary education in rural areas is now largely carried on in a consolidated school, often remote from the student's home and alien to his daily home life. [The] values and programs of the modern secondary school are in sharp conflict with the fundamental mode of life mandated by the Amish religion; modern laws requiring compulsory secondary education have accordingly engendered great concern and conflict. The conclusion is inescapable that secondary schooling, by exposing Amish children to worldly influences in terms of attitudes, goals, and values contrary to beliefs, and by substantially interfering with the religious development of the Amish child and his integration into the way of life of the Amish faith community at the crucial adolescent stage of development, contravenes the basic religious tenets and practice of the Amish faith, both as to the parent and the child.

The impact of the compulsory-attendance law on respondents' practice of the Amish religion is not only severe, but inescapable, for the Wisconsin law affirmatively compels them, under threat of criminal sanction, to perform acts undeniably at odds with fundamental tenets of their religious beliefs. Nor is the impact of the compulsory-attendance law confined to grave interference with important Amish religious tenets from a subjective point of view. It carries with it precisely the kind of objective danger to the free exercise of religion that the First Amendment was designed to prevent. [Compulsory] school attendance to age 16 for Amish children carries with it a very real threat of undermining the Amish community and religious practice as they exist today; they must either abandon belief and be assimilated into society at large, or be forced to migrate to some other and more tolerant region.

III

[Wisconsin's] position is that the State's interest in universal compulsory formal secondary education to age 16 is so great that it is paramount to the undisputed claims of respondents that their mode of preparing their youth for Amish life, after the traditional elementary education, is an essential part of their religious belief and practice. . . .

Wisconsin [argues] that "actions," even though religiously grounded, are outside the protection of the First Amendment. But our decisions have rejected the idea that religiously grounded conduct is always outside the protection of the Free Exercise Clause. It is true that activities of individuals, even when religiously based, are often subject to regulation by the States in the exercise of their undoubted power to promote the health, safety, and general welfare, or the Federal Government in the exercise of its delegated powers. *See, e.g., Reynolds v. United States* (1878) [*supra* this chapter]. But to agree that religiously grounded conduct must often be subject to the broad police power of the State is not to deny that there are areas of conduct protected by the Free Exercise Clause of the First Amendment and thus beyond the power of the State to control, even under regulations of general applicability. *E.g., Sherbert v. Verner* (1963)....

Nor can this case be disposed of on the grounds that Wisconsin's requirement for school attendance to age 16 applies uniformly to all citizens of the State and does not, on its face, discriminate against religions or a particular religion, or that it is motivated by legitimate secular concerns. A regulation neutral on its face may, in its application, nonetheless offend the constitutional requirement for governmental neutrality if it unduly burdens the free exercise of religion....

[Wisconsin argues] that its interest in its system of compulsory education is so compelling that even the established religious practices of the Amish must give way. Where fundamental claims of religious freedom are at stake, however, we cannot accept such a sweeping claim; despite its admitted validity in the generality of cases, we must searchingly examine the interests that the State seeks to promote by its requirement for compulsory education to age 16, and the impediment to those objectives that would flow from recognizing the claimed Amish exemption.

The State advances two primary arguments in support of its system of compulsory education. It notes [that] some degree of education is necessary to prepare citizens to participate effectively and intelligently in our open political system if we are to preserve freedom and independence. Further, education prepares individuals to be self-reliant and self-sufficient participants in society. We accept these propositions.

However, the evidence adduced by the Amish in this case is persuasively to the effect that an additional one or two years of formal high school for Amish children in place of their long-established program of informal vocational education would do little to serve those interests.... It is one thing to say that compulsory education for a year or two beyond the eighth grade may be necessary when its goal is the preparation of the child for life in modern society as the majority live, but it is quite another if the goal of education be viewed as the preparation of the child for life in the separated agrarian community that is the keystone of the Amish faith.

The State attacks respondents' position as one fostering "ignorance" from which the child must be protected by the State. No one can question the State's duty to protect children from ignorance but this argument does not square with the facts disclosed in the record. Whatever their idiosyncrasies as seen by the majority, [the] Amish community has been a highly successful social unit within our society, even if apart from the conventional "mainstream." Its members are productive and very law-abiding members of society; they reject public welfare in any of its usual modern forms. The Congress itself recognized their self-sufficiency by authorizing exemption of such groups as the Amish from the obligation to pay social security taxes. It is neither fair nor correct to suggest that the Amish are opposed to education beyond the eighth grade level. [They] are opposed to conventional formal education of the type provided by a certified high school because it comes at the child's crucial adolescent period of religious development. [One expert] testified that their system of learning-by-doing was an "ideal system" of education in terms of preparing Amish children for life as adults in the Amish community....

The State [posits] the possibility that some such children will choose to leave the Amish community, and that if this occurs they will be ill-equipped for life. . . . [That] argument is highly speculative. There is no specific evidence of the loss of Amish adherents by attrition, nor is there any showing that upon leaving the Amish community Amish children, with their practical agricultural training and habits of industry and self-reliance, would become burdens on society because of educational short-comings. . . . There is nothing in this record to suggest that the Amish qualities of reliability, self-reliance, and dedication to work would fail to find ready markets in today's society. . . . [Nor] is there any basis in the record to warrant a finding that an additional one or two years of formal school education beyond the eighth grade would serve to eliminate any such problem that might exist. Insofar as the State's claim rests on the view that a brief additional period of formal education is imperative to enable the Amish to participate effectively and intelligently in our democratic process, it must fall. The Amish alternative to formal secondary school education has enabled them to function effectively in their day-to-day life under self-imposed limitations on relations with the world, and to survive and prosper in contemporary society as a separate, sharply identifiable and highly self-sufficient community for more than 200 years in this country. [This] is strong evidence that they are capable of fulfilling the social and political responsibilities of citizenship without compelled attendance beyond the eighth grade at the price of jeopardizing their free exercise of religious belief. . . .

We should also note that compulsory education and child labor laws find their historical origin in common humanitarian instincts, and that the age limits of both laws have been coordinated to achieve their related objectives. . . . [Wisconsin's] interest in compelling the school attendance of Amish children to age 16 emerges as somewhat less substantial than requiring such attendance for children generally. For, while agricultural employment is not totally outside the legitimate concerns of the child labor laws, employment of children under parental guidance and on the family farm from age 14 to age 16 is an ancient tradition that lies at the periphery of the objectives of such laws. There is no intimation that the Amish employment of their children on family farms is in any way deleterious to their health or that Amish parents exploit children at tender years. . . .

IV

Finally, the State, on authority of *Prince v. Massachusetts*, argues that a decision exempting Amish children from the State's requirement fails to recognize the substantive right of the Amish child to a secondary education, and fails to give due regard to the power of the State as *parens patriae* to extend the benefit of secondary education to children regardless of the wishes of their parents. . . . [However, the Court] later took great care to confine *Prince* to a narrow scope in *Sherbert v. Verner*, when it stated [that in the cases rejecting challenges under the Free Exercise Clause, the conduct or actions regulated by the state] have invariably posed some substantial threat to public safety, peace or order. . . .

Contrary to the suggestion of the dissenting opinion of Mr. Justice Douglas, our holding today in no degree depends on the assertion of the religious interest of the child as contrasted with that of the parents. It is the parents who are subject to prosecution here for failing to cause their children to attend school, and it is their right of free exercise, not that of their children, that must determine Wisconsin's power to impose criminal penalties on the parent. . . . Our holding in no way determines the proper resolution of possible competing interests of parents, children, and the State in an appropriate state court proceeding in which the power of the State is asserted on the theory that Amish parents are preventing their minor children from attending high school despite their expressed desires to the contrary. . . . On this record we neither reach nor decide those issues.

The State's argument proceeds without reliance on any actual conflict between the wishes of parents and children. . . . Indeed it seems clear that if the State is empowered, as *parens patriae*, to "save" a child from himself or his Amish parents by requiring an additional two years of compulsory formal high school education, the State will in large measure influence, if not determine, the religious future of the child. Even more markedly than in *Prince*, therefore, this case involves the fundamental interest of parents, as contrasted with that of the State, to guide the religious future and education of their children. The history and culture of Western civilization reflect a strong tradition of parental concern for the nurture and upbringing of their children. This primary role of the parents in the upbringing of their children is now established beyond debate as an enduring American tradition. . . . And, when the interests of parenthood are combined with a free exercise claim of the nature revealed by this record, more than merely a "reasonable relation to some purpose within the competency of the State" is required to sustain the validity of the State's requirement under the First Amendment. . . . In the face of our consistent emphasis on the central values underlying the Religion Clauses in our constitutional scheme of government, we cannot accept a *parens patriae* claim of such all-encompassing scope and with such sweeping potential for broad and unforeseeable application as that urged by the State.

V

For the reasons stated we hold, with the Supreme Court of Wisconsin, that the First and Fourteenth Amendments prevent the State from compelling respondents to cause their children to attend formal high school to age 16. . . . Nothing we hold is intended to undermine the general applicability of the State's compulsory school-attendance statutes or to limit the power of the State to promulgate reasonable standards that, while not impairing the free exercise of religion, provide for continuing agricultural vocational education under parental and church guidance by the Old Order Amish or others similarly situated. The States have had a long history of amicable and effective relationships with church-sponsored schools, and there is no basis for assuming that, in this related context, reasonable standards cannot be established concerning the content of the continuing vocational education of Amish children under parental guidance, provided always that state regulations are not inconsistent with what we have said in this opinion.

Affirmed.

MR. JUSTICE POWELL and MR. JUSTICE REHNQUIST took no part in the consideration or decision of this case.

MR. JUSTICE STEWART, with whom MR. JUSTICE BRENNAN joins, concurring. [Omitted.]

MR. JUSTICE WHITE, with whom MR. JUSTICE BRENNAN and MR. JUSTICE STEWART join, concurring. [Omitted.]

MR. JUSTICE DOUGLAS, dissenting in part. [Omitted.]

Employment Division v. Smith
494 U.S. 872 (1990)

JUSTICE SCALIA delivered the opinion of the Court.

This case requires us to decide whether the Free Exercise Clause of the First Amendment permits the State of Oregon to include religiously inspired peyote use within the reach of its general criminal prohibition on use of that drug, and thus permits the State to deny unemployment benefits to persons dismissed from their jobs because of such religiously inspired use.

I

Oregon law prohibits the knowing or intentional possession of a "controlled substance" unless the substance has been prescribed by a medical practitioner. . . . Persons who violate this provision by possessing a controlled substance listed on Schedule I are "guilty of a Class B felony." [Schedule I] contains the drug peyote, a hallucinogen derived from the plant *Lophophora williamsii Lemaire.*

Respondents [were] fired from their jobs with a private drug rehabilitation organization because they ingested peyote for sacramental purposes at a ceremony of the Native American Church, of which both are members. When respondents applied to petitioner Employment Division for unemployment compensation, they were determined to be ineligible for benefits because they had been discharged for work-related "misconduct." . . .

[The Oregon Court of Appeals reversed that determination. On appeal, the Oregon Supreme Court held that the denial of benefits violated respondents' free exercise rights under the First and Fourteenth Amendments. We granted certiorari, vacated the judgment, and remanded for further consideration whether the sacramental use of peyote was in fact proscribed by Oregon's controlled substance law—an issue that had not been decided and a matter of dispute between the parties. *Employment Div. v. Smith,* 485 U.S. 660 (1988) (*Smith I*). On remand, the Oregon Supreme Court held that religiously inspired use of peyote fell within the prohibition of the Oregon statute and went on to reaffirm its previous ruling that the State could not deny unemployment benefits to respondents for having engaged in that practice.] We again granted certiorari.

II

Respondents' claim for relief rests on our decisions in *Sherbert v. Verner* (1963) [*supra* this chapter], *Thomas v. Review Bd. of Indiana Employment Security Div.*, 450 U.S. 707 (1981), and *Hobbie v. Unemployment Appeals Comm'n of Florida*, 480 U.S. 136 (1987), in which we held that a State could not condition the availability of unemployment insurance on an individual's willingness to forgo conduct required by his religion. As we observed in *Smith I*, however, the conduct at issue in those cases was not prohibited by law. We held that distinction to be critical. . . . Now that the Oregon Supreme Court has confirmed that Oregon does prohibit the religious use of peyote, we proceed to consider whether that prohibition is permissible under the Free Exercise Clause.

[The] free exercise of religion means, first and foremost, the right to believe and profess whatever religious doctrine one desires. . . . But the "exercise of religion" often involves not only belief and profession but the performance of (or abstention from) physical acts: assembling with others for a worship service, participating in sacramental use of bread and wine, proselytizing, abstaining from certain foods or certain modes of transportation. It would be true, we think (though no case of ours has involved the point), that a State would be "prohibiting the free exercise [of religion]" if it sought to ban such acts or abstentions only when they are engaged in for religious reasons, or only because of the religious belief that they display. It would doubtless be unconstitutional, for example, to ban the casting of "statues that are to be used for worship purposes," or to prohibit bowing down before a golden calf.

Respondents [seek] to carry the meaning of "prohibiting the free exercise [of religion]" one large step further. They contend that their religious motivation for using peyote places them beyond the reach of a criminal law that is not specifically directed at their religious practice, and that is concededly constitutional as applied to those who use the drug for other reasons. They assert [that] "prohibiting the free exercise [of religion]" includes requiring any individual to observe a generally applicable law that requires (or forbids) the performance of an act that his religious belief forbids (or requires). As a textual matter, we do not think the words must be given that meaning. . . .

[W]e have never held that an individual's religious beliefs excuse him from compliance with an otherwise valid law prohibiting conduct that the State is free to regulate. On the contrary, the record of more than a century of our free exercise jurisprudence contradicts that proposition. [In] *Reynolds v. United States* (1878) [*supra* this chapter], [we] rejected the claim that criminal laws against polygamy could not be constitutionally applied to those whose religion commanded the practice. . . . Subsequent decisions have consistently held that the right of free exercise does not relieve an individual of the obligation to comply with a "valid and neutral law of general applicability on the ground that the law proscribes (or prescribes) conduct that his religion prescribes (or proscribes)." *United States v. Lee*, 455 U.S. 263 n.3 (1982) (Stevens, J., concurring in the opinion). . . .

The only decisions in which we have held that the First Amendment bars application of a neutral, generally applicable law to religiously motivated action have involved not the Free Exercise Clause alone, but the Free Exercise Clause in conjunction with other constitutional protections, such as freedom of speech and of the press, *see Cantwell v. Connecticut* (1940) [Chapter 8] (invalidating a licensing system for religious and charitable solicitations under which the administrator had discretion to deny a license to any cause he deemed nonreligious); *Murdock v. Pennsylvania*, 319 U.S. 105 (1943) (invalidating a flat tax on solicitation as applied to the dissemination of religious ideas); *Follett v. McCormick*, 321 U.S. 573 (1944) (same), or the right of parents, acknowledged in *Pierce v. Society of Sisters*, 268 U.S. 510 (1925), to direct the education of their children, *see Wisconsin v. Yoder* (1972) [*supra* this chapter] (invalidating compulsory school-attendance laws as applied to Amish parents who refused on religious grounds to send their children to school). Some of our cases prohibiting compelled expression, decided exclusively upon free speech grounds, have also involved freedom of religion, *cf. Wooley v. Maynard* (1977) [Chapter 9] (invalidating compelled display of a license plate slogan that offended individual religious beliefs); *West Virginia Bd. of Education v. Barnette* (1943) [Chapter 9] (invalidating compulsory flag salute statute challenged by religious objectors). And it is easy to envision a case in which a challenge on freedom of association grounds would likewise be reinforced by Free Exercise Clause concerns. *Cf. Roberts v. United States Jaycees* (1984) [Chapter 10].

The present case does not present such a hybrid situation, but a free exercise claim unconnected with any communicative activity or parental right. Respondents urge us to hold, quite simply, that when otherwise prohibitable conduct is accompanied by religious convictions, not only the convictions but the conduct itself must be free from governmental regulation. We have never held that, and decline to do so now. There being no contention that Oregon's drug law represents an attempt to regulate religious beliefs, the communication of religious beliefs, or the raising of one's children in those beliefs, the rule to which we have adhered ever since *Reynolds* plainly controls. . . .

Respondents argue that even though exemption from generally applicable criminal laws need not automatically be extended to religiously motivated actors, at least the claim for a religious exemption must be evaluated under the balancing test set forth in *Sherbert v. Verner*. Under the *Sherbert* test, governmental actions that substantially burden a religious practice must be justified by a compelling governmental interest. Applying that test we have, on three occasions, invalidated state unemployment compensation rules that conditioned the availability of benefits upon an applicant's willingness to work under conditions forbidden by his religion. We have never invalidated any governmental action on the basis of the *Sherbert* test except the denial of unemployment compensation. Although we have sometimes purported to apply the *Sherbert* test in contexts other than that, we have always found the test satisfied. In recent years we have abstained from applying the *Sherbert* test (outside the unemployment compensation field) at all. . . .

Even if we were inclined to breathe into *Sherbert* some life beyond the unemployment compensation field, we would not apply it to require exemptions from a generally applicable criminal law. The *Sherbert* test, it must be recalled, was developed in a context that lent itself to individualized governmental assessment of the reasons for the relevant conduct. [Our] decisions in the unemployment cases stand for the proposition that where the State has in place a system of individual exemptions, it may not refuse to extend that system to cases of "religious hardship" without compelling reason.

Whether or not the decisions are that limited, they at least have nothing to do with an across-the-board criminal prohibition on a particular form of conduct. . . . We conclude today that the sounder approach, and the approach in accord with the vast majority of our precedents, is to hold the [*Sherbert*] test inapplicable to such challenges. The government's ability to enforce generally applicable prohibitions of socially harmful conduct, like its ability to carry out other aspects of public policy, "cannot depend on measuring the effects of a governmental action on a religious objector's spiritual development." To make an individual's obligation to obey such a law contingent upon the law's coincidence with his religious beliefs, except where the State's interest is "compelling"—permitting him, by virtue of his beliefs, "to become a law unto himself," *Reynolds v. United States*—contradicts both constitutional tradition and common sense.

The "compelling government interest" requirement seems benign, because it is familiar from other fields. But using it as the standard that must be met before the government may accord different treatment on the basis of race, or before the government may regulate the content of speech, is not remotely comparable to using it for the purpose asserted here. What it produces in those other fields—equality of treatment and an unrestricted flow of contending speech—are constitutional norms; what it would produce here—a private right to ignore generally applicable laws—is a constitutional anomaly.

Nor is it possible to limit the impact of respondents' proposal by requiring a "compelling state interest" only when the conduct prohibited is "central" to the individual's religion. It is no more appropriate for judges to determine the "centrality" of religious beliefs before applying a "compelling interest" test in the free exercise field, than it would be for them to determine the "importance" of ideas before applying the "compelling interest" test in the free speech field. What principle of law or logic can be brought to bear to contradict a believer's assertion that a particular act is "central" to his personal faith? . . . Repeatedly and in many different contexts, we have warned that courts must not presume to determine the place of a particular belief in a religion or the plausibility of a religious claim. *See, e.g., United States v. Ballard* (1944) [*supra* this chapter].

If the "compelling interest" test is to be applied at all, then, it must be applied across the board, to all actions thought to be religiously commanded. Moreover, if "compelling interest" really means what it says (and watering it down here would subvert its rigor in the other fields where it is applied), many laws will not meet the test. Any society adopting such a system would be courting anarchy, but that danger increases in direct proportion to the society's diversity of religious beliefs, and its determination to coerce or suppress none of them. . . . The rule respondents favor would open the prospect of constitutionally required religious exemptions from civic obligations of almost every conceivable kind—ranging from compulsory military service to the payment of taxes, to health and safety regulation such as manslaughter and child neglect laws, compulsory vaccination laws, drug laws, and traffic laws, to social welfare legislation such as minimum wage laws, child labor laws, animal cruelty laws, environmental protection laws, and laws providing for equality of opportunity for the races. The First Amendment's protection of religious liberty does not require this.

Values that are protected against government interference through enshrinement in the Bill of Rights are not thereby banished from the political process. [A] society that believes in the negative protection accorded to religious belief [by the First Amendment] can be expected to be solicitous of that value in its legislation as well. It is therefore not surprising that a number of States have made an exception to their drug laws for sacramental peyote use. But to say that a nondiscriminatory religious-practice exemption is permitted, or even that it is desirable, is not to say that it is constitutionally required, and that the appropriate occasions for its creation can be discerned by the courts. It may fairly be said that leaving accommodation to the political process will place at a relative disadvantage those religious practices that are not widely engaged in; but that unavoidable consequence of democratic government must be preferred to a system in which each conscience is a law unto itself or in which judges weigh the social importance of all laws against the centrality of all religious beliefs.

Because respondents' ingestion of peyote was prohibited under Oregon law, and because that prohibition is constitutional, Oregon may, consistent with the Free Exercise Clause, deny respondents unemployment compensation when their dismissal results from use of the drug. The decision of the Oregon Supreme Court is accordingly reversed.

JUSTICE O'CONNOR, with whom JUSTICE BRENNAN, JUSTICE MARSHALL, and JUSTICE BLACKMUN join as to Parts I and II, concurring in the judgment.*

Although I agree with the result the Court reaches in this case, I cannot join its opinion. In my view, today's holding dramatically departs from well-settled First Amendment jurisprudence, appears unnecessary to resolve the question presented, and is incompatible with our Nation's fundamental commitment to individual religious liberty. . . .

II

. . . [The] "free *exercise*" of religion often, if not invariably, requires the performance of (or abstention from) certain acts. Because the First Amendment does not distinguish between religious belief and religious conduct, conduct motivated by sincere religious belief, like the belief itself, must be at least presumptively protected by the Free Exercise Clause.

---

* Although Justice Brennan, Justice Marshall, and Justice Blackmun join Parts I and II of this opinion, they do not concur in the judgment.

The Court today, however, interprets the Clause to permit the government to prohibit, without justification, conduct mandated by an individual's religious beliefs, so long as that prohibition is generally applicable. But a law that prohibits certain conduct—conduct that happens to be an act of worship for someone—manifestly does prohibit that person's free exercise of his religion. A person who is barred from engaging in religiously motivated conduct is barred from freely exercising his religion. Moreover, that person is barred from freely exercising his religion regardless of whether the law prohibits the conduct only when engaged in for religious reasons, only by members of that religion, or by all persons. It is difficult to deny that a law that prohibits religiously motivated conduct, even if the law is generally applicable, does not at least implicate First Amendment concerns.

The Court responds that generally applicable laws are "one large step" removed from laws aimed at specific religious practices. The First Amendment, however, does not distinguish between laws that are generally applicable and laws that target particular religious practices. Indeed, few States would be so naive as to enact a law directly prohibiting or burdening a religious practice as such. Our free exercise cases have all concerned generally applicable laws that had the effect of significantly burdening a religious practice. If the First Amendment is to have any vitality, it ought not be construed to cover only the extreme and hypothetical situation in which a State directly targets a religious practice. . . .

To say that a person's right to free exercise has been burdened, of course, does not mean that he has an absolute right to engage in the conduct. Under our established First Amendment jurisprudence, we have recognized that the freedom to act, unlike the freedom to believe, cannot be absolute. Instead, we have respected both the First Amendment's express textual mandate and the governmental interest in regulation of conduct by requiring the government to justify any substantial burden on religiously motivated conduct by a compelling state interest and by means narrowly tailored to achieve that interest. . . .

[In] *Yoder* we expressly rejected the interpretation the Court now adopts: "A regulation neutral on its face may, in its application, nonetheless offend the constitutional requirement for government neutrality if it unduly burdens the free exercise of religion."

. . . In my view, [the] essence of a free exercise claim is relief from a burden imposed by government on religious practices or beliefs, whether the burden is imposed directly through laws that prohibit or compel specific religious practices, or indirectly through laws that, in effect, make abandonment of one's own religion or conformity to the religious beliefs of others the price of an equal place in the civil community. . . . A State that makes criminal an individual's religiously motivated conduct burdens that individual's free exercise of religion in the severest manner possible. . . . I would have thought it beyond argument that such laws implicate free exercise concerns.

[We] have never distinguished between cases in which a State conditions receipt of a benefit on conduct prohibited by religious beliefs and cases in which a State affirmatively prohibits such conduct. The *Sherbert* compelling interest test applies in both kinds of cases. . . . I would reaffirm that principle today: A neutral criminal law prohibiting conduct that a State may legitimately regulate is, if anything, more burdensome than a neutral civil statute placing legitimate conditions on the award of a state benefit. . . . To me, the sounder approach — the approach more consistent with our role as judges to decide each case on its individual merits — is to apply this test in each case to determine whether the burden on the specific plaintiffs before us is constitutionally significant and whether the particular criminal interest asserted by the State before us is compelling. . . . Given the range of conduct that a State might legitimately make criminal, we cannot assume, merely because a law carries criminal sanctions and is generally applicable, that the First Amendment never requires the State to grant a limited exemption for religiously motivated conduct. . . .

The Court today gives no convincing reason to depart from settled First Amendment jurisprudence. There is nothing talismanic about neutral laws of general applicability or general criminal prohibitions, for laws neutral toward religion can coerce a person to violate his religious conscience or intrude upon his religious duties just as effectively as laws aimed at religion. . . .

[The] Court today suggests that the disfavoring of minority religions is an "unavoidable consequence" under our system of government and that accommodation of such religions must be left to the political process. In my view, however, the First Amendment was enacted precisely to protect the rights of those whose religious practices are not shared by the majority and may be viewed with hostility. The history of our free exercise doctrine amply demonstrates the harsh impact majoritarian rule has had on unpopular or emerging religious groups such as the Jehovah's Witnesses and the Amish. . . . The compelling interest test reflects the First Amendment's mandate of preserving religious liberty to the fullest extent possible in a pluralistic society. . . .

III

The Court's holding today [appears] to be unnecessary to this case. I would reach the same result applying our established free exercise jurisprudence.

There is no dispute that Oregon's criminal prohibition of peyote places a severe burden on the ability of respondents to freely exercise their religion. Peyote is a sacrament of the Native American Church and is regarded as vital to respondents' ability to practice their religion. . . .

There is also no dispute that Oregon has a significant interest in enforcing laws that control the possession and use of controlled substances by its citizens. . . .

Although the question is close, I would conclude, [in] view of the societal interest in preventing trafficking in controlled substances, uniform application of the criminal prohibition at issue is essential to the effectiveness of Oregon's stated interest in preventing any possession of peyote.

For these reasons, I believe that granting a selective exemption in this case would seriously impair Oregon's compelling interest in prohibiting possession of peyote by its citizens. Under such circumstances, the Free Exercise Clause does not require the State to accommodate respondents' religiously motivated conduct. . . .

I would therefore adhere to our established free exercise jurisprudence and hold that the State in this case has a compelling interest in regulating peyote use by its citizens and that accommodating respondents' religiously motivated conduct "will unduly interfere with fulfillment of the governmental interest." Accordingly, I concur in the judgment of the Court.

Justice Blackmun, with whom Justice Brennan and Justice Marshall join, dissenting.

This Court over the years painstakingly has developed a consistent and exacting standard to test the constitutionality of a state statute that burdens the free exercise of religion. Such a statute may stand only if the law in general, and the State's refusal to allow a religious exemption in particular, are justified by a compelling interest that cannot be served by less restrictive means.

[I] agree with Justice O'Connor's analysis of the applicable free exercise doctrine, and I join parts I and II of her opinion. As she points out, "the critical question in this case is whether exempting respondents from the State's general criminal prohibition 'will unduly interfere with fulfillment of the governmental interest.'" I do disagree, however, with her specific answer to that question.

In weighing the clear interest of respondents [in] the free exercise of their religion against Oregon's asserted interest in enforcing its drug laws, it is important to articulate in precise terms the state interest involved. It is not the State's broad interest in fighting the critical "war on drugs" that must be weighed against respondents' claim, but the State's narrow interest in refusing to make an exception for the religious, ceremonial use of peyote. Failure to reduce the competing interests to the same plane of generality tends to distort the weighing process in the State's favor.

[In] this case, the State actually has not evinced any concrete interest in enforcing its drug laws against religious users of peyote. Oregon has never sought to prosecute respondents, and does not claim that it has made significant enforcement efforts against other religious users of peyote. The State's asserted interest thus amounts only to the symbolic preservation of an unenforced prohibition. . . .

The State proclaims an interest in protecting the health and safety of its citizens from the dangers of unlawful drugs. It offers, however, no evidence that the religious use of peyote has ever harmed anyone. The factual findings of other courts cast doubt on the State's assumption that religious use of peyote is harmful. The Federal Government, which created the classifications of unlawful drugs from which Oregon's drug laws are derived, apparently does not find peyote so dangerous as to preclude an exemption for religious use. . . . Moreover, 23 States, including many that have significant Native American populations, have statutory or judicially crafted exemptions in their drug laws for religious use of peyote. Although this does not prove that Oregon must have such an exception too, it is significant that these States, and the Federal Government, all find their (presumably compelling) interests in controlling the use of dangerous drugs compatible with an exemption for religious use of peyote.

The carefully circumscribed ritual context in which respondents used peyote is far removed from the irresponsible and unrestricted recreational use of unlawful drugs. The Native American Church's internal restrictions on, and supervision of, its members' use of peyote substantially obviate the State's health and safety concerns. In this respect, respondents' use of peyote seems closely analogous to the sacramental use of wine by the Roman Catholic Church. During Prohibition, the Federal Government exempted such use of wine from its general ban on possession and use of alcohol. However compelling the Government's then general interest in prohibiting the use of alcohol may have been, it could not plausibly have asserted an interest sufficiently compelling to outweigh Catholics' right to take communion. . . .

The State also seeks to support its refusal to make an exception for religious use of peyote by invoking its interest in abolishing drug trafficking. There is, however, practically no illegal traffic in peyote. [Peyote] simply is not a popular drug; its distribution for use in religious rituals has nothing to do with the vast and violent traffic in illegal narcotics that plagues this country.

[The] State argues that granting an exception for religious peyote use would erode its interest in the uniform, fair, and certain enforcement of its drug laws. The State fears that, if it grants an exemption for religious peyote use, a flood of other claims to religious exemptions will follow. . . . This Court, however, consistently has rejected similar arguments in past free exercise cases, and it should do so here as well. The State's apprehension of a flood of other religious claims is purely speculative. Almost half the States, and the Federal Government, have maintained an exemption for religious peyote use for many years, and apparently have not found themselves overwhelmed by claims to other religious exemptions. Allowing an exemption for religious peyote use would not necessarily oblige the State to grant a similar exemption to other religious groups. The unusual circumstances that make the religious use of peyote compatible with the State's interests in health and safety and in preventing drug trafficking would not apply to other religious claims. Some religions, for example, might not restrict drug use to a limited ceremonial context, as does the Native American Church. Some religious claims involve drugs such as marijuana and heroin, in which there is significant illegal traffic, with its attendant greed and violence, so that it would be difficult to grant a religious exemption without seriously compromising law enforcement efforts. That the State might grant an exemption for religious peyote use, but deny other religious claims arising in different circumstances, would not violate the Establishment Clause. Though the State must treat all religions equally, and not favor one over another, this obligation is fulfilled by the uniform application of the "compelling interest" test to all free exercise claims, not by reaching uniform results as to all claims. A showing that religious peyote use does not unduly interfere with the State's interests is "one that probably few other religious groups or sects could make"; this does not mean that an exemption limited to peyote use is tantamount to an establishment of religion.

Finally, although I agree [that] courts should refrain from delving into questions whether, as a matter of religious doctrine, a particular practice is "central" to the religion, I do not think this means that the courts must turn a blind eye to the severe impact of a State's restrictions on the adherents of a minority religion. Respondents believe, and their sincerity has never been at issue, that the peyote plant embodies their deity, and eating it is an act of worship and communion. Without peyote, they could not enact the essential ritual of their religion. [This] Court must scrupulously apply its free exercise analysis to the religious claims of Native Americans, however unorthodox they may be. Otherwise, [the] First Amendment [will] offer to Native Americans merely an unfulfilled and hollow promise.

For these reasons, I conclude that Oregon's interest in enforcing its drug laws against religious use of peyote is not sufficiently compelling to outweigh respondents' right to the free exercise of their religion. Since the State could not constitutionally enforce its criminal prohibition against respondents, the interests underlying the State's drug laws cannot justify its denial of unemployment benefits. . . . The State of Oregon cannot, consistently with the Free Exercise Clause, deny respondents unemployment benefits. I dissent.

———

Note: Statutory Protections of the Exercise of Religion

1. In 1994, Congress revised the federal drug policy for American Indians, to follow the previous policy in several of the states — the policy that the state of Oregon expressly rejected on remand after *Smith I* to set the stage for the Supreme Court's decision in *Smith II*, the principal case above — by amending the American Indian Religious Freedom Act in 1994 to protect the religious use of peyote by Native Americans. 42 U.S.C. § 1996a.

2. The *Religious Freedom Restoration Act of 1993*, 42 U.S.C. § 2000bb ("RFRA"), was adopted to undo the effect of the holding in *Employment Division v. Smith* by creating a statutory cause of action for appropriate relief as a substitute for a cause of action under the Free Exercise Clause. Congress explicitly stated its purpose to restore the compelling interest analysis in the *Sherbert-Yoder* line of cases by this provision:

> Government shall not substantially burden a person's exercise of religion even if the burden results from a rule of general applicability, except [government] may substantially burden a person's exercise of religion only if it demonstrates that application of the burden to the person (1) is in furtherance of a compelling government interest; and (2) is the least restrictive means of furthering that compelling interest.

Furthermore, in more than half the states, either because the state legislature enacted a mini-RFRA statute or because the state constitution has been interpreted to afford greater protection than the *Smith II* holding, a Free Exercise-type state law claim in state court will trigger something like the heightened scrutiny of the *Sherbert-Yoder* analysis.

3. In *City of Boerne v. Flores*, 521 U.S. 507 (1997), the Supreme Court invalidated RFRA as exceeding the scope of congressional power under the Fourteenth

Amendment. Section 5 of the Fourteenth Amendment empowers Congress "to enforce" that amendment against the states. However, the Supreme Court held that Congress can legislate under § 5 only to protect a right previously recognized and defined by the courts. The Court found that by enacting RFRA Congress was attempting to create a new right or was attempting to enlarge the scope of the right to free exercise of religion. Justice O'Connor, joined by Justice Breyer, dissented. Justice O'Connor did not dispute the Court's view of Congress's § 5 power; rather, she called for the judicial overruling of *Smith*. She insisted that "the decision has harmed religious liberty" because "lower courts applying *Smith* no longer find necessary a searching judicial inquiry into the possibility of reasonably accommodating religious practice."

The *City of Boerne v. Flores* holding declared RFRA unconstitutional vis-à-vis state and local governments under the Fourteenth Amendment. But the Fourteenth Amendment does not apply to the federal government, and the RFRA statute as amended applies to any "branch, department, agency, instrumentality, and official [of] the United States." 42 U.S.C. § 2000bb-2. Therefore, RFRA's statutory regime of heightened strict scrutiny analysis is still in place for claims that the federal government has substantially burdened rights under the Free Exercise Clause.

4. In *Gonzales v. O Centro Espirita Beneficente União do Vegetal*, 546 U.S. 418 (2006), the small American branch of a Christian spiritualist sect ("UDV") with origins in the Amazon Rainforest successfully invoked RFRA to obtain a preliminary injunction prohibiting the enforcement of the federal drug laws against their communion ritual. As part of their religious service, UDV members drink "hoasca," a sacramental tea brewed from plants unique to that region which contains a hallucinogen that is a Schedule I substance and otherwise illegal under the federal Controlled Substances Act. The Government conceded that its application of the federal law would substantially burden a sincere exercise of religion by UDV adherents. The Government argued, however, that this burden did not violate RFRA, because it was the least restrictive means of advancing the compelling governmental interests underlying the federal drug laws. Writing for a unanimous Court (Justice Alito did not participate), Chief Justice Roberts explicitly reaffirmed *Smith* as a First Amendment precedent. Under RFRA's heightened statutory standard, however, the Court ruled in favor of the UDV and against the Government:

> UDV effectively demonstrated that its sincere exercise of religion was substantially burdened, and the Government failed to demonstrate that the application of the burden to the UDV would, more likely than not, be justified by the asserted compelling interests. . . . [RFRA] requires the Government to demonstrate that the compelling interest test is satisfied through application of the challenged law "to the person"—the particular claimant whose sincere exercise of religion is being substantially burdened. . . .
>
> RFRA . . . plainly contemplates that courts would recognize exceptions—that is how the law works. See 42 U.S.C. § 2000bb-1(c) ("A person whose religious exercise has been burdened in violation of this section may assert that

violation as a claim or defense in a judicial proceeding and obtain appropriate relief against a government"). . . . [The congressional] findings of the Controlled Substances Act do not preclude exceptions altogether; RFRA makes clear that it is the obligation of the courts to consider whether exceptions are required under the test set forth by Congress. . . .

Here the Government's argument for uniformity . . . rests not so much on the particular statutory program at issue as on slippery-slope concerns that could be invoked in response to any RFRA claim for an exception to a generally applicable law. The Government's argument echoes the classic rejoinder of bureaucrats throughout history: If I make an exception for you, I'll have to make one for everybody, so no exceptions. But RFRA operates by mandating consideration, under the compelling interest test, of exceptions to "rules of general applicability." 42 U.S.C. § 2000bb-1(a). Congress determined that the legislated test "is a workable test for striking sensible balances between religious liberty and competing prior governmental interests." § 2000bb(a)(5). . . .

We do not doubt that there may be instances in which a need for uniformity precludes the recognition of exceptions to generally applicable laws under RFRA. But it would have been surprising to find that this was such a case, given the longstanding exemption from the Controlled Substances Act for religious use of peyote [by Native Americans], and the fact that the very reason Congress enacted RFRA was to respond to a decision denying a claimed right to sacramental use of a controlled substance [in *Smith*]. And in fact the Government has not offered evidence demonstrating that granting the UDV an exemption would cause the kind of administrative harm recognized as a compelling interest in [any of our previous cases]. . . .

The Government repeatedly invokes Congress' findings and purposes underlying the Controlled Substances Act, but Congress had a reason for enacting RFRA, too. Congress recognized that "laws neutral toward religion may burden religious exercise as surely as laws intended to interfere with religious exercise," and legislated "the compelling interest test" as the means for the courts to "strike sensible balances between religious liberty and competing prior governmental interests." 42 U.S.C. §§ 2000bb(a)(2), (5).

We have no cause to pretend that the task assigned by Congress to the courts under RFRA is an easy one. . . . But Congress has determined that courts should strike sensible balances, pursuant to a compelling interest test that requires the Government to address the particular practice at issue. Applying that [statutory] test, we conclude that the courts below did not err in determining that the Government failed to demonstrate, at the preliminary injunction stage, a compelling interest in barring the UDV's sacramental use of hoasca.

5. *Burwell v. Hobby Lobby Stores, Inc.*, 134 S. Ct. 2751 (2014), involved Department of Health and Human Services (HHS) regulations under the Affordable Care Act of

2010 (ACA), which required specified employers' group health plans to provide coverage for all the contraceptive methods approved by the Food and Drug Administration (FDA), including some methods that have the effect of preventing an already fertilized egg from attaching to the uterus and developing any further. Religious employers, such as churches, were exempted from this contraceptive mandate, as were religious non-profit organizations with religious objections to providing contraceptive services and employers with fewer than 50 employees.

The owners of three closely held for-profit corporations challenged the regulations because their Christian beliefs were that life begins at conception and that their faith prohibited them from facilitating the contraceptive methods that operated after fertilization/conception. The sincerity of their beliefs was not questioned by anyone. The three family-owned companies were of considerable size: Hobby Lobby has 500 stores and 13,000 employees; Conestoga Wood Specialties has 950 employees; Mardel operates 35 Christian bookstores and employs 400 people. In both lawsuits, the two district courts denied a preliminary injunction. On separate appeals, the Third Circuit affirmed but the Tenth Circuit reversed and struck down the regulations. The Supreme Court divided 5 to 4 to hold that the HHS regulations violated RFRA. That statutory holding made it unnecessary to reach the First Amendment claims.

Justice Alito wrote the majority opinion joined by Chief Justice Roberts and Justices Scalia, Kennedy, and Thomas. The majority rehearsed the legislative history of RFRA and then tracked the text of the statute. First, RFRA applies to a "person's" exercise of religion. The majority concluded that Congress intended to protect religious liberty broadly to include the religious liberty of for-profit corporations in order to protect religious liberty for their shareholders, officers, and employees. Second, RFRA protects "any exercise of religion, whether or not compelled by, or central to, a system of religious belief." The majority understood RFRA to protect more religious liberty than does the First Amendment, although the majority did not explain just how much more or specifically what else the statute covers. The owners of the plaintiff corporations had a lawful right to pursue profits in conformity with their sincere individual religious beliefs. Third, the majority had "little trouble" concluding that the HHS contraceptive mandate was a "substantial burden," in the wording of the statute, on their exercise of religion. The mandate required the owners to engage in conduct that seriously violated their sincere religious beliefs under the threatened penalty of severe economic consequences, i.e., millions of dollars in fines. The majority explained that the case involved the "difficult and important question of religion and moral philosophy, namely, the circumstances under which it is wrong for a person [the owners] to perform an act that is innocent in itself but that has the effect of enabling or facilitating the commission of an immoral act by another [the employees]." Fourth, the majority applied the statutory two-pronged standard—the "compelling government interest" and "least restrictive means" analysis. The majority finessed the issue whether the government's interest in guaranteeing cost-free access to the four challenged contraceptive methods was "compelling within the meaning of RFRA" by assuming that it was. Therefore, "least restrictive means" analysis was outcome determinative:

The least-restrictive-means standard is exceptionally demanding, and it is not satisfied here. HHS has not shown that it lacks other means of achieving its desired goal without imposing a substantial burden on the exercise of religion by the objecting parties in these cases. . . . [The] most straightforward way of doing this would be for the Government to assume the cost of providing the four contraceptives at issue to any women who are unable to obtain them under their health-insurance policies due to their employers' religious objections. This would certainly be less restrictive of the plaintiffs' religious liberty, and HHS has not shown that this is not a viable alternative. . . . If, as HHS tells us, providing all women with cost-free access to all FDA-approved methods of contraception is a Government interest of the highest order, it is hard to understand HHS's argument that it cannot be required under RFRA to pay anything in order to achieve this important goal. . . .

In the end, however, we need not rely on the option of a new, government-funded program in order to conclude that the HHS regulations fail the least-restrictive-means test. HHS itself has demonstrated that it has at its disposal an approach that is less restrictive than requiring employers to fund contraceptive methods that violate their religious beliefs. As we [have] explained, HHS has already established an accommodation for nonprofit organizations with religious objections. Under that accommodation, the organization can self-certify that it opposes providing coverage for particular contraceptive services. If the organization makes such a certification, the organization's insurance issuer or third-party administrator must "expressly exclude contraceptive coverage from the group health insurance coverage provided in connection with the group health plan" and "provide separate payments for any contraceptive services required to be covered" without imposing "any cost-sharing requirements . . . on the eligible organization, the group health plan, or plan participants or beneficiaries." [We] do not decide today whether an approach of this type complies with RFRA for purposes of all religious claims. At a minimum, however, it does not impinge on the plaintiffs' religious belief that providing insurance coverage for the contraceptives at issue here violates their religion, and it serves HHS's stated interests equally well.

The majority refuted the dissent's concern that invidious discrimination in hiring could be robed in religious practice with the observation that "[the] Government has a compelling interest in providing an equal opportunity to participate in the workforce without regard to race, and prohibitions on racial discrimination are precisely tailored to achieve that critical goal." Ultimately, the majority suspected that the dissenters' "fundamental objection" was that the federal courts will be obliged to consider "a host of claims by litigants seeking a religious exemption from generally applicable laws"—a role the dissent believed is at odds with the Religion Clauses— but the majority countered that Congress enacted RFRA and Congress thus assigned that statutory role to the Third Branch.

Justice Kennedy wrote a concurring opinion that endorsed the majority's interpretation and application of RFRA statutory strict scrutiny and emphasized religious liberty. Justice Ginsburg wrote a dissenting opinion, joined by Justices Breyer, Kagan, and Sotomayor. She agreed that "[any] First Amendment Free Exercise Clause claim [the plaintiffs] might assert is foreclosed by this Court's decision in *Employment Div., Dept. of Human Resources of Ore. v. Smith* [*supra* this chapter]." In a portion of her dissent joined only by Justice Sotomayor, she squarely rejected the majority's interpretation of RFRA to apply to for-profit corporations. She further maintained that "the connection between the families' religious objections and the contraceptive coverage requirement is too attenuated to rank as substantial [under the statute]." She believed that the government's purpose to provide birth control to employees did satisfy the "compelling interest" prong of the statute. She was persuaded that [the] Government has shown that there is no less restrictive, equally effective means that would both (1) satisfy the challengers' religious objections to providing insurance coverage for certain contraceptives (which they believe cause abortions); and (2) carry out the objective of the ACA's contraceptive coverage requirement, to ensure that female employees receive, at no cost to them, the preventive care needed to safeguard their health and well-being. She cautioned the majority:

> There is an overriding interest, I believe, in keeping the courts "out of the business of evaluating the relative merits of differing religious claims," or the sincerity with which an asserted religious belief is held. Indeed, approving some religious claims while deeming others unworthy of accommodation could be "perceived as favoring one religion over another," the very "risk the Establishment Clause was designed to preclude." The Court, I fear, has ventured into a minefield, by its immoderate reading of RFRA. I would confine religious exemptions under that Act to organizations formed "for a religious purpose," "engaged primarily in carrying out that religious purpose," and not "engaged . . . substantially in the exchange of goods or services for money beyond nominal amounts."

Justices Breyer and Kagan also filed a short dissenting opinion declining to vote either with the majority opinion ("yes") or with Justice Ginsburg's dissent ("no") on the question whether for-profit corporations or their owners may bring claims under RFRA.

6. In 2000, Congress enacted the *Religious Land Use and Institutionalized Persons Act*, 42 U.S.C. § 2000cc ("RLUIPA"). This statute requires that the government satisfy the strict scrutiny test when it significantly burdens religion in two specific contexts: land use regulations and the treatment of institutionalized persons. Congress expressly invoked its Spending Clause and Commerce Clause powers as the basis for enactment, in order to distinguish RFRA and the Fourteenth Amendment holding in *City of Boerne v. Flores*. And in *Cutter v. Wilkinson*, 544 U.S. 709 (2005), the Supreme Court unanimously upheld the institutionalized persons provision of RLUIPA as a valid religious accommodation that did not violate the Establishment Clause. Defendant state corrections officials had challenged RLUIPA on its face to defend against a suit brought by prisoners of several non-mainstream religions (the Satanist, Wicca, Asatru religions, and the Church of Jesus Christ Christian). The prisoners were challenging various prison regulations and practices that they claimed substantially burdened their free exercise rights protected by the statute.

7. In *Holt v. Hobbs*, 135 S. Ct. 853 (2015), the Court unanimously ruled in favor of a prisoner who sought a religious exemption under RLUIPA from a state prison regulation prohibiting beards. Petitioner Gregory Holt, also known as Abdul Maalik Muhammad, was a devout Muslim. He objected to the Arkansas Department of Corrections' [Department] grooming policy, which provided that "no inmates will be permitted to wear facial hair other than a neatly trimmed mustache that does not extend beyond the corner of the mouth or over the lip." The policy made no exception for inmates who object on religious grounds, but it did include an exemption for prisoners with a medically diagnosed dermatological problem to allow facial hair no longer than 1/4 of an inch. Although he believed that his faith required him not to trim his beard at all, petitioner requested that he be permitted to grow a 1/2-inch beard. When the prison officials denied his request, petitioner filed a pro se complaint in U.S. District Court challenging the grooming policy under RLUIPA. The District Court ruled against the petitioner and upheld the prison regulation. The U.S. Court of Appeals for the Eighth Circuit affirmed in a brief per curiam opinion, holding that the Department had satisfied its statutory burden of showing that the grooming policy was the least restrictive means of furthering its compelling security interests. The Court of Appeals emphasized that the prison officials deserved judicial deference due to their expertise and experience. The Supreme Court reversed by a unanimous vote. Justice Alito wrote for the Court. Justices Ginsburg and Sotomayor joined the opinion of the Court but wrote short concurring opinions.

The Court's opinion underscored the expansive protection for religious liberty under RLUIPA — in comparison to the narrower protection afforded under the Free Exercise Clause. The Department's regulation that required petitioner to shave his beard or suffer serious disciplinary action substantially burdened his sincere religious belief. It mattered not that the Department had accommodated petitioner's other religious exercises, for example, to use a prayer rug, to adhere to dietary restrictions, and to observe religious holidays. The Department could not argue that the burden was insignificant because petitioner's religion would somehow "credit" him for attempting to grow a beard and being forced to shave. The Department could not argue that some Muslim men do not believe they have a religious duty to grow their beard. Even if that were so, the protection of RLUIPA, like the protection of the Free Exercise Clause, is not limited to only those beliefs that are accepted by all members of a religious sect.

Once the petitioner met his burden to show that the grooming policy substantially burdened his exercise of religion, the burden shifted to the Department to demonstrate that the ban on beards was the least restrictive means of furthering a compelling government interest. The Department argued that the Court should defer to the expertise and experience of the prison officials in general. The Court countered that

"RLUIPA, like RFRA, contemplates a 'more focused' inquiry and 'requires the Government to demonstrate that the compelling interest test is satisfied through application of the challenged law "to the person"—the particular claimant whose sincere exercise of religion is being substantially burdened.'" The Court continued its focused inquiry:

> We readily agree that the Department has a compelling interest in staunching the flow of contraband into and within its facilities, but the argument that this interest would be seriously compromised by allowing an inmate to grow a 1/2-inch beard is hard to take seriously. . . . An item of contraband would have to be very small indeed to be concealed by a 1/2-inch beard, and a prisoner seeking to hide an item in such a short beard would have to find a way to prevent the item from falling out. Since the Department does not demand that inmates have shaved heads or short crew cuts, it is hard to see why an inmate would seek to hide contraband in a 1/2-inch beard rather than in the longer hair on his head. . . . [The] Department failed to establish that it could not satisfy its security concerns by simply searching petitioner's beard. The Department already searches prisoners' hair and clothing, and it presumably examines the 1/4-inch beards of inmates with dermatological conditions. . . . [The] Department's interest in eliminating contraband cannot sustain its refusal to allow petitioner to grow a 1/2-inch beard.

The second compelling interest put forward by the Department was "preventing prisoners from disguising their identities." According to the prison officials, "bearded inmates could shave their beards and change their appearance in order to enter restricted areas within the prison, to escape, and to evade apprehension after escaping." The Court acknowledged that this was also a compelling government interest but concluded that the no-beard policy was not the least restrictive means because the Department could photograph the prisoner with and without a beard even though the Department argued that practice would not be sufficient. The Court went further to conclude that the no-beard policy was "substantially under-inclusive" under RLUIPA. The Department already allowed 1/4-inch beards and haircuts longer than 1/2-inch. Therefore, the Court concluded that "[although] the Department's proclaimed objectives are to stop the flow of contraband and to facilitate prisoner identification, 'the proffered objectives are not pursued with respect to analogous nonreligious conduct,' which suggests that 'those interests could be achieved by narrower ordinances that burdened religion to a far lesser degree.' *Church of Lukumi Babalu Aye, Inc. v. Hialeah* (1993) [*infra* this chapter]." Finally, the Court challenged correctional officials to accept their general obligation under the federal statute to protect the religious practices of prisoners while maintaining the security and safety of prisons:

> We emphasize that although RLUIPA provides substantial protection for the religious exercise of institutionalized persons, it also affords prison officials ample ability to maintain security. We highlight three ways in which this is so. First, in applying RLUIPA's statutory standard, courts should not blind themselves to the fact that the analysis is conducted in the prison setting.

Second, if an institution suspects that an inmate is using religious activity to cloak illicit conduct, "prison officials may appropriately question whether a prisoner's religiosity, asserted as the basis for a requested accommodation, is authentic." *Cutter v. Wilkinson* [*supra* this Note]. *See also Hobby Lobby* [*supra* this Note]. Third, even if a claimant's religious belief is sincere, an institution might be entitled to withdraw an accommodation if the claimant abuses the exemption in a manner that undermines the prison's compelling interests.

Justice Sotomayor's concurring opinion sounded more supportive of prison officials generally but, at the same time, was skeptical of this particular no-beard policy. Justice Ginsburg's one-paragraph separate concurring opinion cited her dissenting opinion in *Burwell v. Hobby Lobby* (*supra* this Note) in which she previously sounded a caution about judicially-determined religious exemptions under the companion free exercise exemption statute (RFRA).

8. Title VII of the Civil Rights Act of 1964 makes it an unlawful employment practice to discriminate against someone on the basis of race, color, religion, national origin, or sex. The Equal Employment Opportunity Commission has jurisdiction over religious discrimination in the workplace. Title VII also requires that employers reasonably accommodate applicants' and employees' sincerely held religious practices, unless doing so would impose an undue hardship on the operation of the employer's business. The *EEOC Online Fact Sheet* (2017) provides this overview:

Title VII of the Civil Rights Act of 1964 prohibits employers from discriminating against individuals because of their religion (or lack of religious belief) in hiring, firing, or any other terms and conditions of employment. The law also prohibits job segregation based on religion, such as assigning an employee to a non-customer contact position because of actual or feared customer preference.

In addition, the Act requires employers to reasonably accommodate the religious beliefs and practices of applicants and employees, unless doing so would cause more than a minimal burden on the operation of the employer's business. A reasonable religious accommodation is any adjustment to the work environment that will allow the employee to practice his religion. Flexible scheduling, voluntary shift substitutions or swaps, job reassignments lateral transfers, and exceptions to dress or grooming rules are examples of accommodating an employee's religious beliefs.

Whether a particular accommodation would pose an undue hardship on the employer's business depends on the individual circumstances. For example, an accommodation may cause undue hardship if it is costly, compromises workplace safety, decreases workplace efficiency, infringes on the rights of other employees, or requires other employees to do more than their share of potentially hazardous or burdensome work. Undue hardship also may be shown if the request for an accommodation violates others' job rights established through a collective bargaining agreement or seniority system.

Title VII also prohibits religious harassment of employees, such as offensive remarks about a person's religious beliefs or practices. Although the law doesn't prohibit simple teasing, offhand comments, or isolated incidents that aren't very serious, harassment can be unlawful when it is so frequent or severe that it creates a hostile or offensive work environment or when it results in an adverse employment decision (such as the victim being fired or demoted).

It is also unlawful to retaliate against an individual for opposing employment practices that discriminate based on religion or for filing a discrimination charge, testifying, or participating in any way in an investigation, proceeding, or litigation under Title VII.

9. Congress has declared a commitment to furthering religious freedom as part of the official foreign policy of the United States. The *International Religious Freedom Act of 1998*, Pub. L. No. 105-292, 112 Stat. 2787, was passed unanimously and signed into law by President Clinton. That statute (sometimes referred to as "IRFA") mandated the establishment of an Office of International Religious Freedom within the Department of State, headed by an Ambassador-at-Large who acts as the principal advisor to the President and Secretary of State in matters concerning religious freedom abroad. The President is required to apply sanctions of various kinds to violator countries. The statute also established the United States Commission on International Religious Freedom and created a Special Adviser on International Religious Freedom at the National Security Council.

10. What do you make of these related phenomena: Congress and state legislatures seem willing to go out of their way to protect a robust version of individual religious liberty, while at the same time the Justices seem to be backing away from vigorous judicial review to promote the values underlying the Free Exercise Clause? What are the possible reasons for this constitutional role reversal? What, if any, are the implications of these legislative initiatives for judicial interpretation of the Free Exercise Clause? How do you judge the judges? In these cases interpreting and applying the federal free exercise exemption statutes—RFRA and RLUIPA—are the Justices merely respecting congressional policy favoring religious exercise or are the Justices coming close to indirectly violating the Establishment Clause? We will explore the interrelationships among the clauses in the next chapter.

C. Discrimination against Religion

Government cannot regulate religion, except as the incidental effect of neutral and generally applicable law, or to serve the compelling interest by the least restrictive means. Laws are subject to the compelling interest test if they overtly discriminate against religion, if they are enacted because of an anti-religious motive, or if their anti-religious effect is exclusive or dominant instead of merely incidental.

Those are the opening lines from the *Brief of Petitioner*— the prevailing party—in the next case. Is that a complete and accurate statement of the law of the Free Exercise Clause? When is a law or regulation "neutral"? When is a law or regulation of "general applicability"? What is "overt discrimination"? What is an "anti-religious motive"? How do you determine when there is an unconstitutional, objectively unequal treatment of religious practices and analogous non-religious conduct?

Church of the Lukumi Babalu Aye, Inc. v. City of Hialeah
508 U.S. 520 (1993)

Justice Kennedy delivered the opinion of the Court, except as to Part II-A-2.*

The principle that government may not enact laws that suppress religious belief or practice is so well understood that few violations are recorded in our opinions. [This] fundamental nonpersecution principle of the First Amendment was implicated here. . . . [The] laws in question were enacted by officials who did not understand, failed to perceive, or chose to ignore the fact that their official actions violated the Nation's essential commitment to religious freedom. The challenged laws had an impermissible object; and in all events the principle of general applicability was violated because the secular ends asserted in defense of the laws were pursued only with respect to conduct motivated by religious beliefs. We invalidate the challenged enactments. . . .

I

A

This case involves practices of the Santeria religion, which originated in the 19th century. When hundreds of thousands of members of the Yoruba people were brought as slaves from western Africa to Cuba, their traditional African religion absorbed significant elements of Roman Catholicism. The resulting syncretion, or fusion, is Santeria, "the way of the saints." The Cuban Yoruba express their devotion to spirits, called *orishas*, through the iconography of Catholic saints, Catholic symbols are often present at Santeria rites, and Santeria devotees attend the Catholic sacraments.

The Santeria faith teaches that every individual has a destiny from God, a destiny fulfilled with the aid and energy of the *orishas*. The basis of the Santeria religion is the nurture of a personal relation with the *orishas*, and one of the principal forms of devotion is an animal sacrifice. . . . According to Santeria teaching, the *orishas* are powerful but not immortal. They depend for survival on the sacrifice. Sacrifices are performed at birth, marriage, and death rites, for the cure of the sick, for the initiation of new members and priests, and during an annual celebration. Animals sacrificed in Santeria rituals include chickens, pigeons, doves, ducks, guinea pigs, goats,

---

* The Chief Justice, Justice Scalia, and Justice Thomas join all but Part II-A-2 of this opinion. Justice White joins all but Part II-A of this opinion. Justice Souter joins only Parts I, III, and IV of this opinion.

sheep, and turtles. The animals are killed by the cutting of the carotid arteries in the neck. The sacrificed animal is cooked and eaten, except after healing and death rituals.

Santeria adherents faced widespread persecution in Cuba, so the religion and its rituals were practiced in secret. The open practice of Santeria and its rites remains infrequent. The religion was brought to this Nation most often by exiles from the Cuban revolution. [There] are at least 50,000 practitioners in South Florida today.

B

Petitioner Church of the Lukumi Babalu Aye, Inc. (Church), is a not-for-profit corporation organized under Florida law in 1973. The Church and its congregants practice the Santeria religion. The president of the Church is petitioner Ernesto Pichardo, who is also the Church's priest and holds the religious title of *Italero*, the second highest in the Santeria faith. In April 1987, the Church leased land in the city of Hialeah, Florida, and announced plans to establish a house of worship as well as a school, cultural center, and museum. Pichardo indicated that the Church's goal was to bring the practice of the Santeria faith, including its ritual of animal sacrifice, into the open. The Church began the process of obtaining utility service and receiving the necessary licensing, inspection, and zoning approvals. . . .

The prospect of a Santeria church in their midst was distressing to many members of the Hialeah community, and the announcement of the plans to open a Santeria church in Hialeah prompted the city council to hold an emergency public session on June 9, 1987. . . . First, the city council adopted Resolution 87-66, which noted the "concern" expressed by residents of the city "that certain religions may propose to engage in practices which are inconsistent with public morals, peace or safety," and declared that "the City reiterates its commitment to a prohibition against any and all acts of any and all religious groups which are inconsistent with public morals, peace or safety." Next, the council approved an emergency ordinance, Ordinance 87-40, which incorporated in full, except as to penalty, Florida's animal cruelty laws. Among other things, the incorporated state law subjected to criminal punishment "whoever . . . unnecessarily or cruelly . . . kills any animal."

The city council desired to undertake further legislative action, but Florida law prohibited a municipality from enacting legislation relating to animal cruelty that conflicted with state law. To obtain clarification, Hialeah's city attorney requested an opinion from the attorney general of Florida as to whether [the existing state statute] prohibited "a religious group from sacrificing an animal in a religious ritual or practice" and whether the city could enact ordinances "making religious animal sacrifice unlawful." The attorney general responded [that] the "ritual sacrifice of animals for purposes other than food consumption" was not a "necessary" killing and so was prohibited. . . . He advised [that] a city ordinance prohibiting it would not be in conflict.

The city council responded at first with a hortatory enactment, Resolution 87-90, that noted its residents' "great concern regarding the possibility of public ritualistic animal sacrifices" and the state-law prohibition. The resolution declared the city policy "to oppose the ritual sacrifices of animals" within Hialeah and announced that any person or organization practicing animal sacrifice "will be prosecuted."

In September 1987, the city council adopted three substantive ordinances addressing the issue of religious animal sacrifice. Ordinance 87-52 defined "sacrifice" as "to unnecessarily kill, torment, torture, or mutilate an animal in a public or private ritual or ceremony not for the primary purpose of food consumption," and prohibited owning or possessing an animal "intending to use such animal for food purposes." It restricted application of this prohibition, however, to any individual or group that "kills, slaughters or sacrifices animals for any type of ritual, regardless of whether or not the flesh or blood of the animal is to be consumed." The ordinance contained an exemption for slaughtering by "licensed establishment[s]" of animals "specifically raised for food purposes." Declaring, moreover, that the city council "has determined that the sacrificing of animals within the city limits is contrary to the public health, safety, welfare and morals of the community," the city council adopted Ordinance 87-71. That ordinance defined "sacrifice" as had Ordinance 87-52, and then provided that "it shall be unlawful for any person, persons, corporations or associations to sacrifice any animal within the corporate limits of the City of Hialeah, Florida." The final Ordinance, 87-72, defined "slaughter" as "the killing of animals for food" and prohibited slaughter outside of areas zoned for slaughterhouse use. The ordinance provided an exemption, however, for the slaughter or processing for sale of "small numbers of hogs and/or cattle per week in accordance with an exemption provided by state law." All ordinances and resolutions passed the city council by unanimous vote. Violations of each of the four ordinances were punishable by fines not exceeding $500 or imprisonment not exceeding 60 days, or both.

Following enactment of these ordinances, the Church and Pichardo filed this action. . . . [The] District Court ruled for the city, finding no violation of petitioners' rights under the Free Exercise Clause. . . . The Court of Appeals for the Eleventh Circuit affirmed in a one-paragraph *per curiam* opinion. . . .

II

. . . The city does not argue that Santeria is not a "religion" within the meaning of the First Amendment. Nor could it. Although the practice of animal sacrifice may seem abhorrent to some, "religious beliefs need not be acceptable, logical, consistent, or comprehensible to others in order to merit First Amendment protection." Given the historical association between animal sacrifice and religious worship, petitioners' assertion that animal sacrifice is an integral part of their religion "cannot be deemed bizarre or incredible." Neither the city nor the courts below, moreover, have questioned the sincerity of petitioners' professed desire to conduct animal sacrifices for religious reasons. . . .

[Our] cases establish the general proposition that a law that is neutral and of general applicability need not be justified by a compelling governmental interest even if the law has the incidental effect of burdening a particular religious practice. *Employment Division v. Smith* (1990) [*supra* this chapter]. Neutrality and general applicability are interrelated. . . . A law failing to satisfy these requirements must be justified by a compelling governmental interest and must be narrowly tailored to advance that interest. These ordinances fail to satisfy the *Smith* requirements. . . .

A

[The] First Amendment forbids an official purpose to disapprove of a particular religion or of religion in general. These cases, however, for the most part have addressed governmental efforts to benefit religion or particular religions. . . . Petitioners allege an attempt to disfavor their religion. . . .

At a minimum, the protections of the Free Exercise Clause pertain if the law at issue discriminates against some or all religious beliefs or regulates or prohibits conduct because it is undertaken for religious reasons. Indeed, it was "historical instances of religious persecution and intolerance that gave concern to those who drafted the Free Exercise Clause." These principles, though not often at issue in our Free Exercise Clause cases, have played a role in some. In *McDaniel v. Paty*, 435 U.S. 618 (1978), for example, we invalidated a state law that disqualified members of the clergy from holding certain public offices, because it "impose[d] special disabilities on the basis of . . . religious status." On the same principle, in *Fowler v. Rhode Island*, 345 U.S. 67 (1953), we found that a municipal ordinance was applied in an unconstitutional manner when interpreted to prohibit preaching in a public park by a Jehovah's Witness but to permit preaching during the course of a Catholic mass or Protestant church service.

1

Although a law targeting religious beliefs as such is never permissible, if the object of a law is to infringe upon or restrict practices because of their religious motivation, the law is not neutral; and it is invalid unless it is justified by a compelling interest and is narrowly tailored to advance that interest. There are, of course, many ways of demonstrating that the object or purpose of a law is the suppression of religion or religious conduct. To determine the object of a law, we must begin with its text, for the minimum requirement of neutrality is that a law not discriminate on its face. A law lacks facial neutrality if it refers to a religious practice without a secular meaning discernible from the language or context. Petitioners contend that three of the ordinances fail this test of facial neutrality because they use the words "sacrifice" and "ritual," words with strong religious connotations. We agree that these words are consistent with the claim of facial discrimination, but the argument is not conclusive. The words "sacrifice" and "ritual" have a religious origin, but current use admits also of secular meanings. The ordinances, furthermore, define "sacrifice" in secular terms, without referring to religious practices.

We reject the contention advanced by the city that our inquiry must end with the text of the laws at issue. Facial neutrality is not determinative. The Free Exercise Clause, like the Establishment Clause, extends beyond facial discrimination. The Clause "forbids subtle departures from neutrality," and "covert suppression of particular religious beliefs." Official action that targets religious conduct for distinctive treatment cannot be shielded by mere compliance with the requirement of facial neutrality. The Free Exercise Clause protects against governmental hostility which is masked as well as overt. . . .

The record in this case compels the conclusion that suppression of the central element of the Santeria worship service was the object of the ordinances. First, though use of the words "sacrifice" and "ritual" does not compel a finding of improper targeting of the Santeria religion, the choice of these words is support for our conclusion. [The] text of the city council's enactments discloses the improper attempt to target Santeria. Resolution 87-66 [recited] that "residents and citizens of the City of Hialeah have expressed their concern that certain religions may propose to engage in practices which are inconsistent with public morals, peace or safety," and "reiterate[d]" the city's commitment to prohibit "any and all [such] acts of any and all religious groups." No one suggests, and on this record it cannot be maintained, that city officials had in mind a religion other than Santeria.

It becomes evident that these ordinances target Santeria sacrifice when the ordinances' operation is considered. Apart from the text, the effect of a law in its real operation is strong evidence of its object. To be sure, adverse impact will not always lead to a finding of impermissible targeting. . . . The subject at hand does implicate, of course, multiple concerns unrelated to religious animosity, for example, the suffering or mistreatment visited upon the sacrificed animals and health hazards from improper disposal. But the ordinances when considered together disclose an object remote from these legitimate concerns. The design of these laws accomplishes instead a "religious gerrymander," an impermissible attempt to target petitioners and their religious practices.

It is a necessary conclusion that almost the only conduct subject to Ordinances 87-40, 87-52, and 87-71 is the religious exercise of Santeria church members. The texts show that they were drafted in tandem to achieve this result.

Ordinance 87-71 [prohibits] the sacrifice of animals, but defines sacrifice as "to unnecessarily kill . . . an animal in a public or private ritual or ceremony not for the primary purpose of food consumption." The definition excludes almost all killings of animals except for religious sacrifice, and the primary purpose requirement narrows the proscribed category even further, in particular by exempting kosher slaughter. We need not discuss whether this differential treatment of two religions is itself an independent constitutional violation. It suffices to recite this feature of the law as support for our conclusion that Santeria alone was the exclusive legislative concern. The net result of the gerrymander is that few if any killings of animals are prohibited other than Santeria sacrifice, which is proscribed because it occurs during a ritual or ceremony and its primary purpose is to make an offering to the *orishas*, not food consumption. Indeed, careful drafting ensured that, although Santeria sacrifice is prohibited, killings that are no more necessary or humane in almost all other circumstances are unpunished.

Ordinance 87-52 [prohibits] the "possession, sacrifice, or slaughter" of an animal with the "intent to use such animal for food purposes." This prohibition, extending to the keeping of an animal as well as the killing itself, applies if the animal is killed in "any type of ritual" and there is an intent to use the animal for food, whether or not it is in fact consumed for food. The ordinance exempts, however, "any licensed [food] establishment" with regard to "any animals which are specifically raised for food purposes," if the activity is permitted by zoning and other laws. This exception, too, seems intended to cover kosher slaughter. Again, the burden of the ordinance, in practical terms, falls on Santeria adherents but almost no others: If the killing is — unlike most Santeria sacrifices — unaccompanied by the intent to use the animal for food, then it is not [prohibited]; if the killing is specifically for food but does not occur during the course of "any type of ritual," it again falls outside the prohibition; and if the killing is for food and occurs during the course of a ritual, it is still exempted if it occurs in a properly zoned and licensed establishment and involves animals "specifically raised for food purposes." A pattern of exemptions parallels the pattern of narrow prohibitions. Each contributes to the gerrymander.

Ordinance 87-40 incorporates the Florida animal cruelty statute, Fla. Stat. § 828.12 (1987). Its prohibition is broad on its face, punishing "whoever . . . unnecessarily . . . kills any animal." The city claims that this ordinance is the epitome of a neutral prohibition. The problem, however, is the interpretation given to the ordinance by respondent and the Florida attorney general. Killings for religious reasons are deemed unnecessary, whereas most other killings fall outside the prohibition. The city, on what seems to be a *per se* basis, deems hunting, slaughter of animals for food, eradication of insects and pests, and euthanasia as necessary. There is no indication in the record that respondent has concluded that hunting or fishing for sport is unnecessary. . . . Further, because it requires an evaluation of the particular justification for the killing, this ordinance represents a system of "individualized governmental assessment of the reasons for the relevant conduct." *Employment Division v. Smith* (1990). [In] circumstances in which individualized exemptions from a general requirement are available, the government "may not refuse to extend that system to cases of 'religious hardship' without compelling reason." Respondent's application of the ordinance's test of necessity devalues religious reasons for killing by judging them to be of lesser import than nonreligious reasons. Thus, religious practice is being singled out for discriminatory treatment. . . .

The legitimate governmental interests in protecting the public health and preventing cruelty to animals could be addressed by restrictions stopping far short of a flat prohibition of all Santeria sacrificial practice. If improper disposal, not the sacrifice itself, is the harm to be prevented, the city could have imposed a general regulation on the disposal of organic garbage. It did not do so. Indeed, counsel for the city conceded at oral argument that, under the ordinances, Santeria sacrifices would be illegal even if they occurred in licensed, inspected, and zoned slaughterhouses. Thus, these broad ordinances prohibit Santeria sacrifice even when it does not threaten the city's interest in the public health. . . . The neutrality of a law is suspect if First Amendment freedoms are curtailed to prevent isolated collateral harms not themselves prohibited by direct regulation.

Under similar analysis, narrower regulation would achieve the city's interest in preventing cruelty to animals. With regard to the city's interest in ensuring the adequate care of animals, regulation of conditions and treatment, regardless of why an animal is kept, is the logical response to the city's concern, not a prohibition on possession for the purpose of sacrifice. The same is true for the city's interest in prohibiting cruel methods of killing. [Killing] an animal by the "simultaneous and instantaneous severance of the carotid arteries with a sharp instrument"—the method used in kosher slaughter—is approved as humane. [Although] Santeria sacrifice also results in severance of the carotid arteries, the method used during sacrifice is less reliable and therefore [is deemed] not humane. If the city has a real concern that other methods are less humane, however, the subject of the regulation should be the method of slaughter itself, not a religious classification that is said to bear some general relation to it.

Ordinance 87-72—unlike the three other ordinances—does appear to apply to substantial nonreligious conduct and not to be overbroad. For our purposes here, however, the four substantive ordinances may be treated as a group for neutrality purposes. Ordinance 87-72 was passed the same day as Ordinance 87-71 and was enacted, as were the three others, in direct response to the opening of the Church. It would be implausible to suggest that the three other ordinances, but not Ordinance 87-72, had as their object the suppression of religion. We need not decide whether Ordinance 87-72 could survive constitutional scrutiny if it existed separately; it must be invalidated because it functions, with the rest of the enactments in question, to suppress Santeria religious worship.

2*

[We] may determine the city council's object from both direct and circumstantial evidence. Relevant evidence includes, among other things, the historical background of the decision under challenge, the specific series of events leading to the enactment or official policy in question, and the legislative or administrative history, including contemporaneous statements made by members of the decisionmaking body. These objective factors bear on the question of discriminatory object.

That the ordinances were enacted "'because of,' not merely 'in spite of,'" their suppression of Santeria religious practice is revealed by the events preceding their enactment. [Here the opinion detailed the public controversy, citizen testimony, and statements made by the members of the city council at the hearings and meetings leading to the enactment of the ordinances.] This [legislative] history discloses the object of the ordinances to target animal sacrifice by Santeria worshippers because of its religious motivation.

3

In sum, the neutrality inquiry leads to one conclusion: The ordinances had as their object the suppression of religion. The pattern we have recited discloses animosity to Santeria adherents and their religious practices; the ordinances by their own terms

---

* [*Editor's note.* Only Justice Stevens joined this part of Justice Kennedy's opinion.]

target this religious exercise; the texts of the ordinances were gerrymandered with care to proscribe religious killings of animals but to exclude almost all secular killings; and the ordinances suppress much more religious conduct than is necessary in order to achieve the legitimate ends asserted in their defense. These ordinances are not neutral. . . .

B

We turn next to a second requirement of the Free Exercise Clause, the rule that laws burdening religious practice must be of general applicability. *Employment Division v. Smith* (1990). . . . The Free Exercise Clause "protect[s] religious observers against unequal treatment," and inequality results when a legislature decides that the governmental interests it seeks to advance are worthy of being pursued only against conduct with a religious motivation. . . .

Respondent claims that Ordinances 87-40, 87-52, and 87-71 advance two interests: protecting the public health and preventing cruelty to animals. The ordinances are underinclusive for those ends. They fail to prohibit nonreligious conduct that endangers these interests in a similar or greater degree than Santeria sacrifice does. . . .

Despite the city's proffered interest in preventing cruelty to animals, the ordinances are drafted with care to forbid few killings but those occasioned by religious sacrifice. Many types of animal deaths or kills for nonreligious reasons are either not prohibited or approved by express provision. For example, fishing [is] legal. Extermination of mice and rats within a home is also permitted. Florida law incorporated by Ordinance 87-40 sanctions euthanasia of "stray, neglected, abandoned, or unwanted animals"; destruction of animals judicially removed from their owners "for humanitarian reasons" or when the animal "is of no commercial value"; the infliction of pain or suffering "in the interest of medical science"; the placing of poison in one's yard or enclosure; and the use of a live animal "to pursue or take wildlife or to participate in any hunting"; and "to hunt wild hogs."

[The city] asserts, however, that animal sacrifice is "different" from the animal killings that are permitted by law. According to the city, it is "self-evident" that killing animals for food is "important"; the eradication of insects and pests is "obviously justified"; and the euthanasia of excess animals "makes sense." These *ipse dixits* do not explain why religion alone must bear the burden of the ordinances, when many of these secular killings fall within the city's interest in preventing the cruel treatment of animals.

The ordinances are also underinclusive with regard to the city's interest in public health, which is threatened by the disposal of animal carcasses in open public places and the consumption of uninspected meat. Neither interest is pursued by respondent with regard to conduct that is not motivated by religious conviction. The health risks posed by the improper disposal of animal carcasses are the same whether Santeria sacrifice or some nonreligious killing preceded it. The city does not, however, prohibit hunters from bringing their kill to their houses, nor does it regulate disposal after their activity. Despite substantial testimony at trial that the same public health hazards result from improper disposal of garbage by restaurants, restaurants are outside the scope of the ordinances. Improper disposal is a general problem that causes substantial health risks, but which respondent addresses only when it results from religious exercise.

The ordinances are underinclusive as well with regard to the health risk posed by consumption of uninspected meat. Under the city's ordinances, hunters may eat their kill and fishermen may eat their catch without undergoing governmental inspection. . . . The asserted interest in inspected meat is not pursued in contexts similar to that of religious animal sacrifice.

Ordinance 87-72, which prohibits the slaughter of animals outside of areas zoned for slaughterhouses, is underinclusive on its face. The ordinance includes an exemption for "any person, group, or organization" that "slaughters or processes for sale, small numbers of hogs and/or cattle per week in accordance with an exemption provided by state law." Respondent has not explained why commercial operations that slaughter "small numbers" of hogs and cattle do not implicate its professed desire to prevent cruelty to animals and preserve the public health. Although the city has classified Santeria sacrifice as slaughter, subjecting it to this ordinance, it does not regulate other killings for food in like manner.

We conclude, in sum, that each of Hialeah's ordinances pursues the city's governmental interests only against conduct motivated by religious belief. The ordinances "have every appearance of a prohibition that society is prepared to impose upon [Santeria worshippers] but not upon itself." This precise evil is what the requirement of general applicability is designed to prevent.

III

A law burdening religious practice that is not neutral or not of general application must undergo the most rigorous of scrutiny. To satisfy the commands of the First Amendment, a law restrictive of religious practice must advance "'interests of the highest order'" and must be narrowly tailored in pursuit of those interests. . . . A law that targets religious conduct for distinctive treatment or advances legitimate governmental interests only against conduct with a religious motivation will survive strict scrutiny only in rare cases. It follows from what we have already said that these ordinances cannot withstand this scrutiny.

First, even were the governmental interests compelling, the ordinances are not drawn in narrow terms to accomplish those interests. [All] four ordinances are overbroad or underinclusive in substantial respects. The proffered objectives are not pursued with respect to analogous nonreligious conduct, and those interests could be achieved by narrower ordinances that burdened religion to a far lesser degree. The absence of narrow tailoring suffices to establish the invalidity of the ordinances.

Respondent has not demonstrated, moreover, that, in the context of these ordinances, its governmental interests are compelling. Where government restricts only conduct protected by the First Amendment and fails to enact feasible measures to restrict other conduct producing substantial harm or alleged harm of the same sort, the interest given in justification of the restriction is not compelling. It is established in our strict scrutiny jurisprudence that "a law cannot be regarded as protecting an interest 'of the highest order' . . . when it leaves appreciable damage to that supposedly vital interest unprohibited." [The] ordinances are underinclusive to a substantial extent with respect to each of the interests that respondent has asserted, and it is only conduct motivated by religious conviction that bears the weight of the governmental restrictions. There can be no serious claim that those interests justify the ordinances.

IV

The Free Exercise Clause commits government itself to religious tolerance, and upon even slight suspicion that proposals for state intervention stem from animosity to religion or distrust of its practices, all officials must pause to remember their own high duty to the Constitution and to the rights it secures. Those in office must be resolute in resisting importunate demands and must ensure that the sole reasons for imposing the burdens of law and regulation are secular. Legislators may not devise mechanisms, overt or disguised, designed to persecute or oppress a religion or its practices. The laws here in question were enacted contrary to these constitutional principles, and they are void.

Reversed.

JUSTICE SCALIA, with whom THE CHIEF JUSTICE joins, concurring in part and concurring in the judgment. [Omitted. Justice Scalia objected to the judicial inquiry into the subjective motivations of lawmakers generally and of the Hialeah City Council in this case.]

JUSTICE SOUTER, concurring in part and concurring in the judgment. [Omitted. Justice Souter sought to distinguish *Employment Division v. Smith* (1990) and called for a reexamination of that decision.]

JUSTICE BLACKMUN, with whom JUSTICE O'CONNOR joins, concurring in the judgment.

The Court holds today that the city of Hialeah violated the First and Fourteenth Amendments when it passed a set of restrictive ordinances explicitly directed at petitioners' religious practice. With this holding I agree. I write separately to emphasize that the First Amendment's protection of religion extends beyond those rare occasions on which the government explicitly targets religion (or a particular religion) for disfavored treatment, as is done in this case. . . . I continue to believe that *Employment Division v. Smith* (1990) was wrongly decided, because it ignored the value of religious freedom as an affirmative individual liberty and treated the Free Exercise Clause as no more than an antidiscrimination principle. . . .

When the State enacts legislation that intentionally or unintentionally places a burden upon religiously motivated practice, it must justify that burden by "showing that it is the least restrictive means of achieving some compelling state interest." A State may no more create an underinclusive statute, one that fails truly to promote its purported compelling interest, than it may create an overinclusive statute, one that encompasses more protected conduct than necessary to achieve its goal. In the latter circumstance, the broad scope of the statute is unnecessary to serve the interest, and the statute fails for that reason. In the former situation, the fact that allegedly harmful conduct falls outside the statute's scope belies a governmental assertion that it has genuinely pursued an interest "of the highest order." . . .

In this case, the ordinances at issue are both overinclusive and underinclusive in relation to the state interests they purportedly serve. They are overinclusive, as the majority correctly explains, because the "legitimate governmental interests in protecting the public health and preventing cruelty to animals could be addressed by restrictions stopping far short of a flat prohibition of all Santeria sacrificial practice." They are underinclusive as well, because "despite the city's proffered interest in preventing cruelty to animals, the ordinances are drafted with care to forbid few killings but those occasioned by religious sacrifice." Moreover, the "ordinances are also underinclusive with regard to the city's interest in public health. . . ."

When a law discriminates against religion as such, as do the ordinances in this case, it automatically will fail strict scrutiny under *Sherbert v. Verner* (1963) [*supra* this chapter]. This is true because a law that targets religious practice for disfavored treatment both burdens the free exercise of religion and, by definition, is not precisely tailored to a compelling governmental interest.

Thus, unlike the majority, I do not believe that "[a] law burdening religious practice that is not neutral or not of general application must undergo the most rigorous of scrutiny." In my view, regulation that targets religion in this way, *ipso facto*, fails strict scrutiny. It is for this reason that a statute that explicitly restricts religious practices violates the First Amendment. Otherwise, however, "the First Amendment . . . does not distinguish between laws that are generally applicable and laws that target particular religious practices."

It is only in the rare case that a state or local legislature will enact a law directly burdening religious practice as such. Because respondent here does single out religion in this way, the present case is an easy one to decide. . . .

———

Problem: Police Grooming Regulation

Laws that discriminate against religion and single out religious practices for unique disadvantage, like the Hialeah ordinances, are unconstitutional. But is the *Lukumi* precedent limited only to such obviously discriminatory laws? Consider this hypothetical under the *Smith-Lukumi* analysis. A police department regulation requires male officers to be clean-shaven in order to maintain a uniform appearance and present a professional image to the public. "Neatly trimmed mustaches and sideburns" are permitted, but "beards or other facial hair" are generally prohibited. The regulation contains only two exceptions: "undercover officers on assignment" and officers with "a medical condition substantiated by a physician" may grow a beard.

Suppose some police officers bring a lawsuit to challenge the no-beard regulation, alleging that they are devout Sunni Muslims whose sincere religious beliefs oblige them to grow their beards. They further allege that for a Sunni man not to grow a beard, even under the instruction of an employer, is a serious sin. How should the court rule and why?

Chapter 19

Interrelationships among the Clauses

The Religion Clauses are succinct but Delphic: "Congress shall make no law respecting the establishment of religion, or prohibiting the free exercise thereof." Traditional thinking about the Religion Clauses conceptualizes them not as articulating two separate and independent principles, but as entrenching two closely related values that would fundamentally contradict one another if both were taken to their logical extreme. The Establishment Clause has been understood to *proscribe* government aid, support, and some accommodations of religion. The Free Exercise Clause has been understood to *prescribe* some governmental accommodations of religion. Favoritism and discrimination are equally improper government agendas; the First Amendment contemplates freedom *from* religion and freedom *for* religion.

As we have seen in the preceding two chapters, the Establishment Clause and the Free Exercise Clause have each generated its own body of interpretative case law. In this chapter we explore the interrelationships of the two Religion Clauses as well as the interplay between those clauses and the Free Speech Clause. First, however, we examine a more fundamental question: how to define "religion."

A. Definition of Religion

The Religion Clauses have in common the term "religion." So, whatever *it* is that can be exercised freely by the individual cannot be established by the government and presumably *vice versa*.

Perhaps not surprisingly, the Supreme Court has not attempted to promulgate a formal dictionary definition. The theological reason is that there is no single characteristic, or even a set of characteristics, that all religious belief systems have in common. Not even the concept of "God" is common to all the world's great religions. The constitutional reason is that for the Court to formally define "religion" would necessarily raise serious establishment concerns. Furthermore, the Justices have resisted giving in completely to the push and pull of the two clauses. As Justice Rutledge once pointed out: "'Religion' appears only once in the Amendment. But the word governs two prohibitions and governs them alike. It does not have two meanings, one narrow to forbid 'an establishment' and another, much broader, for securing 'the free exercise thereof.'" *Everson v. Board of Education*, 330 U.S. 1, 32 (1947) (Rutledge, J., dissenting).

Finally, as we have learned, the Supreme Court has consistently interpreted the Religion Clauses against the background principles of neutrality and equality to protect the religious, the irreligious, and the areligious — all alike. Consequently, the First Amendment term "religion" has some settled content but remains a contested concept.

Torcaso v. Watkins

367 U.S. 488 (1961)

Mr. Justice Black delivered the opinion of the Court.

Article 37 of the Declaration of Rights of the Maryland Constitution provides:

> No religious test ought ever to be required as a qualification for any office of profit or trust in this State, other than a declaration of belief in the existence of God. . . .

The appellant Torcaso was appointed to the office of Notary Public by the Governor of Maryland but was refused a commission to serve because he would not declare his belief in God. He then brought this action in a Maryland Circuit Court to compel issuance of his commission, charging that the State's requirement that he declare this belief violated "the First and Fourteenth Amendments to the Constitution of the United States . . . ."[1] The Circuit Court rejected [these] contentions, and the highest court of the State, the Court of Appeals, affirmed, holding that the state constitutional provision is self-executing and requires declaration of belief in God as a qualification for office without need for implementing legislation. The case is [here] on appeal. . . .

There is, and can be, no dispute about the purpose or effect of the Maryland Declaration of Rights requirement before us — it sets up a religious test which was designed to and, if valid, does bar every person who refuses to declare a belief in God from holding a public "office of profit or trust" in Maryland. The power and authority of the State of Maryland thus is put on the side of one particular sort of believers — those who are willing to say they believe in "the existence of God." It is true that there is much historical precedent for such laws. Indeed, it was largely to escape religious test oaths and declarations that a great many of the early colonists left Europe and came here hoping to worship in their own way. It soon developed, however, that many of those who had fled to escape religious test oaths turned out to be perfectly willing, when they had the power to do so, to force dissenters from their faith to take test oaths in conformity with that faith. This brought on a host of laws in the new Colonies imposing burdens and disabilities of various kinds upon varied beliefs depending largely upon what group happened to be politically strong enough to legislate in favor of its own beliefs. The effect of all this was the

---

1. Appellant also claimed that the State's test oath requirement violates the provision of Art. VI of the Federal Constitution that "no religious Test shall ever be required as a Qualification to any Office or public Trust under the United States." Because we are reversing the judgment on other grounds, we find it unnecessary to consider appellant's contention that this provision applies to state as well as federal offices.

formal or practical "establishment" of particular religious faiths in most of the Colonies, with consequent burdens imposed on the free exercise of the faiths of nonfavored believers.

There were, however, wise and far-seeing men in the Colonies—too many to mention—who spoke out against test oaths and all the philosophy of intolerance behind them. . . . When our Constitution was adopted, the desire to put the people "securely beyond the reach" of religious test oaths brought about the inclusion in Article VI of that document of a provision that "no religious Test shall ever be required as a Qualification to any Office or public Trust under the United States." Article VI supports [the] observation that "the test oath is abhorrent to our tradition." Not satisfied, however, with Article VI and other guarantees in the original Constitution, the First Congress proposed and the States very shortly thereafter adopted our Bill of Rights, including the First Amendment. That Amendment broke new constitutional ground in the protection it sought to afford to freedom of religion, speech, press, petition and assembly. . . . What was said in our prior cases we think controls our decision here.

We repeat and again reaffirm that neither a State nor the Federal Government can constitutionally force a person "to profess a belief or disbelief in any religion." Neither can constitutionally pass laws or impose requirements which aid all religions as against non-believers, and neither can aid those religions based on a belief in the existence of God as against those religions founded on different beliefs. . . .[11]

In upholding the State's religious test for public office the highest court of Maryland said: "The petitioner is not compelled to believe or disbelieve, under threat of punishment or other compulsion. True, unless he makes the declaration of belief he cannot hold public office in Maryland, but he is not compelled to hold office." The fact, however, that a person is not compelled to hold public office cannot possibly be an excuse for barring him from office by state-imposed criteria forbidden by the Constitution.

This Maryland religious test for public office unconstitutionally invades the appellant's freedom of belief and religion and therefore cannot be enforced against him. The judgment of the Court of Appeals of Maryland is accordingly reversed and the cause is remanded for further proceedings not inconsistent with this opinion.

MR. JUSTICE FRANKFURTER and MR. JUSTICE HARLAN concur in the result.

United States v. Seeger

380 U.S. 163 (1965)

MR. JUSTICE CLARK delivered the opinion of the Court.

These [three] cases involve claims of conscientious objectors under §6(j) of the Universal Military Training and Service Act, which exempts from combatant training and service in the armed forces of the United States those persons who by reason of

---

11. Among religions in this country which do not teach what would generally be considered a belief in the existence of God are Buddhism, Taoism, Ethical Culture, Secular Humanism and others.

their religious training and belief are conscientiously opposed to participation in war in any form. The cases were consolidated for argument and we consider them together although each involves different facts and circumstances. The parties raise the basic question of the constitutionality of the section which defines the term "religious training and belief," as used in the Act, as "an individual's belief in a relation to a Supreme Being involving duties superior to those arising from any human relation, but [not including] essentially political, sociological, or philosophical views or a merely personal moral code." . . .

[In case No. 50, Seeger was convicted in the District Court of refusing to submit to induction into the armed forces. Although he did not adopt verbatim the printed Selective Service System form, he declared that he was conscientiously opposed to participation in war in any form by reason of his "religious" belief; that he preferred to leave the question as to his belief in a Supreme Being "open"; that his "skepticism or disbelief in the existence of God" did "not necessarily mean lack of faith in anything whatsoever"; that his was a "belief in and devotion to goodness and virtue for their own sakes, and a religious faith in a purely ethical creed." He cited Plato, Aristotle and Spinoza for support of his ethical belief in intellectual and moral integrity "without belief in God, except in the remotest sense." Seeger's belief was found to be sincere, honest, and made in good faith, but his claim was denied solely because it was not based upon a "belief in a relation to a Supreme Being" as required by § 6(j) of the Act. At trial, defense counsel admitted that Seeger's belief was not in relation to a Supreme Being as commonly understood, but contended that he was nonetheless entitled to the exemption under the statute. The Court of Appeals reversed the conviction. Case No. 51, Arno Sascha Jakobson, and Case No. 29, Forest Britt Peter, involved similar facts and issues.]

[The] Draft Act of 1917 afforded exemptions to conscientious objectors who were affiliated with a "well-recognized religious sect or organization [then] organized and existing and whose existing creed or principles [forbade] its members to participate in war in any form . . . ." [In 1940,] Congress broadened the exemption [by] making it unnecessary to belong to a pacifist religious sect if the claimant's own opposition to war was based on "religious training and belief." . . .

The crux of the problem lies in the phrase "religious training and belief" which Congress has defined as "belief in a relation to a Supreme Being involving duties superior to those arising from any human relation." . . . The section excludes those persons who, disavowing religious belief, decide on the basis of essentially political, sociological or economic considerations that war is wrong and that they will have no part of it. . . . The statute further excludes those whose opposition to war stems from a "merely personal moral code." . . . No party claims to be an atheist or attacks the statute on this ground. . . . Nor do the parties claim the monotheistic belief that there is but one God; what they claim [is] that they adhere to theism, which is the "Belief in the existence of a god or gods; . . . Belief in superhuman powers or spiritual agencies in one or many gods," as opposed to atheism. Our question, therefore, is the narrow one: Does the term "Supreme Being" as used in § 6(j) mean the orthodox God or the broader concept of a power or being, or a faith, "to which all else is subordinate or upon which all else is ultimately dependent"? . . .

. . . [In] no field of human endeavor has the tool of language proved so inadequate in the communication of ideas as it has in dealing with the fundamental questions of man's predicament in life, in death or in final judgment and retribution. This fact makes the task of discerning the intent of Congress in using the phrase "Supreme Being" a complex one. Nor is it made the easier by the richness and variety of spiritual life in our country. Over 250 sects inhabit our land. Some believe in a purely personal God, some in a supernatural deity; others think of religion as a way of life envisioning as its ultimate goal the day when all men can live together in perfect understanding and peace. There are those who think of God as the depth of our being; others, such as the Buddhists, strive for a state of lasting rest through self-denial and inner purification; in Hindu philosophy, the Supreme Being is the transcendental reality which is truth, knowledge and bliss. Even those religious groups which have traditionally opposed war in every form have splintered into various denominations . . . . This vast panoply of beliefs reveals the magnitude of the problem which faced the Congress when it set about providing an exemption from armed service. It also emphasizes the care that Congress realized was necessary in the fashioning of an exemption which would be in keeping with its long-established policy of not picking and choosing among religious beliefs.

. . . [We] are not without certain guidelines. In amending the 1940 Act, Congress adopted almost intact the language of Chief Justice Hughes [dissenting] in *United States v. Macintosh* (1931): "The essence of religion is belief in a relation to *God* involving duties superior to those arising from any human relation." (Emphasis supplied.) By comparing the statutory definition with those words, however, it becomes readily apparent that the Congress deliberately broadened them by substituting the phrase "Supreme Being" for the appellation "God." And in so doing it is also significant that Congress did not elaborate on the form or nature of this higher authority which it chose to designate as "Supreme Being." By so refraining it must have had in mind the admonitions of the Chief Justice when he said in the same opinion that even the word "God" had myriad meanings . . . .

Moreover, the Senate Report on the bill specifically states that § 6(j) was intended to re-enact "substantially the same provisions as were found" in the 1940 Act. . . . Under the 1940 Act it was necessary only to have a conviction based upon religious training and belief . . . . Within that phrase would come all sincere religious beliefs which are based upon a power or being, or upon a faith, to which all else is subordinate or upon which all else is ultimately dependent. The test might be stated in these words: A sincere and meaningful belief which occupies in the life of its possessor a place parallel to that filled by the God of those admittedly qualifying for the exemption comes within the statutory definition. This construction avoids imputing to Congress an intent to classify different religious beliefs, exempting some and excluding others, and is in accord with the well-established congressional policy of equal treatment for those whose opposition to service is grounded in their religious tenets. Thus the history of the Act belies the notion that it was to be restrictive in application and available only to those believing in a traditional God. . . .

. . . [We] believe this construction embraces the ever-broadening understanding of the modern religious community. . . . Moreover, it must be remembered that in resolving these exemption problems one deals with the beliefs of different individuals who will articulate them in a multitude of ways. In such an intensely personal area, of course, the claim of the registrant that his belief is an essential part of a religious faith must be given great weight. . . . The validity of what [the registrant] believes cannot be questioned. Some theologians, and indeed some examiners, might be tempted to question the existence of the registrant's "Supreme Being" or the truth of his concepts. But these are inquiries foreclosed to Government. . . . Local boards and courts in this sense are not free to reject beliefs because they consider them "incomprehensible." Their task is to decide whether the beliefs professed by a registrant are sincerely held and whether they are, in his own scheme of things, religious. [While] the "truth" of a belief is not open to question, there remains the significant question whether it is "truly held." This is the threshold question of sincerity which must be resolved in every case. It is, of course, a question of fact . . . .

. . . The records in these cases [show] that at no time did any one of the applicants suggest that his objection was based on a "merely personal moral code." Indeed at the outset each of them claimed in his application that his objection was based on a religious belief. We have construed the statutory definition broadly and it follows that any exception to it must be interpreted narrowly. The use by Congress of the words "merely personal" seems to us to restrict the exception to a moral code which is not only personal but which is the sole basis for the registrant's belief and is in no way related to a Supreme Being. . . .

[Seeger] professed "religious belief" and "religious faith." He did not disavow any belief "in a relation to a Supreme Being"; indeed he stated that "the cosmic order does, perhaps, suggest a creative intelligence." He decried the tremendous "spiritual" price man must pay for his willingness to destroy human life. [We] think the Board, had it applied the test we propose today, would have granted him the exemption. . . . It may be that Seeger did not clearly demonstrate what his beliefs were with regard to the usual understanding of the term "Supreme Being." But as we have said Congress did not intend that to be the test. We therefore affirm the judgment in No. 50.

In *Jakobson*, No. 51, the Court of Appeals found that the registrant demonstrated that his belief as to opposition to war was related to a Supreme Being. We agree and affirm that judgment. We reach a like conclusion in *Peter*, No. 29, [because the registrant] acknowledged "some power manifest in nature . . . the supreme expression" that helps man in ordering his life. As to whether he would call that belief in a Supreme Being, he replied, "you could call that a belief in the Supreme Being or God. These just do not happen to be the words I use." We think that under the test we establish here the Board would grant the exemption to [him] and we therefore reverse the judgment in No. 29.

Mr. Justice Douglas, concurring.

. . . The legislative history of this Act leaves much in the dark. But it is, in my opinion, not a *tour de force* if we construe the words "Supreme Being" to include the cosmos, as well as an anthropomorphic entity. If it is a *tour de force* so to hold, it is no more so than other instances where we have gone to extremes to construe an Act of Congress to save it from demise on constitutional grounds. . . .

The words "a Supreme Being" have no narrow technical meaning in the field of religion. Long before the birth of our Judeo-Christian civilization the idea of God had taken hold in many forms. Mention of only two — Hinduism and Buddhism — illustrates the fluidity and evanescent scope of the concept.

In the Hindu *religion* the Supreme Being is conceived in the forms of several cult Deities. The chief of these, which stand for the Hindu Triad, are Brahma, Vishnu and Siva. . . . Though Hindu religion encompasses the worship of many Deities, it believes in only one single God, the eternally existent One Being with his manifold attributes and manifestations. . . .

Indian *philosophy*, which comprises several schools of thought, has advanced different theories of the nature of the Supreme Being. According to the Upanisads, Hindu sacred texts, the Supreme Being is described as the power which creates and sustains everything, and to which the created things return upon dissolution. The word which is commonly used [to] indicate the Supreme Being is Brahman. Philosophically, the Supreme Being is the transcendental Reality which is Truth, Knowledge, and Bliss. It is the source of the entire universe. . . . But, in the view of one school of thought [even] this is an imperfect and limited conception of Brahman which must be transcended. . . . Ultimately, mystically, Brahman must be understood as without attributes, as *neti neti* (not this, not that).

Buddhism — whose advent marked the reform of Hinduism — continued somewhat the same concept. . . . Does a Buddhist believe in "God" or a "Supreme Being"? That, of course, depends on how one defines "God." . . . [If] "God" is taken to mean a personal Creator of the universe, then the Buddhist has no interest in the concept. But if "God" means something like the state of oneness with God as described by some Christian mystics, then the Buddhist surely believes in "God," since this state is almost indistinguishable from the Buddhist concept of Nirvana, "the supreme Reality; . . . the eternal, hidden and incomprehensible Peace." And finally, if "God" means one of the many Deities in an at least superficially polytheistic religion like Hinduism, then Buddhism tolerates a belief in many Gods. . . .

When the present Act was adopted in 1948 we were a nation of Buddhists, Confucianists, and Taoists, as well as Christians. . . . When the Congress spoke in the vague general terms of a [Supreme Being] I would attribute tolerance and sophistication to the Congress, commensurate with the religious complexion of our communities. [Any] person opposed to war on the basis of a sincere belief, which in his life fills the same place as a belief in God fills in the life of an orthodox religionist, is entitled to exemption under the statute. . . .

———

Note: Freedom of Conscience and the Constitution

1. In *United States v. Seeger*, the Supreme Court majority self-consciously emphasized it was interpreting only the draft exemption statute, i.e., the Military Selective Service Act §6(j), and not the First Amendment. Congress defined the term "religious training and belief" to mean "an individual's belief in a relation to a Supreme Being involving duties superior to those arising from any human relation, but [not including] essentially political, sociological, or philosophical views or merely a personal moral code." The majority attributed this understanding of religion to Congress: "A sincere and meaningful belief which occupies in the life of its possessor a place parallel to that filled by the God of those admittedly qualifying for the exemption comes within the statutory definition."

2. In *Welsh v. United States*, 398 U.S. 333 (1970), the Court extended the *Seeger* precedent and held that test was satisfied even though the person seeking the conscientious exemption from the draft had crossed out the words "religious training" on his application. There was no majority opinion. Justice Black, joined by Justices Douglas, Brennan and Marshall, deemed the facts to be virtually indistinguishable from *Seeger* because Welsh's beliefs "play[ed] the role of religion and function[ed] as a religion in [his] life." Section 6(j) was intended to "exempt from military service all those whose consciences, spurred by deeply held moral, ethical, or religious beliefs, would give them no rest or peace if they allowed themselves to become a part of an instrument of war." The Court set aside Welsh's conviction for refusing to submit to induction into the Armed Services.

3. Justice Harlan concurred in the judgment. In his separate opinion, he candidly admitted that the results in *Seeger* and *Welsh* contradicted the language of the statute and those decisions only made sense as First Amendment holdings:

> Candor requires me to say that I joined the Court's opinion in *United States v. Seeger* (1965), only with the gravest misgivings as to whether it was a legitimate exercise in statutory construction, and today's decision convinces me that in doing so I made a mistake which I should now acknowledge.... I therefore find myself unable to escape facing the constitutional issue that this case squarely presents: whether §6(j) in limiting this draft exemption to those opposed to war in general because of theistic beliefs runs afoul of the religious clauses of the First Amendment. [I] believe it does, and on that basis I concur in the judgment reversing this conviction, and adopt the test announced by Mr. Justice Black, not as a matter of statutory construction, but as the touchstone for salvaging a congressional policy of long standing that would otherwise have to be nullified....
>
> The [statutory issue is] whether Welsh's opposition to war is founded on "religious training and belief" and hence "belief in a relation to a Supreme Being" as *Congress* used those words. It is of course true that certain words are more plastic in meaning than others. "Supreme Being" is a concept of

theology and philosophy, not a technical term, and consequently may be, in some circumstances, capable of bearing a contemporary construction as notions of theology and philosophy evolve. This language appears, however, in a congressional enactment; it is not a phrase of the Constitution, like "religion" or "speech," which this Court is freer to construe in light of evolving needs and circumstances. . . . It is Congress' will that must here be divined. . . . The natural reading of § 6(j), which quite evidently draws a distinction between theistic and nontheistic religions, is the only one that is consistent with the legislative history.

Against this legislative history it is a remarkable feat of judicial surgery to remove, as did *Seeger*, the theistic requirement of § 6(j). The prevailing opinion today, however, in the name of interpreting the will of Congress, has performed a lobotomy and completely transformed the statute by reading out of it any distinction between religiously acquired beliefs and those deriving from "essentially political, sociological, or philosophical views or a merely personal moral code." . . .

Unless we are to assume an Alice-in-Wonderland world where words have no meaning, I think it fair to say that Congress' choice of language cannot fail to convey to the discerning reader the very policy choice that the prevailing opinion today completely obliterates: that between conventional religions that usually have an organized and formal structure and dogma and a cohesive group identity, even when nontheistic, and cults that represent schools of thought and in the usual case are without formal structure or are, at most, loose and informal associations of individuals who share common ethical, moral, or intellectual views. . . .

The constitutional question that must be faced in this case is whether a statute that defers to the individual's conscience only when his views emanate from adherence to theistic religious beliefs is within the power of Congress. Congress, of course, could, entirely consistently with the requirements of the Constitution, eliminate *all* exemptions for conscientious objectors. Such a course would be wholly "neutral" and, in my view, would not offend the Free Exercise Clause. . . . However, having chosen to exempt, it cannot draw the line between theistic or nontheistic religious beliefs on the one hand and secular beliefs on the other. Any such distinctions are not, in my view, compatible with the Establishment Clause of the First Amendment. The implementation of the neutrality principle of these cases [requires] "an equal protection mode of analysis. The Court must survey meticulously the circumstances of governmental categories to eliminate, as it were, religious gerrymanders. In any particular case the critical questions is whether the scope of the legislation encircles a class so broad that it can be fairly concluded that [all groups that] could be thought to fall within the natural perimeter [are included]."

The "radius" of this legislation is the conscientiousness with which an individual opposes war in general, yet the statute, as I think it must be construed, excludes from its "scope" individuals motivated by teachings of non-theistic religions, and individuals guided by an inner ethical voice that bespeaks secular and not "religious" reflection. It not only accords a preference to the "religious" but also disadvantages adherents of religions that do not worship a Supreme Being. The constitutional infirmity cannot be cured, moreover, even by an impermissible construction that eliminates the theistic requirement and simply draws the line between religious and nonreligious. This in my view offends the Establishment Clause and is that kind of classification that this Court has condemned.

If the exemption is to be given application, it must encompass the class of individuals it purports to exclude, those whose beliefs emanate from a purely moral, ethical, or philosophical source. The common denominator must be the intensity of moral conviction with which a belief is held. Common experience teaches that among "religious" individuals some are weak and others strong adherents to tenets and this is no less true of individuals whose lives are guided by personal ethical considerations. . . .

The policy of exempting religious conscientious objectors is one of long-standing tradition in this country and accords recognition to what is, in a diverse and "open" society, the important value of reconciling individuality of belief with practical exigencies whenever possible. It dates back to colonial times and has been perpetuated in state and federal conscription statutes. That it has been phrased in religious terms reflects, I assume, the fact that ethics and morals, while the concern of secular philosophy, have traditionally been matters taught by organized religion and that for most individuals spiritual and ethical nourishment is derived from that source. It further reflects, I would suppose, the assumption that beliefs emanating from a religious source are probably held with great intensity.

When a policy has roots so deeply embedded in history, there is a compelling reason for a court to hazard the necessary statutory repairs if they can be made within the administrative framework of the statute and without impairing other legislative goals, even though they entail, not simply eliminating an offending section, but rather building upon it. Thus I am prepared to accept the prevailing opinion's conscientious objector test, not as a reflection of congressional statutory intent but as patchwork of judicial making that cures the defect of underinclusion in §6(j) and can be administered by local boards in the usual course of business. Like the prevailing opinion, I also conclude that petitioner's beliefs are held with the required intensity and consequently vote to reverse the judgment of conviction.

4. Justice White, joined by Chief Justice Burger and Justice Stewart, dissented to insist that extending the draft exemption to Welsh directly contradicted the statute and violated the intent of Congress. The dissent concluded that Welsh's conviction

should be upheld under the Establishment Clause and the Free Exercise Clause. Justice Blackmun took no part in the case.

5. Is Justice Harlan correct to observe above that "Congress, of course, could, entirely consistently with the requirements of the Constitution, eliminate *all* exemptions for conscientious objectors"? Why does he concur in setting aside Welsh's conviction?

6. In these draft exemption cases, the Justices deploy an analogy to define "religion" in the statute as "[a] sincere and meaningful belief which occupies in the life of its possessor a place parallel to that filled by the God of those admittedly qualifying for the exemption." The extended opinions contain footnote references to several notable theologians in the "modern religious community," among them Paul Tillich. Tillich's definition of religion is "ultimate concern" by which he means a psychological, emotional, and spiritual aspect of human nature that is absolute, unconditional, and unqualified. For Tillich, religion is thus a deeply-personal individuated construct and every person has one that is unique to that person. Would Tillich's definition work for the Religion Clauses?

Note: Dogma, Heresy, and Schism

1. Recall *United States v. Ballard* (1944) (Chapter 18), involving the "I Am" cult and a federal prosecution for fraud. There the Supreme Court held that the courts could determine only whether the individual's beliefs are sincere and not whether they are true or false. Likewise, the Court has refused to come between a believer and his or her religion. An individual may exercise a sincere religious belief even though it is idiosyncratic and inconsistent with the doctrines of his or her religion and even though other members of the same religion do not share the stated belief. *Thomas v. Review Bd. of Ind. Employment Sec. Div.*, 450 U.S. 707 (1981) (holding it was immaterial that the Jehovah's Witness faith did not require that a member quit his job instead of working to manufacture armaments); *Frazee v. Ill. Dep't of Employment Sec.*, 489 U.S. 829 (1989) (Sabbatarian's decision to quit his job instead of working on Sundays was protected even though other Sabbatarians did not do so).

2. Likewise, the Supreme Court has proclaimed that secular courts may not declare which side is correct in a religious dispute within a religious organization or community. To do so would simultaneously violate the Establishment Clause by ruling in favor of the "winners" and violate the Free Exercise Clause by ruling against the "losers." Property disputes may be resolved under settled principles of state law following two neutral constitutional rules: (1) for a dispute within an independent, congregationalist church the will of the majority of its members is controlling and determinative; and (2) for a dispute between a local congregation and its general church with which it is affiliated, the court will defer to the hierarchical ecclesiastical authority. This line of cases goes back to 1872; for a modern example, see *Jones v. Wolf*, 443 U.S. 595 (1979).

3. What assumptions about "religion" is the Court operating under in these rules? What values of the Religion Clauses are preserved by these rules?

Hosanna-Tabor Evangelical Lutheran Church and School v. EEOC

565 U.S. 171 (2012)

CHIEF JUSTICE ROBERTS delivered the opinion of the Court.

Certain employment discrimination laws authorize employees who have been wrongfully terminated to sue their employers for reinstatement and damages. The question presented is whether the Establishment and Free Exercise Clauses of the First Amendment bar such an action when the employer is a religious group and the employee is one of the group's ministers.

I

A

Petitioner Hosanna-Tabor Evangelical Lutheran Church and School is a member congregation of the Lutheran Church-Missouri Synod, the second largest Lutheran denomination in America. Hosanna-Tabor operated a small school in Redford, Michigan, offering a "Christ-centered education" to students in kindergarten through eighth grade.

The Synod classifies teachers into two categories: "called" and "lay." "Called" teachers are regarded as having been called to their vocation by God through a congregation. To be eligible to receive a call from a congregation, a teacher must satisfy certain academic requirements. One way of doing so is by completing a "colloquy" program [of study] at a Lutheran college or university. . . . Once called, a teacher receives the formal title "Minister of Religion, Commissioned." A commissioned minister serves for an open-ended term; at Hosanna-Tabor, a call could be rescinded only for cause and by a supermajority vote of the congregation.

"Lay" or "contract" teachers, by contrast, are not required to be trained by the Synod or even to be Lutheran. At Hosanna-Tabor, they were appointed by the school board, without a vote of the congregation, to one-year renewable terms. Although teachers at the school generally performed the same duties regardless of whether they were lay or called, lay teachers were hired only when called teachers were unavailable.

Respondent Cheryl Perich was first employed by Hosanna-Tabor as a lay teacher in 1999. After Perich completed her colloquy later that school year, Hosanna-Tabor asked her to become a called teacher. Perich accepted the call and received a "diploma of vocation" designating her a commissioned minister.

Perich taught kindergarten during her first four years at Hosanna-Tabor and fourth grade during the 2003–2004 school year. She taught math, language arts, social studies, science, gym, art, and music. She also taught a religion class four days a week, led the students in prayer and devotional exercises each day, and attended a weekly school-wide chapel service. Perich led the chapel service herself about twice a year.

Perich became ill in June 2004 with what was eventually diagnosed as narcolepsy. Symptoms included sudden and deep sleeps from which she could not be roused. Because of her illness, Perich began the 2004–2005 school year on disability leave. On January 27, 2005, however, Perich notified the school principal . . . that she would be able to report to work the following month. [The principal] responded that the school had already contracted with a lay teacher to fill Perich's position for the remainder of the school year [and] also expressed concern that [she] was not yet ready to return to the classroom.

On January 30, Hosanna-Tabor held a meeting of its congregation at which school administrators stated that Perich was unlikely to be physically capable of returning to work that school year or the next. The congregation voted to offer Perich a "peaceful release" from her call, whereby the congregation would pay a portion of her health insurance premiums in exchange for her resignation as a called teacher. Perich refused to resign and produced a note from her doctor stating that she would be able to return to work on February 22. The school board urged Perich to reconsider, informing her that the school no longer had a position for her, but Perich stood by her decision not to resign.

On the morning of February 22 . . . Perich presented herself at the school. [The principal] asked her to leave but she would not do so until she obtained written documentation that she had reported to work. Later that afternoon, [the principal] called Perich at home and told her that she would likely be fired. Perich responded that she had spoken with an attorney and intended to assert her legal rights.

Following a school board meeting that evening, [the] board chairman sent Perich a letter stating that Hosanna-Tabor was reviewing the process for rescinding her call in light of her "regrettable" actions. [He] subsequently followed up with a letter advising Perich that the congregation would consider whether to rescind her call at its next meeting. As grounds for termination, the letter cited Perich's "insubordination and disruptive behavior" on February 22, as well as the damage she had done to her "working relationship" with the school by "threatening to take legal action." The congregation voted to rescind Perich's call on April 10, and Hosanna-Tabor sent her a letter of termination the next day.

B

Perich filed a charge with the Equal Employment Opportunity Commission, alleging that her employment had been terminated in violation of the Americans with Disabilities Act, 42 U.S.C. §12101 *et seq.* (1990). The ADA prohibits an employer from discriminating against a qualified individual on the basis of disability. It also prohibits an employer from retaliating "against any individual . . . because such individual made a charge, testified, assisted, or participated in any manner in an investigation, proceeding, or hearing under [the ADA]."

The EEOC brought suit against Hosanna-Tabor, alleging that Perich had been fired in retaliation for threatening to file an ADA lawsuit. Perich intervened in the litigation, claiming unlawful retaliation under both the ADA and the Michigan Persons with Disabilities Civil Rights Act. . . . Hosanna-Tabor moved for summary judgment. Invoking what is known as the "ministerial exception," the Church argued that the suit was barred by the First Amendment because the claims at issue concerned the employment relationship between a religious institution and one of its ministers. According to the

Church, Perich was a minister, and she had been fired for a religious reason — namely that her threat to sue the Church violated the Synod's belief that Christians should resolve their disputes internally.

The District Court agreed that the suit was barred by the ministerial exception and granted summary judgment in Hosanna-Tabor's favor. . . . The Court of Appeals for the Sixth Circuit vacated and remanded . . . . The court concluded . . . that Perich did not qualify as a "minister" under the exception. . . . We granted certiorari.

II

[We] have said that . . . there can be "internal tension . . . between the Establishment Clause and the Free Exercise Clause." Not so here. Both Religion Clauses bar the government from interfering with the decision of a religious group to fire one of its ministers.

A

Controversy between church and state over religious offices is hardly new. [Here the Chief Justice highlighted the English and colonial history of that relationship.]

It was against this background that the First Amendment was adopted. Familiar with life under the established Church of England, the founding generation sought to foreclose the possibility of a national church. By forbidding the "establishment of religion" and guaranteeing the "free exercise thereof," the Religion Clauses ensured that the new Federal Government — unlike the English Crown — would have no role in filling ecclesiastical offices. The Establishment Clause prevents the Government from appointing ministers, and the Free Exercise Clause prevents it from interfering with the freedom of religious groups to select their own.

B

Given this understanding of the Religion Clauses — and the absence of government employment regulation generally — it was some time before questions about government interference with a church's ability to select its own ministers came before the courts. This Court touched upon the issue indirectly, however, in the context of disputes over church property. Our decisions in that area confirm that it is impermissible for the government to contradict a church's determination of who can act as its ministers. [Our prior opinions] "radiate[] . . . a spirit of freedom for religious organizations, an independence from secular control or manipulation — in short, power to decide for themselves, free from state interference, matters of church government as well as those of faith and doctrine." *Kedroff v. Saint Nicholas Cathedral of Russian Orthodox Church in North America*, 344 U.S. 94, 116 (1952).

C

Until today, we have not had occasion to consider whether this freedom of a religious organization to select its ministers is implicated by a suit alleging discrimination in employment. The Courts of Appeals, in contrast, have had extensive experience with this issue. Since the passage of Title VII of the Civil Rights Act of 1964, and other employment discrimination laws, the Courts of Appeals have uniformly recognized the existence of a "ministerial exception," grounded in the First Amendment, that precludes application of such legislation to claims concerning the employment relationship between a religious institution and its ministers.

We agree that there is such a ministerial exception. The members of a religious group put their faith in the hands of their ministers. Requiring a church to accept or retain an unwanted minister, or punishing a church for failing to do so, intrudes upon more than a mere employment decision. Such action interferes with the internal governance of the church, depriving the church of control over the selection of those who will personify its beliefs. By imposing an unwanted minister, the state infringes the Free Exercise Clause, which protects a religious group's right to shape its own faith and mission through its appointments. According the state the power to determine which individuals will minister to the faithful also violates the Establishment Clause, which prohibits government involvement in such ecclesiastical decisions.

The EEOC and Perich acknowledge that employment discrimination laws would be unconstitutional as applied to religious groups in certain circumstances. They grant, for example, that it would violate the First Amendment for courts to apply such laws to compel the ordination of women by the Catholic Church or by an Orthodox Jewish seminary. According to the EEOC and Perich, religious organizations could successfully defend against employment discrimination claims in those circumstances by invoking the constitutional right to freedom of association — a right "implicit" in the First Amendment. *Roberts v. United States Jaycees* (1984) [Chapter 10]. The EEOC and Perich thus see no need — and no basis — for a special rule for ministers grounded in the Religion Clauses themselves.

We find this position untenable. The right to freedom of association is a right enjoyed by religious and secular groups alike. It follows under the EEOC's and Perich's view that the First Amendment analysis should be the same, whether the association in question is the Lutheran Church, a labor union, or a social club. That result is hard to square with the text of the First Amendment itself, which gives special solicitude to the rights of religious organizations. We cannot accept the remarkable view that the Religion Clauses have nothing to say about a religious organization's freedom to select its own ministers.

The EEOC and Perich also contend that our decision in *Employment Div., Dept. of Human Resources of Ore. v. Smith* (1990) [Chapter 18], precludes recognition of a ministerial exception. In *Smith*, two members of the Native American Church were denied state unemployment benefits after it was determined that they had been fired from their jobs for ingesting peyote, a crime under Oregon law. We held that this did not violate the Free Exercise Clause, even though the peyote had been ingested for sacramental purposes, because the "right of free exercise does not relieve an individual of the obligation to comply with a valid and neutral law of general applicability on the ground that the law proscribes (or prescribes) conduct that his religion prescribes (or proscribes)."

It is true that the ADA's prohibition on retaliation, like Oregon's prohibition on peyote use, is a valid and neutral law of general applicability. But a church's selection of its ministers is unlike an individual's ingestion of peyote. *Smith* involved government regulation of only outward physical acts. The present case, in contrast, concerns government interference with an internal church decision that affects the faith and mission of the church itself. The contention that *Smith* forecloses recognition of a ministerial exception rooted in the Religion Clauses has no merit.

III

Having concluded that there is a ministerial exception grounded in the Religion Clauses of the First Amendment, we consider whether the exception applies in this case. We hold that it does.

Every Court of Appeals to have considered the question has concluded that the ministerial exception is not limited to the head of a religious congregation, and we agree. We are reluctant, however, to adopt a rigid formula for deciding when an employee qualifies as a minister. It is enough for us to conclude, in this our first case involving the ministerial exception, that the exception covers Perich, given all the circumstances of her employment.

To begin with, Hosanna-Tabor held Perich out as a minister, with a role distinct from that of most of its members. . . . Perich's title as a minister reflected a significant degree of religious training followed by a formal process of commissioning. . . . Perich held herself out as a minister of the Church by accepting the formal call to religious service, according to its terms. She did so in other ways as well. For example, she claimed a special housing allowance on her taxes that was available only to employees earning their compensation "'in the exercise of the ministry.'" In a form she submitted to the Synod following her termination, Perich again indicated that she regarded herself as a minister at Hosanna-Tabor, stating: "I feel that God is leading me to serve in the teaching ministry . . . . I am anxious to be in the teaching ministry again soon."

Perich's job duties reflected a role in conveying the Church's message and carrying out its mission. Hosanna-Tabor expressly charged her with "lead[ing] others toward Christian maturity" and "teach[ing] faithfully the Word of God, the Sacred Scriptures, in its truth and purity and as set forth in all the symbolical books of the Evangelical Lutheran Church." In fulfilling these responsibilities, Perich taught her students religion four days a week, and led them in prayer three times a day. Once a week, she took her students to a school-wide chapel service, and—about twice a year—she took her turn leading it, choosing the liturgy, selecting the hymns, and delivering a short message based on verses from the Bible. During her last year of teaching, Perich also led her fourth graders in a brief devotional exercise each morning. As a source of religious instruction, Perich performed an important role in transmitting the Lutheran faith to the next generation.

In light of these considerations—the formal title given Perich by the Church, the substance reflected in that title, her own use of that title, and the important religious functions she performed for the Church—we conclude that Perich was a minister covered by the ministerial exception. . . .

Because Perich was a minister within the meaning of the exception, the First Amendment requires dismissal of this employment discrimination suit against her religious employer. The EEOC and Perich originally sought an order reinstating Perich to her former position as a called teacher. By requiring the Church to accept a minister it did not want, such an order would have plainly violated the Church's freedom under the Religion Clauses to select its own ministers. . . .

The EEOC and Perich suggest that Hosanna-Tabor's asserted religious reason for firing Perich—that she violated the Synod's commitment to internal dispute resolution—was pretextual. That suggestion misses the point of the ministerial exception. The purpose of the exception is not to safeguard a church's decision to fire a minister only when it is made for a religious reason. The exception instead ensures that the authority to select and control who will minister to the faithful—a matter "strictly ecclesiastical,"—is the church's alone.[4]

IV

[The] case before us is an employment discrimination suit brought on behalf of a minister, challenging her church's decision to fire her. Today we hold only that the ministerial exception bars such a suit. We express no view on whether the exception bars other types of suits, including actions by employees alleging breach of contract or tortious conduct by their religious employers. There will be time enough to address the applicability of the exception to other circumstances if and when they arise.

The interest of society in the enforcement of employment discrimination statutes is undoubtedly important. But so too is the interest of religious groups in choosing who will preach their beliefs, teach their faith, and carry out their mission. When a minister who has been fired sues her church alleging that her termination was discriminatory, the First Amendment has struck the balance for us. The church must be free to choose those who will guide it on its way.

The judgment of the Court of Appeals for the Sixth Circuit is reversed.

It is so ordered.

Justice Thomas, concurring.

. . . The Court thoroughly sets forth the facts that lead to its conclusion that Cheryl Perich was one of Hosanna-Tabor's ministers, and I agree that these facts amply demonstrate Perich's ministerial role. But the evidence demonstrates that Hosanna-Tabor sincerely considered Perich a minister. That would be sufficient for me to conclude that Perich's suit is properly barred by the ministerial exception.

Justice Alito, with whom Justice Kagan joins, concurring.

---

4. A conflict has arisen in the Courts of Appeals over whether the ministerial exception is a jurisdictional bar or a defense on the merits. We conclude that the exception operates as an affirmative defense to an otherwise cognizable claim, not a jurisdictional bar. . . . District courts have power to consider ADA claims in cases of this sort, and to decide whether the claim can proceed or is instead barred by the ministerial exception.

I join the Court's opinion, but I write separately to clarify my understanding of the significance of formal ordination and designation as a "minister" in determining whether an "employee" of a religious group falls within the so-called "ministerial" exception. The term "minister" is commonly used by many Protestant denominations to refer to members of their clergy, but the term is rarely if ever used in this way by Catholics, Jews, Muslims, Hindus, or Buddhists. In addition, the concept of ordination as understood by most Christian churches and by Judaism has no clear counterpart in some Christian denominations and some other religions. Because virtually every religion in the world is represented in the population of the United States, it would be a mistake if the term "minister" or the concept of ordination were viewed as central to the important issue of religious autonomy that is presented in cases like this one. Instead, courts should focus on the function performed by persons who work for religious bodies.

The First Amendment protects the freedom of religious groups to engage in certain key religious activities, including the conducting of worship services and other religious ceremonies and rituals, as well as the critical process of communicating the faith. Accordingly, religious groups must be free to choose the personnel who are essential to the performance of these functions.

The "ministerial" exception should be tailored to this purpose. It should apply to any "employee" who leads a religious organization, conducts worship services or important religious ceremonies or rituals, or serves as a messenger or teacher of its faith. If a religious group believes that the ability of such an employee to perform these key functions has been compromised, then the constitutional guarantee of religious freedom protects the group's right to remove the employee from his or her position.

I

. . . Religious autonomy means that religious authorities must be free to determine who is qualified to serve in positions of substantial religious importance. Different religions will have different views on exactly what qualifies as an important religious position, but it is nonetheless possible to identify a general category of "employees" whose functions are essential to the independence of practically all religious groups. These include those who serve in positions of leadership, those who perform important functions in worship services and in the performance of religious ceremonies and rituals, and those who are entrusted with teaching and conveying the tenets of the faith to the next generation.

Applying the protection of the First Amendment to roles of religious leadership, worship, ritual, and expression focuses on the objective functions that are important for the autonomy of any religious group, regardless of its beliefs. . . . Religious groups are the archetype of associations formed for expressive purposes, and their fundamental rights surely include the freedom to choose who is qualified to serve as a voice for their faith. . . .

The connection between church governance and the free dissemination of religious doctrine has deep roots in our legal tradition. . . . The "ministerial" exception gives concrete protection to the free "expression and dissemination of any religious doctrine." The Constitution leaves it to the collective conscience of each religious group to determine for itself who is qualified to serve as a teacher or messenger of its faith.

II

A

The Court's opinion today holds that the "ministerial" exception applies to Cheryl Perich (hereinafter respondent), who is regarded by the Lutheran Church-Missouri Synod as a commissioned minister. But while a ministerial title is undoubtedly relevant in applying the First Amendment rule at issue, such a title is neither necessary nor sufficient. As previously noted, most faiths do not employ the term "minister," and some eschew the concept of formal ordination.[3] And at the opposite end of the spectrum, some faiths consider the ministry to consist of all or a very large percentage of their members.[4] Perhaps this explains why, although every circuit to consider the issue has recognized the "ministerial" exception, no circuit has made ordination status or formal title determinative of the exception's applicability. . . .

B

The ministerial exception applies to respondent because, as the Court notes, she played a substantial role in "conveying the Church's message and carrying out its mission." She taught religion to her students four days a week and took them to chapel on the fifth day. She led them in daily devotional exercises, and led them in prayer three times a day. She also alternated with the other teachers in planning and leading worship services at the school chapel, choosing liturgies, hymns, and readings, and composing and delivering a message based on Scripture.

It makes no difference that respondent also taught secular subjects. While a purely secular teacher would not qualify for the "ministerial" exception, the constitutional protection of religious teachers is not somehow diminished when they take on secular functions in addition to their religious ones. What matters is that respondent played an important role as an instrument of her church's religious message and as a leader of its worship activities. Because of these important religious functions, Hosanna-Tabor had the right to decide for itself whether respondent was religiously qualified to remain in her office.

Hosanna-Tabor discharged respondent because she threatened to file suit against the church in a civil court. This threat contravened the Lutheran doctrine that disputes among Christians should be resolved internally without resort to the civil court system and all the legal wrangling it entails.[5] In Hosanna-Tabor's view, respondent's

---

3. In Islam, for example, "every Muslim can perform the religious rites, so there is no class or profession of ordained clergy. Yet there are religious leaders who are recognized for their learning and their ability to lead communities of Muslims in prayer, study, and living according to the teaching of the Qur'an and Muslim law."

4. For instance, Jehovah's Witnesses consider all baptized disciples to be ministers.

5. *See* The Lutheran Church-Missouri Synod, Commission on Theology and Church Relations, 1 *Corinthians* 6:1–11: An Exegetical Study, at 10 (Apr. 1991) (stating that instead of suing each other, Christians should seek "an amicable settlement of differences by means of a decision by fellow

disregard for this doctrine compromised her religious function, disqualifying her from serving effectively as a voice for the church's faith. Respondent does not dispute that the Lutheran Church subscribes to a doctrine of internal dispute resolution, but she argues that this was a mere pretext for her firing, which was really done for nonreligious reasons.

For civil courts to engage in the pretext inquiry that respondent and the Solicitor General urge us to sanction would dangerously undermine the religious autonomy that lower court case law has now protected for nearly four decades. In order to probe the *real* reason for respondent's firing, a civil court — and perhaps a jury — would be required to make a judgment about church doctrine. The credibility of Hosanna-Tabor's asserted reason for terminating respondent's employment could not be assessed without taking into account both the importance that the Lutheran Church attaches to the doctrine of internal dispute resolution and the degree to which that tenet compromised respondent's religious function. . . . [W]hatever the truth of the matter might be, the mere adjudication of such questions would pose grave problems for religious autonomy: It would require calling witnesses to testify about the importance and priority of the religious doctrine in question, with a civil factfinder sitting in ultimate judgment of what the accused church really believes, and how important that belief is to the church's overall mission. . . .

What matters in the present case is that Hosanna-Tabor believes that the religious function that respondent performed made it essential that she abide by the doctrine of internal dispute resolution; and the civil courts are in no position to second-guess that assessment. This conclusion rests not on respondent's ordination status or her formal title, but rather on her functional status as the type of employee that a church must be free to appoint or dismiss in order to exercise the religious liberty that the First Amendment guarantees.

Problem: Peremptory Challenges

The Supreme Court has held that peremptory challenges based upon the race or sex of the prospective juror violate the Fourteenth Amendment. *J.E.B. v. Alabama*, 511 U.S. 127 (1994); *Batson v. Kentucky*, 476 U.S. 79 (1986). Should this line of precedent be extended to prohibit religion-related peremptory challenges? Is your answer based on the Establishment Clause or the Free Exercise Clause or both? What would qualify as a religiously-based peremptory challenge? Give some examples.

B. Tensions between the Religion Clauses

The Justices have self-consciously sought to harmonize the Establishment Clause with the Free Exercise Clause in countless individual cases. They have been unwilling

---

Christians"). *See also* 1 *Corinthians* 6:1–7 ("If any of you has a dispute with another, dare he take it before the ungodly for judgment instead of before the saints?").

or unable, however, to attempt a once-and-for-all reconciliation of the contradictions between the two clauses:

> The Court has struggled to find a neutral course between the two Religion Clauses, both of which are cast in absolute terms, and either of which, if expanded to a logical extreme, would tend to clash with the other.... The course of constitutional neutrality in this area cannot be an absolutely straight line; rigidity could well defeat the basic purpose of these provisions, which is to insure that no religion be sponsored or favored, none commanded, and none inhibited. The general principle deducible from the First Amendment and all that has been said by the Court is this: that we will not tolerate either governmentally established religion or governmental interference with religion. Short of those expressly proscribed governmental acts there is room for play in the joints productive of a benevolent neutrality which will permit religious exercise to exist without sponsorship and without interference.

Walz v. Tax Comm'n, 397 U.S. 664, 668–69 (1970). This section considers the "play in the joints" between the two clauses. Does thinking about the two clauses together make it easier or more difficult to understand what they mean?

Locke v. Davey

540 U.S. 712 (2004)

Chief Justice Rehnquist delivered the opinion of the Court.

The Washington State Legislature [created] the Promise Scholarship Program, which provides a scholarship, renewable for one year, to eligible students for postsecondary education expenses. Students may spend their funds on any education-related expense.... The scholarships are funded through the State's general fund, and their amount varies each year depending on the annual appropriation, which is evenly prorated among the eligible students. The scholarship was worth $1,125 for academic year 1999–2000 and $1,542 for 2000–2001.

To be eligible for the scholarship, a student must [graduate] from a Washington public or private high school and either graduate in the top 15% of his graduating class, or attain on the first attempt a cumulative score of 1,200 or better on the Scholastic Assessment Test I or a score of 27 or better on the American College Test. The student's family income must be less than 135% of the State's median. Finally, the student must enroll "at least half time in an eligible postsecondary institution in the state of Washington," [either public or accredited private,] and may not pursue a degree in theology at that institution while receiving the scholarship. A "degree in theology" is not defined in the statute, but, as both parties concede, the statute simply codifies the State's constitutional prohibition on providing funds to students to pursue degrees that are "devotional in nature or designed to induce religious faith."... The institution, rather than the State, determines whether the student's major is devotional. If the student meets the enrollment requirements, the scholarship funds are sent to the institution for distribution to the student....

Respondent, Joshua Davey, was awarded a Promise Scholarship, and chose to attend Northwest College, [a] private, Christian college affiliated with the Assemblies of God denomination, and [an] eligible institution.... Davey had "planned for many years to attend a Bible college and to prepare [himself] through that college training for a lifetime of ministry, specifically as a church pastor." To that end, when he enrolled in Northwest College, he decided to pursue a double major in pastoral ministries and business management/administration. There is no dispute that the pastoral ministries degree is devotional and therefore excluded under the Promise Scholarship Program.

[Davey sued in District Court alleging that the denial of his scholarship based on his decision to pursue a theology degree violated, *inter alia*, the Free Exercise, Establishment, and Free Speech Clauses of the First Amendment, as incorporated by the Fourteenth Amendment, and the Equal Protection Clause of the Fourteenth Amendment. After the District Court rejected Davey's constitutional claims and granted summary judgment in favor of the State, a divided panel of the Court of Appeals for the Ninth Circuit reversed.] We granted certiorari and now reverse.

The Religion Clauses of the First Amendment, [the] Establishment Clause and the Free Exercise Clause, are frequently in tension. Yet we have long said that "there is room for play in the joints" between them. In other words, there are some state actions permitted by the Establishment Clause but not required by the Free Exercise Clause.

This case involves that "play in the joints".... Under our Establishment Clause precedent, the link between government funds and religious training is broken by the independent and private choice of recipients. *See Zelman v. Simmons-Harris* (2002) [Chapter 17]. As such, there is no doubt that the State could, consistent with the Federal Constitution, permit Promise Scholars to pursue a degree in devotional theology, and the State does not contend otherwise. The question before us, however, is whether Washington, pursuant to its own constitution,[2] which has been authoritatively interpreted as prohibiting even indirectly funding religious instruction that will prepare students for the ministry, *see Witters v. Commission for Blind*, 112 Wash. 2d 363 (1989), can deny them such funding without violating the Free Exercise Clause.

Davey [contends] that under the rule we enunciated in *Church of Lukumi Babalu Aye, Inc. v. Hialeah* (1993) [Chapter 18], the program is presumptively unconstitutional because it is not facially neutral with respect to religion.[3] We reject his claim of

---

2. The relevant provision of the WASHINGTON CONSTITUTION, Art. I, § 11, states:
    Religious Freedom. Absolute freedom of conscience in all matters of religious sentiment, belief and worship, shall be guaranteed to every individual, and no one shall be molested or disturbed in person or property on account of religion; but the liberty of conscience hereby secured shall not be so construed as to excuse acts of licentiousness or justify practices inconsistent with the peace and safety of the state. No public money or property shall be appropriated for or applied to any religious worship, exercise or instruction, or the support of any religious establishment.
3. Davey, relying on *Rosenberger v. Rector and Visitors of Univ. of Va.* (1995) [*infra* this chapter], contends that the Promise Scholarship Program is an unconstitutional viewpoint restriction on speech. But the Promise Scholarship Program is not a forum for speech. The purpose of the Promise Scholarship Program is to assist students from low- and middle-income families with the cost of

presumptive unconstitutionality, however; to do otherwise would extend the *Lukumi* line of cases well beyond not only their facts but their reasoning. . . . In the present case, the State's disfavor of religion (if it can be called that) is of a far milder kind. It imposes neither criminal nor civil sanctions on any type of religious service or rite. It does not deny to ministers the right to participate in the political affairs of the community. And it does not require students to choose between their religious beliefs and receiving a government benefit. The State has merely chosen not to fund a distinct category of instruction.

Justice Scalia argues [in his dissent], however, that generally available benefits are part of the "baseline against which burdens on religion are measured." Because the Promise Scholarship Program funds training for all secular professions, Justice Scalia contends the State must also fund training for religious professions. But training for religious professions and training for secular professions are not fungible. Training someone to lead a congregation is an essentially religious endeavor. Indeed, majoring in devotional theology is akin to a religious calling as well as an academic pursuit. And the subject of religion is one in which both the United States and state constitutions embody distinct views — in favor of free exercise, but opposed to establishment — that find no counterpart with respect to other callings or professions. That a State would deal differently with religious education for the ministry than with education for other callings is a product of these views, not evidence of hostility toward religion.

Even though the differently worded Washington Constitution draws a more stringent line than that drawn by the United States Constitution, the interest it seeks to further is scarcely novel. In fact, we can think of few areas in which a State's antiestablishment interests come more into play. Since the founding of our country, there have been popular uprisings against procuring taxpayer funds to support church leaders, which was one of the hallmarks of an "established" religion.

Most States that sought to avoid an establishment of religion around the time of the founding placed in their constitutions formal prohibitions against using tax funds to support the ministry. [Here the Chief Justice cited to the Constitutions of Georgia, Pennsylvania, New Jersey, Delaware, Kentucky, Vermont, Tennessee, and Ohio.] The plain text of these constitutional provisions prohibited any tax dollars from supporting the clergy. . . . That early state constitutions saw no problem in explicitly excluding *only* the ministry from receiving state dollars reinforces our conclusion that religious instruction is of a different ilk.

Far from evincing the hostility toward religion which was manifest in *Lukumi*, we believe that the entirety of the Promise Scholarship Program goes a long way toward including religion in its benefits. The program permits students to attend

---

postsecondary education, not to "'encourage a diversity of views from private speakers.'" Our cases dealing with speech forums are simply inapplicable.

Davey also argues that the Equal Protection Clause protects against discrimination on the basis of religion. Because we hold that the program is not a violation of the Free Exercise Clause, however, we apply rational-basis scrutiny to his equal protection claims. For the reasons stated herein, the program passes such review.

pervasively religious schools, so long as they are accredited. . . . And under the Promise Scholarship Program's current guidelines, students are still eligible to take devotional theology courses. . . . [We] find neither in the history or text of Article I, § 11 of the Washington Constitution, nor in the operation of the Promise Scholarship Program, anything that suggests animus towards religion. Given the historic and substantial state interest at issue, we therefore cannot conclude that the denial of funding for vocational religious instruction alone is inherently constitutionally suspect.

Without a presumption of unconstitutionality, Davey's claim must fail. The State's interest in not funding the pursuit of devotional degrees is substantial and the exclusion of such funding places a relatively minor burden on Promise Scholars. If any room exists between the two Religion Clauses, it must be here. We need not venture further into this difficult area in order to uphold the Promise Scholarship Program as currently operated by the State of Washington.

The judgment of the Court of Appeals is therefore reversed.

JUSTICE SCALIA, with whom JUSTICE THOMAS joins, dissenting.

In [*Lukumi*], the majority opinion held that "[a] law burdening religious practice that is not neutral . . . must undergo the most rigorous of scrutiny," and that "the minimum requirement of neutrality is that a law not discriminate on its face." The concurrence of [Justices Blackmun and O'Connor] stated that "[w]hen a law discriminates against religion as such, . . . it automatically will fail strict scrutiny." And the concurrence of [Justice Souter] endorsed the "noncontroversial principle" that "formal neutrality" is a "necessary conditio[n] for free-exercise constitutionality." These opinions are irreconcilable with today's decision, which sustains a public benefits program that facially discriminates against religion.

When the State makes a public benefit generally available, that benefit becomes part of the baseline against which burdens on religion are measured; and when the State withholds that benefit from some individuals solely on the basis of religion, it violates the Free Exercise Clause no less than if it had imposed a special tax. That is precisely what the State of Washington has done here. It has created a generally available public benefit, whose receipt is conditioned only on academic performance, income, and attendance at an accredited school. It has then carved out a solitary course of study for exclusion: theology. No field of study but religion is singled out for disfavor in this fashion. Davey is not asking for a special benefit to which others are not entitled. He seeks only equal treatment—the right to direct his scholarship to his chosen course of study, a right every other Promise Scholar enjoys. . . .

The Court's reference to historical "popular uprisings against procuring taxpayer funds to support church leaders" is therefore quite misplaced. That history involved not the inclusion of religious ministers in public benefits programs like the one at issue here, but laws that singled them out for financial aid. . . . One can concede the Framers' hostility to funding the clergy *specifically*, but that says nothing about whether the clergy had to be excluded from benefits the State made available to all.

No one would seriously contend, for example, that the Framers would have barred ministers from using public roads on their way to church.

The Court does not dispute that the Free Exercise Clause places some constraints on public benefits programs, but finds none here, based on a principle of "'play in the joints.'" I use the term "principle" loosely, for that is not so much a legal principle as a refusal to apply *any* principle when faced with competing constitutional directives. There is nothing anomalous about constitutional commands that abut. A municipality hiring public contractors may not discriminate *against* blacks or *in favor of* them; it cannot discriminate a little bit each way and then plead "play in the joints" when haled into court. If the Religion Clauses demand neutrality, we must enforce them, in hard cases as well as easy ones.

Even if "play in the joints" were a valid legal principle, surely it would apply only when it was a close call whether complying with one of the Religion Clauses would violate the other. But that is not the case here. It is not just that "the State could, consistent with the Federal Constitution, permit Promise Scholars to pursue a degree in devotional theology." The establishment question *would not even be close*, as is evident from the fact that this Court's decision in *Witters v. Washington Dept. of Servs. for Blind*, 474 U.S. 481 (1986), was unanimous [holding that the First Amendment did not preclude a state from extending benefits under its vocational rehabilitation program to a blind person who chose to study at a Christian college to become a pastor, missionary, or youth director]. Perhaps some formally neutral public benefits programs are so gerrymandered and devoid of plausible secular purpose that they might raise specters of state aid to religion, but an evenhanded Promise Scholarship Program is not among them.

In any case, the State already has all the play in the joints it needs. There are any number of ways it could respect both its unusually sensitive concern for the conscience of its taxpayers *and* the Federal Free Exercise Clause. It could make the scholarships redeemable only at public universities (where it sets the curriculum), or only for select courses of study. Either option would replace a program that facially discriminates against religion with one that just happens not to subsidize it. The State could also simply abandon the scholarship program altogether. If that seems a dear price to pay for freedom of conscience, it is only because the State has defined that freedom so broadly that it would be offended by a program with such an incidental, indirect religious effect.

What is the nature of the State's asserted interest here? It cannot be protecting the pocketbooks of its citizens; given the tiny fraction of Promise Scholars who would pursue theology degrees, the amount of any citizen's tax bill at stake is *de minimis*. It cannot be preventing mistaken appearance of endorsement; where a State merely declines to penalize students for selecting a religious major, "no reasonable observer is likely to draw . . . an inference that the State itself is endorsing a religious practice or belief." Nor can Washington's exclusion be defended as a means of assuring that the State will neither favor nor disfavor Davey in his religious calling. Davey will throughout his life contribute to the public fisc through sales taxes on personal purchases, property taxes on his home, and so on; and nothing in the Court's opinion turns on whether Davey winds up a net winner or loser in the State's tax-and-spend scheme.

No, the interest to which the Court defers [is] a pure philosophical preference: the State's opinion that it would violate taxpayers' freedom of conscience *not* to discriminate against candidates for the ministry. This sort of protection of "freedom of conscience" has no logical limit and can justify the singling out of religion for exclusion from public programs in virtually any context. The Court never says whether it deems this interest compelling [but], self-evidently, it is not.

The Court [identifies] two features thought to render its discrimination less offensive. The first is the lightness of Davey's burden. [But the] indignity of being singled out for special burdens on the basis of one's religious calling is so profound that the concrete harm produced can never be dismissed as insubstantial. The Court has not required proof of "substantial" concrete harm with other forms of discrimination, and it should not do so here. Even if there were some threshold quantum-of-harm requirement, surely Davey has satisfied it. The First Amendment, after all, guarantees *free* exercise of religion, and when the State exacts a financial penalty of almost $3,000 for religious exercise — whether by tax or by forfeiture of an otherwise available benefit — religious practice is anything *but* free. . . . The other reason the Court thinks this particular facial discrimination less offensive is that the scholarship program was not motivated by animus toward religion. The Court does not explain why the legislature's motive matters, and I fail to see why it should. . . . It is sufficient that the citizen's rights have been infringed.

[Let] there be no doubt: This case is about discrimination against a religious minority. Most citizens of this country identify themselves as professing some religious belief, but the State's policy poses no obstacle to practitioners of only a tepid, civic version of faith. Those the statutory exclusion actually affects — those whose belief in their religion is so strong that they dedicate their study and their lives to its ministry — are a far narrower set. One need not delve too far into modern popular culture to perceive a trendy disdain for deep religious conviction. . . . When the public's freedom of conscience is invoked to justify denial of equal treatment, benevolent motives shade into indifference and ultimately into repression. Having accepted the justification in this case, the Court is less well equipped to fend it off in the future. I respectfully dissent.

JUSTICE THOMAS, dissenting. [Omitted.]

————

Note: The Blaine Amendments

The original Blaine amendment was an 1875 proposal to revise the First Amendment sponsored by Representative James Blaine of Maine:

> No State shall make any law respecting an establishment of religion or prohibiting the free exercise thereof; and no money raised by taxation in any State for the support of public schools, or derived from any public fund

therefore, nor any public lands devoted thereto, shall ever be under the control of any religious sect, nor shall any money so raised or lands so devoted be divided between religious sects or denominations.

As the text suggests, the two purposes of the proposal were: first, to apply the Religion Clauses to the states, and second, to prohibit state aid to private religious schools. It originated in the politics of the day—Congressman Blaine wanted to run for President—and from the contest between Protestants and Catholics to dominate the common public schools and the related subsequent controversy over funding of private, mostly Catholic, parochial schools. The measure was also fueled by nativist prejudice against immigrants and anti-Catholic sentiment. Much later, of course, the Supreme Court's Incorporation Doctrine would accomplish the first purpose to apply the Religion Clauses to the states via the Fourteenth Amendment. *See supra* Chapter 16, section B. Note: The Incorporation Doctrine. The proposed federal amendment failed to get the two-thirds majority in Congress, however, and never made it to the states for consideration. *See* U.S. Const. art. V.

Proponents then shifted their attention to the states and more than 30 states adopted "Blaine amendments" to their state constitutions by 1890. Many states acted on their own initiative, but Congress did compel several Western states to adopt the measure as a condition for being admitted into the Union. There was considerable variation in the language of the provisions, but the common purpose behind the state Blaine amendments was to expressly prohibit any form of public assistance to sectarian schools.

In *Locke v. Davey*, the majority was careful to drop a footnote and go on record that the State of Washington had consistently maintained—and Respondent Davey did not dispute—that the particular provision being challenged, Wash. Const. art. I, § 11, was not in fact one of the Blaine amendments from this era; therefore, the issue of their constitutionality was not before the Court. In *Mitchell v. Helms* (2000) (Chapter 17), Justice Thomas, writing for a plurality that included Chief Justice Rehnquist and Justices Scalia and Kennedy, referred disapprovingly to the state Blaine amendments as having been "born of bigotry."

If a proper constitutional challenge to a state Blaine amendment were presented to the Supreme Court, how should the Justices go about analyzing the question under the Religion Clauses?

Trinity Lutheran Church of Columbia, Inc. v. Comer

137 S. Ct. 2012 (2017)

Chief Justice Roberts delivered the opinion of the Court, except as to footnote 3.

The Missouri Department of Natural Resources offers state grants to help public and private schools, nonprofit daycare centers, and other nonprofit entities purchase rubber playground surfaces made from recycled tires. Trinity Lutheran Church applied for such a grant for its preschool and daycare center and would have received one, but for the fact that Trinity Lutheran is a church. The Department had a policy of categorically disqualifying churches and other religious organizations from receiving grants under its playground resurfacing program. The question presented is whether the Department's policy violated the rights of Trinity Lutheran under the Free Exercise Clause of the First Amendment.

I

[The Trinity Lutheran Church Child Learning Center is a preschool and daycare center. The Center began as a nonprofit organization in 1980, it merged with Trinity Lutheran Church in 1985, and it currently operates under the Church's auspices on church property. The Center admits students of any religion, and enrollment stands at about 90 children ranging from age two to five. The Center includes a playground, which has coarse pea gravel beneath the play equipment. In 2012, the Center sought to replace the gravel with a pour-in-place rubber surface by participating in Missouri's Scrap Tire Program. That program is administered by Missouri's Department of Natural Resources and is intended to reduce the number of used tires disposed of in landfills and dump sites. The program offers reimbursement grants to qualifying non-profit organizations that purchase playground surfaces made from recycled tires. It is funded through a fee imposed on the sale of new tires in the State. The Department adhered to a strict and express policy of denying grants to any applicant owned or controlled by a religious entity. It believed that this policy was compelled by Article I, Section 7 of the Missouri Constitution, which provides:

> That no money shall ever be taken from the public treasury, directly or indirectly, in aid of any church, sect or denomination of religion, or in aid of any priest, preacher, minister or teacher thereof, as such; and that no preference shall be given to nor any discrimination made against any church, sect or creed of religion, or any form of religious faith or worship.

In a letter rejecting the Center's application, the program director explained that, under Article I, Section 7, the Department could not provide financial assistance directly to a church. The Department awarded 14 grants in 2012. Although the Center ranked fifth out of 44 applicants, it did not receive a grant because it is a church.

Trinity Lutheran sued the Director of the Department in U.S. District Court alleging that the Department's rejection of the Church's grant application violated the Free Exercise Clause. The District Court granted the Department's motion to dismiss, citing *Locke v. Davey*, 540 U.S. 712 (2004). The Court of Appeals for the Eighth Circuit agreed and affirmed. The Eighth Circuit recognized that it was "rather clear" that Missouri could award a scrap tire grant to Trinity Lutheran without running afoul of the Establishment Clause of the United States Constitution, but explained that did not mean the Free Exercise Clause necessarily compelled the State to disregard the antiestablishment principle reflected in its own Constitution. Viewing a monetary grant to a religious institution as a "hallmark of an established religion," the Eighth Circuit concluded that the State could rely on an applicant's religious status to deny its application. We granted certiorari and now reverse.]

II

The First Amendment provides, in part, that "Congress shall make no law respecting an establishment of religion, or prohibiting the free exercise thereof." The parties agree that the Establishment Clause of that Amendment does not prevent Missouri from including Trinity Lutheran in the Scrap Tire Program. That does not, however, answer the question under the Free Exercise Clause, because we have recognized that there is "play in the joints" between what the Establishment Clause permits and the Free Exercise Clause compels. *Locke v. Davey* (2004) [*supra* this chapter].

The Free Exercise Clause "protect[s] religious observers against unequal treatment" and subjects to the strictest scrutiny laws that target the religious for "special disabilities" based on their "religious status." *Church of Lukumi Babalu Aye, Inc. v. Hialeah* (1993) [Chapter 18]. Applying that basic principle, this Court has repeatedly confirmed that denying a generally available benefit solely on account of religious identity imposes a penalty on the free exercise of religion that can be justified only by a state interest "of the highest order."

In *Everson v. Board of Education of Ewing* (1947) [Chapter 17], for example, we upheld against an Establishment Clause challenge a New Jersey law enabling a local school district to reimburse parents for the public transportation costs of sending their children to public and private schools, including parochial schools. In the course of ruling that the Establishment Clause allowed New Jersey to extend that public benefit to all its citizens regardless of their religious belief, we explained that a State "cannot hamper its citizens in the free exercise of their own religion. Consequently, it cannot exclude individual Catholics, Lutherans, Mohammedans, Baptists, Jews, Methodists, Non-believers, Presbyterians, or the members of any other faith, *because of their faith, or lack of it*, from receiving the benefits of public welfare legislation." *Id.* . . .

In recent years, when this Court has rejected free exercise challenges, the laws in question have been neutral and generally applicable without regard to religion. We have been careful to distinguish such laws from those that single out the religious for disfavored treatment. . . . In *Employment Division, Department of Human Resources of Oregon v. Smith* (1990) [Chapter 18], we rejected a free exercise claim brought by two members of a Native American church denied unemployment benefits because they had violated Oregon's drug laws by ingesting peyote for sacramental purposes. [We] held that the Free Exercise Clause did not entitle the church members to a special dispensation from the general criminal laws on account of their religion. At the same time, we again made clear that the Free Exercise Clause *did* guard against the government's imposition of "special disabilities on the basis of religious views or religious status."[2]

---

2. This is not to say that any application of a valid and neutral law of general applicability is necessarily constitutional under the Free Exercise Clause. Recently, in *Hosanna-Tabor Evangelical Lutheran Church and School v. EEOC* (2012) [*supra* this chapter], this Court held that the Religion Clauses required a ministerial exception to the neutral prohibition on employment retaliation contained in the Americans with Disabilities Act. Distinguishing *Smith*, we explained that while that case

[In] *Church of Lukumi Babalu Aye, Inc. v. Hialeah*, we struck down three facially neutral city ordinances that outlawed certain forms of animal slaughter. Members of the Santeria religion challenged the ordinances under the Free Exercise Clause, alleging that despite their facial neutrality, the ordinances had a discriminatory purpose easy to ferret out: prohibiting sacrificial rituals integral to Santeria but distasteful to local residents. We agreed. Before explaining why the challenged ordinances were not, in fact, neutral or generally applicable, the Court recounted the fundamentals of our free exercise jurisprudence. A law, we said, may not discriminate against "some or all religious beliefs." Nor may a law regulate or outlaw conduct because it is religiously motivated. And we restated the now-familiar refrain: The Free Exercise Clause protects against laws that "impose special disabilities on the basis of . . . religious status."

III

A

The Department's policy expressly discriminates against otherwise eligible recipients by disqualifying them from a public benefit solely because of their religious character. If the cases just described make one thing clear, it is that such a policy imposes a penalty on the free exercise of religion that triggers the most exacting scrutiny. *Lukumi Babalu Aye, Inc.* . . . [The] Department's policy puts Trinity Lutheran to a choice: It may participate in an otherwise available benefit program or remain a religious institution. Of course, Trinity Lutheran is free to continue operating as a church . . . . But that freedom comes at the cost of automatic and absolute exclusion from the benefits of a public program for which the Center is otherwise fully qualified. And when the State conditions a benefit in this way, [the] State has punished the free exercise of religion . . . .

The Department contends that merely declining to extend funds to Trinity Lutheran does not *prohibit* the Church from engaging in any religious conduct or otherwise exercising its religious rights. In this sense, says the Department, its policy is unlike the ordinances struck down in *Lukumi*, which outlawed rituals central to Santeria. Here the Department has simply declined to allocate to Trinity Lutheran a subsidy the State had no obligation to provide in the first place. That decision does not meaningfully burden the Church's free exercise rights. And absent any such burden, the argument continues, the Department is free to heed the State's antiestablishment objection to providing funds directly to a church.

It is true the Department has not criminalized the way Trinity Lutheran worships or told the Church that it cannot subscribe to a certain view of the Gospel. But, as the Department itself acknowledges, the Free Exercise Clause protects against "indirect coercion or penalties on the free exercise of religion, not just outright prohibitions." As the Court put it more than 50 years ago, "[i]t is too late in

---

concerned government regulation of physical acts, "[t]he present case, in contrast, concerns government interference with an internal church decision that affects the faith and mission of the church itself."

the day to doubt that the liberties of religion and expression may be infringed by the denial of or placing of conditions upon a benefit or privilege." *Sherbert v. Verner* (1963) [Chapter 18].

Trinity Lutheran is not claiming any entitlement to a subsidy. It instead asserts a right to participate in a government benefit program without having to disavow its religious character. The "imposition of such a condition upon even a gratuitous benefit inevitably deter[s] or discourage[s] the exercise of First Amendment rights." *Sherbert*. The express discrimination against religious exercise here is not the denial of a grant, but rather the refusal to allow the Church — solely because it is a church — to compete with secular organizations for a grant. Trinity Lutheran is a member of the community too, and the State's decision to exclude it for purposes of this public program must withstand the strictest scrutiny.

B

The Department attempts to get out from under the weight of our precedents by arguing that the free exercise question in this case is instead controlled by our decision in *Locke v. Davey*. It is not. In *Locke*, the State of Washington created a scholarship program to assist high-achieving students with the costs of postsecondary education. The scholarships were paid out of the State's general fund, and eligibility was based on criteria such as an applicant's score on college admission tests and family income. While scholarship recipients were free to use the money at accredited religious and non-religious schools alike, they were not permitted to use the funds to pursue a devotional theology degree — one "devotional in nature or designed to induce religious faith." *Id.* Davey was selected for a scholarship but was denied the funds when he refused to certify that he would not use them toward a devotional degree. He sued, arguing that the State's refusal to allow its scholarship money to go toward such degrees violated his free exercise rights.

This Court disagreed. It began by explaining what was *not* at issue. Washington's selective funding program was not comparable to the free exercise violations found in the "*Lukumi* line of cases," including those striking down laws requiring individuals to "choose between their religious beliefs and receiving a government benefit." *Id.* At the outset, then, the Court made clear that *Locke* was not like the case now before us.

Washington's restriction on the use of its scholarship funds was different. According to the Court, the State had "merely chosen not to fund a distinct category of instruction." *Id.* Davey was not denied a scholarship because of who he *was*; he was denied a scholarship because of what he proposed *to do* — use the funds to prepare for the ministry. Here there is no question that Trinity Lutheran was denied a grant simply because of what it is — a church.

The Court in *Locke* also stated that Washington's choice was in keeping with the State's antiestablishment interest in not using taxpayer funds to pay for the training of clergy; in fact, the Court could "think of few areas in which a State's antiestablishment interests come more into play." *Id.* The claimant in *Locke* sought funding for an "essentially religious endeavor" . . . and opposition to such funding "to support church leaders" lay at the historic core of the Religion Clauses. *Id.* Here nothing of the sort can be said about a program to use recycled tires to resurface playgrounds.

Relying on *Locke*, the Department nonetheless emphasizes Missouri's similar constitutional tradition of not furnishing taxpayer money directly to churches. But *Locke* took account of Washington's antiestablishment interest only after determining, as noted, that the scholarship program did not "require students to choose between their religious beliefs and receiving a government benefit." *Id.* As the Court put it, Washington's scholarship program went "a long way toward including religion in its benefits." *Id.* Students in the program were free to use their scholarships at "pervasively religious schools." Davey could use his scholarship to pursue a secular degree at one institution while studying devotional theology at another. *Id.* He could also use his scholarship money to attend a religious college and take devotional theology courses there. *Id.* The only thing he could not do was use the scholarship to pursue a degree in that subject.

In this case, there is no dispute that Trinity Lutheran *is* put to the choice between being a church and receiving a government benefit. The rule is simple: No churches need apply.[3]

C

The State in this case expressly requires Trinity Lutheran to renounce its religious character in order to participate in an otherwise generally available public benefit program, for which it is fully qualified. Our cases make clear that such a condition imposes a penalty on the free exercise of religion that must be subjected to the "most rigorous" scrutiny. *Lukumi v. Babalue Aye, Inc.*[4]

Under that stringent standard, only a state interest "of the highest order" can justify the Department's discriminatory policy. Yet the Department offers nothing more than Missouri's policy preference for skating as far as possible from religious establishment concerns. In the face of the clear infringement on free exercise before us, that interest cannot qualify as compelling. The State has pursued its preferred policy to the point of expressly denying a qualified religious entity a public benefit solely because of its religious character. Under our precedents, that goes too far. The Department's policy violates the Free Exercise Clause.[5]

* * *

The consequence [of the policy of the Missouri Department of Natural Resources] is, in all likelihood, a few extra scraped knees. But the exclusion of Trinity Lutheran

---

3. This case involves express discrimination based on religious identity with respect to playground resurfacing. We do not address religious uses of funding or other forms of discrimination.

4. We have held that "a law targeting religious beliefs as such is never permissible." *Id.* We do not need to decide whether the condition Missouri imposes in this case falls within the scope of that rule, because it cannot survive strict scrutiny in any event.

5. Based on this holding, we need not reach the Church's claim that the policy also violates the Equal Protection Clause.

from a public benefit for which it is otherwise qualified, solely because it is a church, is odious to our Constitution all the same, and cannot stand.

The judgment of the United States Court of Appeals for the Eighth Circuit is reversed, and the case is remanded for further proceedings consistent with this opinion.

It is so ordered.

JUSTICE THOMAS, with whom JUSTICE GORSUCH joins, concurring in part.

[This] Court's endorsement in *Locke* of even a "mil[d] kind" of discrimination against religion remains troubling. *See Locke v. Davey* (2004) (Scalia, J., dissenting) [*supra* this chapter]. But because the Court today appropriately construes *Locke* narrowly, see Part III-B, *ante*, and because no party has asked us to reconsider it, I join nearly all of the Court's opinion. I do not, however, join footnote 3, for the reasons expressed by Justice Gorsuch, *post*, (opinion concurring in part).

JUSTICE GORSUCH, with whom JUSTICE THOMAS joins, concurring in part.

Missouri's law bars Trinity Lutheran from participating in a public benefits program only because it is a church. I agree this violates the First Amendment and I am pleased to join nearly all of the Court's opinion. I offer only two modest qualifications.

First, the Court leaves open the possibility a useful distinction might be drawn between laws that discriminate on the basis of religious *status* and religious *use. See ante.* Respectfully, I harbor doubts about the stability of such a line. . . . Is it a religious group that built the playground? Or did a group build the playground so it might be used to advance a religious mission? The distinction blurs . . . when stared at too long . . . . Often enough the same facts can be described both ways.

Neither do I see why the First Amendment's Free Exercise Clause should care. After all, that Clause guarantees the free *exercise* of religion, not just the right to inward belief (or status). . . . Generally the government may not force people to choose between participation in a public program and their right to free exercise of religion. I don't see why it should matter whether we describe that benefit, say, as closed to Lutherans (status) or closed to people who do Lutheran things (use). It is free exercise either way.

For these reasons, reliance on the status-use distinction does not suffice for me to distinguish *Locke v. Davey* (2004) [*supra* this chapter]. In that case, this Court upheld a funding restriction barring a student from using a scholarship to pursue a degree in devotional theology. But can it really matter whether the restriction in *Locke* was phrased in terms of use instead of status (for was it a student who wanted a vocational degree in religion? or was it a religious student who wanted the necessary education for his chosen vocation?). If that case can be correct and distinguished, it seems it might be only because of the opinion's claim of a long tradition against the use of public funds for training of the clergy, a tradition the Court correctly explains has no analogue here.

Second and for similar reasons, I am unable to join the footnoted observation, *ante* n.3, that "[t]his case involves express discrimination based on religious identity with respect to playground resurfacing." Of course the footnote is entirely correct, but I worry that some might mistakenly read it to suggest that only "playground resurfacing" cases, or only those with some association with children's safety or health, or perhaps some other social good we find sufficiently worthy, are governed by the legal rules recounted in and faithfully applied by the Court's opinion. Such a reading would be unreasonable for our cases are "governed by general principles, rather than *ad hoc* improvisations." And the general principles here do not permit discrimination against religious exercise—whether on the playground or anywhere else.

JUSTICE BREYER, concurring in the judgment.

I agree with much of what the Court says and with its result. But I find relevant, and would emphasize, the particular nature of the "public benefit" here at issue.

The Court stated in *Everson v. Board of Ed. of Ewing* (1947) [Chapter 17], that "cutting off church schools from" such "general government services as ordinary police and fire protection . . . is obviously not the purpose of the First Amendment." Here, the State would cut Trinity Lutheran off from participation in a general program designed to secure or to improve the health and safety of children. I see no significant difference. . . . The sole reason advanced that explains the difference is faith. And it is that last-mentioned fact that calls the Free Exercise Clause into play. We need not go further. Public benefits come in many shapes and sizes. I would leave the application of the Free Exercise Clause to other kinds of public benefits for another day.

JUSTICE SOTOMAYOR, with whom JUSTICE GINSBURG joins, dissenting.

[This] case is about nothing less than the relationship between religious institutions and the civil government—that is, between church and state. The Court today profoundly changes that relationship by holding, for the first time, that the Constitution requires the government to provide public funds directly to a church. Its decision slights both our precedents and our history, and its reasoning weakens this country's longstanding commitment to a separation of church and state beneficial to both.

I

Founded in 1922, Trinity Lutheran Church (Church) "operates . . . for the express purpose of carrying out the commission of . . . Jesus Christ as directed to His church on earth." *Our Story*, http://www.trinity-lcms.org/story. The Church uses "preaching, teaching, worship, witness, service, and fellowship according to the Word of God" to carry out its mission "to 'make disciples.'" *Mission Statement*, http://www.trinity-lcms.org/mission (quoting *Matthew* 28:18–20). The Learning Center serves as "a ministry of the Church and incorporates daily religion and developmentally appropriate activities into . . . [its] program." *Id.* In this way, "[t]hrough the Learning Center, the Church teaches a Christian world view to children of members of the Church, as well as children of non-member residents" of the area. *Id.* These activities represent the Church's "sincere religious belief . . . to use [the Learning Center] to teach the Gospel to children of its members, as well to bring the Gospel message to non-members." *Id.*

II

Properly understood then, this is a case about whether Missouri can decline to fund improvements to the facilities the Church uses to practice and spread its religious views. This Court has repeatedly warned that funding of exactly this kind—payments from the government to a house of worship—would cross the line drawn by the Establishment Clause. *See, e.g., Rosenberger v. Rector and Visitors of Univ. of Va.* (1995) [*infra* this chapter]; *Mitchell v. Helms* (2000) (O'Connor, J., concurring in judgment) [Chapter 17]. So it is surprising that the Court mentions the Establishment Clause only to note the parties' agreement that it "does not prevent Missouri from including Trinity Lutheran in the Scrap Tire Program." *Ante.* Constitutional questions are decided by this Court, not the parties' concessions. The Establishment Clause does not allow Missouri to grant the Church's funding request because the Church uses the Learning Center, including its playground, in conjunction with its religious mission. The Court's silence on this front signals either its misunderstanding of the facts of this case or a startling departure from our precedents.

A

The government may not directly fund religious exercise. Put in doctrinal terms, such funding violates the Establishment Clause because it impermissibly "advances . . . religion."[1] *Agostini v. Felton* (1997) [Chapter 17].

Nowhere is this rule more clearly implicated than when funds flow directly from the public treasury to a house of worship.[2] A house of worship exists to foster and further religious exercise. . . . Within its walls, worshippers gather to practice and reaffirm their faith. And from its base, the faithful reach out to those not yet convinced of the group's beliefs. When a government funds a house of worship, it underwrites this religious exercise.

[The] Church seeks state funds to improve the Learning Center's facilities, which, by the Church's own avowed description, are used to assist the spiritual growth of the children of its members and to spread the Church's faith to the children of nonmembers. The Church's playground surface—like a Sunday School room's walls or the sanctuary's pews—are integrated with and integral to its religious mission. The conclusion that the funding the Church seeks would impermissibly advance religion is inescapable.

True, this Court has found some direct government funding of religious institutions to be consistent with the Establishment Clause. But the funding in those cases

---

1. Government aid that has the "purpose" or "effect of advancing or inhibiting religion" violates the Establishment Clause. *Agostini v. Felton* (1997). Whether government aid has such an effect turns on whether it "results in governmental indoctrination," "defines its recipients by reference to religion," or "creates an excessive entanglement" between the government and religion. *Id.* (same considerations speak to whether the aid can "reasonably be viewed as an endorsement of religion").

2. Because Missouri decides which Scrap Tire Program applicants receive state funding, this case does not implicate a line of decisions about indirect aid programs in which aid reaches religious institutions "only as a result of the genuine and independent choices of private individuals." *Zelman v. Simmons-Harris* (2002) [Chapter 17].

came with assurances that public funds would not be used for religious activity, despite the religious nature of the institution. *See, e.g., Rosenberger* (Souter, J., dissenting) (chronicling cases) [*infra* this chapter]. The Church has not [provided] and cannot provide such assurances here. The Church has a religious mission, one that it pursues through the Learning Center. The playground surface cannot be confined to secular use any more than lumber used to frame the Church's walls, glass stained and used to form its windows, or nails used to build its altar.

B

The Court may simply disagree with this account of the facts and think that the Church does not put its playground to religious use. If so, its mistake is limited to this case. But if it agrees that the State's funding would further religious activity and sees no Establishment Clause problem, then it must be implicitly applying a rule other than the one agreed to in our precedents.

When the Court last addressed direct funding of religious institutions, in *Mitchell v. Helms*, it adhered to the rule that the Establishment Clause prohibits the direct funding of religious activities. At issue was a federal program that helped state and local agencies lend educational materials to public and private schools, including religious schools. *Id.* (plurality opinion). The controlling concurrence assured itself that the program would not lead to the public funding of religious activity. It pointed out that the program allocated secular aid, that it did so "on the basis of neutral, secular criteria," that the aid would not "supplant non-[program] funds," that "no . . . funds ever reach the coffers of religious schools," that "evidence of actual diversion is *de minimis*," and that the program had "adequate safeguards" to police violations. *Id.* (O'Connor, J., concurring in judgment). Those factors, it concluded, were "sufficient to find that the program . . . [did] not have the impermissible effect of advancing religion." *Id.*

A plurality would have instead upheld the program based only on the secular nature of the aid and the program's "neutrality" as to the religious or secular nature of the recipient. *See Mitchell* (plurality opinion). [However,] the controlling concurrence rejected that approach. It viewed the plurality's test—"secular content aid . . . distributed on the basis of wholly neutral criteria"—as constitutionally insufficient. *Id.* (O'Connor, J., concurring in the judgment). This test, explained the concurrence, ignored whether the public funds subsidize religion, the touchstone of establishment jurisprudence.

Today's opinion suggests the Court has made the leap the *Mitchell* plurality could not. For if it agrees that the funding here will finance religious activities, then only a rule that considers that fact irrelevant could support a conclusion of constitutionality. The problems of the "secular and neutral" approach have been aired [in Justice Souter's dissent in *Mitchell*]. *See, e.g., id.* (Souter, J., dissenting). It has no basis in the history to which the Court has repeatedly turned to inform its understanding of the Establishment Clause. It permits direct subsidies for religious indoctrination, with all the attendant concerns that led to the Establishment Clause. And it favors certain religious groups, those with a belief system that allows them to compete for public dollars and those well-organized and well-funded enough to do so successfully.

Such a break with precedent would mark a radical mistake. The Establishment Clause protects both religion and government from the dangers that result when the two become entwined, "*not* by providing every religion with an *equal opportunity* (say, to secure state funding or to pray in the public schools), but by drawing fairly clear lines of *separation* between church and state—at least where the heartland of religious belief, such as primary religious [worship], is at issue." *Zelman v. Simmons-Harris* (2002) (Breyer, J., dissenting) [Chapter 17].

III

Even assuming the absence of an Establishment Clause violation and proceeding on the Court's preferred front—the Free Exercise Clause—the Court errs. It claims that the government may not draw lines based on an entity's religious "status." But we have repeatedly said that it can. When confronted with government action that draws such a line, we have carefully considered whether the interests embodied in the Religion Clauses justify that line. The question here is thus whether those interests support the line drawn in Missouri's Article I, § 7, separating the State's treasury from those of houses of worship. They unquestionably do.

A

The Establishment Clause prohibits laws "respecting an establishment of religion" and the Free Exercise Clause prohibits laws "prohibiting the free exercise thereof." U.S. Const., Amdt. 1. "[I]f expanded to a logical extreme," these prohibitions "would tend to clash with the other." *Walz v. Tax Comm'n* (1970). Even in the absence of a violation of one of the Religion Clauses, the interaction of government and religion can raise concerns that sound in both Clauses. For that reason, the government may sometimes act to accommodate those concerns, even when not required to do so by the Free Exercise Clause, without violating the Establishment Clause. And the government may sometimes act to accommodate those concerns, even when not required to do so by the Establishment Clause, without violating the Free Exercise Clause. "[T]here is room for play in the joints productive of a benevolent neutrality which will permit religious exercise to exist without sponsorship and without interference." *Id.* This space between the two Clauses gives government some room to recognize the unique status of religious entities and to single them out on that basis for exclusion from otherwise generally applicable laws.

Invoking this principle, this Court has held that the government may sometimes relieve religious entities from the requirements of government programs. A State need not, for example, require nonprofit houses of worship to pay property taxes. . . . But the government may not invoke the space between the Religion Clauses in a manner that "devolve[s] into an unlawful fostering of religion." *Cutter v. Wilkinson* (2005).

Invoking this same principle, this Court has held that the government may sometimes close off certain government aid programs to religious entities. The State need not, for example, fund the training of a religious group's leaders . . . . It may instead avoid the historic "antiestablishment interests" raised by the use of "taxpayer funds to support church leaders." *Locke v. Davey* (2004) [*supra* this chapter]. When reviewing a law that, like this one, singles out religious entities for exclusion from its reach, we thus have not myopically focused on the fact that a law singles out religious entities, but on the reasons that it does so.

B

Missouri has decided that the unique status of houses of worship requires a special rule when it comes to public funds. Its Constitution reflects that choice [as provided in Article I, Section 7.] Missouri's decision, which has deep roots in our Nation's history, reflects a reasonable and constitutional judgment.

1

This Court has consistently looked to history for guidance when applying the Constitution's Religion Clauses. Those Clauses guard against a return to the past, and so that past properly informs their meaning. . . .

This Nation's early experience with, and eventual rejection of, established religion—shorthand for "sponsorship, financial support, and active involvement of the sovereign in religious activity"—defies easy summary. No two States' experiences were the same. In some a religious establishment never took hold. In others establishment varied in terms of the sect (or sects) supported, the nature and extent of that support, and the uniformity of that support across the State. Where establishment did take hold, it lost its grip at different times and at different speeds. *See* T. Cobb, The Rise of Religious Liberty in America 510–11 (1970).

Despite this rich diversity of experience, the story relevant here is one of consistency. The use of public funds to support core religious institutions can safely be described as a hallmark of the States' early experiences with religious establishment. Every state establishment saw laws passed to raise public funds and direct them toward houses of worship and ministers. And as the States all disestablished, one by one, they all undid those laws.[5]

Those who fought to end the public funding of religion based their opposition on a powerful set of arguments, all stemming from the basic premise that the practice harmed both civil government and religion. The civil government, they maintained, could claim no authority over religious belief. For them, support for religion compelled by the State marked an overstep of authority that would only lead to more. Equally troubling, it risked divisiveness by giving religions reason to compete for the State's beneficence. Faith, they believed, was a personal matter, entirely between an individual and his god. Religion was best served when sects reached out on the basis of their tenets alone, unsullied by outside forces, allowing adherents to come to their faith voluntarily. Over and over, these arguments gained acceptance and led to the end of state laws exacting payment for the support of religion. . . .

---

5. This Court did not hold that the Religion Clauses applied, through the Fourteenth Amendment, to the States until the 1940's. *See Cantwell v. Connecticut* (1940) (Free Exercise Clause); *Everson v. Board of Ed. of Ewing* (1947) (Establishment Clause). When the States dismantled their religious establishments, as all had by the 1830's, they did so on their own accord, in response to the lessons taught by their experiences with religious establishments.

The course of this history shows that those who lived under the laws and practices that formed religious establishments made a considered decision that civil government should not fund ministers and their houses of worship. To us, their debates may seem abstract and this history remote. That is only because we live in a society that has long benefited from decisions made in response to these now centuries-old arguments, a society that those not so fortunate fought hard to build.

2

In *Locke*, this Court expressed an understanding of, and respect for, this history. *Locke* involved a provision of the State of Washington's Constitution that, like Missouri's nearly identical Article I, § 7, barred the use of public funds for houses of worship or ministers. Consistent with this denial of funds to ministers, the State's college scholarship program did not allow funds to be used for devotional theology degrees. When asked whether this violated the would-be minister's free exercise rights, the Court invoked the play in the joints principle and answered no. The Establishment Clause did not require the prohibition because "the link between government funds and religious training [was] broken by the independent and private choice of [scholarship] recipients." Nonetheless, the denial did not violate the Free Exercise Clause because a "historic and substantial state interest" supported the constitutional provision. The Court could "think of few areas in which a State's antiestablishment interests come more into play" than the "procuring [of] taxpayer funds to support church leaders." *Id.*

The same is true of this case, about directing taxpayer funds to houses of worship. Like the use of public dollars for ministers at issue in *Locke*, turning over public funds to houses of worship implicates serious antiestablishment and free exercise interests. The history just discussed fully supports this conclusion. As states disestablished, they repealed laws allowing taxation to support religion because the practice threatened other forms of government support for, involved some government control over, and weakened supporters' control of religion. Common sense also supports this conclusion. Recall that a state may not fund religious activities without violating the Establishment Clause. *See* Part II-A, *supra*. A state can reasonably use status as a "house of worship" as a stand-in for "religious activities." Inside a house of worship, dividing the religious from the secular would require intrusive line-drawing by government, and monitoring those lines would entangle government with the house of worship's activities. . . . Finally, and of course, such funding implicates the free exercise rights of taxpayers by denying them the chance to decide for themselves whether and how to fund religion. If there is any "'room for play in the joints' between" the Religion Clauses, it is here.

As was true in *Locke*, a prophylactic rule against the use of public funds for houses of worship is a permissible accommodation of these weighty interests. The [Missouri] rule has a historical pedigree identical to that of the [Washington] provision in *Locke*. Almost all of the States that ratified the Religion Clauses [in 1791] operated under this rule. . . . Today, thirty-eight States have a counterpart to Missouri's Article I, § 7. [Footnoted lists of the referenced States are omitted.] [That] so many States have for so long drawn a line that prohibits public funding for houses of worship, based on principles rooted in this Nation's understanding of how best to foster religious liberty, supports the conclusion that public funding of houses of worship "is of a different ilk." *Locke v. Davey*.

And as in *Locke*, Missouri's Article I, § 7, is closely tied to the state interests it protects. A straightforward reading of Article I, § 7, prohibits funding only for "any church, sect, or denomination of religion, or in aid of any priest, preacher, minister or teacher thereof, as such." The Missouri courts have not read the State's Constitution to reach more broadly, to prohibit funding for other religiously affiliated institutions, or more broadly still, to prohibit the funding of religious believers. . . . Article I, § 7, thus stops Missouri only from funding specific entities, ones that set and enforce religious doctrine for their adherents. These are the entities that most acutely raise the establishment and free exercise concerns that arise when public funds flow to religion.

Missouri has recognized the simple truth that, even absent an Establishment Clause violation, the transfer of public funds to houses of worship raises concerns that sit exactly between the Religion Clauses. To avoid those concerns, and only those concerns, it has prohibited such funding. In doing so, it made the same choice made by the earliest States centuries ago and many other States in the years since. The Constitution permits this choice.

3

[The] Constitution creates specific rules that control how the government may interact with religious entities. And so of course a government may act based on a religious entity's "status" as such. It is that very status that implicates the interests protected by the Religion Clauses. Sometimes a religious entity's unique status requires the government to act. Other times, it merely permits the government to act. In all cases, the dispositive issue is not whether religious "status" matters — it does, or the Religion Clauses would not be at issue — but whether the government must, or may, act on that basis.

Start where the Court stays silent. Its opinion does not acknowledge that our precedents have expressly approved of a government's choice to draw lines based on an entity's religious status. Those cases did not deploy strict scrutiny to create a presumption of unconstitutionality, as the Court does today. Instead, they asked whether the government had offered a strong enough reason to justify drawing a line based on that status.

The Court takes two steps to avoid these precedents. First, it recasts *Locke* as a case about a restriction that prohibited the would-be minister from "us[ing] the funds to prepare for the ministry." *Ante*. A faithful reading of *Locke* gives it a broader reach. *Locke* stands for the reasonable proposition that the government may, but need not, choose not to fund certain religious entities (there, ministers) where doing so raises "historic and substantial" establishment and free exercise concerns. *Id*. Second, it suggests that this case is different because it involves "discrimination" in the form of the denial of access to a possible benefit. *Ante*. But in this area of law, a decision to treat entities differently based on distinctions that the Religion Clauses make relevant does not amount to discrimination. To understand why, keep in mind that "the Court has unambiguously concluded that the individual freedom of conscience protected by the First Amendment embraces the right to select any religious faith or none at all." *Wallace v. Jaffree* (1985) [Chapter 17]. If the denial of a benefit others may receive is discrimination that violates the Free Exercise Clause, then the accommodations of religious entities we have approved would violate the free exercise rights of nonreligious entities. We have, with good reason, rejected that idea and instead focused on whether the government has provided a good enough reason, based in the values the Religion Clauses protect, for its decision. [A] State's decision not to fund houses of worship does not disfavor religion; rather, it represents a valid choice to remain secular in the face of serious establishment and free exercise concerns. . . .

Justice Breyer's concurrence offers a narrower rule that would limit the effects of today's decision, but that rule does not resolve this case. Justice Breyer, like the Court, thinks that "denying a generally available benefit solely on account of religious identity imposes a penalty on the free exercise of religion that can be justified only by a state interest of the highest order," *ante* (majority opinion). *See ante* (Breyer, J., concurring in judgment). Few would disagree with a literal interpretation of this statement. To fence out religious persons or entities from a truly generally available public benefit—one provided to all, no questions asked, such as police or fire protections—would violate the Free Exercise Clause. This explains why Missouri does not apply its constitutional provision in that manner. Nor has it done so here. The Scrap Tire Program offers not a generally available benefit but a selective benefit for a few recipients each year. In this context, the comparison to truly generally available benefits is inapt.

On top of all of this, the Court's application of its new rule here is mistaken. In concluding that Missouri's Article I, § 7, cannot withstand strict scrutiny, the Court describes Missouri's interest as a mere "policy preference for skating as far as possible from religious establishment concerns." *Ante.* The constitutional provisions of thirty-nine States—all but invalidated today—the weighty interests they protect, and the history they draw on deserve more than this judicial brush aside.[14] Today's decision discounts centuries of history and jeopardizes the government's ability to remain secular. . . .

IV

The Religion Clauses of the First Amendment contain a promise from our government and a backstop that disables our government from breaking it. The Free Exercise Clause extends the promise. We each retain our inalienable right to "the free

---

14. In the end, the soundness of today's decision may matter less than what it might enable tomorrow. The principle it establishes can be manipulated to call for a similar fate for lines drawn on the basis of religious use. *See ante* (Gorsuch, J., concurring in part); *see also ante* (Thomas, J., concurring in part) (going further and suggesting that lines drawn on the basis of religious status amount to *per se* unconstitutional discrimination on the basis of religious belief). It is enough for today to explain why the Court's decision is wrong. The error of the concurrences' hoped-for decisions can be left for tomorrow. . . .

exercise" of religion, to choose for ourselves whether to believe and how to worship. And the Establishment Clause erects the backstop. Government cannot, through the enactment of a "law respecting an establishment of religion," start us down the path to the past, when this right was routinely abridged.

The Court today dismantles a core protection for religious freedom provided in these Clauses. It holds not just that a government may support houses of worship with taxpayer funds, but that—at least in this case and perhaps in others, *see ante* n.3—it must do so whenever it decides to create a funding program. History shows that the Religion Clauses separate the public treasury from religious coffers as one measure to secure the kind of freedom of conscience that benefits both religion and government. If this separation means anything, it means that the government cannot, or at the very least need not, tax its citizens and turn that money over to houses of worship. The Court today blinds itself to the outcome this history requires and leads us instead to a place where separation of church and state is a constitutional slogan, not a constitutional commitment. I dissent.

———

Problem: The Good Friday School Holiday

Suppose you are a U.S. District Judge. Finish drafting this opinion by explaining who should win and why, taking into account both Religion Clauses:

Christians believe that Jesus Christ was crucified on a Friday afternoon in the spring and that he rose from the dead the following Sunday. The crucifixion is commemorated on Good Friday, the resurrection on Easter Sunday. In 1941, the State made Good Friday a state holiday; state facilities, including schools (but not colleges or universities), were to be closed on that day. There is no contemporaneous legislative history. In 1989, the State legislature rescinded Good Friday as a state holiday but retained it as a school holiday, and so it remains. 105 State Stat. § 5/24-2. All public schools (below the college level) in the state are closed that day but the teachers are paid just as for other holidays. Schoolchildren are excused from attending school on other days if their religion requires their absence and some school districts, apparently without thereby violating any state law, close for major Jewish holidays. But apart from Christmas and Thanksgiving, Good Friday is the only holiday of religious origin or character on which all the public schools of the state are closed, by virtue of the statute being attacked here in a suit under 42 U.S.C. § 1983 by a public school teacher who objects, among other things, to the use of public funds from taxes that she pays to pay teachers for the Good Friday holiday. . . .

C. Religious Speech

Our precedent establishes that private religious speech, far from being a First Amendment orphan, is as fully protected under the Free Speech Clause as secular private expression. Indeed, in Anglo-American history, at least, government suppression of speech has so commonly been directed *precisely* at religious speech that a free-speech clause without religion would be Hamlet without the prince. Accordingly, we have not excluded from free-speech protections religious proselytizing or even acts of worship.

Capitol Square Review & Advisory Bd. v. Pinette, 515 U.S. 753, 760 (1995) (plurality opinion). From a litigation perspective, religious speech cases generally fall into two broad categories. In one category, the government has denied access to facilities or funding to a speaker or group who wants to engage in religious speech, and the speaker or group is suing the government. In the other category, the government has authorized or facilitated the religious speech, and someone else is suing the government to complain of an improper endorsement.

The relevant principle of the First Amendment that governs both categories of cases can be simply stated: "there is a crucial difference between *government* speech endorsing religion, which the Establishment Clause forbids, and *private* speech endorsing religion, which the Free Speech and Free Exercise Clauses protect." *Bd. of Educ. of Westside Cmty. Schools (Dist. 66) v. Mergens*, 496 U.S. 226, 250 (1990) (plurality opinion). Everyone, on and off the Court, accepts that basic distinction as a constitutional given. However, a pervasive feature of modern life—perhaps best understood as an aspect of the so-called culture wars—is that both sides are quick to go to court to litigate governmental action that they believe falls on the wrong side of the line. Those seeking to restrict religious speech in public places always try to make out a case of government sponsorship; those seeking to expand religious speech in public places always try to make out a case of private prayer. Consequently, the public square today is a deeply contested space regarding the issue of religious speech. (Also recall the concept of government speech from Chapter 13.)

———

Note: The Free Speech-Public Forum Overlay

A relatively recent development in litigation over the Religion Clauses has been the introduction of free speech claims. In part, this development has been a reaction to a series of Supreme Court decisions holding that access to particular government facilities for religious speakers not only was permitted by the Establishment Clause, but was required by the Free Speech Clause. This Free Speech-Public Forum Overlay is subtle and complex.

As was explored more fully in Chapter 8, Free Speech Clause doctrine distinguishes among three kinds of government-owned property: (1) traditional or quintessential public forums; (2) designated or limited public forums; and (3) non-forum public property. In *Int'l Soc'y of Krishna Consciousness v. Lee*, 505 U.S. 672, 678–79 (1992), Chief Justice Rehnquist briefly summarized the rules applicable to each of the three categories:

Under [the forum-based] approach, regulation of speech on government property that has traditionally been available for public expression is subject to the highest scrutiny. Such regulations survive only if they are narrowly drawn to achieve a compelling state interest. The second category of public property is the designated public forum, whether of a limited or unlimited character—property that the State has opened for expressive activity by part or all of the public. Regulation of such property is subject to the same limitations as that governing a traditional public forum. Finally, there is all remaining public property. Limitations on expressive activity conducted on this last category of property must survive only a much more limited review. The challenged regulation need only be reasonable, as long as the regulation is not an effort to suppress the speaker's activity due to disagreement with the speaker's view.

The important free speech difference is that the second and third categories—the designated or limited public forum and the non-forum public property—can be opened to private speakers with limitations based either on the subject matter of the speech or on the identity of the speaker, i.e., content discrimination is permissible. The government may never discriminate on the basis of viewpoint, however, even in a non-forum government property.

The upshot of this doctrine is that whether a religious speaker may constitutionally be excluded from a public place often depends on whether the exclusion is deemed to be based on content or viewpoint. On that point there is no dispute within the Court. But the Justices often disagree sharply as to which type of discrimination is being practiced in a given case.

Rosenberger v. Rector and Visitors of the University of Virginia
515 U.S. 819 (1995)

Justice Kennedy delivered the opinion of the Court.

The University of Virginia, an instrumentality of the Commonwealth and thus bound by the First and Fourteenth Amendments, authorizes the payment of outside contractors for the printing costs of a variety of student publications [from its Student Activities Fund ("SAF")]. It withheld any authorization for payments on behalf of petitioners for the sole reason that their student paper "primarily promotes or manifests a particular belief in or about a deity or an ultimate reality." That the paper *Wide Awake: A Christian Perspective at the University of Virginia* did in fact fall within this defined exclusion [in the funding regulations] seems plain enough. The challenge is to the University's regulation and its denial of authorization, the case raising issues under the Speech and Establishment Clauses of the First Amendment.

[Petitioners' organization, Wide Awake Productions ("WAP"), and three of its editors and members filed suit challenging the withholding of funds. The District Court rejected their claims and ruled for the University; the U.S. Court of Appeals for the Fourth Circuit affirmed, concluding that the discrimination by the University was justified by the "compelling interest in maintaining strict separation of church and state."] We granted certiorari.

II

It is axiomatic that the government may not regulate speech based on its substantive content or the message it conveys. *Police Department of Chicago v. Mosely* (1972) [Chapter 5]. Other principles follow from this precept. In the realm of private speech or expression, government regulation may not favor one speaker over another. Discrimination against speech because of its message is presumed to be unconstitutional. . . . When the government targets not subject matter, but particular views taken by speakers on a subject, the violation of the First Amendment is all the more blatant. *R.A.V. v. City of St. Paul* (1992) [Chapter 15]. Viewpoint discrimination is thus an egregious form of content discrimination. The government must abstain from regulating speech when the specific motivating ideology or the opinion or perspective of the speaker is the rationale for the restriction.

These principles provide the framework forbidding the State from exercising viewpoint discrimination, even when the limited public forum is one of its own creation. In a case involving a school district's provision of school facilities for private uses, we declared that "there is no question that the District, like the private owner of property, may legally preserve the property under its control for the use to which it is dedicated." *Lamb's Chapel v. Center Moriches Union Free School Dist.*, 508 U.S. 384 (1993). The necessities of confining a forum to the limited and legitimate purposes for which it was created may justify the State in reserving it for certain groups or for the discussion of certain topics. Once it has opened a limited forum, however, the State must respect the lawful boundaries it has itself set. The State may not exclude speech where its distinction is not "reasonable in light of the purpose served by the forum," nor may it discriminate against speech on the basis of its viewpoint. Thus, in determining whether the State is acting to preserve the limits of the forum it has created so that the exclusion of a class of speech is legitimate, we have observed a distinction between, on the one hand, content discrimination, which may be permissible if it preserves the purposes of that limited forum, and, on the other hand, viewpoint discrimination, which is presumed impermissible when directed against speech otherwise within the forum's limitations.

The SAF is a forum more in a metaphysical than in a spatial or geographic sense, but the same principles are applicable. The most recent and most apposite case is our decision in *Lamb's Chapel*. There, a school district had opened school facilities for use after school hours by community groups for a wide variety of social, civic, and recreational purposes. The district, however, had enacted a formal policy against opening facilities to groups for religious purposes. Invoking its policy, the district rejected a request from a group desiring to show a film series addressing various child-rearing questions from a "Christian perspective." . . . Our conclusion was unanimous: "It discriminates on the basis of viewpoint to permit school property to be used for the presentation of all views about family issues and child rearing except those dealing with the subject matter from a religious standpoint."

The University ... [insists] that this case does not present that issue because the Guidelines draw lines based on content, not viewpoint. ... It is, in a sense, something of an understatement to speak of religious thought and discussion as just a viewpoint, as distinct from a comprehensive body of thought. The nature of our origins and destiny and their dependence upon the existence of a divine being have been subjects of philosophic inquiry throughout human history. ... Religion may be a vast area of inquiry, but it also provides, as it did here, a specific premise, a perspective, a standpoint from which a variety of subjects may be discussed and considered. ...

The University's denial of WAP's request for third-party payments in the present case is based upon viewpoint discrimination not unlike the discrimination the school district relied upon in *Lamb's Chapel* and that we found invalid. ... [Just] as the school district in *Lamb's Chapel* pointed to nothing but the religious views of the group as the rationale for excluding its message, so in this case the University justifies its denial of SAF participation to WAP on the ground that the contents of *Wide Awake* reveal an avowed religious perspective. ...

The University tries to escape the consequences of our holding in *Lamb's Chapel* by urging that this case involves the provision of funds rather than access to facilities. ... It does not follow, however, [that] viewpoint-based restrictions are proper when the University does not itself speak or subsidize transmittal of a message it favors but instead expends funds to encourage a diversity of views from private speakers. A holding that the University may not discriminate based on the viewpoint of private persons whose speech it facilitates does not restrict the University's own speech, which is controlled by different principles. ... The University's regulation now before us, however, has a speech-based restriction as its sole rationale and operative principle.

The distinction between the University's own favored message and the private speech of students is evident in the case before us. ... The University declares that the student groups eligible for SAF support are not the University's agents, are not subject to its control, and are not its responsibility. Having offered to pay the third-party contractors on behalf of private speakers who convey their own messages, the University may not silence the expression of selected viewpoints. ...

Vital First Amendment speech principles are at stake here. The first danger to liberty lies in granting the State the power to examine publications to determine whether or not they are based on some ultimate idea and, if so, for the State to classify them. The second, and corollary, danger is to speech from the chilling of individual thought and expression. That danger is especially real in the University setting, where the State acts against a background and tradition of thought and experiment that is at the center of our intellectual and philosophic tradition. ... For the University, by regulation, to cast disapproval on particular viewpoints of its students risks the suppression of free speech and creative inquiry in one of the vital centers for the Nation's intellectual life, its college and university campuses. The Guideline invoked by the University to deny third-party contractor payments on behalf of WAP effects a sweeping restriction on student thought and student inquiry in the context of University sponsored publications. . . .

Based on the principles we have discussed, we hold that the regulation invoked to deny SAF support, both in its terms and in its application to these petitioners, is a denial of their right of free speech guaranteed by the First Amendment. It remains to be considered whether the violation following from the University's action is excused by the necessity of complying with the Constitution's prohibition against state establishment of religion. We turn to that question.

III

[The University argued] at all stages of the litigation that inclusion of [Wide Awake Productions' outside printing] contractors in SAF funding authorization would violate the Establishment Clause. . . . We granted certiorari on this question: "Whether the Establishment Clause compels a state university to exclude an otherwise eligible student publication from participation in the student activities fund, solely on the basis of its religious viewpoint, where such exclusion would violate the Speech and Press Clauses if the viewpoint of the publication were nonreligious." . . .

A central lesson of our decisions is that a significant factor in upholding governmental programs in the face of Establishment Clause attack is their neutrality towards religion. We have decided a series of cases addressing the receipt of government benefits where religion or religious views are implicated in some degree. . . . We have held that the guarantee of neutrality is respected, not offended, when the government, following neutral criteria and evenhanded policies, extends benefits to recipients whose ideologies and viewpoints, including religious ones, are broad and diverse. More than once have we rejected the position that the Establishment Clause even justifies, much less requires, a refusal to extend free speech rights to religious speakers who participate in broad-reaching government programs neutral in design.

The governmental program here is neutral toward religion. There is no suggestion that the University created it to advance religion or adopted some ingenious device with the purpose of aiding a religious cause. The object of the SAF is to open a forum for speech and to support various student enterprises, including the publication of newspapers, in recognition of the diversity and creativity of student life. The University's SAF Guidelines have a separate classification for, and do not make third-party payments on behalf of, "religious organizations," which are those "whose purpose is to practice a devotion to an acknowledged ultimate reality or deity." The category of support here is for "student news, information, opinion, entertainment, or academic communications media groups." . . . WAP did not seek a subsidy because of its Christian editorial viewpoint; it sought funding as a student journal, which it was.

The neutrality of the program distinguishes the student fees from a tax levied for the direct support of a church or group of churches. A tax of that sort, of course, would run contrary to Establishment Clause concerns dating from the earliest days of the Republic. The apprehensions of our predecessors involved the levying of taxes upon the public for the sole and exclusive purpose of establishing and supporting specific sects. The exaction here, by contrast, is a student activity fee designed to reflect the reality that student life in its many dimensions includes the necessity of wide-ranging speech and inquiry and that student expression is an integral part of the University's educational mission. . . . Here, the disbursements from the fund go to private contractors for the cost of printing that which is protected under the Speech Clause of the First Amendment. This is a far cry from a general public assessment designed and effected to provide financial support for a church.

Government neutrality is apparent in the State's overall scheme in a further meaningful respect. The program respects the critical difference "between *government* speech endorsing religion, which the Establishment Clause forbids, and *private* speech endorsing religion, which the Free Speech and Free Exercise Clauses protect." In this case, "the government has not fostered or encouraged" any mistaken impression that the student newspapers speak for the University. The University has taken pains to disassociate itself from the private speech involved in this case. . . .

It does not violate the Establishment Clause for a public university to grant access to its facilities on a religion-neutral basis to a wide spectrum of student groups. . . . [It] follows that a public university may maintain its own computer facility and give student groups access to that facility, including the use of the printers, on a religion neutral, say first-come-first-served, basis. If a religious student organization obtained access on that religion-neutral basis and used a computer to compose or a printer or copy machine to print speech with a religious content or viewpoint, the State's action in providing the group with access would [not] violate the Establishment Clause. . . . There is no difference in logic or principle, and no difference of constitutional significance, between a school using its funds to operate a facility to which students have access, and a school paying a third-party contractor to operate the facility on its behalf. The latter occurs here. The University provides printing services to a broad spectrum of student newspapers. . . . Any benefit to religion is incidental to the government's provision of secular services for secular purposes on a religion-neutral basis. Printing is a routine, secular, and recurring attribute of student life. By paying outside printers, the University in fact attains a further degree of separation from the student publication, for it avoids the duties of supervision, escapes the costs of upkeep, repair, and replacement attributable to student use, and has a clear record of costs. . . .

To obey the Establishment Clause, it was not necessary for the University to deny eligibility to student publications because of their viewpoint. . . . There is no Establishment Clause violation in the University's honoring its duties under the Free Speech Clause.

The judgment of the Court of Appeals must be, and is, reversed.

Justice O'Connor, concurring.

. . . This case lies at the intersection of the principle of government neutrality and the prohibition on state funding of religious activities. It is clear that the University has established a generally applicable program to encourage the free exchange of ideas by its students, an expressive marketplace that includes [student] publications with predictably divergent viewpoints. It is equally clear that petitioners' viewpoint is religious and that publication of *Wide Awake* is a religious activity. . . . Not to finance *Wide Awake*, according to petitioners, violates the principle of neutrality by sending a message of hostility toward religion. To finance *Wide Awake*, argues the University, violates the prohibition on direct state funding of religious activities. . . . [In this case, certain] considerations specific to the program at issue lead me to conclude that by providing the same assistance to *Wide Awake* that it does to other publications, the University would not be endorsing the magazine's religious perspective.

First, the student organizations, at the University's insistence, remain strictly independent of the University. And the agreement requires that student organizations include in every letter, contract, publication, or other written materials the following disclaimer:

> Although this organization has members who are University of Virginia students (faculty) (employees), the organization is independent of the corporation which is the University and which is not responsible for the organization's contracts, acts or omissions.

Any reader of *Wide Awake* would be on notice of the publication's independence from the University.

Second, financial assistance is distributed in a manner that ensures its use only for [the] University's purpose in maintaining a free and robust marketplace of ideas, from whatever perspective. . . .

Third, assistance is provided to the religious publication in a context that makes improbable any perception of government endorsement of the religious message. *Wide Awake* . . . [competes] with 15 other magazines and newspapers. . . . The widely divergent viewpoints of these many purveyors of opinion, all supported on an equal basis by the University, significantly diminishes the danger that the message of any one publication is perceived as endorsed by the University. [For] example, the University has provided support to *The Yellow Journal*, a humor magazine that has targeted Christianity as a subject of satire. . . . Given this wide array of nonreligious, anti-religious and competing religious viewpoints in the forum supported by the University, any perception that the University endorses one particular viewpoint would be illogical. This is not the harder case where religious speech threatens to dominate the forum.

The Court's decision today therefore neither trumpets the supremacy of the neutrality principle nor signals the demise of the funding prohibition in Establishment Clause jurisprudence. . . . When bedrock principles collide, they test the limits of categorical obstinacy and expose the flaws and dangers of a Grand Unified Theory that may turn out to be neither grand nor unified. The Court today does only what courts must do in many Establishment Clause cases—focus on specific features of a particular government action to ensure that it does not violate the Constitution. By withholding from *Wide Awake* assistance that the University provides generally to all other student publications, the University has discriminated on the basis of the magazine's religious viewpoint in violation of the Free Speech Clause. And particular features of the University's program [convince] me that providing such assistance in this case would not carry the danger of impermissible use of public funds to endorse *Wide Awake*'s religious message.

JUSTICE THOMAS, concurring. [Omitted.]

JUSTICE SOUTER, with whom JUSTICE STEVENS, JUSTICE GINSBURG, and JUSTICE BREYER join, dissenting.

The Court today, for the first time, approves direct funding of core religious activities by an arm of the State. [I] would hold that the University's refusal to support petitioners' religious activities is compelled by the Establishment Clause. I would therefore affirm.

I

The central question in this case is whether a grant from the Student Activities Fund to pay *Wide Awake*'s printing expenses would violate the Establishment Clause. Although the Court does not dwell on the details of *Wide Awake*'s message, it recognizes something sufficiently religious in the publication to demand Establishment Clause scrutiny.... The Court's difficulties will be all the more clear after a closer look at *Wide Awake* than the majority opinion affords. [Here the dissent summarized and quoted from past issues of *Wide Awake*.]

This writing is no merely descriptive examination of religious doctrine or even of ideal Christian practice in confronting life's social and personal problems. Nor is it merely the expression of editorial opinion that incidentally coincides with Christian ethics and reflects a Christian view of human obligation. It is straightforward exhortation to enter into a relationship with God as revealed in Jesus Christ, and to satisfy a series of moral obligations derived from the teachings of Jesus Christ. These are not the words of "student news, information, opinion, entertainment, or academic communication ..." (in the language of the University's funding criterion) but the words of "challenge [to] Christians to live, in word and deed, according to the faith they proclaim and ... to consider what a personal relationship with Jesus Christ means" (in the language of *Wide Awake*'s founder)....

Using public funds for the direct subsidization of preaching the word is categorically forbidden under the Establishment Clause, and if the Clause was meant to accomplish nothing else, it was meant to bar this use of public money....

The principle against direct funding with public money is patently violated by the contested use of today's student activity fee. Like today's taxes generally, the [$14.00 per semester] fee is Madison's threepence. The University exercises the power of the State to compel a student to pay it, and the use of any part of it for the direct support of religious activity thus strikes at what we have repeatedly held to be the heart of the prohibition on establishment....

... The Court starts with the [forum-access] cases, in which religious groups were held to be entitled to access for speaking in government buildings open generally for that purpose. The Court reasons that the availability of a forum has economic value (the government built and maintained the building, while the speakers saved the rent for a hall); and that economically there is no difference between the University's provision of the value of the room and the value, say, of the University's printing equipment; and that therefore the University must be able to provide the use of the latter. Since it may do that, the argument goes, it would be unduly formalistic to draw the line at paying for an outside printer, who simply does what the magazine's publishers could have done with the University's own printing equipment.

The argument is as unsound as it is simple, and the first of its troubles emerges from an examination of the cases relied upon to support it. The common factual thread running through [the forum-access cases] is that a governmental institution created a limited forum for the use of students in a school or college, or for the public at large, but sought to exclude speakers with religious messages. In each case the restriction was struck down either as an impermissible attempt to regulate the content of speech in an open forum . . . or to suppress a particular religious viewpoint . . . . In each case, to be sure, the religious speaker's use of the room passed muster as an incident of a plan to facilitate speech generally for a secular purpose, entailing neither secular entanglement with religion nor risk that the religious speech would be taken to be the speech of the government or that the government's endorsement of a religious message would be inferred. But each case drew ultimately on unexceptionable Speech Clause doctrine treating the evangelist, the Salvation Army, the millennialist, or the Hare Krishna like any other speaker in a public forum. It was the preservation of free speech on the model of the street corner that supplied the justification going beyond the requirement of evenhandedness.

The Court's claim of support from these forum-access cases is ruled out by the very scope of their holdings. While they do indeed allow a limited benefit to religious speakers, they rest on the recognition that all speakers are entitled to use the street corner (even though the State paves the roads and provides police protection to everyone on the street) and on the analogy between the public street corner and open classroom space. Thus, the Court found it significant that the classroom speakers would engage in traditional speech activities in these forums, too, even though the rooms (like street corners) require some incidental state spending to maintain them. The analogy breaks down entirely, however, if the cases are read more broadly than the Court wrote them, to cover more than forums for literal speaking. There is no traditional street corner printing provided by the government on equal terms to all comers, and the forum cases cannot be lifted to a higher plane of generalization without admitting that new economic benefits are being extended directly to religion in clear violation of the principle barring direct aid. The argument from economic equivalence thus breaks down on recognizing that the direct state aid it would support is not mitigated by the street corner analogy in the service of free speech. Absent that, the rule against direct aid stands as a bar to printing services as well as printers.

Nothing in the Court's opinion would lead me to end this enquiry into the application of the Establishment Clause any differently from the way I began it. The Court is ordering an instrumentality of the State to support religious evangelism with direct funding. This is a flat violation of the Establishment Clause.

II

Given the dispositive effect of the Establishment Clause's bar to funding the magazine, there should be no need to decide whether in the absence of this bar the University would violate the Free Speech Clause by limiting funding as it has done. But the Court's speech analysis may have independent application, and its flaws should not pass unremarked.

The Court acknowledges the necessity for a university to make judgments based on the content of what may be said or taught when it decides, in the absence of unlimited amounts of money or other resources, how to honor its educational responsibilities. Nor does the Court generally question that in allocating public funds a state university enjoys spacious discretion. Accordingly, the Court recognizes that the relevant enquiry in this case is not merely whether the University bases its funding decisions on the subject matter of student speech; if there is an infirmity in the basis for the University's funding decision, it must be that the University is impermissibly distinguishing among competing viewpoints.

The issue whether a distinction is based on viewpoint does not turn simply on whether a government regulation happens to be applied to a speaker who seeks to advance a particular viewpoint; the issue, of course, turns on whether the burden on speech is explained by reference to viewpoint. . . . Accordingly, the prohibition on viewpoint discrimination serves that important purpose of the Free Speech Clause, which is to bar the government from skewing public debate. Other things being equal, viewpoint discrimination occurs when government allows one message while prohibiting the messages of those who can reasonably be expected to respond. It is precisely this element of taking sides in a public debate that identifies viewpoint discrimination and makes it the most pernicious of all distinctions based on content. Thus, if government assists those espousing one point of view, neutrality requires it to assist those espousing opposing points of view, as well.

There is no viewpoint discrimination in the University's application of its Guidelines to deny funding to *Wide Awake*. Under those Guidelines, a "religious activity," which is not eligible for funding, is "an activity which primarily promotes or manifests a particular belief(s) in or about a deity or an ultimate reality." It is clear that this is the basis on which Wide Awake Productions was denied funding. [My previous] discussion of *Wide Awake*'s content shows beyond any question that it "primarily promotes or manifests a particular belief(s) in or about a deity," in the very specific sense that its manifest function is to call students to repentance, to commitment to Jesus Christ, and to particular moral action because of its Christian character.

If the Guidelines were written or applied so as to limit only such Christian advocacy and no other evangelical efforts that might compete with it, the discrimination would be based on viewpoint. But that is not what the regulation authorizes; it applies to Muslim and Jewish and Buddhist advocacy as well as to Christian. And since it limits funding to activities promoting or manifesting a particular belief not only "in" but "about" a deity or ultimate reality, it applies to agnostics and atheists as well as it does to deists and theists (as the University maintained at oral argument, and as the Court recognizes). The Guidelines, and their application to *Wide Awake*, thus do not skew debate by funding one position but not its competitors. As understood by their application to *Wide Awake*, they simply deny funding for hortatory speech that "primarily promotes or manifests" any view on the merits of religion; they deny funding for the entire subject matter of religious apologetics. The Court, of course, reads the Guidelines differently, but while I believe the Court is wrong in construing their breadth, the important point is that even on the Court's own construction the Guidelines impose no viewpoint discrimination.

. . . [It] was unremarkable that in *Lamb's Chapel* we unanimously determined that the access restriction, as applied to a speaker wishing to discuss family values from a Christian perspective, impermissibly distinguished between speakers on the basis of viewpoint. Equally obvious is the distinction between that case and this one, where the regulation is being applied, not to deny funding for those who discuss issues in general from a religious viewpoint, but to those engaged in promoting or opposing religious conversion and religious observances as such. If this amounts to viewpoint discrimination, the Court has all but eviscerated the line between viewpoint and content.

. . . [The] Court's decision equating a categorical exclusion of both sides of the religious debate with viewpoint discrimination suggests the Court has concluded that primarily religious and antireligious speech, grouped together, always provides an opposing (and not merely a related) viewpoint to any speech about any secular topic. Thus, the Court's reasoning requires a university that funds private publications about any primarily nonreligious topic also to fund publications primarily espousing adherence to or rejection of religion. But a university's decision to fund a magazine about racism, and not to fund publications aimed at urging repentance before God does not skew the debate either about racism or the desirability of religious conversion. The Court's contrary holding amounts to a significant reformulation of our viewpoint discrimination precedents and will significantly expand access to limited-access forums. . . .

I respectfully dissent.

Good News Club v. Milford Central School

533 U.S. 98 (2001)

JUSTICE THOMAS delivered the opinion of the Court.

This case presents two questions. The first question is whether Milford Central School violated the free speech rights of the Good News Club when it excluded the Club from meeting after hours at the school. The second question is whether any such violation is justified by Milford's concern that permitting the Club's activities would violate the Establishment Clause. We conclude that Milford's restriction violates the Club's free speech rights and that no Establishment Clause concern justifies that violation.

I

The State of New York authorizes local school boards to adopt regulations governing the use of their school facilities. In particular, [N.Y. Educ. Law § 414] enumerates several purposes for which local boards may open their schools to public use. In 1992, respondent Milford Central School (Milford) enacted a community use policy adopting seven of § 414's purposes for which its building could be used after school. Two of the stated purposes are relevant here. First, district residents may use the school for "instruction in any branch of education, learning or the arts." Second, the school is available for "social, civic and recreational meetings and entertainment events, and other uses pertaining to the welfare of the community, provided that such uses shall be nonexclusive and shall be opened to the general public."

Stephen and Darleen Fournier reside within Milford's district and therefore are eligible to use the school's facilities as long as their proposed use is approved by the school. Together they are sponsors of the local Good News Club, a private Christian organization for children ages 6 to 12. Pursuant to Milford's policy, in September 1996 the Fourniers [requested] permission to hold the Club's weekly afterschool meetings in the school cafeteria.

[The] Club sent a set of materials used or distributed at the meetings and the following description of its meeting:

> The Club opens its session with Ms. Fournier taking attendance. As she calls a child's name, if the child recites a Bible verse the child receives a treat. After attendance, the Club sings songs. Next Club members engage in games that involve, *inter alia*, learning Bible verses. Ms. Fournier then relates a Bible story and explains how it applies to Club members' lives. The Club closes with prayer. Finally, Ms. Fournier distributes treats and the Bible verses for memorization.

[Milford's] attorney reviewed the materials and concluded that "the kinds of activities proposed to be engaged in by the Good News Club were not a discussion of secular subjects such as child rearing, development of character and development of morals from a religious perspective, but were in fact the equivalent of religious instruction itself." In February 1997, the Milford Board of Education adopted a resolution rejecting the Club's request to use Milford's facilities "for the purpose of conducting religious instruction and Bible study."

[In March 1997, petitioners, the Good News Club, Ms. Fournier, and her daughter Andrea Fournier (collectively, the Club), filed an action under 42 U.S.C. § 1983 against Milford in federal court. The District Court held that because the school had not permitted other groups that provided religious instruction to use its limited public forum, the school could deny access to the Club without engaging in unconstitutional viewpoint discrimination. The Second Circuit affirmed.] There is a conflict among the Courts of Appeals on the question whether speech can be excluded from a limited public forum on the basis of the religious nature of the speech.... We granted certiorari to resolve this conflict.

II

The standards that we apply to determine whether a State has unconstitutionally excluded a private speaker from use of a public forum depend on the nature of the forum. *See Perry Ed. Assn. v. Perry Local Educators' Assn.* (1983) [Chapter 8 Note]. If the forum is a traditional or open public forum, the State's restrictions on speech are subject to stricter scrutiny than are restrictions in a limited public forum. We have previously declined to decide whether a school district's opening of its facilities pursuant to N.Y. Educ. Law § 414 creates a limited or a traditional public forum. [*Lamb's Chapel v. Center Moriches Union Free School Dist.*, 508 U.S. 384 (1993).] Because the parties have agreed that Milford created a limited public forum when it opened its facilities in 1992, we need not resolve the issue here. Instead, we simply will assume that Milford operates a limited public forum.

When the State establishes a limited public forum, the State is not required to and does not allow persons to engage in every type of speech. The State may be justified "in reserving [its forum] for certain groups or for the discussion of certain topics." *Rosenberger v. Rector and Visitors of Univ. of Va.* (1995) [*supra* this chapter]. The State's power to restrict speech, however, is not without limits. The restriction must not discriminate against speech on the basis of viewpoint, and the restriction must be "reasonable in light of the purpose served by the forum."

III

Applying this test, we first address whether the exclusion constituted viewpoint discrimination. We are guided in our analysis by two of our prior opinions, *Lamb's Chapel* and *Rosenberger*. In *Lamb's Chapel*, we held that a school district violated the Free Speech Clause of the First Amendment when it excluded a private group from presenting films at the school based solely on the films' discussions of family values from a religious perspective. Likewise, in *Rosenberger*, we held that a university's refusal to fund a student publication because the publication addressed issues from a religious perspective violated the Free Speech Clause. Concluding that Milford's exclusion of the Good News Club based on its religious nature is indistinguishable from the exclusions in these cases, we hold that the exclusion constitutes viewpoint discrimination. Because the restriction is viewpoint discriminatory, we need not decide whether it is unreasonable in light of the purposes served by the forum.

Milford has opened its limited public forum to activities that serve a variety of purposes, including events "pertaining to the welfare of the community." Milford interprets its policy to permit discussions of subjects such as child rearing, and of "the development of character and morals from a religious perspective." . . . In short, any group that "promotes the moral and character development of children" is eligible to use the school building.

Just as there is no question that teaching morals and character development to children is a permissible purpose under Milford's policy, it is clear that the Club teaches morals and character development to children. For example, no one disputes that the Club instructs children to overcome feelings of jealousy, to treat others well regardless of how they treat the children, and to be obedient, even if it does so in a nonsecular way. Nonetheless, because Milford found the Club's activities to be religious in nature—"the equivalent of religious instruction itself"—it excluded the Club from use of its facilities.

Applying *Lamb's Chapel*, we find it quite clear that Milford engaged in viewpoint discrimination when it excluded the Club from the afterschool forum. In *Lamb's Chapel*, the local New York school district similarly had adopted §414's "social, civic or recreational use" category as a permitted use in its limited public forum. The district also prohibited use "by any group for religious purposes." Citing this prohibition, the school district excluded a church that wanted to present films teaching family values from a Christian perspective. We held that, because the films "no doubt dealt with a subject otherwise permissible" under the rule, the teaching of family values, the district's exclusion of the church was unconstitutional viewpoint discrimination.

Like the church in *Lamb's Chapel*, the Club seeks to address a subject otherwise permitted under the rule, the teaching of morals and character, from a religious standpoint. . . . The only apparent difference between the activity of Lamb's Chapel and the activities of the Good News Club is that the Club chooses to teach moral lessons from a Christian perspective through live storytelling and prayer, whereas Lamb's Chapel taught lessons through films. This distinction is inconsequential. Both modes of speech use a religious viewpoint. Thus, the exclusion of the Good News Club's activities, like the exclusion of Lamb's Chapel's films, constitutes unconstitutional viewpoint discrimination.

Our opinion in *Rosenberger* also is dispositive. In *Rosenberger*, a student organization at the University of Virginia was denied funding for printing expenses because its publication, *Wide Awake*, offered a Christian viewpoint. . . . [We] concluded simply that the university's denial of funding to print *Wide Awake* was viewpoint discrimination, just as the school district's refusal to allow Lamb's Chapel to show its films was viewpoint discrimination. [We] cannot say that the Club's activities are any more "religious" or deserve any less First Amendment protection than did the publication of *Wide Awake* in *Rosenberger*.

Despite our holdings in *Lamb's Chapel* and *Rosenberger*, the Court of Appeals, like Milford, believed that its characterization of the Club's activities as religious in nature warranted treating the Club's activities as different in kind from the other activities permitted by the school. The "Christian viewpoint" is unique, according to the court, because it contains an "additional layer" that other kinds of viewpoints do not. That is, the Club "is focused on teaching children how to cultivate their relationship with God through Jesus Christ," which it characterized as "quintessentially religious." With these observations, the [lower] court concluded that, because the Club's activities "fall outside the bounds of pure 'moral and character development,'" the exclusion did not constitute viewpoint discrimination.

We disagree that something that is "quintessentially religious" or "decidedly religious in nature" cannot also be characterized properly as the teaching of morals and character development from a particular viewpoint. What matters for purposes of the Free Speech Clause is that we can see no logical difference in kind between the invocation of Christianity by the Club and the invocation of teamwork, loyalty, or patriotism by other associations to provide a foundation for their lessons. It is apparent that the unstated principle of the Court of Appeals' reasoning is its conclusion that any time religious instruction and prayer are used to discuss morals and character, the discussion is simply not a "pure" discussion of those issues. According to the Court of Appeals, reliance on Christian principles taints moral and character instruction in a way that other foundations for thought or viewpoints do not. We, however, have never reached such a conclusion. Instead, we reaffirm our holdings in *Lamb's Chapel* and *Rosenberger* that speech discussing otherwise permissible subjects cannot be excluded from a limited public forum on the ground that the subject is discussed from a religious viewpoint. Thus, we conclude that Milford's exclusion of the Club from use of the school, pursuant to its community use policy, constitutes impermissible viewpoint discrimination.

IV

Milford argues that, even if its restriction constitutes viewpoint discrimination, its interest in not violating the Establishment Clause outweighs the Club's interest in gaining equal access to the school's facilities. In other words, according to Milford, its restriction was required to avoid violating the Establishment Clause. We disagree.

We have said that a state interest in avoiding an Establishment Clause violation "may be characterized as compelling," and therefore may justify content-based discrimination. However, it is not clear whether a State's interest in avoiding an Establishment Clause violation would justify viewpoint discrimination. We need not, however, confront the issue in this case, because we conclude that the school has no valid Establishment Clause interest. [*See supra* this chapter, section B.]

V

When Milford denied the Good News Club access to the school's limited public forum on the ground that the Club was religious in nature, it discriminated against the Club because of its religious viewpoint in violation of the Free Speech Clause of the First Amendment. Because Milford has not raised a valid Establishment Clause claim, we do not address the question whether such a claim could excuse Milford's viewpoint discrimination.

The judgment of the Court of Appeals is reversed, and the case is remanded for further proceedings consistent with this opinion.

Justice Scalia, concurring.

As I understand it, the point of disagreement between the Court and the dissenters (and the Court of Appeals) with regard to petitioner's Free Speech Clause claim is not whether the Good News Club must be permitted to present religious viewpoints on morals and character in respondent's forum, which has been opened to secular discussions of that subject. . . . The disagreement, rather, regards the portions of the Club's meetings that are not "purely" "discussions" of morality and character from a religious viewpoint. The Club, for example, urges children "who already believe in the Lord Jesus as their Savior" to "stop and ask God for the strength and the 'want' . . . to obey Him," and it invites children who "don't know Jesus as Savior" to "trust the Lord Jesus to be [their] Savior from sin." The dissenters and the Second Circuit say that the presence of such additional speech, because it is purely religious, transforms the Club's meetings into something different in kind from other, nonreligious activities that teach moral and character development. Therefore, the argument goes, excluding the Club is not viewpoint discrimination. I disagree.

[Respondent] has agreed that groups engaged in the endeavor of developing character may use its forum. . . . When the Club attempted to teach Biblical-based moral values, however, it was excluded because its activities "did not involve merely a religious perspective on the secular subject of morality" and because "it [was] clear from the conduct of the meetings that the Good News Club goes far beyond merely stating its viewpoint."

From no other group does respondent require the sterility of speech that it demands of petitioners. The Boy Scouts could undoubtedly buttress their exhortations to keep "morally straight" and live "clean" lives, by giving reasons why that is a good idea—because parents want and expect it, because it will make the scouts "better" and "more successful" people, because it will emulate such admired past Scouts as former President Gerald Ford. The Club, however, may only discuss morals and character, and cannot give its reasons why they should be fostered—because God wants and expects it, because it will make the Club members "saintly" people, and because it emulates Jesus Christ. The Club may not, in other words, independently discuss the religious premise on which its views are based—that God exists and His assistance is necessary to morality. It may not defend the premise, and it absolutely must not seek to persuade the children that the premise is true. The children must, so to say, take it on faith. This is blatant viewpoint discrimination. . . .

In *Rosenberger*, we struck down a similar viewpoint restriction. . . . The right to present a viewpoint based on a religion premise [carries] with it the right to defend the premise. The dissenters emphasize that the religious speech used by the Club as the foundation for its views on morals and character is not just any type of religious speech—although they cannot agree exactly what type of religious speech it is. In Justice Stevens' view, it is speech "aimed principally at proselytizing or inculcating belief in a particular religious faith." This does not, to begin with, distinguish *Rosenberger*, which also involved proselytizing speech. . . . But in addition, it does not distinguish the Club's activities from those of the other groups using respondent's forum—which have not, as Justice Stevens suggests, been restricted to roundtable "discussions" of moral issues. Those groups may seek to inculcate children with their beliefs, and they may furthermore "recruit others to join their respective groups." The Club must therefore have liberty to do the same, even if, as Justice Stevens fears without support in the record, its actions may prove (shudder!) divisive.

Justice Souter, while agreeing that the Club's religious speech "may be characterized as proselytizing," thinks that it is even more clearly excludable from respondent's forum because it is essentially "an evangelical service of worship." But we have previously rejected the attempt to distinguish worship from other religious speech, saying that "the distinction has [no] intelligible content," and further, no "*relevance*" to the constitutional issue. Those holdings are surely proved correct today by the dissenters' inability to agree, even between themselves, into which subcategory of religious speech the Club's activities fell. If the distinction did have content, it would be beyond the courts' competence to administer. And if courts (and other government officials) were competent, applying the distinction would require state monitoring of private, religious speech with a degree of pervasiveness that we have previously found unacceptable. I will not endorse an approach that suffers such a wondrous diversity of flaws.

JUSTICE BREYER, concurring in part [addressed the Establishment Clause question].

JUSTICE STEVENS, dissenting.

The Milford Central School has invited the public to use its facilities for educational and recreational purposes, but not for "religious purposes." Speech for "religious purposes" may reasonably be understood to encompass three different categories. First, there is religious speech that is simply speech about a particular topic from a religious point of view. . . . Second, there is religious speech that amounts to worship, or its equivalent. . . . Third, there is an intermediate category that is aimed principally at proselytizing or inculcating belief in a particular religious faith.

A public entity may not generally exclude even religious worship from an open public forum. Similarly, a public entity that creates a limited public forum for the discussion of certain specified topics may not exclude a speaker simply because she approaches those topics from a religious point of view. . . . But, while a public entity may not censor speech about an authorized topic based on the point of view expressed by the speaker, it has broad discretion to "preserve the property under its control for the use to which it is lawfully dedicated." Accordingly, "control over access to a nonpublic forum can be based on subject matter and speaker identity so long as the distinctions drawn are reasonable in light of the purpose served by the forum and are viewpoint neutral." *Cornelius v. NAACP Legal Defense & Ed. Fund, Inc.* (1985) [Chapter 8]. The novel question that this case presents concerns the constitutionality of a public school's attempt to limit the scope of a public forum it has created. More specifically, the question is whether a school can, consistently with the First Amendment, create a limited public forum that admits the first type of religious speech without allowing the other two.

Distinguishing speech from a religious viewpoint, on the one hand, from religious proselytizing, on the other, is comparable to distinguishing meetings to discuss political issues from meetings whose principal purpose is to recruit new members to join a political organization. If a school decides to authorize after school discussions of current events in its classrooms, it may not exclude people from expressing their views simply because it dislikes their particular political opinions. But must it therefore allow organized political groups — for example, the Democratic Party, the Libertarian Party, or the Ku Klux Klan — to hold meetings, the principal purpose of which is not to discuss the current-events topic from their own unique point of view but rather to recruit others to join their respective groups? I think not. Such recruiting meetings may introduce divisiveness and tend to separate young children into cliques that undermine the school's educational mission.

School officials may reasonably believe that evangelical meetings designed to convert children to a particular religious faith pose the same risk. And, just as a school may allow meetings to discuss current events from a political perspective without also allowing organized political recruitment, so too can a school allow discussion of topics such as moral development from a religious (or nonreligious) perspective without thereby opening its forum to religious proselytizing or worship. . . .

The particular limitation of the forum at issue in this case is one that prohibits the use of the school's facilities for "religious purposes." It is clear that, by "religious purposes," the school district did not intend to exclude all speech from a religious point of view. Instead, it sought only to exclude religious speech whose principal goal is to "promote the gospel." In other words, the school sought to allow the first type of religious speech while excluding the second and third types. As long as this is done in an even handed manner, I see no constitutional violation in such an effort. The line between the various categories of religious speech may be difficult to draw, but I think that the distinctions are valid, and that a school, particularly an elementary school, must be permitted to draw them.

This case is undoubtedly close. Nonetheless, regardless of whether the Good News Club's activities amount to "worship," it does seem clear, based on the facts in the record, that the school district correctly classified those activities as falling within the third category of religious speech and therefore beyond the scope of the school's limited public forum. In short, I am persuaded that the school district could (and did) permissibly exclude from its limited public forum proselytizing religious speech that does not rise to the level of actual worship. I would therefore affirm the judgment of the Court of Appeals. . . . Accordingly, I respectfully dissent.

JUSTICE SOUTER, with whom JUSTICE GINSBURG joins, dissenting.

. . . The sole question before the District Court [was] whether, in refusing to allow Good News's intended use, Milford was misapplying its unchallenged restriction in a way that amounted to imposing a viewpoint-based restriction on what could be said or done by a group entitled to use the forum for an educational, civic, or other permitted purpose. The question was whether Good News was being disqualified when it merely sought to use the school property the same way that the Milford Boy and Girl Scouts and the 4-H Club did. The District Court held on the basis of undisputed facts that Good News's activity was essentially unlike the presentation of views on secular issues from a religious standpoint [and] was instead activity precluded by Milford's unchallenged policy against religious use, even under the narrowest definition of that term. The Court of Appeals understood the issue the same way. . . . A sampling of those facts shows why both courts were correct.

Good News's classes open and close with prayer. In a sample lesson considered by the District Court, children are instructed that "the Bible tells us how we can have our sins forgiven by receiving the Lord Jesus Christ. It tells us how to live to please Him . . . . If you have received the Lord Jesus as your Saviour from sin, you belong to God's special group—His family." The lesson plan instructs the teacher to "lead a child to Christ," and, when reading a Bible verse, to "emphasize that this verse is from the Bible, God's Word" and is "important—and true—because God said it." The lesson further exhorts the teacher to "be sure to give an opportunity for the 'unsaved' children in your class to respond to the Gospel" and cautions against "neglecting this responsibility."

While Good News's program utilizes songs and games, the heart of the meeting is the "challenge" and "invitation," which are repeated at various times throughout the lesson. During the challenge, "saved" children who "already believe in the Lord Jesus as their Savior" are challenged to "'stop and ask God for the strength and the "want" . . . to obey Him.'" They are instructed that

> if you know Jesus as your Savior, you need to place God first in your life. And if you don't know Jesus as Savior and if you would like to, then we will—we will pray with you separately, individually . . . . And the challenge would be, those of you who know Jesus as Savior, you can rely on God's strength to obey Him.

During the invitation, the teacher "invites" the "unsaved" children "'to trust the Lord Jesus to be your Savior from sin,'" and "'receive [him] as your Savior from sin.'" The children are then instructed that

> if you believe what God's Word says about your sin and how Jesus died and rose again for you, you can have His forever life today. Please bow your heads and close your eyes. If you have never believed on the Lord Jesus as your Savior and would like to do that, please show me by raising your hand. If you raised your hand to show me you want to believe on the Lord Jesus, please meet me so I can show you from God's Word how you can receive His everlasting life.

It is beyond question that Good News intends to use the public school premises not for the mere discussion of a subject from a particular, Christian point of view, but for an evangelical service of worship calling children to commit themselves in an act of Christian conversion. The majority avoids this reality only by resorting to the bland and general characterization of Good News's activity as "teaching of morals and character, from a religious standpoint." If the majority's statement ignores reality, as it surely does, then today's holding may be understood only in equally generic terms. Otherwise, indeed, this case would stand for the remarkable proposition that any public school opened for civic meetings must be opened for use as a church, synagogue, or mosque. . . .

Justice Stevens distinguishes between proselytizing and worship, and distinguishes each from discussion reflecting a religious point of view. I agree with Justice Stevens that Good News's activities may be characterized as proselytizing and therefore as outside the purpose of Milford's limited forum. Like the Court of Appeals, I also believe Good News's meetings have elements of worship that put the club's activities further afield of Milford's limited forum policy, the legitimacy of which was unchallenged. . . .

Problem: "Whom Do I Arrest?"

You are the County Attorney for Zion County. It is Saturday afternoon. When you check your voicemail, you hear this message from the Sheriff of the county:

> Hey Counsel. This is Sheriff Rick Grimes. Where the hell are you? You need to answer your phone! We have a situation. This is the weekend of the annual Arab Heritage and Cultural Festival downtown at City Park. A bunch of yahoos from out of town are walking around provoking the sponsors and the attendees. Call me back right away: 555-4720.

You are familiar with the festival because you worked on the official permitting and you attended last year. Zion County is home to one of the largest populations of Arab Americans in the country comprised of both Christian and Muslim families from several Arab nations. Now in its tenth year, the festival occupies the entire City Park and is free and open to the public. The festival features Middle Eastern food, music, artisan booths, cultural performances, music, and other amusements, including carnival rides. A principal purpose of the festival is to promote cultural exchange. The largest gathering of its kind in the United States, the festival attracts people from all over; last year more than 300,000 people attended over the course of three days.

When you call the Sheriff back, he briefs you over the phone on the situation as follows:

- A group of about 12 self-described Christian evangelicals who called themselves "Bible Followers" showed up this morning.

- The founder and leader of the group, Reverend Gabriel Stokes, announced that he and his followers were there "to convert non-believers and to call sinners to repent."

- The Bible Followers wore T-shirts and carried posters and signs with messages such as: "Islam Is a Religion of Blood and Murder," "Jesus Is the Way, the Truth, and the Life. All Others Are Thieves and Robbers," "Only Jesus Christ Can Save You from Sin and Hell," "Turn or Burn," and "Fear God."

- One of the Bible Followers carried a severed pig's head on a spike, because, in Reverend Stokes's own words, it would "keep the Muslims at bay" since "they are kind of petrified of that animal."

- At first, few festival attendees paid much attention other than to wonder curiously at the odd assembly following around a man carrying the head of a pig on a pole.

- Then Reverend Stokes began street preaching to the crowd using a megaphone: he hollered that they should not follow "a false prophet," who was nothing but a "liar and an imposter" and "a wicked pedophile" and he yelled at a large group of passing teenagers that "your religion will send you to hell."

- When a crowd of about 50 to 100 onlookers formed, he taunted, "You believe in a prophet who is a pervert. Your prophet was a child molester," and "God will reject you. God will put your religion into hellfire when you die."

- After approximately 10 minutes of this harangue, some elements of the crowd began to express their anger by throwing bottles and rocks at the Bible Followers but stopped when several deputies threatened them with arrest for assault and battery.

- A number of small confrontations formed between members of the larger crowd of onlookers, which had continued to grow, and individual Bible Followers.

- Some of these small confrontations quickly turned into angry shouting and cursing face-offs with a few individuals on each side actually pushing and shoving each other and sympathizers pulling them apart but there were no actual fisticuffs or personal injury.

- At this point, the deputies physically separated the opposing groups.

- The deputies took the Bible Followers aside and warned them that the deputies could no longer protect them from the larger crowd and strongly urged them to leave for their own safety and for the safety of the deputies.

- The Bible Followers eventually, but reluctantly, agreed to leave but they defiantly vowed to return tomorrow to attend the closing ceremony of the festival and continue their proselytizing.

- As he was leaving, Reverend Stokes pointedly warned the deputies that tomorrow they had better be prepared to protect his followers and their constitutional rights to free speech and free exercise "no matter what" and he promised they would record videos of everything that happens.

- One of the planners of the festival, a leader in the Arab community, called the Sheriff and advised him that the events of the day had galvanized many of the Arab youths in the community, particularly some of the Muslim teenagers, who were all over social media urging each other to attend the closing ceremony and vowing to confront the Bible Followers physically if they returned and continued to disrespect Islam and defame the Prophet Mohammed.

At the end of his briefing, the Sheriff tells you, "I assigned some of my best and most experienced deputies to the festival. As many deputies as were detailed when the presidential candidates came to town. My deputies do not believe they can maintain order. They believe that a lot of people are going to get seriously hurt tomorrow. And I think they are right. Realistically, we cannot arrest hundreds of festival attendees, but we can arrest a dozen outside agitators easily enough. So, if the Bible Followers show up and if they start acting out again to provoke our Muslim neighbors, we are planning on arresting them for disorderly conduct. Before things get out of control."

What do you tell the Sheriff?

———————

Note: A Postscript on the Religion Clauses

The First Amendment has erected a wall between church and state. That wall must be kept high and impregnable. We could not approve the slightest breach.   — *Everson v. Bd. of Educ.* (1947)

We are a religious people whose institutions presuppose a Supreme Being.
                                                      — *Zorach v. Clauson* (1952)

Our cases, Janus-like, point in two directions. . . . One face looks toward the strong role played by religion and religious traditions throughout our Nation's history. . . . The other face looks toward the principle that governmental intervention in religious matters can itself endanger religious freedom.

                                                      — *Van Orden v. Perry* (2005)

Appendix A

The Constitution of the United States

(Excerpts)

We the people of the United States, in order to form a more perfect union, establish justice, insure domestic tranquility, provide for the common defense, promote the general welfare, and secure the blessings of liberty to ourselves and our posterity, do ordain and establish this Constitution for the United States of America.

ARTICLE I

Section 1.

All legislative powers herein granted shall be vested in a Congress of the United States, which shall consist of a Senate and House of Representatives.

. . .

Section 9.

The migration or importation of such persons as any of the states now existing shall think proper to admit, shall not be prohibited by the Congress prior to the year one thousand eight hundred and eight, but a tax or duty may be imposed on such importation, not exceeding ten dollars for each person.

The privilege of the writ of habeas corpus shall not be suspended, unless when in cases of rebellion or invasion the public safety may require it.

No bill of attainder or ex post facto Law shall be passed.

No capitation, or other direct, tax shall be laid, unless in proportion to the census or enumeration herein before directed to be taken.

No tax or duty shall be laid on articles exported from any state.

No preference shall be given by any regulation of commerce or revenue to the ports of one state over those of another: nor shall vessels bound to, or from, one state, be obliged to enter, clear or pay duties in another.

No money shall be drawn from the treasury, but in consequence of appropriations made by law; and a regular statement and account of receipts and expenditures of all public money shall be published from time to time.

No title of nobility shall be granted by the United States: and no person holding any office of profit or trust under them, shall, without the consent of the Congress, accept of any present, emolument, office, or title, of any kind whatever, from any king, prince, or foreign state.

Section 10.

No state shall enter into any treaty, alliance, or confederation; grant letters of marque and reprisal; coin money; emit bills of credit; make anything but gold and silver coin a tender in payment of debts; pass any bill of attainder, ex post facto law, or law impairing the obligation of contracts, or grant any title of nobility.

No state shall, without the consent of the Congress, lay any imposts or duties on imports or exports, except what may be absolutely necessary for executing it's inspection laws: and the net produce of all duties and imposts, laid by any state on imports or exports, shall be for the use of the treasury of the United States; and all such laws shall be subject to the revision and control of the Congress.

No state shall, without the consent of Congress, lay any duty of tonnage, keep troops, or ships of war in time of peace, enter into any agreement or compact with another state, or with a foreign power, or engage in war, unless actually invaded, or in such imminent danger as will not admit of delay.

ARTICLE II

Section 1.

The executive power shall be vested in a President of the United States of America.

. . .

ARTICLE III

Section 1.

The judicial power of the United States, shall be vested in one Supreme Court, and in such inferior courts as the Congress may from time to time ordain and establish. The judges, both of the supreme and inferior courts, shall hold their offices during good behaviour, and shall, at stated times, receive for their services, a compensation, which shall not be diminished during their continuance in office.

Section 2.

The judicial power shall extend to all cases, in law and equity, arising under this Constitution, the laws of the United States, and treaties made, or which shall be made, under their authority;—to all cases affecting ambassadors, other public ministers and consuls;—to all cases of admiralty and maritime jurisdiction;—to controversies to which the United States shall be a party;—to controversies between two or more states;—between a state and citizens of another state;—between citizens of different states;—between citizens of the same state claiming lands under grants of different states, and between a state, or the citizens thereof, and foreign states, citizens or subjects.

In all cases affecting ambassadors, other public ministers and consuls, and those in which a state shall be party, the Supreme Court shall have original jurisdiction. In all the other cases before mentioned, the Supreme Court shall have appellate jurisdiction, both as to law and fact, with such exceptions, and under such regulations as the Congress shall make.

The trial of all crimes, except in cases of impeachment, shall be by jury; and such trial shall be held in the state where the said crimes shall have been committed; but when not committed within any state, the trial shall be at such place or places as the Congress may by law have directed.

Section 3.

Treason against the United States, shall consist only in levying war against them, or in adhering to their enemies, giving them aid and comfort. No person shall be convicted of treason unless on the testimony of two witnesses to the same overt act, or on confession in open court.

The Congress shall have power to declare the punishment of treason, but no attainder of treason shall work corruption of blood, or forfeiture except during the life of the person attainted.

ARTICLE IV

Section 1

Full faith and credit shall be given in each state to the public acts, records, and judicial proceedings of every other state. And the Congress may by general laws prescribe the manner in which such acts, records, and proceedings shall be proved, and the effect thereof.

Section 2.

The citizens of each state shall be entitled to all privileges and immunities of citizens in the several states.

A person charged in any state with treason, felony, or other crime, who shall flee from justice, and be found in another state, shall on demand of the executive authority of the state from which he fled, be delivered up, to be removed to the state having jurisdiction of the crime.

No person held to service or labor in one state, under the laws thereof, escaping into another, shall, in consequence of any law or regulation therein, be discharged from such service or labor, but shall be delivered up on claim of the party to whom such service or labor may be due.

. . .

Section 4.

The United States shall guarantee to every state in this union a republican form of government, and shall protect each of them against invasion; and on application of the legislature, or of the executive (when the legislature cannot be convened) against domestic violence.

ARTICLE V

The Congress, whenever two thirds of both houses shall deem it necessary, shall propose amendments to this Constitution, or, on the application of the legislatures of two thirds of the several states, shall call a convention for proposing amendments, which, in either case, shall be valid to all intents and purposes, as part of this Constitution, when ratified by the legislatures of three fourths of the several states, or by conventions in three fourths thereof, as the one or the other mode of ratification may be proposed by the Congress; provided that no amendment which may be made prior to the year one thousand eight hundred and eight shall in any manner affect the first and fourth clauses in the ninth section of the first article; and that no state, without its consent, shall be deprived of its equal suffrage in the Senate.

ARTICLE VI

All debts contracted and engagements entered into, before the adoption of this Constitution, shall be as valid against the United States under this Constitution, as under the Confederation.

This Constitution, and the laws of the United States which shall be made in pursuance thereof; and all treaties made, or which shall be made, under the authority of the United States, shall be the supreme law of the land; and the judges in every state shall be bound thereby, anything in the Constitution or laws of any State to the contrary notwithstanding.

The Senators and Representatives before mentioned, and the members of the several state legislatures, and all executive and judicial officers, both of the United States and of the several states, shall be bound by oath or affirmation, to support this Constitution; but no religious test shall ever be required as a qualification to any office or public trust under the United States.

. . .

AMENDMENT I

Congress shall make no law respecting an establishment of religion, or prohibiting the free exercise thereof; or abridging the freedom of speech, or of the press; or the right of the people peaceably to assemble, and to petition the government for a redress of grievances.

AMENDMENT II

A well regulated militia, being necessary to the security of a free state, the right of the people to keep and bear arms, shall not be infringed.

AMENDMENT III

No soldier shall, in time of peace be quartered in any house, without the consent of the owner, nor in time of war, but in a manner to be prescribed by law.

AMENDMENT IV

The right of the people to be secure in their persons, houses, papers, and effects, against unreasonable searches and seizures, shall not be violated, and no warrants shall issue, but upon probable cause, supported by oath or affirmation, and particularly describing the place to be searched, and the persons or things to be seized.

AMENDMENT V

No person shall be held to answer for a capital, or otherwise infamous crime, unless on a presentment or indictment of a grand jury, except in cases arising in the land or naval forces, or in the militia, when in actual service in time of war or public danger; nor shall any person be subject for the same offense to be twice put in jeopardy of life or limb; nor shall be compelled in any criminal case to be a witness against himself, nor be deprived of life, liberty, or property, without due process of law; nor shall private property be taken for public use, without just compensation.

AMENDMENT VI

In all criminal prosecutions, the accused shall enjoy the right to a speedy and public trial, by an impartial jury of the state and district wherein the crime shall have been committed, which district shall have been previously ascertained by law, and to be informed of the nature and cause of the accusation; to be confronted with the witnesses against him; to have compulsory process for obtaining witnesses in his favor, and to have the assistance of counsel for his defense.

AMENDMENT VII

In suits at common law, where the value in controversy shall exceed twenty dollars, the right of trial by jury shall be preserved, and no fact tried by a jury, shall be otherwise reexamined in any court of the United States, than according to the rules of the common law.

AMENDMENT VIII

Excessive bail shall not be required, nor excessive fines imposed, nor cruel and unusual punishments inflicted.

AMENDMENT IX

The enumeration in the Constitution, of certain rights, shall not be construed to deny or disparage others retained by the people.

AMENDMENT X

The powers not delegated to the United States by the Constitution, nor prohibited by it to the states, are reserved to the states respectively, or to the people.

AMENDMENT XI
(1798)

The judicial power of the United States shall not be construed to extend to any suit in law or equity, commenced or prosecuted against one of the United States by citizens of another state, or by citizens or subjects of any foreign state.

. . .

AMENDMENT XIII
(1865)

Section 1.

Neither slavery nor involuntary servitude, except as a punishment for crime whereof the party shall have been duly convicted, shall exist within the United States, or any place subject to their jurisdiction.

Section 2.

Congress shall have power to enforce this article by appropriate legislation.

AMENDMENT XIV
(1868)

Section 1.

All persons born or naturalized in the United States, and subject to the jurisdiction thereof, are citizens of the United States and of the state wherein they reside. No state shall make or enforce any law which shall abridge the privileges or immunities of citizens of the United States; nor shall any state deprive any person of life, liberty, or property, without due process of law; nor deny to any person within its jurisdiction the equal protection of the laws.

Section 2.

Representatives shall be apportioned among the several states according to their respective numbers, counting the whole number of persons in each state, excluding Indians not taxed. But when the right to vote at any election for the choice of electors for President and Vice President of the United States, Representatives in Congress, the executive and judicial officers of a state, or the members of the legislature thereof, is denied to any of the male inhabitants of such state, being twenty-one years of age, and citizens of the United States, or in any way abridged, except for participation in rebellion, or other crime, the basis of representation therein shall be reduced in the proportion which the number of such male citizens shall bear to the whole number of male citizens twenty-one years of age in such state.

. . .

Section 5.

The Congress shall have power to enforce, by appropriate legislation, the provisions of this article.

AMENDMENT XV
(1870)

Section 1.

The right of citizens of the United States to vote shall not be denied or abridged by the United States or by any state on account of race, color, or previous condition of servitude.

Section 2.

The Congress shall have power to enforce this article by appropriate legislation.

. . .

AMENDMENT XVII
(1913)

The Senate of the United States shall be composed of two Senators from each state, elected by the people thereof, for six years; and each Senator shall have one vote. The electors in each state shall have the qualifications requisite for electors of the most numerous branch of the state legislatures.

When vacancies happen in the representation of any state in the Senate, the executive authority of such state shall issue writs of election to fill such vacancies: Provided, that the legislature of any state may empower the executive thereof to make temporary appointments until the people fill the vacancies by election as the legislature may direct.

This amendment shall not be so construed as to affect the election or term of any Senator chosen before it becomes valid as part of the Constitution.

AMENDMENT XVIII
(1919)

Section 1.

After one year from the ratification of this article the manufacture, sale, or transportation of intoxicating liquors within, the importation thereof into, or the exportation thereof from the United States and all territory subject to the jurisdiction thereof for beverage purposes is hereby prohibited.

Section 2.

The Congress and the several states shall have concurrent power to enforce this article by appropriate legislation.

. . .

Section 3.

This article shall be inoperative unless it shall have been ratified as an amendment to the Constitution by the legislatures of the several states, as provided in the Constitution, within seven years from the date of the submission hereof to the states by the Congress.

AMENDMENT XIX
(1920)

The right of citizens of the United States to vote shall not be denied or abridged by the United States or by any state on account of sex.

Congress shall have power to enforce this article by appropriate legislation.

. . .

AMENDMENT XXI
(1933)

Section 1.

The eighteenth article of amendment to the Constitution of the United States is hereby repealed.

Section 2.

The transportation or importation into any state, territory, or possession of the United States for delivery or use therein of intoxicating liquors, in violation of the laws thereof, is hereby prohibited.

. . .

AMENDMENT XXIV
(1964)

Section 1.

The right of citizens of the United States to vote in any primary or other election for President or Vice President, for electors for President or Vice President, or for Senator or Representative in Congress, shall not be denied or abridged by the United States or any state by reason of failure to pay any poll tax or other tax.

Section 2.

The Congress shall have power to enforce this article by appropriate legislation.

. . .

AMENDMENT XXVI
(1971)

Section 1.

The right of citizens of the United States, who are 18 years of age or older, to vote, shall not be denied or abridged by the United States or any state on account of age.

Section 2.

The Congress shall have the power to enforce this article by appropriate legislation.

AMENDMENT XXVII
(1992)

No law varying the compensation for the services of the Senators and Representatives shall take effect until an election of Representatives shall have intervened.

Appendix B

The Justices of the United States Supreme Court, 1946–2016 Terms

U.S. Reports	Term*	The Court**
329–332[1]	1946	**Vinson**, Black, Reed, Frankfurter, Douglas, Murphy, Jackson, Rutledge, Burton
332[1]–335[2]	1947	"
335[2]–338[3]	1948	"
338[3]–339	1949	Vinson, Black, Reed, Frankfurter, Douglas, Jackson, Burton, Clark, Minton
340–341	1950	"
342–343	1951	"
344–346[4]	1952	"
346[4]–347	1953	**Warren**, Black, Reed, Frankfurter, Douglas, Jackson, Burton, Clark, Minton
348–349	1954	Warren, Black, Reed, Frankfurter, Douglas, Burton, Clark, Minton, Harlan[5]
350–351	1955	"
352–354	1956	Warren, Black, Reed,[6] Frankfurter, Douglas, Burton, Clark, Harlan, Brennan, Whittaker[7]
355–357	1957	Warren, Black, Frankfurter, Douglas, Burton, Clark, Harlan, Brennan, Whittaker
358–360	1958	Warren, Black, Frankfurter, Douglas, Clark, Harlan, Brennan, Whittaker, Stewart
361–364[8]	1959	"
364[8]–367	1960	"

---

* Rule 3 of the Supreme Court's Rules provides in part: "The Court holds a continuous annual Term commencing on the first Monday in October and ending on the day before the first Monday in October of the following year."

** Justices are listed in order of seniority. Boldface indicates a new Chief Justice.

1. The 1947 Term begins at 332 U.S. 371.
2. The 1948 Term begins at 335 U.S. 281.
3. The 1949 Term begins at 338 U.S. 217.
4. The 1953 Term begins at 346 U.S. 325.
5. Participation begins with 349 U.S.
6. Participation ends with 352 U.S. 564.
7. Participation begins with 353 U.S.
8. The 1960 Term begins with 364 U.S. 285.

U.S. Reports	Term	The Court*
368–370	1961	Warren, Black, Frankfurter,[9] Douglas, Clark, Harlan, Brennan, Whittaker,[10] Stewart, White[11]
371–374	1962	Warren, Black, Douglas, Clark, Harlan, Brennan, Stewart, White, Goldberg
375–378	1963	"
379–381	1964	"
382–384	1965	Warren, Black, Douglas, Clark, Harlan, Brennan, Stewart, White, Fortas
385–388	1966	"
389–392	1967	Warren, Black, Douglas, Harlan, Brennan, Stewart, White, Fortas, Marshall
393–395	1968	Warren, Black, Douglas, Harlan, Brennan, Stewart, White, Fortas,[12] Marshall
396–399	1969	**Burger**, Black, Douglas, Harlan, Brennan, Stewart, White, Marshall, [vacancy]
400–403	1970	Burger, Black, Douglas, Harlan, Brennan, Stewart, White, Marshall, Blackmun
404–408	1971	Burger, Douglas, Brennan, Stewart, White, Marshall, Blackmun, Powell,[13] Rehnquist[13]
409–413	1972	"
414–418	1973	"
419–422	1974	"
423–428	1975	Burger, Brennan, Stewart, White, Marshall, Blackmun, Powell, Rehnquist, Stevens[14]
429–433	1976	"
434–438	1977	"
439–443	1978	"
444–448	1979	"
449–453	1980	"
454–458	1981	Burger, Brennan, White, Marshall, Blackmun, Powell, Rehnquist, Stevens, O'Connor
459–463	1982	"
464–468	1983	"
469–473	1984	"
474–478	1985	"
479–483	1986	**Rehnquist**, Brennan, White, Marshall, Blackmun, Powell, Stevens, O'Connor, Scalia
484–487	1987	"

* Justices are listed in order of seniority. Boldface indicates a new Chief Justice.
 9. Participation ends with 369 U.S. 422.
10. Participation ends with 369 U.S. 120.
11. Participation begins with 370 U.S.
12. Participation ends with 394 U.S.
13. Participation begins with 405 U.S.
14. Participation begins with 424 U.S.

U.S. Reports	Term	The Court*
488–492	1988	Rehnquist, Brennan, White, Marshall, Blackmun, Stevens, O'Connor, Scalia, Kennedy
493–497	1989	"
498–501	1990	Rehnquist, White, Marshall, Blackmun, Stevens, O'Connor, Scalia, Kennedy, Souter
502–505	1991	Rehnquist, White, Blackmun, Stevens, O'Connor, Scalia, Kennedy, Souter, Thomas
506–509	1992	"
510–512	1993	Rehnquist, Blackmun, Stevens, O'Connor, Scalia, Kennedy, Souter, Thomas, Ginsburg
513–515	1994	Rehnquist, Stevens, O'Connor, Scalia, Kennedy, Souter, Thomas, Ginsburg, Breyer
516–518	1995	"
519–521	1996	"
522–524	1997	"
525–527	1998	"
528–530	1999	"
531–533	2000	"
534–536	2001	"
537–539	2002	"
540–542	2003	"
543–545	2004[15]	Rehnquist, Stevens, O'Connor, Scalia, Kennedy, Souter, Thomas, Ginsburg, Breyer
546–548	2005	**Roberts**, Stevens, O'Connor,[16] Scalia, Kennedy, Souter, Thomas, Ginsburg, Breyer, Alito[17]
549–551	2006	Roberts, Stevens, Scalia, Kennedy, Souter, Thomas, Ginsburg, Breyer, Alito
552–554	2007	"
555–557	2008	"
558–561	2009	Roberts, Stevens, Scalia, Kennedy, Thomas, Ginsburg, Breyer, Alito, Sotomayor
562–564	2010	Roberts, Scalia, Kennedy, Thomas, Ginsburg, Breyer, Alito, Sotomayor, Kagan
565–567	2011	"
568–570	2012	"
571–573	2013	"
574–576	2014	"

* Justices are listed in order of seniority. Boldface indicates a new Chief Justice.

15. Chief Justice Rehnquist died on Sept. 3, 2005, shortly before the 2004 Term officially concluded, but after all opinions from that Term had been delivered.

16. Participation ends with 546 U.S. 417.

17. Participation begins with 547 U.S.

U.S. Reports	Term	The Court*
577–579	2015	Roberts, Scalia,[18] Kennedy, Thomas, Ginsburg, Breyer, Alito, Sotomayor, Kagan
580–582	2016	Roberts, Kennedy, Thomas, Ginsburg, Breyer, Alito, Sotomayor, Kagan, Gorsuch[19]

---

* Justices are listed in order of seniority. Boldface indicates a new Chief Justice.

18. Justice Scalia died on February 13, 2016, before most of the cases argued in the 2015 Term were decided. His participation ended with 136 S. Ct. 760.

19. Justice Gorsuch joined the Court on April 10, 2017. He took no part in any of the cases discussed in this casebook except *Trinity Lutheran Church of Columbia, Inc. v. Comer* (Chapter 19).

Index